THE BUILDINGS OF ENGLAND

FOUNDING EDITOR: NIKOLAUS PEVSNER

SUFFOLK: WEST

JAMES BETTLEY
AND
NIKOLAUS PEVSNER

West Suffolk

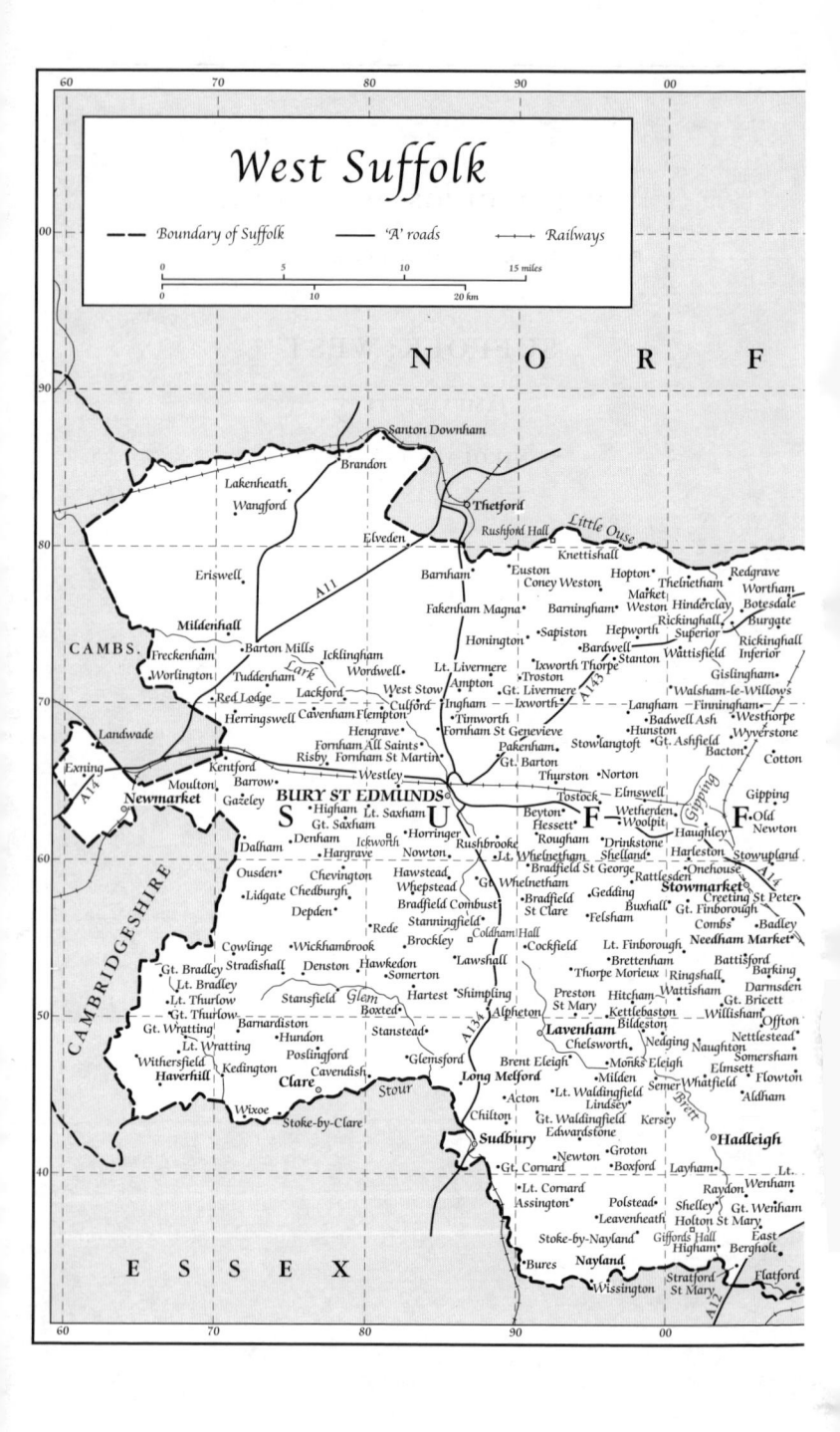

— — — Boundary of Suffolk   ——— 'A' roads   +—+—+ Railways

0   5   10   15 miles
0   10   20 km

10
20
30
40
50
Breydon Water
Great Yarmouth
Burgh Castle
Yare
Bradwell
Belton
Fritton
A12
Hopton-on-Sea
00
St Olaves
Ashby
Lound
Herringfleet
Corton
Blundeston
Somerleyton
Flixton
Gunton
Oulton
Waveney
Lowestoft
O
L
K
Oulton Broad
Kirkley
Mettingham
Beccles
Carlton Colville
Pakefield
Shipmeadow
Bungay
Barsham
Worlingham
Barnby
North Cove
90
Gisleham
Ilketshall St John
Ringsfield
Weston
Mutford
Rushmere
Ilketshall St Andrew
Flixton
Ilketshall St Margaret
Ellough
Kessingland
Homersfield
S. Elmham St Peter
S. Elmham All Saints
Redisham
Henstead
Sotterley
S. Elmham St Cross
Ilketshall St Lawrence
Benacre
Shadingfield
Mendham
S. Elmham St Margaret
S. Elmham St Michael
Wrentham
Frostenden
Withersdale
Brampton
Stoven
Covehithe
Rumburgh
Spexhall
Westhall
Uggeshall
South Cove
Metfield
A140
Waveney
Weybread
S. Elmham St James
80
Sotherton
Wangford
Palgrave
Wissett
Syleham
Linstead Parva
Chediston
Holton
Stuston
Oakley
Henham
Reydon
Brome
Hoxne
Fressingfield
Linstead Magna
Halesworth
Blyford
Thrandeston
Wingfield
Cookley
Wenhaston
Southwold
Cratfield
Yaxley
Eye
Denham
Thorpe Hall
Walpole
Blythburgh
Mellis
Walberswick
Stradbroke
Huntingfield
Thornham Parva
Blyth
Bramfield
Thorington
Horham
Braiseworth
Laxfield
Redlingfield
Wilby
Heveningham
Thornham Magna
Athelington
Ubbeston
Dunwich
Stoke Ash
Occold
70
Brundish
Darsham
Wickham Skeith
Thorndon
Southolt
Peasenhall
Sibton
Westleton
Rishangles
Bedingfield
Worlingworth
Badingham
Yoxford
Thwaite
Tannington
Middleton
Wetheringsett
A12
Bedfield
Bruisyard
Dennington
Minsmere
Mendlesham
Kenton
Alde
Theberton
Aspall
Monk Soham
Saxtead
Cransford
Rendham
Kelsale
Debenham
Carlton
Gt. Glemham
Saxmundham
Leiston
Sizewell
Earl Soham
Ashfield
Framlingham
Deben
Sweffling
Benhall
Knodishall
Mickfield
Winston
Brandeston
Parham
Stratford St Andrew
Sternfield
Friston
Aldringham
Lt. Stonham
Cretingham
Farnham
60
Stonham Aspal
Framsden
Kettleburgh
Hacheston
Thorpeness
Easton
Earl Stonham
Pettaugh
Monewden
Hoo
Marlesford
Lt. Glemham
Snape
Creeting St Mary
Crowfield
Letheringham
Glevering Hall
Helmingham
Charsfield
Wickham Market
Blaxhall
Aldeburgh
Gosbeck
Otley
Clopton
Campsea Ashe
Iken
Coddenham
Pettistree
Tunstall
Ashbocking
Debach
Dallinghoo
Loudham Hall
Hemingstone
Swilland
Bredfield
Rendlesham
Sudbourne
Shrubland Park
Boulge
Wantisden
Barham
Witnesham
Ufford
Chillesford
Henley
Burgh
Eyke
Baylham
Grundisburgh
Melton
Butley
Gt. Blakenham
Hasketon
Bromeswell
Orford
Claydon
Seckford Hall
Woodbridge
50
Akenham
Tuddenham St Martin
Culpho
Gt. Bealings
Capel St Andrew
Lt. Blakenham
Playford
Lt. Bealings
Whitton
Westerfield
Boyton
Bramford
Rushmere St Andrew
Martlesham
Sutton
Ore
Sproughton
Kesgrave
Waldringfield
Shottisham
Burstall
IPSWICH
Foxhall
Newbourne
Hollesley
Chattisham
Brightwell
Hintlesham
Ramsholt
Shingle Street
Washbrook
Hemley
Copdock
Bucklesham
Alderton
Belstead
Bawdsey
Nacton
40
Freston
Levington
Kirton
Falkenham
A14
Bentley
Woolverstone
Orwell
Trimley St Martin
Capel St Mary
Tattingstone
Chelmondiston
Trimley St Mary
Holbrook
North Sea
Stutton
Harkstead
Shotley
Walton
Brantham
Erwarton
Felixstowe
Stour
Harwich

PEVSNER ARCHITECTURAL GUIDES

The *Buildings of England* series was created and largely written by Sir Nikolaus Pevsner (1902–83). First editions of the county volumes were published by Penguin Books between 1951 and 1974. The continuing programme of revisions and new volumes was supported between 1994 and 2011 by research financed through the Pevsner Books Trust. That responsibility has now been assumed by the Paul Mellon Centre for Studies in British Art.

Suffolk: West

BY
JAMES BETTLEY
AND
NIKOLAUS PEVSNER

THE BUILDINGS OF ENGLAND

YALE UNIVERSITY PRESS
NEW HAVEN AND LONDON

YALE UNIVERSITY PRESS
NEW HAVEN AND LONDON

302 Temple Street, New Haven CT 06511
47 Bedford Square, London WC1B 3DP
www.pevsner.co.uk
www.lookingatbuildings.org.uk
www.yalebooks.co.uk
www.yalebooks.com

Published by Yale University Press 2015
2 4 6 8 10 9 7 5 3 1

ISBN 978 0 300 19655 9

Copyright © Nikolaus Pevsner, 1961, 1974 and
Copyright © Enid Radcliffe, 1974
Copyright © James Bettley, 2015

Printed in China
through World Print
Set in Monotype Plantin

All rights reserved.
This book may not be reproduced
in whole or in part, in any form (beyond that
copying permitted by Sections 107 and 108 of the
U.S. Copyright Law and except by reviewers
for the public press), without written
permission from the publishers

The dedication of *Suffolk* was
TO THE MEMORY OF
PETER FLOUD

The dedication of *Suffolk: West* is
TO THE MEMORY OF
A WEST SUFFOLK WEEKEND
Little Saxham, 1–3 February 1985

CONTENTS

LIST OF TEXT FIGURES AND MAPS	x
PHOTOGRAPHIC ACKNOWLEDGEMENTS	xiv
MAP REFERENCES	xv
FOREWORD AND ACKNOWLEDGEMENTS	xvi
INTRODUCTION	1
GEOLOGY AND BUILDING MATERIALS	3
THE PREHISTORY OF SUFFOLK, BY EDWARD MARTIN	8
ROMAN SUFFOLK, BY JUDITH PLOUVIEZ	15
SUFFOLK: WEST	20
ANGLO-SAXON	22
MEDIEVAL CHURCHES	23
MEDIEVAL SECULAR BUILDINGS	35
CHURCHES AND CHAPELS 1540–1840	39
SECULAR BUILDINGS 1540–1840	44
ARCHITECTURE 1840–1914	51
ARCHITECTURE SINCE 1914	59
FURTHER READING	65
GAZETTEER	75
GLOSSARY	577
INDEX OF ARCHITECTS, ARTISTS, PATRONS AND RESIDENTS	603
INDEX OF PLACES	624

LIST OF TEXT FIGURES AND MAPS

Every effort has been made to contact or trace all copyright holders. The publishers will be glad to make good any errors or omissions brought to our attention in future editions.

Suffolk Soil map (N. Scarfe, *The Suffolk Landscape*, 2002)	3
Great Cornard, Abbas Hall, details of timber framing by Cecil Hewett (Suffolk Historic Buildings Group, *Historic Buildings of Suffolk*, vol. 1, 1998)	6
Roman Suffolk (adapted from *An Historical Atlas of Suffolk*, 3rd edn, 1999)	16
Woodbridge, St Mary, mid-C15 flushwork monogram of the Virgin and device of Thomas Aldryche, drawing by J. Blatchly, 2005 (J. Blatchly and P. Northeast, *Decoding Flint Flushwork*, 2005). Courtesy of J. Blatchly and the late P. Northeast	29
Shrubland, Old Hall, terracotta tile unit (*East Anglia's History: Studies in Honour of Norman Scarfe*, ed. C. Harper-Bill, C. Rawcliffe, and R. G. Wilson, 2002)	30
Down Hall, Preston St Mary, timber framing (*Regional Variation in Timber-Framed Building in England and Wales down to 1550*, Essex County Council, 1998)	37
Brantham, Bull Bridge, engraving (*Illustrated London News*, 20 June 1846)	52
Finningham, Old Rectory, design by E. C. Frere (*Academy Architecture*, vol. 34, 1908)	58
Acton, All Saints, brass of Sir Robert de Bures †1331 © Martin Stuchfield	76
Bildeston, St Mary Magdalene, arcade, drawing by Birkin Haward (B. Haward, *Suffolk Medieval Church Arcades*, 1993)	96
Boxford, St Mary, brass to David Birde †1606 © Martin Stuchfield	101
Boxford House (former rectory), design by M. G. Thompson, 1818 (SROB 806/2/3). Courtesy of Suffolk Record Office, Bury St Edmunds	103
Bures, vicarage, design by M. G. Thompson, 1821 (SROB 806/2/4). Courtesy of Suffolk Record Office, Bury St Edmunds	119
Burgate, St Mary, brass to Sir William de Burgate †1409 and wife Eleanor © Martin Stuchfield	123

LIST OF TEXT FIGURES AND MAPS

Bury St Edmunds, Abbey and precincts, plan
(after *English Heritage guidebook*, 1992)
© Crown copyright. English Heritage — 129

Bury St Edmunds, railway station, engraving, 1852
(S. Tymms, *Handbook of Bury St Edmunds*, 1854) — 148

Bury St Edmunds, town plan (after Bernard Gauthiez, British Archaeological Association Conference Transactions 20, 1998) — 149

Bury St Edmunds, Cupola House, elevation, drawn by P. Aitkens, 1999, reproduced courtesy of Philip Aitkens — 155

Bury St Edmunds, Hardwick House, engraving, 1852
(S. Tymms, *Handbook of Bury St Edmunds*, 1854) — 173

Cavenham Hall, stables, design by A. N. Prentice
(H. Muthesius, *Das englische Haus*, vol. ii, 1904–5) — 181

Chelsworth, The Grange, porch, measured drawing, 1910 (B. Oliver, *Old Houses and Village Buildings in East Anglia*, 1912) — 184

Chilton Hall, gateway, drawing by I. Johnson, Private Collection — 188

Copdock, Felcourt (former rectory), design by E. B. Lamb, 1858 (SROI FF1/24/1). Courtesy of Suffolk Record Office, Ipswich — 203

Cowlinge, Branches Park, lithograph, *c.* 1820, © Diocese of St Edmundsbury and Ipswich, SROB E3/10/5.5 — 206

Dalham Hall, unexecuted design for additions by C. E. Mallows (*The Studio*, vol. 54, 1908) — 213

Elveden Hall, design by John Norton
(*The Builder*, 18 Nov 1871) — 226

Flempton, St Catherine, engraving, 1827 (T. England, *A Concise Description of Bury St Edmund's and its Environs: within the distance of ten miles*, 1827) — 239

Giffords Hall, plan (*Proceedings of the Suffolk Institute of Archaeology and History*, vol. 30, 1965) — 246

Gipping, Chapel of St Nicholas, flushwork emblems, drawing by J. Blatchly, 2005 (J. Blatchly and P. Northeast, *Decoding Flint Flushwork*, 2005). Courtesy of J. Blatchly and the late P. Northeast — 248

Hadleigh, design for cottages on smallholdings by R. W. Schultz (*The Builder*, 19 December 1913) — 284

Hawkedon, Thurston End Hall, drawing by J. S. Corder (*The Builder*, 20 January 1894) — 296

Hawstead Place, engraving (J. Gage, *History and Antiquities of Suffolk: Thingoe Hundred*, 1838) — 300

Hengrave Hall, plan (*Recent English Domestic Architecture*, 1909) — 301

Hengrave, St John Lateran, monument to Countess of Bath †1562 (J. Gage, *History and Antiquities of Suffolk: Thingoe Hundred*, 1838) — 305

Higham, Chauffeurs Cottage, design by W. H. Atkin Berry (*Academy Architecture*, vol. 2, 1890) — 313

xii LIST OF TEXT FIGURES AND MAPS

Ickworth House, plan (adapted from *National Trust guidebook*, 2011) © National Trust Images	326
Ickworth, Rotunda, drawing by I. Johnson, 1817, by permission of Suffolk Record Office, Ipswich	328
Ickworth Park, plan (adapted from *National Trust guidebook*, 2011) © National Trust Images	332
Lakenheath, The Retreat, design by A. N. Prentice (*Academy Architecture* vol. 17, 1900)	347
Lavenham, Wool Hall, drawing by J. S. Corder, 1888 (*The Builder*, 23 March 1889)	361
Little Wenham Hall, plan (*Proceedings of the Suffolk Institute of Archaeology and History*, vol. 38, 1998)	376
Little Wenham, All Saints, brass to Thomas Brewse †1514 and wife Jane © Martin Stuchfield	378
Long Melford, Holy Trinity, plan by B. Haward, 1989 (B. Haward, *Suffolk Medieval Church Arcades*, 1993)	381
Long Melford, Holy Trinity, inscription (E. L. Conder, *The Church of the Holy Trinity, Long Melford*, 1887)	383
Long Melford, Melford Hall, plan (*National Trust guidebook*, 2009) © National Trust Images	395
Long Melford, Long Wall, plan (S. Cantacuzino, *Modern Houses of the World*, 1964)	399
Mendlesham, St Mary, brass to John Knyvet †1417 © Martin Stuchfield	404
Nayland, Alston Court, plan (*Architectural Review*, vol. 21, 1907)	417
Nettlestead Chace, gateway, etching by H. Davy, 1824 (H. Davy, *A Series of Etchings Illustrative of the Architectural Antiquities of Suffolk*, 1827)	427
Newmarket, Prince's Lodging, drawing by I. Jones, c. 1616, RIBA Library Drawings & Archives Collections	431
Newmarket, Palace, reconstruction, drawing by Stephen Conlin (*Country Life*, 24 April 2008) © Stephen Conlin	432
Newmarket, Murray Lodge, design by A. N. Prentice (*Academy Architecture*, vol. 27, 1905)	437
Newmarket, Exeter House Stables, covered ride, engraving (G. Tattersall, *Sporting Architecture*, 1841)	439
Nowton Cottage, engraving (*Frost's New Town and Country Ladies Memorandum Book and Fashionable Repository for* 1835)	446
Pakenham, St Mary, before restoration (*Proceedings of the Suffolk Institute of Archaeology and History*, vol. 1, 1850)	451
Poslingford, St Mary, E end of nave in 1881 (*Proceedings of the Suffolk Institute of Archaeology and History*, vol. 1, 1893)	458
Rushbrooke Hall, engraving © Diocese of St Edmundsbury and Ipswich. SROB 1511/204(d)	477
Stoke-by-Nayland, St Mary, brass to Sir William Tendring †1408 © Martin Stuchfield	497
Stoke-by-Nayland, Tendring Hall, design by J. Soane, 1784. Courtesy of the Soane Museum	499

LIST OF TEXT FIGURES AND MAPS

Stowmarket, Milton House, etching by W. Hagreen after F. Russel (A. G. H. Hollingsworth, *The History of Stowmarket, the ancient county town of Suffolk*, 1844)	506
Stowmarket, Edgar's Farm, timber framing, drawing by Cecil Hewett (*Historic Buildings of Suffolk*, vol. 1, 1998)	511
Sudbury, bank, design by B. Binyon (*Building News*, 8 August 1879)	524
Thurston, St Peter, collapsed tower, drawing by Rev. R. S. Fox, 1860 (*Ilam Anastatic Drawing Society*, 1867)	538
Whepstead, Plumpton House, engraving by G. Hollis (J. Gage, *History and Antiquities of Suffolk: Thingoe Hundred*, 1838)	557
Wordwell, All Saints, engraving after J. G. Lenny (*The Gentleman's Magazine*, April 1824)	570

MAPS

West Suffolk	ii–iii
Bury St Edmunds Town Centre	151
Bury St Edmunds Outer	166
Clare	193
Hadleigh	277
Lavenham	356
Newmarket	434
Stowmarket	507
Sudbury	523

PHOTOGRAPHIC ACKNOWLEDGEMENTS

The photographs were almost all taken by Paul Highnam (© Paul Highnam). We are also grateful for permission to reproduce the remaining photographs from the sources as shown below.

Colchester & Ipswich Museum Service: 76

© Country Life: 10, 11, 55, 59, 60

© English Heritage Images: 25

Kevin Pengelly, courtesy of Haughley Park: 66

Landmark Trust: 24, 41

© National Trust Images/Andrew Butler: 85

© National Trust Images/Andreas von Einsiedel: 87

© National Trust Images/Dennis Gilbert: 91

© National Trust Images/Arnhel de Serra: 86

© National Trust Images/Rod Edwards: 46

© National Trust Images/Rupert Truman: 58

© The Churches Conservation Trust, Andy Marshall: 13, 27

© The Churches Conservation Trust, Steve Cole: 67, 73

The Perry Lithgow Partnership Ltd: 12

VIEW Pictures Ltd / Alamy: 117

MAP REFERENCES

The numbers printed in italic type in the margin against the place names in the gazetteer of the book indicate the position of the place in question on the index map (pp. ii–iii), which is divided into sections by the 10-kilometre reference lines of the National Grid. The reference given here omits the two initial letters which in a full grid reference refer to the 100-kilometre squares into which the county is divided. The first two numbers indicate the *western* boundary, and the last two the *southern* boundary, of the 10-kilometre square in which the place in question is situated. For example, Acton (reference 8040) will be found in the 10-kilometre square bounded by grid lines 80 (on the *west*) and 90, and 40 (on the *south*) and 50; Yaxley (reference 1070) in the square bounded by the grid lines 10 (on the *west*) and 20, and 70 (on the *south*) and 80.

The map contains all those places, whether towns, villages or isolated buildings, which are the subject of separate entries in the text.

FOREWORD AND ACKNOWLEDGEMENTS

'Work in Suffolk has been a pleasure throughout. The weather was clement, the natives friendly, the scenery and the buildings a delight.' These words opened the foreword to the first edition of *Suffolk*, published in 1961, and they are just as valid for this new foreword. Only the observation about the weather needs a little qualification, because Pevsner's tour of Suffolk (with his wife, Lola) took place in August 1957, which was notably warm, dry and sunny, whereas preparation of the third edition was spread over six years and all seasons.

Pevsner's first action on returning to London was to write to Aspall (E)* and ask to be sent a crate or two of dry cider. Two days later he had the less welcome task of writing to the owner of Assington Hall (W) to commiserate with him about the fire which had all but destroyed the house about three weeks after his visit. Only then did the work of fact-checking commence, and it seems to have taken longer than usual for *Suffolk* to come out. The text did not go to the typesetters until late in 1959, galley proofs were ready the following March (these were sent out in batches to vicars so that they could check the entries for their churches), and *Suffolk* was published early in 1961. Letters with comments and corrections arrived within days, and Pevsner accepted them with his usual humility, as we all must. His entry for Assington Hall – already drafted before his return to London – had of course been revised to take account of the fire; not so the entry for Haughley Park (W), gutted by fire almost as the first copies of *Suffolk* were going on sale. Later the same year Hobland Hall, Bradwell (E) also burnt down, and Rushbrooke Hall (W) was demolished. The process of revision started almost immediately.

The second edition, although dated 1974, was published in 1975, and had been revised by Enid Radcliffe. As was the norm for these early revisions, the second edition did not involve revisiting – Pevsner was still too busy working on the first editions of other counties – but took account of material that had been sent in since 1961, not just correcting mistakes but incorporating the results of new research as well as adding a number of new buildings that had caught Pevsner's eye in the architectural press.

Preparation of the third edition has been a different process, and has resulted in a considerably expanded account of Suffolk's buildings, to the extent that it has been necessary to split the county into two volumes. How to divide a county is potentially controversial, and complicated in the case of Suffolk by the fact

---

* (E) and (W) following place names denotes whether they appear in *Suffolk: East* or *Suffolk: West*.

that between 1888 and 1974 East Suffolk and West Suffolk were separate administrative counties. To have perpetuated that division might have seemed the obvious course, but the boundary between the two is gradually being forgotten, and in any case would have resulted in volumes of unequal size. It was therefore decided to keep to an E–W split, but to draw the boundary along the line of the A12 where it crosses the River Stour from Essex at Stratford St Mary, continuing along the A14 round the W side of Ipswich, and then following the A140 N to the Norfolk border. This boundary has the merit of being easy to identify on a road map, and the small number of towns and villages on the route almost always fall clearly one side or the other. The determining factor is the location of the parish church, with the sole exception of Stratford St Mary (W), where the bypassing of the village has resulted in the church being separated from the village by the A12.

The local government reorganization of 1974 left Suffolk relatively unscathed. Five parishes in the far NE of the county – Belton, Bradwell, Burgh Castle, Fritton and St Olaves, and Hopton-on-Sea – were transferred to Norfolk, thus joining Gorleston, which had been absorbed into Great Yarmouth in the C19. Norman Scarfe wrote witheringly in *The Suffolk Landscape* that 'the great Roman fortress at Burgh Castle is now reckoned by the Norfolk Archaeological Trust as one of the most striking attractions of "Norfolk's past"!', adding that 'the stout flint walls . . . remain a part of my understanding of the Suffolk landscape' – as they do for many, and for present purposes Burgh Castle and the other four parishes remain in Suffolk. The only other change of this nature concerns Landwade, a parish in Cambridgeshire that was transferred to the civil parish of Exning in 1994. It seemed expedient to include Landwade in both *Suffolk: West* and the second edition of *Cambridgeshire* (2014).

Other places meriting new entries are Red Lodge (W) and Capel St Andrew, Shingle Street and St Olaves (all E). Trimley (E) has been split into its separate parishes, St Martin and St Mary. The entry for Lowestoft (E) has been reorganized to reflect the status of Gunton, Kirkley and Pakefield as once-separate parishes that are now suburbs, and also to take account of Oulton Broad as a suburb with its own distinct character. The treatment of Ipswich (E) is generally unchanged, except that there is now a separate entry for Whitton. A few country houses and other isolated buildings that previously had separate entries are now to be found under their parishes; one new entry in this category is Thorpe Hall (E).

The principle of this revision has been to keep as much as possible of what Pevsner wrote in the first and second editions, and to add rather than alter. All the buildings included in the first and second editions have been visited, and many more besides. Suffolk has always been well populated with antiquaries, but particularly so, it would seem, in recent years, and new research has greatly increased knowledge of the county's buildings, not just those on which Pevsner tended to concentrate – medieval churches and larger houses – but also, or perhaps especially, those which he was liable to overlook, and above all vernacular buildings, which in Suffolk are almost invariably timber-framed. Increased study of these buildings, combined with the science of dendrochronology or tree-ring dating, has resulted in the inclusion of many more examples, and in the case of those which Pevsner did mention, thorough reassessment. A glance at Further Reading (p. 65) will show how much material published since 1974 has had to be taken into account.

Generally, the criteria for inclusion remain the same. All Anglican and Roman Catholic churches built before 1914, and Nonconformist churches and chapels before 1840, should be included, as well as a high proportion of those built since. Most church furnishings of any importance have been included, especially for Anglican churches, but not bells and plate nor, as a rule, chairs or other easily movable objects, or organs. Castles and larger houses are all included. In the case of the latter, access has not always been possible, but most owners and custodians have been extraordinarily welcoming, and it is only fair to them to state clearly that inclusion of a building in this volume does not imply any form of public access. However, many houses in Suffolk participate in 'Invitation to View', an initiative, now national, that started in Suffolk in 1998 and provides access on specified days to a growing number of private houses.

For smaller houses, such as the farmhouses and cottages in which Suffolk abounds, selection has had to be very rigorous. All buildings listed Grade I and II* should have been included, and the remainder are either especially eye-catching for one reason or another, or have some particular feature that makes them stand out from the crowd. An effort has also been made to include more C19 and C20 buildings, particularly those by local architects, who were collectively responsible for a major body of work that has tended be overlooked by national studies.

The friendly natives of Suffolk have been hugely welcoming to an outsider and generous in their offers of information and help of all kinds. First in a very long list, and not just for alphabetical reasons, must be Julia Abel Smith, a daughter of Suffolk but, like me, an adopted resident of Essex, whose vicarious enthusiasm for the project got me off to a good start, and who also lent me a number of useful reference books from the library of her father, the late J. C. Wolton. She led me to John Blatchly, who has kept me supplied with a constant stream of useful information, and also arranged for the loan of a long run of the invaluable *Proceedings* of the Suffolk Institute of Archaeology and History. Edward Martin has also willingly shared his immense knowledge of the history of Suffolk of all ages, and contributed 'The Prehistory of Suffolk' to the Introduction as well as revising those parts of the Gazetteer dealing with prehistory. Judith Plouviez kindly did the same for Roman Suffolk. Both contributions take account of a general policy to include less information in the Gazetteer about prehistoric and Roman sites of which there are no visible remains.

For help on a wide range of subjects across the whole county I am most grateful to Philip Aitkens, Leigh Alston, Andrew

FOREWORD AND ACKNOWLEDGEMENTS

Anderson, Ian Anderson, Michael Archer, Guy Barefoot, Mark Barnard, John Barnes, Ron Baxter, Jon Bayliss, Richard Benny, Rodney Black, James Blackie, Geoff Brandwood, Michael Breen, Michael Brook, Cynthia Brown, Tim Buxbaum, Ralph Carpenter, Bob Carr, Muriel Carrick, Adrian Corder-Birch, Peter Cormack, Rosemary Cramp, the late Colin Cunningham, David Dymond, Timothy Easton, Anthony Edwards, John Fitch, Claire Gapper, Angela Goedicke, Brian Golds, the late Andor Gomme, Jane Gosling, Tim Grass, Michael Hall, Robert Halliday, James Halsall, Alec Hamilton, John Harris, Martin Harrison, Stephen Hart, Birkin Haward Jun., Peter Howell, Peter Kay, Shawn Kholucy, Paul Kievenaar, Bob Kindred, Ian McKechnie, Alison Maguire, Hugh Martin, Joanna Martin, Peter Minter, Charles Morris, the late Peter Northeast, Clive Paine, Lynn Pearson, Hugh Pilkington, Kenneth Powell, Tony Redman, John Martin Robinson, Arthur Rope, Marion Scantlebury, David Sherlock, Christopher Starr, Alan Teulon, Charles Tracy, Roy Tricker, Paul Tritton, John Walker, Lynn Walker, Brenda and Elphin Watkin, Roger White, Tom Williamson and David Whymark. Particular mention must be made of the following, who made available comprehensive lists of Suffolk material in their respective fields, much of it unpublished: Geoffrey Fisher and Adam White (church monuments, their attributions denoted GF and AW in the Gazetteer), Michael Kerney (stained glass), Andrea Kirkham (domestic wall paintings) and Martin Stuchfield (brasses). I must also make a general acknowledgement to the hard work and expertise of members and officers, past and present, of the Suffolk Institute of Archaeology and History and the Suffolk Historic Buildings Group, whose publications and programmes of lectures and visits, as well as general friendliness and willingness to share information, have been of enormous help.

Churchwardens, incumbents, house owners and others who have provided access and information, often without prior notice, are too numerous to list here, and indeed some remain anonymous; but those who were conspicuously helpful in the places covered by this volume include Sir George Agnew, Sue Andrews, Richard Ballard, Joseph Barrere, Anne Bent, Andrew Boyce, Marcia Brocklebank and the late Charles Brocklebank, Hugh Bunbury, David Burnett, Rev. David Burrell, Jonathan Burton, Jan Byrne, Lynn Cardale, Sir Kenneth Carlisle, Mark Champion, Edward Coales, Ben Crossman, Andrew Didham, Rev. John Eley, James and Jacko Fanshawe, Eddie Farrell, Nigel Farthing, Charles and Sara Fenwick, Canon Brian Findlay, Henry Freeland, Rev. John Fulton, Leslie Geddes-Brown, Peter Gibbs, Simon Gibson, Jonathan Glancey, Brian Golds, Anthony and Moira Goldstaub, Anthony Goode, David Gordon-Lennox, the late Duke of Grafton and the Dowager Duchess of Grafton, Rev. Philip Gray, Veere Grenney, Colin Hart, Lord and Lady Hart, Christopher Hawkins, Lady Henniker, Rev. Simon Hill, John Hodge, Anne Holden, Alan Horsfall, Roz Howling, Sir Richard Hyde Parker, Lord Iveagh, Roger Kennell, Pat Knock, Gerald and Rosemary Knox, Frank Lawrenson, Martin Lightfoot, the late Corbett Macadam, the late Richard Macaire, Tom

McKenny, Rev. Peter Macleod-Miller, David Martin, Stephen Mattick, Alan Medlock, Jan Michalak, Peter and Elisabeth Mimpriss, Martin Mitchell, Christopher Moore, Pat Murrell, Mark and Maryanne Nicholls, Philip Orchard, Daisy Palmer, Matthew Parker, Stephen Partridge-Hicks, Lady Laura Paul, Evelyn Payne, Warwick Pethers, Patrick Phillips, Geoffrey Probert, Dominic Richards, Father Bernard Rolls, John Rowe, Andrew Scott, Dan Scott, Arland Shawe-Taylor, Jean Sheehan, Rob and Emily Shelley, Angela Sills, Charles Spicer, Christopher Spicer, Hew Stevenson, Lionel Stirgess, Janet Swann, Anne Templeton, Quinlan Terry, George and Rachel Vestey, Barry Wall, Robert Williams, Mary and the late John Wolton, Francis Woodman, Christopher and Patricia Woods, Mike Woolley and Edward Wortley.

Staff at the three branches of the Suffolk Record Office, in Bury St Edmunds, Ipswich and Lowestoft, have been unfailingly helpful, as have those at Norfolk Record Office, where some diocesan records relating to Suffolk before 1914 are still located. Museums in Bury St Edmunds (Moyse's Hall), Newmarket (National Horseracing Museum), Stowmarket (Museum of East Anglian Life) and Woolpit have also provided useful information that would have been hard to find elsewhere. Anna Forrest (National Trust) kindly arranged access to research files on Ickworth and other properties.

At Yale University Press Charles O'Brien has been an encouraging and perceptive editor, and has saved the reader from some of my lengthier digressions. The reader is also indebted (as I am) to the copy editor, Katy Carter, whose searching questions revealed many errors and inconsistencies in the text. Paul Highnam rose enthusiastically to the challenge of taking the new photographs. Phoebe Lowndes has shown equal enthusiasm in sorting out the other illustrations, and both she and Martin Brown, who prepared the maps and plans, have been very patient. Judith Wardman had the unenviable task of preparing the indexes, and Catherine Bankhurst masterminded the whole magical process of turning the disparate elements into the finished book. I am grateful also to Sally Salvesen for her support as publisher throughout.

In spite of the many people acknowledged, there will still be errors, for which the responsibility is mine alone; as Pevsner wrote to the West Suffolk County Archivist in February 1961, 'it is very disappointing indeed to realise that whatever trouble you take, the resident expert will always be able to find mistakes'. The author and publishers will, as ever, be grateful to be told of errors and omissions.

James Bettley
October 2014

INTRODUCTION

In area Suffolk is seventh among English counties, covering some 940,000 acres (380,400 ha), and of the seven largest counties it is, with a population of about 730,000, the most densely populated. This gives a misleading impression, because Suffolk is still a county of small towns and villages. Its largest town, Ipswich, has only about 133,000 inhabitants, Lowestoft just under 57,000, Bury St Edmunds a little over 40,000. It is still predominantly an agricultural county, and historically much of its wealth has been derived from the land and many of its industries were connected with the soil (woollen cloth manufacture, agricultural machinery, fertilizers). The rural landscape and the architecture associated with it (picturesque cottages as well as impressive churches) have attracted tourists for at least two centuries; 'Constable Country', the landscape of the River Stour around East Bergholt, Flatford and Nayland, was famous during the painter's own lifetime. Tourists go chiefly to the coast, which in Suffolk is a mix of ancient heathland, salt marsh, reed beds and muddy estuaries; the beaches are mainly of uncomfortable shingle. The Broads (known loosely as the Norfolk Broads) reach down to include the northern edge of Suffolk along the River Waveney, but are less of a holiday destination in the C21 than they were in the C20; the extensive pine plantations in the NW of the county, round Elveden and Brandon and including Thetford Forest, are becoming more visited.

One of the chief attractions of Suffolk, perversely, is that it is not very easily accessible by road. The A12 from Essex is discouraging, and although it continues N from Ipswich to Lowestoft, for much of its length in Suffolk it is a single carriageway. The M11, originally intended to go from London to Norwich, stopped short at Cambridge, and thus Suffolk is one of the few English counties not to contain a motorway. The main traffic artery of the county is the A14, which links the container port of Felixstowe to the Midlands; along the way it connects (and bypasses) Ipswich, Stowmarket, Bury St Edmunds and Newmarket. Reaching some of the smaller towns such as Bungay, Debenham, Eye, Framlingham or Hadleigh is a slow business, although enjoyable enough if one is not in a hurry.

The administrative history of Suffolk is a little complicated but does need to be understood. Suffolk, meaning 'south folk', was the southern part of the C6–C10 kingdom of East Anglia. In the Middle Ages its twenty-five hundreds (reduced to twenty-one by the C19) were grouped into administrative areas known as franchises or liberties, and the Geldable. The Geldable was subject to land tax (geld) payable to the Crown, and covered much of the eastern part of the county; its chief towns were Ipswich in the S and Beccles in the N. The Liberty of St Etheldreda comprised six hundreds grouped around the Alde and Deben estuaries; its chief town was first Sudbourne, then Wickham Market, then Melton and finally Woodbridge (hence the Shire Hall at Woodbridge). Here royal jurisdiction was delegated to the prior of Ely. The western part of the county, the Liberty of St Edmund, comprised eight hundreds; it was centred on Bury St Edmunds and power rested with the abbey there. Changes were necessarily made as a result of the Dissolution of the Monasteries, but the basic divisions remained until the Local Government Act of 1888 replaced all this with two separate administrative counties, East Suffolk and West Suffolk, the latter with Bury St Edmunds as its county town and covering the same area as the Liberty of St Edmund. Ipswich was just large enough to be made a county borough. Local government reorganization in 1974 brought the two counties together under a single administration, with Ipswich as the county town. Five parishes in the far NE of the county – Belton, Bradwell, Burgh Castle, Fritton and Hopton – were transferred to Norfolk; their loss was deeply felt, but they were only following Gorleston, which had been lost to Great Yarmouth in the C19.[*]

As far as ecclesiastical administration is concerned, the whole of Suffolk was in the diocese of Norwich from 1094 until 1836. Before that it had been in the East Anglian diocese established by St Felix c. 630 at Dommoc (probably Dunwich, although possibly Walton Castle) and split in the later C7 with seats at Dommoc and Elmham (either South Elmham, Suffolk, or North Elmham, Norfolk) (all E).[†] In about 1125 Suffolk was split into two archdeaconries, Sudbury in the W and Suffolk in the E. The archdeaconry of Sudbury was transferred to the diocese of Ely in 1837, but the two were reunited in 1914 in the new diocese of St Edmundsbury and Ipswich, with the cathedral at Bury St Edmunds (W) and bishop's residence at Ipswich (E).

A more ancient and deeply rooted cultural division of the county is the so-called 'Gipping Divide' identified by Edward Martin. Unlike the other divisions this is N–S rather than E–W. It follows the River Gipping but is also similar to the Late Iron Age boundary between the Trinovantes (S) and the Iceni (N), and may reflect the greater influence of the English in S Suffolk and Essex, as opposed to the Scandinavians in N Suffolk and Norfolk. Evidence of the Gipping Divide is found in field systems and patterns of land holding, in place names, in medieval dialect and in vernacular carpentry traditions.

---

[*] For present purposes the five parishes are still treated as being in Suffolk.
[†] (E) and (W) following place names in the introduction and gazetteer denotes whether they appear in *Suffolk: East* or *Suffolk: West*.

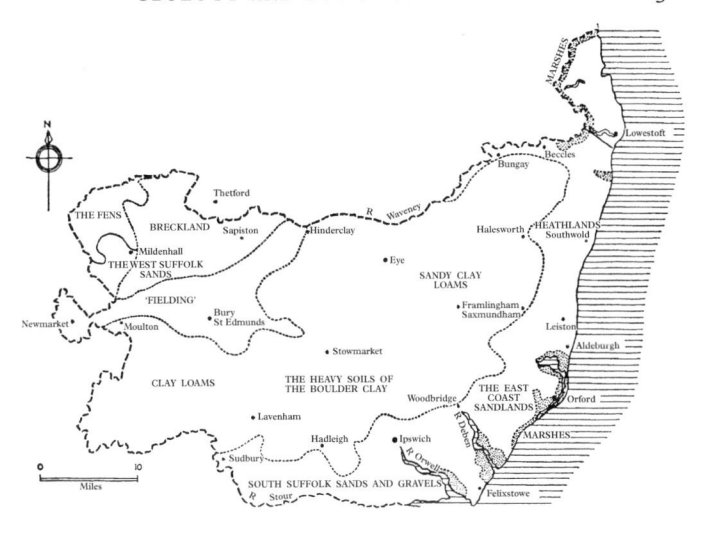

Suffolk Soil map

GEOLOGY AND BUILDING MATERIALS

The landscape of Suffolk is not especially varied. Much of it can be summed up as rolling countryside. There are no great hills. The highest point above sea level is just 420 ft (128 metres) in Depden, in the far W of the county, but there is no sense of being on high ground. The steeply sloping village street in Kersey (W), that for a moment reminds one of Dorset or Devon, is exceptional. About two-thirds of the county, a broad band from the SW to the NE, is covered by the claylands of High Suffolk, good farming land, although no longer characterized by small fields and thick hedges. High Suffolk also forms the county's watershed. Streams flow N and E into the Lark, the Black Bourn and the Dove, and thence to the Great Ouse, Little Ouse and Waveney. To the S and E are the streams that feed the Stour, Gipping, Deben, Alde and Blyth rivers.

To either side of the claylands are much flatter areas of sandy soil. In the NW of the county this is known as Breckland, which beyond Mildenhall merges into the Fens. Breckland consisted principally of open heathland, much of it given over to rabbit warrens in the Middle Ages; the processing of rabbits, for meat and fur, continued to be an important industry in Mildenhall and Brandon (both W) into the C20. After the First World War much of the heathland was planted up with conifers or converted to agricultural land. The story is much the same with the corresponding area in the E of the county, particularly between the Orwell and the Alde, known as the Sandlings, although along the coast more heathland is preserved.

This landscape, or rather the topsoil that dictates its character, is made up of glacial deposits of the Quaternary or Pleistocene period. The underlying geology is rather simple. The whole county has a substratum of the familiar English chalk, but only in the NW region, round Mildenhall, Bury St Edmunds, Newmarket and Brandon, does it come to the surface. Elsewhere the chalk basement is covered either by a few score feet of Eocene sands or clays (the 'London Clay' formation, mainly); or by the thin patchy drifts of red and buff shelly sands known locally as 'crag', particularly Coralline Crag, that were formed in the Pliocene period.

As a result of this somewhat unexciting substructure Suffolk is not rich in BUILDING MATERIALS other than flint and brick, for which suitable clays are almost ubiquitous. Direct quarrying for building stone was possible only in the chalk (but here with the severe limitation that chalk 'clunch' needs protection from wear and the weather); a notable concentration of farm buildings built of clunch has been identified at Exning, but it was also used for the higher-quality Wamil Hall, Mildenhall (both W). The occasional harder varieties of Coralline Crag can be seen in many of the older buildings in the E of the county, particularly in the small area between the Alde and Ore rivers. The church towers of Chillesford and Wantisden are built entirely of Coralline Crag, and it is found also at Butley, Eyke, Iken, Orford Castle and Tunstall (all E). Crag pits abound, for example at Crag Farm, Sudbourne (E). For the rest, stone has either to be imported – as in the case of Cretaceous ironstone at Lakenheath (W) – or collected from certain 'host rocks'. Thus what is perhaps the most characteristic Suffolk building material, flint – the most usual in the Middle Ages, and already used by the Anglo-Saxons and the Romans – can either be extracted directly from the chalk matrix (as from prehistoric times has been done at Brandon), or got from the seashore storm-beaches, or from glacial gravel beds like those at Westleton (E).

FLINT became the normal material for Suffolk churches throughout the Middle Ages, and for that reason is not normally specified in the gazetteer. In its rough undressed state flint leaves much to be desired aesthetically, and no material makes uglier ruins. But in the course of time many refinements were introduced: regular coursing was achieved by selecting stones (often pebble-flints) of about the same size, which were sometimes inclined to l. and r. in alternate courses. The introduction of knapped (fractured) flints, which could be squared or trimmed to more elaborate shapes if desired, marked another great artistic advance. The knapper hits a flint with his hammer so skilfully in strength and direction that the flint breaks into two halves with a perfectly straight, smooth cleft. Walling is then done so that these even surfaces form the outside. FLUSHWORK is the combination of such knapped flint surfaces with freestone to form chequer patterns or lozenge patterns or blank arcading or indeed whole blank windows. The first known occurrence of flushwork in Suffolk is at Butley Priory (E), *c.* 1320, equalled elsewhere only by the (probably) slightly earlier St Ethelbert's Gate, Norwich. The use of flushwork reached great heights of sophistication in the mid C15–C16 (*see* p. 29). Brandon (W) was the centre of the flint industry – for gunflints as well as knapping – and some of the craftsmen are known by name: Henry Curson left his initials at Eye (E) in 1856, *Joseph Needham* and *Henry Ashley* at Icklingham (W) in 1866.

But flint was not employed for the humbler types of house until wood became scarce in the C17. Similarly, the smooth grey or brown clay-limestone nodules of the London Clay ('septaria') were formerly dredged from the foreshores or river estuaries and incorporated, usually with other stones, into foundations and walls, as in the keep of Orford Castle (E). At Boyton (E) it is even used for the steps of the church tower, something for which it is singularly unsuited. Finally, the 'erratic blocks' of the glacial deposits, often gathered together in field-clearance, were used either as cornerstones (e.g. Bramford and Washbrook, both W), since some of them were fairly large, or in the main walling, so that at Wherstead (E), for example, the church is a kind of geological museum, with boulders of granite, gneiss and quartzite, some very likely brought down by the ice from Scandinavia or Scotland. Conventional FREESTONE is thus something of an exception in Suffolk, and was reserved for the most important buildings. Examples are Long Melford church, the nave of Lavenham, and the S sides of the two main churches of Bury St Edmunds, not forgetting the old abbey church (all W); and Orford Castle, the tower of Beccles and the clerestory of St Margaret, Ipswich (all E).

TIMBER must have been used extensively, much more no doubt in the early centuries than we now know. Suffolk was not in fact heavily wooded – only about 15 per cent of the county was woodland in 1086, and this had fallen to 5 per cent by 1349 – but what woodland there was, was intensively managed by coppicing. Timber was used in its green unseasoned state, within a few months of felling; if suitable timbers are available the science of dendrochronology (tree-ring dating) is able to determine a felling date, which is usually a reliable indicator of when the building was erected.

The glory of timber is of course the church roofs, and much will be said about them later. It is mostly porches where one finds external timberwork; Crowfield (E) is exceptional in having a timber-framed chancel. In houses timber remained the main structural material to the end of the Middle Ages, and on this subject also more is said below, but it should be noted here that the oldest identified timber-framed house is at Cookley (E), *c.* 1200. The earliest house to be tree-ring dated is Abbas Hall, Great Cornard, 1289–90, and Purton Green, Stansfield is much the same age (both W). The greatest display of timber-framed houses is to be found at Lavenham (W): nowhere else have they survived in such numbers, thanks to the decline in the town's prosperity from the mid C16. In E Suffolk one should go to Debenham. Here and there, after the mid C15, the original

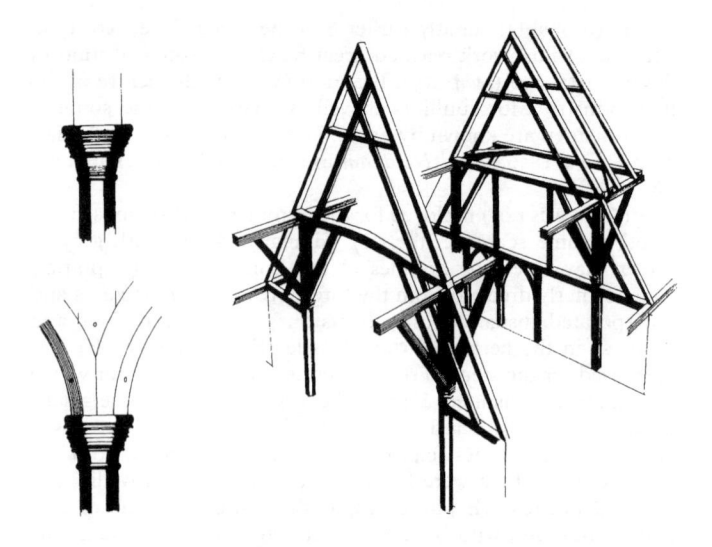

Great Cornard, Abbas Hall, details of timber framing.
Drawing by Cecil Hewett

wattle-and-daub infillings gave place to brick-nogging. Or the framing might be entirely masked by a smart new front of Georgian brick. Frequently in Suffolk, timber-framed houses were wholly plastered over, only to be 'restored' in the C20 to a black-and-white state never intended by their first builders. In some places this trend has been reversed, and a better understanding of how timber-framed buildings originally looked has resulted in their being colourwashed all over (e.g. Little Hall, Lavenham (W)). The plaster was more often colourwashed in Suffolk than in other counties, with a special affection for a shade of pink; and occasionally ornamentation was added in the form of pargetting, either incised or in relief, of which the Ancient House at Clare (W) and the Ancient House at Ipswich (E) furnish spectacular instances. Weatherboarding, although less common than in Essex, is also in some places a feature of the scenery, especially on farm buildings, watermills and windmills.

For English BRICK Suffolk is exceptionally important. The fact is that – curious as it may seem – England pretty much lost the art of brick- and tile-making which the Romans had possessed, and which the High Middle Ages on the Continent had recovered to such an extent as to make it possible for such gigantic Romanesque churches as St Sernin at Toulouse or the North Italian cathedrals or, somewhat later, the Hanseatic parish churches, to be built exclusively of brick. The Anglo-Saxon builders made ample use of Roman bricks, which they must have trusted more than their own rubble, but only on rare occasions is it thought that they made their own: St Gregory, Sudbury (W), contains brick that is probably Saxon. The place most associated with early medieval bricks is Coggeshall Abbey in Essex, where they are not thought to have been made before about 1160, but at Polstead (W) there are arches of bricks that are not Roman and date from very much the same time. The Coggeshall bricks measure 12 in. by 6 in. by 1¾ in., the Polstead bricks 10–11 in. by 5–7 in. by 1¾ in. The Roman brick size is 18 in. by 12 in. The Polstead bricks are followed by those at Little Wenham Hall (W), late C12, and St Olave's Priory (E), *c.* 1300 – still extremely early dates, as far as England is concerned. Little Wenham Hall can claim to be the earliest house in England to be constructed largely of brick.

Suffolk is one of the best counties in which to enjoy Tudor brickwork. Among the favourite ornamental motifs, nearly always produced with the aid of moulds, were recessed panels with cusped-arched heads, trefoils and quatrefoils set in horizontal bands, finials with various raised designs, and crocketed pinnacles. Some of the moulded brick chimneys of the Tudor period, like the group of four that crowns Cliftons at Clare (W), must rank among the most exuberant ever made. Unadorned chimneystacks, rising massively from the centre of the roof ridge, add dignity, as in Kent, to many other houses of quite modest size, and also sometimes provide the best clue to the true age of a house covered by a later façade. In addition to red bricks, some parts of Suffolk also produced the 'white' variety. In fact they are usually pale yellow or buff, and when 'white brick' is used in this book it should not be taken as an adjective describing simply colour. Such bricks can even be seen at Little Wenham Hall, and large numbers were used between 1525 and 1538 at Hengrave Hall (W), where they blend very well with the richly carved central oriel in the King's Cliffe oolite, specially brought from Northamptonshire. But the heyday of 'white' bricks was in the C19, when an important centre of production was Woolpit (W), where brickmaking is first recorded in the C16. White's *Directory*, 1844, described Woolpit brick as 'a very white and durable kind of brick, equal in beauty to stone . . . Many mansions in various parts of the county have been built of it.' Woolverstone Hall (E) is just one example. Mathematical tiles (or 'weather tiles') were also made at Woolpit, but their use in Suffolk seems to have been rare. The supreme example (possibly anywhere) is at Culford Hall (W), and they were also used at Helmingham Hall (E) and Livermere Hall, Great Livermere (W; dem.), as well as on a handful of smaller houses elsewhere in the county. The differences in the clay needed to make bricks of different colours varied locally – at Woolpit there was a pit for white brick-earth on one side of the road and one for red on the other.

At certain places in the N and W of the county the grey boulder clays were also a source of CLAY LUMP. The wet clay, with an admixture of straw, was pressed into moulds and left to dry out. These outsize but unfired bricks are seldom visible, as they had to be rendered for purposes of preservation, but, next to Norfolk, this is the county in which they were most used. There are examples of such houses at Barningham and Palgrave (both W). At Buxhall (W) the squarson, Rev. Copinger Hill, built cottages of cob, and described the method in a prize essay published in the *Journal of the Royal Agricultural Society*, 1843.

The lack of good indigenous building materials led to other instances of ingenuity and invention. In the early C19 *William Lockwood* of Woodbridge (E) invented a type of Portland or Roman CEMENT which he used to build a house in that town (The Castle, dem.). An employee, *James Pulham*, went on to develop a form of ARTIFICIAL STONE ('Pulhamite') that achieved considerable commercial success, particularly for rockeries and other garden features: it was used extensively at Bawdsey Manor (E). *William Ranger* patented another artificial stone or cement in 1832 and in 1834 a concrete block as a substitute for masonry; his church at Westley (W), 1835–6, is built mainly of poured concrete. There was a large cement works at Waldringfield (E) and some workers' houses in the village seem to be built of concrete. Other unexpected instances of CONCRETE construction are the former vicarage at Wherstead, 1880, and the village hall at Bawdsey, 1886 (both E).

Suffolk is believed to keep a higher proportion of thatched roofs than any other county, including some twenty-seven churches and chapels (but Norfolk has many more of these). Reed, usually from Norfolk, is steadily replacing straw as the latter becomes ever more difficult to obtain – straw of suitable length is no longer a by-product of wheat production, but has to be grown specially. But the large majority of Suffolk roofs are tiled. Both plain tiles and pantiles are used extensively. Their delightful reds are most common, but black is found also, sometimes glazed; and occasionally black and red are mixed, as at Little Glemham (E), to good effect.

THE PREHISTORY OF SUFFOLK

BY EDWARD MARTIN

Suffolk has a special place in the human perception of its past, for it was at Hoxne (E), in 1797, that the antiquary John Frere observed flint implements from a brick pit and deduced from their stratigraphic position that they must belong 'to a very remote period, indeed, even beyond that of the present world'. His letter detailing his observations was published by the Society of Antiquaries in 1800 and is the earliest published recognition of the great antiquity of humankind. Sadly his letter was ignored until 1859 when Sir John Evans saw, by chance, Frere's flint tools in a display case at the Society and 'was absolutely horror-struck' to see that they precisely resembled implements he had just seen at St Acheul in France that came from an undeniably very ancient provenance. He and Sir Joseph Prestwich hurried up to Hoxne and confirmed Frere's observations. Their subsequent lectures and publications set in train a major reassessment of human origins that coincided with the publication of Charles Darwin's *Origin of Species*.

We now know that the brick-earth deposits at Hoxne came from a lake that had formed in a hollow left by the Anglian Glaciation. Around 450,000 years ago this great glaciation had covered most of England as far S as Essex. When it retreated it left a thick deposit of boulder clay (Lowestoft Till) on the central part of Suffolk. The Hoxne lake infilled with silt in the subsequent warm period, around 400,000 years ago, that has, since 1956, been known as the 'Hoxnian Interglacial'. Later excavations indicate that the flint handaxes and other tools were deposited on the edge of the lake in a late stage of the Hoxnian Interglacial, about 370,000 years ago.

The Anglian Glaciation wiped away earlier landscapes, but in 2000 pre-Anglian humanly worked flints were discovered in the Cromer Forest-bed Formation, dating from around 700,000 years ago, at the base of the cliffs at Pakefield, near Lowestoft (E). At the time of discovery this was the earliest evidence for humans in northern Europe. More recently, even earlier evidence for humans, pre-dating the last magnetic reversal around 780,000 years ago, has been discovered a little further up the coast at Happisburgh in Norfolk.

The most prolific area in Suffolk for PALAEOLITHIC sites is Mildenhall (W). At High Lodge a C19 brick pit revealed lake or river silts containing Lower Palaeolithic worked flints of a unifacial scraper industry dating from 500,000 to 450,000 years ago. A raft of these silts had been transported and re-deposited by the great ice-sheet of the Anglian Glaciation. At Warren Hill C19 gravel workings produced a large number of Palaeolithic flint handaxes that may be contemporary with the High Lodge site. Not far away at Barnham, Palaeolithic implements including over two hundred handaxes, many cores and scrapers were found in the 1940s and early 1950s. Excavations by the British Museum and others in the nearby East Farm Brick Pit in the 1980s and 1990s yielded evidence of the contemporaneity of Clactonian and Acheulian industries.

At least two substantial cold periods followed the Anglian, but none of the ice-sheets reached Suffolk. The last interglacial, around 125,000 years ago, is named the Ipswichian after the type-site outside Ipswich at Bobbits Hole in Wherstead (E). There is no evidence for a human presence during this interglacial, but a hunter's bone barbed point from Sproughton, radio-carbon-dated to 11,440±120 B.C., indicates that humans were again active in the region before the end of the last ice age, about 10,000 years ago. At this time there was a land bridge linking East Anglia to the Continent, but the gradually rising sea level submerged it around 6000 B.C.

Around 4500 B.C. the techniques of both farming and pottery manufacture were imported from the Continent, beginning the

NEOLITHIC period. People began to use stone axes to clear the woodland to make the first fields and many of those axes have been picked up in the fields of Suffolk – some made of the local flint, but others sourced from distant axe factories, implying significant trade networks. The people of NW Suffolk looked principally towards Cumberland for their supplies, but those in the SE looked to Cornwall for theirs, presaging later cultural divisions in the county.

A significant early Neolithic settlement site at Hurst Fen, Mildenhall (W), was excavated in the 1950s. It contained numerous pits, and is the type-site for Mildenhall Ware, a form of decorated Neolithic pottery of the fourth millennium B.C. But it was the development of aerial surveys in the 1960s that brought the greatest discoveries, particularly three CAUSEWAYED ENCLOSURES at Fornham All Saints (W), Potash Farm, Freston (E) and Kedington (W). The purpose of these enclosures is still debated. Some contain human remains, but they do not appear to have a primary funerary function; rather they seem to be *foci* for community activities that include ritual practices. The Freston enclosure is roughly circular, measuring 320 yds by 340 yds (290 metres by 310 metres), and covers 21 acres (8.55 ha). Within it are cropmarks indicating a possible Neolithic long house measuring *c*. 125 ft by 33 ft (38 metres by 10 metres).

The Fornham causewayed enclosures, a main enclosure measuring about 300 yds by 355 yds (274 metres by 325 metres) covering an area of 20 acres (8.93 ha), and a subsidiary enclosure *c*. 355 yds (325 metres) in diameter, are overlaid by the cropmarks of a later Neolithic monument – a CURSUS, so-called because early antiquaries thought these monuments to be racecourses; modern thought tends to regard them as procession ways. This cursus runs for 1.2 m. beside the River Lark, and around its SE terminal are four cropmark rings that are probably yet more Neolithic 'ritual' monuments, this time related to henges. Other smaller cursus monuments are recorded at Stratford St Mary and Bures (both W). The Stratford St Mary enclosure was identified from the air in 1966 and was 320 yds (290 metres) long by 75 yds (68 metres) wide, but it was severely truncated by the building of the A12 bypass the same year and only the SE terminal survives to the E of the road. A number of ring ditches are recorded clustered around it, and to the W there is an oval cropmark 115 yds by 26 yds (106 metres by 24 metres) that probably indicates a flattened Neolithic long barrow.

Upstanding Neolithic LONG BARROWS are not recorded in Suffolk, but there are a number of cropmarks of oval enclosures that might represent flattened barrows. An example is the oval cropmark at Stratford St Mary. The first certain Neolithic long barrow in Suffolk was identified in 2006–7 in an excavation on the gravel terrace of the River Waveney at Hall Quarry in Flixton near Bungay (E). Here an oval ditch, 130 ft by 50 ft (40 metres by 15 metres), has at its eastern end a line of post-holes that suggests a façade of wooden posts, and behind them a trough 36 ft by 4 ft 3 in. (11 metres by 1.3 metres) that was probably part of a wooden burial chamber. But no bodies were found because of the acid gravel soil.

The excavations at Flixton have also revealed three post-hole circles, suggesting the timber equivalent of the stone circles found elsewhere. The first, found in 1998, was 59 ft (18 metres) in diameter and yielded a radiocarbon date of 2575–2464 B.C. The second, found in 2009, was 39 ft (12 metres) in diameter, with a cremation burial at its centre. The third, 44 ft (13.5 metres) in diameter, was found in 2010 and formed the innermost part of a complex funerary monument, being surrounded by three overlapping ring ditches. Central to all this was a large burial pit that contained a male inhumation accompanied by a Beaker pot, an archer's stone wrist-guard and two amber toggle-like objects, suggesting a burial date towards the end of the third millennium B.C. Another remarkable Beaker burial was discovered at Great Cornard (W) in 2009. Two of a group of four ring ditches were excavated. One was 121 ft 4 in. (37 metres) in diameter and had an off-centre cremation with bone tweezers; the other, 70 yds away, was a double ring ditch with a maximum diameter of 82 ft (25 metres). This contained a deep primary grave with the crouched inhumation burial of a young adult female accompanied by an Early Bronze Age beaker, a copper pin and a necklace consisting of about 412 small black jet and white shell beads, with 42 larger amber beads. There was also a secondary grave of a child, aged about four years.

The users of Beaker pottery are associated with the introduction of copper metallurgy and a sharply increasing prevalence of burial under round barrows. These BRONZE AGE ROUND BARROWS are the oldest upstanding man-made features in the Suffolk landscape, and just over a hundred survive as visible earthworks (e.g. Pole Hill in Foxhall (E) and How Hill in Icklingham (W)). But many more are visible from the air as cropmark ring ditches, bringing the combined total, in 2012, to 1,346. The main concentrations are in the light sandy soil areas of Breckland and the Sandlings, and in the river valleys. Some barrows are grouped into substantial cemeteries, one of the largest being the 'Seven Hills' that, despite its name, is a group of no fewer than fourteen mounds straddling the Bucklesham, Foxhall and Nacton parish boundaries (E). Another 'Seven Hills' exists on the border of Little Livermere and Ingham (W), but only three mounds survive. At Hall Quarry, Flixton, excavations since the 1990s have revealed the ring ditches of a dispersed cemetery of at least fourteen flattened round barrows, including the one mentioned above.

In the mid second millennium B.C. 'flat' cremation cemeteries or 'urnfields' appear, the cremated remains being buried in pits either in or under inverted pottery urns. The pits may originally have been marked by small mounds and some are surrounded by miniature ring ditches. These cemeteries occur mainly in the Stour valley (with an important excavated example at Ardleigh on the Essex side) and in the coastal strip. Excavations at Aldham Mill Hill, Hadleigh (W), in 2000 revealed two Bronze Age ring ditches with urned cremation burials. The S ring also had some Anglo-Saxon secondary burials on its W margin. The distribution was widened in 2011 with the discovery of thirty cremations with Bucket Urns at Wangford in NE Suffolk (radiocarbon-dated to 1485–1310 B.C.). The same site also revealed an Early Bronze Age ring ditch and a number of non-barrow Beaker graves.

Settlement sites of the Bronze Age are much more elusive than burials. In 1999 excavations at Cavenham (W) in the Lark valley uncovered six shallow hollows surrounded by seemingly random post-holes that might represent possible structures. These are associated with Beaker pottery (with a radiocarbon date of 2200–2050 B.C.) and although they are difficult to reconstruct as houses they are noteworthy because Beaker-period 'houses' are a national rarity. A more certain Bronze Age house was excavated at West Row Fen in Mildenhall (W). Here the erosion of peat has revealed sand-hills with evidence of Early Bronze Age settlements. Excavations in the 1980s uncovered the post-holes of three small roundhouses, *c.* 16 ft 6 in. (5 metres) in diameter, with porches, that date from *c.* 1700–1500 B.C. – the first Bronze Age houses to be discovered in Suffolk. The inhabitants were farmers growing wheat, barley and flax, and they kept cows, sheep, pigs, dogs and horses. Hunting was a minor pursuit, but included the aurochs or wild ox (*Bos primigenius*). Specimens from the area of Mildenhall and Burwell and Littleport (Cambs.) are amongst the latest known in the British Isles for this giant but now extinct mammal. The inhabitants of West Row Fen used Beaker and collared urn pottery, had numerous bone and flint tools, and used small jet toggles as personal ornaments, probably in their ears. Cuts on preserved wood indicate they also had metal axes, though none were found. Houses comparable with those at Mildenhall have subsequently been identified at Sutton Hoo (E) and Barnham (W). At Barnham, a large number of features were found, mainly pits containing charcoal and burnt flint, and also the likely outline of a roundhouse also 16 ft 6 in. (5 metres) in diameter. Around the village, a number of barrows have been excavated, yielding Bronze Age and later finds. In a barrow about 50 yds NE of the windmill an incense or pygmy cup was found in 1957 with a female inhumation, and another barrow about 1 m. NE of the church contained an urn and over one hundred pieces of worked flint, as well as a secondary Anglo-Saxon burial with grave goods including a sword, spearhead and shield. Excavations on the E edge of Brandon (W) in 1994 produced evidence of a Middle to Late Bronze Age settlement with enclosure ditches and four sub-circular post-built structures.

Iron was introduced into Britain between 800 and 650 B.C., but the pottery of the later Bronze Age forms a continuous series with that of the earlier IRON AGE, suggesting a continuity of population. Iron Age houses continued to be round, but larger, with diameters in the range of 23–39 ft (7–12 metres). A roundhouse excavated in 1979 on a hilltop overlooking the Gipping valley at Barham (E) is associated with an oven that has been radiocarbon dated to 845–795 B.C. It is a slightly oval setting of seventeen post-holes measuring 33 by 36 ft (10 by 11 metres). Another, with a diameter of 36 ft (11 metres) was found in one corner of an Iron Age enclosure excavated in 1990–1 at Foxhall (E). The enclosure itself measured c. 71 yds by 60 yds (65 metres by 55 metres), surrounded by a ditch, with an entrance in the middle of the E side. Entrances to the houses are also usually on the E side and mostly without external porches. The houses are often accompanied by square four-post structures 6½–10 ft (2–3 metres) across that are probably granaries. Several such combinations have been found in the excavations at Hall Quarry, Flixton.

In the lighter soil areas Iron Age settlements are fairly regularly spaced along valley sides at intervals of c. ½ m. (700–1,000 metres). These settlements were either unenclosed or very simply enclosed with modest ditches. These 'open' settlements were probably farmsteads and contrast with the HILL-FORTS that are a defining feature of Iron Age settlements in western England. The closest thing to a hill-fort in Suffolk is the double-ditched and banked rectangular enclosure at Burgh in SE Suffolk. It covers 17 acres (7 ha) and housed a wealthy population in the early C1 A.D. Another double-ditched enclosure of similar date, but covering only about 2.5 acres (1 ha), is recorded at Barnham in NW Suffolk. In both cases there is a suggestion of a religious dimension to the sites. At Barnham, where the site has been assigned a radiocarbon date of 180 B.C.–A.D. 20, an articulated human leg was found beside a large post on the corner, together with a nearby clay-lined trough and a horse jaw in the ditch.

In the 1980s claims were advanced that extensive areas of co-axial fields (characterized by long lines of roughly parallel field boundaries) in N Suffolk were Iron Age in origin, but more recent work has suggested that these field systems are more likely to be Late Saxon or early medieval. The excavations at Flixton (E) have revealed ditches of rectangular 'fields' of Iron Age/Roman date that are 2.5–3.5 acres (1–2.5 ha) in size. Similarly sized land units have been identified at Sutton Hoo in SE Suffolk.

In contrast to the Bronze Age, Iron Age burials are rare, with only a few scattered inhumation and cremation burials, largely without grave goods that, by association, are likely to be Iron Age. However, two Late Iron Age cremation cemeteries, 550 yds (500 metres) apart, have been found in S Suffolk at Polstead (W), though often described as being from Boxford. The cremations were contained within 'Belgic' pots dating from the early C1 A.D. Both the pottery and the burial practice connect these cemeteries with cultural groups to the S. The term 'Belgic' is used to describe pottery made using new techniques introduced into southern England in the Late Iron Age from Gallia Belgica (modern-day

Belgium and northern France) and is the first wheel-thrown pottery in Britain.

Coins also came to Britain via Gallia Belgica, around 100 B.C. Inscribed issues with the names of rulers, tribes and places started to appear towards the end of the CI and these are an important supplement to the writings of the classical authors that provide a thin history of Late Iron Age Britain. From them we gain the names of the tribes inhabiting this region – the Iceni in the N, the Trinovantes in the S and the Catuvellauni at its SW edge. The Trinovantes had their capital at Camulodunum (Colchester, Essex) but seem to have been taken over by Catuvellaunian rulers from Verulamium (St Albans) at the end of the CI B.C.; jointly they then expanded their territory in the early CI A.D. under their powerful ruler, Cunobelinus.

The mapping of the coinages gives a closer indication of the tribal territories: the Iceni were in Norfolk, N Suffolk and parts of N Cambridgeshire; the Trinovantes were in Essex and S Suffolk; and the Catuvellauni were centred in Hertfordshire, Bedfordshire and S Cambridgeshire. Exact lines are not possible, but within Suffolk, the boundary between the Iceni and the Trinovantes seems to have run along the Lark valley, across the top of the Gipping valley in the vicinity of Stowmarket, and then eastward towards Aldeburgh on the coast. This division echoes the earlier, very tentative, Neolithic divisions and is also a possible forerunner of the much later 'Gipping Divide' (*see* p. 2).

The wealth of the region is shown by finds like the Ipswich gold torcs (neck rings) and the Dallinghoo coin hoard. The six torcs were found in Belstead (E) on the S edge of Ipswich in 1968–70 and date from *c.* 75 B.C. The Dallinghoo (E) hoard of 840 gold coins, found in 2008, is one of the largest Iron Age coin hoards ever found in England. Curiously this mainly Icenian coin hoard lies in what should be a Trinovantian area. Its likely deposition date of *c.* A.D. 15 coincides with the period of Catuvellaunian/Trinovantian expansion under Cunobelinus and suggests that the tribal boundary may have fluctuated. The fortified site at Burgh (E) is nearby and this was certainly importing Belgic pottery from Camulodunum in the first half of the CI A.D., but apparently not in its earliest phase, suggesting a possible take-over by the followers of Cunobelinus. A group of late Icenian coin hoards in NW Suffolk may be linked to the hounding of the Iceni by the Romans after the failure of the uprising led by their queen, Boudica, in A.D. 60/61. Two such hoards were found at Lakenheath in 1959 and 1960.

There is an echo of Boudica and her warriors in the numerous finds of chariot fittings in the county. A splendid hoard of bronze terret (rein) rings decorated with red enamel was found at Westhall (E) in 1855. Similar rings are recorded from Weybread and Rushmere and fragments of clay moulds for the manufacture of terrets were found at Waldringfield in 1984/5 (all E). A decorated lynch pin from a chariot wheel was found at Eye (E) in 2008.

ROMAN SUFFOLK

BY JUDITH PLOUVIEZ

The invasion of Britain in A.D. 43 led to the inclusion of the S of Suffolk, the tribal kingdom of the Trinovantes, within the new Roman province. A legionary fortress and subsequent city (Colonia Victricensis) at Colchester continued the pattern of control of this area already established in the Late Iron Age by Cunobelinus and his predecessors. Auxiliary forts have been identified at Baylham Mill, Coddenham (E), and probably Long Melford (W). To the N the rest of Suffolk and Norfolk, the lands of the Iceni, retained a degree of independence as a client kingdom because they had submitted to the emperor at an early stage in the invasion. Despite an unsuccessful minor revolt in A.D. 47, perhaps focused in their western lands around Stonea in Cambridgeshire, the Iceni retained their king, Prasutagus, until his death in A.D. 60. Both areas saw change and exploitation in these early years; it is recorded that the Iceni were lent large sums of money by the Romans. Evidence of the acquisition of Roman goods, and perhaps customs, is seen in hoards such as a group of bronze drinking vessels found in Brandon (W) that included both Continental and native British-made pieces. In A.D. 60 the Roman takeover of the Icenian area, involving the flogging of Prasutagus's widow, Boudica, and the rape of their daughters, led to a serious revolt involving both the local tribes and spreading rapidly across southern Britain. Boudica's revolt was eventually defeated in the Midlands and inevitably eastern England suffered occupation by the Roman army and some redistribution of landholdings, particularly in the core Icenian area. Roads and forts were established across East Anglia, with auxiliary troops again stationed at Coddenham and also at Pakenham (W), just S of Ixworth village, for several years.

The fort at Pakenham was identified by aerial photography in the 1950s and partially excavated in 1984–5. It had triple ditches, but there is no evidence of ramparts. It was constructed in the C1 following the Boudican uprising and was operational for only a few years, although there is evidence of non-military occupation up to the end of the C4. The area in and beyond the fort developed as a small town, with mainly timber buildings along the main and subsidiary roads. Two pottery kilns were excavated in the 1985 area, and others had been discovered previously to the E, at Grimstone End; all produced C2–C3 pottery, including colour-coated tableware.

The ROAD network is the most visible survival of the Roman period in the Suffolk landscape, still followed by several major routes like the modern A140 between Coddenham and Norwich, and the A12 on the same route S to Colchester. E–W routes included one from Coddenham to Peasenhall (both E), much of it now the A1120. The pattern of roads also stimulated the development of small towns at junctions and at river crossings. These were the local trade, manufacture and probably administrative centres between the later C1 and C4. Some, including Pakenham (W), developed over the forts that had been briefly but effectively occupied in the A.D. 60s. The town at Hacheston (E) was discovered in 1964 on Bridge Farm and partly excavated over the following ten years. Like others it may have been a smaller Late Iron Age settlement that benefited from its roadside location. It may have covered up to 90 acres (37 ha). Numerous pottery kilns were identified producing wares of C1–C3 types, including some red tableware, as well as evidence for iron- and bronze-working. A gravel road was flanked by small timber buildings and an oak-lined well.

A large settlement at Icklingham, adjacent to a Roman road from Pakenham, may be the site of Camboricum, mentioned in the Antonine Itinerary as lying between Venta Icenorum and Durolipons (Cambridge). Its extent was confirmed by geophysical survey in the 1990s, but had been indicated by a number of finds. In 1877 partial excavation of a villa revealed part of a hypocaust containing a coin of Carausius (286–93). In the vicinity were found considerable numbers of brooches, pins and bracelets. Ploughing in 1940 uncovered further building material and coins. Nearby the discovery of lead cisterns with Christian symbols (Alpha and Omega and Chi-Rho) in 1939 and 1971 was followed by the excavation in 1974 and 1977 of a C4 Christian cemetery adjacent to a small rectangular building, perhaps a church with detached baptistery. A group of C3 Roman kilns was found in 1937.

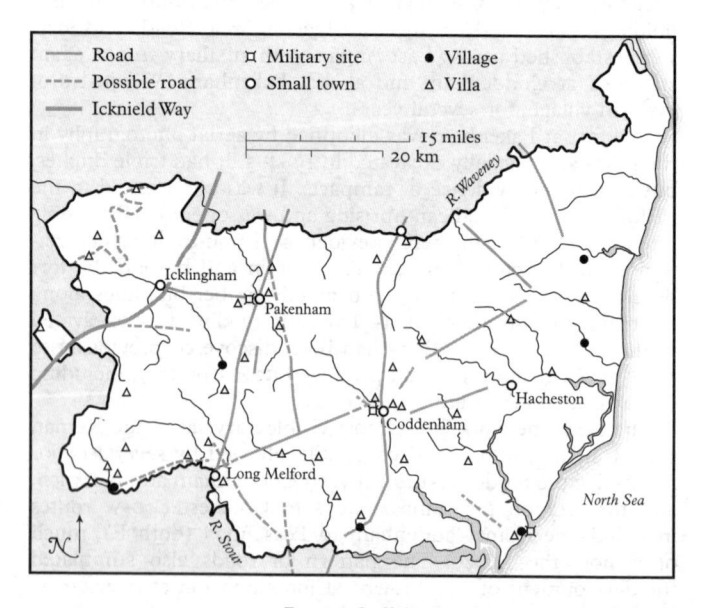

Roman Suffolk

The small Roman town of Combretovium (Coddenham), situated in the Gipping valley at the junction of several roads, was more complex, incorporating both a Late Iron Age centre and subsequent military and civilian establishments. Since 1823, much material has come from the river N and S of Baylham Mill, and the camps were located by air photographs in the vicinity of Baylham House Farm. N of the forts a section cut in 1953 across the road from Camulodunum (Colchester, Essex) to Venta Icenorum (Caistor St Edmund, Norfolk) produced a coin of c. A.D. 70. A statuette of the Emperor Nero (in the British Museum, said to be have been found on land of Barking Hall) indicates a possible imperial shrine, although a mirror case depicting Nero addressing his troops might have come from a burial near the forts. Further excavation prior to construction of the A14, c. 1973–5, uncovered early Roman ditches, pits and a pottery kiln. To the SE a kiln was found containing stamped mortaria of potters known also at Colchester.

The countryside saw more gradual change. By the C1 there were farmsteads all across the landscape, surrounded by areas of managed woodland, pasture and cultivated fields. Almost all rural buildings changed in style from the traditional roundhouse to rectangular during the C1, generally built entirely in timber. At Valley Farm, Coddenham, excavations have revealed evidence of a Roman farm. Finds include coins ranging from the time of Vespasian (A.D. 69–79) to the later C4. At Park Quarry, Flixton (E), the evidence of continued occupation of this site has been shown by post-holes of a substantial Roman building, 46 ft by 36 ft (14 metres by 11 metres), that may be a granary, and a grave containing the bodies of three adults (one male, two females) and a teenager who appear to have met with violent deaths – the male was decapitated and one female has cuts to her head – during the C1.

From the C2 onwards some of the farmhouses can be described as VILLAS. These have flint wall foundations, often for a timber superstructure, but were occasionally entirely built of flint with brick courses. The roofs were tiled or thatched; the plastered walls might be brightly painted and the floors could be tiled or tessellated. Only occasional rooms in the more extravagant villas had patterned mosaic floors, but many had small bath houses either incorporated in a wing of the main building or as a separate structure. The largest and most affluent of the Suffolk villas was at Castle Hill, Ipswich (E), discovered in 1854. Finds included a mosaic floor of geometric design (now in Ipswich Museum) as well as other tessellated floors, pottery and coins of the C1–C4 A.D. and a jet plaque depicting the god Atys. Partial excavation in 1928–9 and rescue work in 1946–50 revealed the complex multi-phase plan of the central building and traces of several subsidiary buildings, one with a roof of stone slates. A separate bath house and an aisled building with a cobbled yard between them were excavated in 1989. The earliest phase of the villa building is probably C2 but the complex was extended and remodelled at least once in the C4. Anglo-Saxon pottery in the robbed-out rooms of the bath house shows that activity continued in the immediate vicinity of this very wealthy establishment after the end of the Roman period.

Another important villa was at Exning (W), sometimes referred to as the Landwade Villa. Excavated in 1904 and 1957–8, it was of tripartite plan with flanking corridors and a N block containing a hypocaust and bath. Four phases were represented. There were C1 A.D. ditches, and a C2 A.D. aisled building, 100 ft (30.5 metres) long and constructed on a timber frame, which was rebuilt on flint and mortar footings with an integral bath house in the late C2–C3 A.D. Further stone walls and a heated room were added later. The building was probably abandoned during the second half of the C4 A.D. A fine semicircular mosaic with a guilloche border and geometrical pattern found in 1904 was removed to what is now the Cambridge Museum of Archaeology and Anthropology.

Another bath house has been found attached to a villa at Stanton (W) that was discovered in 1933. Partial excavation of the SW edge of the settlement revealed a wing c. 300 ft (90 metres) long consisting of an aisled building joined to a double apsidal bath block. It is thought to have been started before c. A.D. 130. The interior of what seems to have been a large estate building included painted rooms with glazed windows and coins ranging from Nero to Honorius, suggesting that it was in use until the end of the C4. The robbed remains of a C3 bath house were excavated at Stonham Aspal (E) in 1962–5. There were two rooms each 10 ft (3 metres) long by 8 ft (2.5 metres) wide. The bath house originally consisted of a cold room with a plunge bath attached and an apsidal heated room. In the last phase the functions of the two rooms were reversed, and a plunge bath and water tank were added. The building was apparently timber-framed on stone footings, with a tiled roof, glazed windows and brightly painted walls.

A villa was found at Ixworth (W) in 1834. Excavations in 1849 revealed an apsidal building with a pillared hypocaust and a coin of Constantine I (307–37). Further excavations in 1948 uncovered another building, with a furnace and a channelled hypocaust. Evidence of destruction and finds of the Saxon period were also recovered; a nearby well contained much Roman debris. Geophysical survey has shown part of a probably contemporary double-ditched enclosure. Nearby, a villa was identified at Redcastle Farm, Pakenham in 1776 and excavated in 1951–2. What was probably a late C1 phase of less substantial buildings was replaced in the C2 by a winged building with a central apsidal-ended room that contained a circular mosaic in a surround of red tesserae (now destroyed). It was apparently occupied until around the C4. At Lidgate (W), Roman remains were ploughed up in 1971 and aerial photography showed the outline of a winged corridor villa, with a buttressed outbuilding nearby and boundary ditches. Aerial photography has also revealed the outline of a square courtyard plan on the S side of Long Melford (W). Another villa has been identified at Brandon (W). Here quantities of building material, including tesserae, fragments of marble, and parts of stone capitals have been found.

At Capel St Mary (W) is the site of what was probably a villa, overlooking the valley above Lattinford Bridge, where there was a roadside settlement on the line of the Roman road to Venta Icenorum (Caistor St Edmund, Norfolk). Two bronze figures of crouching lions, probably ornamental furniture fittings, were found in 1928, and excavation in 1946–7 resulted in finds of window glass, painted plaster fragments, C1/C2 A.D. pottery, and a large number of glass mosaic cubes. In 1963 further tesserae of glass and Samian ware were found associated with kiln debris, and in 1967, about 60 yds E of the 1928 discovery, a cobbled yard was found which was partly overlaid by the *opus signinum* floor of an outbuilding.

At Stanstead (W) remains have been found in a field about ½ m. E of the village of what appears to have been a substantial and well-appointed building. Finds include part of two walls and fragments of hypocaust tiles, *opus signinum* flooring and tesserae. There is also evidence for other buildings nearby, and magnetometry survey has shown that the complex is one of the largest in Suffolk, with several areas of flint and brick building debris and a probable timber aisled building within rectangular ditched enclosures.

Evidence for burial practices in the countryside is sporadic, but an exceptional high-status example is the four burial mounds alongside a road and close to a villa at Rougham (W). More commonly groups of burials are found around the small towns, such as a group of cremation burials discovered in the 1980s at Gallows Hill, Hacheston (E), and several areas of inhumation burials at both Icklingham and Long Melford (both W).

Rural industries included brewing, smithing and salt extraction on the coastal estuaries, probably alongside the collection and efficient distribution of oysters over large distances. Numerous pottery kilns have been identified in the parishes around Wattisfield (W) which span the whole period, and indeed the potting industry was re-established here later in the medieval period.

There were small temples and shrines in both the small towns and the countryside where native, Roman and more exotic deities were celebrated. The C4 Christian church and cemetery at Icklingham, mentioned earlier, probably replaced the temple site to the S at Lackford (W) where a set of bronze priestly head-dresses, known as the Cavenham Crowns, were discovered.

Activity diminished markedly in the E of the county after the middle of the C4, probably reflecting insecurity due to coastal piracy and raiding. From the later C3 the large forts of the Saxon Shore were established around S and E Britain, including Burgh Castle and Walton Castle in Suffolk (both E). Inland there may have been troops based at some of the small towns such as Icklingham in the later C4, but the strongest indication of insecurity by the early C5 is the concealing and non-recovery of numerous precious metal hoards. Many of these consist of a few hundred silver coins, perhaps with a gold ring as at Tuddenham St Martin (E); at Icklingham a hoard of pewter was discovered in 1956 comprising nine vessels, including a pointed oval dish depicting a fish, an iron key, a saw blade and a sherd of *terra sigillata*. Much greater wealth is represented by the Mildenhall Treasure (W), discovered in 1942. Ploughing in a field 30 yds from the site of a two-roomed building, with hypocaust and pottery of C4 A.D. date, revealed the great hoard of thirty-four pieces of elaborate Roman silver tableware (now in the British Museum), also C4. The largest object was the Great Dish, *c.* 2 ft (61 cm.) in diameter, depicting scenes of Bacchic revelry with a central image of Oceanus. This, together with a pair of platters with rustic scenes of satyrs and maenads, may well have been made in Rome. Also important are five baptismal spoons, three of which are engraved with Christian Alpha and Omega and Chi-Rho symbols (cf. those of later date found in the Sutton Hoo ship burial). At Hoxne (E) a boxful of gold and silver coins, spoons and jewellery was found in 1992. The coins in the Hoxne hoard show that it was hidden after the final withdrawal of Roman authority from Britain in A.D. 410. In the C5 the local elite might either retreat to estates and relatives elsewhere in W Britain and the Continent or attempt to maintain their authority locally by employing mercenary soldiers, probably including the earliest Germanic settlers.

SUFFOLK: WEST

The remainder of the Introduction deals principally with the area covered by this volume, the western half of the county. As explained in the Foreword, this includes the whole administrative county of West Suffolk that existed between 1888 and 1974 – the area that corresponds to the medieval Liberty of St Edmund – as well as a band of the Geldable that includes Stowmarket and Needham Market. Whereas Ipswich is tucked away in one corner of E Suffolk, Bury St Edmunds lies at the heart of W Suffolk, with major roads radiating from it in all directions connecting it to the other market towns – Stowmarket, Hadleigh, Sudbury, Haverhill, Newmarket and Mildenhall (and, just over the border in Norfolk, Thetford).

Bury St Edmunds lies on the NW edge of High Suffolk, and most of W Suffolk is composed of this fertile farmland. There are, however, two parts of W Suffolk that have particular characteristics that have shaped the way they have developed. The first is not perhaps immediately obvious, but comprises a stretch of country between Glemsford and East Bergholt (E) that, from the late C13, was a major centre of the woollen cloth industry, and included the towns of Lavenham and Sudbury. A muster roll for the Hundred of Babergh in 1522 recorded sixty weavers in

Boxford, thirty-four clothiers in Lavenham, twenty in Glemsford and fourteen in Nayland. Fullers were concentrated in Long Melford, shearmen in Nayland. The prosperity brought by this industry resulted in some of Suffolk's greatest churches (e.g. Lavenham, Long Melford) as well as a large number of high-quality timber-framed houses. Lavenham is rightly celebrated both for its magnificent church and for its quaint old houses, but it should be understood as a manufacturing town rather than a picture-postcard village. The broadcloth trade declined in the mid C16 but was succeeded by other industries of a similar nature, which grew to considerable proportions in the C19: straw-plaiting, the weaving of silk and horsehair and coconut fibre, the manufacture of drabbet for agricultural smocks. There are still silk mills in Sudbury and a clothing factory in Haverhill.

It is no coincidence that Haverhill and Sudbury (to be precise, its close neighbour Great Cornard) were chosen, after the Second World War, for 'London overspill' housing. The other Suffolk towns to be accorded this dubious honour were Mildenhall and Brandon, which lie in the second distinct area of W Suffolk: the Breckland, NW of Bury St Edmunds. The characteristics of this flat area are the sandy soil, originally covered with heathland and good for little beyond the grazing of sheep and farming of rabbits. Big changes came in the C19 with improvements in agricultural methods that enabled much of this area to be turned into productive farmland, which saw the building up of large estates at Culford and Elveden. The latter in particular was renowned also as a sporting estate, just as some of the estates on the corresponding land on the E side of county, such as Sudbourne, were. A further transformation of the landscape occurred in the C20, after the First World War and the setting up of the Forestry Commission in 1919, when large areas were planted with conifers. In more recent years these have been transformed into country parks and are the principal centres for recreation in W Suffolk. Also in the NW corner of the county, Mildenhall and Lakenheath are better known to the wider world as airbases, opened in 1934 and 1941 respectively and still in operational use (by the United States Air Force). Of great historical interest is the former atomic bomb store at Barnham, c. 1952–5.

A third distinct area also needs to be mentioned, a much smaller one, comprising the town of Newmarket and the parish out of which it grew, Exning. They stick out in a little bubble on the W side of the county, surrounded on all sides by Cambridgeshire and connected to Moulton and the rest of Suffolk only by the old turnpike road (the Icknield Way) and a strip of land about 300 yds (274 metres) wide. Newmarket is of course dominated by horseracing and bloodstock and has a character all of its own, and its presence is felt also in the surrounding countryside, which is largely given over to stud farms with their distinctive paddocks and immaculate grassland and fencing. Since 1994 the bubble has also included Landwade, transferred from Cambridgeshire in that year.

ANGLO-SAXON

The confused account of history and archaeology following the departure of the Romans begins with Vortigern's ill-advised invitation for further settlers in eastern England, against the Picts and Saxons. That Romanized elements remained is clear from coin hoards deposited *c.* 450 at Icklingham (and also near Ipswich in the E of the county), as well as from some of the pottery deposited in the Lackford cemetery, where more than 390 cremations have been discovered. At Undley, in Lakenheath, a gold bracteate (now in the British Museum) was found in 1981. It dates from *c.* A.D. 475. The design is based on a Roman coin, but with a runic inscription that is the oldest known example of Anglo-Saxon writing; its meaning is not clear. The sub-Roman population, if not the last of the Romans themselves, may have been responsible for the linear earthworks such as the Devil's Dyke, along the edge of Newmarket Heath (*see Buildings of England: Cambridgeshire*). It was built across the Icknield Way, the ancient trackway from Dorset to Norfolk that crosses the NW corner of the county. Suffolk's only examples of these earthworks, the Black Ditches at Cavenham, were also possibly intended as an obstacle against the spread of the erstwhile *foederati*, although they may have been constructed as W boundaries for the later Wuffingas kingdom (of which more is said in *Suffolk: East*).

By the mid C5 the valleys of the Lark, Black Bourn and Little Ouse in the NW of Suffolk had been settled by a mixed group of immigrants of Anglian, Saxon and Frisian origin. The settlement at West Stow, on the N bank of the Lark and occupied between *c.* 420 and 650, has been comprehensively excavated and, to a certain extent, re-created, but other SETTLEMENTS have been at least partially excavated at Honington and Pakenham. About 500 a group of North Jutish settlers, practising inhumation and using square-headed brooches, made for Breckland; evidence for them comes from cemeteries at Mildenhall and Lakenheath. An Early Saxon cemetery was discovered at Eriswell in 1957 during construction work at Lakenheath Airfield, when thirty-two burials were excavated. A much larger cemetery nearby was excavated in 1997: a total of 261 graves, including a horse burial, were uncovered. Finds included numerous brooches, beads, spears, shields and iron knives.

The end of the settlement at West Stow corresponds to a general shift in occupation that followed the death of the East Anglian King Anna in 654 and the increasing dominance of Mercia to the W. Over the next two centuries the pattern of towns and villages was established that remains today, with towns at Bury St Edmunds, Clare, Haverhill and Sudbury (the latter mentioned in the Anglo-Saxon Chronicle for 797–8). One of the most extensive Middle Saxon settlements to have been excavated (in 1895–6 and more extensively in 1980–88) is at Brandon. The settlement, which lasted from the mid C7 to the late C9, was originally on a small island in the river. It had at least fifty-two buildings, including a timber church, and the cemetery contained 220 inhumations.

Generally, however, Suffolk is poor in visible Anglo-Saxon ARCHITECTURE. The most conspicuous structures that are often considered to be Saxon are ROUND CHURCH TOWERS, but these are predominantly in the E of the county, and of the eleven in W Suffolk it is doubtful whether any date from before the Conquest. The structural reason for the preference for round as against square towers is the absence in Suffolk of good building stone. Without ashlar, firm corners are hard to build, and the Saxon technique of long-and-short work, that is one large cornerstone laid horizontally to bond deep into both walls and then one yet larger cornerstone set up vertically to cover the angle without worthwhile bonding, did not make for durability. Long-and-short work is found at one round-tower church, Little Bradley, where the age of the tower itself is disputed, and Little Wratting seems to be late Anglo-Saxon. Other churches with long-and-short work are Fakenham Magna and Little Livermere, or what remains of it. Notable SCULPTURAL REMAINS are the crosses at Great Ashfield and Kedington, and the carved panel at Wickhambrook, although the latter is (to judge by the shape of the shield) more likely to be post-Conquest. Other churches with sculptural and decorative fragments (some doubtful) are Aldham, Bury St Edmunds (built into the ruined outer wall of the ambulatory of the abbey), Gedding, Hunston and Thornham Parva.

MEDIEVAL CHURCHES

Norman religious buildings

The distinction between Anglo-Saxon and Norman architecture is not always an easy one to make, and in a sense 1086 is a more important date than 1066, because of the picture that Domesday Book provides of the state of the county in that year. The most remarkable single fact is that about 418 of Suffolk's churches – four out of five of the county's surviving medieval churches – had been founded by then, although most have been rebuilt to a greater or lesser extent. This compares with 274 churches in Norfolk. Suffolk's Domesday churches are spread pretty evenly over the county. By way of further background, the state of MONASTICISM should first be considered, because the major monument of Norman architecture in the county, and one of the mightiest houses of England, was the Benedictine monastery of Bury St Edmunds. In wealth at the time of the Dissolution Bury was inferior only to Westminster, Glastonbury, Canterbury Cathedral, St Albans and Abingdon, and about equal with Peterborough, Ramsey, Reading, Tewkesbury, Winchester and St Mary, York. Other Benedictine houses in W Suffolk were at Edwardstone (very small), Sudbury and Wickham Skeith.

Nearly all of these were founded in the C12. In addition there were three alien cells of the Benedictine house of Bec: Clare, Great Blakenham and Stoke-by-Clare, the first two established in or about 1090. The Cluniac Benedictines had a single priory at Wangford, a mid-C15 foundation. The Augustinian canons are well represented, with houses at Chipley (Poslingford), Ixworth (where some vaulted rooms can still be seen and the plan has been excavated), and Kersey. In addition there was one alien cell (of Saint-Léonard, near Limoges) at Great Bricett, and of that parts of the church and some extremely interesting monastic remains are extant. It was founded *c.* 1110. For completeness' sake the houses of mendicant friars may also be recorded here, although they are of course all of somewhat later foundation. At Bury St Edmunds there was a house of the Franciscans (Greyfriars), and there was a house of the Dominicans (Blackfriars) at Sudbury. The Austin Friars were at Clare (founded 1248), and Crutched Friars at Little Whelnetham (1274). Finally the Templars had a preceptory at Gislingham and the Hospitallers one at Battisford.

To return after this digression to NORMAN ARCHITECTURE in W Suffolk, the abbey church at Bury St Edmunds was certainly one of the major monuments in East Anglia. It was begun in the 1080s and was largely complete by 1140. It was 505 ft (154 metres) long and had an E end with ambulatory and three radiating chapels, N and S transepts with E aisles and a chapel attached to each, a central tower, and a W front probably in its original state more spectacular than any other in England. It had a commanding tower like that of Ely, a W transept like that of Ely, and, as a late C12 addition, octagonal angle towers which gave the front an unparalleled width of 246 ft (75 metres). Of this only the scantiest and least elegant fragments stand upright. What does stand, however, four-square and proudly attired, is the Norman Tower, which served as both as a gate to the abbey church and as a campanile for St James's Church. It was built *c.* 1130. For other substantial evidence of Norman work one can only turn to Polstead, with its surviving Norman arcades. They have piers with nook-shafts, the arches with the early English bricks already mentioned, and a Norman clerestory above them, also with brick arches. Otherwise the Norman churches which remain in Suffolk are unaisled. There are no churches with cruciform plans in W Suffolk, but a longitudinally tripartite plan, i.e. with a raised, tower-like central compartment, exists in its most complete state at Ousden, with others at Pakenham and, probably, Lakenheath. At Wissington, which has nave, chancel and apse, the chancel compartment is tunnel-vaulted and may have carried a tower. More elaborate plans are rare and without exception recorded only by excavation. The ambulatory and radiating chapels of Bury St Edmunds have already been mentioned. Great Bricett Priory had apses E of the transepts and (in all probability) the main apse.

In elevation much of Norman work is visible, but little of it is of more than local interest. The bulk of what survives is purely masonry, not as a rule commented on in the gazetteer, or such minor features as angles with nook-shafts (Great Thurlow, Moulton), or towers or chancel arches or doorways. There are more Norman doorways by far than can here be listed, but especially sumptuous are those of Great Bricett, Honington, Polstead (W door), Poslingford and Wissington. At Poslingford the tympanum of the S doorway is notable, and appears to have been carved in the same workshop that produced the font at Preston St Mary. The doorways at Wordwell also have carved tympana. Of chancel arches it is enough to note Wissington. Round towers have been commented on in connection with Anglo-Saxon architecture. The most spectacular Norman round tower is at Little Saxham (with blank arcading round the bell-stage). The round tower at Wortham is the largest in England, with a diameter of 29 ft (9 metres).

p. 570

8

E.E. and Decorated churches

Of the C13 very little needs recording, and no consistent picture emerges. Nowhere does work of national interest survive. Plans were aisled or unaisled and some evidence of transepts remains (Pakenham, also of the early C14 Earl Stonham). Arcade piers were circular (Hinderclay, Mendlesham) or alternatingly circular and octagonal (Hintlesham). For architectural quality, the first place goes to the N chapel and the chancel of Mildenhall, work, it seems, of Ely Cathedral masons. The good mid-C13 E wall of Little Blakenham, with its deep shafted and trefoiled niches, and the good late C13 N transept of Hunston are also worth a mention. A special minor feature which adds to the attractiveness of chancels is ANGLE PISCINAS, i.e. piscinas placed across the angle of a chancel S window so that the lower part of the jamb and adjoining wall are cut out and the angle of the jamb is caught up by a colonnette. There are examples at Coney Weston, Eriswell, Hinderclay, Ickworth (not *in situ*), Little Wenham, Rickinghall Inferior, Thelnetham and Thornham Magna. Both Eriswell and Thelnetham have two, one in the chancel, another in the S aisle or chapel.

p. 451

11

With the early C14 and the coming of the DECORATED STYLE architectural events began to gather momentum in Suffolk, as prosperity from the woollen cloth trade grew. It becomes less easy to select what ought to figure in a summary such as this. Motifs first, whole buildings second. Window tracery can be followed in many examples from the late Geometrical to the flowing Decorated, by such transitional stages as the Y-form, intersection, cusped intersection, intersection broken by a top circle, etc. The most usual Dec form, i.e. a form with ogee curves, is that known as reticulated. Flowing forms also occur, but Suffolk cannot here compete with such counties as Lincolnshire. A particularly good example of the pre-ogee stage is the E window of Mildenhall, and a particularly good ogee example is the E window of Cotton. A typical Suffolk motif is the

14

four-petalled flower or crossing of two figures of eight. The first datable example of this is on the Great Gate at Bury St Edmunds (begun by 1346). It occurs in many places (e.g. Badwell Ash, Barton Mills, Cowlinge, Flowton, Langham, Stansfield, Troston, Wickhambrook) and not always in the C14 only (Cavendish). After tracery, towers. Spires are extremely rare. Polstead has one of stone of the C14, Hadleigh a lead-covered spire. At Cotton the ground floor of the tower is open in a giant arch to the W, with the nave window appearing at the back of the deep niche thus formed.

Piers are of several forms, the octagonal being the most frequent. A characteristic detail which occurs here and there is one or two blank arch-heads at the top of each side of an octagonal pier. They can be pointed-trefoiled (Lakenheath, Worlington) or have ogee curves (Norton, Walsham-le-Willows). The piers at Burstall have a most unusual, finely detailed section. At Sproughton filleted main shafts and keeled subsidiary diagonal shafts alternate. Rickinghall Inferior, although small, is a nice ensemble with its early C14 S aisle, S porch, and the tower top. But there are plenty of very fine aisleless churches, with tall naves and tall windows, followed sometimes by tall chancels.

Of the celebrated roofs of Suffolk many must go back to the C14, and some may well be of the C13. But as none of them are securely dated, they will be discussed together with their Perp progeny. On the other hand timber porches can by their detail sometimes be assigned C14 dates with certainty. The simple, robust porch of Somersham may even be of before 1300. Of the early C14 porches the most beautiful is that of Boxford with its flowing tracery, its cusped bargeboarding and its vault with flying ribs.

Perpendicular churches

That the PERPENDICULAR STYLE starts in the 1330s is familiar. The first places where it can be found are in London and Gloucester. When it first appeared in Suffolk, it is hard to say. As much of the general impression one receives of Suffolk churches is bound up with the Perp style, a few very general remarks may first be made. Uncommonly many churches in the county lie outside the villages, sometimes at least close to the manor house, sometimes away even from that. That nearly all Suffolk churches are of flint has already been said. Quite a good number are thatched. A surprising quantity of churches are in ruins or marked by the well-known black-letter 'remains of' on Ordnance Survey maps, but there is not the same extent of receding prosperity and depopulation that is evident on the E coast. That was one centre of Golden Age Suffolk; the other was near the Stour and Essex border, the cause of prosperity being the woollen cloth already mentioned. It is true that the two largest parish churches in the county are in neither area but in the shadow of Bury Abbey – St Mary with a length of

213 ft (65 metres) and St James (now the cathedral) with 195 ft (59 metres) – but then follow Lavenham with 156 ft (48 metres) and Long Melford with 153 ft (47 metres). Mildenhall, 168 ft (51 metres) long, is an outlier towards Cambridge. In the same two regions naturally one must look for the same ornate work. It is due usually to merchants, and they not infrequently saw to it that their names were immortalized on the buildings or parts for which they had given money. Thus it is with the Cloptons at Long Melford, the Springs and Branches at Lavenham, the Goldings and Mundys at Glemsford, the Mors, Smyths and others at Stratford St Mary. We are uncommonly well informed on this generosity, as many wills have been published, and it is thanks to the researches of Adrian Allan and Peter Northeast, who have identified hundreds of BEQUESTS to churches in the late medieval period, that we know even more about the construction history of many of these churches than can be read on their walls. Frequent reference is made in the gazetteer to bequests, which often (as at Long Melford) corroborate other evidence. Certain parts of buildings were particularly favoured when it came to leaving money. Towers that can be dated by bequests include Kersey (1430–72; completed 1481), Rougham (1444–88) and Stoke-by-Nayland (1439–76). Money was also left for building porches at Boxford (1441–80) and Stratford St Mary (1510–26). A bequest to Earl Stonham in 1534 to have the church 'new hallowed' was probably prompted by the completion of the church's magnificent hammerbeam roof. The setting of little mirrors in the vaulting over the tomb of John Baret in St Mary, Bury St Edmunds, is specified in his will of 1463. A frequent object for donations was the rood loft, commonly referred to as the 'candlebeam' in wills, and in particular for the painting of it. Although few have survived, they can be a useful indication of the date of the rood screen. A bequest in 1478 for the rood loft at Clare refers to a contract with the carver, *Thomas Goche (Gooch)* of Sudbury.

Now the architecture of Perpendicular churches must be summarized, starting with their plans. That most of them have aisles and many chancel aisles or chapels goes without saying. That aisles are wide and plans close to unmitigated rectangles is also no more than would be expected. A speciality, however, are wide and airy aisleless naves (Copdock, Stowlangtoft), which may nonetheless have clerestories (Wyverstone). They have tall wide windows, as have the Perp aisles too.

TOWERS are usually to the W. Four medieval churches in W Suffolk have S porch towers, noticeably fewer than E Suffolk's sixteen. Of these the one at Stanton may originally have been free-standing; Haughley's is separated from the nave by the S aisle and almost appears to be. PORCHES are among the greatest glories of Suffolk church architecture. The most elaborate of them, such as Woolpit's, appear with the full orchestration of traceried windows, battlements, niches above the entrance, and carved decoration in the spandrels. Not much less overblown is Yaxley; Kersey is more typical. Among the most usual motifs are a Wild Man with a club, said to represent St George, as well as more conventional depictions of St George or St Michael, and the emblems of the Trinity and the Passion. Many porches have upper storeys. That at Mendlesham served as the village armoury, and its door is suitably strengthened (the armoury still contains a fine collection of armour, first assembled c. 1593, and ranging in date from c. 1470 to c. 1640). At Mildenhall (as at Fordham across the Cambridgeshire border) the upper floor is open to the church and served as a Lady Chapel. The Lady Chapel at Long Melford is of the most unusual shape, the chapel itself being surrounded on all four sides by a cloister or ambulatory.

Regarding the elevations, nothing is more typical, not of Suffolk, but of East Anglia, than the CLERESTORY in major churches with closely set windows to a number twice that of the arcade bays below. Such it is at Long Melford, where the nave has nine bays and there are eighteen clerestory windows on either side, at St Mary, Bury St Edmunds, at Lavenham and at Woolpit. Lavenham displays as a crowning crest lacy openwork BATTLEMENTS, and the same *tour de force* was accomplished by the carvers of the Woolpit porch and the clerestory and N aisle at Hessett. But the supreme skill of the carvers went into the CHANTRY CHAPELS built by the richest of the merchants, notably the Clopton Chantry Chapel at Long Melford of the 1490s.

Of individual Perp motifs only a few can be singled out. PIERS occur in a variety of forms, the most usual remaining the octagon, already equally popular in the C14. It comes as a rule with double-chamfered arches and stands for the bread and butter of Perp design. However, many more complex shapes with slender shafts and thin hollows are to be found, usually developed from the motif of shafts attached to a lozenge-shaped core of which often the four sides are hollowed out to a concave shape. A customary refinement (also already popular in the C14) is the withdrawal of capitals from all shafts except those towards the arch openings. Of particular interest are certain forms of piers with carved capitals, some with trails or foliage or vines, others with demi-figures of angels with overlapping spread wings. Variations of these can be seen at Bildeston, Hengrave and Higham, attributed by Birkin Haward to master mason *Hawes* of Occold, although it may simply be that Hawes (known from a contract for work at Wingfield (E)) was just one particularly skilled practitioner of a local tradition. Another motif attached to Hawes is that of windows with stepped transoms, i.e. with transoms crossing the centre light at a higher level than the side lights and with arches below them (e.g. Bildeston, Gislingham). But this is typical of Norfolk too.

As well as Hawes, a handful of other medieval masons are known by name. *William Leyr (Layer)* of Bury St Edmunds owned property in Rougham and left money for the church tower; it is thought he may have designed it, but that it was built by his apprentice *John Forster*. Layer himself seems to have been the mason for work at St Mary, Bury St Edmunds, in the second quarter of the C15. Work at Cavendish has been attributed by John Harvey to *Reginald Ely*, although it might equally be by his apprentice *John Melford* of Sudbury. Both have also been connected with Long Melford, and Melford with Boxford. *Simon Clerk*, the master mason of Bury Abbey who also worked at Eton College and King's College, Cambridge, was granted a thirty-five-year lease of Hessett by the abbey in 1445 and is thought to have rebuilt much of the church there; work at Denston and Long Melford is also attributed to him. *John Wastell*, who worked with Clerk (and may have been his apprentice), lived in Bury St Edmunds in the late C15 and may have worked at St James, Bury St Edmunds, Great Barton, Lavenham (in partnership with Clerk), Nayland and Rattlesden, as well as on Bury St Edmunds Guildhall. A mason known to have worked at Lavenham is *John Rogers*.

Finally, as a postscript, a couple of odd but charming features. First, the way in which the PRIEST'S DOORWAY at Bures is set in a buttress, a motif found elsewhere in Suffolk and East Anglia; second, the placing of ROOD-LOFT STAIRS so that they climb up in the window recess, at Barningham and Whepstead.

So far no distinction has been made between the various MATERIALS used in Perp churches. From all that has been said before readers must have assumed that FLINT held sway, and indeed that is so; carved stone remained rare and has been commented on here and there on the preceding pages. But a feature that was responsible for many of the finest and most characteristic effects of Perp architecture in Suffolk is FLUSHWORK. The technique has already been described (*see* p. 4), and although it originated in the early C14 there was a great change in about 1440 with the introduction of decorative panels, usually square, often including letters and other symbols, which made reference to the Virgin Mary, Jesus, the Holy Trinity, saints, donors etc. One is hard put to it to decide on preferences, but Long Melford

Woodbridge (E), St Mary, flushwork monogram of
the Virgin and device of Thomas Aldryche.
Drawing by J. Blatchly, 2005

must be among them and, without any doubt, that little gem the chapel of Gipping, built as a detached private chapel at the end of the C15 to serve a mansion of which no stone remains. It appears the most dainty glasshouse inside, and has a most odd N annexe. One master of the art of flushwork was *Thomas Aldryche* of North Lopham, Norfolk, who had his own geometrical device, an orb with fleur-de-lys finial in a circle, that can be found on a number of churches and which, together with other stylistic features, links him to the towers of Badwell Ash, Earl Stonham, Elmswell, Ixworth, Mendlesham and Rougham, as well as the clerestories of Bacton, Redgrave, Walsham-le-Willows and Wortham.

BRICK, it will be remembered, had been in use in Suffolk from the C12, if not earlier. But it remained quite rare and only came into its own about 1500. It was used mostly in the rebuilding of towers, but also for porches, of which the best are Great Bradley and Ixworth Thorpe. Even window frames and tracery were occasionally made of brick, and in the 1520s a new material made its appearance: TERRACOTTA. A group of buildings have windows with moulded terracotta frames, apparently made by the same band of itinerant craftsmen, who appear to have first worked at Layer Marney, Essex, and then made their way up to Norfolk. The Suffolk buildings are Barking and (in E Suffolk) Shrubland Old Hall and the churches at Barham and Henley.

As for TIMBER, there is no shortage of porches, but for open TIMBER ROOFS Suffolk stands supreme. There are splendours in other counties as well, especially the other counties of East Anglia and also Somerset. But no county is richer *in toto* or has more varieties of type. Birkin Haward and Philip Aitkens distinguished nine main types of church roof, of which the largest

Shrubland Old Hall (E), terracotta tile unit.
Drawing by B. Haward, 1997

across the county as a whole is the single hammerbeam, popular from the late C14 to the C16, although less numerous in the W than the E. Earl Stonham can without hesitation be called the most beautiful single hammerbeam roof in England. Other good examples include Bardwell, Palgrave and Rougham. Bardwell's is a rare example of a dated roof (1421). Money was left for painting Palgrave's roof in 1471, so presumably it had then been recently finished. Money was left for the hammerbeam roofs at Burstall (1510), and we know from a bequest that Hawstead's roof was still being built as late as 1552. Double hammerbeam roofs are even more celebrated, and can be divided into true and false; the latter are called false because the upper hammers carry no vertical posts. Double hammerbeams are even more concentrated in Suffolk: there are thirty-two in England as a whole, of which twenty-one are in Suffolk, four in Norfolk, four in Essex and three in Cambridgeshire. True double hammerbeams are Hepworth, Hitcham, Little Stonham, and the hall of Giffords Hall, Stoke-by-Nayland. False double hammerbeams are concentrated in a small area that includes Bacton, Cotton, Gislingham, Rattlesden, Tostock, Wetherden and, perhaps the finest, Woolpit; there is another further away at Kedington. Within the overall category of hammerbeam roofs variations occur, such as alternating between hammerbeams and tie-beams (Badwell Ash, Redgrave, Walsham-le-Willows), or between normal arched braces and hammerbeams on arched braces (St Mary, Bury St Edmunds, Hawstead, Kersey, Wyverstone) or between normal arched braces and double hammerbeams on arched braces (Cotton, Tostock). Moreover, much could be done by sheer ornament or other decoration, such as the long and incomprehensible story that runs along the wall-plate at Kersey (and is incidentally carved in stone), or the scenes in the spandrels at Mildenhall, or the pretty conceits in the splendid double hammerbeam roof of Giffords Hall. Of other types of roof, the cambered tie-beam roof is one particularly found in W Suffolk, in the churches built with the profits of the woollen cloth trade (Cavendish, Lavenham, Long Melford, Nayland etc). Lakenheath and Mildenhall (and a few others) have roofs with queenposts on tie-beams, a form popular in NW Norfolk. The arch-braced collar roof is less common in the W of the county than the E, but occurs here and there (Rushbrooke, Yaxley).

One roof, finally, stands on its own: Needham Market. To understand it, it must be seen and its description (p. 421) read. Perhaps it should primarily be called a hammerbeam roof with vertical posts standing on the hammers and running up to a collar. But the feet of the hammerbeams are longitudinally connected by raking-out boarding, and the rafters do not continue at their regular pitch from the level of the collars upward but are caught by a strong purlin on which a clerestory with ample windows is erected; on this, high above the collars, is a low-pitched tie-beam roof. The space between the posts standing on the hammerbeams and the unusually tall ashlar struts running from the wall-plate to the rafters is like an aisle suspended in mid-air, to which the clerestory is in the right relation, contributing to the designer's achievement of an entire make-believe church floating high above the one in which we stand.

Medieval church furnishings and monuments

Among CHURCH FURNISHINGS, FONTS should be considered first as there are far more of them than of anything else and because they alone spread over all the medieval centuries from the C11 or C12. Of Norman fonts, none is of more than county interest. Those with carving include a small group at Hawkedon, Little Thurlow and Preston St Mary, with square bowls with angle shafts, the faces carved with foliage and, at Preston, more complex motifs. Others with carving, but not part of the same group, are at Kettlebaston and, of the late C12, the wild font at Great Bricett. A purer E.E. form with gables and stiff-leaf foliage is at Lakenheath. For the late C12 and C13 the most characteristic products are the mass-produced square or octagonal font bowls of Purbeck marble with very shallow blank, round or pointed arches along the sides, of which there are seven in W Suffolk (at Layham, unusually, hexagonal). For the C14 the most characteristic designs have arcading, and there is a whole little group of bowls with panels decorated by what might be described as very shallow blank windows with their appropriate tracery. The earliest of these, at Gazeley, need not be later than 1300. The others are at Barningham, Barton Mills, Coney Weston, All Saints, Icklingham, and Rickinghall Inferior.

But the type which H. M. Cautley calls East Anglian pure and simple, and of which indeed, in its various minor modifications, the county numbers more than a hundred, is Perp. It is characterized by the following motifs which need not all be present in all examples: a stem with four seated lions set against it, or with four lions and four Wild Men (or woodwoses); a bowl often supported by angels with spread wings and occasionally by heads with contemporary head-dresses instead; and an octagonal bowl with on its panels the Emblems of the four Evangelists and four angels or demi-figures of angels holding shields with armorial bearings, or simply shields with the arms of donors or other dignitaries, or the Emblems of Christ's Passion or the Trinity, or flowers, or any combination of these motifs. There are few in the western third of the county, i.e. W say of Woolpit, but Pakenham is an excellent example. They bear out one's impression of Perp England: much lavish display going with much standardization. The most ambitious Perp fonts are those with reliefs of the Seven Sacraments, of which there is just one example in W Suffolk, at Denston. As the sacraments could account for only seven of the eight panels of the octagonal bowl an eighth scene was necessary, in this case the Crucifixion, and all the panels here have rayed backgrounds. At Finningham the font is made more prominent by being raised on two steps, the upper step forming a Maltese cross. At Hessett there is an inscription on the step naming the donors; the font is thought to have been made in Norwich *c.* 1451.

The mason's work on the font was crowned by the carpenter's work on the FONT COVER, and Suffolk possesses some of the finest and giddiest of England, canopies of great height and intricacy. St Gregory, Sudbury, is outstanding. Hepworth has pretty little men coming seemingly out of pretty little doors. Of probably the same time, *c.* 1500–20, is Bramford; and Finningham, though much less ambitious, has very curious tracery motifs worth pondering over. A little smaller but charming also is the font cover at Barking.

By and large, however, the wood carver's highest achievement was not in font covers but in SCREENS. Again, as in fonts, the C15 and early C16 were more sumptuous than the C14 had been. The earliest wooden screens, at Badley (as far as one can tell), Brent Eleigh, Burstall, Eriswell, Harleston, Lavenham, Santon Downham and Westhorpe have round shafts with capitals instead of mullions and simple flowing tracery. One fine stone screen of the early C14 survives, at Bramford, over-restored unfortunately in its upper parts. Of Perp screens there is a glut. The most gorgeous perhaps are those of the Spring Chapel at Lavenham, again restored but carefully so, and the rood screen at Barking. The latter has the coving for its loft preserved, and can be dated by a bequest for rood figures to 1464. Walsham-le-Willows can be dated by bequests for the rood beam in 1441 and 1448. It was mentioned above that *Thomas Gooch* of Sudbury was named in a will of 1478 as the maker of the rood loft at Clare. Tim Howson has identified other screens, at Kersey, Stradishall, and All Saints and St Peter, Sudbury, as the products of Gooch's workshop, and notes a similarity between tracery on the screens and that on the pulpit at Newton. Howson has also identified a larger group of related screens likely to have come from one workshop, comprising five in a relatively small area of Suffolk (Great Livermere, Langham, Rickinghall Inferior, Risby and Stowlangtoft) and seven in Norfolk, up to thirty miles away.

In the panels of the dados of Suffolk (and Norfolk) screens there are often painted figures of saints, apostles and occasionally donors. The aesthetic quality of these paintings is almost without exception low. Wyverstone is unusual in that the panels, which show the Annunciation, Nativity, Magi, Mass of St Gregory, and Visitation, are not painted but carved in relief. WALL PAINTING as a rule is no better. The Doom of Stanningfield is an example. Churches were extensively painted with figures, scenes and ornament, and often no doubt all over their interiors. Here again subjects are oddly standardized: St Christopher facing the main door, the Seven Deadly Sins (growing on a tree), the Seven Works of Mercy, the Three Quick and the Three Dead. A so-called Christ of the Trades is at Hessett. Early wall paintings survive at Risby (early C13) and Wissington (mid C13). An especially good series of *c.* 1300 is at Little Wenham. Analysis of the paintings at Lakenheath during conservation in 2009 identified five separate phases of painting, dating back to *c.* 1200, with schemes being overpainted to reflect changing liturgy and taste. A similar situation can be observed at Troston, with its fine late C14 St George and the Dragon. The supreme item of painted work in a Suffolk church is the retable at Thornham Parva. The style is East Anglian and it was most probably painted in Norwich, perhaps for the Blackfriars at Thetford, established in 1335.

There are many scattered fragments of medieval STAINED GLASS, the most impressive ensemble being at Long Melford, although the late C15 glass was assembled in the C19 and re-set in the C20. An exceptional single piece in the same church is the mid-C14(?) lily crucifix. Churches with complete figures include Bardwell, Drinkstone, Norton and Rushbrooke. A rarity is the window with grisaille foliage at Hunston, which may be C13, and the charming birds at Great Whelnetham, holding texts in their beaks, are also unusual.

Now we must return to WOODWORK, and to the job which at the end of the Middle Ages brought results almost as fine and varied as screens: BENCHES. Suffolk benches are many; some churches have whole series. They have poppyheads and ends decorated excellently or less excellently with tracery patterns. In addition backs and fronts can be carved, or traceried, and so on. On the arms and sometimes the very poppyheads there can be seen figures, monsters, animals, human beings, kneeling or seated, and angels. At Finningham one can see the Vices, at Ixworth Thorpe the thatcher with his comb, at Withersfield in the poppyheads St George and the Dragon and St Michael weighing souls, and so on. A bench at Earl Stonham has the remains of an inscription asking for prayers for the soul of Necolai Houk. CHOIR STALLS are of less interest, though here and there also are occasionally fine traceried ends (Stowlangtoft) and genre figures on the arms (at Norton a boy being beaten, at Earl Stonham a bagpiper), and there are in addition MISERICORDS with scenes such as St Martin and the Beggar, the Martyrdom of St Thomas (both Fornham St Martin, not *in situ*), and the Martyrdom of St Edmund and St Andrew (both Norton). WOODEN DOORS with decoration are something of a speciality. Blank tracery is to be found on many, and on fewer doors a border of quatrefoils (e.g. Thorpe Morieux) or a border of foliage trails (e.g. Brettenham, Clare) or linenfold panelling (e.g. Lavenham, Nayland), or indeed small figures (Stoke-by-Nayland). No PULPITS of special beauty or elaboration need notice. One of the best is that at Stoke-by-Clare, money for making which was bequeathed in 1498. The pulpit at Newton has an inscription asking for prayers for the donors. Only a small selection of CHESTS is included in the gazetteer. That at Chevington is notable for its elaborately carved front, Icklingham for its wrought-iron scrollwork and to a lesser extent Poslingford, the latter tree-ring-dated to the last quarter of the C13, making it the oldest dated chest in Suffolk (although a date of 1199 has been claimed for Norton). Earl Stonham is decorated with a pattern of roundels that places it in a group with others in Cambridgeshire (Longstanton), Surrey and West Sussex (including Chichester Cathedral). Mendlesham has a collection of no fewer than six, and there was formerly at least one more. They are kept in the armoury that occupies the upper storey of the porch, its door iron-bound for security. There are similarly strengthened doors to the towers at Hopton and Stowlangtoft, the latter completely iron-clad. As for other METALWORK, there are the stately brass LECTERNS at Cavendish, Clare and Woolpit.

Rare survivals from pre-Reformation England are the C16 SINDON or pyx-veil that belongs to Hessett, and the same church's early C14 BURSE. The SEXTON'S WHEEL at Yaxley, dating from not long before the Reformation, was used to choose the Lady Day for starting a fast that lasted for a year, one day a week. One other example is known. Even rarer, not to say unique, is the HEAD of Archbishop Simon Sudbury, cut off by the rebels in the Peasants' Revolt and preserved in St Gregory, Sudbury. This really brings us to FUNERAL MONUMENTS. We may indeed begin with brasses, for W Suffolk possesses one of the earliest and finest in England, the Bures brass at Acton of *c.* 1320. Other outstanding brasses, all of the early C15, are those of the Burgates at Burgate, John Knyvet at Mendlesham, and Sir William Tendring at Stoke-by-Nayland. Oaken effigies start a little later than brasses, stone effigies considerably later. Of the early C14 is the wooden Knight at Bures. The Poleys rendered in wood at Boxted are as late as *c.* 1587.

p. 76
p. 123
p. 404
p. 497

At the beginning of the series of stone effigies stands that venerable fragment of a coffin-lid with the lower part of the figure of Aubrey †1441, master chamberlain of England, at St Stephen's Chapel, Bures, which comes from Colne Priory, Essex. The next de Vere there is of the 5th Earl of Oxford †1296. The effigy lies on a tomb-chest, with small fine figures of the early C14, which does not belong to the figure and seems to be part of a former shrine. There is nothing else of importance from the C13 or early C14 except perhaps a lady of the early C14 at Newton, but one might mention the impressive tomb recess at Chelsworth as an example of how these monuments were given beautiful settings and were often an integral part of the building. Of the late C14 and early C15 the de Veres of *c.* 1371 and 1417 at Bures may be mentioned. More of between the mid C15 and the mid C16: Sir William Clopton †1446 and John Clopton †1497 at Long Melford, Sir Thomas Barnardiston †1503 at Kedington. The Middle Ages died hard, even as Renaissance designs were taking hold: the monuments of *c.* 1568 and *c.* 1569 at Lakenheath and Mellis respectively have no Renaissance motif whatever, although the former does have Roman lettering.

15

MEDIEVAL SECULAR BUILDINGS

Domesday Book recorded MARKETS in W Suffolk at Bury St Edmunds, Clare, Haverhill, Stowmarket and Sudbury. Most of the remaining markets date from the C13–C14, e.g. Mildenhall

1220, Nayland 1227/8, Toppesfield (Hadleigh) 1252, Brandon 1319/20, and Ixworth 1384. Mendlesham (1280) and Bildeston (by 1348) are good examples of towns where the market place has been largely built over, but its former extent can still be deduced from the present street pattern. Newmarket (first recorded in 1219), Botesdale (1227) and Needham Market (1226) all began as markets established on busy roads in outlying parts of their respective parishes, Exning, Redgrave and Barking. But it is noticeable that there are relatively few markets within easy reach of Bury St Edmunds, the abbey perhaps being careful not to allow markets that would take business away from its own. As far as Bury itself is concerned, not the least remarkable aspect of the town, and one rarely taken in by visitors, is its TOWN PLAN, for it was laid out by Abbot Baldwin, who ruled from 1065 to 1097, on a grid system that relates directly to the layout and dimensions of the abbey church. One substantially intact stone-built house of the late C12, Moyse's Hall, survives from Norman Bury St Edmunds, and a number of other houses scattered about the centre of the town contain remains of Norman stone fabric within them, notably Norman House, Guildhall Street, with a complete Norman doorway.

The CASTLES in the western part of Suffolk were of the motte-and-bailey variety. Those at Clare and Haughley were built soon after the Conquest as the *caput* or administrative centre of the estates of Richard de Clare and Hugh de Montfort respectively. Both had stonework, but only part of the C13 shell-keep of Clare survives. Another motte-and-bailey castle with stonework was at Freckenham. Other remaining mottes are at Gazeley (Denham Castle), Great Ashfield, Groton, Lindsey and Milden, as well as a ditched mound at Lidgate. At Chevington the ditches show that the vanished C13 or C14 palace of the abbots of Bury was at least semi-fortified, as was Little Wenham Hall: that is to say, it was fortified, but was first and foremost a manor house and not a keep. It was built in the 1270s or 1280s. It is also of interest for being built largely of brick, and may be the earliest domestic brick building in England. It is L-shaped, and on its principal floor hall and chapel join and are connected by a very pretty tripartite arrangement of doorway and windows. It is assumed that there was a free-standing, timber-framed hall. The same change from fortress to house occurs at the same moment at Stokesay and Acton Burnell in Shropshire, though in different forms. One can say that by 1300 the foundations were laid for the development of the English manor house.

The stone-built houses of Bury St Edmunds were very much the exception, in terms both of the material used and their great age. Otherwise the general rule was TIMBER FRAMING, and for this we can go back as far as the late C13. The earliest house that can be dated with any accuracy (by tree-ring dating) is Abbas Hall, Great Cornard, timbers for which were felled in 1289–90. The prior's house at Great Bricett and Purton Green, Stansfield, are of similar date. One of the most characteristic features of the timber-framed manor house is the arrangement of hall, screens passage, and doorways to service rooms and staircase, clearly in evidence at both Great Bricett and Purton Green. The hall at Purton Green is aisled, as was originally Abbas Hall. A slightly later aisled hall was that of mid-C14 Edgar's Farm, Stowmarket (now in the Museum of East Anglian Life). A significant development in the late C13 was the raised-aisle hall, where the normal structure of the aisle hall is raised up on a tie-beam, thus clearing the floor of arcade posts; the upper truss usually carries a crown-post. Although these do occur elsewhere in England, notably in Essex, most of the known examples are in E Suffolk, concentrated in an area around Stradbroke, but there are a few in the western part of the county: Boynton Hall, Capel St Mary (C14), Peyton Hall, Hadleigh (c. 1300), Nos. 87–88 High Street, Lavenham (late C14 or early C15), and Down Hall, Preston St Mary (c. 1400). Crown-posts, incidentally, also emerge in about 1300; before that date there are none known in Suffolk, but in the C14 they are the main roof type. They are found mainly in the middle of the county, in the rich commercial and agricultural regions, with very few in the towns and villages along the E and W fringes. There is a crown-post with a finely carved capital in the mid-C14 range of St Clare Hall, Bradfield St Clare. This range was once longer and its two floors were undivided, leading to the suggestion that it may have been an exceptionally early example of a manorial court hall.

The halls of LATE MEDIEVAL HOUSES share the high quality of timberwork with the churches. Giffords Hall, Stoke-by-Nayland, has already been introduced. It is delightful in every other respect as well. It shares its name with Giffords Hall, Wickhambrook, a late C15 house made especially picturesque by its moat. The same can be said for Columbine Hall, Stowupland, the oldest parts of which are late C14. Domestic MOATS are found across the claylands of High Suffolk, where the soil is particularly suitable for them, and there are over 900 moated sites in the county, a figure approached only by Essex. They

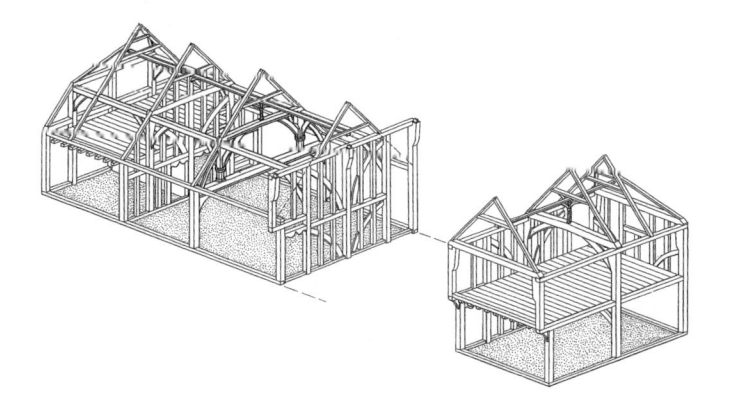

Down Hall, Preston St Mary, timber framing.

date from the later C12 to the mid C16, but mostly belong to the period 1200–1325. The earliest are circular but most are rectangular, and the size of the moat platform was a reflection of status: an acre was the norm for the lord of the manor or for a monastic property, half an acre for a parsonage or for lesser freemen. Both can be seen by the church at Brockley. Moats were not primarily defensive: the spoil from digging a moat was used not to make a bank, but to raise the platform and thus improve drainage and make the house more visible. There was often a subsidiary moat to enclose barns and other farm buildings, which seldom occupied the same platform as the house. At Shelley Hall is the unusual case of a moated enclosure that contains a pleasure garden and is thought to have been built as such in the early C16 rather than adapted from the site of an earlier house.

For TOWN AND VILLAGE HOUSES there is nothing to beat Lavenham in numbers or variety, closely followed by Nayland. The principal ornamental motifs of these houses are thin buttress-shafts, carved corner-posts with brackets, carved bressumers, carved oriel sills and carved bargeboards (e.g. Salter's Hall, Sudbury). But it is important to remember that most of these houses were places of business as well as homes, with a workshop occupying part of the front (usually in the front service room, to one side of the hall and screens passage), private accommodation above, and warehouses and workshops further back. A house that illustrates this on a grand scale, as well being visually a delight, is Alston Court, Nayland. Sometimes houses have retained their original shop windows, as at Nos. 10–11 Lady Street, Lavenham. Bildeston Hall contains the remains of early C16 tenements with workshops that fronted the town's market place. Also in Bildeston (Nos. 23–39 Chapel Street) is an example of early C16 'renters', small timber-framed hall houses built for renting out. Others that have been identified include late C14 examples in Nayland (No. 17 Court Street) and Sudbury (Nos. 51–52 Church Street). A particular type of house, more commonly found in towns and villages than the countryside, is the Wealden house, that is to say with cross-wings and a recessed centre under a single roof. The oldest in Suffolk seems to be Hill House, Woolpit, which may be as early as the third quarter of the C14; the oldest known example in Kent, where Wealden houses are most numerous, has been tree-ring-dated 1379/80 (Chart Hall, Chart Sutton). There is an unusually large example in Stowmarket (Nos. 22–26 Stowupland Street), and an unusually small one in Clare (the Cock Inn), their halls 56 ft (17 metres) and 11 ft (3.4 metres) long respectively. The distinctive Wealden structure at Clare is concealed by a later front, as is that of c. 1420 behind the brick front of the Blue Boar, Walsham-le-Willows. A particularly fine example is Street Farm, Barton Mills, of c. 1500, with high-quality timberwork including octagonal crown-posts; the open hall had a brick chimneystack from the start, something of an innovation in 1500.

An important building type of towns and large villages was GUILDHALLS, mostly built during the hundred years before guilds were suppressed in 1548. Most parishes in W Suffolk had guilds, and the majority at least two. Guildhalls are usually found near the church, jettied towards it, and often remained in some form of public use after the Reformation and the abolition of guilds, e.g. as almshouses or, later, parish workhouses. Two of the best known are those in Hadleigh, *c.* 1451, and Lavenham, built on a site given in 1529 – one of five guildhalls in that town. Lavenham Guildhall had a relatively small hall on the ground floor, which was unheated, indicating that it was for public rather than domestic use. The upper floor was subdivided and probably used for storage. Hadleigh was more typical in having its hall on the upper storey. Examples of smaller guildhalls are at Bardwell (late C15), Hawstead (*c.* 1478), Nayland (*c.* 1530), Walsham-le-Willows (*c.* 1500) and Yaxley (early C16). Similar to guildhalls were church houses, forerunners of village halls: an example is at Cockfield, on the edge of the churchyard, jettied with exposed timbers and brick-nogging towards the church.

Before we leave timber framing something should also be said about BARNS, because aisled barns, both medieval and later, are a particular feature of W Suffolk. Many have been rebuilt or demolished – the C14 barn next to St Bartholomew's Chapel, Sudbury, was burnt down only in 2011 – but substantial early survivals are Old Hall Farm, Alpheton (late C13 or earlier), and Manor Farm, Great Barton (second half of the C13). The barn at Desning Hall, Gazeley, also dates back to the C13.

EARLY TUDOR BRICK can be seen first in the Deanery Tower at Hadleigh, built by Archdeacon Pykenham probably in about 1485. It has panelled polygonal corner turrets and friezes of little trefoiled arches. All these are current motifs of that moment in England (Buckden Palace, Hunts., Faulkbourne Hall, Essex, Oxburgh, Norfolk, and Someries Castle, Beds.). It was a freestanding gatehouse rather than a fragment of an unbuilt or demolished mansion, a display of the archdeacon's wealth and power. The dovecote at Stoke-by-Clare, placed in a prominent location and with emblems of status in its brickwork, was perhaps intended to convey a similar message. There are several more early Tudor gatehouses of brick in Suffolk, the finest no doubt those of Giffords Hall, Stoke-by-Nayland (*c.* 1520–5), and West Stow Hall (*c.* 1530). Gedding Hall is probably earlier (1480s); Shelley Hall was built by 1533. They must be looked at in conjunction with the brick mansions and houses of Norfolk and Essex, and, like them, continue straight into the Renaissance, if the introduction of occasional Italian motifs justifies the use of that term.

CHURCHES AND CHAPELS 1540–1840

As far as actual CHURCH BUILDING is concerned, this came to a standstill at the Reformation as everywhere in England, and did not recover for a long time. The late Middle Ages had built so much that no new needs arose right into the C19. What can be mentioned is almost without exception small fry: the Perp chancel of 1617 at Clare, the rebuilt chancel of Boxted with its Jacobean hammerbeam roof, the similar roof at Wickhambrook. The exception, however, is an important one, the church at Euston, built in 1676 on an elongated central plan of the type undoubtedly derived from Wren's work in the City of London. For the C18 there is equally little: Shelland, remodelled in 1767, and towers added to Cowlinge (1733) and Redgrave (1784). On the other hand the NONCONFORMISTS, who could only in the C17 begin to build freely, contributed a few chapels which ought to find space in any book dealing with their architecture nationally and not locally. In W Suffolk the finest such building is the Unitarian meeting house in Bury St Edmunds, built by the Presbyterians in 1711, with its fine red brick front, tall arched windows and galleried interior. Other early chapels are those in Whiting Street, Bury St Edmunds, *c.* 1700, but rebuilt in 1802; Long Melford, 1725–6; and Wickhambrook, 1733–5. The Friends built modest meeting houses in Needham Market *c.* 1704, Bury St Edmunds 1749–50, and Sudbury 1804. ROMAN CATHOLICS had to wait longer, until the Catholic Relief Act of 1791 allowed them to build churches under licence (without bells or steeples). The chapel at Bury St Edmunds was illegal when it was built in 1762, hidden from the street by the presbytery; it now forms a side chapel to the monumental and severely classical church of 1836–7 by *Charles Day* of Worcester. Much simpler is the church at Withermarsh Green, Stoke-by-Nayland, 1825–7.

Of CHURCH FURNISHINGS there is nothing to note until the C17, with the exception of the ROYAL ARMS at Preston St Mary. They are Elizabethan, of which few survive, and magnificently painted. The arms of Henry VIII at Rushbrooke were introduced in the C19 and must be treated with caution. Otherwise one must wait until the Jacobean (or Carolean) PULPITS. Here the decoration, apart from blank arches, is by means of panels with arabesques and dolphins or monsters and by raised diamond-cut knobs or the raised motifs which look like exclamation marks. No development can be recognized between the dated examples in W Suffolk: Great Ashfield (1619), Mendlesham (1630), Yaxley (1635). Yaxley is the richest, but for Mendlesham there is the added interest of knowing who made it: *John Turner*, who at the same time was commissioned to make the FONT COVER, a fanciful piece with columns, pediments and obelisks. Another good font cover is at Boxford, of cupboard type with painted texts on scrolls inside. For complete interiors there is nothing until Euston, with the furnishing of the new church in 1676. Besides the pulpit, the WOODWORK here includes a reredos and screens. Of similar date is the woodwork at Great Waldingfield, both in the church and the rectory, which was removed from St Michael, Cornhill, in the City of London in the C19. The pulpit at Great Livermere of *c.* 1700, with its frieze of

CHURCHES AND CHAPELS 1540–1840 41

acanthus foliage, is also noteworthy. The contrast between the low chancel screen at Euston and a 'Jacobean' screen such as that of Kedington, dated 1619, is as patent as it is in pulpits, and the new spirit is seen also in, for example, the COMMUNION RAILS at Kedington (strongly moulded balusters) and Boxted (twisted balusters). Both sets have survived in their original three-sided form; others are at Brent Eleigh, Elmsett, Great Livermere, Ixworth Thorpe, Lindsey and Polstead. BENCHES in the C17 continued in the medieval traditions. One can even find C17 poppyheads (Great Livermere, 1601).

To Georgian church furnishings Suffolk makes little contribution. Gipping Chapel was very prettily refurnished and decorated in about 1743, and the original furnishings at Shelland are intact. The interiors of churches such as Kedington and Gislingham, the latter with box pews of 1810 and three-decker pulpit of 1802, are still essentially Georgian in character. C18 box pews at Brent Eleigh, as elsewhere, incorporate parts of medieval benches. For complete contrast one should travel to Rushbrooke and see the results of *Col. Robert Rushbrooke*'s antiquarian taste: a reordering in the 1820s, with woodwork carved and assembled by himself incorporating old materials of high quality pieced together with whatever came to hand. He also installed fragments of old stained glass, but most of his collection, gathered from monasteries in Brussels between 1801 and 1804, went to Nowton. Admirers of *John Constable* will seek out his painting of Christ blessing bread and wine at Nayland (1809).

As we saw with Lakenheath and Mellis, the influence of the Renaissance was slow to make itself felt in CHURCH MONUMENTS. But there are glimpses. The Codington monument at Ixworth (†1567) is a chest tomb of medieval form but with prettily decorated pilasters and, on the back wall, a round arch with leaf carving of a very pure Italian style. Also of the 1560s the monument to the Countess of Bath at Hengrave (†1562) has the full accompaniment of a heavy Tuscan six-column canopy – Elizabethan at its sturdiest and without any Gothic hangover. But monuments on that scale still remained rare in Suffolk. The only comparable one before 1600 is Sir William Cordell †1581 at Long Melford, also with detached columns. Then the pace quickens, and for the years between 1600 and 1620 a number of monuments ought to be considered here. The Lewkenor monument (†1605) at Denham and Sir Thomas Kytson †1603 (erected 1608) at Hengrave are more six-posters. Elizabeth Drury †1610 at Hawstead, Sir Robert Gardener †1619 at Elmswell and Sir John Cotton †1620 at Landwade are represented not recumbent, but stiffly reclining on their sides. Other big monuments, Jacobean in date or style, may be noted at Bures (†1613), Stoke-by-Nayland (†1615), Little Thurlow (†1619; very good), Milden (†1627; also very good), and Denham (†1634, by *John & Matthias Christmas*, 1638). A familiar Elizabethan and Jacobean type of monument has kneeling instead of recumbent effigies, the most interesting perhaps being those where, above figures kneeling in profile, the principal figure is kneeling frontally. Such it is in the

Paul D'Ewes monument at Stowlangtoft and the Crane monument at Chilton. The former is known to be by *Jan Janssen* (contract of 1624 for £16 10s.), the latter by *Gerard Christmas* (contract of 1626 for £50). So here monuments cease to be anonymous for us, even if the individuality of the Janssens and Christmases is hardly worth special study.

It is different with *Nicholas Stone*. We can follow him closely from 1613 onwards, when he returned to England from Holland where he had studied his art, and his work always repays attention, partly for reasons of sculptural quality and partly for reasons of iconography. In Suffolk his accomplishment as a sculptor is patent in all its purity in the earliest dated work in the county, the Bacon monument of 1616 at Redgrave, for which he and *James White* received £200. They deserved it. There is no novel conceit here. The effigy is recumbent, and architecture plays no part. Yet a great nobility is achieved. Some other works by Stone in w Suffolk are minor (Redgrave †1621, †1626), but two others are of considerable iconographical interest as illustrating the most progressive trends in monument design in England. The Whettell monument (†1628/9) at Ampton has a frontal bust and the Drury monument (†1615) at Hawstead a frontal demi-figure in an oval niche. These two forms are matched or imitated by the frontal busts in shallow relief placed in oval niches of the Stuteville monument (†1631) at Dalham, the frontal bust in a circular niche of the Eldred monument of 1632 at Great Saxham, the two frontal demi-figures in circular niches of the Calthorpes of 1638 at Ampton (by the *Christmas* brothers), the two demi-figures turning to one another of the Tyrell monument (†1641) at Stowmarket (attributed to *Edward Marshall*), the two demi-figures of the Sayers (†1625 and †1647) at Nettlestead, the three demi-figures of the Gurdons of 1648 at Assington, and the demi-figures of the Barnardistons (†1653 and †1669) at Kedington. But the most surprising work of the years with which we are now concerned is the Timperley monument (†1629/30) at Hintlesham (also attributed to *Marshall*), an upright figure engraved with great swagger on a slab of slate – it originally formed the top of a tomb-chest.

With the 1650s names become more frequent. Nicholas Stone has already been discussed and Edward Marshall mentioned. In addition there are two tablets by *John Stone* (Barrow 1650 and Hessett †1653; Redgrave †1652 is also attributed to him) and a monument with a seated figure at Culford (1655–8) by *Thomas Stanton*. Seated figures were something rare at that time. Stanton received £300 for it.

There is no clear break in the decades following 1660 such as we shall find in domestic architecture. The break had been made before. Reclining figures had been the standard for large monuments in the earlier C17; they remain so still, but again with the new relaxation in attitude and the new effusiveness of sentiment. As examples one can quote the white marble figure of Maurice Barrow †1666 at Westhorpe, his hand on his heart, the two figures of the Crofts (he died in 1677) by *Abraham*

CHURCHES AND CHAPELS 1540–1840   43

Storey at Little Saxham, where he lies above and behind her, Thomas Jermyn †1692 at Rushbrooke with one hand resting on a skull, and then in the C18 the Colman monument of 1743 at Brent Eleigh which is by *Thomas Dunn*.

New or relatively new types are rarer. Without any figure and quite unlike anything else is the Cullum monument at Hawstead by *Diacinto Cawcy*, who left his name and the date (1675) not on the monument but on the chancel arch nearby. It is an altogether extraordinary piece, not least for its use of scagliola – then a rare material in England – and plaster painted in imitation of *pietra dura*. His work can be seen also at Mildenhall †1671 and Westhorpe †1666. Busts, formerly placed in niches, are now used free-standing – at Cockfield (†1723) by *N. Royce* of Bury St Edmunds. The standing figure, a great exception before the late C17, is now the centre of the uncommonly excellent monument to Sir John Poley †1638 at Boxted, made in about 1680. The contrast to his wife's monument, also with a standing figure but not set up until 1725, is revealing. It is much less rhetorical, and altogether restraint is characteristic of one trend of the 1720s and 1730s – see e.g. the Davers monument without any effigy at Rushbrooke (†1722–43), and the Cullum (†1720) at Hawstead by *Robert Singleton* of Bury St Edmunds. For the seated figure we have had C17 precedent in the Culford monument by Stanton. The two cases in which it occurs in the C18 are, however, part of a different tradition. They both represent judges, and here the *ex cathedra* posture was customary. The Holt (†1710) at Redgrave is by *Thomas Green* of Camberwell, the Reynolds (†1739) at Bury St Edmunds is unsigned. Seated also are Francis Dickins †1747 and wife at Cowlinge. They have an urn on a pedestal between them and wear Roman dress. The monument is signed by *Peter Scheemakers*.

72

71

73

78

With him we have reached the great mid-C18 trio, but in W Suffolk there is no work by Roubiliac, nor by Rysbrack, as the bust of Tillemans made by him for Little Haugh Hall, Norton, is now in the Yale Center for British Art. For the second half of the C18 memorable sculpture can indeed be listed by names. First in date comes *John Golden*'s pretty white and pink marble monument at Finningham (†1781), then *R. Westmacott Sen.*'s monument (†1771) at Shimpling and *John Bacon Sen.*'s at Hawstead (†1793) and Finningham (†1794, dated 1797). *Thomas Singleton* of Bury St Edmunds signs monuments at Horringer (†1750) and Walsham-le-Willows (†1726 but erected later). There is a little more after 1800: *John Bacon Jun.* at Assington †1817, Edwardstone †1808, Hawstead †1810 (and others by *Bacon* and *S. Manning*), Market Weston †1789, Mildenhall †1821 and Nowton †1811, Stoke-by-Nayland erected 1813, and St Gregory, Sudbury, †1814. At Thornham Magna is one of *J. J. P. Kendrick*'s most ambitious works (†1821), and another simpler one (†1823). At the end of the age comes the dignified monument by *Sir Richard Westmacott* at Great Finborough (†1833). The Singletons of Bury St Edmunds have been mentioned. When Thomas Singleton retired shortly before his death

95

in 1792 he sold his business to *John* and *Robert de Carle*, the latter remaining in Norwich to run the business there and John setting up in Bury. The firm were responsible for a good number of monuments, none of them very ambitious, as well as carrying out the stonework on such major buildings as Culford Hall, Great Saxham Hall and Ickworth House (including the obelisk in the park).

Before finally leaving the C18 we should take the opportunity to consider a miscellany of items found in churches that have nothing in common but their ODDITY AND CURIOSITY. To this category belong the thirty-four leather FIRE BUCKETS at Haughley, dating from 1725; the BRAZIERS at Barking; the stoneware GOTCHES or beer jugs (for the bellringers) at Clare (1729, four gallons) and Hinderclay (1724, two gallons); and the two BIERS (one child-size) and surveyor's ODOMETER at Mendlesham.

SECULAR BUILDINGS 1540–1840

The terracotta windows at Barking and elsewhere, mentioned above, are the first signs in the county of the new ornamental fashion which came from Italy and appeared in England between 1510 and 1520 in works done for Henry VIII (the monument to Henry VII in Westminster Abbey) and Wolsey (Hampton Court). But in DOMESTIC ARCHITECTURE as in church monuments it was slow to catch on outside London. Hengrave Hall, built *c.* 1525–38, is essentially still of the late medieval type, with turreted gatehouse, courtyard, and hall opposite the gatehouse. Its exceedingly pretty oriel window over the gateway is of a design invented it seems about 1500 at Windsor and especially popular for ambitious jobs of *c.* 1500–20, but found also on Henry VIII's Nonsuch Palace, begun in the same year, 1538, that the Hengrave gatehouse is dated. Yet the detail of the oriel is Italian, even if not a particularly knowledgeably handled Italian. The big bay window of the hall with mullions and transoms and arched lights is still entirely Perp, but the cloister-like corridor round three sides of the courtyard is a remarkably progressive motif. A similar corridor is known to have existed at Westhorpe Hall, a house of *c.* 1526–33 much closer to Court circles than Hengrave; at Westhorpe, incidentally, terracotta was used for architectural features and decorative panels.

Not the least remarkable aspect of Hengrave Hall is that it was built of white brick. All other houses and mansions to be noted over the next hundred years and more will be of red brick. The favourite plan for LARGE ELIZABETHAN HOUSES becomes that with two far-projecting wings: Kentwell Hall, Long Melford, in stages *c.* 1500–80, and Rushbrooke Hall *c.* 1550 (dem.); Melford Hall, however, began as a courtyard house, and did not achieve its present shape until the E range was taken down in the C18.

All three shared the features of a porch in the centre of the hall range, and symmetrically placed stair-turrets attached to the wings in varying positions. The dating of the porch at Melford Hall is uncertain – it may be a mid-C17 reconstruction of one built a hundred years earlier by Sir William Cordell – but it incorporates the composition of superimposed orders that is found also at Coldham Hall of 1574 (and formerly at Rushbrooke Hall). The stair-turrets at Melford Hall have stone ogee tops decorated with semicircular shell-gables, an Italian Quattrocento motif found elsewhere in England in the 1520s, e.g. at Layer Marney, Essex. Other E-plan houses include Hintlesham Hall, built in the 1570s and remodelled in the C18. Quite a number of Elizabethan and Jacobean houses are only partly preserved, and that makes it hard to judge their complete original plans: early C17 Baylham Hall may have been E-plan, but mid-C16 Smallbridge Hall, Bures, was probably quadrangular.

The only new motif in JACOBEAN HOUSES, which seems to have been introduced about 1620, is the shaped gable, a gable the sides of which are composed of convex, concave or double-curved parts. Newe House, Pakenham, 1621–2, is a dated example. But shaped gables are less prevalent in W Suffolk than in the E, perhaps indicating a failure of the Dutch and N German influence to penetrate far inland. So-called Dutch gables, i.e. with pediments rather than curved tops, are found at Brettenham Park (1661). For the most part straight gables remained the norm (Kentwell Hall, and the former schoolhouse, Little Thurlow, 1614), with a few examples of stepped gables (West Stow Hall *c.* 1530, the demolished Redgrave Hall 1545–54, and Haughley Park *c.* 1620).

For changes more thorough than this, Ipswich and the Suffolk countryside had to wait until after 1630 and as a rule after 1670. In INTERIOR DECORATION the change between 1500 and the Elizabethan and Jacobean decades was much more thorough-going. The ribbed ceilings at Troston Hall (late C16) and Clock House, Little Stonham (*c.* 1600), have no pre-Elizabethan precedent in the county, and display a wide variety of patterns and motifs. Painted decoration is also found, not just in major houses such as West Stow Hall with its entertaining scheme of the Four Ages of Man, *c.* 1575, but also in more modest houses relatively far down the social scale. Two phases of such decoration have been identified by Andrea Kirkham, the first (*c.* 1575–1610/20) much more elaborate than the second (1610/20–1670/80). The first phase made much use of rich pattern and grotesque work, often in imitation of the tapestries and other cloth hangings that few could afford; the later phase is plainer, and typically makes use of the timber-framed structure of the building, with exposed internal timbers painted and elaborated as columns in a single colour. The greatest concentration of surviving schemes is in Bury St Edmunds, e.g. at Baret House (Chequer Square), No. 5 Honey Hill, No. 5 Sparhawk Street (including a text panel dated 1600), and in Whiting Street No. 6 (pattern of interlocking octagons based on a Serlio ceiling design) and No. 83. The late C17 panels at Finningham are delightful examples of external plasterwork or pargetting.

In architecture a new world was ushered in by Inigo Jones, whose truly epoch-making works started in 1616. By the beginning of the Civil War his reform had been achieved, even if it took another twenty years and more to convince more than a few patrons of it. The impetus was greatest near the Court, especially after Charles I had ascended the throne, and the Court came to one town in Suffolk, Newmarket, for the sport of kings. James I had lodgings built in 1614–15, and in 1619–20 *Inigo Jones* himself built the Prince's Lodgings. Almost everything was demolished during the Civil War, although some fragments may remain. After the Restoration Charles II had a new palace built by *William Samwell*, and of this a small part, the King's Lodging of 1668–71, does survive (as Palace House), as well as parts of Charles II's stables. Restoration of Palace House in 1996–8 revealed the earliest known example of a counterbalanced sliding sash window in England.

Otherwise, as far as architectural innovation was concerned, the provinces hesitated, and Suffolk as a whole had now turned very provincial. Little is reflected of the new style in architecture, and what there is, is late. Thus Cupola House at Bury St Edmunds corresponds with its belvedere on the roof to such houses as Coleshill of *c.* 1650 and yet is dated 1693. The most metropolitan design is perhaps the church at Euston of 1676, mentioned earlier as the one example of an echo of Christopher Wren in Suffolk. Euston Hall, the house to go with the church, was built *c.* 1666–71 but does not survive in that state. It was simple and undecorated except for the somewhat awkward giant pilasters of the porch, a motif which also occurs at Clopton Hall, Rattlesden, remodelled in the late C17. King Charles's Gate at Euston belongs to the provincial mid-C17 Baroque rather than the Jones–Webb–Wren style. On the other hand the summerhouse at Ickworth, *c.* 1702, is a sophisticated work on a small scale, and is attributed to *William Talman*. As far as INTERIORS are concerned, mention must be made of the plaster ceiling at Hintlesham Hall of *c.* 1686, among the best of its date in East Anglia, and more was done here externally and internally from 1724 onwards. Little Haugh Hall, Norton, has inside some splendid luxuriant carving and also ceiling paintings, part of a programme of work that lasted from 1715 until at least 1745.

With the Temple which *William Kent*, the most imaginative of the earlier Palladians, designed for Euston in 1746, we are once again in the main stream of English developments among GEORGIAN COUNTRY HOUSES. It is an exceedingly fine piece. Kent had also sketched a design for rebuilding the house at Euston, but he died in 1748, and instead it was remodelled and enlarged by *Matthew Brettingham*, another of the leading Palladians. *Robert Adam* is represented by Moreton Hall, 1773–6, a compact country house overlooking Bury St Edmunds from the E, with at least two interiors still in something like their original condition. His work of 1774 at Great Saxham Hall was destroyed by fire after only five years, and most of the present house is by *Joseph Patience*, 1796–8. *James Wyatt*'s Fornham Hall, Fornham St Genevieve, 1776–85, has been demolished, although his stables and other ancillary buildings survive. There is also evidence that he worked at Culford Hall, but here most of the credit for the remodelling of 1790–6 goes to *Samuel Wyatt*, who clad the red brick Tudor house with white mathematical tiles in a thoroughly convincing manner. He also used mathematical tiles at Livermere Hall, Great Livermere, 1795–6, but this too has been demolished, as has Tendring Hall, Stoke-by-Nayland, an early work of *Sir John Soane*, 1784–8, and a major loss – the survival of Soane's modest Wiston Hall, Wissington, 1791, hardly compensates, pleasing though it is in its simplicity. Another significant loss, although its architects are not known, was Branches Park, Cowlinge, which before overwhelming additions in 1904–8 was a very attractive house of *c.* 1720 with wings added later in the C18.

But the grandest of Suffolk's Georgian houses is without question Ickworth, built by that erratic prelate the Earl of Bristol. Initial designs by *Mario Asprucci*, 1794–5, were modified and executed by *Francis Sandys* and his brother *Rev. Joseph Sandys*, the Earl-Bishop's domestic chaplain. The centre is a huge domed oval to which quadrant wings and long side pavilions are attached. The idea is bold, but it has not resulted in much beauty either outside or indeed inside, where the oddest shapes of rooms had to be coped with. The interior was got ready only after the Earl-Bishop's death, and the most impressive interior feature, the staircase hall, has existed in its present form only since the early C20, as part of alterations by *A. C. Blomfield*.

Sandys benefited greatly from his association with the Bristols. At the same time as working at Ickworth he built Finborough Hall, Great Finborough, 1795, and settled for a while in Bury St Edmunds, where he is thought to have remodelled Nos. 5–6 St Mary's Square and to have built No. 4, *c.* 1804. This brings us to the early years of the C19 and the REGENCY PERIOD, and a rather mixed picture. *Thomas Hopper* worked at Melford Hall in 1813 and again in 1840, and at Kentwell Hall *c.* 1825–7; his only new house in W Suffolk, Rougham Hall, *c.* 1821–6, was gutted in 1940. Hopper's picturesque Neo-Gothic design has ended up as a picturesque ruin, something that many lovers of Gothic would not altogether regret. The word picturesque can also be applied to Nowton Court, or rather 'Nowton Cottage' as it was first called, a large-scale *cottage orné* of the early C19 remodelled and coarsened first by *G. R. French*, 1837–9, and then by *H. F. Bacon*, 1880–2. French was also responsible for remodelling Hardwick House, Bury St Edmunds, in the 1840s (dem.). All that undoubtedly remains of French's work there is a lodge, although it is possible that he was responsible also for the charming and decorative estate buildings nearby and also in Hawstead and Horringer, built for Rev. Sir Thomas Gery Cullum between 1831 and 1855. Another demolished house that belongs to this period by virtue of extensive remodelling was Thornham Hall,

Thonham Magna, altered and extended first by *Sydney Smirke*, 1837–9, and then by *E. B. Lamb*, *c.* 1856–7. The remodelling here, as at Hardwick House, was in a style based on the early C17 originals, rather more fantastical in the case of Thornham than of Hardwick.

Country houses do not of course vanish without trace, and various surviving ancillary buildings have been mentioned. PARKS too usually survive in one form or another, as at Redgrave Hall, where *Capability Brown* was employed by Rowland Holt between 1763 and 1773. The house, which he remodelled by encasing it in white Woolpit brick, has been demolished, but the stables remain, and the park is still an exemplary Brown landscape, with its serpentine lake and a domed pavilion as an eyecatcher. Brown's hand can also be detected, to a greater or lesser degree, at Branches Park, Cowlinge, 1763–5, Euston Hall, 1767–71, and Fornham Hall, 1782. He was also employed at Ickworth between 1769 and 1776, although it is uncertain how much work he actually did; but if the house at Ickworth lacks charm, the same cannot be said for the park, which is a constant delight and a triumph in the way that the surroundings of the house progress from formal gardens to sheltered walks to open parkland, with strategic planting of trees (mainly in the first half of the C19) and carefully placed buildings, notably the 50-ft (15-metre) obelisk, erected as a monument to the Earl-Bishop in 1817. *Humphry Repton* produced Red Books for Livermere Hall (1790), Tendring Hall (1790–1) and Culford Hall (1792). Only at the last of these were his proposals carried out to any extent, with the creation of kitchen gardens and a lake, perhaps building on the work of *Thomas Wright* in the 1740s. Most of the improvements at Livermere Hall had taken place forty or fifty years earlier, when Baptist Lee took the unusual step of collaborating with his neighbour, James Calthorpe of Ampton Hall, to create a long serpentine lake from a mere that spread across their two estates. Some ornamental buildings in parks have already been mentioned. The best house for these is Great Saxham Hall, with its tea house, Temple of Dido, and the delicate Gothick Umbrello, the latter by *Coade & Sealy*, *c.* 1800. At Tendring Hall is the exceedingly pretty mid-C18 Temple or fishing lodge, attributed to *Sir Robert Taylor*, that stands at the head of a canal. There are pure FOLLIES in the grounds of Boxted Hall, Thornham Hall (C19, restored as a 'hermitage' in the late C20) and Nowton Court (the remains of the S porch of St Mary, Bury St Edmunds), as well as a dilapidated folly in the form of a church tower near Yaxley Hall. Connected with Fornham Hall are the MODEL FARMS at Fornham St Genevieve and (probably) Fornham St Martin by *Robert Abraham*, *c.* 1824.

As far as MEDIUM-SIZED HOUSES are concerned, the first house of a pure C18 type, Bramford House, is as early as 1693–4, of seven bays and two storeys with a carved eaves cornice and hipped roof. The red brick front is newer than what lies behind, as is so often the case with such houses; Gainsborough's House in Sudbury is another such example, the façade of *c.* 1722 concealing two timber-framed houses that had been joined together about two hundred years earlier. In most small towns and villages the best C18 houses are the former RECTORIES, the best examples from the C18 being Ketton House, Kedington, c. 1723, Jacob's Manor, Withersfield, 1726, Drinkstone, c. 1760, and Tostock, 1796–8. At Whatfield the rectory of 1657 was remodelled by the splendid Rev. John Clubbe, rector 1735–73, who was painted by Gainsborough and wrote a spoof antiquarian history of the village; he also laid out the grounds. In the early decades of the C19 comes a spate of parsonages whose architects (many of them local) are known: *William Brown* of Ipswich at Barking (1819), Earl Stonham (1820) and Elmsett (1818); *Arthur Browne* of Norwich at Hepworth (1820); *William Dudley* of Bury St Edmunds at Beyton (1840), Poslingford (1838) and Risby (1839–40); *Robert Heffer* of Ixworth at Great Livermere (1812–13) and Wetherden (1816); *William Lambert* at Felsham (1814); *Clark Rampling* at Brandon (1818); *M. G. Thompson* at Boxford (1818– 21), Bures (1820) and Hartest (1821); *John Whiting* of Ipswich at Creeting St Peter (1826). Most of these are Georgian or Regency in style, but William Dudley tended towards the Elizabethan, and at Long Melford (1832–3), perhaps out of deference to the adjacent Trinity Hospital, is an early example of the use of Neo-Tudor for parsonages; the architect is not known, but *Thomas Hopper* is a strong possibility.

p. 103
p. 119

Of TOWN HOUSES generally there is, however, little. Although the royal palace at Newmarket was maintained until 1819, the Hanoverian kings did not share the Stuarts' love of racing, and there are only a few C18 houses of any importance, mostly towards the SW end of the High Street, as well as the Rutland Arms Hotel at the opposite end. Bury St Edmunds, however, is essentially Georgian in character, despite its medieval layout and the medieval timber framing that lies behind the façades of so many houses. This character can best be appreciated, in a relatively modest way, in Chequer Square and along Crown Street, and on a slightly grander scale in Northgate Street. Individual houses all over the town have what seems to be a favourite motif, a doorway set in a segmental-arched recess with little columns *in antis*. The grandest of all town houses in Bury St Edmunds is Manor House, Honey Hill, 1736–8 by *James Burrough* for the Countess of Bristol. It looks across the churchyard to the Clopton Asylum (now Deanery), built between 1735 and 1744 on a comparable scale and by the same bricklayer, *Thomas Steele*. Bury was well endowed generally with PUBLIC BUILDINGS. As well as the Clopton Asylum, and the William Barnaby Almshouses in College Street by *William Steggles*, 1826, there is the Market Cross by *Robert Adam*, 1774–7; a hotel of the new gentlemanly type, the Angel, by *John Redgrave*, 1774–6; the Athenaeum as modified in 1789 and (by *Francis Sandys*) in 1802–5; the gaol by *George Byfield*, 1801–5, of which only parts survive, but once a famous building designed on the most up-to-date principles; and the Theatre Royal by *William Wilkins*, 1819, restored in 2005–7 to its original function. Elsewhere are the

91

Metcalfe Almshouses at Hawstead (1811), and the Colman Cottages at Brent Eleigh (1731). At Sudbury the Town Hall by *A. J. Johnston*, 1828, is a relatively rare surviving example of a town hall that pre-dates the Municipal Reform Act of 1835. A Suffolk speciality are the HOUSES OF INDUSTRY or workhouses. Under the Elizabethan Poor Laws parishes were required to provide accommodation for paupers, and in the mid C18 the idea of grouping parishes together for this purpose was widely discussed. It was first put into practice at Nacton in 1758 (E) and taken up slowly in W Suffolk, with examples at Onehouse for the Stow Hundred (1779–81), and Semer for Cosford Hundred (1781). The latter has mostly been demolished, but the former, designed by *Thomas Fulcher*, survives as flats; it was described in 1810 as 'having more the appearance of a gentleman's seat than a receptacle for paupers'.

ROADS had improved somewhat in the C18 with the introduction of turnpikes. The earliest in Suffolk, 1711–12, principally covered Ipswich to Scole, but also had branches to Wickham Market and Stowmarket. A turnpike connected Newmarket to Cambridge and London, 1724, and extended NE towards Norwich in 1768. Other important routes were from Sudbury to Bury St Edmunds, 1762 (surviving toll house at Sicklesmere, Great Whelnetham), and from Bury to Scole, 1769 (toll house at Botesdale). Transport of heavy goods was made very much easier by the creation of NAVIGATIONS, the first being the improvement of the River Lark under an Act of Parliament of 1700: this made the river navigable as far as Fornham All Saints and thus created a connection between Bury St Edmunds and King's Lynn, as the Lark is a tributary of the Great Ouse. A number of locks (mostly staunches or flash locks) remain, e.g. at Mildenhall. In the S of the county the Stour Navigation was established under an act of 1705, connecting Sudbury to the coast. The Ipswich & Stowmarket (or Gipping) Navigation opened in 1793, with surviving locks at Baylham, Creeting and Needham Market (Bosmere). The navigation was surveyed by *Isaac Lenny* of Norwich and the route approved by the engineer *William Jessop*, on the basis of which an act was passed in 1790. *James Smith* of Reading was appointed resident engineer, being succeeded in 1792 by *Richard Coates*, with *John Rennie* as surveyor.

The Stour Navigation was of particular benefit to the brickyards of Ballingdon, and maltings soon sprang up at Stowmarket beside the river there. Mention has already been made of the particular INDUSTRIES of Brandon and Mildenhall (flint, rabbits) and Babergh and Cosford hundreds (woollen cloth, silk, horsehair), but otherwise W Suffolk is noticeably less industrial than the E of the county. An interesting survival, in terms of buildings although not the business, is the tannery at Combs, established in 1711, although most of the surviving buildings are of the first half of the C19. Early IRON foundries included *Woods & Co.* of Stowmarket (1812), but two early cast-iron bridges, at Brent Eleigh and Clare, were made by *Ransome &*

Son of Ipswich (1813), to designs by *William Cubitt*. These are not as remarkable as the bridge in the park of Culford Hall, fabricated from tubular sections of cast iron, the only known example of a design patented by *Samuel Wyatt* in 1800 and cast in 1804 by *William Hawks & Sons* of Gateshead. An unusual early use of cast iron can be seen at Barningham, Hepworth and Market Weston, where *George Bloomfield*, millwright and engineer of Thelnetham, used tie-rods and clamps to restore the churches in 1834, 1828 and 1844–5 respectively. At Market Weston the work was directed by *L. N. Cottingham* (*Cottingham & Son*), and involved fixing iron bars across the nave that were heated, tightened and contracted as they cooled, and thus brought the leaning nave walls back to the perpendicular. Cast iron was also used innovatively for the roof of Westley in 1835–6.

Of WINDMILLS and WATERMILLS there is no shortage. The latter are to be found mainly along the Stour at Brundon (Sudbury), Bures, Great Cornard, Kedington, Wissington and Wixoe, and the Gipping at Baylham, Brantham (E), Needham Market and Sproughton. Special mention should be made of the watermill at Euston, designed by *William Kent* in 1731 and disguised as a church; as well as grinding corn it raised water for fountains in the ornamental gardens. Kersey Mill, on the Brett, forms a particularly impressive group. Pakenham boasts a watermill and a windmill that are both in working order, the former recorded in Domesday Book and dating in its current state from 1814, the latter (a tower mill) built in 1830. Another working windmill is at Stanton (a post mill), built in 1751 and moved to its present site *c.* 1818; the tower mill at Thelnetham, probably by *George Bloomfield*, 1819, with cast-iron windshaft by *J. Aickman* of King's Lynn, 1832, has also been fully restored. The single most remarkable site is at Drinkstone, where there is a post mill with timbers dating back to 1586, and a horse mill converted to a smock mill in the late C18.

ARCHITECTURE 1840–1914

The impact of the VICTORIAN AGE is less apparent in W Suffolk than in the E. W Suffolk has no towns to rival Felixstowe, Ipswich or Lowestoft in terms of C19 expansion, and today Bury St Edmunds, Hadleigh and Lavenham seem almost untouched by the Victorians, although if one could travel back in time, and see them as they were a hundred years ago, it would be clear how false that impression is, and how much noisy and smoky industry these picturesque places formerly supported. Only Newmarket and Exning have retained a Victorian character, which is just another aspect of their highly unusual nature, and must be attributed not just to the architecture but also to the ubiquitous presence and smell of horses, common in the C19 but now rare in a town.

The first RAILWAY in Suffolk was in the far NW corner, where the main line from London to Norwich crossed the county in 1845, with stations at Brandon and Lakenheath. This was followed in 1846 by the line from Ipswich to Bury St Edmunds (resident engineer *Peter Bruff*, contractor *Thomas Brassey*), with its excellent stations by *Frederick Barnes* at Needham Market, Stowmarket and Thurston, as well as *Sancton Wood*'s at Bury. Barnes also designed the stations at Raydon and Hadleigh, on the branch line from Bentley that opened in 1847. The Ipswich–Bury line was continued to Newmarket in 1854, thus enabling travel from Ipswich to Cambridge and thence to the Midlands. The closure of the Hadleigh and other smaller branch lines (Sudbury to Long Melford and on to Clare and Haverhill, Lavenham and Bury) has contributed to the obscuring of the semi-industrial character of these places. The very large former maltings next to the old station at Long Melford are a reminder of this.

The lesser impact of the Victorian age in W Suffolk is seen also in the relatively small number of ARCHITECTS who were based in that half of the county. The only architect of any distinction to practise in Bury St Edmunds in the C19 was *John Johnson* (1811–91, and not to be confused with at least two London architects of the same name). He is remembered mainly for church restorations (Glemsford 1860, Great Barton 1856–8, Mellis 1858–9, Rougham 1856, Yaxley 1854) and schools (Cavendish

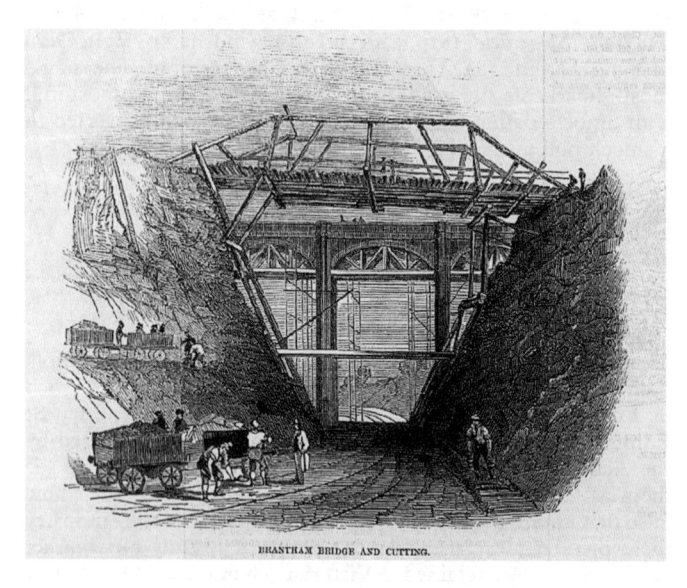

Brantham (E), Bull Bridge.
Engraving, 1846

1863, Wattisfield 1861–2). *William Steggles Jun.* (1777–1859) was a builder in succession to his father of the same name (1752–1834), but was County Surveyor for W Suffolk and designed the Police Station at Clare (1847) as well as some parsonages, so may be considered an architect as well. *Edward Salter* practised as an architect in London and Sudbury but also owned the Chilton Brickworks near Sudbury; after being declared bankrupt in 1873 he was in partnership with *W. R. Firmin*. Most church and school work was otherwise done mainly by Ipswich architects – *Frederick Barnes*, *E. F. Bisshopp* and *R. M. Phipson*. Newmarket had more resident architects than Bury St Edmunds, who were probably rather better at judging horseflesh than at designing buildings: *J. F. Clark* (*Clark & Holland*), *John Flatman* and *W. C. Manning*. Only Clark & Holland did much beyond Newmarket and Exning, including church restorations at Moulton (1851), Ousden (1861–2), Wickhambrook (1862–3, also school, 1877–8), and Withersfield (1867, also school, 1865), and the school at Clare (1858–62, one of their more appealing efforts). *J. D. Wyatt*, although not resident in Suffolk, was responsible for a number of church restorations in W Suffolk, as well as a new church at Beck Row, Mildenhall (1875–6), and was consulting architect to the Incorporated Church Building Society for the archdeaconry of Sudbury; and *W. M. Fawcett* of Cambridge also did much church work on the W side of the county, particularly after his appointment in 1871 as diocesan surveyor for Ely (which included the archdeaconry of Sudbury from 1837 to 1914). The situation began to change somewhat towards the end of the C19, with *Archie Ainsworth Hunt* practising in Sudbury from 1889 until 1908, when he moved to Bury St Edmunds; he was West Suffolk County Surveyor 1900–11. (His predecessor as County Surveyor (1889–1900) was *Frank Whitmore*, son of the millwright John Whitmore of Wickham Market (*see Suffolk: East*) and pupil of R. M. Phipson.) *Sidney Naish* set up practice in the town in 1905.

The lack of resident architects in Bury St Edmunds is apparent when it comes to the town's PUBLIC BUILDINGS. *Benjamin Backhouse* of Ipswich was responsible for the town's first Corn Exchange (1836), although it was enlarged in 1848 by *John Johnson*. Backhouse also built Bury's workhouse in Hospital Road (1836; dem.) and altered the Market Cross (1840). The second Corn Exchange, 1861–2, was by a London firm, *Ellis & Woodward*. The Shire Hall was built in 1841–2 by *W. McIntosh Brookes* but rebuilt in 1906–7 by *A. A. Hunt*. Elsewhere in W Suffolk, there are TOWN HALLS at Hadleigh by *W. P. Ribbans* of Ipswich, 1851, and Haverhill by *Edward Sharman*, 1883–4; CORN EXCHANGES in Haverhill, 1857 and 1889 (the latter by *Frank Whitmore*), Stowmarket, 1872 by *F. Barnes*, and Sudbury, 1841 by *H. E. Kendall Sen.*, the best of the lot. The village hall at Hartest (Hartest and Boxted Club) is an interesting early work by *Reginald Blomfield* (1888).

As well as at Bury St Edmunds, WORKHOUSES were built in Kedington (1855–6 by *J. F. Clark*; dem.), Mildenhall (1894–5 by

F. *Whitmore*; dem.), Newmarket (1836 by *William P. Roote*) and Sudbury (1836–7 by *John Brown* of Norwich). Bury had a HOSPITAL from 1826, but all the C19 buildings have been demolished. St Leonard's Hospital, Sudbury, by *Edward Salter*, 1867–8, was the first cottage hospital to be built on the pavilion plan and impressed Horace Swete, who used it as a model in his *Handy Book of Cottage Hospitals* (1870). In Newmarket, Rous Memorial Court by *F. W. Roper*, 1878–9, was built as a hospital and ALMSHOUSES; other C19 almshouses include those at College Square, Bury St Edmunds, 1908 by *A. A. Hunt*, Hadleigh, 1887 by *H. J. Wright*, Nowton, 1877 by *H. F. Bacon*, and Rougham, 1876 by *John Taylor*. Trinity Hospital, Long Melford, founded in 1573, was substantially rebuilt in 1847, but entirely sympathetically. An unusual example of what in the C21 is called sheltered housing is the Fennell Memorial Homes in Bury St Edmunds, a block of four flats on two storeys by *Brightwen Binyon*, 1873–4, for Quaker women.

More than anything else, new SCHOOLS were built in the C19, first the National Schools built by the Church of England in most villages, modest affairs on the whole (Boxford 1839 by *William Howe*), some more ambitious (Baylham 1860 by *F. Barnes*, Finningham 1872 by *Edmund Catchpole*, Hadleigh 1853–4 by *Barnes*, Hopton 1854–5 by *Thomas Farrow*, Kedington 1875–6 by *R. Kent*, Tuddenham by *L. N. Cottingham* 1846). Following the 1870 Education Act most schools were built by school boards, but architects easily made the transition, e.g. *Barnes* at Stratford St Mary, 1877. Other good examples are by *F. Whitmore* at Haverhill (1875–6) and Whepstead (1874), and by *Henry Lovegrove* at Combs (1875–60), Lakenheath (1876–8) and Beck Row, Mildenhall (1876–7). The Board School at Glemsford by *Salter & Firmin*, 1872, was unusually large (for 520 children), an indication of the extent of industrial activity in this village in the C19. Outside the normal system are the Guildhall Feoffment School, Bury St Edmunds, by *H. E. Kendall Jun.*, 1843, a pretty Tudor-Gothic design that he included in his book *Designs for Schools and School Houses, Parochial and National* (1847); the Grammar School, Sudbury, by *R. P. Pope*, 1857–8; and the King Edward VI Grammar School, Bury St Edmunds, by *A. W. Blomfield*, 1882–3.

CHURCHES in W Suffolk as everywhere else in the country were the subject of innumerable restorations, and those architects mainly responsible have already been named: *F. Barnes, E. F. Bisshopp, W. M. Fawcett, R. M. Phipson, J. D. Wyatt*. Other architects who carried out significant restoration were *L. N. Cottingham* (St Mary, Bury St Edmunds, 1842–9; Horringer, 1845–6), *Anthony Salvin* (Nowton, 1842–3), *George Gilbert Scott* (St James, Bury St Edmunds, 1862–9; Gazeley, 1856–7), *S. S. Teulon* (Ampton, c. 1848; Pakenham, 1847–50; possibly Wordwell, 1857). *William Butterfield* worked on six churches in W Suffolk, notably at Bacton, 1860–4; Great Waldingfield, 1865–9; and St Peter, Sudbury, 1854–9. Scott's restoration of Gazeley led to his new church at Higham, 1858–61, a satisfyingly complete little building

ARCHITECTURE 1840–1914

with its round tower; the latter was completed by his former assistant, *J. D. Wyatt*, in 1870. The parsonage at Higham might be by either Scott or Wyatt; but Scott did design the vicarage at Great Bricett, 1874. Other new churches are two by *William Ranger*, St John, Bury St Edmunds (1840–1), and Westley (1835–6), neither of them distinguished but the latter interesting for its use of concrete and cast iron. *Phipson*'s church at Great Finborough was a complete rebuilding, 1874–7, retaining only the C15 porch, and is distinguished for its exceptionally tall spire, but stylistically belongs to an earlier generation. St Agnes, Newmarket, by *R. H. Carpenter*, 1886, is modest externally and reserves all its effect for the interior, especially the reredos by *Sir Edgar Boehm*. *W. D. Caröe*'s work at Elveden, 1904–6, comprised substantial additions to the existing church in a highly individual manner, which were followed in 1919–22 by the erection of a memorial tower outside the churchyard but connected to the church by a cloister walk, an extraordinary concept for which it is hard to think of a precedent. Also of this later phase of church work is *Charles Spooner*'s restoration of the little Row Chapel, Hadleigh (1891), an exemplary piece of work in the Arts and Crafts tradition, with a painted reredos by his wife, *Minnie Dibdin Spooner*. Spooner's uncle was rector of Hadleigh, and both he and his wife did further work at the parish church *c.* 1911–35.

There are two ROMAN CATHOLIC CHURCHES of significance, at Stowmarket and Sudbury. The former, by *A. E. Purdie*, 1883–4, was originally designed as a school (hence the unexpected two storeys) that would have been an adjunct to the largest R.C. church in Suffolk, but the scheme foundered, and the church has been comprehensively reordered. The church at Sudbury, by *Leonard Stokes*, 1893 but looking later, is little more than its ritual W front, but that is a very pleasing composition; what a pity that the interior has been gutted, and that Stokes was not able to design the attached presbytery too. Of NONCONFORMIST CHURCHES AND CHAPELS there is no shortage, but little to get excited about. Outside the ordinary run are the charming little Baptist church at Whepstead (1844), in a very rustic version of Gothick; the exuberant Primitive Methodist chapel at Ousden (1872), with its decorative brickwork and brightly coloured glass; the Baptist church in Sudbury by *Eade & Johns* of Ipswich (1889–90); and, literally towering over everything else, the Old Independent Church, Haverhill (1884–5), by *Charles Bell*, a prolific designer of Wesleyan chapels. It is equally impressive inside, with its unaltered seating, galleries and organ, and is by far the best building in Haverhill, having lived down Pevsner's description of it in 1961 as a horror.

Among Victorian CHURCH FURNISHINGS are some surprises. At Thornham Magna is a screen designed by *Joseph Clarke* for a church in Surrey and made by *Henry Ringham* of Ipswich; it was exhibited at the Great Exhibition where it was bought by Lord Henniker. Otherwise there is very much less work by Ringham (e.g. benches at Wattisham 1847–8) than in E Suffolk.

The beautiful chancel organ at Stowlangtoft, supplied by *Gray & Davison* in 1869, is almost identical to the organs designed for the firm by *J. P. Seddon* and shown at the International Exhibition of 1862. The interior of St Agnes, Newmarket, has been mentioned, with its reredos; further decoration is provided by Spanish-style tiles, and mosaic by *Salviati*, and there is a complete scheme of stained glass by *Clayton & Bell*. Another good Victorian interior is Edwardstone, restored by *G. F. Bodley* in 1877–8, with decorative painting by *William Powell* of *F. R. Leach & Sons*, Cambridge, stained glass by *Burlison & Grylls* and a reredos by Bodley's partner *C. G. Hare* (1910). The interior of Elveden is as rich as one would expect, with much carving by *Nathaniel Hitch*, especially the alabaster reredos (1906–7), densely populated with saints as well as the Supper at Emmaus. Other individual furnishings of note include the rood and parclose screens by *G. H. Fellowes Prynne* at Rattlesden (1909 and 1916), both with coved lofts and connected to the original stair, and the reredos by *Ninian Comper* at Cavendish, made in 1895 for the private chapel of Athelstan Riley's house in London and incorporating a C16 Flemish alabaster relief of the Crucifixion.

Some STAINED GLASS has been mentioned. Complete schemes are rare, but one was supplied by *Lavers & Barraud* to *A. W. Blomfield*'s church at Culford Heath, 1864–5 (now a private house). The major firms are all well represented. Less common are windows by *J. B. Capronnier* of Brussels at Stoke-by-Nayland (1868–9, highly pictorial), *N. J. Cottingham* at Barrow (1848) and Redgrave (1853), *Alfred Gérente* at St Mary, Bury St Edmunds (1857), *George Hedgeland* at Hadleigh (1857, Nazarene, based on a painting by *Overbeck*), and *Leonard Walker* at Brandon (1900 and *c*. 1913). At Herringswell is a fine group of windows, in particular four given in 1901–2 and made by *Christopher Whall* and his pupils *Paul Woodroffe* and *Jasper Brett*; the tradition was maintained with windows by *James Clark* (1916–17 and 1923). There were no firms making stained glass in w Suffolk, but there were two amateurs, *Lucy Marriott* and *Lucy Rickards*, both daughters of clergymen, and Lucy Marriott was also married to one: she may have designed windows at Onehouse when her husband was curate there in the 1840s, and the w window at Woolpit is by her. The unusual painted monument to Lucy Marriott and her husband at Woolpit (1901) is by their daughter, also Lucy. Lucy Rickards designed and made windows at Market Weston (1845) and Stowlangtoft, where her father was rector 1832–64. *Rev. Charles Rawlins* designed windows at Creeting St Peter (1847) that were probably made by *John King* of Ipswich; he was curate of Creeting St Mary and designed chancel windows installed in 1846 but later replaced. Good MONUMENTS are rare, but that at Culford to Countess Cadogan †1907 by *Countess Feodora Gleichen* is exceptional, a white marble effigy on a tomb-chest in its own vaulted chapel, as good in its way as any monument of any age. The monument to Thomas Hallifax †1850 at Shimpling combines piety and sentiment in a characteristically Victorian way; it is unsigned, but probably by

R. Westmacott Jun. The family mausoleum in the churchyard (1842) looks strangely utilitarian. There are good churchyard monuments at Assington (Gurdon family, 1850s) and Nettlestead (†1855 by *F. B. Russel*, executed by *Henry Ringham*). Outside churchyards, for reasons unknown, are two mausolea at Brandon, one at North Court Lodge (1830) and the other at Brandon Park (*c.* 1845). Public memorial sculpture is to be found at Bury St Edmunds (Boer War memorial by *A. G. Walker*, 1904; monument to the novelist Ouida †1908 by *E. G. Gillick*); Newmarket (Cooper Memorial Fountain by *E. A. Rickards* and *Henry Poole*, 1910); and Sudbury (statue of Thomas Gainsborough by *Bertram Mackennal*, 1913).

VICTORIAN COUNTRY HOUSES in W Suffolk are represented by two supreme examples, Elveden Hall and Culford Hall, both of significance as much for their dependent buildings as for the houses themselves. Elveden developed principally as a sporting estate. The moderately sized Georgian house was rebuilt in 1869–71 for the Maharajah Duleep Singh by *John Norton*, rather dull externally but lavishly fitted out in Rajput style. After Duleep Singh's death in 1893 the estate was bought by Lord Iveagh of Guinness fame and fortune, who employed *William Young* to make large additions that included the spectacular Marble Hall, designed by *Sir Caspar Purdon Clarke* of the South Kensington Museum. Lord Iveagh also rebuilt most of the village as well, as we have seen, as transforming the church. At Culford Hall the estate came in 1839 to Rev. E. R. Benyon, who held it until his death in 1883 and used his position to make great improvements to the estate buildings, not just in Culford but in the surrounding villages of Ingham, Timworth, West Stow and Wordwell, restoring the churches and building schools, almshouses and cottages. He seems to have done nothing to the house itself; that was left to his successor, the 5th Earl Cadogan, who employed *William Young* to make additions in 1894–6 and 1904, with a result that reminds one that Young's best-known building is the old War Office in Whitehall. Well down the scale is Stowlangtoft Hall by *J. H. Hakewill*, 1859, its white brick very stark and without enough detail to provide interest, but with an impressive domed conservatory It is hard to believe that only four years later *W. E. Nesfield* was building Sproughton Manor, also in white brick but enlivened by patterned brickwork and half-hipped roofs with tile-hanging. He also designed the entrance lodge to Bradfield Hall, Bradfield Combust (1865). It is also perhaps unreasonable to compare Hakewill with *E. B. Lamb*, who in 1858 built the highly original rectory at Copdock.

MEDIUM-SIZED HOUSES become more plentiful in the last decade of the C19 and the first decade of the C20, although it is very regrettable that *A. N. Prentice*'s Cavenham Hall (1898–9) has been demolished (although lodges and stables survive) and that The Retreat, Lakenheath (*c.* 1900; now Lakenheath Hall), has been mutilated beyond recognition. Cavenham Hall was widely published when new, not least by Hermann Muthesius in his influential study *Das englische Haus* (1904–5). Fortunately

Prentice's Murray Lodge, Newmarket (1905), is intact, and Newmarket (by this date fashionable again if still not entirely respectable, thanks to the interest of the Prince of Wales, later Edward VII) at last began to produce some decent buildings. These include a few large 'Queen Anne' houses by *R. W. Edis*, 1898 and 1903–4; Edis was probably responsible for additions to the Jockey Club Rooms in 1882, and was a safe establishment figure. His lodges for Cheveley Park (p. 438) still stand in Newmarket; the house itself, 1896–8, has been demolished (*see Buildings of England: Cambridgeshire*). Beyond Newmarket, but still within its orbit, *Philip Webb* made Baroque additions to the Early Georgian Exning House, 1895–6. Lanwades Park, Moulton, was built in 1907 with the proceeds of a 100–1 bet on the client's own Derby winner in 1898. The architect is unknown; the house is a near-replica of Horham Hall, Essex. A scheme for Dalham Hall by *C. E. Mallows*, prepared in 1901 for Cecil Rhodes, was unexecuted, as was the greater part of a scheme by *Edwin Lutyens*, but his gates and lodge, 1903, were built. Lutyens had recently (1897–9) been working at Stoke College, Stoke-by-Clare, making alterations for Lord Loch.

Late Victorian picturesqueness is evident on a small scale in Higham, near Stratford St Mary (Chauffeurs Cottage by *W. H. Atkin Berry*, 1887), in contrast to the houses at Ixworth for Thingoe Rural District Council by *Frank Whitmore* (1892–4). These were built in the wake of the Housing of the Working Classes Act 1890 and may be the earliest surviving examples of rural council housing. The rectory at Finningham by *E. C. Frere* (1907–8) is of a very sophisticated simplicity; the removal in 2012 of its foundation stone, with lettering by *Eric Gill*, was an act of vandalism.

Finningham, Old Rectory.
Design by E.C. Frere, published 1908

COMMERCIAL BUILDINGS are to be found principally in Bury St Edmunds, one of them the exceptional Savings Bank by *L. N. Cottingham*, 1846–7, in Tudor-Gothic. The contractor was *Thomas Farrow*, an enterprising builder and stonemason who was also a capable architect; he extended Cottingham's building in the same style but with rather more elaborate detail, as his own premises and also as an advertisement for his abilities. It is worth comparing this with the premises that *Lot Jackaman*, Farrow's equally competent foreman, built for himself in Westgate Street in 1884. Cottingham's bank has nothing about it to suggest its function, unlike later bank buildings, such as *John Gibson*'s reassuringly sober and classical National Provincial Bank (1868) in Abbeygate Street. *Brightwen Binyon*'s bank in Sudbury (1879) is 'Queen Anne', almost next door to the Neo-Georgian London & County Bank by *Cheston & Perkin* (1907), nicely illustrating changing fashions for such buildings. The Alliance Assurance Co.'s building in Bury St Edmunds by *J. S. Corder*, 1890–1, is more exuberant in its carving, but not to the riotous extent of *M. V. Treleaven*'s building for Boots the Chemist (1910–11) round the corner in Cornhill.

A different sort of commerce is represented by the STABLES of Newmarket and Exning. They were designed by specialist firms of architects, and although they can be decorative, they were not generally built for display, unlike country-house stables. Practicality was the key, as was security, given the money to be made from betting. In terms of planning, loose boxes opening on to a courtyard were preferred to stalls opening on to a corridor, which was the country-house model. Some provided covered rides, an early example being at Exeter House Stables, Newmarket, designed by *George Tattersall* and illustrated in his *Sporting Architecture* (1841). Harraton Court, Exning, is a particularly extensive establishment built for the Earl of Durham from the 1880s, with a racing yard, trainer's house and other staff accommodation. *Heaton & Gibb*, a Newmarket firm who specialized in such things, were at least partially responsible; they also built the Earl of Derby's Stanley House and stables in Newmarket, 1900–1. Machell Place Stables by *W. C. Manning* (1884) were considered exemplary in their day.

ARCHITECTURE SINCE 1914

The impact of the C20 on Suffolk is felt less than in many other counties, and less so on the W side of the county than the E. Adrian Bell's book *Corduroy* (1930), in which Bradfield St George is thinly disguised as Benfield St George, may seem to depict a vanished way of rural life, but in many respects it corresponds to the persisting popular view of Suffolk, and Bury St Edmunds ('Stambury') is still recognizable from his description. Many villages still feel almost untouched by the C20, the main change being that the cottages are lived in not by farmworkers but by professionals, and are in better condition (as are parish churches) than ever before. Yet the county of West Suffolk (as it then was) was the fastest growing county in the country by 1971, its population having increased by 27 per cent in the previous ten years.

Much of the history of architecture in the C20 in Suffolk has had more to do with the PRESERVATION of old buildings than the construction of new ones. Awareness of the threat to timber-framed buildings grew in the early years of the C20 as the result of some notorious cases. In 1908 an early C16 house in Lady Street, Lavenham, was dismantled and moved to Walberswick (E) by *Frank Jennings*. In 1911 *J. A. Sherman* (then still *Scheuermann*) was responsible for moving the C15 Hammond's Farmhouse, Hawstead, to Clacton-on-Sea (*see Buildings of England: Essex*, p. 244), and also arranged for a house at Thwaite to be shipped to Connecticut for the American architect Isaac Newton Phelps Stokes, who re-erected it there for his own occupation. When in 1912 workmen started taking down the early C16 Wool Hall, Lavenham, for Princess Louise there was a public outcry; work was stopped, materials that had been taken away were returned, and the building was reinstated by *William Weir*. This was not quite the turning point it is sometimes thought to have been, for a very similar situation occurred in 1926, with De Vere House, Water Street, Lavenham: in this case the house was reconstructed but without one of its fine timber ceilings, which went to America. The trade in old buildings and their components was of course a reflection of taste and fashion which, for example, led *W. G. Probert* to extend and embellish his house, Great Bevills, Bures (completed 1928), with reused timbers and brick. It was also the result of the desirable houses being thought to be in the wrong places, Lavenham not being considered a desirable village in the way that it became after the Second World War. The same attitude resulted in a C15 house being moved from Kersey to Bures in 1926 (Dunstead House); Old Hadleigh, Capel St Mary, on the other hand, was moved from Hadleigh in 1934 to save it from a road-widening scheme. The Society for the Protection of Ancient Buildings intervened on behalf of many buildings in Lavenham and elsewhere, including Lavenham Guildhall, the subject of what they considered a very unsympathetic restoration (by *Kemp & How*) in 1913. This building, which has become so iconic, had a very chequered history before it was finally vested in the National Trust in 1951. A significant development for the county was the foundation of the Suffolk Preservation Society in 1929 by Muriel Schofield, whose son *Sydney Schofield* restored Sun Court, Hadleigh, and Clock House, Little Stonham, for her in the 1920s, as well as High House, Otley (E).

The most representative C20 architect in w Suffolk was *Basil Oliver*, a member of the Sudbury brewing family whose business was taken over by Greene King in 1919. Although his office was in London his roots were firmly in Suffolk, and in 1912 he published *Old Houses and Village Buildings in East Anglia, Norfolk, Suffolk & Essex*, beautifully illustrated with his own measured drawings and sketches as well as photographs (including Lavenham Guildhall as the frontispiece). Old houses that he himself restored include The Grange, Chelsworth (1926–7), the Old Rectory, Great Whelnetham (1934), Castling's Hall, Groton (1933–4), Langley's Newhouse, Hawkedon (1930s), and Manston Hall, Whepstead (1938). He was also adept at Neo-Georgian, seen in his rebuilding of Beyton House (1936–7) and the Borough Offices, Bury St Edmunds (1935–7). He is also remembered as an expert on the design of pubs, but in that connection his work in Suffolk appears to be restricted to the inn sign of the Fox, Bury St Edmunds (but cf. the Rushbrooke Arms, Great Whelnetham); he may have had more influence behind the scenes at Greene King, and was probably responsible for *George Kruger Gray* being commissioned to design the glazed stoneware plaque (made by *Doulton & Co.*) that was fixed to all Greene King pubs from 1933. His versatility is further demonstrated by the *moderne* road sign known as the Pillar of Salt on Angel Hill, Bury St Edmunds (1935).

p. 184

2

2

The Fox Inn, Bury St Edmunds, was restored in 1922–3 by *Sidney Naish*, the town's leading resident architect from 1905 until his death in 1925. He was latterly in partnership with *William Henry Mitchell*, who practised as *Naish & Mitchell* until the late 1930s, then as *Mitchell & Houghton* (with *John Sanderson Houghton*) and finally as *Mitchell & Weston* (with *Norman Weston*). Mitchell collaborated with Oliver on the Borough Offices in Bury; otherwise Naish & Mitchell's major project was the old West Suffolk Hospital, Bury St Edmunds, in the 1920s and 1930s.

PRIVATE HOUSES were almost without exception traditional (Neo-Tudor or Neo-Georgian) up to the Second World War; the Modern Movement might never have existed as far as W Suffolk was concerned. The situation was generally very different after 1945, although from time to time traditional buildings are evoked, as at Tye House, Monks Eleigh, by *Sandon & Harding* (1968–9), which uses the form of a Suffolk farmhouse with hall range and cross-wings. *Eric Sandon* claimed the same inspiration for his Stratford Hills, Stratford St Mary (1960), with its jettied upper storey and central full-height hall, but in a more Modernist idiom. Purely Modernist are Second Pits, Monks Eleigh (1959), and Long Wall, Long Melford (1962–3), both by *Philip Dowson* (the former with *Steane, Shipman & Cantacuzino*, the latter with *Peter Foggo*), and *Aldington & Craig*'s Miesian Ketelfield, Higham (1974–6). At Wissington, Rosemary and Gerald Knox commissioned two houses from *Edward Cullinan*, New Maltings (1963–4) and Maltings Chase (1969–71), the latter with *Julyan Wickham*. Former members of Cullinan's office have also worked at Wissington: *Sunand Prasad* (*Penoyre & Prasad*) and *Simon Knox* (*Knox Bhavan Architects*) at New Maltings, and *Jeremy Stacey* building Chase Cottage (2007–8) for Mr and Mrs Knox. Other individual Modernist houses of note are Crystal Palace, Bury St Edmunds (1978), by *Michael & Patty Hopkins*, built soon after

p. 399

113

112

the similar house they had built for themselves in Downshire Hill, Hampstead, and the uncompromising extension by *James Gorst Architects* to the C16 Wakelins, Wickhambrook (2002–3). The latter could not be further in spirit from *Rodney Black*'s Wood Farm, Gipping (2000–4), a small C16 timber-framed house extended romantically over a pond. Cottars Hall, Hopton (1990–1), is an authentic timber-framed house, traditional in appearance and construction, by *Alan Horsfall*. Holm House, Drinkstone, by *KLH Architects* (2007–9) is an unusually elaborate example of a house that appears to have grown over the centuries, and would fulfil the desire of many to live in a traditional house but without any of the accompanying inconveniences.

LARGER-SCALE DEVELOPMENTS are inevitably of variable quality. The Mildenhall Estate, Bury St Edmunds, *c.* 1945–51 (by *Mitchell & Houghton* and the Borough Surveyor *N. C. Goldsmith*) stuck to pre-war Neo-Georgian. Cosford Rural District Council were equally conservative in appointing *Raymond Erith* to design housing at Cockfield, Hitcham and Polstead, *c.* 1949–58, as were Clare R.D.C. in appointing *A. E. Richardson* (*Richardson & Houfe*) for housing at Barnardiston, Hundon and Wickhambrook, 1950. Private clients could perhaps afford to take greater risks, and Lord Rothschild's rebuilding of the estate village at Rushbrooke, commissioned in 1950 from *Llewelyn-Davies & Weeks* and built in phases between then and 1963, was a remarkably bold undertaking. The mainly single-storey, white-painted houses with monopitch roofs contrast tellingly with the traditional thatched cottages of 1939 by *W. H. Mitchell*, and indeed the thatched Home Farm of *c.* 1938–9.

PUBLIC HOUSING on a large scale came to Suffolk with 'London overspill', first to Haverhill from 1955 and to Great Cornard from 1961, where most of the estates were designed by the *London County Council* (*Greater London Council* from 1965) under their architects *Sir Hubert Bennett* (1956–71) and *Sir Roger Walters* (1971–8). Brandon and Mildenhall were also considerably expanded in the 1960s and 1970s. The most interesting large-scale development, however, was Studlands Park, Newmarket, by *Ralph Erskine* (1968–75), comprising about 500 houses laid out round a large green, with enough variety and quirky detail to add interest. Conspicuous among the many housing schemes of the late C20 and early C21 is Clay Field, Elmswell, by *Riches Hawley Mikhail Architects*, 2005–8, where priority was given to affordability and sustainability. The materials used in their construction included hemp, which had been pioneered by *Modece Architects* in two experimental houses at Teasel Close, Haverhill, in 2001 and also used by the same architects at The Foundry, Lawshall (2005–6). Environmental concerns were also an important factor in the design of flats in Parkway and King's Road, Bury St Edmunds, by *Studio MGM* (2007–8), where the front is screened by a timber grid covered with climbing plants.

SCHOOLS on the 'London overspill' estates were left to *Suffolk County Architect's Dept*, first West Suffolk under *Jack Digby*, 1964–73, succeeded by *J. Brian Jackson*, 1973–4, who then became architect for the whole county, 1974–85. Digby came to Suffolk from Hertfordshire, with its strong reputation for school building, and very soon signed the county up to the South Eastern Architects' Collaboration (SEAC), a prefabricated modular building system initiated in Hertfordshire and developed in collaboration with Kent and Essex. In Suffolk it replaced the Derwent system used at Thurston (1965–6) and Risby (1967–8). Hartest (1965–6) was the first school with which Digby was personally involved, and it received a Civic Trust Commendation in 1968. The first school built using SEAC was Howard Primary School, Bury St Edmunds (1967), other notable examples being Bildeston (1967–8), Great Waldingfield (1969–70) and Hopton (1971–3) (all with *James Blackie* as project architect); Westley Middle School, Bury St Edmunds (1968–71); and secondary schools at Sudbury (1969–72), Thurston (1969–73), Mildenhall (1973–8) and Stowupland (1976–80). The last of these, with its black weatherboarding and pitched pantiles roofs, shows how SEAC could be adapted to suit the prevailing taste (in 1976) for vernacular forms, although Hartest, with its dormers and gabled roofs, had similarly been thought to be deferential to its village setting ten years earlier. Mildenhall is mainly of interest for its sports hall, a concrete 'parashell' that was erected in a single day in 1977. *Johns, Slater & Haward*, so prolific in and around Ipswich, designed a primary school at Hadleigh (1965–8) that uses *Birkin Haward*'s preferred 12-ft (3.7-metre) structural grid and pyramidal timber shell roofs, and the King Edward VI School, Bury St Edmunds, has a sports hall of 1968, a timber barrel vault designed in conjunction with consultant engineers *Stepien & Winiarski* similar in concept to the 'activity domes' that Haward built in Ipswich and Woodbridge (E). As with houses, schools have come to be designed with sustainability as an ever-greater priority, such as those at Hadleigh (2003) and Red Lodge (2011–12).

For COMMERCIAL AND PUBLIC BUILDINGS one again looks to Bury St Edmunds. The Borough Offices have been mentioned, and the new Shire Hall by *McMorran & Whitby*, 1958–68, is very much in the same tradition, albeit on a larger scale and in a very stripped-down, Soanean style of classical architecture. A quite different approach was taken by *Arup Associates* for Babergh District Council's offices at Hadleigh (1978–82), which integrated existing historic buildings into a varied and irregular complex. In addition to schools, notable work by the West Suffolk County Architect's Dept included the conversion of the Corn Exchange in Sudbury to a public library in 1968, and police housing in Maynewater Lane, Bury St Edmunds (1971–2). Elsewhere in Bury the old West Suffolk Hospital was replaced in 1969–73 by *Howard Goodman*, chief architect at the Department of Health & Social Security, with the first of a series of so-called 'Best Buy' hospitals, designed to be cheap to build and run. Blomfield House Health Centre, Bury, by *Johns, Slater & Haward*, won a Civic Trust Commendation in 1968 but was later castigated by Marcus Binney for being 'in what might be termed the official "pissoir" style – clad in shiny white tiles [and] designed with callous disregard for neighbouring buildings and the existing street pattern'; it has since been re-clad in red brick, and no longer seems quite so intrusive as, for example, the *Building Design Partnership*'s Cornhill Walk (1986–8). The buildings of Westgate Brewery may be out of scale but they nonetheless do not jar; the massive brewhouse by *W. H. Mitchell* (1936–9) makes an effort to reduce its impact on the street by having its upper floors set back. The brewery's Modernist buildings by *Lyster, Grillet & Harding* (1974) and *Michael Hopkins* (1978–81) are almost invisible. Mitchell also designed the Prior's Inn, Bury St Edmunds, for Greene King (1933), singled out for praise by Basil Oliver in his book *The Renaissance of the English Public House* (1947). An account of Bury's commercial buildings can end on a very positive note thanks to the ARC shopping centre by *Hopkins Architects* (2007–9) on the site of the town's cattle market, with new streets of traditional scale, using traditional materials but in a contemporary way, leading to a public square with civic auditorium and the emphatically non-traditional, curved, aluminium-clad Debenhams store.

Newmarket offers the Jockey Club Rooms, remodelled by *A. E. Richardson* (*Richardson & Gill*) in 1933–6 to provide luxurious accommodation for owners and trainers (but not jockeys). The same architects' Sale Ring at Tattersalls (1965) is, like so much else at Newmarket, *sui generis*, and the soaring Millennium Grandstand by *The Goddard Wybor Practice* (1998–2000) is the most exhilarating of the otherwise rather low-key racecourse buildings.

There is generally little to note as far as C20 CHURCHES are concerned. The most impressive new church was Our Lady Immaculate and St Etheldreda (R.C.), Newmarket, by *J. B. S. Comper*, 1966, a large brick basilica. *Inkpen Downie*'s new church at Clare Priory, 2011–13, is a successful Modernist extension to the medieval infirmary that had been adapted for use as a church in 1953–4. The United Reformed church, Stowmarket, by *A. D. Cooke* (1953–5), is nicely detailed but is not really suited to its surroundings. Bildeston and Stowmarket both had new spires by *Andrew Anderson*; in the former case the old tower collapsed in 1975, and the resulting pile of rubble can still be seen.

There is a general paucity too of good CHURCH FURNISHINGS. The continuing Suffolk tradition in seating is nowhere better illustrated than at Mildenhall, its nave filled with benches made by *Ernest Barnes* of Ipswich with carving by *H. Brown*, 1959–60, designed by *H. M. Cautley* and given by his wife Mabel. The chancel of Chevington shows that reordering (by *Keith Murray* with *Whitworth, Hall & Thomas*, 1983–4) can be most successful when bold rather than tactful. Burgate and Hitcham have very idiosyncratic reorderings of *c.* 1926–31 and 1934–49 respectively, the former including an extraordinary war memorial 'shrine' erected by *Rev. Benjamin Appleyard*, with altar ornaments made from shell cases by patients at the casualty clearing station in Belgium where he had been chaplain. A more conventional and equally impressive First World War memorial is in

St Mary, Bury St Edmunds, by *William A. Pite, Son & Fairweather*, with sculpture by *C. Whiffen*. Unusual memorials are those by *E. Sylvia Packard* at Bramford, *Charles Spooner* and *Minnie Dibdin Spooner* at Hadleigh, *Miss Rope* at Stowupland, and *Hon. Marion Saumarez* at Tostock, all of which include painting rather than carved lettering or sculpture. Outdoor memorials include the tall column by *Clyde Young* that stands at the point where the parishes of Elveden, Eriswell and Icklingham meet, and the cenotaph in Hadleigh by *Charles Spooner*. The best STAINED GLASS is by (or after) *Rosemary Rutherford*, at Boxford, Hinderclay and Walsham-le-Willows. As for SCULPTURE, Great and Little Thurlow each have maquettes by *Elisabeth Frink*, that at Little Thurlow (where she was born) for the statue of St Edmund (1976) that stands near the old W front of the abbey church in Bury St Edmunds. There is another sculpture by her inside the cathedral.

Which brings us to what is without doubt the greatest architectural achievement, the transformation of St James, Bury St Edmunds, into the cathedral for the diocese of St Edmundsbury and Ipswich that was created in 1914. *S. E. Dykes Bower* was appointed architect in 1945 and by 1970 had added the NW porch, the first phase of the cloisters, the choir, chapels, transepts and crossing, followed by the Cathedral Centre in 1988–90. When he died in 1994 he left money for the completion of the crossing tower, which was carried out between 1999 and 2005 by the *Gothic Design Practice* (*Hugh Mathew* and *Warwick Pethers*). The cloister and N transept were also extended and an outer N chapel built. Furnishings by Dykes Bower (and also by *F. E. Howard*, 1927) contributed also to the creation of an interior that, while not especially large, feels utterly cathedral-like, thanks to Dykes Bower's understanding of the importance of retaining a sense of mystery and revealing gradually rather than in a single sweep. The tower, significantly modified by Pethers, is in the very best Gothic tradition, largely but not entirely Suffolk in inspiration, and providing the visual climax that the cathedral, and indeed the town, previously lacked.

FURTHER READING

It is surprising that Suffolk's extensive bibliography does not include an early county history to rival Morant's *Essex*. The earliest useful work is *The Suffolk Traveller* by John Kirby of Wickham Market, published in 1735 (2nd edn 1764; facsimile of 1st edn published by the Suffolk Records Society, 2004). John Gage embarked upon *The History and Antiquities of Suffolk* but completed only one volume (1838), on the Thingoe Hundred W of Bury St Edmunds, and the two volumes of Alfred Suckling's admirable *The History and Antiquities of the County of Suffolk* (1846–8) covered only the hundreds of Wangford, Lothingland

and Mutford, as well as Leiston, all in the NE of the county. Two volumes of the *Victoria County History* were published in 1907 and 1911, with the first volume covering natural history, archaeology (now out of date, but the section on the Roman period has useful information on early discoveries) and the Domesday survey, and the second volume ecclesiastical history (including details of religious houses), schools, industry and other general topics. Older topographical works that remain useful include H. R. Barker's *West Suffolk, Illustrated* (1907) and *East Suffolk, Illustrated* (1908–9), partly for the sake of their photographs. Nor should county directories be overlooked, particularly for information about buildings recently erected; as well as Kelly's Post Office Directories there is William White's *History, Gazetteer, and Directory, of Suffolk*, first published in 1844 (facsimile reprint 1970), with new editions in 1855, 1874, 1885 and 1891–2. It goes without saying that the *Proceedings* of the Suffolk Institute of Archaeology and History (*PSIAH*), established in 1848, are indispensable (available online at *suffolkinstitute.pdfsrv. co.uk*). As well as the longer articles, the more recent volumes also contain detailed reports of excursions that often provide the most up-to-date accounts generally available of churches and other buildings.

The best general introduction to the county is *A History of Suffolk* by David Dymond and Peter Northeast (1995), supplemented by *An Historical Atlas of Suffolk*, edited by D. Dymond and Edward Martin (3rd edn 1999). The latter is a mine of information, presented in maps as well as words, on topics as wide-ranging as place-name patterns, rabbit warrens, crown-post roofs and airfields of the two world wars, with a comprehensive guide to further information. Norman Scarfe's *The Suffolk Landscape* (1972, revised editions 1987 and 2002) is essential for an understanding of how the county's landscape has been shaped by its inhabitants from earliest times, and places buildings in their wider context. Scarfe's interest in buildings and his unrivalled broad knowledge of them is evident in his excellent *Shell Guide*, first published in 1960 (new edns 1966, 1976 and (as *The Suffolk Guide*) 1988). This would be the right moment to mention *East Anglia's History: Studies in Honour of Norman Scarfe*, edited by C. Harper-Bill, C. Rawcliffe and R. G. Wilson (2002), which includes a number of chapters that will be referred to below.

David W. Lloyd's *Historic Towns of East Anglia* (1989) provides perceptive walks around twenty-seven Suffolk towns and larger villages. Eric Sandon did something similar for fifteen villages in *A View into the Village: a Study in Suffolk Building* (1969), although it has become something of a period piece and one might no longer share his enthusiasm for some of the recent buildings he mentions. The Suffolk Preservation Society has published an excellent series of booklets of guided walks, including *A Walk around Lavenham* (1977), *About Hadleigh* (1981), *Along Melford* (1983; 3rd edn 2000), and *Clare: the Place, the People* (1998). The same format has been used for *A Walk around*

Historic Nayland, published by the Nayland with Wissington Conservation Society (2000). Substantial works on individual places include *Bury St Edmunds: Medieval Art, Architecture, Archaeology and Economy* edited by Antonia Gransden (British Archaeological Association Conference Transactions 20, 1998) and *The Book of Bury St Edmunds* by Margaret Statham (1988, revised edn 1996); *The Culford Estate, 1780–1935* by Clive Paine (1993); *Hartest: A Village History* edited by Paine (1984); and by Barry Wall *Long Melford through the Ages: a Guide to the Buildings and Streets* (1986) and *Sudbury: History & Guide* (2004).

The archaeology of Suffolk is introduced well in the books mentioned in the previous paragraph, and in *Aspects of East Anglian Pre-history*, edited by Christopher Barringer (1984). The detailed evidence is to be found in the pages of *PSIAH* and in the series *East Anglian Archaeology*, published since 1975. The latter consists mainly of reports on single sites, but more general volumes include *Settlements on Hill-tops: Seven Prehistoric Sites in Suffolk* (1993), *A Corpus of Anglo-Saxon Material from Suffolk* (1998), *'Wheare most inclosures be': East Anglian Fields: History, Morphology and Management* (2008), and *Middle Saxon Animal Husbandry in East Anglia* (2012). *'Wheare most inclosures be'* includes Edward Martin's explanation of the Gipping Divide, which can be found also in 'Norfolk, Suffolk and Essex: Medieval Settlement in "Greater East Anglia"', in *Medieval Rural Settlement: Britain and Ireland, AD 800–1600*, edited by N. Christie and P. Stamper (2012). The Roman period is covered by *The Archaeology of Roman Suffolk* (1988) by Ivan E. Moore.

For CHURCHES the standard work remains H. Munro Cautley's *Suffolk Churches and their Treasures*, first published in 1937, although it is essential to have the fifth edition, 1982, which includes not only Cautley's own revisions from intermediate editions, but a considerably revised gazetteer to take account of his almost total disregard of churches built since the Reformation and furnishings later than the c18, as well as supplements on Victorian churches (by Anne Riches) and lost and ruined churches (by John Blatchly and Peter Northeast). Alongside Cautley stands D. P. Mortlock's *Guide to Suffolk Churches* (2009), superseding his three separate volumes published in 1988, 1990 and 1992. This provides readable accounts of practically every Anglican church in the county, including the most recent and least architecturally distinguished, but not churches of other denominations or redundant churches. For comprehensive coverage of churches and chapels of all denominations, including redundant churches as well as ruins and other remains, there is Simon Knott's website *www.suffolkchurches.co.uk*, with good photographs and a personal, sometimes polemical account of each one. *Suffolk Churches: a Pocket Guide*, published by the Suffolk Historic Churches Trust in 1976, remains a very handy introduction, with distinguished contributors and an introduction by Kenneth Clark, as does *Selig Suffolk: a Catalogue of Religious Art*, published by Ipswich Borough Council *c.* 1974. Stephen Hart's *The Round Church Towers of England* (2003) obviously includes the Suffolk examples, as do his books *Flint Architecture of East Anglia* (2000) and *Flint Flushwork: a Medieval Masonry Art* (2008). Round towers are also discussed by Steven J. Plunkett in 'Anglo-Saxon Stone Sculpture and Architecture in Suffolk', in *A Corpus of Anglo-Saxon Material from Suffolk*, edited by Stanley E. West (East Anglian Archaeology 84, 1998).

Many individual churches have first-class guidebooks; a great number have been written by Roy Tricker, and where these exist it is seldom necessary to look elsewhere for further information. Clive Paine is almost as prolific, and his accounts are to be found also in *PSIAH*. For Nonconformist churches there is Christopher Stell's *Inventory of Nonconformist Chapels and Meeting-Houses in Eastern England* (2002), and for individual denominations *'There my friends and kindred dwell': the Strict Baptist Chapels of Suffolk and Norfolk* by Tim Grass (2012) and *The Story of Ninety Years: Methodism in the Ipswich Circuit 1909–98* by Elizabeth Watthews and Janet Lumley (2001).

Books on specific aspects of Suffolk churches are dominated by Birkin Haward, who embarked upon a second career after retiring from architectural practice in 1977. First came *Nineteenth Century Suffolk Stained Glass* (1989), which certainly concentrated on the C19 in its explanatory text, but details stained glass of all periods in its gazetteer. It is largely owing to his pioneering work that much research since 1989 has been able to confirm (and occasionally correct) his attributions. In the present gazetteer Haward's attributions have only rarely been cited, on the grounds that to include them all would take up too much space, and those who are interested in the subject will wish to have Haward's book with them. *Stained Glass* was followed in 1993 by *Suffolk Medieval Church Arcades, 1150–1550*, an analysis of arcades and, in particular, their mouldings and piers, accompanied by meticulous measured drawings, in which he paid particular attention to the work of individual masons (many of whom can be found also in the 1987 edition of John Harvey's *English Medieval Architects: a Biographical Dictionary down to 1500*). This theme Haward developed in *Master Mason Hawes of Occold, Suffolk & John Hore Master Carpenter of Diss* (2000). He also compiled a mainly photographic survey of *Suffolk Medieval Church Roof Carvings* (1999), invaluable for providing images of details seldom visible from the ground.

As noted earlier, the researches of Adrian Allan and Peter Northeast have enabled many late medieval churches (or parts of them) to be dated with a degree of accuracy that was hitherto impossible. Northeast's notes are in the Suffolk Record Office and some of the results of his research were published in *East Anglia's History* ('Suffolk Churches in the Later Middle Ages: the Evidence of Wills'), but he was generous with his findings and many authors (including the present one) have made use of them. He also collaborated with John Blatchly on *Decoding Flint Flushwork on Suffolk and Norfolk Churches* (2005), which fully explains for the first time the meaning of the various symbols and initials to be found on so many Suffolk churches (addenda in

PSIAH 42, 2011, 347–56). Will evidence also provides the basis for 'Medieval Rood Screens in Suffolk: their Construction and Painting Dates' by S. Cotton, H. E. Lunnon and L. J. Wrapson (*PSIAH* 43, 2014).* Further work on rood screens has been done by Audrey Baker (*English Panel Paintings 1400–1558: a Survey of Figure Paintings on East Anglian Rood Screens*, 2011) and Tim Howson ('Suffolk Church Screens: their Production in the Late Middle Ages and their Conservation Today', unpublished thesis for the Architectural Association Postgraduate Diploma in Building Conservation, 2009). David Sherlock's *Suffolk Church Chests* (2008) makes up for their somewhat sparse coverage in the present volume, but has enabled the most important to be identified and included. For church monuments the principal guide is Ingrid Roscoe's *Biographical Dictionary of Sculptors in Britain, 1660–1851* (2009; available also as an online database via *www.henry-moore.org/hmi/library*), which builds on the *Dictionary* by Rupert Gunnis that had been the standard work of reference since it was first published in 1953. Adam White's 'Biographical Dictionary of London Tomb Sculptors *c.* 1560–*c.* 1660' (Walpole Society, 61 (1999) and 71 (2009)) takes the story further back. For brasses one still turns to Edmund Farrer's *List of Monumental Brasses Remaining in the County of Suffolk* (1903), as well as three books by T. M. Felgate, *Knights on Suffolk Brasses* (1976), *Suffolk Heraldic Brasses* (1978), and *Ladies on Suffolk Brasses* (1989). The Monumental Brass Society's volume on Suffolk is in preparation.† Roger Rosewell's *Medieval Wall Paintings* (2008) includes many Suffolk examples, as does, not surprisingly, H. M. Cautley's *Royal Arms and Commandments in our Churches* (1934, reissued 1974; supplemented by D. MacCulloch in *PSIAH* 32 (1971–2), 193–7 and 279). For church furnishings generally, over fifty churches have now been recorded by NADFAS Church Recorders, their inventories deposited in Suffolk Record Office, the English Heritage Archive and elsewhere.

Public Sculpture of Norfolk and Suffolk by Richard Cocke (2013) catalogues and illustrates a few church monuments, but is mostly concerned with free-standing outdoor sculpture, and architectural sculpture that is an integral part of the building it adorns. The content is also available on a website, *www.rucns.co.uk*.

For COUNTRY HOUSES, the equivalent of Cautley's book on churches is Eric Sandon's *Suffolk Houses: a Study of Domestic Architecture* (1977): equivalent, because Sandon, like Cautley, was an architect, who had worked on many of the buildings he described. It is comprehensive in its coverage, ranging from the greatest country houses down to farmhouses and cottages, and even includes a short postscript on C20 houses. Sandon's conclusions do not always stand up to scrutiny – his analysis of Alston Court, Nayland, for example, is flawed – but the book is an

---

*Forthcoming at the time of writing; I am grateful to the authors for allowing me to read and make use of the article before publication.
†I am grateful to H. Martin Stuchfield for providing me with a draft.

essential first port of call, and its illustrations include photographs of interiors that might otherwise be inaccessible. Another good starting point is the East Anglian volume of *Burke's and Savills Guide to Country Houses* (1981), the Suffolk section of which was written by Peter Reid. A dozen Suffolk houses are covered by Anthony Emery's *Greater Medieval Houses of England and Wales, 1300–1500* (vol. 2, *East Anglia, Central England and Wales*, 2000) and more are analysed in Andor Gomme and Alison Maguire's *Design and Plan in the Country House: from Castle Donjons to Palladian Boxes* (2008). Many individual houses have been written up over the years for *Country Life*. Others are to be found in the pages of older works, the value of which is mixed. Henry Davy's *Views of the Seats of Noblemen and Gentlemen in Suffolk* (1827) can help to identify later alterations and additions, as well as documenting houses that have been demolished. The latter are the melancholy subject of W. M. Roberts's *Lost Country Houses of Suffolk* (2010), which covers forty demolished between 1914 and 2002. Another work containing useful references, but more for information about owners than houses themselves, is W. A. Copinger's *The Manors of Suffolk* (7 vols, 1905–11). Thanks to the good survival of plans in the Suffolk Record Office the county features strongly in *The English Parsonage in the Early Nineteenth Century* by Timothy Brittain-Catlin (2008).

The setting of country houses is covered by Tom Williamson's *Suffolk's Gardens and Parks: Designed Landscapes from the Tudors to the Victorians* (2000). Detailed studies of aspects of the subject include *'Pastime of Pleasure': a Celebration of Suffolk Gardens from the Seventeenth Century to the Present Day* (Suffolk Gardens Trust and Manor House Museum, Bury St Edmunds, 2000), and essays by Edward Martin ('Garden Canals in Suffolk') and Tom Williamson ('Shrubland before Barry: a House and its Landscape 1660–1880') in *East Anglia's History*.

For HOUSES further down the social scale, Basil Oliver's *Old Houses and Village Buildings in East Anglia* (1912) is still of great value, not least for its magnificent photographs and Oliver's own measured drawings. There are a few Suffolk examples in Eric Mercer's *English Vernacular Houses: a Study of Traditional Farmhouses and Cottages* (1975), and Matthew Johnson's *Housing Culture: Traditional Architecture in an English Landscape* (1993) is a study of vernacular houses in W Suffolk. The understanding of vernacular buildings generally, and timber-framed buildings in particular, has changed enormously in recent years. There is no overall account of the subject for Suffolk, and one has to look in a variety of places, first and foremost *Eavesdropper*, the newsletter (but substantial and well illustrated) of the Suffolk Historic Buildings Group, published since 1994; a twentieth-anniversary selection was published in 2013. Their journal, *Historic Buildings of Suffolk*, unfortunately appeared only once, in 1998. Other contributions to the subject can be found in *Regional Variation in Timber-Framed Building in England and Wales down to 1550* (Essex County Council, 1998), *The English*

Medieval Roof: Crownpost to Kingpost (Essex Historic Buildings Group, 2011) and *The Vernacular Workshop: from Craft to Industry* (Council for British Archaeology Research Report 140, 2004). Leigh Alston's notes for those attending the conference of the Vernacular Architecture Group (Spring 2001) contain analyses of a number of buildings in Badley, Bedfield, Bury St Edmunds, Debenham, Lavenham, Nayland and Needham Market. *Vernacular Architecture* includes summaries of the latest tree-ring datings. Much of the above applies equally to farm buildings, together with articles by Philip Aitkens and Susanna Wade Martins in the *Journal of the Historic Farm Buildings Group* 3 (1989) and 13 (1999). Those interested in dovecotes need look no further than *The Dovecotes of Suffolk* by John McCann (1998). The hitherto neglected subject of internal painted decoration is introduced by Timothy Easton in 'The Internal Decorative Treatment of 16th- and 17th-century Brick in Suffolk', in *Post-Medieval Archaeology* 20 (1986), and Andrea Kirkham in 'Pattern and Colour in Late 16th- and 17th-century Secular Wall and Panel Paintings in Suffolk: an Overview', in *All Manner of Murals: the History, Techniques and Conservation of Wall Paintings*, edited by R. Gowing and R. Pender (2007).

For the practitioners of 'polite' architecture one turns of course to H. M. Colvin's *Biographical Dictionary of British Architects, 1600–1840* (4th edn, 2008). Suffolk is exceptionally fortunate in having a sequel in the shape of the *Dictionary of Architects of Suffolk Buildings, 1800–1914* (1991), compiled by Cynthia Brown, Birkin Haward and Robert Kindred, and modestly subtitled 'a working document'. Unlike the RIBA's *Directory of British Architects, 1834–1914* (2001), the Suffolk dictionary includes – indeed, consists principally of – lists of buildings, with relatively brief biographical summaries, but for local architects these usually provide the only readily available information on their subjects. Where it should be treated as a working document, and therefore with some caution, is that the lists of buildings are not selective and depend very much on the availability of source material (e.g. plans deposited with the local planning authority), and no systematic attempt was made to establish whether designs were executed and, if so, whether buildings have subsequently been altered or demolished – although that information is indeed frequently provided, when known. But it is an exemplary work that should be the envy of every other county, and has revealed just how much good architecture of the period there is in a county not generally renowned for it.

For the TWENTIETH CENTURY the evidence has to be pieced together from a number of sources, starting perhaps with the Twentieth Century Society's journal *Twentieth Century Architecture* and its 'Gazetteer of Modern Houses' (vol. 2, 1996), 'Places of Christian Worship 1914–1990' (vol. 3, 1998) and 'List of Architect-designed Houses in England 1945–1975' (vol. 4, 2000, which also includes articles by Hugh Pilkington on Long Wall, Long Melford, and by Richard Gray on John Penn's Suffolk houses). The Society has also organized a number of tours to

Suffolk (as has the Victorian Society) for which comprehensive notes by Alan Powers et al. were provided for those attending. A narrower period is covered by Charles McKean's *Architectural Guide to Cambridge and East Anglia since 1920*, published in 1982, which has a strong emphasis on the 1960s and 1970s. Much the same period is covered by the RIBA's *Recent East Anglian Buildings*, published between 1977 and 1980, and *ERA*, a journal published by the RIBA Eastern Region between 1968 and 1977. Issue 45 (1977) was devoted to Ipswich and includes articles on the architects H. M. Cautley, E. T. Johns, R. M. Phipson and J. A. Sherman. Useful sources of information about public architecture are *A Century of Service: the County Councils of Suffolk 1889–1989*, which includes lists of the various county surveyors and architects, and two publications of *The Work of the Suffolk County Architect's Department* covering 1974–9 and 1974–84. The problems of conservation, and the difficulty of designing new buildings that harmonize with old, are addressed by Celia Jennings in *The Identity of Suffolk* (1980), written to mark the fiftieth anniversary of the Suffolk Preservation Society, and *Patterns for Suffolk Buildings: a Simple Design Guide* (1993). An interesting study of conservation issues in Lavenham and Sudbury is J. S. Michalak's unpublished thesis 'A Tale of Two Small Towns: Conservation, Commerce and the Property Market and their Impact on Timber-framed Buildings in the Twentieth Century' (MA in Conservation Studies, University of York Department of Archaeology, 2000), themes explored also in James Bettley's 'The Wool Hall, Lavenham: an episode in the history of preservation', in *Transactions of the Ancient Monuments Society* 57 (2013).

INDUSTRIAL ARCHAEOLOGY (the quantity of which may surprise those who think of Suffolk as consisting entirely of thatched cottages and wool churches) is well covered in *The Batsford Guide to the Industrial Archaeology of East Anglia* by David Alderton and John Booker (1980) and (less comprehensively, but in more detail) Peter Cross-Rudkin's *Civil Engineering Heritage: East Anglia* (2010). The many books on windmills include Brian Flint's *Suffolk Windmills* (2012). A guide to industry in general is provided by *Suffolk Enterprise: a Guide to the County's Companies and their Historical Records* by Christine Clark and Roger Munting (*c.* 2000). The progress of railways across the county is detailed in *Railways of Britain: Norfolk and Suffolk* by Colin and David McCarthy (2007), and Gordon Biddle's *Britain's Historic Railway Buildings* (2003) covers the important Suffolk stations. Patrick Taylor's *The Toll-Houses of Suffolk* (2009) throws some light on road travel and includes a useful list of 'impostors' – lodges and other cottages (usually round) generally mistaken for toll houses.

Mention should also be made of English Heritage's useful monographs, of which *Cold War: Building for Nuclear Confrontation 1946–1989* (2003) by Wayne D. Cocroft and Roger J. C. Thomas (2003), *English Prisons: an Architectural History* by Allan Brodie et al. (2002) and *The Workhouse: a Study of Poor-Law Buildings in*

England by Kathryn Morrison (1999) contain much Suffolk material. *England's Schools 1962–88: a Thematic Study* by Geraint Franklin et al. (Research Report Series no. 33-2012) includes important sections on local authority schools in West Suffolk and Ipswich.

For listed buildings, scheduled monuments, and registered parks and gardens the most up-to-date version of the National Heritage List is on the English Heritage website, *www.englishheritage.org.uk*. Heritage Gateway (*www.heritagegateway.org.uk*) provides access not just to the National Heritage List but also to related databases such as PastScape (*www.pastscape.org.uk*) and the Suffolk Historic Environment Record, which contain much more detailed information about individual sites, including archaeology. Images of England (*www.imagesofengland.org.uk*) gives the list descriptions of all listed buildings as at 2000 and an exterior photograph of most.

Among other useful WEBSITES, *www.suffolkchurches.co.uk* has already been mentioned. The Corpus of Romanesque Sculpture (*www.crsbi.ac.uk*) includes records for nearly 150 Suffolk churches. Information about the great majority of work to churches in the C19 and C20 can be found at *www.churchplansonline.org.uk*, the database of the archive of the Incorporated Church Building Society at Lambeth Palace Library. Suffolk Heritage Direct (*www.suffolkheritagedirect.org.uk*) gives access to a number of heritage organizations, including the Suffolk Record Office and its online catalogue. Suffolk Painters (*suffolkpainters.co.uk*) provides information on a great many artists who worked closely with or were themselves architects. Many of the books referred to in Further Reading have been digitized and are available online, including White's *Directory* and the works of Copinger and Suckling, as well as the *PSIAH*. Finally, Pevsner in Suffolk (*www.pevsnersuffolk.co.uk*) is an unofficial website that consists principally of photographs of buildings mentioned in the second edition.

GAZETTEER

ACTON

ALL SAINTS. Restored by *W. M. Fawcett*, 1885–6, except for the s porch, restored some twenty years earlier, and the w tower, the upper part of which was taken down and only rebuilt (by *Hunt & Coates*) in 1923. Base of tower *c.* 1300, also the s aisle and s chapel (Y-tracery). s chapel continued E for the Jennens monument, *c.* 1726 (*see* below). N doorway and N chapel Dec; N chapel E window 1885–6. Arcades with piers with four polygonal shafts, those to the nave and aisles broader and stronger and without capitals. Between the chancel and the N chapel a big Dec MONUMENT, the tomb-chest of Andrew and Sir Robert de Bures, †1360 and †1361; on top a slab with indents of a foliated cross and shields; cusped arch, and ogee gable. – COMMUNION RAIL. Late C17, with turned balusters. – BENCH ENDS with poppyheads, one of them with a pair of moorhens. – ROYAL ARMS. Hanoverian. Carved wood. – TILES. A few medieval floor tiles (N chapel). – CURIOSUM. A bomb dropped by a Zeppelin, 1916 (w tower). – STAINED GLASS. E window by *Heaton, Butler & Bayne*, 1871. – BRASSES. The brass to Sir Robert de Bures †1331 is one of the oldest and finest in England. It may have been engraved before his death, perhaps *c.* 1320. The figure is nearly 6 ft 7 in. (200 cm.) tall. He wears chain-mail, over his head as well, no helmet, and a long surcoat. His legs are crossed and the feet are on a lion. His hands are in prayer. Exquisite engraving. – Alice de Bryan †1435. Under a triple canopy. The figure is 4 ft 9 in. (145 cm.) long. – Henry Bures †1528. Long-legged 36-in. (92-cm.) figure, in armour. – Edmund Daniel †1569. 15-in. (38-cm.) figure, in civilian dress, with wife, Margaret. – John Daniel †1598. 15-in. (38-cm.) figure, in civilian dress. – MONUMENT. Robert Jennens †1725/6, adjutant to the Duke of Marlborough. It was put up, and the little vaulted chapel built for it, by Jennens's widow, Ann. Standing wall monument. Reredos background with Corinthian pilasters. He reclines comfortably on a mattress. His elbow rests on a pillow and his head is propped up by his hand. He looks towards his wife, who is seated

Acton, All Saints, brass of Sir Robert de Bures †1331.
Rubbing by M. Stuchfield, 2014

by his feet. Minute details of the dress very competently carved. Emotionally the figures are perhaps less convincing. Attributed to the partnership of *Henry Scheemakers* and *Henry Cheere* (GF).

ACTON PLACE. Robert Jennens had commissioned *James Gibbs* to design a very large mansion ½ m. NW of the church, but it remained unfinished at Jennens's death. It consisted of a four-storey centre, eleven bays wide with three-bay pediment and hipped roof, connected by single-storey quadrants to two-storey, nine-bay pavilions. The main house was demolished in 1825, one of the pavilions about twenty years later, and the remaining pavilion in 1960. The site is now an industrial park.

OLD VICARAGE, ½ m. SSE. Rebuilt 1852 by *Ewan Christian*, following a fire. Knapped flint with cast stone dressings. The plan seems to follow that of the old timber-framed house, with central hall entered by a gabled porch, and gabled cross-wings.

LONG WALL, Newman's Green. *See* Long Melford, p. 399.

ALDHAM

0040

No obvious village; just the church and hall, perched on the side of a valley.

ST MARY. Very much restored. In 1883–5 *W.M. Fawcett* rebuilt the s wall of the nave, as well as a large part of the N wall, and all but 20 ft (6 metres) of the round flint tower; new chancel arch, roofs and s porch. The E wall of the chancel was rebuilt by *H. M. Cautley*, 1933–4. Nave and chancel have windows in the style of *c.* 1300. – REREDOS. By *Cautley*, with niches l. and r. of the window. – Also by *Cautley* most of the woodwork, too much of it and too heavy for this rural church, including BENCHES with poppyheads; older restored ones at the W end, one with a panel dated 1537. – LECTERN. Restored 1885; the base at least is medieval. – SCULPTURE. Built into the jamb of a nave S window, a fragment of an Anglo-Saxon grave-slab with interlace ornament. Another fragment, with ribbon ornament, is built into the SW corner of the nave as a quoin. – ROYAL ARMS. Two sets: George III and Elizabeth II. – STAINED GLASS. E window by *Horace Wilkinson*, 1933.

ALDHAM HALL. Timber-framed and plastered. At the s end a hall range of *c.* 1420. Extending N an early C16 range, jettied on both sides. Evidence has been found of a fine oriel window on the W side, facing into the courtyard.

OLD RECTORY, 1 m. NW. Alterations by *William Rogers*, 1849–50. Two-storey L-plan addition to existing building. Red brick with stone dressings. Tudor-style straight gables.

ALDHAM MILL, and MONUMENT on Aldham Common. *See* Hadleigh, p. 283.

ALPHETON

8050

ST PETER AND ST PAUL. Nave and chancel, and quite a substantial Perp W tower. Pretty s doorway with fleuron decoration. Dec SEDILIA and PISCINA composition damaged by a later window. The piscina is in the angle of the window. Niches l. and r. of the chancel arch, the one to the N fixed higher in 1839, when the squint to the pulpit was inserted in the pier.

The niches have vaulting and remains of colouring, and the one to the N a Bacchic mask. Scissor roof in nave; crown-post roof in the C15 timber-framed S porch. Porch restored by *G.A.T. Middleton*, 1911–13, with new doors. General restoration by *Hunt & Coates*, 1936–8. – ALTAR. By *Rev. Ernest Geldart*, 1902, made by *Taylor & Clifton*. The front was meant to have painted panels. Also PRIESTS' STALLS, 1903, made by *T. Cadge*. The seat on the N side is medieval in origin, its back made up of two misericords. – PULPIT. Jacobean, the base 1906. – BENCHES. Some ends with medieval poppyheads, copied for new CHOIR STALLS by *John & Henry Leeks* of Long Melford, *c.* 1853. – PAINTING. Late C14 St Christopher on the N wall; dim. – ROYAL ARMS. Of Charles II, on boards. Charmingly rustic. – STAINED GLASS. E window by *Pippa Blackall*, 2000. Incorporating C18 or C19 quarries.

The aisled BARN of OLD HALL FARM, next to the church, is mainly C16, but has at its E end three bays that are C13 or possibly C12. Part of the original aisle structure survives unaltered.

MILL HOUSE, Bridge Street, ¾ m. SSE. C15, timber-framed and plastered. Gabled cross-wings, the one to the r. jettied. Crown-post roof with smoke-blackened timbers. Chimney inserted *c.* 1500; red brick panel over fireplace with arcade of trefoiled arches. Hall floored in the early C17 (tree-ring date 1618). Restored scheme of polychrome painted decoration.

AMPTON

ST PETER. Nave, chancel and W tower. Restored by *S.S. Teulon*, *c.* 1848, and *Balfour & Turner* in 1888–9. The latter restoration seems to have left more of a mark, including a new N vestry, re-seating, new nave roof, and 'perfecting' the chancel roof. This is late C15, boarded and painted with C17 strapwork decoration. N chantry chapel at the E end of the nave built, according to its inscription, as a Capella Perpetue Cantarie Joh'is Coket. The foundation was granted in 1479. Four-centred arch from the church with brattishing over. The arch is panelled inside. – COMMUNION RAIL. Late C18. – PULPIT. Early C18, simply panelled, with tester; remodelled in 1889. – CHEST. Oak, heavily bound with iron and large-headed nails; *c.* 1420. – ROYAL ARMS. Of Charles I, probably 1636. Fretwork, painted, originally fixed to the top of the rood beam (now at W end). Badges of Scotland and England alongside. – STAINED GLASS. By *Burlison & Grylls*, 1889. In thanksgiving for the fact that no lives were lost when Ampton Hall burnt down (*see* below): small scene of Shadrach, Meshach and Abednego in the burning fiery furnace. – MONUMENTS. Brasses probably of Cokets: kneeling Civilian and Wife, *c.* 1480 (17½ in. (44.5 cm.)); Lady of *c.* 1480 (17 in. (43 cm.)); Lady of *c.* 1490

(12 in. (30 cm.); palimpsest of portion of a Lady of *c.* 1470); two sons (only 6 in. (15 cm.)), *c.* 1490. – William Whettell †1628/9 by *Nicholas Stone*. Rather flatly modelled frontal bust in an arched niche. Good, with beautiful detailing of his ruff and lace cap. – Sir Henry Calthorpe and wife, Dorothy, by *John & Matthias Christmas*, 1638. Two frontal demi-figures holding hands; in a circular niche. Small figures of children in the 'predella' below. Two columns support a broken segmental pediment. – Dorothy Calthorpe †1693. Kneeling figure in an arched niche, a conservative motif. Attributed to *William Stanton* (GF). – James Calthorpe †1702. Marble oval, with elaborate surround of drapery, foliage and cherubs' heads. – James Calthorpe †1784. Oval medallion with head in profile, before an obelisk. By *John Bacon Sen.* (*PSIAH* vol. 1 (1853) p. 195), but not signed. – Lt B.W.T. Wickham †1917. *Opus sectile* figure of St George by *Powell & Sons*, in one of the panels of the entrance to the Coket Chapel. In the facing panel a corresponding figure of St Christopher, 1919 (designed by *Read*), commemorating the use of Ampton Hall as a Red Cross hospital.

AMPTON HALL. Burnt down in 1885 and rebuilt in a restrained Tudor style by *Balfour & Turner* in 1885–9. Red brick with stone dressings. Two storeys. The entrance front, facing the church, follows the character of the old house: mullioned-and-transomed windows with pediments, and crowstepped gables. Simpler E front, with two broad canted bays. Flint and brick STABLES to the S survived the fire; *Teulon* may have had a hand. Fine wrought-iron GATES, said to have come from Livermere Hall, Great Livermere (q.v., also for the PARK).*

Small estate VILLAGE. S of the church the OLD SCHOOLHOUSE, founded by James Calthorpe in 1692 and built in 1705–6. Painted brick front, otherwise of flint and red brick. Two storeys and attics. Four widely spaced bays. N of the church former ALMSHOUSES of 1693, founded by James's sister Dorothy Calthorpe for six spinsters. Single-storey. In the centre a projecting bay with rusticated brick quoins and pediment. Beyond it a wall of flint with white brick dressings, including rusticated piers and good rusticated ARCHWAY with pediment and inscription ET VOLUPTATI PLURIMUM ET SALUTI: it refers to Ampton Hall's kitchen garden, supplying both great pleasure and health. At the N end of the village, a former LODGE and entrance to Livermere Hall.

ASSINGTON

ST EDMUND. Perp, predominantly flint, with four-bay arcades. Tall S porch built with a bequest of 1396, its side windows now

---

*There was in the park a domed Doric TEMPLE by *Robert Browne*, exhibited at the Royal Academy in 1793.

blocked up. Thoroughly but attractively restored by the incumbent, *Rev. Philip Gurdon*, in 1863: the W tower and chancel were rebuilt, the N vestry added, the nave re-roofed and re-seated. – SOUTH DOORS. With tracery and a border of foliage trails. Something of a puzzle. They seem Perp, but the churchwardens' accounts for 1766 record payment of £13 3s. to *Thomas Elliston* for church doors, as well as £1 5s. 6d. for locks and bolts and 2s. carriage from London. Expenditure on bricks etc. indicates quite a lot of work to the church that year. – SCULPTURE. Renewal of Life by *Richard Heseltine*, 1996–7. – STAINED GLASS. E window, probably by *Clayton & Bell*, part of the 1863 restoration, together with the carved oak REREDOS, which incorporates some old work. Chancel S and tower window by *Powell & Sons*, 1863. – MONUMENTS. Brass to Robert Taylboys †1506 and wife Letitia. 30-in. (76-cm.) figures. – A fine sequence of monuments to the Gurdons of Assington Hall, beginning with Robert †1577 and wife and John †1623 and wife. Double monument of *c.* 1625 with two pairs of the usual kneeling figures facing one another across a prayer-desk. Children in the 'predella'. – Brampton Gurdon, dated 1648. His demi-figure and those of his two wives; represented frontally. He is flanked by columns. Top with a handsome pedimental arrangement. Attributed to *John & Matthias Christmas* (GF). – Nathaniel Gurdon †1696. Cartouche with drapery, cherubs' heads and skull. Attributed to *James Hardy* (GF). – Similar monuments to John Gurdon †1758 and his wife Lettitia †1710, and John Gurdon †1777. – Rev. Philip Gurdon †1817 and wife. Tablet by *John Bacon Jun.* – Large monument to Bridget Gurdon †1826 and others by *D.W. Willson*. Various symbols of death. Another by Willson to Rev. John Hallward †1826. – War memorial. White marble tablet by *Basil Oliver*, 1920, executed by *Joseph Armitage*. – In churchyard, further Gurdon monuments: one of coffin-lid type (†1854, deeply carved with floriated cross), another of churchyard-cross type (†1859, column on tapering octagonal base, with kneeling angels on top).

ASSINGTON HALL. The late C16 red brick house N of the church was almost completely destroyed by fire in 1957. It had been significantly altered *c.* 1770 and in 1817. What remains is the shell of the two-storey porch, two polygonal clasping buttresses with ogee tops from either end of the entrance front, and part of the servants' wing. To the W, the former stables and coach house: early C19 white brick with two-storey pedimented centre.

HOME FARM, 700 yds N. Octagonal, timber-framed and plastered, and thatched. Late C18 or early C19, no doubt connected with Assington Hall.

ASSINGTON HOUSE, ¾ m. ESE. Timber-framed, with a nice C18 gault-brick front of seven bays. Doorcase with open pediment.

ASSINGTON MILL, 1¼ m. S. Probably the watermill mentioned in Domesday and again in 1588. Stopped working in 1868;

no surviving machinery, but a steel wheel was installed in 2006 to generate electricity. Weatherboarded, with mansard roof. Late C17 house, also timber-framed, restored and extended 2004–6 by *Hilary Brightman*. Ancillary buildings include four constructed of straw bales, 2005–11. Plastered inside and out. One circular with thatched roof, another of two storeys.

BACTON

ST MARY. Dec W tower. The bell-openings have Y-tracery and also flowing tracery, which is unusual for towers. Early C16 stair-turret of brick. Aisles and S porch Perp. Inscription on the S aisle seeking prayers for the souls of Sir James Hobart, Attorney-General under Henry VII, his wife Margaret, and their parents; on the N aisle, for Robert Goche and his wife Agnes, who gave plate to the church in 1485. Clerestory with doubled windows. The arches with intermittent radially placed bricks. The windows are of two lights with panel tracery. A variety of flushwork emblems between them, including initials of C15 abbots of Bury and the *Aldryche* device. The arcade is of five bays and has octagonal piers and double-chamfered arches. Nave roof with false double hammerbeams, the figures sawn off. Big square flowers on the wall-plates. Colouring over the rood bays. The aisle roofs also have decorated wall-plates. The chancel roof is cambered and has arched braces. The E bays have coloured stylized symmetrical leaves or palmettes. The roofs were restored by *William Butterfield*, 1860–4, with painting by *Herbert Orsbourn* of Bacton; repainting by *Jenny Goater* of Palgrave, 1995–6. Butterfield also took down a W gallery, restored the chancel and added the N vestry. W end of nave reordered by the *Whitworth Co-Partnership*, 2009–11, with meeting room and organ gallery. – FONT. Octagonal, Perp. Against the stem two tiers of shields and square flowers. Against the bowl angels with shields, a shield, and square flowers. – COMMUNION RAIL and PULPIT. By *Butterfield*. – SCREEN. With one-light divisions, ogee arches, and close panel tracery above them. Originally a parclose screen to the S aisle chapel, moved by Butterfield. – BENCHES. Two, with carved backs, poppyheads, and on the arms three animals and one kneeling figure. Restored by Butterfield, who designed new benches for the aisles. – WALL PAINTING. Doom over the chancel arch, discovered in 1854 and cleaned in 1968. Including St Peter in papal tiara receiving the righteous. C15. – STAINED GLASS. E window by *Morris & Co.*, 1922 (war memorial). Including figures designed by (or adapted from designs by) *Burne-Jones* and *J. H. Dearle*. – Chancel S †1858 by *O'Connor*. – MONUMENTS. Thomas Smyth †1702 and wife Dorothy †1728. Inscription with coat of arms and *trompe l'œil* drapery, very nicely painted on the respond at the E end of the N arcade.

– George Pretyman †1732 and widow Jane †1738. Two good cartouches facing each other across the nave.
MANOR HOUSE, 350 yds w. Built by George Pretyman, *c.* 1720. Red brick with chequer of dark blue headers. Two storeys and attics. Hipped roof. Five-bay centre and two-bay slightly projecting wings. Three-bay pediment, with coat of arms and lively garlands added *c.* 1738. Doorway with broken segmental pediment on carved brackets. In the pediment a bust of Mercury. C19 and C20 additions to rear. Staircase with twisted balusters to the first floor, turned balusters to the attics. Ground- and first-floor rooms panelled, formerly with overmantel paintings said to be by *Thomas Bardwell*. One, dated 1741, depicted the house itself, showing single-storey two-bay wings to l. and r.*
BACTON GRANGE, 1 m. SW. Built as the rectory for Rev. A. B. Hemsworth, 1860, by *Witherden Young*. White brick. 'Elizabethan', according to the *Ipswich Journal* (8 December 1860), but not in a way that the C16 would have recognized.

BADLEY

ST MARY (Churches Conservation Trust). A lonely church, and one left happily unnoticed by the Victorian restorers; it remains very much as described by D. E. Davy in 1827, and as drawn by H. Davy in 1841. w tower unbuttressed, with brick top, and with a huge Perp w window put in later than the tower was built. Nave and chancel. In the chancel an early C13 slit lancet. In the nave a s doorway of the same time. Simple pointed arch with one slight chamfer. Rough wooden s porch with sheep-gate. The interior is memorable for its untreated, bleached woodwork – a beautifully pale, silvery tone. Crownpost roof with four-way struts. – FONT. Of Purbeck marble, C13, octagonal, with the customary two flat blank pointed arches on each side. – SCREEN. Only the dado, used as one side of a C17 pew. Other pews incorporate tracery, datable to the C14, that may have formed part of the screen. The colouring of the dado may or may not be original. – Two-decker PULPIT, also C17. – BENCHES. Rough, with poppyheads and animals on the arms. – COMMUNION RAIL. Of iron, *c.* 1830. – STAINED GLASS. E window by *F. Preedy*, 1866. – MONUMENTS. Edward Poley †1548 and others. With obelisks. – Dorothy Poley †1625. Ledger stone in sanctuary. The inscription should be read. – Henry Poley †1707. Inscription flanked by pilasters. Open segmental pediment. – Henrietta Robins †1728. Outside the chancel s wall. Elaborate framing of a sarcophagus.†

---

*Reproduced in Eric Sandon, *Suffolk Houses* (1977), p. 226; no longer in the house.
†CHEST now at Redgrave (q.v.).

BADLEY HALL, N of the church, was a substantial courtyard house built c. 1520 by Edmund Poley. In 1735 it was sold to Abraham Crowley of Barking, who at the same time bought the adjoining Combs Hall estate; and like Combs Hall, Badley Hall was largely demolished by Crowley's successors, some of its timbers being offered for sale in 1759. The present timber-framed, L-plan house is the SW corner of the Tudor house, part of the service range. It is mostly plastered, but has a panel of brick-nogging with diapering, emphasized by painting. Around this, carved buttress-shafts and bressumer. The main hall adjoined to the N. S of the present house a former BAKEHOUSE, and E of that a late C16 DOVECOTE. Its construction is unusual in that the oak boards that form the sides of the nest boxes also function as studding for the timber frame. Other buildings include a C15 or early C16 BARN with queenpost roof. The extent of the house is known from an estate map of 1741, which also shows a double avenue, 1,500 yds (1,370 metres) long, running straight from the front of the house, past the N side of the church, to the road; the line of this remains, as well as two distinctively shaped groves halfway along.

BADWELL ASH

ST MARY. Right in the centre of the village. Perp W tower with an inscription on the battlements asking for prayers for John Fincham and his wife Margaret. Money for the tower was bequeathed (not by the Finchams) in 1476–87. Flushwork emblems on the buttresses and base, including what seems to be a group of farm implements (N of the W door) and mason's tools (S of the door). Perp also the S porch. This has a façade with flushwork panelling all over. In the spandrels of the entrance arch St George and the Dragon. More flushwork emblems, including blacksmith's tools on the r. buttress, and on the E side the *Aldryche* device. One niche above the entrance. The PISCINA in the S aisle is of c. 1300, i.e. has no ogee forms yet. The arcade between nave and aisle with tallish octagonal piers and double chamfered arches. The chancel is Dec too. The tracery in the two-light windows has the motif of the four-petalled flower. The nave N windows are Perp, tall, of two lights. On the S side at that time the clerestory was built or rebuilt with seven windows as against the four bays below. Roof with alternating hammerbeams and tie-beams on short arched braces. Both rest on wall-posts with small figures. Against the hammerbeams large angels. The tie-beams are dated 1703 and may have been added to prevent the spread of the roof. Chancel roof of 1867–8, when there was a general restoration and re-seating. – FONT. Octagonal, Dec. Shields on the stem. On the bowl, ogee arches carried by heads. Embattled top. – STAINED GLASS. E window by *Powell & Sons*, designed by *Penwarden*, 1920. S aisle E by *Heaton, Butler & Bayne*, 1920 (war memorial). – MONUMENTS. Three by *M.W. Johnson* to members of the Norgate family: Dr Thomas †1818, Sophia Mary Ann †1831, Rev. James †1841. The earliest, with draped urn, is the best.

THE WURLIE, 250 yds NE. Large U-plan building, dating back to the C15; now three dwellings. The range along the street incorporates an open hall, now floored, with crown-post roof. The central range, two storeys from the start, has a two-bay hall with original service doorways and large Tudor brick fireplace. Some original windows. Queenpost roof. The further range was probably originally detached, and joined to the main range in the C17.

BADWELL ASH HALL (also known as High House), 1 m. E. Remains (perhaps half) of a three-storey, red brick Elizabethan house. Mullioned-and-transomed windows, some pedimented; stone dressings. Entrance on the W side, which has a projecting stair-wing, battlemented and with polygonal corner turrets. To the r. of this three narrow bays, the central bay a chimney with three fine decorated shafts and crenellated tops. S gable-end also with polygonal turrets, windows of six, five and four lights, and crowstepped gable. To the r. of this a Victorian extension in matching style. The N gable-end is of C19 brick and the Elizabethan house no doubt extended further in this direction. At the back, a low timber-framed and plastered wing extending E, probably C17, perhaps reusing timbers from the house that preceded the Elizabethan one.

BALLINGDON see SUDBURY

BARDWELL

Bardwell has the biggest church in the neighbourhood. The best approach is from the SW, up a short steep path past BELL COTTAGE, C16 with delightful early C19 ogee-headed windows.

ST PETER AND ST PAUL. Tall Perp W tower with spike (money bequeathed in 1409). Fine, tall Perp S porch with the arms of Sir William Berdewell who died in 1434. A will of 1460 left 2s. for its repair. Good flushwork decoration, chequerboard and panelling. Entrance with two orders of fleurons. Three niches around it. Side windows with fine tracery. Lofty nave with tall two-light Dec windows. Excellent hammerbeam roof, in which Birkin Haward detected the hand of *John Hore*. Thin arched braces. Arched braces also below the ridge. No collarbeams. Of the angel figures which originally held the roof only four remain, one with the date 1421 on the open pages of a book. Much original colouring, including the charming trails on the rafters. Restoration, particularly affecting the chancel, by *H. F. Bacon*, 1852–3, executed and superintended by *T. Farrow*. – SCREEN. Four panels of a finely traceried dado. Money was left for the rood beam in 1498–1504. – WALL PAINTINGS. Discovered in 1853 but plastered over again. Visible fragments of the Deposition (nave N wall) and the Seven Deadly Sins (S wall), both late C14 or early C15. Other subjects recorded in 1853 included the Legend of St Catharine, the Last Judgment (over chancel arch), St Christopher, and the King of Terrors. – STAINED GLASS. Three kneeling early C15 figures, the largest no doubt Sir William Berdewell. Also some C15 figures, including a German Pietà. Chancel windows by *O'Connor*, 1863–9. Nave S †1895, and probably also its neighbour, by *W. G. Taylor*. – MONUMENTS. Cecilia, wife of Sir Charles Crofts, †1626, and his daughter Elizabeth †1633. No figures; the later one with upturned torches and other symbols of mortality. Both erected by Sir Charles, whose name is much more prominent than those whom he sought to commemorate (cf. Ixworth Thorpe). – Thomas Read and wife, dated 1652. Kneeling figures facing each other. In the 'predella' seven children, one lying on its side, two next to it forming a pretty little group. – Sir Charles Crofts †1660 and Charles Crofts Read †1690. Two fronts of a tomb-chest, placed one on each side of the sanctuary in 1853. – Thomas Read †1678. With swan-neck pediment. – Rev. James Welton †1772 and wife Mary Stracey †1784. By *Joshua Cushing* of Norwich. An unusual piece, with sarcophagus.* – Simple Crimean War memorial, 1854–5. Seven names. – Anna Maria Dunlap †1854 by *R. Brown*. Inscription within a cusped arch. – Sarah Jones †1864 and Sarah Hill †1866. Identical monuments to faithful servants by *John Darkin*. – Rev. A. P. Dunlap, rector 1852–89. Mural brass, in the form of a cross, by *Jones & Willis*. – War memorial by *F. H. Goddard*, 1920. Marble tablet inserted into N doorway. Twenty-three names.

Former BAPTIST CHURCH, Low Street. 1824. Red brick with pyramidal slate roof. Entirely domestic in appearance. Front with two doors, sash window between them, and two smaller sash windows lighting the gallery. Closed 2003.

PRIMARY SCHOOL, School Lane. By *Bacon* and *Farrow* (as at the church), 1854–5, followed by the teacher's house. Flint with stucco dressings and 'Tudor' windows.

Most of the village is contained within a square of roads with the church in the middle of the W side. In the SE corner of the

---

*Jon Bayliss points out that the same design is used by Cushing for a monument to Harriet Stracey †1817 at Rackheath, Norfolk.

churchyard, the former GUILDHALL. Late C15, converted to almshouses at the Reformation, and to two houses *c.* 1962. Timber-framed and plastered, L-plan. Large internal chimneystacks, the brickwork of one left exposed by the 1960s conversion. To the E, in Up Street, the OLD RECTORY, C16 timber-framed and plastered with white brick additions of *c.* 1815. To its S CROFT HOUSE, mid-C15, with exposed timbers and thatched half-hipped roof.

In Low Street, on the way to Bardwell Hall, MOTHERSOLES, late C15 with some exposed timbers. Jettied cross-wing to l., early C17 extension to r. Opposite, PELHAM HOUSE is probably C15, with a C17 red brick shaped gable at one end. Early C19 wall and gatepiers of moulded brick.

BARDWELL HALL, ⅔ m. S. Early C16. Heavily and closely timber-framed. N and S diapered brick ends, crowstepped and with chimneystacks. Jettied front with brick ground floor and brick-nogging on first floor. Two two-storey brick projections, one for the entrance, one for the stairs. They both have four- and five-light stuccoed windows with transoms and pediments, and a timber-framed, gabled third storey added in the C17. The back of the house irregular, all brick-nogged. At the S end, two single-storey porch-like extensions, also with stepped gables, and at this end also medieval stone fragments that may be part of an earlier house, or may have been brought in from elsewhere.

BARDWELL MANOR, 1 m. SSW. Large red brick house of 1884–5, described in sale particulars of 1918 as 'a modern, compact mansion in the Elizabethan style'.

WINDMILL, School Lane. Tarred red brick tower mill, described as new in 1830. Restored.

WATERMILL, ½ m. NW. Early C19. Three storeys, weatherboarding above a white-brick ground floor, with lucam. Most machinery removed.

BARKING

0050

A large parish, extending to the River Gipping, of which Needham Market was originally a hamlet, and which still contains the hamlet of Darmsden (q.v.).

ST MARY. Late C13 S porch with typical mouldings to the entrance and typical side windows. Of the same time the S doorway, which has one order of shafts and one continuous chamfer. Hoodmould on headstops. Of the same time also the chancel. The E window is a good example of cusped intersected tracery. Attached to the chancel is a two-storeyed vestry. A little later than the chancel windows, i.e. Dec, the S arcade with octagonal piers and double-hollow-chamfered arches, the N doorway and the unbuttressed W tower (with polygonal buttresses), the upper parts of which were rebuilt in 1870. Perp N arcade, N windows and S windows, and clerestory. The latest of the windows, one on the N side, goes beyond the Perp style. The tracery is Perp, but the mullions and jambs are in the Early Italian Renaissance style, c. 1525, made of terracotta by the same craftsmen who did the windows of Henley, Barham and Shrubland Old Hall (E). The same moulds were used throughout. Here there are, in addition, vertical panels on the jambs inside. Simple tie-beam roof with arched braces and crown-posts with four-way struts. Much finer N aisle roof. Traceried arched braces, carved purlins. The design alternates in detail. General restoration by *E. F. Bisshopp*, 1895. Chancel restored by *Bisshopp & Cautley*, 1905, including new ceiling, and in 1928–9 by *W.A. Forsyth*. – FONT. Octagonal, Perp. Against the stem four lions and four Wild Men; against the bowl the Emblems of the Evangelists and four angels. – FONT COVER. Very pretty; late C15 (restored). Two tiers of arches with flying buttresses and pinnacles, with central crocketed pinnacle. – PULPIT. Incorporating one Flemish late C16 or early C17 relief. – SCREENS. Very fine, complete N and S parclose screens with delicate cresting. The rood screen is complete too and has three-light divisions and coving. All have been restored, but retain a significant amount of original colouring. The chancel screen can be dated by a bequest for rood figures in 1464. – DOORS. The W, S and vestry doors are traceried. In the case of the W door, the tracery is arranged in panels as on bench ends. There is an inner vestry door for additional security. – COMMUNION RAILS. Late C17, with tapering twisted balusters. – BENCHES. A few, with poppyheads. In the chancel a large pew made up from various fragments, including what may be the front of the rood loft. – CURIOSUM. Two iron braziers, for heating. – ROYAL ARMS. Of Charles II, on panels. – STAINED GLASS. Some medieval glass in the top of the NE window and the terracotta window. – MONUMENTS. Theobald Gascoyne †1714. Grey marble, with the inscription on a white marble urn. – Crowley family, 1771. Of white, grey and pink marble. No figures, but an elegant design.

OLD RECTORY, N of the church. By *William Brown* of Ipswich, 1819, for Rev. Charles Davy. White brick on the two important fronts, the rest red. Five bays, two storeys. The middle bay is emphasized rather heavily by giant Tuscan columns *in antis* and a pediment. Octagonal hall with geometric staircase. Good cedars in the garden and churchyard, one at least said to have been planted in 1712 by the botanist Robert Uvedale, rector 1700–22.

BARKING HALL, which stood behind the wall on the SW side of the churchyard, was demolished in 1926. The name has been taken by the nursing home that now occupies the C18 stables.

CREETING LOCK and BRIDGE, 1¾ m. ENE, for the Ipswich & Stowmarket Navigation (*see* Introduction, p. 50). No gates, but otherwise restored.

BARNARDISTON

ALL SAINTS. Flint and stone rubble with some Roman brick. C13 chancel, C14 nave and W tower. Handsome C14 N doorway with castellated canopy and pinnacles. C15 N porch with exceptionally tall entrance. – PULPIT. Simple; Jacobean. The iron stand for the HOURGLASS on the wall beside it. – READER'S DESK. With the same panels as the pulpit. – SCREEN. One-light divisions, ogee arches with tracery over. – PANELLING in the chancel, Jacobean. – COMMUNION RAIL. C17. – NORTH DOOR. C15, with ogee-headed wicket. – BENCHES. Simple, with straight tops and some blank tracery. – GRAFFITO. Of a windmill, on the sill of the chancel SW window.

OLD RECTORY, ENE of the church. By *Clark & Holland*, 1855–7. Red brick with white-brick corner pilasters and dressings.

N of the church some HOUSING for Clare Rural District Council by *A. E. Richardson* (*Richardson & Houfe*), 1950. A rather formal composition in pairs of Neo-Georgian red brick houses. The corner house is lower and has a mansard-pyramid roof. Cf. Hundon, Wickhambrook.

OLD CHAPEL, 300 yds NW. Mid-C19. Red brick, three bays square, with Gothick windows.

BARNHAM

ST GREGORY. Flint rubble W tower, nave and chancel, all with Y-tracery, i.e. *c.* 1300. N transept *c.* 1840; N aisle and vestry 1863–4, together with a thorough restoration. The best feature is inside, the PISCINA of the late C13 with a pointed-trefoiled arch and a pointed trefoil in bar tracery over it. – STAINED GLASS. E window and a nave S window by *A. K. Nicholson*, 1912.

ST MARTIN, 250 yds NW. Only three walls of the tower remain, almost completely covered with ivy. The parish was consolidated with St Gregory in 1639 and the church was ruinous by the end of the C17.

OLD PARSONAGE, W of St Gregory. Red brick. By *J. H. Hakewill*, 1861. Might he also have restored the church? The former SCHOOL, E of the church, is of about the same date. Red brick with white-brick dressings.

YE OLDE HOUSE, 250 yds SW. C16. Not quite in the centre is a gabled and jettied cross-wing with exposed studwork, the oldest part of the building. It formerly carried a date of 1553, which might well be the true one. The rest of the house mostly plastered, with C18 red brick gable-ends.

WINDMILL, 400 yds WSW. Painted brick tower mill, dated 1821. Three storeys. Now part of a house; no sails etc.

Former ATOMIC BOMB STORE (now Gorse Industrial Estate), 1¼ m. WNW. Built *c.* 1952–5. Pentagonal compound with observation towers at the corners. Three large stores for non-nuclear components (of which one dem.) with reinforced concrete frames, blockwork walls, and concrete roofs, set in deep earth banks. Four groups of small separate stores for the fissile cores. Ancillary buildings including two 'Seco' huts, a prefabricated building system of hollow plywood beams and columns, here clad with asbestos cement sheeting.

BARNINGHAM

9070

ST ANDREW. Dec chancel. The E window has flowing tracery. On the S side a lowside window with an embattled transom. The nave has tall Perp two-light windows. Inside it should be noticed how the rood stair ascends in the window. W tower under construction, according to bequests, in 1431–41. Restoration by *Satchell & Edwards*, 1877, confined to the interior, and especially the chancel furnishings. In 1834 the church had been 'screwed together' by *George Bloomfield*, i.e. by means of tie-rods. – FONT. Octagonal, Dec. With tracery patterns, e.g. a rose of eight radiating arches and a wheel of three mouchettes. Late C15 COVER with crocketed buttresses sweeping up to a finial. – SCREEN. Very good and well preserved. One-light ogee arches with panel tracery; cresting. Remains of gesso and painted decoration. Early C17 gates. Of the former rood beam the cut-off ends remain in the walls. Money was left for the new rood beam in 1469. – REREDOS. 1877. Carved oak, with a copy of *Leonardo da Vinci*'s Last Supper by *Eliza Edwards*, sister of the rector. By her also the copy of *Murillo*'s Return of the Prodigal Son (nave W wall). – PULPIT. The tester looks mid-C17, the body later. – BENCHES. A whole set. With tracery panels against the ends, carved backs, and poppyheads and animals on the arms, also birds, monsters, one kneeling figure, etc. At the front, reused C17 ALTAR RAIL with turned balusters. – STAINED GLASS. E window by *Heaton, Butler & Bayne*, 1877. – MONUMENTS. Brass of William Goche, rector of Barningham, †1499. 13-in. (33-cm.) figure. – Mural brasses by *Gawthorp* to Rev. George Hunt †1853 and Rev. James Edwards †1875 and wife Eliza †1864.

CHURCH COTTAGE, SW of the church, is early C19. Of clay lump, rendered, with thatched roof and chimney of moulded white bricks. Then THE BEECHES, equally but differently *orné*. Knapped flint with white-brick dressings. Stone cusped ogee arches over the ground-floor windows. S of that the SCHOOL, 1856–9 by *Robert Smith* of Dickleburgh. Red brick with white-brick dressings and curly bargeboards. On the E side of the road THE ROYAL GEORGE, C15 and early C17, EVERGREEN HALL, early C17, and CHURCH FARM HOUSE, late C15 with smoke-blackened timbers; all timber-framed and plastered with thatched roofs.

Former STEAM MILL, 200 yds E. Three storeys. Timber-framed, mainly weatherboarded and mainly C19, although the lower part at the S end is C18 in origin. Lucam on the W side. Converted to housing.

BARROW

ALL SAINTS. One Norman window on the N side; other windows here Perp. Unbuttressed W tower, early C13, raised in the C14. Dec S aisle with four-bay arcade (octagonal piers, double-chamfered arches, dying into the W and E responds), W window a lancet, E window Dec. At the E end of the aisle a curious arrangement of two SEDILIA in the S wall followed by a canopied RECESS for a tomb or Easter sepulchre, with DOUBLE PISCINA on the E wall. In the chancel E window, three tall single-chamfered stepped lancets under one arch, renewed but correct. The chancel's DOUBLE PISCINA and SEDILIA clearly belong to the same time, i.e. the mid C13, but are no longer of value as evidence. N vestry 1845, chancel restored 1846–8, nave and aisles 1852, by *L. N. Cottingham*, completed by *N. J. Cottingham*. – FONT. Perp, octagonal, with eight shields and panels. Given in 1401 by the Despenser family. – STALLS. Rearranged in 1848, with returns, but reusing medieval work, including poppyheads (some carved with heads) and perhaps the dado of the screen. – BENCHES. Two with traceried ends and carved backs. One inscribed with the name of John Prycke, apparently the carpenter who made them (and who died in 1551); another inscription, now lost, appears to have commemorated Thomas Plesance †1541.* – WALL PAINTINGS. In the jambs of the Norman window two small agile figures, said to be musicians. – SCULPTURE. Text, 'Glory to God', carved on stone by *Eric Gill*. – STAINED GLASS. E window by *N. J. Cottingham*, 1848. Patterns of medallions. – MONUMENTS. Tomb-chest with cusped and decorated lozenges. Niche with lintel on small quadrant arches and cresting. Panelled sides. The whole of Purbeck marble and supposed to belong together with the Elizabethan brasses against the back wall. These commemorate Sir Clement Heigham †1570 and his two wives. Long poem, worth reading, as it describes his life in doggerel. But the monument, with its total absence of Renaissance detail, cannot be so late, even in Suffolk. It is more likely of *c.* 1500. – Sir John Heigham †1626. By *John Stone*, set up in 1650. Tablet with inscription flanked by heavy volutes supported by square brackets. Open segmental pediment. – Other C17 Heigham monuments were crudely painted *c.* 1969, a misfortune that also affected the font.

---

*Information from David Sherlock.

– Second World War memorial. 1949 by *Francis Cooper*. Brass, with figure of St George.
CAVE ADULLAM BAPTIST CHAPEL, The Street. Originally Congregational; registered 1837. Flint with red brick dressings. Lancets, with three grouped under a hoodmould on the gabled front.
PRIMARY SCHOOL, Church Road. 1846. Neo-Tudor. Knapped flint with white-brick dressings.
The village is centred on a large green ¾ m. S of the church. In THE STREET, N of the Green, No. 34, timber-framed and thatched, is C17 or earlier, with a schoolroom added at one end in 1872. In BURY ROAD, NE of the Green, FELTONS, flint and red brick with a white-brick front of *c.* 1840; then GABLES COTTAGE, about the same date but Gothick, a top-heavy composition with a narrow three-and-a-half-storey centre flanked by two-storey wings, hung with fish-scale slates; then another cottage in different style but the same spirit, red brick with white-brick pilasters and other dressings, wrought-iron casements and Tudoresque chimneys.

BARTON MILLS

7070

Along the S bank of the River Lark. The watermill was at the E end of the village, next to the Norwich road; it was demolished in 1949, the late C20 house on the site made to look like a conversion. The church is at the opposite end of the village.

ST MARY. Mostly Dec, the W tower perhaps a little earlier. Five-light E window with a reticulated arrangement in which the top motif is a pointed oval rather than having ogee top and bottom. The lowside window on the S side of the chancel has tracery with a four-petalled flower in the top. Arcade of four bays, with octagonal piers, double-chamfered arches, and hoodmoulds on heads. The clerestory windows are above the spandrels, not the apexes of the arcade. Re-roofed 1866. Transeptal N organ chamber (now chapel) 1870. S porch restored 1901. Restoration by *G. F. Bodley*, 1902–5, including painted chancel ceiling and CHOIR STALLS. – FONT. Octagonal, with flat Dec arch and tracery motifs, almost a mason's pattern-book of such motifs (cf. Icklingham, All Saints). – PULPIT. Jacobean, on stone base of 1905. – WALL PAINTING. Over chancel arch, the Good Shepherd and background of foliage, sacred monograms, etc. By *Giles Gilbert Scott*, 1911, executed by *Powell & Sons*. – MOSAICS. On sanctuary walls, by *Rust & Co.*, *c.* 1884. – STAINED GLASS. Original C14 fragments in the S aisle, also nearly complete (though headless) figures. E window †1866 by *Clayton & Bell*. Chancel S †1867 by *H. Hughes* (*Ward & Hughes*). Chancel S *c.* 1894 and N †1907 by *Heaton, Butler & Bayne*, the latter in the (by then antiquated)

Walter Crane style. – MONUMENTS. War memorial by *C. G. Hare*, 1919. Alabaster, with bronze wreath. Swan-neck pediment. Similar design used for the Second World War, 1948.

RECTORY, sw of the church. By *Peter Cleverly*, *c.* 1978–80. It reuses the flint and white-brick façade of Glebe Cottage, *c.* 1800. Castellated, with a raised centre. In this a circular window. The other windows Gothick.

MIDDLEFIELD MANOR (residential home, formerly Barton Hall), 200 yds NE. Mid-C18 stuccoed brick house. Two storeys. Seven-bay garden front with pilasters and parapet. Alterations by *Oliver Hill*, 1926–30.

Along the village street to the E, on the s side the BAPTIST CHURCH of 1844. White brick. Three-bay gabled front. Two tiers of windows with cast-iron frames. At the back, the cheaper local material is used – knapped flint. Then on the N side STREET FARM, a Wealden-type house of *c.* 1500, jettied at both ends. Extensively restored, but the high-quality timberwork largely intact, including two-bay roof with octagonal crown-posts. The open hall had a brick chimneystack from the start; the floor was inserted within a few years, its timbers richly carved and moulded. Original cross-passage screen. Further E, LORD MAYOR'S COTTAGE, mostly C17 and picturesquely altered in the early C19, but the cross-wing may date back to the C15. At the E end of the village a charming corner with THE BULL INN, with shaped end gable, facing THE MILL HOUSE. The latter, timber-framed and plastered, has tall brick chimneystacks with two elongated blank arches, a Vanbrughian effect, but one is dated 1668. Behind it the river, lock, and site of the watermill.

BRONZE AGE BARROW, Chalk Hill, about 1 m. sw of the church. Completely excavated in 1923 and then rebuilt about 15 ft (4.5 metres) NW of its original location. It yielded three inhumations and a central cremation associated with both Food Vessel and Cinerary Urn pottery, and a bone crescentic necklace perhaps imitating the form more common in jet. It was originally one of a group of four in line, and there were two others excavated in 1868 which revealed two inhumations and a cremation. It also contained Beaker pottery.

BATTISFORD

ST MARY. Nave and chancel. There was once a w tower, but there is now only the oddest red brick and rubble buttress, climbing up the w wall with five set-offs. It may date from 1784, when a faculty was granted for the sale of two bells to repair the steeple. Perched on top a timber bell-turret with saddleback roof, probably part of the general restoration of 1902. Nave and s porch early C14. Chancel of the same time – see the E window. NE vestry probably C19, with a reused Perp window. On the N side of the nave a small attachment which used to contain family pews and may be medieval in origin. Roof with crown-posts with four-way struts, braced collars and ashlar-pieces. – FONT. Bowl with nice cusped tracery; all designs, with the exception of one, are Dec. – PULPIT. 1902, reusing an C18 two-decker. – WEST GALLERY. 1841 by *William Reeve* of Needham Market. The front replaced, perhaps in 1902. – WALL PAINTING. Two fragments of decoration on the nave S wall. – MONUMENTS. Edward Salter †1724 and John Lewis †1724. Two identical monuments l. and r. of the E window. No effigies, but a trumpeting putto on top of the usual obelisk.

On the N side of the churchyard, a timber-framed and plastered COTTAGE dating back to the mid C14. It was the priest's house, and until it was floored *c.* 1520 consisted of an open hall with 'croglofft' or sleeping platform at one end. Against the W wall a C16 brick chimneystack and against that a small SCHOOLROOM of 1843. White brick, with hipped slate roof, pointed-arched openings and Gothick glazing.

ST JOHN'S MANOR HOUSE, ½ m. W. A Preceptory or Commandery of the Knights of St John of Jerusalem was founded at Battisford in the second half of the C12. At the Dissolution the property was granted first to Andrew Judde and then in 1544 to Sir Richard Gresham (cf. Ringshall). The present house was almost entirely faced in white brick in the mid C19, but seems to have been built in the later C16, perhaps by Sir Thomas Gresham †1579, reusing timbers from an earlier house. Hall with moulded beams. Built into the base of the chimney (now inside) was a terracotta panel with the head of St John the Baptist on a platter; another panel, also *ex situ*, dated 1529 with the arms of Giles Russell, one of the last preceptors or masters. At the N end an early C16 service wing. Moated site.

HOLLY FARM, 1,500 yds W. Early C17 timber-framed lobby-entrance farmhouse with an interesting scheme of coloured decoration of the wall studs: grey for the lobby and stairway, red for the parlour, yellow for the parlour chamber. The unpainted hall may have been hung with cloth, or panelled.

BAYLHAM

ST PETER. Unbuttressed W tower of knapped flint. Blocked Norman N nave doorway. Most other windows Dec, or imitation Dec. Thoroughly restored by *F. Barnes*, 1870, including the addition of N and S transepts, and new S porch. The two Perp windows in the N wall were moved as part of the work. – FONT. Octagonal, Perp. With shields on the bowl. – TOWER SCREEN. 1870. With reused tracery of the rood screen. Other parts incorporated in the READING DESK. – TILES. By *Maw*

& Co. In the sanctuary, and an especially good display at the crossing. – STAINED GLASS. E window by *Clayton & Bell*, 1870. – MONUMENTS. John and Elizabeth Acton. C17, with the usual kneeling figures facing each other across a prayer-desk, but in the background a less usual skeleton. Alabaster. The inscription records the day and month of Elizabeth's death, but not the year, and nothing is said about John; Elizabeth Lamb married John Acton who inherited in 1663 and died in 1695. – On s side of chancel, three chest tombs, one still with its deeply carved limestone panels. Mid-C18, also of a member of the Acton family.

Former NATIONAL SCHOOL, in SE corner of churchyard. 1860, also by *Barnes*. Flint, with red brick dressings.

BAYLHAM HALL, ⅔ m. WNW. Fragment of a brick mansion, taxed on twenty-two hearths in 1674, and owned by the Actons from 1626. The fragment is of T-shape. The early C17 front range has shaped gable-ends (two convex curves each side). The elevation is irregular with, in the l. part, angle pilasters in two orders. The windows are all altered, but the back range, which is probably earlier, has a number of mullioned-and-transomed as well as cross-windows of brick, and spiked dentil friezes. The front range probably continued northwards. Fine open-well staircase with carved newels and four square balusters to each flight. Spacious outbuildings, especially a fine mid-C16 STABLE range to the SE. Brick ground floor, with openings with four-centred arches. Timber-framed upper storey (lodgings), partly weatherboarded, partly with exposed timbers and brick-nogging. Crown-post roof.

RODWELL HOUSE, ⅔ m. ENE, on the main road. Georgian, red brick, of five bays and two storeys. Pedimented doorcase. Venetian windows on the rear elevation.

WATERMILL, 1 m. NE. Picturesque in its elevation and its position by the humpback bridge over the Gipping. Early to mid-C19 weatherboarded mill, with cast-iron breast-shot waterwheel and intact machinery. Adjoining it a low, two-bay timber-framed and plastered range, probably medieval, and then the C19 white-brick MILL HOUSE. Above the bridge, remains of a LOCK on the Ipswich & Stowmarket Navigation (*see* Introduction, p. 50).

BEYTON

ALL SAINTS. Round tower with Perp w window and two massive buttresses. Top stage rebuilt 1780. Simple Norman N doorway, re-set. Nave rebuilt by *John Johnson* of Bury, 1853–4, with the addition of a N aisle to replace the w gallery that had been erected twenty years earlier. Chancel rebuilt and lengthened by *A. W. Blomfield*, 1884. Poorly sited vestry with glazed link SE of the chancel; by *Whitworth, Hall & Thomas*, 1973, extended by the *Whitworth Co-Partnership*, 1992. – REREDOS. *Opus sectile* Last Supper by *Powell & Sons*, 1884. – CHOIR STALLS. With poppyheads and animals on the arms (mostly renewed), some traceried ends, and carved backs. Ten shillings was left for 'stooling' the church in 1480. – STAINED GLASS. E window by *Powell & Sons*, designed by *C. Hardgrave*, 1885. – In N aisle, Second World War memorial window by *M. Meredith Williams*, 1948, probably made by *Lowndes & Drury*. – Another by *Goddard & Gibbs*, 1970.

OLD RECTORY, S of the church. Mostly of 1840 by *William Dudley*. 'Elizabethan', with chimneys of moulded white brick.

BEYTON HOUSE, ¼ m. SE. Almost completely rebuilt by *Basil Oliver*, 1936–7, following a fire. Very agreeable Neo-Georgian. Red brick. Two storeys. Seven-bay garden front. Main doorway recessed behind a pedimented entrance. Part of the servants' wing, of flint with red brick dressings, survived.

BILDESTON

9040

The woollen cloth industry made Bildeston a prosperous little town in the later Middle Ages, centred on the market place off the road from Stowmarket to Hadleigh. The parish church stands on a hilltop ½ m. W, now surrounded by fields but originally at the centre of the early medieval village.

ST MARY MAGDALENE. Dec chancel with inventive five-light E window. Dec N aisle E window with reticulated tracery. Perp W tower. The W doorway big with three niches over. The tower collapsed in 1975; rebuilt by *Andrew Anderson*, the lower masonry stage in 1990, timber belfry and spirelet in 1996–7. Large Perp aisle windows with segmental arches and stepped transoms. Clerestory with twice as many windows as bays of the arcade. S porch with flushwork, entrance with fleuron decoration. The S doorway is excellently decorated with crowns, shields, etc. Hoodmoulds on seated lions. Spandrels with shields. The arcade of five bays has piers with four filleted shafts and small spurs without capitals in the diagonals. The abaci have rows of small angels or leaf motifs. The moulded arches. All this points to master mason *Hawes* of Occold, and may be the new work mentioned in a bequest of 1420. No division between nave and chancel. Continuous roof with alternating tie-beams and hammerbeams, restored by *E. F. Bisshopp*, 1878–9. It is remarkable for a total absence of collar-beams. General restoration by *W. M. Fawcett*, including renewal of most of the windows, 1883–5. Carving by *John Groom & Son* of Ipswich, which presumably included the stone SEDILIA. – FONT. Octagonal, Perp. Damaged stem. Bowl with the four Emblems of the Evangelists and four demi-angels. – COMMUNION RAIL. Slim turned balusters. – STALLS with

p. 96

Bildeston, St Mary Magdalene, arcade.
Drawing by B. Haward, 1993

simple MISERICORDS, heads, etc., all defaced. – REREDOS in s chapel. Part of the dado of the screen from Wattisham (q.v., closed 1977). Panels with four male and four female saints, thoroughly repainted. ALTAR and COMMUNION RAIL also from Wattisham. – SOUTH DOOR. With tracery and foliage-trail border. – STAINED GLASS. E window by *Goldie & Child*, made by *Wailes & Strang*, c. 1873. Scenes only in the tracery heads. Chancel s by *Chance Bros*, 1856. One s window by *Kempe*, 1892. Typical of his early work. S aisle w by *Philippa Heskett (Pippa Blackall)*, 1981. – MONUMENTS. Brass to William Wade †1599 and wife Elizabeth. Only her figure, 22 in. (56 cm.) with hat, and two sons and two daughters. – R. Wilson

†1834 and R. P. Wilson †1837. Both by *E. Gaffin*, the latter a cartouche and more decorative than the usual austere tablet. – John Parker †1833. By *J. H. Elmes*. An open book ('this durable volume'), with his three deceased children listed on the opposite page. – Growse family memorial, 1881, in the form of a stone triptych. By *John Wiles* of Cambridge. – War memorial by *Basil Hatcher*, 1921. White marble tablet with ornate scrolly pediment.

BAPTIST CHURCH, Duke Street. 1844. Red brick. Polygonal clasping buttresses and funny rusticated ones on the front. Doors and windows with four-centred arches. Church originally formed in 1737, the earliest surviving Baptist cause in Suffolk.

PRIMARY SCHOOL, Newberry Road. By *West Suffolk County Architect's Dept* (job architect *J. Blackie*), 1967–8. U-plan, built round an existing tree. On the SEAC system, with stained weatherboarding.

The MARKET PLACE is now a small square on the W side of the High Street, but originally covered the whole area between Duke Street and Chapel Street. In the middle stands the incongruous CLOCK TOWER of 1864.* By *J. S. Moye*. White and red brick. Three stages, the bottom one arched. Pyramidal roof, bell-turret and spirelet. WAR MEMORIAL alongside by *E. E. Saunders*, 1920. Portland stone. Ball on Ionic column. The actual buildings are better, an attractive mix, of which two stand out. On the N side CHRISTMAS HALL, a stately three-bay house of the early C19. White brick, Greek Doric porch. Red brick stable block to the rear. In the NE corner RED HOUSE (No. 126 High Street), Georgian, of seven bays and two storeys with an open pediment and a Venetian window below. Later top floor with parapet and blind windows. Behind the front an older timber-framed building. Along the HIGH STREET to the N No. 130, C16 timber-framed and plastered with an C18 pedimented doorcase on thickly carved brackets. Then a row of nice timber-framed houses, some with exposed timbers, and one on the corner of Wattisham Road jettied on two sides with a large corner-post.

s of the Market Place THE BILDESTON CROWN. Late C15. Handsome, timber-framed, with jettied front and exposed timbers on the upper storey. Crown-post roof. Much restored, most recently in 2004–5 by *Wincer Kievenaar*, with harmonious rear additions of 2007–8. Towards the far s end No. 22, C15–C16, the surviving part of a once larger house. It has several rare and pretty features, especially the small carved porch, two small mullioned windows with carved top and sill, and a doorway with a four-centred arch, a carved lintel and carved spandrels. Plastered jettied front. No. 14 is by *John Weller*, 1960. Painted brick. Pitched roof. The front is split, with one side set back and part weatherboarded, reducing its bulk. Weller also designed the two-storey building at the SEWAGE WORKS,

---

*Pevsner, with his usual distaste for the 1860s, called it 'hideous'.

Chelsworth Road, 1976. More vernacular and domestic, with pitched roof and traditional materials, than such buildings usually are.

CHAPEL STREET runs from the SW corner of the Market Place, its name derived from a medieval chapel that stood on the S side. The older houses are of course all on the S side, facing what was the larger market place. CARLISLE HOUSE (Nos. 11–13) has an unusual doorcase, pedimented, with Ionic pilasters, but the pilasters are carved with Early Renaissance ornament like strapwork. Nos. 15–17 is a small hall house, with gabled and jettied cross-wings. Then a long row, Nos. 23–33, with jettied front and exposed timbers, and a shorter similar row, Nos. 35–39, of which the end house has been refronted. Arched doorway to No. 35. Early C16, identified by Leigh Alston as 'renters', i.e. small houses built for letting.

Chapel Street leads round into DUKE STREET, which has BILDESTON HALL at its W end. This now looks predominantly of c. 1840, with its red brick gabled front, but contains the remains of early C16 tenements with workshops that fronted the market place. More timber-framed houses along the N side of Duke Street, running back up to the Market Place.

BENTONS, ½ m. NE of the Market Place. By *John Johnson* of Bury, 1849–50, as the rectory, for Rev. Joseph Gedge. White brick. Two storeys. Four bays square. Bow window, Ionic porch. Johnson also designed the National School, 1853 (Chapel Street, mostly dem.).

BOTESDALE

Botesdale (i.e. Botolph's Dale) was a hamlet in the parish of Redgrave, but assumed greater importance because of its position on the route from Bury to Norwich and Lowestoft (cf. Needham Market and Barking). A weekly market and annual fair were granted a charter in 1227. The first recorded reference to the chapel occurs in 1338.

CHAPEL OF ST BOTOLPH. The building is called new in 1494 and 1506. The windows are Perp, one of them cutting into the flushwork inscription (attributed to *Thomas Aldryche*) over the door. This records the generosity of John Shrive or Sheriff († c. 1480), his wife Juliana, and Margaret Wykes, which made it a chantry chapel. It was accordingly suppressed in 1547, but in 1561 Sir Nicholas Bacon of Redgrave founded a grammar school in the old chapel and added to the W end a house for the schoolmaster (now CHAPEL HOUSE). Chapel mainly of flint, the house timber-framed and plastered, all under one roof. The school closed in 1878 and the chapel reverted to ecclesiastical use in 1883. Simple interior, without division between nave and chancel. At the W end a rough SCREEN like a hall-screen forming a lobby under the gallery. Undecorated muntins and boards.

NE of the chapel THE PRIORY. Red brick five-bay Georgian front with a Doric doorway with metope frieze. The windows have Gothick casements. Timber-framed behind this, dating back to the late C15 or early C16, and also additions of 1877. Across Mill Road STREET FARMHOUSE. Early C15, with many alterations and additions; refronted in red brick *c.* 1833. Opposite, HILL TOP is early C19, built of shuttered clay with slate cladding. It has cast-iron floor joists.

SW from the chapel the road slopes attractively down towards the triangular MARKET PLACE. This has across its base at the NE end CHILVERS (former drapery), with shop windows on the ground floor and three-bay white-brick upper storey. Early C19. Behind it HONISTER HOUSE, C17 with a Tudor façade of *c.* 1830. Along the NW side THE OLD SADDLERS, late C15 or early C16, altered in 1637 according to a date formerly in the plaster. Cross-wing to l. jettied on two sides. On the SE side, OSMOND HOUSE, Late Georgian, of white brick, three bays wide, with a nice pedimented doorway. Then THE GREYHOUND. Timber-framed, late C15, refronted in the mid C19. Five bays of red brick with quoin-like strips of white brick, and hoodmoulded windows. To the l. of this a square bay fully glazed with Gothic lights and a smaller square bay on the upper storey.

After the Market Place THE STREET continues SW. On the SE side ST CATHERINE'S, mid-C15, timber-framed and plastered. Two-bay hall and cross-wing to the l.; there was originally another to the r. For buildings SW of here, *see* Rickinghall Inferior.

In Bridewell Lane, off The Street to the SE, THE BRIDEWELL (former house of correction), 1799–1800. Red brick. Three bays and two storeys under hipped roof (i.e., just like the private house it now is). Rear garden whose side walls extend forward to the road, with piers and ball finials.

BOTESDALE LODGE, nearly 1 m. SE. White-brick front range of *c.* 1810. Two storeys. Five bays with the centre breaking forward. Pointed-arched entrance. Windows with hoodmoulds and, on the ground floor, casements with cusped Gothic heads. Corner pilaster strips. Behind this was a timber-framed C16 range, completely rebuilt (but still timber-framed) by *Andrew Smith Associates*, *c.* 2002–3.

TOLLGATE HOUSE, 400 yds NE. White brick. Octagonal. Single-storey. Round-arched windows with simple tracery, in arched recesses.

BOXFORD

A pleasant village, about halfway between Sudbury and Hadleigh, whose buildings have more of the character of a small town, and which has benefited greatly from the construction of a bypass. The Box, little more than a stream, flows through it; the two principal streets (Swan Street and Broad Street) are on its N side, the church just to the S.

ST MARY. Quite a big church. Its most interesting feature is the timber-built N porch. It is C14 and may well be the earliest timber porch in the county (but cf. Somersham). Big Dec two-light windows, and a rib-vault, now a skeleton only but originally with filled-in cells of boarding or lath and plaster. There are diagonal ribs, ridge ribs, and one pair of tiercerons to each side. The S porch is the very opposite, Late Perp, stone-faced, and exceedingly swagger. Money was left for its building at various times between 1441 and 1480. Four-light windows in two bays, of two different designs, plenty of decorations on the front, the buttresses and parapet, head-stops, gargoyles, etc., all rather wild. Inside the porch the mullions are continued down below the windows as far as the stone benches and there are niches in the reveals. C14 W tower. Money was left for a pinnacle or lantern in 1465/6 (and for repairs to it in 1535), although the present timber and lead spirelet is probably early C19. Perp aisles and chancel chapels. Money was left towards building a new aisle in 1468 and 1469, which may, according to Birkin Haward, refer to the S chapel; money for the N chapel was left in 1487/8, 'the new part of the church on the N side' is mentioned in a will of 1495, and the 'new aisle' in 1498. Perp clerestory of closely set windows. Perp the pretty doorways on the W and the N side. Perp arcades of four bays. Piers with four shafts and four hollows, finely moulded arches. Chancel chapel arcades of two bays, the S details similar to those of the nave arcades. The flatter form on the N side is similar to the piers at Cavendish and attributed by Haward to *John Melford* of Sudbury. At the E end of the S chapel niches in two tiers l. and r. of the window. The church was repaired in 1864 (rainwater heads), with a major internal restoration by *Reginald Blomfield* in 1886–7. The latter included re-seating, and a new chancel roof. – FONT. Only the panelled stem of the Perp font. – FONT COVER. C17, cupboard type, with ogee cap. Painted inside with texts on scrolls. – PULPIT. Nice C18 piece. The staircase with finely twisted balusters, two to the tread. – PANELLING. Some linenfold panelling (S chapel). – DOORS. S door with tracery and border with quatrefoils. – N door with only a quatrefoil border. – W door with a border of vine trails. – WEST GALLERY. Handsome, with cusped panels. – WALL PAINTINGS. Above the chancel arch small demi-figure of Christ, and l. and r. large figures of angels with wings spread. C15. On E wall of S chapel, outlines of painted figures in the stone niches, and a painted crowned figure (probably St Edmund) in a painted niche. – STAINED GLASS. E window (Transfiguration) by *Rosemary Rutherford*, 1973, made by *Lowndes & Drury* (installed posthumously). – BRASS. David Birde, son of the rector, †1606 aged 22 weeks. Touching little

Boxford, St Mary, brass to David Birde †1606.
Rubbing by M. Stuchfield, 2014

picture of the child in his cot. – MONUMENTS (churchyard). Daniel Tiffen †1861. Stone spirelet on octagonal base. – War memorial. 1919. Portland stone crucifix with canopy over the corpus. Prominently positioned right by the N porch, the main entrance from the village.

PRIMARY SCHOOL, SE of the church, includes the old National School, signed and dated on a nice little plaque by *William Howe*, 1839. Red brick with decorative bargeboards.

PERAMBULATION. In CHURCH STREET, facing the W end of the church, a pretty row of timber-framed houses. The OLD CHEQUERS is much restored, but has a carved bressumer along part of its front. To the S, up SCHOOL HILL, KNOLLGATE, with a curious C19 white-brick front and C16 timber-framed parts to the rear. The front has a square bay with hipped roof in the centre, and flat-roofed bays to l. and r., one square and one canted. Further S, OLD SCHOOL HOUSE, formerly the grammar school, founded in 1596. Timber-framed and plastered, of two storeys and attics, with cross-wing at one end. Large chimneystack. Round the corner, on the main road, THE ARC, 2007–9 by *SEArch Architects*. Irregular fan-shaped plan, with glazed s-facing rooms, for maximum solar gain, and high-density aggregate-block walls mainly on the N side for good insulation. Curved sloping roof of recycled aluminium.

On the N side of the Box is the centre of the village, where Church Street meets Swan Street and Broad Street. It is all very lovely. SWAN STREET leads NW, mostly of timber-framed houses, many refronted. The only slight blot is ASHLEY HOUSE on the r., *c.* 1879 by *J. S. Moye*, whose father kept the White Hart (*see* below). Although Picturesque by the standards of the day it is out of place here, in red brick with bands of black and various gables and panels of stamped plaster. A little way up on the l. HENDRICK HOUSE, with an C18 plastered front and a pedimented gable. Further on the same side OLD CASTLE HOUSE, timber-framed with cross-wings dressed up in the C19 with castellated gables and castellated porch. It is coarse work, but fun. Next to it VICTORIA COTTAGE. White brick. Two storeys and two bays, the windows and door set in shallow recesses with semicircular heads. Within the arches plaster strips carrying the name and 'built 1839'. Gothick glazing bars. Then KINGSBURY HOUSE (No. 29), with a red brick Georgian front of five bays and two storeys. Doorway with open pediment and ornamental fanlight, and above it an arched window with Gothick glazing. Further out on the same side the EDWARDSTONE ALMSHOUSES, rebuilt 1855. Red brick with white-brick dressings, unfortunately all now painted. Single-storey, quite plain apart from hoodmoulds. Finally the former Congregational chapel (now BOX HOUSE), 1823. Red brick. Two storeys and three bays. Only the wide entrance, and the OLD MANSE next door, suggest its original purpose. Less of individual interest on the other side of the street, but the overall effect is very good, with the church tower showing above the houses as one returns to the centre.

BROAD STREET runs E from the top of Church Street. On the N side the main building is the FLEECE HOTEL, with a stately pedimented doorway on Ionic columns. On the S side RIVERSIDE HOUSE (Nos. 7–9), actually on the S side of the Box, a pair of Early Georgian three-bay houses. They have a mansard roof, quoins, and doorways with Gibbs surrounds and pediments. To their E, back on the N side of the river, the OLD ENGINE HOUSE of 1823. White brick, two Gothick arches side by side. Built to house a fire engine, but one half was taken over by the police as a lock-up, *c.* 1845; now a shelter. Then the WHITE HART, timber-framed and plastered with two gabled cross-wings. Further on, Broad Street becomes Ellis Street. At the junction, off to the l., BUTCHER'S LANE, narrow, with some good timber-framed houses with jettied upper floors and exposed timbers. Along ELLIS STREET, on the S side, RIVER HALL, just like Hendrick House with its pedimented gable, and a doorway with a very upright and rather comic version of a swan-neck pediment. Nos. 16–18, opposite, stand at right angles to the street, large and with some exposed timbers. Finally, on the corner of Cox Hill, the former POLICE STATION, 1848. Red brick. U-plan, and quite large, but domestic in character.

BOXFORD HOUSE, 400 yds S, was the rectory, and before the bypass was built its park-like grounds extended all the way to the churchyard. By *M. G. Thompson*, 1818–21, for Rev. Thomas Thurlow. Stuccoed. Main range of two storeys and five bays, but not symmetrical. The roof is hidden behind a high parapet, which is castellated over the middle three bays. Castellated polygonal corner turrets. Hoodmoulded windows. Arched entrance, not central, but in the r.-hand bay. To the r. of that a lower wing of four bays, also with polygonal turrets. But the

Boxford House, former rectory.
Design by M. G. Thompson, 1818

back is more conventionally Georgian, and inside is a curved geometrical staircase behind an Ionic screen. Across the road to the E THE PARSONAGE, once the rectory and later a farmhouse. In the grounds a canal, probably early C18 and formed from an arm of the medieval moat, and N of the house a DOVECOTE. Red brick. Cylindrical, with conical roof and cupola. Rebuilt in the 1970s by *Ray Williams*.

At STONE STREET, ½ m. s, a number of good timber-framed houses that seem almost to meet across the narrow roadway.

BOXTED

8050

Boxted Hall has been occupied by the Poley family since the late C14, and the same might be said of the church, which is full of their monuments. The church stands on the hill above and to the w of the house, which lies in the Glem valley.

HOLY TRINITY. Much restored in 1885 (one of his earliest commissions) by *Reginald Blomfield*, including rebuilding the s porch. Unbuttressed, battlemented w tower; money was left for its construction in 1440–57. Perp nave with clerestory and N aisle. Low arcade with octagonal piers and double-chamfered arches. The chancel was rebuilt in the C17, probably at the same time as the N (Poley) chapel was added, and this was described as new in 1658. Its red brick is continued as battlements along the N aisle. Interesting hammerbeam roof in the chancel, interesting because Jacobean. Nave roof of c. 1505 (bequest for 'leading of the church'), restored 1885. Of the latter date also the chancel arch, with three arched openings in timber over it, and the tower SCREEN and gallery. – PULPIT. Jacobean. Octagonal, with back panel. Tester with pendants and date, 1618. – POLEY PEW. Taken out of the E end of the N aisle, with a round-headed doorway from the Poley Chapel. Parclose screen filling the first bay of the arcade, with balusters carrying arches and achievements on top. Similar screen in the second bay, appropriated for use by Boxted Hall servants in 1853–4. – COMMUNION RAIL. Three-sided, with twisted balusters. – STAINED GLASS. Some original glass in the E window of the Poley Chapel, e.g. the figure of a king, incorporated in window of 1936 by *W. Aikman*. Aikman probably also responsible for the chancel E window †1942. – MONUMENTS. The Poley family monuments are the most interesting feature of the church. The earliest is in the chancel: William †1587 and wife Alice †1577. Two recumbent effigies, a late example of oak carving for a funeral purpose. He is in armour. – Later monuments in the Poley Chapel, notably Sir John †1638 (of Wormegay, Norfolk) and his wife Abigail †1652. Both have standing effigies in arched niches and crowning pediments with rounded centres, both are of alabaster, and both were erected many years after their deaths. In all else they differ characteristically. Sir John's monument is of *c.* 1680 and has been attributed to *William Stanton* by Geoffrey Fisher, who considers it his masterpiece. Sir John stands with one hand on his hip, in a self-assured and a slightly mannered attitude, and he has a gold frog in one ear. The costume is that of his day, not of that of the sculptor. To the l. and r. standing putti pull away a big drapery which seems to hang from the top of the monument. The top of the niche has a shell pattern. All the decoration is rich and lively – garlands, foliage borders, etc. Dame Abigail's monument was not erected until 1725 and is, according to K. A. Esdaile, the last English monument in alabaster. It is demonstratively less demonstrative than Sir John's and has only flanking pilasters; the head of the niche is undecorated. – Also attributed to *Stanton* are several ledger stones, notably that to Elizabeth Poley †1677 with armorial inlay in white marble, and the family PEDIGREE on the W wall: an open book crowned with an urn, and a scroll with seal below it. A second scroll was added in the C18, and the pedigree is complete from the C14 to 1976. – George Weller Poley †1849. By *de Carle*. Gothic, but insignificant by comparison with the earlier monuments. – In chancel, Philip Hamond and wife Martha, both †1679. With scrolled pediment and arms. Erected by Edward Plume of Hawkedon; there are marked similarities between the inscription plate and that of the Everard monument at Hawkedon (q.v.).

BOXTED HALL. The house is surrounded by a moat, fed by the Glem which runs past on its E side, so that it feels more as if it is on an island in the river. The present house, of two storeys and attics, is mid C16, probably the rebuilding soon after 1561 of an existing house, and the four-arched brick bridge leading to it is older. Externally, the oldest visible parts are the external chimneystacks; the house was taxed on twenty-two hearths in 1674. It was remodelled between 1754 and 1767 by George Weller (later Weller Poley), when it was stuccoed and fitted with sash windows. Two single-storey semicircular bays were added to the W front, to l. and r. of the three-bay centre. The house was given its present appearance between 1900 and 1905, when it was faced in red brick with rather crudely applied false timbers. The windows on the bays received hoodmoulds, and the windows above them were set in half-timbered gables. A third gable was inserted over the porch, which was rebuilt in Tudor-Gothic style and alone has stone dressings. The entrance remained off-centre, as one would expect in a C16 house; to its r. a tripartite window, its centre arched with Gothick tracery – an impure Serlian form. At the S end of the house a polygonal red brick extension, C18, leading into a single-storey late C19 billiard room. On the E side of the house a wing, mainly of red brick, extends N beyond the main part. It has large tripartite windows with pilasters and an open pediment over the centre. Inside, the principal room is the hall, with carved and moulded beams and mainly C17 panelling. On its N side the dining room, remodelled in the C18 with a curved recess at the E end echoing the curve of the bay window. Most of the other rooms are panelled, but the original timber frame is occasionally exposed.

On the E bank of the Glem, a WALLED GARDEN built by George Weller (brick dated 1756), with two PAVILIONS in the E wall. Both of red brick with rusticated quoins, and pedimented with semicircular windows in the tympana. The front of the S one is open, its centre with a squashed arch on Tuscan columns and a little balustrade to either side of the opening, another Serlian effect. N of the house a BRIDGE over the Glem dated 1760. STABLES NW of the house, the main range C18. Two storeys with gabled centre and clock turret. N range dated 1851. An estate map of 1767 shows a number of other structures, practical and decorative, including an obelisk, of which nothing remains, at the head of an avenue of lime trees WSW of the house. At the E end of this avenue one wall of a brick and flint FOLLY. At the E entrance to the park a single-storey white-brick LODGE with pyramid roof and deep eaves: 'This lodge built, and road diverted anno domini 1843; G.W. Poley.'

Former NATIONAL SCHOOL, built by Mrs Weller Poley in 1852, and estate cottages W of the church. Flint with white-brick dressings.

BRADFIELD COMBUST

8050

ALL SAINTS. Nave and broad S aisle, together almost square on plan, with shallow chancel. The nave is C12, with a blocked N door round-headed on the inside. C14 arcade with octagonal piers and double-chamfered arches. S wall with datestone 1721 denoting repairs. Nave W wall, with bellcote and a third bell set in a little arch below it, part of the restoration by F.C. Penrose, 1868–9, which also included virtual rebuilding of the chancel walls, with much use of tiles laid flat among the flint. – FONT. Square, Norman, with scalloped underside. Angle volutes, carved (perhaps later) as human heads. Also later (C14?) the quatrefoil on one face of the bowl. – SCREEN. Two sections, traceried, reused for the back of the C19 organ seat. – WALL PAINTINGS. Large, once splendid St George of *c.* 1400, with plumed helmet; and a very large St Christopher with hermit, fisherman and sprouting staff. – STAINED GLASS. E window, 1869, commemorating Arthur Young (1741–1820), 'in agriculture and political economy pre-eminent', in the words of his tomb which stands E of the chancel. By *Lavers, Barraud & Westlake*, who also did the chancel S and S aisle W windows, 1870, and probably also the S windows. S aisle E by *Powell & Sons*, 1900. – MONUMENTS. A number to the Young family, including Rev. Arthur Young †1759. With obelisk, cartouche with arms, flaming urn and lamps, and winged cherub's head.

THE MANGER pub, almost in the churchyard, is late C15 in its oldest parts, with some exposed timbers. To the N a little green with, on the N side, BRADFIELD HOUSE (former rectory). Early C18, with later C18 and C19 alterations and additions. The timber frame exposed, although surely never meant to be; the front is otherwise Georgian, of two storeys and five bays. Hipped mansard roof. Further N, along the main road to Bury, a few estate cottages, including a pair dated 1866, and former SCHOOL, 1856.

BRADFIELD HALL. Seat of the agriculturalist Arthur Young, but rebuilt in 1857 by Arthur John Young. Knapped flint with red brick dressings. Shaped gables. V-shaped oriel over the front door, two-storey canted bay on W front. Circular corner turret with conical roof. Now flats. To its W the moated site of the medieval house, originally a grange of the abbot of Bury. Many good trees in the surrounding park, including an avenue planted by Rev. Arthur Young, *c.* 1725. – ENTRANCE LODGE by *W. E. Nesfield*. Half-timbered gables with pargetting that includes the date, 1865, and crude flowers set with black pebbles and pieces of glass or ceramic.

METHODIST CHURCH, ¾ m. SSW. 1867. Pedimented front of white brick; sides of red brick with white-brick pilasters. Tall round-arched windows.

9050

BRADFIELD ST CLARE

ST CLARE. The name comes from the family of St Clare or Cleers; the pre-Reformation dedication was to All Saints. W tower, nave and chancel. The appearance is C15, restored in 1873 (presumably by *W. M. Fawcett*) following the collapse of part of the tower, but parts of the fabric are C13. Porch restored 1921. The best feature is the chancel roof, which has arched

braces reaching high up to a collar. – BENCHES. Some simple ones, with poppyheads. – MONUMENTS. Rev. Richard Grandorge †1619. Touchstone tablet with alabaster frame. – Rev. Robert Davers †1853. Plain marble tablet by *de Carle*.
Former RECTORY, ½ m. NW. By *W. M. Fawcett*, 1874. Red brick. Two-storeyed porch with pedimented gable.
ST CLARE HALL, ⅔ m. E. Timber-framed and plastered house on a moated site. The main front, facing W, is jettied, and dates to the second quarter of the C16; it contains a parlour (with C16 panelling) and hall. To the r. is a cross-wing, rebuilt a century later. To the l. is the earliest part of the house, a two-bay range of the mid C14 that originally continued further E. Its two floors were undivided and it may have been a manorial court hall – if so, it would be an exceptionally early example. Roof with octagonal crown-posts, of which one is well preserved and has a finely carved capital.

BRADFIELD ST GEORGE

9050

ST GEORGE. A Norman window in the nave on the S side. Chancel with E.E. doorway and lancets. A very charming Dec nave S doorway with a much-moulded ogee arch. Perp three-bay arcade (four shafts and four fine hollows) and diverse Perp windows. Perp W tower. Diagonal buttresses with carved inscriptions picked out in black flint; one mentions John Bacon, no doubt a donor, and no doubt the same John Bacon (†1513) who paid for the tower at Hessett (q.v.). William Cowper also made a bequest for the tower in 1496, providing the work started within four years. Following the tower the nave roof was rebuilt, with money left for it in 1520. Of low pitch with arched braces. Their spandrels have tracery, two with carvings of dragons. Church restored 1863–4, with addition of N vestry. – FONT. Octagonal, Perp, simple. – REREDOS. By *F. L. Pearson*, 1919. A lavish Nativity, richly carved, painted and gilded. – PULPIT. Jacobean, with two tiers of short blank arches. Iron HOURGLASS STAND on wall nearby. – BENCHES. With poppyheads and traceried backs. – SCULPTURE. In the jamb of the porch's E window, a carved hand raised in blessing, perhaps associated with a stoup. – St George by *C. Blakeman*, 1949. Plaster, painted. – STAINED GLASS. Lustrous E window, 1913, designed by *E. A. Fellowes Prynne*, made by *John Jennings*.
WEST LODGE, ½ m. WSW. 1870. 'A fine mansion of red brick in the Domestic Gothic style' (Kelly's). An unspoilt specimen of its type.
YEOMAN'S ACRE, ½ m. ENE. C15 timber-framed and plastered hall house with jettied cross-wing to the l. Restored and enlarged *c.* 1963, when a new, larger cross-wing (of plastered brick) was added to the r. The original hall, with crown-post

roof, was opened up and its C16 inserted floor reused in the new cross-wing. Matching thatched garage.

BRADFIELD AND ROUGHAM BAPTIST CHURCH, Kingshall Green. *See* Rougham.

BRAMFORD

ST MARY. An impressive and interesting church with a spectacular N façade of Late Perp date. This has much stone decoration to heighten the effect of its flint walls. All parapets of aisle, clerestory, and porch of stone with pretty blank panelling. Short pinnacles with figures of supporters. Tall porch. This porch however was only heightened in the Perp age. Its two-centred entrance arch, with its typical sunk wave mouldings, and its E window are early C14. Niche above the entrance. Two lions as stops of the hoodmould of the entrance arch. The W window of the porch is Perp, of the same design as the aisle windows. In fact much of the church is of the early C14 and late C13. Of the latter date the chancel – see the one S window with its tracery and rere-arch, the plain PISCINA and SEDILIA, and the priest's doorway. Of the early C14 most of the rest, namely both arcades – three bays, octagonal piers, double-chamfered arches – though the capitals on the S side were renewed in the Perp style, the N aisle W window (intersected tracery), the S doorway (fine, filleted continuous mouldings), and the W tower (Dec bell-openings and quatrefoil windows in circles below them). The tower has very big angle buttresses, a niche with a little vault in the W wall, a NW stair-turret lower than the parapet, and a recessed lead spire rebuilt in the C18. Though the tower is Dec and the arcades are early C14, the former must have been built later than the latter, as its buttressing cuts into their W arches. The NE buttress sits on a large glacial boulder. What remains obscure is why the tall tower arch is not axial with the nave. Perp, apart from the N front already described, are the clerestory, which has six windows against the three arcade arches below and tracery of the same lively type as the aisles, and the fine roofs of nave, chancel and S aisle. The former two have hammerbeams. The tower must once have been vaulted; three corbels remain. The vestry was added on the N side by *Cheston & Perkin* in 1894–6. It repeats the style of the aisle successfully. The principal restoration was in 1862–6, begun by *F. Barnes* and completed by *Ewan Christian*, which included the patently Victorian chancel arch.

FURNISHINGS. ROOD SCREEN. Of stone and *c.* 1300 in date, so rather part of the architecture than of the furnishing, and highly unusual for this part of the world. Three even arches with shafts carrying capitals left unfinished. The arches have two wave mouldings. The quatrefoil openings and the battlement coping are of the 1860s. – FONT. Octagonal, Perp. Against the bowl four angels and four shields. Traceried stem. – FONT COVER. A very fine early C16 piece. Of cupboard type, with doors folding back. On their panels groups of three little plinths arranged like the oriel windows of Hengrave Hall. Domed crocketed top. – REREDOS. By *W.D. Caröe*, 1901. Carved oak. The crucifix and gilding are later, and it has also been lowered. – Also by Caröe the CHOIR STALLS, now in the S aisle, and sanctuary PANELLING, *c.* 1897–9. – PULPIT. C16, with linenfold panelling. – INSCRIPTION. On SW pier of nave arcade, incised and coloured:

> Remember ye pore
> The scripture doth record
> What to them is geven
> Is lent unto the Lord
> 1591

– STAINED GLASS. E window by *Kempe*, 1904, replacing one of 1865 by *Chance Bros*; some of this reused in the W window. N aisle W designed by *Samuel Evans* of Smethwick, made by *D. & E. Haggar* of Ipswich, 1874. – ENGRAVED GLASS DOORS to S porch by *Jennifer Conway*, 1987–8. – MONUMENTS. Elizabeth Dade †1648. Rather clumsily classical, with dumpy pilasters and broken pediment, and with many Latin inscriptions as was then the fashion. – William Alston †1749 and wife Elizabeth †1741. More sophisticated classical, with two little urns. The tradition continued well in the monument to Sir Edward Packard †1932, with broken segmental pediment. – War memorial by *John Daymond & Son*, 1920. Marble, with small angels at top and bottom. A similar, smaller memorial for the Second World War. – Another war memorial, made for E. Packard & Co.'s works by *E. Sylvia Packard*, 1922. A touching piece. It commemorates all employees who fought as well as those who died, including two members of the Packard family. Mahogany triptych. In the centre panel an illuminated list of names, with small portraits of fourteen of the men. The side panels have large figures of a soldier and a medieval knight. Above the centre, Britannia and two angels look down.

METHODIST CHURCH, The Street. 1873 by *Cattermole & Eade*. Red brick with white-brick dressings. Pedimented gable to street with triple-arched window. Rusticated corner pilasters and pronounced dentils. Small porches in return walls and schoolroom at rear.

Former SCHOOL, NW of the church. By *F. Barnes*, 1860, enlarged 1873 and 1897. A picturesque range, of black knapped flint with red brick dressings. Teacher's house at the N end and classrooms stretching towards the church. Gothic windows.

The village is in two parts, one to the N of the church along the River Gipping, the other W of this along The Street. On the N side of the churchyard is CHURCH GREEN. At the far end Nos. 2–8, mid-C16 with exposed timbers (now colourwashed) and long-wall jetty with four thin carved pre-Reformation brackets. Originally an inn, floored throughout. Carved and moulded hall ceiling, and remains of painted decoration. C17 extension at S end. Across Ship Lane, BRAMFORD HOUSE, of 1693–4 according to deeds. This may refer to the remodelling of a timber-framed house. It sits back behind a high red brick wall, so from the road one sees only the entrance, through a pedestrian gateway, and the upper part of the house, and it is here that the effort is concentrated. The very fine façade is of red brick, plain on the ground floor but chequered on the first with burnt headers. Seven bays and two storeys with pitched roof on a richly carved eaves cornice with modillions. The modillions run rhythmically in groups of 4–3–3–4–4–3–3–4. Ogee guttering with lion masks. The Ionic porch is a later C18 addition. Entrance hall with the staircase placed inside it. The third of the three flights propped up awkwardly by two (later) pillars. Handrail and upper gallery rails with slender twisted balusters.

Along MILL LANE, behind Bramford House, MILL HOUSE, originally a small hall house with single-bay open hall of the late C15, floored and extended in the C17 and refronted in the early C19. Next to it the large gatepiers of MILLBANK, built c. 1754 but much altered in the C19. Timber-framed and plastered, the original three-bay entrance front encased in white brick. Mid-C19 sashes with cast-iron lintels. Then BRIDGE HOUSE, mid-C19 flint with white-brick dressings.

A few timber-framed houses scattered along THE STREET, the best-preserved Nos. 6–10 at the S end. C15 two-bay hall in the centre, floored in the C16. Jettied cross-wings, the N c. 1400, the S late C15 or early C16. Inside, C17 painted decoration in the form of imitation textile hanging, no longer *in situ*. Further N, on the W side, a row of C15–C16 cottages and houses, including two jettied cross-wings.

BRAMFORD HALL, 1 m. WNW. Mostly dem. 1956. Three-storey, seven-bay stuccoed house, with two-storey, two-bay wing to one side. Principally mid-C18, but probably incorporating parts of a house built for John Acton, High Sheriff of Suffolk in 1631. Alterations and additions by *Morgan & Phipson*, 1857–8, *R.W. Collier*, 1895, and *Richardson & Gill*, 1934–8.

Former FISONS WORKS, Paper Mill Lane, 1 m. N. Edward Packard established the world's first complete factory for the production of chemical fertilizers (superphosphates) at Bramford between 1851 and 1854, followed in 1858 by Joseph Fison on a site immediately N. Some original buildings from Fison's works, which later amalgamated with Packard's, survive, considerably altered in the late C19 or early C20. Main block (North Warehouse) about 100 yds (30.5 metres) long, mostly weatherboarded but with tarred red brick ground floor along the W side. Four storeys, of which the upper two are part of the alterations, with segmental felt-clad roof. Heavy timber floors on cast-iron columns. Continuous glazing on the upper floors of the side walls. Similar, shorter range alongside at the s end.* The Packards lived at GROVE HOUSE, ⅓ m. s of the works. Early C19 red brick with later C19 additions, one dated 1889. The original house of two storeys and three bays, the centre stepping slightly forward with pediment. Broad segmental windows.

RUSHBROOK MILL, Paper Mill Lane, 1¼ m. N. C19 watermill, converted to flats and extended by *Barefoot & Gilles*, 2005–7. Two and three storeys. Red brick ground floor, the upper parts weatherboarded. Three-storey extension (for offices) mainly red brick.

BRANDON

Brandon was the centre of the East Anglian craft of flint-knapping and gunflint production. The most famous site associated with this is Grimes Graves, Norfolk,† but there were gunflint mines at Lingheath Farm, 1¼ m. SE of Brandon church, and W of Spruce Covert in Brandon Park, about 2 m. SSE, the former C18 and the latter probably C17 or earlier. Knapped flint is extensively used on the town's buildings of all ages. The railway arrived in 1845. The town was greatly expanded to the E in the 1970s by 'London overspill' housing and light industry.

ST PETER. Early Dec chancel with two pretty E turrets with spirelets. For the dating see the windows and the chancel arch. The E window is of five lights, segment-headed, and has an irregular design with reticulated elements. Of the same time probably the W tower. Its doorway and window however are Perp. Of the same time also the five-bay arcade with unusually slim quatrefoil piers and arches with two small quadrant hollows. Perp N and S sides, Perp S chapel. Restored by *J. D. Wyatt*, 1873, including new nave roof and re-seating. – FONT. Plain, octagonal, C14. The stem has an octagonal core with eight detached shafts. – REREDOS. 1873, executed by *Thomas Earp*. Marble and alabaster. – SCREEN. With one-light divisions. Rather arid. Only the lower parts original, with renewed colouring. – STALLS. With traceried fronts and poppyheads. – BENCHES. Some with poppyheads. – STAINED GLASS. E and W windows by *Ward & Hughes*, 1873. Two chancel N windows by *Leonard Walker*, 1900 and †1913. – S aisle by *Heaton, Butler & Bayne*, 1921.

The church lies ½ m. SW of the centre; the only remaining building of interest near it is the former WORKHOUSE to the W. 1673, repaired or rebuilt 1778, converted to National School 1843. Five bays and two storeys. Clunch, with dressings of

---

*Plans submitted in 2012 for redevelopment as offices and homes, preserving the North Warehouse and other historic buildings.
†See *Buildings of England: Norfolk 2: North-West and South*, pp. 756–7.

white and red brick. BRANDON HALL, 700 yds w, dates from the late C17, but is mainly of *c.* 1730. Two storeys, three bays wide with two-storey wings projecting slightly. Knapped flint with red brick headers and dressings. Shell-hood. FOORD HOUSE, ½ m. NW, was built as the rectory, presumably the design by *Clark Rampling* (born at Brandon) exhibited at the Royal Academy in 1818. White-brick front with two two-storey bows and one return wall of very fine knapped and squared flint with another bow. A new rectory was built in 1902 by *E. C. Shearman* in Victoria Avenue, 600 yds ENE of the church (now Abbots Court).

The town developed along the main road either side of the BRIDGE (rebuilt 1953–4, faced with flint) over the Little Ouse. The best houses are at this end of the HIGH STREET. N of the bridge, BRANDON HOUSE (hotel), Georgian, red brick, of five bays and two and a half storeys, with lower wings. Porch with Doric columns carrying an open pediment, and above this a Venetian window in an arch. s of the bridge THE LIMES, with an open segmental pediment on Doric columns, and on the W side CONNAUGHT HOUSE, two storeys with mansard roof, of white brick with an Ionic porch. Further s, on the same side, GRAFTON HOUSE has a C19 stuccoed elevation to the street with crowstepped gable, main elevation of white brick, and a mid-C16 core. Beyond it, also at right angles to the street, HELLESDON HOUSE, late C18 white brick. Facing up the High Street at its s end the SCHOOL by *J. T. Lee*, 1877–8. Red brick, Gothic, with an asymmetrical façade and clock tower, and not attractive. Additions by *E. Boardman & Son*, 1897.

BRANDON PARK, I m. SE. The house (now a nursing home) was built in 1826 for Edward Bliss. Seven bays and two storeys, with a low tetrastyle Doric portico on the garden front (no pediment). Stuccoed. Bliss, who died in 1845, erected for himself and his wife a Gothic MAUSOLEUM 250 yds WSW of the house. A full-size, chapel-like building of knapped flint with white-brick and stone dressings. Now in Brandon Country Park, with other remains of the estate including walled garden and lake.

NORTH COURT LODGE, 1½ m. SW. The house was demolished *c.* 1970, but in the grounds is a MAUSOLEUM, built for Capt. J. P. M. Kenyon †1830 by his wife and consecrated that year. She died 1856 and is immured there also. Knapped flint with stone dressings, the exterior Gothic but the interior classical, with a domed ceiling.

BRENT ELEIGH

ST MARY. Dec nave with Perp N windows. Perp W tower. Chancel E window 1859–60, when the library of 1720 built against the E wall was removed. Its free-standing replacement was demolished in 1988. – FONT. Octagonal Purbeck bowl, two blank pointed arches to each side. – FONT COVER. Jacobean, pretty; finial added by *Cecil B. Smith*, 1960. – PULPIT. Jacobean, tall, with carved panels and book-rest. – BOX PEWS. Some are Jacobean, the majority C18. Some incorporate parts of medieval benches, including one with poppyhead. – SCREEN to the SE chapel. Early C14 with shafts with capitals instead of mullions, and ogee arches. With painted medallions of uncertain date; C15? – SOUTH DOOR. A rare piece, early C14 with blank reticulated tracery. – COMMUNION RAIL. Three-sided, with twisted balusters. Early Georgian. – WALL PAINTINGS. An important group on the E wall, discovered in 1960.* In the middle, as a reredos, the Crucifixion with the Virgin and St John. Of high quality. Red on a green background. On the N side, censing angels adoring a lost carved figure, doubtless the Virgin and Child. On the S side, the remains of a Harrowing of Hell, including the figure of the donor, a tonsured priest. The three paintings have been dated *c.* 1270–1330, the side panels earlier than the central one. – STAINED GLASS. E window †1857, and probably also the chancel SE, by *O'Connor*. – MONUMENTS. Edward Colman †1739. By *Thomas Dunn*, 1743. Standing wall monument. Reredos background with open pediment. Reclining figure in loose dress, one hand outstretched towards us. Above a putto with a crown. Two more putti reclining on the pediment. – Dr Thomas Brown †1852. Severely classical. By *E. G. Physick*. – Dionesse Colman †1697 and husband Robert †1730. Chest tomb in churchyard, against chancel S wall. With elaborate carving, including a skeleton holding an hourglass.

BRENT ELEIGH HALL. An attractive house, wholly Georgian in appearance. It is stuccoed, of two storeys and attics, with two far-reaching wings on the S side, away from the church. In 1607 the property was bought from Sir Robert Jermyn of Rushbrooke by Samuel Colman, grandfather of Edward Colman whose monument is in the church. Samuel either built a new house or improved an existing one. The story is complicated by a number of Samuel's descendants dying in quick succession without issue, but a major remodelling, giving the house its present basic shape, seems to have taken place in the second decade of the C18. This must be the date of the N front, which has a five-bay pedimented centre, slightly projecting, another bay to either side enclosed by pilasters, and beyond them a broad bay with single window corresponding to the cross-wings of the original house. The staircase also belongs to this time, with two twisted balusters to the tread. The ceiling above it has a painted oval surrounded by a rich stucco garland. In the spandrels of the oblong ceiling branches with foliage. The centre panel, with Barnardiston arms and putti, was added in the 1780s, following the dismantling of the Barnardistons'

---

*When the Early Georgian REREDOS noted by Pevsner was taken down for repair and not returned.

Kedington Hall; Mary Barnardiston had married Edward Goate, who inherited from the Colmans in 1739. Another set of Barnardiston arms, in stone, also from Kedington, was added to the pediment of the N front. The S front also belongs to this campaign of alterations, with canted bays added to the ends of the wings and a giant Tuscan portico placed between them. This remained the main entrance to the house until *c.* 1877. *Sir Edwin Lutyens* was busy at Brent Eleigh Hall in 1933–4. The principal external change was the Early Georgian-looking entrance doorway, and a new kitchen wing on the W side. He remodelled the entrance hall, enlarged the dining room, and made the fireplaces in the hall and dining room. – ENTRANCE GATES with tall slender piers dated 1763* and good 1920s lodge.

OLD RECTORY, opposite the church. 1861 by *Ewan Christian*. Red brick with bands of black, but otherwise rather plain.

The village lies mostly on the S side of the River Brett, along what was the main road but now is mercifully bypassed. CORNER FARM is prominent, with its exposed timbers and brick-nogging, much restored but still splendid. C16, the tall centre and lower cross-wings all jettied. Opposite, the former SCHOOL (now village hall), 1876, very good of its kind. Red brick with black-and-white brick ornamentation and prettily composed roofs and gables. Along the street to the W COLMAN COTTAGES, a two-storey terrace of six almshouses built by Edward Colman in 1731. Segment-headed windows. Small central pediment with inscription tablet in the tympanum. A few more good timber-framed houses, including two that date back to the C14: HIGH BANK with exposed timbers on the jettied cross-wing, and STREET FARM, the front altered in 1880 but with some exposed timbers at the back. Many original features including a moulded C14 crown-post.

WELLS HALL, ½ m. SE. C17 timber-framed and plastered house on an older moated site. By the road a good C16 brick gateway with wall to either side. Arched entrance. The top battlemented with three finials set diagonally.

BRIDGE, ½ m. W. 1813. Cast iron, with seven ribs of 13-ft (4-metre) span. By *William Cubitt*, made by *Ransome & Son* (cf. Clare). Disused; formerly carried the main road over the Brett.

BRETTENHAM

ST MARY THE VIRGIN. Essentially C14, with a S porch tower. Nave W window with flowing tracery. Dec PISCINA in the chancel with the arms of Stafford and Buckingham. But Perp chancel windows. Restored by *A. W. Blomfield*, 1866, who

---

*Not original to the house.

rebuilt the chancel S wall, E gable and chancel arch. 'The interior wears an entirely new face, the architect having left not a single point untouched' (*Ipswich Journal*). – FONT. C14, octagonal, with crocketed ogee gables in the panels (cf. Rattlesden, Walsham-le-Willows). – COMMUNION RAIL. With twisted balusters. – SOUTH DOOR. With a foliage-trail border. – PAINTING. On E wall, two slate panels painted with scenes of the Three Wise Men and Christ on the Road to Emmaus. 1880–1 by *Powell & Sons*, designed by *Miss H. L. Beale* of Brettenham Park. – STAINED GLASS. E window, chancel N and nave S by *Ward & Hughes*, 1866; also chancel S, 1882. – MONUMENTS. Elizabeth Wenyeve †1751. Ledger stone by *Charles Bottomley*.

Former RECTORY, N of the church. White brick. Mostly a rebuilding of 1860–1 by *T. J. Willson*, but keeping to its Georgian character.

CHURCH FARM, 100 yds SE. C19 front of red brick with white-brick dressings. Behind this, and visible at the sides, timber-framed. Jettied gable-end with exposed timbers and carved bressumer dated 1587.

POPPLES FARM, 1¼ m. SW. Picturesque timber-framed C15 house overhanging the moat on one side. Exposed timbers, thatched. Carved bressumer, one original doorway and some original windows. Restored by *Marshall Sisson*, 1957, when the larger of the two E wings was added.

BRETTENHAM PARK
(Old Buckenham Hall School)

A large red brick house built by Sir George Wenyeve, whose family had been in the parish since the middle of the C15. It was taxed on fourteen hearths in 1674, and the date given for its construction is 1661. It descended to Lt-Col. John Carnac, husband of Henrietta Wenyeve, who made alterations between 1814 and his death in 1831. After that the house passed through various hands, and was occupied by tenants who included Joseph Bonaparte, ex-king of Spain and brother of Napoleon. Further alterations and additions were made in 1902–3 by (Sir) Courtenay Warner; his architect was *John Dunn*, who had been working on the development of the Warner estate in Walthamstow. Warner's grandson sold Brettenham Park in 1956 to Old Buckenham Hall School, named after the house the school occupied in Norfolk until it was gutted by fire in 1952.*

The evidence of the earliest part is on the N side: the row of five Dutch gables with concave sides and pediments. They are of two and three bays wide and of varying depths. Against one of the gables a one-and-a-half-storey extension of 1977 with a further single-storey extension of 2005 by *Wincer Kievenaar*. The sympathetic gables are not enough to overcome the

---

*In 1953–6 the school occupied Merton Hall, Norfolk, until that too suffered a bad fire.

misfortune of an extension in such a prominent position. Chimneys with octagonal shafts rise in ranks above the old part. To the l. of this a large E range dated 1903 built against the original entrance front. More Dutch gables. In the angle between the old and new blocks a three-storey tower with higher polygonal stair-turret and projecting entrance porch set at an angle. On the S front, the 1903 E range of two bays followed by three steps back to a five-bay centre that is the principal sign of the early C19 alterations. It has a bowed three-bay centre and the outer bays on the first floor have windows with semicircular heads (one blind). Deep parapet with one actual and four blind windows. Ground-floor loggia, following the curve of the bow, with unfluted Doric columns and triglyph frieze. The interiors seem mainly to be of 1902–3, notably the entrance hall with stained-glass windows and a full-height galleried staircase hall. The ground-floor room with the bow has rather Rococo plasterwork, painted ceiling, and painted overdoors that might well belong to the occupancy of Joseph Bonaparte, 1837.

Adaptation of the house for use as a school was by *W. A. E. & Rosemary W. Sewell*, who designed the single-storey range of classrooms and gym E of the house, 1957. It is linked to the house by a covered walkway supported on antique columns salvaged from Old Buckenham Hall. NE of the house a classroom block, 2003, and Britten Hall, 2005, by *Wincer Kievenaar*. Curved, with sweeping slate roof. Part red brick, part timber cladding. W of the house the former STABLES, adapted for use as classrooms, etc., with new block (Sewell) by *Huggins & Bromage*, 2001. Walled kitchen garden beyond the stable yard, not rectangular but lozenge-shaped. On its N side, SQUASH COURTS by *R. S. Hollins*, c. 1983. Red brick, made more interesting by diapering and shallow buttresses.

Many good trees in the surrounding PARK, including avenues leading NE towards Park Farm and village, and W to the main entrance with gates and a pair of mid-C19 LODGES. Red brick with tall chimneys, decorative gables, and windows with diamond-latticed glazing bars. A similar lodge, later C19, SE of the house on Bury Road.

BROCKLEY

ST ANDREW. W tower with buttresses carrying flushwork panelling. Money was left for it in 1504. On the base of the S wall an inscription commemorating Ricardus Coppyng, who left money for the tower's completion in 1521. But the battlements are of 1899. Nave of c. 1300, chancel Dec and originally shorter than at present (Norman?) – see the remains of former quoins, N and S. Plain DOUBLE PISCINA. Piscinae also in the sills of N and S nave windows. In the S wall inside a big ogee-headed

recess, possibly for the tomb of Sir Alexander de Walsham
†1335. Restored 1866, including re-seating and re-roofing of
nave. – REREDOS. 1866? With figures of saints painted on metal
panels. – SOUTH DOOR. With interesting closing ring and
escutcheon, probably early C14. – STAINED GLASS. E window
by *Ward & Hughes*, 1871. – In churchyard, base of a medieval
CROSS.

BROCKLEY HALL. Aisled hall with contemporary cross-wing to
the l. and early C18 cross-wing to the r. High-quality carpentry
in the earlier parts, including a pair of octagonal arcade posts
with moulded capitals. Timbers tree-ring-dated 1317–19,
seeming to confirm the supposition that the house was built
for Sir Alexander de Walsham. Hall floored in the C16. Red
brick chimneystack with crowstepping against l. return wall.
Complete moat. A smaller moated site NE of the church may
have contained the parsonage.

SUTTONS FARM, nearly ½ m. NNE. Late C16 timber-framed and
plastered farmhouse. Original staircase with solid treads and,
in the attic, the unusual feature of a smoke-curing chamber
built round the chimneystack.

BROCKLEY PLACE, a little further N. Built as the rectory, 1843–4,
for Rev. J. D. Sprigge. White brick. Two-storey, five-bay front,
the centre bay breaking forward. Greek Doric porch. Ground-
floor windows with cornices on consoles. Enlarged 1847.

BURES

9030

Properly, Bures St Mary, to distinguish it from Bures Hamlet,
which is part of the same settlement but lies across the River
Stour in Essex.* St Edmund was consecrated king of the East
Angles at Bures on Christmas Day 856.

ST MARY. A stately church, built mostly of flint. Late C13 to early
C14 W tower with Dec bell-openings. Tomb recess in the outer
N wall. Also C14 the tower arch towards the nave with three
chamfers dying into the imposts. Inside the tower, springers
of a projected vault with fine faces and grotesques; reordering
by *Whitworth, Hall & Thomas*, 1989–90. The tower originally
carried a spire, destroyed by lightning in 1733. C14 N porch
of big timbers. C14 arcades of three bays (octagonal piers,
double-chamfered arches), the S side rebuilt as part of *Ewan
Christian*'s restoration of 1862–3. Perp aisle and clerestory, with
the line of the earlier, steeper roof visible on the outer E face
of the tower. Ornate Perp S chapel (Waldegrave Chapel),
founded by Sir William Waldegrave in 1514. Brick, with flushwork battlements to the E. Big windows, two to the S. In the
buttress between them a small priest's doorway. The piers of

---

*See *Buildings of England: Essex*, p. 188.

the arcade towards the chancel are square with four half-columns with fillets. Of about the same time the big founder's MONUMENT in the chancel and the elegantly decorated doorway next to it. The doorway has fleurons, the tomb a chest with shields in cusped foils. The lid appears to be reused, as it has indents of brasses that are probably those of Sir Richard Waldegrave †1410 and his wife; he founded a chapel on the N side of the chancel. Arch above and big angel corbels l. and r. Early C16 S porch of brick, the side windows with brick tracery. The inner doorway, however, belongs to the C14 work. Battlements and crowstepped gables. An ecclesiological curiosity is the PISCINA high up on the S side of the chancel arch, to serve the rood loft. – FONT. Octagonal, Perp. Stem with four tracery panels and at the angles the four Emblems of the Evangelists. Bowl with panels with demi-figures of angels. On the shields the arms of England, de Vere, Fitzralph, Mortimer, de Cornerthe, Waldegrave, de Bures and Mortimer of Clare. – STOUP. Inside the S porch. On it two male demi-figures, one a bishop. – SOUTH DOOR, With tracery and a trail border. – STAINED GLASS. The E and tower windows, probably by *Ward & Hughes*, belong to Christian's restoration, as does the elaborate carved stone REREDOS with painted panels of the Annunciation. S chapel E by *Horace Wilkinson*, 1940, to the Waldegrave and Probert families. – MONUMENTS. For the chancel N side see above. – In a N window on the sill a beautiful oaken effigy of a knight, cross-legged, early C14. Probably Sir Richard de Cornerthe. – In the S chapel, a tomb-chest with shields on lozenges in square panels. The top rises like a lectern towards the window sill. Indents of brasses on it. It seems to be made up from former tombs of Sir William Waldegrave †1527/8 and his son Sir George †1528. – Also in the S chapel, against the W wall, a small tomb-chest with shields in cusped foils, and a free-standing monument to Sir William Waldegrave †1613 and his first wife Elizabeth Mildmay †1581. Erected 1581. Big square base and recessed square top with coupled columns and pediments. The only figures are the row of small kneeling children on the N side. – In the churchyard, WAR MEMORIAL by *W. S. Deanes*, 1921, in the form of a wayside cross with roof. Oak cross on Portland stone base.

On the S side of the churchyard, the former VICARAGE by *M. G. Thompson*, 1820. White brick. Three bays, two storeys, with simple doorcase. Lower two-bay service wing to the r. CHURCH SQUARE frames the E view of the church nicely; round the corner in NAYLAND ROAD an attractive row of houses on the NE side, including No. 4, C16 with tall jettied gable, exposed timbers, and carved bressumer, originally a gatehouse. No. 2, with smaller gable, was the mid-C14 service bay, with workshop at the front, of a hall house, the hall rebuilt in the C16. But the best houses are in the HIGH STREET, N of the church: the OLD BAKERY on the N side, opposite the MALTHOUSE. The former consists of a C16 house with jettied cross-wing to the l., lower hall range, and then a C17 house also jettied and

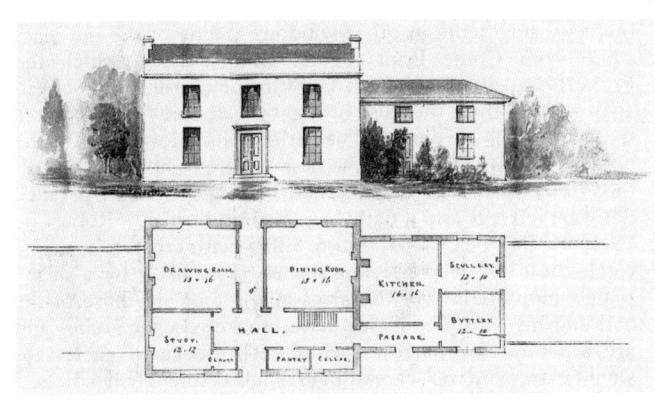

Bures, vicarage.
Design by M. G. Thompson, 1821

with a jettied gable. The Malthouse, C16–C17, has a jettied front, partly underbuilt and partly with exposed timbers. Its glory is the boldly carved bressumer: crown and Tudor rose, big leaves, animals, and a figure (the butcher at his block? the smith at the anvil? a carver?). The actual malthouse projects from the rear, an C18 range of red brick with burnt headers. Two storeys with long row of dormers. Next to it the BAPTIST CHURCH of 1834, enlarged 1862 by *Edward Salter*. Red brick with white-brick front. Pedimented gable. Five bays, separated by pilasters, with three round-headed windows. BRITISH SCHOOL, 1854, alongside. Further out, up Cuckoo Hill, a modest group of ALMSHOUSES of 1866. Diapered red brick with stone dressings. Single-storey, on three sides of a courtyard.

BRIDGE, NW of the church, over the Stour. 1881. Segmental cast-iron arch with five ribs, cast by *Rownson, Drew & Co*.

BURES MILL, 700 yds SE. Four-storey weatherboarded water-mill with C18 painted-brick mill house.

Further from the centre:

ST STEPHEN'S CHAPEL, ¾ m. NE. A private memorial chapel built for Sir Gilbert de Tany †1221. Dedicated by Archbishop Stephen Langton between 1213 and 1221; the traditional date is 1218. Still in use as a chapel in the 1520s, it later became a barn. Lancet windows and three stepped lancets at the E end, shafted inside. Of rubble, mainly rendered, with a timber-framed W attachment, all thatched. In *c*. 1931–4 it was restored by its owner Isabel Baynes Badcock and Col. W. G. Carwardine-Probert, the latter perhaps acting as architect (cf. Great Bevills, below), and a two-storey addition was made to the N side, with gallery looking down into the chapel. – STAINED GLASS. E window by *Horace Wilkinson*, 1934, to complement medieval fragments in other windows. Some of the old glass came from Colne Priory, Earls Colne, Essex, which the Proberts had inherited from Carwardine cousins and sold in 1935. – From there they also brought the de Vere MONUMENTS that almost fill the chapel. The earliest is the lower half of the coffin-lid of Aubrey †1141, the first de Vere to hold the hereditary office of master chamberlain of England. With parallel, flatly carved legs and a flatly ornamented border. – Robert de Vere, 5th Earl of Oxford, †1296. Effigy with crossed legs. The tomb-chest has deep kneeling niches, more likely for a shrine than a monument, but the arms at the foot are those of the earl and his wife. The niches have crocketed ogee arches and are separated by narrow niches with crocketed gables for small, extremely well-carved figures, unfortunately headless. – Thomas, 8th Earl, †1371. Alabaster. Effigy with the de Vere mullet carved on the jupon. Against the side walls of the tomb-chest pairs of mourners under broad depressed nodding ogee arches (the alabaster end panels come from the base of the next tomb). A C17 drawing indicates that the tomb-chest was originally broader and may have been intended for two effigies. – Richard, 11th Earl, †1417 and wife Alice. Alabaster. She wears a horned head-dress. Pet dogs playing at her feet. Against the tomb-chest alternating, rather flat frontal figures of angels holding shields, and tracery strips in two tiers.

DUNSTEAD HOUSE, 1½ m. NNW. From Kersey, re-erected here in 1926. The main range is probably a late C15 hall house, with a cross-wing at one end. Exposed timbers, with some brick-nogging. Part of the main front is jettied.

FYSH HOUSE, ⅔ m. NE. Large C18 red brick house with remains of an earlier, timber-framed house, and later additions. Two-storey bays, one square and one canted. Parapet with balustrading above the windows.

GREAT BEVILLS, ½ m. N. Two-storey timber-framed house of c. 1500 with brick-nogging and jettied along the whole front. It consisted of a single range, one room deep. Some additions to the rear were made (or rebuilt) in the mid C19 but the present appearance is due to *W. G. Probert* (later Carwardine-Probert), who acquired the property in 1894. At first he commissioned his brother-in-law *Baynes Badcock* to build a small red brick wing at the SE corner, 1895–6, utterly unsympathetic in form and materials. For the rest of the work he acted as his own architect, using both his antiquarian knowledge and reused materials to create a wholly convincing and spectacular result, completed 1928. He extended the main range to N and S, with two timber-framed gables facing W and brick ends with crowstepped gables, octagonal turrets with pinnacles, and brick windows with hoodmoulds. The interior was treated in similar vein with much imported woodwork, so that it is hard to be sure what is original and what C20. He also restored the BARN N of the house and contemporary with it; also timber-framed with brick-nogging, although the latter is not original.

HOLD FARM, 1 m. E. Red brick ground floor, timber-framed first floor. Roof with six (originally seven) in-line crown-posts. The unexpected feature of the house is a pair of opposing early C16 brick archways, from which Leigh Alston deduced that this was originally a watermill, associated with Smallbridge Hall; the archways framed the mill race.

SAWYERS FARM, 2 m. N. Timber-framed farmhouse with some exposed timbers. The oldest part dates from *c.* 1400 and was originally the detached kitchen or bakehouse of a now-vanished house. It was jettied along one side. In the late C16 it became the service range of a new hall and parlour that now forms the E cross-wing of the house. Late C17 or early C18 timber-framed and plastered wing at the W end of the earlier range.

SMALLBRIDGE HALL, 1½ m. ESE. The Waldegrave family acquired the manor of Smallbridge in the C14 (licence to crenellate 1383) and the house was rebuilt in the mid C16 by (Sir) William Waldegrave †1613, who came of age in 1561 and in the same year hosted a visit of Queen Elizabeth I. A piece of armorial glass dated 1572 may relate to a later phase of construction. The house was probably quadrangular (it had a hall, gallery and chapel) and in 1674 was assessed as having forty-four hearths, making it one of the largest houses in the county. It declined sharply in the C18, and throughout the C19 was described as a farmhouse, although extensive work is said to have taken place in 1874. It was restored and extended for the Marchioness of Bristol by *Harvey G. Frost*, 1930. The entrance (N) front is mainly of the latter date, red brick like everything else but hard and with cement dressings. Two projecting wings with only a narrow space between them. S front with four straight-gabled full dormers. Hall behind this. Mullioned-and-transomed brick windows. Tall chimneys with some original octagonal shafts. The interior mostly altered, but several good panelled rooms, especially on the first floor. Surrounded by a moat. FARM BUILDINGS to the N built for George Wythes, 1851, of red brick with white-brick dressings. Two-storey front range with pedimented centre and tall semi-circular archway.

BURGATE

ST MARY OF PITY. Dec W tower with small upper circular windows with quatrefoils. Above the bell-openings small quatrefoil windows as well as blind windows in flushwork. Dec chancel with pretty PISCINA. Nave N windows Dec, S windows Perp. Restoration by *R. M. Phipson*, the nave in 1865, the chancel in 1872, including new chancel windows, raised chancel walls, nave BENCHES with reused poppyheads, and new roofs. Elaborate timber chancel arch with lobed cusps on deeply carved foliated stone corbels. Idiosyncratic reordering by *Rev. Benjamin Appleyard*, 1926–31. Across the nave, E of the entrance, a low solid screen with carved figures by *H. A. Miller* of Norwich. In the middle of the galilee thus created, the organ, with chapel on its N side and vestry on the S. Altar-like screen on the E side of the organ forming a backdrop to the font. – FONT. Octagonal, Perp. Against the stem four lions. The figures against the bowl have been hacked off, but the arms of Sir William de Burgate remain. His donation is recorded in the inscription on the two-step base. – PULPIT. Square, Jacobean. – ROYAL ARMS. Of George II, 1735. – STAINED GLASS. C15 bits in a N window. – Chancel S by *Lavers, Barraud & Westlake*, 1872. – MONUMENTS. Sir William de Burgate †1409 and wife Eleanor. The best brasses of their date in Suffolk and placed on a fine tomb-chest in front of the high altar. The figures are 4 ft 7 in. (140 cm.) long and placed under ogee canopies. The engraving is uncommonly bold and economical. The tomb-chest has on its long sides eleven ogee-headed niches with crockets and little buttresses. In five of them on one side hearts with wings, on the other shields. – War memorial. 1927. In the unusual form of a shrine, in a recess against the chancel N wall. Carved oak, with altar ornaments made from shell cases 'by soldiers of the Great War at Godwearsvelde [i.e. Godewaersvelde], Belgium, during the winter of 1917, while patients of No. XI C. C. S.', the casualty clearing station where Appleyard was chaplain. This and other chancel fittings, including the COMMUNION RAIL with its sturdy balusters, designed by *Appleyard*, made by *Potter & Sons* of Wortham. – CHURCHYARD CROSS, E of chancel. 1933 by *H. M. Cautley*.

Former SCHOOL, 300 yds N (now village hall and house). By *George E. Wright*, 1872. Red brick. Casements with arched tops.

OLD RECTORY, ¼ m. E. For Rev. William Pemberton, rector 1806–28. Red brick. Eight-bay garden front with off-centre full-height bow. Another full-height bow to the r., in front of the service wing.

HALL FARM, 300 yds W. Timber-framed and plastered, with both fronts jettied. It is thought to have been built *c.* 1400, so perhaps for Sir William de Burgate, but was remodelled and partly demolished in 1587. Crown-post roof. Moated site.

BURSTALL

ST MARY. Essentially of the C14, probably late C14 in the case of the most uncommon N arcade of four bays. Very finely moulded piers, their front mouldings running continuously into the arches, their mouldings towards the arch openings interrupted by capital bands with fleurons. Steep arches. N windows with finely moulded rere-arches seem a little earlier.

Burgate, St Mary, brass to
Sir William de Burgate †1409 and wife Eleanor.
Rubbing by M. Stuchfield, 2014

Niches under ogee arches l. and r. of the E window. The flint-work externally has large panels of black flints like a chequerboard; can it be original? Nave and chancel early C14 externally, although the chancel has a lancet in the N wall. The W tower also seems earlier, perhaps mid-C13. The bell-openings are cusped lancets, and below them are quatrefoil windows in circles. Finely moulded nave S doorway (continuous mouldings). Perp S porch of timber with cusped side openings and decorated bargeboards. Perp hammerbeam roof in the nave. There were two bequests for the roof in 1510. Restored and re-seated 1847. Further restorations of 1866 and 1870 by *F. Barnes*, including addition of angels by *Thomas Stopher* of Ipswich to the nave roof. – SCREENS. Of the Perp rood screen only the dado and part of one upright survive (bequest for rood loft 1515). More interesting is the N parclose screen. This belongs to the C14. It has shafts instead of mullions and several simple patterns of flowing tracery that reflect the tracery of the N aisle windows. – STAINED GLASS. Nave S by *Heaton, Butler & Bayne*, 1922 (war memorial). By them also, perhaps, the E window of 1913.

VILLAGE HALL, E of the church. 1910, and good of its kind, with half-timbering and Tudor-style chimneystacks of diapered red brick. Curious little detached clock tower, also half-timbered. The donor lived at 'Burstall Cottage', SW of the church; its LODGE remains, also half-timbered, and picturesquely thatched. In similar vein BURSTALL HOUSE, 200 yds ENE, dated 1912.

BURY ST EDMUNDS

Introduction	124
The Abbey	127
Cathedral Church of St James	134
Churches	137
Public Buildings	142
Perambulations	149
1. Angel Hill, Abbeygate Street and Cornhill	150
2. Churchgate Street, Guildhall Street and adjoining streets	156
3. Crown Street, Honey Hill, Southgate and Westgate	160
4. King's Road to Risbygate Street	164
5. Mustow Street, Eastgate and Northgate	168
Outlying Buildings	173

INTRODUCTION

Daniel Defoe seems to have had mixed feelings about Bury St Edmunds. He described it as 'a town famed for its pleasant situation and wholesome air, the Montpelier of Suffolk, and perhaps of England', but he thought it 'perhaps a little too much' talked of. Cobbett noted that locals boasted it was 'the nicest town in the world', and did not disagree. It is certainly hard to think of a more attractive town of its size in the east of England. The architectural character of Bury is predominantly Georgian, pleasant and quiet, perhaps a little sleepy. There is no spectacular older timber-framed architecture left, nor any spectacular brickwork, and only the occasional later C19 and C20 surprise (and mostly pleasant surprises at that). There are also a few older surprises, hidden from general view.

The Anglo-Saxon town of *Bedericesworth* was transformed by the arrival of the remains of St Edmund in 903 and the growth of the abbey, described in detail below. It is generally, although not universally, agreed that King Edmund gave the town to the abbey in 945, and this area was a *banleuca* that came under the direct control of the abbot – a tremendously privileged position. The fortunes of the town and the abbey were intertwined, resulting from time to time in disagreement and outright hostility, not least because the abbots exacted a payment of 100 marks (£66 13s. 4d.) upon the election of each new abbot. This situation was largely resolved by John (Jankyn) Smyth, who on his death in 1481 bequeathed to the town 238 acres (96 ha) of land, the income from which could be used to pay this charge and thus relieve the citizens of the burden. Further bequests were made by Margaret Odeham †1492 and others, and the funds were administered by the Guildhall Feoffment Trust. The trust took on many of the responsibilities of a corporation or town council, and is still a visible presence in the town, notably through the provision of a number of almshouses; it also owns the Guildhall and Moyse's Hall.

The town grew rapidly after the Norman Conquest (a process described in further detail below), and by the Dissolution had a population of about 4,500. Although the majority of the medieval buildings were refaced in the C18 and C19, many survive to a greater or lesser extent behind their fronts. There was a devastating fire in 1215 that no doubt led to much redevelopment. The oldest known timber-framed building in Bury stands at the corner of Churchgate Street and College Street, and dates from the second half of the C13. But Bury also boasts something much rarer in East Anglia, a stone house in the shape of Moyse's Hall (late C12), and fragments of stone buildings of similar date have been found in houses scattered about the centre. Perhaps the most notable of these is Norman House in Guildhall Street, which contains a complete Norman doorway. Many timber-framed houses in the vicinity of the Great Market were destroyed in another fire in 1608.

Bury flourished in the C18. It was a prosperous market town, and trade was helped by improvements to the River Lark, made navigable to Fornham St Martin on the northern edge of the town, under an Act of 1700; this provided a link via the Great Ouse to King's Lynn and the North Sea. But its chief character (as Defoe noticed in the 1720s) was as a cultural and social centre for the surrounding countryside, epitomized by the opening of an assembly room in 1713, the remodelling of the Market Cross as a theatre by *Robert Adam* in 1774–7, and the construction of a number of large town houses, foremost among them Manor House, Honey Hill, for the Countess of Bristol in 1736–8. By 1801, the population stood at 7,655.

Great changes in the C19 – including a doubling of the population, by 1901, to 16,255 – seem to have been relatively benign as far as the character of the town was concerned. The usual public buildings were erected – gaol 1801–5, hospital 1826 onwards, workhouse 1836, corn exchanges 1836 and 1861–2 – and there were signs of industry: the railway arrived in 1846, maltings grew up around the station and elsewhere, and on the S side of the centre were two breweries (Greene's and King's) that merged in 1887; the Westgate Brewery remains a strong and welcome presence that helps to keep Bury a working town and not just a dormitory or shopping centre. But most of the building in the C19 stayed on a sympathetic scale, in the hands of local builders like *William Steggles*, who was responsible for large numbers of very agreeable white-brick houses. What most people would think of as Victorian buildings in Bury are few and far between, and by architects not of the town but who had not travelled far: *L. N. Cottingham* (Savings Bank, Crown Street, 1846–7), was born in Laxfield, and *Brightwen Binyon* (Fennell Memorial Homes, St Andrew's Street North, 1873–4) practised in Ipswich, as did *E. F. Bisshopp* (West Suffolk County Club, Abbeygate Street, 1883) and *J. S. Corder* (Alliance Assurance Co., Abbeygate Street, 1890–1). In fact, unless one counts Steggles, *Thomas Farrow* and *Lot Jackaman* as architects (and they certainly proved themselves very able designers on occasions), Bury had only one resident architect of any distinction, *John Johnson*, until the C20, and even then the only practice to leave its mark was that of *Sidney Naish* (1872–1925), latterly in partnership with *W. H. Mitchell* (1881–1965), who in turn was in partnership with *J. S. Houghton*. It is surprising that there is not more work by *Basil Oliver*, given his family connections with the brewers Greene King, although he may have exerted a benign influence (and some of Mitchell's buildings have been wrongly attributed to him).

Bury became the county town of West Suffolk when that administrative unit was created in 1888, although this was effectively a continuation of Bury's position as the chief town of the Liberty of St Edmund, a territorial unit that dated back to the C11 and possibly even the C7. This required the building of new county offices in 1906–7 and more in the 1960s. A further honour was the selection of St James's Church as the cathedral of the new diocese of St Edmundsbury and Ipswich in 1914. Developments in the C20 included the building of the sugar beet factory N of the town in 1924–5 (by *Oscar Faber*) and municipal housing in the W (Priors Estate, 1928–35). More housing was built immediately after the Second World War (Mildenhall Estate, *c.* 1945–51), but the biggest change came with the construction of the bypass in 1972–3 and the development, in its wake, of a huge area to the E (Moreton Hall, still in progress). Norman

Scarfe, in 1976, lamented this proposed doubling of the town from 20,000 to 40,000 inhabitants, 'relentlessly changing both its heart and its country setting', coming only two years after the loss of county town status under the administrative changes of 1974. But anyone visiting the town for the first time would think that it has fared much better than most. The ARC shopping centre on the site of the town's cattle market, completed in 2009, seems to have given the town a new lease of life, and not to have had the deadening effect of an out-of-town shopping centre, as well as providing the town with some world-class C21 architecture. Another boost was given to the town by the completion of the tower of the cathedral in 2005. This means that the cathedral now has a visible presence from a distance, something to draw the attention of motorists driving past on the A14 and to challenge the dominance of the sugar beet factory.

THE ABBEY

St Edmundsbury was one of the six most powerful and wealthy Benedictine monasteries in England. A small religious community was apparently founded c. 633. In 903 the remains of King Edmund, martyred by the Danes in 869, were brought here. In the C10 the community was of secular priests, but these were replaced in 1020–2 by twenty Benedictine monks. William the Conqueror in 1081 confirmed and increased the abbey's privileges and the number of monks was raised to eighty. Soon after this Abbot Baldwin, who ruled from 1065 to 1097, began to rebuild the church, and in 1095 the relics of St Edmund were translated to the new presbytery. In the next twenty years the parts round the cloister were built. The building programme was, as usual, from E to W. The crossing tower was begun c. 1105 and completed by Abbot Anselm (1120–48). It was damaged in 1210 and rebuilt in the course of twenty-six years, beginning in 1361. The nave followed, and the W front was built by the famous Samson, first as sacrist and then (1182–1211) as abbot. It was well in hand by 1142, when the upper N chapel was consecrated. The W doors were made before 1148. The crowning glory was the mighty W tower in the centre of the W front, a feature corresponding to Norman Winchester (begun in 1079) and to Ely, completed by Samson's successor as sacrist, Walter de Banham (c. 1200–11). Eric Fernie has demonstrated that, like most of the great Norman churches in England, Bury was built using a system of proportion based on the relationship between the side of a square to its diagonal (one to the square root of two), and that this was applied also to the layout of the town (*see* Perambulations). The abbey continued to prosper in the C13, but it was twice plundered in the C14: in 1327 following the death of Edward II, and 1381 during the Peasants' Revolt. The former especially, in the course of which the abbey was sacked and much was burnt, necessitated some rebuilding, including the Great Gate, as did collapses of part of the fabric in 1430–1 and a serious

p. 129

fire in 1465. The abbey was dissolved in 1539, following which most of the buildings were demolished and quarried for building materials. The abbot's house survived as a house until 1720.

What now remains of the abbey are two mighty gates into the precinct, the greater part of the precinct wall built mostly by Abbot Anselm *c.* 1130, and inside it various fragments. But the precinct is not built over: most of it is within a public garden (established in 1820), and its extent can be visualized without effort. It is about 1,500 ft (450 metres) from N to S and about 1,000 ft (300 metres) from W to E. The W boundary is along Angel Hill and Crown Street, the N boundary at Mustow Street, the S boundary by Honey Hill, and the E boundary along the original course of the River Linnet (not the Lark, which is further E). In addition, the two parish churches of St James (now the cathedral) and St Mary, described separately below, stand within the precinct, their W fronts projecting beyond the line of the wall. The abbey is described in two sections: first the S part of the precinct, entered by the Norman Tower, including the abbey church and claustral buildings, and then the N part, entered by the Great Gate, consisting mainly of the Great Court and abbot's house.

Norman Tower, abbey church and claustral buildings

6 The NORMAN TOWER, on the S side of the cathedral, served both as a gate to the abbey church and as a campanile for St James's Church. It was built under Abbot Anselm, i.e. between 1120 and 1148, and is a splendid piece of proudly decorated architecture of its date. The face to the town (W) is more ornate than the others. Big gateway, not vaulted inside. Heavy block capitals of the columns. The inner order on the W side has sculpture. Big roll mouldings. The arch projects like a porch and has a gable with fish-scale decoration. To the l. and r. are niches with billet decoration. Above these are short buttresses with intersected arches and pyramid roofs and corbel frieze of carved heads. On the first floor are two small two-light windows in much taller blank arches. The blank fields are decorated with a kind of vertical folding motif. The second and third floors are taken together by giant shafts with arches. These three arches have windows in their top part and, below, three times two-light blank arches. At the top stage there are again giant shafts and arches, but this time the lower motif is roundels (cf. Norwich Cathedral). Apart from the rich decoration on the lower stages of the W side, all four sides are essentially the same. The tower had battlements until its restoration in 1842–6 by *L. N. Cottingham* (cf. St Mary, below), who decided they were not original. The tympanum on the W side was removed in 1789 to allow carts through; the original ground level, as can be seen, was considerably lower.

Directly ahead is the ABBEY CHURCH. That more of the W front survives than of any other part of the church is due to the fact

BURY ST EDMUNDS: THE ABBEY 129

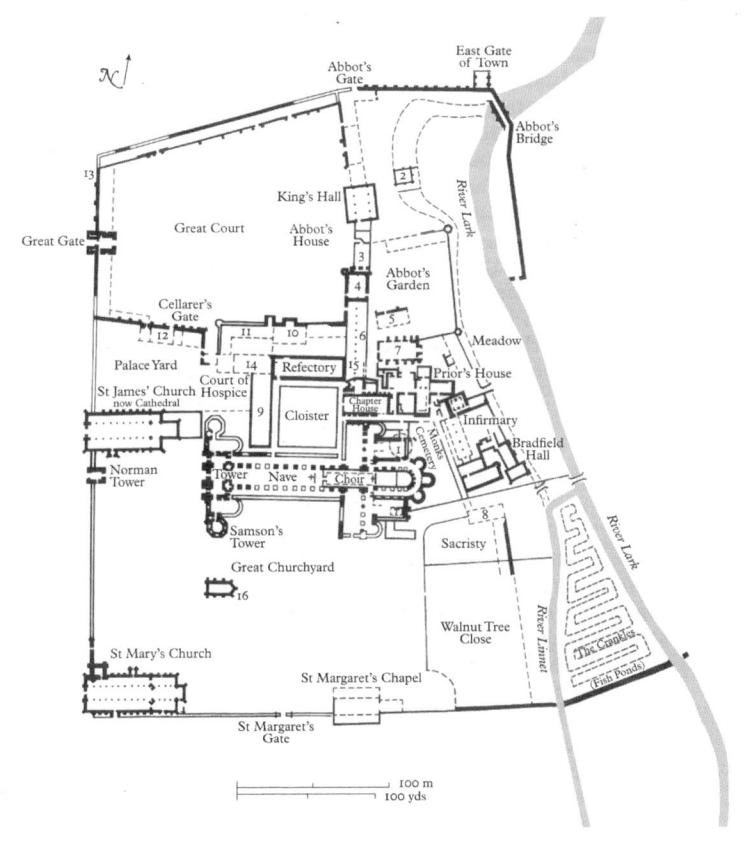

1 Chapel of St Edmund within round church (1020–32)
2 Watermill
3 Abbot's Hall over Cellar
4 Queen's Chamber over Larder & Wardrobe
5 Chapel
6 Dormitory
7 Reredorter
8 St Andrew's Chapel
9 Great Hall over Cellar
10 Kitchen
11 Cellarer's Range
12 Hall of Pleas
13 Buttressed Wall c. 1150, heightened after 1327
14 Black Hostry
15 Warming House
16 Charnel House

Bury St Edmunds, Abbey and precincts.
Plan

that in the C17, C18 and early C19 a number of small houses were built into the structure, to great picturesque effect. The enormous scale of this front can still be appreciated, despite the fact that (as with the Norman Tower) the original ground level was about 10 ft (3 metres) below what it is today, and the N end is now obscured by the E end of the cathedral. It stretched out 246 ft (75 metres), a width unmatched by any other English medieval church (Ely *c.* 160 ft (49 metres), Lincoln *c.* 175 ft (53 metres)), and lies along the line of the main N–S street of the Anglo-Saxon town (*see* Perambulations). The centre of the front, corresponding to nave and aisles, had three deep giant niches, the outlines of which can still be discerned; this is a motif peculiar to England, even if developed from Carolingian and Ottonian German precedent, and to be found at Lincoln and Peterborough. These niches have been filled in to provide the fronts of the houses, the smoother flint contrasting with the craggy medieval work. The upper floor of the central house merges into the stump of the great W tower. There were in addition apsed chapels N and S of this centre, with further chapels over them. The octagonal N corner tower, of which nothing is to be seen, was probably built at the same time as the tower, i.e. *c.* 1200–11, followed by a corresponding S tower, a substantial portion of which (known as SAMSON'S TOWER) still stands. It has walls of tightly packed flint, and Neo-Romanesque windows inserted in 1863 when the tower was converted to the town's probate registry by *William Rednall*.

The W front was restored as five houses by *Nicholas Jacob Architects*, 2005–6. Their backs are a charming jumble of medieval and later work, and the W end of the nave and aisles is still largely buried under their gardens, so that the length of the church – 485 ft (148 metres) internally, about 50 ft (15 metres) longer than Norwich and 30 ft (9 metres) shorter than Winchester – is more difficult to appreciate than the width. But the rest of the abbey church is discernible: the E parts of the nave, the crossing and transepts, and especially the crypt at the E end, which has been completely excavated. Most of the building was of Barnack stone, but ashlar remains only at base level; the rest is core flint work.

The NAVE was twelve bays long (St Albans thirteen, Ely twelve, Norwich fourteen). It had an arcade 26 ft (8 metres) in height, and groin-vaulted aisles, but only the stumps of the N arcade can be seen. There was a gallery, probably unsubdivided in its openings and 19 ft (5.8 metres) high, and a clerestory. The nave was not vaulted. A change of plan, perhaps following the arrival of St Edmund's relics in 1095, seems to lie behind the fact that the nave is about 3 ft (0.9 metres) wider at the W end than at the crossing. The TRANSEPTS projected far N and S; the N wall of the N transept survives to nearly its full extent, including a window opening, as do the piers of the CROSSING. The transepts each had an E aisle, and each had two apsed chapels to the E, although the inner N chapel was replaced by a more spacious, straight-ended LADY CHAPEL in 1275; when this was being built, remains were found of a small ROTUNDA, built under Canute in 1020–32 as an addition to the earlier church. E of the inner S chapel a further chapel (St Botolph's) was added by 1300. The CHANCEL was five bays long, the W bay being a little different from the rest and marking the beginning of the second phase of the building programme. The E end had an ambulatory and three radiating chapels over the crypt, on the pattern of French *chevets*. The pattern was not usual in Normandy, but existed *c.* 1030 at Rouen Cathedral. In England it first appeared in William's Battle Abbey, begun in 1070, at St Augustine's, Canterbury, begun in the same year or one or two years later, and at Winchester, begun in 1079. The transept inner chapels were two-storeyed, and it seems that the radiating chapels were even on three floors.

The CLOISTER lay to the N of the nave. It has been almost entirely lost. The site of the W range is now gardens. Here were the cellars or store houses, above which was originally the old guests' hall, or the hall of the abbot's lodgings, and between this and the church lay the PARLOUR, of which a fragment of wall remains. More clearly understandable is the REFECTORY which filled the N side, where three bare walls stand to sill height. This range was continued to the W by the Black Hostry or the new guesthouse, opening on to Palace Yard on the N side of St James's Church (the present cathedral). N of the refectory was the monks' KITCHEN; there is the fragment of the N wall of the LARDER and to the W, buried under a bank, are foundations which include a fireplace and W of that a porch. W of the kitchen were the cellarer's quarters and cellarer's gate into the Great Court.

The E range of the cloister abutted the N transept, on the N side of which was first the passage to the parts E of the church – its name at Bury was Trayledore or Trayle – then the CHAPTER HOUSE, built *c.* 1105 but rebuilt *c.* 1215–25, the lower parts of its walls still standing. Inside at the E end are the remains of the pulpitum or raised platform. N of the chapter house were the DORMITORY STAIRS (the dormitory filled the upper floor of the E range of the cloister and extended N beyond it), and beyond it the concave apsidal entrance to the TREASURY. In the apse, bases of four small columns, two each side, on continuous plinths. The N wall of the treasury is bent to give access to the WARMING HOUSE beyond.

Remains to the E of the cloister and church are even more fragmentary and hard to follow on the ground. The REREDORTER was E of and at right angles to the dormitory (bases of its N wall are visible) and connected with it probably by a bridge. S of this and E of the E range of the cloister was the intricate group of smaller apartments which formed the PRIOR'S HOUSE. Its small garden was immediately E of the chapter house. It had a hall and a chapel. Adjoining these to the SE (now largely under tennis courts) was the INFIRMARY. It was placed at an angle to the uniformly axial buildings so far described and was reached by the Trayle, which here turned SE, running along the original or old infirmary hall, built *c.* 1107–10, and on to the SE quarters of the monastery. E of the old hall was a garden and on the N side of this are remains of the infirmary chapel of St Benedict, built as the abbot's chapel by Abbot Uvius (1020–44). It had a clerestoried centre 14 ft by 20 ft (4.3 metres by 6.1 metres) in size, and a tunnel-vaulted passage 8 ft (2.4 metres) wide and 12 ft (3.7 metres) high along its four sides. To the E of this was St Michael's Chapel.

S of the infirmary were two more buildings: Bradfield Hall, to which Edward II retired on visits to Bury, and Bradfield Spanne, a kind of convalescent home for monks after bloodletting. The latter was built *c.* 1260. S of these and again reached by the Trayle were the sacrist's quarters. A little further S still was the S wall, continuing E the S side of St Mary's Church. There is a stretch of the Norman wall of *c.* 1130, continued by a short length of C13 walling. This ends at the River Linnet, but is continued E of the River Lark by the S wall of the abbey vineyard (*see* below). The Song School was just E of St Mary's, and the grammar school on the site of the Old Shire Hall. Between them stood St Margaret's Gate.

S and W of the site of the abbey church is the GREAT CHURCHYARD. The main medieval survival here is the ruinous CHARNEL HOUSE SE of the Norman Tower, built by Abbot John Northwold (1279–1301). Originally two-storeyed, of flint and reused ashlar, with a triangular E end, but now with an C18 pedimented front and surrounded by very fine C18 railings. Its walls carry C18 and C19 monuments, indeed the whole churchyard is crowded with headstones, chest tombs etc. of the C17 onwards, including those of the Steggles and de Carle families of Bury stonemasons (SW corner). Also the MONUMENT to the Protestant Martyrs of 1555–8 by *Hanchet*, 1903 (stone obelisk with Gothic detailing and ball finial) and, in the middle of a lawn cleared of gravestones, a bronze STATUE of St Edmund by *Elisabeth Frink*, 1976.

NW of the charnel house, on the N side of the churchyard, is the DEANERY, built as the Clopton Asylum (i.e. almshouses) under the will of Dr Poley Clopton †1730. The site was purchased in 1735 and the first residents chosen in 1744; the cost (including the site) was £1,894 0s. 2d. No architect is known, but the largest payment was to the bricklayer *Thomas Steele*, who was working at the same time on Manor House, Honey Hill (*see* Perambulation 3). Red brick with stone quoins. Long, two-storey seven-bay front with two-bay projecting wings, two bays deep. Three-bay pedimented centre breaking forward slightly, with Clopton arms in the pediment by *Thomas Singleton*. In the NE corner of the churchyard a mid-C19 house of flint with red brick dressings, bargeboards and windows with Gothick cast-iron casements. In the SE corner ST MARGARET'S HOUSE. Early Georgian, of seven bays, red brick with rubbed brick trim, two and a half storeys. Giant angle pilasters, and giant pilasters to mark the pedimented centre bay. Staircase with three slender balusters to the step and carved tread-ends. S side rebuilt in the early C20. The precinct wall of the abbey runs through the building, and can also be seen externally at the SE corner.

Great Gate, Great Court and abbot's house

The abbot's house was on the N side of the precinct, on the E side of the Great Court. This was entered by the GREAT GATE, the business access to the abbey. It was begun after the riots of 1327 and before 1346, and completed after 1353. Strong, and still defensive (see the arrow loops), yet as exquisitely decorated as only that moment in medieval English architecture could do. A very broad, embattled structure. On the town façade, a broad segmental arch. Over this three niches, the whole crowned by a big ogee gable with foiled circles l. and r. Big buttresses flank this centre. They have ogee-headed and steeply gabled niches in three tiers, two for the ground floor so far described, and the third corresponding to a centre composition of five tall blank niches of which the centre one is wider and taller and has a crocketed gable. It is again flanked by circles, but inscribed into them are six-pointed stars. The arch leads from the town into a first part of the passage. There is then an inner gate and a longer second chamber. The side walls of these two passages have blank arches on a large scale, the W bay of the second chamber with the boldest flowing tracery, the E bay composed of three ogee-headed blank arches. Both parts were vaulted with ribs and tiercerons; the clustered springers have survived the collapse of the vault. The transverse arches did not differ in section or gauge from the ribs. To the abbey side the ground floor has a shafted doorway, the shafts with leaf capitals, the arch with a double quadrant moulding; the first floor has a large transomed three-light window with at the top a figure of a four-petalled flower. This upper room has a fireplace.

The GREAT COURT was about 600 ft (183 metres) from E to W and up to about 450 ft (137 metres) from N to S. It was laid out as a botanic garden in 1831, and most of the medieval enclosing wall can be seen. The W wall N of the Great Gate is of c. 1150, heightened after the riot of 1327. The buttressed N wall, S of Mustow Street, contains lancets (now blocked) that date it to the early C13. The S wall has a keeled string course and flat buttresses of c. 1200 and added buttresses of after 1327. Against this wall, on its s side, stood the Hall of Pleas. On the W side of the Great Court were the stables (N) and the almonry (s). Against the N wall were the bakery, brewery, granary, etc. The DRINKING FOUNTAIN was originally a horse trough, erected 1870 in The Traverse, and moved to the garden in 1939. By *Kirk & Parry*. Above the bowl an enriched Ionic column surmounted by a sundial and then an urn.

From the NE angle of the Great Court the ABBOT'S HOUSE ran N–S, and a C14 part of its buttressed W wall remains as the W wall of ALWYNE HOUSE, built between 1823 and 1834. Two storeys. Five-bay E front of flint with red brick dressings and battlemented Gothick porch. Its S end is a canted bay with stone quoins and dressings, battlements and hoodmoulds. S of this lay the King's Hall (no visible remains), and S of that the

QUEEN'S CHAMBER, with angle stair-turret and some walls still standing around a wooded knoll. SE of this the ABBOT'S CHAPEL, of which the N wall can be seen. The free-standing chapel was in the abbot's garden, which was walled with hexagonal DOVECOTES at the two outer corners. The N one of these is largely intact, with to the W of it fragments of a wing of rooms. The dovecote would have stood right at the edge of the River Linnet; to its N is the site of a watermill.

The buttressed outer wall continues E from the N end of the abbot's house, with at its start clasping buttresses of the late C12. It crosses the River Lark (just after it was joined by the Linnet) on the ABBOT'S BRIDGE. This consists of the bridge proper (visible from the W), which dates from the late C12, and the wall carried across it with two added C14 breakwaters, chamfered ribs in the arches, and exterior buttresses and flying buttresses (best seen from the E). The inner arches originally contained portcullises, to prevent access by water. The wall then turns S towards the large abbey vineyard that lay on the E bank of the Lark. Part of the S wall of the vineyard can be seen, with an incomplete C14 gateway at its W end. Between the Lark and the Linnet at this point were fishponds, known because of their shape as the Crankles.

CATHEDRAL CHURCH OF ST JAMES
(ST EDMUNDSBURY CATHEDRAL)

The diocese of St Edmundsbury and Ipswich was created in 1914 and the parish church of St James was chosen as St Edmundsbury Cathedral. A church had been built on the site in the C11, replaced in the C12. A new chancel was built c. 1390–1402. Rebuilding of the nave began c. 1503, but was completed only under Edward VI, who gave £200 towards it. The designer may well have been *John Wastell*, who designed the vaults and upper parts of King's College Chapel at Cambridge, lived at Bury, and died c. 1518. The chancel was rebuilt in 1711 and again in 1865–9, by *G. G. Scott*, who also re-roofed the nave, 1862–4. In 1945 *S. E. Dykes Bower* was appointed architect for enlarging the cathedral, and it is to him that we owe much of its present appearance. His NW porch and first phase of cloisters were built in 1959–61, followed in 1963–70 by the choir, N and S chapels, transepts and crossing in place of Scott's chancel, and the Cathedral Centre in 1988–90. Dykes Bower died in 1994 and bequeathed money for the completion of the crossing tower, which was carried out between 1999 and 2005 by the *Gothic Design Practice* (*Hugh Mathew* and *Warwick Pethers*). This also included extending the cloister and N transept, and building an outer N chapel (Chapel of the Transfiguration) connecting the N chapel to the Cathedral Centre (completed 2008). The result is a building which, without being much larger than many of the other great Perp churches of Suffolk, has a truly cathedral-like appearance and character, both inside and out, something not easy to achieve when upgrading a parish church. Glimpses through to the partly screened N and S chapels, the flood of light down into the crossing, and the half-hidden stairs to the N transept gallery all contribute to the feeling of mystery that was so important for Dykes Bower, and give the impression that the building is larger than it really is. Construction of the N and W sides of the cloister would complete the vision.

The building is essentially Perp. The original W front is ashlar-faced with embattled aisles. The gable was added by *Scott* to accommodate his nave roof. Original transomed seven-light window below, and original transomed five-light aisle W windows. Decorated base, decorated buttresses, tall niches l. and r. of the doorway. To the N *Dykes Bower*'s porch, 1960, with first-floor library, making a continuous street front with, beyond, the houses built against the outer wall of the abbey precinct. Doorway with quatrefoils in the spandrels, above that a panelled frieze echoing the base of the main W front. The first floor is divided into three bays, with paired two-light windows over the door and blind arcading to l. and r. Parapet with more blind arcading. The N and S aisles have three-light transomed windows, and the clerestory windows are double in number. The S side also ashlar-faced. Dykes Bower's crossing and choir are enriched with flushwork, including blind tracery between the choir's tall clerestory windows. The E window is of three times two lights, an unusual configuration dictated by Dykes Bower's wish to reuse *Kempe*'s stained glass. On the N side of the nave, below the aisle windows, is the flat-roofed cloister by Dykes Bower that leads off from his porch. Each bay is of two times three lights, their arched tops straightened like pediments within an outer rectangular frame. The cloister continues beneath the *Gothic Design Practice*'s extension of the N transept (which again has flushwork, as well as flint diapering on the return walls). On the N side of the choir is the Cathedral Centre of 1988–90, including the Song School; elevations by Dykes Bower, interior by the executant architects, the *Whitworth Co-Partnership*. It is faced in pale brown brick, with stone dressings, vaguely Tudor in style. The cloister continues along its W wall, extended by the Gothic Design Practice but following Dykes Bower's original. Between the Cathedral Centre and the choir rises an elegant octagonal chimney, C16 in inspiration but C21 in construction and function.

The crossing TOWER is an impressive last (or late?) roar of the Gothic Revival. *Dykes Bower*'s design, prepared in 1962, proposed a concave-sided roof rising to a flèche. This was modified by *Warwick Pethers*, leaving the tower itself approximately the same height (150 ft (45.7 metres)) but terminating in a more traditional Suffolk-style top with decorated balustrade and pinnacles. It evokes not only Wastell's Bell Harry Tower at Canterbury Cathedral, but also the towers of Long Melford by Bodley, and Cattistock, Dorset, by G. G. Scott Jun., architects whom Dykes Bower greatly admired. The core of Dykes Bower's base, to just above the level of the nave and chancel roofs, is reinforced concrete, but the remainder is of load-bearing brick faced with stone, principally Clipsham and Barnack, with tall two-light windows on each side.

Inside, the early C16 nave is of nine bays, with very tall arcades, the piers of lozenge shape with four thin shafts and four broad hollows in the diagonals. Only the shafts to the arch openings have capitals. The shafts towards the nave rise right up to *Scott*'s hammerbeam roof, which has painted decoration by *Dykes Bower*, 1948–82. The panelled ceilings of the transepts and chancel are also richly decorated. The piers of the crossing are by Dykes Bower, and the glorious fan-vault of painted and gilded timber is by *Freeland Rees Roberts*, 2009–10, based on *Hugh Mathew*'s design. In the chancel the arcades are much simpler in form, with moulded arches dying into square piers. Between the arcades and the tall clerestory windows a band of openwork tracery, with blind arcades on the solid wall above the piers. In the Chapel of the Transfiguration the relationship to Gothic precedent is even looser, with round columns that have pronounced entasis. The chapel is overlooked by the timber oriel of an upper room in the Cathedral Centre. Below it is the Treasury (originally intended as a crypt chapel), converted from Dykes Bower's boiler house.

FURNISHINGS. REREDOS (High Altar). By *Dykes Bower*, 1984, made by *Norman Furneaux*. Wrought-iron sunburst set with semi-precious stones. – ALTAR CROSS. By *W. D. Caröe*, 1931. Matching candlesticks by *Dykes Bower*, 1955. – BISHOP'S THRONE. By *F. E. Howard*, c. 1927. With elaborate Gothic canopy, echoing his font cover (*see* below). – SEDILIA. Reused from *Scott*'s chancel. Crocketed and pinnacled, with nodding ogee canopies. – REREDOS (N chapel). Painted and gilded in Florentine style, as a setting for a panel painting of the Virgin and Child with St Anne.* German, c. 1510 (School of *Hans Burgkmair*). – ALTAR (Chapel of the Transfiguration). By *Henry Freeland*, 2009. Medieval mensa from Mistley, Essex (dem. c. 1735), on cruciform stone base. – SCREENS to N and S chapels. By *Dykes Bower*, made by *Norman Furneaux*. Wrought iron, that on the N incorporating C19 cast-iron floor gratings from a Manchester church. – STALLS. Two, with desks. By *Dykes Bower*, from Birch, Essex. – ORGAN. Two cases, facing W and S, 2010. By *John Bucknall*, based on designs by *Alan Rome*, painted by *Campbell, Smith & Co.* – PULPIT. By *Scott*, made by *Rattee & Kett*. – FONT. By *Scott*, 1870, reusing the octagonal shaft of the old one. Caen stone, with Purbeck marble columns, made by *Farmer & Brindley*. – FONT COVER by *F. E. Howard*, 1927. Both with painted decoration by *Dykes Bower*, 1960. – SCULPTURE. Christ Crucified by *Elisabeth Frink*, acquired in 1995 (Chapel of the Transfiguration). – Figures of Mary and Jesus, given in 1997 (S chapel) and St Edmund, 2007 (N Chapel) by *Leonard Goff*. – In garden N

---

*Formerly in the S chapel, and free-standing; the base with predella described by Pevsner has gone.

of the Cathedral Centre, God Speed V by *Jonathan Clarke*, 2001. – ROYAL ARMS. Stuart (probably Charles II). Carved and painted wood. Above them a cherub kneeling on a cloud blowing a trumpet, *c.* 1730, from an organ that formerly stood at the W end. – STAINED GLASS. In S aisle, first window from the W, good assembly of early C16 French or Flemish fragments depicting *inter alia* the Story of Susanna and parts of a Tree of Jesse. Remaining aisle windows by *Clayton & Bell*, 1882–1925, including the W windows (S, Tree of Jesse, N, Creation). Nave W window by *Hardman*, 1869. – E window and chancel S made up from *Kempe*'s original chancel windows of 1867, 1874, etc., i.e. very early in his career; *Dykes Bower* designed the lower lights (behind tracery), made by *Goddard & Gibbs*. – N chapel E. The remains of a window of *c.* 1852 by *Wailes*, all but the figures broken up and rearranged like a C13 mosaic window. – S transept S †1837 by *William Warrington*. On stairs to Song School, a window by *Pippa Blackall*, 2008. – MONUMENTS. Surprisingly few, but two of importance against the W wall. S of the doorway, James Reynolds, Chief Justice of the Exchequer, †1739. White and black marble. Seated frontally on a plinth in robe and wig. Two putti l. and r. No columns. Open pediment on consoles. – N of the doorway, his wife Mary Reynolds †1736. No figure, but instead a sarcophagus with obelisk background and l. and r. two urns on pedestals. Attributed to *Henry Cheere* (GF). – War memorial (King Edward VI School) by *Basil Oliver*, 1921. Stone tablet with modillion cornice. Repeated for Second World War. – In the cloister, Rev. E. V. Blomfield †1816. With portrait medallion by *Chantrey*, and scholarly accoutrements. – B. H. Malkin †1842. By *J. G. Lough*. With bas-relief profile.

CHURCHES

ST MARY, Crown Street. A church was built on this site in the first half of the C12, but nothing of that survives. The tower stands on the N side, a little E of the W front. It is broad and sturdy, late C14 in its lower part (bequest 'if it shall be built' 1393). Attached to its NW corner is a short stretch of the abbey precinct wall, showing that the W front of the church projected forward of it. Earlier C14 the simple N doorway of the church, and Dec the chancel – see the chancel arch. Rebuilding of the church itself was begun in 1424, supported by numerous bequests over the next two decades, e.g. for the rood loft 1436, for the porches 1438, for the battlements 1442–5. *William Layer* was very likely the mason. The chancel chapels and sanctuary were added by Jankyn Smyth, who died in 1481. The main C19 restorations were by *L. N. Cottingham*, 1842–9, and *A. W. Blomfield*, 1866–7.

The façade is similar to that of the cathedral: stone facing, embattled aisles, gabled nave. The windows are also transomed, though only of four and five lights, and there are niches l. and r. of the doorway. The stone facing continues down the s side of the nave, with all windows identical from W to E: three lights with transom, under four-centred arches. The S porch was taken down in 1831 and re-erected at Nowton Court (*see* p. 447). The clerestory has twice as many windows as the aisle. At the nave's E end rise two rood-stair turrets with little crocketed spires and finials. With the S chapel, the windows change to two-centred arches, and this and the whole of the E and N sides are of flint and stone. The windows on the N side match those on the S. Also on the N side is the porch bequeathed by the will of John Notyngham (†1439/40) and commemorating him and his wife. It is placed unusually far E, connected with the position of the church in the abbey precinct. The porch is stone-faced, has pinnacles on diagonal buttresses, a gable with crockets, and three niches above the entrance. Inside it has a charming stone ceiling panelled with a wheel of blank arches, the hub of which is an openwork pendant that conceals a carved head of God surrounded by ministering angels.

The interior is very impressive, partly as a result of C19 reorderings; *Cottingham*'s work included removing earlier C19 galleries (although some remained until 1880), and restoring the nave roof; *Blomfield* re-seated the nave. Ten bays to the chancel arch. The piers have single shafts to the nave and aisles, thin triple shafts to the arch openings, and broad hollows in the diagonals. The nave shafts rise to the roof, and also branch off into roll mouldings over the arches. Also a shaft rises to the roof from the apex of each arch. The roof is rightly famous. Essentially a roof with principal rafters and tenoned purlins; the principals are strengthened with hammerbeams with large angel figures against them, alternating with moulded arch braces. The eastern pair of angels were coloured by Cottingham, according to traces he found. The intermediate arch braces have 'embryo hammerbeams, not projecting beyond the braces but clamping them and disguised as carved grotesques' (Cautley). The spandrels of the braces are carved with dragons, unicorns, birds, fishes, etc., while the collar-beams carry dainty arches with tracery. On the wall-plate are demi-figures of saints, martyrs, prophets and kings. At the E end of the nave is a window above the chancel arch, part of Cottingham's restoration. The N and S chapels are of four bays. Their piers are slenderer and simpler, but of the same type as in the nave. The chancel roof is a single-framed, straight-braced rafter roof, panelled. The panels are cusped and have bosses. Among the scenes on the bosses a fox preaching to chickens, a dog carrying two flasks, two dogs fighting. Coved cornice painted with angels holding scrolls with verses of the Te Deum, repainted by *A. Mackintosh* of *Burlison & Grylls* in 1880. The N chapel was reordered by *Ninian Comper* in 1935 as the Suffolk Regimental Chapel, including panelling and wrought-iron gates. The chancel and Baret chantry roofs were repaired and repainted as part of restoration by *Robert Potter*, 1963–8, and in 1995–7 the tower was converted by the

Whitworth Co-Partnership to provide four floors of vestries, offices, etc.

FURNISHINGS. FONT. Octagonal, Perp, the base with four seated lions and four small standing figures. 20s. was bequeathed for making it in 1512. The bowl's original carvings were defaced in 1783. – ALTAR, THRONES and PULPIT, and W entrance SCREEN with ROYAL ARMS. All part of *Cottingham*'s restoration, with carving by *S. A. Nash*; the entrance screen originally wider. – CHOIR STALLS. With poppyheads and animals on the arms; some on the S side with traceried backs, reused medieval work. Reconstructed as part of chancel alterations (including floor) by *G. F. Bodley*, supervised by *A. A. Hunt*, 1901. – ROOD SCREEN. 1913, by *Hicks & Charlewood*. In typical Suffolk Perp style. – CHEST. Oak, with four panels of linenfold of unusual design. Probably late C16, possibly Flemish. – PAINTINGS. C18 figures of Moses and Aaron (tower). Interior of the church, after 1707, showing box pews and N gallery (N aisle). The Incarnation by *John Williams*, 1982 (S chapel). – STAINED GLASS. Cottingham introduced glass by *Thomas Willement*, of which the window over the chancel arch survives (Martyrdom of St Edmund), and armorial glass in various N chapel and N aisle windows, originally in the W window. The latter replaced by *Heaton & Butler*, 1859, who also did the N chapel E window, 1857, and (as *Heaton, Butler & Bayne*) the S aisle W window, 1865, and seven S windows, 1881 and 1893, following the removal of the galleries. – Sanctuary: E window by *Percy Bacon & Bros*, c. 1914 and 1935, N (and originally S) by *Clutterbuck*, 1857. – S chapel: E window by *Alfred Gérente*, 1857. S, from E to W: by *Clayton & Bell*, 1881, given by Queen Victoria in memory of Princess Mary Tudor (*see* Monuments); *H. Hughes*, †1872; *Clutterbuck*, 1854 (over S door); and *W. H. Constable*, 1881. – N chapel: N windows by *Comper*, with additional panels by *Whitefriars* and *Chapel Studio*. – N aisle: Ascension by *Ward & Hughes*, 1884, W of the tower N window by *Hughes*, 1869, and W by Ward & Hughes, 1868.

MONUMENTS. John Baret †1467 (S aisle E end). Tomb-chest with small shields in lozenge and quatrefoil fields. On it a cadaver with this inscription:

> He that will sadly beholde me with his ie
> May se his owyn merowr and lerne for to die.

Other inscriptions about the tomb, including his motto 'Grace me Governe' held by Baret fully dressed and wearing his SS collar. Especially noteworthy the one on the pedestal (copied here from Tymms):

> Wrappid in a selure as a ful rewli wrecche
> No mor of al myn good to me ward wil strecche
> From erhe I kam and on to erthe I am browht
> This js my nature, for of erthe I was wrowht;

Thus erthe on to erthe to gedit now is knet
So endeth each creature Q'd John Baret
Qwerfor ze pupil in weye of charite
Wt zor good payeris I prey zu help me
For lych as I am right so schal ze all be
Now God on my sowle have m'cy & pite. Amen.

Above the monument, which must have stood in a large chantry area (see the adjacent PISCINA), the aisle roof is panelled, set with small mirrors (a wonderful effect) and painted, including his motto and the Lancastrian SS. – Brass with male and female kneeling figures, each 24 in. (61 cm.), traditionally taken to be John (Jankyn) Smyth †1481 and his wife (S chapel). – Brass of John Fyner, Archdeacon of Sudbury, †1509. 35-in. (89-cm.) figure (N chapel). – Sir William Carew †1501. Big tomb-chest with shields in richly cusped quatrefoils. Two recumbent effigies (chancel N). – Sir Robert Drury †1536 (chancel S), almost a copy of the previous. – Mary Tudor †1533 (chancel N side). The sister of Henry VIII, married to King Louis XII of France, and after his death to Charles Brandon, Duke of Suffolk (*see* Westhorpe Hall). Her embalmed body was transferred from Bury Abbey in 1539; the plain slab is an old altar stone. – Thomas Bedingfield †1764 (nave). By *Thomas Paty*. Urn and tablet on background of coloured marble. – James Oakes †1829 (S chapel). By *W. Steggles*. Grecian-style tablet. – Many monuments were tidied away to the internal wall of the tower, presumably in the C19, and make a good display, including Anne Warren †1732, classical with pediment and portrait bust, and Lt-Col. Collier †1814 by *Robert de Carle*, with symbols of mortality and military impedimenta. – Cenotaph (Suffolk Regiment memorial, St Wolstan's Chapel). By *William A. Pite, Son & Fairweather*, 1920, with bas-relief angels by *C. Whiffen*. Marble and alabaster.

ALL SAINTS, Park Road. 1962, by *Cecil B. Smith*. Red brick. Tall windows rising through the eaves as flat-topped half-dormers, and inside cutting into the vaulted ceiling. Flèche. W extension by the *Whitworth Co-Partnership*, 2007, connecting to earlier hall.

ST GEORGE, Anselm Avenue. *See* Perambulation 5.

ST JOHN THE EVANGELIST, St John's Street. By *William Ranger*, 1840–1. White Woolpit brick and Bath stone dressings, with a W tower and an ignorant spire. Gaunt recessed porch, under the spire. The style of the church is E.E. Clerestory with three stepped lancets per bay. Timber rib-vault. The W end is canted towards the tower. The E end redone by *J. D. Wyatt* in 1875, including the REREDOS (figures and coloured decoration added 1947); he also added the vestry, 1879, extended 1908. – STATIONS OF THE CROSS and S aisle REREDOS. By *Iain McKillop*, 2007–8. Painted on arched boards. – STAINED GLASS. E window †1856 by *Forrest & Bromley*, the panels re-set in 1960. S aisle E †1863 by *Heaton, Butler & Bayne*, as is a N aisle window of 1902. Another N aisle window †1900 by *Kempe*.

– ST JOHN'S CENTRE, S of the church. Built as schools by *Ranger*, 1841, with additions of 1875, 1883 and 1899, but homogeneous. White brick with stone dressings.

ST PETER, Hospital Road. 1856–8 by *J. H. Hakewill*. Flint, with Caen stone dressings and bands of knapped flint on the lower part of the walls. Transitional style, E.E. to Dec. Nave, chancel, and two-bay N aisle, extended 1898 for vestry. S porch tower with splay-foot spire. Interior reordered by the *Whitworth Co-Partnership*, 1996–2007, preserving Hakewill's stone PULPIT and LECTERN which formed part of a low chancel wall. – STAINED GLASS. E window by *Clayton & Bell*, 1902. Nave S by *Hugh Easton*, 1955.

ST EDMUND (R.C.), Westgate Street. 1836–7 by *Charles Day*. Grecian. Red brick with stone-faced façade. Three bays with projecting pedimented centre. Two tall fluted Ionic columns *in antis*. Coved ceiling, the coving partly glazed. W gallery. Short sanctuary behind a screen of two Ionic columns, with concealed skylight. On the wall of the apse a PAINTING on copper of the Ascension by *Robert Park* of Preston, Lancs.; part of a comprehensive decorative scheme by *Rev. I. C. Scoles*, 1876, that has otherwise been obliterated. At the W end of the nave two grand doorcases of *c.* 1735 from Rushbrooke Hall (dem. 1961), on the N side used as an altar surround, on the S as an entrance to the BLESSED SACRAMENT CHAPEL. This is the original chapel on the site, built illegally in 1762 and hidden from the street by the presbytery. Pretty Gothick cornice but otherwise plain, with sash windows. Also from Rushbrooke the surround to the main doors, once a marble chimneypiece in the hall. It may be a composite piece: the supports (outward-facing terms) Dutch mid-C17, the frieze probably slightly earlier, Tuscan (?), with emblems of the Farnese and della Rovere families. – PAINTING. Martyrdom of St Edmund by *Charles Delafosse*. C19 copy. – MONUMENT. Hon. Charles Petre †1854. Bas relief of the Raising of Lazarus. By *R. Brown* of London.

BAPTIST CHURCH, Garland Street. 1834, by *W. Steggles*. Red brick with white-brick front. Five bays, with two tiers of arched windows, the three-bay centre breaking forward slightly. Original gallery on three sides, extended on fourth side 1842, reordered 1874–6 and (by the *Whitworth Co-Partnership*) in 1997. Sunday School, opposite, by *J. E. Sears*, 1892. White-brick front with stone dressings and a very free interpretation of a Venetian window.

CONGREGATIONAL CHAPEL, Northgate Street. *See* Perambulation 5.

FRIENDS' MEETING HOUSE, St John's Street. 1749–50. Timber-framed and plastered, the white-brick front added in 1870: three bays wide, with hipped roof. Central Venetian window. Contrasting extension by *Modece Architects*, 2007–8.

SALVATION ARMY CITADEL, St John's Street. 1889 by *J. W. Dunford*. Painted brick. Stepped gabled front, lacking its original turrets.

SEVENTH-DAY ADVENTIST CHURCH, Fornham Road. Built as the Railway Mission 1900, extended 1903. Tin tabernacle with Gothic windows and decorative bargeboards.

TRINITY METHODIST CHURCH, Brentgovel Street. By *Alexander Louder*, 1877–8, enlarged 1885. E.E. Red brick with stone dressings. Front largely obscured by flat-roofed three-storey block of 1975–7 by *Maurice Whalley & Partners*.

UNITARIAN MEETING HOUSE, Churchgate Street. Built by the Presbyterians, 1711. A stately chapel surpassed in Suffolk only by that at Ipswich. Red brick with rubbed red brick trimmings. The bonding of the brickwork is still English. Three-bay façade with big arched windows. Doorway with pilasters carrying a big, broken segmental pediment with urn. The top parapet is raised over the entrance; there was originally a one-bay pediment, removed in the early C20. Three galleries inside, supported on columns continuing up to the roof, which is also supported by a (later) central column. Fine hexagonal pulpit with large canopy facing the entrance, reached by a spiral staircase with clerk's desk below. Restored 1967–91.

UNITED REFORMED CHURCH, Whiting Street. Independent chapel, later Congregational, built on a site acquired in 1697. Timber-framed and plastered with cross-windows and hipped roof. 'Rebuilt upon a much larger scale' (*Bury & Norwich Post*) in 1802; front and internal refitting by *Bacon & Bell*, 1866, adjoining Sunday School by *H. F. Bacon*, 1887, both in white brick with stone dressings. Late Gothic. – MONUMENT to Nonconformist martyrs of 1583. By *Hanchet*, 1904. Churchyard cross, a smaller version of the one by the cathedral.

CEMETERY, King's Road. Chapel, entrance lodge and gateway by *Cooper & Peck*, 1854–5. Stone, coursed on the chapel, random on the lodge. The Dec chapel has a small bell-tower with slender spire and lucarnes.

PUBLIC BUILDINGS

GUILDHALL, Guildhall Street. Documented in 1279 and in civic use until 1966. The front was refaced in white brick in 1806, but the E wall is of coursed flint rubble that has all the appearance of being late C12. One can be more certain about the early to mid-C13 doorway with three orders of colonnettes and much dogtooth ornament. It is protected by the late C15 porch, which is of two storeys with angle turrets. Flint and stone, on the upper floor also brick bands. Embattled parapet with quatrefoils. It has been attributed to *John Wastell*. The single-storey ranges to l. and r. were faced in white brick in 1806, but the roof over its whole length is C14, with a combination of kingposts and queenposts. This work was carried out as a result of the bequest to the town of John Smyth (known as Jankyn Smyth) who died in 1481 (cf. St Mary's Church). Inside, two large rooms, the Court Room to the N and Banqueting Room to the S. The Banqueting Room was remodelled in the C18 with a segmental tunnel vault and an elaborate overmantel with broken pediment framing a portrait of Jankyn Smyth. E of the Banqueting Room and connected to it by a passage is what was originally a detached kitchen, rebuilt in the mid C19 but with some Tudor brick remaining. In the Court Room the lower trusses of the roof are visible below the ceiling. Good ROYAL ARMS of James I and also his portrait. Gallery along the E wall connecting to the council chamber, on the first floor of the two-storey E wing that was rebuilt in 1806. The architect appears to have been *Henry Wilkins*. It is built largely of reused materials, including stonework from the E wall of Moyse's Hall (*see* p. 145). The council chamber was converted in 1939 to a control room for the Royal Observer Corps, with galleries still in place.

OLD SHIRE HALL (Magistrates' Courts), Honey Hill. 1906–7 by *A. A. Hunt*. Free classical. Red brick with yellow stone dressings. Three storeys. Three-bay centre with rusticated base, giant columns and an open segmental pediment within a straight one. Single bays to l. and r. and then three-bay pavilions. It replaced a two-storey building in the style of a Greek temple by *W. McIntosh Brookes*, 1841–2. It is rather overpowering – perhaps that was the intention – especially in relation to St Margaret's House, which adjoins it on the E side (*see* p. 132).

SHIRE HALL, Raingate Street. By *McMorran & Whitby*. A promising group of buildings, in pale brick with Portland stone lintels and other details, but scaled down as the result of budget cuts and further compromised by *Donald McMorran*'s death in 1965. He was appointed in 1958 and produced detailed plans in 1959–60. The first parts to be completed were the separate POLICE STATION, 1962–4, and the COUNTY LIBRARY (now Record Office), 1962–5. The library is particularly charming, with single-storey Soanean arcades along the sides and rectangular lantern, but was intended to extend much further W and to have contained the council chamber. Two-storey, five-bay front with large sash windows. The Police Station has a long front with segmental-arched openings. Work did not start on the main offices until 1966 (opened 1968); they were completed by *George Whitby* and his senior assistant *Tibor Cselko*. Main elevation of three storeys and thirteen bays. Under McMorran's plan the N end should have been a five-bay pedimented centre with cupola, continued N to join up with the Old Shire Hall and involving the demolition of St Margaret's House. The Shire Hall was superseded in 2009 by West Suffolk House (*see* below) and by 2013 had been partly converted to flats, with an additional block by *Milburn Leverington Thurlow (MLT Architects)*.

Former BOROUGH OFFICES (now partly Town Council), Angel Hill. 1935–7 by *Naish & Mitchell* (i.e. *W. H. Mitchell*) and *Basil Oliver*. Tactful Neo-Georgian. Designed as council offices at the front, with clinic (entered from Lower Baxter Street) to the rear. Red brick, nine bays, two storeys, with three-bay pediment. Borough arms in pediment carved by *Laurence Turner*. Inside, elegant curved staircase, and windows with roundels of

STAINED GLASS by *E. M. Dinkel* depicting the months of the year. Stone SCULPTURE, The Healing Waters of St Edmund, by *Denise de Cordova*, *c.* 1990. Three-storey extension fronting Lower Baxter Street by the Borough Surveyor, *George S. Standley*, 1965–6; remodelled and converted to flats, with additional storey, by *Milburn Leverington Thurlow*, 2009–11.

WEST SUFFOLK HOUSE, Western Way (Suffolk County Council and St Edmundsbury Borough Council). By *Pick Everard*, 2007–9, the first phase of a proposed 'public service village'. Three and four storeys, linked by an atrium. Red brick, with terracotta rain-screen panels. The distinguishing feature is the zinc-clad oval block housing the council chamber and other ceremonial spaces.

MARKET CROSS, Cornhill. The finest post-medieval building in Bury, dating from rebuilding after the fire in 1608. Its original appearance is known from paintings. In 1774–7 the whole building was remodelled by *Robert Adam*, beginning with the S front, but retaining the basic timber-framed structure. (Robert Adam was commissioned in 1774, but the final payment of £42 in 1777 was to Robert & *James Adam*.) The ground floor remained open for corn dealing, with two small shops at the N end, and the first floor continued as a theatre, for which use it had been adapted in 1734. Oblong cruciform plan. White brick with stone dressings, the ground floor with stone rustication. Each of the four projections has two giant columns with typical Adam capitals and a pediment. Between them on the upper floor a delicately decorated Venetian window. To the N and S in the recessed angle bays trophy panels on the ground floor, urns in niches on the upper floor. The panels (masks representing Comedy and Tragedy) were carved by *Thomas Singleton*, who was also the builder; most of the other decorative details are of *Coade* stone. Upper floor superseded as a theatre in 1819 (*see* below, Theatre Royal) and converted by *William Wilkins* to a concert room. The ground floor was mostly enclosed in 1840 by *Benjamin Backhouse*, and the upper floor then put to use as the Town Hall; there was a major fire in 1908. In 1970–1 the archways on the W and N sides were opened up to make arcades, and a new shopfront was built within the W arcade (architect: *Mark A. Pawling*). The upper floor has become an art gallery; little survives by way of interior decoration, although the space remains impressive.

Former CORN EXCHANGE, Cornhill. There are two. The first building S of the Market Cross is by *Benjamin Backhouse*, 1836, and succeeded the corn-dealing area on the ground floor of the Market Cross. Enlarged by *John Johnson* of Bury in 1848, converted to a provision market in 1863 and remodelled in 1899 for additional use as a school of art (later Public Library) and Fire Station (see the inscription over its S entrance). White brick. Two-storeyed S front on the falling ground, the other sides one-storeyed. Attached Doric porticoes to E and W. Converted to shops after 1983. The second building, to the S of the first and facing Abbeygate Street, is of 1861–2 by *Ellis*

& *Woodward*. White brick and stone. The contractor was *Lot Jackaman*, with ironwork by *Ransomes & Sims*. One-storeyed, with a six-column giant Ionic portico to Abbeygate Street, arched windows and giant pilasters to the E and W sides. Pediment with profile of Queen Victoria and male and female figures representing Agriculture. At the N end a pediment with the arms of the Earl of Bristol who was responsible for building the Butcher's Shambles in 1761. The Tuscan colonnade from this is the basis of the lower range along the building's N side. In 1969–70 the building was converted into shops with a hall above.

FIRE STATION, Parkway. By the *County Architect's Dept*, 1984–7. Two-storey offices at one end. Red brick plinth with corrugated metal cladding and red columns.

Former GAOL, Southgate Street. Built in 1801–5, with its spectacular stuccoed façade. The centre is raised and contains the entrance. It is given vermiculated rustication, and the arch and jambs slope inwards. This centre is crowned with a pediment. To the l. and r. forbidding rusticated wings with broad semicircular windows, a motif familiar from the French style of 1760–1800, but also from George Dance's Newgate Prison, London. This front range has been converted to flats. The gaol itself lay behind it, and consisted of four detached wings (dem.) radiating from a central block that contained the governor's rooms with a chapel on the first floor (now THE FORT). Red brick. Three storeys. Square, with bevelled corners from which projected walkways connecting to the wings. Ground-floor windows in arched recesses. The architect was *George Byfield*, working closely with the governor John Orridge, who in turn was influenced by the prison reformer John Howard. In 1819 Orridge published a book about the ideas behind the design and management of the prison, together with a design for a prison for the Emperor of Russia. He also illustrated a treadwheel designed by *William Cubitt* that was tried out at Bury and widely adopted by other prisons.

PUBLIC LIBRARY, Sergeants Walk. 1982–3 by *Suffolk County Council*, refurbished with new entrance 2009–10. Red brick, in a traditional idiom with straight gables and two-storey square bays.

MOYSE'S HALL MUSEUM, Cornhill. The oldest domestic building of Bury. Said in the past to have been built by a rich Jew, and to have housed a synagogue, but this is now generally discredited. It was probably connected with the abbey, and dates from the late C12. In 1626 it was bought by the Guildhall Feoffees for use as the town gaol, and in 1836 a room was fitted up as the town's first Police Station; from 1892 to 1898 it was used as a parcels office by the Great Eastern Railway. Meanwhile the W part was annexed by the Castle Inn. The two parts were reunited and opened as the Borough Museum in 1899, which saved the interior from being cleared to accommodate the borough's fire engine. No. 41 Cornhill was incorporated into the museum in 1971–4; a further extension opened in 2002. The building is of two storeys, of flint and stone. The s front has two gables towards Cornhill. The w part has a two-light traceried window of which the sill at least, with carved head of St Edmund, is original C15. The E part has broad, flat buttresses, typically Norman. On the first floor two original windows. They are rectangular with a roll moulding and stand under arches, resting on colonnettes with crocket capitals. The date seems to be *c.* 1180. Other features, including the clock and bell-turret, belong to the restoration of 1858 by *G. G. Scott*, then in the middle of restoring St James's Church. The E wall was rebuilt after collapsing in 1804; now almost bare, it was of three bays separated by flat buttresses and had three two-light windows under arches. Interior of two rooms, E and W, on each of two floors. On the ground floor the E part is vaulted in two rows of three bays. Circular piers with simple capitals made, it seems, for cruciform piers. Broad N–S arches, single-chamfered E–W arches, groin-vaults. The W part is vaulted in a single row of three bays. The red brick arch between the two rooms is Perp. On the first floor were the hall and solar, each with C16 fireplaces, and the range to the rear of the E part has a C16 roof. As part of the conversion to a museum in 1898–9 by the Borough Surveyor, *J. Campbell Smith*, the ground-floor windows of the W part of the S front were restored, a new 'Norman' window was inserted in the E wall, and a stone staircase was added in a small extension against the N wall.

THEATRE ROYAL, Westgate Street. Built in 1819 to designs by *William Wilkins*, best known as the architect of the National Gallery and Downing College but also, like his father William Wilkins, the lessee of various East Anglian theatres. Wilkins Sen. leased the theatre in the Market Cross (*see* above) in 1799 and his son took over in 1808. He persuaded the corporation to allow him to erect a new building, taking the old fittings with him. It has an unassuming rendered front. Nine-bay arcade, the centre three bays projecting as a heavy porch with plain pilasters and Doric frieze. Exceptionally fine interior, restored 2005–7 by *Levitt Bernstein Associates* for the National Trust with new foyer building on the E side. Four levels of seating: the pit, and two tiers of boxes arranged in a horseshoe with gallery on top. Rectangular proscenium arch flanked by pilasters that frame curved doors (giving access to the forestage) and *trompe l'œil* vases in niches; this and other scenic painting by *Meg & Kit Surrey*. Between 1925 and 1962 it was used as a barrel store by Greene King (*see* p. 162, Westgate Brewery).

LEISURE CENTRE, Beetons Way. By *Suffolk County Architect's Dept* (*J. Brian Jackson* in succession to *Jack Digby*; job architect *Henk Pieksma*), 1973–5; rebuilt 1980–1 following a fire. In the architect's own words, 'simply conceived as a rectangular box, executed in high quality modern materials'. Lower walls of brick, the rest with metal cladding. The simplicity of the original design was lost in the rebuilding, but along the S side the concept was preserved of the steel members supporting the roof, exposed 'to give a feeling of rhythm and scale' like flying buttresses.

WEST SUFFOLK COLLEGE, Out Risbygate. On the site of Gibraltar Barracks (*see also* Perambulation 4). The landmark building is THE GATEWAY by *Pick Everard*, 2012–13, which lives up to its name and gives to the college, which is set quite a way back from the street, a presence that it might otherwise lack. By the same architects LEONARDO HOUSE, 2005–7, to the N, and refurbishment and landscaping of existing buildings to give coherence to the institution. SUFFOLK HOUSE (University Campus Suffolk), E of The Gateway, was one of the original College of Further Education buildings, by *Johns, Slater & Haward*, 1963, also refurbished by Pick Everard.

GUILDHALL FEOFFMENT SCHOOL, Bridewell Lane. By *H. E. Kendall Jun.*, 1843. Tudor-Gothic. Red brick. White brick not only for dressings but also for pinnacles, parapets and buttresses, which have panels of knapped flint. This was the Poor Boys' School. The Commercial School, opened in 1842, also by Kendall and in similar style, faces College Street; originally separate, now joined. The Poor Girls' School was in Well Street (*see* Perambulation 5).

KING EDWARD VI SCHOOL, Grove Road. Built as the Silver Jubilee Schools for Boys and Girls, 1935–6 (King Edward VI School since 1972; for its earlier homes, *see* Perambulation 5). Red brick with pantiled roof. Two storeys. Main range of nineteen bays, including three-bay centre with quoins, pedimented doorcase, and parapet with flaming urns. The architect was probably *W. H. Mitchell*. NE of the main block a SPORTS HALL by *Johns, Slater & Haward*, 1968 (in collaboration with the County Architect, *Jack Digby*; consultant engineers *Stepien & Winiarski*). Timber barrel vault, with ends of the same curvature as the sides, creating a segmental barrel vault shell and enclosing an area of 72,000 sq. ft (6,689 sq. metres).

ST EDMUNDSBURY PRIMARY SCHOOL, Grove Road. 1937, probably by *W. H. Mitchell* (cf. King Edward VI School, above). Red brick with pantiles and stone quoins. Single-storey. Twenty-one bays, with three-bay pedimented centre. Oval window in the pediment and a pretty round-arched doorway with fanlight.

WESTLEY MIDDLE SCHOOL, Oliver Road. By *West Suffolk County Architect's Dept* (county architect *Jack Digby*), designed 1968, built 1970–1. On the SEAC system, with white walling panels and black window frames. Planned round internal courts; in one of these, a series of nine aluminium panels by *Geoffrey Clarke*, c. 1970. Other schools built under Digby and using the SEAC system included HOWARD PRIMARY SCHOOL, St Olaves Road, 1967, and WESTGATE PRIMARY SCHOOL, Brooklands Close, 1968–9 (tile-hung); also HARDWICK MIDDLE SCHOOL, Mayfield Road, 1976 (incorporating solar panels), by *Suffolk County Architect's Dept* under Digby's successor, *J. Brian Jackson*.

ABBOTS GREEN PRIMARY SCHOOL, Airfield Road, Moreton Hall. 2005 by *Nick Loomes* of Suffolk County Council. Formal entrance with white-painted render and vertical timber boarding. Elsewhere more timber and coloured render. Low-pitched sedum roofs.

ST EDMUNDS HOSPITAL, St Mary's Square. *See* Perambulation 3.

WEST SUFFOLK HOSPITAL, Hardwick Lane. 1969–73 by *Howard Goodman*, chief architect, Dept of Health and Social Security; superintending architect *John Ward*, consultant architect *Paul James*, in association with *Hospital Design Partnership*. This and Frimley, Surrey, were the first of a series of so-called 'Best Buy' hospitals, designed to be cheap to build and run, and domestic rather than institutional in character. Two storeys, planned round landscaped courtyards. Prefabricated concrete frame with load-bearing walls of aerated concrete panels. The wards, all on the first floor, have projecting bay windows.

BLOMFIELD HOUSE HEALTH CENTRE, Looms Lane. By *Johns, Slater & Haward*, 1964–5, originally faced with white faience tiles and more popular with the critics (Civic Trust Commendation, 1968) than with the public. Remodelled and clad in red brick in 1987.

RAILWAY STATION, Station Hill. 1847. The architect was *Sancton Wood*, the contractor Thomas Brassey. Red and white brick with stone dressings; 'its style is pure Elizabethan' (*Bury and Norwich Post*, 24 November 1847). Two storeys (the line is elevated), including an impressive house for the station master, originally with shaped gables. Two 'Free Renaissance' towers with lead domes at the ends of the platforms. Much altered,

Bury St Edmunds, railway station.
Engraving, 1852

and lacking the shed roof that originally spanned the four tracks, but a programme of general restoration was completed in 1995. Immediately E of the station a very fine skew BRIDGE of 1846. Single 50-ft (14.24-metre) span over Out Northgate. Yellow brick with stone dressings. Contemporary accounts credit *Charles Russell*, assistant to the resident engineer Peter Bruff, but *F. Barnes* was also working for Bruff at this time and is likely to have been involved. W of the station a well-preserved timber SIGNAL BOX of 1888.

PERAMBULATIONS

The Anglo-Saxon town lay along a N–S road that included modern Northgate and Southgate Streets and probably also what is now Sparhawk Street. At the S end of Sparhawk Street was the market place (now St Mary's Square), which was also entered from the W by modern Westgate Street. The same Abbot Baldwin who began the rebuilding of the abbey church also built houses: 342 had been built by 1086 on what had until 1066 been fields. The plan of the town is a grid, still readily recognizable in the area between the abbey and St Andrew's Street, and it is directly related to the abbey church. This has led to the conclusion that, like the abbey, it was planned by Baldwin, although other evidence suggests that – like the abbey church itself – the plan evolved over two or three centuries. The central axis is Churchgate Street, on the same axis as the Norman Tower and the abbey church. The distance from the Norman Tower to the W front of the abbey church is the same as the distance from the Norman Tower to the junction of Churchgate Street and Angel Lane, and from Whiting Street to Guildhall

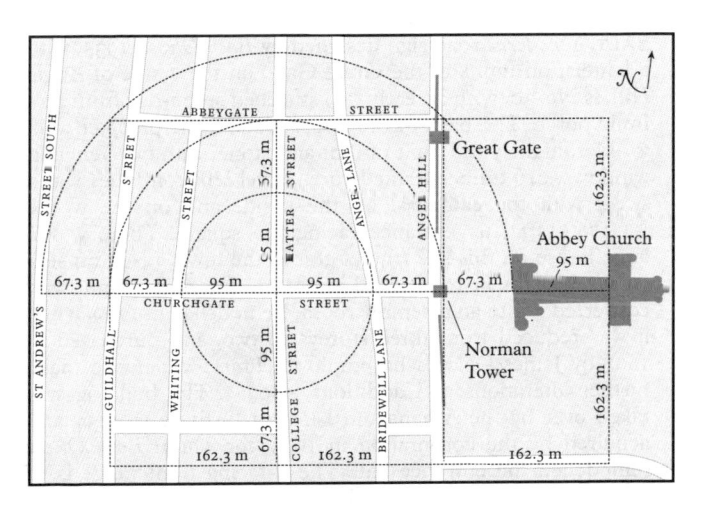

Bury St Edmunds, Norman town.
Plan

Street. The distance from the W front to the crossing of the abbey church is the same as the distance from Angel Lane to Hatter Street, and from Hatter Street to Whiting Street. The N–S layout is less regular, but Hatter Street and the N section of Whiting Street are the same length as the distance from the Norman Tower to the crossing. A further example of deliberate planning is that three of the gates in the town wall – Westgate, Risbygate, and Northgate – are equally spaced, while Northgate and Southgate are equidistant from the Norman Tower. A few towns in Normandy have been identified as having comparable layouts, notably Rouen.

The two main E–W thoroughfares, Abbeygate Street and Churchgate Street, form the basis for the first two perambulations. The remaining perambulations are based on the outer gates of the town – Southgate, Westgate, Risbygate, Eastgate and Northgate – and take us beyond the centre. It is useful to know that street numbering in Bury is usually consecutive, up one side and then down the other, rather than the more usual arrangement of odd numbers on one side and even on the other.

1. Angel Hill, Abbeygate Street and Cornhill

Abbeygate Street leads from the Great Gate of the abbey to the Great Market, as it was once known. The Great Gate is not quite in line with Abbeygate Street, because it was built to replace the gate damaged by the riots in 1327; presumably its predecessor had been in line. Between the Great Gate and Abbeygate Street, however, lies ANGEL HILL, a large and delightful open space. Cars have not been entirely banished, but they do not dominate, and to cars is owed what is perhaps Angel Hill's most unusual feature, the so-called PILLAR OF SALT, a *moderne* road sign designed by *Basil Oliver*, 1935, with a lantern on top. S of the Great Gate, on the E side of Angel Hill, is No. 30, with an early C19 stuccoed seven-bay front and Ionic porch. The back of the house, behind the precinct wall, is older, higher, and built of flint and stone, with two Venetian windows. C16 timber-framed core. Angel Hill continues S as a street with the cathedral on the E side and on the W the ATHENAEUM, its entrance facing the square. There was a large house on this site (the largest in the town, taxed on seventeen hearths in 1674), sold in 1713 to James Eastland, who converted it into an assembly room. Remodelled in 1789, when it was reduced from three storeys to two, and purchased in 1801 by James Oakes who employed *Francis Sandys* to make further alterations and additions, 1802–5. The building was taken over by the Athenaeum Literary Institute in 1854 and acquired by the corporation in 1935, for whom *Basil Oliver* remodelled the entrance hall. The N-facing front range is of 1802–5. Rendered, seven wide bays, parapet raised over the centre. Doric tetrastyle porch with balcony. Behind the parapet a copper-covered observatory dome added in 1859. E front of

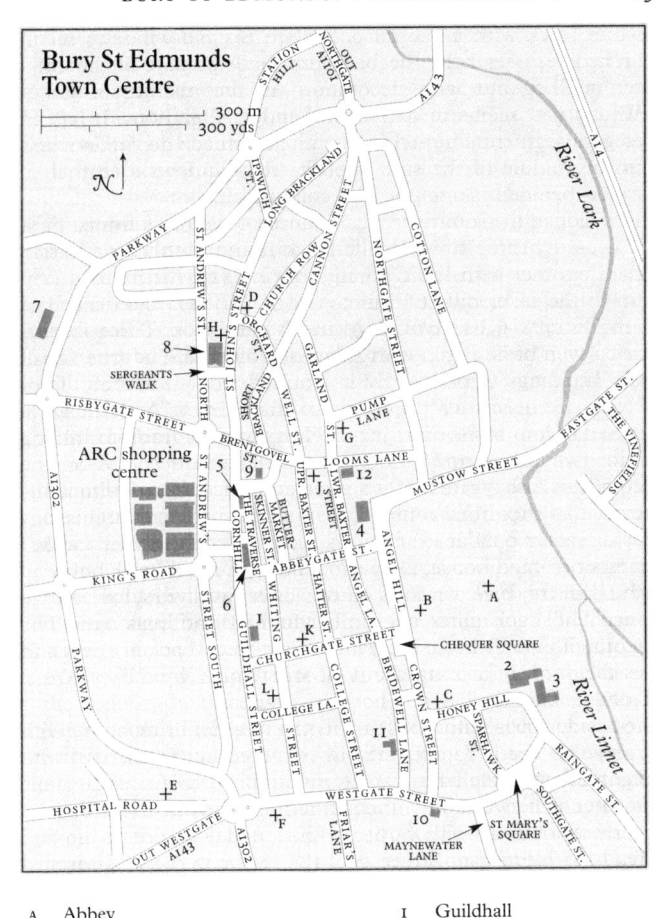

A Abbey
B Cathedral
C St Mary
D St John the Evangelist
E St Peter
F St Edmund (R.C.)
G Baptist Church
H Friends' Meeting House
J Trinity Methodist Church
K Unitarian Meeting House
L United Reformed Church

1 Guildhall
2 Old Shire Hall
3 Shire Hall
4 Borough Offices (former)
5 Market Cross
6 Corn Exchange
7 Fire Station
8 Public Library
9 Moyse's Hall Museum
10 Theatre Royal
11 Guildhall Feoffment School
12 Blomfield House Health Centre

white brick with a central pediment. Six tall windows set in arched recesses light the ballroom, built as part of the 1789 remodelling but with decoration (in the manner of James Wyatt) that seems to date from Sandys' alterations. It has an elegant segmental tunnel vault with fine stucco decoration, and in the middle of the side opposite the windows a segmental recess behind a screen of four columns.

The w side of the square proper is mostly quiet brick fronts. First a five-bay, three-storey white-brick house with Doric porch, then another with Ionic porch; both *c.* 1815. After that a step up to the taller but still quiet ANGEL HOTEL, the main part rebuilt 1774–6 by *John Redgrave*. White brick. Three storeys and seven bays. Porch with Adamish columns. The true age of the buildings is proved by its vaulted C13 undercroft. Two-storey extension with archway to the l. by *W. Steggles*, 1818, raised to four storeys in 1921–2. Next a timber-framed building with two gables and C18 (or C18-style) features, and on the corner of Abbeygate Street a three-storey C18 house with a fine early C19 shopfront composed of unfluted Ionic columns carrying rather ponderous capitals. N of Abbeygate Street another timber-framed house, early C17, and then a red brick house of the late C17. Five windows on the lower two floors, four on the top. The back parts are timber-framed and plastered. The Council Offices (*see* p. 143) are set modestly back at the N end of the w side; in front, the WAR MEMORIAL by *Sidney Naish*, 1921–2. Celtic cross of Clipsham stone.

The N side starts with ANGEL CORNER, a red brick house with rainwater heads dated 1702 but refronted in the mid C19 with canted bays. Five bays, two storeys, hipped roof. Beside it the former stables also of *c.* 1702. A terrace of white-brick houses, early C19 but all with earlier origins, makes a nice group and leads to Northgate Street; No. 18, on the corner, has arched windows on the ground floor and Ionic doorcases. (For Northgate Street and Mustow Street, *see* Perambulation 5.) The character of the s side of this section of Angel Hill is more varied, starting at the E end (opposite Northgate Street) with a timber-framed building of the late C15 and early C16 with exposed timbers and jettied front. The taller section to the r. originally had another jettied storey – the ends of the joists can be seen below the eaves. Moving back up the hill the long range that includes THE ONE BULL pub is also timber-framed, C16, but plastered. Turning the corner back into the square is an early C19 three-storey block of eight bays with three-bay curved centre.

ABBEYGATE STREET has retained the character of an old-fashioned shopping street, with a number of good shopfronts. One of these, on the corner of Angel Hill, has been mentioned. Soon after it, also on the s side and on the corner of Angel Lane, another with small glazing panes. Above can be seen the red brick front of a house of *c.* 1700, and inside C16 timbers. On the other side of ANGEL LANE the corner building (No. 37) was formerly jettied (see the joist ends above the shopfront) and the rear parts along the lane have exposed timbers and jetties. Similar remains of timber framing opposite along LOWER BAXTER STREET and at the next corner along HIGH BAXTER STREET. But before that, on the s side, commercial architecture of the later C19 intrudes – a row of four shops with alternating Dutch and straight gables in red brick by *H. F. Bacon*, 1882. Opposite, No. 16 was built to his own design by photographer *William Stanton*, c. 1863. White brick and stucco. Four storeys and three bays. Segmental pediments to the first-floor windows. Back on the s side, on the corner of Hatter Street, the former WEST SUFFOLK COUNTY CLUB by *E. F. Bisshopp*, 1883. Red brick, loosely Queen Anne. Two storeys. Three bays to Abbeygate Street, ten to Hatter Street. Arched entrance in Hatter Street, and arched windows to the upper storey. (For Hatter Street itself, see Perambulation 2.) w of High Baxter Street, on the N side, another tall white-brick building of the mid C19 with chemist's pestle and mortar between the first-floor windows, and then another good Georgian shop with six arched Gothick shop windows. These were inserted into an early C17 timber-framed house, its top floor jettied with three gables.

Towards the w end the buildings get increasingly townish, demonstrated clearly by Nos. 50–52, the E half built in 1856 by *H. F. Bacon* for Gurneys Bank, the w half added in 1880–2 by *J. B. Pearce* of Norwich. Three storeys, in a quiet Renaissance style. After this there is a further change because the N side of the rest of Abbeygate Street is the old market place, bounded on the E by Buttermarket and on the N and W by Cornhill, and including buildings along Skinner Street and The Traverse that have over the centuries filled up much of the open space. A market in this position is first mentioned in documents of the C13. First, the remainder of the s side of Abbeygate Street. After No. 52 comes another bank, HSBC, in a building remodelled and extended in 1914 by *T. B. Whinney* for the London, City & Midland Bank. Stone ground floor with attached Doric columns and arched openings. Above this red brick with stone cornice and red brick parapet. The three bays to the l. are early C18, the three to the r. 1914. Then timber-framed houses either side of the entrance to Whiting Street. On the E side No. 56 dates to the late C15 and has a carved corner-post (now inside the shop window) carved with figures of a man and a woman in early C16 dress. On the w side No. 57 is of less interest, but No. 58 is early C16 and also has a corner-post but at the back (and not normally visible). It is carved with a centaur-like creature and others including a seated figure playing an organ. None of this could be guessed from the plain exterior. Then, by way of complete contrast, No. 59 by *J. S. Corder* for the Alliance Assurance Co., 1890–1. Red brick, the ground storey of red sandstone. Three storeys. Five bays, including two canted bays with Dutch gables. Between the ground and first floor a frieze of red rubbers carved with foliage etc. and coats of arms. It is followed by *John Gibson*'s soberly classical stone-fronted National Provincial Bank of 1868 (now SANTANDER). On the N side, a picturesque late C15 timber-framed house with overhang between Skinner Street and The Traverse, and then the first of a sequence of three former public buildings between here and the market place to the N: the two corn exchanges and the Market Cross (for which *see* p. 144). The buildings round the edge of the market place begin with the W side of CORNHILL. Most of this is commonplace rebuilding of the C20, and the former Everards Hotel, facing Abbeygate Street, has been rebuilt behind the façade, although it retains its doorway with Roman Doric columns *in antis* and big hood. Three buildings stand out, in a row facing the Market Cross. First BURTON of 1933, presumably by their in-house architect *Harry Wilson*, with good Art Deco detailing. Then the former BOOTS store (now W. H. Smith) by the company architect *M. V. Treleaven*, 1910–11. It is a riotous and glorious fantasy, with lots of timber framing, gables and stucco ornamentation. On the first floor niches with statues of Agricola, St Edmund and Kings Edward I and Edward II; in the centre gable a panel depicting Canute 'rebuking his flatterers'. The subjects may have connections with Bury, but stylistically the building is utterly unconcerned with the spirit of the town. Finally the POST OFFICE of 1894–5 by *H. Tanner* of H.M. Office of Works, a pleasant building, of red brick with stone dressings, well detailed. Three storeys, three bays. Ground-floor windows with trefoiled heads. Little gable with pinnacles and the royal arms. On the N side only Moyse's Hall is of particular note (*see* p. 145), but in the middle of what remains of the market place the BOER WAR MEMORIAL by *A. G. Walker*, 1904. Bronze figure of a bare-headed soldier sitting on a rock, on a stone sarcophagus.

E of the Corn Exchange etc. is the row of buildings with their fronts in The Traverse and their backs in Skinner Street. The important building here is CUPOLA HOUSE – or was, for it was gutted by fire in 2012 and its elevation to Skinner Street destroyed.* It was the best C17 building in Bury, remodelled by Thomas Macro Jun. and his wife, Susan Macro, in 1693 (date and initials on weathervane) and described by Celia Fiennes in 1698. Macro, like his father before him, was an apothecary (also styled grocer), alderman and chief magistrate of the town, and father of Cox Macro of Little Haugh Hall, Norton (q.v.). Thomas Macro Sen. is documented as owning the property in 1653, and it seems likely that the date 1693 records major alterations, including the addition of the attic storey and the eponymous cupola. The house was three-storeyed, of five bays, plastered and with quoins. Pitched roof and on it the cupola or belvedere, a fashionable feature in the second half of the C17 (cf. Coleshill, Ashdown, Belton). Inside the cupola a seat round as in a gazebo. Celia Fiennes praised

---

*Proposals for reconstruction being developed (2014) by *Purcell*.

Bury St Edmunds, Cupola House, elevation.
Drawing by P. Aitkens, 1999

the 'pleasing prospect' to be had from it, once the sixty steps had been climbed. In the roof three dormers with alternating steep triangular and semicircular pediments, again a typical later C17 feature. The carved brackets carrying the second-floor balcony are typical too. Tall back in Skinner Street with two gables. Pretty staircase inside with strong twisted balusters, parts of which survived the fire.

In BUTTERMARKET, the E side of the old market place, the E side of the street is dominated by the former Greyhound Inn, later Suffolk Hotel (now WATERSTONE'S and EDINBURGH WOOLLEN MILL). Three storeys, stuccoed, eight bays wide. Late C15 Wealden house, refronted 1833 and considerably altered *c.* 1872–3 by *John Watson* of Bury for G. J. Oliver & Son. The visible result of this is the ground floor, with Corinthian pilasters and arched windows with colonnettes of polished pink granite with Romanesquoid capitals. On the w side LLOYDS BANK, rebuilt *c.* 1795–7 with alterations by *Edward Maufe*, *c.* 1919. White brick with stone dressings, the latter supplied by *J. de Carle*. Three storeys and five bays. Three large ground-floor windows with elliptical heads and delicate glazing in the heads, and two doors with fanlights.

2. Churchgate Street, Guildhall Street and adjoining streets

The second perambulation starts in front of the Norman Tower (*see* p. 128), facing CHEQUER SQUARE. In the middle of the square a late C18 stone OBELISK. The E side (actually Crown Street, for which *see also* Perambulation 3) has as its first building NORMAN TOWER HOUSE, built as the Savings Bank in 1846–7 by *L. N. Cottingham*. Tudor-Gothic, irregular. Red brick with diapering and stone dressings. Gabled bay with oriel towards Churchgate Street. The slightly plainer range to the S (No. 2 Crown Street) is an addition of 1858 by *W. Rednall*. Facing the churchyard a separate building (TOWER COTTAGE) that was built to his own design and as his own premises by *Thomas Farrow*, who was the contractor for the Savings Bank. It is in the same style, but Farrow was clearly trying to out-do Cottingham as an advertisement for his own abilities. It has a more elaborate oriel and a slender square tower; in the spandrels of the doorway the initials TF and mason's tools. Both Norman Tower House and Tower Cottage have lost some of their original pinnacles and other embellishments.

On the S side of Chequer Square Nos. 1–2 were built in 1840. Rendered brick. Three storeys. Arched windows to the ground and first floors, the latter with cast-iron balconies. Along the W side, first BARET HOUSE, once the property of John Baret †1467 whose monument is in St Mary's Church. The front is white brick, part of repairs carried out by *W. Steggles* when he leased the house in 1813. Five bays wide. Central doorway with fanlight and fluted columns, set in a segmental-arched recess – a feature to be found on many houses in Bury. The back is faced in red brick. Inside, there is evidence for C12–C14 buildings, including a C14 stone doorway that survives from an open stone hall. At the back is a timber-framed range built by Baret before 1463 as lodgings for priests from St James's and St Mary's churches. The hall range was rebuilt *c.* 1500, probably by Baret's nephew and heir, William Baret; ceiling with moulded beams and joists, and evidence of a jetty behind the C19 brick. Soon after 1500 a chimneystack was inserted in the lodging range, decorated with brick arcades. There is also surviving painted decoration, both pre-Reformation and of *c.* 1600. CHEQUER HOUSE, to its N, is mainly early C19, white brick, of three storeys. On the first floor a cast-iron iron balcony, and windows set in blank arches.

The N side of Chequer Square is the start of CHURCHGATE STREET. No. 35, Georgian, of five bays, red brick with white-brick quoins and platband, has a Gibbs surround to the doorway. No. 38, opposite, is earlier, *c.* 1700, with an apsed door hood on carved brackets. The street continues in its pleasantly varied, low-key way. On the corner of Angel Lane, No. 34 is early C18, timber-framed and plastered; inside a fine staircase with twisted balusters leading to a first-floor room with good panelling and painted overmantel of a hunting scene. The white-brick front of No. 28, five bays wide, is dated 1835 on the lintel of a second-floor window. Next to it a two-storey, four-bay house, timber-framed with a late C17 front of dark brick and dressings of a lighter red brick that join up to form continuous vertical panels. Then an early C16 timber-framed house with jettied front. On the S side, a half-timbered commercial building by *H. S. Watling*, *c.* 1904, with a wide carriage arch at the W end. After that Nos. 48–49, including No. 1 COLLEGE STREET, contains the remains of an aisled hall with contemporary cross-wing, dating from the second half of the C13, the earliest timber-framed building known in Bury. The two-storey cross-wing was jettied on both sides, again a very early example of such a feature, and its roof incorporated double tie-beams which clasp the wall-plates, a method of construction normally associated with base crucks, i.e. alien to this part of the country. These parts were mostly rebuilt in the C16, but enough remains to be able to determine their original form.

That brings us to the junction with College Street (*see* below) and Hatter Street. In HATTER STREET a number of nice houses, some timber-framed and plastered, others with white-brick or painted brick fronts. On the E side Nos. 7–8 with a late C18 white-brick front, three-storeyed with five bays, the two outer bays to l. and r. pedimented. The recessed centre has the curious arrangement of a pair of arched doorways with attached Doric columns separated by a window. Above that a Venetian window and above that a single sash window with small circular windows l. and r. But as with so many buildings in Bury, the front conceals much older origins. The roof (raised in 1788) contains reused C12 timbers, and the flint rubble back wall of the house may be of that date also. No. 5 is Georgian red brick with a pedimented doorcase and fanlight. A little further on the ABBEYGATE PICTUREHOUSE manages the near-impossible, discreetly fitting a cinema among the neighbouring houses. Opened 1924, rebuilt following a fire in 1930. It occupies the site of the southern half of a house, of which the centre bay with arched doorway and recessed columns survives, as well as the northern three bays with C20 door and Georgian-style bows. No. 25, almost opposite, has a broad recessed doorway with Ionic columns, the windows to l. and r. also with segmental arches. The rear wall of the building is medieval, possibly Norman.

At this point, rather than returning to Churchgate Street, one can cut through LANGTON PLACE (a pleasant enough development of the mid 1980s by *Heaton Abbott Swales*) to WHITING STREET. No. 6, to the N on the E side, has an early C19 front of white brick with plastered panel to the l., to which are fixed an outsize auctioneer's gavel and dumpy level in teak by *E. W. Turner* for H. C. Wolton & Son, *c.* 1948. The interior is timber-framed, C17, including an excellent panel of painted decoration with a pattern of interlocking octagons based on a Serlio ceiling design. Remains of painted decoration also in No. 83 on the W side: *c.* 1530, including foliate decoration with pomegranates, and texts in yellow and white Gothic lettering. Plain rendered C18 front. Further S, on the same side, Nos. 76–78 is a nice early C19 white-brick terrace of two storeys with the now familiar arched doorways with recessed columns; the builder was *W. Steggles*. Back on the E side, the MASONS ARMS pub stands out with its weatherboarding, straight and wavy; the front is C19, the rest early C16, formerly a hall house with two cross-wings.

Whiting Street continues S of Churchgate Street, but first we shall complete the latter. The section E of Whiting Street is of interest principally for the Unitarian meeting house (*see* p. 142), and there is nothing of especial significance in the short remaining stretch W up to GUILDHALL STREET. Here, opposite the end of Churchgate Street, is No. 79, with a conventional C18 plastered front of five bays and two storeys. But it is called NORMAN HOUSE, and the back wall of the front rooms is of stone and contains, opposite the front door, a Norman doorway. Roll-moulded arch. Nook-shafts with volutes on the capitals. Another doorway has a pointed arch. To the N on the same side No. 80, a conventional red brick Georgian house of five bays and three storeys, and then No. 81, an early C18 house altered and enlarged in 1789–91 by *John Soane* for James Oakes, yarn merchant and banker. Oakes's accounts record the mason as *Thomas Ingleton*, bricklayer and plasterer *John Hill*, and carpenter *Samuel Lyon*; the total cost was £263 9s. 6d. For this Soane added two wings, that on the l. for a family dining room, that on the r. for a banking hall, with a dining room on the first floor in which to entertain clients. Red brick. Five-bay centre. Doric doorcase with open pediment and fanlight. Soane's wings are of one broad bay, pedimented, with a circular window in the tympanum. On the ground floor a tripartite sash window under a blank segmental arch. The geometrical staircase in the older part of the house may also be by Soane.

The Guildhall stands opposite (*see* p. 142), followed by a few good houses along the remaining stretch up to Cornhill, e.g. No. 84 with its doorway and first-floor balconies, and the doorway to No. 88 with Gibbs surround. Guildhall Street S of Churchgate Street has timber-framed houses with jettied fronts occurring intermittently on both sides. On the W side No. 74, Early Georgian red brick and a pedimented doorcase with Gibbs surround, then a more rustic pair whose fronts are plastered in large panels. No. 72 is early C19 white brick with a Doric doorcase, No. 70 C18 red brick, the windows laced with white. The jettied upper floor of Nos. 66–67 is supported on scroll brackets and has a Georgian shopfront. A room at the back has an unexpectedly ornate plaster ceiling.

College Lane, on the E side of Guildhall Street opposite the Black Boy pub, leads through to the southern part of WHITING STREET. Immediately on the W side, on the corner of College Lane, Nos. 61–63, an interesting complex that once extended further S. At this end is a gabled and jettied cross-wing of the early C14; against the S wall a C16 chimneystack with sawtooth chimneys. N of this a mid-C15 two-bay hall range, replacing the original C14 hall, and early C15 N cross-wing with exposed timbers on the jettied gable-end. (The rear wall of the cross-wing is partly stone and in this a three-light Norman window was found during restoration in the 1960s.) Opposite, a white brick terrace of two-storey houses by *W. Steggles & Sons*, 1838. To the S, more timber-framed houses on both sides of the street, including No. 60 on the W side with jettied front (GREYFRIARS), and on the E side a varied group including Nos. 32 and 38 with jettied gables; the latter was formerly the cross-wing of a C15 house. No. 59 has picturesquely exposed timbers, and No. 56 (ST MARY'S HOUSE) a nice arched doorway with recessed columns and fanlight. N of College Lane the United Reformed church (*see* p. 142) and then, set back on the W side, the OLD SNUFF FACTORY, probably originally stables; late C18, red brick and flint, three storeys. Converted to a house by *Jeremy Sheppard*, 1999–2001. Between here and Churchgate Street, good doorcases to Nos. 68 (Gibbs surround; also quoins) and 19 (Doric, disproportionately big).

We continue E down COLLEGE LANE, passing COLLEGE SQUARE almshouses by *A. A. Hunt*, 1909. Red brick with pebbledashed gables. Two-storey centre and two one-storey wings. So into COLLEGE STREET. Nothing outstanding, by Bury's high standard, to the S; on the E side the Commercial School of 1842 by *H. E. Kendall*, now part of the Guildhall Feoffment School (*see* p. 147). To the N, on the E side, the former WILLIAM BARNABY ALMSHOUSES, rebuilt 1826 by *W. Steggles*. White brick with stone dressings. Two-storeyed, of twelve bays (eight windows only on upper storey). 'Tudor' windows with hoodmoulds, but a classical four-bay pedimented centre. Across the front an act of vandalism that has now, like medieval graffiti, acquired its own charm: large painted letters advertising Marlow & Co. Ltd, timber merchants and builders' supplies, who occupied the building from 1954 to 1978. Converted to four houses by *Charles Morris*, 1980. Opposite is the site of the Borough Workhouse, 1748–1884. OLD DAIRY YARD, a two-storey red brick and flint range at right angles to the street, is the surviving fragment; converted to houses by *John Atkins*, c. 2004–5. Soon after this we are back at Churchgate Street, and not far from the start of this perambulation and also of the next.

3. Crown Street, Honey Hill, Southgate and Westgate

CROWN STREET s of Chequer Square (*see* Perambulation 2) has a fine row of large houses facing the churchyard and St Mary's. No. 49 has a white-brick front of five bays and three and a half storeys with a pedimented doorcase and pretty fanlight; it was remodelled in the 1770s for Michael Otley, licensee of the Angel Hotel, so is very possibly the work of *John Redgrave*. Nos. 45–45A are red brick, a single house divided in two *c.* 1900 when the doorcase with Adamesque columns was carefully doubled. Between Nos. 43 and 44 a short diversion up Tuns Lane allows a view of Nos. 16–18 BRIDEWELL LANE, a timber-framed and plastered C15 hall house with gabled cross-wings. The oversize Doric doorcase on the s cross-wing came from Blomfield House, Looms Lane. Back in Crown Street, typical doorways on Nos. 37–38, with segmental fanlights and recessed columns, and another such on No. 30. Then the attractive DOG AND PARTRIDGE, timber-framed and with a gable at the N end and a long carved bressumer along the rest of the façade; C17 brackets. After this, buildings of the Westgate Brewery, to which we shall return later.

HONEY HILL runs E along the s side of St Mary's Church. Immediately past the church Nos. 1–2, semi-detached houses designed as one. Early C19 white brick. Three broad bays under a pedimented gable with urns. In the tympanum a lunette. Below this a large arched recess with a segmental-arched window and paired doors. No. 3 has the same feature of the arched recess but is otherwise more conventional. On the s side No. 6 (ST DENYS) dates back to the C15 but has a conspicuous ashlar front. This was the home of the stonemason and sculptor Thomas Singleton, who sold his business and premises to John and Robert de Carle shortly before his death in 1792 (John ran the Bury end of the business, Robert remained in Norwich). Whether the stone front was erected by Singleton or de Carle is debatable, but in either case it would have served as an advertisement. Two storeys and three broad bays. Recessed porch with paired pilasters joined together by bands of vermiculated rustication. The small building on the corner of Sparhawk Street was added in the early C19, its return wall of red brick with stone offcuts.

MANOR HOUSE is the principal building in Honey Hill and indeed the finest town house in Bury. It was built for Elizabeth Hervey, wife of the 1st Earl of Bristol, 1736–8, by *James Burrough*, the son of a local doctor. The house is on a grand scale and seems to have been designed for entertaining and display rather than extended residence. Red brick with stone dressings, including quoins. Nine bays wide, two-storeyed,

BURY ST EDMUNDS: PERAMBULATION 3   161

with three-bay pediment that originally contained stone arms by *Robert Singleton* (Thomas's uncle). Big doorway with segmental pediment on brackets and broad steps. On the ground floor is a large entrance hall, with dining room to the l. (with Corinthian screen at one end) and another room to the r. (library?) with the Hervey arms in the plaster ceiling. On the first floor l. a large saloon that runs from front to back. Ceiling with a flat coffered centre above a deep plain cove. Next to Manor House No. 5, a mid-C16 timber-framed house remodelled at the end of the C16 and containing remains of painted decoration of that date and the late C17. Two-storey, three-bay front. Three-light windows with transoms and hoodmoulds.

ST MARY'S SQUARE is the next destination, and can be reached via Raingate Street and Swan Lane – passing various public buildings, including the Magistrates' Courts (Old Shire Hall), former Shire Hall, Record Office and Police Station – or via Sparhawk Street (No. 5, timber-framed and plastered with jettied front, is late C16 with a painted panel inside dated 1600). St Mary's Square is a relatively recent designation: on C18 maps it is shown as Horse Market, and it is the site of the Saxon market that was superseded by the Norman market at the W end of Abbeygate Street. The fact that it is (and probably always has been) crossed diagonally by the main road out of Bury to the S detracts from its loveliness, as do the sheer brick walls of the Westgate Brewery (*see* p. 162) on its W side. But there are good houses on the other sides, and in the little GARDEN a nice group of terracotta URNS by *M. H. Blanchard*, London, 1874: one large central urn (pedestal and base replaced by *Catalano*, 2010) with a tiled surround, and four smaller ones. On the N side the easternmost house is a former Methodist chapel of 1811. Red brick, with arched windows and hipped pantiled roof. After 1878 it became a stay manufactory and it is now a house. On the E side Nos. 5–6, a nine-bay house of two and a half storeys. White brick with red brick dressings, including quoins and vertical lacing between the windows. Early C16 (timber frame visible internally), remodelled in the early C18, and again in the early C19, when it was divided in two. *Francis Sandys* owned the building *c.* 1803–16 and was probably responsible, also for adding the two storey extension set slightly back at the N end. To its S, set back, No. 4 was built *c.* 1804 and is also thought to be by Sandys. Red brick, of three bays and two and a half storeys. Tripartite windows with segmental heads, and Tuscan porch. On the S side of the square a timber-framed and plastered house mainly of the mid C18 but with elements of the mid C17 internally. Doorcase with open pediment and fanlight, both delicately detailed. Behind it Nos. 9–10 by *Hawkins Brown*, *c.* 1996–7. Two red brick one-and-half-storey houses. L-plan, forming courtyards with full-height glazed and galleried areas looking into them. Then in the SW corner of the square the garden wall of ST EDMUNDS HOSPITAL (St Mary's Square House), an early Georgian house enlarged in the early C19. Red brick.

Three storeys. Seven bays, with Ionic porch. Small LODGE of flint with white-brick dressings.

SOUTHGATE STREET starts at the SE corner of St Mary's Square. Some good timber-framed houses with jettied fronts. No. 149 (GRAMERCY COTTAGE), with exposed timbers, was much restored in the 1960s, when its southern end (No. 148) was rebuilt. Of Georgian houses, No. 131, also on the W side, is of red brick with dressings and pilasters of a lighter red. Two storeys and five bays, the windows with segmental heads. C19 two-bay extension to the l. Then on the E side LINNET HOUSE, C17 timber-framed and rendered. Five bays. Two storeys and attics, with three gabled dormers. After that No. 34, an early Victorian white-brick villa with Tuscan porch, and behind it a converted three-storey steam corn mill and kiln of former maltings. The latter is unusually large, square at the base but developing into a cone, with tiers of gabled dormers. Still on the E side, up to the corner with St Botolph's Lane, Nos. 42–43, a large red brick house of three storeys and nine bays. Front range and parallel rear range. Mainly C18, but with remains of late C15 or early C16 timber framing, and C19 alterations and additions. Back on the W side another good timber-framed house, WEAVERS HOUSE (No. 80), with carved bressumer, arched entrance, and remains of carved oriel bases.

Now back to MAYNEWATER LANE, which curves round the grounds of St Edmunds Hospital to join Westgate Street. On the SW side MAYNEWATER HOUSE, built as police housing by *West Suffolk County Architect's Dept* (project architect *James Blackie*), 1971–2. Pale buff brick. Two storeys, with external corridor along the street front to provide sound insulation. After this we come to MAYNEWATER SQUARE, 1868, built for workers at the Westgate Brewery (*see* below). Sixteen two-storey houses on three sides of a quadrangle. Red brick with white-brick dressings. N of this No. 32 Maynewater Lane, BATH COTTAGE, and round the corner No. 1 WESTGATE STREET, are by *Lot Jackaman*, 1870 and 1884 respectively. Jackaman, builder and stonemason, was also proprietor of a swimming bath on the site. Both houses of flint with stone dressings. Bath Cottage has a doorway with attached columns and arched hood. Arched windows with little panels of stained glass with his initials, mason's tools etc. The walls of the later house incorporate many fragments of dressed and carved stone etc., including the apposite inscription 'Waste Not Want Not'. The Theatre Royal (*see* p. 146) is just along from this and the adjacent house (No. 6 Westgate Street) may also be by *William Wilkins*. White-brick front, the main block of three bays. Broad bow and doorway both with Doric frieze.

The theatre and house both sit quite happily among the buildings of the WESTGATE BREWERY. Benjamin Green came to Bury in 1799 and in 1806 entered into partnership with William Buck to take over Wright's Brewery in Westgate. The business was much expanded after 1836 by Edward Greene, and in 1887 merged with Frederick King's neighbouring St Edmund's

Brewery to form Greene, King & Sons. The complex dominates the N side of Westgate Street and the two-storey building on the corner with St Mary's Square is the oldest part, with a C17 range along Westgate Street and a C16 range facing the square, both timber-framed and encased in red brick in the C19. N of the earlier range the red brick Barley Store by *Evans & Son*, 1914. Four bays and five storeys with two lucams. Back in Westgate Street is the original brewhouse of King's St Edmund's Brewery, five storeys of white brick, succeeded by the principal BREWHOUSE of 1936–9 by *W. H. Mitchell* (*Mitchell & Houghton*; consulting engineer *Mark Jennings*). Red brick, with channelled rustication on the ground floor. Three-bay centre with full-height arched windows, and further parts set back to reduce their impact on the narrow street. Diminutive beside this, on the corner of Crown Street, a two-storey range dated 1881, of red brick with white-brick dressings and exposed timbers in the gable with decorative bargeboards. Its style is seen also in the buildings W of Crown Street that form the nucleus of Edward Greene's Westgate Brewery (WESTGATE YARD, with repositioned stone inscription dated 1800). Along CROWN STREET, a terrace of workers' housing built in 1859. Red brick with white-brick dressings and diapering. Shaped gables and latticed casements. Doorways with semicircular hoods. W of Westgate Yard, along BRIDEWELL LANE, a brewhouse with mansard roof. Red brick, with sections of flint and rubble. Dated 1789 in the N gable, but largely of 1846; the S gable remodelled with half-timbering and bargeboards. Opposite Bridewell Lane, on the S side of Westgate Street, OFFICES by *H. M. Cautley*, 1914. Red brick with stone dressings. Two storeys. Asymmetric front with quoined and pedimented entrance bay. On the chimney-breast an example of the stoneware plaque fixed to all Greene King pubs, designed by *George Kruger Gray* (made by *Doulton & Co.*, 1933–56, thereafter by *Carter* of Poole).

Back on the N side of Westgate Street, an impressive range of former maltings built by Edward and Walter Greene in 1880, now converted to housing and extended. Red brick with white-brick dressings. Three storeys. Irregular eight-bay front with archway and half-timbered lucam. WESTGATE HOUSE, opposite, was built by Edward Greene for himself, 1865 (rainwater head); white brick, six bays, three storeys. W of College Street HIGHBURY HOUSE, with a rather plain plastered front masking an early C17 house with some exposed timbers. Opposite, down FRIAR'S LANE, No. 5, a minimalist, High-Tech single-storey house (CRYSTAL PALACE) by *Michael & Patty Hopkins*, 1978, sensitively refurbished by *Project Orange*, 2013. Large areas of glazing, flat roof, and internal demountable walls. Further W along Westgate Street, No. 17 on the S side has a good doorcase with open pediment and fanlight. No. 24, opposite Guildhall Street, has a three-storey, seven-bay stuccoed front with quoins. Late C17–C18. The end of Westgate is marked, somewhat abruptly, by the roundabouts of Cullum Road and Parkway. On the NE corner a development of old people's flats by the *Borough Architects' Dept*, c. 1978, built round a courtyard. White brick and pantiles, with varying roof pitches, appropriate to the surroundings. Between Cullum Road and Westgate Street, Greene King's WINE & SPIRIT STORE by *Lyster, Grillet & Harding*, 1974, a minimalist steel box, extended by *Michael Hopkins Architects*, 1979–81, and a High-Tech DISTRIBUTION WAREHOUSE by Hopkins, 1978–80.

OUT WESTGATE is the continuation beyond the line of the town walls. On the S side a white-brick terrace with arched windows and nicely punctuated inscription, 'Albert Buildings, 1840'. On the N side ST PETER'S VINEYARD, Lot Jackaman's yard. C18 house of flint with red brick dressings with lower C19 range at the S end that incorporates reused stone. In the angle between the two parts an open porch and over that plaster casts of the figures of Agriculture from the Corn Exchange of 1861–2, for which Jackaman was contractor (*see* Public Buildings). About 500 yds further out, at the junction of Vinery Road, MONUMENT to the novelist Ouida (Marie Louise de la Ramée) †1908, by *E. G. Gillick*. Rectangular stone basin (animal drinking trough) with cenotaph carrying a bronze profile portrait, with standing figures of Courage and Sympathy.

HOSPITAL ROAD starts at the same point as Out Westgate but goes off at an acute angle to it. A few nice houses along the N side: No. 14 was Ouida's birthplace, one half of an early C19 semi-detached pair that share a gable with scalloped bargeboards. Little evidence of the workhouse (*B. Backhouse*, 1836) and hospital (1826 onwards). On the S side of the road the former nurses' home of 1924–5 by *S. Naish*, and on the N side the Bristol Annex (ward block, now Cornwallis Court), 1938–40, by *Naish & Mitchell* (later *Mitchell & Houghton*), both red brick and Neo-Georgian.

A brief foray into ST ANDREW'S STREET SOUTH, N from the E end of Hospital Road and Out Westgate, completes this perambulation. On the W side is ST ANDREW'S CASTLE, built in the first quarter of the C19. Rubble, with stone dressings. Two storeys, with battlemented parapet. Sash windows with modest Gothick tracery and hoodmoulds. On the entrance front a stuccoed porch and to its S a round tower whose top rises above the parapet. At the NE corner of the house a small turret. Vaulted entrance hall. Gateway and entrance lodge in similar style, but red brick with white-brick and stone dressings. S of the entrance a pair of C17–C18 cottages that were probably remodelled at the same time or a little later.

4. King's Road to Risbygate Street

The area bounded by King's Road, Parkway, Risbygate Street and St Andrew's Street was the site of the town's cattle market from 1828 to 1999.* The site was redeveloped in 2007–9 as a shopping centre (ARC), which had a significant and, it would seem, beneficial impact upon the town. By *Hopkins Architects*. 265,000 sq. ft (25,000 sq. metres) of retail space, including a large department store, as well as sixty-two flats and a civic auditorium. The beauty of the scheme is that it does not feel like a vast mall, but is based on a number of new pedestrian streets with a public square at the centre that in effect extends the medieval grid. The only regret is that the alleys linking the new quarter to the old are so insignificant, and there is nothing to draw one through from Cornhill. The buildings along the new streets are of traditional scale and gabled. Three storeys, the first floor set back behind balconies supported on concrete columns, with the ground-floor shops set further back behind them. The colouring is subdued: lime render and grey timber cladding. On the E side of the central square is THE APEX, a multi-purpose theatre with a glass foyer and galleried wings projecting into the square. Beautifully finished interior, the auditorium almost entirely of timber. The real surprise lies in the SW corner of the square in the shape of DEBENHAMS. That shape is a clamshell, entirely curved and clad in diamonds of cast aluminium. Windowless, apart from the glass entrance, and with three floors, although the shape makes it hard to judge its size.

KING'S ROAD can be reached via an alley on the E side of Debenhams that leads to a little square. On the W side of this is No. 155 King's Road, a mid-C19 stone-fronted house once the premises (as an inscription proclaims) of A. H. Hanchet, monumental mason, followed by No. 147, a three-bay house of 1813 altered and raised to three storeys in 1880. Typical doorway with recessed columns and fanlight. Not much else of interest until the W side of Parkway. On the NW corner of the junction a low-cost, low-energy block of twelve flats by *Studio MGM*, 2007–8. Built of timber, the main elevation an open grid like a giant pergola and overgrown with climbing plants in order to reduce solar gain in summer. The plants also help to filter pollutants from the road. On the SW corner, and extending W along the S side of King's Road, houses converted from the former barracks of the West Suffolk Militia by *Morgan & Phipson*, 1857. Red brick with burnt headers, and limited decorative detailing. King's Road leads to the cemetery (*see* p. 142), immediately to the W of which is the PRIOR'S ESTATE (council housing), 1928–35. Its principal building is the PRIOR'S INN, Prior's Avenue, by *W. H. Mitchell*, 1933, for Greene King; praised by Basil Oliver in *The Renaissance of the English Public House* (1947) as being 'in conformity with local tradition' (red brick, long and low) but closed in 2013. A church (All Saints) was built in 1962 (*see* p. 140).

---

*Octagonal timber Settling House, 1864, moved to the Museum of East Anglian Life, Stowmarket (q.v.).

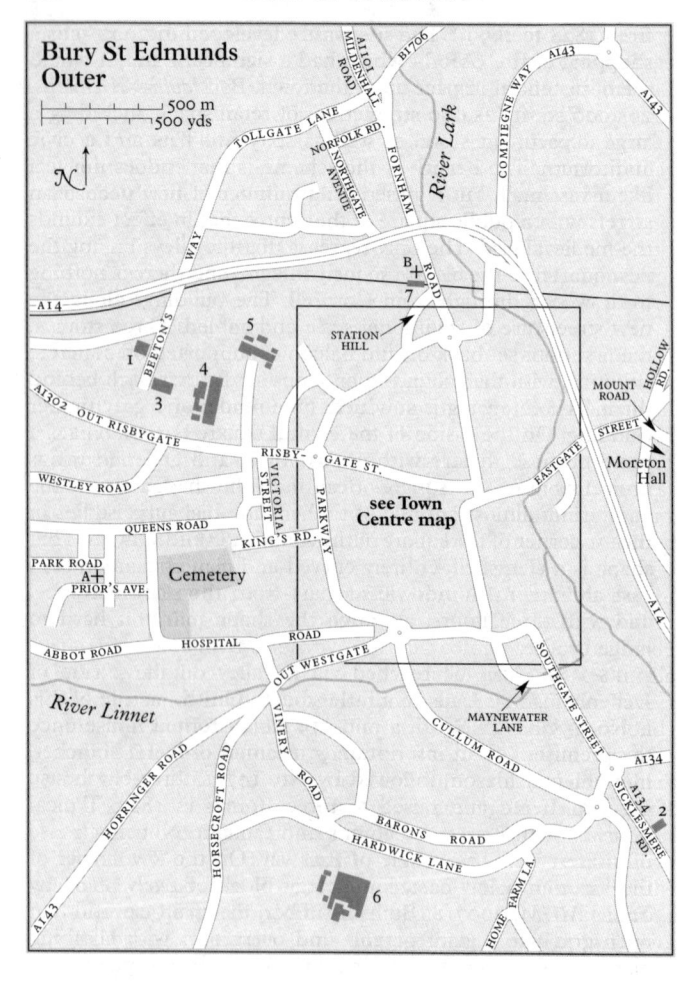

A   All Saints
B   Seventh Day Adventist
    Church

1   West Suffolk House
2   Gaol (former)
3   Leisure Centre
4   West Suffolk College
5   King Edward VI School
6   West Suffolk Hospital
7   Railway Station

PARKWAY, constructed c. 1974–8, seems to have been deliberately designed to discourage pedestrians, although for the benefit of motorists two roundabouts are enlivened by steel SCULPTURES: at King's Road, With the Grain by *Roy Porter*, 2013, and at Risbygate Street, St Edmund by *Emmanuel O'Brien*, 2011, both made by *Nigel Kaines*. For those on foot it is preferable to take one of the quiet residential streets such as Victoria Street or Albert Crescent and Street N from King's Road to reach OUT RISBYGATE. On the N side, 650 yds W of Parkway, THE KEEP and part of the perimeter wall, all that remains of Gibraltar Barracks, built in 1878 to designs by *Major H. C. Seddon R.E.* Red brick, with some white-brick decoration, in the toy-fort style. Three storeys, with water tower at one corner. Originally the armoury; now Suffolk Regiment Museum. The rest of the site is occupied by West Suffolk College (see p. 147). On the grass in front of the college, the stone base of a medieval CROSS. It was probably one of the four crosses that marked the boundary of the area governed by the abbot; not *in situ*. Opposite, a pair of semi-detached red brick houses (SUFFOLK REGIMENT COTTAGE HOMES) by *A. A. Hunt*, 1903, as a Boer War memorial.

Nothing special between here and Parkway, but the character changes E of that in RISBYGATE STREET. First, on the N side, Nos. 81–82 by *W. Steggles*, 1834. White-brick fronts. Two and a half storeys. The l.-hand part is grander, its doorway with arched fanlight on recessed columns. Then a long range with jettied front and exposed timbers, C16–C17 but heavily restored in the 1930s. No. 90, white brick, has a similar doorway to No. 81 and bows to l. and r., originally full height but now only at first-floor level. Off Risbygate Street to the N, Elsey's Yard leads to THE MALTHOUSE, converted to community use by *Milburn Leverington Thurlow* in 2006–7 with the addition of courtyard flats. Barn of *c.* 1620, converted to maltings *c.* 1700. Flint rubble and red brick ground floor, timber-framed and plastered upper floor. Back in Risbygate Street ST EDMUNDS TAVERN (formerly Rising Sun), picturesquely jettied and gabled with some exposed timbers and a doorway with carving of a bird in the spandrels. C15 in its earliest parts. Then No. 100, despite its early C19 white-brick front C17. The segmental oriels may, like those of No. 90, originally have come down to the ground. Further on, Nos. 104–108, a mid-C19 terrace of two-storey houses, of red brick with white-brick pilasters and a pierced parapet. Ionic doorways. Good strong cast-iron railings in front. On the S side, a nice recessed doorway with fluted columns at No. 19.

At the E end of Risbygate Street two corners of the crossroads have retained their early C19 character. On the SW corner No. 1 Risbygate Street turns into No. 56 ST ANDREW'S STREET SOUTH, white brick and each with the characteristic doorway with recessed columns and fanlight. On the NE corner (Brentgovel Street and St Andrew's Street North) THE GRAPES, white brick, with the corner subtly articulated by means of a slightly recessed quadrant. Addition to the N, facing St Andrew's Street North, dated 1837: carriage entrance and, on the first floor, two large windows with semicircular heads. ST ANDREW'S STREET NORTH is increasingly depressing as one heads N but spirits should be lifted by the FENNELL MEMORIAL HOMES opposite the dreadful government offices. 1873–4 by *Brightwen Binyon*. Red brick with white and black brick decoration. Two prominent gables with timber bracing, and a decorative opening in each. Four flats on two storeys, the upper flats reached by a covered external stair at either end. Built for Quaker women, and backing on to the meeting house in St John's Street (*see* p. 141).

5. *Mustow Street, Eastgate and Northgate*

MUSTOW STREET leads E from the junction of Angel Hill and Northgate Street. On the N side MUSTOW HOUSE (subdivided), with a Late Georgian nine-bay, three-storey, red brick front. Entrance hall with a richly patterned Victorian encaustic tiled floor and a good C17 open-well staircase. Part of the timber frame of the original C16 front wall is exposed internally. THE DUTCH HOUSE, to its E, single-storey with an elaborate shaped gable, may have been the coach house. On the S side, some cottages and then the precinct wall of the abbey and the Abbot's Bridge (*see* p. 134). Just before the bridge, on the N side, No. 17 is a curiosity, built in 1926 reusing timbers from a house demolished for road widening. Upper storey jettied on two sides with traceried angle-post and traceried panels.

EASTGATE STREET is the continuation E, with the River Lark running along its S side for a short stretch; on its S bank a little *cottage orné* dated 1862, of random stone and knapped flint with bands of knapped flint, and beyond it the former ST JAMES'S INFANT SCHOOL, 1872, in much the same style albeit with large plate-traceried windows. On the N side a pleasant little open space, THE BROADWAY. Facing this along the W side the FOX INN, a late C15 timber-framed and plastered hall house. Two gabled cross-wings, both jettied, the S along Eastgate Street as well. Restored by *Sidney Naish*, 1922–3; cut-out metal sign by *Basil Oliver*. E of the Lark (white-brick BRIDGE signed by *Steggles & Son*, 1840), a row of mainly timber-framed houses, culminating in No. 33 on the corner of Barn Lane. C15. Two gabled and jettied cross-wings, the E cross-wing jettied also along Barn Lane. Some exposed buttress posts on the ground floor, and an angle-post carved with the figure of an angel. Generally taken to be the first home of the King Edward VI Grammar School, 1550–1665. EASTGATE HOUSE, on the S side, stands at right angles to the street. C17 with an early C19 white-brick front of three bays and three storeys. Doorway with recessed columns and segmental fanlight. 300 yds to the S, in THE VINEFIELDS, the former KING EDWARD VI GRAMMAR SCHOOL by *A. W. Blomfield*, 1882–3. From its style one might say it was by his nephew, the future Sir Reginald Blomfield, who was just then training in his uncle's office. Red brick with tile-hung top floor, clearly under the influence of Norman Shaw. The school had previously been in Northgate Street (*see* below), and moved in 1972 to Grove Road (*see* p. 147).

The bridge carrying the A14 across Eastgate Street makes this feel like the end of the town in this direction, but 400 yds further on, at the fork of HOLLOW ROAD and Barton Road, is an unusually picturesque sight – picturesque in the original English C18 sense – that amply rewards the additional effort: a church window with its tracery against the sky and a big cedar tree overshadowing it. The window came from the former Leper Hospital of St Petronilla that stood by Southgate Green and was demolished in the C19. It now forms part of the garden wall of ST NICHOLAS, a house on the site of the former Hospital of St Nicholas. There were five hospitals at Bury (for the Hospital of St Saviour *see* below). The window is Dec, of three lights, and can be clearly seen in old prints of St Petronilla's. Of the Hospital of St Nicholas there remains a red brick chimneystack on the W side of the house. This has diapering on its base and an arcaded panel of seven tall thin bays higher up. The top rebuilt with crowsteps. To the r. of the chimney a section with exposed timbers and brick-nogging, above a base of stone rubble. The rest is a mainly C19 confection, in a variety of materials, and including some pseudo-Romanesque arched windows. The boundary walls and also the cottages to the N along Hollow Road contain a good deal of reused stonework. For Moreton Hall, ½ m. ESE of the A14 bridge, *see* p. 174.

We now retrace our steps to the S end of NORTHGATE STREET, which contains Bury's grandest town houses. Nos. 1–3, with their Ionic doorcases, are a continuation of No. 18 Angel Hill. Then the former CONGREGATIONAL CHAPEL of 1829, refronted in 1867–8 by *Bacon & Bell*. White brick. Venetian Gothic. Three pairs of arched windows and a small square turret. N of Looms Lane No. 7, a timber-framed and plastered house of *c.* 1500. Jettied front with C18 windows, pedimented doorcase and dentilled cornice. No. 8 is of red brick with stone quoins, seven bays wide, with a recessed centre. This is only one bay wide, but taller than the wings. It has a pediment, below this a Venetian window, and on the ground floor an odd porch with clustered pilasters, behind which the doorway appears; its entablature, rising to a point in the centre, suggests the façade is Early Georgian. There is in fact a rainwater head dated 1713. Inside, however, a moulded beam of the C16 indicates the house's true age, and one room has reused Jacobean panelling. On the garden front the windows are more closely spaced, eleven bays, with segmental heads. Nos. 9–11 present an even more complex history. The front is white brick, of 1823. Gabled centre projecting over a shallow tetrastyle Tuscan porch that contains three doorways with Gothick fanlights. Canted oriel window above. Three broad bays l. and r. of the centre. The interior is complex, but behind the front of No. 9 is a C14 three-bay storeyed range with crown-post roof, connected with an open hall that was rebuilt in the late C14 and now lies behind the front of No. 10 (Bury Farmers' Club). In the hall a C16 fireplace, and Jacobean panelling, screen, and staircase with splat balusters. The screen and its gallery represent the original cross-passage, entered from a stone porch now in No. 9. Also inside No. 9 a section of flint and stone walling.

The houses on the E side are of less interest individually, but make an impressive group. No. 111 is timber-framed with an early C18 front, subtly varied with different shades of brick and a mix of Flemish and English bond. Tuscan doorway with open pediment to No. 110, occupied by the County School from 1907; extension to the r. (assembly hall) by *A. A. Hunt*, 1909, with entrance and arched window in oxblood red tiles. Back on the W side, an unexpected pair of red brick Victorian villas of *c.* 1870 before No. 18, home of King Edward VI Grammar School from 1665 to 1883 (now flats). Timber-framed and plastered. Hipped roof with dormers. The original 1665 (N) part of seven bays and two storeys and cross-windows, mostly replaced. The ground-floor windows have been lowered from schoolroom to domestic level. Over the doorway an arched niche (formerly with bust of Edward VI) and inscription. The S part added in 1762 to provide boarding accommodation. Porch with Ionic columns *in antis* and balcony. Further out, No. 28 has a good Corinthian porch, and stands opposite single-storey almshouses (LONG ROW) by *Sidney Naish*, 1911. Red brick. Tall central archway with knapped flint in the gable.

Northgate Street is brought to a dreary end by a roundabout, part of road improvements connected with the opening of the town's bypass in 1973. It continues N as Out Northgate, but with little of interest until the railway bridge (*see* p. 149) and just beyond it the remains of ST SAVIOUR'S HOSPITAL in FORNHAM ROAD. This was founded in 1184/5 by Abbot Samson. What remains is the W end of a range 100 ft (30.5 metres) long. Two-centred entrance arch, looking early C14. Of the large window above only the lower half of the frame survives. The base of much of the walling beyond the front has been exposed, showing that the building comprised two separate chambers, the eastern one a chapel.

Another ½ m. further out, at the beginning of MILDENHALL ROAD, THE PRIORY HOTEL stands on the remains of Babwell Priory, the Franciscan house of Bury. The order had arrived in 1257, but in 1262 was forced by the envious abbey to pull down its building. The abbey then gave the site at Babwell. Of the Franciscan buildings nothing stands above ground, though the position and shape of the church (a plain aisleless oblong) are known. The house now on the site is C16 to C17. The red brick end to the street has a shaped gable with integral chimneys and two small Elizabethan or Jacobean windows. The main range behind this is timber-framed, the S front of five bays Georgianized with Tuscan porch. Inside, on the first floor, can be seen close studding, a blocked three-light window and a carved bressumer. Much of the boundary walls of the friary remain. ¼ m. along Mildenhall Road a large range of red brick MALTINGS converted to flats by *Milburn Leverington Thurlow*, 2013. Tie-rod plates dated 1851 with the initials of Rev. Sir Thomas Gery Cullum of Hardwick House (*see* p. 173) show that the building was originally associated with the Lark Navigation that lies to the E (cf. Mildenhall, p. 412); it was served by a canal arm. On the W side of the road is the MILDENHALL ESTATE, begun immediately after the Second World War. By the Borough Surveyor, *N. C. Goldsmith*, but with the first phase of housing by *Mitchell & Houghton* and in an attractive pre-war-style Neo-Georgian. Brick and pantiles with sash windows and pedimented doorcases, e.g. along ANSELM AVENUE, where a community centre opened in 1951. Enlarged and converted to a church (ST GEORGE) by *Wearing & Hastings*, 1967.

The walk back to the centre may be extended by a diversion along NORFOLK ROAD, off the W side of Fornham Road. Good Edwardian houses on both corners, that on the NW corner identified as THE CABIN, 1904, by a beaten brass plaque in a red brick frame. Probably by *H. S. Watling* while working for Arthur Rutter & Son. More good houses of similar date in NORTHGATE AVENUE, at the W end of Norfolk Road, including No. 8 of 1905 with red brick ground floor and pebbledashed first floor. Large asymmetric gables, one with Diocletian window on the ground floor and a small canted oriel above. It may be the house designed by *J. C. Ridley* for himself. HIGHLANDS and NEWMAN HOUSE, opposite, was built as a large red brick house by *William Eade*, 1880, occupied the following year by the East Anglian Middle School, and extended over the years by *Eade & Johns* and *Johns & Slater*. Closed 1972; part converted back to housing, 2000.

Back on the S side of the railway bridge, we can return to the centre by way of STATION HILL, mostly cleared of its early industrial buildings but with one remaining GRAIN MILL by *H. R. Hooper* for G. Burlingham & Sons, 1911. Red brick. Four storeys. Remains of steam engine house. S of Tayfen Road, Ipswich Street leads to a complicated knot of streets, as different from the grid of the Norman town as could possibly be. LONG BRACKLAND doubles back to the NE, worth a quick look for No. 50, a warehouse by *H. A. King* of Sudbury, 1896–7. Red brick with stone dressings. Two storeys of five bays, with a further floor in a huge shaped gable. Between No. 50 and Ipswich Street, St Martin's Street leads SE through to CANNON STREET and a triangular open space known as PEA PORRIDGE GREEN, all white brick, very understated but worth treasuring. On the E side a mid-C19 pub and stable yard, and on the S side a small terrace of houses (CANNON PLACE) by *W. Steggles*, 1825. From the SW corner CHURCH ROW leads up to St John's church (*see* p. 140) and ST JOHN'S STREET. No. 33, opposite St John's, seems entirely Victorian, with its false exposed timbers; but the Victorian bargeboards are reused, as is the carved bressumer dated 1630. To the S, the character of the street is increasingly medieval, with timber-framed houses on both sides, some with jettied fronts, and including two half-Wealden houses (Nos. 7–9); but among them the towering former Police Station of 1891 by *Frank Whitmore*. Red brick with red stone dressings. Three storeys. Three bays. Pedimented gables on the broader outer bays, a little Dutch gable on the centre.

At the risk of trying the user's patience, it would be better now to return to St John's church and go SE along Orchard Street. In the angle between Short Brackland and Well Street the former POOR GIRLS' SCHOOL by *H. E. Kendall*, 1852. White brick, and very much more modest than Kendall's other buildings for the Guildhall Feoffment (*see* p. 147). The main reason for this less than straightforward route is WELL STREET, with its lovely early to mid-C19 houses. No. 20, knapped flint with white-brick dressings and pretty fanlight, is set back behind railings. Nos. 14 and 15, on the W side, are a detached pair, red brick with white-brick fronts. But most of the E side is a terrace, or rather groups of houses giving the overall impression of a terrace, all white brick, the best section Nos. 35–37, with pediment across No. 36 and each with a doorway with recessed columns and segmental fanlight. It is worth looking back, as well, for what is perhaps the most flattering view of the spire of St John's.

Towards the S end of Well Street the side of CORNHILL WALK shopping centre by *Building Design Partnership*, 1986–8, comes as a nasty surprise – one of the few in the centre of Bury. The mass is broken down into separate gabled units, with staggered street-line, and the red brick is relieved by bands and corners of stone, but none of this really helps, and the obligatory glass and metal entrance to the two-storey mall (in BRENTGOVEL STREET) is simply not the right way to close a vista that, from the S, includes Moyse's Hall.

E along Brentgovel Street is the S end of GARLAND STREET. This has a good white-brick house attached to the S side of the Baptist church, and may well be of the same date (1834) and also by *Steggles*. Three bays and three storeys. Doorcase with Doric pilasters and frieze. Further N up Garland Street on the same side No. 62 (HORNDON HOUSE), C17 timber-framed and rendered. Two storeys and five bays, with three dormers in the steep-pitched roof. On the W side a two-storey white-brick terrace, much more modest than its counterpart in Well Street, but with a three-bay pedimented section, with arched windows, built as a Primitive Methodist chapel in 1851. Now back to Brentgovel Street, or rather its continuation E, LOOMS LANE. On the S side Blomfield House (*see* p. 148); on the N, behind a high red brick wall that is in part Tudor, REGENCY HOUSE HOTEL. Early C19 white brick with stuccoed front. Two storeys, three bays, with a nice cast-iron veranda along the front with curved lead roof. At the E end of Looms Lane we are back near the S end of Northgate Street and Angel Hill.

Bury St Edmunds, Hardwick House.
Engraving, 1852

OUTLYING BUILDINGS

CLARICE HOUSE (residential spa), Horringer Road, 1⅓ m. SW of Angel Hill. A house known as Horringer Red House was rebuilt *c.* 1898 for E. R. Hawkins and renamed Horringer Court. Red brick with stone dressings. Elizabethan, with straight gables. Entrance with deep flat canopy on Doric columns. Expensive interiors with much panelling and stained glass.

HARDWICK HOUSE, Hardwick Lane, 1¼ m. SSW. The house was demolished in 1926–7 but associated buildings remain.* Since 1609 it had been owned by the Drury and Cullum families, together with Hawstead Place (q.v.), and was built (or rebuilt) *c.* 1612 by Sir Robert Drury, with considerable alterations in 1681 for Sir Dudley Cullum, and for Rev. Sir Thomas Gery Cullum in the 1830s and 1840s. As part of the latter campaign *G. R. French* made a design for remodelling the S front, and the single-storey LODGE at the N entrance to the park in Hardwick Lane is his work. Plastered, with tall decorative white brick chimneys. Gothic bargeboards and little oriel windows with cast-iron casements. In the PARK S of the West Suffolk Hospital, off Sharp Road, HARDWICK MANOR, 1926–7 by *Kersey, Gale & Spooner,* is the considerable enlargement in Tudor style of the gardener's cottage that had been built on the site of the original dower house. Ground floor of

*The sale of contents, 1924, included the Jacobean painted closet, originally at Hawstead Place, now in Christchurch Mansion, Ipswich (E). Demolition sale, 1926, included wrought-iron gates and turret clock now at Coldham Hall (q.v.).

flint with brick and stone dressings. Jettied upper storey with exposed timbers (reusing old materials from elsewhere), gabled two-storey porch, and four tall red brick chimneys. Two smaller gables on the garden front. The interior incorporates panelling and the staircase from Hardwick House and Hawstead Place. The contractor was *Harvey G. Frost*, who designed and built for himself a Neo-Tudor house in the NW corner of the park (STONEBRIDGE, Horsecroft Road).

E of the site of the house, in Home Farm Lane, HOME FARM HOUSE. 1838, for Rev. Sir T. G. Cullum. White brick, with panels of knapped flint. To its N DAIRY COTTAGE (formerly Swiss Cottage), a highly picturesque thatched building of about the same date. It has a large two-storey half-timbered porch on one side, with elaborate bargeboards, that might be considered Swiss. In HARDWICK LANE, W of the lodge, No. 112 is one of a number of distinctive Y-plan estate cottages erected by Rev. Sir T. G. Cullum. Flint, with red brick dressings. Ornamental red brick chimneys. Cast-iron casements. For other examples, see Hawstead and Horringer.

MORETON HALL (preparatory school), Mount Road, 1 m. E. Originally St Edmund's Hill, and built on high ground overlooking the town. 1773–6 by *Robert Adam* for John Symonds, Professor of Modern History at Cambridge. White brick. A small, square house, only three bays by three, but two and a half storeys high with cellars and attics. Pediments on each front. On the N front giant pilasters of the 'Spalatro' order between the first and second floors. The pilasters themselves are painted timber, the capitals, frieze and string courses of *Coade* or similar material. The porch and flanking tripartite windows, with their stone dressings, are C19 additions; Adam's plans* show a smaller enclosed porch. Against the W (and, originally, the E) front a two-storey segmental bow with balustrade and above it a Diocletian window. On the S front a central doorway (originally with a small open porch) with Venetian windows in round-arched recesses l. and r. Pyramidal roof with chimneys at the apex; chimneys also on the pediments. Two-storey, five-bay E wing, probably added by John Josselyn, *c*. 1850, with Venetian window on the N front lighting the staircase. Inside, two ground-floor rooms have (largely) original decoration with plaster ceilings: Symonds's study in the SE corner, and across the W front the Eating Room, which has screens of two columns on its N and S sides. On the first floor, over the Eating Room, the drawing room, and the principal bedchamber over the study, with secondary bedrooms on the second floor. (François de la Rochefoucauld stayed with Symonds in 1784 and complained of having to climb sixty-four stairs to his room, four or five times a day.) Entrance hall with Neo-Jacobean woodwork and staircase of 1891. STABLES E of the house. Nine bays with round-arched openings. Single-storey with three-bay two-storey centre with pedimented gable.

---

*In the Soane Museum.

Mid-C19 LODGE to N with round-arched windows in arched recesses and porch with pedimented gable. Remains of ICE HOUSE W of the lodge.

Moreton Hall has given its name to a large housing estate with a population of some 7,000 in 2011. Plans were announced in 1973 and development started in 1975, with the first houses being built in 1978. Moreton Hall is also the name of a pub, 350 yds SE of the Adam house, converted from an attractive group of buildings that was once Mount Farm. Nearby are CHRIST CHURCH by *Modece Architects*, 1992–4, a rather plain building of pale buff brick and pantiles, and a COMMUNITY CENTRE, 2000.

BUXHALL

Dominated by the Copinger and Hill families, lords of the manor and patrons of the living. Twelve Copingers or Hills were also rectors between 1569 and 1948, in addition to William Copinger, rector 1411–36. The families combined when the last Copinger heiress, Sarah, married Rev. Dr Thomas Hill (rector 1709–43).

ST MARY. Nave, chancel and W tower. All Dec. Money was left for the tower in 1392 but it is still Dec. Wide nave and chancel. Tall two-light windows. Only the E window is bigger – a good piece of five lights with flowing tracery. Double PISCINA with ogee arches and steep gable. The SEDILIA which were set against the window are mostly broken off. Dec S porch with two-light windows. Niche over the entrance. Battlements with flushwork chequerboard decoration. Chancel re-roofed in 1656. Restorations in 1875–7 (mainly internal, including re-seating, but also new N vestry) and 1922–3 (including new nave roof by *S. J. Bury*, successor to *J. S. Corder*). – FONT. Octagonal. Early C14. Simple arches under gables, much use made of the encircled quatrefoil. Embattled top. No ogees. – BENCHES. A few in the chancel with poppyheads. Restored 1875–7, with carving by *Robert Fairweather* of Ipswich, although *Agnes Emily Hill* also executed some carving in the church, and her father *Rev. Henry Hill* seems to have acted as architect. – STAINED GLASS. Medieval fragments in several window heads. – MONUMENT. Robert Maltyward †1796. By *Tovell*, Ipswich. Little ornament. His chest tomb, rather more ornamented, stands outside against the nave S wall.

COPINGER HALL. *De facto* the rectory, although not built as such, and the E and N sides of the church can only be inspected from its grounds. The house is often said to have been built for Thomas Hill in 1710, but it has an older timber-framed core. The back is still plastered and the tall red brick chimneys with octagonal shafts look C17. Dog-leg stair with twisted balusters. Refronted in white Woolpit brick for Rev. Copinger Hill,

1854, with cornice and parapet. Eight-bay E front. Five-bay S front including a three-bay bow.

MAYPOLE FARM, 150 yds NE. Mid-C16 range by the road, probably built as the parlour wing of a medieval hall. The new range was jettied to the N, although this is now obscured by a C19 addition. Red brick gable with diapering and two ornate chimneys added later. The original hall range was rebuilt in the C17.

A few nice cottages further along RECTORY ROAD, including THE OLD FORGE and ROSE COTTAGE. Built of cob for Rev. Copinger Hill, who described the method in a prize essay published in the *Journal of the Royal Agricultural Society*, 1843. Thatched. Another of his cob buildings is POUND COTTAGE, Valley Lane, S of the church, but it has been much altered.

BUXHALL VALE, ¾ m. NNE. Early C19, plastered, seven bays wide. Greek Doric porch. Older timber-framed core.

FASBOURN HALL, ¾ m. SW. The cross-wing and half the main range of an early C17 red brick house. Two storeys and attics. In front of the house a brick BRIDGE, also C17, over the remaining arm of the medieval moat. Two arches.

WINDMILL, ½ m. W. Seven-storey tower mill, 1860. Tarred red brick. Sails and machinery removed. Beside it the former PRIMITIVE METHODIST CHAPEL, 1875.

CAPEL ST MARY

ST MARY. Restored 1869. The nave N wall may be C12. Mainly flint rubble, partly rendered, including also some Roman brick. The chancel is Dec, the windows on the S side with spurs between the foils or cusps of the tracery. Pretty Dec chancel doorway with foliage decoration. Perp E window. Perp also the S aisle and S porch (outer doorway with fleuron decoration). Sturdy W tower, until 1818 with a spire. Plain arcade with octagonal piers and double-chamfered arches. False hammerbeam roof, without hammerposts. The arched braces rest directly on the hammerbeams. Brick extension with link to N doorway by the *Whitworth Co-Partnership*, 1990. Two storeys, the upper within the pyramidal roof. – PULPIT. C18, with renewed tester. Painted in imitation of inlay. – SCULPTURE. Limewood rood figures, 1912, and angels on chancel roof, 1913, by *Lang* of Oberammergau. – STAINED GLASS. S aisle: E by *F. C. Eden*, 1925, S by *G. Maile & Son*, 1984. – MONUMENT. William Press †1807. By *Coade & Sealy*, 1809. *Trompe l'œil* drapery.

METHODIST CHURCH, The Street. By *W. Eade*, 1883. Red brick with white-brick dressings. Gabled front, with pediment outlined in white brick and round-headed doors and windows.

Former SCHOOL, The Street. By *F. Barnes*, 1854. Only the house remains. Flint with red brick dressings. Pointed-arched windows.

Some timber-framed COTTAGES close to the churchyard, but otherwise the village has been overwhelmed by housing of the 1960s and 70s.

OLD HADLEIGH, London Road. C15 timber-framed house with brick-nogging, moved here from George Street, Hadleigh, in 1934, complete with early C20 rear extension. Two storeys. Jettied front with gabled cross-wing to l. Bressumer with date 1424. Corner-post with carved figure holding a scroll. Inside, good panelling etc., and plasterwork in first-floor rooms dated 1649.

BOYNTON HALL, Old London Road. Timber-framed and plastered house with C14 raised-aisle hall, floored in the C16 and with later alterations and additions. Most of the internal structure is hidden, but two octagonal aisle-posts with moulded capitals and bases are visible.

CAVENDISH

The village is strung out along the road which runs parallel to and a little N of the Stour. Towards the W end a large green slopes up towards the church, whose tower appears above and behind a picturesque group of thatched cottages – a deservedly famous view.

ST MARY. Early C14 W tower. The SE stair-turret rises higher than the tower top and carries a triangular bell-frame and a weathervane on top of a tall pole. There is also a chimney, for the upper floor has a fireplace. The ground floor is vaulted, with a Green Man at the intersection of the heavy single-chamfered ribs. Low tower arch. The S porch is also early C14, an unusually early date for such a porch. The side windows are flanked inside by shafts with moulded capitals. Structurally the aisles are Dec, proved by the modest N doorway, but their windows are later. Those on the S side, with the motif of the four-petalled flower in their tracery, have been attributed by John Harvey to *Reginald Ely*, on account of the similarity to the windows at Burwell, Cambs., although it must be remembered that Burwell itself is a stylistic attribution, based on Ely's work at King's College, Cambridge. Money was left for the S aisle in 1471, the year of Ely's death, leading Birkin Haward to conclude that his apprentice, *John Melford* of Sudbury, is more likely to have been responsible (cf. Long Melford). The PISCINA inside the chancel looks Dec too, though the chancel was built by the will of Sir John Cavendish who died in 1381. It is in a very original idiom. Flint chequerwork base that continues up the side of the priest's doorway. This doorway has an *anse de panier* arch. The tracery of the side windows especially pretty. The E window is ordinary, but very large (seven lights). Fine Late Perp five-bay arcades with slim piers with single shafts to nave and aisle, triple shafts to the arch openings, and dainty mouldings in the diagonals. These may be the work for which money was left in 1484, and the quality again suggests the involvement of John Melford. Clerestory with three-light windows and a good cambered roof. The walls are panelled with flushwork outside. It was erected by the Smyth family. Late Perp also the N aisle windows. *William White* restored the chancel, 1865, adding the N vestry (on the foundations of a chapel discovered during the work) and chancel aisle. Boldly painted sanctuary ceiling. Nave restored 1869, not by White. Small nave N extension by the *Whitworth Co-Partnership*, 2006. – FONT. Octagonal, Perp. Panelled stem, bowl with Emblems of the Evangelists, shields and flowers. – LECTERNS. One big, of brass, with eagle, the same type as Woolpit (q.v.) and also Upwell (Norfolk), Croft (Lincs.), Chipping Camden (Glos.) and Corpus Christi College, Oxford. The other of wood, C16. – SCULPTURE. C16 Flemish relief of the Crucifixion. Alabaster, painted and gilded. Incorporated in a reredos designed by *Ninian Comper*, 1895, for the private chapel of Athelstan Riley's house, No. 2 Kensington Court, London. – STAINED GLASS. Original bits in several windows, especially the E. S aisle E and S by *Cox & Sons*, 1873. – MONUMENTS. Sir George Colt †1570. Tomb-chest with shields in cartouches. Canopied niche above with, on its bracket, two angels carrying the soul of the deceased. Is the niche earlier than the monument? – Shadrach Brise †1699 and descendants. By *John Soward*, 1810. With wreath and drapery. – Thirteen First World War wooden crosses (base of tower). A rare survival in such quantity.

UNITED REFORMED CHURCH (Congregational), Lower Street. White-brick front, one side wall white and the other red. Tall lancets.

MEMORIAL HALL, Melford Road. By *Edward Salter*, 1869. Built as a lecture hall etc. at the expense of J. S. Garrett, Cavendish's maltster and miller, and erected by his workmen. Tudor-Gothic windows with hoodmoulds and gables with elaborately carved bargeboards.

PERAMBULATION. Immediately N of the church, CHURCH FARM has a jettied gable at its S end. Opposite, the entrance to OVER HALL, built as the rectory by *W. M. Fawcett*, 1863. Red brick with two-storey gabled porch, of which the upper part is half-timbered. Two-storey bay on the garden front with half-hipped roof with gablet. In the grounds, a fragment of a substantial medieval, probably moated, house. Brick ground floor and jettied, timber-framed upper floor. N of Church Farm, NETHER HALL, C16 with exposed timbers. Two storeys, with two-storey porch. Jettied at the E end.

THE GREEN is wide and irregular in shape. On it a few trees and the WAR MEMORIAL by *Leonard Crowfoot*, 1920. Portland stone cross. Along the N side the FIVE BELLS with neat thatched roof, and then the PRIMARY SCHOOL, 1863 by *John Johnson* of Bury. Red brick. Two projecting wings with straight gables. Centre with canted porch and bellcote. s of the church, CHURCH COTTAGES, mentioned earlier. C16–C17. L-plan, the varying heights of the roofs adding to their charm. Restored by *J. E. M. MacGregor*, 1958, and again in 1971–2 following a fire. At the bottom of The Green, on the sw side, a little row including THE GREYS, jettied along the front with carved bressumer, and GREEN END, early C19 white brick. Three-bay front divided by pilasters. The hoodmoulds look like a later embellishment. The SE side, really a continuation of the High Street, is continuously built up, in an attractively varied and unpretentious way. The best building is MANOR COTTAGES, a C16 timber-framed and plastered house set back behind a small garden. Centre and jettied cross-wings of equal width, all three parts gabled. Oriel windows with mullions and transoms to the cross-wings. The centre sashed with pedimented doorcase. A panelled room in the r. cross-wing. To its r. THE GRAPE VINE, also C16, also with a pedimented doorcase, and a panel of pargetting (rose, foliage, etc.). To its l. the OLD GRAMMAR SCHOOL, founded by Rev. Thomas Grey in 1696. Timber-framed and plastered. Two storeys and attics. Three bays wide, originally with a further three to the l. Sash windows and pedimented doorcase.

The HIGH STREET is similarly varied, with no outstanding houses. On the N side, CAVENDISH HOUSE, early C19 white brick, has a distinctive rounded corner in which is set an Ionic portico *in antis*. Distinctive also the wavy cast-iron railings in front. Behind it, backing on to the churchyard, a three-storey former mill (now part of THE MALTINGS) dated 1841 with the initials of J. S. Garrett. White brick with weatherboarded lucam. Pairs of tall arched windows. On the s side, set back from the High Street, DEVONSHIRE HOUSE (former Old Rectory). C16. Exposed timbers. Gabled cross-wings, one jettied. Lower jettied rear wing. Much altered and extended, most recently (as a care home) by *Bennetts* (*Richard Bennett*), 2009–10. By contrast, also on the s side, a terrace of five C19 red brick cottages, with tall chimneys and triangular bays. Further E, on the N side, another timber-framed hall house with both cross-wings jettied, and subdivided (PEACOCKS and MELCOTT HOUSE).

BLACKLANDS HALL, Water Lane, 750 yds NE of St Mary's. Large timber-framed and plastered house, probably C16, much altered in the C19. According to *White's Directory* it was rebuilt *c.* 1850; in 1853 it was purchased by J. S. Garrett, and the style of the decorated bargeboards and arched windows suggest that *Edward Salter* remodelled it for him, and built the lodge on Melford Road (E of the Memorial Hall). Hall range with large window of five lights and two transoms. To its l. a gabled and jettied two-storey porch. Gabled cross-wing to the l. and taller cross-wing to the r. with two-storey canted bay.

CAVENDISH HALL, ¾ m. SW (Landmark Trust). Elegant white-brick house, built for Thomas Hallifax (cf. Shimpling), a London banker, in 1801–2. Two storeys. Three-bay entrance front. Tall ground-floor windows set in arched panels. Broad porch with pediment on four Ionic columns. On the W front two full-height bows. Lower service range to rear with octagonal bell-turret and weathervane. White-brick LODGE on the W side of the entrance gateway. The slate roof extends at the front to form a curved veranda on columns. Mid-C20 counterpart opposite in the same spirit.

CAVENHAM

ST ANDREW. Small. Unbuttressed W tower, formerly with a two-storey erection in front (cf. Lakenheath). The faculty for taking it down in 1729 calls it a chantry chapel (perhaps this was on the upper floor). C13 chancel, but with a good Dec PISCINA in the angle of the SE window. Angle shafts and crocketed gable. The nave windows minor Dec. Restored 1870. – FONT. A curious affair, with a crude bowl sitting on what looks like the lower part of an octagonal pier. – SCREEN. Humble, with one-light divisions, the entrance arch repaired c. 1600. – PULPIT. Jacobean. – WALL PAINTING. On the N wall, a crowned man holding a scythe, identified as St Walstan, whose shrine was at Bawburgh, near Norwich. Kneeling figures below him. Clothing and hairstyles date it to c. 1465–85. – STAINED GLASS. E window †1872, probably by *William Wailes*. Nave S by *Jones & Willis*, 1921 (war memorial). – MONUMENTS. H. S. Waddington †1864. Old-fashioned classical design by *Jackaman* of Bury. Copied by *Hanchet* of Bury for H. S. Waddington †1895.

CAVENHAM HALL. Sold three years after H. S. Waddington's death in 1895 to H. E. M. Davies, for whom *A. N. Prentice* designed a new house in a Late Renaissance style, completed in 1899, the year of Davies's death (cf. Herringswell). It was used as an exemplar by Hermann Muthesius in *Das englische Haus*, but that did not save it from demolition in 1949. The STABLE BLOCK and COACHMAN'S COTTAGE survive, as do the ENTRANCE GATE and LODGE S of the house. The latter follows the style of the main house. The stable block is also red brick, but with Baroque stonework round the archway towards the house, while the coachman's cottage is thatched with half-timbering.

Along the VILLAGE STREET a series of boxy COTTAGES, dated 1902–14. Red brick and overhanging upper storey with exposed timbers and pebbledash. VILLAGE HALL, 1902, in similar vein. All for the new owner of the Hall, the banker A. B. H. Goldschmidt, and very possibly by *P. M. Beaumont*, who was working at the church in 1912. Also the former SCHOOL, 1871 with addition of 1905, of knapped flint with white-brick dressings; and a very long range of red brick FARM BUILDINGS erected by Goldschmidt in 1902.

Cavenham Hall, stables.
Design by A. N. Prentice, *c.* 1899

PORTER'S LODGE, ½ m. SW of St Andrew's. An early C19 lodge of the old Cavenham Hall, superseded by Prentice's lodge. Knapped flint with white brick dressings. Windows set in arched panels. The end to the former drive is elliptical, with a rectangular loggia. Alterations and additions from 1989 by *Lionel Stirgess* for himself, including the woodland GARDEN. This is a Désert de Retz or Villa d'Este in miniature, with a variety of pavilions including a banqueting house, and a WATER ORGAN by *Rodney Briscoe*.

PACKHORSE BRIDGE, 300 yds SE. Probably C16. A single arch of red brick.

BLACK DITCHES. A boundary (?) ditch and bank now visible in two sections. First the S section, traceable for 1½ m. across Risby Poor's Heath to the S and extending over the parish boundary. The section along the edge of Long Plantation takes advantage of the slope above Cavenham Brook. It is lost in the arable land SE of the common, though an old hedgerow continues the line of the dyke nearly to Barrow Bottom. Secondly, the N section, 1,100 yds (1,000 metres) long, lies on Cavenham Heath and extends from just S of Oak Plantation to the River Lark. As with all the East Anglian dykes, the date and purpose of the Black Ditches are unknown, but they are in all likelihood of post-Roman date (see Introduction, p. 22). The S section covers the Icknield Way to the N and its crossing of the Lark at Lackford.

CHATTISHAM

ALL SAINTS AND ST MARGARET. Nave, chancel and W tower. The latter was reduced in height in 1770, when the roof was also lowered and most of the chancel arch removed. Restorations of 1869 and 1908 failed to reverse this damage. Otherwise the church appears to be early C14, with two Y-traceried as well as Perp windows. – POOR BOX. Octagonal, 8 in. (20 cm.) high, made of a solid piece of wood. – SCULPTURE. Elm figure of St Margaret of Antioch by *Derek Jarman* of Ipswich, 1986. – BRASS. Marie Revers †1592, with indent of her husband John. 13-in. (33-cm.) figure.

OLD RECTORY, NW of the church. C16 timber-framed house with C18 additions. Pargetted front of *c.* 1935, including porch with reused embattled timbers.

Former METHODIST CHAPEL, ¼ m. W. 1875. Red brick with white-brick dressings and bands. Closed 1954; now residential.

CHEDBURGH

ALL SAINTS. Nave and chancel of septaria and flint rubble. Nave of *c.* 1300 with renewed lancet and Y-tracery windows. Original shafting of one S window. Pretty quatrefoil W window. Chancel and S vestry by *William Dudley* of Bury, 1839; the old E window, with reticulated tracery, was largely reused. NW tower, *c.* 1840–2, of white brick. Battlemented parapet and recessed octagonal spire. It originally served also as a porch. S porch 1872, part of a restoration by *Thomas Cadge* of Hartest under the supervision of the rector, *Rev. H. K. Creed*. – STAINED GLASS. E window †1923 by *F. C. Eden*, incorporating some C15 fragments.

CHELSWORTH

ALL SAINTS. Curiously proportioned, with early C14 W tower, short, wide nave and aisle and small Dec chancel (one S window). This is the result of considerable enlargement in the C15, when the aisles, clerestory and S porch were added, but rebuilding was taken no further. Of the Perp features the best are the S porch and the S doorway. The porch is tall and has Perp side windows. Diagonal buttresses with lions as finials. Battlements, continued along S aisle. Handsome ceiling. The doorway is uncommonly ambitious. Hoodmould on angel busts. Fleurons in jambs and arch. Ogee gable and two niches l. and r. These hold statues added when the porch was converted to a vestry in 1843 by *Peter Gage* of Chelsworth. Gage also added the outer doors, to match the inner SOUTH DOORS with their tracery and border of quatrefoils, and in 1853 rebuilt the N porch. Nave arcade of three bays. Tall piers with four attached shafts and moulded arches. The C15 alterations included moving the church's outstanding feature, an early C14 TOMB RECESS now in the N aisle, possibly for Sir John de St Philibert †1334. It projects to the outside, and has here a flat flint wall with diagonal buttresses. Top frieze of ballflower and two circular pinnacles. Inside, the recess has a depressed two-centred arch under a normal two-centred arch below a gable. The arches are carried on short shafts, still with naturalistic foliage. Between the two arches is a big, somewhat squashed trefoil, and between the upper arch and the gable is a slimmer pointed trefoil. The spandrel surfaces are diapered. Buttresses l. and r., diapered also in their lower parts, and ending in finials. The main gable is crocketed and carries a finial too. The interior of the niche has a rib-vault with finely moulded ribs. The style is that of the royal court, just before the introduction of ogee forms. The buttresses prevent the adjoining small lancets (presumably reused from the earlier nave) from having evenly spaced jambs on the l. and the r. Similar lancets also in the S aisle. – FONT. C14, with cusped, crocketed little arches. – WALL PAINTING. Doom over the chancel arch, discovered and badly restored in 1849. Part of a scene depicting St George and the Dragon was also found by the tower arch, but has not survived. – FLOOR TILES. Medieval, at foot of rood stair. – STAINED GLASS. C17 fragments gathered in the S porch. – N and S aisle lancets by *R. B. King* of Ipswich, 1853. – Later C19 glass apparently by *Hardman* (E *c.* 1875, chancel S †1880), *Nathaniel Westlake* for *Lavers & Barraud* (chancel S †1862) and, less certainly, *Heaton, Butler & Bayne* (N aisle E †1897). – N aisle W by *Paul Quail*, 2000. – MONUMENTS. Elizabeth Fowke †1820. By *H. Rouw*. With draped urn. – Major General George Stracey Smith †1823. With bas-relief profile portrait. Unsigned. – Sir Robert Pocklington †1840. With draped urn and militaria. Unsigned. – Charles Peck †1917 (war memorial). *Opus sectile* panel by *Powell & Sons*, 1920.

THE GRANGE, N of the church. Picturesque timber-framed and plastered house, restored in 1926–7 by *Basil Oliver* but essentially unchanged since 1689, the date recorded in a plaster cartouche in the gable of the porch. Probably also of that date the r. cross-wing (rebuilt parlour wing), although to the rear of this remains of an earlier structure, possibly C14. Central hall, with smoke-blackened timbers and crown-post roof, of *c.* 1450, floored in the C16. Contemporary jettied service cross-wing to the l., extended in the early C16 by a parlour wing facing the church. Courtyard with an early C16 four-bay building, built with reused timbers, extended by two bays later in the C16; no doubt a bakehouse and brewhouse, possibly also maltings.

Very pretty village street with houses almost entirely on the N side facing the trees and the River Brett. Especially attractive some of the houses opposite the bridge, E of the church, e.g. Nos. 18–20 (former rectory), timber-framed with two

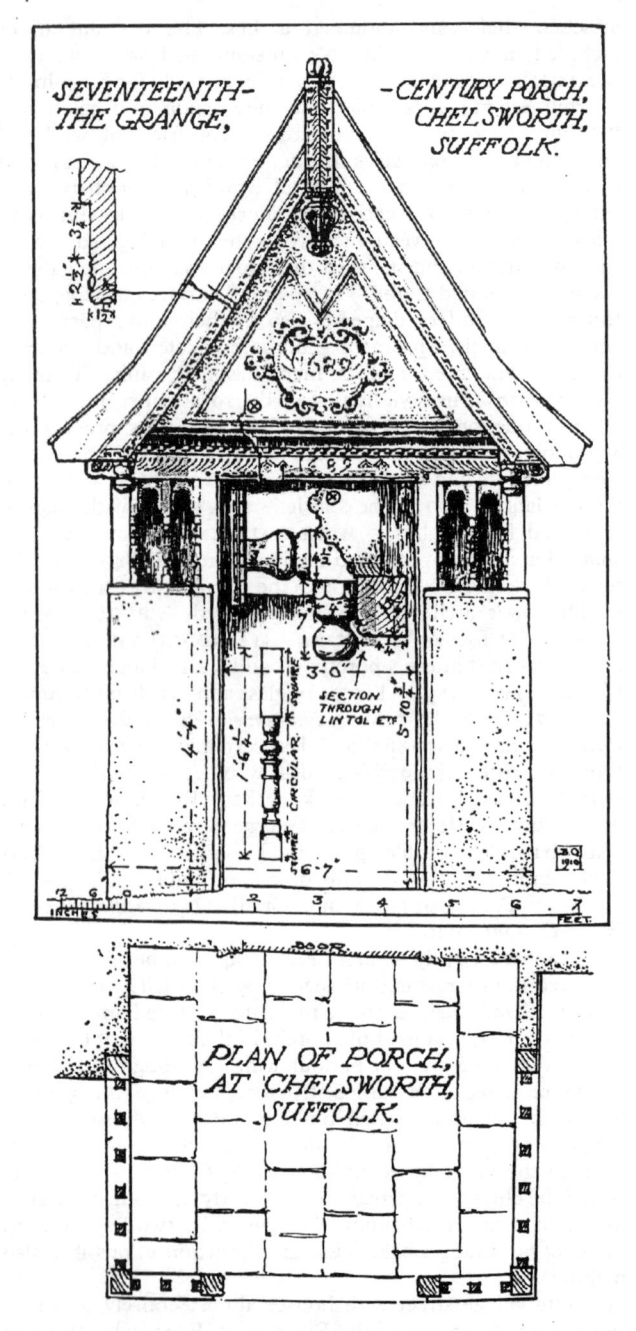

Chelsworth, The Grange, porch.
Measured drawing by Basil Oliver, 1910

projecting wings but with a Late Georgian painted brick front, and Nos. 10–12, thatched with exposed timbers and a cross-wing overhanging the street. The BRIDGE is really two short hump-backed bridges of red brick. The S half is dated 1754; the N half is probably older. Across it, BRIDGE HOUSE, its N side looking C18, but jettied along its S side.

At the entrance to the village from the W, Nos. 91–93 The Street has at one end a finely carved corner-post, suggesting a house once much larger and more important than what is there now.

CHEVINGTON

The manor of Chevington belonged to Bury Abbey from soon after the Conquest to the Reformation, and in 1716 was bought by John Hervey, 1st Earl of Bristol. In 1814 the 5th Earl closed the old route from Chevington to Bury because it crossed his park, building instead New Road W of the church.

ALL SAINTS. Of flint and septaria. Transitional nave – see the S doorway, which has a round arch, one order of shafts with thick crocket capitals, and an outer arch order of dogtooth, repeated in the outer order of the jambs. One small Norman N window also preserved, and the plain single-chamfered N doorway. The nave has one C13 window with plate tracery on the S side; another with slightly later tracery on the N side, and Perp windows otherwise. C16 brick battlements. E.E. chancel, reduced in height and length in 1697, although the straight-headed E window with five arched lights is by *Fawcett & Atkinson*, 1908–9, as part of a general restoration that included re-seating and removing a W gallery. The C13 chancel arch is very original and successful. Tall and rather narrow on moulded corbels and two completely plain side arches, no doubt to put altars in. The W tower is Perp. Money was left for it in 1444, in 1475 for a window and buttress, and in 1475–6 for bells. Base with flushwork panelling. The top stage, which is open to the sky, and the parapet with its tall crocketed pinnacles were added in 1817 by the Earl of Bristol, no doubt to act as an eyecatcher from Ickworth (q.v.). The nave roof has supplementary carved beams dated 1590 and 1638; restored by *E. F. Bisshopp*, 1886. Chancel reordered by *Keith Murray* with *Whitworth, Hall & Thomas*, 1983–4: Portland stone ALTAR with four plain columns and central cruciform shaft, on a projecting semicircular plinth, and an iron TABERNACLE on a single column to one side. – FONT. Perp, octagonal. – BENCHES. Broad with blank tracery and poppyheads, some of them figures with musical instruments. – CHEST. Oak, C14. Front panel elaborately carved with Dec tracery with pinnacles. Between the pinnacles birds and other creatures and flowers. Stile to the l. with four carved panels: a pair of monkeys; a pair of confronting birds; a wyvern or behemoth; and two bunches of grapes. There would originally have been a similar stile on the r. (cf. e.g. Alnwick, Northumberland; Brancepeth, Co. Durham; Kirkleatham, Yorkshire, North Riding; St Peter, Derby). – MONUMENT. Ann Burch †1764. Pretty marble cartouche.

CHEVINGTON HALL. Rebuilt by the 1st Earl of Bristol, *c.* 1720, reusing late C16 timbers; partly encased in brick. Behind it are the foundations of the C13–C14 palace of the abbots of Bury, and the surroundings reflect the status of the manor under their ownership. Deep water-filled ditch on three sides, about 40 ft (12 metres) wide, with inner rampart or bank between 10 and 15 ft (3–5 metres) high. On the E side, two large ponds on either side of the entrance causeway. Between the house and moat, on the W side, was an orchard, and outside the moat to the N a deer park. LODGE FARM, ½ m. NW, mid-C16 timber-framed and plastered and now standing behind a house of 1872–4, may have begun as a hunting lodge.

Former SCHOOL, S of the church. 1847, by *Thomas Farrow*. Tudor. Flint pebbles with stone dressings and red brick chimneys.

OLD RECTORY, 700 yds SW. Late Georgian white-brick front. Five bays and two storeys with parapet. Mid-C16 timber-framed range to rear.

MOAT FARM, 1½ m. SE. Early to mid-C15, with exposed timbers. Two-bay open hall with crown-post roof and smoke-blackened timbers. In-line service and parlour bays. Early C17 hall ceiling and brick chimney, with stair-tower to the rear of the chimney. RUFFINS FARM, to its S, is a late C15 Wealden-type hall house. Two-bay open hall with crown-post roof, floored in the mid C16, with two-storey jettied ends. Behind and between them RUFFINS HOUSE, built for John Worlledge, a Bury banker, *c.* 1850. Domestic Gothic. Flint with red brick dressings. Of about the same date, and ¼ m. to its N, HOLLYBUSH GREEN FARM, formerly part of the Ickworth estate. Red brick with white-brick dressings, including diapering on the chimneystacks. Hoodmoulded windows and steeply gabled dormers.

CHILTON

ST MARY (Churches Conservation Trust). Approached on foot, from Chilton Hall to the N, the church still seems to be in the middle of fields; but it is now on the edge of an industrial estate that joins it to Sudbury. Flint nave and chancel. Red brick N chapel founded by Robert Crane †1500. W tower also brick and a little later, its flint battlements and pinnacles probably C19. Moreover a brick window in the nave N wall, next to a very tall transomed straight-headed stone window also of two lights. The S windows are equally tall and transomed, but of three lights and arched, of the same design as the S aisle windows at Long Melford. Restored in stages by *George Grimwood*, 1860–75. S porch *c.* 1930. – FONT. Perp, octagonal, simple. – SCREEN. Only the dado survives. Robert Crane's bequest of 1500 included money for making the rood loft, and also for seating. – STAINED GLASS. In the tracery of the E window of the Crane Chapel two original figures, St Apollonia and St Michael. – MONUMENTS. In the Crane Chapel, George Crane †1491, and in the archway between chapel and chancel, his parents, Robert †1500 and Anne †1521. Alabaster effigies on tomb-chests, their sides with shields in lozenge and quatrefoil panels. Canopies taken down in 1868; fragment against N wall of chapel. – Sir Robert Crane †1643 with his two wives, Dorothy †1624 and Susan †1681. Commissioned from *Gerard Christmas* in 1626; the price in the contract is £50. Tripartite composition of 'Venetian window' shape. Columns of touch. Three niches with kneeling figures. In the middle Sir Robert facing outwards, in the other two his wives facing him. – Sarah Freeland †1839 and her son Rev. W. C. Freeland †1852. Standard designs by *Harding* of Ballingdon and *Keogh & Son* of Sudbury respectively.

CHILTON HALL. The seat of the Crane family from 1400 to 1643. The house, of which the principal N range was demolished at the end of the C18, is described as newly built in the will of Robert Crane IV †1591, and is shown on an estate map of 1597. It was surrounded by a moat that was crossed by a brick bridge on the S side and a smaller bridge on the E – all well preserved, apart from the superstructure of the smaller bridge. There was a gatehouse (late C15, to judge by a watercolour of *c.* 1790) on the N side of the brick bridge, and a base court on the S side, of which nothing remains. The present house may have been built as a guest range, and is presumably the building shown on the 1597 map running down the E side of the island. Its E wall drops sheer into the moat. Late C16. Red brick, with traces of painted diapering both outside and inside. The diapering inside, most unusually, is white rather than black. Two storeys with cellar and attic, with a suite of high-ceilinged chambers on the upper floor – see the evidence in the brickwork of large windows, since blocked, in the E and S walls. At the SE corner a polygonal stair-turret with battlements, and at the SW corner a polygonal clasping buttress. Between them a straight gable, although this and the top of the turret were rebuilt in the 1920s. The W wall was rebuilt at the end of the C18, with sash windows and coved eaves. At the N end a lower service range, probably mid-C16 and reduced in height in the C18. Outside the moat to the W a walled garden. Part of the wall has capping that gives the effect of crenellation.

p. 188

Chilton Hall, gateway.
Drawing by I. Johnson, *c.* 1790

Gateway with four-centred arch; also three arched recesses. Two fishponds just outside the wall.

CLARE

Clare is now an exceptionally attractive small town. In the Middle Ages it was one of considerable importance. After the Conquest the land round Clare was granted to Richard fitz Gilbert, known as Richard de Clare, the first of a rich and powerful dynasty, whose descendants became Earls of Hertford and Gloucester. By 1090 Richard or his son had built a castle, and the town became an administrative as well as a trading centre; its importance was increased by the founding of the priory in 1248. Clare enjoyed something of a golden age under Elizabeth de Burgh, Countess of Ulster, founder of Clare College, Cambridge, whose principal home was Clare Castle from 1317 until her death in 1360. From the late C13, and particularly in the C15 and C16, Clare also profited greatly from the woollen industry. Trade declined after the C17, and although Clare continued as a market town the arrival of the railway in 1865 did not attract business, but made it easier to do business elsewhere. This has helped to preserve the character that is so appealing today.

The commercial and administrative aspects of Clare have determined its shape and layout. On the N side of the town is the earthwork known as Clare Camp, while the Castle is on the S side by the river. Between the two is essentially a long market place, partly filled in over the centuries to create the separate High Street and Market Hill, with the parish church at its centre.

CHURCHES

ST PETER AND ST PAUL. Large and externally Late Perp, but the W tower is C13 and, unfortunately, a little short for the church. W doorway with two orders of shafts and a hoodmould with nailhead decoration. Lancet windows higher up. The W window of five lights is of course Perp, as is the frieze with shields and quatrefoils below it. Inside, the arcade piers (six bays) are C14 and reused in the remodelling. They are quatrefoiled and keeled. Of the C14 also the S porch with its windows with Y-tracery. It is vaulted and has carved bosses. The second bay of vaulting was half cut off when the aisle of the C14 building was widened. E of the porch is the contemporary St John's Chapel (cf. St Gregory, Sudbury, etc.), and the arch of this towards the aisle is again C14. Beneath this chapel and the porch is a vaulted bone-hole. N porch also C14 and, like the S, reduced by the widening of the aisles. The rest of the church is mostly Early Tudor, except for the chancel, which was all but rebuilt in 1617, an example of the effortless Perp survival of those years. There are few (if characteristic) differences between the C15 and C17 work. The motif of the stepped arches of the lights in the three-light windows is carried through, but simplified in the chancel. At the E end of the nave is the most easily remembered feature of the church, the two rood-stair turrets with their crocketed spirelets (cf. Lavenham). The clerestory windows are not doubled, as in so many East Anglian churches, but as all the windows of aisles and clerestory are slender and closely set, the effect has the same erectness as at Long Melford and Lavenham. The remodelling of the interior made it very airy. The C14 shafts received castellated capitals, the arches crocketed hoodmoulds. Shafts rise from the piers to the roof. Above the arches a string course with demi-figures of angels and fleurons. Chancel arch and chapel arches go with the nave. Nave roof repaired by *Robert Martin*, carpenter, 1804, according to an inscription on one of the beams. General restoration in phases, c. 1877–83, by *J. P. St Aubyn*. Tower restored by *Detmar Blow*, under the auspices of the Society for the Protection of Ancient Buildings, 1898–9. This involved replacing the inner structure of the tower with concrete and tiles, with bonds of blue Staffordshire bricks, leaving the outer walls undisturbed. A nicely lettered plaque records the work. Blow also restored the chancel, 1907–8.

FURNISHINGS. FONT. Simple, octagonal, Perp. – SCREENS. Remains of the rood screen reused at the entrance to the S chapel. Money was left for the rood loft in 1465–6, and a bequest of 1478 refers to a contract with *Thomas Goche* (*Gooch*) of Sudbury, carver. – Parclose screen at the E end of the S aisle.

Fine wide one-light divisions. Cresting with griffins, pomegranates and monograms of Maria. – STALLS. Clergy stalls of 1617, with Jacobean poppyheads. Matching choir stalls by *Blow*. – GALLERY in St John's Chapel. Jacobean with balusters. Taken down in 1883, rebuilt 1914. – ALTAR. 1946, by the *Warham Guild*, with painted riddel-posts. – COMMUNION RAIL. With twisted balusters; late C17. – DOORS. N and S doors and chancel S door with tracery and a border of foliage trail. – LECTERN. Brass, with a big eagle. The same type as at St Margaret, King's Lynn, and Redenhall (Norfolk). Late C15 or early C16. – CURIOSA. On the S porch a SUNDIAL dated 1790 with what seems a rather bossy injunction, 'Go about your business'. – GOTCH, or stoneware pitcher, given for the use of the bellringers in 1729 (cf. Hinderclay). It could hold four gallons (18 litres) of beer. – STAINED GLASS. In the E window, heraldic glass of 1617 commemorating some of those who paid for rebuilding the chancel. S aisle, by *W. G. Taylor*, 1884. N aisle, by *F. C. Eden*, 1921 (war memorial). In St John's Chapel, by *Ward & Hughes*, 1885, and *Powell & Sons*, 1905. – MONUMENTS. Elisabeth Ruggles †1776. Marble sarcophagus, built into the sill of the S chapel E window. – Mary Sayer †1823. By *C. R. Smith*. With minimal decoration. – Rev. J. C. Coleman †1868. Frame of Gothic moulding with carved flowers and emblems. By *Keogh* of Sudbury. – Prince Leopold, Duke of Albany and Earl of Clarence, †1884. Elaborate brass plaque. He was master of the local freemasons' lodge.

OUR LADY OF GOOD COUNSEL (R.C.). *See* Clare Priory.

BAPTIST CHURCH, High Street. 1859. White brick with giant pilasters and round-arched windows. Pedimented three-bay front.

UNITED REFORMED CHURCH, Nethergate Street. 1841, set well back from the street. Red brick with domestic windows on two levels. Interior remodelled by *Eade & Johns*, 1906. – MONUMENT. Ruth Kemp †1817. White-brick chest tomb. Cast-iron top with gadrooned edges.

CLARE PRIORY

Founded for Austin Friars in 1248 by Richard de Clare, 6th Earl of Gloucester and 5th Earl of Hertford. It was the earliest house in England of the order, which would eventually number thirty-four. The site chosen for it was close to the Castle (*see* below), by the River Stour, which the friars diverted ('New Cut' etc.). The original priory was rebuilt in the first half of the C14, with the new church being consecrated in 1338. The priory was dissolved in 1538 and the following year given by Henry VIII to Richard Frende, the king's trumpeter. In 1596 it was acquired by a branch of the Barnardiston family, of Kedington, and remained in their hands and those of a connected family, the Barkers, until 1953. It was then returned to the Austin Friars, by whom it is run as a parish and retreat centre.

Although a great part of the priory buildings have been demolished, the layout of the complex can be readily understood. The CHURCH stood on the N side. It was 168 ft (41.2 metres) long and had a chancel of six bays with a S chapel (St Vincent) and S vestry, a narrow central tower, and a nave of six bays with N aisle but no S aisle. The last two bays of the N aisle were a chapel (Annunciation or Lady Chapel). Of the church most of the S wall survives, including a doorway from the nave to the cloister, a nave PISCINA, the SEDILIA with curious cusped blank arches against the back wall, and the blocked doorway to St Vincent's Chapel. The monument to Joan of Acre, daughter of Edward I and mother of Elizabeth de Burgh and who died in 1307, lay between the chancel and St Vincent's Chapel, which she founded. Of the domestic buildings of the priory, the walls of the CLOISTER remain on the S side of the church. In the E wall are the entrances to the chapter house, built, it is known, by Elizabeth de Burgh between 1310 and 1314, and the dormitory stairs.

The PRIOR'S LODGING stands on the W side of the cloister. Built in the second half of the C14, it comprised a guest hall on the ground floor with prior's lodging above. It was upgraded *c.* 1500 and retained as a house after the Dissolution; there was further remodelling in the early C17, and restoration by *Detmar Blow* in 1902–3. C14 doorway with original door on the W front. Of *c.* 1500 are the low mullioned windows with arched lights. The larger mullioned-and-transomed windows are Elizabethan, as is the square bay (of stone, not flint) at the back. Inside, the main room (so-called Cellarer's Hall) has heavily carved beams of *c.* 1500 and a fireplace of the same date against the E wall. To the N a parlour (now oratory), and service rooms to the S. On the upper floor a room with fine panelling of 1604. S of the service rooms a little stone-vaulted chamber with one two-light window (single-chamfered ribs) and a door that led into the refectory. In the window, fragments of C15 STAINED GLASS. S of the vaulted chamber an irregular little courtyard with, on its W side, a covered walk with open sides but lined with diamond mullions. This seems to have been a passage to a detached kitchen, and now leads to the simple SHRINE OF OUR LADY OF GOOD COUNSEL, with relief of the Mother of Good Counsel by *Mother Concordia OSB, c.* 1998. Of the refectory, which formed the S side of the main cloister, parts of the walls are standing. In the S wall is a projection for the reader's pulpit, and at the W end of the N wall was the lavatorium, or friars' hand-washing place, whose arches can still be seen. At the E end of the refectory range a large room, added in 1908 as a billiard room, with pyramidal ogee roof.

The friars' dormitory – a unique case – lay 12 ft (3.7 metres) E of the S end of the cloister, separated from it by an irregular quadrangular courtyard. It overlapped at its S end with the infirmary, a two-storey building with reredorter (i.e. lavatories) at the E end and at right angles to it, conveniently close to the river. The upper floor of the infirmary has closely set windows in blank arches; these may have lit cubicles for scholars or novices. After the Dissolution the building was used as a barn and later as a school, and at some point lost most of its floor; it was adapted in 1953–4 by *Patrick Elliott* as a parish church (OUR LADY OF GOOD COUNSEL). This was remodelled in 2011–13 by *Inkpen Downie*, with the old church becoming the narthex for a new church on the S side, a successful juxtaposition of medieval and modern. The new parts of white brick and stone, and large windows with vertical timber screening. Altar in the SW corner.

S of the priory buildings a C16 FARMHOUSE. Timber-framed and plastered, with thatched roof. Extended in the C19 and C20.

CASTLE

Motte-and-bailey castle built, as mentioned earlier, by Richard de Clare or his son Gilbert. It is first recorded in 1090, when Gilbert granted the collegiate church of St John in the Castle to the Abbey of Bec, Normandy (the monks were moved to Stoke-by-Clare in 1124). The castle was gradually enlarged until it had, apart from the keep on its mound, two baileys, both E of the keep. On the mound stands an impressive fragment of the C13 shell-keep, with three buttresses. Much is known of the castle during its occupation by Elizabeth de Burgh in the C14. In the inner (S) bailey there were numerous timber buildings, including several chapels, two great halls, and a barn which had previously been the Great Hall, as well as the usual service buildings. The outer (N) bailey was a large garden and also housed Elizabeth's huntsmen and dogs. After Elizabeth's death in 1360 the Castle declined in importance and probably fell into ruins during the latter part of the C15. In 1865 it suffered the indignity of having the railway run through the inner bailey. Following the closure of the railway, Clare Castle Country Park was created in 1972, comprising the Castle and baileys, as well as sections of the railway and station buildings (*see* Perambulation).

PERAMBULATION

At the SW corner of the churchyard lies THE ANCIENT HOUSE. It was the priest's house and has a jettied gabled cross-wing with brackets and shafts, a window with carved arms and supporters, an original doorway, and much bold later pargetting. This includes a date, 1473, which is about right for the cross-wing; the hall range may be C14. Given to the town in 1938 and opened as a museum in 1979; restored and part converted to a holiday flat by the *Whitworth Co-Partnership*, 1999. On its E side ALMSHOUSES of 1865. Red brick with white-brick dressings and Gothic doorways. The W side of the churchyard is the upper part of the HIGH STREET, and opposite the W door of the church Nos. 20–21, with jettied front, is the former

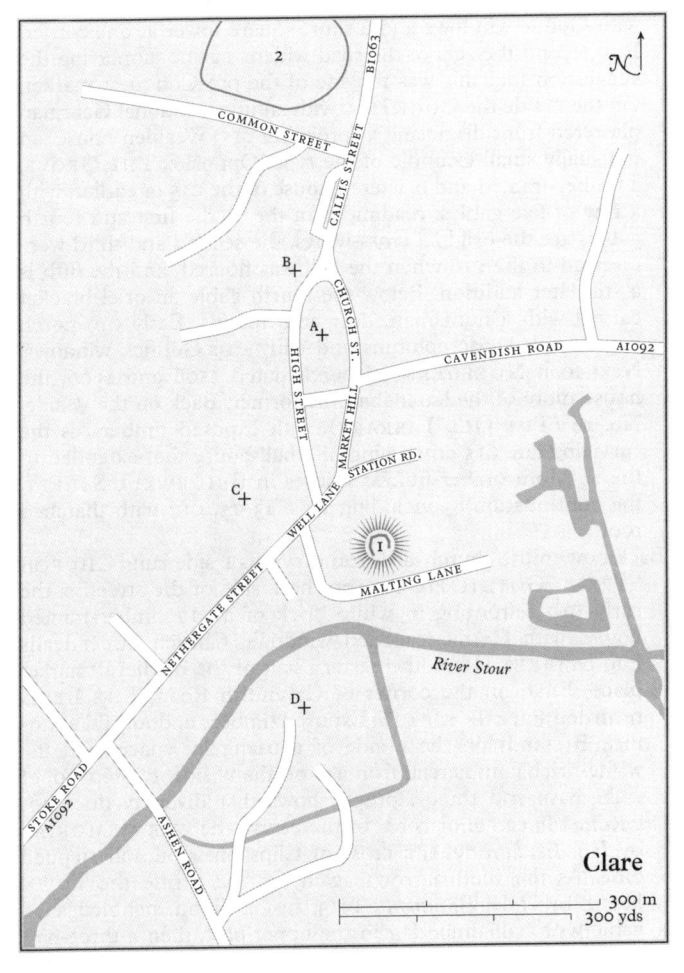

A   St Peter & St Paul
B   Baptist Church
C   United Reformed Church
D   Clare Priory

1   Castle
2   Clare Camp

guildhall. C14, with crown-post roof and smoke-blackened timbers. To its N, CHURCH FARM, also with jettied front, c. 1510. Behind it a mid-C16 DOVECOTE. Timber-framed and plastered. Hipped roof with gablets. It was moved on rollers to make way for the road to the CEMETERY (opened 1887). At the N end of the churchyard the High Street becomes CALLIS STREET, the width of the road reduced by the former SCHOOL (now community centre) by *Clark & Holland*, 1858–62. Red brick with white-brick dressings and some diapering. Gables with Gothic windows and a short square tower at one corner. But beyond the school the road widens again, supporting the suggestion that this was the site of the pre-Conquest market. On the W side the COCK INN, with an unexceptional Georgian plastered front disguising a (probably C15) Wealden house, an unusually small example of the type. Opposite, THE GROVE, a timber-framed and plastered house of the C15 or earlier, with a row of five gables: reading from the N, the first and fourth gables are the original cross-wings, the second and third were inserted in the C16 when the hall was floored, and the fifth is a still later addition. Below the fourth gable an oriel bracket carved with a huntsman, deer and hounds. Early C19 porch with Greek Doric columns and early C19 Gothick windows. Next to it NORFOLKS, its porch dated 1506 and 1906, the house more of the latter than the former. Back on the W side, No. 14 (THE OLD LIBRARY), with exposed timbers, is the surviving late C15 cross-wing of a hall house that extended to the N. More timber-framed houses in BRIDEWELL STREET, the continuation N, including Nos. 13–15, C17 with thatched roof.

Back now to the churchyard, and down its E side runs CHURCH STREET. GOTHIC HOUSE, on the E side of the street, is the early C19 refronting in white brick of a C17 timber-framed house, with Gothic-traceried windows. Church Street leads into MARKET HILL, the eastern half of the medieval market place. First, on the corner of Cavendish Road, THE BELL, recorded since the late C16. Exposed timbers of doubtful antiquity. It stands on the E side of a triangular space, and the white-brick commercial frontage on the W side, c. 1860–70, of eight bays and three storeys, shows that diversity does not necessarily create discord. In the centre the WAR MEMORIAL by F. J. Lindley, 1921, a cross of Clipsham stone on stepped base. As the road narrows again, on the E side the TOWN HALL by P. M. Beaumont, 1913, just a broad, pebbledashed gable with half-timbering in the upper part, then a three-bay, three-storey, white-brick building of the early to mid C19. But the most interesting building of Market Hill is the least conspicuous: No. 4, on the W side, on the corner of Pashlers Alley, which has a C14 stone-vaulted undercroft with a central octagonal pier. Facing back up Market Hill from the S, SADDLERS COTTAGE is part of a hall house, with a C14 cross-wing. The hall was rebuilt in the first half of the C17, reusing some old timbers, with decorative wall painting of the mid C17 in an upper room. An original two-light window among the C18 sashes. The other cross-wing of the original house is now a separate property.

STATION ROAD leads off to the E at this point and provides a change of mood. On the S side, a short terrace of three houses built of red brick in rat-trap bond, 1840, and at the end a pair of 'Model Cottages', 1849, of flint with white-brick dressings and decorative bargeboards. The former STATION (now in the country park) was built in the inner bailey of the Castle in 1865 and closed in 1967. Red brick with white-brick dressings. On the opposite platform a waiting room and, to the w, the goods shed, with crane formerly at Glemsford.

The buildings between Market Hill and the High Street are a typical late medieval island development of permanent houses and shops in place of temporary market stalls. So the w side of the lower part of the HIGH STREET would have been the w side of the original market place. The highlight here is the SWAN INN, late C16 (see the chimney), which has for its sign the bracket of a large oriel window. It is thought to have come from the Castle, and is probably early C15; the central figure of the chained swan was the badge of Henry IV, and the dating is supported by the arms, royal on the l. and Mortimer impaling de Burgh on the r. N, back towards the church, Nos. 11–13, late C15 or early C16 with exposed timbers, and No. 15 (SIGORS), C16, plastered, with cross-wing at the N end and C19 additions. S of the Swan, a good C19 shopfront with raised lettering on the fascia ('IRONMONGER. OIL & COLOURMAN') and then No. 2, formerly the Half Moon, C15 with jettied front and, at the rear, the remains of an inn gallery.

The staggered junction of roads at the s end of the High Street and Market Hill, all slightly curving, is another of the town's attractive features, offering tantalizing glimpses of what lies round the next corner. WELL LANE is the main thoroughfare at this point, with Saddlers (noted above) at the NE end, and opposite, where Well Lane turns into Market Hill, a row of painted brick houses of *c.* 1840 with the curious feature of a blocked opening with Doric columns and entablature on the canted corner. SW, past the s end of the High Street, another little widening into BROADWAY, with a C15 house that extends down MALTING LANE with elaborate old pargetting. Further down Malting Lane the character is more industrial, with the former BYFORD'S MILL (gas-powered) of 1908. Red brick with dressings of blue engineering bricks. Three storeys and five bays, extended by three bays to the s.

NETHERGATE STREET, the continuation of Well Lane after Malting Lane, contains Clare's best houses. At first narrow, it soon broadens out, with grass on both sides. On the SE side CLARENCE HOUSE, early C19 red brick with a white-brick front, three bays with distyle porch *in antis*, and then NETHERGATE HOUSE, *c.* 1500, originally with an open hall between a parlour cross-wing and in-line service range. These outer parts are jettied, with carved bressumers. Centre remodelled in the C17 (rear dormer dated 1644), with tall cross-windows. Doorway with later C17 pediment. Chimneys with star tops, rebuilt by *H. M. Cautley* as part of a general restoration, 1906–12. Staircase of *c.* 1644 with turned balusters and carved newels; another of the late C17. Beyond Nethergate House the WHITE HOUSE, C18 timber-framed and plastered, seven bays with pedimented doorcase.

On the NW side, just past the entrance to the United Reformed church (*see* p. 190), STONEHALL, a plaque showing it to be the almost complete rebuilding in 1931 of a hall recorded in 1309, but the oldest surviving parts are C16. Then a very varied and pretty row of timber-framed houses leading up to the RED HOUSE, with an C18 red brick front of five bays and two storeys. Doorcase with open pediment. Beyond it, NETHERIDGE, C15, with two later wings set back from the street, one with extravagant C17-style pargetting. Next, THE OLD COURT, built as the Police Station and Court House by *William Steggles Jun.*, 1847–8. White-brick front with giant pilasters, red brick behind. Three bays with pedimented centre and Doric portico. Further broad bay to the l. It fits perfectly into the otherwise residential street. Beside it a lane leads up to two large C16 barns, one thatched, both now converted to houses, alongside two houses by *Stephen Mattick* in the Suffolk vernacular, 1987–8: one red brick, the other pargetted.

After the lane the grandest house of the street, CLIFTONS. The plastered front is C18, as symmetrical as a C16 timber-framed house can be made to be while retaining its richly decorated cluster of four chimneys. Four-bay centre, its doorway with open pediment squeezed in near the middle, and low pavilions l. and r. linked to the centre by single-storey wings with round-arched doorways. Jacobean panelling in a ground-floor room and fragment of Tudor wall painting (imitation textile) in another. An C18 owner of Cliftons removed the houses opposite, but then on the corner of Ashen Road is THORNTON HOUSE, C16 with jettied front and early C19 Gothic windows like triple lancets. STOKE ROAD is the continuation of Nethergate Street sw of Ashen Road, with two good houses on the SE side, both early C16 and both jettied along the front: STOUR HOUSE, thatched, has a carved bressumer, and RIVERSIDE has the curious peculiarity of the panels between the posts being plastered so as to appear rusticated.

A short distance along ASHEN ROAD, a BRIDGE over the Stour. Cast iron, dated 1813. By *William Cubitt*, made by *Ransome & Son* (cf. Brent Eleigh). Three elliptical arches with spans of 11 ft, 13 ft 6 in. and 11 ft (3.35 metres, 4.11 metres and 3.35 metres). Seven ribs, with an additional rib on the w face, and parapet railings. Short brick walls at either end with cast-iron cappings by *Ward & Silver* – an addition, as the foundry was not established until 1843.

OLD CHAPEL COTTAGE, about ¾ m. N of the church. A late C12 chapel, converted to a dwelling at the Reformation; it was dedicated to St Mary Magdalene, and may have been a leper chapel (sometimes identified with Wentford Chapel). In the N wall an original doorway. One order of (missing) shafts with capitals with curly decoration and a round arch. This must have had a tympanum, but the tympanum was in the C13 or C14 opened into a pointed chamfered arch. Remains of Norman windows in the E gable.

CHILTON STREET, 1¼ m NW, is a hamlet of Clare. Around HOME FARM, a little group of disused C19 industrial buildings: former MALTINGS (now a house), with square kiln of red brick with slate roof; large weatherboarded STEAM MILL, with octagonal red-and-white-brick chimney; and the red brick shell of a TOWER MILL. CHILTON HALL, 250 yds W of Home Farm, is timber-framed and plastered, probably C16, but with an C18 exterior. Good early C19(?) wrought-iron gates with cast-iron piers.

CLARE CAMP, at the N end of the town, behind the W side of Bridewell Street. D-shaped enclosure of about 12 acres (5 ha), surrounded by a double bank and ditch, measuring internally about 210 yds by 165 yds (190 metres by 150 metres). The N side is the most complete, with ramparts and counterscarps of about 10–15 ft (3–5 metres). The S and E sides are much depleted owing to building and gardens; two entrances, possibly original, lie N and S. Suggested but not yet proved to be Iron Age in date. It was called Erbury ('earth fortification') in the Middle Ages and was certainly then used as an agricultural and administrative centre for the manor of Clare-cum-Chilton. Only slight earthwork traces survive of the many buildings recorded on the site in the C13 and C14, but a geophysical survey in the 1990s confirmed their presence.

COCKFIELD

9050

A fragmented village, with a number of small settlements clustered round greens, of which CROSS GREEN, ¾ m. NW of the church, is the most generally attractive. The church, Church Cottage, Church Farm and the school form a little group of their own.

ST PETER. Quite big. Dec W tower with flushwork chequer pattern on the buttresses. The top was adapted for use as an observatory by Rev. William Ludlam, rector 1767–88; the scars of the openings he cut in the walls can still be seen. Dec N aisle. Early C14 chancel: see the outlines of the windows outside, the buttresses with ogee-headed niches, the PISCINA, and the splendid if grossly over-restored Easter sepulchre. Niche with three stepped gables with blank quatrefoils. Cusped and sub-cusped arches with crockets. Angle buttresses. Hardly any ogee forms yet (cf. e.g. Edmund Crouchback, Westminster Abbey). S porch with a front with flushwork panelling. It may be the 'vestibulum' for which money was bequeathed in 1468. Three niches round the entrance. Doorway with fleurons and shields. Battlemented parapet. Side windows of 1878–80 by *W. M. Fawcett*, who restored the church in stages 1869–80. Perp S aisle with elaborate battlements and fine roof with carved beams. Carved dates record repairs in 1643 and 1795. Perp clerestory. John Hersent left money for two of the clerestory windows in 1509. Tall Perp chancel windows. Rood-loft stair, red brick on the outside, built with the help of a bequest of 1483. Two-storey N vestry also C15. Base of tower reordered with organ gallery by *Philip Orchard* (*Whitworth Co-Partnership*), 2007. – FONTS. A plain octagonal font of the C14, and a C14-style font of 1874–5 by *Elizabeth Farrow* to *Fawcett*'s design. – AUMBRY. On W wall of N aisle, *c.* 1200. Trefoil arch with ogee top and trails of foliage carved in the spandrels. Against the column next to it the pillar of a PILLAR PISCINA. – PULPIT. Jacobean, with arches carved with leaf patterns, and deep book-rest. The pedestal is C15. – STALLS. Not much survives, but it includes ends with tracery and poppyheads and some minor MISERICORDS. – COMMUNION RAIL. With twisted balusters; late C17. Rearranged in 1867; four of the balusters appear to have been reused for the LECTERN of 1871 by *Rattee & Kett*, designed by *Fawcett*. – STAINED GLASS. Various medieval fragments, including four C14–C15 heads, rearranged by *Constable* of Cambridge during Fawcett's restoration. E window by *Kempe*, 1889–90. N aisle E by *Rosemary Everett*, made by *Lowndes & Drury*, 1963–4. – MONUMENTS. James Harvey †1723 while an undergraduate at Clare College, Cambridge. By *N. Royce* of Bury. It is his only recorded work, but an accomplished one. Standing wall monument. Coupled Corinthian columns against coupled Corinthian pilasters. Pediment. Bust on short black sarcophagus. – Rev. George Belgrave †1831. Plain tablet by *de Carle*.

Church Cottage and Church Farm form a very pretty approach to the church from the S. CHURCH COTTAGE was the church house, i.e. a forerunner of the village hall, used for parish festivals and holidays, especially after the Act of 1571 forbade the use of the church itself for feasting. Timber-framed, C15, plastered on the S side but with exposed timbers on the N, towards the church, with brick-nogging. It is also jettied along most of this front. One original doorway. CHURCH FARM is timber-framed and plastered, C16, jettied to the front. To their S the PRIMARY SCHOOL by *William Mills* of Long Melford, *c.* 1856. Red brick with white-brick and stone dressings. Much altered and extended, especially in 1975–6, with the addition of VILLAGE HALL.

CONGREGATIONAL CHURCH, ¾ m. ENE. Red brick with white-brick dressings and decorative bargeboards. 1841, considerably enlarged in 1860, with schoolroom of 1867.

At PARSONAGE GREEN, ½ m. E, the OLD RECTORY. Late Georgian white brick. Three-bay N front, the ground-floor windows with semicircular heads in semicircular recesses. Doorway with open pediment. Partly moated.

At GREAT GREEN, 1 m. NE, GREAT GREEN HOUSE on the S side, C16, has jettied cross-wings, one with exposed timbers, and a large chimneystack with four octagonal shafts. To its E, in GREEN LANE, three pairs of houses for Cosford Rural

District Council by *Raymond Erith, c.* 1949–51. Red brick, with shallow brick porches. Cf. Hitcham, Polstead.
WINDMILL, ¾ m. S. Tower mill (tower only) of 1891. Tarred brick.

COLDHAM HALL
¾ m. WSW of Stanningfield

8050

Built in 1574 by Robert Rookwood (or Rokewood) †1600. The family had held the manor of Stanningfield since 1359 and Coldham Hall since 1388, occupying a house closer to Stanningfield church. At the Reformation they remained Roman Catholic and one of Robert's sons, Ambrose, was executed for his part in the Gunpowder Plot. Coldham Hall became a focus for Roman Catholic worship, with successive chapels, and after the family (by then Rokewode Gage) sold the estate to Richard Holt-Lomax in 1869 a new church was built in Lawshall (q.v.).

The house is H-plan, of red brick with some diapering. The windows are mullioned and transomed, of rendered brick. Many of them have low pediments. The front faces NW and neither the centre nor the wings are symmetrical. The front walls of the wings are treated quite differently, and the SW part of the centre is dominated by the hall's big bay window with four transoms. The three-storey porch is somewhat barbarically detailed, with two orders of fluted pilasters tapering so strongly that they seem almost obelisks. Pediments sit between rather than on the pilasters, and seem detached from the doorway and window.

(The porch leads into the double-height hall which has its big original fireplace – see the chimney-breast on the E side. Inside on the ground floor in the NW wing a room with a fireplace and a good plaster ceiling. The beams are exposed, and each panel has a large oblong principal motif. Above the hall all along the house runs a long gallery. Off it the former CHAPEL, with pretty Gothick decoration of the 1770s. It was superseded by a free-standing chapel E of the house, 1794 (EMANCIPATION CHAPEL). Part red brick, part flint with red brick dressings. Three-light transomed stone windows with round-arched tops. Its interior also Gothick.)

Later additions include STABLES etc. to the E, 1871, and the pair of LODGES at the main entrance from the NW, 1872. On one of the outbuildings a very pretty, tall clock turret and cupola, dated 1851, with clock by *W. N. Last* of Bury St Edmunds. From Hardwick House (*see* p. 173), 1927.

DOVECOTE, 140 yds S. Early C19, circular. Red brick with white-brick dressings. The first stage is battered and has a pedimented entrance. Above that the walls are vertical with arched windows, five false and one real. Below the eaves an arcade of white bricks, resembling machicolations, three of the arches left open as flight holes. Conical tiled roof. Inside, twenty-two tiers of nest boxes, thirty-seven to each tier, and incomplete potence.

COMBS

ST MARY. Now closer to Stowmarket than it is to the village. Quite a big church. Built up against one side of the churchyard, so the big Dec W tower has N and S archways and no W entrance. The archways have three continuous chamfers. Flushwork at the base only. The bell-openings are Perp. Dec chancel. E window with plain intersected tracery, but two ogee-arched niches to l. and r. of it inside. The SW and NW windows treated as lowsides with a transom. On the S side also a circular window, not quatrefoiled but with a four-petal motif. SEDILIA and PISCINA are mostly the result of restoration (see below) but were clearly Dec. Pretty Dec N doorway with two thin shafts with foliage capitals and hoodmould on headstops. Perp S aisle windows (except for the W window which is early C14). Wills of 1447 and 1449 left money for the making of an aisle; one of 1452 'to the making of a new window in the aisle of the Holy Trinity'; and another of 1472 towards the making of the E window of the S aisle. Perp N aisle windows, Perp clerestory. A stone string course connects them horizontally. Brick S porch, described as new in a will of 1531; crowstepped gable and polygonal corner turrets that want pinnacles. Its entrance was altered in the late C17. Six-bay arcade with octagonal piers and double-chamfered arches. Restoration by *H. J. Green*, 1885–6, including new chancel roof and chancel arch, and re-seating; also the uncovering and restoration of the chancel niches and sedilia. Reordering of W end, with screens in the aisles, by *Peter Cleverly*, 1995. – FONT. Probably C14. Stem with ogee-arched panels. On the bowl knobbly foliage in fields variously detailed. – ROOD SCREEN. Only the dado. Money was left towards the rood beam in a will of 1462, and for rood stairs in 1472. – PARCLOSE SCREENS. At E ends of N and S aisles. – PULPIT. Jacobean, with scrolly book-rests. – BENCHES. With traceried ends, poppyheads, and men, beasts and birds on the arms. Much restored in 1885–6. – STAINED GLASS. In several S windows a good deal of C14 and C15 glass, assembled in 1952 by *Joan Howson*. Parts from a life of St Margaret, also from the Seven Works of Mercy and from a Tree of Jesse. – MONUMENT. Hon. & Rev. Richard Ashburnham †1882. Gothic. By *Heathcote*, London.

COMBS HALL stood to the S of the church. It was rebuilt in 1724 by Orlando Bridgeman, who may have been his own architect. It was of two storeys and seventeen bays, the façade stepping forward in three stages with a three-bay pedimented centre. At the W end were stables at right angles. Bridgeman died in 1731 and the house was demolished in 1775–6 (cf. Badley Hall). The present house on the site was a small service range. Bridgeman laid out elaborate and extensive GARDENS which surrounded the churchyard on three sides, including a rectangular lake or basin and an ornamental canal. The earthworks associated with these gardens are clearly visible.

The VILLAGE is ½ m. SW of the church. The best of the older houses is THE OLD HALL, with a hall range of the late C14 or early C15, and C16 gabled cross-wing. The hall has a crown-post roof and was floored in the C16. Carved gable tie-beam and bargeboards on the cross-wing.

The TANNERY, S of the Old Hall, was established in 1711; now a business park. The main range along the road was built as a house for Lankester Webb, c. 1855. White brick with stone dressings. Two storeys, with six bays along the road. Return of four bays, with canted bay and pedimented doorway. The rear range is timber-framed, C17 or C18. Three early industrial buildings survive, probably all from the first half of the C19, the largest the BARK BARN. Clay-lump walls. Queenpost roof of unusually broad span. Next to it the LEATHER WAREHOUSE or drying shed. Red brick ground floor and two weatherboarded storeys, the weatherboarding louvred for ventilation. Then the GLOVERS' LEATHER WAREHOUSE. Red brick. Three storeys, with continuous glazing under the eaves. Across the road a large park-like field and N of that a MODEL FARM (now converted to housing) built by Webb in 1867. A plaque records that it was designed by *J. O. Fraser*, architect *O. Andrews*, builders *Andrews & Son*. Red brick with white-brick dressings. Tall central gateway with tall timber lantern. Five gables to either side, the outer two representing long ranges running back with a large barn across the far end.

Former BOARD SCHOOL, E of the model farm. By *Henry Lovegrove*, 1875–6. White brick, with red brick bands and red and white voussoirs. A restless composition, with a variety of pitched, hipped and half-hipped roofs.

OLD RECTORY, 1 m. SW of the church. Mostly of 1836 by *Ephraim Rednall*. Two storeys. Pedimented five-bay front.

CONEY WESTON

ST MARY. Outside the village. Nave and chancel, both Dec, the nave thatched. The W tower fell in 1690; blocked square-headed windows in W wall of about that date. Evidence also of a demolished two-bay N chancel chapel. The nave S wall and the S porch have knapped flint walls, and the porch has battlements with chequered flushwork. In the outside chancel S wall a low tomb recess. Inside there are two cusped niches to the l. of the chancel arch, and two not quite so tall ones to its r. Angle PISCINA in the chancel with angle shaft and a gable starting with vertical pieces. Remains of a remarkably large niche in the corner between the piscina and the E window. Restoration by *Satchell & Edwards*, 1884–6, including re-seating; chancel re-roofed 1891. – FONT. Octagonal, Dec. With a number of tracery motifs of the date and also a panel with twelve roses and two with big square leaves. – ALTAR. 1909. Six panels on the front reused from the medieval chancel screen, with repainted figures of saints. Two new panels on each of the sides. – TILES. A few medieval tiles in the NW corner of the nave, originally in the chancel. – WALL PAINTINGS. Indistinct remains on nave N wall. – PAINTING. Two angels, on zinc, in niches to r. of chancel arch. By *Eliza Edwards* (cf. Barningham), 1886. – MONUMENT. Maurice Dreyer †1786. White and grey marble, with obelisk.

Former PRIMITIVE METHODIST CHAPEL, 1 m. SW, i.e. more in the middle of the village. 1862. Red brick with white-brick dressings. Gabled front with arched entrance and two arched windows.

CONEY WESTON HALL. ½ m. WSW. Painted brick. Two storeys. The earliest parts are C17. Remodelled and enlarged *c.* 1805, and further enlarged 1891. Principal (E) front of seven bays with three-bay pedimented centre divided by pilasters. Roof of black glazed pantiles. Kitchen garden to NW with crinkle-crankle wall.

THE OLD PARSONAGE, The Street. Timber-framed and plastered, with thatched roof. Two storeys and attics. On the three dormers, the date 1713 and initials of Rev. Maurice Alexander †1733/4.

COPDOCK

The village lies along what was once the main road, partly Roman, from London to Ipswich and Stowmarket, with the hall and church a little off the road to the E.

ST PETER. Quite an impressive church with its aisleless nave, its tall three-light Perp windows, its various doorways – their jambs and arches decorated with fleurons, crowns, and shields – its N transept separated from the nave by a tall arch, again decorated with shields, and its W tower with flushwork panelling on the diagonal buttresses. Money was left for the fabric of the W entrance in 1478. Roofs restored 1901. General restoration by *Brown & Burgess*, 1909, including reordering of chancel, new N vestry and conversion of old vestry to organ chamber. – FONT. Octagonal, Perp, but heavily restored and re-cut. – REREDOS. 1853. Caen stone, including a relief panel of the Last Supper. – BENCHES of the same date. With poppyheads and low doors. – WEST GALLERY. 1909, incorporating some Elizabethan panels with figures and ornament (e.g. Edward VI on horseback). – DOOR. N door with tracery. – STAINED GLASS. Chancel N by *H. Hughes*, 1874. – MONUMENTS. Rev. Arnald de Grey †1889. Large white marble slab, like a ledger stone, with a very elaborate floriated cross and lettering in relief. – War memorial by *H. M. Cautley*, 1920. – In churchyard, headstone of John Marven †1789, a noted bell-ringer. With relief of a reclining female, one elbow resting on a bell, based on a design by *Francesco Bartolozzi* for the Ancient Society of College Youths.

COPDOCK HALL, W of the church, has a spectacular late C16 red brick BARN of ten bays. Stepped gables at the ends. Diapering with blue headers. Three tiers of ventilation slits arranged chessboard-wise. C17 gabled midstrey on the W side. The hall itself, timber-framed and plastered, seems to date to the C17.

PRIMARY SCHOOL. By *Barnes & Bisshopp*, 1874–5. Red brick. With a large three-light window set in what looks like a chimney-breast but turns into a small square bell-turret.

FELCOURT, 600 yds SW. Built as the rectory for the Hon. and Rev. Frederick de Grey, 1858, by *E. B. Lamb*. Red brick. Chunky detailing, including windows with heavy stone frames and lights with depressed arched heads. Three storeys. Steeply pitched roofs. L-plan. Asymmetric entrance front (SW) with a split gable. The r. half is set back, with a projection for the back stairs. On the l. the gable continues downwards, with a step at each storey, to include the porch against the return wall. On the NW front the r. slope of the gable continues downwards in a similar way over the window of the main stairs. Single-storey service range extending SW, ending in a kitchen with pyramidal roof and lantern (*à la* Abbot's Kitchen, Glastonbury, but square rather than octagonal).

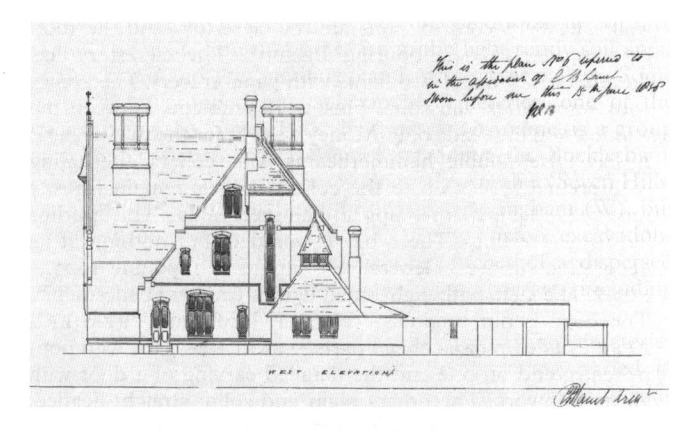

Copdock, Felcourt (former rectory).
Design by E. B. Lamb, 1858

MILL, 500 yds NNE. Late C19 watermill of red brick with white-brick dressings. The adjacent house is timber-framed and plastered, late C15 or early C16. Two-bay, two-storey block with jettied front and crown-post roof. Lower range to the r.

COTTON

ST ANDREW. The startling feature of the church is the W tower. Its W side is opened by a tall arch taking all the height which is usually occupied by doorway and window (cf. Wetheringsett (E)). At its E, however, there is no doorway, only a fine Dec three-light window, so that it serves only as quite a spectacular ringing chamber. The church is almost entirely Dec. Chancel with an original tracery design. Five lights, above them four rounded triangles, forming the main ogee arches, and above them one large reticulation unit. The side windows of the chancel are segment-headed. To the l. and r. of the E window niches outside. Above them pinnacles. Inside, ogee-arched PISCINA and SEDILIA. Of the sedilia the arches of the two seats in front of the window are broken off. Aisles with segment-headed two-light windows, either with one rounded triangle or with reticulation motifs treated very originally. The latter type of window also in the S porch. Its front has flushwork decoration. Porch entrance with leaf capitals. Delightful S doorway with three orders of shafts all with leaf capitals. In the arch one order closely carved with leaves. The hoodmould also treated in this way. It rests on the l. on a big lizard. There is exceptionally much of the original colour preserved. The five-bay aisle arcades have the typical early C14 piers: quatrefoil with fine diagonal spurs. The arch is moulded in two waves. Ogee-arched recess in the N aisle N wall. The Perp contributions are the clerestory and the roof, both similar to neighbouring Bacton's. The clerestory has doubled windows, of two lights with panel tracery. The arches with some brick voussoirs. Flushwork emblems between the windows on the S side only. Money was left for the roof in 1471. It has false double hammerbeams with collars alternating with arched braces up to the collars. Angels remain (mostly renewed) against the upper hammerbeams. The purlins have fine crestings. The E bay is boarded, but nothing of its decoration survives. General restorations in 1890 and 1903. – FONT. The stem with eight small figures (monks? bedesmen?). The bowl is not original. – PULPIT. Jacobean. – READER'S DESK. Made up of Jacobean parts. – BENCHES. One with poppyheads, and on one end the detailed carving of a door with all its ironwork. The others plain and solid, straight-headed. Money was left for seating in 1477. – COMMUNION RAIL. With turned balusters; C17. – DOORS. The S door with tracery of reticulation motifs. – The door to the tower stairs is all iron-faced (cf. Westhorpe). – STAINED GLASS. Fragments in the aisles and in the N clerestory.

Former NATIONAL SCHOOL, NE of the church. By *Alfred Hubert*, 1874–5, enlarged by *I. A. Clarke*, 1897. Red brick with black-and-white-brick decoration.

METHODIST CHURCH, ½ m. WNW. 1877 by *Cattermole & Eade*. A busy little building, of red brick with white-brick dressings, nicely detailed. Lancets and plate tracery.

HEMPNALL'S HALL, ¾ m. NE. Timber-framed and plastered house of the late C16, with a small C18 rear wing and unobtrusive early C21 extension at the E end. At the W end a C16 red brick crowstepped gable with integral chimneystack and blocked windows. Medieval moat crossed by an early C18 red brick bridge of one arch on the N side. By the moat on the S side a red brick PRIVY with original seating; probably C19.

PARK FARM COTTAGE, ¾ m. NNE. Timber-framed and plastered, with a handsome oval panel over the door. It contains flowers, initials and the date 1691.

COWLINGE 7050

ST MARGARET. Austere red brick tower built by Francis Dickins in 1733. Good classical inscription tablet with swan-neck pediment on the nave W wall inside, behind the W gallery. The medieval church incorporates a good deal of septaria and brick. It dates from the early C14. Arcade of octagonal piers with broadly moulded arches. Extensive medieval GRAFFITI on the pillars, including a ship. Aisle windows with nice flowing tracery (motif of four-petalled flowers). Simple Perp N porch, clerestory with quatrefoil windows (at least the first N and S from the W; the others Perp), Perp E window. Crown-post roofs in nave and chancel, the former original, the latter part of the restoration by *Detmar Blow*, 1913–14. – FONT. Perp, octagonal. Quatrefoils on the bowl, stem with traceried panels. – SCREENS. Rood screen Perp. Simple, with one-light divisions. The original gates are preserved. Parclose screen of crude workmanship. – BENCHES. At W end of N aisle, very plain tiered seating, but later than the seats 'for the Use of the Keeper of the Correction House' referred to in the inscription panel of 1618 above them. – WALL PAINTINGS. Weighing of Souls, above the chancel arch. An unusual representation. Large St Michael on the r. with feathered body, large Virgin on the l. reaching across with a long rod to tip the balance. In S aisle, upper part of the figure of a saint. – ROYAL ARMS. 1731. A fine set, on canvas, the frame painted with columns and other decoration (W gallery). – STAINED GLASS. S aisle E by *Christopher Webb*, 1931. A colourful ship, representing the Christian church. – MONUMENTS. Brass of Robert Higham †1571 and wife Margaret †1599. 18½-in. (47-cm.) figures, with

Cowlinge, Branches Park.
Lithograph, *c.* 1820

five sons and five daughters. – Francis Dickins †1747, signed by *Peter Scheemakers*. Base and reredos background with open pediment on brackets. Seated figures of Dickins and his wife in Roman dress l. and r. of an urn on a tall pedestal. White marble and grey-veined white marble. Noble, if cool. – Henry Usborne †1840. By *T. Denman*. Classical, with upturned torches. Also the smaller tablet to his daughter Elizabeth †1837.

BRANCHES PARK. The house, built by Francis Dickins *c.* 1720, was demolished in 1957. Wings had been added later in the C18, with further considerable additions of 1904–8 by *G. Hornblower* for G. A. Tonge. The COACH HOUSE or stables of *c.* 1720 remains W of the site. Red brick. Two storeys. Projecting wings with hipped roofs. Pedimented centre with clock turret and domed octagonal cupola. W of this a lozenge-shaped walled garden. *Capability Brown* landscaped the park for Ambrose Dickins in 1763–5. N and S LODGES probably by Hornblower. Red brick and tile-hanging.

The VILLAGE is mainly clustered around the S entrance to Branches Park. Opposite, PARSONAGE FARMHOUSE is C16 with central hall and cross-wings, one jettied. S, in Queen Street, the OLD VICARAGE by *Percy Holland & Son*, 1884. Red brick, with pointed relieving arches. Opposite it, OLD COLLEGE HOUSE, former 'College School' of 1865–7 by *Edward Dru Drury*. Red brick with stone dressings. Two-storey cross-wings at each end and Gothic centre with bell-turret.

KILN COTTAGE, ¾ m. S of the church. C17 timber-framed and weatherboarded building with thatched roof. At one end a square C18 kiln, now rendered, with pyramidal slate roof.

HIGHPOINT PRISON. *See* Stradishall.

CREETING ST MARY

Creeting St Mary was formerly three parishes, with Creeting St Peter (*see* below), also known as West Creeting, making a fourth. The other two churches have disappeared.

ST MARY. S doorway Norman, with one order of colonnettes, scalloped capitals, and one arch with a band of scallop or lunette forms. W tower in its lower parts C14, heavily buttressed at the corners in C18 red brick. C15 S porch with a front panelled with flushwork. A niche above the entrance with Bath stone SCULPTURE of the Virgin and Child by *John A. Green* of Burstall, 1961. Restoration by *C. J. Kohler*, including new N aisle (to replace transept of 1801, built to compensate for the loss of All Saints), organ chamber and vestry, 1884; upper part of tower rebuilt 1887. – FONT. Octagonal, with four lions against the stem, and four angels and the four Emblems of the Evangelists against the bowl. – PANELLING in chancel by *A. G. Humphry*, 1911. – STAINED GLASS. Six windows of 1886–1931 by *Kempe* (some signed with his wheat sheaf) and *C. E. Kempe & Co.* (with the later wheat sheaf and tower). The contrasting N aisle window comes as something of a relief: 1958 by *Brian Thomas*, made by *Powell & Sons*. Colourful and lively. – On the N side of the churchyard, former SCHOOLROOM of 1837. White brick. Arched doorway and windows with nice Gothick cast-iron tracery.

ALL SAINTS stood only a few yards SW of St Mary's; it was demolished following storm damage in 1800.* ST OLAVE, about ¾ m. NE, fell out of use in the C16 and had disappeared by the mid C17. Both St Mary and St Olave were small alien priories of Benedictine monks.

CREETING HOUSE, 125 yds SE. Built as the rectory by *Henry Woodyer* for his brother-in-law, Rev. William Eliot, 1862–3. Flint, with red brick dressings and stone windows, in a very attractive version of Domestic Gothic. Two storeys and attics. Ten bedrooms. The previous rectory (technically All Saints') had burnt down, but the low wing at the NW corner is a remnant.

PRIMARY SCHOOL, 250 yds NE. 1871 by *Henry Godfrey* of Needham Market. Red brick with white-brick dressings. Sympathetic addition of 1995.

ALL SAINTS HALL, 2/3 yds NNW. Mid-C16, timber-framed and plastered, with three C17 extensions, including a parlour block. Inside this remains of a fine scheme of painted decoration, including grotesque ornament with candelabra motif. Taxed on seventeen hearths in 1674.

At ALDER CARR FARM, on the outskirts of Needham Market nearly 1 m. SSW, a two-storey black-weatherboarded building, now a farm shop. Built in 1796 as the buck of a post mill,

---

*FONT now in Holy Trinity, Stowupland (q.v.).

moved in 1860 and converted to a dovecote, and moved a short distance to its present site in 1996. Tiled hipped roof with gablets. This is the last reused post mill body on the ground to survive in the country.

CREETING LOCK and BRIDGE, 1½ m. SE. *See* Barking, p. 87.

CREETING ST PETER

ST PETER. The nave N doorway minimum Norman. Early C14 W tower. The W doorway has two continuous chamfers. Nave and chancel with Dec and Perp windows, completely unrestored, it seems. A restoration of 1861, by *Henry Godfrey* of Needham Market, was largely confined to the interior, including the W gallery and nave roof. C19 N vestry rebuilt on a slightly larger scale in 1999. – FONT. Octagonal. Four lions against the stem. Demi-figures of angels supporting the bowl. Four angels with shields round the bowl, and panels with square interlace, a rose, a heart set in foliage, and a flower or pomegranate set in a wreath. – PULPIT. Perp, with two-light ogee-arched panels. Seven-sided. – WALL PAINTING. Remains of a large St Christopher. C15. Above the saint's head a long inscribed scroll, and the upper part of a border. Also a small figure, now separate. – STAINED GLASS. E window, and presumably also the other chancel windows, by *Rev. Charles Rawlins*, 1847; thought by Birkin Haward to have been made by *John King* of Ipswich. Rawlins was curate of Creeting St Mary, where he designed chancel windows installed in 1846 but later replaced.

OLD RECTORY, E of the church. 1826 by *John Whiting* for Edward Paske, rector 1818–85. White brick. Two-storey, three-bay front facing the church, with a further two bays set back. Doric porch. Stable block.

ROYDON HALL, ½ m. NNE. Mid to late C16 timber-framed and plastered house, Georgianized externally. In front of it a ten-bay weatherboarded BARN, floored at one end to provide stabling and loft. What makes it unusual is the roof, with two tiers of queenposts – necessitated by the broad span of about 28 ft (8.5 metres).

CULFORD

Culford is (or was) an estate village, its houses spread out along the turnpike road of 1804. On the W side of the road is Culford Hall, with the parish church in its grounds. The estate descended from the Bacons to the Cornwallis family, from whom it was bought in 1824 by Richard Benyon de Beauvoir. In 1839 he presented the estate for life to his nephew, Rev. Edward Richard Benyon, who had been instituted as rector earlier that year (having been curate of Wordwell since 1826); from then until his death in 1883 he was a squarson on a grand scale, responsible for a considerable amount of building not just in Culford but in the adjoining villages of Ingham, Timworth, West Stow and Wordwell. After E. R. Benyon's death the estate was sold to the 5th Earl Cadogan, who was an equally active builder, but after he died in 1933 the 11,000-acre estate was broken up. The Hall was purchased in 1935 as new premises for the East Anglian School for Boys, Bury St Edmunds.

ST MARY. Rebuilt for E. R. Benyon by *W. G. Habershon*, 1856–7, all except the medieval tower which was heightened and faced with flint pebbles and Bath stone to match the rest. E.E., nicely detailed. N aisle by *Clyde Young*, 1907, as a memorial to Lady Cadogan (*see* below). Hammerbeam roof in chancel. – STAINED GLASS. E window †1909, possibly by *J. Dudley Forsyth*, who did the N aisle windows, *c.* 1907–8. Chancel N and S †1876 by *Hardman*, who may also have done the previous E window of *c.* 1857. – MONUMENTS. Jane, Lady Bacon, †1659. 1655–8 (i.e. before her death) by *Thomas Stanton*, who was paid £300 to do it 'alle in whit and black marble without the addition of any other ston whatsoever'. A large standing wall monument, in its original position (other C17 monuments repositioned in the tower). She is seated frontally in a deep arched recess and holds a small child on her lap. Five more kneel frontally to her l. and r. one behind another: a sincere, not at all aristocratic, rather Dutch group. Segmental pediment within a scrolled pediment, framing a cartouche. Below the main group lies her son Sir Nicholas Bacon †1660, on his side and elbow. – Her husband Sir Nathaniel Bacon, the amateur painter, †1627. Lozenge-shaped tablet with, in the middle, an oval recess with portrait bust. Garlands l. and r. and also two palettes. Attributed to *Nicholas Stone* (AW). – Margaret, Lady Cornwallis, †1669. By *Joshua Marshall*. Two tablets framed by Corinthian columns with segmental pediments. Wreathed skulls above, swags of fruit below. – Various nicely carved ledger stones of the Cornwallis family, mid-C17. Charles, 2nd Marquess Cornwallis, †1823. By *E. H. Baily*. White urn before a black obelisk; nothing special. – Beatrix Jane Craven, Countess Cadogan, †1907. By *Countess Feodora Gleichen*. Recumbent effigy of white marble on a tomb-chest. It lies in a vaulted chapel at the E end of the N aisle, behind low wrought-iron screens and gates. Putti, a cross, and large vine trails on the E wall.

CULFORD HALL. The first Culford Hall was built by Sir Nathaniel Bacon's father, Nicholas, who purchased the estate in 1586. This was remodelled for the 1st Marquess Cornwallis, 1790–6, by *Samuel Wyatt*; the stonemasons were *de Carle* of

Bury.* Wyatt clad the red brick exterior with white mathematical tiles, made locally, and roofed over a central courtyard, as well as adding new wings in white brick. The S and W fronts of this house can still be seen; the S front, originally the entrance, is of seven bays and two and a half storeys, with a three-bay pediment and little enrichment. A portico was added in 1828, but most of this was taken down in 1947. The N and E fronts of Wyatt's house, however, were swallowed up by gargantuan enlargements of 1894–6 by *William Young* for Lord Cadogan, with further additions (including winter garden, now demolished) by 1904. These are of white brick, in a weak Italianate style, with an asymmetrically placed tower and large *porte cochère*. Inside, Cadogan's rooms are as large and richly decorated as one would expect, but rather commonplace, although the hall has a painted frieze of busts, trophies, etc., that probably came from Caversham Park, the Cadogans' seat in Berkshire, and may be by *G. A. Pellegrini*, c. 1719. Surprisingly, most of Wyatt's interiors have survived, with fine stucco ceilings in the principal downstairs rooms, chimneypieces, and original bookcases in the library. Also in the library, unusually positioned over the windows, are grisaille mythological panels in the manner of *Biagio Rebecca*. The three-storey staircase hall has a coffered dome with glazed centre, stucco work almost certainly by *Joseph Rose*, and a lead and iron balustrade with anthemion ornament. Wyatt's E office wing, behind the 1894 N front, was sunk one storey below ground level, but it was demolished in 1980 to make way for the monstrous Centenary Hall. Other school buildings include the HEADMASTER'S LODGE, 1936, which contains a chimneypiece from the dining room of Wyatt's house, with three inset *Wedgwood* plaques.

Thomas Wright made a plan of the garden in 1742 and designed a temple for it c. 1745, but if anything was carried out, little has survived. The grounds were improved by *Humphry Repton* in a Red Book of 1792. This resulted in the creation of kitchen gardens and the long serpentine lake S of the Hall, the latter perhaps a reshaping and extension of one devised by Wright. It is crossed by a remarkable BRIDGE. This is of one span, fabricated from tubular sections of cast iron, following a design patented by *Samuel Wyatt* in 1800 and cast in 1804 by *William Hawks & Sons* of Gateshead. Stone balustrades with urns and balls. Within the park, notable buildings include the picturesque, single-storey WIDOWS HOUSES opposite the church, 1856 (by *Habershon*?), and, NE of the Hall, the STABLE BLOCK of 1889–90, built by Lord Cadogan. Mostly red brick, with some half-timbering and pebbledash, the entrance modelled on the gatehouse of West Stow Hall. Of about the same date the former LAUNDRY, E of the Hall.

---

*There is, however, evidence that *James Wyatt* was involved in the initial stages, but was sacked in 1790. A curved Doric portico added by *George Wyatt*, 1806–8, was removed in 1894.

Outside the park, to the S, HOME FARM includes an C18 timber-framed barn but is chiefly of interest for the alterations and additions of 1890 by Lord Cadogan, who had a prize herd of Jersey cows. Feed was prepared using machinery driven by a water wheel and delivered to the cowhouse by a tramway, and there were turntables in the corners of the yard. Along the main road, various ESTATE COTTAGES, the earlier ones in local white brick with panels of knapped flint, some with pediments, dating back to 1825, and probably designed by *James Ilsley*, the estate carpenter. Mostly with slate roofs, but REDE LODGE is thatched. Lord Cadogan's buildings are of red brick with half-timbered gables, including the former SCHOOL, 1895–6, and READING ROOM (now Culford Club), 1891–2. WAR MEMORIAL, in front of the village hall, by *Sidney Naish*, 1921. Portland stone obelisk.

At CULFORD HEATH, 3 m. NNE, E. R. Benyon built a CHAPEL OF EASE in 1840–1, converted to a school and cottage (enlarged 1881) when ST PETER was built by *A. W. Blomfield*, 1864–5. E.E., nave and chancel in one. Bellcote between nave and chancel, originally with flèche. Flint, with stone dressings and a band of knapped flint below the eaves. W porch and above it a large rose window. Redundant 1976; now a private house. – STAINED GLASS. By *Lavers & Barraud*, a complete scheme of 1864–5, with monochrome panels in N and S walls.

In addition to the former school, a small group of estate cottages, one dated 1823, another with a READING ROOM added in 1905. On the main road, ⅔ m. ESE of St Peter's, the former PARSONAGE,* 1864–5 but still wholly Georgian in character, with Tuscan porch and tall sash windows. Flint with white-brick dressings.

BARROW, about ⅔ m. SW of St Mary's on the edge of Dixon's Covert. Although scheduled as a Bronze Age round barrow, the location of this large mound – over 8 ft (2.62 metres) tall and 92 ft (28 metres) in diameter – coincides with that of a circular tree-covered feature on a 1742 estate map. This forms the terminus of an axis that runs through the middle of the S front of Culford Hall and along the length of a now-infilled garden canal, strongly suggesting that this is a prospect mound for views to and from Culford Hall. A more certainly genuine barrow is the HILL OF HEALTH, ⅔ m. NNE in a private garden. This is 72 ft (22 metres) in diameter and 11 ft (3.48 metres) high.

DALHAM

Church and Hall are quite separate from the village, about ⅓ m. NNE of it, and the churchyard is like another compartment of the

---

*In Ingham CP.

Hall's formal gardens. The Stutevilles held the manor from 1417 to 1627, the Afflecks from 1714 to 1901. The house was then bought by Cecil Rhodes, who died before he could take up residence, but his family lived there until 1927, when it was bought by Sir Laurence Philipps.

ST MARY. C14 chancel (see the S doorway – the windows are Perp) and S aisle (see one window and the doorway). C14 arcade with octagonal piers and double-chamfered arches. Perp N aisle and lower part of the W tower (flushwork ornament on the buttresses). But most of the tower was rebuilt in 1625 by Sir Martin Stuteville and the rector, Dr Thomas Warner, as is recorded in a huge inscription inside ('this steeple was reedified') and on the parapet to the N. On the W side it says 'Deo Trin Uni Sacrum', but on the S side 'Keepe my Sabbaths'. That was for the villagers. There was a spire, but it blew down in 1658. The Perp window must be of 1625, unless it was reused. The Perp chancel S window was made under the will of Thomas Stuteville, 1466, who also left money for the repair of the old tower. N chapel (now open to the sky) inserted by the Afflecks between the N aisle and vestry. Chancel restored by *Benjamin Burrell*, 1867, and *Sir Arthur Blomfield & Sons*, 1899–1900; on the latter occasion the E wall was rebuilt, with new E window. S aisle restored 1905, N aisle 1908. – FONT. 1625. – SCREEN. Only the dado, with arabesque paintings. – BENCHES. By *Burrell*, 1866. With poppyheads. Those on the S side of the nave have animals on the arms. – WALL PAINTINGS. On the nave N wall traces of the Seven Deadly Sins (l.) and the Seven Works of Mercy (r.). Over the chancel arch apparently scenes from the Passion. – ROYAL ARMS. Hanoverian (1714–1801); carved and painted wood. – SCULPTURE. Madonna and Child. Plaster relief after *Antonio Rossellino*. – HELM. Over the monument to Sir Martin Stuteville. – STAINED GLASS. E window by *H. W. Bryans*, 1908, in the manner of his master, Kempe. S aisle E by *Willement*, 1859. Tower window †1882 by *Ward & Hughes*. – MONUMENTS. Thomas Stutevyle †1571. Inscription tablet flanked by two Ionic columns. It stands in front of the chancel S window, on a C15 tomb-chest with three shields in strapwork cartouches. – Sir Martin Stuteville †1631. Three oval niches, the middle one raised, for Sir Martin and his two wives. Frontal busts in flat relief. Black columns l. and r. and entablature with semicircularly raised centre. The children kneel in the 'predella'. – In the churchyard, obelisk to General Sir James Affleck †1833. Presumably by *de Carle*, i.e. *Robert de Carle IV*, who signs the corresponding monument inside.

DALHAM HALL. Built in 1704–5 by Bishop Patrick of Ely. Originally of two and a half storeys and attics, but the top storey removed *c.* 1955 following a fire. Red brick. Dressings in a lighter shade of red, with plastered and painted keystones. On the garden front (s) this treatment has been extended to the quoins and platband. The entrance and garden fronts of

Dalham Hall.
Unexecuted design by C. E. Mallows, 1908

seven bays, the three-bay centres projecting slightly on the garden front, more so on the entrance front, which has also a C19 or C20 three-bay glazed porch. No pediments. Ground-floor windows altered on the garden front. C19 flat-roofed extension on the W side, enlarged and remodelled *c.* 1927, possibly by *H. S. Goodhart-Rendel*. Interior much altered, but still with original staircase. Two twisted balusters per tread. Good STABLES to NW, of ten bays, with two three-bay projections and segment-headed windows. The materials and general appearance correspond to the garden front of the house. They used to have a central clock turret and cupola. Alterations and additions of 1906. Large walled garden on the S side of the house, shown on an C18 estate map as 'Middle Court' and 'Nether Court'. Further formal gardens to the NE, although a scheme prepared by *T. H. Mawson* with *Mallows & Grocock* for Sir Richard Affleck, 1901, was dropped by Cecil Rhodes's executors, as were proposed additions to the house itself by Mallows. He was superseded by *Lutyens*, whose own proposals for the house (for Col F. F. Rhodes) were unexecuted, apart from GATES and LODGE ¾ m. WNW, 1903. Red brick with heavy stone rustication. Curved screen walls with niches and bands of tiles laid herringbone-wise.

OLD RECTORY, S of the church. By *Burrell*, 1863–70. Red and white brick, very plain.

In the VILLAGE some thatched estate cottages, one pair with a rustic porch dated 1817. Opposite, a red brick conical MALTING KILN. Along Stores Hill, W of the centre, a terrace of four 'COTTAGE HOMES' by *James Watts*, 1914. Pebbledashed, with red brick dressings. Three gables, and shallow curved bays.

LOWER MILL, 300 yds w of the village. Late c18 smock mill. Beehive cap with gallery. In use until 1926, with three pairs of stones. Sails and fantail removed.

DARMSDEN
Barking

ST ANDREW. Completely rebuilt by *H. J. Green*, 1880, although on the same scale as the old church. In the Dec style, with small s porch and w bellcote. Good set of contemporary FURNISHINGS, especially the carved wood REREDOS. Redundant 1979, but preserved as a place of worship.

DENHAM

ST MARY. 'Repaired and partly reseated in 1846, and has since at various times undergone a thorough restoration' (White's *Directory*, 1874). That work included rebuilding the w tower. N doorway plainest Norman. E window slightly less plain Dec. The interest lies in the brick NE chapel, built to house the MONUMENT of Sir Edward Lewkenor and his wife Susan †1605. They died of smallpox within two days of each other. Big six-poster with kneeling family, ten of them, in double file, facing E. Big superstructure with obelisks and strapwork. Not good. – His grandson, also Edward †1634 (incorrectly given as 1635), also of smallpox. Signed by *John & Matthias Christmas*, 1638. White and black marble. Recumbent effigy in armour, his head on a half-rolled-up straw mat. Tomb-chest with cartouches with shields and columns around it. Back wall with columns carrying an entablature rising in a semicircle in the middle. Cherubs and a skull on top. – STAINED GLASS. E window by *Dixon, Frampton & Hean*, *c.* 1876.

DENHAM HALL. C16 timber-framed, with four gables at the rear, but the front faced in red brick in the C19. Sash windows with hoodmoulds and Gothick glazing bars. Moat with ruin of gazebo at one corner. Late C16 or early C17 brick with stone dressings.

DENHAM CASTLE. *See* Gazeley.

DENSTON

ST NICHOLAS. Apart from the short w tower, which is probably late C14, this excellent church is all of a piece and was rebuilt in accordance with the will of John Denston of Denston Hall who died in 1473 or 1474. He endowed a chantry college (letters patent issued 1475), with provision for three priests, who probably lived in CHURCH COTTAGE W of the church. Circumstantial and stylistic evidence makes it very likely that the master mason was *Simon Clerk*. Nave, aisle, chapels and clerestory have three-light windows, only those of the clerestory without transoms. The windows are tall and fairly close to each other. S porch with fan-vault inside and a pretty crocketed and vaulted niche and a castellated stoup outside. The N rood-stair turret and all the buttresses are of stone, not of flint with stone trim. Arcade of seven bays running without a break from W to E. Piers of lozenge section with concave-sided polygonal shafts without capitals towards the nave, i.e. running right up to the roof. They are crossed by a string course below the clerestory windows. Good cambered nave roof and lean-to aisle roofs. In the nave alternate tie-beams are unbraced. Wall-plates have affronted lions, hounds, hares and harts, as well as a manticore. The arched braces of the nave have carving too. – FONT. Perp. On the bowl the Seven Sacraments and the Crucifixion in small figures against a rayed background. The figures are defaced. – PULPIT. Jacobean; very simple. – SCREENS. The dado only of the rood screen, which continues across both aisles; much restored. Still with its central gates. Above the centre a portion of the ROOD BEAM, a moulded embattled beam: a rare survival. Parclose screens to the chapels. C15 tower screen. – STALLS and BENCHES with animal poppyheads and animals on the armrests. The stalls, which return against the screen, have traceried fronts. Four MISERICORDS are preserved. One of them has a fine figure of a crane. – C18 BOX PEWS in the S aisle. – SOUTH DOOR with tracery, C15. – COMMUNION RAIL. With slender twisted balusters; C17. – STAINED GLASS. The whole E window consists of bits of old glass. S chapel E by *Martin Travers*, 1932. S aisle †1914 by *Heaton, Butler & Bayne*. – MONUMENTS. On N side of the sanctuary, an open-sided tomb-chest in which are two shrouded corpses lying on a floor of red and black tiles. Death is shown more frighteningly in him than in her. Good quality. In the slab above them the indents of brasses. Late C15. Probably John Denston and his wife Katherine Clopton. – Balancing tomb-chest on S side of the Robinson family of Denston Hall. By *de Carle* of Bury, 1822. In the S chapel, suspended ARMOUR (tabard, helmet and sword) of Sir John Robinson †1704. The GATES to this chapel are C18, of wood made to look like iron. – Brasses to Henry Everard †1524 and wife Margaret. 25½-in. (65-cm.) figures. He is in armour with tabard of arms, his head resting against his crested and mantled helmet; she in heraldic mantle. – Brass to a Lady of the Drury family, *c*. 1530; 18 in. (45 cm.). – Robert Robinson †1822. By *Charles Randall*. With draped urn.

CHANTRY FARMHOUSE, E of the church. Rebuilt by Henry Everard, who was granted the lease in 1521. Timber-framed and plastered, the centre part of the S front jettied. Lobby entrance, with a later wing against the entrance. The hall, W of the large stack, has moulded beams and joists. CHANTRY FARM BARN, N, converted and extended by *Hudson Architects*, 2010–11. Two linked barns, at right angles, dating back to the early C16.

DENSTON HALL. The present house was built by Sir John Robinson in about 1690–1700. It replaced – although not entirely, as we shall see – an early Tudor house whose appearance is known from old illustrations. It was a courtyard house, surrounded by a moat, and had on its E side a tall brick gatehouse with angle turrets. Either side of this were the gable-ends of timber-framed ranges, and then low embattled walls leading to turrets at the corners of the moat platform. Nothing survives of this side of the old house. Robinson's replacement is of red brick with blue headers, of two storeys and attics. E front of five bays with two-storey wings two bays deep. Ionic porch. Staircases with twisted balusters. Much of the interior remodelled *c.* 1780, including the circular entrance hall and the rooms to l. and r. of it. The room on the l. has a screen of two columns at the far end. Over it a grisaille panel giving a very convincing impression of bas relief. In the entrance hall, two *Coade* stone female figures, dated 1790 and 1800, from Grovelands, Southgate. On the S front, an Ionic orangery by *Ronald Geary*, 2000, with Soanean interior. This slots unobtrusively between Robinson's house and the surviving service range of the earlier house, the two connected by a narrow passage with C17 gables. The Tudor range is also of red brick and the windows and doorways (not all of them original) have hoodmoulds. One room in the middle was the kitchen and the remainder seem to have been for storage with, on the first floor, lodgings for servants. At the S end is a room that was fitted out *c.* 1923 with moulded beams and other C15–C16 woodwork. On the S and W sides of this range is the remaining portion of the moat. S of the house a lozenge-shaped walled garden, partly C18; straight canals outside it on three sides. The lake to the E of the house is late C20. Elaborate entrance gates to N *c.* 1896. Wrought iron, with stone pillars.

ROUND HOUSE, ½ m. ENE of Denston Hall and originally a lodge to it. Octagonal, with thatched roof and eaves supported on timber posts to form veranda.

DEPDEN

Not a noticeably hilly parish, but it contains the highest point above sea level in Suffolk, ¾ m. SE of the church: 420 ft (128 metres).

ST MARY. In the middle of fields, with no road to it. Footpath from the NE, off the Bury road. Its survival is all the more surprising in that the nave was gutted by fire in 1984, and the opportunity might have been taken to abandon it; but it was restored by the *Whitworth Co-Partnership*, 1985, with a modern arch-braced roof. Walls of septaria and flint. Norman S doorway with one order of single-scalloped capitals and one chevron in the arch. Beautiful late C13 PISCINA in the chancel, of two lights, cusped, with a quatrefoiled circle. The tracery of nave and chancel, insofar as it represents the original, is of the same date; the nave S windows are C19, those on the N side original. There were restorations in *c.* 1837, probably by *H. E. Kendall Sen.*, and in 1855–65, including the addition of a S porch. E window Dec (reticulated tracery). Diagonal buttresses continued upwards as pinnacles. Perp W tower, for which money was left in 1451. N porch timber, C17, with side balusters, badly treated. – FONT. Octagonal, early C18 with shields in cartouches. – BENCHES. A few remaining after the fire, with poppyheads and blank panels of good tracery. – STAINED GLASS. E window probably by *S. C. Yarington* of Norwich, *c.* 1838–40. Heraldic glass of that date at the top; below that original late C14 canopies, chiefly dark yellow and green. Beneath this, early C16 panels and roundels of early C16 glass from Steinfeld Abbey, near Cologne. Nave S by *Heaton, Butler & Bayne*, 1911. – MONUMENTS. Anne Drewry †1572 with her husbands, George Waldegrave of Smallbridge Hall, Bures, and Sir Thomas Jermyn of Rushbrooke. Kneeling brass figures in a stone frame with two arches. – Sarah Loretta Lloyd †1838. Draped sarcophagus by *de Carle*. – In churchyard, NE of the chancel, an OBELISK erected in 1837 commemorating five members of a family of seven who died of cholera in 1832.

BEECH HALL, 400 yds NE. Built as the rectory by *Kendall*, 1844–7, but greatly altered. C19 planting of yews and other evergreens joining up with the churchyard.

DEPDEN HALL, 400 yds NW. Timber-framed and plastered house of possibly C14 origins, although the exterior is C18, with Tuscan porch. Large C16 weatherboarded barn to SE, now converted to dwelling. Complete moat with brick revetting, some of it probably Tudor.

DEPDEN GREEN, N of the Hall, has a number of attractive timber-framed houses round its edges, mostly plastered and thatched.

DRINKSTONE

9060

ALL SAINTS. W tower 1694 (see inscription), of red brick with burnt headers. Angle buttresses and crenellated parapet. Two of its six BELLS cast by *Henry Pleasant* of Sudbury, 1696. The rest mainly Dec, restored by *E. C. Hakewill* in 1866–7. E window of that date, the old one (of three lights with flowing tracery) reused, it seems, on the s side. Dec N aisle E and W windows with segmental heads. Dec arcades, N and S, with octagonal piers and double-chamfered arches. Perp aisle windows. Hakewill also re-roofed the nave and aisles and added the quatrefoil clerestory windows. S porch rebuilt 1872. Ringing chamber and balcony by the *Whitworth Co-Partnership*, 2002. – FONT. Norman, of Purbeck marble. Octagonal. Re-cut in the C13 with the usual pair of flat blank arches on each side. – SCREEN. Tall, one-light divisions, with ogee arches. Close panel tracery above them. Original cresting and a good deal of original colouring. Restored by *Hakewill*; it had been supporting a W gallery. – REREDOS. 1870, carved by *James Wormald*. C17 PANELLING to either side installed 1913. – BENCHES. Of 1867, with poppyheads, some reusing medieval carved backs. Probably made by *Wormald*. – TILES. A few medieval tiles at the E end of the nave (N side). – STAINED GLASS. Medieval fragments in chancel and aisles, notably a seated Virgin (chancel N), and several whole figures (chancel S). Restored by *Hakewill*. E window by *Lavers & Barraud*, 1867; also no doubt the tower window. – MONUMENTS. In the NE corner of the nave, a platform which seems to be a very low tomb-chest or part of an Easter sepulchre. The front is decorated with circles with two, three or four mouchettes; early or mid-C14 probably. – Joshua Grigby of Drinkstone Park †1798 and wife Jane †1789. A pair of elegant urns. – George Grigby †1811. Sarcophagus. By *Joseph Kendrick*. – Anna Grigby †1853. Similar, but less fine. By *Edward Simpson* of Stowmarket. – Rev. Henry Patteson †1824. By *W. Steggles*. White marble on grey background with shield of arms.

Opposite the church, THE OLD ALMSHOUSES, C16, timber-framed and plastered; originally a guildhall. Large chimney at one end of a wing that once continued further towards the road. On N side of the churchyard, former SCHOOL and teacher's house by *John Y. Rednall* of Woolpit, 1859. Red brick, with some paired lancets. Closed 1986 and converted to a private house.

DRINKSTONE LODGE, 100 yds S. White-brick front range, dated 1815. Three bays and two storeys with porch on slender Tuscan columns. Boxy C20 extensions to l. and r. The rear parts of the house timber-framed, C17 or earlier.

OLD RECTORY, 200 yds N. Built *c.* 1760 for Rev. Richard Moseley. Red brick, two storeys, five bays. Quoins of brick. Doorway with segmental pediment on brackets, a Venetian window above. Lower service range set back to l.

HOME FARM, 100 yds NW. C17. Timber-framed, with red brick front, extended in the C19. Early C19 stable with pigeon loft. Flint and stone rubble with brick quoins. Gambrel roof.

DRINKSTONE PARK was demolished in 1951. It was built in 1760 for Joshua Grigby and stood ¾ m. W of the church. The stables, of white brick like the house, have been converted to dwellings. Lake below the site of the house.

STOTTS COTTAGE, Cross Street, ¾ m. s. Timber-framed and plastered house of *c.* 1500, extended later in the C16. In 1919 it was chosen by the Society for the Protection of Ancient Buildings as a model scheme to demonstrate that repair (carried out by *William Weir*, including small rear extension, and published by the society in 1921) was cheaper than the new houses then being built by the government and less wasteful of resources.

HOLM HOUSE, Garden House Lane, 1¼ m. SSE. By *KLH Architects*, 2007–9. Pastiche on a grand scale, giving the impression of a house that has evolved over the centuries. H-plan. Front range of red brick. Two storeys and attics. Four bays, doorcase with segmental pediment. One-bay 'extension' to l. with single-storey canted bay, and a similar bay on the return wall to the r. The remainder of the house is 'timber-framed and plastered', with a gabled and jettied wing forming the other leg of the H. Between the two legs a single-storey conservatory, perhaps 'an early C21 addition'. Gardens by *Janey Auchincloss*.

WINDMILLS, ½ m. NE. A remarkable site, portraying the history of country milling over five centuries. First the POST MILL, the oldest surviving in the county. It carries a date of 1689, but this seems to refer to rebuilding, because the timbers are earlier: the main post has been tree-ring-dated 1586–7, and others 1541–73 and 1543–74. Timber-framed and weatherboarded buck. Early C19 roundhouse of flint rubble and brick. Fantail added in the 1960s. Below it a former SMOCK MILL. Originally a horse mill, sixteen-sided, converted to smock mill in the late C18 when the eight-sided weatherboarded upper part was added. Gutted for use as an engine mill *c.* 1900, the present oil engine installed 1932. Early C19 MILL COTTAGE, timber-framed and plastered with mansard roof.

EARL STONHAM
(Stonham Earl)

1050

ST MARY THE VIRGIN. The splendour of the church is its nave roof. But there are signs of an older history first to be inspected. One lancet in the chancel N wall. Dec the present arrangement of crossing and transepts; for Earl Stonham is a cruciform church, although it has no crossing tower. The crossing arches look early C14. Those to the N and S have fleuron decoration. Above the S transept arch a tiny quatrefoil window to throw light on to the rood. Money was left for the rood in 1526. Dec transept windows, two in the S transept with Y-tracery. Handsome inner hoodmould to the N transept E window, which has reticulated tracery. Dec also the E half of the chancel. Fine gabled PISCINA, yet without ogee arch. The SEDILIA form a window seat. The arm is of stone with a pet dog (decapitated) lying on it. Dec also the W window in the tower, obviously the reused W window, before the tower existed. Dec finally the S porch with its strong, simple entrance mouldings. The exterior of the lower parts of the church is unfortunately cemented. Above this commonplace zone rise the clerestory and the tower. The clerestory – a significant addition in a church without aisles (all the glory to the roof) – has on the S side flushwork arcading between the closely set windows. As for the tower, it has flushwork on the base and the buttresses and culminates in a parapet with flushwork quatrefoils and battlements with tall blank flushwork arcading, including the *Aldryche* device. W doorway with two orders of fleurons, shields, crowns, etc., and three-light bell-openings. Principal restoration by *Cory & Ferguson*, 1874–5, including rebuilding the N wall of the N transept.

And now we can enter the nave and look at the ROOF, one of the finest in a county rich in rich roofs. A bequest of 1534 to have the church 'new hallowed' may have been prompted by its completion. It is a hammerbeam roof in which trusses with pendant hammerposts (i.e. the ends of the hammerbeams are tenoned into them) alternate with trusses in which the hammerpost stands on a hammerbeam in the form of a (decapitated) prone angel. Arched braces to the collar-beams. From their middles hang pendants, and on their middles stand kingposts. All spandrels are carved, a number with fools or jesters. The wall-posts have figures, the wall-plates much decoration (three tiers, the first and the third of angels with spread-out wings). Arched braces rise and fall in a W–E direction from wall-post to wall-post. Embattled collar-beams, embattled ribs and embattled purlins. Even the common rafters are moulded. The chancel roof is lower and a little simpler, and was thoroughly restored in 1874–5. It has fine tracery above the hammerbeams. Transept roofs of 1874–5.

FURNISHINGS. FONT. Octagonal. The figures against the stem have disappeared. Against the bowl four angels and a flower, the Crown of Thorns, Sacred Heart, etc. – PULPIT. Jacobean. It had four HOUR GLASSES beside it (not on view), three together (for a quarter, a half and one hour) and one separate in its iron holder. – BENCHES. Of 1874–5, made by *James Gibbons*, with carving by *Robert Godbold*, incorporating some medieval work. Poppyheads in the nave; in the chancel figures in relief against the fronts of ends, e.g. a bagpipe player, a pelican, a man with an axe, etc. One poppyhead is a *signum triciput*. A detached original bench has on the arm-rest the inscription 'Orate pro [anima] Necolai Houk'. – WEST DOOR with tracery. – CHEST. Oak, *c.* 1300, with chip-carved decorative roundels. – WALL PAINTINGS. The wall paintings of Earl Stonham as recorded in 1874 by *Hamlet Watling* were interesting and instructive. There is a Doom above the chancel arch, and St George on the W wall of the S transept. There were in addition a Martyrdom of St Thomas Becket (converted under Henry VIII into a Martyrdom of St Catherine), also in the S transept, and in the N transept a Journey of the Magi and Adoration of the Magi. – STAINED GLASS. E window by *H. Hughes* (*Ward & Hughes*), 1875.

EARL STONHAM HOUSE, ½ m. N. Former rectory, rebuilt by *William Brown* of Ipswich, 1820. White brick. Five-bay front with tall ground-floor windows.

DEERBOLT HALL, 750 yds SE. A Queen Anne front of red and blue chequered brick. Nine bays, two and a half storeys. The three-bay centre with giant stuccoed pilasters and pediment was part of an early C19 remodelling, which also included a slate roof with deep eaves and paired modillions. Associated with Deerbolt Hall is THE LODGE, 650 yds NE on the A140. Early C19, three bays, white brick. Giant pilasters, also in brick but with enriched Ionic pilasters and paterae of what looks like, and probably is, *Coade* stone. Greek Doric porch.

WEYLANDS COTTAGE, Wicks Green, 1 m. NW. Timber-framed and plastered house with thatched roof. Early C16, remodelled *c.* 1550, with a wing at right angles that was originally a separate dwelling. Gable towards the road with carved bressumer and carved arch braces. In the wing remains of painted decoration, including roll-moulded beams with red and white barber-pole stripes.

YEWTREE HOUSE, Forward Green, nearly 1 m. NW. Well-preserved hall house of the early C15. Timber-framed and plastered with thatched roof. In-line parlour bay, its chamber originally lit by an early type of dormer window. Hall floored in the late C16, when a wing was also added.

EDWARDSTONE

9040

ST MARY THE VIRGIN. W tower, nave and N aisle (described as new in 1462); no clerestory. The chancel windows, if reliably restored, point to *c.* 1300. The piers of the arcade Perp: quatrefoil with fillets. The same type between chancel and N chapel. NE vestry built with a bequest of 1506. C19 red brick S porch-cum-shed. Restoration by *G. F. Bodley*, 1877–8, apparent mostly in the FURNISHINGS, detailed below, but also in the fine roofs, from which he removed plaster ceilings: in the nave, C14, with crown-posts on five tie-beams; in the chancel, boarded, with cornice, painted by *William Powell* of *F. R. Leach & Sons*, Cambridge (repainted to the same design, 1973). – REREDOS. By *C. G. Hare*, 1910. With three panels, the figures carved by *Robert Bridgeman* of Lichfield, coloured by *Harper* of London. – PULPIT. Jacobean, good and big, with back panel and tester. Restored by *Rattee & Kett*, 1877–8. – SEATING. Nave benches with stepped ends modelled on a few surviving old ones, choir stalls made by *Robert Hawkins* of Monks Eleigh, 1878. – PANELLING. In nave, 1877–8; in sanctuary, 1898. – BENEFACTIONS and COMMANDMENTS BOARDS. By

Watts & Co., 1878. In the form of triptychs. – ORGAN CASE. 1879 by *Bodley*, painted by *Leach*, with wing panels carved by *John McCulloch*. The instrument was originally made for the Sheldonian Theatre, Oxford, by *Bernard Schmidt (Father Smith)*, 1671. – Wrought-iron CHANDELIERS thought to be by *W. Bainbridge Reynolds*. – WALL PAINTING. Above w window of N aisle, the figure of a censing angel. Not medieval, but possibly a repainting. – STAINED GLASS. E window by *Burlison & Grylls*, the tracery 1878, the remainder 1897. They are also recorded as having made the two nave s windows †1877 (designed by *Bodley*) and 1921. – MONUMENTS. Benjamin Brand †1636, wife Elizabeth and groups of children. Brasses in the medieval tradition, his figure in civilian dress 26½ in. (67 cm.) tall. The inscription tells us that husband and wife were by 'Providence after 35 yeares conjunction divided', and 'after 12 dayes divorcement reunited', and that she had twelve children 'all nursed with her unborrowed milk'. – Thomas Dawson †1807. By *John Bacon Jun.*, 1808. With elegant white urn in front of a grey obelisk. – Also by Bacon, Dawson's son-in-law William Shepherd †1815. With urn. – G. A. Dawson †1848. By *de Carle*. Austerely monumental tablet. – Major R. W. Magenis †1863. By *T. Gaffin*, with flags and other militaria. – Another by Gaffin to Ann Lovell Shepherd †1864, with classical ornament.

EDWARDSTONE HALL, the seat of the Brands and Dawsons, stood to the E of the church; dem. 1952. It had been rebuilt by Charles Dawson *c.* 1832 in Tudor-Gothic style. The red brick COACH HOUSE was spared (converted to a house in 1995), as was the GATEHOUSE with castellated polygonal turret (known as Temple Bar, but bearing no resemblance to that structure).

WAR MEMORIAL, 700 yds E. Wayside cross, at the meeting of three roads. 1920, by *Farmer & Brindley* and *F. J. Lindley*.

At SHERBOURNE STREET, 1 m. SE, EDWARDSTONE HOUSE, timber-framed and plastered with some exposed timbers on the s wing. Georgianized front with sash windows and nicely crooked doorcase. Large late C19 N wing, of red brick with stone dressings. Tudor-Gothic, with tall moulded brick chimneys. To its N EDWARDSTONE COTTAGE by *Frank Saunders & Partners*, 1973, white-painted with double monopitch roof; SIDEWAYS, C17 with exposed timbers; and EDWARDSTONE LODGE, early C19 white brick, four bays wide, the outer bays stepping slightly forward and with pedimented gables.

ELMSETT

ST PETER. Two blocked lancets (C12) in the nave, other windows with Y-tracery and Dec. W tower of the C13; also the s porch, with cruck-style arch and original bargeboards. Chancel Dec,

ELMSETT · ELMSWELL

the E window with flowing tracery of a standard pattern. Restored 1900, including new nave roof. – FONT. Square, Norman, of Purbeck marble and originally with the usual flat blank round arches. – FONT COVER. Simple, conical, C17. – PULPIT. Jacobean; from St Mary-at-the-Quay, Ipswich. – COMMUNION RAIL. – Three-sided, with turned balusters. Later C17. – PANELLING. Some Jacobean panelling, perhaps from former pews. – ORGAN. By *John Gray*; early C19. Gothick. From St Peter, Ubbeston (E). On C18 WEST GALLERY. – DOOR. S door with late C12 ironwork. C-hinges and barbed straps. – ROYAL ARMS. Painted on board. Of Queen Anne, updated for George II and dated 1758. On the back, Prince of Wales' feathers within a sun in splendour, presumably for the future George III, and suggesting that they originally hung in the chancel arch. – TABLE OF KINDRED AND AFFINITY. C18, painted on board; also the more usual COMMANDMENTS etc. – MONUMENTS. Edward Sherland †1609. The usual kneeling figure in an aedicule; alabaster. – Rev. William Talbot †1811. Simple sarcophagus, on animal's paws. Considerably more space is devoted to describing its erection, and the need to keep it 'free from injury' and 'in a perfectly legible state'.

TITHE MONUMENT, provocatively placed opposite the entrance to the churchyard. Concrete monolith with inscription, 1935. It records the seizure of goods 'including baby's bed & blankets' at Elmsett Hall for non-payment of tithe (cf. Wortham).

LAUREL COTTAGE, 300 yds SE. Early C19 white-brick front of two storeys and three bays. The centre bay projects slightly and continues above the eaves, flat-topped but with an elliptical arch framing the first-floor window. The rear parts timber-framed and plastered of the C16.

In the centre of the village, ½ m. SW, the METHODIST CHURCH by *Basil & David Hatcher*, 1962. Pale buff brick. Re-roofed and extended by *Michael Croughton*, 2003. To its N the OLD RECTORY, part timber-framed and plastered, part red brick. C16 with various alterations and additions, including work by *William Brown* of Ipswich, 1818, and *Rodney Black*, 2008.

ELMSWELL

9060

ST JOHN THE DIVINE. The W tower, and to a lesser extent the S porch, have an unusually comprehensive series of flushwork devices; the former is attributed to *Thomas Aldryche*. Panelling on the tower battlements as well as emblems. The principal benefactor of the tower was Margery Walter, who bequeathed 40s. in 1476; her first husband, William Hert †1472, left money for roofing the aisle. He and her second husband, Edmund Walter, are commemorated by monograms, and Hert's merchant's mark can also be found. There is an inscription and two chalices for Sir William Moundevyle (rector

1488–1503) and what may be the monogram of Richard Crowe, who left a mark (13s. 4d.) for the building in 1541. Robert Scot, abbot of Bury 1469–74, is also mentioned. S aisle rebuilt by *Hakewill* (probably *J. H.*), 1862–3; no window in the E wall but a very bold flushwork pattern of linked crosses. Dec chancel, restored 1864 by *R. J. Withers*, including new N vestry. N aisle, organ chamber and new nave roof by *J. D. Wyatt*, 1872. Five-bay arcade, original Perp on the S side, copied for the N. The clerestory not with double the number of windows. Inside below the windows a fleuron frieze. On this wall-shafts of the former roof. W end reordered by the *Whitworth Co-Partnership*, 1990–3, including meeting rooms and gallery, as well as a small N extension. – FONT. Base with ox, two eagles, pelican. Bowl with shields in foiled shapes. On the shields the letters of the name I. (John) Hedge, one of Margery Walter's executors, donor of the font and probably also of the S porch. Retooled by *Rattee & Kett*, 1872. – REREDOS. By *Withers*, 1864; 'rather ungainly' (*The Ecclesiologist*). Stone. Paintings in the panels by *Rev. W. F. Francis*, 1872, who also painted the shields on the nave roof. – CHANCEL SCREEN. Low stone screen by *Withers*; wrought-iron upper part 1884. Wrought-iron gates by *W. H. Syer* of Great Saxham, 1872. – PULPIT. 1872. Carved openwork by *Lot Jackaman*; stone base, with shafts of Cornish serpentine marble, by *Mrs Elizabeth Farrow* of Bury. – PARCLOSE SCREENS. To S chapel. Good, with two-light divisions. Little creatures in the spandrels of the dado. On the N side, painted figures of 1904, mercifully on removable panels. – BENCH ENDS. Some with poppyheads and blank tracery; one with carved back. Other benches of 1872. – STAINED GLASS. E window by *Lavers & Barraud*, 1864. Chancel S by *Alexander Gibbs*, 1868. – MONUMENT. Sir Robert Gardener †1619. Standing monument with stiff reclining figure. By his feet a rhinoceros, his crest. To the l. his son, kneeling. At the foot of the monument lie Sir Robert's robes and part of his armour. Two columns carry a large and tall coffered arch. Attributed to *William Wright* (AW). – E of chancel, Samuel, Robert and George Jackson †1850, 1852 and 1855 respectively, each described as 'Gent. From Woolpit'. Slab with raised iron lettering, protected by a heavy iron cage as if from bodysnatchers. – CHURCHYARD CROSS. The base is old, perhaps C14, and has good carvings. Restored 1904.

ALMSHOUSES. Founded by Sir Robert Gardener 'for six poore women widows', 1614. Red brick, single-storey, with a steep central gable in which are a sundial and inscription. Five doorways, four groups of chimneys. The windows of are two lights with an architrave over.

HILL COURT. By *R. J. Withers*, *c.* 1864, as the rectory. 'The style is Pointed, of a most simple character, depending for its effect on the moulded chimneys' (*The Ecclesiologist*, which also noted that the walls were 'double, for protection against the weather, the situation being an exposed one'). Red brick, with Ancaster stone dressings. Sash windows set in arched recesses. Withers also designed the National School, 1865, but this has been demolished.

METHODIST CHURCH, School Road. By *Eade & Johns*, 1898, replacing chapel of 1804. Red brick with white-brick and stone dressings. Gabled front with pinnacles, large round plate-traceried window and gabled porch. Adjoining hall 1955–6.

RAILWAY STATION. Opened 1846. The main building, by *F. Barnes*, was demolished in 1974, but a platform shelter survives on the S side, restored 1995. Good canopy on cast-iron columns by *G. B. Gibbons & Co.*, Ipswich.

THE OLD BANK HOUSE, N of the station. Long-wall jettied house of *c.* 1500 or a little earlier. Early C17 red brick chimney with four (rebuilt) octagonal shafts, and evidence that it once had a timber chimney, as well as a crown-post roof.

CLAY FIELD, Thedwastre Close, ¾ m. E of St John's. By *Riches Hawley Mikhail Architects*, 2005–8. Twenty-six homes, a mixture of houses and flats, in four groups, both affordable and sustainable. Structural timber frame, filled with Hemcrete (lime and hemp), partly lime-rendered and partly cedar-clad. Pitched roofs of cedar shingles, shallow on one face, near-vertical on the other. The buildings, of airtight construction, are oriented for maximum solar gain, use a biomass district heating system, and collect rainwater.

ELVEDEN

ST ANDREW AND ST PATRICK. The medieval church, dedicated to St Andrew, consisted of nave and chancel with a W tower. The nave was Norman (see one S window), the chancel Dec (four-light E window with flowing tracery shafted inside), the tower early C15 with flushwork panelling at the foot; Thomas Crowe left money for its completion in 1421. The church was restored for the Maharajah Duleep Singh, a favourite of Queen Victoria, in 1869, presumably by *John Norton* (*see* below). Then, in 1904–6, Lord Iveagh employed *W. D. Caröe* to raise the church to the standard of Elveden Hall. He added a new N nave and chancel, dedicated to St Patrick, relegating the old church to the status of S aisle and S chapel. All his detail is of the most ornate Gothic, that version of *c.* 1900 which can be called Art Nouveau Gothic. It is full of unexpected and unauthorized turns. The new front e.g. has a small NW turret to balance at the S end the projecting tower of the old church. The piers between the new and old naves defy description. The roof is of the double hammerbeam type with large angels, but the chancel is so low that the effect is completely different from that in medieval predecessors. Caröe also replaced the old nave roof, supported in part on corbels that cut wilfully into the old S windows and with tracery above the arch-braced tie-beams. In 1919–22 he built a separate TOWER just outside the churchyard but connected to the SE corner of the church by a long vaulted and traceried cloister walk, as a memorial to Countess Iveagh †1916. The tower is more correct, but sumptuously decorated with flushwork. – REREDOS. 1906–7. Alabaster. With the Supper at Emmaus, two principal tiers of statues and a number of smaller figures. Executed by *Nathaniel Hitch*, who also carved the figures on the exterior as well as poppyheads and other woodwork. – STAINED GLASS. E window, 1910, and chancel S, by *Clayton & Bell*. – W window by *Frank Brangwyn*, 1937. – S chapel E †1894 by *Kempe*, S by *Clayton & Bell*, 1902 (Boer War memorial). – In S aisle, two windows by *Hugh Easton* (Second World War memorials) and one by *Lawrence Lee*, 1971. – MONUMENTS. Augustus, Viscount Keppel, †1786. With a bas-relief profile. Unsigned. – Rev. Thomas Bull †1841, by *Thomas Farrow* of Diss, and William Newton †1862, by *G. Maile*. Both very plain. – War memorial by *H. M. Cautley*, 1948. Gothic, in the spirit of Caröe.

ELVEDEN HALL, SE of the church, was a Georgian house of moderate size. It may have been built by Admiral Keppel, who purchased the estate in 1766, although Kirby's map of that year shows a house on the site. In 1862 it became the seat of Duleep Singh, who in 1869 commissioned *John Norton* to enlarge the existing house, but ended up rebuilding. Externally the result, published in 1871, was more that of town house than country house. Red brick with heavy Ancaster stone dressings, three storeys, the ground floor rusticated and with rusticated quoins. Three-bay centre with segmental pediment, two bays set slightly back, and three-bay ends coming forward again with two-storey canted bays. The interior was fitted out in the most exotic Rajput style, executed in plaster, and coloured and gilded by *Holzmann*, with mirrored decorations by *Powell & Sons* and inlays by *Maw & Co*.

Elveden Hall.
Design by John Norton, 1871

Duleep Singh died in 1893 and the estate was acquired by Lord Iveagh, who used his Guinness fortune to create an even more extravagant Oriental palace. On the exterior, he stuck to the rather pedestrian style of Duleep Singh's mansion, his choice of architect being the establishment figure of *William Young*, whose *magnum opus* is the former War Office in Whitehall. The existing house was almost exactly replicated to the E, the two halves joined by a new entrance with giant portico and *porte cochère*. On the garden front the centre is also pedimented but with a large bow on the ground floor with coupled columns. Above all this rises a dome, covering the greatest extravagance of all. The new entrance hall was fine enough, octagonal, panelled, with Cipollino columns and vaulted Adamesque ceiling, but the Marble Hall beyond it quite eclipsed any of Duleep Singh's efforts. It is full height, with galleries, and the aforementioned dome, with a lower half-dome at the garden end, almost entirely constructed of the purest white marble. It cost over £70,000. The carving was done by *Farmer & Brindley*, and *Sir Caspar Purdon Clarke* of the South Kensington Museum, who had trained as an architect, was responsible for the details. In spite of Clarke's credentials as an Indian expert the design is far from pure – motifs and styles from various Indian and Islamic traditions are freely mixed – but the effect is breathtaking. Duleep Singh's rooms were brought into line and their decorations painted over. The additions were on the site of Duleep Singh's service wing and a new one was built further E, but this has been demolished.

Lord Iveagh's alterations were completed by 1903; William Young had died in 1900 and the work was continued by his son *Clyde*. Elveden Hall was (and is) the centre of a 23,000-acre (9,300-ha) estate and at the same time as work on the house, much of the estate VILLAGE along the London Road was rebuilt, as well as lodges etc., all in a homely style with half-timbered gables. Buildings include the SCHOOL and FIRE STATION, both 1899, the latter (now a house) with a brick tower overlooking the churchyard, and COTTAGE HOMES (almshouses). SW of the Hall an Italianate WATER TOWER, 1895, and large STABLE BLOCK, 1903. Older estate buildings include SOUTH LODGE, ¼ m. S of the Hall. Flint with white-brick dressings and Gothick windows, mid-C19.

WAR MEMORIAL, 2½ m. SW of the church. By *Clyde Young*, 1921. Tall Composite column with urn, erected at the point where the parishes of Elveden, Eriswell and Icklingham meet.

ERISWELL

Eriswell had two medieval churches: St Peter, which fell into disuse at the Reformation, and a dependent chapel, St Laurence, 1¾ m. S. Most of the houses are now near St Laurence, an estate village largely rebuilt in the first half of the C19 by the New England Co. The Bedingfield family estate had been seized by Oliver Cromwell, and was sold in 1649 to the newly formed Society for the Propagation of the Gospel in New England and Parts Adjacent in America. It was bought by the Maharajah Duleep Singh in 1869, and in 1894 by Lord Iveagh (cf. Elveden).

ST LAURENCE. Late C13 S aisle and S chapel, presumably the extent of the original church. The rest Dec. Angle PISCINAS in chancel and S chapel, both with stiff-leaf decoration but more elaborate in the S chapel. The chapel has on its S side two lancets. Pier towards the chancel with deeply hollowed-out quatrefoil section and double-chamfered arches. The S aisle has uncusped intersected tracery. One window deserves special notice. It is small and square, and its tracery is a centre with four diagonally radiating cusped arches. Inside there is a seat (or credence table?) below it and a piscina. Low gabled outer tomb recess in the S aisle. Dec chancel, with an E window where two intersected ogee arches carry a pointed oval. The nave and chancel side windows are of two lights and of the same date. Arcade with octagonal piers and arches with a moulding of two sunk quadrants. The same in the chancel arch, including the responds. Across the chancel NE corner is a strange stone fitment with two openings. It looks like a double aumbry, but the bottom is considerably deeper than the foot of the doors. It may originally have been a niche for a statue, the cupboards added later. Restored by *J. D. Wyatt*, 1873–4, including new roof and seating. – FONT. Octagonal, with quatrefoil decoration but on an octagonal middle support and eight attached shafts with moulded capitals. They are clearly early C14; so this type of decoration of the font bowl goes back as far as that. – SCREEN. Much restored, but apparently Dec. Shafts and mullions, Dec tracery. – PULPIT, COMMUNION RAIL, READING DESK and CHOIR DESKS. Pine and wrought iron. By *Rev. W. F. Francis*, 1874, made by *W. H. Syer* of Great Saxham (cf. Elmswell). – BENCH ENDS. Simple, with small poppyheads. – STAINED GLASS. Bits of original glass in the chancel N windows and the square S aisle window. – MONUMENT. James Paul †1820. A North American Indian brought over to Eriswell by the New England Co. as an apprentice carpenter and builder. The original headstone is preserved inside the church.

ST PETER (Eriswell Hall Barns). The only survivals are parts of the N and S flint walls of the nave.* In the N wall, most of a Perp window and part of a C13 lancet. These remains were incorporated in a dovecote, 1754, the rest of the structure part white brick, part timber-framed with brick-nogging. Hipped roof with gablets.

The village buildings are mainly of flint with red or white brick trim. Next to the church the former SCHOOL, 1856; it became

---

*Some of the materials appear to have been reused at Lakenheath (q.v.).

a reading room when a new school was built ⅔ m. N by Lord Iveagh, 1895–6, designed by *William Young*. The latter of red brick, with shaped gables and timber cupola. Separate teacher's house. COTTAGES include a terrace, Victoria Place, 1837, and another dated 1842. Among them, set back on the E side, the former METHODIST CHAPEL, 1843–4. Inscription over the door: WESLEYS DOCTRINE.

OLD RECTORY, 1¼ m. N of St Laurence's. Alterations and additions in Tudor style by *Thomas Jeckyll*, 1854, with half-timbered gables, bays and tall chimneys. The original building (hall range and N cross-wing) timber-framed, C16.

WAR MEMORIAL. *See* Elveden.

A RING DITCH, 70 ft 6 in. (21.5 metres) in diameter and probably Early Bronze Age, was excavated at RAF Lakenheath in 2005. It contained a central grave with the remains of four individuals: the semi-articulated remains of an elderly woman overlying the inhumation of a baby with a small pot, the inhumation of a young female aged about 16 years in a sitting crouched position, and the crouched inhumation of an older female, the last three all within individual cuts in the grave; no grave goods. To the S a shallow circular depression about 33 ft (10 metres) in diameter (possibly a type of 'pond barrow') had the unurned cremation of a mature male at its centre.

BARROW at Upper Chamberlain's Farm, 1½ m. SE of St Laurence's. Excavations in 1965–6 of the barrow, surrounded by a chalk ring and a ditch, revealed various Bronze Age cremation burials and a secondary inhumation burial. Neolithic pottery was also found.

EUSTON

EUSTON HALL. The Euston estate, owned by the Rookwoods from the early C15 and briefly, in the mid C17, by the Earl of Desmond, was acquired by Henry Bennet, Lord Arlington, in 1666. Arlington, as Secretary of State, was one of King Charles II's most influential ministers, and was created Baron in 1665 and Earl in 1672, the same year that his daughter Isabella was betrothed to Henry FitzRoy, one of the illegitimate sons of the king and Barbara Villiers, later Duchess of Cleveland. Soon after the betrothal FitzRoy was created Earl of Euston, and in 1675 1st Duke of Grafton.

Between 1666 and 1671 Arlington rebuilt the house on three sides of a courtyard open to the E. It had domed pavilions at the corners 'after the French', as John Evelyn observed, and at the centre a tall porch with giant angle pilasters. The architect of the house is not known; it has been attributed to *William Samwell*, who was then working for Charles II at Newmarket (q.v.), but the evidence is only circumstantial. The principal rooms and staircase were decorated by *Antonio Verrio*, but nothing of this survives. Arlington also, in 1676, rebuilt the parish church, and moved the village to its present position just outside the park. The 2nd Duke of Grafton engaged *William Kent* to make major alterations to the house and park, c. 1730, and perhaps only Kent's death in 1748 prevented a completely new house, for which he sketched a design, being built on a site to the E. Kent was succeeded by the more sober *Matthew Brettingham*, who completely remodelled the exterior of the house in 1750–6. He removed the domes and replaced them with low pyramid roofs, so that they looked like those at Holkham and other country houses of the strict Palladian observance. The W range, containing the main entrance, was given a pedimented centre on its E side, and Brettingham also doubled the width of the N wing. Further alterations were made to the house in the second half of the C19, but it was seriously damaged by a fire in 1902 that destroyed the W and S wings. These were rebuilt in 1905 but mostly demolished in 1950–2 by *Mitchell & Weston* for the 10th Duke, leaving the N wing and three bays of the seven-bay W range.

Since 1952 the entrance to the house has been on the N side. To reach it one passes under the STABLES, which are of Arlington's time, altered and extended by *Brettingham*. Red brick, of two storeys, with hipped roof and octagonal clock turret with ogee dome. Short wings extending towards the house and blank arcades with Diocletian windows in the arches. Inside, two staircases remain, with plain turned balusters. Brettingham added three-bay pedimented pavilions at either end, as well as a range of service buildings along the W side of the courtyard that continue the arcade of the original stables. The symmetry is spoilt by the addition of an upper storey along part of this range in the C19.

The N front of the HOUSE, nine bays wide with a central porch, is exceedingly restrained. Although basically by Brettingham, it was heightened in the second half of the C19, when the balustrade was added and the attic storey rebuilt. Behind this range can be seen the two surviving pavilions with Brettingham's pyramid roofs. The appearance of the S front is less straightforward. At the E end is one of the three-storey pavilions, of red brick with stone quoins and cornice. Then the five-bay S front of the N wing, again as remodelled by Brettingham. At the W end is the stump of the W range, which was thicker than the N and S wings: the first bay is the full depth of the original, the remainder narrower. The S elevation has a pediment reused by *Mitchell & Weston* from the 1905 rebuilding, and a single-storey canted bay. On the W front the three bays of the W range, as rebuilt in 1905, can be more clearly seen, followed by the other corner pavilion, and then a single-storey billiard room added in the second half of the C19. Beyond it the W side of Brettingham's stable range, its symmetry more apparent than when seen from the courtyard.

The importance of the interior lies in its superb collection of portraits, which were rescued from the fire of 1902. What is now the main staircase is late C17, a survival from Arlington's house, with vertically symmetrical balusters.

The grounds to the E, W and S of the house were laid out after 1671 by *John Evelyn*, although very little of his work survives. The forecourt of Arlington's house was bounded to the E by KING CHARLES'S GATE and railings. The date must be the 1670s, although the design is of an earlier style, the mid-C17 Baroque. The stone piers are pierced by elongated arches and carry little segmental pediments above which are elongated vases. The design is small and busy. The gate is in line with the centre of the old W wing, and beyond it, to the E, was an avenue laid out by Evelyn. On the same axis, 650 yds W of the house, PORTER'S LODGE, built in 1752 but corresponding to a sketch of *c.* 1740 by *Kent*. White brick with stone dressings. Pedimented archway flanked by single-storey lodges, altered in the C19; the two lodges now joined by a glazed link. To the S a contemporary WASHHOUSE. Three bays with pediment. Now converted to residential use. In the park and surrounding farmland are numerous clumps of trees, typical of Kent's planting.

S of the house, in line with the middle of the S front, *Evelyn* constructed a polygonal BASIN fed by the Black Bourn that in turn fed a straight CANAL. This ran past the W front of the house to the WATERMILL, which as well as grinding corn also raised water for fountains, a scheme devised by *Sir Samuel Morland*. The present building was designed in 1731 by *Kent*, with the millrace coming straight off the river, at which time Evelyn's canal was filled in. Red brick with burnt headers, in the form of a church with an embattled tower at the water's edge. Machinery by *C. Burrell* of Thetford, 1859, restored to working order 2000–1. Further widening of the river by *Capability Brown*, who carried out alterations to the park for the 3rd Duke in 1767–71. Kent had created a series of small lakes along the river, with a wooden bridge by *Lord Burlington*; Brown joined these into one larger lake SW of the house, as well as making a new lake further upstream called the Broad Water. BRIDGE over the Black Bourn by *Christiani & Nielsen*, 1925. Reinforced concrete, including the balustrade.

In the formal garden E of the house a little wooden SUMMERHOUSE after a design by *Kent*. N of the house, extensive walled gardens. Beside them GARDEN HOUSE, early C17, remodelled probably by Lord Arlington. Eight bays and two storeys, flint with red brick dressings and a hipped roof. Now two dwellings.

THE TEMPLE, 600 yds SE of the house, was *Kent*'s *tour de force* at Euston, a fine mature design, dated inside 1746. It was originally planned to sit on the skyline E of the new house that Kent proposed, and was designed for the 2nd Duke as a banqueting house and also as a vantage point from which to watch his racehorses being exercised. It still sits on high ground, raised higher by the excavation of the ice house that lies beneath it. The centre is octagonal, or rather, square with chamfered corners, and domed. The cardinal faces of the octagon are pedimented below the dome. Two short lower one-bay extensions with Palladian half- or lean-to pediments. The most noteworthy feature of the temple is the rustication of quoins and principal accents by pieces of white or light grey flint. Kent must have loved putting a local material to this Serlian and Palladian use.* The main structure is white brick. The centre has a pedimented principal window to front and back, and this is placed in a niche also surrounded by this flint rustication. The lower parts have arched niches towards the house, and windows on the other side. Two open staircases lead up to the main room. It has arched openings to the side parts (now converted into doorways) and a finely carved cornice. The dome itself had to be reconstructed after a fire, and the decoration up to the eight former ribs was left out. Below this room is a lower one with four free-standing Tuscan columns.

ST GENEVIEVE, 300 yds SE of the house. Rebuilt in 1676 by Lord Arlington. Rendered, with stone quoins and dressings. Of the medieval church, the two lower stages of the tower remain and perhaps some of the outer walls. The new church is an important document of its date, designed in full knowledge of Wren's City churches (1670 onwards) and finished with craftsmen as good as his. The architect is not recorded, but *Henry Bell* of King's Lynn has been suggested on stylistic grounds. The plan is a nave of two oblong groin-vaulted bays, a chancel of two oblong groin-vaulted bays, and between them a bay of identical shape but with square groin-vaulted transepts l. and r. The nave has circular clerestory windows. The second bay of the S aisle was the family pew and has some stucco decoration in the ceiling and, at the back, a large marble inscription tablet, like a standing monument with scroll pediment, volutes and cherubs, commemorating Lord Arlington's rebuilding. Attributed to *Jasper Latham* (GF). Beneath this bay is the family vault. Arched windows, also in the old W tower. The larger ones have simple posthumously Gothic tracery: two lights with round arches and a circle over (what one calls Lombardic tracery). – PULPIT. Exquisitely carved in the style of Gibbons and the City churches. Equally fine the REREDOS (with C19 panel of the Last Supper), low CHANCEL SCREEN with openwork carving, and low SCREEN to N transept. – FONT. 1884. Square, with chamfered corners, on central support and four corner shafts. What seems to be its late C17 marble predecessor sits in the churchyard. – STAINED GLASS. Chancel S and N transept by *Mayer & Co.*, c. 1896. S transept by *Powell & Sons*, 1890–2, designed by *H. E. Wooldridge* in C17 style. Remains of painted decoration on the reveals. Chancel N by *Clayton & Bell*, 1911; their E window of c. 1864 was removed in 1971[†] and replaced with clear

---

*He did the same thing on the Triumphal Arch at Holkham Hall, Norfolk, designed in 1739 but not completed until 1752.
[†]Now in St Matthew, Grafton, New South Wales, Australia.

glass. – BRASSES. Civilian and Lady, probably Roger Rookwood and wife Alice, 1482. 35-in. (89-cm.) figures. – Civilian (lower part lost) and Lady (head gone), *c.* 1520; figures *c.* 18½ in. (47 cm.). – Lady, *c.* 1520; 16-in. (41-cm.) figure. – Knight in armour (lower part lost), wife and indent of another wife, probably Edmund Rookwood †*c.* 1535; figures *c.* 23½ in. (60 cm.). – MONUMENTS. Various coffin-plates taken from the coffins in the vault, starting with that of Lord Arlington †1685. – Many conventional monuments to the FitzRoys, by the usual names: *Bacon & Manning* (1828), *J. Theakston* (1829), *S. Manning* (1835). More adventurous are those to the 3rd Duke of Grafton †1811 by *Behnes* and the 6th Duke of Grafton †1882 by *Gaffin*, but neither could be described as beautiful. – Edward Henry FitzRoy †1917. Marble, enamel and silica, with a figure of St George. By *Powell & Sons*, 1919.

The VILLAGE stands outside the park to the N. Some COTTAGES probably date from Lord Arlington's time, the remainder being mostly C19, but one (long, low, thatched) is dated 1949. Also the former SCHOOL and house, *c.* 1850. Knapped flint with white-brick dressings, arched windows and black glazed pantiles. Opposite, GRANGE FARM, early C18, of flint with red brick diapering and dressings. By the river, the former RECTORY. Front range of knapped flint with white-brick dressings, *c.* 1830, with a later C19 two-storey canted bay at one end. White-brick rear range of the late C18.

BLACKBOURNE HOUSE, ¼ m. SSW. C17, probably timber-framed, clad in the early C19 in an attractive mix of flint and red brick, particularly as seen on the end chimneystacks.

THE RACING STABLES, 2 m. SE. Converted to a house in the 1970s. Red brick with black pantiled roof. Ground floor of blank arcades, seven bays by five, the ends of the long sides projecting slightly. Small windows to the upper floor under semicircular roofs that break the line of the overhanging eaves. The style is close to *Brettingham*'s stables at Euston Hall, i.e. *c.* 1750.

ESTATE COTTAGES, Rymer Point, 2¾ m. SW. 1828. D-plan. One and a half storeys. Flint with white-brick dressings.

RUSHFORD HALL. See p. 477.

EXNING

The old parish of Exning included much of what is now Newmarket, and horses dominate here as well, although the connection has been somewhat damaged by the construction of the A14. This forms the southern boundary of the civil parish, which also includes Landwade (q.v.).

ST MARTIN. Much renewed, with restorations in 1868 and (by *Temple Moore*) in 1911. E.E. chancel with lancet windows on the N and S sides and plain DOUBLE PISCINA. The E window cannot be trusted. W tower late C13 to early C14. Triple-chamfered tower arch with continuous mouldings, W window with reticulated tracery, S transept Dec. The four-light S window also reticulated. The N transept has the same forms, but they seem all new. C14 arcade of four bays with octagonal piers and double-chamfered arches. In the S transept, AUMBRY and PISCINA with dogtooth carving, *c.* 1300, and in the S wall a double HEART SHRINE. Ogee-headed recess divided into two compartments with cusped openings. – PULPIT. C18 with very tall back and tester; simple. – STALL. C15, with traceried front and poppyheads. – BENCH ENDS. Straight-headed, with linen-fold panelling; C16. – COMMUNION RAIL. C18, with slender turned balusters; now painted, unfortunately. – SCULPTURE. St Martin by *Charlie Hull*, 1998. In a C14 canopied niche by the N door. – ROYAL ARMS. Of George II; painted on canvas by *Peter Cattee*, 1734. Another set, on wood, of George III, 1817. – STAINED GLASS. E window by *Heaton, Butler & Bayne*, 1901. – MONUMENT. Francis Robartson of 'Reiseaprice' (Rise ap Rise, Fishtoft, Lincs.). Mid-C17 memorial board, charmingly painted. Achievement of arms between pilasters with verse below.

OLD VICARAGE, Church Lane. By *H. Hakewill*, 1820–1, enlarged by *W. M. Fawcett*, 1903. Hakewill's modest white-brick house, of two storeys and attics, was three bays wide, quite plain, with a semicircular porch. To this Fawcett added two more bays on the E side and a central pediment, and enlarged the ground-floor windows.

W of Church Lane, extending through to Chapel Street, HARRATON COURT, a large racing establishment built by the Earl of Durham in the 1880s, and probably designed by *Heaton & Gibb*, who made additions in 1900. Mostly of white brick with red brick dressings. Main house (partially dem.) at the N of the site, and in the middle a large racing yard with a three-storey tower and pavilion roof topped with an open metalwork crown and weathervane. Trainer's house (HARRATON LODGE) at the S end of the E range, as well as other staff houses. QUEEN ALEXANDRA STABLES, in the SW part of the site, was originally the stud yard. Adjoining it a large clunch BARN of 1811–21.

EXNING HOUSE, Cotton End Road. Fine Early Georgian red brick house. Two and a half storeys and seven bays, with three-bay pediment. Stone quoins to the angles and also to the angles of the centre. Porch with segmental pediment on well-carved Corinthian columns, and similar doorcase on the garden front. *Andrews Jelfe*, mason-contractor, added a doorcase in 1734, but it is not known whether his contribution extended further. Elliptical staircase with slender twisted balusters. Large Baroque additions to the N by *Philip Webb*, 1895–6, which left the old house alone but otherwise paid it few compliments, with floor levels at different heights and the brick not quite matching. The additions included a new main entrance, dining room and billiard room, and extensive service wing. Mostly two-storey, but with a three-storey block of domestic offices at the NE corner that has rendered upper walls. Now subdivided, and the interiors much altered. In the garden, two sets of mid-C18 wrought-iron gates. On the W side of Cotton End Road, a large complex of estate buildings and stables, including an early C19 BARN of painted clunch with half-hipped slate roof.

GEORGE GIBSON CLOSE, Windmill Hill. By *Fitzroy Robinson & Partners*, 1965. Group of sixteen semi-detached single-storey houses and one two-storey house. Agreeable Neo-Georgian in red brick; the layout rigidly symmetrical, facing the back of Exning House but, annoyingly, not quite on an axis with it.

NORTHMORE STUD, North End. A two-cell, lobby-entrance, timber-framed and plastered house of the late C16 or early C17, enlarged out of all recognition *c.* 1930. Some impressive clunch walling along the road and behind the house two weatherboarded and thatched BARNS, one early C17 of seven bays with aisles, one C18 of three bays. More good outbuildings to the S at ORCHARD FARM, including an early C19 barn of clunch, and at ROSE HALL, including a large white-brick-and-flint barn of *c.* 1870–80.

At MARSH STABLES, Church Street, 100 yds SSE, a C17 or C18 DOVECOTE. Of clunch, with red brick dressings, and hipped roof with large gablets. Across the road to the E, at EXETER STUD, a C17 BARN, now converted, also of clunch but painted. Half-hipped pantiled roof.

EXNING CEMETERY. *See* Newmarket.

FAKENHAM MAGNA

9070

ST PETER. The E angles of the nave with long-and-short work prove the Saxon origin of this part of the church. One blocked N and one blocked S window Norman, the latter just W of the porch gable. In the chancel a pair of C13 lancets. W tower, nave windows and most chancel windows Dec. N vestry perhaps 1859, when the church was restored and re-seated. – SCREEN. Much restored; with one-light divisions. – MONUMENT. Reynolds Taylor †1692. Tomb-chest of black and white marble. Pilasters with shields of arms.

N of the church FAKENHAM HALL, now two houses: the S wing (Church Lodge) timber-framed, encased in brick in the mid C19 when the N wing (Northern House) was added. Here the brick is diapered, and the windows have hoodmoulds. Further N, FIELD FARMHOUSE. Late C16 timber-framed and plastered with a cross-wing at the N end, all unusually of three storeys. At the S end a two-storey early C19 range with a cast-iron openwork porch. Then RECTORY COTTAGE, knapped flint with white-brick dressings, and the OLD RECTORY, altered and enlarged in 1857, mostly white brick but with a front in the same materials as the cottage.

FAKENHAM PARVA lay on the N side of the Black Bourn valley from Fakenham Magna, but had been absorbed into Euston by the mid C18; the site of its church is not known.

EARTHWORK in Burnthall Plantation, 600 yds S of the church, on the N bank of the Black Bourn. There is a circular ditch and bank, about 100 yds in diameter, with an entrance to the W where the N end of the rampart broadens. It has no recorded history before the C18, but is probably a Norman ringwork built by the de Valognes family, descended from Peter de Valognes, Sheriff of Essex and Hertfordshire in 1086.

FELSHAM

ST PETER. A will of 1423 refers to the new tower, but its tracery is still Dec. Dec also the wide nave with tall two-light windows. Panelled battlements. No aisles. N porch with much flushwork panelling on the buttresses and the battlements. Side windows with tracery. Money for their glass was left in 1470 and 1471. Entrance with three orders of fleurons. Three niches round the entrance. Shields in the spandrels and seated lions as headstops. Chancel rebuilt in 1873. Nave restored by *H. J. Green*, 1878, including removal of W gallery and re-seating. – FONT. Really two fonts; for the base is clearly the mutilated bowl of a font. On it animals, human faces, etc., below ogee arches. On the other bowl demi-figures of angels on the underside and tracery patterns on the eight sides. – ROYAL ARMS. Of George III, updated for George IV in 1820, painted on board. The lion on the crown has a very human face, and there are two little faces peeping out from the scrollwork of the motto. – STAINED GLASS. *Messrs Pepper* were responsible for reglazing the nave in 1878, and the tower window †1894 may be by them also. – LYCHGATE. 1901–2 by *P. J. Turner*, a pupil of J. S. Corder.

Former NATIONAL SCHOOL (now village hall), E of church. By *J. Flatman*, 1897–8. Red brick with white brick dressings. Half-hipped slate roof. One large window with Gothic tracery.

OLD RECTORY, 300 yds E. Timber-framed, probably C17, remodelled in 1814 by *William Lambert* of Cowes, although the deposited plans do not correspond exactly to the present building. Three-bay, two-storey front with full-height semicircular bays at each end. Partially clad in mathematical tiles. Doric porch.

MAUSOLEUM HOUSE, 100 yds W. 1794. White brick. Three bays and two storeys. The MAUSOLEUM after which it is named stands in the middle of a field 300 yds to its S. According to John Wesley, who saw it in 1771, it was built *c.* 1755 by John Reynolds, High Sheriff in 1735, for his only child, whose death was followed two years later by that of his wife; two years after that, in 1759, Reynold himself died. Now an indistinct ruin; according to Pevsner (1961) of yellow brick with red brick dressings and blank windows.

FELSHAM HOUSE, ½ m. NNW. Large mid-C19 white-brick house. At one end of the garden front a broad single-storey bow with first-floor Venetian window. Built by Rev. Thomas Anderson, rector and patron 1822–72, for his son. Alterations and additions by *Peter Cleverly*, *c.* 1964.

HILL FARM, ¾ m. ENE. Farmhouse with some exposed timbers. Two-storey mid-C16 hall with large early C16 cross-wing to the l. Both parts jettied. Some original windows.

FINNINGHAM

ST BARTHOLOMEW. Partly of the early C14, partly Perp. The W tower is of the earlier date. Bell-openings with Y-tracery, but that to the E a quatrefoil in a circle. The chancel S doorway and nave S doorway also of the earlier date. The rest of the S side Perp. N side all Perp with a simple porch of red brick with diapering. The S porch is the only ornate piece. It has flushwork panelling, three niches round the entrance, and a parapet nicely decorated with alternating quatrefoils placed upright and diagonally. It was restored in 1885, as was the rest of the church, between 1880 and 1889, by *J. A. Reeve* – most noticeably the chancel. – FONT. Octagonal, Perp. Simple. The base is of two steps, the upper in the form of a Maltese cross. – FONT COVER. Early C16. A pinnacle, but not a high one. The principal decoration is some oblong panels with squares flanked by little arches. In the squares an interesting combination of squares and circles, e.g. a square set within a square. All three touch. Or a circle set within a square set within a circle set within a square. All squares and circles touch. It all looks connected with the masons' mysteries of proportion. – REREDOS and WEST GALLERY. 1888 by *Reeve*. – BENCH ENDS. With tracery and poppyheads, reused in 1886. On the arms figures seated not towards the E as usual but towards the gangway. – STAINED GLASS. Some, in the E window. – MONUMENTS. John Williamson †1781. By *John Golden* of Holborn. A pretty tablet of white and pink marble, Neoclassical in style. No figures. – Sir John Fenn, editor of the Paston letters, †1794. By *John Bacon Sen.* Exhibited 1795, dated 1797. With a woman kneeling over a tomb-chest. – His widow Ellenor Fenn *née* Frere †1813. By *Tomson* of Cambridge. Tablet within an ogee arch with two children's heads as stops. – Rev. Edward Frere †1841. Marble oval with painted coat of arms, above marble scroll with inscription. – Hatley Frere †1868. Floral wreath of white marble. By *Currie*, Oxford Street. – John Frere, the antiquary, †1807. Oval slate tablet with inscription and a replica of the flint handaxe found by him at Hoxne in 1797. By the *Cardozo-Kindersley Workshop*, 1999.

FORMER NATIONAL SCHOOL, 525 yds NNW. By *Edmund Catchpole*, 1872, including two-storey teacher's house. Red brick. Windows with narrow cusped lights. Gables with wavy bargeboards.

OLD RECTORY, 200 yds NNE. 1907–8 by *E. C. Frere* for Rev. L. H. Frere, built with funds provided by Rev. Temple Frere, rector of Finningham 1805–29.* L-plan, with the entrance in the angle. Red brick ground floor, the upper storey plastered and slightly overhanging.

YEW TREE HOUSE and AMBERLEY, N of the church. Mid-C16 timber-framed and plastered house, with service cross-wing added to the l. in the late C17. On the main range two large oval panels of late C17 pargetting, perhaps the most handsome in Suffolk. On one panel a vine, on the other a fig tree.

GREEN FARM, 100 yds S. C16, timber-framed and plastered. Parlour cross-wing to the l., longer dairy cross-wing to the r., both C17 additions for the Freres, who purchased the farm in 1593.

FLEMPTON

ST CATHERINE. Much renewed. W tower rebuilt in 1839, part of a general restoration by *J. C. & G. Buckler*. Further internal restoration by *James Fowler*, 1885–6, including re-seating, and removal of W gallery of 1839. The details of the nave and chancel are late C13 to early C14. The best original feature is the chancel PISCINA with a two-light reticulated head. E window of three lights with minor flowing tracery. One chancel S window has a transom and beneath it a lowside window. Nave N vestry 1911 by *J. Flatman*. – PULPIT. Jacobean. – COMMUNION RAIL. With turned balusters. Late C17. – DOOR with tracery. – ROYAL ARMS. Of George III. Painted on canvas by *Ed. Boyton*, Bury, 1763. – STAINED GLASS. Chancel windows probably by *Clayton & Bell*, after 1895. – Nave N †1927 by *F. C. Eden*, nave S †1951 by *G. E. R. Smith*. – Tower window by *T. F. Curtis, Ward & Hughes*, 1902. Christ crowning the young Queen Victoria, attended by Faith, Hope, Charity and Gentleness. – MONUMENT. J. H. Powell †1849. By *M. W. Johnson*. With an urn and Graeco-Egyptian ornament. – LYCHGATE. 1931. Good carving to the gable.

St Catherine's was the parish church for Hengrave (q.v.). At the edge of the village, on the Hengrave side, the former SCHOOL for both villages, built by Rev. W. R. Bain, 1866. 'Elizabethan', of flint with white-brick dressings.

---

*Recorded on a foundation stone with lettering by *Eric Gill*, removed from the house and sold in 2012.

Flempton, St Catherine.
Engraving, 1827

BUS SHELTER next to the churchyard by *Eric Sandon*, 1955. Like the one at Hengrave, but with a tiled roof.

BARROWS. A group of four, Bronze Age, around the NE corner of Risby Poor's Heath, half in Flempton and half in Risby (q.v.). The most easterly was excavated in 1964 revealing two ditches c. 79 and 75 ft (24 and 23 metres) in diameter surrounding eight inhumation burials (including a child with beaker/food vessel; one in the remains of a tree-trunk coffin; one with jet beads; one with a beaker; one with a food vessel) and fragments of others. Barrow now scarcely visible in an arable field. The other barrow is close by in the same field, adjacent to a trackway, and is c. 95 ft (29 metres) in diameter but only 16 in. (0.4 metres) high.

FLOWTON

ST MARY. A church with individuality in various details. Of c. 1300, except for the big early C16 s window no doubt inserted to light the rood screen (which has not survived). Panel tracery in red brick. Unbuttressed W tower of knapped flint. It has a S, not a W doorway. W window with Y-tracery flanked by two deep and large cusped niches. Small circular quatrefoiled windows above. Top stage rebuilt in red brick c. 1748, with pyramid roof. Charming E window. It is of three lights with reticulated tracery, but each reticulation unit is filled by the motif of a four-petalled flower. Rough tie-beam roof with crown-posts and four-way struts. Restored and re-seated 1878–9. – FONT. Octagonal, of Purbeck type, C13, with two flat pointed arches to each side. – PULPIT. By *H. M. Cautley*, made by *Ernest Barnes*, 1957–8. – WALL PAINTING. Fragment of C14 decoration (nave S wall).

OLD RECTORY, E of the church. 1845 by *J. M. Clark*. 'Elizabethan', of red brick with diapering and carved bargeboards.

FORNHAM ALL SAINTS

The village overlies part of a Neolithic cursus (*see* Introduction, p. 10), 1.2 m. (1,900 metres) long and 25–40 yds (23–36.5 metres) wide, that runs alongside the River Lark. The church stands within its projected course, at the NE end of the long narrow village green.

ALL SAINTS. Restored by *A. W. Blomfield*, 1863–4: 'so complete has been the restoration that any casual observer would imagine it to have been entirely rebuilt' (*Bury & Norwich Post*). Norman S doorway with one order of shafts. Early C13 W tower, unbuttressed, with lancets and a small single-chamfered doorway towards the nave. Parapet and pinnacles of 1863–4. Nave of *c.* 1300 – see one window with Y-tracery. Tall Dec chancel, the E window reticulated. Stepped SEDILIA in the S window with PISCINA between the window and the priest's door, i.e. W rather than the usual E of the sedilia. Perp S aisle attached to the E wall of the S porch, the latter refaced with knapped flint in 1863–4. The aisle was built by Thomas Edward, and completed by his son William; their wills (proved in 1500 and 1509 respectively) ask to be buried in it. Flushwork initials, shields, etc., on the battlements spell out their names. Simpler Perp N aisle and N transept. The S arcade has two bays, with a further opening from the S chapel into the chancel; the N arcade three bays, with an opening from the N transept into the nave. Shafts with capitals to the arches only. In the S chapel the Perp E window has a niche to its r. in the SE angle. There was also one in the NE angle. Small N extension by the *Whitworth Co-Partnership*, 2007. – BENCHES. With poppyheads, and two with animals on the arms. – COMMANDMENT BOARDS. Two, now at the W end. C18. Painted to imitate hinged panels, complete with *trompe l'œil* hinges. – STAINED GLASS. E window by *Hardman*, 1912. It cost £125. – BRASS. Thomas Barwick †1599. Only the upper part of the figure, now mural; 8 in. (20 cm.).

OLD RECTORY, on the E side of the Green. C16, timber-framed and plastered, with gabled cross-wings: that on the r. jettied, that on the l. with an early C19 lattice-work porch. Against the r. return wall a single-storey bow. At the l. end of the house a three-bay, two-storey addition of *c.* 1830, also timber-framed and plastered.

FORNHAM ST GENEVIEVE

ST GENEVIEVE. Money was left for the repair of the W tower in 1452, and that is now all that remains of the church. Unbuttressed, with a lancet on the ground floor and a top parapet. The remainder was destroyed by fire in 1775: 'this accident was occasioned by a man's shooting at some jackdaws upon the steeple' (*Ipswich Journal*, 20 May 1775).
FORNHAM HALL, which stood just to the E, has also now gone (dem. 1951). It was built for Charles Kent by *James Wyatt*, 1776–85, enlarged *c.* 1824 by *Robert Abraham* for the 12th Duke of Norfolk, and further enlarged later in the C19. Wyatt's STABLE BLOCK and other outbuildings remain, as well as the Agent's and Head Gardener's Houses, all in white brick; now converted to housing. Beyond them to the NW the walled KITCHEN GARDEN, surrounded by a secondary or slip wall. ICE HOUSE a little further out. Another walled garden 500 yds WNW, open on its fourth side to the River Lark. Kent enclosed the PARK and in 1782 sought the advice of *Capability Brown*, although it is not clear what, if anything, was carried out as a result.
PARK FARM, ½ m. SE. Model farm by *Abraham* for the Duke of Norfolk. Red brick and flint quadrangle. Across one end a five-bay two-storey house with two-bay one-and-a-half-storey pavilions with pedimented gables. Flint with some red and some white-brick dressings, including rusticated quoins. *See also* Hall Farm, Fornham St Martin.

FORNHAM ST MARTIN

ST MARTIN. Perp, with a S aisle of 1870–1 by *A. W. Blomfield*, replacing one of 1846. Twenty marks (£13 6s. 8d.) was left for the W tower in 1425. Unusually it has tall two-light bell-openings with a transom. Flushwork chequerboard decoration on the battlements and at the base. Nave tracery with straight-headed arches. N porch of brick with a stepped gable. – FONT. Perp, octagonal, simple. – MISERICORDS. Two, reused in lectern and reader's desk, 1871. They represent St Martin and the Beggar and the Martyrdom of St Thomas Becket. – STAINED GLASS. E window †1846 by *William Wailes*; nave N †1860 by *Wailes & Strang*, 1873; probably also two S aisle windows and the W window †1858. – Nave N †1973–4 by *R. F. Ashmead* (*Abbott & Co.*).
Almost opposite the church the OLD RECTORY. Early C19 white brick. Three bays and two storeys. Doric porch. Next to the church THE WOOLPACK, late C19 white brick with two canted bays and pedimented gable-ends. In the garden, overlooking the churchyard, a small red brick early C19 GAZEBO. Further

N on the same side a terrace of COTTAGES, 1873, built by William Gilstrap of Fornham Hall (*see* Fornham St Genevieve). He also enlarged the SCHOOL, 1887, originally built by the Duke of Norfolk, 1836. Flint with white-brick dressings. Then the OLD PARSONAGE, Georgian and partly red brick but mostly concealed by C19 white brick. Opposite, KRISTIE COTTAGE, *c.* 1840. Flint with red brick dressings, panels of moulded bricks, and ornamental cast-iron casements. Connected by screen walls to the wall of FORNHAM HOUSE. This is of white brick, early to mid-C19, but greatly altered and extended as a residential home. STABLES with clock turret and GATE COTTAGE of red brick with white-brick dressings and decorative detailing, similar to Kristie Cottage.

Most of Fornham St Martin belonged to the Fornham Hall estate. A pair of estate cottages at the N end of the village (FLINT COTTAGES), and behind the Old Rectory RECTORY COTTAGE and LITTLE PARK. All early C19, of flint with white-brick dressings. Rectory Cottage and Little Park have Gothick windows, Little Park has a three-bay centre and projecting canted bays at each end. Very probably by *Robert Abraham*, who designed HALL FARM, ¾ m. ENE, for the Duke of Norfolk, *c.* 1824. Flint with white-brick dressings. Two-storey, five-bay farmhouse, much plainer than Park Farm, Fornham St Genevieve.

FRECKENHAM

The village is strung out along the Fordham–Mildenhall road, with the church and manor house tucked away to the S.

ST ANDREW. Over-restored by *G. E. Street*, 1867–9. The W tower fell in 1882 and was rebuilt by *J. D. Wyatt*, 1884. One window with Y-tracery in the vestry, two two-light Perp windows used as a kind of dormer to light the rood. E window of three stepped lancet lights under one arch, shafted inside, i.e. *c.* 1300. Arcade with piers of keeled quatrefoil section and arches with one chamfer and one recessed chamfer, i.e. also *c.* 1300. Nice Perp canted wagon roofs in nave and chancel, with bosses. – FONT. Octagonal, Perp, plain. – FONT COVER. By *Jack Penton*, 1972. Scrolls, painted. – PULPIT. 1884. Stone.– BENCHES. A mix of medieval and C19 work. With poppyheads, some in the form of praying figures, one with the devil dropping a priest into the jaws of hell. – SCULPTURE. Alabaster relief from a former altar, a scene from the Life of St Eligius. C15. – COMMANDMENTS. Painted on canvas by *Samuel Rolfe* of Mildenhall, 1845. – STAINED GLASS. E window probably by *Hardman*, *c.* 1867. Chancel S †1899 (Annunciation) by *H. W. Lonsdale*.

OLD RECTORY, s of the church. Late C16, enlarged in 1760 and 1830. White brick, including cladding of the older timber-framed parts. Gothick detailing to the 1830 range.

MANOR HOUSE, 150 yds NE. Late C17 red brick. Two storeys. Wide four-bay front. Timber-framed and plastered rear wing with C17 staircase. Another rear wing enlarged 1934.

BEACON MOUND, opposite Manor House. A small motte-and-bailey castle. Mound about 15 ft (4.5 metres) high. Rectangular bailey on NW side with ditch on its N side. Of uncertain date.

GAZELEY

7060

ALL SAINTS. Mostly of the later C13. The chancel is an interesting and individual work. The E window has three lights, the outer ones a little taller and narrower than the middle one. On them stands not a circle but a rounded triangle with a sexfoil set in, three foils being pointed and large, the other three round and small. The whole window is not simply arched, but the outer arches of the outer lights form part of its outline, which is then continued by the sides of the rounded triangle, forming a normal arch-head. Inside, the arch has a normal rere-arch, but there are in addition tall arched panels in the jambs. The side windows have quatrefoils on pointed-trefoiled lights. The westernmost chancel windows are transomed lowside windows. PISCINA with oddly double-cusped arch on shafts. The adjoining SEDILIA are two stepped seats in the window sill, separated by a simple arm with a (defaced) lion *couchant*. On the N side of the chancel a deep gabled niche. The chancel arch and four-bay arcade were rebuilt in 1856–7 by *G. G. Scott*, but in correct late C13 style. Quatrefoil piers and boldly moulded capitals. The chancel roof is an early C16 canted wagon roof and has small cusped panels and many carved bosses. The W tower was largely rebuilt in 1884, but its Perp W doorway seems in order. Perp also the aisles and clerestory. Tree-ring analysis of the timbers of the S aisle roof shows that it was built in the first half of the C15. *J. D. Wyatt* restored the nave roof in 1888, and the chancel and S porch 1890–1. – FONT. Octagonal. The sides have plainly represented tracery motifs, all usual about 1300 (e.g. three stepped lancets under one arch, three-light intersected, three lancets of the same size, Y-tracery in a round arch, and pointed quatrefoils). – FONT COVER. C17. – PULPIT. Perp, with cusped-arched panels. – SCREEN. Much restored; with one-light divisions. It was sufficiently admired in 1520 (and was presumably then quite new) to have been specified as one of the models for a new rood loft for Great St Mary's, Cambridge. – BENCH ENDS. Some with poppyheads, others with straight tops with simple tracery and buttresses. Some backs have pierced tracery and one an inscription, much damaged, that seems to read 'Salamon Sayet'. Some of the bench ends may be reused panels from the screen. – STAINED GLASS. E window, c. 1886, probably by *Burlison & Grylls*. Aisle E windows by *Lavers & Barraud*: N 1859, designed by *H. Stacy Marks*, S 1865. W window by *Clutterbuck*, 1867. – MONUMENTS. Early C16 tomb recess in the S aisle. Tomb-chest with small lozenge panels. The arch above the recess is nearly a lintel. Top with cresting. The brasses inside are lost. – Chalice brass, c. 1530. Inscription lost. – Edmond Heigham †1604 and wife Alice †1599. Kneeling figures, facing in the same direction, between Ionic columns. Strapwork pediment.

OLD RECTORY, 100 yds N. By *William Rogers*, 1856. White brick, and rather urban. For Rev. William Cooke, vicar 1856–66, who also paid for the work done to the church in the 1880s.

(At DESNING HALL, 1 m. SE, an aisled BARN dating back to the C13 but principally late C14. Nine bays, two gabled midstreys.)

WINDMILL, 850 yds NNW. A tower mill of 1844, converted into a house by *H. C. Hughes* in the early 1950s and extended c. 2000. C19 flint and red brick cottages nearby, one pair with Gothick windows and doors.

DENHAM CASTLE, 2 m. ESE. A motte-and-bailey castle, the mound much reduced in height. Surrounded by a ditch, enlarged to a pond on one side. Also known as Castle Holes.

BARROWS. A group of three, on the S side of the old Newmarket Road (Icknield Way), about 1½ m. N of the village, and now spread by ploughing. Another about ½ m. further NE, at Pin Farm, was excavated in 1969; sixteen burials were found.

GEDDING

ST MARY. Nave and chancel. W tower with flushwork on two diagonal buttresses, probably paid for by a bequest of 1470. The upper parts finished much later in red brick. In the nave two Norman windows, one N, one S. The S window has a monolithic arched top with beading, and jambs with chevron decoration that may have been reused from a larger (Saxon?) opening. Nave N doorway of c. 1200. The remaining details are Dec. The most interesting feature is the chancel arch. It is double-chamfered with continuous mouldings and flanked by one tall cusped lancet-like niche l. and one r. The side arches have on their E face crocketed hoodmoulds added by *E. F. Bisshopp*, part of his restoration of 1884 which included taking down a white-brick S porch; his plans for a new porch, and for rebuilding the tower, were not executed. Roof with scissor-bracing below and above the collars. – FONT. Octagonal, Perp, with simple cusped blank arches and shields. – BENCHES. Very simple. Four, C15, with poppyheads and carved backs. Another probably C17.

ST MARY'S HOUSE, on s side of churchyard. Late C16, timber-framed and plastered, extended to the r. in the early C18. C17 sawtooth chimneystack.

GEDDING HALL, NE of the church and visible from the churchyard. The fragment of a moated courtyard house, built probably in the 1480s by Sir Robert Chamberlain, a leading Yorkist executed by Henry VII in 1491. What remains of this time is the gatehouse. Red brick, with a very tall four-centred archway (filled in) and two polygonal turrets whose top parts are not preserved and instead have gables. At the height of the springing of the archway they have a frieze of a kind of ballflower. Two-light windows. Stepped gable-ends to the return walls. To the r. a lower wing, contemporary or a little later, leading to additions of 1897 by *Arthur Wakerley* of Leicester, who had bought the house for his own occupation. Large square tower on the corner and service range beyond. The tower has diapered brickwork, a parapet that rises to accommodate an oculus, and a taller stair-turret with ogee dome. It does not pretend to look older than it is. The moat is said to have been built in 1273.

GIFFORDS HALL

2 m. NE of Stoke-by-Nayland

Giffords Hall, as it stands, is one of the loveliest houses of its date in England, neither small nor overwhelmingly grand; warm and varied, happy in scale and in the proportions between its materials. The manor was held by the Gifford family in the second half of the C13 (first recorded 1287), and the earliest parts of the house date from the late C13 or early C14. It was acquired by Philip Mannock in 1428. Some rebuilding took place in the mid C15 but the greater part of the present house was built between about 1490 and 1520 (perhaps following the marriage of George Mannock to Catherine Waldegrave in about 1494), with some modernization *c.* 1730–40. The house remained with the Mannock family until 1883, after which it was restored and extended; further alterations and additions were made following its purchase by C. G. Brocklebank in 1934.

On the S side of the house, but not in the middle, is a brick gatehouse. It is only two storeys high, but has angle turrets that give a vertical emphasis and make it seem taller. To the outside, a four-centred arch, blank tracery in the spandrels, cusped tracery friezes above. One of them occurs identically at Layer Marney in Essex, *c.* 1520–5. Windows with four-centred heads to the lights. The turrets with angle strips and trefoiled corbel-friezes at the tops of the panels. Three-step battlements and brick pinnacles. Brick pinnacles had been used at Faulkbourne in Essex somewhat earlier, and are to be found *c.* 1530 at West

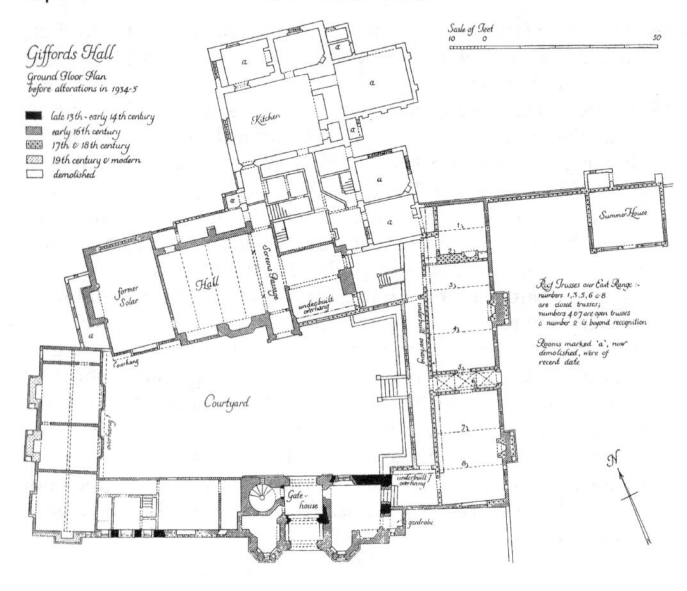

Giffords Hall.
Plan before alterations in 1934–5

Stow Hall. The walls are diapered, although not extensively, and the archway and window surrounds were plastered in imitation of stone. Stone was actually used for the middle archway, and on the inner w wall of the gatehouse is a small (re-set?) early C14 stone doorway. The DOORS, with linenfold panelling, belong to the C16. CLOCK by *Thomas Moore* of Ipswich, mid-C18.

The courtyard is delightful. The gatehouse looks broader and lower on the inside and altogether more domestic, and has three stepped brick gables and half-gables at the ends. The small pinnacles are set diagonally. Brickwork with extensive diapering but, at the E end, a large area of older flint walling. Opposite the gatehouse is the hall. It has a brick porch with four-centred entrance. The timber-framed upper storey, with its charming oriel window and bargeboarding, was added *c.* 1890. To the w the big chimney-breast with a two-light upper window in it, the flues being conducted to its l. and r. Polygonal chimneys with star tops. The hall bay was replaced *c.* 1730–40 by a brick wall with a Venetian window and a (blank) circular window over. Another Venetian window in the plastered wall E of the hall porch. The rooms behind here were remodelled internally in the mid C18, as was the solar block beyond the hall to the w; but the latter was refronted in the late C19 in the style of the timber-framed W range. The W range was then embellished with oriels and brick-nogging, but has its original jettied upper storey. The S range back to the gatehouse also has exposed timbers, with plaster between the studs, although its s (exterior) wall has sections of older flint. The E range, originally the service range, was extensively altered c. 1730–40, including lowering the floor to gain ceiling height for reception rooms, but an original doorway has been exposed inside, there are crown-posts in the roof, and the original massive external chimney-breasts remain on the garden side. The crown-posts suggest that this might be the earliest phase of the Mannocks' rebuilding, and the chimney-breasts might relate to a contract of 1459 for the purchase of 60,000 bricks by John Mannock. Two more big chimneystacks on the exterior of the W range, with star tops, but here of 1934–5. Of this date also the large service wing on the N side of the house, replacing what was almost certainly the original kitchen that had been extended in the late C19.

Inside, the hall has a splendid double hammerbeam roof with nice carving in the three sets of arched braces and tracery in the spandrels. In the spandrels also some pretty carvings of mainly domestic subjects: a fish on a plate, a mouse running into a pitcher, a cauldron, a lute. The gallery front has late C17 twisted balusters. The staircase to the gallery, which was moved and altered in the 1930s, has earlier parts, probably of c. 1630. The ground-floor rooms of the W range have finely carved beams.

Opposite the gatehouse, the CHAPEL OF ST NICHOLAS. The flint building, in ruins, consists of nave and chancel only and has a flat E end. It is supposed to date from the early C13. No more detail survives than the surround of the W window.

On the E side of the house, attached to it by a wall, a delightful mid-C18 ORANGERY of red and white brick. Three bays, with tall sashes. NE of the house a square timber-framed and plastered DOVECOTE with wattle-and-daub nesting boxes. Hipped roof with gablets. The timber frame appears C16.

GIPPING

CHAPEL OF ST NICHOLAS. The private chapel[*] of Sir James Tyrell, who was beheaded in 1502. His mansion, demolished in the mid C19, stood about 200 yds to the E. A chapel is recorded in 1340, but a bequest of 1474 may be a *terminus post quem* for rebuilding. It became a Free Chapel, administered by trustees, in 1743. The plain stuccoed W tower, probably C16 or early C17, spoils what would otherwise be a singularly perfect piece of late medieval Suffolk architecture – nave and chancel and a curious N annexe added within a few years, certainly before 1502. This annexe has a fireplace in its N wall, and for that reason it has been assumed that originally it was the

[*] Hence no burials or monuments, which are to be found at Stowmarket.

Gipping, Chapel of St Nicholas, flushwork emblems.
Drawing by J. Blatchly, 2005

chaplain's dwelling. The wall behind the fireplace is treated as a dummy bay window. It is canted, and the one-light, three-light, one-light rhythm with transoms is all made up of flushwork. W entrance to the room with inscription 'Pray for Sr Jamys Tirell: Dame Anne his wyf'. Flushwork decoration, which is generously applied to walls, buttresses, etc., incorporates the Tyrell emblem (the triquetra of the Trinity), Tyrell motto, and Lombardic letters 'AMLA', apparently referring to Tyrell's wife, Anne Arundel. The composition of N and S doorways is identical, and they are charming pieces too. Whereas the other windows are of three lights and transomed, there are here four lights and the lower part of the middle two is taken up by the doorways. The lower parts to their l. and r. are again flushwork, and in the upper parts flushwork is also inserted between the two l. and two r. lights. On the S side, but not on the N, and for no obvious reason, the windows are of different heights. E wall with polygonal buttresses. Five-light E window. The interior is as translucent as a glasshouse. What effect the original glass must have had is hard to guess. – BENCHES. Some of the C15, thought to have come from Stowmarket church, including one with an end of quite exceptional, very simple shape, with the Tyrell triquetra. Twisted-leaf frieze along the back of the seat. – Other FURNISHINGS of *c.* 1743, including COMMUNION RAIL, PULPIT and BENCHES, all painted. Also of that date the ALTAR, with marble slab and fitted red velvet cover, and *trompe l'œil* PAINTING on E wall of columns and drapery. – STAINED GLASS. Five figures and jumbled fragments of the late C15 and early C16, as well as a piece dated 1756, re-set by *Townshend & Howson*, 1938–9.

CHAPEL FARM, W of the church. C16, timber-framed and plastered, the front mostly jettied. Chimney rebuilt 1967. 150 yds W of the house a DOVECOTE. Octagonal. Timber-framed, probably C17, covered with clay daub and later lined with brick.

GIPPING LONE, 600 yds N. L-plan timber-framed and plastered house. Lower range late C15, main range added *c.* 1600. At the S end of the main range a gable with overhanging tie-beam and carved decoration that incorporated the Tyrell arms. Central chimneystack with four ornamental shafts.

WOOD FARM, 1 m. SE. Small C16 timber-framed house, tactfully restored and imaginatively extended over a pond by *Rodney Black*, 2000–4. S of the house a range of farm buildings to which Black added, 2008–9, a traditional five-bay timber-framed BARN for entertaining etc.

GISLINGHAM

0070

ST MARY. Mid-C13 chancel with Dec windows. Good four-light E window with depressed arch and reticulation motifs. Good N porch with an inscription commemorating Robert Chapman and his wife Rose. The entrance arch has little shields in the outer and inner mouldings. The hoodmould rests on seated lions. Perp nave, nearly 24 ft (7.3 metres) wide, wider than the one it replaced. Three-light windows with stepped transoms. One of the mullions of the SW window has been craftily replaced in oak at some point. Red brick W tower of 1639–40 by *John Rusel*; the bricklayer was *Edmund Petto* of Bramford and John Darby gave £100 towards the cost. The W door was reused from the old tower, which was built *c*. 1386 (bequest of 20s.) and fell in 1599. False double hammerbeam roof. – FONT. Perp. Four lions against the stem. The Emblems of the Evangelists and four shields against the bowl. Inscription against the top step of the base also referring to the Chapman family. – REREDOS. With painted slate panels. Probably of 1874, when the chancel was restored. – COMMUNION RAIL. 1712 by *Matthew Tanner*. With turned balusters. – SCREEN. Four panels from the base (chancel wall). – PULPIT. A three-decker, including tester, built by *Richard Rednall* in 1802 for £14 1s. HOURGLASS STAND nearby. – BENCHES. Seventeen with poppyheads, C15. Others incorporated in the BOX PEWS. Fifteen of the original nineteen, for which *John Legget* was paid £29 15s. 5d. in 1810. – WEST GALLERY. Mid-C18, very plain. – WALL PAINTINGS. In nave, two C15 consecration crosses and remains of C17 texts. – Under tower, PANELS giving the names of the bellringers in 1717. Also a slate plaque recording a peal in 1822, giving the names of the ringers and depicting the tools of their various trades. – STAINED GLASS. Many fragments in N and S windows. In the nave NE window a headless St Catherine, and C15 shields set in wreaths of columbine and other flowers. – MONUMENTS. John Darby †1639. Alabaster, with a little obelisk. By the same mason a separate oval monument to his wife Mary †1646. They paid for the school in Mill Street (*see* Foundation House below). – Anthony Bedingfield †1652. Large kneeling figure, of indifferent quality, framed by Corinthian columns and broken segmental pediment. The inscription is in Latin with Greek admixtures. – Rev. Thomas Collyer †1850 and his son of the same name †1890, both rectors. Identical monuments in crocketed niches.

N of the church, in Mellis Road, IVY HOUSE FARM, late C15 or early C16 with carved tie-beam in the gable. C17 brick chimney with four hexagonal shafts. To the W in MILL STREET, on the S side FOUNDATION HOUSE, originally the school built in 1641 on land given by Mary Darby. Timber-framed and plastered lobby-entrance house with thatched roof. Opposite, the OLD GUILDHALL, also thatched. Late C15, originally with open hall. Cambered tie-beam on arched braces carrying crown-post roof, and smoke-blackened timbers over hall and solar. Floored *c.* 1600. Attached to it at right angles OAK FARM COTTAGE, C16 with C19 addition along the street. ½ m. further out, at LITTLE GREEN, MANOR FARM HOUSE, dating back to the late C15. The original range has at its S end an addition of *c.* 1500, containing the parlour, with jettied upper storey, buttress-shafts, and corner-post with minor decoration.

At the S end of the village the OLD RECTORY of 1791. Red brick, with glazed pantiled roof. Five bays and two and a half storeys, with simple pedimented doorway. THE LITTLE HOUSE, next to it, has the same roof construction as the Old Guildhall, and like it was originally a two-bay open hall with storeyed solar bay; no surviving service bay.

GLEMSFORD

8040

In the Middle Ages Glemsford, like nearby Long Melford and Sudbury, had its part to play in the cloth industry, as some of the surviving medieval houses, and parts of the church, testify. The industry revived in the C19, with the opening of a silk mill in 1824. A horsehair factory opened in 1844, and others followed, as well as a firm that manufactured umbrella silk and a number that produced coconut matting. The factories have all closed and have mostly been demolished, but their legacy is the large number of terraces of workers' housing dotted about the village, as well as the surprisingly large school. The church stands at the NE corner of the village, in a commanding position looking down over the Glem valley.

ST MARY THE VIRGIN. Dec W tower, rebuilt by *John Johnson* of Bury in 1860, prompted by the collapse of Thurston (q.v.). Dec nave arcades (octagonal piers, double-chamfered arches, the N side apparently earlier than the S). Perp aisle walls and windows, chancel chapels, and porches. The S aisle, S chapel, S porch and N chapel have flushwork panelling, the N aisle and N porch not. S doorway with tiny canopied niches in one arch moulding. On the S chapel, inscription recording gift of John

GLEMSFORD

Golding and wife Joan, 1497; on the N chapel, of John Mundys, wife Margaret and their son John and his wife Elizabeth, 1525. The men were clothiers. Large three-light windows, mostly transomed. Money was left for a S window in 1447, a N window in 1452 and N clerestory windows in 1474 (following the design of one already installed). Another will refers to the new aisle, 1517, and money was left for paving the N aisle in 1534. Good N aisle roof with carved beams. Nave and chancel restored 1864–7, including renewal of clerestory walls and windows, and re-seating. – FONT. Octagonal, Perp. Panelled stem with four small figures. Bowl with two Emblems of the Evangelists, head with crown, head with mitre, angel with shield, and (?) Virgin of the Annunciation. – REREDOS. 1913, by *Cecil G. Hare*. Carved wood, with Annunciation. – What it presumably replaced, C18, now in N aisle. Commandments etc. on panels separated by pilasters. – PULPIT. Jacobean. With blank arches and other characteristic decoration. – LECTERN. By *Jack Penton*, 1961. – SOUTH DOOR. With tracery and a scroll along the edge. – MONUMENTS. Captain Nicholas Kerrington, merchant, †1687. White marble surround with pilasters, urns, swags, winged cherub's heads, crossed bones, etc. – War memorial by *George Kruger Gray*, 1920. Carved, painted and gilded oak, including Christus Rex crucifix.

PRIMARY SCHOOL, Lion Road. Board School by *Salter & Firmin*, 1872. Built at a cost of over £3,000, for 520 children. Red brick, with white-brick and stone dressings. Squat clock tower at one end, with gables on all four sides, and teacher's house at the other. The design is wild, with pointed windows set in relieving arches within crowsteps within gables, and other such eccentricities.

Glemsford boasts a number of worthwhile buildings, but they are widely scattered. On the S side of the church, a little group starting with PARK FARM. C18, timber-framed and plastered. Five bays, two storeys and attics. Then Nos. 14–16 CHURCHGATE, probably C16, partly jettied on two sides. On the W side of the little green, CHURCHGATE FARMHOUSE, early to mid-C19 red brick of two storeys and three bays. In LOW STREET, 500 yds N of the church down the hill, MONKS HALL, an impressive house with exposed timbers with a C15 core. Two storeys and attics. Two gabled cross-wings and, in the middle of the centre, a full-height gabled bay dated 1614.

o of the church, Churchgate leads into BELLS LANE, which has on its S side the former HORSEHAIR FACTORY of 1844, now converted to housing. Some flint, but mainly red brick. Two and a half storeys. Eighteen-bay range along the street and two nine-bay blocks at right angles; also a two-storey, four-bay house facing the street. BROOK STREET runs off Bells Lane to the N, and at the end of the village in this direction the former CROWN INN, timber-framed and plastered with jettied cross-wing. In CHEQUERS LANE, alongside, a house of comparable size and quality to Monks Hall, CHEQUERS, with gabled and jettied cross-wings. Additional gable to one side of the hall range with a modern date of 1617.

Bells Lane continues as Broadway and Lion Road, past the school (*see above*) to TYE GREEN, with PEVERELLS on its W side. Probably C15. Exposed timbers. Hall, floored in the C16 or C17, with jettied and gabled cross-wings. Off the N side COLDHAMS HOUSE, the former rectory by *William Steggles Jun.*, 1834–5. White brick. Two storeys, the main part three bays by three.

From Tye Green, Hunts Hill runs S into EGREMONT STREET. First of note are Nos. 4–8, an L-plan timber-framed and plastered house jettied towards the street. Then the ANGEL INN and ANGEL HOUSE, with two wings extending towards the street. C15, possibly originally a guildhall. The N part (now the pub) is plastered and partly Georgianized, but the S part has exposed timbers and the projecting wing is jettied on two sides. Corner-post with a fine carving of the Archangel Michael with his dragon, and below him a smaller angel with outstretched wings. Next to it the former EBENEZER BAPTIST CHAPEL of 1829. Rendered walls of red brick plinth and hipped slate roof. Further S, on the same side, more exposed timber framing at THE GREYHOUND COTTAGE, C15, and then on the E side Nos. 91–97, a C15 hall house with jettied and gabled cross-wings, divided into four houses. Finally, on the same side, SKATES HILL HOUSE. Jettied front with exposed timbers towards the street, but early C19 painted brick on the S side. Three bays, with Ionic porch.

GREAT ASHFIELD

ALL SAINTS. Finely moulded C13 S doorway. One C13 lancet in the chancel. Original ogee-arched niche to the l. of the E window. Nave and N aisle Perp. The arcade piers have four semi-octagonal shafts. The capitals are treated as one band. Double-chamfered arches. The piers (and the plain FONT; cf. Worlington) sit on the base of the original N wall. S porch Perp, unusually of red brick with flushwork panelling. W tower of knapped flint with a spike; money for tower and bells bequeathed 1458–71. Base-frieze of flushwork panelling. Dec W window. Restoration by *Lot Jackaman*, 1870, which included rebuilding the chancel and the S wall of the nave between the chancel and the porch, and extending the N aisle to provide a vestry. – PULPIT. On short bulbous legs. The body square, not polygonal. One tier of the familiar Elizabethan short blank arches, a tier with simple lozenge panels below. Back panel and tester. On the tester the date 1619 and initials of William Fyrmage. – BENCHES. C15 originals, with poppyheads and animals on the arms, restored and replicated in 1870. One end with carved panel of blacksmith's tools reused in reading desk. – PANELLING. Behind the altar, in the style of the pulpit. – COMMUNION RAIL. With twisted balusters, *c.* 1700 (not original to the church). – ALTAR and REREDOS (N aisle). By H. M. *Cautley*, 1945 (U.S. Air Force memorial). – CHARITY BOARD. Recording the bequest of 'Nicholaus Fyrmage', 1620. In the form of a long, narrow board, painted to resemble an unrolled scroll. – STAINED GLASS. E window by *A. K. Nicholson*, 1926. N aisle N by *Rowland & Surinder Warboys*, 1991. – MONUMENT. Sir H. C. Blake Bt †1880. By *Jackaman*. White marble scroll.

Former SCHOOL (now village hall), ½ m. SSE. By *Jackaman*, 1875. Red brick with white-brick dressings. One large window with hoodmould. Pointed-arched doorway in gabled porch. Prominent chimney.

ASHFIELD LODGE (now Ashfield Grange, subdivided) and ASHFIELD HOUSE, ¼ m. NE, were both built in the late C18 by Lord Chancellor Thurlow (1731–1806), son of the rector. Both of white brick, five bays and two storeys, and extended in the C19. The Lodge, on the N side of the road, has a pedimented centre with tetrastyle Doric portico. Tall ground-floor windows set in arched recesses. Ashfield House, on the S side of the road, is plainer, and seems to have been used simultaneously by Thurlow as a private retreat. In the grounds a CROSS, formerly in the churchyard. About 10 ft (3 metres) high, with original socket stone, on C18 plinth. Probably mid- to late C10. Carved with scroll decoration and remains of an inscription, probably Latin. Thurlow erected it in a corner of the grounds, in front of a summerhouse (which has not survived) from which he could contemplate it.

CASTLE HILL, ½ m. SW. Motte, about 12–15 ft (3.5–4.5 metres) high, with a wet ditch. The bailey has been detected as a soil mark, and field walking indicates occupation during the C12–C14.

GREAT BARTON

8060

The village consists of a few houses along the main Bury–Norwich road, and a much greater number of houses built in what was the park of Barton Hall. The church is happily sited ½ m. S of all this down a quiet lane.

HOLY INNOCENTS. Late C13 chancel with interesting window details. The E window has three lancet lights with three circles at the top that have quatrefoils set back from the face of the tracery moulding. N and S windows with plate tracery, a lozenge, also with recessed quatrefoils. At the E angles polygonal buttresses with obelisk roofs. The priest's doorway has an arch on thin shafts, and to its E an external founder's tomb under a heavy gable on big corbels. The chancel arch inside has friezes of leaves on the two capitals. The PISCINA has an ogee gable. The s aisle has an early C14 E window, and the arcade inside also belongs to that style. Four bays, slender octagonal pier and two circular piers, fleurons on the capitals, moulded arches. Its other windows Perp. Perp also the N aisle of knapped flint, probably the subject of a large bequest (£6 13s. 4d.) in 1472. It has been attributed to *John Wastell*, both on stylistic grounds and because the manor of Great Barton belonged to Bury Abbey. Arcade with attached shafts and capitals only towards the arch openings, also with fleurons. Big W tower, of knapped flint and stone, built with bequests of 1440–86. Flushwork decoration at the top: quatrefoil frieze and panelled battlements. It was followed by the clerestory, double the number of arcade bays. The hammerbeam roof in the nave is nothing special. Bequests of 1515 for battlementing the church, of 1521 for pammenting. Restorations by *John Johnson* of Bury, 1856–8 (interior, including re-seating), and *W. M. Fawcett*, 1880. – FONT. C13. Octagonal, plain, with central shaft and four columns. – BENCHES. 1856, with reused traceried ends and poppyheads. Animals on the arms of the front pair. – SCREEN. Part of rood screen or parclose screen, reused for vestry at W end of s aisle. – STAINED GLASS. In the N aisle Perp canopies. Much late C19 and early C20 stained glass, notably two s aisle windows. Queen Victoria's Golden Jubilee, 1887, probably by *Heaton, Butler & Bayne*. In the centre light her portrait bust and royal arms. In the side lights figures of the Queen of Sheba and Queen Esther. Next to it a window of 1913 by *Morris & Co.*, with figures of Faith, Charity and Hope designed by *Burne-Jones* and painted by *Stokes, Titcomb* and *Edge* respectively; other details by *Knight* and *Watson*. It commemorates Frank Riley-Smith (*see* below). – MONUMENTS. H. W. Bunbury (the caricaturist) †1811. Simple scroll, hanging over a black marble tablet. By *Magnus*, London. – Louisa, Lady Bunbury, †1828. By *Thomas Milnes*. Another scroll, this time hanging from the branch of a tree. – Lt-Gen. Sir Henry Bunbury †1860. Large Gothic standing monument, like a founder's tomb, against the chancel N wall. Base with arcade of six cusped arches. On top a large arch with inner order of colonnettes. – In churchyard, N of the church, Frank Riley-Smith †1912. By *Ernest G. Gillick*. Tall stone shaft with figure of Christ under a traceried canopy with little angels, looking down on a large, plain slab. – War memorial by *Hunt & Coates*, 1921. Stone cross with octagonal shaft on octagonal base.

PRIMARY SCHOOL. By *West Suffolk County Architect's Dept* (job architect *E. M. Stow*), 1966–7. Single-storey. White brick, with black weatherboarding and black water tank. Large hall with laminated timber beams on brick piers, creating a cloister effect. Courts on two sides that separate the hall from the five classrooms.

BARTON HALL burnt down in 1914; a few fragments still standing. The house was probably built in the late C16 or early C17 by the Audleys, and was from 1746 the seat of the Bunbury family. Among other alterations and additions in the C18 and C19, a library was added by *Sir William Chambers* in 1767–8. The park has since been developed for housing, mostly following existing roads, but with a more considered 1960s planned layout s of the site of the house, DIOMED DRIVE. Of the individual houses one of distinction, No. 8 (MATSUDANA) by *Jack Digby*, 1966, for himself, sensitively extended *c.* 1999. Single-storey, flat-roofed. White-painted brick walls, with windows mainly looking inwards to courtyards and garden, and narrow dark clerestory.

Round the perimeter of the park, a few C19 estate cottages, lodges etc., to a greater or lesser extent *ornés*, including a pair built on a Y-plan at the crossroads of Mill Road and Livermere Road. The best is THE LODGE on the main road, thatched, with tall (rebuilt) brick chimneys. One end hexagonal. Gables with decorative bargeboards, one gable filled with a jumble of antler-like branches. It dates from 1826, when this section of turnpike was built. NE of the Lodge FORGE BUNGALOWS, four almshouses ('The Widow's Home') of 1830. Random flint and stone with white-brick dressings. Single-storey with two-storey central porch with round-arched entrance and window above. Canted bays below the eaves. THE FORGE itself is C17, timber-framed, the smithy weatherboarded and the attached house faced in knapped flint with white-brick dressings. Then, set back from the road, THE ELMS, a C17 timber-framed and plastered house. Large chimneystack with panelled base and sides. Inside a room with extensive and complex apotropaic candle-smoke marks on the ceiling that date from *c.* 1660.

At MANOR FARM, ¼ m. N of the church, a fine aisled BARN dating to the second half of the C13. It was modified *c.* 1600, when queenposts were added, and the aisles were faced in flint and brick in 1834. Main roof thatched, the aisles slate. Now in commercial use.

BARTON MERE HOUSE, 1½ m. ENE. C16 timber-framed house with cross-wing, gabled to E and W, at the N end. Across the S end a mid-C18 five-bay range of white brick. Central doorway with open pediment and single-storey bays to l. and r. Two-storey red brick LODGE of *c.* 1870, with round-arched windows and one canted and one triangular bay.

GREAT BLAKENHAM

ST MARY. Norman probably the unbuttressed W tower in its lower parts and Norman certainly the nave – see the two remaining s windows, the simple s doorway and the simple blocked N doorway. Chancel E.E. with three stepped separated lancets at the E end and small N and S windows, the latter now only visible internally. Late C12 PISCINA. C14 the upper parts of the tower, C15 the timber S porch. This still has its carved wooden figure of the figure of the Virgin over the entrance, albeit worn. The single-framed rafter roofs probably belong to the early C14. Restoration by *Cory & Ferguson*, 1876–7, including addition of N organ chamber. S vestry 1931. – FONT. Octagonal, Perp, with panels decorated by various foiled motifs, framing Emblems of the Passion. – PULPIT. Jacobean, with backboard and tester. – COMMUNION RAIL. 1877, but incorporating C15 tracery from the rood screen. – BENCHES. 1877. A good set, with poppyheads, made by *James Gibbons*, with carving by *Robert Godbold* (cf. Earl Stonham, on which they are said to have been based). – MONUMENT. Richard Swift †1645. Tomb-chest with backplate supported by kneeling cherubs, unfortunately consigned to the base of the tower in 1877. The rhymed inscription is an acrostic:

> Reader knowe, this narrow earth
> Incloses one, whose name and worth
> Can live, when marble falls to dust,
> Honoured abroad for wise, and just,
> Ask the Russe, and Sweden, theis
> Report his prudence with their peace.
> Deare when at home, to his faith given
> Stedfast as earth, devout to heaven,
> Wise merchant he (some storms endurd)
> In the best porte his soul securd.
> For fear, thou shouldst forgett his name
> 'Tis the first epitaph of fame.

OLD RECTORY, on S side of churchyard. By *Richard Day*, 1849–50. Red brick with bands of black. Hoodmoulded windows and a castellated bay. Curiously lopsided.

GIPPING WEIR, 100 yds E. Built about 1800. Grey brick, three widely spaced bays, two storeys, low hipped roof. Nice doorway with semicircular fanlight.

ENERGY-FROM-WASTE FACILITY, ¾ m. SSE. By *Grimshaw*, 2011–14. The dominant element is the turbine hall, where electricity is generated from household waste. Clad in polycarbonate and silver-blue metal louvres.

GREAT BRADLEY

ST MARY. Late Norman N and S doorways. The S doorway has spiral-fluted shafts, decorated capitals, and several chevrons in the arch. The tympanum decoration has disappeared. At the top of the jambs two corbels with projecting human heads, half-turned outwards, a motif found on the prior's door at Ely Cathedral and also at Kirtling (Cambs.). N doorway much simpler, with scalloped capitals to the shafts. Late Norman also the jambs of the chancel arch, with imposts with a slight notch between the vertical and the diagonal member. The arch itself is pointed but has only one slight chamfer; rebuilt as part of restoration by F. J. Smith, 1892–4.* Chancel in its present form mostly c. 1300; shortened c. 1730. One bay of fine SEDILIA remains, but the chancel is over-restored. Recesses at E end of nave to accommodate rood screen. C14 W tower. On the first set of set-offs of the buttresses carved shields and lions for the Botetourt family. Perp W doorway and window. Inside, a fireplace and an elementary smoke-outlet in the N wall with an odd baffle in front. Higher SE stair-turret. Early Tudor S porch of red brick with a stepped gable containing six niches. Brick porch windows. – FONT. Octagonal, Perp. Carved with quatrefoils and fleurons. Traces of colouring. – PULPIT. C18, with back panel and tester. – STAINED GLASS. E window, 1920. War memorial, based on *James Clark*'s 'The Great Sacrifice'. Nave S by *Powell & Sons*, c. 1952.

GREAT BRADLEY HALL, SW of the church. Painted brick. Late C17, extended c. 1730 (rebuilt 2002–4) and in the mid C19. Between the Hall and the Stour, on the S side of the churchyard, remains of the large moat of an earlier house.

OLD RECTORY, ½ m. W. 1876 by *J. W. Holland*, extended after 1965. Painted brick. Various gables and bays, but otherwise plain.

SUGAR LOAF, The Street. Small timber-framed cottage, probably C17, with mansard roof. Large monopitch extension by *C. J. Bourne*, 1972, of painted brick.

GREAT BRICETT

A priory of Augustinian canons, dedicated to St Leonard, was founded c. 1110 by Ralph Fitzbrian and his wife Emma. It later became a cell of Nobiliac (now Saint-Léonard-de-Noblat), near Limoges. As an alien priory it came into the hands of the crown and formed part of the original endowment by Henry VI of King's College, Cambridge, in 1444. The church and hall are the remains of the priory buildings, and are still physically joined to each other.

ST MARY AND ST LAWRENCE. A long plain oblong, the nave and choir of the priory church. It once had transepts, and these had E apses. Their existence has been proved by excavation, and a main E apse within the present E wall can be surmised

---

*F. J. Smith (1845–1912) lived in Great Bradley and is buried near the S porch.

with certainty. That was the plan in the C12. Towards the end of the C12 the E end was made straight; second transepts, containing chapels, were built to its N and S, with a presbytery against the E wall. The responds and arches of the chapels are still visible in the walls. Of the early transepts only traces can be detected. The only impressive Norman piece is the S doorway. It is not *in situ*, but originally stood a little further E. One order of shafts, decorated but defaced, an inner order of jambs and one with close decoration. Chevrons in the arch. Down the W jamb, and partly on the E, a carved inscription, probably mixed up, but including the word LEONARDUS. One blocked Norman slit window in the N wall, one taller round-arched window in the S wall. A blocked arch in the W wall shows that a tower was either built or intended. Other windows of *c.* 1300. The big five-light E window with flowing tracery is Dec. The E wall was rebuilt in 1868, but the window is most probably a copy of what was there before. Tie-beam roof with crown-posts and four-way struts. Restoration by *E. H. Sedding*, 1905–7, including bellcote at W end. – FONT. Square, Norman, with intersected arches on two sides, trefoil arches on columns on the third, and very oddly pointed-trefoil arches on the fourth. – PULPIT. A very unusual piece; probably Victorian. Octagonal, its faces (each square) carved with tracery elements – cusped lancets, quatrefoils, etc. – but arranged as in a catalogue, not in a coherent pattern. – MONUMENT. John Bright of Tollemache Hall, Little Bricett (*see* Offton) and wife Mary, erected 1680. With an elaborately carved alabaster surround, including segmental pediment and flaming urns. Attributed to *Jasper Latham* (GF). – STAINED GLASS. In a nave S window, fine figures of the four Evangelists, early C14; from the tracery of the E window. Chancel windows, including perhaps the present tracery of the E window, by *Robert King* of Ipswich, *c.* 1853. Nave S †1975 by *G. Maile*.

The church formed the S side of the cloister, with the prior's house in the W range. This is now the main wing of THE HALL, although its external appearance, and much of the interior also, is C18. But embedded in the fabric, and rediscovered in 1956, is the C13 frame of the wall of the cross-entry, at the N end of what was a two-bay open hall. The wall has four arched doorways of timber, three of the same size and a smaller one with dogtooth ornament on jambs and arch (cf. Purton Green, Stansfield). The larger arches have shafts with moulded capitals, but the arch mouldings have unfortunately been hacked off. The wall above has bold cross-bracing. At the S end of the hall was a storeyed bay, extended at the SW corner in the C14 and further extended W *c.* 1600.

ST PETER'S COURT, E of the church. Fully exposed timber frame. A Wealden-type house of *c.* 1500, modified more than once in the course of the C16.

OLD VICARAGE, 300 yds N. By *G. G. Scott*, 1874. Red brick, with no adornment and no symmetry. Windows set in segmental-arched recesses.

GREAT CORNARD

The village near which Gainsborough painted Cornard Wood is now more or less a suburb of Sudbury. A large amount of 'London overspill' housing was built from 1961 onwards, with accompanying factories and schools.

ST ANDREW. C14 W tower. It has diagonally placed niches l. and r. of the W window and carries a C19 shingled broach spire. Unusual and rather charming stair-turret on the N side, like the S porch of C16 red brick. Nave and chancel predominantly C15, encased in flint in 1853. Restoration by *Edward Salter*, 1862, including addition of N vestry; S aisle by *Arthur Grimwood*, 1887; further restoration by *Leonard Crowfoot*, 1908, including new nave roof. Low N arcade with piers of the Sudbury type (St Gregory, All Saints), copied on the S side. – FONT. Simple, octagonal, Perp, with shields in quatrefoils. C19 stem. – CHOIR STALLS. C19, with reused poppyheads. – STAINED GLASS. S aisle E by *James Clark*, made by *A. J. Dix*, 1927, a strong pictorial design. Its qualities show up the pedestrian window of the same year by *Jones & Willis* in the N aisle. – MONUMENT. Against the chancel S wall, the front of a tomb-chest, probably to a C16 member of the Downes family. The other side was until 1853 visible in the outside wall. – In the churchyard, mid-C19 cast-iron GATES by *Barton & Co.*, Sudbury, and war memorial CROSS by *Earee & Haslewood*, 1920.

S of the church, along BURES ROAD, some substantial late C19 and early C20 villas, and on the W side the former CONGREGATIONAL CHAPEL (now village hall) by *Charles Pertwee*, 1875–6. Red brick with white-brick dressings and round-arched windows. In MILL TYE, between the railway and the River Stour, extensive former MILL BUILDINGS. Timber-framed watermill, encased in white brick in the late C19 and converted to a roller mill, with a four-storey white-brick steam mill of 1911. Now converted as part of a large commercial and residential development. C18 MILL HOUSE with C19 additions.

OVERSPILL ESTATES. The initial development, by *Sir Hubert Bennett* and his staff at the *London County Council* and *Greater London Council*, was completed in 1970, and comprised 728 houses, shops, maisonettes and six unit factories. Their impact can be felt E of the church along Pot Kiln Road and Poplar Road. Off Pot Kiln Road, in RAYDON WAY and HARTEST WAY, 166 prefabricated 'Anglia' houses (cf. Haverhill). In Head Road, THOMAS GAINSBOROUGH SCHOOL (former Upper School) by *Suffolk County Architect's Dept*, 1974–8, on the SEAC system.

ABBAS HALL, 1 m. E. Owned by the abbess of West Malling, Kent. Hall house, the hall originally aisled. It retains two arched doorways that formed part of the screens passage, and tree-ring dating has shown that the timbers were felled in 1289–90. Much of the original roof structure also survives. Hall floored in the mid C16 (felling date 1548/9), the massive brick fireplace apparently inserted a few years later – perhaps at the same time as the late C16 cross-wing at the W end. This and part of the older range faced in brick, but all rendered and painted, with mainly C18 and C19 windows.

POPLARS FARM, 1¼ m. ENE. Timber-framed and plastered house of the C16 or C17 with cross-wing at one end. The other end has a gabled jetty and the whole of the SE front is also jettied. Big central chimneystack with four octagonal shafts, and another stack with two shafts against the cross-wing.

GREAT FINBOROUGH

ST ANDREW. Rebuilt by *R. M. Phipson*, 1874–7, at the behest of R. J. Pettiward of Finborough Hall. An expensive building, although it has no aisles, just a transeptal N chapel for the Pettiwards. The S porch of the old building was kept, and the two western nave windows appear also to have been reused. The porch, mentioned in wills of 1422 and 1445, has chequered flushwork on the base and panelling on the buttresses. Niche over the entrance. Walls raised by Phipson and turrets added. The rest of the church in keeping. What made it really expensive, and obviously not a restoration of a medieval building, was the W tower. It starts square, with diagonal buttresses, but the belfry is octagonal. The buttresses continue upwards, flying across the gap between the square and the octagon. Above the belfry a tall octagonal stone spire, with irregular bands of red and white sandstone – High Victorian, but ten or twenty years behind the times. Small N organ chamber of 1914. – FONT. Beneath the Gothic cladding an C18 white marble bowl on a fluted stem. – SCREEN. By *Leonard Leeper*, 1925 (war memorial). – STAINED GLASS. A good set. E window †1892 by *Clayton & Bell*, who presumably were responsible for seven other windows, up to *c.* 1927. – MONUMENTS. A number from the old church, mostly in the N chapel. Charlton Wollaston †1729. Over-life-size putto unrolling a scroll. – William and Elizabeth Wollaston, erected 1769. With two portrait medallions, facing each other. Vase on top. – Robert Wollaston †1778. Circular, with the inscription in the centre, surrounded by swords, cannon, etc. – William Wollaston †1797. White marble tablet with draped urn against a black pyramid. By *John de Carle* (cf. Tyrell monument, Stowmarket). – Roger Pettiward †1833. By *Sir Richard Westmacott*. Very large relief of the Good Samaritan in a pedimented surround. – Jane Seymour, widow of Roger Pettiward and Admiral Sir William Hotham, †1855. Grandiosely classical for its date. With a palette, mallet and other tools, and the capital of a column, indicating her accomplishments. – From another monument remain three big putti hanging a garland round an urn with the profile head of a lady. – Under the tower, two C14 coffin-lids, one with a floriated cross.

FINBOROUGH HALL. A house was built by Sir John Gilbert in the C16 (a carved beam dated 1575 survives, not *in situ*), sold by his descendants to William Wollaston in 1656. Col. William Wollaston, M.P. for Ipswich, sold the house in 1794 to Roger Pettiward of Onehouse. It burnt down in 1795 and a new house was built about 25 yds N of the old one, to designs by *Francis Sandys*. Sandys was then already involved with the Earl of Bristol, although work at Finborough may have got under way before the building at Ickworth. The Pettiwards owned the estate until 1936, making many additions to the house over the years. It then became the offices of the East Anglia Electric Supply Co., and has been a school since 1980, both organizations making further additions.

Sandys's building, white brick, of two storeys, was relatively modest. It faced E. Five bays with pedimented centre on four giant attached Tuscan columns, the middle interstice being wider than the others. Far-projecting eaves (which is also a 'Tuscan', i.e. Etruscan, motif). On the returns three-bay bows with a bay to l. and r. Not long afterwards, and by 1824, the entrance had been moved to the N side, through one of the bows, to which a colonnade of six Tuscan columns was added. By this time there was also an orangery at the W end of the S front, but this was rebuilt later in the C19, at first of four bays, eventually seven. Behind it a long C19 service range ending in a square water tower. W of this is a little building that was originally separate and, to judge by its eaves, may have been part of Sandys's design, perhaps a garden house of some kind. Two storeys, the ground floor a series of arches and probably originally open. Decorated with stone panels with roundels, swags, etc., and Pettiward's arms. C20 additions more apparent on the N side: a utilitarian office block of *c.* 1936, and slightly better school block of 1981. The interiors are mostly institutionalized, but the central staircase hall with octagonal lantern remains impressive. Geometrical staircase with wrought-iron balustrade. Bas reliefs with classical scenes over the doors.

Across the lawn S of the house, and linked to it by a tunnel (now blocked), former STABLES. Red brick, with a Dutch gable at one end, possibly C17. Between here and the road the C19 walls of a large kitchen garden, now filled with houses. The PARK is largely given over to a golf course, but something of its character survives, with a long curving drive down to Rattlesden River and up the other side to the N entrance.

The Hall's SOUTH LODGE, of red brick with elaborate white-brick decoration and dated 1883 in the brickwork, is the first of a succession of similar buildings in the village: from E to W, the very large WHITE HORSE HOUSE, 1880; the only slightly less large PRIMARY SCHOOL and house, 1881; and cottages, 1889.

BUXHALL LODGE, 150 yds SW of the primary school, has an early C18 plastered front of five bays and two storeys, with doorway with Gibbs surround.

THE BUTTERFLY, 2 m. SW. Timber-framed and plastered farmhouse of c. 1600, with cross-wing at the N end added twenty years or so later. Of the latter date also a dog-leg staircase. Remains of late C17 or early painted wall decoration, imitation textile in stripes of red and blue-grey. The new wing was built against the service gable of the original house and thus preserved some strapwork pargetting, a rare survival for its date.

GREAT LIVERMERE

ST PETER. The W tower stands only to roof height.* Above that a weatherboarded top with pyramid roof. The stone parts are Dec – see the W window and the tower arch. Dec also the chancel in its present form, though blocked lancets tell of an earlier, C13, state. Dec E window of three lights. Four-centred arch. The tracery consists of arch-heads upon the three arch-heads of the lights and in the two main shapes thus produced two small cusped reticulation motifs, one below the other. Inside, niches l. and r. of the window. Thatched nave, its windows Dec too, though the simple N doorway seems to be of c. 1200. A large niche inside, in the N wall, Perp. Also the outline of a Perp Easter sepulchre in the chancel N wall. The chancel roof has beautifully carved broad wall-plates with various leaf and tracery patterns. Early C19 N vestry. – FONT. Octagonal, Perp, with tracery patterns. – PULPIT. A three-decker of the rare date c. 1700; panelled, with friezes of acanthus foliage. – BENCHES. In chancel, one end with elaborate tracery. Three later ones with very coarse, under-developed poppyheads. One of them is dated 1601. In nave, more with coarse poppyheads, the rest by *T. D. Atkinson*, 1897, part of a general reordering. – SCREEN. With broad one-light divisions and ogee tops. – COMMUNION RAIL. Three-sided. Very thin, twisted balusters, with Composite capitals at the corners; Georgian. – WALL PAINTING. Two standing C14 figures, perhaps part of the story of the Three Quick and the Three Dead (nave N wall). Also a Noli me tangere, much faded (nave S wall), and some scrollwork (chancel S wall). – ROYAL ARMS. Of Queen Victoria, 1874. Rather crudely carved, in deep relief. – LADDER to belfry. Dated 1681. Not for the faint-hearted. – MONUMENT. Richard Coke †1688. With urn and skull. From

---

*Repton's Red Book for Livermere Hall shows it with a further stage and cupola. The top is said to have collapsed in 1871.

Little Livermere. – By s door, headstone of William Sakings †1689, 'forkner [falconer] to King Charles ye 1 King Charles ye 2d King James ye 2d'.

LIVERMERE HALL (former rectory), s of the church. Painted brick. Three storeys. Five-bay front with Greek Doric porch. *Robert Heffer* of Ixworth drew plans for partial rebuilding, 1812–13; further improvements recorded *c.* 1824–9.

The old LIVERMERE HALL was demolished in 1923, but Great Livermere still has the air of an estate village, with flint and white-brick LODGES between the church and the former rectory. There are conflicting accounts of the Hall's history, but it seems to have been rebuilt by the Cooke family in the C17. Thomas Lee of Kensington bought Little Livermere in 1709 and Great Livermere in 1715, and was succeeded by his son Baptist Lee in 1724. Baptist won £30,000 in the state lottery and used his new fortune to add to the existing house and to create a PARK, enclosed in 1733–5. With what Arthur Young, writing in 1769, called 'a harmony very unusual', Lee collaborated with his neighbour, James Calthorpe of Ampton (q.v.), in extending the existing mere and creating a long serpentine LAKE that runs along the parish boundary, and crossed by a timber BRIDGE in 1753 (since rebuilt). The estate passed in 1768 to Nathaniel Lee Acton, who continued to develop the park (about 16,000 trees were planted in 1771) and in 1790 commissioned a Red Book from *Humphry Repton*, although little of what he suggested seems to have been carried out. More work was done to the house, attributed to *Samuel Wyatt*, 1795–6, including cladding in white mathematical tiles. Further proposals for the park were made by *Lewis Kennedy* in 1815.

About 400 yds sw of the church is the partly moated site of a former manor house, latterly the kitchen garden. There is another C19 LODGE at the w (Ampton) entrance to the park.

GREAT SAXHAM

7060

ST ANDREW. Rebuilt in 1798 by Thomas Mills, i.e. at the same time as Great Saxham Hall. The s wall of the chancel revealed as brick, the remainder mostly flint rubble. The tower and the s porch are medieval. A will of 1441 left money for work on the tower; the front is Perp, the lower parts perhaps earlier. In addition two humble Norman doorways are preserved, N and s. 'Restored', i.e. gothicized, by 1869, with new nave windows, N 'organ chapel', and sw vestry. Flushwork initials and symbols on the E and N walls date from this time. *F. Preedy* was responsible. – FONT. Octagonal, Perp, simple. – PULPIT. Jacobean, with two tiers of the usual blank arches. – STALLS. With C18 panels, including the Mills family stall E of the chancel arch. – BENCHES. Some with primitive, elongated poppyheads. – STAINED GLASS. In the E window some extremely good early C16 German glass, mixed up with much that seems Flemish and Swiss. In the W window glass from the monastery at Rapperswil on Lake Zurich. Installed in 1815. Nave S †1859 by *Preedy*. – MONUMENTS. Monument and brass to John Eldred, 1632, a merchant who, as can be read in the inscriptions, had travelled to Egypt, Arabia, Syria and – as it is called – Babilon. The monument has a painted frontal bust in a circular niche and no date of death inscribed. The brass is of the traditional medieval composition, with 27½-in. (70-cm.) figure. The brass and its slab, now on the chancel floor, originally formed the top of a tomb-chest. Monument attributed to *James White* of Long Acre, brass to *Edward Marshall* (GF).

GREAT SAXHAM HALL. John Eldred built a house E of the church which he called Nutmeg Hall, after the spice which he introduced to England. The estate was purchased in 1745 by Hutchison Mure, who in 1762 commissioned a new house from *Robert Adam*. Various designs were produced but in the end the old house was greatly enlarged in Adam's castle style in 1774. Five years later, in 1779, this was destroyed by fire. Adam produced further schemes for rebuilding, including a D-plan house, and work began on converting the former stables to a house, but stopped when Mure was declared bankrupt in 1793. The estate was bought in 1795 by Thomas Mills, for whom *Joseph Patience* completed the rebuilding, on the site of the stables E of the old house, in 1796–8; the stonework was executed by *de Carle* of Bury. The servants' wing on the N side of the main house was rebuilt in the mid C19 (with octagonal water tower); an Edwardian addition at the N end of the garden front was demolished *c.* 1925.

The house is of two storeys, rendered. Centre with a portico of four giant columns with Adam-style capitals (a version of Ionic) in *Coade* stone, and a pediment with palm branches and a coat of arms, also Coade and dated 1797. To the l. and r. one recessed bay and then wider pavilion bays with attached pairs of one pier and one column. Tripartite windows on the ground floor between them, that on the r. now of Venetian shape. It formerly had a Coade roundel ('Autumn'), of which its counterpart ('Spring') survives on the l. Over the other ground-floor windows were rectangular Coade plaques, removed when the first-floor windows were lowered (probably by William Mills, who inherited in 1834). At the same time pediments or mouldings on consoles were added to all the windows. On the shorter S side a single-storey bow. On the W front, two-storey canted bays at each end, then single-storey bows, and in the middle a three-storey octagon. The ceiling of the top-floor room is painted in Adam style, with plaques containing portraits of the Muses in the style of Angelica Kauffmann. But the floor was inserted in the 1920s, and this seems to have been originally a double-height music room. A chimneypiece in the drawing room on the S side of the house includes a marble panel that is another Coade design, 'A Phrygian Shepherd and Shepherdess'.

The park was carefully laid out with a serpentine lake in a wooded dell to the E; above it the octagonal TEA HOUSE, of stuccoed brick with four Tuscan porches. SW of the house, and likewise visible from it, the TEMPLE OF DIDO, hexagonal, red brick with rusticated flint quoins and three gabled porches. Converted to a house and extended by *Charles Morris*, *c.* 1980. At the S end of the serpentine, a larger expanse of water, China Pond, and E of that the Gothick UMBRELLO by *Coade & Sealy*, therefore after 1799, and not recorded on an estate survey of 1801. A graceful, octagonal structure, with crocketed ogee arches on clustered columns and balustrade with obelisks. Based on two designs from *Batty Langley*'s *Gothic Architecture Improved* (1747), 'Gothic Temple' and 'an octangular Umbrello to terminate a view'. It lost its leaded dome in the 1960s and is now in poor condition.

W of the house, a group of mid-C19 farm buildings, and next to them, along one side of the churchyard, the former SCHOOL, 1862. To the N, an early C19 LODGE, single-storey with tetrastyle Ionic portico; it may be the lodge that *Anne Mills* designed for her father-in-law in 1819. Beyond it estate cottages, including the OLD SMITHY with decorative bargeboards and ornamental chimneys.

SYMOND'S FARMHOUSE, 1¾ m. N. Three-bay, three-storey C18 brick façade. Pediment with urns; blank roundel in the tympanum. One, formerly two single-storey lean-tos, also with blank roundel. Segment-headed windows. The house ruinous.

GREAT THURLOW

6050

ALL SAINTS. The chancel is structurally Norman; see the nook-shafts at the E end. But the impression of the church is entirely Perp. Battlemented W tower; a will suggests it was under construction in 1378. Pretty lead bell-turret. The arcade has lozenge-shaped piers, the arches dying into them. The principal restoration was by *W. M. Fawcett*, 1879–80, which included removal of plaster ceilings and W gallery, and rebenching. – FONT. Norman. Square, with nook-shafts. On the sides, blank arches of curious detail: three on the W side, two on the other three. – PULPIT. Jacobean. – REREDOS. By *Laurence H. Bond*, 1956, part of a programme of 'repair and beautification' for the Vesteys, 1953–66, including construction of a burial vault. – SCREENS to S chapel. 1960–2, incorporating woodwork dated 1616 that probably formed part of the Warren family pew. – ORGAN SCREEN. 1964–5. – TOWER SCREEN. 1955–7, when the ringers' floor was built. With Jacobean-style balustrade. – SCULPTURE. Bronze maquette by *Elisabeth Frink* of Paternoster (Shepherd and Sheep), 1975, given in 1990.

– CHANDELIERS. Three, in the nave, of silver, each of eight branches, with very ornate decoration. Probably Russian, mid-C19; given in 1956. Two in the sanctuary by *W. Frank Knight*, 1957. Silver-plated bronze. – STAINED GLASS. E window by *Harry Harvey*, 1957–8. S chapel E attributed by Michael Archer to *William Price the Younger*. Elaborate coat of arms (with grotesque faces hidden in the mantling, typical of Price's work), and inscription recording restoration by James Vernon, 1741. This and the chancel S window rearranged by *Joan Howson*, 1956–7, with new glass recording the Vesteys' restoration. S aisle windows †1899 by *J. Cameron* and †1922 by *Heaton, Butler & Bayne*. – MONUMENTS. Headless brass of a Lady, *c.* 1460, 19-in. (48-cm.) figure (in safe). – Brass to a Knight and Lady, possibly John Gedding †1469 and wife Margery; 25-in. (83.5-cm.) figures. – Brass of John Bladwell †1534, in armour, and wife Anne; 18-in. (46-cm.) figures, his lower half missing. – In churchyard, headstone of Mary Traylen †1797. With carved relief of Death being driven away from the corpse.

HALL. A handsome mid-Georgian building of red brick, now stuccoed. Stone base with vermiculated rustication. Two and a half storeys. Three fronts of five bays with slightly projecting three-bay pedimented centres. Only the SW front, with giant Ionic pilasters, is in its original state. The SE front has two single-storey canted bays added in the late C19 or early C20. On the NW front the entrance was remodelled in the 1950s and the porch, with coupled Ionic columns, reduced in width. Fine staircase with three turned balusters to each tread and carved tread-ends. Nice late C18 plasterwork. Long two-storey service and stable wing extending from the NE corner. Broad pedimented carriage entrance with Ionic columns. Through this red brick FARM BUILDINGS dated 1846, as well as an C18 weatherboarded BARN. E of the farm buildings a late C17 DOVECOTE. Timber-framed and plastered. Hipped roof with gablets. Good fittings, mainly of Baltic pine, including flight platform and pipe.

In the village, a number of late C19 estate COTTAGES, as well as a RECREATION AND READING ROOM, 1904, with gabled bays and bell-turret. Over the Stour, a cast-iron BRIDGE by *R. Garrett & Son* of Leiston, 1851, with simple but attractive balustrade.

WINDMILL, ⅔ m. SW. Smock mill, 1807. Tarred brick base. Sails removed *c.* 1920. Restored 1962 and 2011. Machinery intact. Near it the OLD VICARAGE by *William Steggles Jun.*, 1837. Two-storey, three-bay, white-brick front with Tuscan porch.

GREAT WALDINGFIELD

ST LAWRENCE. Perp, with some flushwork decoration, chiefly of a chequerboard pattern. W tower with diagonal buttresses of five set-offs. W doorway with shields in the spandrels. Three-light transomed W window. Niches with little fan-vaults to l. and r. Nave and aisles. Tall arcades. Piers with four shafts and four small hollows. Clerestory with single, not double windows. Inscription on the S side in the battlements seeking prayers for Thomas Malcher and his wives Joan and Agnes. Malcher left 5 marks (£3 6s. 8d.) for the 'new fabric' of the church in 1458. Much of the rest had been paid for by John Appleton, c. 1400. S porch with flushwork. Its entrance and the S doorway have fleurons in the jambs and arches. The N porch seems to be of the restoration of 1827–9 by *Rev. Robert Kedington* of Babergh Hall. Chancel rebuilt by *W. Butterfield*, 1865–9. Flint walls set with tiles on edge, exaggerating a feature found on the older parts. Inside, the chancel walls are polychromatized with tiles, and mosaic panels made up from pieces of marble 'collected in the ruins of the heathen temples in old Rome' by Emily and Louisa Baily, sisters of the rector. Butterfield also restored the N chapel, 1875, but the nave was done by *J. H. Hakewill*, 1875–7. NE vestry, projecting beyond the chancel, by *W. M. Fawcett*, 1887. – FONT. Octagonal, Perp, with heavy quatrefoils. – ROYAL ARMS. Hanoverian. Carved and painted. – COMMUNION RAIL. By *William Cleere*, c. 1672, for St Michael, Cornhill, in the City of London, removed during the restoration by G. G. Scott in 1857–60 (*see* also the former rectory, below). With twisted balusters, and enriched with leaves and garlands. More balusters reused for the fronts of the STALLS and on the READING DESK.* – PULPIT. By *Butterfield*. – BENCH ENDS. Some with poppyheads, reused in 1875–6. – STAINED GLASS. E window and chancel S, 1869, and W window, 1875, by *Alexander Gibbs*. Three N aisle windows by *Lavers, Barraud & Westlake* (one dated 1887), and another †1882 in the S aisle. In the S aisle E window, fragments of C15 glass.

OLD RECTORY, S of the church. Medieval in origin, but largely rebuilt by *Ewan Christian*, 1859–61; entrance and the range to its r. of white brick with red brick dressings, the remainder partly timber-framed and clad in white brick. In one room, more reused woodwork from St Michael, Cornhill (cf. communion rail, above), principally the REREDOS by *Cleere*, 1672–3, dismantled c. 1858; also additional woodwork from the reredos of St Peter, Sudbury (q.v.), removed during Butterfield's restoration of that church in 1854–9. Arched recesses (converted to bookshelves) with a seraph and cherubim in the spandrels. Composite columns to l. and r. Swags, drops of carved foliage, etc. In the recesses the Ten Commandments, painted by *Robert Streater*, and on another wall the Creed and Lord's Prayer. The chimneypiece seems to incorporate woodwork from the same source.

The older and more interesting part of the village is clustered round the church and quite separate from the rest. Between

---

*The old three-sided communion rail was reused for the balustrade of the rectory staircase.

the church and the rectory a few nice thatched cottages and CHURCH GATE (formerly High Trees), C17 timber-framed and partly faced in brick. Cross-wing at one end with carved bressumer dated 1670, and stack of three chimneys with octagonal shafts and star tops. NW of the church THE LODGE. C17 timber-framed and plastered range, with gabled and jettied end on the road and Greek Doric doorcase. At right angles a white-brick Georgian range, which has red brick Victorian additions including bay windows and two-storey porch. N of the church the former SCHOOL. Gothic, of flint with white-brick dressings. 1851–2, with house by *T. F. Ray*, 1866.

PRIMARY SCHOOL, ½ m. SW, in the newer part of the village. 1969–70 by *West Suffolk County Architect's Dept* (job architect *J. Blackie*). Space-frame roof with deep overhang, supported on steel columns. The roof construction permitted flexibility in the layout of the teaching areas, around a central assembly hall and covered court. Lightweight timber curtain walls (since replaced), with brick walls for the kitchen, boiler room and offices.

BABERGH HALL, ⅔ m. NW. Mid-C16 timber-framed U-plan house. White-brick Georgian front of two storeys and nine bays. Three-bay gabled centre with pedimented Ionic doorcase.

GREAT WENHAM

ST JOHN THE EVANGELIST. Fine Perp W tower with flushwork decoration on base and buttresses. The rest alas plastered, but C14. Three stepped lancets at the E end with pointed-trefoiled heads. Other windows either lancets or with Y-tracery. On the N side a lowside window. Restored 1842, when the S vestry was built, and 1867–8, when the nave was re-seated and the ORGAN by *Thomas Lewis* installed in the base of the tower. – REREDOS. In memory of Rev. Daniel Whalley †1869, responsible for the 1867–8 restoration. With painted panels of Lord's Prayer, Creed and Commandments. – TILES. Many in the chancel, and a few more in the vestry, probably of the C15. – ROYAL ARMS. Of George II. Large, painted on board. – HAT or WIG RACK. C18. Metal rail with pegs along the whole of the nave N wall. – STAINED GLASS. Chancel N and S by *Lavers, Barraud & Westlake*, 1875. – MONUMENT. John Bailey †1813. Marble sarcophagus, standing on lion's paws. By *Robert Ashton* of Piccadilly.*

OLD RECTORY, opposite the church. C16 or earlier with exposed timbers. Deep, two-storey, gabled and jettied porch. Georgian and Victorian additions to rear.

---

*HELMET with crest, sword and shield of the East family stolen in 2006.

PRIORY FARM, 250 yds ENE. Timber-framed and plastered, with some exposed timbers. Hall and cross-wing probably C15, with two taller cross-wings at the W end. These have between them a large square chimneystack dated 1699. The principal ground-floor and corresponding first-floor rooms in the outer W wing have plaster ceilings of c. 1600 divided into panels, on the ground floor with arabesque scrolls. Also a good open-well staircase with heavy turned balusters.

WENHAM PLACE, ¼ m. s. Interesting remains of a brick mansion of the early C16. One projecting wing survives on the N side with dark blue diapering, polygonal angle buttresses, gable and pinnacles. Mullioned-and-transomed brick windows with arched lights. The upper storey of the main range has exposed timbers with brick-nogging on the N side. The S side of the house was refronted in the C19, with straight gables and hood-moulds. Inside, the hall fireplace can be seen, and a brick spiral staircase. – GREENWAYS to N (100 yds WSW of church) by *Raymond Erith*, 1954. Red brick farm cottage. Three bays and two storeys with catslide roof to rear. Ground-floor windows with segmental heads.

WENHAM HILL, ½ m. SSE. C16 timber-framed and plastered. H-plan, with two-storey canted bays added to the fronts of the cross-wings. A fine collection of external chimneystacks: two to the l., of three and two shafts, one to the r. of three shafts, and one to the rear of three, mostly octagonal. Early C17 BARN to N, originally three bays, extended to five in the mid to late C18 by the insertion of extra bays in the centre.

GREAT WHELNETHAM

8050

ST THOMAS À BECKET. Small. The W tower blew down in 1658 and was replaced in 1749 by the present weatherboarded bell-turret. The chancel is C13 with N lancets, and finely if simply detailed SEDILIA and PISCINA. The nave perhaps of the same date. Circular, quatrefoiled W window. Tiny clerestory. Two-bay Dec arcade to the N aisle, the aisle itself rebuilt in 1839 by *William Dench Major* (wheelwright and victualler, Rushbrooke Arms) with *William Dudley* of Bury. Restorations by *C. H. Bullen* of Bury, 1883 (including removal of W gallery of 1839), and *J. Flatman*, 1964. – FONT. Perp, octagonal. Roses etc. in quatrefoil panels. – PULPIT. With panels of c. 1500. – SCULPTURE. On one of the nave SE quoins the carving of a serpent; possibly Saxon or Norman. – STAINED GLASS. Plenty of medieval fragments in the chancel SE window, including some charming birds holding texts in their beaks. – E window by *Burlison & Grylls*, designed by *Eleanor Fortescue-Brickdale*, 1917–18 (war memorial). – MONUMENTS. Richard Gipps †1660. Inscription plate with alabaster surround. Broken segmental pediment. Skull and crossbones. – Charles Battely

†1722 and wife Elizabeth †1752. Coloured marble sarcophagus against *trompe l'œil* drapery. – John Plume †1911. Panel of 102 red opaque glass tiles by *Powell & Sons*, one with inscription and others with Voyseyesque motifs.

PRIMARY SCHOOL. 1849. Red brick with white brick dressings. Windows with hoodmoulds. Interesting addition by *Nick Loomes* of Suffolk County Council, 2005, with large clerestory window and vertical timber boarding.

GREAT WHELNETHAM HALL, 300 yds SE. Timber-framed and plastered. Early C17, refaced in the C18. Five bays wide. With a complicated system of moats.

OLD RECTORY, 475 yds SSW. C17 timber-framed and plastered, with alterations in the C18 and by *Basil Oliver*, 1934.

WINDMILL (Tutelina Mill), 600 yds N. Red brick tower mill, 1865. No sails.

SICKLESMERE is the part of the parish that lies along the main road to Bury, marked by the so-called ROUND HOUSE, an early C19 toll house. Octagonal, white brick, with Gothick arched windows. Beside it the RUSHBROOKE ARMS. C16, timber-framed and plastered and thatched. Mid-C20 alterations in the style of *Basil Oliver*. To the r. an extension of 1987 that was a C15 barn from Wetherden Hall, Hitcham (q.v.). To the S, SICKLESMERE HOUSE. Late C18. Timber-framed and plastered but with a white-brick front. Two storeys, three bays. The heads of the windows are segmental on the first floor and ogee-arched on the ground floor.

GREAT WRATTING

ST MARY. Septaria and flint. Nave and chancel and battlemented W tower. Nice Perp S doorway. Good E.E. chancel with lancets. Triple-shafted SEDILIA. The corbels under the chancel arch originally supported the rood beam. Restored 1887, at the expense of W. H. Smith of Great Thurlow. W end reordered by the *Whitworth Co-Partnership*, 1989, to provide a meeting room. – SCREEN. 1877. One-light divisions with tracery, and broad central opening. The openings are cusped, with little carved heads on each point. Loft with coving. – STAINED GLASS. E window (three lancets) and other chancel windows by *W. H. Constable*, 1870s.

OLD RECTORY, W of the church. 1873. Red brick, and relatively modest.

A few red brick ESTATE COTTAGES dotted about the village, including two pairs E of the church with terracotta plaques commemorating Queen Victoria's Golden Jubilee, 1887, erected by W. H. Smith.

WEATHERCOCK COTTAGE, ½ m. ENE. Mid-C19 almshouses, built on a cruciform plan for three widows, with a shared kitchen. Painted brick. Now a single house.

GROTON

One of the founding fathers of New England, John Winthrop (1588–1649), was lord of the manor of Groton before emigrating to North America in 1630, having been chosen as governor of the Massachusetts Bay Company. His descendant, Robert C. Winthrop, visited Groton in 1847 and 1878, and the family have since done much to perpetuate the memory of their ancestor. It is thought that the Winthrops lived at Groton Place (*see* below).

ST BARTHOLOMEW. Chancel E window with reticulated tracery; Dec. The W tower contemporary or a little earlier. Flushwork panelling in the battlements. Otherwise Perp. Nave and tall clerestory, aisles, S porch. All embattled except for the chancel. Arcade of four bays. Oddly shaped piers with polygonal shafts, with capitals to the arch openings but not to the nave. Chancel restored 1873; further restoration and organ chamber *c.* 1880–2. Roofs restored 1912–13 by *Caröe & Passmore*; timbers in porch dated 1690 and 1912. – STAINED GLASS. E window by *Daniel Bell*, 1875, commemorating John Winthrop. A chancel S window, put in at the same time, commemorates his two wives. In the heads of the S aisle S windows, and at the W end, five armorial lights by *William Miller*, 1855, also relating to the Winthrops; similar lights in the N aisle added later. – Chancel S (Faith and Charity) by *J. Cameron*, 1883. – S aisle E, 1869, and tower window, 1870, by *O'Connor*. – S aisle S (Emblems of the Evangelists) and corresponding N aisle window (stamped quarries) by *Powell & Sons*, 1854. – MONUMENT. Adam Winthrop †1562. Brass inscription, restored to the church 1878 with a commemorative brass plaque by *Cox & Sons*.

GROTON HALL, on the S side of the churchyard. C16 timber-framed and plastered house with cross-wings at each end. Good chimneystack with four octagonal shafts and star tops.

In the street W of the church, the OLD SCHOOL, 1854. Flint pebbles with white-brick dressings. To the N, a large timber-framed and plastered house, now three dwellings. C15, of one build. Two-bay hall with gabled and jettied cross-wings. The wings stretch back to the rear, with the kitchen on the N side beyond the service rooms, and lodgings on the S side beyond the parlour. Further along the OLD RECTORY, timber-framed of the C15–C16 (roof with crown-post dated 1490) but faced in red brick. Additions by *Salter & Firmin*, 1873. Finally GROTON PLACE, now subdivided. Also timber-framed, but the front Georgianized with sash windows, pedimented doorcase, and parapets. Two storeys. Five-bay centre, the doorway not central but aligned with the original cross-entry. One-bay wings, one bay deep, with plastered quoins.

GROTON HOUSE, ½ m. NNE. 1705, incorporating a C15 timber-framed house. Damaged by fire in 1981 and reduced in size. E of the house PITCHES or PYTCHES MOUNT, a Norman castle

CASTLING'S HALL, 1¼ m. NE. C16 timber-framed house. Two storeys with lower cross-wing at the E end, both parts jettied. Restored by *Basil Oliver*, 1933–4, who exposed the jetty (which had been underbuilt) and most of the timbers, and reinstated the windows, distinguishing between original work (with ovolo moulding) and new work (with a simple chamfer). Original carving including bressumer, brackets, sills and buttresses. Oliver's porch does not sit well, cutting into the jetty.

HADLEIGH

Hadleigh was a very prosperous town in the Middle Ages and into the C17, thanks to the cloth trade: its coat of arms includes three woolsacks. As a result the town has a great number of high-quality medieval timber-framed houses along all its principal streets, many concealed by later fronts, although a decline in the town's prosperity in the C18 meant there was not as much rebuilding as there might otherwise have been. But there was also industry in the form of maltings and a large silk mill, and fortunes were somewhat revived by the coming of the railway in 1847 (closed 1965). The establishment of an industrial estate to the NE of the centre in the 1960s, followed by a considerable amount of new housing, has greatly increased the population of the town, but without unduly affecting the historic centre. The High Street runs N–S through the town, parallel to the River Brett, and between the two lie the parish church and other buildings that indicate the town's prosperity. It needs to be understood that the rector of Hadleigh is co-dean of Bocking (Essex), for reasons connected with the parish's status as a peculiar of the Archbishop of Canterbury until 1838.

CHURCHES

ST MARY. The church is 163 ft (49.7 metres) long and has a tower which is crowned by a lead splay-foot spire, 135 ft (41.1 metres) high; re-covered in 1926–7, when a battlemented parapet round the base (of 1854–7) was removed. Externally mostly Perp, except for the tower, which is clearly of the early C14 but in its lower parts may be C13 or even late C12. To the l. and r. of the bell-openings, which have three-light intersected tracery, are circular openings. On the E side is an external BELL, probably of the late C13 and the earliest in the county. It is thought to have come from Butley Priory (E). Of the C14 also a tomb recess in the S aisle (ogee arch cusped); so the S aisle wall is also of that period. There may be more of it (e.g. the chancel walls) but the windows are Perp, large in the aisles, larger still in the E end, where three windows look down Church Street, smaller, in pairs of two lights each, in the nave clerestory (renewed). At the E end to the N a two-storey vestry, vaulted below. S porch of two bays with side windows and three niches above the entrance. In the porch, springers of vaulting that seems not to have been completed. Arcades of five wide bays. The piers have polygonal shafts, carrying capitals only towards the arch openings. The clerestory windows are not above the apexes of the arches, but above the spandrels. Chancel arch and two-bay arcades of the chancel chapels of the same type. Restoration of the exterior by *F. Barnes*, 1854–7, of chancel by *G. E. Pritchett*, 1859–60 (including restored roof, with stone corbels by *William Farmer*), and of the interior of the nave (including re-seating) by *J. D. Wyatt*, 1871–2. Further work by *Charles Spooner*, c. 1911–35, including reordering of the sanctuary and chapels; his uncle was rector, 1875–99.

FURNISHINGS. FONT. Perp, octagonal, with finely detailed blank niches, two to each side, with feigned rib-vaults. Restored 1871. – FONT COVER. By *Spooner*, 1925. Tall and slender spire. Small figure of St John the Baptist within by *Holzer* of Titisee, Germany, 2007. – SCREENS. Perp, to the N and S chapels. Tower screen by *H. M. Cautley*, 1950. – BENCH END. Late C14. With a representation which has been interpreted as the wolf finding the head of St Edmund, although the hind feet are cloven and something quite other may be intended. – PULPIT. 1871, by *Wyatt*. Oak, carved by *John Spurgeon* of Stowmarket, on vaulted stone base with marble columns by *Farmer & Brindley*. – SOUTH DOOR. With tracery and a border of quatrefoils. – BIBLE BOX. Dated 1626, with decorative panels on the sides. – ORGAN. A fine large instrument in an impressive case, built in 1687 by *Bernard Schmidt (Father Smith)*. Made for East Donyland Hall, Essex, and brought to Hadleigh in 1738. – SCULPTURE. Lepine stone Mother and Child by *Derek Jarman* of Ipswich, 1996. – PAINTING. Head of Christ by *Maggi Hambling*, 1986. – STAINED GLASS. Odd bits in the N chapel E window, rearranged and supplemented by *George Hedgeland*; more in tower window. By Hedgeland the S chapel E window, 1857, very Nazarene. Christ blessing the little children, after *Overbeck*. A number of other windows by *Ward & Hughes*, including the E, 1875, and six in the S aisle, c. 1885–1908, the later ones by *T. F. Curtis*. N aisle by *Alfred Fisher (Chapel Studio)*, 1988, designed by *John O'Connor*. – BRASSES. Thomas Alabaster †1592. Kneeling figure in civilian dress within an arch. – Anne Alabaster, wife of Rev. John Still, †1593. 23-in. (59-cm.) figure. – John Alabaster †1637. Similar to Thomas's, but finer. – Richard Glanfield and wife Elizabeth, both †1637. Three-quarter-length figures, holding hands. Mounted on board. – MONUMENTS. Between sanctuary and N chapel, Purbeck marble tomb-chest with three shields in quatrefoils separated by small niches for weepers. Superstructure restored 1859, including 'Late Perp' vaulted canopy of painted limestone. Indents of lost brasses on W and E sides of opening. The main indent appears to be the figure of a cleric, taken to be Archdeacon William Pykenham †1497. The monument also no doubt served as an Easter sepulchre. – Sarah Johnson †1793 by *Regnart*. With two putti by an urn. – Dean Fryer †1910 by *Spooner*. With bas relief of Lamb and Flag. – War memorial. By *Spooner*, 1921. Painted roll of honour in oak frame. Figure of crucified Christ in tempera by Spooner's wife *Minnie Dibdin Spooner*. By them both also the nearby monument to Grace Mary Strange †1920. Tablet with painted Virgin and Child. – Dean Carter †1935 and wife Sibella †1940. Tablets by *Eric Gill*.

ROW CHAPEL, George Street. Restored by *Charles Spooner* in 1891, when a date of 1498 (thought to be a repair) was found on one of the roof timbers. Timber-framed with brick-nogging. PULPIT and STALL made from pieces of old furnishings brought from St Mary's; remaining fittings by Spooner, including very sturdy BENCHES, and a painted REREDOS of the rising sun by *Minnie Dibdin Spooner*.

ST JOSEPH (R.C.), Long Bessels. By *Eric Sandon*, 1965–6. Rather dreary, of buff-coloured brick. Nave with chancel and transepts of equal length. Lantern with flèche at the crossing. Soon after completion the church was reoriented, with the new nave running N–S across the transepts and the old nave screened off as a hall. – SCULPTURE. Madonna and Child by *Peter Watts*, 1971. Clipsham stone. Also a stone relief of the Deposition (Joseph of Arimathea supporting Christ) by *Dom Hubert van Zeller*.

BAPTIST CHURCH, George Street. 1830. Red brick, with two tiers of windows set in blank giant arches. Mostly obscured by brick additions of 1985 etc.

UNITED REFORMED CHURCH (Independent, later Congregational), Market Place. 1832. White brick with upper arched windows and broad heavy Grecian entrance below. Corner pilasters. Interior refitted by *Eade & Johns*, 1890. Large hall (originally school) 1863.

CEMETERY, Friars Road. 1856. Picturesque LODGE of knapped flint with white-brick and stone dressings. Gothic arched windows, gables, and tall chimneys with diamond flues. L-plan, with open gabled timber porch in the angle.

PUBLIC BUILDINGS

GUILDHALL (Town Council). The complex of buildings known as the Guildhall lies between the Town Hall of 1851 and the churchyard, and includes the Market Hall, built between 1438 and 1451, which faces the S side of the church and is the most visible component of the group. This is what one sees from the churchyard – a three-storey timber-framed building with two jetties, with two-storey ranges to E and W. The W range was rebuilt in the late C19, in place of a building known as the Market House that was erected between 1419 and 1433 and damaged by a gale in 1884. The E range was originally the same height as the centre, but the first floor was converted to an assembly hall in the late C18, extended further E with an apsidal end, and the jetty underbuilt with brick. The top storey was removed to allow for a barrel-vaulted ceiling and small musicians' gallery at one end (now council chamber). The dragon posts from the NE and SE corners of the original building are preserved inside. On the ground floor was an open passageway linking the market place and the churchyard; this had shops on either side, and the front of one of these can be seen inside the building. Characteristic thin buttress posts. The first floor had oriels towards the church. Crown-post roof. Chimney inserted in the C16. In a room on the top floor is a SCREEN with linenfold panelling, salvaged from No. 50 High Street. The Guildhall proper lies at right angles to the Market Hall and was originally free-standing; the two were linked in the C16. The Guildhall was erected c. 1451 and has a brick cellar, brick ground floor, and timber-framed first floor jettied along both sides; the E side was underbuilt in the C18. The ground floor originally had a cross-passage towards the S end. The large room on the upper floor has an impressive roof with seven crown-posts, inserted after the link to the Market Hall was constructed and no doubt reused from elsewhere. At about the same time a stair-tower, later removed, was built in the SW angle between the Market Hall and Guildhall, and two large chimneystacks were built against the W wall in the mid C17. Part of the S end of the Guildhall was demolished when the Town Hall was built in 1851. In the garden, ruins of a detached medieval kitchen.

TOWN HALL. 1851 by *W. P. Ribbans*. Two storeys. Red brick with stone dressings and quoins, the ground floor treated as a basement and faced in white brick. Five bays, with two tall arched doorways at either end. Three tall arched windows on the upper floor, the middle one Venetian and added c. 1925, when the original lantern over the Grand Hall on the upper floor was removed. Ground floor intended as Police Station, later offices, now dining room. The building connects on the S side to the Guildhall (q.v.).

BABERGH DISTRICT COUNCIL OFFICES, Corks Lane. By *Arup Associates*, 1978–82. A large complex of irregular plan, of the right scale (mostly two storeys) and materials (red brick and pantiles) to sit well in its location. A number of listed buildings, mostly C18 and early C19, were incorporated into the scheme: a two-storey, three-bay red brick house facing the river; a timber-framed and plastered cottage next to it; a two-storey, seven-bay house on Bridge Street, with an C18 front of blue brick (all headers) with red brick dressings, nice doorway, and central segment-headed window; and maltings with attached house at the N end of the site. These were fully integrated with and linked to the new buildings, which include a square, pavilion-like block of three storeys with platform roof, and, at the core, an octagonal, slate-roofed council chamber. This forms one side of an internal courtyard garden, most of the other three sides being the older buildings.

BEAUMONT COMMUNITY PRIMARY SCHOOL, Durrant Road. 2003 by *Rob King* of Suffolk County Council, designed as a model of sustainability. Of timber construction, clad in untreated western cedar, insulated with recycled newspaper. Green roof with rainwater recovery system. Energy supplied by wind turbine, photovoltaic panels, and solar heat collector panels.

HADLEIGH COMMUNITY PRIMARY SCHOOL, Station Road. 1904. Red brick. Tudor-Gothic, with straight gables and big windows with arched lights. Probably by *Eade & Johns*.

ST MARY'S CHURCH OF ENGLAND PRIMARY SCHOOL, Stonehouse Road. By *Johns, Slater & Haward* (partner in charge *J. L. Harding*), 1965–8. One large and seven smaller linked pavilions with pyramidal timber-shell roofs, clad in vertical cedar boarding.

PERAMBULATIONS

1. North of the Market Place

The CHURCHYARD contains the town's most spectacular buildings, and if one treats the church as essentially C15, then those three buildings belong to the same century but could hardly be more different one from the other: one built of stone, one of timber, and one of brick. The Market Hall stands opposite the S side of the church (*see* p. 274), and Gainsborough's painting of the church, 1748, shows a second porch in the middle of the S side to the E of the present one that was originally for the use of the guilds. It was taken down in the C19 and bits of it can be found in the wall along the W side of the churchyard, to the S of the splendid DEANERY TOWER. This was built by William Pykenham, who died in 1497. He was a churchman and lawyer, who held some sixteen ecclesiastical posts, including that of rector of Hadleigh (1470) and archdeacon of Suffolk (1472). The traditional date given for the building is 1495, but it seems probable that it is ten years or so earlier than that, and very close in date and character to the gatehouse of Oxburgh in Norfolk, completed by 1487, with which it shares many characteristics. It is also apparent that Pykenham's gatehouse was intended to be free-standing, a splendid display of wealth and power but not the beginning of an uncompleted project nor the remaining fragment of a vanished mansion. It was, rather, a lodging that would have functioned as an appendage to the existing parsonage that lay between the church and the river, a timber-framed building that is also visible in Gainsborough's painting and which stood until the C19. The gatehouse is of red brick with black diapering. The middle part is three-storeyed with a four-centred archway. This was filled in in 1831–3 and the oriel window above it is of this date also. Polygonal turrets to either side, of

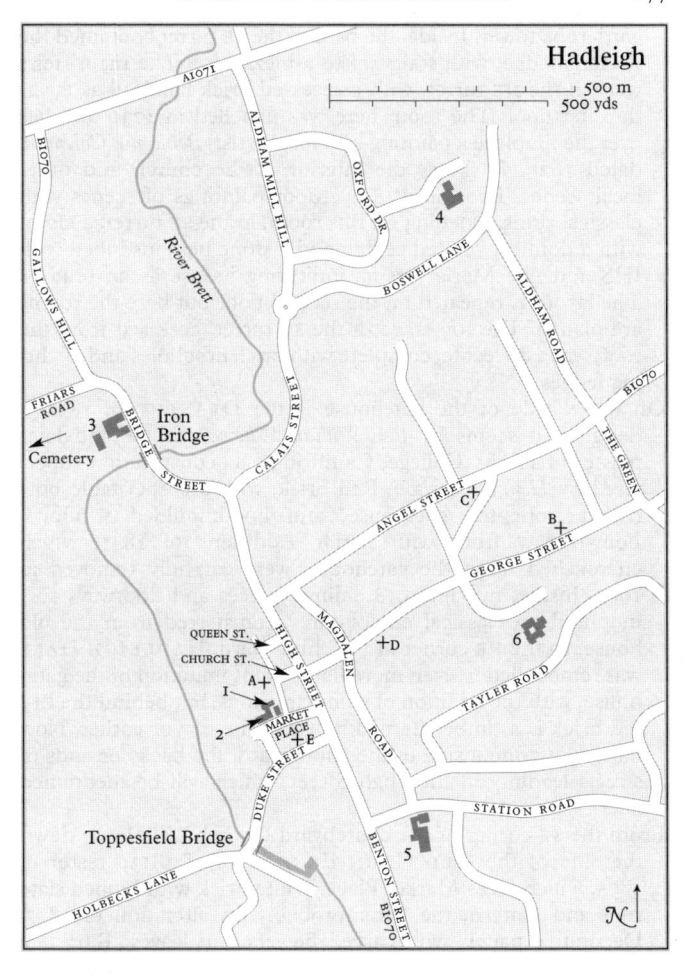

A St Mary
B Row Chapel
C St Joseph (R.C.)
D Baptist Church
E United Reformed Church

1 Guildhall
2 Town Hall
3 Babergh District Council Offices
4 Beaumont Community Primary School
5 Hadleigh Community Primary School
6 St Mary's Church of England Primary School

six stages. The turrets are divided into panels with pairs of trefoiled arches in each. Battlemented tops. The turrets are repeated on the W or inner face of the gatehouse but here start only at the level of the corbel table. The ornate chimneys are of 1833 and 1961, three of them dummies. On the S side is a garderobe tower. Inside, the base of the SE turret contained the porter's lodge, with stairs up to a mezzanine. The main stairs were in the NE turret, with a recessed brick handrail as far as the first floor. The room here was panelled in 1730 and has over the fireplace a painting by a local artist, *Benjamin Coleman*, dated 1629. It shows the interior of the church and other local scenes. Two mid-C18 overdoor paintings of scenes with classical ruins. Opening off this room, in the SE turret, a closet with a domical vaulted ceiling and a stone boss inscribed with IHS and Ave Maria Gratia, indicating its use as an oratory. The layout is repeated on the second floor but here the rooms are plainer. The top stage of the SE turret, accessed from the roof, was a dovecote, complete with brick nest holes and alighting ledges.

On the N side of the gatehouse is the DEANERY of 1831–3, designed it seems by *Rev. William Whewell*, fellow and later master of Trinity College, Cambridge, its construction supervised by *Henry Harrison*. Red brick, with a corbel table borrowed from the gatehouse, and hoodmoulded windows. Four-bay W front with porch. Additions of 1841, which encroached upon the gatehouse, were carefully removed in 1961. Inside, two fine C18 chimneypieces and doorways surmounted by classical entablatures, transferred from the old house. In the NE corner of the churchyard, HADLEIGH HALL was remodelled in even more flamboyant imitation of the gatehouse, with the addition of stone dressings, but behind the C19 red brick is a timber-framed house of the C17 or earlier. Now flats. Along the E side of the churchyard, the backs or ends of streets leading off the High Street, which will be mentioned later.

From the SE corner of the churchyard Church Walk leads down the side of the OLD CORN EXCHANGE of 1813, 'restored' 1895, which faces Market Place. White brick with hipped slate roof and lantern, the latter probably an alteration of 1873. Decorative panels with carved flowers and leaves. Tetrastyle Greek Doric portico. To its W is the Town Hall (*see* p. 275), in front of which stands a painted cast-iron PUMP by *Ransomes*. Beyond it TOPPESFIELD HALL, a timber-framed former manor house refronted in white brick in 1829. Portions survive of its red brick boundary walls, mentioned in 1496. Opposite the Corn Exchange the United Reformed church (*see* p. 274). To its E, a pair of three-bay, two-and-a-half-storey houses (Nos. 6–8) on the N side. Late C18, timber-framed and plastered. Pedimented doorcases and a little arched window on the top floor. Beyond it, as Market Place opens out, a C19 warehouse of red brick with black-brick detailing, converted and extended by *Wincer Kievenaar*, 1982, as their offices. VICTORIA HOUSE dominates the main Market Place, facing E towards the High Street. Early C19. White brick, of two and a half storeys. Three broad bays, the pedimented centre breaking forward. But the back, which was originally the front, has been Victorianized, with later C19 canted bays and a heavy Tuscan porch.

The HIGH STREET is remarkable for having retained nearly all its old buildings unspoilt while remaining busy and commercial. The result, not easily achieved, is of an overall harmony, yet with enormous variety between individual buildings. On the E side, opposite the Market Place, is the former WHITE LION HOTEL (now flats) with a widely spaced seven-bay front of brick, rendered and painted. As with many of Hadleigh's buildings, the C18 front conceals an earlier timber-framed structure. To its N, Nos. 46–48 has some humble C17 pargetting on the front, which was originally jettied. Inside, a good plaster ceiling and contemporary wall paintings with imitation panelled dado and scenes from the story of Joseph based on Crispijn de Passe, after 1612. Opposite, Nos. 45–49 date from the C14, with C18 shopfronts below the jetty and an original doorway at one end. We then come to a crossroads, with Church Street to the W and George Street to the E; on one corner an C18 obelisk MILESTONE with distances to other Suffolk towns and London (64 miles). CHURCH STREET, leading up to the E end of the church, can be quickly covered; its principal building is the RED HOUSE at the far end, its front C19 Neo-Tudor with straight gables and hoodmoulds, but along its W flank original C16 brickwork can be seen including two large chimneystacks.

After George Street (*see* below) comes Nos. 62–66, the finest house in the street. Two storeys and attics. The first floor, which originally projected, has six times repeated the so-called 'Ipswich window', the rectangular window with a Venetian window set in and outlined by casements found at the Ancient House, Ipswich (E). In the leading of a window (3rd from l.) the date 1676. Deep carved eaves. At the back, three gables and more windows of the same type can be seen from Magdalen Road. Staircase with vase balusters, with matching painted balustrade on the wall. Restored by *Marshall Sisson*, 1956–7. Then a look into QUEEN STREET, which runs to the churchyard, a pleasing unified composition of *c.* 1838–41, built by *Wilkinson & Parsons*. White-brick fronts. Two storeys rising to two and a half, and the last two houses before the churchyard closer together. The narrowing is stressed by rounded corners, and rounded shop windows on the ground floor; to the churchyard their sides are red brick.

Continuing N along the High Street, Nos. 79–83 is a hall house with two long cross-wings, probably C15 but with a date 1693 and swag in the plaster. No. 89 is late C18, a seven-bay front of plastered and painted brick, the centre breaking forward with a semicircular Doric porch and window above it set in a segmental-arched recess.

N of Angel Street (for which *see* below), three more outstanding hall houses in the High Street, all with two gabled cross-wings, and probably C15. First, on the W side, Nos. 97–99, with delightful C17 pargetting including royal arms, Tudor roses and the date 1618. Then SUN COURT (No. 107). The usual plastered front with gabled and jettied cross-wings; an original two-light window in the return wall of the S cross-wing. Mid-C15, with the sympathetic additions of a C16 bay in front of the hall and C20 garage doors in the S cross-wing. To the rear an early C16 wing, timber-framed with brick-nogging and a jettied and gabled cross-wing at one end, which has below the jetty two bays on brick plinths. Transomed windows of five, six and eight lights as well as frieze windows. Rear doorway with spandrels carved with de Vere and Bourchier emblems. The building was restored 1927–9 by *Sydney Schofield*, one of his mother Muriel's rescue projects (cf. High House, Otley (E), and Clock House, Little Stonham). On the High Street's E side, Nos. 108–110 (THE GABLES) is distinguished by having a third gable on the hall range, with carved bressumer dated 1649. But there are quieter houses to enjoy also – No. 104 (BEECH HOUSE), with arched rusticated doorway and canted bays below the jetty; No. 106 timber-framed with a red brick front, described as new built in 1796, pedimented doorcase, and (false) Gothick arched window; No. 116 set back from the front, early C19 white brick with Ionic porch – as well as the humble weatherboarded GARAGE showroom and workshop at No. 115.

From the far end of the High Street BRIDGE STREET runs W. On the S side the former NATIONAL SCHOOL and teacher's house by *F. Barnes*, 1853–4. Red brick with Tudor detailing. Then a row of timber-framed houses, with some overhangs and exposed timbers, before HADLEIGH IRON BRIDGE crosses the Brett. Rebuilt 1843 by *George Hurwood* of St Peter's Foundry, Ipswich. Six cast-iron arches on brick pillars. The original construction is apparent on the NE side and a section of the cast-iron beams and deck-plates is displayed nearby. Widened and refurbished by Suffolk County Council (county surveyor *J. J. Stansfield*), 1988. Across the bridge, No. 21 and other houses, now part of the offices of Babergh District Council, on the W side (*see* p. 275), and on the E Nos. 12–16, another SUN COURT, C16 timber-framed and plastered, partly jettied, with a brick gable facing the road. At the top of the street, the WHITE HART, C15 or C16, timber-framed and plastered with some exposed timbers on the lower jettied cross-wing.

Two streets running E from the High Street involve longer diversions. The main part of GEORGE STREET is cut off from the centre by Magdalen Road, opened in 1973 to relieve the High Street of some of its traffic. E of Magdalen Road, the Baptist church (*see* p. 274) and some houses with exposed timbers opposite and to the E, including Nos. 22–26, with gabled cross-wings and plasterwork dated 1585. Further E, on the S side, EAST HOUSE has a seven-bay Georgian red brick front (two storeys, parapet, Doric porch with triglyph frieze) but the other sides were rebuilt or refaced in the C19 with plain and crow-stepped gables. Nos. 40–42, with a date of 1663, has the only remaining thatched roof in the town. No. 48 is a curious remnant of a timber-framed hall house of *c.* 1400, encased in red brick *c.* 1580. Two gables on the front, one with a projecting stair-turret, and a large chimneystack between them. Three gables to the rear. Windows of up to six lights, transomed on the ground floor. Inside, late C16 panelling, and a complete crown-post roof to the parlour cross-wing. This roof is painted red, and there are remains of C16 painted decoration elsewhere in the house. Just beyond it the former METHODIST CHAPEL of 1875, now a private house. No. 111, on the N side, is a C15 hall house with one jettied cross-wing, exposed timbers, and crown-post roof. Wide chimneystack in the angle between the two ranges. Finally, set back on the N side, the PYKENHAM ALMSHOUSES, founded by William Pykenham, who died in 1497. Rebuilt in 1887 by *H. J. Wright*. Red brick, single-storey. Main range designed as seven linked 'houses', the centre one gabled, the others with half-hipped roofs. Three additional houses by *Eric Sandon*, 1972–3. Between them and the road the Row Chapel (*see* p. 274).

ANGEL STREET has several good timber-framed houses, including Nos. 63–79, about 300 yds from the High Street, an attractive and varied row, one house with pargetting and date-panel 1596; Nos. 95–99, on a corner, with a large chimneystack with octagonal shafts on the return wall; and Nos. 149–151, with jettied front, carriage entrance at one end, and date-panel 1713, 600 yds E of the High Street.

2. *South of the Market Place*

The HIGH STREET s of the Market Place starts strongly with No. 40 (BARCLAYS BANK), at the s end of the White Lion, an early C19 three-storey house of white brick with a bow window taking three of its five bays. In front of the whole ground floor a loggia of six baseless Doric columns. On the W side, No. 29 (now PUBLIC LIBRARY), Late Georgian red brick with doorcase with baseless columns, converted 1854–5 by *F. Barnes* for the Police Station. It stands on the corner of DUKE STREET, which has a few worthwhile houses and, on the s side, former C19 maltings, but above all leads to TOPPESFIELD BRIDGE, over the Brett, 300 yds SW of the High Street. Probably C14. Red brick. Three slightly pointed arches, with stone ribs on the SE side. Parapet on this side with datestone 1624. Widened on the NW side in 1812.

Further down the High Street, No. 15 is a good example of the style of c. 1830: white brick with stucco dressings, three bays with projecting centre and a little pediment on the roof, Greek Doric portico *in antis*, and pedimented gable on the return wall. On the E side, less of interest until the last house, No. 2 (EDGE HALL), its mid-C18 red brick front with five widely spaced windows and Doric doorcase with open pediment and decorative fanlight. We have now reached the junction of Station Road, opposite which stands the WAR MEMORIAL by *Charles Spooner*, 1921. Stone cenotaph, square with diminishing stages and pyramidal top. Behind it CROSS MALTINGS (now residential), red brick, *c.* 1850, the main range of nine bays separated by pilasters, with former kiln at the far end.

In STATION ROAD, on the corner of Benton Street, a timber-framed house with early C19 Y-traceried windows looking back up the High Street. Beyond the primary school (*see* p. 276), more maltings converted to housing and additional buildings in similar style, and hidden among them the former STATION of 1847 by *F. Barnes*, of red brick with lavish white-brick dressings. Round-arched windows, including the Venetian type. Flat canopy over entrance on ornate cast-iron brackets. The gables were originally Jacobean rather than straight.

BENTON STREET is the continuation s of the High Street. Its narrowness, gentle curves and jettied houses create a picturesqueness that is unfortunately almost outweighed by traffic and overhead electricity cables. A Georgian bay beneath the jetty distinguishes Nos. 31–35. No. 43 has a Georgian-Gothic doorcase, an open pediment on triple shafts with shaft-rings instead of columns. Another good group at Nos. 69–75 with some timbers exposed. Nos. 77–81 was refronted in the C18, its roof partly concealed by a parapet with dentilled cornice, the plastered front with pedimented doorcase and sashes; but in the N return wall an 'Ipswich window' as on Nos. 62–66 High Street, and on the s return exposed timbers. A little further on, still on the E side, THE OLD MONKEY (former King's Arms pub, now residential) has two cross-wings. Jetties to one cross-wing and the main block, which also has two small gables.

On the W side, nothing much until No. 86, with some exposed timbers and a date-panel of 1714, then No. 90, THE OLD MANSE, intriguingly set back behind its walled garden. Red brick. Three-bay, two-storey front. Doric doorcase with open pediment and above it a lovely Gothick Venetian window. Single-storey extensions to either side. The back has a similar doorcase, a non-Venetian Gothick window, two canted bays that start on the ground floor and carry on down to the cellar, and a datestone of 1790. S of Raven Way, Nos. 92–94, known as the FLYING CHARIOT, with a richly decorated C17 front including some decayed pargetting. Elaborate carving on the pediment of the doorcase, on the brackets supporting the three oriels, on the eaves board (dated 1653) and on the eaves brackets. Painted decoration inside including imitation panelling and an imitation overmantel of three arches supported on columns. Restored by *Marshall Sisson, c.* 1937–8. Nos. 110–118 are the RAVEN ALMSHOUSES of 1555, single-storey with a two-storey cross-wing at the N end. Back on the E side, PRIORY HALL. The original part, probably C16, lies closest to the road, and has a crown-post roof. This was greatly enlarged to the E in the 1930s in the same style, i.e. with exposed timbers, jetties, and gables, perhaps by *Titchmarsh & Goodwin*, who extended the service wing in 1938. Such is the depth of the later range that much of the roof is in fact flat, behind the tiled slopes of normal pitch and height. At the E end a Great Hall, a reused barn from elsewhere.

BENTON END HOUSE, ¾ m. SE. C16 timber-framed and plastered house. The front is C18 in character but has at the N end an octagonal brick pier. A wing extending to the rear has exposed timbers and brick-nogging and a gabled brick end wall with octagonal piers. Home of Sir Cedric Morris, painter and gardener, 1940–82, and his East Anglian School of Painting and Drawing. Range of C17 and C18 farm buildings to the S including a red brick granary, almost square, with hipped roof.

PEYTON HALL, ¾ m. NNW. Former manor house. Timber-framed and plastered, with raised-aisle hall of *c.* 1300. Cross-wing at W end, which itself has a cross-wing across the S end. 150 yds downstream, ALDHAM MILL, 1764. Timber-framed with mansard roof and faced in red brick.

POND HALL, 1½ m. ESE. Former manor house, probably C15; a chapel was licensed in 1466. Long W front (nine bays) with exposed timbers, jettied the entire length. Farm buildings to the W, mainly early C19, include remains of a red brick BARN of the late C15 or early C16. Further W, on the S side of the road, a small COTTAGE by *R. Weir Schultz*, 1907, one of a number built on smallholdings by Felix Cobbold, and based on a design by *F. W. Troup* for Letchworth. Timber-framed and weatherboarded. Other similar cottages further E towards Hintlesham. *p. 284*

MONUMENT, Aldham Common, 1 m. NE. Elongated obelisk, erected 1819, to Rev. Rowland Taylor, martyred in 1555. On the plinth a verse by Nathan Drake. On the W side, an unhewn stone with carved inscription, the original late C16 memorial.

HARGRAVE

7060

ST EDMUND. Plain Tudor brick tower with diagonal buttresses and a Perp stone window. Nave with very simple Transitional S doorway. One two-light brick window. The chancel windows E.E. but renewed as part of the restoration by *Ralph Chamberlain* in 1868–9, when the humble N aisle was added. – SCREEN, Perp, rather raw; the top parts must have been odd. On the E face carvings of a dragon, a fox, fishes, a unicorn, a pair of wyverns, a Turk's head, etc. Carved rood beam above.

A long way from the village, but with the Old Rectory on the S side of the churchyard and Hargrave Hall to the SW. RECTORY rebuilt by *Chamberlain*, 1868, for Rev. Samuel Chamberlain, whose wife was patron. Painted brick. Windows with depressed arches. HARGRAVE HALL is mid-C16, timber-framed, encased in early C19 red brick.

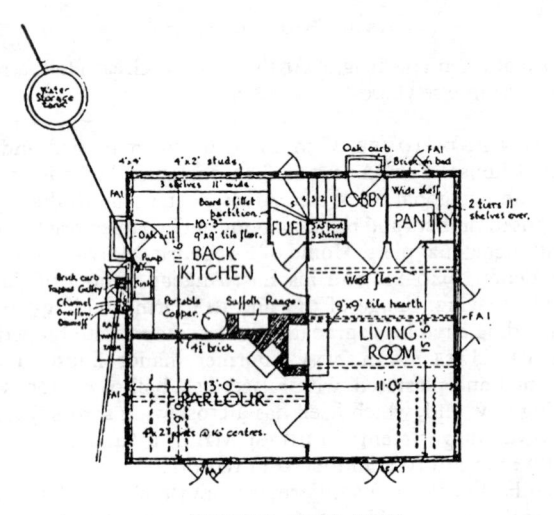

GROUND FLOOR PLAN

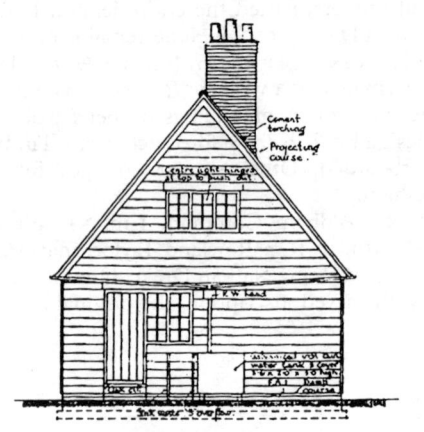

NORTH ELEVATION

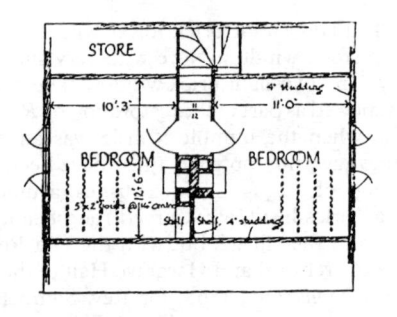

FIRST FLOOR PLAN

Hadleigh, design for cottages on smallholdings.
Drawing by R. Weir Schultz, published 1913

HARLESTON

St Augustine. Nave and chancel in one, under a thatched roof. Norman nave. Plain Norman s doorway and fragments of the N doorway. C13 chancel with one remaining s lancet. In the nave also a lancet. Restored in 1860: see the E and W walls, the latter with its very Victorian timber bell-turret. Reordered and furnished 1931, according to a plaque inside. – SCREEN. An interesting early or mid-C14 piece, still with shafts instead of mullions. In the spandrels between the ogee arches circles with three mouchettes. – The return STALLS, with weeping angels on the arms, look more 1931 than 1860.

Harleston Hall, 250 yds w. Front dated 1832, with the initials of Roger and Jane Pettiward of Great Finborough. Red brick with white-brick dressings and very curvaceous gables. An external chimneystack and internal timber framing of the late C16. Farm buildings between the house and the road in similar style, dated 1879, for Charles Tyrell of Haughley.

HARTEST

All Saints. All Perp. C14 chancel, s chapel and s aisle, C15 N chapel and aisle. Arcades with octagonal piers and double-chamfered arches. Porches of knapped squared flint, over-restored in 1890. The N porch has three niches over the entrance, and shields l. and r. These include the initials of John Philipson, who in 1546 asked to be buried within the porch. W tower rebuilt with much red brick by *Thomas Moore* of East Bergholt, 1652–3, following its collapse in 1650. At the same time the nave roof was rebuilt (without its clerestory); roof renewed as part of general restoration by *J. D. Wyatt*, 1879–80, which also included a new E window (replacing two lancets), re-seating and new FONT. – PULPIT. Jacobean, good, with two tiers of the usual short blank arches. – SCREEN to s chapel by *Andrew Anderson*, 2003–4. Glass and metal. s door replaced by a plate-glass window at the same time. – STAINED GLASS. E window by *Burlison & Grylls*, 1880. – MONUMENTS. Mary Carter †1799 and her husband Thomas Barwell Carter †1803. Two monuments, almost identical, with bas-relief figure of Hope (with anchor) beneath a gilded sunburst. – Lt J. G. Harrington R. N. †1812, buried near Mahon, Minorca. Various nautical paraphernalia, including a sail on which the inscription is written. By *Henry Westmacott*.

The church is nicely placed in a dip, at the SE corner of a large and very attractive GREEN dotted with limes and other trees. Behind the church the former RECTORY by *M. G. Thompson*, 1821. White brick. Three bays wide. Originally two storeys, a third added later in the C19. Doric portico. Red brick stable block backing on to the churchyard. w of All Saints the CROWN INN, formerly Hartest Hall. C16, timber-framed and plastered. Large wing projecting N, originally free-standing, jettied on two sides. But none of these have much visual impact, being set back from the Green. The NE side is a different matter, a delightfully varied yet utterly harmonious row: some red brick, some painted brick, but above all plastered timber-framed houses, some jettied, some thatched, brightly but contrastingly painted. Even the C20 garage at the far end, of corrugated iron, fits in. In the middle, the former CONGREGATIONAL CHAPEL: a C17 timber-framed house, later cottages, used as a chapel (when the floor was removed) between 1864 and 1980, now once more a house. Two tall round-headed windows. At the NW corner of the Green, PLACE FARM, its E gable dated 1688 (and 1800) in the plaster. Chimneystack with three octagonal shafts. Later wing to the W of the cross-wing. To its S, facing E across the Green, SPURGEON'S HALL, C17 with gabled and jettied cross-wing at the S end, much restored. Then HARTEST AND BOXTED CLUB (village hall), 1888 by *Reginald Blomfield*. Red brick. On the front a tall central chimney with large oriel windows l. and r. that rise through the eaves and end in half-timbered gables. Hipped roof with tile-hanging in the gable-ends. Restored and enlarged by *Modece Architects*, 2002. On the Green itself, the WAR MEMORIAL (Portland stone obelisk), 1920, and the HARTEST STONE, a large glacial erratic apparently brought to the Green in 1713 to celebrate the Treaty of Utrecht and the end of the War of the Spanish Succession.

PRIMARY SCHOOL, S of the village hall. By *West Suffolk County Architect's Dept* (job architects *Jack Digby* and *Dudley Baylis*), 1965–6. Single-storey. Pale buff brick and weatherboarding. Considered at the time, with its dormers and gabled roofs, to harmonize with the other village buildings, but subsequent additions, unexceptional in themselves, have detracted from the effect.

CAWSTONS, ½ m. SE. Thatched, timber-framed and plastered farmhouse, probably C17. Parallel rear range by *Modece Architects*, 1997–9. Opposite, FOSTERS, of similar date with some exposed timbers and chimneystack with four octagonal shafts. Weatherboarded barn to one side converted by *Modece Architects* for their own offices, 2007–8.

STOWE HILL, 1 m. NNW. Timber-framed house of *c.* 1792, with various C19 alterations and additions. White-brick front. Three broad bays, the outer bays breaking very slightly forward. Across the whole front a glazed cast-iron veranda. Single-storey wings to l. and r. with crenellated parapets. Home of the sculptor *Geoffrey Clarke*, 1955–2009, who considerably altered the interior to create studios. Behind the house, HANGAR, 1963 by Clarke, intended partly as a gallery. Ground floor rendered, upper storey weatherboarded.

In Hartest Wood, 600 yds NE of All Saints, a SCULPTURE by *Geoffrey Clarke* ('The Gift'), 2000. Bronze, on granite base.

A group of abstract figures, one taller and looking over the rest.

HAUGHLEY

Haughley was the *caput*, or centre, of the Suffolk estate of Hugh de Montfort, who was Duke William's constable in Normandy and took part in the Battle of Hastings. The impressive remains of his motte-and-bailey castle are still visible, and the shape of the village is largely determined by its outer defences. The church, which was in existence before 1066, stands inside the outer bailey.

ST MARY (Assumption of the Blessed Virgin Mary). All of c. 1330–40. Nave and chancel, S aisle and S porch tower, which appears almost to be free-standing. Inside the tower a good doorway with two orders of slender shafts and finely moulded arch. The S aisle E window has a very pretty enrichment of the usual reticulation motif. Each unit has a lozenge in the middle held by four bars. The W window has two cusped spherical triangles above the even three lights. The N windows of the nave are segment-headed, again with reticulation motifs. The five-bay arcade which separates the nave from the wide S aisle has octagonal piers and double-hollow-chamfered arches. Beautiful nave roof with alternating castellated tie-beams on arched braces and arched braces meeting at the ridge. Large bosses. S aisle roof on demi-figures of angels. Smaller angels on the wall-plate as well. Nave roof restored 1866 (*Frederick Andrews*, carpenter), when the N wall of the nave was rebuilt. General restoration by *Augustus Frere*, 1877–8, including new barrel roof in the chancel, chancel arch, re-seating, and addition of organ chamber and NW vestry. Extension to vestry by *D. Whymark*, 2013. – FONT. Perp. Against the stem four ferocious seated lions and four Wild Men. Against the bowl the Emblems of the Evangelists, and angels holding shields with symbols of the Trinity, the Mass, St George, and Bury Abbey. – CURIOSA. Thirty-four leather fire buckets, dating from 1725. – STAINED GLASS. S aisle E window by *J. & J. King* of Norwich, designed by *T. J. Scott*, 1870. – MONUMENTS. Mary Smyth †1728. Quite small, but with nice lettering. Broken pediment and arms. – William Crawford of Haughley Park †1835. By *de Carle*. White marble sarcophagus on black ground, the design copied extensively for other members of the family, including Elizabeth Crawford †1828 and Rev. W. H. Crawford †1868 (cf. Wetherden); later examples by *Simpson* of Stowmarket. – War memorial by *J. Crowe*, 1920. Churchyard cross with Crucifixion at the head.

The CASTLE, N of the church, was taken in 1173 and was then probably about a century old (cf. Eye (E), Clare). It occupies

7 acres (2.8 ha) and the motte is 213 ft (65 metres) at the base and 47 ft 6 in. (14.5 metres) high from the bottom of the moat. The bailey is rectangular and has its own well-preserved moat. To the W of the bailey another moated enclosure, part of a larger outer bailey that contained the church and the land to its S; the street known as The Folly follows the line of the ditch, traces of which have also been found by the school in Green Road.

The centre of the village is THE GREEN, which starts as a large triangle SE of the church and tapers off along Old Street to the E. At the NW tip, on the corner of DUKE STREET, a red brick group (including the POST OFFICE) with white-brick dressings built as almshouses, c. 1870. Next to it, facing E across the Green, ANTRIM HOUSE and THE OLD COUNTING HOUSE. Timber-framed and plastered, the lower part to the r. C14, the higher centre mid-C16. On the S side HAUGHLEY HOUSE is C16, with a sashed front and a surprisingly stately straight door hood on carved brackets. The rear parts remodelled in the mid C19 with bays, oriels and bargeboards. W along The Folly the VILLAGE HALL, converted in 1907 from maltings. E, on the S side of the Green, DIAL FARM, mid-C16, with a carved porch of c. 1500 and a ceiling with moulded beams. Nos. 32–34 OLD STREET are late C16, refronted in the early C18, with two doorways with Gibbs surrounds. On the Green itself the parish COAL HOUSE, 1861 (cf. Shimpling). Built by Rev. W. H. Crawford of Haughley Park, whose other benefactions included the SCHOOL in Green Road, 1866. Both of red brick, with crowstepped gables.

At HAUGHLEY GREEN, 1 m. NNE, WALNUT TREE MANOR, a C17 timber-framed farmhouse. Red brick, some original, but mostly C18 and C19. Remains of original painted decoration inside. NEW BELLS FARM, ⅓ m. to its E, is of c. 1530, with two gabled cross-wings. The r. cross-wing is jettied to the front and side, and has exposed timbers with brick-nogging. Additions by *Rodney Black*, 2012. Complete moat.

PLASHWOOD, ½ m. WNW. Rebuilt after 1892 for Benjamin B. Booth. Red brick with stone dressings. Straight gables with ball finials and small round bartizans. Late C18 STABLES between the house and the road (now converted). Timber-framed and plastered, with Diocletian windows.

HAUGHLEY PARK

Over 1 m. W of the village, and closer to Wetherden, where monuments of the Sulyards (and some later owners) are to be found. John Sulyard of Eye had bought Wetherden Hall in the 1460s. The family flourished under the Tudors, particularly under Queen Mary, and remained Roman Catholic. Sir John Sulyard, the grandson of Sir John who died in 1575 (*see* Wetherden), was responsible for building Haughley Park c. 1620. It remained in the family until 1818, when it was sold to William Crawford; his son, Rev. W. H. Crawford, added a stable wing at the SW corner. Following his death in 1868 it passed through a number of hands before being acquired in 1956 by Alfred Williams for use both as a private house and for his poultry-processing business. The S end of the house was converted to offices and a factory was built in the grounds SW of the house. In 1961, during the conversion and restoration, most of the house was gutted by fire, but it was faithfully rebuilt over the following three years by *Eric Sandon*.

The house is of red brick with cement dressings. Impressive symmetrical E façade on an E-plan. The projecting wings have tall stepped gables, the porch a narrower (but equally tall) stepped gable. All three gables have finials. In the recessed parts two two-storey canted bays. Above them dormers, also with stepped gables and finials, that had been removed in the C19 but were known from earlier drawings, and were reinstated by *Sandon*. Mullioned-and-transomed windows, all the more important ones with pediments. Of three lights in the wings and the porch, of two lights, i.e., the cross-type, in the bay windows. Doorway in the porch also with pediment. Two circular windows above it. Stepped gables at the back too. Star-topped chimneys. The N front, by contrast, was remodelled in the early C19, with two broad bows and a castellated parapet. Inside, only one surviving room of importance, on the first floor of the S wing. This has complete C17 panelling with Ionic pilasters. Fine well staircase with solid treads reproduced after the 1961 fire; the original, which was totally destroyed, may have come from Wetherden Hall, as it appeared to have been adapted to fit the new house.

Walled KITCHEN GARDEN SE of the house, and E of that a C17 BARN, also of the same date as the house, partly red brick, partly timber-framed; converted in 1977 to a conference centre. In the grounds, a series of glass SCULPTURES by *Danny Lane*, installed 2006.

SW of the house the FACTORY, built originally as an egg-packing station by *Johns, Slater & Haward*, 1957. It has a timber hyperbolic paraboloid roof, used by the firm for schools (e.g. the contemporary Sprites Lane Primary School, Ipswich (E)), but here on a much larger scale.

HAVERHILL

Haverhill was, by the C16, a prosperous market town, although most of its medieval buildings were destroyed by a disastrous fire in 1667. In the C18 it developed as an important centre for weaving, the most prominent firm being that of Daniel Gurteen & Sons, founded in 1784. Their products included drabbet (a coarse linen) and the agricultural labourers' smocks that were made from it. The decline of the industry in the C20 was balanced, after the Second World War, by the expansion of the town

CHURCHES

ST MARY. Badly damaged in the fire of 1667, repaired then, and restored in 1866–7 by *Elmslie & Franey*. W tower Dec below (see the arch towards the nave) and Perp higher up. Stair-turret at the SE corner (rebuilt 1851) rising higher than the tower. Nave and aisle (aisle described as new in wills of 1474–5), clerestory, S chapel and chancel all Perp, except for a blocked C13 lancet in the chancel. Pinnacles on the S aisle. N doorway, restored 1866–7, decorated with fleurons, etc. The nave arcades were rebuilt in 1866–7, when the bricked-up arches between the chancel and S chapel (moulding with four shafts and four hollows, arches with two-wave moulding) were reopened. N vestries by *H. B. Thake* of Haverhill, 1907–9. W end of nave reordered by the *Whitworth Co-Partnership*, 1999, to form meeting room. – FONT COVER. By *Sir Frederick Gibberd*, after 1967. Tall, with curved ribs sweeping upwards. – CHESTS. Flemish 'Armada' chest of *c.* 1550. Iron plated, further protected with iron bands. Also an oak chest with linenfold panels, *c.* 1500. – STAINED GLASS. S chapel E by *Shrigley & Hunt*, 1897. Two S aisle and one N aisle by *Percy Bacon*, *c.* 1900. Tower window by *Gibbs & Howard*, late C19. – MONUMENTS. John Ward †1602, Puritan preacher. Tablet with oddly steep gable with strapwork. Latin inscription framed by mottos such as Watch, Warde, Lights here, Starrs hereafter. – John Neville †1773. Simple lettering painted on boards, an unusual survival. – Johanna Howland †1815. By *Atkinson & Browne*. With draped sarcophagus. – Rev. Robert Roberts †1875. Pediment with antefixae. By *E. M. Green* of Haverhill.

ST FELIX (R.C.), Princess Way. By *NPS Group*, 2011–12. White brick inside and out. Half-octagon plan, under a monopitch roof, with a rectangular entrance block opposite the altar. Between the two parts a circular baptistery at the foot of a short tower. Over the font a hanging glass SCULPTURE by *Derek Hunt*.

BAPTIST CHAPEL, Upper Downs Slade, off Camps Road. 1828. Red brick, and very modest. Wide doorway with reeded pilasters and lunette window above. Hipped roof. Vestry and gallery added *c.* 1860.

OLD INDEPENDENT CHURCH (United Reformed church), Hamlet Road. By *Charles Bell*, 1884–5.* A remarkable building, that shows just how prosperous a manufacturing town Haverhill had become. Very tall, slender S porch tower and spire, paid for by Daniel Gurteen. Pinnacles at base of spire. High nave with three gabled transepts along each side. Soaring above the pavement, a vast W window with Geometric tracery, framed in

---

*Described as a 'horror' by Pevsner.

a larger arch carried on very tall clustered shafts that start just above the pavement. Galleried interior with original fittings. – MONUMENT. Daniel Gurteen †1893 and wife Caroline †1884. By *J. S. Corder*, executed by *Harry Hems*. Marble and alabaster. Two Gothic arches under an ogee gable. – Behind the church, an earlier chapel of 1843, now a hall. White brick front with lancets. Altered and enlarged 1875, including gallery with cast-iron front.

WEST END CONGREGATIONAL CHURCH, Withersfield Road. 1891 by *Searle & Son*. Red brick with Bath stone dressings. Gothic. Large chapel with gabled front and two porches, linked to a two-storey block of hall and classrooms. MANSE to l., 1894.

CEMETERY, Withersfield Road. Twin chapels by *Elmslie & Franey*, 1867. Dec. Red brick with stone dressings. The link between the chapels looks as if it should once have carried a bell-turret.

PUBLIC BUILDINGS

Former TOWN HALL, High Street. 1883–4 by *Edward Sharman*, given to the town by Daniel Gurteen. Pretty terrible Gothic, from the purist's viewpoint, but giving a much-needed lift to an otherwise dreary street. Red brick with stone dressings and a band of glazed tiles. Windows with cast-iron latticing. Three-bay front with projecting three-storey gabled porch. Large galleried hall on first floor with barrel roof. Enlarged 1909. Converted to arts centre, 1993–4. STAINED GLASS in porch by *Catrin Jones*, 1998.

COUNCIL OFFICES, Lower Downs Slade. By *Peter Barefoot*, 1963–4. Two storeys. Ground floor red brick, the upper floor – which cantilevers over the pavement of Queen Street – clad with white tiles.

PERAMBULATION

The church stands on the S side of the Market Place. The only other building of any prominence is on the E side, the former CO-OP by *Goodey & Cressall*, 1897. Red brick with stone dressings. Three storeys. Segmental pediment within a straight gable and domed corner turret. SE of the church the former CORN EXCHANGE of 1857, superseded in 1889 (*see* below). Red brick with white-brick dressings. Two storeys, with round-arched windows on the ground floor. Extension with small pediment towards the High Street, but before that really begins, opening off it is the entrance to CHAUNTRY MILLS, built by Daniel Gurteen & Sons in 1856 and greatly enlarged in 1865. The original steam factory is fronted by a three-storey red brick warehouse, and beyond it the taller, later building, also red brick but with stone dressings and some carved ornament. Long E façade of fourteen bays punctuated by seven straight gables each with a pointed window. Two-bay gabled returns. In the HIGH STREET, a former CHAPEL of 1839, red brick with arched windows and giant pilasters, the ground floor completely altered, and s of Quaker's Lane CHAUNTRY HOUSE, built for Daniel Gurteen in the mid C19. Two storeys and attic, the ground floor again converted to shops. White brick with stone front. Rusticated quoins and deep eaves. Two canted bays and between them a narrower recessed bay that rises through the eaves to a pedimented dormer.

On the other side of the High Street, BARCLAYS BANK has a nice white-brick front of 1822 with a Roman Doric porch. Otherwise, apart from the former Town Hall (*see* p. 291), the mood is predominantly 1970s, with two buildings looming particularly large: GLASSWELLS by *Basil & David Hatcher*, on the corner of Jubilee Walk, *c.* 1977, with the rounded corners and rounded windows typical of that time, and opposite it the former Provincial Insurance (now AXA) by *Murray Ward & Partners* in red brick, overhanging the pavement in a threatening way.

Once past the s end of the High Street, which continues as Hamlet Road, the C19 character of Haverhill can be appreciated. Off Hamlet Road to the NE, EDEN ROAD and DUDDERY ROAD have good terraces of late C19 red brick workers' housing; of particular interest are three-storey blocks in WAVENEY TERRACE, *c.* 1885, each block with three gables comprising five houses. Decorative brickwork in the gables. Off Hamlet Road to the SW, in COLNE VALLEY ROAD, the former VANNERS SILK FACTORY, 1865. Red brick. Three storeys. Thirteen bays with three-bay pedimented centre and two-bay houses projecting slightly at each end.

In HAMLET ROAD, first the Old Independent Church (*see* p. 290) and then HEAZWORTH HOUSE, which has a nice early C19 white-brick front with a Tudoresque doorway, Gothick sashes and a canted oriel. Opposite it, the spuriously named ANNE OF CLEVES HOUSE, a good-quality timber-framed house of *c.* 1630, probably built for John Mortlock, a local merchant. Long jettied front with exposed close studding. Much altered later in the C17, when the large red brick chimneystacks with star tops were added. These correspond to two fine panelled rooms inside, with chimneypieces dated 1656 and 1657 and with the initials of Thomas and Anne Mortlock. Floral wall painting of similar date over the fireplace of a first-floor room. At the back of the house, an early C19 staircase hall, probably dating from when the house became the vicarage; about the same time the house was given an extraordinary but endearing Tudor-Gothic façade, castellated and with a castellated veranda, that was unfortunately removed as part of restoration by *Hardy, Cochrane & Partners*, 1974–5.

At the far end of Hamlet Road, HAMLET HOUSE, early C18 timber-framed encased in brick and rendered. Two storeys with attic and basement. Three bays, with a nice fanlight over the front door. Attached to it a three-storey, eleven-bay FACTORY, built *c.* 1828 as a silk mill. Timber-framed, rendered, with wide sash windows on the upper floors. Taken over by

Atterton & Ellis, 1882, who built timber workshops with round-headed cast-iron windows. Red brick showroom and warehouse of *c.* 1892. A little further on, at the start of STURMER ROAD, VALE PLACE. Probably built in 1795 (date-stone in garden wall). Red brick, with white-brick front and stone portico with Doric columns. Two storeys with attic and basement, the hipped roof unusually high. Ground-floor windows in shallow arched recesses.

There are a few buildings N and W of St Mary's. QUEEN STREET, N of the Market Place, has largely kept its C19 character, while the QUEEN'S HEAD is late C15, timber-framed, with a crown-post roof. On the NE side, QUEENS SQUARE opened in 1962, a flat-roofed shopping parade faced mostly in white brick and good of its kind. Stainless-steel GATES at either end of Queen Street, 2010, by students of the Samuel Ward Academy under *Neil Williams.* Where Queen Street becomes WITHERSFIELD ROAD, on the corner of Wratting Road, very extensive former BOARD SCHOOL, 1875–6 by *Frank Whitmore* and enlarged by him in 1886. Red brick with stone dressings. Long and low, with many gables, and distinction provided by a slender clock turret with spirelet. Almost opposite, the town's second CORN EXCHANGE of 1889, also by *Whitmore,* in a 'Free Renaissance' style. Red brick with a stuccoed entrance. Pedimented gable front. For West End Congregational Church and cemetery, further N, *see* p. 291.

CAMPS ROAD runs W from the Market Place. On the N side the former BRITISH SCHOOL, 1851. Half-H-plan. Red brick with stone and white-brick dressings. HEALTH CENTRE, opposite, by *Suffolk County Architect's Dept,* 1976–7. Two storeys with flat roof. Traditional construction, faced in pale brown brick. Some of the windows with pre-cast concrete surrounds. At BURTON END, ½ m. from the centre, WEAVERS ROW, a mid-C19 terrace of twelve three-storey houses with large first-floor windows to light the workshops. ¼ m. further on, on the S side, ROPE HOUSE (No. 117), associated with former rope works. Knapped flint with painted brick dressings, *c.* 1840.[*]

OVERSPILL ESTATES

In 1955, when Haverhill was chosen as one of the towns to take London's overspill, an increase in population from 4,222 to 9,750 over twenty years was planned. Building of new factories began in 1956 and housing in 1957, most of the estates being designed by the *London County Council* (*LCC; Greater London Council* (*GLC*) from 1965) under their architects *Sir Hubert Bennett* (1956–71) and *Sir Roger Walters* (1971–8). By 1962 the target had risen to 18,500. In 1971 a master plan by *Sir Frederick Gibberd* was published, restricting the overall growth of the town and trying to bring some order to the centre by

---

[*]Winding gear from the rope walk now at the Museum of East Anglian Life, Stowmarket.

pedestrianizing the High Street and Queen Street. Gibberd hoped that the population might rise to 30,000, and in 2011 it stood at just over 27,000. The Town Development Agreement with the GLC ended in 1983, although development had in fact stopped some years before.

PARKWAY ESTATE, ⅝ m. w of the church between Withersfield Road and Burton End, had been started by the Co-operative Building Society, followed by Haverhill Urban District Council, in 1948 (houses in ASH GROVE), and in 1957 became the first area to be developed by the *LCC*. 540 houses, some semi-detached, and some in terraces, designed in courts off cul-de-sacs achieving a degree of pedestrian segregation. Mainly white brick, some red, and all with occasional weatherboarding; pitched roofs, some split. Characteristic layouts can be seen e.g. along THE CAUSEWAY. In CAMBRIDGE WAY, off Withersfield Road, an interesting group of eighty houses designed by *Harding & Horsman* for Calder Homes, 1964: prefabricated timber boxes (two forming the ground floor, two the upper) set on concrete bases. The layout (by LCC/GLC architects) is in terraces grouped round a series of linked play areas. Most of the houses have been re-clad. In TEASEL CLOSE, off the NE side of Park Road, experimental houses by *Modece Architects* for the Suffolk Housing Society, 2001. Two houses with walls of rendered hemp panels (Nos. 11–12) were built alongside two traditional brick houses, to compare their energy efficiency and other properties.

CLEMENTS ESTATE, ½ m. SW of the church on the S side of Burton End, was begun in 1962 and essentially complete in 1966. 997 dwellings with 100 per cent garage provision. Here there was complete segregation of pedestrians and traffic, as well as a greater mixture of house types and more varied layouts. Some white brick, some coloured render. Refurbished 1988 onwards. On the S side of the estate, off Greenfields Way (PARKSIDE and LADYGATE), eighty-five prefabricated 'Anglia' houses, developed by the *LCC* with *Anglia Housing Ltd* in 1964. White brick and weatherboarding, with concrete slabs exposed on the end walls. Staggered pitched roofs.

CHALKSTONE ESTATE, ⅜ m. NE of the church along Wratting Road, was started in 1966, with about 750 houses grouped round open landscaped courts, designed in terraces along the contours of the sloping site. Densities were reduced as a result of *Gibberd*'s 1971 report. The estate was substantially completed in 1977.

New SCHOOLS were designed by *West Suffolk* (*Suffolk* from 1974) *County Architect's Dept*; the first was the three-storey secondary school (now CASTLE MANOR ACADEMY), Eastern Avenue, opened 1959. Later buildings include WESTFIELD PRIMARY SCHOOL, Manor Road, 1976, which incorporated controlled environment and energy-conserving features that had been developed by Essex County Council, and SAMUEL WARD ACADEMY (former Upper School), Chalkstone Way, built on the SEAC system, 1978. COUPALS PRIMARY SCHOOL,

Chalkstone Way, 1982, represented a move away from system building and open-plan layouts, reverting to separate classrooms and using traditional white brick, as well as Postmodern elements such as pediment-like end gables and balls on piers. CLEMENTS PRIMARY SCHOOL, Greenfields Way, was rebuilt 2010–11 by *Suffolk County Council* (project architects *Matthew Self* and *David Garrard*). Double-height central circulation and activity area linking single-storey classrooms. Varied elevations with a mixed of coloured render, black bricks and timber cladding. Some of the roofs with sedum plants.

The principal industrial area for the newly expanded town lies ½ m. s of the church, along DUDDERY HILL and HOLLANDS ROAD. Although many of the original factory buildings have been redeveloped, a few characteristic buildings can still be seen, with exposed concrete, white-brick infilling and high-level glazing.

HAWKEDON

ST MARY. The church lies in the middle of a wide green edged with houses. Mainly C14, although a bequest by John Hucton of Hawkedon in 1452 for new bells indicates that alterations were then in progress. Nave, chancel and battlemented w tower. The most notable external feature is the s porch with a brick top. Pretty trefoil frieze. The porch has an outer stoup, as well as three niches over the entrance, and good carved C15 roof. – FONT. Square, Norman, with angle shafts and big coarse leaf motifs. By the same carvers as the font at Little Thurlow. – PULPIT. Plain, Jacobean. – SCREEN. Dado with fine tracery. The painted figures are almost obliterated. Money was left for rood figures in 1472. – STALLS. The front of the stalls with tracery survives on the S side. – BENCHES. A whole set, with poppyheads (some carved with faces) and unusual seat details. C15.– COMMUNION RAIL. With twisted balusters; C18. – WEST GALLERY. By *Detmar Blow*, 1912. With organ. – WALL PAINTINGS. Transfiguration; above the E window, almost unrecognizable. Also a fragment of St Christopher opposite the S door. – ROYAL ARMS. Of Charles II, altered in 1704 and 1750. On board. A dignified set – STAINED GLASS. Considerable fragments in the E window, rearranged by *Dennis King*, 1958. Chancel s †1857, probably by *Hardman*. – MONUMENTS. Brasses of Civilian and Wife, *c.* 1510. 16½-in. (42-cm.) figures, much rubbed off, with children. – Richard and Dorothy Everard †1670 and †1678. Large tablet across the NW corner of the chancel. Framed inscription flanked by Corinthian columns and standing putti. Above the entablature achievement of arms with swags of fruit and a single flaming urn. Drapery and a skull below. On the wall beneath, a row of hat pegs.

HAWKEDON HALL, s of the church. c18 plastered front, seven bays wide with pedimented doorcase, but inside parts of a kingpost roof and a ceiling with moulded beams, i.e. work of the c15. In the garden the base and part of the shaft of the former VILLAGE CROSS, c14 or c15.

HAWKEDON HOUSE, ⅔ m. NNE. Built as the rectory by *W. G. & E. Habershon*, 1850. It cost £3,000, including stabling, and is correspondingly impressive. Black flint with red brick dressings. Two storeys with steep roofs and tall chimneys. Built by H. J. Oakes of Thurston End Hall (*see* below) for his son.

LANGLEY'S NEWHOUSE, ¾ m. NE. Timber-framed and plastered house, probably built by John Langley, rector of Hawkedon from 1554. Stack of four round chimneys, amply decorated with moulded patterns and star tops. Inside, a painted plaster overmantel with vine trail and other decoration, and original screen with vertical plank panelling. Well restored by *Basil Oliver* in the 1930s.

THURSTON END HALL, ¾ m. SSW. Quite a showpiece, in spite of being considerably restored between 1823 and 1836 (when it reached its present appearance) and again in the 1920s. Principally early to mid-c16. Exposed timbers with bricknogging. Broad front with two gabled bays, taller gabled porch between them, and gabled cross-wing to the r. which is jettied at both ends. The porch and cross-wing have windows lighting the attics. At the back of the house an impressively large chimneystack with four ornate flues. The porch carries the date 1607, but on part of an elaborate carved surround to the

Hawkedon, Thurston End Hall.
Drawing by J. S. Corder, 1893

entrance introduced between 1823 and 1836; the same date (1607) is, however, also recorded on a chimneypiece.

SWAN'S HALL, ¼ m. s of Thurston End Hall. Timber-framed, with exposed timbers, partly with brick-nogging. Two ranges at right angles. The older range at the w end now forms a cross-wing, and is C16. The main range is early C17, and has at its E end a double-jettied show gable with carved window surrounds, brackets and bressumers.

HAWSTEAD

8050

ALL SAINTS. Norman doorways, N and S, with one order of shafts and one of chevron in the arch. Chancel of *c.* 1300 (see the chancel arch and the side windows), but with a Perp E window. Perp W tower, N and S sides, and S porch. The porch has flushwork decoration on the buttresses. Money was left for the tower in 1446 and 1519, but the main expense must have been borne by the Drurys, whose arms appear on the frieze of shields over the W doorway and whose emblems feature in flushwork both on the battlements and at the base. Higher SE stair-turret. Tower restored, especially the top parts, by *E. P. Warren*, 1887. Very tall tower arch. The nave has windows whose sills form seats. The nave roof must once have been very fine, but it was over-restored (by *Rattee & Kett*) in 1858. It is latest Perp, and money was still being given for building it in 1552. Alternating hammerbeams with angel figures against them and arched braces. Good carvings including grotesque heads against the braces. Wall-plates with shields and small quatrefoils. Chancel roof, canted and panelled, prettily painted by *C. F. M. Cleverly* to Warren's design, 1887. Floral background and, within a wreath, the IHS monogram; over the altar, the Agnus Dei and chalice.

FURNISHINGS. FONT. Plain, square, bowl, probably Norman, on Neo-Norman base. – REREDOS. By *Warren*, 1887, made by *Farmer & Brindley*, painted and gilded by *W. O. Powell*. Alabaster panels of the Crucifixion and saints in oak surround. – SCREEN. Late C15 (bequest for painting rood loft 1477), restored 1858. Fixed to it in the C17 is the pre-Reformation SANCTUS BELL. Rood figures 1905–6, carved in Florence. – PULPIT. Early C16; on heraldic evidence (Drury and Calthorpe arms) between 1509 and 1533. – LECTERN. With two book-rests, *c.* 1500; minor. – COMMUNION RAIL. C17 with turned balusters; now under the tower. – STALLS. With blank tracery along the fronts and poppyheads. – BENCHES. Mostly of 1858, by *Rattee & Kett*, but a few original poppyheads. – FAMILY PEW. Jacobean, with some marquetry work; now at back of nave. – ORGAN. 1858 by *George Sturgeon* of Hartest. Enlarged 1887 with new case designed by *Warren*, made by *G. F. Wright* and *John McCulloch*, painted and gilded by *W. O. Powell*. Restored and repainted 1976 by *Leslie Brewins* and *Elsa Kilpatrick*. – WALL PAINTING. In NW corner of nave, an obscure figure, possibly the Resurrected Christ. – STAINED GLASS. Some C15 and later glass in a nave N window and the chancel SW window. The nave window includes a panel (Crucifixion) dated 1630 with monogram of *Abraham Wirth* of Lichtensteig, Switzerland. E window by *Heaton & Butler*, 1856, said to be the firm's earliest work. Four windows by *Powell & Sons*: chancel S by *Penwarden*, 1908; nave S by *Mann* (St Michael), 1898, and *Holiday* (Faith, Hope and Charity, and Suffer the Little Children), 1885. The last commemorates John Powell of Hawstead (1661–1725) and was given by his descendants, who included James Powell. W window by *Burlison & Grylls*, 1886. Chancel N (over N door) designed by *Warren*, 1899, made by *A. A. Orr* for *A. J. Dix*. Chancel N by *A. K. Nicholson*, 1923.

Few churches in Suffolk possess as many MONUMENTS as Hawstead. They belong to the Drury and Cullum families (mostly in the chancel) and the Metcalfes (in the nave), and to the already crowded walls the last of the Cullums, Gery Milner-Gibson-Cullum (†1921), added more to members of the family buried elsewhere. – Cross-legged knight, late C13, thought to be Sir Eustace Fitz Eustace †1271 (chancel N). Fine carving. The effigy lies on an early C14 tomb-chest with blank pointed-trefoiled arcading (below the present floor level) in an early C14 niche. The niche is richly adorned with thick foliation along the arch moulding and has big buttresses l. and r. and a top cresting. – Brasses to a boy of *c.* 1500 (10 in. (25 cm.)), a girl of *c.* 1500 (7 in. (18 cm.)), and Ursula Allington †*c.* 1530 (17 in. (43 cm.)). – Tomb-chest for Sir William Drury †1557/8. Lozenges on the tomb-chest, which appears to have been built in at least two stages. Brasses on the lid of Drury and his wives Joan †1517 and Elizabeth †1573, his figure 23½ in. (60 cm.). – Elizabeth Drury †1610 aged 15, daughter of Sir Robert (*see below*). Reclining figure. Alabaster. Good allegorical figure (Pomona?) seated frontally on top of the back arch against a rayed background. Under the back arch a fine cartouche. *John Donne* wrote two elegies for Elizabeth and the Latin verse on the cartouche may well be his work. The monument was attributed by K. A. Esdaile to *Gerard Christmas*, but this is not universally accepted. – Sir Robert Drury †1615, the last of his line. By *Nicholas Stone*. Black and white marble. Big black sarcophagus raised on plinths and between two columns carrying arches that spring from a richly carved bracket in the centre. Above the spandrel between the two, high up, demi-figure in oval niche of Sir Robert's father, Sir William, †1589/90. The oval is held by two allegorical figures. Latin epitaph by *John Donne*. It all cost £140; Sir Robert left £100 for the bust of his father. – Sir Thomas Cullum †1664. An extraordinary, highly coloured piece by *Diacinto Cawcy*, who carved his name and the date (1675) on the NE side of the chancel arch. Sarcophagus on a tomb-chest. Black fluted Ionic pilasters to l. and r. and a strangely voluted top. In the middle at the top arms and crest that, as J. Blatchly and G. Fisher have written, 'seem to threaten the viewer below like some frightful monster rearing up in the semi-darkness'.* On the wall to l. and r. wreaths with more arms. The material is chiefly painted plaster, much of it in imitation of *pietra dura*, but the sarcophagus, and the step in front of the monument, include panels of scagliola patterns – a rare occurrence in late C17 England, but used also at this time for a fireplace at Ham House, Surrey. – Sir Dudley Cullum †1720. By *Robert Singleton* of Bury (£125 5s.). Quite elaborate. White and coloured marble. Three panels with Composite columns in the middle and pilasters l. and r. The centre panel has drapery gathered up at the top. Above it a weeping putto holding a skull, standing in an aedicule with broken segmental pediment. – A group of late C18 to early C19 tablets, all variations on the same theme of the urn with or without mourning allegorical figures. The earliest is the finest: Lucy Metcalfe †1793. Signed by *John Bacon Sen.* Relief of seated figure of Benevolence on the base of an urn. – Mary Buckley, Viscountess Carleton, †1810. Sarcophagus, on which lies a rather alluring female figure holding a scroll. By *John Bacon Jun.* – Christopher Metcalfe †1794. A woman mourns over a sarcophagus. By *Bacon Jun.* and *S. Manning Sen.* – Signed by the same, C. B. Metcalfe †1801, Philip Metcalfe †1818, and Frances Jane Metcalfe †1830. – Mary Anne Cullum †1830. By *J. J. Sanders*, and quite a drop in standards. Very plain. – Emma Colvile †1840. By *Robert de Carle IV.* Gothick. – Clara Colvile †1849. By *E. H. Baily.* A scroll, casually draped over a tablet. – Sophia Metcalfe and Ellen Frances Metcalfe †1855 and †1858. By *S. Manning Jun.* Gothick. – In churchyard, base and part of the shaft of a churchyard CROSS. Early C16.

CHURCH HOUSE, opposite. Originally the Guildhall of St James, described as newly built in 1478. Timber-framed and plastered. Three-bay open hall with crown-post roof. Floor inserted in the C17.

OLD RECTORY, 300 yds ESE. By *Alfred R. Mason*, 1853–4. 'Tudor'. Red brick with some stone dressings. Many gables and bay windows.

Former SCHOOL, E of the rectory. 1845. Y-plan, with the schoolroom in the stem. Flint rubble with red brick dressings. Elaborately shaped gables. Gabled porch. Windows with hoodmoulds and decorative glazing. Ornamental red brick chimneys. Built by Rev. Sir Thomas Gery Cullum. Estate cottage in similar style, also Y-plan, 1845, 2 m. NNW of the church (Horsecroft Road). Cf. Hardwick House, Bury St Edmunds (p. 173), and Horringer.

METCALFE ALMSHOUSES, The Pound, 600 yds E. Erected 1811 by Philip Metcalfe 'for the benefit of the Aged, and Deserving, Poor'. A hungry-looking job of white brick, two storeys high

*PSIAH vol. 40 (2004), p. 443.

and eleven bays wide, castellated and with pointed windows. The two middle doorways are taken together under one ogee arch – the one plum in the cake. Originally six, now four houses.

HAWSTEAD HOUSE, 600 yds SE, was the seat of the Metcalfes. 1783, burnt down 1916, rebuilt in the 1930s.

HAWSTEAD PLACE, 1 m. NW. Only fragments remain of the seat of the Drurys. Roger Drury of Rougham bought the manor of Bokenham alias Talmache in 1463/4. A chapel is mentioned in 1494 (licensed 1501), and a licence to crenellate was granted in 1510. The house was greatly altered and enlarged for a visit by Queen Elizabeth in 1578. Together with Hardwick House (*see* p. 173) it was sold in 1656 to Sir Thomas Cullum. Sir Robert Drury †1615 had already made Hardwick his principal residence, and from the mid C18 Hawstead Place was gradually demolished, finally disappearing *c.* 1827. What remains is the rectangular MOAT, lined with Tudor brick, that surrounded the courtyard house. A limestone STATUE was erected in the courtyard for Queen Elizabeth's visit, taken to Hardwick in 1827, and returned and restored in 1978 (not *in situ*). It is of a Wild Man (sometimes called Hercules) with a club over his shoulder, and, for the entertainment of the queen, passed water. Red brick garden walls SW of the moat with two GATEWAYS. The larger has piers with arched niches in their base. These contain initials that date the piers to 1675. The base court lay to the S of the moat and the present HOUSE, C18–C19, stands at the N end of the W side. To its S a C15 BARN. Three bays with crown-post roof and aisle on one side. Other farm buildings of the C17–C19. A series of fishponds to the S and E.

At PINFORD END, ½ m. E of the church, PINFORD END FARM-HOUSE. Timber-framed and plastered. Early C16 hall house,

Hawstead Place.
Engraving, 1838

mostly rebuilt in the C17, with a two-storey Tudor-Gothic porch of the early C19. HAMMONDS, s, is mid C15. Thatched. Two-bay hall with crown-post roof and smoke-blackened timbers.

HENGRAVE

HENGRAVE HALL is one of the most important and externally one of the most impressive houses of the later years of Henry VIII, in spite of much alteration which tends to confuse the visible history of the building. It was the creation of Sir Thomas Kytson (1485–1540), a London merchant who dealt in broadcloth, Lancashire cotton, and other fabrics. Alongside this he had a conventional civic career, and was knighted in

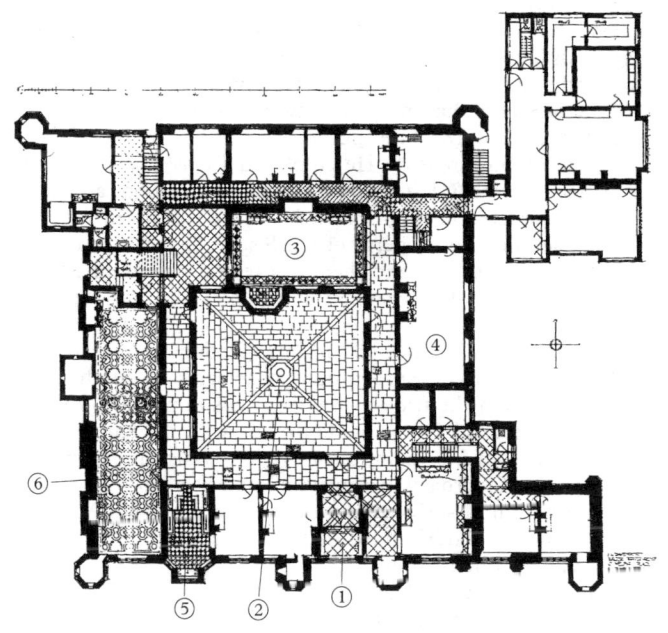

1 Gatehouse
2 Courtyard
3 Hall
4 Dining Room
5 Chapel
6 Long Gallery

Hengrave Hall.
Plan, 1909

1533. At his death his goods were valued at £3,142 17s. 1d., and he spent a little more than that – over £3,500 – building Hengrave. He had bought the manor in 1521 from the Duke of Buckingham, who was executed later the same year; Henry VIII backdated the attainder of Buckingham's property, and it must have taken all Kytson's skill as a negotiator to hold on to his new possession. He began rebuilding in 1525, and part of the existing house may have been preserved in the NE wing (dem. 1775). The date on the gatehouse, 1538, marks the effective completion of the new house. Licence to crenellate was granted in 1540. The house was taxed on fifty-one hearths in 1674, making it the largest house in Suffolk by that measure. The 'ruler of the building' was *Robert Watson*, and the names of a number of the craftsmen are known from the original bills: masons *John Eastawe* (contracted 1525), *John Spark* and *William Ponyard*; bricklayer *Richard Kyrbe*, carpenter and joiner *Thomas Neker* (contract for panelling, 1538), another joiner, *Thomas Dyriche*, and a carver, *Davy*. Kytson's son, also Sir Thomas, died in 1603 without a male heir, and the estate descended via the Darcys of Chiche to the Gages of Firle Place, Sussex. Sir Thomas Gage, who inherited in 1767 and died in 1796, made considerable alterations to the Hall and grounds between 1775 and 1780, including demolishing the old NE wing and remodelling part of the main front. The widow of the last Gage baronet (Sir Edward Rokewood Gage) died in 1887 and in 1897 the house was bought by John Wood, created baronet in 1918. He employed *Walter Tapper* (then in partnership with *J. L. Davenport*) to make alterations and additions, completed in 1899. Following Wood's death in 1951 the house became the property of the Sisters of the Assumption, used first as a school and then as a retreat centre. In 2005 it returned to private ownership and is now run as a wedding venue.

The S side is a spectacular introduction to the HOUSE. The main material is, surprisingly, white brick, one of the earliest instances of the use of white brick, as opposed to red, on such a large scale. It was made to tone with the King's Cliffe limestone from Northamptonshire that is also much in evidence. As the project progressed, materials for reuse were acquired from dissolved monastic houses: Bromehill Abbey in 1536, Ixworth and Thetford in 1537. The S side as originally built was symmetrical, with polygonal angle turrets, a central gatehouse, and canted bay window in the middle of the distance between this and the angle turret l. as well as r. The r. bay however was removed during the 1775 alterations, when the r. end of the façade was also stone-faced and embattled (instead of the original gables), and the N and E ranges were largely rebuilt.

The showpiece of the façade is the bay window above the gateway. It is dated 1538 and is the work of *William Ponyard*, whose name appears in the accounts for 1536 and who three years earlier had been paid for the domes on the angle turrets.

Whereas the gateway has a four-centred arch, Perp mouldings and Gothic foliage in the spandrels, and whereas the turrets flank the entrance in a way familiar from Hampton Court (1515 etc.), Thornbury (c. 1511 etc.) and many others, the bay window includes significant Renaissance detail. In its curious trefoiled plan it is pre-Renaissance; for that shape goes back to the oriel windows of Henry VII's tower of c. 1500 at Windsor Castle, was repeated on the garden side at Thornbury (c. 1511 etc.), and is incidentally also echoed in Henry VII's Chapel at Westminster Abbey, begun in 1503 (a building known to Ponyard, who was working at Westminster in 1532). The most striking comparison, however, is with the oriel in the gateway of Henry VIII's Nonsuch Palace, Surrey, begun in the same year, 1538. The windows with their arched lights – the shape used throughout the original work at Hengrave – the fantastical, crocketed, scale-covered half-ogee caps of the three parts of the bay: all this is Gothic; but the multiform mouldings at the foot of the bay are certainly meant to be antique, and the little cherubs below who hold the shields with coats of arms are also Italian in origin and intention. The heraldry (repainted in 2000) was altered by Sir Thomas Kytson II after 1583 to emphasize his aristocratic connections and play down the mercantile origins of his wealth.

Through the archway one enters the square COURTYARD. This has a two-storey corridor round three sides, a most unusual and progressive feature for its time that allowed movement from one part of the house to another without either going outside or going through other rooms; although if one thinks of it as a two-storey cloister, like the one at Chetham's School, Manchester, it is perhaps less surprising. The walls of the courtyard are stone-faced. They have quatrefoil friezes near the ground; mullioned windows on two floors, the upper one being more prominent and slightly projected, like oriel windows in stone; and top battlements. The chimneys are of red brick, circular in plan and decorated with spirals or raised brick ornament. The N side of the courtyard is different from the others. It contains the HALL, which has the height of the two storeys of the other ranges, and a large canted bay window, the work of *John Spark*. The original entrance to the hall, against the customary schemes of composition, was not in line with the gateway. It was actually entered from the corridor, a unique arrangement. The entrance led into the normal screens passage and from here, again in the normal way, a corridor led to the kitchen (in the pulled-down NE wing). The interior of the hall, with its hammerbeam roof, is as remodelled by *Tapper*. Original, however, is the charming fan-vaulting of the bay window and the stone panelling of the broad arch between it and the hall. Another surprising and prophetic feature is the placing of rooms behind the hall – in double pile, as the C17 called it. Normally the hall of the C16 fills completely the depth of the range in which it lies. On the site of the NE wing Tapper added a new service range, dated 1899 on rainwater heads; this was extended to the E, in plain fashion, for the Sisters of the Assumption.

Other notable features of the interior are an Elizabethan stone fireplace in the DINING ROOM (E range) with Ionic pilasters and a painted overmantel with strapwork and mermaids etc., and the little CHAPEL which lies behind the bay window of the S front. Its tall windows have a total of twenty-one lights of STAINED GLASS that was made in France, shipped to England in 1527, and installed by *Robert Wright* of Bury St Edmunds in 1540. It represents scenes from Genesis and from the life of Christ. It is pre-Renaissance in style except for one piece of quite undated classical ornament. Restored by *T. F. Curtis* (*Ward & Hughes*) when the chapel was refitted by *Tapper*. The latter at the same time created out of three smaller rooms the LONG GALLERY in the W wing, with a good Tudor-style plaster ceiling by *Laurence Turner*. The rest of the interior, including staircases, is redolent of the 1890s. Armorial stained glass throughout the house may include that supplied by *Willement*, 1825–53, but there was also new armorial glass by *Victor Milner*, as well as decorative painting by *Charles Powell*.

The pretty CHURCH (ST JOHN LATERAN) stands just to the E of the house, tiny by comparison and almost a garden ornament. It ceased to be the parish church in 1589 and became a mausoleum for the owners of the Hall; reopened as a private chapel following restoration by *H. J. Green*, 1898–9, for John Wood. Round tower of *c.* 1200. Chancel of *c.* 1300, or perhaps earlier with windows of *c.* 1300. Nave altered and N aisle added by Sir Thomas de Hemgrave †1419, whose name appears over the S doorway. Tall Perp S windows with transom and segmental heads. Arcade piers delicate with four semi-polygonal shafts and spurs in the diagonals. A demi-figure of an angel at the apex of each arch. S porch of knapped flint and a delightful S doorway with dainty fleurons, etc., in the hoodmould. The style of the work, e.g. the frieze of angels on the capitals of the arcade piers, suggests the hand of master mason *Hawes* of Occold.

The N chapel was built by Sir Thomas Kytson in time for his burial in 1540. Here and in the chancel crowd the MONUMENTS of the Kytsons and their relations. Kytson's own tomb, made by *William Ponyard*, was replaced by, or absorbed into, that of his second wife, Margaret, Countess of Bath, †1562. Six-poster with stubby Tuscan columns. Big superstructure. On the slab, recumbent effigies of Margaret and her third husband, John Bourchier, Earl of Bath, †1561. Below it a tomb-chest and in front of this the recumbent effigy of Sir Thomas. – John Bourchier, Lord Fitzwarren, †1556. Tomb-chest with shields in roundels. No effigy. – Sir Thomas Kytson †1603, erected 1608. Six-poster like that of his mother. Very big superstructure with much strapwork. Recumbent effigies of husband and two wives. Poor quality. – Thomas, Lord Darcy, †1614 aged twenty-two. Big kneeling figure between

Hengrave, St John Lateran, monument to Countess of Bath †1562.
Engraving, 1838

columns. On the broken segmental pediment two small allegorical figures. At the foot a shrouded skeleton. Attributed to *William Wright* (GF; cf. Ousden). – Sir Edward Gage †1707. Low tomb-chest with black marble slab. Against the chest cartouches. – Sir Thomas Gage †1741. Hanging monument. Bust before grey pyramid. By *Benjamin Palmer*, 1742. – STAINED GLASS. Two nave s windows †1927 by *F. C. Eden*. Two small round windows in base of tower by *Paul Quail*.

Former STABLES, NW of the house, are contemporary with it and built mostly of similar white brick. Straight gables and some windows with hoodmoulds.

On the w side of the house a formal GARDEN was laid out c. 1858–63 by *James Howe*, of which the general layout, with stone steps etc., survives. At the N end of the terrace by the house, a substantial GARDEN ROOM with exposed timbers, white brick-nogging, and hipped roof with gablets.

Further afield, a 300-acre (120-ha) PARK was formed in 1587. The principal surviving feature is a long avenue running SE from the house, the earliest known in Suffolk and one of the earliest in England. It now passes between two remaining sections of the moat, most of which was filled in by Sir Thomas Gage as part of his improvements in the 1770s. In 1777 he consulted *Richard Woods*, whose plans for pleasure gardens round the house, with numerous little buildings, were not carried out, but who seems to have been responsible for the belt of woodland that surrounds the park. At the E entrance to the park a picturesque LODGE of 1848 in keeping with the style of the house, and entrance gates with brick piers imitating the house's angle turrets.

The VILLAGE consists mainly of a few houses along the road NE of Hengrave Hall, and owes much of its character to work carried out for Sir Thomas Rokewode Gage in the mid C19 – for example the very attractive THATCHED COTTAGE NW of the lodge, with decorative iron casements and trellising. Beyond it a row of four ALMSHOUSES built by Sir Thomas Kytson †1603. The circular BUS SHELTER a short distance SE of the entrance to Hengrave Hall is by *Eric Sandon*, 1955. Thatched, faced with flint pebbles, and built of white brick reused from the demolished Tendring Hall, Stoke-by-Nayland (q.v.). There is a similar one at Flempton.

GRANGE FARM, 600 yds NNW of Hengrave Hall, and STANCHIL'S FARM, ¾ m. SW, were both built by Sir Thomas Gage, in 1777 and 1775 respectively. Red brick. W of Grange Farm a red brick BARN rebuilt by Sir Thomas Rokewode Gage in 1849. Projecting from its E side is a polygonal wheel-house in which a horse worked the threshing engine.

HEPWORTH

ST PETER. W tower for which money was left in 1417. The tower arch is completely unmoulded and may well indicate that the lower parts of the tower were early C13. Higher up Dec windows of quatrefoils in circles. The top stage was probably removed in 1677, the date of the iron wall-plates on the W face. The ironwork clamping the diagonal buttresses was added in 1828 by *George Bloomfield* of Thelnetham. Chancel Dec. Nave with tall two-light Perp windows. Inside the church two loose stones, a capital and a voussoir, from a C12 doorway. Badly damaged by fire in 1898 and restored by *J. S. Corder*, including the fine double hammerbeam roof in the nave. – FONT COVER. An admirable piece that must be of *c.* 1500–20. A tall pinnacle. On the lowest floor (which opens like a cupboard) panelling projecting in five little lobes like the oriel window of the Hengrave gatehouse (q.v.) or the windows of Henry VII's Chapel at Westminster Abbey. They are meant to represent whole structures, for tiny men come out of tiny doors as in the familiar German weather-boxes. Restored by *W. J. Brooke* of Hopton, 1855, when layers of paint were removed, some panels replaced, and the cross added. – BENCH ENDS. C15, with poppyheads, incorporated in choir stalls. – STAINED GLASS. Chancel N by *Powell & Sons*, designed by *Penwarden*, 1902. In two nave S windows, panels by *Bronwen Gordon*, 1998 and 2001.

CHURCH HOUSE, 300 yds SW. Former Primitive Methodist chapel, opened 1867, closed 1974. Timber-framed and plastered. Continuous range with small square chapel between two-storey cottages. The chapel part has sash windows and a small hexagonal window in the centre. The cottage parts have windows with cast-iron casements.

OLD RECTORY, 600 yds NW. 1820 by *Arthur Browne* of Norwich, round a mid-C16 core. Timber-framed and plastered with white-brick front. Two storeys and four bays. Canted bay in the middle of the ground floor and front door to its l., both covered by a later C19 wrought-iron veranda. Mid-C19 dairy building on E side of red brick with white-brick dressings.

Former NATIONAL SCHOOL, N of the Old Rectory. 1852. Flint with white-brick dressings. Straight gables with kneelers.

HEPWORTH HOUSE, ¾ m. NNW. By *E. F. Bisshopp*, *c.* 1880–4. Large, red brick, made picturesque in the fashion of the day with bays, half-timbered gables, tall chimneys, timber cupola, etc.

REEVES HALL, ⅔ m. NW. Mid-C16 timber-framed and plastered house with jettied front. Crown-post roof.

HERRINGSWELL

7060

ST ETHELBERT. Restored 1869–70 by *A. W. Blomfield*, following a major fire. Repairs had just been completed, including rethatching the roof. Blomfield's restoration preserved the medieval walls, but substituted tiles for thatch. New window tracery throughout. Nave and chancel C12, C14 transeptal S chapel, S porch and W tower. The tower has a curious arrangement of two big heavy buttresses sticking out N and S, a buttress reaching up the middle of the W side, and inside, two octagonal piers to carry the E angles of the tower and a kind of inner flying buttresses to make them safer. The mid-C19 N vestry survived the fire. – STAINED GLASS. A remarkable collection, the first four windows, 1901–2, given in memory of H. E. M. Davies †1899, whose MONUMENT, with broken column and mourning female, stands by the path to the S door. Two large windows by *Christopher Whall*, the E (Good

Shepherd) and nave S (Resurrection). The E window includes sheep drawn by *Alice Chaplin*, Whall's sister-in-law, from Davies's own flock. Two windows by pupils of Whall: chancel N by *Paul Woodroffe* and chancel S by *Jasper Brett*. Also by *Whall* the chancel SW window to Dr W. E. Image †1903. – S chapel S and nave N by *James Clark*, made by *A. J. Dix*, 1916–17. Landscapes of Herringswell in spring and autumn. Also by *Clark* the window under the tower, 1923 (St Francis). – Later windows struggle to continue the pictorial tradition: nave N by *Luxford Studios*, 1954, and S chapel W by *Dean Cullum* (*Cambridge Stained Glass*), 1992.

CHURCH FARM. E of the church, an early C19 weatherboarded GRANARY, standing on twelve staddle-stones.

HERRINGSWELL MANOR, ⅔ m. N. Rebuilt 1906–7 by *J. S. Corder* for A. W. Ballance. Rambling Elizabethan-style house. Ground floor of red brick with stone dressings, first floor half-timbered. Now flats. COACH HOUSE to NE. E of the house a Japanese TEMPLE, ARCHERY COURT and TEA HOUSE, 1986, also now converted, built round a Japanese GARDEN for the Shi-Tennoji School. Along the road E of the grounds a row of estate COTTAGES, WATER TOWER and COACH HOUSES in the same style as the main house.

HESSETT

Simon Clerk, the master mason of Bury Abbey, who is also known to have worked at Eton College and King's College, Cambridge, among other places, was granted a thirty-year lease of Hessett by the abbey in 1445, and for that reason, as well as on stylistic grounds, the rebuilding of the nave and aisles of the church is generally taken to be his work.

ST ETHELBERT. All Perp, apart from the chancel, which is Dec and has an E window with flowing tracery. Attached to the chancel a two-storey vestry with barred windows. The lower room has a small three-light window. The upper room is reached by an original ladder with solid steps. There is a fireplace too. Along the vestry and part of the aisle runs a long inscription recording that John Hoo and his wife, 'the quweche hath mad y chapel, a very deyl heyteynd y westry & batylementyd y hele'. So with his money he built the N chapel, added the upper storey of the vestry, and embattled the whole. John Hoo died in 1492. The N aisle indeed has battlements, which are of very pretty openwork stone-carving. The clerestory has the same, though the pattern differs. Three-light windows with transoms. Clerestory windows of the same width and pattern but without transoms. The S aisle is similar to the N aisle and again has openwork battlements. Excellent S porch, partly faced with stone, partly with knapped flint.

Entrance arch with St George and the Dragon in the spandrels. Three canopied niches. Flushwork decoration on the base and buttresses, including the initials of John Bacon, who died in 1513. His initials appear also on the W tower (cf. Bradfield St George). Battlemented parapet with small shields, pinnacles at the corners and angels midway. Below it a frieze with larger shields. The arcades inside are typically Perp. A slender shaft to the nave with capital, wide diagonal hollows and shafts to the arch openings with capitals. There are four bays, and in addition the one-bay chapel to the N to which reference has already been made (now the organ chamber, unfortunately). Aisle roofs with arched braces and a little carving. Money was left for leading the church in 1521, indicating completion of the roof.

FURNISHINGS. FONT. Panelled stem. Bowl with flowers in cusped quatrefoils and similar decoration. The inscription on the step refers to the donors, Robert Hoo and his wife Agnes; the font is thought to have been made in Norwich, *c.* 1451. – SCREEN. Tall, with one-light divisions with broad ogee arches. Simple panel tracery over; cresting. Some original colouring and gold gesso decoration, but the dado has lost its saints. – BENCHES. A complete square-headed set in the nave. In the S aisle, one with a poppyhead in the form of a shield with arms of Bacon impaling Rous, *c.* 1513. – CHOIR STALLS, including return stalls against the screen. With poppyheads and traceried fronts. Also one extremely richly carved bench with a frieze of birds on the back. – DOOR. To vestry, with iron boss and ring. – WALL PAINTINGS. Much better understood since conservation in 1997. Over the S door, St Michael weighing souls and, nearby, a devil. Over the N door, St Christopher. Between two N windows, the Seven Deadly Sins (*c.* 1370) and, below them, Christ of the Trades (*c.* 1430), with thirty-eight tools depicted (e.g. awl, shuttle, spokeshave, chisel). At the E end of the S aisle, St Barbara (patron saint of architects) holding a tower. – ROYAL ARMS. Of Charles II. Altered for Queen Anne, but the overpainting removed during mid-C20 restoration by *M. C. Farrar Bell*. – SINDON or pyx-veil. C16. Of white linen, embroidered all over to form a regular openwork pattern. Fringe of red and yellow silk. A great rarity, and the only surviving example of this technique in English medieval embroidery. The church also possesses a BURSE, i.e. a case for the corporal, the cloth on which the wafer lies during Mass. Linen, painted in gold, silver and colours. On one side the Head of Christ in an ogee quatrefoil, on the other the Lamb of God. It dates from *c.* 1400–30.* – TILES. A few medieval encaustic tiles in the vestry floor. – STAINED GLASS. Much medieval glass is preserved, but not *in situ* and mostly jumbled. The best is in the E window of the S aisle, thought to have started as the Three Marys; in the middle, St Mary Cleopas (now with the head and shoulders of a bishop), with her four children at her

---

*Neither object is kept in the church, but photographs are displayed.

feet, including St James the Less holding a fuller's club. Chancel E window by *William Warrington*, *c*. 1855. Chancel S †1867 by *O'Connor*. – MONUMENTS. Lionel and Ann Bacon, both †1653. By *John Stone*. Tablet with inscription in an exuberantly carved cartouche with drapery, a shield in another cartouche, two smaller shields, skulls, an urn at the top and a pinecone at the bottom. It cost £30. – John Bacon †1513. Coped burial stone E of the porch. Its companion presumably that of his wife Margery. – SW of the church, the stump of a C15 limestone CROSS.

OLD RECTORY, NE of the church. By *S. I. Ladds*, 1904–5. Roughcast, with weatherboarded gables. It superseded the rectory of 1850 by *W. G. Habershon* (now HESSETT HOUSE, ½ m. ENE).

Former NATIONAL SCHOOL, 175 yds N. By *John Darkin*, 1847. Flint with red brick dressings.

A few nice houses along the street by the church. The unusual inn sign of the Five Bells is a red brick pier thought to have come from Hessett Hall, which burnt down in the C18. The moated site is 800 yds SW.

HIGHAM

2 m. NW of Gazeley

Part of Gazeley, until the church was opened in 1861; it did not become a separate civil parish until 1894. The prime mover was Rev. William Cooke, vicar of Gazeley.

ST STEPHEN. 1858–61 by *G. G. Scott*, who had just restored Gazeley. In the style of the early C13, with plate tracery. Flint, with Ancaster stone dressings. Nave and N aisle, chancel and N organ chamber and vestry. Scott gave himself the pleasure of a round tower, no doubt a nod to the nearby towers of Risby and, especially, Little Saxham. Its top stage has an arcade, the Gothic equivalent of Little Saxham's Norman one. Conical roof. In the base the rib-vaulted baptistery, an agreeable touch of fancy. Only two stages of the tower had been built by the time of the consecration; completed 1870 by *J. D. Wyatt*, who had worked on the church while still in Scott's office, and kept to his master's design. – FONT and PULPIT by *William Farmer*. – REREDOS by *William Field*. – Other carving by *Rattee & Kett*. – STAINED GLASS. E window and three others of *c*. 1873, probably by *Clayton & Bell*.

OLD PARSONAGE HOUSE, next to the church, and a little later than it. Flint, with stone dressings, and quoins and bands of red brick. Domestic Gothic. Oriel over the entrance, corbelled out on bricks. Attributed to *Scott*, but the evidence is only circumstantial; it might equally be by *Wyatt*.

Former SCHOOL, at the S end of the village. 1861, enlarged 1892. Flint, with red brick dressings. Two-storey porch-cum-clock tower.

Former RAILWAY STATION, ⅓ m. N. 1854. Large white brick goods shed, with arched openings. Just to the N. on the old main road, a hexagonal COTTAGE of clunch. Early C19. Apparently not a toll house.

HIGHAM
1 m. WNW of Stratford St Mary

ST MARY. Simple heavy W tower with small upper windows indicating a C13 date. The tower arch double-chamfered and dying into the imposts may well be *c.* 1300. Otherwise early Perp. The chief point of interest is the N aisle with its four-bay arcade, very similar to the arcades at Otley, Debenham (both E) and Bildeston which have been attributed to master mason *Hawes* of Occold. The piers quatrefoil with the foils filleted and the fillets not set off from the foils but running into them in an ogee curve. In the re-entrant angles thin octagonal shafts. The abaci carved alternately with vine band and single fleurons. Many-moulded arches, hoodmoulds on heads. *E. F. Bisshopp* restored the church in 1888, including new seating. His hand is most visible at the chancel arch, with wooden figures of St Peter and St Peter in canopies at the springing. Timber N porch by *W. H. Atkin Berry*, *c.* 1892. – FONT. Perp, octagonal, damaged, disused. – REREDOS. 1892. Gold design on a blue mosaic background and rather gaudy pink tiles, in an alabaster surround. – STAINED GLASS. E window by *Clayton & Bell*, 1891; two nave S by *Powell & Sons*, 1899 (figures of Faith and Charity by *Henry Holiday*) and 1920 (war memorial, designed by *J. Hogan*). – MONUMENT. Robert Hoy †1811 aged 10 years 3 months and 19 days. By *C. Regnart*. Seated woman clasping an urn. The grave is nearby, a large chest tomb with sharply tapering sides and an urn.

HIGHAM HALL, by the church. White-brick front, one room deep, of 1811. Five bays and two storeys, with three-bay pediment and deep eaves. Doric porch. The windows are tied together by giant segmental arches, but although the overall effect is symmetrical the pilasters between the bays are not all the same width. At the rear, evidence of an early C17 red brick house, but with a two-storey bow of *c.* 1811. Stone staircase with iron balusters lit by an octagonal lantern.

HIGHAM HOUSE, 400 yds NW, and HIGHAM LODGE, ½ m. NNE, are of about the same date as the front of Higham Hall and share many of its characteristics. Higham House has a three-bay N (entrance) front with one-bay pediment. The seven-bay S front, with three-bay pedimented centre breaking slightly forward, is by *Quinlan Terry*, 2003, replacing Victorian additions. He also added the Doric porches (semicircular on the E front), and built the red brick and weatherboarded staff cottage sw of the house. Higham Lodge has on the three-bay entrance front broad tripartite windows recessed beneath segmental relieving arches. Round-headed dormers behind parapet. In the same tradition is DRUMLINS, Upper Street, designed by *Terry*, c. 2004, but not built under his supervision. Two-storey, five-bay white-brick house with central one-bay pediment and deep eaves on modillions.

HIGHAM PLACE (formerly Barhams Manor), at the main crossing in the village. The two-storey, seven-bay front dates from 1795 and was the work of *Kingsbury* of Boxford. One-bay pedimented centre and two-bay wings, painted and rendered. This masks a C15 timber-framed house, built by the Mannocks of Giffords Hall (q.v.), with C16 and later additions. These include a small bay window on the S side of c. 1860 with Gothic windows, and on the W side a two-storey grain store of 1810 converted and given a large doorcase with Gibbs surround, part of various late C20 alterations to the house and gardens carried out with the advice of *George Carter*. Inside, one first-floor room has a wall painting based on the familiar Serlian design of interlaced octagons with fruit motifs; early C17. Remodelling of entrance hall, with three-bay round-arched screen, attributed to *Lutyens*, 1936.*

OLDEN MANOR (formerly Tudor House), N of Higham House. C16, much restored. Exposed timbers with brick-nogging. Two jettied and gabled cross-wings with carved bressumers and bargeboards.

CHAUFFEURS COTTAGE, Lower Street. 1887, by *W. H. Atkin Berry*. Picturesque, with tile-hanging and half-timbered gables. It belonged to Higham House.

KETELFIELD, Hadleigh Road. By *Aldington & Craig*, 1974–6. Single-storey steel and glass house, after the manner of Mies van der Rohe's Farnsworth House (Plano, Illinois). It stands clear of the ground, apparently floating, supported by eight columns. Steel frame and columns painted matt black.

TEA CADDY COTTAGE, Hadleigh Road. Early C19 red brick. Two storeys, with bowed ends, and pointed windows with Gothick glazing on the first floor.

HINDERCLAY

ST MARY. Simple N doorway, its mouldings and hint of a point to the arch suggesting very early C13 rather than C12. Early C13 S arcade of four bays with short circular piers, round abaci and double-hollow-chamfered arches. Dec chancel with reticulated

---

*Lutyens had been employed by the Fenwicks, owners of Higham Place, at Temple Dinsley, Herts.

Higham, Chauffeurs Cottage.
Drawing by W. H. Atkin Berry, 1889

E window. The SW window is treated as a lowside window, with a transom. Angle PISCINA with altered shaft. Perp W tower with tall bell-openings, the part below the transom blocked and with chequer flushwork. Battlements with flushwork panelling. Nave and S aisle Perp. Timber S porch with its original C14 outer arch. Tower restored by *W. M. Fawcett*, c. 1896. – SCREEN. C19, incorporating C15 traceried panels and moulded beam. Remains of ROOD BEAM, cut off flush with the N wall. – BENCHES. At the back of the nave, a number with diamond-shaped poppyheads, one dated 1617. – C18 BOX PEWS towards the front and in S aisle. – CURIOSUM. The church possesses a GOTCH or pitcher of stoneware, to hold about two gallons of beer for the bellringers (cf. Clare). Inscription with date 1724.* – STAINED GLASS. In S aisle, four windows from designs by *Rosemary Rutherford* (†1972), adapted by her brother *Rev. John Rutherford* (rector 1975–86). E window 1975, two S windows 1981, W window 1994, the last with *Rowland & Surinder Warboys*. Elongated figures, at first sight almost abstract. Also in tracery of chancel E window. – MONUMENT. Rev. George Thompson †1711. With putti l. and r. and cherubs' heads at the foot.

Former NATIONAL SCHOOL, WSW of the church. By *Richard Cornish* of Botesdale, builder, 1872–3. Red brick. Just Gothic, but considerably altered.

*On loan to Moyse's Hall Museum, Bury St Edmunds.

HINDERCLAY HALL, S of the church. Mostly early C19 white brick. Two storeys. Four-bay entrance front, facing NE, with three-bay return. Early timber-framed parts behind, C16–C17.

OLD RECTORY, ¾ m. WSW. Small timber-framed and plastered house, enlarged by *Robert Sword* of Botesdale, 1836, in the same materials, the plaster jointed and coloured in imitation of Portland stone. Further additions in brick by *W. M. Fawcett*, 1880, and *Isaac Clarke* of Walsham-le-Willows, 1886.

HINTLESHAM

ST NICHOLAS. Lancets in the chancel N wall. E.E. arcades of four bays. The piers are circular–octagonal–circular on the S side, octagonal–circular–octagonal on the N. Double-chamfered arches. Dec S aisle. Perp W tower and clerestory, obscured on the N side by the raising of the aisle roof in the C17. S aisle roof dated 1759. Perp timber porch, restored 1911. General restoration *c.* 1849–51; tower top rebuilt 1899. – FONT. From Shipmeadow. Octagonal, Perp. Four lions against the stem. Against the bowl flowers and armorial shields. Below the bowl alternating lions' and angels' heads. The old font went to St Edmund, Felixstowe (E). – COMMUNION RAIL. With twisted balusters. – WALL PAINTINGS. On nave N wall, a faded St Christopher and other fragments. More remains also on the N wall of the S aisle. – MONUMENTS. Thomas Tympley †1593/4, his wife Etheldreda (Audrey) and his son Nicholas's family. Erected by Nicholas, whose date of death was never entered. Two groups of small kneeling figures in the usual arrangement across prayer-desks. The monument was built into an existing recess that presumably contained SEDILIA. – Capt. John Timperley †1629/30. A fine, elegant, upright figure, engraved like a brass on a large slate slab. It was the top of a tomb-chest, dismantled *c.* 1824. The figure has an engraved architectural frame with tympanum and trophies l. and r. Attributed to *Edward Marshall* (GF). – Sir Thomas Tymperley †1651 and Michael Tymperley †1653. No figures. A diptych with two inscriptions, framed by columns and a broken pediment. Attributed to *Martin Morley* of Ipswich (GF).

PRIMARY SCHOOL, E of the church. By *F. Barnes*, 1873. Red brick with a little black decoration. Cross-wing at one end with tall three-light window and bell-turret. Enlarged 1898 and 2001.

OLD HALL FARM, 1½ m. WNW. C16, with exposed timbers and long-wall jetty. Good ceiling with moulded beams in the parlour.

PRIORY FARM, 1½ m. NW. Front of mid-C19 red brick with hoodmoulded windows and a full-height canted bay not in the middle. Beneath the brick a timber-framed house of the C16 or earlier, and a room with grotesque antiquework painted decoration of the C17.

HINTLESHAM HALL

Built in the 1570s by Thomas Tympley, i.e. Timperley, whose family had come to Hintlesham in the early C15. His mother was a daughter of the 3rd Duke of Norfolk, and he was the 4th Duke's comptroller and M.P. for Bramber and Great Yarmouth. He was a recusant, so his career did not continue to prosper after Elizabeth came to the throne, but the family's fortunes revived briefly under James II, allowing significant alterations to be made by Henry Timperley after he inherited in 1686. Henry died in exile in 1690 and in 1720 his son sold the house to Richard Powys, whose son, also Richard and M.P. for Orford, remodelled the front of the house after inheriting in 1724. He died in 1743 and his widow sold to Richard Lloyd, whose descendants (latterly Lloyd-Anstruther) remained at Hintlesham until 1909. It has been a hotel since 1972, with various alterations by *Wincer Kievenaar*.

The house as built in the 1570s was the usual E-plan, of red brick. This can readily be seen on the S and E fronts. Here are the large chimney-breasts of the Elizabethan house, and a certain amount of diapering. On the W front, the wings projected quite far, and there would have been a central porch, but this was removed by Powys and replaced by a two-storey link between the wings. The doll's-house-like façade is now plastered and painted, of two storeys with quoins, parapet and hipped roof. The ground floor of the recessed centre is rusticated in the French banded way and has four arched windows, originally forming an open arcade (filled in in 1819). Entrance with coupled unfluted Ionic columns. First floor with rather curiously spaced and mean-looking Corinthian pilasters and a central Venetian window. Pediment against the parapet. The two-bay wings project by four bays and have in the middle of each side a pedimented doorway with Ionic pilasters.

Inside, the finest room is on the first floor of the S wing. This is not of Powys's time, but of Henry Timperley's, i.e. 1686 or very soon after. The plaster ceiling of this room is among the best of the late C17 anywhere in East Anglia. Timperley's initials are included in the design. It has a central oval panel and square and oblong panels along the four sides, and the finesse of modelling and boldness of undercutting are prodigious. The work is remarkably similar to that at Melton Constable and Felbrigg, both in Norfolk and dated 1687. Also of about this date is the staircase in the N wing. This has carved newel posts with big vases on top, a carved string, and balusters with the bulb near the foot decorated with leaves. Of Powys's time, i.e. the later 1720s, the long and narrow entrance hall with apsed ends and the corresponding gallery above it. Behind this the double-height Saloon, formed out of the hall of the Elizabethan house. Panelling, overmantel with broken pediment, and at the W end a large doorcase with Corinthian columns and pediment. This leads to the S staircase, with slim twisted balusters, two to each tread, and unusually long carved tread-ends.

Attached to the N side of the house, an C18 SERVICE RANGE. Red brick. Seven bays and two storeys, the centre three bays breaking forward and the eaves rising to form a pediment. Oculus in the pediment. Beyond that a further range connected by a brick archway, at right angles, to the STABLES. Mainly C17, of red brick with burnt headers, extended in the C18 and containing a C16 timber-framed structure. Two storeys. Small square bell-turret. 150 yds N, the walls of the former KITCHEN GARDEN; on its E side the GOLF CLUB-HOUSE by *Wincer Kievenaar*, 1991. Low, with cedar boarding, large hardwood windows and cedar shingle roof, reminiscent of a colonial bungalow. On the garden's S side, a house (now health club) of 1985 incorporating an existing ORANGERY. In HOME WOOD, E of the kitchen garden, a circular pond with boathouse, two further ponds and an ice house. Late C18 or early C19 GATEWAY and railings at the S entrance to the park, with a surprisingly plain two-storey red brick LODGE of the mid C18.

HITCHAM

ALL SAINTS. Quite large; at the far S end of the village. Nave with clerestory and aisles, W tower, S porch, and a chancel with two-storey N vestry. The chancel is Dec, its S and E walls rebuilt during the restoration by *G. E. Pritchett*, 1878. N aisle doorway Dec, aisle windows Dec with segmental heads. Arcades of five bays with octagonal piers and double-chamfered arches. The clerestory has quatrefoil windows on the N side. Sturdy C15 W tower with stair-turret not going externally to the top. W doorway with niches l. and r. Perp S porch with flushwork panelling, restored 1882–3. Entrance with motifs of crowns and lions and a niche over the arch. Shields and other motifs on the inner mouldings of the arch. Perp S doorway of the same style with crowns and shields. Hoodmould on seated lions. Fine nave and lean-to aisle roofs rebuilt or greatly reworked in the early C17 (monograms of James I and Charles I). The nave roof alternates between double hammerbeams and arched braces masquerading as hammerbeams. Against the lower hammerbeam ends big emblems such as roses, shields, a sun with crowns over. Hammerbeam roof in chancel concealed by coved timber ceiling. Idiosyncratic reordering by Rt Rev. M. H. Maxwell-Gumbleton, rector 1934–49, including clergy stalls and bishop's throne (for himself) in the chancel, with choir stalls in front of the organ at the W end of the nave flanked by churchwarden's stalls. – FONT. 1878. Octagonal, with panelled sides. Good COVER of *c.* 1943. Carved and painted, with pinnacles and crocketing. – SCREEN. Dado with eight painted figures of angels with Instruments of the Passion. Mid-C15. – PULPIT. C18. Octagonal, plainly panelled. The base looks older. Tester *c.* 1935. – SOUTH DOOR with tracery and a border of foliage panels. – BENCHES. Ends with poppyheads and remains of beasts on the arms. Restored and augmented *c.* 1935. – ROYAL ARMS. Of George VI, 1937. Carved, painted and gilded. – MONUMENTS. Sir George Waldegrave †1636. With little Corinthian columns and broken pediment. – Rev. J. S. Henslow †1861, Professor of Botany at Cambridge and Charles Darwin's mentor. By *Thomas Woolner*, who was born in Hadleigh. White and red marble, disappointingly plain.

THE OLD GUILDHALL, by the churchyard gate. Money was left for it in 1452 and 1461. Plastered front range rebuilt in the latter part of the C17. Cross-windows. Long jettied rear range, with exposed timbers.

HITCHAM HOUSE, ½ m. SW. Former rectory, rebuilt 1814 by *James Spiller* for Rev. J. S. Mathews. White brick. Two storeys. Front of three wide bays with bows to l. and r. Small pediment over the centre. Two-storey pigeon tower SW of house, also white brick and presumably of the same date.

BRICK HOUSE FARM, 600 yds NW. A puzzling house. The lower parts of the N and S walls, and the whole of the end E wall, are of Tudor red brick. The latter has polygonal turrets at the corners which may have gone higher. At the W end is a fragment of another turret. The brickwork is decorated with diapering and, on the S wall, flushwork, seldom found on domestic buildings. The upper part of the house is timber-framed, late C16 or early C17. Another oddity of the house is its lobby-entrance plan, an early instance. The parlour ceiling has fleur-de-lys and other floral decoration of *c.* 1600. There was formerly a chapel E of the house, which may be connected with it, and Edward Martin suggests a link with the bishops of Ely, as a hospice or lodgings, possibly as early as the 1490s.

WETHERDEN HALL, ¾ m. W. Originally, it would seem, the service range of a larger house that belonged to the Waldegraves. Now fourteen bays long, until 1984 twenty-one, and possibly once longer. Timber-framed, its roof dated to *c.* 1570. The western end is weatherboarded and consisted of barns and other farm buildings.* The site is moated, and the house stands on the northern edge; it may originally have extended all the way across the N side.

At HITCHAM CAUSEWAY, ½ m. NNE, a small estate of houses for Cosford Rural District Council by *Raymond Erith*, *c.* 1949–58 (cf. Cockfield, Polstead).

---

*A C15 barn moved in 1987 to Great Whelnetham (q.v.).

HOLTON ST MARY

St Mary. Flint and stone. Big incomplete w tower with brick battlements. C13 chancel (see the PISCINA). Aisleless C14 nave (see the doorways with their small quadrant mouldings and the big headstops of the hoodmould). E end of chancel rebuilt *c.* 1863, general restoration 1881–2. – FONT. Octagonal, Perp. – PAINTING. Sign for the school established by Rev. Stephen White, 29 August 1748. With the figure of a schoolboy, church and school in the background, and motto 'Not Slothful in Business / Serving the LORD'. Painted, it seems, by *Thomas Gainsborough*, then aged twenty-one. The school building (now a private house) stands on the s side of the churchyard; mainly late C16 or early C17. – STAINED GLASS. A chancel s window †1899 signed by *Heaton, Butler & Bayne*, who also probably did the E and W windows, *c.* 1881.

Lark Hall, ½ m. WNW. Early C15 timber-framed and plastered hall house with crown-post roof, floored in the C16. Jettied cross-wing to l., r. cross-wing added as part of sympathetic restoration by *Marshall Sisson*, 1939–40. Large weatherboarded and thatched BARN, with a pantiled single-storey lean-to between the two large midstreys, nicely converted to a house *c.* 1980.

HONINGTON

All Saints. Norman s doorway with two orders of shafts. They are decorated with chevron, and the r. one in addition with three square blocks or bands, also decorated. Hoodmoulds on beasts' heads. Norman chancel arch. Nook-shafts, well preserved, and impost with sawtooth carving that presumably extended further, perhaps into the nave. The s side of the nave seems early C14, the N side remodelled Perp. Dec w tower with a stair-turret of brick. Dec chancel. Perp s porch (ready for glazing in 1487) with flushwork panelling; initials, etc., very similar to neighbouring Troston's (q.v.). Entrance with shields and leaf motifs. Three niches above the entrance. Restored 1864, and again in 1909 by *Fawcett & Atkinson*. – FONT. Octagonal, Dec. Panelled stem. On the bowl Dec tracery including three blank rose windows (one High Gothic, one with six mouchettes) and a Crucifixion. – COMMUNION RAIL. Late C17, with twisted balusters. – BENCHES. In chancel, four with poppyheads, and animals on the arms. The rest of the church re-seated in 1864. – WALL PAINTINGS. On s wall. Described as the story of St Nicholas and Martyrdom of St Thomas of Canterbury. Now covered over. – STAINED GLASS. Nave N by *Pippa Blackall*, 2004–6. – MONUMENTS. Brass of George Duke †1594. 24-in. (61-cm.) figure in civilian dress. – Robert Rushbrooke †1753. Simple, but with exquisite italic lettering. – In churchyard, SE of chancel, headstone of Richard Shepherd †1843. Signed by *Edward Ruddock* of Barningham, equally nicely done in its own way.

The church sits right in the middle of the little village. On the W side of the churchyard the former SCHOOL of 1863, enlarged 1926. Red brick with white-brick dressings. Porch with arched entrance and bellcote. NW, on the main road, HONINGTON HOUSE (former rectory), C18; timber-framed and plastered with roof of black glazed pantiles. MANOR FARM, opposite, uses the same materials, but dates back to the C16. It was re-roofed and refronted in the C18, but the windows with their hoodmoulds must be later. N of the church, in Sapiston Road, two pairs of semi-detached ESTATE COTTAGES. Red brick and black glazed pantiles, with cast-iron casements of the same pattern as New Cottages, Sapiston (q.v., 1867).

WINDMILL, ½ m. SSW. Roundhouse of early C19 post mill. Converted to a house by 1936.

HOPTON

ALL SAINTS. S aisle of the late C13 – see the W window with plate tracery (two pointed-trefoiled lights and an enriched quatrefoil). Dec E window. Perp widening. The arcade is pre-Perp, with octagonal piers and double-chamfered arches. Dec W tower with a pretty C18 top. Tall arched bell-openings, and the walls all of flushwork in a chequerboard pattern. The chancel is of *c*. 1300 or earlier – see the N doorway. Perp N aisle (bequest of 1461). Late Perp clerestory of brick with two-light windows and a fine roof. Brick shafts help to carry it. Against these small seated figures. The roof is of the hammerbeam type. Against the hammerbeams figures holding a book, a chalice, musical instruments, etc. Carved wall-plate. Colouring by the rector's daughters, 1879. General restoration that year by *Satchell & Edwards*, including removal of W gallery, re-seating and rebuilt S porch. – ROOD BEAM. Cut off flush with the walls. – DOOR To tower, reinforced with iron bands. – STAINED GLASS. E window by *Ward & Hughes*, 1890. Including portraits of those commemorated. S aisle E by *Kempe*, 1905. – MONUMENTS. Thomas Raymond †1680. With broken pediment, and skull at the foot. Signed by *John Fellows* of King's Lynn, and almost identical to his monument to Sarah Raymond †1700 at Foulden, Norfolk. Both erected by Burham Raymond †1728 (Thomas's son, Sarah's husband), and closer to 1728 than 1700. – Two nicely lettered tablets signed by *T. Ruddock* of North Lopham, Norfolk: Frances Elizabeth Beales †1808 (tower) and Martha Stone †1838 (chancel).

PRIMARY SCHOOL, Thelnetham Road. By *West Suffolk County Architect's Dept* (job architect *J. Blackie*), 1971–3. A development of the Great Waldingfield school design (q.v.), using the SEAC system. Four semi-open-plan teaching areas round a sunken central hall. Flat metal roof-deck on steel stanchions with lightweight window-walling.

OLD RECTORY, NE of church. Timber-framed, C16, but remodelled in the C18 with painted brick front, sash windows and doorcase.

Former NATIONAL SCHOOL, Nethergate Street. By *Thomas Farrow*, 1854–5. Tudor-Gothic. Knapped flint with stone dressings.

COTTARS HALL, Nethergate Street. 1990–1 by *Alan Horsfall* for himself. Fully timber-framed in green oak, with jettied cross-wings, in the manner of the C16. Plinth and external stack of reused red bricks.

HORRINGER

A corruption of Horningsheath, by which name it was formerly known.

ST LEONARD. Dec chancel with E window of four lights with reticulated tracery. W tower Perp, with pretty fleurons on the capitals of the arch towards the nave. The top was rebuilt in 1703, and the parapet and pinnacles in 1912–13 by *Nicholson & Corlette*, who also rebuilt the nave parapets and removed stucco from the walls of the tower, nave and porch. S porch Perp, for which money was left 1464–74; much flushwork decoration, chequerboard as well as panel designs. A S chapel is attached to its E wall. The restoration of 1818 by 'London artificers', following which 'nothing remains of the former edifice, but the plain masonry of the walls' (*Bury and Norwich Post*, 14 October 1818), was undone by later restorations, first by *L. N. Cottingham & Son*, 1845–6, who added the N aisle and N vestry. *J. D. Wyatt*, 1866–7, restored and partly rebuilt the chancel, and rebuilt the N vestry to join up with Cottingham's N aisle. S chapel restored 1876, possibly also by Wyatt. Nave re-seated *c.* 1883–6. – SCREEN. Upper part of the rood screen, reused as a low screen to the S chapel. Money was left for the new rood loft in 1485. – SCULPTURE. Bronze figure of St Leonard by *Richard Rome*, 2006, in niche over porch entrance. Plaster version (without chains) in N aisle. – STAINED GLASS. E window 1946 by *J. E. Nuttgens*. In the mildly Expressionist style of much C20 English wood-engraving. S chapel E by *Michael Wiley*, 1991, S †1872 by *Clayton & Bell*. – MONUMENTS. Valentine Munbee †1750. By *Thomas Singleton* of Bury. With broken pediment and urn. Cartouche at the foot. – War memorial. By *Sir Charles Nicholson*, 1920. Tablet with heavy moulding, including segmental pediments and scrolled sides.

The church stands on the N side of the green beside the main entrance to Ickworth (q.v.), and although not the estate church, it forms the main feature of Ickworth's estate village which, although not totally rebuilt by the Bristols, was controlled and maintained by them to provide an attractive backdrop to the approach to their park. The road is broad, with deep verges, and the cottages, mostly thatched, look C18 or early C19 even if actually older. The most substantial house is THE OLD RECTORY, timber-framed and plastered with a two-storey, six-bay Georgian front and a further jettied bay to the l.

By the church the former SCHOOL, c. 1846, of white brick with hoodmoulds and other Tudor details. Opposite, along MANOR LANE, the former rectory of 1871–3 by *T. H. Wyatt* (now MANOR GROVE and ST LEONARD'S). Red brick with bands of black. Prominent chimneys and steeply pitched slate roofs with dormers. Opposite, THE GABLES is a Y-plan estate cottage of the type favoured by Rev. Sir Thomas Gery Cullum of Hardwick House (*see* p. 173), here with hoodmoulds and now rendered. Another example, dated 1843, 1 m. SE on Whepstead Road. Flint with red brick dressings and shaped gables (cf. Hawstead).

HORRINGER MANOR, ¼ m E of the church. Built by A. J. Brooke, who was responsible for the 1818 restoration of the church, and originally called Brooke House. Large, of white brick with pilaster strips. Three-bay E front with one-bay pediment. Canted bay on the S side also with pediment. Later C19 Corinthian porch with open segmental pediment. Stable block of flint with red brick dressings and timber clock turret.

HORRINGER HOUSE, ¾ m. S. Some C18 red brick on the two-storey, three-bay W front. S front of white brick, early C19, with canted bay at the W end. At the E end a wholly incongruous four-storey Italianate tower of *c.* 1840. Red brick with white-brick dressings. A single-storey canted bay and little stone balconies to the first- and second-floor windows. Pyramidal slate roof.

THE HOPLEYS, ½ m. ESE. Called Hopleys Cottage in 1844, and 'a tasteful villa' in 1855 (White's *Directory*). Rendered. At the S end a Tudor-Gothic range of *c.* 1833 with hoodmoulds, pinnacles, etc. Large addition to the rear by *David Mikhail Architects*, 2003, including pool house. The same height as the house and entirely glazed on the S front. Thatched LODGE to the E with deep eaves on the front projecting further over the porch. Gothick windows with ogee hoodmoulds.

HORSECROFT HALL, 1 m. E. Early C19 house with white-brick front and glazed Greek Doric porch. Back parts of flint with red brick dressings. It too has a picturesque LODGE, N of the house. Thatched, the eaves at the front supported by rustic posts to form a porch.

OLD FARMHOUSE, Horsecroft, 1¼ m. ESE. 1852 for Rev. Sir T. G. Cullum. Pretty, in the Hardwick House estate style. Flint with red brick dressings. Cast-iron casements. Gabled porch and dormers.

HORRINGER COURT (formerly Horringer Red House, now Clarice House). *See* Bury St Edmunds, p. 173.

HUNDON

ALL SAINTS. Severely damaged by fire in 1914 and restored by *Detmar Blow & Billerey*. The interior is consequently somewhat bleak, and the arcades of low octagonal piers had to be renewed, but from the outside the building appears little different from any other carefully restored medieval church. W tower with higher SW stair-turret. Angle buttresses with prominent set-offs on which crouch little animals. S porch with flushwork panelling, S doorway with small shields in one arch moulding. Clerestory with pretty openwork battlements with quatrefoils, incomplete on the N side. Wills refer to the new S aisle in 1490 and to the new S chapel in 1548. – PANELLING. In S chapel, made up of bench ends and other woodwork salvaged from the fire. – MONUMENT. A wheat sheaf inside the church is all that remains of an ambitious monument to Arethusa Vernon †1728 that stood in a separate building near the porch (dismantled 1984). It consisted of a pyramid on a sarcophagus, carrying a wheat sheaf.

In North Street, W of the church, the OLD SCHOOL HOUSE. C17, timber-framed and plastered, of two storeys and five bays. Pedimented doorcase. To the N, THATCHERS HALL. C15 Wealden house with exposed close studding. Crown-post roof. Stack inserted to serve the open hall in the later C15, with three arched niches over the fireplace and above that a wall painting of the Agnus Dei. Niches and painting separated by C16 floor. N of Thatchers Hall the former CONGREGATIONAL CHAPEL, now a house. 1846. Red brick. Three bays and two storeys, with broad pilasters between the bays.

In Mill Lane, off Church Street, HOUSING for Clare Rural District Council by *A. E. Richardson* (*Richardson & Houfe*), 1950. Neo-Georgian and very formal and townish. Red brick. Semi-detached pairs and terraces of four two-storey houses, with hipped roofs. Cf. Barnardiston, Wickhambrook.

HIGHPOINT PRISON. *See* Stradishall.

HUNSTON

ST MICHAEL. Nave and chancel and W tower. The nave walls are Norman, and built into the base of the wall at the NE corner of the chancel is a fragment of Norman work, part of a decorated window head. Three more similar fragments reused for the threshold of the priest's doorway.* In addition a remarkable S transept. It is of the later C13 and has a W doorway with shafts, two lancets to the E, and a renewed group of three stepped lancets under one arch to the S. Inside, the entry arch is double-chamfered and rests on two corbels which turn into the wall like sections of stove-pipes. In the E wall between the lancets is a niche bordered by huge dogtooth, a dogtooth actually meant to be four petals. Between the petals is some playful stiff-leaf. Hoodmould of stiff-leaf, or at least starting off as stiff-leaf from the l., and after two motifs turning for the rest into much prettier roses. DOUBLE PISCINA in the SE corner on three shafts with trefoil-pointed arches. The chancel is apparently of the same time. It has an E window exactly like the transept S window and a very curious semicircular fully trefoiled-cusped window above the priest's doorway. The chancel arch has shafts with two shaft-rings and primitive capitals with leaves on upright stems. Unbuttressed W tower of knapped flint. Money was left for it in 1472, providing work started that year. Battlemented parapet of 1907. Principal restoration 1878, including re-seating and new S porch. – FONT. Plain bowl, C12 or C13, on C19 columns. – PULPIT. 1878, but the sounding board of its C17 predecessor is preserved (not *in situ*). – SCULPTURE. In S transept, the head of a Saxon cross. Also fragments of a C10–C11 stone grave-slab or cover. – STAINED GLASS. In a chancel S window, grisaille foliage, possibly C13. Chancel N and S by *Heaton, Butler & Bayne*, one a war memorial, 1920. Two more windows, †1890 and 1918, may also be theirs. – MONUMENTS. James Ellis †1824. By *George Tovell* of Stowmarket. Agreeably simple, with broken pediment holding an urn. – Capt. G.T. Heigham †1854 and his son Brevet Major G. H. J. Heigham †1861 at Lucknow. Crisp scroll with swords and regimental insignia. – Grace Hutchinson †1893 aged 18 months. Brass inscription plate in slate surround, an unusual design beautifully done.

A few nice timber-framed houses along THE STREET ¼ m. N of the church, chief among them GUNSTOCKS COTTAGE. Thatched, with exposed timbers and a gabled two-storey porch dated 1619 and jettied on three sides. Decorated bressumer and bargeboards. Not far to its E, TUDOR HOUSE has a similar but less fine porch.

ICKLINGHAM

A village with two churches less than half a mile apart. The two parishes shared a rector from 1786 but they were not

---

*Steven Plunkett suggests that these four fragments might be the heads of belfry or tower lights from a late pre-Conquest structure.

officially combined until 1972, when All Saints was declared redundant.

ALL SAINTS (Churches Conservation Trust). A thatched church, and not a small one. Restored by *W. M. Fawcett*, 1903; the Suffolk Institute, in 1901, had found it 'an extraordinary picture of neglect and desolation'. The nave is structurally Norman (blocked N windows, flint walling), the rest mostly late C13 to early C14. SW tower with windows belonging to that date and including a quatrefoil window in a circle. Dec nave, but with an odd Late Perp W window. Dec S aisle with S windows with cusped and uncusped intersected tracery, a pretty frieze of ballflower and other motifs along the top of the walls, and a splendid five-light E window with reticulated tracery, a hoodmould with fleurons to the inside, and, also inside, two ornate niches l. and r., which differ in their details. The r. one has diapered shafts. Both have traces of original colouring. Dec chancel with a big three-light E window (tracery of 1903) and two lowside windows. Dec arcade with octagonal piers. Perp porch. The interior is impressively bare, with a tiled floor and ancient benches pleasantly left alone. It allows the architecture to speak undisturbedly. Roof with scissor-bracing below and above the collar-beams. – FONT. Early C14, octagonal, with eight different simple motifs of tracery, a veritable mason's pattern-book (cf. Barton Mills). – ROOD SCREEN. The dado only is preserved. With C17 GATE. – PULPIT. Jacobean, the base of 1903. What appears to have been its accompanying READING DESK in the S aisle. – COMMUNION RAIL. Late C17; with flat twisted balusters. – TILES. In the chancel, early C14. Plain and line-impressed, in a variety of colours and designs. Similar to tiles in the floor of Prior Crauden's Chapel, Ely, completed 1324–5. – STAINED GLASS. Something of the original C14 glass remains in the chancel and S aisle, including the upper halves of figures and canopies.

ST JAMES. Chancel of *c.* 1300 – see the E window with cusped intersected tracery and the odd motif of three arches at the foot of the intersecting part. The rest Perp, but with reused Dec windows. Perp arcades, the piers with polygonal attachments towards the nave and aisles which have no capitals. The W tower collapsed at the end of the C18 and was rebuilt in 1808. General restoration by *Bacon & Bell*, 1865–6, including much refacing in black flint; two flints on the N aisle signed by the knappers, *Joseph Needham* and *Henry Ashley*. – FONT. Octagonal, Perp, simple. – CHOIR STALLS. 1866, incorporating parts of the rood screen. – CHEST. From All Saints. An exceptional piece, of *c.* 1300. Oak, covered with elaborate wrought-iron scrollwork. There are strong similarities with the chest at Church Brampton (Northants), and both may have been made in the same workshop for a religious house, perhaps Ely. – STAINED GLASS. E window (and the REREDOS below it) by *Heaton, Butler & Bayne*, 1866. Accompanying plaque with good lettering. Other chancel windows probably also by them. S aisle by *Mayer & Co.*, 1880. – MONUMENT. John Talbot †1689, rector, and daughter Isabella †1704. Plaque with painted inscription and arms.

Former NATIONAL SCHOOL, NW of St James. 1855. Black flint with stone dressings. Schoolroom with bellcote and two-storey house.

OLD RECTORY, NW of All Saints. White-brick front of 1830 added to a house of *c.* 1780. Three bays, with a little pediment.

WAR MEMORIAL. *See* Elveden.

HOW HILL, 2 m. NNW. A Bronze Age round barrow, 92 ft (28 metres) in diameter and 6 ft 6 in. (2 metres) high. An old excavation trench is visible across the mound and a cinerary urn is said to have been found here before 1923. Four other barrows lie ¼ m. NE of Bernersfield Farm: three low mounds in a line and a single mound further N, only one over 3 ft (1 metre) in height.

ROMAN SETTLEMENT. *See* Introduction, p. 16.

ICKWORTH

The parish of Ickworth comprises the church (roughly at its geographical centre), Ickworth House and its dependent buildings, and the park; indeed the park, which still covers about 1,790 acres (725 ha), extends into neighbouring parishes. There is no village as such; Horringer lies just outside the main entrance to the park to the NE.

ICKWORTH HOUSE

The Herveys acquired Ickworth by marriage in the C15. The family prospered under the Tudors and Stuarts and John Hervey (†1751) was created Baron Hervey in 1703 and 1st Earl of Bristol in 1714. Until his day the family lived principally in Ickworth Hall, E of the church, a timber-framed house that had grown into a large W-facing U-plan house comparable to Kentwell Hall, Long Melford. In the C17 it fell into disrepair and John Hervey decided to build a new house. In 1702 he moved into a farmhouse on the estate which became known as Ickworth Lodge (now Dower House), pulled down Ickworth Hall, and consulted first *William Talman* and then *Sir John Vanbrugh*. One hundred and twenty tons of Ketton stone was ordered in 1703, but nothing further came of the scheme, although Vanbrugh was consulted again in 1718. Some work was, however, done to the park and garden. The 2nd Earl (†1775) did nothing more about the house but did consult *Capability Brown*, who was paid for work in the park between 1769 and 1776. It was the 4th Earl, who succeeded in 1779, who set about creating the house we see today. In 1768 he had been made Bishop of Derry, and for that reason is

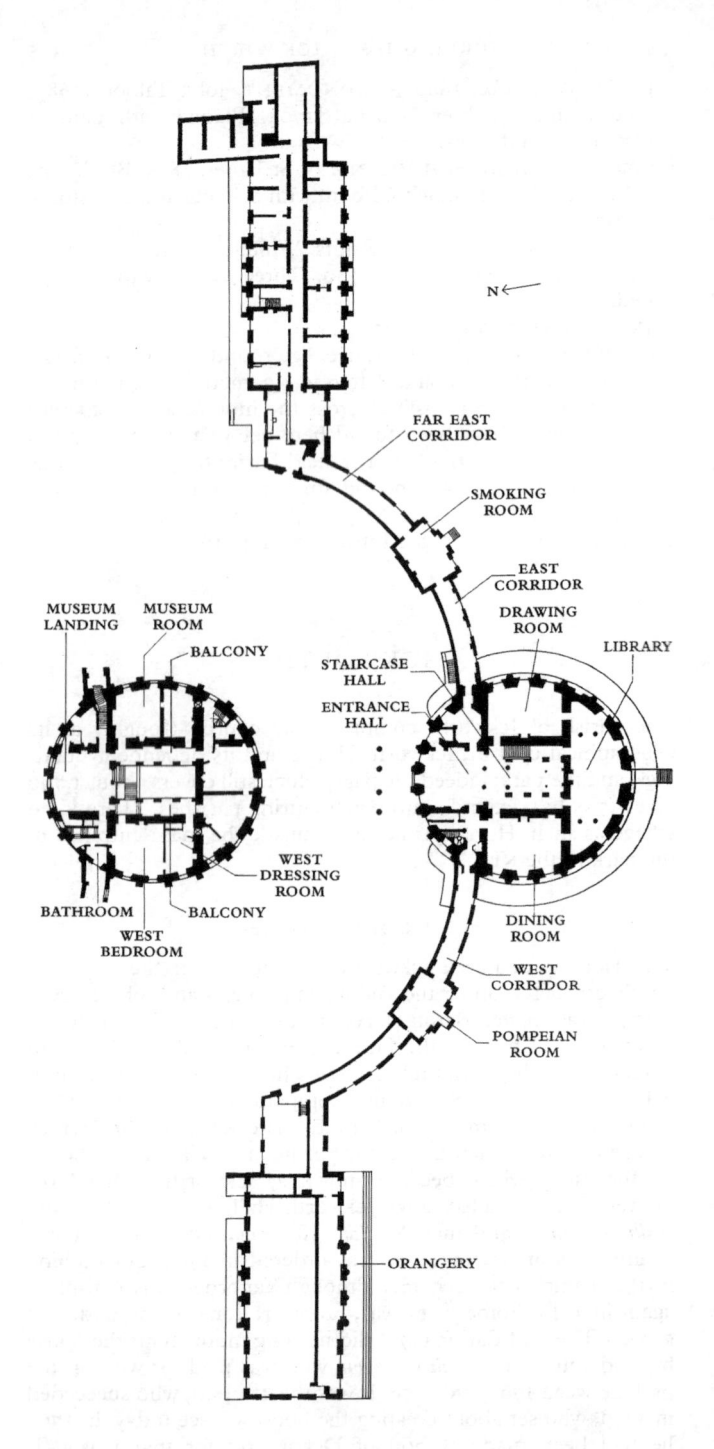

Ickworth House.
Plan

generally known as the Earl-Bishop. He is one of England's eccentrics, and not the most attractive of them. He travelled much and was more at home in Rome than in Ireland or Suffolk. Bristol Hotels all over the world owe their name to him. The chief purpose of his travels was the amassing of a superb collection of works of art, and the other object of his life was the construction of buildings in which to house them. Unfortunately his collection was confiscated in Rome in 1798 by Napoleon's troops, and the rest of his life was devoted unsuccessfully to trying to recover it; it was dispersed by auction in 1804, the year after his death.

In 1781–2 *Brown* was commissioned to design a new house, but this plan was superseded by something much more adventurous. As Bishop of Derry, the Earl-Bishop had begun a house for himself at Ballyscullion, Co. Londonderry, in 1787. Inspired by John Plaw's Belle Isle on Lake Windermere, it had a circular centre connected by quadrants to wings, and was never completed. Ickworth was to be a larger, Neoclassical version of Ballyscullion, and for its design the Earl-Bishop turned to an Italian architect, *Mario Asprucci*; drawings of 1794 and 1795 survive.* Asprucci's design was then modified and executed by *Francis Sandys* and his brother *Rev. Joseph Sandys*, the Earl-Bishop's domestic chaplain, both of whom had worked at Ballyscullion. Joseph made a model in 1796 (on display in the house) which was sent to the Earl-Bishop in Rome for his approval. The most significant modification was moving the quadrants northwards, a concession to the English climate, as it allowed more light and warmth into the principal rooms. Preliminary work is recorded in 1796, with regular bills for building work from 1797, but by the time of the Earl-Bishop's death in 1803 only the Rotunda had been built and the wings and quadrants were barely started. Work continued probably until 1809, when the scaffolding was sold.

Building started again in 1818 while the 5th Earl, who was created 1st Marquess in 1826 and died in 1859, was on the Grand Tour, from which he returned in 1821. His architect was *John Field*, a London builder, who was at the same time rebuilding his town house, No. 6 St James's Square. The Earl-Bishop had intended to live in the Rotunda, with the wings as galleries in which to display his collection. Although the 5th Earl was now putting together his own collection, he wisely decided that the E wing would provide more practical accommodation, and the family moved into it in 1829. Work continued on the Rotunda and its state rooms until 1834, and on the W wing until 1841, although by that date the latter was still a shell; it was really only built for the sake of symmetry. Together the Rotunda and wings are about 625 ft (190 metres) wide. The contractors included *John* and *Benjamin de Carle* and *John Trevethan* of Bury, and *William Hall* and *John Lake* of Ipswich. Further work was done by *W. Ranger*, 1834–40, Trevethan, 1845, and *F. C. Penrose*, 1878–9

*The Earl-Bishop also consulted *C. H. Tatham* in 1794.

and intermittently until 1903, with more substantial alterations by *A. C. Blomfield* in 1907–11 for the 4th Marquess.

Following the death of the 4th Marquess in 1951 the house and park were acquired by the National Trust in 1956, for whom *Raymond Erith* carried out various alterations. The E wing continued to be occupied by the family until the death of the 7th Marquess in 1999, following which it became a hotel with alterations by *Childs & Sulzmann*, 2001–2. The empty W wing was reconstructed internally by *Hopkins Architects* as a visitor centre, etc., opened in 2005. A link from this to the basement of the Rotunda, making a new visitor entrance, was created by *RH Partnership Architects*, 2010–11.

The ROTUNDA is 105 ft (32 metres) high, elliptical, and covered by a segmental dome. It makes for a lumpy appearance from outside and creates very unsatisfactory shapes for most of the rooms inside. On top of the dome is a heavy concrete balustrade, the solid parts of which conceal the chimneys. There are four storeys, including the basement. This is of stone, set in a paved moat-like area. The walls of the principal floors, which are of rendered brick, have unfluted attached columns all the way round, Ionic below, Corinthian above. A terracotta frieze runs above the upper columns, and a second runs below the capitals of the lower. These were copied from *Flaxman*'s designs for Homer by *Casimiro* and *Donato Carabelli* of Milan, who worked also on the façade of Milan Cathedral. They left the friezes unfinished, and they were completed in the 1820s in *Coade* stone. The entrance is marked by a four-column stone portico with pediment, rather inorganically attached. The frieze round the entrance, depicting the Olympic Games, was designed by *Caroline, Lady Wharncliffe*, the Earl-Bishop's granddaughter; originally plaster, since replaced with casts.

Ickworth, Rotunda.
Drawing by I. Johnson, 1817

The ENTRANCE HALL was created by *John Field*, with a pair of giant scagliola Ionic columns supplied by *Coade*. The original staircase was beyond these, behind a wall, but in 1909–11 A. C. Blomfield took this down, inserted a second pair of columns and designed an entirely new STAIRCASE. The stairs are kept behind arcades (and colonnades of coupled Ionic columns on the upper landing) and leave the centre free. This provides a striking setting, top-lit, for *Flaxman*'s most ambitious marble group: 'The Fury of Athamas', commissioned by the Earl-Bishop in 1790 at a price of 600 gns. It is inspired by antique sculpture, notably the Laocoön, and hence not as successful as Flaxman is on a less monumental scale and in a less exacting context. Although it was among the works confiscated in 1798, the 1st Marquess was able to buy it while on his Grand Tour in 1817–21.

The ground-floor rooms are mostly as decorated and furnished by *Field* for the 1st Marquess in 1821–9, with furniture made or supplied by *Banting, France & Co*. The LIBRARY is the most impressive of the suite; it is almost semicircular, occupying the S side of the Rotunda, and has at each end a screen of giant scagliola Ionic columns, again by *Coade*. The chimneypieces in this room and the DINING ROOM are probably Italian, acquired by the Earl-Bishop. The DRAWING ROOM, however, was remodelled by *Blomfield*, with panelling and pedimented doorcases. The first-floor rooms are very modest by comparison, also fitted out by Blomfield. In the MUSEUM ROOM on the E side, mahogany display cases by *Raymond Erith*, 1958, originally in the West Corridor. Erith also converted part of the first floor as a curator's flat, 1956. Further bedrooms on the second floor, and above that vast attics in the space between the roof and the brick dome that supports the central lantern over the stairs. The unfinished state of the dome can be seen through the shallow glass vault over the main staircase. The basement was also largely remodelled by Blomfield, including a FINISHING KITCHEN where food prepared in the main kitchens below the E wing was finished before being sent up to the dining room.

The quadrants and wings, of conventional design, were built by *Field* for the 1st Marquess, and although the foundations had been laid by the Earl-Bishop a fresh start was needed. Field also altered the original scheme and introduced wider rooms halfway along each quadrant. The quadrants are identical externally, single-storey with arched recesses beneath recessed rectangular panels on the N side, and tall arched windows on the S. The EAST CORRIDOR was finished internally in 1826–7 and has a plaster vaulted ceiling. Fitted bookcases by *Banting, France & Co*. The SMOKING ROOM (thus named *c.* 1907) was redecorated in 1998 in the style of the 1820s. The WEST CORRIDOR, however, was left unfinished until 1878–9, when it was decorated for the 3rd Marquess by *F. C. Penrose* and *J. D. Crace* as an approach to their POMPEIAN ROOM. This is in many ways the most successful of the designed interiors. The scheme is based on Roman wall paintings discovered in 1777 at the Villa Negroni, Rome; the Earl-Bishop had actually purchased the figure panels from the original frescoes. The figures here were painted by *Henry Scholz*. Vaulted centre with lantern. Fitted ebony bookcases by Crace.

The wings are each of two storeys and nine bays. Pedimented three-bay centres with attached Ionic columns. In addition on the S side the outer bays are separated by Ionic pilasters, and the S front of the EAST WING is faced in stone rather than stuccoed. The E wing was considerably altered internally by *Blomfield*, 1907–9, who also added the attic storey with mansard roof. Doorway in the centre of the N front by *Purcell & Johnson*, 1958; until then entry was by way of the East Corridor, or a small external door in the W wall. The marble pavement of the entrance hall was brought from No. 6 St James's Square; it is of the same design as the floor of the staircase hall in the Rotunda. Stone CONSERVATORY at the E end probably by *Field* (completed by 1826). From the E end of the E wing a range of outbuildings running NE towards the STABLES and CHAISE HOUSE, all by Field in white brick and surprisingly modest. Inserted into the outbuildings an indoor SWIMMING POOL by *Childs & Sulzmann*, c. 2002.

The WEST WING remained unfinished in 1841, its vast interior undivided. In 1845 *John Trevethan* converted the S side into an ORANGERY; at the same time plans were drawn up for converting the remainder to a real tennis court, but this came to nothing. In 1907 *Blomfield* inserted an engine room (for generating electricity) and racquets court at the E end, but the rest was used for agricultural storage until 1995. Major remodelling of the interior by *Hopkins Architects*, completed in 2005, included inserting two floors, with a large hall on the top floor, its bare brick walls and roof trusses in their original unadorned state.

GARDENS. The SOUTH PLEASURE GROUNDS on the S side of the house are the earliest example of Italianate garden design in England. They were laid out by the 1st Marquess; work seems to have started in 1818 and continued until 1830. The overall plan echoes the shape of the house, and it is divided by hedges into compartments. Domed SUMMERHOUSE of 1823, moved to its present position in 1958. Pedimented, with square columns and antae. The NORTH PLEASURE GROUNDS, also the work of the 1st Marquess, incorporate the BUILDING PLANTATION. This was probably planted as a shelter belt to protect the growing trees nearer the house, but was allowed to remain and thus prevents the house from being seen until the last minute. Within the plantation, two stone piers of CHEVINGTON GATE, originally at a S entrance to the park and moved to their present position in 1966. They are early C18, very fine, with fluted pilasters and vase finials, and very possibly by *William Talman* or *Vanbrugh*. W of the house, the

ALBANA WALK, named after the wife of the 1st Marquess and laid out in 1844. It winds through a belt of ornamental woodland that was planted probably in 1780, and contains a simple white-brick SUMMERHOUSE.

The WALLED GARDEN between the church and the River Linnet, SW of the site of Ickworth Hall, was laid out by the 1st Earl. It seems to have been planned as a pleasure garden, and converted to a kitchen garden in the later C18. Along the S side a broad CANAL fed by the Linnet (described as new in 1717, when the earl nearly drowned in it). Running down to it a garden with red brick walls on three sides, an arrangement that probably dates from 1714. In the middle of the N wall, facing the canal, a red brick SUMMERHOUSE of *c.* 1702, attributed to *Talman*. Three bays with tall sashes and central French window. Over this a broken segmental pediment framing arms. This inner garden sits within a much larger walled area, with a GARDENER'S HOUSE on the W side (early C19, single-storey, with second storey added *c.* 1860–70), and BOTHY of *c.* 1870 in the NE corner.

ST MARY (Ickworth Church Conservation Trust). In the porch, loose, the curved head of a Norman window with saltire-cross decoration. C13 chancel with lancets in the N wall. E wall with three stepped lancets and an oculus over. Double-chamfered reveals and inside jamb pillars with foliated capitals, stiff-leaf, etc. Three-light window with cusping in the nave N wall. Built into it a fine angle PISCINA with cusps and floriated gables that was probably moved to this position when the S aisle was added in 1833. This contains a raised N-facing PEW for the Hervey family over their burial vault. Stuccoed W tower of 1778 in the lancet style. Restoration by *A. C. Blomfield*, 1910–11, who refaced the nave and chancel in knapped flint with stone dressings. His also the open timber roof, nave seating, and the fronts of the Bristol pew and W gallery. Redundant 1984; restored for public opening by *Freeland Rees Roberts Architects*, 2012–13. – FONT. C13, octagonal, entirely plain. – PULPIT. Probably late C17, incorporated in a late C18 triple-decker. – WALL PAINTING. S of the E window a whole-length figure of the Angel of the Annunciation. C14. Discovered in 1910 and much repainted (by *Heaton, Butler & Bayne*). – STAINED GLASS. A number of Flemish roundels. E window by *A. K. Nicholson*, 1911. Two S aisle windows by *Powell & Sons*, 1932 (heraldic). – MONUMENTS. A quantity of grey ledger stones of the Hervey family, mostly re-laid as paving in 1778.

DOWER HOUSE (Ickworth Lodge), ½ m. N of Ickworth House. A farmhouse, enlarged for the 1st Earl in 1702. There seems to be no surviving evidence of the pre-1702 house. By about 1780 it was a large U-plan house with a castellated parapet. After the 1st Marquess moved into Ickworth House in 1829 all but part of the S wing was demolished, leaving a nine-bay, two-storey range of painted brick of Regency character. Segmental three-bay bow in the centre and canted E end.

Canted w end added in the C20. Two-and-a-half-storey w wing of 1853.

A licence for a small PARK at Ickworth was granted by the abbot of St Edmundsbury in 1253, but in its present form the park dates from the time of the 1st Earl, who emparked the area known as Horringer Park, Mansion Meadow and Deer Park, more or less surrounding Ickworth Lodge, between 1702 and 1731. This seems to have required the removal of no more than a dozen households. Although *Capability Brown* was paid for work between 1769 and 1776, there is no documentary

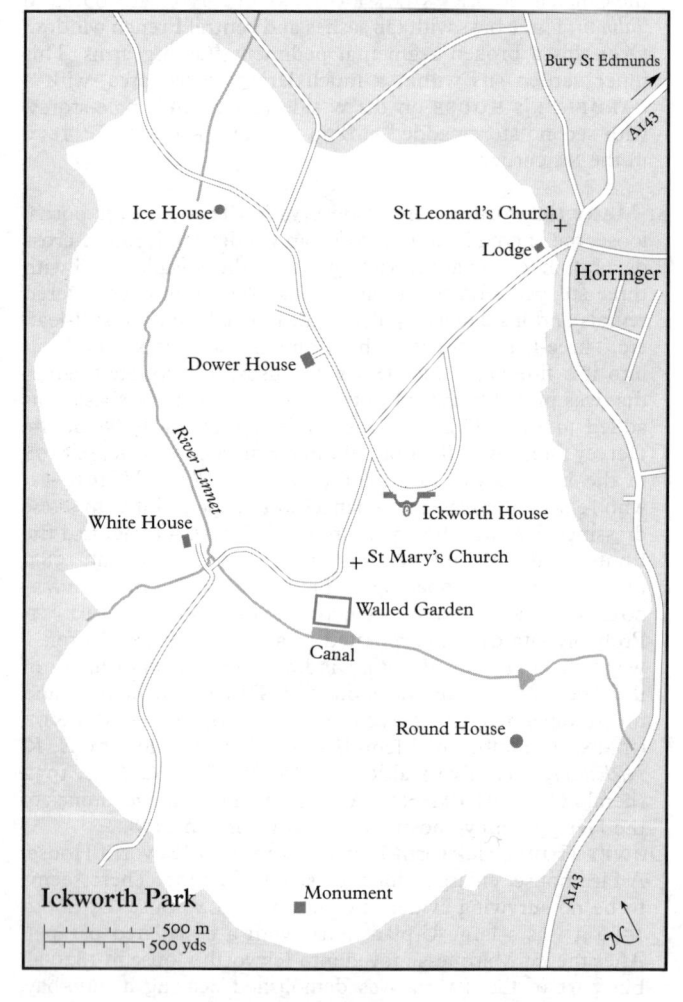

Ickworth Park.
Plan

1. Kersey, Church Hill and The Street (p. 340)

2. Bury St Edmunds, Angel Hill (p. 150)
3. Cavendish, The Green (p. 177)
4. Mildenhall Warren (p. 411)
5. West Stow, Anglo-Saxon village, *c.* 420–650, reconstructed from 1974 (p. 553)

2	4
3	5

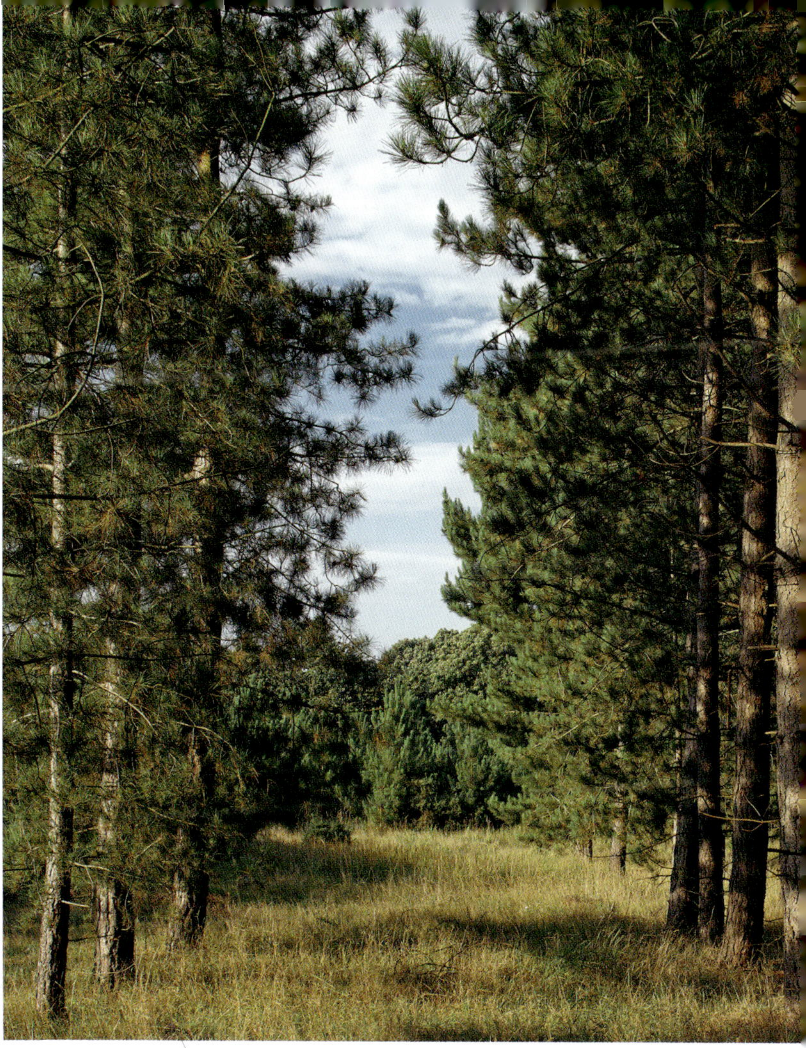

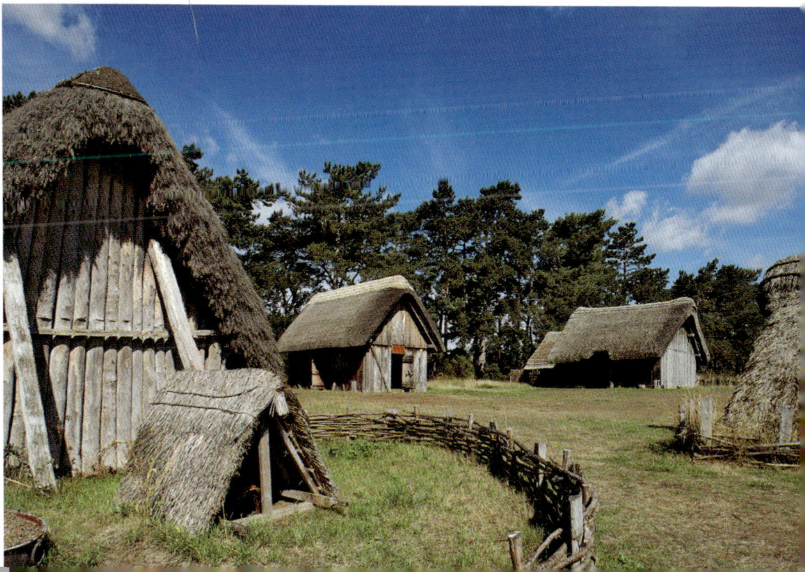

6. Bury St Edmunds, Norman Tower, between 1120 and 1148 (p. 128)
7. Bury St Edmunds, Great Gate, begun between 1327 and 1346, completed after 1353 (p. 133)
8. Little Saxham, St Nicholas, w tower, Norman (p. 369)
9. Polstead, St Mary, c. 1160 (p. 455)

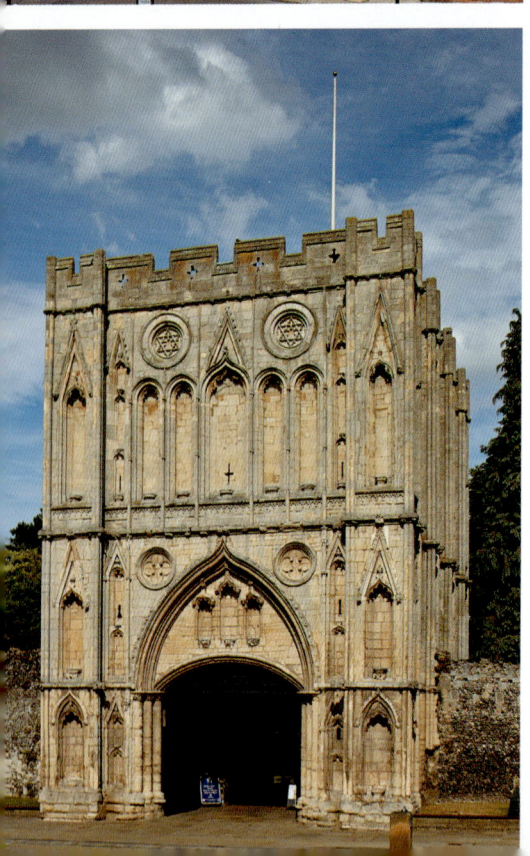

6	8
7	9

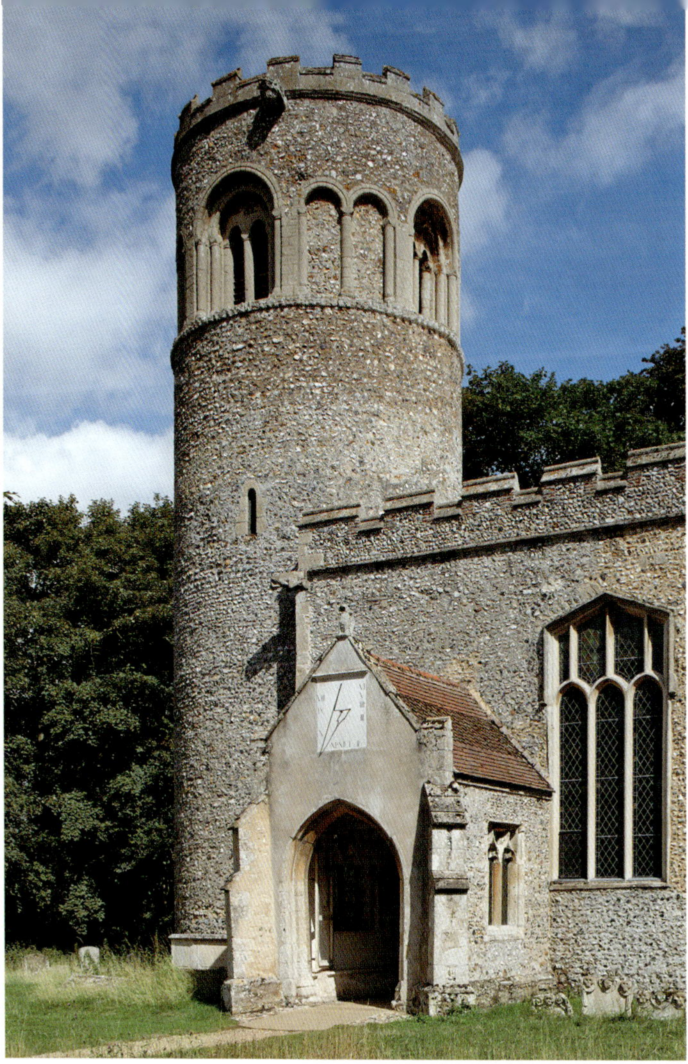

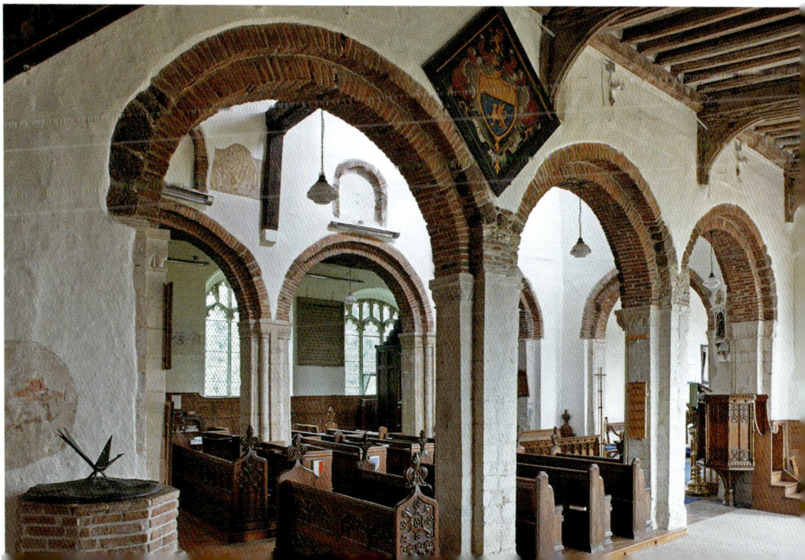

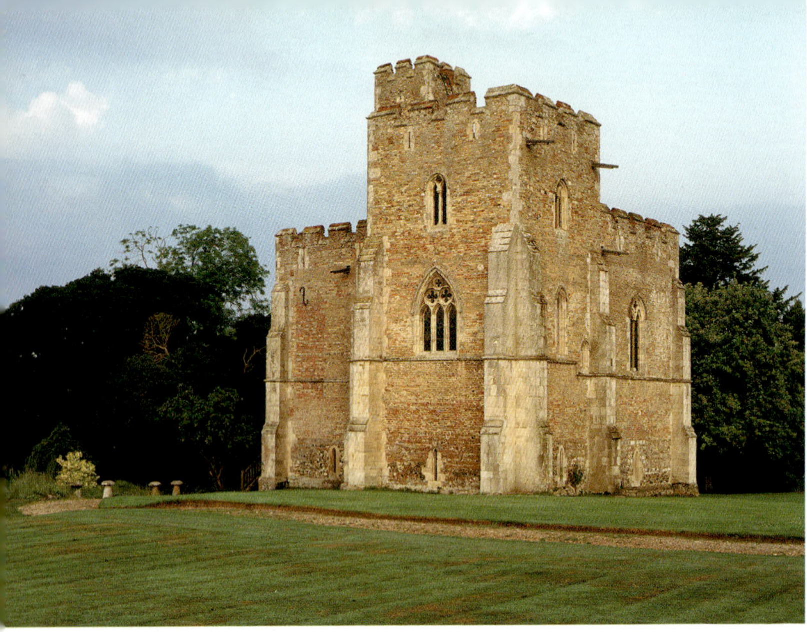

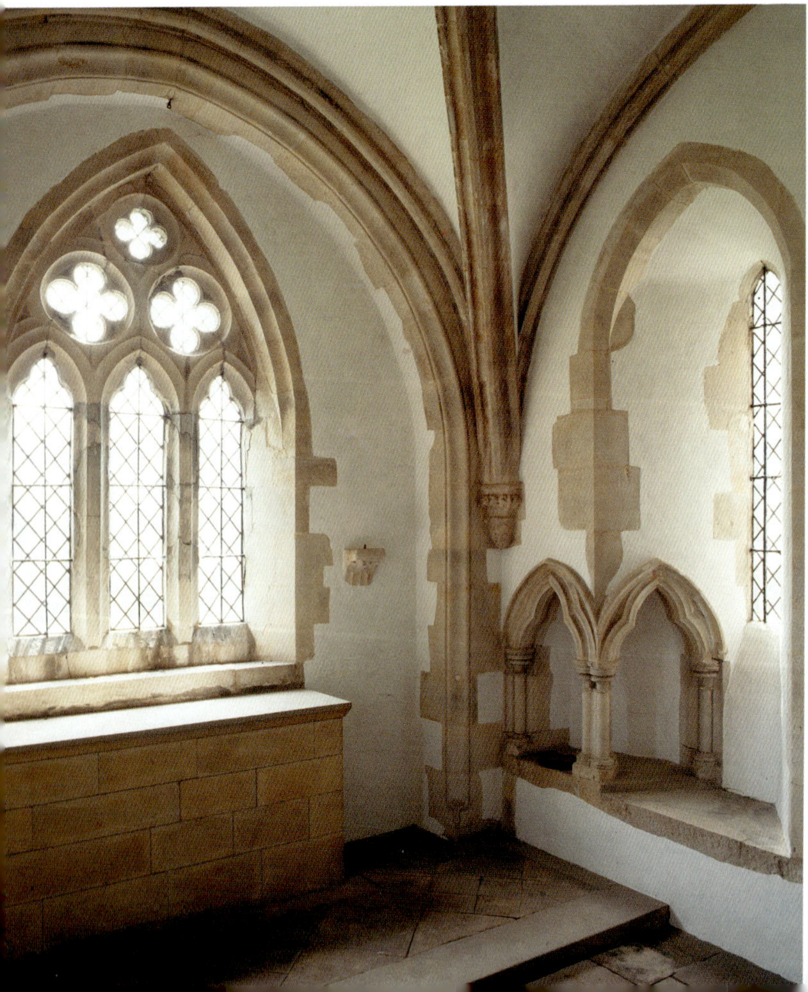

10. Little Wenham Hall, late C13 (p. 375)
11. Little Wenham Hall, chapel, late C13 (p. 375)
12. Lakenheath, St Mary, wall painting, mid-C13, overpainted with Virgin and Child with St Edmund, mid-C14 (p. 346)
13. Little Wenham, All Saints, wall painting, late C13 (p. 379)

10	12
11	13

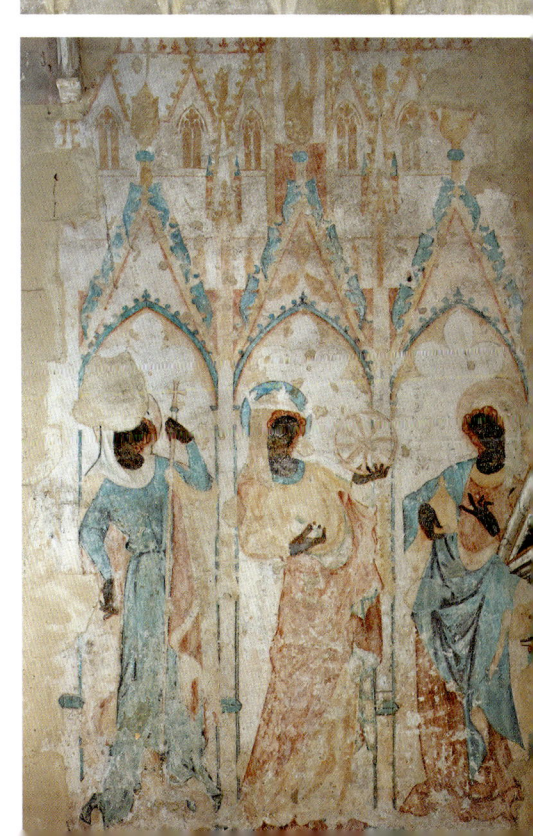

14. Mildenhall, St Mary, E window, c. 1300 (p. 407)
15. Chelsworth, All Saints, tomb recess, possibly for Sir John de St Philibert †1334 (p. 183)
16. Thornham Parva, St Mary, retable, c. 1330–40 (p. 535)

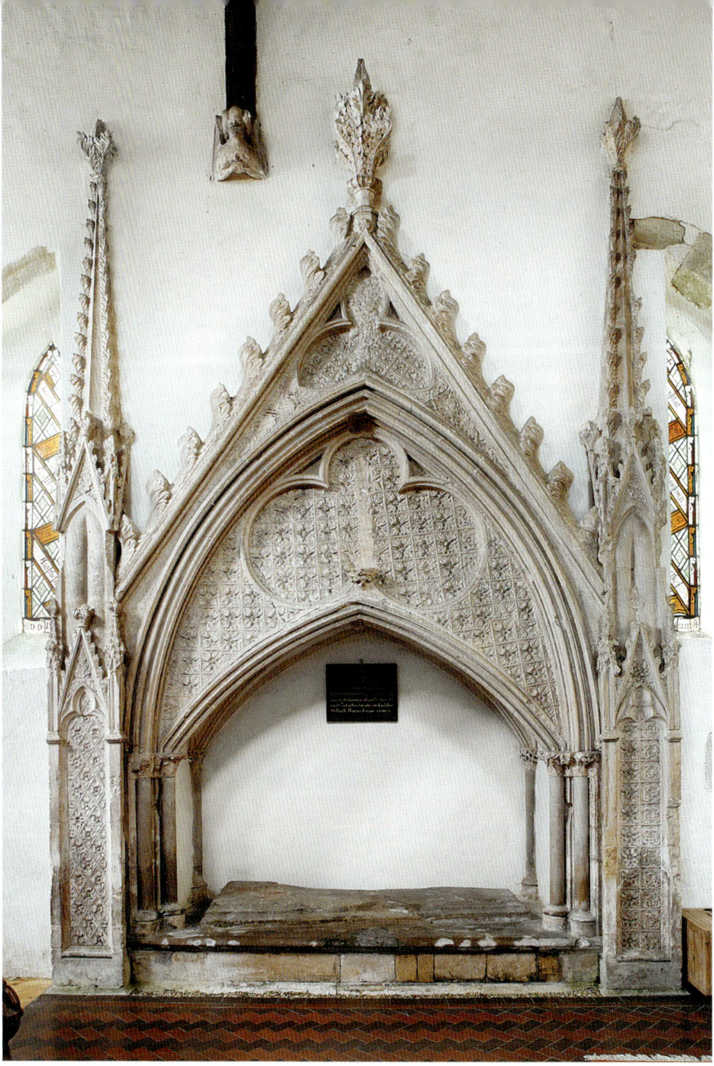

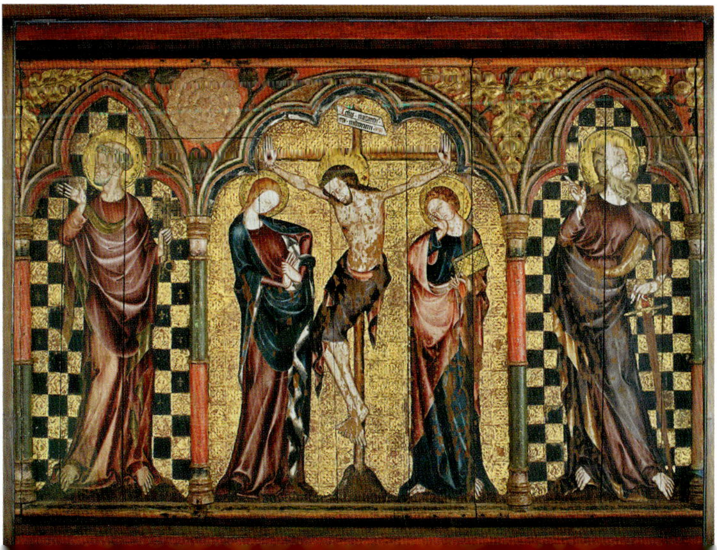

17. Boxford, St Mary, N porch, C14 (p. 100)
18. Long Melford, Holy Trinity, stained glass, late C15 (p. 387)
19. Clare, St Peter and St Paul, N door, Perp (p. 190)
20. Chevington, All Saints, chest, C14 (p. 185)

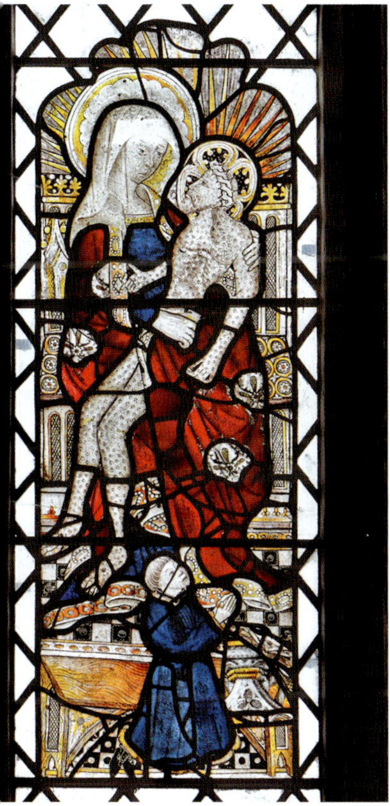

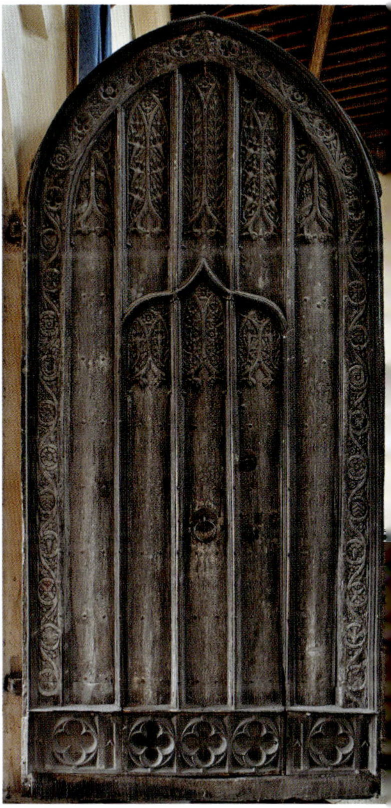

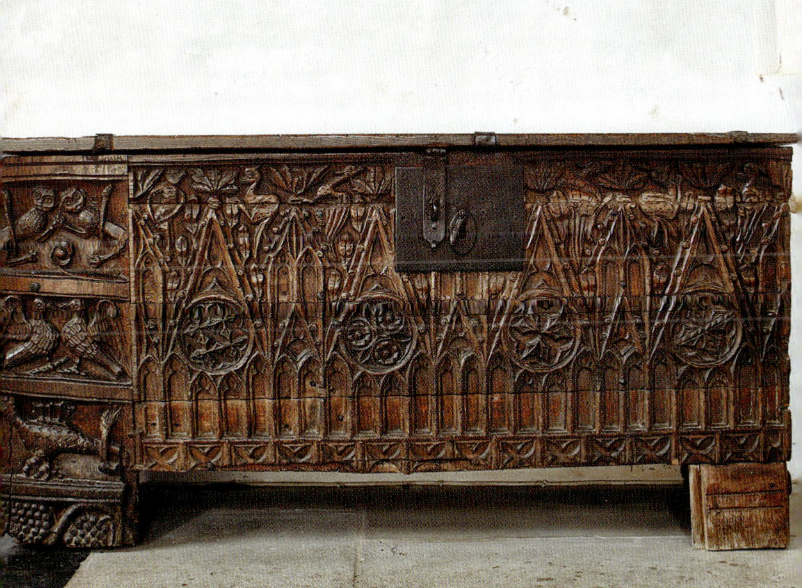

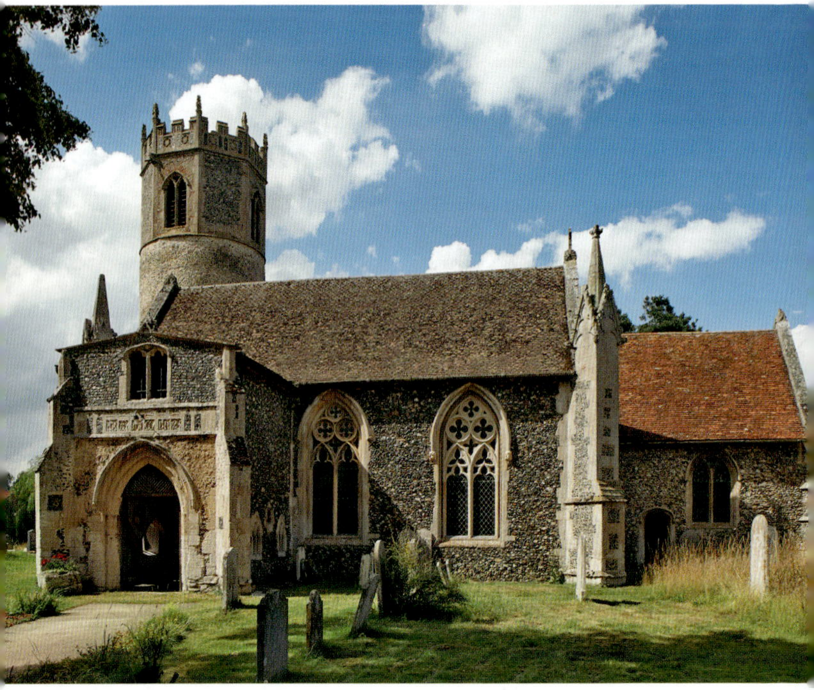

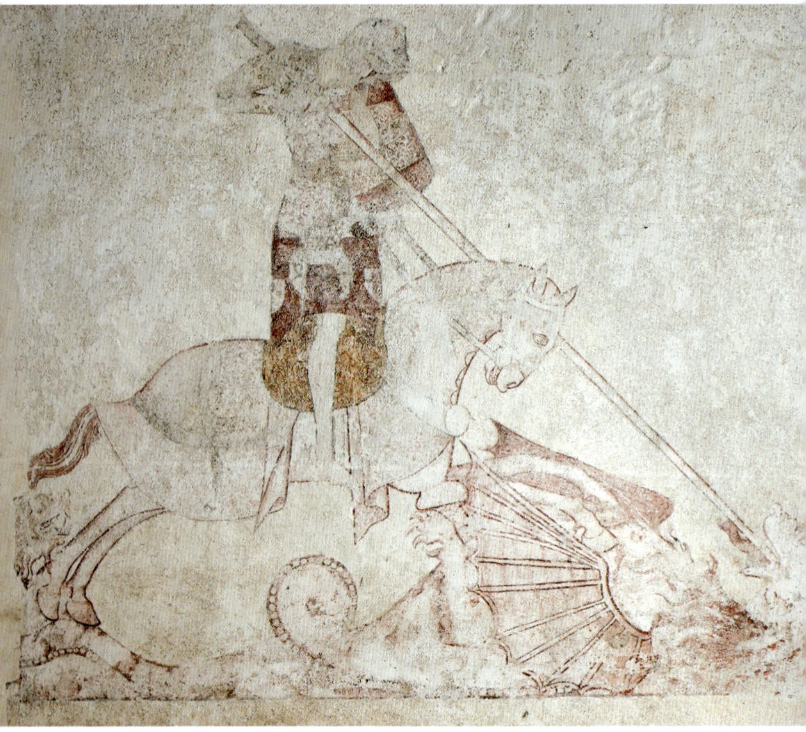

21. Rickinghall Inferior, St Mary, mostly early C14 (p. 467)
22. Troston, St Mary, wall painting, *c.* 1370–90 (p. 542)
23. Hepworth, St Peter, font cover, early C16 (p. 306)

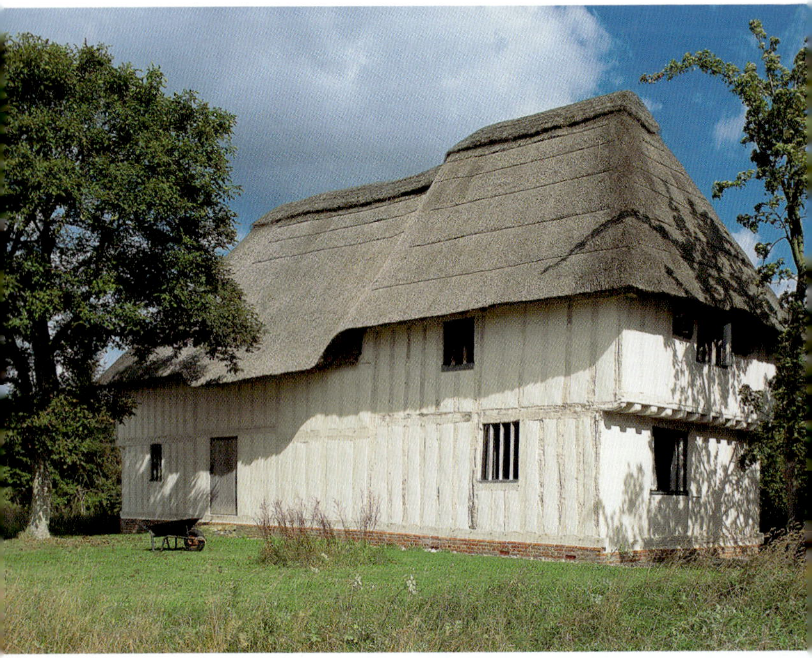

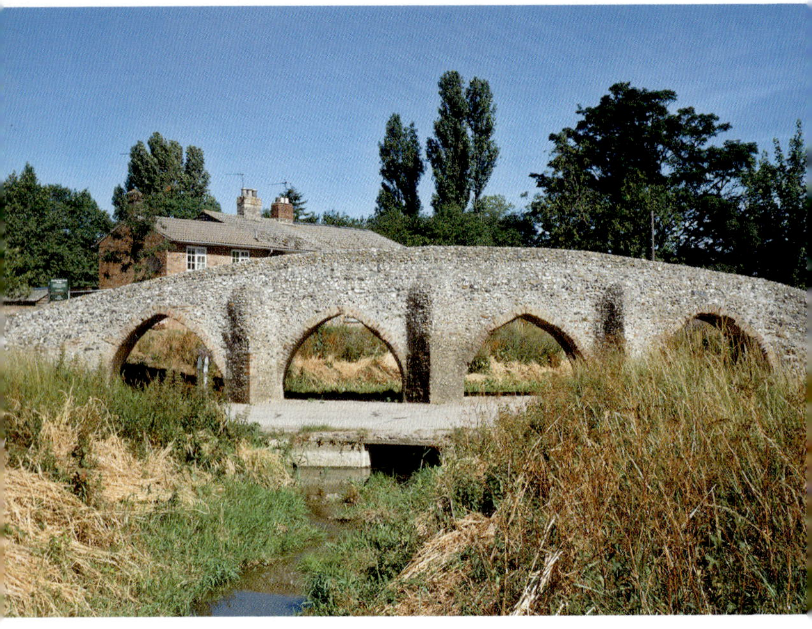

24. Stansfield, Purton Green, late C13 (p. 488)
25. Moulton, packhorse bridge, C14–C15 (p. 414)
26. Stowupland, Columbine Hall, c. 1390 (p. 512)

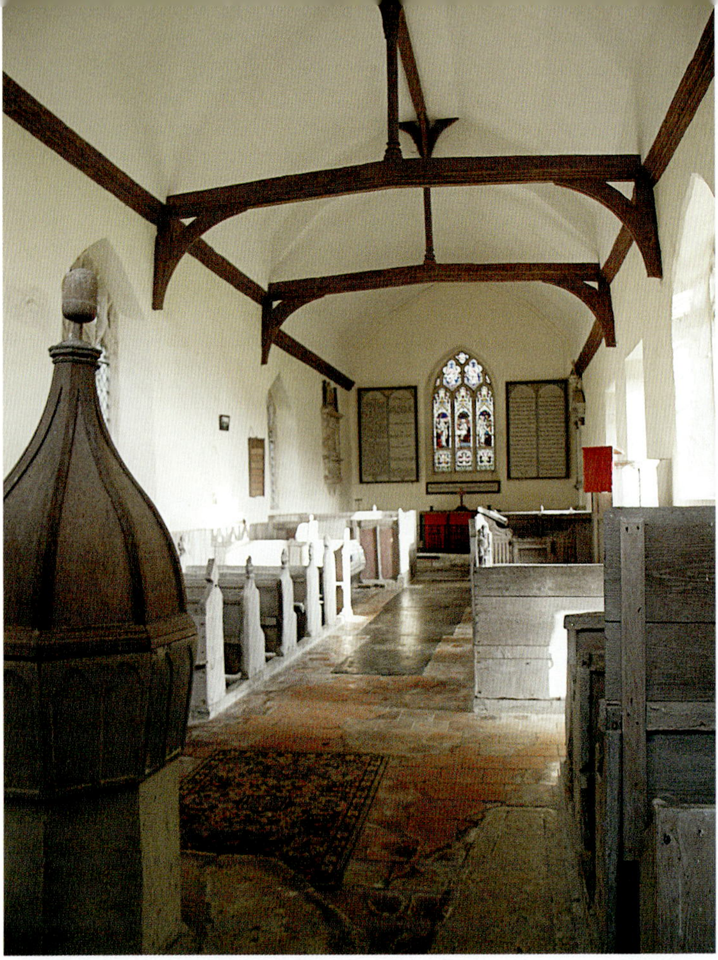

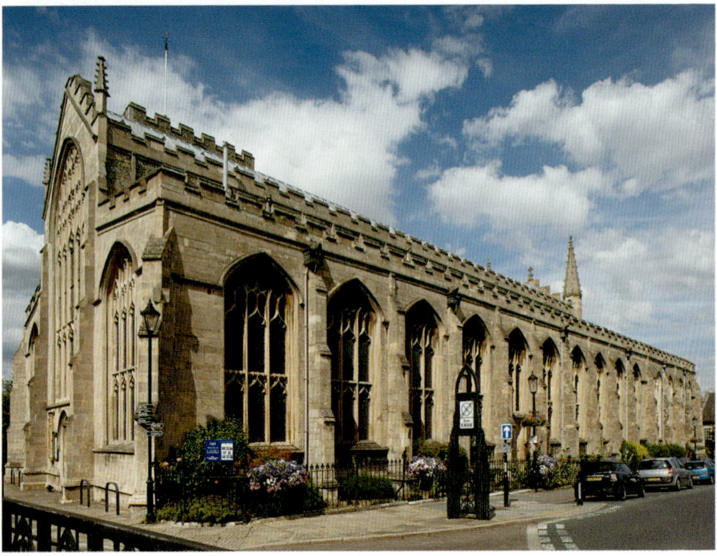

27. Badley, St Mary, C13–C17 (p. 82)
28. Bury St Edmunds, St Mary, rebuilt from 1424 (p. 137)
29. Woolpit, St Mary, s porch, c. 1430–55 (p. 567)
30. Kersey, St Mary, s porch, Perp (p. 341)

| 27 | 29 |
| 28 | 30 |

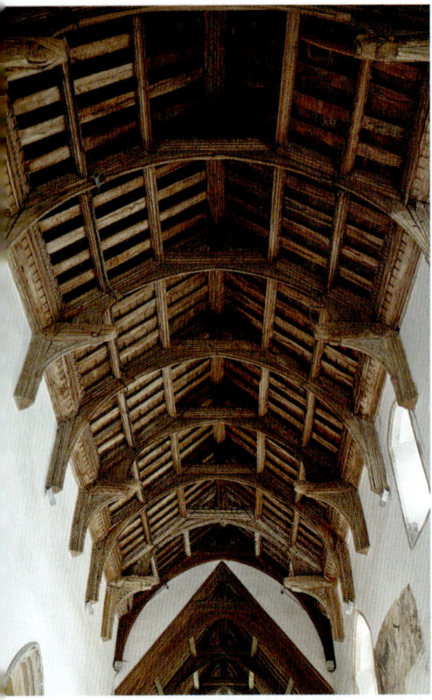
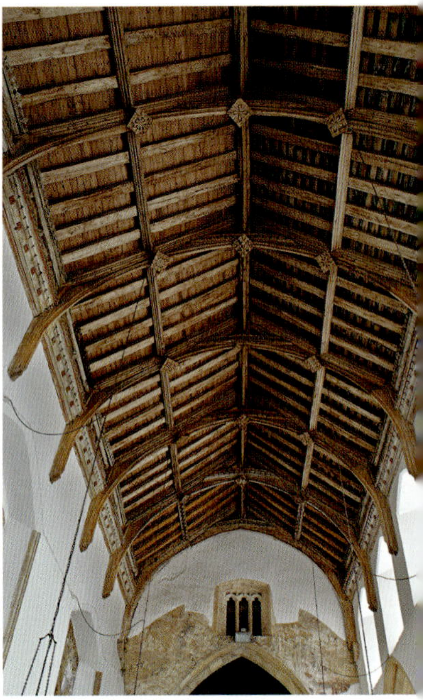
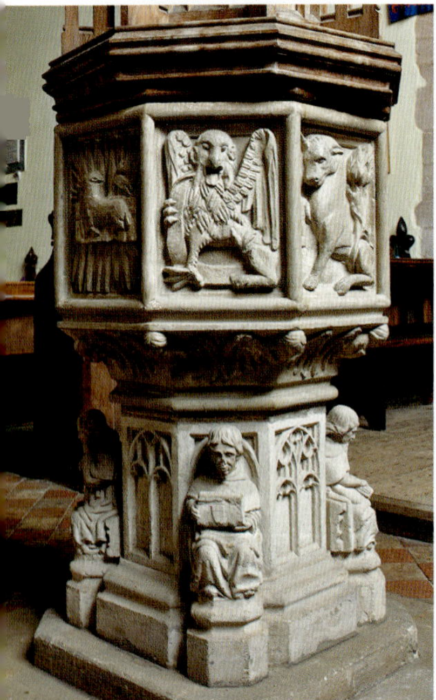
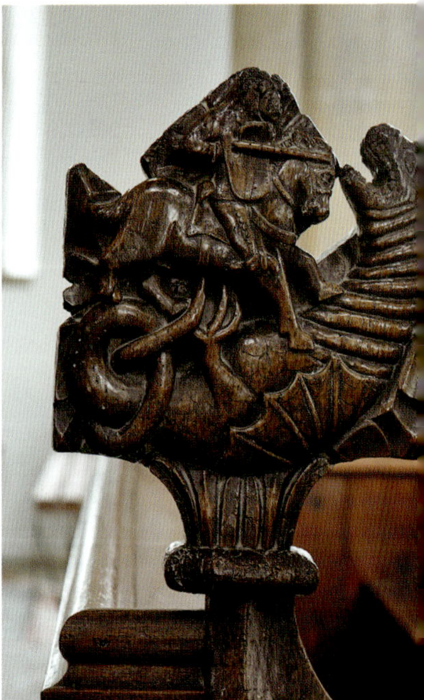

31. Kersey, St Mary, roof of arched braces alternating with hammerbeams, Perp (p. 341)
32. Yaxley, St Mary, arch-braced roof, Perp (p. 574)
33. Pakenham, St Mary, font, Perp (p. 451)
34. Withersfield, St Mary, bench end, C15 (p. 565)
35. Bardwell, St Peter and St Paul, stained glass, early C15, probably Sir William Berdewell †1434 (p. 85)

36. Needham Market, St John the Baptist, roof, late C15, restored by J.H. Hakewill, 1878–80 (p. 421)

37. Long Melford, Holy Trinity, 1467–1507, W tower 1712–25 and 1897–1903 (p. 381)

38. Long Melford, Holy Trinity, Clopton Chantry Chapel, completed by 1494 (p. 387)
39. Gipping, Chapel of St Nicholas, rebuilt before 1474 (p. 247)

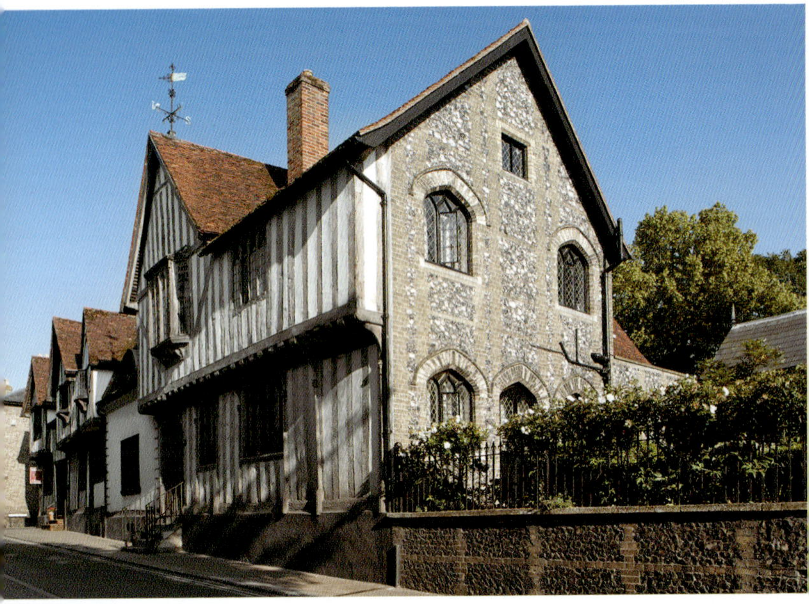

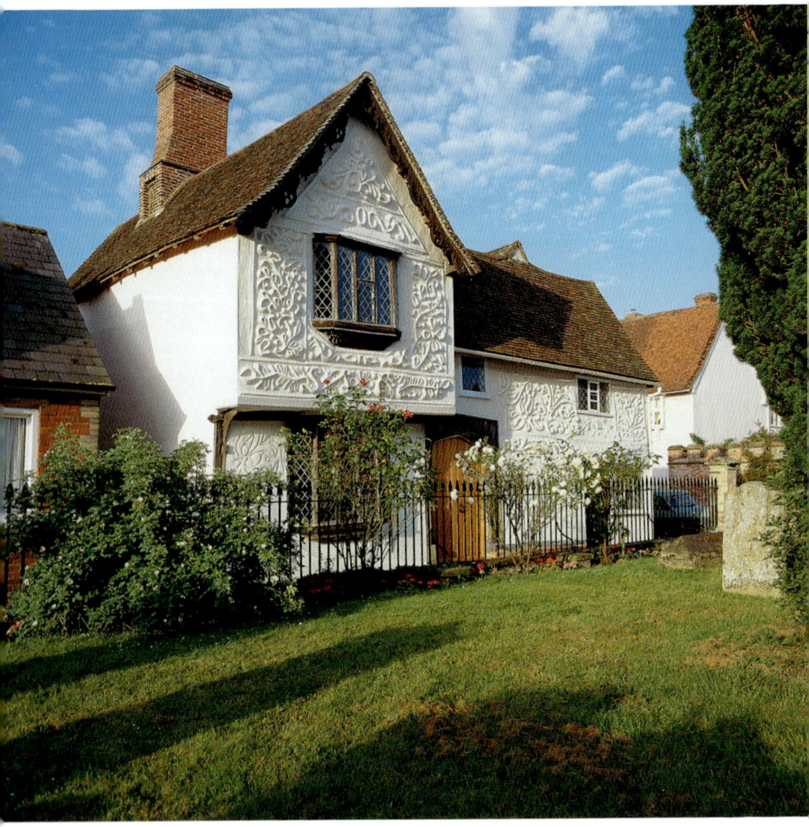

40. Sudbury, Salter's Hall, *c.* 1450 and *c.* 1855 (p. 525)
41. Clare, The Ancient House, C14, cross wing (l.) 1473 (p. 192)
42. Hadleigh, Deanery Tower, *c.* 1485 (p. 276)

43. Stoke-by-Clare, Stoke College, dovecote, between 1485 and 1493 (p. 495)
44. Nayland, Alston Court, W wing (r.) c. 1300, hall and E wing early C15 (p. 417)

45. Lavenham, Wool Hall (l.) and Nos. 10–11 Lady Street, C15–C16 (p. 360)
46. Lavenham, Guildhall, c. 1529 (p. 357)

47. Stoke-by-Clare, St John the Baptist, pulpit, *c.* 1498 (p. 492)
48. Barking, St Mary, nave roof, Perp (p. 87)
49. Fornham St Martin, St Martin, misericord, C15–C16 (p. 241)
50. Great Bradley, St Mary, s porch, Early Tudor (p. 257)

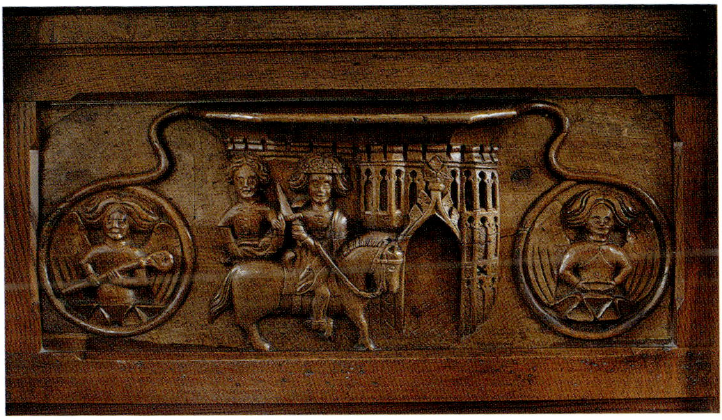

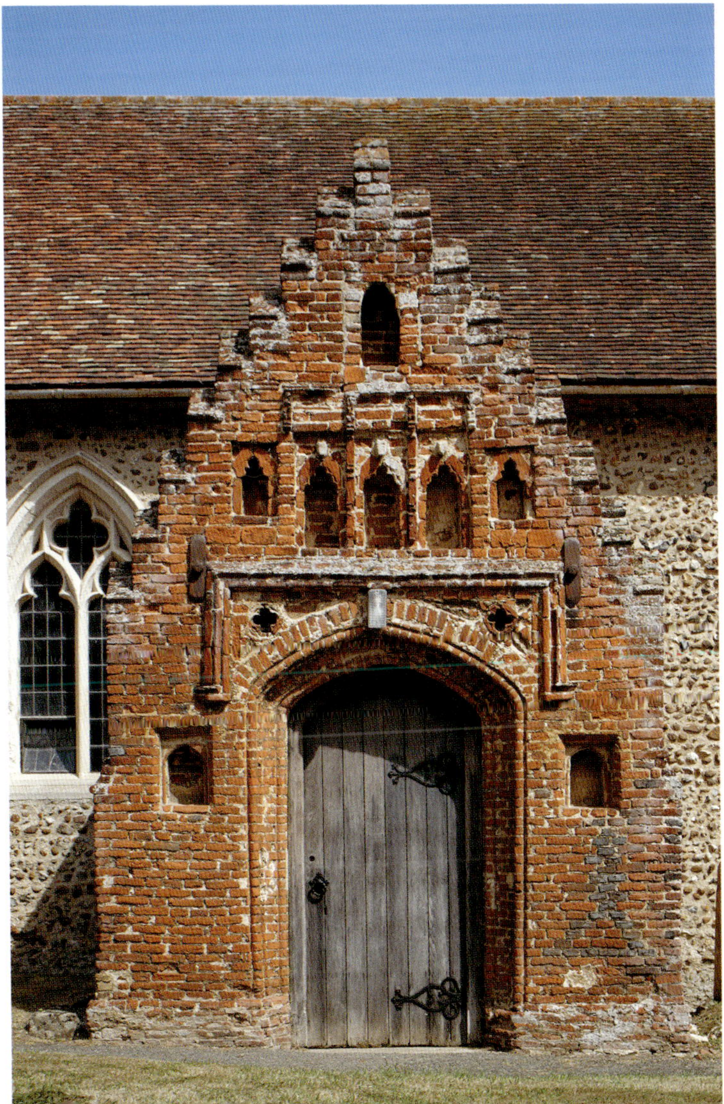

51. Lavenham, St Peter and St Paul, c. 1485–1525 (p. 352)
52. Woolpit, St Mary, false double-hammerbeam roof, Perp, restored by H. Ringham, 1843–4 (p. 567)

53. Stratford St Mary, St Mary, N aisle, *c.* 1500, and N porch, 1532 and 1876–9 (p. 513)
54. Lavenham, St Peter and St Paul, Spring parclose, *c.* 1523 (p. 353)

55. Giffords Hall, c. 1490–1520 and 1730–40 (p. 246)
56. Long Melford, Kentwell Hall, c. 1500–80 (p. 397)
57. West Stow Hall, c. 1530 (p. 552)
58. Long Melford, Melford Hall, early C16, w front, remodelled in the C17 and 1813 (p. 393)

55	57
56	58

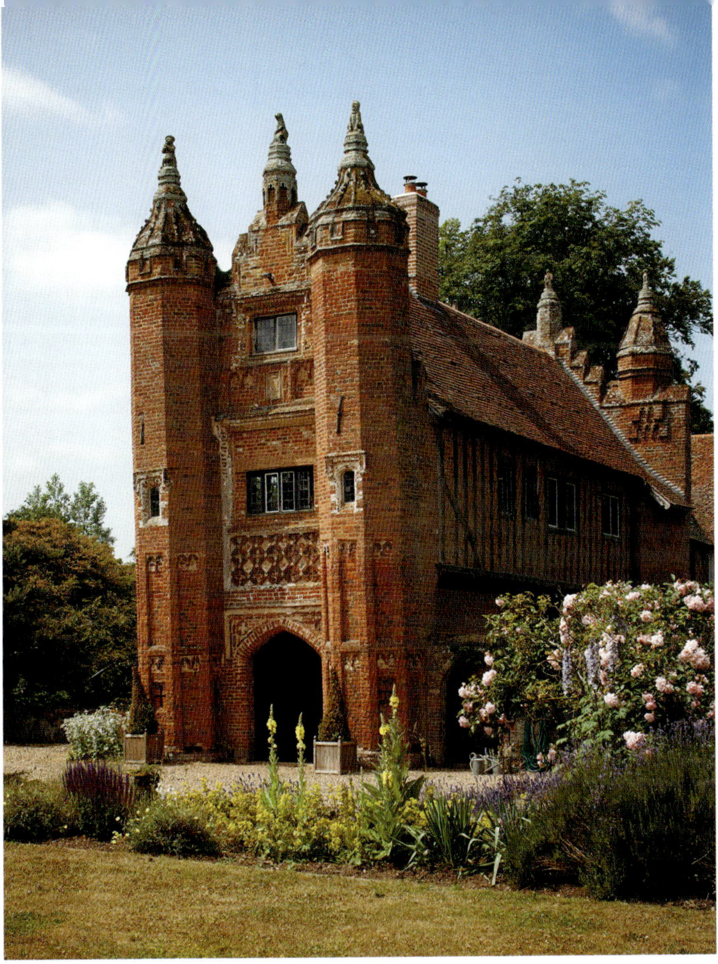

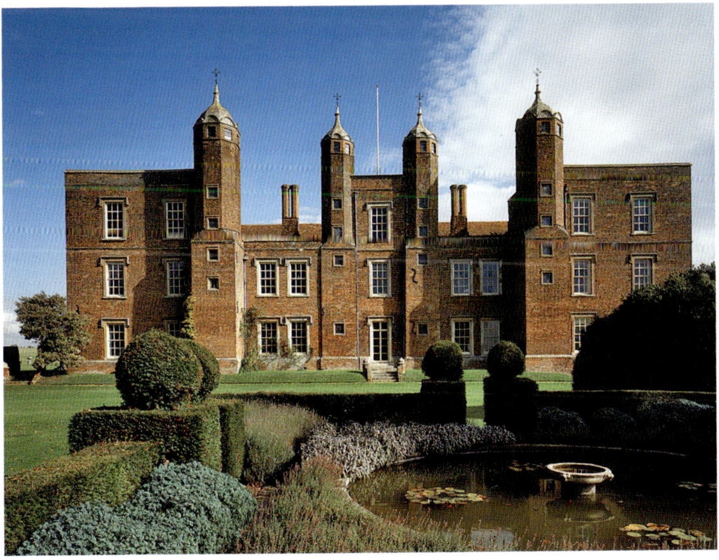

59. Hengrave Hall, s front, 1538, partially remodelled between 1775 and 1780 (p. 302)
60. Hengrave Hall, courtyard, 1538 (p. 303)
61. Long Melford, Holy Trinity, monument to Sir William Cordell †1581 (p. 387)
62. Preston St Mary, St Mary, royal arms of Elizabeth I, after 1588 (p. 460)

| 59 | 61 |
| 60 | 62 |

ELIZABETHA MAGNA · REGINA · ANGLIÆ

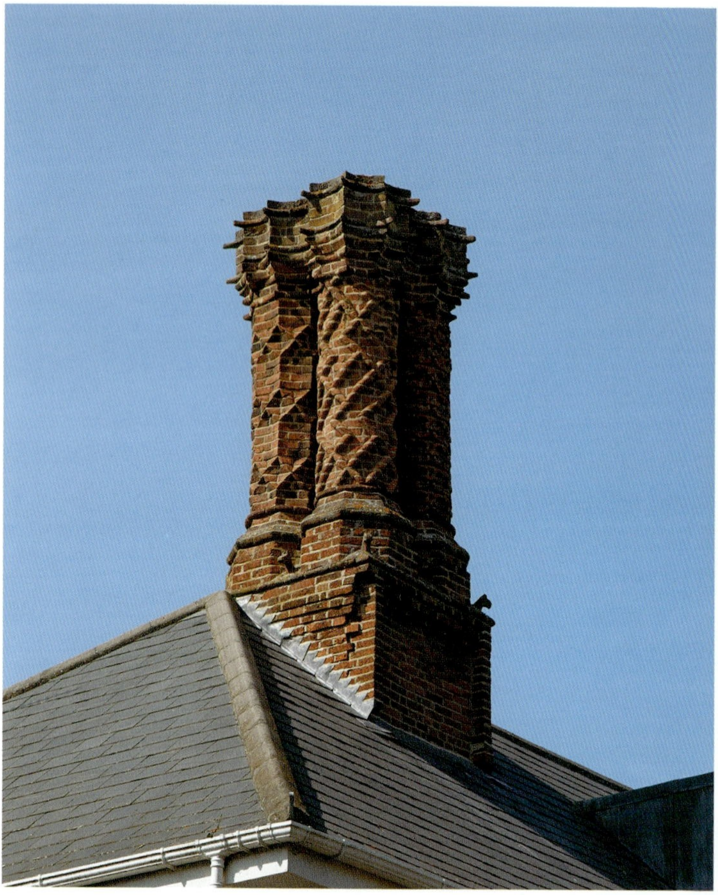

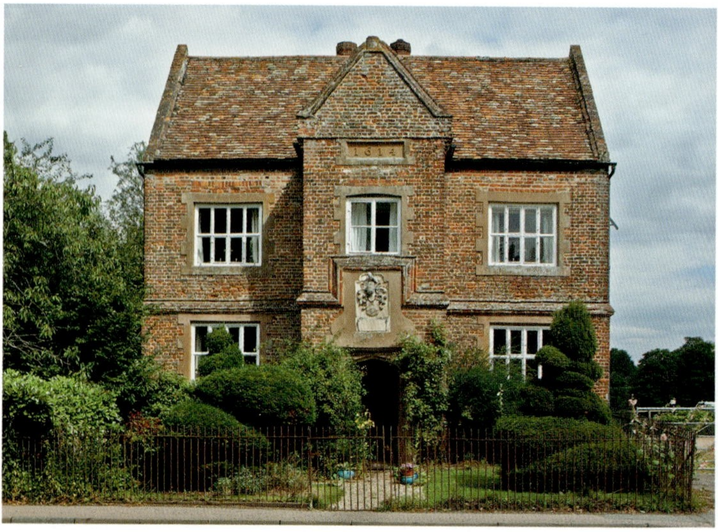
1614

63. Clare, Cliftons, chimneys, C16 (p. 196)
64. Little Thurlow, former schoolhouse, 1614 (p. 373)
65. Pakenham, Newe House, 1621/2 (p. 452)
66. Haughley Park, *c.* 1620, gutted by fire in 1961 and rebuilt by Eric Sandon (p. 289)

63	65
64	66

NICHOLAS BACON KNIGHT AND
LIETH HERE HE TOOKE TO WYFE ANNE
HEYRE TO BVTTS AND HALFE HEYRE TO BVRES
THEY LIVED TOGETHER 52 YEARES WHEN DEATH MAKINGE
THE SEPERATION ON HIR PART HE ERECTED THIS
MONVMENT TO THEM BOTH · AN DMI 1616

67. Redgrave, St Mary the Virgin, monument to Sir Nicholas Bacon †1624 and wife Anne †1616, by Nicholas Stone, James White and Bernard Janssen, 1616–27 (p. 465)
68. Kedington, St Peter and St Paul, Barnardiston Pew and chancel screen, 1619 (p. 338)
69. Great Ashfield, All Saints, pulpit, 1619 (p. 252)

70. Mendlesham, St Mary, font cover, by John Turner, 1630 (p. 403)
71. Boxted, Holy Trinity, monument to Sir John Poley †1638, attributed to William Stanton, *c.* 1680, and wife Abigail †1652, 1725 (p. 104)
72. Hawstead, All Saints, monument to Sir Thomas Cullum †1664, by Diacinto Cawcy, 1675 (p. 298)

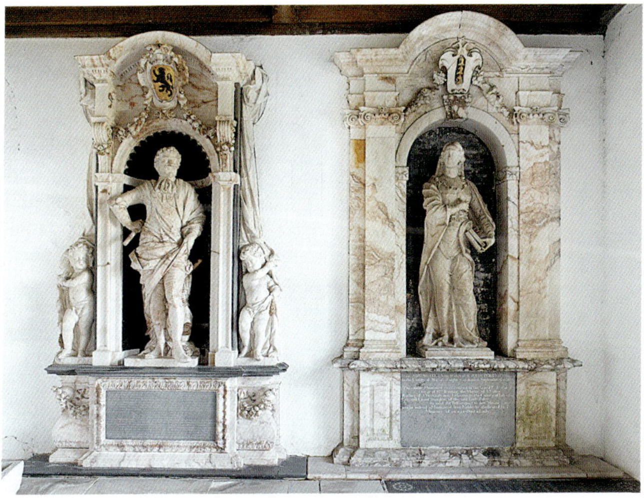

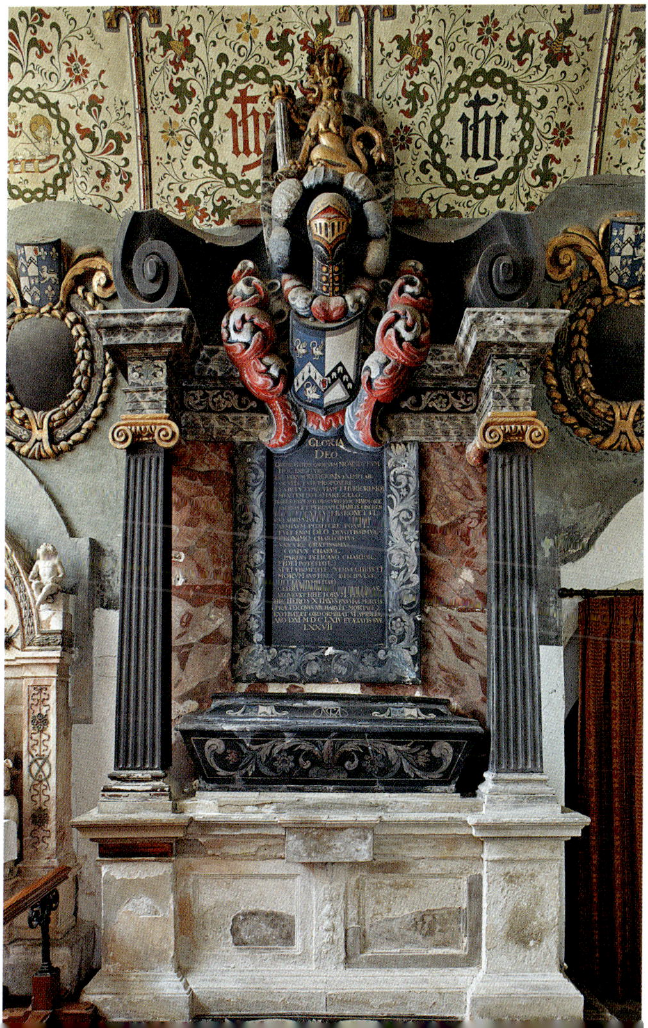

73. Redgrave, St Mary the Virgin, monument to Sir John Holt †1710, by Thomas Green of Camberwell (p. 466)
74. Acton, All Saints, monument to Robert Jennens †1725/6, attributed to Henry Scheemakers and Henry Cheere (p. 75)
75. Bury St Edmunds, Unitarian meeting house, 1711 (p. 142)
76. Hawstead Place, painted closet (detail), early C17, moved to Hardwick House *c.* 1612, now in Christchurch Mansion, Ipswich (p. 173)

73	75
74	76

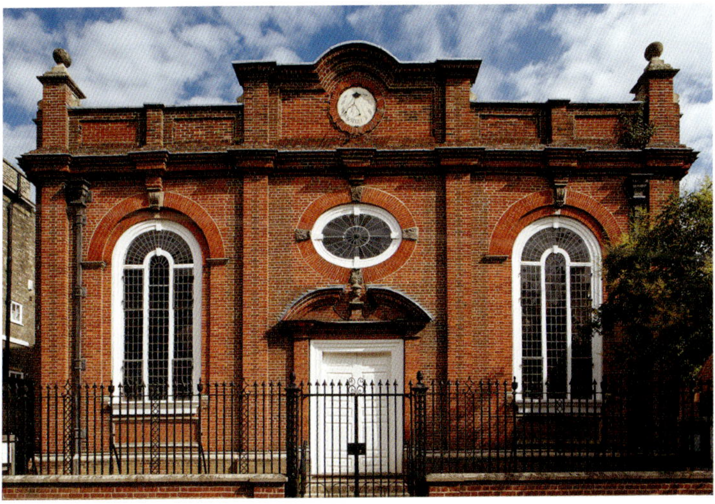

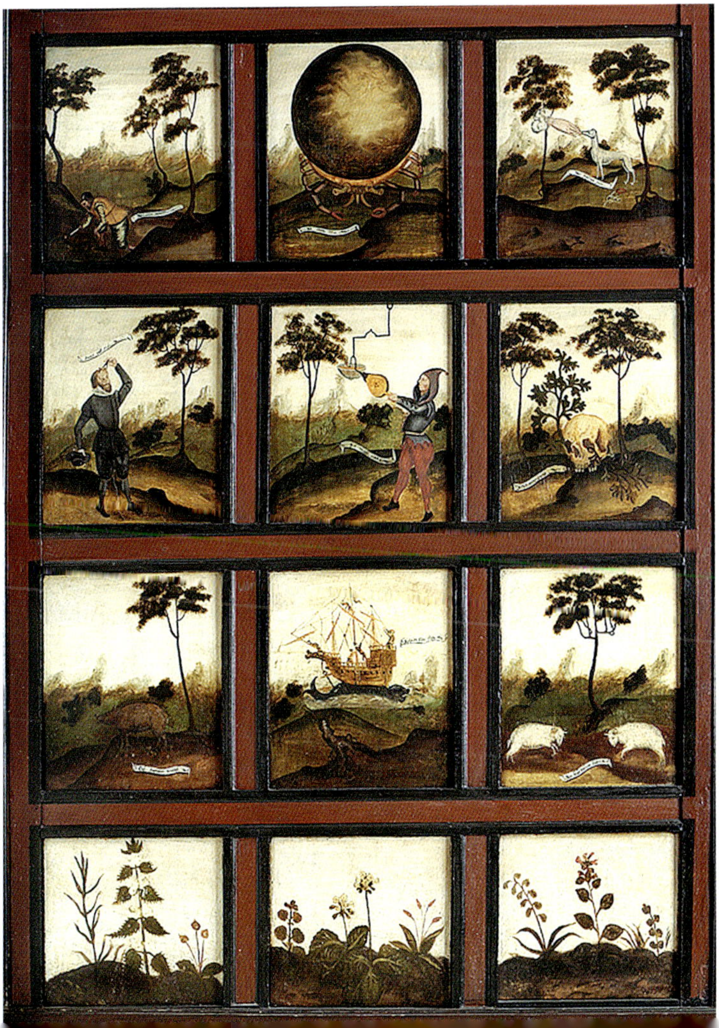

77. Gipping, Chapel of St Nicholas, interior, *c.* 1743 (p. 248)
78. Cowlinge, St Margaret, monument to Francis Dickins †1747, by Peter Scheemakers (p. 206)
79. Shelland, King Charles the Martyr, refitted 1767 (p. 480)

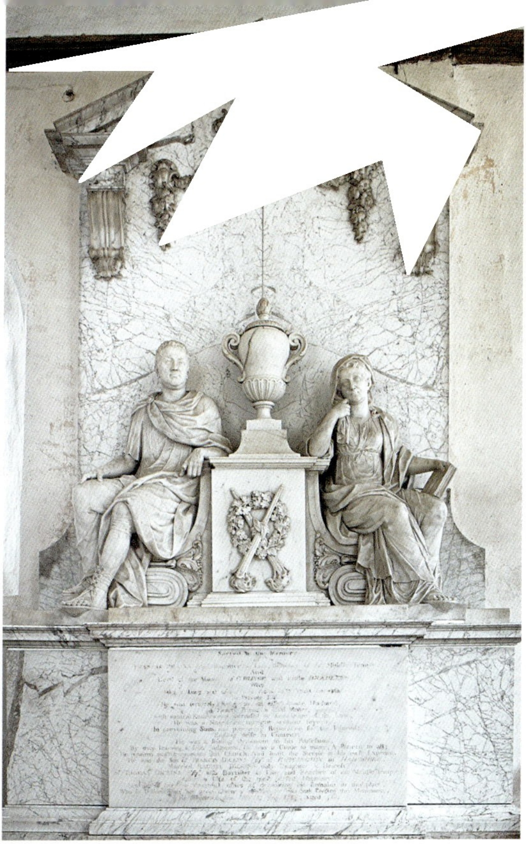

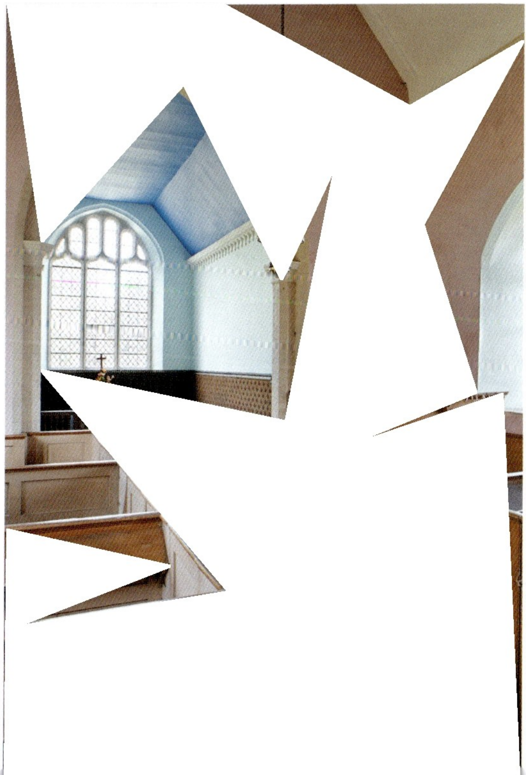

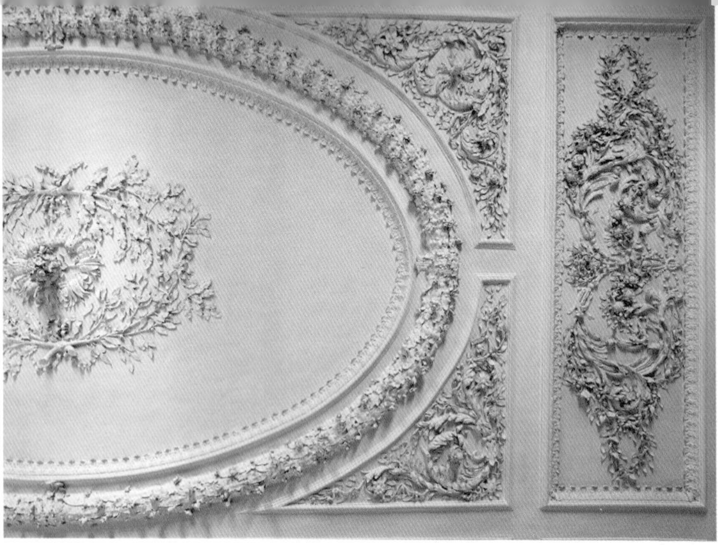

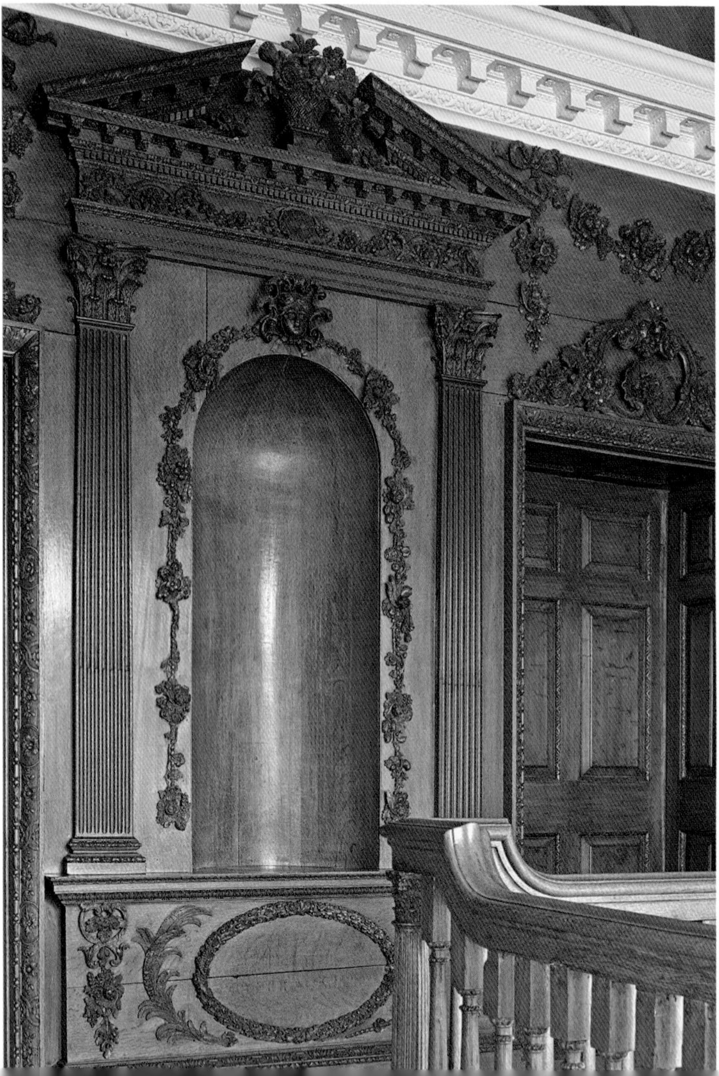

80. Hintlesham Hall, ceiling, *c.* 1686 (p. 315)
81. Norton, Little Haugh Hall, interior remodelled between *c.* 1715 and 1745 (p. 444)
82. Euston Hall, The Temple, by William Kent, 1746 (p. 231)
83. Stoke-by-Nayland, Tendring Hall, The Temple, attributed to Sir Robert Taylor, mid-C18 (p. 500)

80	82
81	83

84. Yaxley Hall, C16 and (l.) 1772 (p. 575)
85. Ickworth, summerhouse, attributed to William Talman, *c.* 1702, and St Mary, w tower, 1778 (p. 331)
86. Ickworth House, Rotunda, by Mario Asprucci, Francis Sandys, and Rev. Joseph Sandys, *c.* 1794–1803 (p. 328)
87. Ickworth House, entrance hall, by John Field, 1820s, and A.C. Blomfield, 1909–11, with 'The Fury of Athamas' by John Flaxman, 1790 (p. 329)

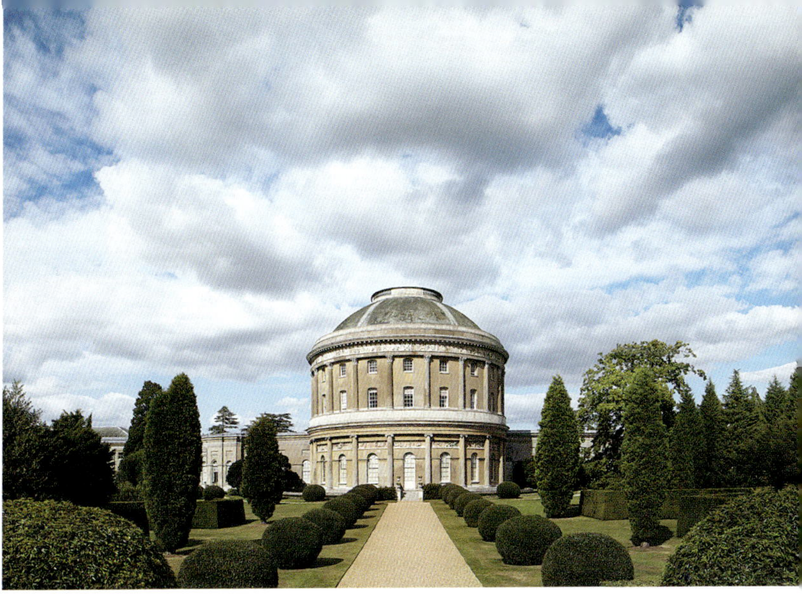

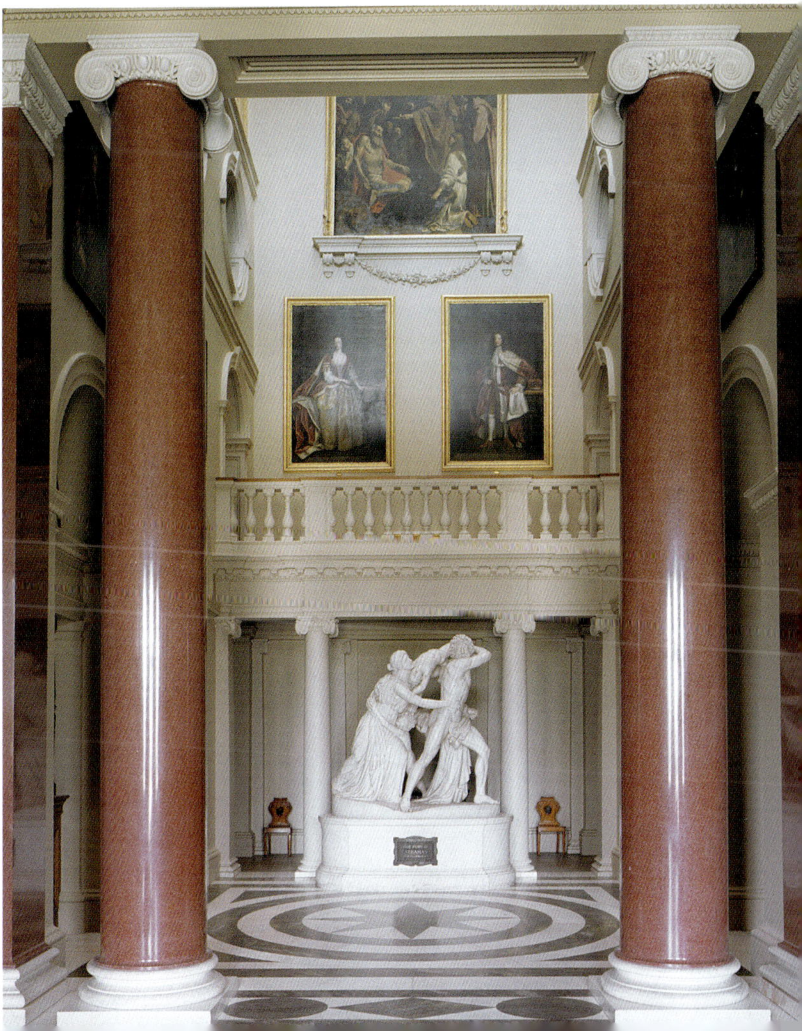

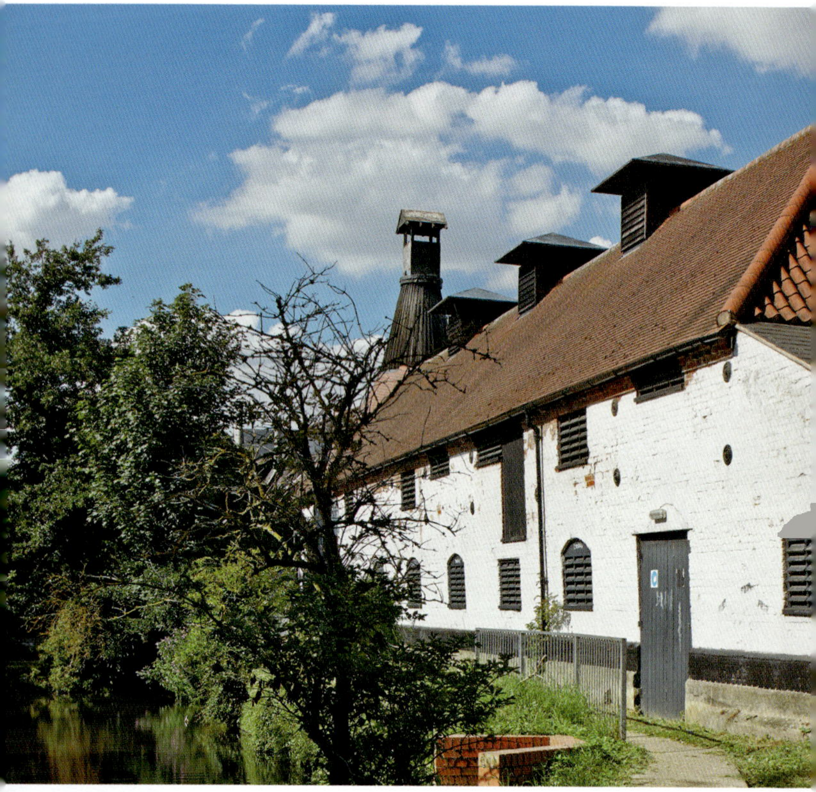

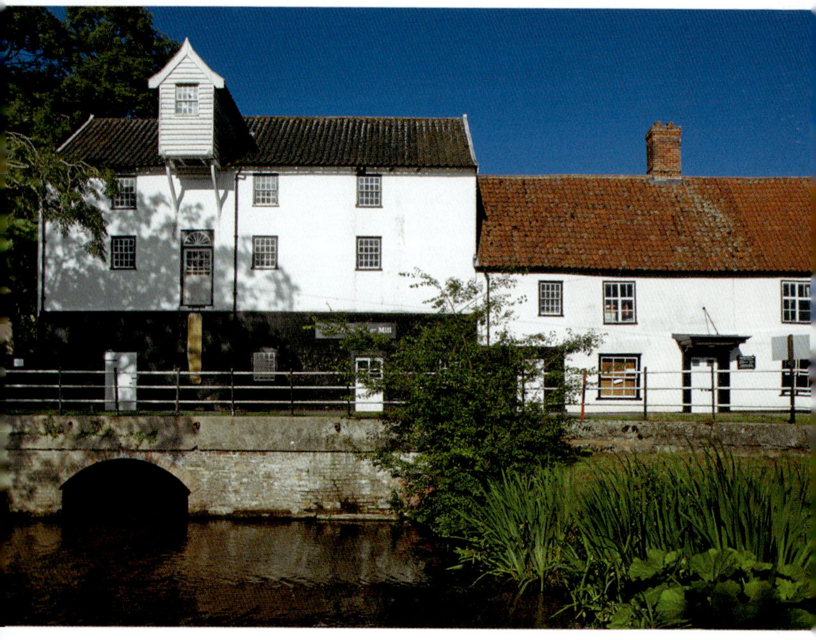

88. Stowmarket, Ipswich & Stowmarket Navigation, 1793, and maltings (p. 508)
89. Pakenham, watermill, rebuilt 1814 (p. 453)
90. Culford Hall, cast-iron bridge by Samuel Wyatt, 1804 (p. 210)
91. Bury St Edmunds, Theatre Royal, by William Wilkins, 1819, restored by Levitt Bernstein Associates, 2005–7 (p. 146)

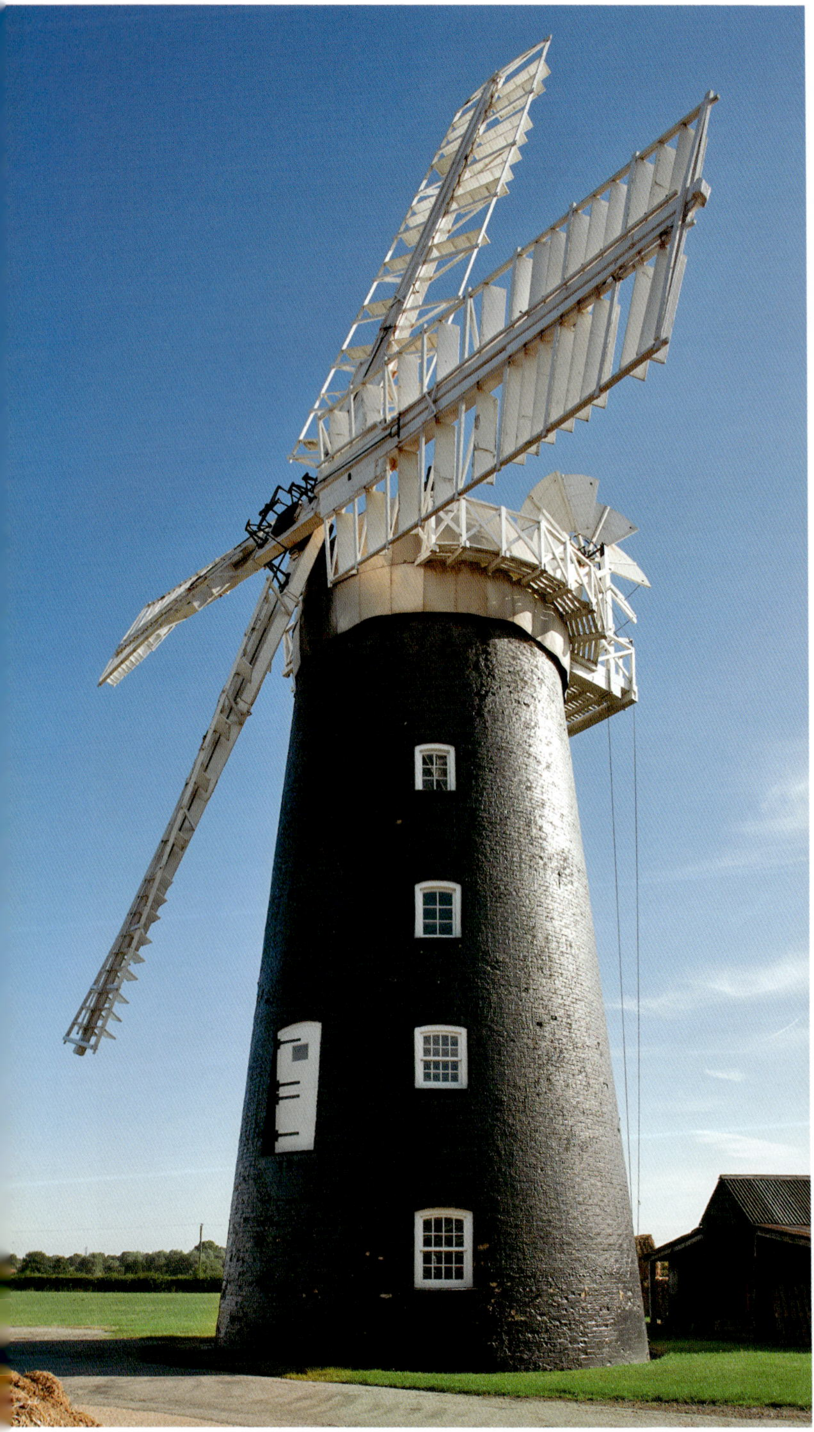

92. Pakenham, windmill, 1830 (p. 453)
93. Thurston, railway station, by F. Barnes, 1846–7 (p. 539)
94. Stowmarket, Museum of East Anglian Life, Robert Boby Building, c. 1877, rebuilt by James Blackie, 1984–5 (p. 511)

SACRED TO THE MEMORY OF
THE RIGHT HON^{BLE} JOHN HENNIKER MAJOR, LORD HENNIKER,
BARON HENNIKER, OF STRATFORD-UPON-SLANEY IN THE COUNTY OF WICKLOW, IN THE KINGDOM OF IRELAND, AND BARONET:

95. Thornham Magna, St Mary, monument to John Henniker Major, 2nd Baron Henniker, †1821 and wife Emily †1819, by J.J.P. Kendrick (p. 533)
96. Rushbrooke, St Nicholas, furnishings by Col. Robert Rushbrooke, 1820s (p. 475)
97. Higham, St Stephen, by G.G. Scott, 1858-61, tower completed by J.D. Wyatt, 1870 (p. 310)

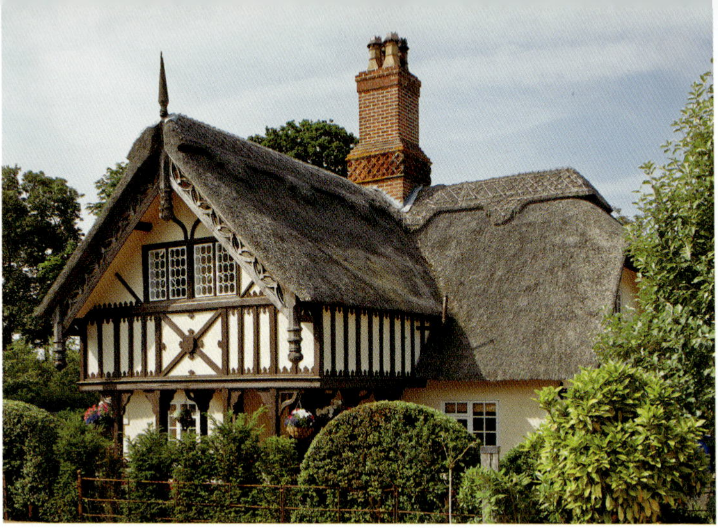
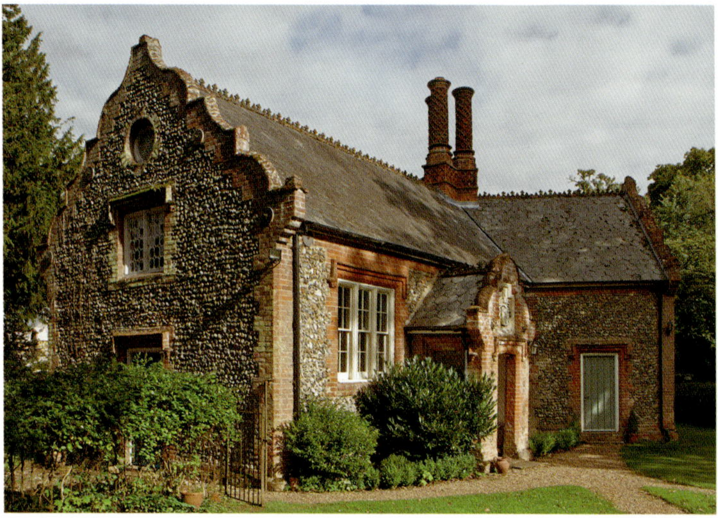
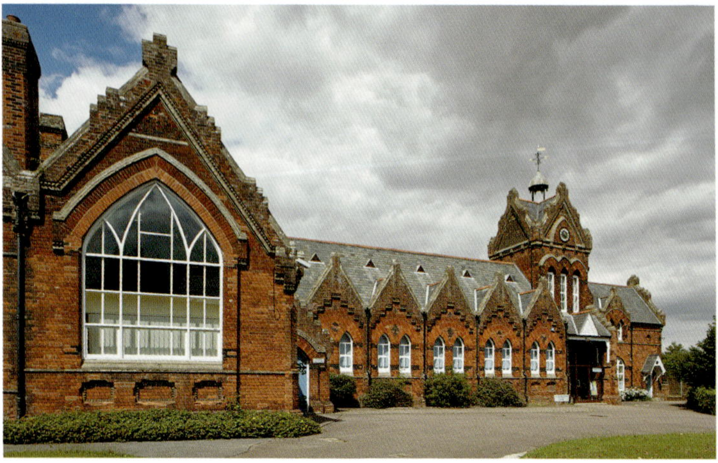

98. Bury St Edmunds, Hardwick House, Dairy Cottage, c. 1840 (p. 174)
99. Hawstead, former school, 1845 (p. 299)
100. Glemsford, Board School, by Salter & Firmin, 1872 (p. 251)
101. Great Finborough, St Andrew, by R.M. Phipson, 1874–7 (p. 260)

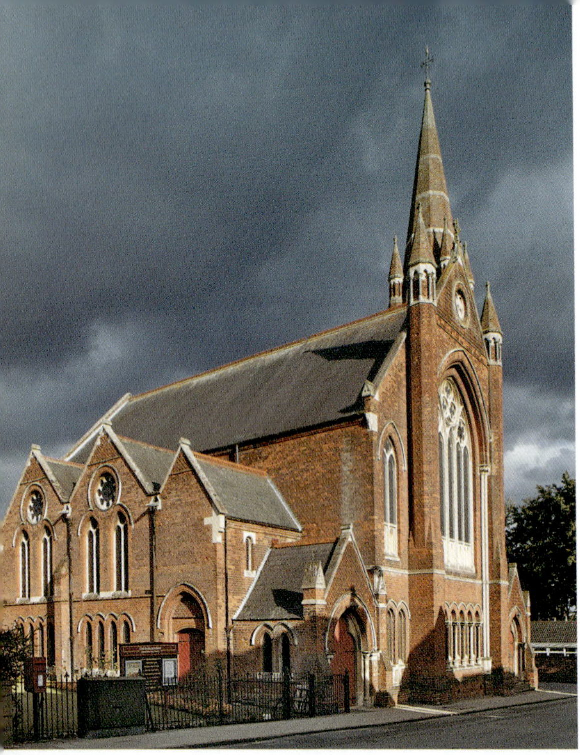

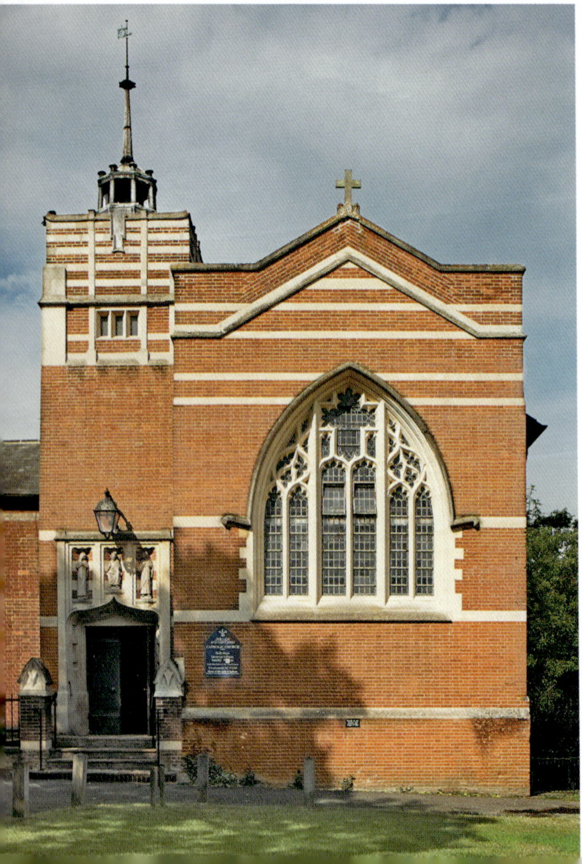

102. Haverhill, Old Independent Church, by Charles Bell, 1884–5 (p. 290)
103. Sudbury, Our Lady and St John (R.C.), by Leonard Stokes, 1893 (p. 520)
104. Newmarket, St Agnes, by R.H. Carpenter, 1886 (p. 430)

105. Exning, Harraton Court, racing yard, probably by Heaton & Gibb, 1880s (p. 234)
106. Culford Hall, N front, by William Young, 1894–6 (p. 210)

107. Elveden, estate village, *c.* 1893–1903 (p. 227)
108. Elveden, St Andrew and St Patrick, chancel by W.D. Caröe, 1904–6, cloister and tower 1919–22 (p. 225)

109. Newmarket, Jockey Club Rooms, 1752, remodelled by A.E. Richardson (Richardson & Gill), 1933–6 (p. 435)
110. Rushbrooke, The Hamlet, by Llewelyn-Davies & Weeks, 1956–9 and 1960–3 (p. 476)

111. Haverhill, Clements Estate, prefabricated 'Anglia' houses, developed by the London County Council with Anglia Housing Ltd, 1964 (p. 294)
112. Wissington, Maltings Chase, by Edward Cullinan with Julyan Wickham, 1969–71 (p. 564)

113. Higham, Ketelfield, by Aldington & Craig, 1974–6 (p. 312)
114. Newmarket, Rowley Mile Course, Millennium Grandstand, by The Goddard Wybor Practice, 1998–2000 (p. 440)

115. Bury St Edmunds, St Edmundsbury Cathedral, crossing tower, begun by S. E. Dykes Bower, 1963–70, completed by the Gothic Design Practice (Hugh Mathew and Warwick Pethers), 1999–2005 (p. 135)

116. Wickhambrook, Wakelins, C16, extended by James Gorst Architects, 2002–3 (p. 559)
117. Bury St Edmunds, ARC shopping centre, by Hopkins Architects, 2007–9 (p. 165)

evidence for what he actually did; it cannot have amounted to much, as he was paid only the relatively small sum of £561. The 1st Marquess was responsible for the planting of most of the woodland belts that surround the park and now define its horizons: stones commemorate the planting of e.g. Adkin's Wood from 1800 to 1812, Downter's Wood in 1804, Fontainebleau Grove in 1845. The most conspicuous structure is the MONUMENT to the Earl-Bishop, erected in 1817 by the inhabitants of Derry, 'grateful for benefits which they can never forget'. Stone obelisk, about 50 ft (15 metres) tall. By *John de Carle*. It stands on high ground 1 m. SW of Ickworth House. WHITE HOUSE, ⅔ m. W, and MORDABOYS COTTAGE, just over 1 m. NNW, both seem to be early to mid-C19, thatched and with ornamental bargeboards. Deliberately picturesque, although less so than the ROUND HOUSE, ¾ m. S of Ickworth House. Plastered and painted brick of *c*. 1850, a gamekeeper's cottage but perhaps originally a shooting lodge. Beneath the eaves of the conical slate roof a band of half-timbering. Picturesque LODGE at the main entrance to the park (at Horringer), with arched windows and entrance. Heavy cast-iron railings and gates. Stone piers with crocketed Gothick finials. All *c*. 1820–30.

ICE HOUSE, about ¾ m. NNW of Ickworth House. Red brick, with domed interior. It was in use by 1806.

INGHAM

ST BARTHOLOMEW. W tower, with diagonal buttresses, battlements and a little flushwork at the base. Money was left for its construction in 1443, 1456 (when it would appear that work had still not started) and 1467. Exceedingly tall, narrow chancel arch on two head corbels. The rest very thoroughly restored for Rev. E. R. Benyon in 1861, perhaps by *W. G. Habershon* (*see* below, and cf. Culford). Five-light Perp E window. The chancel roof, on angel corbels, incorporates C16 carved spandrels. Small N extension, 1989. – FONT. Norman, square, on a round base that curls up round the bowl like a waterleaf capital. – STAINED GLASS. Some C15 fragments in the rebuilt (1861) S porch. – MONUMENTS. Edward and Anna Leedes †1707. With scrolled pediment and skulls-and-crossbones. – Rev. Robert Lowe †1727. With Doric pilasters and pediment.

OLD RECTORY, S of the church. Mostly of 1848, by *W. G. & E. Habershon*. White brick, Georgian in character, with porch on square columns.

The village was part of the Culford Hall estate (*see* p. 209) and includes a number of buildings erected by its owners, including the former SCHOOL, N of the church, built by E. R. Benyon in 1846. A cheerful sight, in flint with white brick dressings. Some remaining diamond window panes. On the W side of the road, plain white-brick ALMSHOUSES, 1867, and the former READING ROOM, 1899, in Lord Cadogan's house style, red brick with half-timbered gable. Estate cottages, e.g. HILLCREST, opposite the rectory, brick and flint (for Benyon), and a red brick pair of 1892 (for Cadogan).

THE PARSONAGE (Culford Heath), Seven Hills, 2¼ m. NNE. See p. 211.

IXWORTH

Ixworth lies on the Roman road that joined Long Melford and Knettishall, which accounts for its long, straight, broad High Street – now happily bypassed. The church lies towards the S end, set back on the W side.

ST MARY. Big W tower. Its construction is well documented. As well as bequests, 1471–84, there are inscriptions on (or formerly on) the tower itself. On the SE buttress is a stone panel with the inscription 'Mast Robert Schot Abot', who was abbot of Bury from 1469 or 1470 to 1474. Also three tiles, now preserved inside the base of the tower. One records Thomas Vyal's bequest of 6 marks (£4) in 1472. The other two name William Densy, prior of Ixworth 1467–84, one dated 1472. In addition, money was left for the nave in 1456, for the chancel in 1458, and for leading the roofs in 1533. The tower has a flushwork frieze at the base (including the *Aldryche* device) and also at the top. Flushwork-panelled battlements. On the NE buttress a panel with mason's tools (cf. Badwell Ash). S porch with flushwork panelling on the front and battlements. Dec W windows in the aisles, Dec doorway in the S aisle. Dec also the chancel, but much rebuilt. Restoration by *J. H. Hakewill*, 1855–6, including re-seating, and extension of the N aisle to the E. Base of tower reordered as meeting room etc. by the *Whitworth Co-Partnership*, 1980. – SCREEN. Only the dado remains. Money was left for painting the rood beam in 1490 and 1496. – STAINED GLASS. E window 1854, probably by *M. & A. O'Connor*. Chancel S by *Lavers & Barraud*, c. 1867. A second window by them, designed by *Westlake*, is now in Ipswich Museum; it was replaced with glass by *Hugh B. Powell*, 1966. – MONUMENT. Richard Codington †1567 and wife Elizabeth †1571. Tomb-chest with decorated pilasters and three shields. At the back a round arch with exceptionally fine Italian leaf carving. Against the back wall brass effigies, brass shields, and inscription plate. This records that Codington was granted the manor of Ixworth by Henry VIII in exchange for Codington in Surrey, where Henry then built Nonsuch Palace.

IXWORTH ABBEY. A priory of Augustinian canons was founded at Ixworth in 1170. The Norman church was cruciform and about 224 ft (68 metres) long with an aisled chancel. The chancel was extended in the C13 and a N aisle added to the nave in the C14. There was probably a W tower. The priory was dissolved in 1537 and granted to Richard Codington; the stone from the church was bought by Sir Nicholas Bacon for use at Redgrave, and the lead by Sir Thomas Kytson for Hengrave. The Codingtons adapted parts of the monastic buildings for a house, which was remodelled and extended in the last quarter of the C17 and in 1821. Foundations of the church and the bases of piers can be seen in the grass N of the house.

The entrance front faces N. It is of five bays and two storeys. White brick, painted. Two parallel ranges, each with a hipped roof. The W range is of 1821, but embedded within the E range is the dormitory range of the monastic buildings, fairly complete except for the chapter house which lay at its N end. The ground floor, which is a few feet lower than ground level, contains the undercroft. This has fine C13 vaulting, and arched windows in the E wall with Gothick glazing. At the N end is the slype, rib-vaulted in three bays. Next is a room of four double bays with three octagonal piers and single-chamfered arches. Finally, at the S end, a room of two double bays with much finer rib mouldings (now a kitchen). The date of this seems to be *c.* 1230. Above, on the first floor at the S end, a room with fine C16–C17 panelling (reused) and a C16 fireplace. In its E wall an original stone lancet, now internal, with remains of simulated stone jointing on the plaster. This now opens into the first-floor chamber of the prior's lodging, a two-storey timber-framed addition of the late C15, faced in red brick, E of and parallel to the dormitory range. On the ground floor a hall with moulded beams that connects to the present kitchen. N of the prior's lodging was perhaps the reredorter, but is now a late C17 wing, extending E from the middle of the dormitory range and lower than it, comprising entrance hall and parlour. Over-sized front door and similarly grandiose internal archway to the undercroft, with rusticated architrave, garlands and open segmental pediment.* Staircase with turned balusters, two to a tread. Ground-floor room with good panelling, including Composite pilasters flanking the fireplace. Of the remaining monastic buildings, there is no trace of the W range; of the S (refectory) range there survives only some walling at the E end with evidence of the pulpit. This walling and other stonework is partly visible externally, and is partly preserved behind panelling in various of the 1821 rooms.

S of the house an early C19 LODGE. White brick, originally single-storey. Ground-floor sash windows with Gothick glazing. 600 yds N, on Thetford Road, THE ROUND HOUSE, also a lodge, timber-framed and plastered with Gothick windows.

---

*Roger White suggests the archway might have been imported from somewhere grander, e.g. Euston Hall.

Conical thatched roof with deep eaves on posts forming a veranda. Restored and extended by *Charles Morris*, 1988–9.

The HIGH STREET is entirely unspoilt and nicely varied. On the N side of the entrance to the churchyard the OLD VICARAGE, 1838 by *Henry Fisk* of Ixworth. White brick, with flint side walls. Two storeys and three bays with round-arched doorway. Further N, on the opposite side, THE PYKKERELL pub has in the yard behind a good late C16 stable block. Two storeys. Red brick ground floor and jettied first floor with exposed timbers and brick-nogging. Crowstepped gable-ends. On the same side, the METHODIST CHURCH by *William Eade*, 1888, making little effort to harmonize with its surroundings: red brick with white-brick dressings, gabled front with three stepped lancets within an arch and arched entrances l. and r. Opposite, Nos. 29–31 are early C19, white brick, with a central bow on the upper storey above an arch. The disused 1930s petrol pumps add to its charm. Back on the E side, No. 48 has an C18 doorcase with segmental pediment. Another, of different design, at THE BEECHES (No. 39), mostly early C19. On the E side again No. 70, with long-wall jetty and pargetting, and No. 72, C16, jettied to the front. Across Crown Lane, CROWN HOUSE, C16 and C17, is jettied down its long side. At the top of the High Street on the W side HILL HOUSE, *c.* 1840. Flint, with white-brick front of three bays and two storeys. Cast-iron lintels.

S of the church, on the E side of the High Street a good row of timber-framed houses: Nos. 20–22 with jettied front, No. 14 with exposed timbers on the first floor and a single red brick shaped gable at the S end, and No. 10, dating back to the late C14, with remains of ornamental ridge tiles. On the W side ROBERT PEEL HOUSE, built as the Police Station, 1878. Tudor-Gothic. White brick (now rendered) with red brick dressings. Then HOLMLEA, C16 with long-wall jetty and little early C19 bow window. The High Street continues round to the r. at this point; on the S side CYDER HOUSE, the main part cased in early C19 white brick, but an early C16 wing still with exposed timbers and jettied front. Brick fireplace with trefoiled arcade. On the other side of the street, one of the lodges to Ixworth Abbey (*see above*).

STOW ROAD branches off the l. at the bottom of the main part of the High Street. On its S side DOVER HOUSE, a C15 Wealden-type house, i.e. with jettied ends and recessed centre under a continuous roof. Pargetted front. Good interior, the original layout largely preserved. Inserted floor in hall, C16 with carving on main beam. Fireplace lintels in hall and parlour with running-leaf designs; brick arcading over the hall fireplace. Crown-post roof. 200 yds further E, on the N side, four pairs of semi-detached COUNCIL HOUSES by *Frank Whitmore*, 1892–4, for Thingoe Rural District Council, following the Housing of the Working Classes Act of 1890. They may be the earliest surviving examples of rural council housing. Red brick with slate roofs, as plain as one would expect.

WATERMILL, ½ m. NNW. Timber-framed and weatherboarded. Three storeys, with lucam at one end. Intact machinery with a timber carved 'I. [John] Lowe 1800'. Attached MILL HOUSE, timber-framed and plastered, dating back to the early C17.

IXWORTH THORPE

ALL SAINTS. Outside the village; small and thatched. Weatherboarded bell-turret on a base of red brick and reused stone. Good brick s porch with stepped gable, and battlements decorated with motifs in flint and brick. Entrance with flint and brick voussoirs. Angle buttresses with crocketed finials. Norman N and S doorways, very plain, the N doorway blocked. Chancel with lancets. Springing of Norman chancel arch on N wall. In the nave some Dec windows. Early C19 E window with wooden tracery. – PULPIT. Jacobean. – COMMUNION RAIL. Three-sided, with late C17 turned balusters. – BENCHES. Reused ends with poppyheads, the arms with animals and figures, a fine set including a mermaid, a unicorn, a thatcher with his comb, and a woman walking a dog. – MONUMENTS. Two erected by Charles Crofts (cf. Bardwell): to his father, Thomas Crofts †1617, and his brother John †1644. Thomas's with inscription set in an arch, arms in another arch above that, on top a small (now headless) naked female figure, one foot on a skull. Little cherubs' heads with winning smiles. John's tablet is called in the inscription 'Marmoriolum hoc'. – John Lamb †1798 of Golden Square, London. Beautifully lettered ledger stone. – E of the church, two identical chest tombs to Thomas Cooke †1822 and family. Columns at each corner. By *de Carle*, ordered 1824.

KEDINGTON

ST PETER AND ST PAUL. There is evidence, not all of it reliable, of a building of great antiquity. Beneath the floor of the nave is Roman building material, discovered in 1933 and thought to be original foundations; but it seems more likely to be reused from a nearby site. The walls contain reused Roman brick and on the S side a section of paving or *opus signinum* can be seen. In the C19 the head and upper shaft of an Anglo-Saxon stone CROSS was dug up in the church (now above the main altar). It is carved with a relief of the Crucifixion and is probably mid-C10. Stone from a Norman church was reused at the base of the tower, and the chancel arch, although late C13, has imposts with a simple, Norman-looking moulding. Late C13 the nave and chancel (see the uncusped and cusped Y-tracery), and a Dec N aisle (W window) and W tower. On the SW diagonal buttress a niche and inscription (no longer legible), 'Dame Amicia', wife of John de Novo Mercato, who built the tower *c.* 1300. Remains of flushwork. The chancel windows are shafted inside. The E window is of course a Perp insertion. The PISCINA (behind C18 panelling) has the weirdest shape – a steep pointed arch cusped by three steep pointed trefoils. Low arcades between nave and aisles. The piers have a big polygonal shaft without capitals to the nave and aisles, as in many other Suffolk churches, but the polygonal shafts to the inside of the arches were painted in the C17 or C18 to simulate fluted columns. There is no clerestory. Yet the impression is not of darkness, for in 1857 skylights were inserted in the roof, completing a restoration begun in 1845. The roof is of false hammerbeam type, given by Lady Elisabeth Barnardiston †1526. Tower restored by *Detmar Blow*, 1920, nave and aisles by *William Weir*, 1930–1.

FURNISHINGS. A delightful diversity, especially in terms of seating, that seldom survived C19 reordering. – FONT. Octagonal, Perp, with quatrefoil decoration. – CHANCEL PANELLING. Probably early C18. – COMMUNION RAIL. Three-sided, with strongly moulded turned balusters; paid for by the bequest (£50) of Sir Samuel Barnardiston †1707. – CHANCEL SCREEN. Dated 1619. Simple, with scrolly ogee tops to the one-light divisions. The centre folds back like a folding door, a highly unusual arrangement. Hanging CRUCIFIX by *George Jack*, 1926. – PULPIT. Of about the same date as the screen. An uncommonly complete three-decker with tester and hour-glass stand. In front, a baluster-shaped WIG STAND. – BARNARDISTON PEW. Opposite the pulpit and again of similar date. It is made up of parts of a screen (probably a parclose screen) of *c.* 1430, with segmental arches and four-plus-four-light tracery over. Painted decoration restored by *Professor E. W. Tristram*, 1931. – BENCHES. Partly Late Perp, straight-headed with buttresses and linenfold panelling, partly C18. – BOX PEWS, of various dates, in the S aisle and more in the nave. – WEST GALLERY, projecting in a semicircle, and CHILDREN'S BENCHES, in rising tiers at the W ends of the two aisles. Both *c.* 1750. Space below the gallery sensitively enclosed by the *Whitworth Co-Partnership*, 2011. – COMMUNICANTS' STALLS. Three, of the late C18, and a rarity. Not *in situ*. – AUMBRY. In N aisle. By *Laurence King*, 1960, made by *Faith Craft*. – BIER. C17, with extending shafts. – COMMANDMENTS etc. Painted on zinc by *Maria E. Syer*, 1861. Originally on sanctuary E wall, now in N aisle; replaced by painted panels by *Tristram*, 1935. – HATCHMENTS. Ten, of the Barnardistons, 1669–1704. – STAINED GLASS. N aisle E †1948 by *J. E. Nuttgens*. Resurrection.

MONUMENTS. Mostly of the Barnardistons of Kedington Hall (dem. at the end of the C18). – Sir Thomas †1503 and Lady Elizabeth †1526 (S aisle, E end). Tomb-chest with shields in lozenges and quatrefoils. The effigies badly worn; he is in armour. Tablet with inscription at their feet. – Tomb-chest with four shields of arms (chancel, N wall). Probably Thomas †1542 and Ann †1560. – Sir Thomas †1619 and Elisabeth †1584 (s side of chancel arch). Big tomb-chest. Two recumbent effigies. Children kneeling small against the chest. Back wall with arms. – Grissel, daughter of Sir Thomas, †1609 (s aisle). Kneeling figure between columns. The inscription runs like this:

Loe heere the Image of Lyfe, new inspyr'd
Too wise: too choice: too olde in youthfull breath:
Too deare to Frendes, too much of men desier'd
Therefore bereaft us by untymely death:
While shee trod Earth, she rais'd her mynd farre Higher
Her Actions faire, unstayn'd of vice, or pride.
Truth was her loade starre, heav'ne was her desier
Christ was her hope & in his Fayth shee dyde.

– Sir Thomas †1610 (son of Sir Thomas †1619) and his two wives, Mary †1594 and Katherine †1632 (s aisle). He recumbent, they kneeling and facing each other. Big superstructure, not refined. In the base a low segment-headed arch in the middle into which a coffin is just being pushed, as if it were a baking oven. On the wall above, his HELMET and gauntlets. – His son Sir Nathaniel †1653 and wife Jane †1669 (N aisle). In an oblong recess with garlands l. and r., two frontal demi-figures, both pensively resting their heads on a hand, her elbow on a pillow, his on his helmet; their other hands joined, resting on a skull. Attributed to *Thomas Stayner*, c. 1690 (GF). – Thomas †1681 (N of chancel arch). Large tablet with cartouche and cherubs' heads. – Thomas †1704 (chancel N wall). Similar to the last, with urns. – Sir Samuel Barnardiston †1707. Inscription (recording his bequest to the church) between terms, with strapwork cresting and obelisks. – Sir Thomas †1698, erected 1724 (N aisle). Without effigy, but with two standing putti holding a skull and a torch outside the pilasters which frame the inscription. – Sophia, Viscountess Wimbaldon [*sic*], †1691 (s aisle) With weeping putti. – Sir Philip Skippon †1691 (N aisle). With urns, putti and cherubs' heads. – Rev. W. H. Syer †1868. By *M. W. Johnson*.

The welcoming and parting touch is the COBBLING of the s porch. Mid-C19 wrought-iron GATES to churchyard by *Ward & Silver* of Long Melford.

PRIMARY SCHOOL. By *West Suffolk County Architect's Dept* (job architects *Brian Grayling* and *Denis Hindson*), 1968–70. Grey brick with black stained window frames and fascias.

The church lies on the N side of the village. Below it, to the sw, an C18 WATERMILL, now a house. Red brick and weather-boarding with lucam. Next to it a nice thatched cottage with three gabled dormers. Further sw, in SCHOOL ROAD, the former NATIONAL SCHOOL by *R. Kent*, 1875–6. Polychromatic brickwork and distinctive chimneys set diagonally.

The centre of the village is 300 yds s of the church, a T-junction with, on its NE corner, PROSPECT TERRACE. 1871. Red brick with white- and black-brick dressings. Beyond it, SUFFOLK HOUSE, early C19 white brick with doorway in arched recess.

KETTON HOUSE, ¾ m. SSE. Built as the parsonage, and described as 'new brick built' in 1723. Red brick with black headers. Segment-headed windows. Two storeys and attics. N and s fronts each with six windows, and a plain doorway squeezed into the middle. Fine staircase with twisted balusters and Rococo plastered ceiling. COACH HOUSE and BARN, both dated 1766, converted to separate houses *c.* 1979.

The former RISBRIDGE UNION WORKHOUSE by *J. F. Clark*, 1855–6, was dem. 1997. It stood 300 yds w of the church.

KENTFORD

ST MARY. All Dec, apart from the brick top of the tower. Much renewed. A brief was issued in 1715 for repairs costing over £1,000 following a fire, and the chancel was restored in 1877. The most individual motif is the rose window of the tower, with a five-petalled rose in a circle. Dec also the chancel doorway and the E window (reticulated tracery). Early C15 s porch with crowstepped gable. – BOX PEWS. C18. – WALL PAINTINGS. Late C14, not easily seen. A badly damaged St Christopher and, better preserved and quite impressive with its big figures, the Legend of the Three Living and the Three Dead. No longer visible are the Seven Deadly Sins and the Seven Works of Mercy (cf. Dalham). – STAINED GLASS. E window by *Burlison & Grylls*, 1919. The centre light is a memorial to Lt H. O. Lord †1916, shown in armour kneeling before Christ on the Cross. Other chancel windows with unusual glass of 1877.

LANWADES PARK. *See* Moulton.

KERSEY

Kersey is the most picturesque village of s Suffolk. The view from the church over the tiled roofs of the houses dipping down to the ford of the River Brett and climbing up the other side is not easily forgotten, and is more characteristic of counties hillier than Suffolk. The church and the priory stand on the high ground at the s and N ends respectively of the village, which is just one long street with a little extension (The Green) by the stream.

ST MARY. Dates are recorded for the completion of the N aisle (1335) and the W tower (1481). Both fit the stylistic evidence.

The N aisle is Dec – see the windows under their almost straight-sided arches and the four-petal motif in the tracery, and the fine, broad, ogee-headed niche between two of them inside. Niches also flank the aisle's E window. Lying between the aisle and chancel are the SEDILIA and PISCINA of the aisle, one straight-headed composition with open-headed vaulted niches. The arch over the first of the sedilia seems to have been cut off, and its vault has miniature ribs. The backs of the three sedilia niches are open in windows to the chancel, surely not an original motif. The N arcade is also of the same period. The piers are octagonal, the arches have one chamfer and one double-wave moulding. Hoodmoulds to nave and aisle with pretty fleurons and leaf trails. Finally the aisle roof resting on an elaborate stone wall-plate, unfortunately ill-preserved. It clearly tells a long story, but what story has not yet been recognized by any student. The roof of the E chapel is ceiled with four big Elizabethan or Jacobean stucco panels. In spite of all these contributions of the early or mid C14, the effect of the church is Perp, thanks to the big W tower, the porches and most of the windows. A start had been made on the tower at the same time as the N aisle, and work resumed c. 1430. It has diagonal buttresses with four set-offs. On them long flushwork panels. Battlements with flushwork tracery. Big W doorway. Three-light W window with transom, flanked by flushwork panels. Also niches l. and r. Bell-openings of two lights with transom. S windows Perp. S porch of two bays with flushwork and pinnacles. Ceiling inside the S porch with sixteen very delicately traceried panels. N porch similar but a little simpler. Remains of wall-plate similar to that in the N aisle. Perp clerestory with just two windows on the S side, the roof with long arched braces meeting at the collar-beam, alternating with hammerbeams. Eastern bay decorated as canopy of honour over the rood. Chancel and N vestry rebuilt 1861–2 by *G. E. Pritchett*, with Dec windows harmonizing with the N aisle's. Restoration of nave and tower by *H. J. Wadling* (*St Aubyn & Wadling*), 1887–9, including removal of W gallery and window repairs.

FURNISHINGS. FONT. Perp, octagonal. Stout stem with quatrefoils. Bowl with four demi-figures of angels. – SCREEN. Dado of former rood screen, now in N chapel. The mouldings and tracery show it was by the workshop of *Thomas Gooch* of Sudbury, i.e. of the last quarter of the C15 (money had been left for painting the rood beam in 1463). With six painted figures, not of high quality. – LECTERN. Wooden shaft with thin buttresses and flying buttresses. C15. The eagle book-desk later, perhaps C16. – WEST DOOR with tracery and a trail border. – SCULPTURE. Fragments of an alabaster altar, e.g. Trinity. Also good bearded heads probably from a reredos (cf. St Cuthbert, Wells, Somerset). From the same perhaps the seated figure of St Anne. – WALL PAINTING. St George and the Dragon, high up on the S wall. – MONUMENTS. A nice group of C18 Thorrowgood monuments in N aisle.

– Marianne Jones †1831. By *J. Milligan*. With simple classical ornament.

PRIORY. Founded *c.* 1218 as a hospital but soon converted to an Augustinian priory. It was granted to King's College Cambridge in 1447. All that remains of the CHURCH is one major fragment, the S chancel chapel. Flint. Two arches to the chancel. Piers with moulded capitals. E wall of transept with lower arch into this chapel and a tall E window, now blocked. The chapel was widened later and received big Perp windows to S and E, of which the surrounds survive. The S windows are segment-headed. The church, which was 156 ft (47.5 metres) long, had a N chancel chapel as well as a N transept, and a crossing tower, nave and S aisle. The cloister stood on the N side. On the W side was the original hospital building, later the prior's house, the timber frame of which survives within the present house. The HALL of *c.* 1300 is divided from an aisle by a single pillar, and the roof truss is of magnificent proportions. Another medieval survival is the square KITCHEN. Originally free-standing, it is now joined to the house, which has a seven-bay white-brick front and Tuscan porch of the C18 or early C19.

VILLAGE. From the church down CHURCH HILL past LITTLE MANOR, a picturesque timber-framed house of the early C15. Two jettied cross-wings and exposed timbers. Some original doorways. Off the hill on this side THE GREEN, with a pretty group of timber-framed and thatched houses. GREENAN, AILSA COTTAGE and GREEN GABLES comprise three C14 cross-wings surviving from former hall houses, together with a house of *c.* 1500. OLDE DRIFT HOUSE has the rare feature of a double timber-framed chimney, between the medieval house and its late C16 extension. Tucked away is the VILLAGE HALL by *George Capon*, 1935. Mostly rendered; old oak timbers reused for the entrance, with brick-nogging. At the bottom of Church Hill RIVER HOUSE, with its surprising Early Elizabethan brick porch. This has angle pilasters with circular and semicircular panels *à la vénitienne*, a round-headed doorway with broad pediment, and a semicircular top with pinnacles l. and r. The rest of the house timber-framed and plastered, *c.* 1500. The S wing, altered in the C18, originally extended further: the end wall, formerly internal, had paintings of figures in Elizabethan dress, no longer visible. Across the river, on the W side, KEDGES END, a large timber-framed house of half-H plan. C15, altered in the C17 (date of 1654 on lintel of doorway). Shallow two-storey bay as well as shallow oriels. Carved bargeboards on N gable. Inside, remains of a scheme of grey painted decoration, with large drop pendants. Then THE STREET runs steeply up with many handsome houses l. and r., e.g. THE BELL pub, late C14, much restored, and Nos. 1–6, an unbroken but varied range with N-facing jetty at one end, a jettied cross-wing halfway along and a jettied front at the top. The climax is the upper end of the street, ANCIENT HOUSES, with exposed timbers: first a house with jettied front, a bay on a red brick plinth below it at one end; then a house with two full-height gabled bays also on deep brick plinths. C15 and C16. BOUTTLES, opposite, is a Wealden-type house that has lost its parlour wing at the N end, leaving just the recessed hall and service wing. A cluster of nice houses at the top where the road bends.

KERSEY MILL, ¾ m. ENE. Large four-storey timber-framed and weatherboarded watermill with lucam; *c.* 1810, replacing an earlier mill. Machinery intact, including three sets of stones and three further sets in a rear addition of *c.* 1880 that were powered by steam. Fine waterwheel by *Whitmore & Binyon* in an attached two-storey wheelhouse. Timber-framed house, probably C17, with an early C18 red brick front. Range of maltings to w, 1852, including conical kiln.

KETTLEBASTON

ST MARY. Norman nave – see one blocked N window, uncovered in 1930. The splays are decorated with three red trails with buds or knobs at the end, familiar from Norman illustration. Transitional s doorway, probably very late C12. The shafts and scalloped capitals are purely Norman, but the arch is decidedly pointed. No chevron; flat row of small triangles instead. Dec chancel and W tower – see the bell-openings, and in the chancel one s window. A document of 1364 records that the church was built anew in 1343. C18 red brick s porch. The reticulated E window is of 1902, but may be a correct replacement; the restoration of the chancel was by *Rev. E. Geldart*, the work overseen by *H. J. Wright*. Also Dec the PISCINA and SEDILIA. Their forms look in fact rather like *c.* 1300, whereas the preserved window has ogee arches, as has also a tomb recess in the N wall. Chancel roof of 1902 with little hammerbeams, but retaining a C17 cornice. – FONT. By the same workmen as the s doorway. Square. The decorative motifs are undisciplined: big chevrons not accurately placed, strips of triangles, etc. – HIGH ALTAR. 1950, by *Rev. Harold Butler*, rector 1929–64, who commissioned much of the decoration of the interior. York stone, made by *Saunders* of Ipswich. – REREDOS and ROOD SCREEN by *Geldart*, 1902, made by *Taylor & Clifton*, coloured by *Patrick Osborne*, 1948–9. Reredos pinnacles, openwork tracery, and figures of angels, Virgin and Child renewed by *Bryan Saunders* of Coggeshall, 1949. Rood figures added 1930. Painted figures of saints on dado of screen by *Enid Chadwick*, 1954. – SCULPTURE. Casts of mid-C14 alabaster panels, the originals discovered in 1864 and presented to the British Museum in 1883. One of them, the Coronation of Our Lady, was re-created in 1947 by *W. J. Drew*; colouring by *Chadwick*, renewed 2006 (in niche on SE buttress of chancel, with wrought-iron gate by *H. Willmington*, who also made the gate to the former rood stair, 1948, designed by *Comper*). – MONUMENT. Joan, Lady Jermy, 'whose arke after a passage of 87. yeres long through this deluge of teares upon ye 6. day of May ano. 1649: rested upon ye mount of joye'. With verses both on the tablet and on her ledger stone. Broken pediment and swag; restored and repainted by *Father Butler*, 1939–40.

KNETTISHALL

ALL SAINTS. Disused and decaying from the early C20; converted to a house, 1984–9. Inserted floor, with dormers in nave roof. Unbuttressed W tower of knapped flint, mentioned in wills of 1453 and 1458. Flushwork decoration of the battlements.*

HALL FARM, ½ m. WNW. The main range early C19, of white brick. Timber-framed parts of the C17. Behind the house a two-storey red brick STEAM MILL. Ten bays long with arched windows. Weatherboarded lucam in one of the gabled end walls.

BRIDGE, 1 m. WNW, over the Little Ouse. Decorative red brick and flint, with stone arch, coping and cutwaters. Probably late C19, perhaps connected with Riddlesworth Hall, Norfolk.

HUT HILL. Bronze Age round barrow on Knettishall Heath, W of the church. There is another barrow about ½ m. to its E in Brickkiln Covert. Also on the heath, about ⅓ m. WNW of Hut Hill, is a low mound surrounded by a circular bank that is probably a post-medieval rabbit warren enclosure.

LACKFORD

ST LAWRENCE. Over-restored in 1868–70. This included rebuilding the N aisle, which had been taken down perhaps in the C16, and adding a N vestry, both with rather minimum windows. Dec W tower with C16 brick battlements. C14 S porch, built mainly of freestone. Nave Norman (see the arch over the S doorway), and the thickening of the walls at its E end shows there was originally a central tower. The present simple S doorway Dec, and also a nave S window shafted inside. The N aisle arcade is original Dec, with its quatrefoil piers, or rather circular piers with four broad semicircular attachments, and its double-chamfered arches. At the E end of the aisle was a chapel, distinguished by leaf capitals which are also original.

---

*Fittings dispersed in 1933, mostly to neighbouring Riddlesworth (*see Buildings of England: Norfolk 2: North-West and South*); the C15 FONT to St Alban, Lakenham, Norwich (*see Buildings of England: Norfolk 1: Norwich and North-East*).

Handsome, large, shafted and gabled squint between the chapel and the chancel, incorporating a PISCINA. Short E.E. chancel, with arcades on both sides. On the S, simple PISCINA and SEDILIA with hoodmould carried over the S window. The pattern is echoed on the N side but with a tomb-recess Easter sepulchre. – FONT. Octagonal, late C13, with big stiff-leaf motifs, but also rose, ivy, etc. – BENCH ENDS. With poppyheads and traceried ends; made up into one long seat along the N aisle. – MONUMENTS. C13 coffin-lid. Coped, with three crosses *alisée patée*. – Rev. William Greaves †1806. Simple sarcophagus. By *de Carle*, Norwich, who presumably supplied the corresponding ledger stone. – STAINED GLASS. E window by *Powell & Sons* (designed by *Holiday*), 1871.

The church stands in the middle of fields E of the village. Rev. J. R. Holden, patron from 1863 and rector 1867–76, was responsible for the restoration, and also built the SCHOOL, 1871, various cottages, and, for himself, LACKFORD MANOR, ½ m. W of the church. Dated 1867, of red brick with stone dressings in Tudor style. Extensive alterations and additions by *Gordon L. Broad*, 1930. More attractive is THE OLD READING ROOM COTTAGE near the school. Early C20, with a half-timbered gable and battered chimney *à la* Voysey.

BARROW, ¾ m. SW of the church, known as Cuckoo Hill. Originally there was a second, opened in 1869 to reveal a pair of cremations. *See also* Risby.

LAKENHEATH 7080

A large parish, second only to Mildenhall in acreage, and like it containing significant prehistoric remains (*see* Introduction) and a major airfield (opened 1941).

ST MARY. An eminently interesting church, whose history is better known as a result of research associated with the conservation of the wall paintings by the *Perry Lithgow Partnership* in 2009 (*see* below).* The chancel arch is Norman (*c.* 1130–50) with three orders of shafts, multi-scalloped capitals, and no other decoration in the arches than rolls. In the chancel N wall one Norman colonnette with the beginning of an arch, which may well indicate blank arcading of the altar space; also a re-set section of string course with deep sawtooth carving. A lancet shows that the chancel was extended in the C13; the length of Norman chancel – unusually long for the date – is clear outside, especially on the S side, with the joint between Norman ironstone conglomerate and flint. Also in the C13 a N chapel was added. The blocked arch from the chancel survives inside, with the former doorway re-set in it. The

---

*I am grateful to Matthew Champion for sharing the results of his research.

Norman church may have had a S aisle (see the bases of the S arcade piers). The N arcade was constructed at the beginning of the C13 and extended W by two bays c. 1250. A piece of solid wall between the third and fourth bays marks the W end of the Norman building; the NW quoins of the Norman nave can be seen on the N side. All the arcade piers are octagonal, but the later pier on the N side is slimmer and has concave sides. The piers of the S arcade were replaced in the C14; they too have concave sides, and have at the top of each side a pointed-trefoiled arch-head (cf. Worlington). The N aisle windows are Dec, with a charming circular E window above the altar, but the S aisle windows are Late Perp. Perp clerestory; also an E window above the chancel arch, unfortunately blocked when the chancel was re-roofed in 1891. The W tower is in its lower parts of the mid C13. It has a single-chamfered E arch and fine W doorway with four-chamfered continuous mouldings. The latter is not usually seen, because it is covered by a two-storey attachment built, it is thought, of material from St Peter, Eriswell (q.v.), probably in the C17. It includes a Perp window, perhaps the E window of St Peter, and was repaired in white brick c. 1800. The upper floor (in which is the niche over the W doorway) was used as a schoolroom, and is also recorded as being the manor office. Fine nave roof with alternating tie-beams and hammerbeams, and big angels against the hammerbeams, queenposts, and tracery above the tie-beams (cf. Mildenhall and also Methwold, Norfolk). Many of the wings were replaced during a general restoration by *W.D. Caröe*, 1904–5; further restoration and reordering, including organ and screen wall against the tower arch, by *H. M. Cautley*, 1925–6.

FURNISHINGS. FONT. The finest C13 font in the county. It was installed when the nave was extended W and probably occupies its original position. Big, octagonal, with gabled arches in each panel and much big stiff-leaf decoration. Octagonal stem with eight detached shafts. – FONT COVER. By *Siegfried Pietzsch*, 1961. He also did the NAVE ALTAR, 1986. – CRUCIFIX. Bog oak, by *William Horrex*, painted by *Mark Cazalet*, 1999. – PULPIT. Perp, with arched panels and trumpet foot. – BENCHES. A delightful set with poppyheads with all sorts of small animals, a unicorn, a tiger, etc., and also a man seated on the ground with his knees pulled up. The bench backs have charming lacework friezes of different patterns. Money was left for the 'stooling' of the church in 1483. – FAMILY PEW (S chapel). Jacobean. – LADDER in W tower. With carved date 1624, but in part at least much older, possibly the original one. – ROYAL ARMS. Of Charles II, 1678. Very large, painted on boards. – WALL PAINTINGS. Five separate phases have been identified. The first, c. 1200–20, on the three eastern bays of the N arcade, with angels in the spandrels, scrollwork on the arches and figures on the piers. Next, c. 1250, a decorative scheme on the newly added western part of the arcade, including a scrollwork pattern, like a vine, on the piece of wall between the third and fourth bays. A century later this important section (opposite the S door) was overpainted with the Harrowing of Hell, scenes from the Passion, and the Virgin and Child with St Edmund. This in turn was overpainted in the late C15 with a figure of St George, although this is the least visible of all the schemes. Also late C15, on the nave E wall, r. of the chancel arch, the Risen Christ with hand raised in blessing (grisaille). On the nave S wall, a framed panel of biblical text, early C17. – STAINED GLASS. E window †1891 by *Heaton, Butler & Bayne*. N aisle E (small round window) by *Powell & Sons*, 1905. – MONUMENTS. Brass of a Civilian and Wife, *c.* 1530, 18-in. (46-cm.) figures. – Simeon Styward †1568 (S chapel). Tomb-chest with lozenges with shields. Niche above with panelled ends and a straight top. All this is purely Perp, but the lettering is Roman. – His wife Joanna Bestney †1583. Tablet with a tree-trunk from which hangs a big shield of arms. A sword at the foot presumably ready to cut the tree. – Earl Kitchener †1916, 'whose ancestors long resided in this parish'. Marble tablet by *E. Guy Dawber*.

ABUNDANT LIFE CHURCH, Back Street. 1815, originally Calvinistic Independent. Knapped flint with white-brick dressings. Three bays, with two tiers of segment-headed windows and arched doorway. Hipped pantiled roof. Similar BAPTIST CHAPEL, Mill Road, 1845. The METHODIST CHURCH, Back Street, 1835, has a gabled white-brick front.

PRIMARY SCHOOL, Mill Road. 1876–8 by *Henry Lovegrove*. White brick with red brick dressings. Straight-topped windows set in stepped lancets, the arches filled with tile-hanging. Extensions of 1969 and 2004.

Lakenheath Hall.
Design by A. N. Prentice, 1900

RAILWAY STATION. By *Francis Thompson*, 1845. Small, plain, white brick. Well-preserved signal box.

LAKENHEATH HALL (originally The Retreat), Station Road. Large butterfly-plan house by *A. N. Prentice*, c. 1900. Mainly flint, with red brick dressings. Picturesque elements, including a loggia in the inner angle beneath a half-timbered projection and, especially, the thatched roof, were lost in a fire; the remainder has been divided into two houses and the grounds built over. The entrance lodge is more intact: semicircular wing with conical roof towards the road.

LANDWADE
Exning*

No village; just the church and the hall.

ST NICHOLAS. Rebuilt by Walter Cotton (†1445) of Landwade Hall, and virtually unaltered since. Coursed flint, partly rendered. Nave, S porch, transepts and chancel; low W tower, its W face repaired and heavily buttressed with brick in 1796. Perp tracery. The E window, and E windows of the transepts (blocked in the S transept), of three lights; the rest of two lights. The transepts are divided from the crossing by an arcade of two bays. The roof rests on original head corbels. – ROOD SCREEN. With two-light divisions, broad ogee arches and Perp tracery with a transom above; well designed. – STOUP. Nice embattled arched niche beside the N doorway. – BENCHES with poppyheads. – PANELLING. Some reused linenfold and some reused Elizabethan panelling (originally with inlay) against the W wall. – STAINED GLASS. Many fragments of original mid-C15 work, part of a unified scheme. Fragmentary figures, and a complete St Margaret (N transept E). Removed in the C19 but returned in 1926–7. E window by *Francis Spear*, 1966. – MONUMENTS. An exceptional number. In the chancel three silent tomb-chests, without evidence of whom they commemorate, although the one in front of the altar is presumably that of Walter Cotton. The motifs of the two others, against the N and S walls, are three and five shields set in lozenges. That on the S has a depressed segmental back arch with quatrefoils in the soffit and cresting, and beneath the arch indents of kneeling brass figures. – S transept: Recess with tomb-chest decorated by four ornately cusped quatrefoils in the front; the arch depressed-pointed with traceried soffit, cresting, and indents for kneeling figures on the back wall. – N transept: Sir John Cotton †1593 and wife Isabel †1578. Six-poster with two recumbent effigies. Top with obelisk and

---

*Transferred from Cambridgeshire in 1994.

achievement surrounded by heavy openwork strap ornament. Strapwork also e.g. on the pilasters of the tomb-chest. – In the s transept three more Cotton monuments: Sir John Cotton †1620 and wife, standing wall monument with his figure lying on his side, propped up on one elbow, one hand on his heart; hers in front of his, supine, a little lower down. Low arch, flanking black columns, broken segmental pediment, white, pink and black marble. Attributed to *Thomas Stanton*, *c.* 1640 (GF). – Sir John Cotton †1689. The same composition and materials, i.e. very reactionary. The figure (rather too big for the arch) now reclining, the pediment straight, broken and ending in volutes. These monuments have original iron railings. – Sir John Cotton †1712 and wife Elizabeth †1714. All of white marble, with obelisk and two putti in front of it holding a double portrait medallion. By *Thomas Adye*. – Sir John Hynde Cotton †1795. Large classical marble wall monument by *R. Westmacott Sen.* (N transept). – Rev. A. A. Cotton †1846. Large mural brass (no figure) like the backplate of a medieval tomb-chest, with friezes and cresting. By *J. W. Archer*.

LANDWADE HALL. The medieval manor house stood within the moat that lies E of the church. It was rebuilt in the early C16, but all that survives is the brick BRIDGE, with three pointed arches, across the moat. The house was rebuilt by *J. C. Buckler*, *c.* 1847–9, but demolished soon after 1854, when the Cottons sold the manor. The present Hall, 200 yds s, incorporates a C17 stone house, of which a gabled section of wall, with mullioned-and-transomed windows, can be seen on the N side. It was extensively remodelled in the C19 and again in 1926, for Lord St Davids, by *Walter Sarel*, when most of it was rendered and Georganized. On its s side a four-bay barn, built of clunch; late C17 or early C18.

LANGHAM

9060

ST MARY. Nave rebuilt by *J. H. Hakewill*, 1877, with bellcote at the W end. A single C13 window, at the NW corner, seems to have determined the style. Flint rubble. Dec chancel, with four tall windows, restored by *Rev. E. Geldart*, 1886–7. The E window is of that date but may well represent what was there before: three lights and a large circle, enclosing four unencircled quatrefoils. Niches l. and r. of the window inside. The side windows have the familiar four-petalled flower in the tracery heads. S organ chamber and vestry also by Geldart, 1889. – FONT. Dec. octagonal, with shields and lions' heads under ogee arches. – SCREEN. Very good, with tracery on the dado, one-light divisions, ogee arches, much close panel tracery above them, and the complete loft parapet towards the W. In 1464 a bequest of a cow was made to pay for lighting the rood beam. – CHOIR STALLS. By *Geldart*, made by *Alfred Taylor* of Ixworth. – FLOOR TILES. In chancel, a vibrant display; by *W.B. Simpson & Sons.* – STAINED GLASS. Nave N by *W. Aikman*, 1919 (war memorial).

The church is prettily placed in the park of LANGHAM HALL, which stands a little to the W on higher ground. Mid-C18 red brick. Two storeys and attics. Principal ranges facing E and S of five bays each. Alterations by Patrick Blake, including three fine Rococo plaster ceilings, one with Chinoiserie decoration, made between his marriage in 1762 and baronetcy in 1772. Two canted bays added to the E front, the pedimented Ionic doorcase brought forward to create a porch between them by the end of the C18. Further alterations and additions, *c.* 1840, including rebuilding the lower service wing. Large walled garden to the N. *John Johnson* exhibited in 1783 a design for a hermitage, but this does not seem to have been executed.

LAVENHAM

Lavenham is rightly celebrated for its timber-framed buildings and for its church. The latter, one of the most famous of the parish churches of Suffolk, was largely rebuilt between about 1485 and 1525, and most of the timber-framed buildings belong to a similar period, *c.* 1460–1530, although the town was already well established by the time of Domesday, and received its market charter in 1257. The wealth that enabled this building came from the manufacture of woollen cloth. In 1524 Lavenham ranked as the fourteenth wealthiest town in England; in that year it contributed over £179 in tax, more than the City of York (Sudbury £60, Long Melford £65). But it declined sharply very soon thereafter, and in the latter part of the C16 many houses were taken down and not replaced. There is little of significance from the C17 and C18. Fortunes revived somewhat in the C19, with the opening of factories for processing horsehair (mainly as seating) and coconut fibre (mainly as matting) from the 1850s, chief among them William W. Roper's. The railway arrived in 1865 (closed 1965). This commercial revival did little to help the medieval domestic buildings, and early photographs show many of them to have been in a desperately poor state of repair. Some were converted to factories; at least one was 'rescued' and re-erected elsewhere. A crisis point was reached in 1912, when dismantling of the Wool Hall, Lady Street, was reversed as a result of local protest. A great deal of restoration took place in the 1920s and 1930s, little of which could be described as conservative or discreet; the fashion then was for exposing timbers and, as often as not, supplementing them. Organized conservation began with the formation of the Lavenham Preservation Committee in 1944.

The village (as it must now be called) has grown a little to the N, in the direction of the railway, but otherwise is concentrated in a surprisingly small area, bounded to the E by the tiny River Brett. The centre is the Market Place, on a little hilltop with streets running down from it to the S and E. The church sits on a separate piece of high ground, about 500 yds SW.

ST PETER AND ST PAUL. As interesting historically as it is rewarding architecturally. In both respects it is a match for Long Melford. The nave of Melford may be the nobler design, but Lavenham has more unity. To the eye it is a Late Perp church throughout, though the chancel and the pretty crocketed spirelet for the sanctus bell are clearly Dec (unknapped flint, Dec window tracery). The church was built by the efforts of the clothiers of Lavenham, chiefly the Springs, and of the lord of the manor, John de Vere, 13th Earl of Oxford. His arms appear on the S porch, and inscriptions record Thomas Spring on the S chapel and Simon Branch on the N chapel. Wills prove that the tower was being built in c. 1486–95 (bequest of £40 by Thomas Spring II, 1486), and its top parts belong to a second campaign of c. 1517–25. In 1523 Thomas Spring III left £200, a large sum, for its completion, over and above what was spent by his executors on the building of a chantry chapel as a monument to himself and his wife, and on the parclose in which he was buried. Other wills indicate building in the church itself between the two tower campaigns, e.g. £200 bequeathed by John Rysby in 1504. It is worth recording also that a niece of Thomas Spring II married the second son of the 15th Earl of Oxford. Thomas Spring III, when he made his will in 1523, owned property in 130 places.

The name of one mason, *John Rogers*, is documented, and on circumstantial and stylistic grounds the nave is attributable to *John Wastell*. The lower parts of the tower may have been the work of *Simon Clerk* in partnership with Wastell (cf. Saffron Walden, Essex). There have been no significant structural alterations to the church since the Reformation. The principal restoration was by *F. C. Penrose*, 1861–7, including re-seating, with further repairs and reordering by *W. D. Caröe*, 1909–10. There were extensive repairs to the roofs by *F. E. Howard* in 1928–32.

Lavenham church makes a perfect picture. Its WEST TOWER is as mighty as its nave is noble. The only criticism is that the tower is, perhaps, a little too substantial for the length of the nave, which is shorter than at Long Melford. Height of the tower 141 ft (43 metres), length of the church 165 ft (50 metres). The tower is of knapped flint. On the plinth the stars and shields of the de Veres, the merchant marks of the Springs, and the crossed keys of St Peter and crossed swords of St Paul. The buttresses are very unusual, broad and clasping but provided on their two fronts with thinner sub-buttresses which look, of course, as if they were normal set-back buttresses. Five set-offs. On them panelling, and lower down canopied niches. Large W doorway with decoration of fleurons and Green Men, ogee gable and flanking buttress-shafts. Four-light W window with battlemented transom. Three-light bell-openings. Parapet with lozenges and, on the corners, shields with arms of Thomas Spring III. His arms, a very recent acquisition when he died, appear thirty-two times. The pinnacles were never built.

The NAVE is faced with Casterton stone. Seven bays with large transomed four-light windows. The clerestory has twelve, not fourteen, windows, owing to the interference of the tower buttresses, and the charming irregularity of the rood turret with spirelet not outside the aisle but between nave and aisle. Aisle buttresses with decoration, aisle battlements with rich openwork decoration, clerestory also with such battlements. A favourite motif is the large tripartite leaves set in panels. The N is essentially the same, although the window tracery is a little different, and there is no porch. The S PORCH is a spectacular piece. Restored in 1865 by *Penrose*, who did the fan-vaulting. The entrance has spandrels with the Oxford boar, above it a niche, a frieze of six shields, again of the de Vere family, and above that openwork battlements of the same design as the aisle. Figures of St Peter and St Paul by *Eric Winters*, 1963.

The S (Spring or Lady) CHAPEL is dated 1525. The inscription on it reads:

[Orate pro Animabus] Thome Spryng armig et Alicie uxoris ejus qui istam capellam fieri fecerunt anno dni MCCCCC vicesimo quinto.

Higher than the aisle, the chapel has flushwork-panelled walls, three large transomed four-light windows with tracery different from that of the aisle, and different battlements too. The N (Branch) CHAPEL corresponds to the S chapel but was built earlier, *c.* 1500. Its inscription is similar:

[Orate pro Animabus] Simonis Branch et Elizabethe uxoris ejus qui istam capellam fieri fecerunt.

Its style is similar too, but the following differences ought to be noted. In the tracery of the Spring Chapel occur ogee arches; in that of the Branch Chapel they do not. The buttresses of the Spring Chapel are more elaborate than those of the Branch Chapel, which are not bonded into the plinth – indicating that the Branch Chapel was probably built on an older foundation. The battlements of the Spring Chapel are of stone similar to those of the S aisle; those of the Branch Chapel have flushwork panelling, similar to those on the low E VESTRY. This is said to date from 1444 and was given by Thomas Spring II whose brass, now inside it (*see* below), was originally on the outside wall.

INTERIOR. The arcades are of six bays. The slender piers have a complex section with four attached shafts which alone carry capitals. The capitals have fleuron decoration and battlements or cresting. The arches have an outer plain roll moulding, and circular shafts rise through the spandrels and from the apexes of the arches to capitals supporting the roof. Below the clerestory windows cresting, a frieze of lozenges with shields, and shields in quatrefoils in the spandrels. Cambered roof on small figures of angels. The E bays, above the former rood, are panelled. The devices on the bosses include Thomas Spring's merchant mark, his monogram, and the de Vere arms. Fine N aisle roof, lean-to, on angel figures. Carved principals. Wall-posts with niches and canopies. Along the N aisle wall below the windows a frieze of fleurons; along the S aisle wall of foliage trails. In the N chapel N wall blank panelling below the windows. Blank panelling also in the tower N, S and W walls. Chancel roof by *Penrose*.

FURNISHINGS. FONT. Perp, octagonal, much decayed. Pairs of standing figures, probably the Apostles, on six sides of the bowl. – REREDOS. By *Penrose*, 1890. Alabaster, marble and stone, executed by *H. Poole*. SEDILIA restored at the same time. – SCREENS. The rood screen is contemporary with the chancel, i.e. of c. 1330–40. Screens that early are rare. Simple two-light divisions with ogee arches and flowing tracery. Original gates, reinstated by *Caröe*. Cresting. Later are the screens to the N and S chapels. Parts of several screens, all good, none outstanding. The best has two-light divisions with gables and fine tracery over. Cresting to S chapel screen dated 1958. – NW nave screen by *Caröe*. Originally choir vestry, reordered as shop 2008. – SPRING PARCLOSE (N aisle E end). Mortuary chapel of Thomas Spring III †1523. The screen is a glorious piece of woodwork, as dark as bronze, although it was originally painted and this is far from the intended effect. The carving is of a high standard, and seems to have been influenced by Flemish work of the type favoured in early C16 court circles, using Italianate and antique forms. Dado with branches instead of tracery. In the two-light arches the tracery has also turned organic, and is alive with putti and other creatures. Shallow canopies with little imitation vaults. Great variety in the buttresses and in the shafts between the openings. Restored for (Sir) Francis Spring by *Harry Hems*, 1906–7, under the supervision of *Temple Moore*, including new figures of St Katharine and St Blaise. – SPOURNE PARCLOSE (S aisle E end). Less fantastical, but equally successful. Three-light divisions with big ogee gables over each six lights. Crested angle buttresses and finials. Most of the tracery belongs to *Caröe*'s restoration, with crocketing on the gables by *Jack Penton*, 1961. It is not known for whom the parclose was erected; the arms of Thomas Spourne are among those displayed. For the monument inside *see* below. – DOORS. W door with tracery, de Vere arms, and chalice and wafer. S door with linenfold panelling and the Oxford boar, no doubt of the same date as the porch. Rood stair with a typical early Tudor motif (cf. S door, Southwold (E)), copied on the S chapel S door. Chancel E end, to C15 vestry, with tracery. – STALLS. Traceried fronts, with poppyheads and animals on the ends. Restored by

H. Ringham, 1861–2, under *Penrose*'s supervision. – MISERI-CORDS. E.g. a man playing a pig as bagpipes, a pelican, a man playing a bellows using tongs as a bow, a woman playing the hurdy-gurdy, and a jester. – SCULPTURE. Virgin and Child by *Neil Godfrey*, 1982 (S chapel). – ROYAL ARMS. Hanoverian, well carved in relief. Also of George II, on canvas, and Elizabeth II. – STAINED GLASS. Seven windows by *Lavers & Barraud*, later *Lavers, Barraud & Westlake*, 1861–89. E window 1861, from cartoons by *James Milner Allen*. Also by Allen the W window, awarded a prize at the International Exhibition of 1862 (re-set following bomb damage in the Second World War), and the N chapel E window, 1864, including the Raising of Lazarus based on Sebastiano del Piombo's painting (the initials are those of the donor, Frederick Thompson). S chapel S windows signed by *N. Westlake*, 1879 and 1889. – BRASSES. Thomas Spring II †1486 (E vestry). 'Resurrection' brass showing Spring, his wife Margaret and children, all in shrouds and rising from their tombs. It also records that Spring 'hoc vestibulum fieri fecit in vita sua'. – Allaine Dister †1534 (nave N wall). Elizabethan plate with kneeling figures of Dister, wife Agnes, and children, and the following inscription:

> A Clothier vertuous while he was
> In Lavenham many a yeare
> For as in lyefe he loved best
> The poore to clothe and feede
> So withe the riche and all the rest
> He neighbourlie agreed
> And did appoint before he died
> A small yearlie rent
> Whiche shoulde be every Whitsontide
> Amonge the poorest spent

– Clopton D'Ewes †1631 (in front of altar). 'Chrysom' brass of a baby in swaddling bands, only 8½ in. (22 cm.) long. – MONUMENTS. John Ponder †1520. Decayed tomb-chest with pitched roof. Originally in the churchyard; moved to the Spourne Parclose 1910. – Henry Copinger †1622 (chancel). Two kneeling figures facing each other across a reading desk, kneeling figures in the 'predella'. Columns l. and r. and two angels standing outside them. – War memorial (S aisle W end). By *Leonard Crowfoot*, 1920. Large tablet with decorative borders. – In churchyard, E of chancel, Rev. Joseph Croker †1892 in the form of a churchyard cross. In addition to the normal inscriptions, lines from hymns with accompanying scores.

CEMETERY, Bridge Street Road. Opened 1893; red brick CHAPEL of 1896. To its N, grave of James Clark †1894. Large headstone carved with a horse in bas relief; at the footstone a dog *couchant gardant*. By *James Shoolbred & Co*. E of the chapel R. G. (John) Gayer-Anderson †1945. Slab with inscription by *Eric Gill*, including Arabic text provided by King Farouk of Egypt.

VILLAGE HALL and LIBRARY, Church Street. 2003–5 by *Wincer Kievenaar*. Horizontal timber cladding, pitched slate roof and exposed gable structure. Two long ranges split by a central atrium with clerestory. Ridgeline of higher range punctuated by industrial-aesthetic vents reminiscent of maltings.

PRIMARY SCHOOL, Barn Street and Bolton Street. By *J. S. Corder*, 1895–6. Red brick. Straight gables, some pedimented, and not quite on the corner a two-storey tower with pyramidal roof.

PERAMBULATION

There is nothing in Suffolk to compete with the timber-framed houses of Lavenham. Most of the village's 200-odd listed buildings can be seen in the course of a relatively compact perambulation, and remembering that most of the timber-framed buildings date from *c.* 1460–1530, many need not be mentioned individually. The church stands apart from its neighbours. SE of it the VILLAGE SIGN by *Neil Rutherford*, 1990, of carved oak, including relief panels of a weaver at his loom and the Guildhall. Opposite, to the SW, the OLD RECTORY, early C18 with alterations and additions by *Joseph Stannard*, 1826. Red brick, the main part of two storeys and attics, five bays wide. Canted bay at one end of the garden front. Down CHURCH STREET towards the centre, first, on the l., No. 81 (FIR TREE HOUSE), the refronting in red brick, *c.* 1750, of a medieval timber-framed house. With two canted bays, the angles oddly stressed by little Doric columns set in. Doorway with open pediment and palm-leaf capitals, Venetian window above this, and open top pediment. On the other side some interesting timber-framed houses (Nos. 13–15, 11–12 and 9–10), but No. 32 (LANEHAM HOUSE), for all its exposed timbers and jettied front, was built in 1935. No. 14, on the corner of Bears Lane, has emblems of the wool trade in its pargetting; there used to be more on the Church Street front. Nos. 9–10, with arched doorway, began as a C15 hall house. Then again on the NW side No. 85, with a floral pargetted panel, and Nos. 88–89, still visibly of Wealden type. No. 91 has an impressive chimney against the cross-wing, with a lean-to extension built round it. Then No. 92 (THE WILLOWS), broadly similar to No. 81 but with antae to the bays, a more elaborate doorcase, and Gothick glazing to the Venetian window.

The HIGH STREET opens with the SWAN HOTEL on the r., the knitting together of a number of separate buildings by *James Hopwood*, 1964–5 and 1967–8. Its cellars are said to date back to the C14. Picturesque front, small rear courtyard. Hopwood's additions include a new dining room with open crown-post roof. Towards Water Street the same pargetted emblems as in Church Street. A good sequence on the W side of the High

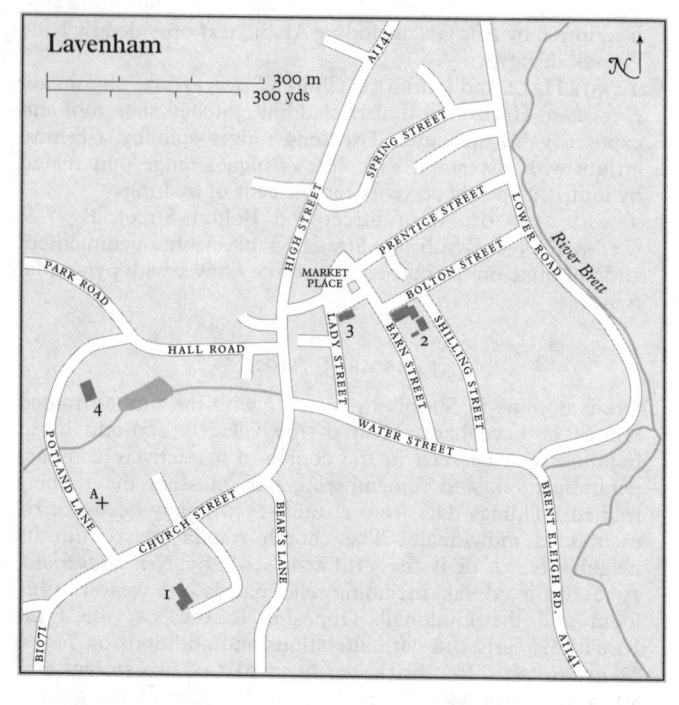

A   St Peter & St Paul

1   Village Hall and Library
2   Primary School
3   Guildhall
4   Lavenham Hall

Street immediately after Hall Road (for Lavenham Hall, *see* below): No. 6, with its two gables with C19 bargeboards; Nos. 7–9, originally a C15 hall house with cross-wings at either end, only the s wing (CROOKED HOUSE) readily recognizable; and then Nos. 10–13, which also began as a hall house. Two crosswings, both with pargetting in geometric patterns. On the E side, after Market Lane, No. 89 (CORDWAINERS), C15, and then Nos. 87–88 (HALL HOUSE), the main range a late C14 or early C15 raised-aisle hall, its single aisle to the rear. C16 gabled and jettied cross-wing.

N of here the C19 influence is more strongly felt, the older houses interspersed with red brick terraces built by Thomas Turner, a worsted manufacturer (dated 1829, 1853, 1856), and W.W. Roper (1885, 1896). The explanation lies in ROPER'S COURT, reached through one end of No. 39: Turner's factory, taken over by Roper *c.* 1864. Three storeys, nine bays. Red brick, with timber lantern on the roof and timber sack hoist on cast-iron brackets. Now converted to housing. A little further, on the r., the former INDEPENDENT CHAPEL of 1827. Painted brick, with arched windows. The classical stuccoed front, with pediment and side porches, may be a later addition.

Now back to Market Lane and MARKET PLACE, which would be a wonderful set piece if it were not used as a car park. As it is, it is hard to enjoy the magnificent sweep of houses on its three sides, with glimpses of the church tower in one direction and in the other open country at the bottom of Prentice Street. In the middle is the MARKET CROSS, set up under the will of William Jacob in 1501; the shaft is a replacement, dated 1725. Near it a C16 cottage on an island; other buildings in the middle were demolished in the C20. The chief attraction of the NW and NE sides is the variety of the buildings, that is, the various ways in which the medieval buildings have been remodelled externally over the centuries, and each in its own way is charming. The ANGEL HOTEL is notable for the first-floor room on the corner of Prentice Street. It is the parlour chamber of a C15 hall house, and has a plaster ceiling of the early C17, as well as earlier wall paintings. On the opposite corner THE GREAT HOUSE looks C18, with its six-bay, two-storey plastered front and Greek Doric doorcase, but this conceals a C15 timber-framed building. Attached to it, on the r., LITTLE HALL, with jettied cross-wing of *c.* 1400 and mid-C15 hall with six-light window. The original hall stood further back. Restored 1926–36 by the Gayer-Anderson twins; *Col. T. G. Gayer-Anderson* seems to have acted as architect, with advice from *A. R. Powys* of the Society for the Protection of Ancient Buildings. Many of the exposed timbers are not original and the parlour end is entirely new. Inside, a good crown-post roof to the hall, and unexpected Oriental elements such as Persian panelling and doors. Owned since 1971 by the Suffolk Preservation Society, and limewashed (including the timbers) a distinctive yellow.

The GUILDHALL and attached buildings (National Trust) extend along most of the SE side of Market Place. The site was given to the guild of Corpus Christi in 1529 and the hall was purpose-built very soon thereafter. After the Reformation the Guildhall served various public functions, including that of jail, before being bought in 1887 by Sir Cuthbert Quilter (cf. Bawdsey (E)). It was partially restored and extended for him by *J. S. Corder*, with a further restoration, more comprehensive and controversial, by *Kemp & How*, 1913, for Quilter's son, also Cuthbert. It has a splendid porch, varied and diversely decorated. Very ornate, with carved angle-posts, carved spandrels, carved friezes, and an overhang. Oriels abound, but only the especially fine one on the ground floor towards Lady Street is original; the rest were added in 1913. At the corner of Lady Street a carved angle-post with a figure with a staff. The layout of the ground floor was essentially domestic, with service room, cross-passage, hall and parlour on the ground floor, and on the first floor small rooms that were probably used as warehouse space. The hall (now combined with the parlour) was relatively small, suggesting that membership of the guild was small, and unheated, proving that it was for public rather than domestic use. Adjoining to the l. a house of similar date to the Guildhall, with higher roof-line. To the l. of that, and lower, another house, the r. part of which was converted for use as a Methodist chapel in 1861 and given a brick front. At the l. end are two medieval arched shop windows, with hinged shutters that are not original.

From the Market Place one should glance first at the top of LADY STREET. No. 1 is about thirty years older than the Guildhall, and became a part of it. Next to it the discreet TOURIST INFORMATION CENTRE by *Babergh District Council* (project architects *Robin Weaver, Roger Rush* and *Aaron Moss*), 1993, with glazed timber-framed front. A little lower down, THE GROVE, timber-framed at the back, but with a Georgian front of white brick. Doorway with open pediment, a Venetian window above it, canted bays to l. and r. (cf. Nos. 81 and 92 Church Street). Back to the Market Place and the top of BARN STREET by the side of Little Hall. Just past the primary school (*see* above), on the other side, MOLET HOUSE, now only one gable wide, but very good, with original doorway, seven-light ground-floor oriel, oversailing first floor, and carved gable bressumer. Restored by *Eric Winters*, 1961. (Buildings further down Lady Street and Barn Street are described below.)

Now we can leave the Market Square by way of PRENTICE STREET. The notable feature on the SE side is BAKER'S MILL, former corn mill and maltings of Thomas Baker (1865, 1868, 1873, 1878) and J.W. & F.W. Baker (1893), converted to housing by *Wincer Kievenaar*, 1986–7. Red brick with white-brick dressings, including a three-storey block with brick decoration that includes shaped brick pendants below the eaves. Square oast house at the far end. MILL HOUSE with canted bays on the street. After all this the street slopes down towards the Brett, with countryside beyond. No. 13, on the l., is earlier than most Lavenham houses, with exposed bracing on the front typical of the mid to late C14, and remains of a hall of that date behind it. The entrance to No. 11 originally opened into the cross-passage, with service wing to the l. extended in the C16. The best house, WOOLSTAPLERS HALL, is on the l. towards the bottom, early C15 or late C14. Two gabled cross-wings at the lower end, their jetties on carved C17 brackets. Opposite, ORANGE COTTAGE by *Project Orange*, 2005–6, and below it No. 26 by *Adrian Palmer*, 1975, both managing to complement their neighbours without copying. At the bottom, along Lower Road, a former GRANARY, probably early C17, originally belonging to Woolstaplers Hall. On the E side of LOWER ROAD, a little to the S, THE ISLAND HOUSE by *Norman Westwater*, 1973. Inspired by traditional mill buildings, with black weatherboarding above a ground floor of red brick and painted render.

A little further S along Lower Road BOLTON STREET returns uphill to the W. It has a few timber-framed houses including No. 28, thought to be the oldest surviving house in Lavenham, dating from c. 1330–40. Near the top on the same side the former METHODIST CHURCH by *Eade & Johns*, 1911. Turning the corner into Shilling Street, PROSPECT HOUSE by *Adrian Palmer*, 1995, taking its cue from Lavenham's C19 rather than C15 industrial heritage. In SHILLING STREET, No. 1 is C17, timber-framed and plastered, extended c. 1975 by Palmer for himself. A nice variety of relatively modest timber-framed houses down both sides, then on the l. SHILLING OLD GRANGE, originally one large house of the C15. It was refronted in the late C17 and remodelled in the C18, with flat plastered front and doorway with open pediment. The r. half was restored c. 1930 by *Percy Green* with jettied front and three gables. Another nice Georgian doorway on ARUNDEL HOUSE, just below.

WATER STREET is perhaps the most rewarding in Lavenham. It is well named, because it follows the line of the stream that feeds the pond in the grounds of Lavenham Hall to the W (*see* below) and continues on to the River Brett. This is now contained in a brick culvert, covered over in the C16, and over which many of the houses on the S side of the street are built. Opposite Shilling Street the LAVENHAM PRESS, a C15 house with carved bressumers to the jetty and C18 canted bays below it. Converted to industrial use and extended in the C19, a rare survival into the C21 of the many medieval houses in Lavenham that were adapted in this way. To its E the site of the former GASWORKS, with a cast-iron gasholder of 1862. Round the corner in Brent Eleigh Road THE BRUSHES, the conversion to housing of a horsehair factory of 1908. Three storeys and eleven bays, of painted brick. W of Shilling Street, an almost unbroken parade of timber-framed houses on both sides. Just before Barn Street, on the N side, a quaint row (Nos. 23–26) known as Weavers' Cottages, but with no historical justification. Large external chimneystack at one end. A short way up BARN STREET the OLD GRAMMAR SCHOOL, built as a house for a wealthy clothier in the C15–C16: late C15 parlour cross-wing to the l., the original hall raised and floored c. 1520. At the same time the house was extended to the r., with a jettied range carrying two display gables (now LOWER HOUSE). It has a broad gateway at the far end; the room between the gateway and the hall may have been the counting house, with the room above the hall, originally lit only by a single narrow window, used as a watchouse. The wing to the rear of the parlour cross-wing was probably also added c. 1520, and contains a brick spiral stair. Carved beam over the hall dais with figures of Christ and Henry VI. Used as the grammar school from the C17 (probably 1647) until the late C19; pupils included John Constable and the agriculturalist Arthur Young. It then entered (or one might say returned to) industrial use, with a three-storey, seven-bay brick factory added to the S end (brick dated 1899), and a two-storey range at the N end round a court. Restored as two houses, 1996, the factory also converted.

Back in Water Street, along the N side to the W a seven-bay, two-storey red brick building, built as a factory by W.W. Roper, 1891; workers' housing of the same date a little further along. On the S side, opposite Barn Street, No. 55 (so-called MANOR HOUSE), C15 but in external detail almost entirely C20. More exposed timbers on No. 58 (former White Horse Inn), then the splendour of DE VERE HOUSE. But here too, little is what it seems. All the brick-nogging is C20. The house was partially dismantled in 1926 for re-erection elsewhere, but the front of the service cross-wing (to the l.) was returned and rebuilt. Carved bressumer, soffit and wall-plate. The medieval hall, set back from the street, was lost. The jettied range to the r. of the cross-wing, with one small and one large gable, is an early C16 addition in front of the hall. The doorway, with carved posts, is of doubtful authenticity; it leads into an internal porch, an early example. Then comes THE PRIORY, never a priory but owned by the priory of Earls Colne, Essex. As with De Vere House, the older part (C13) lies back from the street, behind a red brick wall, with a late C15 range on the present frontage. Remains of elaborate floral pargetting on both parts, and inside painted decoration including interlocking geometric strapwork on a chimney-breast.

Back on the N side, opposite The Priory, Nos. 7–9 is a late C15 merchant's hall house with cross-wings, one still jettied. Remains of painted decoration inside, including antiquework with candelabra grotesques, with tenterhooks remaining from an earlier scheme of cloth hangings. Then the entrance to LADY STREET. On the E corner Nos. 10–11 Lady Street, with the three small arched windows of a medieval shop. The whole front is jettied, with fourteen brackets on shafts with carved capitals. Facing it the WOOL HALL, now part of the Swan Hotel (*see above*). Early C16 hall house, with gabled and jettied cross-wings. The hall is open to the crown-post roof and has a big six-light transomed window. It was the centre of a cause célèbre in 1912 when it was partially dismantled for Princess Louise, who wished to incorporate it in a new house being built for her by Sydney Seymour Lucas at Windlesham, Surrey. As a result of strong local opposition it was restored in 1913–14 by *William Weir*, who omitted a third gable dated 1696 between the two outer ones. The restoration left it with dark exposed timbers, as was then the fashion, whereas the timbers of Nos. 10–11 Lady Street have been limewashed as part of a restoration in the early C21. N of the Wool Hall stood the early C16 Weaver's House, dismantled and moved to Walberswick in 1908.* Finally, along the S side of Water Street, an unexpected building of flint with red brick and stone dressings and mansard roof, late C17 or C18, before a row of houses with jettied front and exposed timbers that leads back into Church Street.

---

*Mercer's Hall, The Street (E), p. 561.

Lavenham, Wool Hall.
Drawing by J. S. Corder, 1888

LAVENHAM HALL, Hall Road, 150 yds N of St Peter and St Paul. Timber-framed and plastered, with an early or mid-C16 crosswing, and main range with timbers of the same date but reassembled here in the C17. Presumably on or near the site of the medieval manor of the de Veres; large fishpond to the S. Opposite the entrance three COTTAGES built to look like one house by William and Mary Anne Biddell of Lavenham Hall, 1873. Red brick, nicely detailed, with gabled cross-wings and two-storey gabled porch.

WINDMILL, ½ m. NNE. Remaining two storeys of red brick tower mill of 1831, on mill mound within retaining wall. White brick MILL HOUSE alongside with Tuscan porch and veranda. The house opposite, FIDDLER SIMPSON'S COTTAGE, with exposed timbers, formerly stood at Washmere Green, 1 m. S of the village.

LAWSHALL

8050

ALL SAINTS. Tall W tower, nave and aisles with clerestory, and S porch all Perp. Bequests of 1383, 1426 and 1444 indicate rebuilding. Arcade of four bays. Piers with four filleted shafts and in the diagonals a thin shaft between two hollows. Castellated capitals. Above the arches a string course with demi-figures of angels. Lower chancel, E.E. in all its details, by

William Butterfield, 1856–7. The nave was also restored. Chancel and base of tower reordered by the *Whitworth Co-Partnership*, 2008. – FONT. C14, with tracery panels, rather garishly painted in the C20. – TILES. In chancel, by *Minton*. – MONUMENT. J. B. van Mesdag, a Dutch RAF pilot †1945. Large inscription plate made up of small tiles. Designed by the distinguished typographer *Jan van Krimpen* and made at the Royal Goedewaagen factory, Gouda. – STAINED GLASS. E window, other chancel windows and S aisle E by *Horwood Bros* of Mells, Somerset, 1857.

PRIMARY SCHOOL. By *J. D. Wyatt*, 1871–2. Red brick with some black-and-white decoration. Attached house with half-hipped roof.

LAWSHALL HALL. Empty for over fifty years, but under restoration in 2013. The manor was bought by Sir William Drury of Hawstead in 1547 and he probably built the Hall as a dower house for his wife Elizabeth; a datestone 1557 is recorded (but has not survived) and he died in 1558. Queen Elizabeth dined there with his son Henry in 1578. The house was then much bigger, and in 1674 was taxed on fourteen hearths, but by 1752 had been reduced, including lowering the roof by three feet (0.9 metres). Red brick two-storey front, mainly rebuilt in the C18. Three bays, the windows with segmental heads. Elsewhere much of the brickwork is diapered. In the W return wall of the front range a stone doorway with Tudor arch and small square windows. N of this a wing with three-light transomed windows.*

LITTLE WEST FARM, ¾ m. W. Timber-framed and plastered house, with thatched roof. Carved date 1592 inside. Intact timber-framed chimney with original brick hearth. Brick chimney added in the C17.

THE FOUNDRY, Bury Road, about 1 m. NW. Timber-framed, originally a mid-C19 barn, relocated and refurbished as offices for an environmental charity by *Modece Architects*, 2005–6. Clad in larch, insulated with lime and hemp.

OUR LADY IMMACULATE AND ST JOSEPH (R.C.), Bury Road, over 1 m. NNW. 1870. Timber-framed and plastered. Simple windows with Y-tracery. An extension to Coldham Cottage at the S end, late C17 or early C18, which had served as the presbytery for the chapel at Coldham Hall. – MONUMENT. Sir Edward Rokewode Gage †1872. Brass tablet by *Vaughan & Co*.

COLDHAM HALL. See p. 199.

LAYHAM

ST ANDREW. Red brick W tower of 1742. It replaced a tower of c. 1300 of which the tower arch remains. The top stage looks

---

*Additional information kindly provided by Edward Martin.

LAYHAM 363

as if it has been rebuilt, but is shown in Henry Davy's print of 1846. The rest of the church is of flint. Windows all of the type of *c.* 1300, but renewed as part of the restoration of 1861 by G. E. *Pritchett*, which also included a new nave roof. S porch, re-seating and PULPIT of 1886, perhaps by *W.M. Fawcett* (see Layham Park below). – FONT. C13. Hexagonal, of Purbeck marble, with two arched blank panels on each side. – REREDOS. 1904. Very elaborate, of stone, extending across the E wall of the sanctuary. In the centre five panels under cusped ogee arches with *opus sectile* figures of Christ, censing angels, St Andrew and St John the Evangelist. Tall niches to l. and r. – SCREEN. Fragment of the dado with simple traceried panels (beside pulpit). Money was left for painting the rood loft in 1441. – STAINED GLASS. E window by *Daniel Bell*, 1886. – MONUMENTS. Ann Roane †1626. An oddity: painted on canvas, in the form of a hatchment (lozenge-shaped), with an inscription below the achievement recording her burial 'at the foot of this wall'. Dated (repainted?) 1730. – Joseph Norman †1840 and children. Plain Gothic tablet by *E. J. Physick*, perhaps as late as 1882. – Good C19 cast-iron RAILINGS and GATES to the churchyard by *Graham & Joslin* of Hadleigh. On the N side the former NATIONAL SCHOOL, 1840. White brick, with hoodmoulds.

NETHERBURY HALL, by the church. Georgian, red brick, of five bays and two storeys, with parapet and Ionic porch.

Some nice houses along the village street SW of the church, and more at UPPER LAYHAM, ⅓ m. E on the other side of the River Brett. On the river a WATERMILL, rebuilt in 1905. Red brick with dressings of white brick and engineering brick. Two storeys, with weatherboarded turret. Iron breast-wheel. C18 timber-framed and plastered MILL HOUSE. Three bays and two and a half storeys, with pedimented doorcase.

HOLBECKS, 1¼ m. NNW. Large timber-framed and plastered house. The estate was acquired by Sir Joshua Rowley of Tendring Hall in 1788 (*see* p. 499) and his son Sir William consulted *Humphry Repton* in 1790; the house's present appearance may date from that time. Two storeys and attics with parapet. Front with two full-height canted bays l. and r. of a single bay. Pedimented Ionic doorway.

LAYHAM PARK, ½ m. NW. Built as the rectory, 1790. Enlarged 1837 and, by *W.M. Fawcett*, in 1885. White brick, later plastered. Four-bay W front with projecting two-storey gabled porch.

MOAT HALL, ¾ m. SW. 'A neat white brick house, erected in 1844, and having tasteful grounds' (White's *Directory*, 1855). Two storeys, three bays, with Greek Doric doorway.

OVERBURY HALL, ½ m. W. Large timber-framed and plastered house of *c.* 1570 and later. Long front of different builds. In the middle a projecting canted bay with pyramidal roof. To the l. of this the upper storey is jettied. Ceiling of close-set moulded beams in the dining room. 'Lately restored and much improved', according to White's *Directory*, 1874, which may

include the two-storey STABLES W of and longer than the house. Red brick with white-brick dressings. Central archway with shaped gable. Venetian window over the arch and attached to the gable a timber nest box.
LAYHAM HALL. *See* Raydon.

LEAVENHEATH

Strung out along the Colchester–Sudbury road, and until 1868 in the parish of Stoke-by-Nayland, to which the church was originally a chapel of ease and school combined.

ST MATTHEW. 1834–5 by *G. R. French*. A modest and pretty enough chapel of plastered brick with Tudor windows and W porch. Wrapped round this were the red brick chancel, S aisle, and bizarre SW tower with pyramid roof and flèche, neither modest nor pretty; by *Satchell & Edwards*, 1882–3.

OLD VICARAGE, E of the church, with a nice round-arched doorway, presumably also of *c.* 1835. Brick, rendered.

HONEY HALL, 1 m. S. Timber-framed and plastered, with jettied and gabled cross-wings. The r. cross-wing is at the service end and of the same date as the hall, *c.* 1400. Extending from it to the rear the kitchen, originally with no direct access to the house. The l. cross-wing is the rebuilding, *c.* 1600, of the parlour end.

LIDGATE

ST MARY. Norman nave, although the only real sign of this is the S doorway, which is of Norman proportions but was given a pointed arch when the aisles were built and the doorway was reused. C13 chancel with nobly spaced lancets on the N side. PISCINA shafted with pointed-trefoiled head. E window Dec with simple flowing tracery. Arcade Dec. Four bays. Tall octagonal piers, double-chamfered arches, W tower late C13 or early C14. Restored in stages between 1853 and 1905. – PULPIT. Jacobean. Octagonal, on a square plinth made from reused C17 woodwork. – SCREENS. Rood screen with simple one-light divisions. Restored 1871, when the gates were added. N parclose screen also with one-light divisions, but prettier tracery. S parclose screen by *W. A. Forsyth*, 1934, with good carving. – BENCHES. Straight-headed, some with linenfold decoration on the ends. – CHANDELIER. Wrought-iron and brass, for twenty-four candles. An unusual and ornate piece, probably C19. – GRAFFITI. A lot, mainly on the clunch pillars of the arcades, dating back to 1547 and including lines of music and four windmills. – STAINED GLASS. E window of 1853 attributed by Birkin Haward to *William Miller*. Chancel S window †1861 and S aisle E †1878 he assigns to *Clayton & Bell*. – BRASS. Figure of a priest, *c*. 1390, in mass vestments; 19½ in. (50 cm.). Top part of head replaced in 1901. Traditionally thought to represent John Lydgate, the poet (cf. Long Melford, p. 387), born in Lidgate *c*. 1370, but now thought more likely to be one of the rectors.

The church stands behind and above the road along which most of the village lies. Its position is explained by the fact that it was built in one of the baileys of the Norman CASTLE, which had a rectangular motte (NE of the church) and three baileys. Some ivy-clad fragments of walls E of the church and a deep ditch on the N and W sides of the churchyard. The castle was in decline by the end of the C13.

Two good houses along the main road S of the church. STREET FARMHOUSE, late C15, is timber-framed and plastered with long-wall jetty. Red brick stack with three chimneys and base with trefoil arcading. SUFFOLK HOUSE is C16, also with long-wall jetty but its timbers exposed and the bressumer partly carved. The NW end of the house is of red brick with crowstep ornamentation in the straight gable and remains of chimneys; moulded brick panelling on the return wall.

OLD RECTORY, 850 yds SE. Two-storey, white-brick house of 1842. Slate roof with deep eaves, but its steep pitch no longer Regency. Gables at each end of the three-bay range, with short gabled projections in the middle of each long side.

MOUSE HOUSE (formerly Round Cottage), ¾ m. NNW. Mid-C19 thatched *cottage orné*. Octagonal, set in a Y-plan range that faces the road (cf. East Lodge, Ousden). Flint with red brick dressings and moulded brick chimneys. Windows with Gothic-arched iron casements.

LINDSEY

9040

ST PETER. The W tower was removed in 1836 and replaced by a weatherboarded bell-turret. Early C14 church – see the segment-headed S aisle and chancel windows. One chancel S window with Y-tracery. The E window, with three cusped lancets under one arch, is of *c*. 1865, by *Francis Betts* of Stowmarket. In the nave on the N side an especially handsome straight-headed two-light window with intersected top like the famous C13 piscina of Jesus College, Cambridge. The window has shafts and niches in the jambs inside, and traces of original colouring. A second of the same type further W is blocked. Simple C14 timber S porch. Arcade inside C14 with octagonal piers and chamfered arches. Roof with tie-beams and crown-posts. – FONT. Of *c*. 1300. Square, with three blank arches on three sides. On the fourth side intersected arches with, in the spandrels, a trefoil, a circle and an encircled trefoil. – FONT COVER. C17. A homely affair, consisting of eight turned balusters leaning up against a central newel. – SCREEN. Fragments of the dado with traceried panels: a bay with original colouring, and a further run of three bays. More tracery seems to have been incorporated in the Jacobean PULPIT. Money was left for the rood beam in 1462. – BOX PEWS. – BENCH with traceried front and poppyheads. – COMMUNION RAIL. Three-sided, with turned balusters. Late C17. – ORGAN. By *Hugh Russell*, 1801. Elegant little chamber organ. From Kersey, 1927; previously at Boxford. – MONUMENT. Nicholas Hobart †1611. Inscription flanked by columns of flowers etc. and cherubs' heads. Festoons and skull below, swan-neck pediment on top.

ST JAMES'S CHAPEL, ⅓ m. S (English Heritage). Early C13, although the walls include some reused stone, which suggests it might be the replacement of a C12 building. The S wall is in its original state, with lancets and a doorway with one slight chamfer. PISCINA late C13 (pointed-trefoiled arch), W doorway early Tudor brick. Re-roofed (and perhaps shortened) in the late C15 or early C16; thatched. The chapel, which was independent and closed down in 1547, no doubt served the CASTLE that stood 350 yds SE. It lay astride a stream, which was probably used to fill its moats. The motte is low, and the arrangement of the baileys complicated. The castle was mentioned in the mid C12, and seems to have been abandoned before the end of the C13.

LITTLE BLAKENHAM

ST MARY. Nave, chancel and unbuttressed W tower. The chancel is E.E. E wall with a window of three stepped lancets under one arch. In the spandrels two pierced trefoils. Inside, l. and r. of the window, deep flat niches with shafts and trefoiled heads (cf. Nettlestead). In the N wall one lancet window with deeply splayed reveals. The other windows Dec (one nave S with elongated sexfoils in the tracery, copied on the N side *c.* 1849–52) or Perp. Restored 1868. – WALL PAINTING. In the jambs of the E.E. lancet two figures, probably originally C13. Discovered *c.* 1850 and completely repainted. Paintings in the niches on the E wall were found at the same time but have been painted over. – ROYAL ARMS. Of James II, 1685, on board.

OLD RECTORY, E of the church. The E front has two shaped gables with convex-concave sides and semicircular tops. They are C17, as is the brickwork of the S front. At the back is the C15 cross-wing of the original hall house, with crown-post roof.

LITTLE BRADLEY

No village to speak of, although earthworks E of the church are evidence that this was once a larger settlement.

ALL SAINTS. The nave and the W part of the chancel in their masonry probably Anglo-Saxon, with long-and-short work at the NW and SW angles. The age of the round W tower is disputed, but it may have pre-dated the nave; if so, Stephen Hart argues for its having been rebuilt in its entirety rather than just the top, which is Perp and octagonal, and was probably built with Thomas Hamvyll's bequest of 6s. 8d. in 1455. Small internal tower doorway on simple imposts. Early Norman E extension of the chancel with E and N windows. Norman also the undecorated S doorway and chancel arch. Restoration by *W. M. Fawcett*, 1879, with new porch, roofs and furnishings. – PULPIT. With C18 tester. – STAINED GLASS. E window 1879, and a number of others by *Heaton, Butler & Bayne*, including a S window of 1881 commemorating John Daye (*see* below). – MONUMENTS. Civilian, probably Thomas Underhill †1508 and Wife. Tudor-arched recess with kneeling brass figures. – Headless brass of a Knight, *c.* 1530, 17 in. (43.5 cm.) remaining; probably Thomas Knighton. – Richard Le Hunt †1540 and his wife Ann Soame †1558. Kneeling figures. Back wall with short columns l. and r. Two blank arches above with achievements. – John Daye †1584, printer of Foxe's Book of Martyrs, his wife and children. Hanging stone monument with kneeling brass figures and punning verse inscription ('Heere lies the Daye that darkness could not blynd / When popish fogges had over cast the sunne' etc.). – Brass of John Le Hunt †1605 and wife Jane. 18-in. (64-cm.) figures. – Thomas Soame †1606, erected by his widow Elizabeth 1612. Mural brass, with kneeling figures. – In churchyard, S of the church, a fine group of C18 headstones.

LITTLE BRADLEY HALL, N of the church, has a nice early C19 octagonal LODGE. Flint with red brick dressings and overhanging eaves supported on rustic timber posts.

LITTLE CORNARD

ALL SAINTS. Flint, of the C14 and C15. W tower with red brick battlements, and a little cupola added in 1803. Nave with brick quoins. S porch with brick windows. Two-storey N vestry. C17, red brick. Restored and re-seated by *R. C. Carpenter*, 1848. – FONT. Simple, Perp. – STAINED GLASS. E window by *Clutterbuck*, 1857. – Tower window by *Heaton, Butler & Bayne*, 1922. – Nave N by *Tim Armstrong*, 2010, incorporating a C15 roundel of an angel. – MONUMENT. Rev. Edwin Sidney †1872.

Gothic. By *Gaffin & Co.* – LYCHGATE and churchyard CROSS by *Earee & Haslewood*, 1921 (war memorials). Some good HEADSTONES, including a dual one of 1800–21 with inset cast-iron cherubs.

PEACOCK HALL, W of the church. Early C18 timber-framed and plastered house. Two storeys and attics. Three-bay fronts to NW and SE with pedimented doorcases.

OLD RECTORY, ⅓ m. W. By *Carpenter* for Rev. Edwin Sidney, 1847, and surprisingly plain. White brick. Three bays. Two storeys and attics, with three dormers in the steep slate roof.

LITTLE FINBOROUGH

ST MARY. Near the HALL (timber-framed and plastered of the C16 with a Georgianized front) but nothing else; no village. Nave, chancel and bellcote. The W wall was rebuilt, and the church generally restored and refitted, by *E. G. Pennington*, 1856–7. The rest mainly C14. – PULPIT. Of 1856–7 and, unusually for the date, a double-decker with READING DESK. – ROYAL ARMS. 1767, painted on board. Displayed on the tympanum over the rood beam, itself a rare survival. – WALL PAINTING. A fragment on the nave N wall. Unidentified figure (St Christopher?), probably C14.

LITTLE LIVERMERE

The village was removed to make way for the park of Livermere Hall, Great Livermere (q.v.). What remains is PARK FARM and beside it the ruins of the church, ST PETER AND ST PAUL. It was abandoned in 1947, the interior stripped out and the roof removed.* Of Saxo-Norman origin (long-and-short work at the NE corner, N doorway with decorated Norman lintel), altered at the E end in the C14 and the W in the C15. Narrow W tower, heightened perhaps in the C18, when much remodelling was done in Strawberry Hill Gothick, including the addition of a N chapel (squire's pew) with plaster vault.

BARROWS. At 'Seven Hills', on the parish boundary about 1¾ m. NW. Only three of the seven remain, and a ring ditch.

---

*Dispersed furnishings include PULPIT of 1755 to St John the Baptist, Egham, Surrey; ALTAR RAIL to Little Saxham (q.v.); SQUIRE'S PEW to Eton College, Bucks. (the former arrangement of BOX PEWS is described by Cautley); MONUMENT (Richard Coke †1688) to Great Livermere (q.v.).

LITTLE SAXHAM

ST NICHOLAS. The most spectacular Norman round tower in Suffolk. Round the top a rhythmical order of arches on columns. In the four main directions they hold deeply recessed two-light bell-openings, in the diagonals two lower blank arches. Billet frieze along the sill level. The tower arch into the nave is tall, and S of it is a blank arch on colonnettes with coarse volute capitals. It appears to be the cut-down reused Norman N doorway, although it shares one stone with the tower arch, making them structurally integral – perhaps explained by the stones of the tower arch being renewed. All these Norman arches have strong roll mouldings. Norman also the S doorway, also with volute capitals and also with a roll moulding and an outer billet frieze. Dec N aisle with its three-bay arcade (very elementary continuous mouldings) and its clerestory windows over. The S porch belongs to the same time. Finally the Perp contribution: the nave and chancel S sides with uncusped, rather bald tracery, the E window, and the N chapel (now vestry). Sir Thomas Lucas (*see* below) built the chapel in 1520, and in his will of 1531 asked for the chancel to be 'renewed' and 'embattled, as the church is'. Restoration by *C. H. Cooper*, 1892–3. – SCREEN. Only the dado survives (under tower arch). – ALTAR RAIL. Mid-C18, curving forward in the centre, with column-on-vase balusters. From Little Livermere, 1947. – PULPIT. Jacobean, with arched panels. Restored 1891, when the tester was added. – STALLS. The fronts have openwork flat tapering balusters, a Jacobean motif. – BENCHES. With reclining animals as poppyheads. One end has a kneeling and praying figure instead, and another has traceried ends. – BIER. C17; a rare survival. – STAINED GLASS. E window by *E. R. Suffling*, 1899; also the adjoining S window, and two nave S windows, one dated 1900. Chancel S by *Heaton, Butler & Bayne*, 1910. – MONUMENTS. Sir Thomas Lucas †1531, solicitor-general to Henry VIII. In the wall between the chancel and his N chapel Lucas placed a four-centred arch with cresting. In the arch he placed a tomb-chest with panels with lozenges and quatrefoils with shields. But he was buried in London, and the tomb-chest was broken up and the panels used to fill in the arch when the main monument in the chapel, to William, Baron Crofts, †1677 and his wife Elizabeth, was erected on the N side of the chancel wall. By *Abraham Storey*, signed by him and with his initials on a badge which the baron holds. Big standing monument of white and black marble. Two reclining effigies, he above and behind her, i.e. a conservative motif in the last quarter of the century. 'Modern' on the other hand the back architecture, with columns carrying a large scrolly pediment. Contrary to normal custom he is wearing his coronet. – Elizabeth Crofts †1642. Lengthy inscription beneath a segmental pediment with cherubs, surmounted by the unexpected feature of a bust with naked breasts. Attributed to *Henry Boughton*. – William Crofts

†1694. Coloured marbles, with swan-neck pediment. – His wife Anne †1727. By *W. Palmer*. Broken segmental pediment on fluted pilasters.

OLD RECTORY, SW of the church. Mostly C19, considerably altered and extended by Rev. W. B. Hall, rector 1852–85. Brick, partly rendered. Irregular E front, W front with five-bay centre flanked by canted bays. It originally stood on the road, but Hall obtained permission to divert this round the other side of the church in 1856. The thatched terrace of C18 timber-framed COTTAGES E of the church lost one end to the new road, with a replacement built at right angles. The older cottages were refurbished when the new ones were built: they have the same metal casements, many with arched heads, and brick chimneys with arched panels. These and other estate buildings belonged to Ickworth; other cottages S of the village on the Saxham Hall estate (Great Saxham). LITTLE SAXHAM HALL, Sir Thomas Lucas's mansion and later the Crofts', was demolished in 1773.

LITTLE STONHAM
(Stonham Parva)

Motorists know Little Stonham for the wrought-iron INN SIGN of The Magpie, supported on a wooden frame over the A140. It is probably C18 in origin, but oft renewed. The church and hall lie ½ m. W of the main road.

ST MARY (Churches Conservation Trust). C14 chancel, although the E window with reticulated tracery is C19. The rest Perp, the stepped gables of the nave and chancel supposed to be original and not part of the restoration of the chancel by *E. F. Bisshopp*, 1886. W tower richly decorated with flushwork. Arched panelling at the base, parapet with quatrefoils, battlements with arched panelling and monogram M (for Mary), and other letters spelling out most of the Ave Maria. W doorway with one order of fleurons in the jambs and arch. Frieze of quatrefoils above the doorway and a shield with the (very worn) Crane arms in the middle. S porch with diagonal buttresses decorated with flushwork. S chapel of one bay added later, to its E. Clerestory with close windows, built at the same time as the fine double hammerbeam roof. Wall-posts with seated figures in nodding ogee niches; carved spandrels. The wall-post and hammerbeam in the SE corner are a richly carved replacement of the C17. The chancel roof belongs to Bisshopp's restoration (good carving by *John Groom & Son*); his also the flying buttress in front of the priest's door (cf. Framlingham (E) etc.). – FONT. Octagonal. Four lions against the stem. Demi-figures of angels supporting the bowl. Against the bowl three angels, two crowned Ms, the Crown of Thorns, a Tudor rose and the Crucifixion. This shows Christ with legs uncrossed, a convention that is rarely found after the C12. – BENCHES. 1928–9 by *H. M. Cautley*, made by *E. Barnes*. – WEST DOOR. With tracery. – WEST GALLERY. C18, on iron columns, with panelled front. – MONUMENT. Gilbert Mouse †1622, buried at St Margaret's, Westminster. Black tablet with demi-figure in an arch. White marble frame with hourglass, skull and crossbones, and other emblems of mortality.

LITTLE STONHAM HALL, NW of the church. C17 timber-framed house, remodelled and enlarged in the early C19, including a parallel range to the rear. Plastered Georgian front of five broad bays. Three-bay centre with broad open pediment and pedimented doorcase.

CLOCK HOUSE, ⅔ m. NNE. A house of the mid to late C15, altered *c.* 1600. Hall range with central two-storey porch-like projection facing the road, and two cross-wings. The hall, which was floored *c.* 1600, has its original crown-post truss. Octagonal post with four-way struts. Also of *c.* 1600 the circular chimneys, decorated with fleur-de-lys and roses, and the good plaster ceiling in the parlour chamber of the S cross-wing. It has geometrical ribbed panels, pendants and other motifs. Elsewhere painted decoration, a free-flowing stem motif in grisaille. Rescued in the 1920s by Muriel Schofield and restored by her son *Sydney Schofield*.

The VILLAGE is strung out along the A140. On the W side of the road the BAPTIST CHURCH of 1816, enlarged 1833. Timber-framed and plastered with gabled front and two tiers of sash windows. On the E side the OLD RECTORY. The four-bay centre is a late C15 timber-framed house of Wealden type. Smoke-blackened crown-post roof to the former open hall. Parlour end to the S rebuilt in the mid C19. THE MAGPIE, already mentioned, stands at the N end of the village. It has a C15 timber-framed range with an early C16 jettied cross-wing extending towards the road; in the angle between them an early C19 range of painted brick.

LITTLE THURLOW

6050

ST PETER. Early C14. The W tower has a W window with intersected-cusped tracery. The top, with a flushwork chequerboard pattern, is Perp. Both aisles have segment-headed Dec windows, the S side also two with uncusped Y-tracery. Clerestory windows trefoiled and C19 on the S side, round and C17 on the N. Arcade with octagonal piers and double-chamfered arches, probably Dec. The N chapel is of brick plastered, the roof inside dated 1621; built by his widow and sons to accommodate the monument to Sir Stephen Soame (*see* below). The soffits of two of the round arches from the chancel and N aisle have Jacobean arabesque decoration. Contemporary FAMILY PEW. The church was restored in 1843 by *William Perry* of Clare, including new chancel roof and BENCHES with poppyheads. – FONT. Square, Norman, with angle shafts. Bold foliage motifs, each different, on three faces, and a cross patonce on the fourth. By the same carvers as the font at Hawkedon. – SCREENS. Of the rood screen only the dado survives, with panels with prettily painted flowers. Tower screen by *Laurence H. Bond*, 1965. – COMMUNION RAIL. Originally three-sided; mid or late C17. – HELM. C17 (Soame Chapel). – SCULPTURE. Bronze maquette* by *Elisabeth Frink* of St Edmund, given by her as a monument to her father, Brigadier H. A. C. Frink †1974. – CHANDELIER. Brass, acquired between 1729 and 1735. Two tiers of six branches. Candlesticks on reading desk of about the same date, but acquired between 1740 and 1747. – WALL PAINTINGS. Slight remains either side of the chancel arch. – STAINED GLASS. Original glass in the oval W window of the Soame Chapel. Chancel S windows probably by *Frederick Preedy*, c. 1865–70. S aisle E by *Geoffrey Webb*, 1937. – MONUMENTS. Brass of a Knight and Lady, c. 1520. 18½-in. (47-cm.) figures. Thought to be William Walpole †1500. – Sir Stephen Soame †1619, Lord Mayor of London and benefactor of Little Thurlow. Large and excellent alabaster structure. Two recumbent effigies, he behind and a little above her. To the l. and r. groups of four columns, two detached, two attached. The children arranged round and between these columns and also on the ground, two kneeling frontally l. and r. of the base, and three in profile in front of the base. The columns carry little pediments from which springs a well-detailed arch, e.g. with a frieze of cherubs' heads. On the top, Father Time l. and Victory r. Original iron railings. Attributed by Jon Bayliss to *Jan Janssen*. – Rev. John Daye †1627. Large pedimented tablet with skull. – Stephen Soame †1771. By *J. Walsh* of London. Strigillated sarcophagus on which is a medallion with a relief of a grieving mother and infant child, representing his widow Frances who wrote the verse on the accompanying inscription plate. Obelisk background. – John Andrews †1794. Painted inscription on wall of bell chamber to a drowned bellringer:

> Beneath his fav'rite Bell poor Andrews lies:
> No pitying Naiade heard his dying cries
> When in the Stour he fell: His spirit rose
> To brighter Climes and left this World of woes.

– Benjamin Preedy †1828. By *T. Tomson* of Cambridge. – Catherine Soame †1882. By *L. Jackaman*.
LITTLE THURLOW HALL. The Elizabethan house, the seat of the Soame family, was rebuilt on a slightly different site in 1847

---

*For the full-size sculpture opposite the old W front of the abbey church, Bury St Edmunds (*see* p. 132).

by *Charles Erswell* of Saffron Walden. White brick. Two storeys. In the middle of the five-bay front a stuccoed porch with pilasters, and over it more pilasters and open pediment. The layout of the gardens is recorded in an estate map of 1735, from which a long canal, a shorter one, and two ponds survive.

A number of good buildings in the village, of which the best are two foundations by Sir Stephen Soame. Both red brick with stuccoed window surrounds. Just outside the village to the N, former ALMSHOUSES for nine poor people, endowed in 1618. Three ranges facing an oblong forecourt. Single-storey, except for the gabled centre. In the middle of the village, the former SCHOOLHOUSE, founded 1614. Two storeys and three bays, the centre bay projecting and gabled. Coat of arms over the door. Between these two, POUND GREEN, with the Hall on the W side and a good C16 timber-framed and plastered house, its main range jettied, on the N. In the street S of the old schoolhouse, THE COCK pub, timber-framed and plastered, its front remodelled in the C18. Over the entrance a window with an elliptical head and Gothick glazing bars. Next to it LAVENDER COTTAGE, C16, timber-framed and plastered with gabled and jettied cross-wings. On the same side of the road, but set back, the octagonal base of a former WINDMILL. Smock mill, 1865; rendered brick.

LITTLE WALDINGFIELD

ST LAWRENCE. Largely C14, altered and given Perp windows in the C15, and unobtrusively restored in 1872. W tower, nave and aisles and clerestory, the walls of flint but mostly rendered. Distinguishing features are the two rood-stair turrets with their crocketed spirelets, and the Tudor brick N porch. This has a stepped gable set in a steep plain gable, with three pinnacles. Beneath the centre one a niche for a statue. S porch of brick and flint, roughly striped. Unusual also the rather fussy decoration over the S aisle windows, which occurs more prominently inside. The arcades have quatrefoil piers with embattled capitals and carry arches of one wave and one hollow with little decorative ogee gables. The same motif over the doorways, that on the S side with crowns, faces and big square fleurons. The E window looks plain C17 Gothic. Evidence of a chapel on the exterior N wall of the chancel: remains of doorway, aumbry and piscina. The roofs in the nave, cambered on arched braces, and in the aisles are original. – FONT. Octagonal, with the Emblems of the Evangelists and four frontal figures of monks with books. Angels round the base of the bowl. Late C14. – PULPIT. Jacobean; good. Panels with the usual blank arches and below them panels with diagonal crosses and acorn pendants. Frieze of stylized foliage at the top and then a carved book-rest on carved brackets. – WEST DOOR. With a band of quatrefoils.

– NORTH DOOR. With a band of foliage trails outside, and a band of shields and quatrefoils inside. Money was left for making new doors in 1466. – CHESTS. One of Baltic oak, its front carved with Perp tracery and, within the tracery, four heads. It probably dates from the third quarter of the C14. Another of *c.* 1300 with coved lid. – STAINED GLASS. S aisle: E window †1895 by *Clayton & Bell*; some C15 fragments in W window. – BRASSES. John Colman †1506, in civilian dress, with six sons and seven daughters and indent of wife; main figure 29 in. (74 cm.). – Robert Appleton †1526, in armour, and wife Mary; 19 in. (48 cm.). – John Wyncoll, clothier †1544, in civilian dress; 18 in. (46 cm.).

CHURCHSIDE, along the W side of the churchyard, is a nice row of C17 or C18 timber-framed and plastered cottages with crowstepped brick gables and chimneystacks at each end, concealed at the N end by an extension. To their W a small former READING ROOM, 1902–3. Red brick with stone dressings. Porch with fretted bargeboards and windows with cusped lights. SE of the church, the former NATIONAL SCHOOL by *Robert Hawkins* of Monks Eleigh, 1875. Red brick, with a little diapering and other black-brick decoration, but otherwise plain.

THE PRIORY, opposite the church. The name of the house appears to be a C19 invention and does not indicate monastic origins. The oldest part is a three-bay range of red brick with crowstepped gables, probably early C16. Two storeys and attics with groin-vaulted brick cellar. Transomed windows of two lights with round-arched heads. Crown-post roof. Three-bay, early C19 painted brick range across the NE end facing the road. Large additions of *c.* 1880 to the rear in the style of the C16 range, and a small NW extension by *Rodney Black*, 2004–5, that bridges the stylistic gap between the early and late C19 parts.

HOLBROOK HALL, ½ m. W. By *Ewan Christian*, 1884. Red brick, partly diapered, with stone dressings. Elizabethan style. Symmetrical garden front with two crowstepped gables. Two more gables on the entrance front, but asymmetrical, with porch on one and chimneystack between them. High roof and higher chimneys. Stables and other outbuildings in similar style. Now Brookwood Manor (care home).

WOOD HALL, ¼ m. N. Timber-framed two-storey L-plan house of the early C16, probably built in two phases: first a range at right angles to the road, jettied along the NE side, followed by the range along the road. Timbers exposed on the inner faces, but the outer faces clad in white brick by Rev. Barrington Syer †1849, who was lord of the manor as well as incumbent. Brick façades of two and a half storeys, divided by pilasters formed of bricks with chevron and nailhead ornament. Five wide bays along the road. Central tetrastyle portico with stiff-leaf capitals. A little to the NE, MALTING FARM, timber-framed and probably also C16 but the front very prettily remodelled in the late C18 or early C19, with decorative plasterwork and a castellated parapet between two gables. At the NE end a tripartite window with plaster moulding to give a Venetian effect. Attached to that end red brick maltings with circular oast. Range of flint and brick outbuildings.

LITTLE WENHAM

Little Wenham Hall and the parish church to its N occupy an isolated site, moated on two sides. Both date from the late C13, when the manor belonged to Sir John de Vaux †1287, but were probably actually built by one of his resident tenants, most likely Master Roger de Holebrok, tenant from 1270/1 to 1294/5.

LITTLE WENHAM HALL (also known as Wenham Castle) is of great historical importance for two reasons. The first is that it is built largely of brick, and represents one of the earliest uses of home-made brick in England. Flint is used, with septaria, only for the base of the walls, and Caen stone for the much rebuilt buttresses and dressings. The character of the brickwork is charmingly crude, the bricks being of several sizes and colours, but predominantly yellow. The quantity of them indicates that they must have been made locally rather than imported from the Low Countries, although Flemish craftsmen may have been employed. The second point of outstanding interest is that the house is a house and not a keep. It is fortified of course, but would not have been able to withstand any serious assault, and it is in its shape and appointment on the way from the fortress to the manor house and so ranks with Stokesay Castle and Acton Burnell (both Shrops.), of about the same date, as one of the incunabula of English domestic architecture.

The house is L-shaped with a spiral staircase in the re-entrant angle. On the ground floor of the main range is a room of three bays, rib-vaulted in brick. The arches and ribs have one hollow chamfer. It has an original outside door at the S end, and another next to it in the W wall which may be entirely later or an original opening remodelled: over it is a stone dated 1569. Opening off the N end, on the E side, is a small square room, also rib-vaulted, with the entrance to the staircase in one corner. On the first floor the principal chamber is slightly larger than the undercroft, because the walls are thinner, and it is well lit, with four windows, all of two lights with plate tracery, including unencircled trefoils and quatrefoils. In the W wall is a fireplace, altered in the C16, and in the S wall a large drain set in a Perp ogee arch. There are outside doors corresponding to those on the ground floor, and another blocked doorway in the E wall. At least one of these doorways, probably the E, must have led originally to a garderobe. From the chamber one enters the CHAPEL at the N end. The doorway is flanked, as if it were that to a miniature chapter house, by two internal

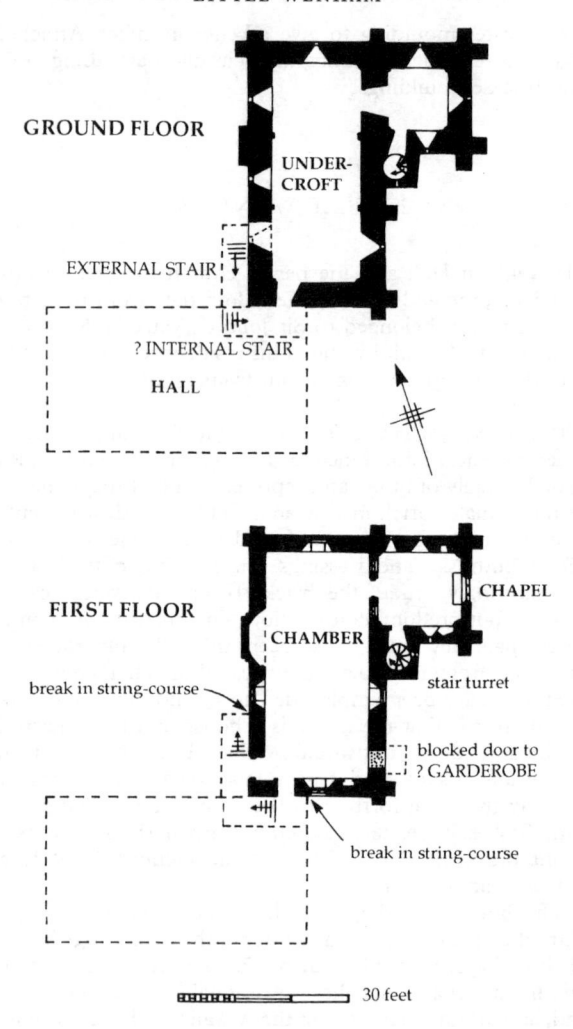

Little Wenham Hall.
Plan, including demolished parts

two-light windows with oddly detailed polygonal shafts and quatrefoils in plate tracery. The chamber was unvaulted – the present ceiling is assigned to the C16 – but the chapel has a rib-vault with a fine profile to the ribs. The vault rests on corbels, and of these the two earlier ones have stiff-leaf capitals. On the boss a crudely carved figure, said to be St Petronilla, an interpretation possibly influenced by the fact that Sir John de Vaux's daughter shared her name. Angle piscina with two pointed-trefoiled arches. E window of three lights with bar tracery of trefoiled circles, a form in advance of those of the chamber. On the N side a lowside window. Above the chapel is a small unheated chamber. This has two windows with Y-tracery on polygonal shafts. The roofs are embattled, although this may date from the C16. The different heights of the main range, chapel range and higher stair-turret create a picturesque skyline.

The way in which the building was used has been much debated.* A description of 1512 refers to 'a hall with a vault of lime and stone, with a tower of the same and different rooms joined on to the hall, and connecting with a kitchen larder-house built under a roof with other rooms under and above'. This other block, which has left no trace and was presumably timber-framed, must have joined at the SW corner of the main range, because either side of this corner there is a clear and deliberate break in the plinth and string course that otherwise run round the entire building, and all the other corners have angle buttresses. If the description is taken at face value, then the main first-floor room would have been the hall, and the room over the chapel the solar. But there is increasing evidence (e.g. Boothby Pagnell, Lincs., and Old Soar, Plaxtol, Kent) of houses with a stone-built chamber block attached to a now-vanished timber-framed hall, and this may well have been the case at Little Wenham: if so the chamber was effectively the solar, or private retiring room (albeit an uncommonly large one) and the room over the chapel was a bedchamber. The alignment of the timber-framed hall range is also debatable, but it is likely to have been E–W, with an internal stair leading to the door in the S wall of the solar; there would also have been an external stair leading to the door in the W wall.

Alterations were made to the Hall, as we have seen, in the C16; with the date 1569 are the initials JB, for Sir John Brewse. The family held the estate until 1695, when it was purchased by John Thurston; his son William is said to have been the last person to inhabit the building, before selling it in 1765. Restoration work was carried out at the end of the C19 by *J. S. Corder* for G. E. Crisp.

W of the Hall, but inside the moat, is a C16 building (now CASTLE HOUSE), timber-framed and plastered, with C18 additions. It may originally have functioned as a service range rather than living accommodation, and may have been converted to a dwelling when the Hall was abandoned in the C18. In 1912 *Corder* built a new house for F. A. Crisp NE of the Hall. Heavily half-timbered with gables, brick chimneys etc., seen also in lodges and other estate houses, one dated 1911. Between the old hall and the church, a group of C17–C19 farm buildings, and W of the church a handsome C16 BARN, timber-framed with brick-nogging.

ALL SAINTS (Churches Conservation Trust). Mainly flint, the nave and chancel contemporary with the Hall. W tower, for which money was left in 1417, with a red brick top probably

* *See PSIAH* vol. 39 (1998), 151–64.

Little Wenham, All Saints,
brass to Thomas Brewse †1514 and wife Jane.
Rubbing by M. Stuchfield, 2014

of the time of Henry VIII. C15 S porch with timber balusters in the W and E walls, probably Jacobean. Windows with fine slender mullions, Y-tracery on the N and S and three unfoiled circles in the head of the E window. Also a lowside lancet. Chancel roof repaired and upper part of E wall rebuilt 1878. General restoration 1901–3, no doubt by *Corder*, when the six-light window high up on the S side of the chancel was inserted. – FONT. Of the same period as the church or a little earlier. Big octagonal bowl on eight polygonal supports. – PULPIT. C18, simple. – SCREEN. Lower part only of a plastered rubble wall. The upper part, described in 1807, had a central arched doorway and four trefoiled arched openings to either side, similar in effect to the entrance to the Hall chapel. It had been taken down by 1828. – BENCHES. Two, with linenfold panelling. – WALL PAINTINGS. On the E wall astonishingly good and well-preserved wall paintings contemporary with the architecture. On the l. Virgin and Child and four Angels, on the r. St Margaret, St Catherine and St Mary Magdalene under a very elaborate canopy that includes a complete building. Also, on the nave N wall, St Christopher, C15, more ordinary in quality. It was painted over an earlier painting of the Virgin and Child. – MONUMENTS. Tomb recess in nave S wall. Late C14, possibly of Gilbert de Debenham, whose will of 1361, proved 1374, requested burial in the S wall. Big cusped and subcusped arch under an ogee gable, set against a panel of tracery and pinnacles on shafts. The tomb-chest is decorated with shields in quatrefoils. – Brass to Thomas Brewse †1514 and wife Jane. 28-in. (70-cm.) figures under a fine and complete double canopy. – Tomb recess, chancel N wall, latest Perp with simple canopy carrying the Brewse arms. Set in it a tablet to John Brewse †1785. – Sir John Brewse †1585. With small kneeling figure in profile in a small arched recess. The surround has columns l. and r. and a pediment, and is painted in imitation of marble. – Alice Walker †1683. Fine cartouche, with cherubs' heads and garland. Attributed to *James Hardy* (GF).

LITTLE WHELNETHAM

ST MARY MAGDALENE. Prettily situated in the garden (or so it feels) of Little Whelnetham Hall. In the churchyard, immediately E of the church, the remains of a circular flint building, perhaps C11. Excavations in 1967 failed to establish its origins and purpose; it seems too insubstantial to be the base of a tower. The church itself is small. W tower and chancel probably C13, but with Dec windows. Lowside window with iron grille in the chancel. Nave mostly Perp. S doorway with the figure of an angel at the apex of the arch. In the S wall a re-set Norman PILLAR PISCINA. Nice Perp brick porch with stepped gable.

There was a restoration by *J. D. Wyatt*, 1879. The nave roof (restored by *H. Ringham*, *c.* 1842) has the unusual rhythm of one pair of principals with hammerbeams and then two simply with arched braces. Lively carvings of grotesque faces etc. In the nave E wall below the roof a sexfoiled circular window. – FONT. Octagonal, Perp, simple. – SCREEN. Only the dado remains. – LECTERN. A very large eagle. C17, probably Dutch. – BENCH ENDS. With poppyheads and tracery. Also restored by *Ringham*. – MONUMENTS. Rev. Edward Agas †1680 and wife Rachel †1677. Ledger stone incised with the shapes of two headstones separated by a Corinthian column with skull and crossbones. Copied for William Bauley †1705 and wife Susan †1718.

CRUTCHED FRIARS, ¾ m. SSW. An interesting and picturesque house. At its NE corner the angle buttress and some flint wall of the chapel of the house of the Crutched Friars, founded by 1274 and later dependent on the London house. In the E wall of the house more of the flint walling. The rest of the house seems to have been rebuilt not long before the Dissolution. U-plan, the chapel originally forming the N side. The E, S and W fronts of red brick with some diapering. Stepped gable at the S end of the E front with re-set terracotta tiles. A row of four small first-floor windows, presumably for brothers' cells. Massive chimneys at either end of the S front, and at the W end another stepped gable. Pretty three-sided courtyard to the N, once the cloister, with timber arcading (now glazed) below the jettied upper storey. W range sensitively extended by the *Whitworth Co-Partnership c.* 2003–4 to balance the E range.

SICKLESMERE. *See* Great Whelnetham.

LITTLE WRATTING

HOLY TRINITY. The C19 W bell-turret with short shingled spire reminds us how close we are to Essex. It is supported internally on Perp timberwork, also more characteristic of Essex than Suffolk. Nave and chancel of septaria and flint. The nave is probably late Anglo-Saxon – see the masonry and the shapes of the N and S doorways. The S doorway has a lintel with a dedication inscription in large letters. It is, unfortunately, incomplete. The E half of the chancel is Dec. E window with minor (rather standardized) flowing tracery. Dec also the PISCINA. The Neo-Norman chancel arch belongs to the restoration of 1895, which also included re-roofing. – BENCHES. Simple, straight-headed, with a little tracery. – One BOX PEW, made up from late C16 panelling. Not *in situ*. – SOUTH DOOR. With Norman C-hinges and other ironwork. – MONUMENT. One kneeling figure from a Jacobean monument. It stood in a former N chapel (Turnour Chapel) which was pulled down in 1710, but of which the Perp W respond survives.

Former SCHOOL, ¼ m. ESE. An eccentric little building, now a house reasonably named The Folly. 1849. Flint, with painted brick dressings. Large shaped gables at each end, and on the porch.

WASH FARM, ⅔ m. ENE. C17 timber-framed and plastered house. Large central chimney with six stacks, now rendered. Inside the house, on the ground and first floors, a wide passageway between the backs of the two fireplaces.

LONG MELFORD

8040

Long Melford is a linear settlement that developed along Peddars Way, one of the two main N–S roads of Roman Suffolk. It is indeed long – 1½ miles from Melford Place to High Street Farm – and halfway between these two extremities are the former mill and site of the ford that give the place the name by which it was known by the mid C15. Long Melford prospered greatly in the later Middle Ages from the cloth trade, which has left a rich legacy of timber-framed houses and, in particular, its magnificent church. In the C19, too, it was surprisingly industrialized: the railway arrived in 1865, and White's *Directory* for 1891–2 mentions the manufacture of horsehair seating and coconut-fibre matting, as well as a large foundry (Ward & Silver, established in 1843) and extensive maltings, all of which have left their mark on the place. In addition, Long Melford possesses two fine Tudor mansions, Melford Hall and Kentwell Hall, both with medieval roots.

HOLY TRINITY

Long Melford church is one of the most moving parish churches in England, large, proud and noble – large certainly with its

Long Melford, Holy Trinity.
Plan, drawn by B. Haward, 1989

length inside nave and chancel of 153 ft (46.6 metres), proud certainly with the many commemorative inscriptions which distinguish it from all others, and noble also without question with the aristocratic proportions of the exterior of its nave and aisles. The layout of its component parts is as complex as that of many cathedrals, and it is necessary to understand the development of the church's plan before considering its appearance.

The oldest parts of the present church date from c. 1380–90: the five W bays of the nave arcades. Between about 1467 and 1507 a major rebuilding took place. It seems likely that *Simon Clerk* was master mason for this work, the progress of which can be followed by bequests but especially by the detailed inscriptions. These record the names of many who gave money to these buildings, and it is illuminating to see how such a major building enterprise was jointly financed by the rich men of the prosperous little town, with John Clopton of Kentwell, it would seem, taking the lead. Unlike most inscriptions on churches at this time (e.g. neighbouring Glemsford), Long Melford's are (with one small exception) in English rather than Latin. Some have been lost, but most are known from a transcription made in 1688 by the rector, Nathaniel Bisbie. They run as follows:*

Clerestory N side:

> Pray for the sowlis of Roberd Sparwe and Marion his wife & for Thomas Cowper and Ma'el his wif, of qwos goodis Mast[er] Gilis Dent Jon Clopton Jon Smyth Roger Smyth with th[e] help of weel disposyd me[n] of this [to]wn dede these sevi[n] archis new repare anno domini milesimo CCCC°i

A further inscription, now lost, recorded the fact that John Clopton built the first four eastern bays.

On the S clerestory, it says over the first twelve windows from the W:

> [Pr]ay for the sowlis of Rogere Moryell Margarett & Kateryn his wyffis of w[h]os goodis the seyd Kateryn John Clopton Mast[er] Wyllyem Qwaytis an[d]John Smyth dede these vi archis new repare and ded make the tabill' at the [h]ye awtere anno domini Millesimo quadringentesimo octogesi[m]o pri[mo].

Further sections on this side are commemorated as follows:

> Pray for the sowl of Thomas Couper the wych th[y]s harch neu repad / Pray for the sowl of law' Martyn and Marion hys wif' & for Rychard Martyn & Elisabeth & Jhone hys

---

*Based on D. Dymond and C. Paine, *Five Centuries of an English Parish Church* (2012), which contains much other valuable information based on documentary sources.

Long Melford, Holy Trinity, inscription.

wyvys & f[r]endis thyat thys Chawncel repared a[nno] do[min]l M°CCCClxx[ix]

On the s side is a series of inscriptions lower down, beginning with a portion w of the porch which was damaged in the fall of the tower and ran:

> Pray for the sowl of Mast[e]r Giles Dent, late pason / John Clopton Maist[er] Rob[er]t Coteler & Thoms Elys did this arch make glase & the ruf wt . . .

On the s porch:

> Pray for the soulis of William Clopton Margery & Marg[er]y / his wifis and for the soule of Alice Clopton & for John Clopto[n] and for / alle thoo soulis tht the seyd John is bou[n]de to prey for

Then over the windows E of the porch:

> Pray for the soule of Rog[er] Moriell' of whos good[es] this arch was made. / Pray for the soule of John Keche and for his fad[er] and mod[er] of whos good[es] this arch was made / P[ra]y for the soull' of Thom[a]s Elys & Jone his wife & for the good sped of Jone Elys mak[er]s h[er]of / Pray for the soulle of John Pie & Alys his wyf of whos good[es] this arch was made & thes twey[n] wy[n]dowys glasid. / Pray for the soulis of John Dist[er] & Alis a[n]d for the good sped of John Dist[er] and Xpĩan mak[er]s h[er]of

Bequests by Thomas Elys and John Pie are also recorded in wills of 1487.

Over the three windows of the s chapel:

> Pray for the soulis of Laurens Martyn & Maryon his wyffe Elysabeth Martyn a[n]d Jone & for the good estat of Richard Martyn & Roger Mar[tyn and the] – wyvis and alle the chyldr[en] of whose good[es] [. . .] made Anno domini . . . Millesimo CCCC°lxxx° & iiii°

Richard Martyn, in his will of 1500, asked to be buried in the s aisle or chapel 'which I did make for me, my wife and my children to lie in'.

Finally, round the Lady Chapel:

> Pray for the sowle of John Hyll and for the sowle of John Clopton Esqwyer and pray for the sowle off Rychard Loveday boteler wythe John Clopton off whos godys thys chappel ys inbaytyllyd by hys excewtors / Pray for the soulis of William Clopto[n] esquyer Margery and Marg[er]y his wifis and for all' ther parentis & childri[n] & for the sowle of Alice Clopton & for John Clopton & for all' his childri[n] / and for all tho soulis that the seid John is bou[n]de to p[ra]y for which deed this chap[e]l newe repare A[nn]o dom[min]i M°CCC°lxxxxvi° Christ[us] sit testis hec me no[n] exhibuisse ut merear laudes set ut spiritus me moretur Roger Smyth and Robert Smyth

So, first after 1467 the nave was extended two bays E, and the chancel was extended E to compensate (completed 1479). The clerestory was built, under a new roof that ran the full length of the church (1481). Rebuilding of the S aisle followed, incorporating the Martyn Chapel (1484). In the last decade of the C15 John Clopton began building the Lady Chapel E of the chancel, dated 1496. The vestry between the Martyn Chapel and the Lady Chapel was built by 1507, according to the will of Geoffrey Foote who had paid for it.

This leaves the Clopton Chapel and Clopton Chantry Chapel, for which there is no firm evidence. The former contains the tomb of Sir William Clopton †1446, but there is no reason to assume that this is in its original position. Stylistically, the Clopton Chapel is comparable to the Martyn Chapel, i.e. of the 1480s. It must be earlier than the Clopton Chantry Chapel, to which it is joined, albeit awkwardly, and the Chantry Chapel is referred to by Clopton in the will he made in 1494. The Chantry Chapel must also pre-date the Lady Chapel, for the presence of the Chantry Chapel explains why the Lady Chapel is placed off-centre.

EXTERIOR. The characteristic feature is the two tall transomed three-light windows for each bay, repeated by the tall transomed clerestory windows. So many thin, wiry perpendiculars are rare even in the Perp style. Once this has been said, attention must however be drawn to the many curious impurities which for some detract from, and for others increase, the pleasure one experiences in approaching along the relatively narrow passage from the S, impurities which can be explained by the way in which the building grew. The Martyn Chapel at the E end of the S aisle has different window tracery and a different rhythm, two wider and between them one narrow window above the priest's doorway. The four-lobed pattern in the heads of the windows occurs also at Burwell, Cambs., attributed to *Reginald Ely*, and the chapel may have been his work or that of his apprentice, *John Melford* (cf. Cavendish). The eastern bay of the S aisle has one window rather than the two found in the other bays, positioned moreover not centrally between the buttresses. This was to allow for the rood screen

LONG MELFORD: HOLY TRINITY 385

and loft that stood behind it; the reason for the asymmetry is more apparent on the N side, where the rood stair projects in a brick turret. The next bay to the W is slightly narrower than the others – more easily discernible in the flushwork between the clerestory windows – and the corresponding bays of the arcades are narrower too. Clive Paine suggests that this may have been the site of the crossing of the original church. The unity is further disturbed by the projecting sanctuary, which has no clerestory and instead an exceedingly tall window to the S (and N); moreover, this has a two-centred arch, but all the clerestory windows have four-centred ones. The sides have eighteen clerestory windows each, corresponding to twelve lower windows. Flint with, on the S side – which is of course the show-front towards the green and the village – much flushwork decoration. The decoration does not obtrude itself, which is another proof of the nobility and purity of the designer. The N side is simpler and has no flushwork on the walls, only on the clerestory and parapet, as if it were going to be seen only from a distance, such as from the Cloptons' Kentwell Hall. Nor does the N side have a porch. The S porch is tall, of two bays, with two-light windows.

The sanctuary projects one bay, and beyond it lies a narrow (priest's) vestry of two storeys. This ends in line with the E end of the Clopton Chantry Chapel on the N side and a low second (choir) vestry on the S side. This looks like a corridor to the Lady Chapel, which is an independently designed, much lower building, with its own separate entrance on the S side as well as a N door (for the Cloptons?). Throughout it has three-light windows with depressed arches and no tracery at all. Flushwork decoration here is less reticent, and rather clumsily continued up into the gables of the three pitched roofs added to the E end in 1680, when the chapel was adapted for use as a school (restored as a chapel in 1888–9); according to a depiction of the church in 1613, the chapel originally had a clerestory over the central part. These C17 roofs cut painfully into the view of the E window from the sanctuary. The Lady Chapel's E end is altogether curious, because the 'nave' seems to be represented not by one big E window, but by two not at all distinguished from the others. There is an internal reason for this, as we shall see.

The unsatisfactory proportions of the tower, similarly, reflect its history, for it is a Georgian structure in Neo-Gothic clothing. The C14 W tower was struck by lightning in 1701, rebuilt by *Daniel Hills* of Long Melford, 1712–25, and heightened and encased in flint and stone by *G. F. Bodley*, 1897–1903. Angle buttresses and pinnacles. Flushwork on the battlements and base. W doorway with ogee arch, shields, and above it a frieze with shields, all in the local tradition.

INTERIOR. Nine-bay arcades and the sanctuary bay. The five earlier W bays have already been mentioned. They have four major and four minor shafts and unmistakable moulded capitals. The others are similar but slimmer and quite characteristically turned Perp. The division between nave and chancel is marked by a step and a modification of the piers to accommodate the rood screen. Roll mouldings to the shafts which rise up from the spandrels and apexes of the arches to the roof principals. The wall below the clerestory windows is panelled so as to seem a blank continuation of the windows. Cambered tie-beam roof, the spandrels pierced with tracery. The nave roof and clerestory were restored by *Rickman & Hutchinson*, 1828, and the church generally was sensitively restored in 1867–9 by *Henry Woodyer*, including the new tower arch. For the Clopton Chantry Chapel, *see* below.

The LADY CHAPEL is internally very unusual. It seems externally a five-bay building with aisles. It is in fact a three-bay chapel with, instead of aisles, what Clopton in a codicil to his will (1497) described as a cloister on all four sides, and which may have functioned as an ambulatory for processions. So the altar has a solid E wall behind, and the first bay is separated from the second by a wall with a doorway (with fleuron decoration) and two two-light windows, just like an external W entrance. Big frieze with shields in quatrefoils above this group, probably not *in situ*, as the wall-post over the centre has been cut off to make way for it. The arcade of the central chapel is low, but above it there are blank panelling and niches with canopies. One must think of this in all its original bright colouring to appreciate it fully, and take into account the fact that the clerestory removed in the C17 would have made it much lighter. Exquisite cambered roofs, especially that of the cloister, where the beams rest on corbels with little figures. Cornice carved after the manner of the Clopton Chantry Chapel (*see* below), but apparently never painted. The cloister character is expressed by the four corner bays having beams set diagonally. The Lady Chapel was repaired by *F. C. Eden*, 1911–16.

FURNISHINGS. FONT. Octagonal, Perp, simple, of Purbeck marble, which is rare in Perp Suffolk. – FONT COVER. By *H. M. Cautley*, 1936. – REREDOS. By *Farmer & Brindley*, 1877. Caen stone. The central panel is partly based on a painting of the Crucifixion by *Dürer*, but also corresponds to a mid-C16 description by Roger Martin of the pre-Reformation reredos. – PULPIT. 1884. Caen stone and marble, with figure carving. – SEAT (Clopton Chapel). Copy of a seat from Granada Cathedral, Spain. With the arms of Ferdinand and Isabella, i.e. late C15. – SCULPTURE (N aisle). Fine alabaster relief, with remains of painting and gilding, of the Adoration of the Magi, the Virgin reclining on a couch. Mid to late C14. – BENCHES (Lady Chapel). By *Richard Almack*, 1833. Simple, with cusped ends and curved fronts to the seats. – CHOIR STALLS and NAVE SEATING by *Woodyer*. – ROYAL ARMS. Very delicate carved limewood; probably George II (over S door; originally on top of the Georgian reredos). – HATCHMENTS. Viscount Savage †1635 (S aisle). The earliest in the county. Two more groups of four, 1807–56. – CLOCK (Lady Chapel).

LONG MELFORD: HOLY TRINITY 387

Tavern clock by *Thomas Moore* of Ipswich. Mid-C18. – STAINED GLASS. The finest collection of medieval stained glass in Suffolk. Gathered in the C19 by R. Almack, re-set in the N aisle by *G. King & Son*, 1957–78. Late C15, including a unique collection of kneeling donors at the W end. Over the N door a Pietà with kneeling figure of a donor, and below it a tiny group of rabbits' heads apparently symbolizing the Trinity. Some C17 glass included in the rearrangement. In the Clopton Chantry Chapel, a small panel with lily crucifix; possibly mid-C14. Clopton Chapel N by *Eden*, 1938. Martyn Chapel S by *Clayton & Bell*, 1880 (Ascension). S aisle eastern window by *H. Hughes*, 1874, then one by *Ward & Hughes*, 1885. In the Lady Chapel, more medieval fragments; also the 'Brownie Window', 2000, by *Léonie Seliger* (*The Cathedral Studio*).

BRASSES. Clopton Chapel: Lady of the Clopton family, *c.* 1420; 18 in. (46 cm.). – Civilian, possibly Thomas Clopton †1420; 18½ in. (47 cm.). – Lady of the Clopton family, probably Margery, mother of John Clopton †1497. In heraldic dress, with kirtle and mantle, and butterfly head-dress, engraved *c.* 1480; 35½ in. (90 cm.). – A similar figure, probably John Clopton's half-sister Alice Harleston, who predeceased him; 36½ in. (93 cm.). – Francis Clopton †1577, in armour; 34½ in. (88 cm.). – Martyn Chapel: Roger Martyn †1615 and two wives; 21 in. (53 cm.). – Richard Martin †1624, three wives and children; 17 in. (44 cm.).

MONUMENTS. The capital monument is the CLOPTON CHANTRY CHAPEL. It is approached from the Clopton Chapel by a tiny vestibule or priest's room with a stone fan-vault so flat that it is almost a panelled ceiling. The room has a fireplace. The chantry has a seven-light E window and towards the chancel the monument to John Clopton †1497. This is a plain sturdy tomb-chest of Purbeck marble with cusped quatrefoils containing shields. No effigy. Ogee arch open to the chancel. In the vault beneath this arch and above the tomb-chest PAINTINGS, especially the Risen Christ. Also kneeling figures of Clopton and his wife. To this arch correspond, as part of the same composition, the SEDILIA and PISCINA. Above this a frieze of shields all along the wall in foiled shields (cf. Lady Chapel), and then a frieze of niches with canopies. Flat ceiling, the cornice painted with a long poem by *John Lydgate*; rope and foliage between the sheets of writing, and at the start of the sequence the hand of God. – Clopton Chapel: Sir William Clopton †1446, father of John Clopton. Knight on a tomb-chest with quatrefoil decoration. Low arch, almost like a lintel; cresting. Heavily restored. – Captain Hyde Parker †1854 in the Crimean War. By *J. Darmanin & Sons*, Malta. Marble, carved with wreath, flags and anchor, and with *pietre dure* laurel leaves, dolphins and tridents. – Sanctuary: Sir William Cordell †1581 of Melford Hall, who was Speaker of the House of Commons and Master of the Rolls. Alabaster. Recumbent effigy on a partly rolled-up mat. Two coffered arches carried on six Corinthian columns.

Back wall with two figures in niches; walls also between the back and the columns to his head and feet. They are pierced by arches with two more figures. The four represent the Virtues (Prudence, Justice, Temperance, Fortitude). Attributed to *Cornelius Cure*. – Martyn Chapel: Lawrence Martyn †1460. Purbeck marble tomb-chest with shields in lozenges. No effigy. – Nave: Jane Faulkner †1832. Perp. By *Denman*. – Similar monument, also by Denman, to Frances Almack †1840. – Elizabeth Parker †1833. By *William Whitelaw*. With mourning female contemplating an urn. – Lt Hyde Parker †1887. Brass plaque with red and black enamel. By *Hart, Son, Peard & Co*. – Revd Nathaniel Bisbie †1695. Transcription of ledger stone, carved on slate by *Denzil J. Reeves*, 1990. – In churchyard, especially on the N side of the church, a large number of C19–C20 cast-iron grave markers by *D. Ward* of Long Melford. – War memorial by *F. E. Howard*, executed by *F. J. Lindley*, 1920. Floriated Clipsham-stone cross on stepped base. – Cast-iron RAILINGS and gate at SE entrance to churchyard by *Ward & Silver*. Mid-C19.

TRINITY HOSPITAL

Founded by Sir William Cordell in 1573 for a warden and twelve brethren, and two honest widows to look after them. It was built of red brick, single-storey, with almshouses on three sides of a quadrangle and hall on the fourth. It was 'new fronted and beautified' in 1847: in fact almost all the visible brickwork, with cement dressings, is of that date, although the character of the old building was faithfully reproduced. The warden at the time was *William Fordham*, a builder by trade, and he may have been responsible for the design; his son was the main contractor. Windows with arched lights and hoodmoulds. Hall range rebuilt as two storeys over the original cellars, with Board Room on the ground floor. Projecting cross-wings also raised to two storeys, with canted oriels on the raised ground floor, straight gables and pinnacles. The centre and the return walls of the cross-wings are embattled; in the middle of the centre a pointed-arched doorway, embattled oriel, and a tall ogee-domed bell-turret based on the original. The other three sides of the quadrangle were kept as single-storey almshouses, with gabled porch facing the church and four large chimneystacks. The red brick garden wall of *c*. 1633, substantially rebuilt in 1981, is also embattled, and has a rendered gateway in the middle of the S side.

PERAMBULATION

At the risk of irritating faithful users, this conducted tour starts not by the church, but 1¼ m. S at MELFORD PLACE, seat of the Martyn family. The advantage of this is that only thus can the climax of the church (to which the Martyns were prominent donors) be brought out fully. Melford Place is late C14, but was largely rebuilt after a fire in 1967; the surviving CHAPEL was added by Roger Martyn †1542. Diapered brickwork, now rendered, but with exposed brick surrounds to the large E window and another blocked window on the N side. Roof with carved ridge-piece and wall-plates. The panelling incorporates a series of Renaissance panels carved with heads and decorative devices, c. 1530, that until the C19 formed part of the Martyn family pew in the church. Fireplace and gallery both probably C17. In the garden, the first of Long Melford's crinkle-crankle walls.

LITTLE ST MARY'S, as the main street is known at this point, is characterized by medieval timber-framed houses too numerous to mention individually, many of them disguised by C18 and C19 refrontings, with relics of industry behind them that occasionally break through to the front. Thus, very soon on the E side, former maltings and granary dated 1840; at its E end a kiln with slate pyramid rood just visible from the road. A little further on, OLD FORGE COTTAGE is conspicuous for being thatched, and is the jettied cross-wing of a hall house, of which a small part of the hall can be seen on the S side. Exposed timber framing of C14 type on the N return wall. CROSSKEYS, with its late C19 or early C20 brick ground floor and tile-hung first floor, is a very thorough remodelling of a C16 or C17 timber-framed house. Beyond the FIRE STATION, a sensitive red brick infill of 1985, is CORPUS CHRISTI (formerly Cadge's House), basically C15 or earlier and with a carved crown-post in the roof, thought to have been a guildhall. Refronted in the C18, when the centre part was rebuilt further forward and the gables of the cross-wings were given hipped roofs. In an upstairs room are remains of wall paintings, and ceiling beams carved in the same way as those in Melford Place chapel and in the Lady Chapel of the church. Carriage entrance at the S end with exposed timber framing inside. About 100 yds on is MANSEL HALL, a handsome mid-Georgian house of five bays and two storeys with a fine doorway (open pediment) and a Venetian window over. Almost opposite, ST CATHERINE'S ROAD leads off the W, a small late C19 suburb of terraced houses with so-called Mission House (ST CATHERINE'S CHURCH) of 1885.

Little St Mary's continues as HALL STREET, with a change of character: the road gradually widens, with patches of grass here and there and also trees, which do not line the street but appear irregularly. Hall Street begins on the E side with very prominent old MALTINGS, a three-bay four-storey gabled front of white brick with timber lucam, its red brick side stretching a long way back. Then the very Victorian INSURANCE OFFICE, a narrow white-brick building with oriel window and pedimented gable to which Robins Row Ltd affixed their name on a wrought-iron frame. Across the yard, MELFORD COURT (now a nursing home), a large white brick house that C. J. N. Row (of Robins Row) built for himself, with a rather unexpected square Italianate tower behind the main block. Opposite, the UNITED REFORMED CHURCH of 1725–6 (originally Presbyterian). Red brick, partly chequered, and with hipped roof. Front with round-arched doorway and two tall arched windows. Rather industrial-looking Sunday School (now PUBLIC LIBRARY) added in 1862. Burial ground to rear with crinkle-crankle wall. C18 timber-framed and plastered MANSE at right angles to the front.

The W side continues with two very heavily disguised timber-framed houses, THE GABLES and ALMACKS, followed by the more obviously medieval TRINITY HOUSE and DRURY HOUSE, with brick-nogging on the cross-wing at the N end. The S cross-wing, with ornamental C19 bargeboards, has rooms with unusually high ceilings for its C16 date, with carved beams. On the E side, after Melford Court, the GEORGE & DRAGON, with long mid-C19 front of white brick with red brick dressings, and then a large timber-framed house refronted in the mid C19 in white brick and divided in two (LINDEN HOUSE and ARDLEY HOUSE). On its S return, a complete Queen Anne doorway with shell-hood under a C19 scalloped canopy. Further up, THE POSTING HOUSE, a late C15 or early C16 timber-framed house with gabled cross-wings. Crown-post roof with unsooted timbers, suggesting there may originally have been a timber-framed chimney. Brick chimney inserted c. 1605. Then CHESTNUT HOUSE, with a good Late Georgian front of white brick and Doric doorcase with open pediment. Opposite, CHIMNEYS has exposed timbers and long-wall jetty, unusual in Long Melford. Probably C16. Two out of three oriels surviving. Then FOUNDRY HOUSE, another C19 white-brick front; Ward & Silver's foundry was in the yard behind. The COCK & BELL has an attractive C18 plastered front with two two-storey canted bays, but greater heights of sophistication are reached at HANWELL HOUSE, with its mid-Georgian red brick front of three bays and two storeys, with four Venetian windows. Doorcase with open pediment and fanlight. That this is a refronting can be seen by looking closely at the Venetian windows, behind whose arched tops the old timbers can be seen. On the corner a cast-iron post or fender by *Ward & Silver*, and along Cock and Bell Lane a crinkle-crankle wall. Behind List House, N of Hanwell House, three ranges of two-storey workshops, now converted to housing, of a horsehair factory.

A few discordant notes now sound: on the E side, CHESTNUT TERRACE, a three-storey row of six artisans' houses, of red brick with bands of black brick and stone lintels, dated 1868, and on the W side the EX-SERVICE & SOCIAL CLUB, opened as a lecture hall in 1872, of red brick with stone dressings and polychromatic voussoirs. Also Victorian in appearance COCOA-NUT HOUSE, 1881, the date referring to its brick refronting and the recent establishment of George Whittle's coconut matting works. It stands opposite THE BULL, a C15 house that had become an inn by the 1520s. The earliest part of the building is the parlour cross-wing on the corner of

Bull Lane; the medieval hall was replaced in the mid C16. Entrance with carved posts dated 1649. The timbers were hidden behind a brick façade until 1935, and the jettied range s of the gabled cross-wing is C20. N of Bull Lane, a little green with an attractive row along the E side leading up to OLD COURT HOUSES, built as the Police Station and Court House in 1849: Tudor style, red brick with white-brick dressings. On the W side, BROOK HOUSE, late C15 with two jettied cross-wings, C19 brick-nogging, and a pretty timber porch dated 1610 that was brought from elsewhere in the C19.

We have now reached the stream, a tributary of the Stour, which divides the two halves of Long Melford (and the ford which gives the place its name), with the picturesque MILL HOUSE, home of the poet Edmund Blunden until his death in 1974; and so come to the point where the Green starts.

MELFORD GREEN is unforgettable. It is large, forms an elongated triangle, and rises gently to the N. On the E side are the moat and yew hedges, and then the wall, octagonal Banqueting House and gateway of Melford Hall (*see* below), the turrets of the house tantalizingly visible. Then the Green itself, with a few trees at the S end, and in a visually quite arbitrary position the C16 brick CONDUIT, square with truncated gables that no doubt once carried pinnacles like the Banqueting House, and which supplied water to the Hall (there were originally two). The buildings along the W side, seen obliquely, form an almost continuous row and draw the eye up to the buildings at the top: the church and, in front of it, Trinity Hospital. This side starts with the old SCHOOL (now community centre), built in 1860, a bad moment for an appreciation of the qualities of Melford, one would think. As it is, the architect, *A. H. Parker*, succeeded in adding to the attractions of the Green. The building, of diapered red brick, is informal, low, and, with its capped little turret based on Melford Hall's, picturesque. Of the houses above it, attention should be drawn to SLOANE COTTAGE, the S cross-wing and extension of a C17 timber-framed house with very pretty early C19 detailing, including an arched doorcase and cast-iron gates, and FALKLAND HOUSE, with three octagonal star-topped chimneys and an C18 doorway. Opposite Fern House, the stone base of the medieval FAIR CROSS.

WESTGATE STREET branches off here, with the BLACK LION HOTEL on the corner. This joins on to, and in its present form is of much the same date as, WESTGATE TERRACE, dated 1839, of white brick and completely urban. It might stand in any street of Cambridge, for example. Seven houses in sixteen bays, the two houses at the far end wider than the others and suggesting a change of plan while construction was under way: the terrace was surely meant to be symmetrical, with pedimented bays at both ends. Further out, WESTGATE HOUSE is in similar style. White brick, of seven bays and two storeys, with deep eaves rising to form a pediment over the centre three bays. Doorway with Gibbs surround. Behind this front range an older, timber-framed structure. WESTGATE PARK, next door, was built as stables, *c.* 1999, converted to a house and extended 2006. By *John Tanner*, for himself. White brick. In classical style and on a classical scale. Between Terrace and House, THATCHED HOUSE, a C15 hall house with brick and flint additions. It has an early to mid-C16 inserted brick stack, but the inserted floor has been removed. Behind Scutchers, SCUTCHERS COTTAGES, a terrace of six early C19 timber-framed and weatherboarded houses. Scutchers worked in the local flax industry, dressing the flax by beating it. Another crinkle-crankle wall along the s side of the street.

Returning to the Black Lion, CHURCH WALK leads to the l. up to the OLD RECTORY of 1832–3, very large Neo-Tudor, red brick with straight gables and polygonal corner turrets, no doubt intended to harmonize with Trinity Hospital across the lane (*see* above). *Thomas Hopper* must be considered as the possible architect, given his involvement at both Melford Hall and Kentwell Hall. After the robust, sturdy red brick of the hospital, the rectory and Melford Hall, the church appears amazingly erect and aristocratic with its cool grey stone and long slim windows.

The perambulation does not quite end here, although it might. From the NE corner of the Green, the through road continues as HIGH STREET, the name here as elsewhere in Suffolk referring to its elevation rather than its status. Discreetly sited on the edge of the Green are exemplary PUBLIC LAVATORIES by *Christopher Chestnutt* of Babergh District Council, *c.* 1981, built of second-hand red bricks with pyramidal tiled roof. On the E side of High Street, CORDELL COTTAGES, begun (in the late C15) as a hall house with cross-wings, enlarged at various times and now eight dwellings. On the W side, a pretty little Gothick cottage at the entrance to Kentwell Hall (*see* p. 396). A curiosity further out: on the wall of No. 60, a panel with the just-legible inscription advertising William Fordham, 'Bricklayer Plain and Ornamental Plasterer', *c.* 1840.

MELFORD HALL

A large and impressive brick mansion, rebuilt in all likelihood by John Reeve, last abbot of Bury St Edmunds, who was elected in 1513. Reeve was a local boy and it would have been natural for him to want to make Melford one of his principal residences. The abbey had held the manor since before 1065. A substantial house at Melford is recorded in 1442, and the park was renowned for its hunting in the time of Abbot Samson (1182– 1211). Reeve's was a courtyard house, with the main entrance on the E side, i.e. facing away from the village and towards the park. There was an outer courtyard on the E side of the house, with a gateway in the middle of the E wall, and a base court on the S side which still exists. At the Dissolution in 1539, Melford Hall was surrendered to the Crown, and in the 1540s it was leased to Sir William Cordell, whose fine monument is in the parish church, and who built Trinity Hospital. He also was local, and had been brought up in the Clopton household at Kentwell, where his father was a principal servant. Sir William was granted Melford Hall by Queen Mary in 1554; Queen Elizabeth visited in 1578. His children all died young, and the next owner of significance was Sir Thomas Savage (†1635), who made alterations and additions to the house for which *John Thorpe* may have been the architect. In 1642, during the Civil War, the house was ransacked by a mob pursuing Savage's widow, Countess Rivers, a supporter of the king. Her son sold the house in 1649 to Robert Cordell, a cousin of Sir William. Robert's great-grandson, Sir Cordell Firebrace, made significant alterations to the house in about 1733–5, demolishing the E range and thus creating the U-plan building we see today. In 1786 the estate was bought by Sir Harry Parker. His son, Sir William, commissioned *Thomas Hopper* to make alterations in 1813; Hopper returned in 1840 to make further alterations for Sir William's brother, Sir Hyde Parker. The N wing was gutted by fire in 1942 and reconstructed after the war by *Sir Albert Richardson* for Sir William Hyde Parker. In 1960 the house passed to the National Trust; the family continue to live in the S wing, which was originally the service wing and was converted in the 1970s: it had kitchens at the W end, probably installed by Savage to replace a free-standing kitchen building in the base court, and offices beyond.

The house is built of red brick with stone dressings, and is mainly of two storeys and attics. The entrance, as we have seen, is on the E side, with a two-storey stone-fronted porch in the middle of the main range. It has superimposed fluted Doric and Ionic pilasters and a semicircular shell-top. The entrance arch is rounded, not depressed or four-centred. It carries the initials of William Cordell, and it is clear from the way it butts against the wall behind it that it is an addition to the original house. Three bays either side of the porch, but not symmetrical, reflecting the internal layout of double-height hall to the r. and staircase to the l. N and S wings projecting forward with straight gables at the ends. C19 mullioned-and-transomed windows, replacing C18 sash windows. On the inner sides of the wings, not quite at their ends, tall staircase turrets. They would have stood at the inner corners when the E side of the courtyard was still there. They have stone ogee tops and are decorated with semicircular shell gables, an Italian Quattrocento motif found elsewhere in England in the 1520s, e.g. at Layer Marney (Essex). On the N side, a projecting two-storey bay with tall stone doorway added by *Richardson* as part of his reconstruction of the N wing. It replaced a large bay window added by *Hopper* in 1840. Then a large external chimneystack; here especially the use of burnt headers is apparent. The windows on this side still C18 sashes but with hoodmoulds added in the C19.

The W front is more easily described than understood. In the middle is a three-storey bay flanked by turrets with ogee tops just like those on the E side. To l. and r. of the centre are two-bay, two-storey blocks, part of *Hopper*'s alterations of 1813; before that the W wall stood further back and the centre was therefore more prominent, as were the further two turrets r. and l. To either side of these outer turrets are two-bay, three-storey blocks. These also were built in front of the original W wall of the house, bits of which, including external brickwork painted with diaper patterns, can be seen inside, behind the structure built against it. The original centre, with its four turrets, would therefore have been very much like a gatehouse, comparable to the main gateway of Hampton Court; it is evident from the brickwork that the doorway and first-floor window were originally much wider. At Melford Hall, however, this cannot have been the main entrance, because it would have led directly into the hall; it might, however, have formed a sort of ceremonial entrance or porch for visitors. An estate map of 1613 by *Samuel Pierse** seems to show the house before the W front was remodelled, in which case the corner blocks probably date from very soon after; a plan by *John Thorpe*, now in the Soane Museum, shows the W front as rebuilt, but it is not clear whether it is a survey or a design. The C17 three-storey blocks provided some additional chambers, and it was probably at this time that garderobes were inserted in the outer turrets. But the alterations very possibly also provided a form of Long Gallery, until then conspicuously absent in the house, but mentioned in a letter of 1619 and said by Sir William Parker in 1873 to have been on the first floor on the W side. Certainly the upper rooms at the SW corner had very large windows on the S side, as can be seen from the brickwork, and may have functioned as viewing points. The ground floor to the l. of the centre is shown on Thorpe's plan as a loggia.

The porch on the E side leads into the screens passage of the HALL, from which it is separated by two Tuscan columns inserted by *Hopper* in 1813 as part of his Neoclassical remodelling of the interior that included the large stone fireplace with its heavy overmantel. The Jacobean panelling, linenfold doors and C16 STAINED GLASS were installed in 1867 to create a more antique atmosphere. Behind the hall is Hopper's LIBRARY, a notable room neatly fitted into the W front and incorporating the base of the centre projection at one end. This part lies beyond a screen of Ionic scagliola columns. Bookcases and other furniture made for the room, including tables probably by *Morant & Co.* and couches attributed to *Gillows*. Opening off the library, in the NW corner of the house, the BLUE DRAWING ROOM, with good early C18 decoration including a glorious Rococo fireplace. The rooms in the N wing, which included some fine C18 plasterwork, were destroyed in 1942. At the E end, where Hopper created a double-height drawing room in 1840, there is evidence that

*At the house, but not on public display.

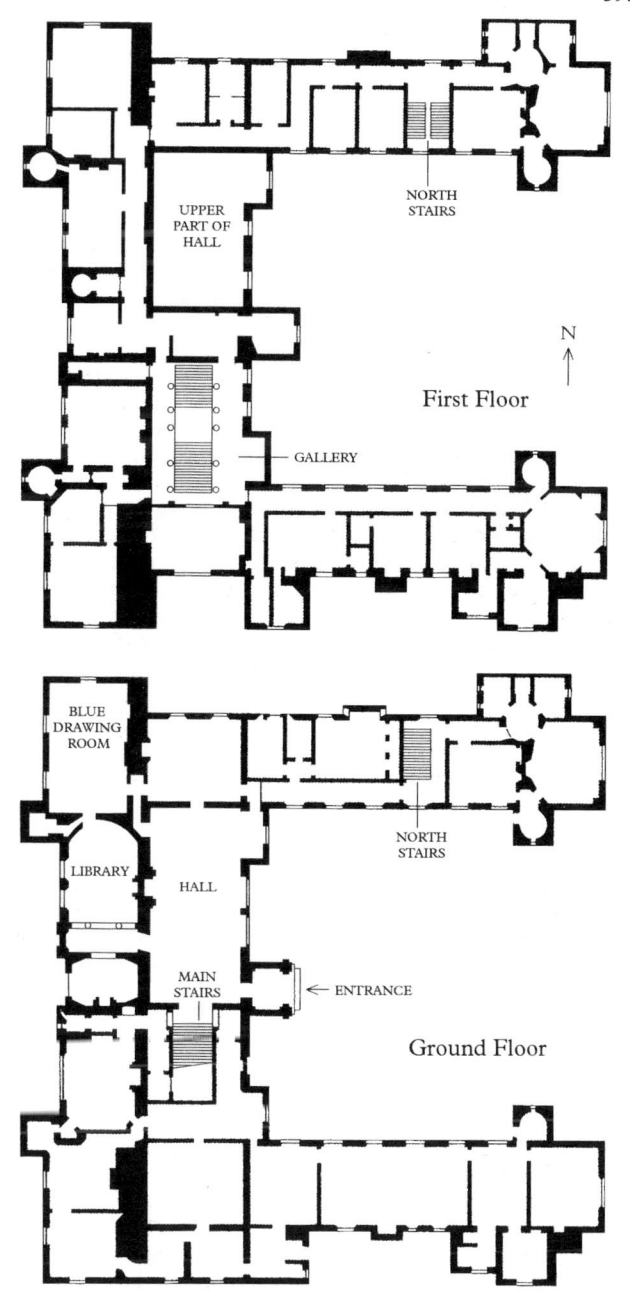

Long Melford, Melford Hall.
Plan

there was a pre-Reformation chapel. *Richardson*'s rebuilding of the wing includes an elegant oval entrance hall from his N door, and a staircase brought from Westoning Manor, Beds. Three balusters to each step, two twisted and one fluted. Carved tread-ends.

Opening off the S side of the hall is the main STAIRCASE, part of *Hopper*'s grand composition of 1813. It ascends with wide steps between solid walls in one straight line with an intermediate landing. On the landings brass grilles for the central heating, supplied by *Moser & Co.*, 'furnishing ironmongers', 1813. On the upper floor a gallery l. and r. with cast-iron balustrade and slender unfluted Ionic columns carrying a noble segmental tunnel vault. After that, the first floor cannot fail to be something of an anticlimax, and there is a feeling that the stairs lead nowhere. On the second floor (not accessible to the public) is what was probably a servants' gallery or garret rather than, as has been suggested, remains of the Long Gallery.

Pierse's map shows formal gardens on the N and W sides of the house. Of these a straight walk on the N side survives, with a BANQUETING HOUSE at its W end that cannot have been built long before 1613. Octagonal, with eight straight gables and simple stumpy pinnacles. Two storeys, the principal upper floor being reached by an outer staircase. Porch with short fluted columns. Might the stairs originally have been covered all the way to the foot? The windows, with their C18 sashes, give views not just of the house and garden but also of the Green and the road, from which the garden is separated by an impressive red brick wall. To the N the GATEWAY from the Green. The lodges were built in 1838 for Sir Hyde Parker by *Col. Robert Rushbrooke* of Rushbrooke Hall. The gateway itself is not shown on Pierse's map but can be seen in an early C19 print, with its turrets copied from the house; it may be part of the E gateway to Reeve's house, moved to its present position in the C18 by Sir Cordell Firebrace. SW of the house the KITCHEN GARDEN, with a crinkle-crankle wall along its N side; another crinkle-crankle wall on the E side of the base court. S of all this large PONDS, also shown by Pierse.

KENTWELL HALL

Kentwell Hall lies ¾ m. N of the church and is not part of Long Melford in the way that Melford Hall is. The house was built in stages by the Clopton family from about 1500. Francis Clopton made payments to mason *John Prynce* in 1571 ('for all his worke done abowghte my new buyldinge') and 1577 (the latter £74), and his brother William paid carpenter *Richard Ward(e)* in 1579. Glazing the window at the lower end of the hall is recorded in 1580. The Cloptons, who had been responsible for so much of the rebuilding of the church, had held the manor of Kentwell since the late C14, as well as other manors including that of Lutons; in fact the present Kentwell Hall is built on the site of

Lutons, and the original Kentwell lay about a mile to the NW. In 1618 the house came by marriage to the antiquary Sir Simonds D'Ewes, and in 1676 it was purchased Sir Thomas Robinson, a successful lawyer, who made a few changes to the Tudor house and also, in 1678, planted the impressive lime tree AVENUE that forms the S approach to the house. Further alterations to the house were carried out by Richard Moore, the owner from 1782 to 1823, but much more was done by his successor, Robert Hart Logan, a Scotsman who had made his fortune in the timber business in Canada. He employed *Thomas Hopper* (cf. Melford Hall) to remodel substantial parts of the interior, *c.* 1825–7. The house has been owned since 1971 by *Patrick Phillips*, who has carried out gradual restoration and some new building acting as his own architect.

The house stands inside a complete moat, crossed by two brick bridges, one in the middle of the S side, the other at the NW corner. The moat was enlarged to the E of the house in the C17 and C18 to take in part of the garden. There is evidence that a gatehouse once stood at the inner end of the S bridge, with an outer gatehouse (about halfway between the moat and the present gates) that presumably formed the entrance to an outer courtyard. The GATES and screen are C18, of wrought iron, brought from Earlham Hall (Norfolk) in 1911. They are flanked by two octagonal GATEHOUSES with ogee roofs of *c.* 1993 containing offices and visitor facilities.

The main house is of red brick with stucco dressings and consists of a centre and two far-projecting wings. These each have an ogee-capped turret at the inner corner of their fronts. It seems that the centre was built first, *c.* 1500, followed by the E wing in two phases (there is a visible break in the brickwork), and the W wing last; it was completed by about 1540, although, as we have seen, work was still being done in the 1570s. The general impression is of symmetry, but this does stand up to close scrutiny. The centre has a buttressed porch in the middle and two large bay windows with five lights and three transoms to either side. The bay to the r. lights the upper end of the hall; the bay to the l. was added to light a staircase that was inserted, in place of the original buttery and pantry, to provide access to the Long Gallery that was built over the hall *c.* 1578. Thus the top floor of the centre is an addition, the lights of its windows square-headed rather than arched. The porch and bays have straight gables and pinnacles. Bays also on the sides and fronts of the wings, and gabled dormers. The courtyard between the wings was laid out as a brick pavement MAZE in the form of a stylized Tudor rose in 1984–5. The other fronts are all quite irregular; the W is the most interesting, with its projecting gabled and pinnacled garderobe towers, and sash windows surviving from C18 alterations. Also on the W side, just detached from the main house, is a range known as the MOAT HOUSE. Red brick, with a timber-framed

56

section jettied over the moat with brick-nogging. It has been identified as an early C16 brewhouse, partly faced in brick later in the century to harmonize with the main house; the timbers of the elevation to the moat were painted to resemble brick.

The porch leads into the screens passage at the W end of the HALL, which was remodelled by *Hopper*. He introduced Gothic panelling and an elaborate Jacobean roof with hammerbeams, pendants and wall-posts made entirely of plaster, painted in imitation of wood. Big stone fireplace of *c.* 1730. Beside it can be seen part of the arch of the original fireplace, lost when the floor was raised to line up with the higher levels of the later wings. STAINED GLASS in the bay window, some of it C15 French, collected and arranged in the C19. W of the hall, the DINING ROOM, a double-height room created by Hopper. Jacobean-style dado of arches and pilasters and above it a decorative scheme of strapwork in arched panels. Massive chimneypiece of grey Bardiglio marble, modelled on the late C15 fireplace in the Bishop's Palace, Exeter. E of the hall the PARLOUR, again remodelled by Hopper but here in more Georgian vein, with a screen of Doric columns. Late C20 painted ceiling with Breughel-esque scenes by *Paul Dufficey*. In the floor of this room and the hall, brass gratings, part of a central heating system by *T. Tapster*, London, 1827. Above the parlour, the STATE BEDROOM and BOUDOIR, created by Hopper from the original Great Parlour, the Boudoir now a Pompeian-style bathroom with murals by Dufficey and painted floorcloth by *Sophie Sarin*. The LONG GALLERY on the top floor was divided up into bedrooms as part of Hopper's alterations.

The E wing contains a fine open-well STAIRCASE of *c.* 1680 with heavy turned balusters, the principal alteration made by Sir Thomas Robinson. The remainder of the wing is taken up with two more of Hopper's rooms, first the BILLIARD ROOM (formerly library) and then the LIBRARY (formerly drawing room). The latter has a Corinthian screen of cast-iron scagliola columns. More STAINED GLASS in the billiard room. The W wing has, at its S end, the KITCHEN, which by the mid C16 had superseded a detached kitchen that stood NW of the house. The remainder of the wing was divided up into sets of chambers with garderobes, the layout of which has been restored; some original panelling.

Beyond the house on the NW side, but still inside the moat, an octagonal GAZEBO adapted as a camera obscura in the late C20. Outside the moat, on the N side, a WALLED GARDEN, originally moated, with one arm remaining as a canal on the W side and a sunken garden on the E. The garden is not aligned to the house and may pre-date it. Just outside it, on the E side, an ICE HOUSE, the mound and brick entrance passage rebuilt 1998–2000 over the original pit. SW of the house, an C18 DOVECOTE. Red brick, square, with pyramidal roof and octagonal cupola. 526 nest holes with potence restored to usable condition.

SE of the house, a range of FARM BUILDINGS mostly by *Patrick Phillips* based on traditional forms, and including a rebuilt C13 aisled barn from Mountnessing (Essex).

OUTLYING BUILDINGS

BRIDGE STREET FARM, 1¼ m. NNE of Holy Trinity. Apparently a standard timber-framed and plastered hall house with jettied and gabled cross-wings, but in fact an altered Wealden-type house, probably C15. Crown-post roof and smoke-blackened timbers. It has particularly tall octagonal chimneys, two pairs and another single one, but these seem to be entirely C19, as are many of the external details. FORD HALL, ½ m. further NW at Bridge Street, dates from the end of the C15. Exposed timbers and single cross-wing, the whole front jettied. For MILL HOUSE, Bridge Street, *see* Alpheton.

CRANMORE GREEN HOUSE, 1 m. NW. Two-storey Regency house of white brick with slate roof. The principal range is rounded at the S end and has a semicircular bay at the N end. Two-storey porch with splayed corners.

LONG WALL, Newman's Green, 2 m. SSE. 1962–3 by *Philip Dowson* with *Peter Foggo*. Single-storey weekend house. Lightweight timber structure, glazed on three sides, with overhanging flat roof. A white-painted brick wall runs through and beyond the house, providing shelter and privacy. Restored by *Hugh Pilkington*, 1995–6, in consultation with Dowson.

Former MALTINGS, off Station Road, 1½ m. SSW. Built by the Lion Brewery Co. in 1878 and described by White as 'fitted up with every modern appliance, and . . . one of the finest malting establishments in the county'. Three-storey range with

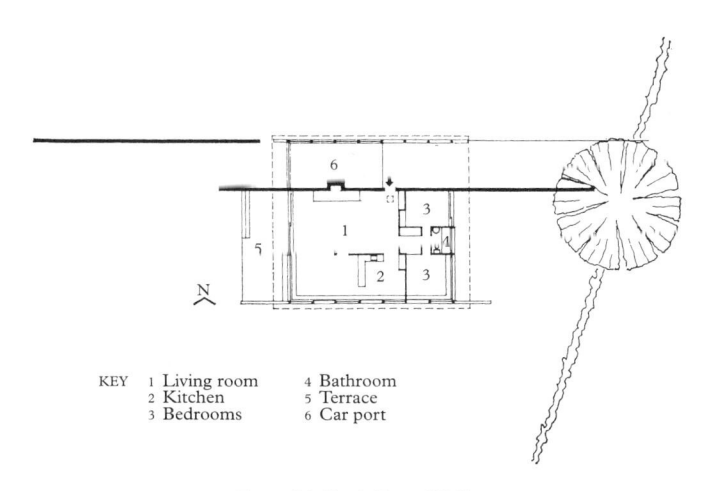

KEY 1 Living room 4 Bathroom
     2 Kitchen   5 Terrace
     3 Bedrooms   6 Car port

Long Melford, Long Wall.
Plan

pedimented centre, originally granary etc., and two taller ranges with kilns. Converted to flats in 1986–90. Of the same materials, red brick with white-brick dressings, the relatively humble former RAILWAY STATION of 1865 behind the maltings.

ROD BRIDGE, 2 m. SSW. Road bridge over the Stour, 1909–11, by *A. A. Hunt* with *Percy J. Sheldon*, Essex County Council Chief Surveyor. Reinforced concrete, with a delicately pierced parapet.

ROMAN SETTLEMENT. Finds were made in 1958 to the S of Liston Lane near Melford Place. They comprised part of a tessellated pavement of white limestone and red tile enclosed in a border of bitumen, limestone, and a moulding of red brick, and also part of a wall, thus indicating a probable bath. Burials and Roman-British occupation material found on both sides of the main street indicate a large settlement, particularly in the C1–C2 A.D., and finds, including an iron sword, suggest C1 military activity. Excavations in Little St Mary's in 1997 identified seven burials dating to the C4 A.D., including one in a stone coffin, probably of Christian Romans.

MARKET WESTON

ST MARY. Dec, except for the good Perp S porch. Tall two-light windows with panel tracery. Front and battlements with flushwork decoration. The entrance has fleuron decoration, and there are three niches, to the l., to the r. and above the entrance. Another niche over the S door. Restored by *L. N. Cottingham* (*Cottingham & Son*), 1844–5, including rebuilding the chancel from the foundations. The leaning nave walls were brought back to perpendicular by means of iron bars (supplied by *George Bloomfield*) that were fixed across the nave, heated, tightened, and contracted as they cooled. Further restoration 1889, when the chancel roof was raised. – FURNISHINGS by *Cottingham*, including CHOIR STALLS, BENCHES, PULPIT and LECTERN. His presumably the Gothick PILLAR PISCINA, a multi-shafted column with a moulded relief of Christ and the woman of Samaria on the wall behind the bowl.* But the FONT is 1889. – BELL. By *Thomas Potter* of Norwich, late C14 or early C15. – STAINED GLASS. Tracery of E window by *Lucy Rickards*, 1845 (cf. Stowlangtoft). – MONUMENTS. Framingham Thruston †1789. An early (and simple) work by *John Bacon Jun.* – Rev. H.T. Wilkinson †1876. Decorative mural brass by *Gawthorp*.

Former NATIONAL SCHOOL (now village hall). By *Henry Angold* of Diss, 1872–3. A modest affair, of red brick with bands of black.

---

*The same relief is used in different ways at Barnby and Wrentham (both E).

MELLIS

Mellis, like nearby Wortham, is distinguished by its large GREEN. Mellis's covers some 235 acres (95 ha) and is the largest grazing common in Suffolk. The Eastern Union Railway cut through one side of it in 1849, resulting in an unexpected cluster of industrial buildings in the middle of an otherwise entirely rural scene. A branch line from Mellis to Eye (E) opened in 1867 (closed 1964). The village's older buildings, including the church, are scattered round the edges of the green, set well back from the through roads and half-hidden by trees.

ST MARY THE VIRGIN. The W tower collapsed in 1730. Substantial parts of its walls remain as buttresses. Dec S porch, originally of two storeys; roof lowered as part of the restoration of the nave by *John Johnson* of Bury, 1858–9.* The nave is wide, with big Perp three-light windows. The E end, including the NE vestry, has a flushwork-panelled base, but above, all is later repair and restoration (chancel restored 1897–8). In the chancel N wall an Easter sepulchre. Five niches with tiny vaulted canopies; over this was a larger canopy, now lost. Above, a Late Perp arched recess with roses on the jambs and in the spandrels. – FONT. Perp, with four lions against the stem, and against the bowl the Emblems of the Evangelists and four Tudor roses. – SCREEN. With one-light divisions, ogee arches, and some tracery over. Original coving, ribbed in a pretty pattern. The colouring, by one of the rector's daughters, dates from 1900. – CHOIR STALLS. 1898, incorporating poppyheads of *c.* 1527 (bequest for new chancel desks) and COMMUNION RAIL of 1637. – STAINED GLASS. In a S window, complete C15 figures in the tracery heads. E window by *Rowland & Surinder Warboys*, 1996. – MONUMENT. Tomb-chest with three lozenges with shields. Indents for brasses on slab. No indication of the Renaissance. For a member of the Yaxley family, perhaps Anthony †1559 or Richard †1569.

OLD PARSONAGE, 250 yds ESE. By *Daniel Penning* of Eye, 1862. Red brick with panels of flint, decoratively arranged. Stables etc. by *W. A. Tagg-Arundell*, 1872. It replaced the previous RECTORY in Earlsford Road (early C19, painted brick), which had ended up on the wrong side of the railway line.

ELM TREE FARM, about ⅔ m. NE. Timber-framed and plastered. Two-cell C16 house. Above the doorway a later embellishment, the sill of a former oriel window, early C16. Carved with an angel holding a shield. On the shield the de la Pole arms. Cross-wing at the W end added in the early C17, reusing what appears to be a C15 structure, perhaps brought from elsewhere. Chimneystack inserted at the same time. The

---

* *E. B. Lamb* also prepared a scheme for restoration; it is not clear why he was replaced by Johnson, although a similar situation occurred at Stuston, where he was superseded by Thomas Jeckyll.

ground-floor room of the cross-wing has an ornamental plaster ceiling with panels of fleur-de-lys and roses, and a border of foliage.

ROBINSON'S MILL, by the railway line. Former mid-C19 steam mill, now flats. Stock brick. Main block of four storeys and attic, three bays wide with straight gables. Chimney on N side and lucam on E.

MENDLESHAM

Mendlesham, now a large village, was formerly a market town, its charter granted by Edward I. The centre consists of two parallel streets, Old Market Street to the N and Front Street to the S; the market would have occupied the space between the two that has been gradually infilled. The parish church, whose ambitious scale is explained by the town's medieval status, stands just SE of the market place.

ST MARY. Much of the C13, but the dominant impression Perp. C13 arcade of six bays, the easternmost separated from the others by a little wall and perhaps representing former transepts. Circular piers, circular abaci, double-chamfered arches. The E responds against the little walls are a fluted corbel on the N side and an oblong one with dogtooth on the S side. The eastern arches stand on short vertical pieces. The same is true of the chancel arch. C13 also the S doorway with three orders of colonnettes and several rolls and hollows in the arch, and the simpler N doorway. Dec S aisle windows. Most of the other windows have two ogee-headed lights under a segmental arch, probably also a C14 form. It applies to the clerestory too. Handsome Perp E window in the N aisle. The middle light is in its lower part blank and contains a niche to the inside. The window is shafted internally. Twenty shillings was left for the 'noth syde ledying' in 1463, perhaps as the N aisle was being completed. But the showpieces of the church are the W tower (which cuts with its E buttresses into the arcade) and the porches. There were bequests for the tower in 1375 and 1431, and then a flurry in 1488–97. W doorway with shields in the spandrels. Carved freestone panels to l. and r., then a frieze of flushwork circles etc., incorporating (here and elsewhere) devices of *Thomas Aldryche*. Diagonal buttresses flush-decorated in their lower parts, and a parapet with flushwork quatrefoils crowned by battlements with flushwork arcading. The S porch has a flushwork-panelled front, above the entrance a frieze of quatrefoils in flushwork, and above that sacred initials. Flush-arcaded battlements. The N porch is two-storeyed. It also has a flushwork front. Three niches l., r. and above the entrance. Two two-light upper windows. Big lions and (at the back) Wild Men serve as pinnacles. Restoration by *Ewan*

Christian, 1864–6, including new nave roof and removal of W gallery.

FURNISHINGS. FONT. Perp, octagonal, plain. Its COVER is a beautiful Jacobean piece with a lower tier open between four elongated Tuscan columns and upper tiers with pediments and spiky obelisks. On top a sort of crown spire. It was made in 1630 by *John Turner*. – The other FONT, in the N porch and adapted for use as a stoup, came from Rishangles (E). It is a curious piece, most probably a self-conscious imitation of Perp East Anglian fonts. The bowl corresponds to what is only too familiar. But against the stem, in niches, standing figures in the costume of 1530. It is said that the font was dated 1599. If that is true, it would be an interestingly early case of medievalism. – PULPIT. Also by *Turner*, 1630. Of the familiar type, with the chief panels treated as short sturdy blank arches; below these, geometrical panels with a central knob, and above small oblong panels with leaf scrolls and grotesques. – COMMUNION RAIL. C17. With turned balusters. From Southolt (E). – BENCHES. Those in the nave with traceried ends, carved backs and poppyheads. The figures on the arms are mostly hacked off. Restored and augmented in 1864–6. Those in the aisles, with poppyheads but otherwise plainer, from Rishangles. – CHESTS. As well as a small oak chest, with iron bands, that came from Southolt, Mendlesham has no fewer than six chests; a seventh is known to have gone missing. Two of the chests were probably made in the 1420s, of Polish pine. Others are of *c.* 1560 and *c.* 1700, and another is dated 1664. They are all located in the ARMOURY on the upper floor of the N porch – the most complete armoury of any English parish church. It was assembled *c.* 1593; in 1594 the room was lined with timber and an iron-bound DOOR fitted. The armour ranges from *c.* 1470 to *c.* 1640. There is also a rare surviving piece of a longbow. – BIERS. Two, probably C18; as well as the usual full-size bier, a smaller one for children, both with original straps. – CURIOSUM. A surveyor's ODOMETER. – ROYAL ARMS. Of George III. From Southolt. – PAINTINGS. In the S porch (now Chapel of the Holy Cross), a series of four depicting the Life of St Helena. By *Cyril Fradan*, 1980. – STAINED GLASS. In the N aisle, pieces of medieval glass from Rishangles and Southolt. Chancel s †1812 by *Mayer & Co.* N aisle by *T. F. Curtis, Ward & Hughes*, 1921 (war memorial). Centre panel based on *James Clark*'s The Great Sacrifice. In the tracery, a medieval figure of St John the Evangelist. – MONUMENTS. Brass of John Knyvet †1417, in armour, his head on a helmet. The figure is 4 ft 7 in. (140 cm.) long. – Brass of Margaret Armgyer, the figure 23½ in. (60 cm.) long (from Southolt). The figure of her husband Robert †1585 missing. – R. C. Chilton †1816. By *Charles Regnart*. Sarcophagus, with a little drapery. – Ann Marriott †1853 and William Cuthbert †1858. Two simple monuments by *S. Manning Jun*. – Rev. E. F. Randolph †1909. By *F. H. Goddard* of Bury. Old-fashioned Gothic.

Mendlesham, St Mary, brass to John Knyvet †1417.
Rubbing by M. Stuchfield, 2014

Of the village houses, the two most striking are on the N side of OLD MARKET STREET, i.e. facing the old market place, both with exposed timbers. TUDOR HOUSE, C16, has a cross-wing at the W end jettied towards the street. WEALD HOUSE is of Wealden type, both ends jettied. Late C15, the hall floored in the C16 and parlour end (E) added *c.* 1600.

MENDLESHAM MANOR, 425 yds ENE. C16 and C17, with exposed timbers. Considerably restored and altered in the C20, including by *Raymond Erith*, 1949.

ELMS FARM, 550 yds SW. Late C15 timber-framed and plastered house of Wealden type, the ends jettied towards the N, with a C19 wing projecting N at the E (parlour) end. High-quality alterations in the second half of the C16, including inserted floor with moulded beams. Extensive remains of painted decoration in two phases, late C16 and early C17. The first phase, in the parlour chamber and hall chamber, includes a trelliswork pattern with stylized flowers and black-letter texts taken from Coverdale's translation of Psalm CXXX. The later phase, in the parlour, includes grey overpainting of studding with pendant motifs between.

HAWKINS FARM, 1¼ m. SW. Timber-framed farmhouse. C16, with C18 additions, encased in white brick *c.* 1900. To its N a seven-bay weatherboarded THRESHING BARN. Softwood frame, with the principal rafters linked to the collars and wall-posts by bolted knee-braces, obviating the need for tie-beams. An inscription records that the barn was raised by John Ottewill on 1 August 1822, the old barn having been burnt down on 8 June; builder, *Francis Betts* of Stowmarket.

TELEVISION MAST, 1½ m. SE. Built by the Independent Television Authority in 1959. 1,000 ft (305 metres) high, at the time the tallest television mast in Europe.

MILDEN

ST PETER. Nave and chancel. The W tower was damaged in a storm in 1827 and taken down in 1840, when the W wall, bell-cote and S porch were built with salvaged stone. Further restoration, and addition of N vestry, 1866. Norman nave – see one S window and the S doorway with chevron arch on plain imposts. The rest has lancet windows, much renewed and perhaps not reliable, and two chancel S windows with Y-tracery. Roof with one slender crown-post (C14). – FONT. Plain, square, Norman. Supported at the corners by later pillars. – PULPIT. Jacobean. – BENCHES. Four, one dated 1685. Four more of the C16 with crude poppyheads. – WALL PAINTINGS. Fragmentary, discovered in 1987. Mainly masonry pattern. – MONUMENTS. James Alington †1627. Excellent recumbent alabaster effigy.

Handsome frames of the two inscription tablets. It was once much more elaborate, with a full canopy and a second effigy below the present one of a shrouded, emaciated figure. – John Canham †1772, erected by his sister Mary †1780. Pedimented tablet with cherubs' heads, vases, etc.

OLD RECTORY, SW of the church, with a very fine cedar in front. C18, timber-framed and plastered, with two full-height canted bays. Single-storey bow on the E return wall.

MILDEN HALL, ¾ m. WSW. Timber-framed house of c. 1520, enlarged in the C17 and remodelled by John Canham c. 1756, the year in which he was High Sheriff. Two storeys. Five-bay centre and one-bay cross-wings, one wider than the other. The narrower (l.) wing appears to have been added in the early C17, and extended to the rear later that century. Enclosed Tuscan porch with ornamental frieze. Above it a Venetian window, repeated on the fronts of the wings. Inside, a wide arched opening leads from the hall to the staircase, which is lit by a large Gothick window. Slender twisted and plain balusters, three to a tread. S of the house a large late C16 aisled BARN, of five bays extended to seven. Exposed studding with brick-nogging. Another similar barn to its E, of five bays with one floored bay at the NE end and a large extension at the SW end. This was linked in the C20 to a C17 granary-cum-cart lodge.

CASTLE (Foxburrow Hill), 900 yds ESE of the Hall. Mound of a C12 motte-and-bailey castle, c. 12 ft (3.7 metres) high. Little or nothing is left of the bailey ditch.

MILDENHALL

The largest parish in Suffolk, situated at the point where the Breckland meets the Fens. Its prosperity was based on rabbits from the former and fish from the latter; the charter for the town's market was granted in 1412. The town is now dominated by the airbase, opened in 1934, and was expanded in the 1960s and 70s to accommodate London 'overspill'. In addition to 'High Town', Mildenhall includes the settlements of Beck Row, Holywell Row and Kenny Hill to the NE (a separate civil parish since 1999), and West Row to the E. Mildenhall also has the greatest concentration of prehistoric sites in the county, although these are only visible, if at all, as field-surface scatters of artefacts (*see* Introduction). Dredging of the River Lark in 1998 uncovered the skull of a wild ox or aurochs (*Bos primigenius*), which became extinct in Britain in the Bronze Age – there have been a number of similar finds in this area, which may have been the last stronghold of this animal. The Mildenhall Treasure, a hoard of Roman silver tableware, was found in 1942 (*see* Introduction, p. 20).

CHURCHES

ST MARY. The most ambitious church in this corner of Suffolk, 168 ft (51.2 metres) long with a tower 120 ft (36.6 metres) high. The earliest parts are to be found at the E end: the chancel and the N chapel, dating back to *c.* 1240–1300. The N chapel comes first, work perhaps of an Ely mason. It is predominantly of limestone, not of flint, two bays long with three lancets at the E end. The chancel windows are of *c.* 1300. Three stepped lancet lights under one arch, but with the lower lights connected with the taller middle one by little token flying buttresses. On the S side these windows alternate enterprisingly with windows with uncusped intersected tracery. The E window is a glorious and quite original design, heralding the later one of Prior Crauden's Chapel at Ely. Seven lights, the first and last continued up and round the arch (as at Ely) by a border of quatrefoils. The next two on each side are taken together as one and have in the spandrel an irregular cusped triangle. Over the middle stands a big pointed oval along the border of which run little quatrefoils again. The centre is an octofoiled figure. The buttresses at the E end of the chancel are also unusual: angle buttresses that become niches with cusped canopies and continue as octagonal pinnacles. The rest of the church is Perp. First the W tower, built with bequests of 1441–78, and restored in 1864 by *John Darkin* of Bury. Angle buttresses with attached shafts carrying little pinnacles (a Somerset motif). Big renewed doorway, big renewed six-light W window with a tier of shields in quatrefoils at its foot. Also Perp the renewed clerestory windows and the big aisle windows. The N side is richer than the S. Battlements on the aisle with panel decoration in two tiers and pinnacles. This is the crowning motif of the N porch too. The porch is long and two-storeyed. Niches in the buttresses, shields above the entrance. The S porch is simpler, largely rebuilt as part of the restoration of the S aisle (by *J. D. Wyatt*? *see* below) in 1875–6. General restoration, mainly interior, but including re-roofing of chancel, by *Thomas Farrow*, 1849–53.

Inside, the ground floor of the N porch is vaulted with ridge ribs, tiercerons and bosses. On the upper floor was the Lady Chapel (as at Fordham, Cambs., a few miles away). Money was left for it in a number of wills between 1513 and 1537. It has a two-bay arcade open to the nave and the doorway to the stair in the NW corner of the N aisle has in its spandrels carvings of the Annunciation. No less unusual is the ground floor of the tower, which has a tunnel-like fan-vault in three bays dating from the second quarter of the C16. Stone benches along each side and canopied niches l. and r. of the arch into the nave. Above the vault a choir gallery with a stone balustrade. Pillar PISCINA, credence shelf and squint at E end of N aisle. The Perp arcades between nave and aisles have very thin piers with finely moulded shafts and capitals only towards the arch openings. Shafts rise from these right up to the roof. This is excellent, of low pitch, with alternating hammerbeams and cambered tie-beams. The depressed arched braces of the tie-beams are traceried, and there is tracery between the queen-posts on the tie-beams. Against the hammerbeams big figures of angels. Angels also against the wall-plate. The aisle roofs have hammerbeams too. In the spandrels of those in the N aisle carved scenes of St George and the Dragon, the Baptism of Christ, the Sacrifice of Isaac, and the Annunciation. Against the wall-posts figures with demi-figures of angels above them serving as canopies.

At the E end of the church we return to the mid C13. The N chapel has an elegant rib-vault in which the transverse arches and the ribs have the same dimensions and profile. The E lancets are shafted inside with detached Purbeck shafts carrying stiff-leaf capitals. The chancel arch is of the same date, a beautiful piece, nicely shafted, with keeling to the shafts, dog-tooth between them, and excellent stiff-leaf and crocket capitals. Also small heads. The PISCINA belongs with all this. It has Purbeck shafts and stiff-leaf capitals. The top of the piscina is not genuine. The SEDILIA are no more than three stepped window seats, separated by simple stone arms. But the windows, as we have seen, are definitely of *c.* 1300, showing that the chancel was built slowly.

FURNISHINGS. FONT. Octagonal, Perp, of Purbeck marble with shields in quatrefoils bearing the arms of Sir Henry Barton and the City of London (*see* below). – SCREEN. By *Walter Tapper*, 1903–4. – PULPIT. By *J. D. Wyatt*, 1875. Replacing the Jacobean one, taken to St John the Evangelist, Beck Row (*see* below), but the sounding board reused as a table (near N door). – BENCHES. In nave, by *H. M. Cautley*, with a bequest by his wife M. S. Cautley †1958; made by *E. Barnes*, 1959–60, with carving by *H. Brown*. Traceried ends and poppyheads. – CHEST. Over 8 ft long. Oak, with iron bands. C14. – NORTH DOOR. With tracery. – ROYAL ARMS. Of George II, 1758 (tower gallery). Exceptionally large. – STAINED GLASS. S aisle E by *H. Hughes*, 1876. A chancel S window †1881 and a S aisle window †1886 by *C. Elliott*. A small window in the tower by *J. Dudley Forsyth* commemorates Mary Anne Jolly †1908 'who for 18 years was a diligent cleaner of this church'.

MONUMENTS. Richard of Wichforde, rector †1344. Slab with Lombardic lettering and indent of floriated cross. – Sir Henry Barton, Lord Mayor of London in 1416 and 1428. Plain tomb-chest, at W end of S aisle. It originally stood in front of the font, which like the tomb-chest carries his arms and those of the City of London. – Brass of Sir Henry Warner †1617. 20-in. (51-cm.) figure, in armour. – Sir Henry North †1620. Alabaster. Two recumbent effigies. The children kneel below, against the tomb-chest. Background with two black columns, two arches, two small obelisks and an achievement. His HELM nearby. – Sir Roger North †1651. Oval touchstone tablet with ornate alabaster surround. Attributed by Adam White to *Joshua Marshall*. – Sir Henry North †1671. By *Diacinto Cawcy*.

With Ionic pilasters and segmental pediment. Black marble and scagliola, including floral ornament (cf. Hawstead). – Lady North. Painted wood tablet, next to and of similar form to the previous monument, but by a different hand. Dated 15 February 1670, i.e. 1671. Was it intended to be temporary? – John Swale †1821 by *John Bacon Jun*. Above it the very much smaller monument erected by Swale to his wife Elizabeth in 1818, also by Bacon. Both white marble on black, quite plain. – William Scott †1831, erected by Sir H. Bunbury, whose steward he was. By *de Carle*. – Boer War memorial. Brass, shield-shaped, by *T. Pratt & Sons*, 1903. – Lt P. S. St P. Bunbury †1916 and Commander E. C. Bunbury †1918. Framed illuminated text by *Isobel Nevill*, 1920.

In the churchyard, the ruined remains of a CHARNEL HOUSE. Over it was a chapel of St Michael, endowed in 1387. Colonized as a memorial by the Read family.

ST JAMES THE GREAT, Kenny Hill. By *Matthew Morley*, 1896. E.E. Flint with white-brick and stone dressings. w porch and short SE bell-tower. Now New Testament Baptist Church.

ST JOHN THE EVANGELIST, Beck Row. 1875–6, by *J. D. Wyatt*. Flint, with stone dressings and bands of red and white brick. Nave, chancel and s transept. Timber bell-turret with short splay-foot spire. – PULPIT. From St Mary. Jacobean.

ST PETER, West Row. E.E. Flint with white-brick dressings. Built as the National School, 1850, with bellcote. Used as a church from 1874; chancel added the following year. – STAINED GLASS. w window †1913 by *J. Dudley Forsyth*.

METHODIST CHURCH, High Street. 1829, 'restored' 1888. White-brick front and sides, the rear elevation (to Queensway) of flint. Two tiers of windows with simple Doric porch. Extension to l.

BAPTIST CHURCH, Chapel Road, West Row. 1815. White brick with hipped slate roof. Rear extension by *A. W. Leonard*, 1911.

METHODIST CHURCH, The Street, Beck Row. 1829, extended by one bay to the front *c.* 1860. White-brick front with pilasters and pedimented gable. Round-arched windows. Other walls of knapped flint with white brick dressings.

METHODIST CHURCH, The Street, Holywell Row. 1955. Behind it, the burial ground of the Friends' meeting house that formerly stood nearby. Boundary walls of white brick with the dates 1754 and 1771 in red brick.

STRICT BAPTIST CHURCH, The Green, West Row. Mid-C19 conversion of an early C19 flint and white-brick barn.

Former WESLEYAN CHAPEL, Beeches Road, West Row. 1841; now a private house. Knapped flint with white-brick dressings. Hipped roof.

PUBLIC BUILDINGS

SWIMMING POOL, Recreation Way. By *George Binns & Associates*, 1972. Brown brick, with clerestory windows lighting the pool.

The roof is carried on straight glulam beams of 40-ft (12.2-metre) span.

DOME LEISURE CENTRE. *See* MILDENHALL COLLEGE ACADEMY.

BECK ROW PRIMARY SCHOOL, The Street. 1876–7 by *Henry Lovegrove*. White brick with red brick dressings. With decorative bargeboards and open bell-turret with flèche.

WEST ROW PRIMARY SCHOOL, Beeches Road. By *J. Young & Son*, 1873–4. White brick with stone dressings and red brick relieving arches. Single-storey schoolroom and two-storey teacher's house.

MILDENHALL COLLEGE ACADEMY (former Upper School), Bury Road. 1973–8 by the *County Architect's Dept*. Built on the SEAC system. Its sports hall (now Dome Leisure Centre) is a concrete 'parashell', 11 metres (36 ft) high, with a diameter of 36 metres (118 ft). It was erected in a single day in 1977 (job architect *Simon Connolly*). Angular extension, 1984.

PERAMBULATION

The parish church stands in the middle of the town, its E end overlooking the High Street. On the W side of the churchyard, a row of four ALMSHOUSES erected by Sir Thomas Hanmer, 1722. Single-storey, red brick, hipped roof. Windows with segmental heads. To their S, THE PRIORY, formerly the workhouse, and also built by Hanmer. Enlarged 1836.* Rendered façade with a shaped gable at each end. Reused stone doorway, C15, with carved frieze of two shields supported by lions and angels respectively. N of the almshouses, a former SCHOOLROOM of 1867. Knapped flint with white-brick dressings. Bellcote and straight-gabled porch. To the W, in the garden of No. 5 Church Walk, the roofless ruin of a flint and clunch DOVECOTE; C14, possibly late C13. Doorway with four-centred arch.

Nothing outstanding in the HIGH STREET, although it remains largely unspoilt in its mix of timber-framed and Georgian brick buildings. Off it on the E side, not quite opposite the church, the MARKET PLACE, its buildings mainly timber-framed and plastered but with some exposed timbers, notably on the corner of the High Street. Mostly rebuilt following a disastrous fire in 1567. At one end the original C15 MARKET CROSS, a hexagonal structure of heavy timbers with a high pole on the lead roof. At the other, an early C19 PUMP in a wooden case with Gothic detailing, surmounted by a lamp standard. The Market Place narrows towards the E, the view closed by a mid-C18 white-brick house. Three bays and two storeys with hipped roof. Doorway with Gibbs surround.

---

*Superseded when a new workhouse was built in Kingsway by *F. Whitmore*, 1894–5; dem.

The Market Place leads through to KING STREET, at the N end of which is the best house in Mildenhall: SHRUBLAND HOUSE. Late Georgian, white brick. Main five-bay block of two storeys with parapet. Pedimented doorcase. One-and-a-half-storey wings to either side, each with shaped gable, smaller pedimented doorcase, and Venetian window set in an arched recess. Near it the WAR MEMORIAL, 1920, with a Portland stone statue of a soldier. Round to the NW in Queensway, facing the top of the High Street, the former COURT HOUSE of *c.* 1851. White brick, with stucco quoins. Two storeys. Five bays, the centre bay projecting forward with stucco rustication on the ground floor. On the first floor the window is recessed and set between attached Tuscan columns.

S of the church, the High Street turns to the SW and continues as MILL STREET. On its S side, No. 13 is mid-C16, timber-framed and rendered, with jettied front. Exposed timbers in the hall and fireplace with brick arcading. A little further on, RIVERSIDE HOTEL, five bays and three storeys with dormers in the hipped roof. Red brick, *c.* 1720, the top floor added *c.* 1900. Staircase with three twisted balusters to each tread. Across the road, PARKERS MILL, former steam and water roller mill of 1887. Four storeys. White brick with red brick dressings. Now flats.

OVERSPILL ESTATES. The expansion of the town to the N in the 1960s and 70s was carried out by the *Greater London Council* under their architects *Sir Hubert Bennett* (1956–71) and *Sir Roger Walters* (1971–8). The centre of the development is an open space with primary school (1968) and community buildings. Housing is grouped in a number of 'closes', with partial segregation of pedestrians, opening off COLLEGE HEATH ROAD. Industrial area on the E side of Field Road. In CHISWICK AVENUE, offices of Kings Forest Housing by *Johns Practice*, 2007–8. Timber-framed and clad with large sloping S-facing windows.

WAMIL HALL, ¾ m. W. Built by Sir Henry Warner in the late C16, but much of it destroyed by fires in the C19 and C20. Two storeys. Main range of clunch, with limestone dressings. Timber-framed service wing with brick-nogging. Straight gables and stone mullioned windows.

WARREN LODGE, 2 m. ENE. The warrens at Mildenhall date back to the early C14. The lodge (for the warrener) is conceivably as old as that, although a mid-C16 date is also suggested, probably later and certainly of lower status than Thetford Warren Lodge, Norfolk.* Two storeys, of flint with stone quoins and windows, like a squat church tower. Partially restored ruin, with pyramidal tiled roof by *Tim Buxbaum*, 2013.

LOCKS. The River Lark is a tributary of the Great Ouse and thus offered the possibility of waterborne access from Bury St Edmunds to King's Lynn and the North Sea. It was made

---

*See *Buildings of England: Norfolk 2: North-West and South*, p. 721.

navigable by Henry Ashley under an Act of Parliament of 1700 as far as Fornham All Saints. Ownership of the navigation descended to Rev. Sir Thomas Gery Cullum of Hardwick House, Bury St Edmunds (*see* p. 173), who rebuilt most of the locks (mostly staunches or flash locks) in the 1830s and 40s. Remains of these can be seen, e.g. by the bridge at the s end of Mill Street. KING'S STAUNCH, about 1¼ m. downstream, has been partially restored, and the LOCK COTTAGE, much altered and extended, has a datestone 1842 and initials T. G. C.

MIDDLE MILL, 5½ m. NW. Octagonal base of a mid-C18 smock mill, used for pumping water from West Row Fen into the River Lark; now part of a house. 600 yds downstream, a white-brick PUMPING STATION dated 1844.

MONKS ELEIGH

ST PETER. A big church. Big Perp w tower with flushwork decoration. Money was left towards its building in a will of 1435. Stair-turret on the s side not at the angle. The bell on top of it used to be in the spire, which was added in 1631 but taken down in 1845. Set-back buttresses continued near the top in polygonal shafts which end in pinnacles. w doorway with animals in the jambs and arch and hoodmould on two big heads. Niches l. and r. Nave and aisles and clerestory. s porch. The chancel and N vestry are of 1845. Internal restoration and re-seating 1867. Interior with arcades differing on the N from the s. s arcade with concave-sided octagonal piers (dated C14 by Cautley). N piers normal octagonal. On the s side double-chamfered arches, on the N one chamfer and one sunk quadrant moulding. Ceilure at the E end of the nave roof. – FONT. An odd form, dated C13 by Cautley, with corner pillars, and an odd C17-looking cartouche. – PULPIT. With Perp traceried panels. – SOUTH DOOR with tracery. – ALMS BOX. Plain square pillar with the date 1636. – STAINED GLASS. A number of windows by *Ward & Hughes*, 1880–*c.* 1900, some with portraits of those commemorated. – MONUMENTS. A few good C18 headstones on the s side of the church with skulls, hourglasses, etc.

UNITED REFORMED CHURCH (Congregational), The Street. 1870. Red brick with white-brick dressings. The former chapel of 1820, next to it, then became the Sunday School. Timber-framed, fronted in brick.

MONKS ELEIGH HALL, s of the church. Timber-framed and plastered. Notable chiefly for its brick chimneystack with six octagonal shafts and the date 1658.

OLD RECTORY, N of the church. Early C19 white brick. Six-bay front towards the church, including full-height canted bay.

The church stands at the top of a green which slopes up towards it, with houses on either side converging as if to focus attention on the tower. None of the houses is very special, but none is out of place either. On the green a cast-iron PUMP by *Ransomes & Sims*, 1854, with a warning to 'boys or other persons' not to damage it. The more interesting houses are along the main street to the E, some of them quite unexpected, such as the former TELEGRAPH OFFICE with its early C19 shopfront with Ionic pilasters, and the terrace of polychromatic brick opposite dated 1868. More characteristic are RUSHBROOKS and then the OLD GUILDHALL on the S side, C16 and C15 respectively, both with jettied cross-wings. Near the end of the village THE CROFT, on the N side, looks entirely C19, but behind its red brick front it is late medieval and timber-framed. PADDOCK HALL, jettied along the front with cross-wing at the N end, looks back down the street.

HIGHLANDS HALL, ½ m. NNE. Timber-framed and plastered house with two cross-wings. The whole front is jettied and the bressumer is carved with the date 1594 and initials of Robert and Elizabeth Munnings.

MANOR FARM, ⅓ m. NW. Timber-framed and plastered house of *c.* 1500, jettied along the E front. S end faced in white brick. Remodelled 1610 (date found inside), including sawtooth chimneystack with six shafts, spiral staircase and painted decoration, a green scheme with drop pendants. Also at this time the house was probably joined to a free-standing kitchen service wing that stands at right angles, rebuilt later in the C17.

SECOND PITS, ¾ m. N. 1959 by *Philip Dowson* with *Steane, Shipman & Cantacuzino*. Timber A-frame with clay-tile roof, on a brick apron. Two storeys at one end, where the gable is weatherboarded, and full-height studio at the other, where the gable is glazed with weatherboarding in the apex. Complementary addition at right angles, barely connected to the original house.

TYE HOUSE, ¾ m. NW. By *Sandon & Harding* (job architect *P. D. Lennard*), 1968–9. Of traditional Suffolk farmhouse form, with central 'hall' and jettied cross-wings, but with contemporary detailing. The centre is open through both storeys but crossed by a gallery.

COBBOLD'S MILL, ½ m. E. Weatherboarded watermill with mansard roof, of C18 appearance but earlier in origin. Miller's house across the end, a five-bay front of painted brick with arched doorway.

At SWINGLETON GREEN, ½ m. SW, is THE FENN, C16 or earlier with an Early Georgian front (1742, according to Norman Scarfe). Blue brick with red brick dressings, the blue brick exclusively in headers. Five bays, two storeys, parapet, central window segment-headed. Older wing with good central chimneystack to the r. E along BACK LANE some good timber-framed houses, especially HOBARTS: early C15, with jettied cross-wing, some exposed timbers, and crown-post roof.

MOULTON

ST PETER. The four corners of the nave are Norman, with nook-shafts and other masonry visible to varying degrees. Late C13 W tower. The tower arch triple-chamfered and dying into the imposts. The rest of the church is Perp, but so restored (by *J. F. Clark*, 1851) to make one think it, at first sight, Victorian. Aisles and transeptal chapels, clerestory. The arcade inside has polygonal shafts with capitals (fleuron and battlement decoration) to the arches, but polygonal attachments without capitals to the nave. The chancel arch corresponds to the former type; so does the W arch of the N transept. The corresponding S arch is lower and heavier. Frieze with fleurons and demi-figures of angels at sill level of the clerestory. Remains of an ANCHORITE'S CELL or ankerhole against the W end of the N aisle. – FONT COVER. C16, with eight curved crocketed buttresses. – BENCH ENDS. With poppyheads and animals on the arms (reused on choir stalls). – SCULPTURE. A detached block of stone carved with a male and a female figure, perhaps of the second half of the C11. The figures are crude and suggestively sexual, but exactly what the sculpture represents, and where it came from, is unexplained. – MONUMENTS. A number of good C18 headstones on the S side of the church.

THE PRIORY, NW of the church. Rebuilt 1846–7 as the rectory. White brick, two storeys. Five-bay garden front with canted bay on the return elevation. It incorporates the fabric of a medieval building. On the far side of its garden the former RECTORY SCHOOL, 1849. Tudor-Gothic. Black flint with white-brick dressings.

BRIDGES. Very impressive packhorse bridge over the River Kennet, on a route from Bury St Edmunds to Cambridge. Four arches. Mainly flint, with brick arches. C14 or C15. Further S another narrow bridge, probably also C15. Single limestone arch.

LANWADES PARK, 1¼ m. NNW. 1907 (rainwater heads). Built by James Larnach with the proceeds of a 100–1 bet on his own Derby winner in 1898. The architect is not known. Red brick with stone dressings. The entrance front is a near-replica of the C16 Horham Hall, Essex. Battlemented 'hall' range with lantern on the ridge. Two-storey porch to the l., full-height six-light canted bay, a skewed bay leading to a wing with crow-stepped gable, and then a four-storey tower with higher stair-turret. The only significant differences are that the wing to the l. of the porch has a shaped gable (straight at Horham) and inside there is no open hall, just two floors of rooms with rather low ceilings, made even darker by extravagant quantities of panelling. Irregular service range with many gables, shaped and crowstepped. Formal sunken garden on the E side. Attractive STABLE BLOCK with tile-hanging and clock turret. Gabled LODGES at the entrances. Owned since 1948 by the Animal Health Trust, with many additional buildings in the grounds. Equine SCULPTURE, Lord Ghyllene, by *Caroline Wallace*, 1999.

WARREN HILL HOUSE, 1¾ m. w. The Neo-Georgian house of 1928 by *Thomas Tyrwhitt* was rebuilt in 1999–2001 by *Julian Bicknell*. Red brick with stone dressings, in the style of *c.* 1700. Two storeys and attics. Three-bay centre. Tripartite stone entrance with segmental pediment over the door. Two-bay wings projecting slightly.

NAUGHTON

ST MARY. Half-hidden by trees on one side of the green, with Naughton Hall more conspicuous on another side. Unbuttressed flint W tower, with what appears to be a blocked Norman window on the S face. The tower arch triple-chamfered and dying into the imposts, i.e. *c.* 1300. Nave and chancel rendered. Late C13 to early C14. On the S side a two-light window, still with plate tracery, and a cusped lancet. In the chancel E window intersected tracery. C14 S porch with original cusped bargeboards. Tie-beam roof with crown-posts and braces springing from wall-posts. Restorations of 1833 (reseated), 1873 (chancel), 1893 (remainder, including removal of gallery), 1906 (roof restored and chancel re-seated), 1911 (interior restored). – FONT. Norman. It was square and decorated with intersected arches, but later made octagonal. – BENCHES. Six C17 ends with rudimentary poppyheads. – ORGAN. By *Robert Gray*, 1777. – WALL PAINTINGS. On the nave N wall, upper half of a large St Christopher. Also an unidentified scene with two women (or angels?) facing each other. – MONUMENT. Rev. William Edge †1871, rector for sixty-one years. Mural brass by *Hart, Son, Peard & Co.*, 1892 (cf. Nedging, a different design).

NAUGHTON HALL. C17, timber-framed and plastered. Gabled and jettied cross-wing with carved bressumer. Good original brick chimneystack with octagonal shafts.

THE OLD MANOR, 300 yds SW. Eminently picturesque with its exposed timber frame, brick-nogging and two-storey gabled porch. The timbers are, it seems, C17, but the house was rebuilt in the early C20. Moated site to the SW.

BRICKHOUSE FARM, 700 yds E. C15–C16. With brick-nogging, like The Old Manor but, being more original, not quite so picturesque. Details of the layout of the house are known from an inventory of 1603. Unusually long range (64 ft (19.5 metres)) of hall, buttery and kitchen. Jettied on both sides, but on the S side underbuilt in red brick. Also on the S side the hall chimneystack. Straight stair with solid treads. There was a backhouse of similar size forming the N side of a courtyard, destroyed in 1987.

NAYLAND

Although Nayland, a chapelry of Stoke, did not become a parish in its own right until 1782, it was a prosperous cloth-making town from the end of the C14, thanks to its position on the banks of the Stour. In 1522 it ranked forty-second in the list of richest towns in the country; only Lavenham, ranked fourteenth, could boast a greater number of wealthy cloth merchants. This has resulted in an astonishing legacy of medieval timber-framed houses, many concealed by later brick and plaster façades, as well as its large church. The original site of the village was probably COURT KNOLL, an earthwork 200 yds S of the church. It is roughly circular, about 120 ft (37 metres) in diameter, but reaches a height of only about 3 ft (0.9 metres).*

ST JAMES. The church is revealed only gradually as one approaches from the High Street, but the unbuttressed W tower is everywhere visible. It is C14, with a recessed spire, lost in 1834, reinstated in 1963. Also C14 are the chancel with its five-light E window displaying flowing tracery, the W window of the N aisle with intersected tracery, and the shape of the blocked window on the S side of the chancel. The rest is Perp. The N porch was rebuilt in accordance with a will of 1441, and wills of 1468 (proved 1493) and 1495 indicate completion of the S aisle. This has a handsome front with rood-stair turret. Arcades of six bays with finely moulded piers, characteristic of the work of *John Wastell* of Bury. Attached shafts with capitals only towards the arch openings. From shields in the spandrels of the arcade rise shafts that divide the clerestory into pairs of windows. The chancel has a clerestory too. Single-bay chapels at the end of the aisles, E of where the rood screen stood although structurally still within the nave. The benefactors seem to have been the Scrope family, whose arms appear in the rich porch attached to the S side of the tower. Built of stone (and largely rebuilt by *A. W. Blomfield*, 1883–4), panelled and castellated, with a vault with many tiercerons but no liernes. – SCREENS. Eight painted panels of *c.* 1500 from the former rood screen are hung up in the S aisle. Indifferent quality. Three arches of the superstructure under the W gallery. – FONT COVER. By *R. Y. Gooden*, after 1945. – WEST GALLERY. Simple C18 work, accommodating the ORGAN by *Samuel Green*, installed during the incumbency of William Jones (1777–1800). On the gallery front, painted cast-iron ROYAL ARMS of 1816–37, probably by *Coleman & Wallis* of Colchester. Another set of arms (William IV) painted on board. – NORTH DOOR. With linenfold panelling and a border of vine trails. – ALTAR PAINTING. Christ blessing bread and wine. By *John Constable*, 1809, and much less tied to the well-tried-out

---

*This account, especially of individual houses, relies heavily upon Leigh Alston's *A Walk around Historic Nayland* (2000).

mannerisms of the late C18 than his picture of 1804 at Brantham (E). – STAINED GLASS. E window by *Baillie & Mayer*, 1869. S aisle †1921 by *Robert Anning Bell*. N aisle W †1907 by *Kempe & Co.* – BRASSES. Large double canopy (N aisle), *c.* 1440. – Wife of John Hacche, *c.* 1485. Upper half of a Lady with butterfly head-dress under a canopy. Original size *c.* 3 ft (90 cm.) (nave). – Richard Davy †1514 and wife Joan with pedimented head-dress. 18-in. (46-cm.) figures (N aisle). – Civilian and Wife under double canopy, probably Richard Pigott †1528 and wife. 37-in. (94-cm.) figures (nave). – MONUMENT. Edward Living †1843. Gothic, with ogee arch and cresting, supported by a little angel. By *C. R. Smith*.

PERAMBULATION. The church is hemmed in by houses on all sides. Being only a chapel of ease it did not originally have a churchyard as such, but stood in the SE corner of what was once a much larger market place, on parts of which houses have been built since the C16. CHURCH LANE runs round the N and E sides, including THE WHITE HOUSE at the SE corner, early C15 with exposed timbers on the cross-wing. This looks down an alley along the S side of the church, at the W end of which is ALSTON COURT, the finest house in Nayland, and an important example of the combination of large house and workplace of which few have survived in anything like their original state. It is a varied house, with great surprises, and until Church Mews was built in the mid C16 commanded the market place to a greater extent than it

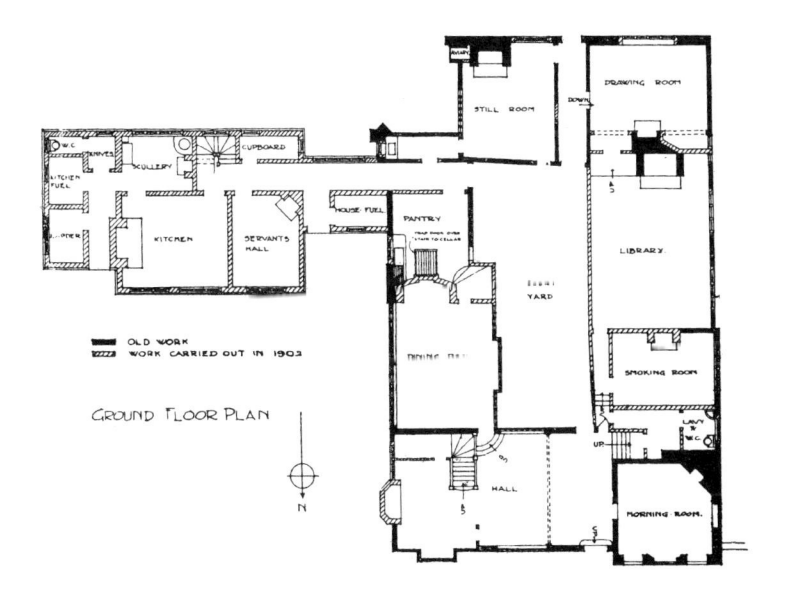

Nayland, Alston Court.
Plan, 1907

does today. The front is plastered and has a W gable, a big doorway of *c.* 1700 with a semicircular, deeply apsed hood on big carved brackets, a spectacular nine-light window with two transoms, and an E gable with jettied upper storey and timbers showing. The E front has the timbers showing too. The first surprise is the great age of the W wing, which dates from *c.* 1300 and was originally jettied to the front – exceptionally early for a floored and jettied building. The aisled hall of which it was the service cross-wing was replaced by the present hall in the early C15, which is also the date of the E cross-wing, although the oriel window here, with its carved sill, was added in the C16 (*c.* 1520). The second surprise is that behind the hall is a fully enclosed courtyard, part of the same C16 improvements. This has on its E side a rear parlour with brick-nogging, and in addition carved bressumers, several oriel windows, and elegant buttress- and angle-posts. The hall has a big eight-light window also towards the courtyard. On the W side, an extension to the service cross-wing, was the service wing, with more exposed timber framing, that included workshops and what was probably a dyehouse. Closing the courtyard at the SE corner a block of *c.* 1500 jettied to the E that appears to be the surviving part of a house which extended to the S.

Inside, the finest rooms begin with the hall, with a tie-beam on arched braces and a crown-post. The braces have traceried spandrels and rest on wall-shafts. The exposed framing of the W wall, however, is of the same date as the earlier cross-wing, with evidence of service doors similar to those at Abbas Hall, Great Cornard (*see* p. 259). In the early C16 windows some interesting and unusual armorial stained glass, mostly original. Then the rear parlour (now dining room), with heavily moulded and carved beams. On a post the carved figure of a soldier, traditionally identified as a German halberdier of *c.* 1471, which has led to this part of the house being considered some fifty years older than it really is. Panelling dated 1630. More armorial stained glass. Above this the beautiful solar with a boarded roof of low pitch supported on generously carved arched braces. They rest on corbels in the shape of human figures. Much carving also of the wall-plate. Painted imitation panelling (cf. Stour House, below). The house was restored in 1902 by *C. J. Blomfield*; before this the hall had been ceiled at eaves level and the windows of the rear parlour and solar facing the courtyard had been plastered over, as had the windows on the street front of the E cross-wing; the rear parlour was in use as the kitchen. Blomfield opened the hall into the parlour of the E cross-wing, with a new staircase, and added a new service wing to the E; the old W service wing was converted to include a library and smoking room.

From Alston Court one looks up the High Street across the market place. First, however, a brief diversion to the S along COURT STREET, which leads to the river and Court Knoll (*see* above). No. 17, on the W side, is an interesting example of a pair of 'renters' (artisans' houses for renting out), dating from the late C14: open halls with cross-passages, floored service rooms and a rear aisle. No. 23 (STOUR HOUSE) has a mid-C16 timber-framed parlour behind a C19 brick façade. Its hall was rebuilt in the C17, and contains decorative wall painting in the form of imitation panelling of the same pattern as that at Alston Court but using different pigments.

Back to the HIGH STREET and CHURCH MEWS, built as a single large house in the mid C16, projecting into the market place on the E side. Its front, now plastered, was originally jettied and had brick-nogging. Beyond it stands an obelisk MILESTONE (nicely lettered '55 miles from London', etc.), then at the entrance to the churchyard No. 14 (ST JAMES's GATE), early C17, designed to face the church, where the cross-wing is jettied on two floors. CHURCH HOUSE, across the lane, also faces the churchyard, and is a Wealden house that was built against an earlier house to its N. On the High Street's W side the OLD GUILDHALL with jettied front, built c. 1530 with an undivided room on the upper storey. The ground floor was a house, with shops or workshops in both the parlour and service bays either side of the hall. To its N the WHITE HART INN, C15 with an C18 stuccoed and sashed front. In a first-floor room are primitive C18 wall paintings, said (but with no authority) to be by *Jack Gainsborough*, brother of the more talented Thomas. Then the former QUEEN's HEAD INN, late C14 or early C15, with carriageway on the site of the cross-passage of the original house. Ogee-headed service doorways. Mostly faced in brick, but some exposed timbers at the N end and especially down the side, along the mill stream.

FEN STREET runs E at this point, a pretty sight. Part of this is due to the mill stream, although this dates only from the C17, and it must have looked very different in the C19 when it was the industrial centre of Nayland, including a tannery and gas factory. On the l., No. 12 (ANCIENT HOUSE), a mid-C16 jettied house added on to a C15 parlour cross-wing. No. 16 is the surviving half of a pair of renters (the other half, No. 14, being rebuilt earlier in the C17); the parlour bay, at the E end, had a workshop with arched windows and narrow doorway at the front. On the r., No. 1 was originally a steam flour mill, c. 1821. Three bays, three storeys. Red brick with segment-headed windows. Of similar date is No. 7, formerly the Congregational Meeting Room. Doorway with Greek Doric columns *in antis* flanked by windows in arched recesses. Beyond it No. 9, surprisingly, is a late C15 hall house, only a little over 9 ft (2.74 metres) to the street including the cross-passage.

MILL STREET is the continuation of the High Street N of the mill stream; on the corner of Fen Street stood the MILL itself, recorded in 1674, rebuilt in the early C18, enlarged to five storeys in 1823 and reduced to two in 1922. Now offices and flats. Along the E side of Mill Street first the miller's house (mid-C18 red brick, three storeys) and counting house (mid-C19 red brick, two storeys), then a C14 merchant's house behind an early C19 white-brick front, of only one storey to the street. It has a large open hall with crown-post. No. 4 Mill Street, with exposed timbers, is early C16.

At the top of Mill Street, Bear Street leads W, and Birch Street E. The N side of BIRCH STREET is an unbroken stretch of timber-framed houses of varying types, each occupying a site about 1½ perches or 25 ft (7.6 metres) wide: No. 4 early C16 with continuous jetty and moulded (and sagging) bressumer; then a pair of renters that was originally of Wealden type but with the area between the jettied ends filled in and the jetty made continuous across the front; then No. 14, similar to No. 4 but with the ground floor built out in brick. No. 16, C15, has a rear workshop wing, jettied towards the courtyard. More exposed timbers on the S side, including No. 17 (OLD MALTINGS), C16 and C17, with jettied front and, inside, painted decoration in the form of large strapwork panels. Further E, in STOKE ROAD, the former CONGREGATIONAL CHAPEL, converted to a house in 1990. By *F. Barnes*, 1864. Red brick with black-brick and stone dressings. E.E., with apsidal E end. The slope of the site enabled schoolrooms to be included beneath the chapel. Finally LONGWOOD HOUSE, with an early C17 cross-wing to the r. of a late C17 hall; the date of 1610 is not contemporary but is approximately accurate. Good chimneystacks with groups of three and four octagonal shafts.

Off Birch Street to the N, in GRAVEL HILL, HILL HOUSE, early C16 but altered over the centuries with canted bays inserted below the jetties of the cross-wings, sash windows and scalloped bargeboards.

Back now to BEAR STREET. No. 5 (BUTCHERS) is jettied with a finely carved bressumer. No. 4, opposite, has a Georgian-looking plastered front but is a mid-C16 merchant's house with remains of painted decoration inside; No. 6 is plastered with the date 1690 in a pargetted cartouche. No. 14 (WEAVERS) has a handsome Georgian red brick front but is timber-framed of the mid C16, as can be understood from the side. BEAR HOUSE, back on the N side, is a late C19 or early C20 dressing-up of a late C15 house, here with applied false timber framing and a little look-out tower. Then No. 27 (THE MANSE), with plastered and jettied front, an early C17 hall replacing a medieval one, and with fragments of a scheme of grotesque decoration inside. On the S side again, No. 34 is a charming mid-C19 cottage, red brick with Gothic windows, dormers, and ornamental bargeboards, opposite Nos. 35–37, another pair of renters (C15). No. 43 (PARKERS) seems to mark the end of the medieval street; the small hall houses further W (Nos. 81 and 106, both C15, and 83, C16–C17) are probably the remnants of a hamlet outside the town on the road to Sudbury. Nos. 95–109 are four pairs of semi-detached houses by *Paul Earee*, c. 1920, with catslide roofs on the outer side of each pair.

NEDGING

Church, hall and rectory comfortably grouped together, 1½ m. SW of the main village (Nedging Tye).

ST MARY. Two Transitional doorways, round-arched, with one order of shafts, the capitals thick crockets with applied decoration or upright leaves. The arches with bobbin ornament like thick rings round the main roll moulding. This unusual feature is found also on parts of Ely Cathedral, and places the doorways in the early C13. On the S side also a hoodmould of dogtooth. The N doorway blocked but with a pretty Gothick window with intersecting tracery. Chancel of *c.* 1300, see the windows (E three-light intersected). Nave and W tower Dec. Nave roof with tie-beams and crown-posts. Restoration by *J. S. Corder*, 1899–1900, completed 1907. – FONT COVER. Jacobean. With the usual curly brackets supporting a central post. – BENCHES with poppyheads. – BELL. By *William Dawe*, 1385. – MONUMENT. Rev. William Edge †1871, rector for forty-nine years. Mural brass by *Hart, Son, Peard & Co.*, 1892 (cf. Naughton, a different design).

NEEDHAM MARKET

In 1226 the Bishop of Ely was granted a charter to hold a market in that part of his manor of Barking that lay along the road between Ipswich and Bury St Edmunds. By 1251 a chapel had been built in part of the market place (cf. Botesdale and Redgrave); it did not become a parish church until 1901, which goes some way towards explaining its unusual external appearance. The market closed in the C17 but prosperity returned with the opening of the Ipswich & Stowmarket Navigation in 1793 and the railway in 1846.

ST JOHN THE BAPTIST. Its roof is 'the climax of English roof construction' (F. H. Crossley), 'the culminating achievement of the English carpenter' (Cautley). No statements could be truer. Earl Stonham or Mildenhall may be richer and of a stronger appeal to the senses, but the intellect must give Needham Market first prize. What the carpenter achieved here was to build a whole church with nave and aisles and clerestory seemingly in the air. The eye scarcely believes what it sees, and has a hard if worthwhile job in working out how this unique effect could be attained. The roof is a hammerbeam roof with hammers coming forward a full 6 ft 6 in. (2 metres). The arched braces supporting them are hidden (as at Framlingham (E)) by a boarded coving with angels with spread-out wings and fleurons. Against the ends of the hammerbeams again angels (added 1892) with alternately swept-upward and spread-out wings. There are also pendants suspended from the hammerbeams. This is done to give the impression that the chief distinguishing structural members of the Needham Market roof – the storey-posts – were not standing on the hammerbeams, but suspended from the top. They are very tall, and carry the cambered tie-beams of the low-pitched roof of the church. But between the hammerbeams and that roof much else is happening. At the point where the arched braces meet the hammerbeams vertical so-called ashlar struts rise, as they do in any canted wagon roof of the single-frame type. And they support, again as in normal canted wagon roofs, the rafters, which reach up like lean-to roofs to the storey-posts. The posts at about one-third of their height are cross-connected, i.e. from W to E, by cambered tie-beams, and at about two-thirds of their height, i.e. just below the place where the lean-to roof reaches them, are transversely connected, i.e. from N to S, by cambered tie-beams on shallow arched braces. Finally, and this is the most astonishing feature, the upper thirds of the storey-posts are cross-connected, i.e. from W to E, by a timber-built clerestory with windows. This feature, as well as the treatment of the ashlar struts and lean-to rafters, creates the impression to which reference was made at the outset, that of a whole church in mid-air. The storey-posts are its piers, the rafters on the ashlar struts its aisle roofs. In addition there is plenty of decoration, even if the storey-posts remain a severely structural feature. The tie-beams are all crenellated, and the arched braces carved. Finally, apart from the aesthetic thrill there is the fact that, as Cautley says, 'it would seem to be the only open type of roof which exerts no outward thrust on the walls'. It was restored by *J. H. Hakewill*, 1878–80, having been hidden by a plaster ceiling.

The roof had to be described in detail to make everybody appreciate what the significance of Needham Market is. For in every other respect the church is a bitter disappointment. Externally it looks like a Nonconformist chapel built in a main street in Victorian times, and with not quite enough money. It was rebuilt by William Grey, Bishop of Ely 1454–78, with the help of bequests made between 1461 and 1500. His arms appear on the chancel S door. The exterior is all Perp. The S buttresses have niches with canopies, the NE buttress is pierced for processions to pass through. The relation of the large windows below and the small timber-framed clerestory above is far from satisfactory, and there is no tower. A W bell-turret was taken down by *Hakewill*, whose restoration was completed, following his death in 1880, by *C. H. M. Mileham*; Hakewill planned a W tower, but instead the S porch, with its ridiculous and miserly spirelet, was put up in 1883 by *H. W. Hayward*,* replacing a C16 brick porch. Single-storey W vestry

---

*Known to Pevsner only as 'some ignorant and insensible architect'. Hayward was chosen after a competition judged by Mileham, who might have made a better job of it.

by *Fawcett & Atkinson*, 1908–10, with upper room 1991–2. – Most of the FURNISHINGS date from 1878–80. – DOORS. Original traceried S and chancel S doors. – SCULPTURE. Two late C15 or early C16 figures of pilgrims, under nodding ogee canopies, on posts. Probably corner-posts from a secular building (S porch, installed 2009). – STAINED GLASS. E window by *Powell & Sons*, 1880, including Crucifixion by *J. W. Brown*.

CHRISTCHURCH (United Reformed church, formerly Congregational), High Street. 1837 by *J. Fenton*. Five-bay white-brick pedimented front. The first bay of the sides is also of white brick, the remainder red. Alterations by *E. T. Johns*, 1913, including three-bay Ionic loggia.

BOSMERE COMMUNITY PRIMARY SCHOOL, Quinton Road. By *Suffolk County Architect's Dept*, 1982. Pale brown brick. A cluster of blocks with opposing monopitch roofs and dormers.

RAILWAY STATION. By *F. Barnes*, and not completed until 1849, although the line opened in 1846; 'a pleasing structure', as the *Illustrated London News* assured its readers. Of red and white brick and Caen stone, in the Jacobean style, with angle towers and gables. Remodelled in 1920, when the Dutch gables (as at Stowmarket) were made straight and the ogee caps on the towers replaced with battlemented parapets.

PERAMBULATION. The church, as noted above, stands on part of what was the market place, and around it were the prosperous merchants' houses and shops. Opposite the S side of the church Nos. 111–113 HIGH STREET (including TUDOR HOUSE), partly faced with C19 painted brick, a Wealden-type house of the late C15 with crown-post roof. Rear wing of *c.* 1600 with some exposed timbers. The house to the r. also C16 but refronted in 1718, according to the date in the plasterwork. Continuing NW, on the far corner of Barrett's Lane, No. 129 (BARCLAYS BANK), again with a front of painted brick but with the hall range and cross-wing jettied along the frontage to the lane. Then No. 131, a big Georgian red brick house somewhat spoilt by the District Council offices of 1965 etc. to which it is now attached. Two and a half storeys. Five bays. Porch with open pediment on Doric columns and a surprising ogee-shaped fanlight. Venetian window on the garden front over a doorcase with open pediment and more conventional fanlight.

Continuing away from the centre, Nos 133–135, early C16 and very effectively disguised in 1870. The date on No. 137, 1482, is spurious, but its jettied front has survived. Then the former METHODIST CHURCH of 1905. Red brick with white-brick dressings. Four-light Dec window. Opposite, the INSTITUTE of 1907, red brick in a version of Tudor-Gothic but with terracotta dressings and some very Edwardian porthole windows. Then, set back on the NW side, 'COTTAGE HOMES' of 1858, also Tudor-Gothic but entirely red brick and with unusually large sash windows set in tall, straight gables.

Now back to No. 131, and down HAWKS MILL STREET opposite, running NE. At the corner of KING WILLIAM

STREET, almost at once, a house with exposed timbers and good angle-posts (THE ANCIENT HOUSE). The date in one of the gables, 1480, is modern and may be as much as a hundred years too late. Two jettied gables, that at the N end jettied on two sides. Hall with crown-post roof, floored in the early to mid C16. A few nice houses further along Hawks Mill Street before the railway: on the r., LONGUEVILLE HOUSE, mostly of red brick, partly of the C18 and partly of the C19, but with a medieval timber-framed core. Beyond the railway, VALLEY HOUSE. Georgian red brick, of five bays and two and a half storeys. Doric doorway. Timber-framed rear range of *c.* 1600 or earlier. Then HAWKS MILL, an impressive watermill of 1884. Red brick with white-brick dressings. Three principal storeys, with attics and two-storey weatherboarded lucam. Five bays, separated by pilasters and with round arches at the top. Lower wings of 1892. Now flats. Contemporary HOUSE to the side. Just past it, the Gipping is crossed by a concrete BRIDGE of 1922 by *George Munday & Sons*.

Back once more to the HIGH STREET, and immediately past the church, on the NE side, No. 92 (PILLAR HOUSE). This has a good white-brick front of *c.* 1820–30, three bays with a Greek Doric porch, but at the back is timber-framed and plastered. The doorway on this side is the entrance to a mid-C14 hall with sooted crown-post roof, and the High Street front is the remodelling of a C15 cross-wing. Opposite this (No. 103) a nice shopfront with canted windows and doorway with Tuscan columns in the middle. The taller bay to the l. is a C16 addition with painted decoration inside imitating bricknogging. After that THE LIMES HOTEL, another medieval timber-framed house with a red brick front. Two storeys and attics. Six bays. Charming wide Georgian doorway with close ornament. Back on the NE side, on the corner of BRIDGE STREET, the former BULL INN, jettied on both frontages. Corner-post carved with an angel with spread-out wings(?) and some tracery. It may have been built as an inn, or as a guildhall; remains of doors and windows (now blocked) of shops. Just beyond it, in Bridge Street, another house with jettied upper floor, brackets, and two thin buttress-shafts at the angles.

In the High Street again No. 93, a five-bay, two-storey house of *c.* 1600 with an early C18 front of yellow brick with red brick dressings. Doorway with broken pediment clearly intended for a bust or other ornament. Then a long low row, punctuated by archways of which one, dated 1772, leads through to the former FRIENDS' MEETING HOUSE and GRAVEYARD. All the tombstones have the same simple design. The plain meeting house, timber-framed and pebbledashed with large sash windows, was built *c.* 1704. After that the long red brick front of Nos. 83–85, six bays in all, effectively disguising an unusually large hall house of the late C14 or early C15 with crown-post roof. No. 81, with plastered front, was the solar block. Further

SE the former ALMS HOUSE, remodelled in 1836 by *F. Harvey* of Ipswich. White brick, with heavy Tudor details. Timber framing of the C16 or C17 inside. On the other corner the former TOWN HALL of 1886 by *F. Barnes*, a sad building of yellow and red brick with lean round arches. THE CAUSEWAY, between the two, led to the parish church at Barking, 1 m. SW. Opposite the Town Hall Nos. 40–44, with an unexceptional roughcast front, is an unusually well-preserved C16 courtyard inn. Parlour, hall and service range along the front, lodgings behind the service range at the S end, a rear parlour of *c.* 1600 at the N end, and along the E side maltings or stables. Behind here, down a little lane, red brick MALTINGS with square kiln at the far end. Further out, on the same side, mid-C19 white-brick MALTINGS at right angles to the street; associated offices (No. 18) an early C17 timber-framed house, encased in the same white brick. At the end of the High Street Nos. 2–4, built as a Free School in accordance the will of Sir Francis Theobald (died 1653). Theobald ordered the old guildhall at Barking to be moved for the purpose, and many of the timbers are indeed reused and of C15–C16 date. Two-storey gabled porch. Some mid-C19 remodelling, e.g. the bargeboards, but not as much as to THE SWAN, opposite, late C16 and 1850. Finally No. 1, C16 with a seven-bay C18 plastered façade.

In CODDENHAM ROAD, behind the old Free School, the RAMPANT HORSE INN, mostly of the C16. A little further out, UVEDALE HALL, early C19 white brick with a pretty tented veranda on the garden front.

HILL HOUSE, 750 yds NW. Red brick. C17, timber-framed, remodelled in the C19. Beside it THE GRANARY, a two-storey red brick building, originally a stable and forming one side of the base court of a more important house than what now remains. The first floor, as well as the attic with dormers, may have been used for banqueting or similar functions. Shaped gables, rebuilt in the C19.

BOSMERE MILL, ½ m. SE. Black-weatherboarded watermill, of four storeys and attics. Now flats; machinery removed, but the breast-shot wheel mounted outside. Behind the mill, the partially restored BOSMERE LOCK of the Ipswich & Stowmarket Navigation, 1793 (*see* Introduction, p. 50). 100 yds NE, THE MUSTARD POT is a former toll house, moved from Brockford, Wetheringsett (E), in 1972. Single-storey. Timber-framed and plastered, with thatched roof.

NETTLESTEAD

ST MARY. A Norman window in the N wall. It has the unusual detail of a closely decorated arch: an outer band of intersected arches, a middle one of scrolls, and an inner one of beads. On the stair-turret of the unbuttressed W tower are three re-set fragments of other Norman window heads, also (but differently) decorated. The other windows mostly Perp. S porch of brick, with a semicircular gable. Over the entrance the arms of its presumed donors, Thomas Wingfield †1632 and Alice Poley †1628. E window of *c.* 1851, with headstops of Queen Victoria and Prince Albert, given by Stephen Jackson (*see below*). Arched recesses l. and r. of the window inside (cf. Little Blakenham). General restoration, including partial rebuilding of nave N wall and re-seating, by *H. J. Green*, 1898. Bomb damage, 1940, restored by *H. M. Cautley*, 1950. – FONT. Against the stem four crowned lions. Against the bowl the uncommon combination of the Emblems of the four Evangelists and figure of St Catherine, and in addition the heads of a bishop, a king and a man sticking his tongue out. – PULPIT. Jacobean. – STALLS. 1898, reusing C15 bench ends with poppyheads. – ROYAL ARMS. Of George IV, on canvas. A good set, with the supporters emerging from behind the shield rather than holding it. – MONUMENTS. Brass of a Knight, *c.* 1500 (nave floor), the figure 17 in. (43 cm.) long. – Samuel Sayer †1625 and his wife Thomasine †1647. Demi-figures holding hands, a skull between them. The whole architectural setting has disappeared. – In the churchyard a triangular monument to Stephen Jackson †1855. By *F. B. Russel*, executed by *Henry Ringham*. In the Gothic style, like an elaborately decorated churchyard cross. Inscription under three gables, the text running round the three sides line after line. On one side a shield depicting the tracery of the E window, with *Jackson*'s initials and architect's compasses, suggesting he designed it, although there is a drawing of it by *R. M. Phipson*.

NETTLESTEAD CHACE, SE of the church. The hall of the Wentworth family was largely rebuilt in the first half of the C19, and has a painted brick front of two storeys and three bays with Tuscan porch. But inside are significant remnants of the Tudor house, which was reduced by the mid C17 and probably extended further E and S; some timbers have been dated 1563. W of the house a late C16 stone ARCHWAY. Round arch, two fluted Doric pilasters on simply decorated bases. Pediment against the attic. Nearby an early C19 thatched SUMMERHOUSE, its domed ceiling covered with shells in an elaborate pattern. Further W, between the former outer court and the churchyard, a large pond or CANAL.

HIGH HALL, ½ m. N. On the Wentworths' estate, and probably built by them as a dower house or, more likely, a hunting lodge, in the last quarter of the C16. The Wentworths sold the manor in 1645 and after that it seems the house was reduced in size, accounting for some of its idiosyncrasies. It is of red brick, double pile, of two and a half storeys. The windows of the top floor are squashed under the eaves, and internal evidence shows that the roof was lowered in the C17 and that the house originally had a full three storeys, and no doubt gables rather than the present hipped roofs with gablets. The ground- and

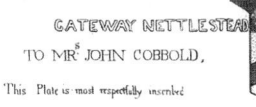

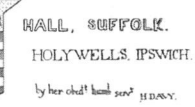

Nettlestead Chace, gateway.
Etching by H. Davy, 1824

first-floor windows are transomed, of five and four lights, and pedimented. The four-light windows belong to the W pile, which is narrower and shorter than the E. The E pile contains two large rooms, presumably hall and parlour, with corresponding rooms on the second floor; the W pile one smaller room on each floor, and the staircase. All three rooms on all three floors have fireplaces. The entrance is on the E side of the hall. Porch with two orders of Tuscan pilasters, its roof now lean-to but originally gabled. The porch is set back from the N front, an unusual position calling, for the sake of symmetry, for a larger range to the E than what is now there, which is a single-storey range to which *H. M. Cautley* added an upper floor in 1929–30. E of that a detached two-storey garage and office by *Maryanne Nicholls* and the *Whitworth Co-Partnership*, 2001, sensitively continuing the line of gables on the S front.

Inside, the parlour has C17 panelling and a good overmantel with two tiers of blank arches separated by stubby fluted pilasters. Well stair with a single sturdy turned baluster to each tread.

Also by *Cautley* two detached COTTAGES W of the house, 1930 and 1935.

TUDOR GRANGE, ½ m. SW. Timber-framed, and highly picturesque. The l. cross-wing is mid C16. The hall range and r. cross-wing were rebuilt in the early C17 on a bigger scale, with red brick on the ground floor. Some of the timbers of the old hall were reused for the stable and hay loft attached to the BARN W of the house. Between the house and the road, a former SERVICE RANGE (dairy and bakehouse) of *c.* 1600, timber-framed with (later) brick-nogging on the upper floor.

LONGLANDS, 300 yds W of Tudor Grange. 1961–2 by *K. G. Pert* (*Hare & Pert*) for his own occupation. Two storeys. The upper floor is clad in timber and overhangs the brick ground floor on all sides, as if a prefab bungalow has been placed on a podium too small for it.

NEWMARKET

Newmarket is synonymous with horseracing, a connection that dates from the C17. The 'new market', established in the southern part of Exning at a convenient spot on the Icknield Way, is first recorded in 1219. Newmarket developed as a coaching town and then, thanks to the facilities provided by Newmarket Heath and to the patronage of Charles II, as the centre of racehorse breeding and one of the centres of racing. The surrounding landscape is highly distinctive – the combination of heath, with its rails and gallops, and neat paddocks – but the architecture is, on the whole, disappointing. The late C19 and early C20 saw a considerable expansion in the racing industry, and the architects who assisted this were mostly local and selected largely, it would seem, for their racing credentials: *John Flatman* was the son of a leading jockey, Nat Flatman; *J. F. Clark* (of *Clark & Holland*) was a judge at the Jockey Club's meetings; *W. C. Manning* was agent to the Jockey Club and a well-known racing official. Racing stables, unlike country-house and hunting stables, were generally not built for display; the business of racing was far too serious for any architectural frivolity.

CHURCHES

ST MARY THE VIRGIN. So restored that practically all is new. C14 S arcade with keeled quatrefoil piers, castellated capitals and double hollow-chamfered arches. Perp W tower with shingled spire behind battlements. Flushwork panelling round the base. Perp S doorway with an angel in the apex of the arch.

The chancel was rebuilt by *J. H. Hakewill* in 1856, but retaining a C13 PISCINA. It has the angle shaft so often met with in Suffolk. N transept replaced in 1867 by a N aisle and vestry by *Clark & Holland*, who also restored the S porch, 1876; further restoration by *Percy Holland & Son*, 1886–7. – TOWER SCREEN (war memorial). Wrought iron, with shield, crossed swords, etc., in other metals. Made by *H. H. Martyn & Co.*, 1919. – PAINTINGS. Virgin and Child with St Elizabeth and St John the Baptist, by *Giovanni Battista Caracciolo* (1578–1635). Christ entering Jerusalem, by *John Wood* (1801–70). – STAINED GLASS. E window by *Heaton, Butler & Bayne*, 1872. S chapel E by *Lavers, Westlake & Co.*, 1887; two S windows, and the first in the S aisle, by *T. J. Marshall & Co.*, 1887. Another S aisle window by *Kempe & Co.*, 1909. Tower window and three in N aisle by *Christopher Webb*, 1930–1.

ALL SAINTS, All Saints Road. Rebuilt 1875–7 by *W. O. Chambers* of Lowestoft, an uninspired choice resulting in an unlovely building. The medieval church was aligned roughly NE–SW; Chambers turned it through 90 degrees, to gain more space, but retained much of the tower (now liturgical SW, with porch), which looks too small for the rest of the building. It had corner pinnacles, taken down in the early C20. The new church Geometrical, flint with stone dressings, and not improved by *W. C. & A. S. Manning*'s vestries of 1907–8, especially the large, ill-proportioned N one. Chancel, originally apsidal, extended 1887. Interior much improved by *Leslie T. Moore*, 1947–9, including refitting of sanctuary as a war memorial. ROOD SCREEN moved to W end, and moved again as part of reordering by *Whitworth, Hall & Thomas*, 1986, to form meeting rooms etc. at W end. – REREDOS and PULPIT. By *Moore*, the latter with painted figures of saints. – STAINED GLASS. Four windows by *W. H. Constable*, 1877: chancel N and S, N aisle, and the main part of the W window. In the lower part of the W wall, five lancets by *C. A. Gibbs*, probably of the same date. – Two N aisle windows by *Powell & Sons*, 1927–9. – MONUMENTS. A few from the old church preserved in the tower. Of historic interest is that to Tregonwell Frampton †1727/8, 'Keeper of ye Running Horses to thr Sacred Majesties King William 3d. Queen Ann. King George 1st. King George 2d'.*

ST AGNES, Bury Road. By *R. H. Carpenter*, 1886. Small, and effectively the private chapel of Caroline Agnes, Duchess of Montrose, of Sefton Lodge, who commissioned it as a lavish memorial to her second husband, the racehorse owner William Stuart Stirling-Crawfurd. The exterior is relatively plain and conventional. Red brick with stone dressings. Nave with narthex, slightly higher chancel with S chapel and N vestry, and an asymmetrically placed spirelet. Blind tracery in place of an E window. Inside, much decoration with Spanish-style TILES, probably *Frederick Garrard*'s 'cuenca' tiles. The

---

*CARTOON by *Burne-Jones*, donated in 1936, sold in 1985 to the family of the donor.

straight E end is made into one composition with tiled dado, MOSAIC by *Salviati*, and a large white marble REREDOS by *Sir Edgar Boehm*, curiously Baroque in the treatment of relief. It represents the Assumption of St Agnes, rising from the Colosseum which was the site of her martyrdom. – STAINED GLASS. Complete scheme by *Clayton & Bell*, including many figures of female saints. – VICARAGE, E of the church, by *E. C. Shearman*, 1897–8. Red brick with tile-hanging and half-timbered gables.

ST PHILIP AND ST ETHELDREDA, Exning Road. Built as the workhouse chapel, 1895. E.E. with apsidal E end. Flint with white-brick dressings. Reordered by *John Marsh* of *MEB Partnership*, 1988, to provide meeting rooms etc. at W end.

OUR LADY IMMACULATE AND ST ETHELDREDA (R.C.), Exeter Road. 1966 by *J. B. S. Comper*. Large, basilica-like church of pale brown brick. Nave clerestory of the same height as the narrow aisles, polygonal sanctuary and NW baptistery, NE Lady Chapel, and narthex below the rose W window. Austere brick interior, although the columns of the arcades (quatrefoil, with square spurs in the diagonals) are of stone. Parish centre on S side opened 2006.

CHRISTCHURCH (Methodist and United Reformed), St Mary's Square. By *Gordon & Gunton*, 1892. Red brick with stone dressings. Polygonal front of five gabled bays and off-centre porch.

EXNING CEMETERY, Cemetery Hill. Entrance gates and lodge by *Percy Holland & Son*, 1886; chapel *c.* 1894. Knapped flint with white-brick dressings.

NEWMARKET CEMETERY, High Street. By *J. F. Clark*, 1858. Twin chapels joined by an archway which carries a bellcote. Knapped flint with white-brick dressings. The C. of E. chapel has a Dec W window and the Nonconformist three lancets, while the E walls have blind arcading of different patterns.

PUBLIC BUILDINGS

KING EDWARD VII MEMORIAL HALL, High Street. 1913 by *A. S. Manning*. Red brick front of two storeys and three bays, the wider centre bay pedimented with first-floor Venetian window.

POLICE STATION, Lisburn Road. By *Frank Whitmore*, 1896, with additions by *A. A. Hunt*, 1905. Free classical. Red brick with stone dressings.

POST OFFICE, High Street. 1951. Red brick, still in the pre-war Neo-Georgian style of the *Office of Works*, as is the white-brick TELEPHONE EXCHANGE of 1947, round the corner in The Avenue.

NATIONAL HORSERACING MUSEUM, High Street. *See* Perambulation 1.

ALL SAINTS PRIMARY SCHOOL, Vicarage Road. By *Johns, Slater & Haward*, designed 1959 but not built until 1974–5. Built of flintwork blocks, with some timber cladding. Single-storey with pyramidal roof over assembly hall. On site of school by *Clark & Holland*, 1869, of which the teacher's house remains.

Former ST MARY'S SCHOOL, Fitzroy Street. National School (now King's Theatre) and house by *J. F. Clark*, 1847. Tudor-Gothic. Knapped flint with white-brick dressings, the house still quite pretty. Separate Board School and house on the corner of Black Bear Lane by *Clark & Holland*, 1874–5. White brick with red brick dressings.

Former NEWMARKET UNION WORKHOUSE, Exning Road. By *William P. Roote*, 1836. White brick, with round-headed windows. Quadrangle of two-storey ranges, of which only three sides remain. Gabled corner pavilions and taller entrance gateway with pedimented gable and cupola. Free-standing block in courtyard part of extensive remodelling, 1899–1902. Latterly a hospital, now residential.

PALACE HOUSE

James I, who probably first visited Newmarket in 1605, built lodgings in 1614–15 on a site between All Saints' Church and the High Street, an area marked on John Chapman's map of 1787 as 'Old King's Yard' (now Kingston Passage). Further work was carried out in the following years by the Surveyor of the King's Works, *Inigo Jones*, most famously the Prince's Lodging of 1619–20. Almost all of the old palace was demolished during the Civil War, but some fragments may remain behind York Buildings (*see* below, Perambulation 1). In 1668 Charles II bought a house on the same side of the High Street but further E and enlarged it as a new palace, with *William Samwell* as architect,

Newmarket, Prince's Lodging.
Design by I. Jones, *c.* 1616

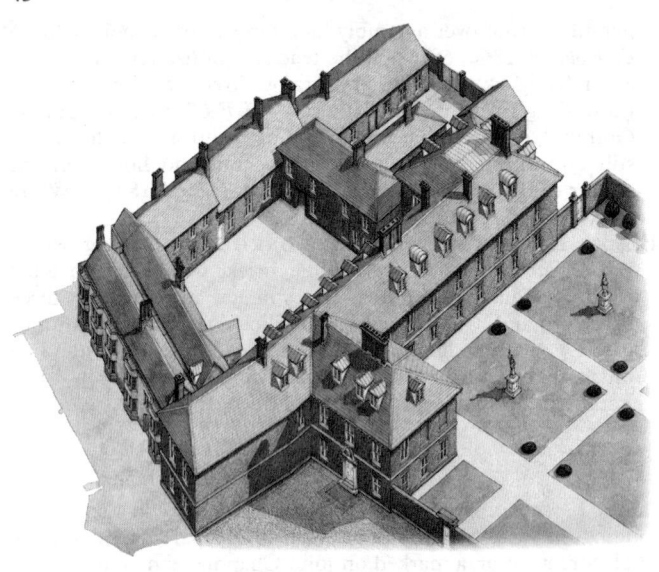

Newmarket, Palace, reconstruction.
Drawing by Stephen Conlin, 2008

1668–71. Samwell added to the existing timber-framed building a red brick range running SE connecting two small, square pavilions: one, nearer the High Street, for the queen, the other, at the far end, for the king. The lodgings opened on to a garden on the SE side; to the NE was a courtyard with further lodgings, kitchens etc. Some alterations were made for Queen Anne in 1705, but most of the palace was demolished after 1819, leaving only the King's Lodging. In 1857 this was bought by Baron Mayer de Rothschild, for whom *George Devey* made additions in 1867. Further additions were made in 1893 by *J. W. Holland*, and in 1897 by *J. Flatman*. This enlarged building, known as Palace House Mansion, was restored in 1996–8 by *Freeland Rees Roberts* for Forest Heath District Council, who removed extensive C19 additions on the NE side of the house and replaced them with a one-bay wing containing a secondary staircase.

Seen from Palace Street, what remains is *Samwell*'s three-bay, two-storey red brick pavilion, with a third storey added by *Devey*. Devey also made a new first-floor entrance, with external stairs, but this was removed in 1996–8 and the original entrance restored. This has a rusticated stone surround of Gibbsian type. On the S (garden) front, two of the three first-floor windows were replaced by *Flatman* with a very large oriel. Beyond that, a three-storey wing added by Devey, including a two-storey canted bay. Inside, the ground floor has plastered groin-vaulting. The king's rooms were on the first floor, with

NEWMARKET: PERAMBULATIONS 433

his bedroom in the large room, to which the oriel was added in 1897. It has a bed alcove. Next to it, in the SE corner of the pavilion, is a small room with a corner fireplace, a feature of Samwell's palace that was noticed in 1670 by John Evelyn as an innovation 'which I do at no hand approve of'. On the N side of the bedroom is the dining room, added by Devey; fully panelled, but truncated by *Freeland Rees Roberts* to allow for the construction of a new principal staircase. Of great archaeological interest is a sash window in the N wall of the room in the NW corner of the pavilion, discovered during the 1996–8 restoration. It is the earliest known example of a counterbalanced sliding sash window in England.

The KINGS YARD STABLES on the E side of Palace Street date in their present form from *c.* 1857–60. Externally of white brick with red brick dressings, but inside the trainer's house a wall partly built of clunch that survives from Charles II's stables. To the E a second yard added by Leopold de Rothschild in 1903. Red brick with terracotta dressings. Central terracotta fountain in the form of an obelisk with spouting dolphins.

Work started in 2014 (by *GWP Architecture*) to create a National Heritage Centre for Horseracing and Sporting Art, with a gallery of British sporting art in Palace House, the National Horseracing Museum in Kings Yard, and live stabling in the Rothschild Yard. Due for completion in 2016.

PERAMBULATIONS

The spine of the town is the long High Street, and this is described first, with one or two minor diversions. The second perambulation covers a much wider area, mainly SE of the High Street and along the roads radiating from the Jubilee Clock Tower, and it is here that most of the stables are to be found.

1. The High Street

The NE end of the High Street is marked by the JUBILEE CLOCK TOWER of 1887.* Flamboyant Gothic, red brick with liberal stone dressings. The builder was *Richard Arber*, who may well have been responsible for the design. The HIGH STREET at this point is very wide, partially enclosed by the side elevation of the Rutland Arms Hotel, to which we shall return. Before that, on the l., a late C19 block on the corner of Rous Road (BELVOIR HOUSE and BUTE HOUSE) with a good shopfront, and in ROUS ROAD No. 5 (ORLANDO VILLA), 1884 by *J. Flatman* for himself. Narrow, white brick with red brick dressings with half-timbered bay and gable. On the other side of the High Street, the WAGGON AND HORSES has a good early C19 front with bold sunk lettering, although timbers inside show it to be C16. Next to it Nos. 38–40, formerly PRIMROSE

---

*Described as 'hideous' by Pevsner.

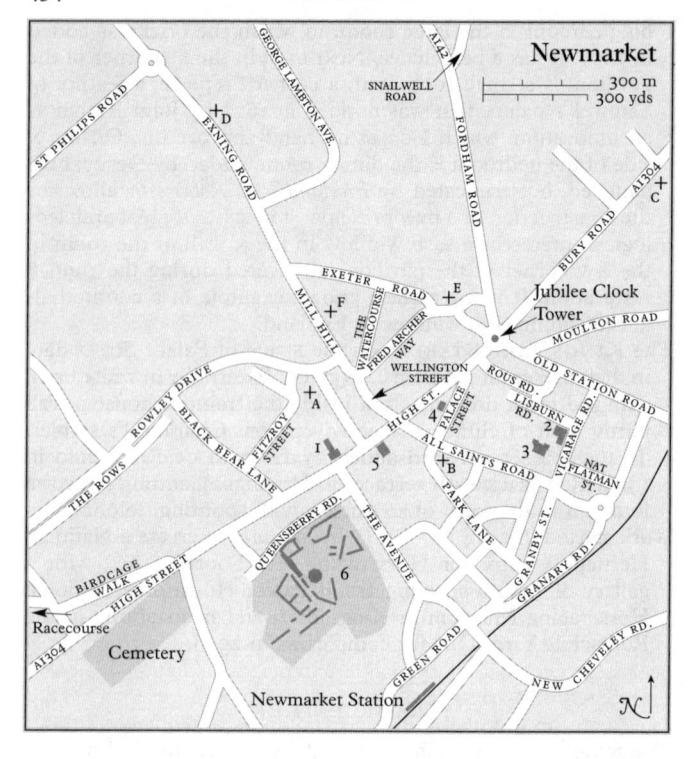

A St Mary the Virgin
B All Saints
C St Agnes
D St Philip & St Etheldreda
E Our Lady Immaculate & St Etheldreda (R.C.)
F Christchurch

1 King Edward VII Memorial Hall
2 Police Station
3 All Saints Primary School
4 Palace House
5 Jockey Club Rooms
6 Tattersalls

HOUSE, also early C19 and with an Adam-style Doric doorway. Opposite this No. 29, on the corner of Palace Street, has a canted façade with large round-headed windows on the first floor. It was built as a theatre by David Fisher, *c.* 1823–5; closed 1848, later a public hall, now a shop. To the S, the RUTLAND ARMS HOTEL, with prominent Late Georgian pedimented façades both to the High Street and towards the NE. The NE's is distinguished by round-headed first-floor windows, the High Street's by having the Rutland arms in the pediment. Behind these red brick fronts lies an inner courtyard of irregular shape, with an C18 timber-framed and plastered range along the SW side and, along Palace Street, an early C18 brick range remodelled and heightened in the late C19. A short distance along PALACE STREET, on the SE side, NELL GWYNNE'S HOUSE and GWYNNE LODGE, probably late

C17 but with a mid-C19 extension at the N end and hood-moulds and other detailing of that date. Mainly timber-framed and plastered. Further along Palace Street is Palace House, described earlier.

Back in the High Street, LLOYDS BANK, opposite the Rutland Arms, by *Flatman*, 1893–4. Red brick with stone dressings, with first-floor oriels and dormers with shaped gables. A few doors down, BARCLAYS BANK is a mid-C18 red brick house, of six bays; doorway with Doric columns, copied on the annex to the l. Behind it, reached by an alleyway, a more modest five-bay house of similar date, the windows with segmental heads. Also behind the High Street on this side, up Market Street, the BUSHEL, a timber-framed pub with a prominent late C18 first-floor bow supported on columns. No. 49 High Street (NATIONWIDE) has a good late C19 shopfront, but otherwise there is little of interest until YORK BUILDINGS on the SE side, dated 1832. White brick, of three storeys and six bays, and taller centre with pedimented gable. Greek Doric doorway and porch on side wall. Behind it, in KINGSTON PASSAGE, a range of early C18 buildings facing the High Street that formed Kingston House, built by the Duke of Kingston on the site of James I's lodgings in the early C18. Some of the brickwork of the garden elevation may well be a surviving part of the Jacobean structure.

SW of York Buildings, set back from the street, the NATIONAL HORSERACING MUSEUM occupies the Subscription Room of 1844.* Painted brick. Single-storey room with blank arcading and central lantern facing the street, two-storey block behind. Adjoining it, the JOCKEY CLUB ROOMS, remodelled by *A. E. Richardson* (*Richardson & Gill*) in 1933–6 in Georgian style. Load-bearing red brick. The Club leased the site in 1752 and built a coffee house (now the Coffee Room), a single-storey building with clerestory that survives behind the centre of the present façade. It retains its original cubicles or booths inside. Alterations and additions were made by *John Johnson*, 1771–2, but these do not seem to have survived later changes, including a new front to the High Street of 1842. The latter was replaced by Richardson & Gill, who provided a three-bay stone arcade in front of the Coffee Room, flanked by projecting bays with very shallow canted bays. Carving by *P. G. Bentham*, including keystones with heads of Hyperion, Mercury and Atalanta. Above the centre a handsome copper-clad Ionic rotunda of eight columns. Statue in courtyard of the racehorse Hyperion by *John Skeaping*, 1961. Richardson & Gill also refronted the rooms behind, providing a new main entrance on the SW side. The single-storey block at the rear, containing the Dining Room, Morning Room and Card Room, was damaged by fire as the work was in progress and had to be rebuilt. Overlooking the garden, a much-gabled range of members' chambers, 1882, very likely by *R. W. Edis*. Red brick,

---

*Due to relocate in 2016.

three storeys and attics. A private entrance with Tuscan portico was added for the use of King Edward VII.

Past the Jockey Club, the Post Office and, and on the NW side, King Edward VII Memorial Hall (*see* p. 430). Next to the Memorial Hall, and opposite The Avenue, the former DORIC CINEMA (ciné-variety theatre, now club) by *Edgar Simmons*, 1937. Neo-Georgian brick front with stucco dressings, with round-headed windows and large off-centre semicircular bay with coupled Doric columns. After The Avenue (*see* Perambulation 2), the character of the High Street is more domestic; on the SE side the pavement rises, and such differences of level are always attractive. No. 119, on this side, is late C18, of five bays with giant angle pilasters and a pedimented doorway. No. 125 (TERRACE HOUSE), also late C18, is improved by early C19 canted bays either side of a broad Doric doorcase. On the NW side, No. 194 (CLARENDON HOUSE), C18 red brick, has a three-storey curved bay. After this, QUEENSBURY [*sic*] COTTAGE and LODGE, the latter formerly the trainer's house for the extensive red brick STABLES behind. They are probably the stables built in 1771 for the Earl of March (later Duke of Queensberry) by *John Johnson*, but although extensive are not architecturally ambitious.*

Back on the SE side, behind a high brick wall, QUEENSBERRY HOUSE by *Edis*, 1898, for Lord Wolverton. Large 'Queen Anne' red brick house (now flats). Symmetrical garden front with six-bay centre and gabled wings with two-storey canted bays. Veranda, with balconies on the wings. Tucked away behind, MURRAY LODGE, Queensberry Road, by *A. N. Prentice*, 1905. Red brick with Dutch gables: two on the entrance front, three on the garden front, the latter separated by two-storey bays. The end of the High Street is marked by the COOPER MEMORIAL FOUNTAIN of 1910 by *E. A. Rickards* and the sculptor *Henry Poole*. It is in the form of a stone baldacchino, oval in plan, surmounted by an urn and decorated with jockeys' caps, saddles, stirrups, etc. Just beyond it, in BIRDCAGE WALK, another house by Edis: GRAHAM HOUSE, 1903–4, similar in style to Queensberry House.

2. *Outer Newmarket*

THE AVENUE runs SE from the High Street. On the W side, on the corner of Queensberry Road, No. 8 by *Roberts & Way*, 1898, with veranda and tile-hanging, and No. 12, also 1898, by *J. Flatman*. The more interesting houses are on the other side, a row of five by *Edis*, 1898. 'Queen Anne' red brick, two repeated designs (Nos. 15 and 19, and 17 and 21) and the last, No. 23, a bigger version of Nos. 17 and 21. They occupy one of the best sites in Newmarket, facing TATTERSALLS (Park Paddocks). Richard Tattersall founded the firm of bloodstock

---

*Derelict and inaccessible in 2012.

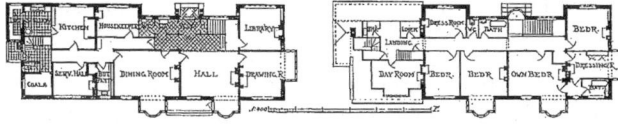

Newmarket, Murray Lodge.
Design by A. N. Prentice, 1905

auctioneers in 1766, at Hyde Park Corner, London. New premises by *Charles Freeman* were built at Knightsbridge Green in 1863–5, damaged by a flying bomb in 1944 and demolished in 1955. Park Paddocks was bought by the firm in 1884 and its rudimentary buildings were redeveloped after 1945. At the centre is the SALE RING by *Sir Albert Richardson* (*Richardson & Houfe*), completed 1965. Octagonal, with large central lantern and weathervane. Reinforced concrete frame with buff-coloured brick and copper roof. The interior, with raked seating round the ring, is functional, apart from the rather kitsch chandelier. Sympathetic extension (Reception) 2006. W of the Sale Ring a Neo-Georgian dining room, like an orangery, 1954, with a matching block to its S and then a two-storey office block, both 1981. N of the Sale Ring the FOX ROTUNDA, originally at Hyde Park Corner, moved from Knightsbridge Green during the war for safe keeping under Richardson's direction. Portland stone cupola on four Ionic columns, *c.* 1780, surmounted by a marble bust of George IV added *c.* 1820. Under the cupola a painted lead fox sitting on a drinking fountain. SE of the Sale Ring, the former entrance ARCH from Knightsbridge Green by Freeman, moved in 1955. Portland stone with Doric columns and pediment.

From The Avenue, various routes can be taken NE to VICARAGE ROAD (for All Saints Primary School and the Police Station *see* p. 430). Off this on the E side, NAT FLATMAN STREET, named after the jockey, with most of the houses (Nos. 1–35 and 10–26) by his son *J. Flatman*, 1899–1900. At the far end of Vicarage Road, ROUS MEMORIAL COURT by *F. W. Roper*, 1878–9. Former hospital and almshouses, now sheltered housing, in 'Queen Anne' style. Red brick. Hospital of five bays, two storeys and attics. Three-bay pedimented centre and pedimented doorcase, both pediments with carved-brick decoration. Segmental pediments on the first-floor windows. Steep roof and clock turret. Originally flanked by wards on the pavilion system, rebuilt in the late C20. In front, two rows of single-storey almshouses. At the end of each row a pedimented gable with carved-brick decoration facing the garden, and facing the street a half-timbered gable with decorative plasterwork.

CLEVELAND HOUSE stands opposite the top of Vicarage Road on OLD STATION ROAD. Originally of c. 1730, remodelled and extended c. 1820. The remodelling was commissioned by Lord Darlington and other racehorse owners as a reward for a successful jockey, Samuel Chiffney Jun. Rendered front of two storeys with four pilasters and a thin cornice. Four-columned Ionic entrance, portico with a decorative railing above. Panelled and partly pierced roof parapet. Large central panel with pediment and flanking scrolls. Inside, the entrance hall and open-well staircase survive from the earlier building, as well as the original drawing room and corresponding first-floor room. To the E, MACHELL PLACE STABLES by *W. C. Manning*, 1884, considered exemplary in its day. On the street, the trainer's house, a picturesque affair with two large and two small gables with decorative bargeboards. Behind this the stables round three sides of a yard, comprising forty-two loose boxes and twelve stalls. In the middle of the far side, a three-bay gateway with Dutch gable. To the W, back towards the High Street, CADLAND HOUSE (35 Old Station Road) has surviving C18 stables, altered, but typical of the earlier, modest stables that once proliferated.

CHEVELEY ROAD is the continuation SE of Old Station Road. Opposite its far end a pair of single-storey red brick LODGES marks the former entrance to Cheveley Park, a house just across the county border that was rebuilt in 1896–8 by *R. W. Edis* and dem. c. 1925 (*see Buildings of England: Cambridgeshire*). The lodges have Dutch gables with carved-brick achievement and initials of the owner, Harry McCalmont. Carved brick also round the doorways, which have flat canopies on elaborate carved brackets.

The NW end of Old Station Road brings us back to the Jubilee Clock Tower, which was the start of the first perambulation. From here BURY ROAD runs NE. It contains a number of large houses and stables, the first, on the E side, SEFTON LODGE by *William Young*, 1872, enlarged by him for the Duchess of Montrose after c. 1883. White brick with red brick dressings. Shallow-pitched roof and deep eaves give an Italianate feel. Trainer's house and stables in similar but plainer style, with additional stabling by *T. H. Smith*, 1905. On the other side, BEDFORD LODGE. Early C19, a hotel since the 1920s and much enlarged. Attached stables (now HIGHFIELD) dated 1864. White brick with red brick dressings. Long, symmetrical range of two storeys with single-storey wings and in the middle an Italianate clock tower. N of Bedford Lodge, set well back from the road, STANLEY HOUSE. Large house and stables by *Heaton & Gibb* for the Earl of Derby, 1900–1. Queen Anne red brick with tall sashes, tall pitched roof and tall chimneys. Stables on three sides of a courtyard with central clock tower. Additions of 1911: to the house by *Romaine-Walker & Jenkins*, to the stables by *T. W. Potter* of Knowsley (Lancs.), 'Architect to the Earl'. Further out, on the E side again, MESNIL WARREN, a large late C19 red brick house purchased by Lord Derby's trainer, the Hon. George Lambton, *c.* 1908. Additional storey with balcony overlooking the gallops by *Owen C. Little*, 1912, and large extension of *c.* 1924–5 by *Sir Edwin Lutyens* to provide guest bedrooms and staff accommodation. Tall narrow windows and hipped roof with dormers. Then ABINGTON PLACE, stables of 1889 on the scale of, and similar in style to, Machell Place, with an elaborately gabled clock tower. Impressive red brick entrance arch with a depressed shaped gable by *J. Flatman*, 1895.

NW from the Clock Tower the layout is confused by Fred Archer Way, but it is worth following Exeter Road as far as THE WATERCOURSE, along one side of which is a COVERED RIDE for Exeter House Stables, the first such in Newmarket, by *George Tattersall*, illustrated in his *Sporting Architecture* (1841). Red brick. Rectangular, with rounded corners, open on the inside. The Watercourse leads to WELLINGTON STREET; on the corner FOLEY HOUSE, with a fine pair of late C18 wrought-iron gates. On the S side of Fred Archer Way, on the wall of The Guineas shopping centre, Lunging Rein by *Geoffrey*

Newmarket, Exeter House Stables, covered ride.
Engraving, 1841

Wickham, 1975. Concrete reliefs of horse and trainer connected by a steel strip. A few nice late C18 and early C19 houses in Wellington Street and MILL HILL, its continuation N.

The final sortie is N from the Clock Tower, along FORDHAM ROAD, which has the same mix of large houses and stables as Bury Road. A short way along on the W side the former DRILL HALL by *J. Flatman*, *c.* 1886–90. A little further on, former MALTINGS by *Richard Hardy*, 1897, with cottages by *Heaton & Gibb*, 1899. Three tall square kilns and a two-storey malthouse. After this, SNAILWELL ROAD branches off to the NE. On its NW side, SOHAM HOUSE by *C. J. Harold Cooper*, 1892, for W. M. Johnstone. Red brick with stone dressings, in a simplified Tudor style. Expensive panelled interiors that originally included two stained-glass windows by *Selwyn Image*.* Beyond here, on the same side, PEGASUS STABLES, originally for Falmouth House (dem.), which was built for the jockey Fred Archer in 1882 by *Clark & Holland*. Red brick with stone dressings. Two storeys. Long range of loose boxes with houses at each end and in the middle an elaborate Tudor-Gothic entrance with clock turret and flèche. Trainer's house by *H. Woodzell*, *c.* 1890.

STUDLANDS PARK, at the far end of Fordham Road, 1½ m. from the Clock Tower, is a development of *c.* 500 houses by *Ralph Erskine*, 1968–75. Cars and pedestrians are segregated, with garage courts at the rear reached via a meandering access road, Hyperion Way. Stepped one- and two-storey terraces of houses and flats, laid out irregularly round a large green. Red brick. Their gabled end walls have apex windows and many are painted: typical Erskine details, as are the little porch canopies of corrugated plastic that have worn less well.

RACECOURSES. Newmarket has two courses. Both are on the heath on the W side of the town and have grown somewhat haphazardly. The ROWLEY MILE COURSE is nearer the town, dominated by the MILLENNIUM GRANDSTAND, 1998–2000 by *The Goddard Wybor Practice*. Four tiers of enclosed lounges with a deep projecting canopy. It dwarfs the adjacent MEMBERS' GRANDSTAND and HEAD-ON STAND, rebuilt by *Lobb Partnership*, 1986–7, rather brutally faced in concrete slabs at the rear. Older buildings on the site include the HONG KONG SUITE (former Weigh Room), red brick with Doric porticoes *in antis* and pantiled roofs, probably by *Walter H. Brierley*, *c.* 1925–6. STATUES of racehorses: Brigadier Gerard by *John Skeaping*, 1973, Eclipse by *James Osborne*, 1989, and Persian Punch by *Philip Blacker*, 2005. The JULY COURSE, on the W side of the heath,† has three large grandstands of *c.* 1930, the area behind them rebuilt by *Limbrick Architecture & Design*, 2006–7, with a series of linked pavilions providing catering and other facilities. On the roundabout leading to the July Course,

---

*Now in the William Morris Gallery, Walthamstow, and the Victoria and Albert Museum.
†In Cambridgeshire.

The Newmarket Stallion, STATUE by *Marcia Aston* and *Allan Sly*, 2000.

DEVIL'S DYKE. The Devil's Dyke (or Ditch) forms part of the boundary between Suffolk and Cambridgeshire for the stretch of about 1¾ m. where it crosses the SW end of Newmarket Heath. It was constructed in the late C6 or early C7, and was the last (and longest) in a series of defensive earthworks designed to protect the East Anglians from the Britons to the W. It is over 7 m. long, 5½ m. of it in a straight line.*

NEWTON

9040

ALL SAINTS. Norman N doorway. Two shafts with scalloped capitals. Chevron in the arch and the hoodmould. Nave of *c.* 1300, see the S doorway and the windows. Chancel Dec with reticulated E window. Dec also the SEDILIA, simple, but with a pretty 'two-light' PISCINA. W tower with red brick battlements. Nave, tower and timber-framed S porch vested in the Redundant Churches Fund (now Churches Conservation Trust), 1975. – FONT. Octagonal, Perp, simple. – PULPIT. Perp, with tracery.† Inscription asking for prayers for the donors Richard Mody and his wife Leticia. – LECTERN. Handsome C17 piece, with mostly consciously used Gothic motifs. – WALL PAINTING. Scenes from the Holy Infancy, including Annunciation, Visitation, Nativity (nave N wall). C14. – MONUMENTS. Lady of the early C14 in low early C14 recess (nave S wall). The effigy was found under the nave floor in the C19. – Margaret Boteler †1410. Effigy under a shallow ogee arch with straight cresting and many shields (chancel N wall).

BUTLERS, N of the church. C17, with exposed timbers on the W front, Georgianized towards the church. Timber-framed and weatherboarded barn to the W. NEWTON HALL, S, also timber-framed, dating back to the C16, but externally mostly C18. C19 castellated white brick porch and some Gothick windows. Some nice houses along the N side of the Green, ½ m. S. ROGUE HOUSE is Georgian, of red brick with white-brick band between the two storeys and white-brick voussoirs. Three bays. Lower range set back to the l., dated 1820 in white brick on the gable-end wall. Further E THE DEANS, C16 timber-framed and plastered with a smart Georgian front. Seven bays. Red brick, partly chequered, and with panels of burnt headers between the windows. Then BROOK FARM, a picturesquely irregular timber-framed house much restored in the C20.

---

*See *Buildings of England: Cambridgeshire*, for a fuller description of this and other dykes forming part of the Anglo-Saxon defences.
†Tim Howson points out the similarity between this tracery and that on screens from the workshop of *Thomas Gooch* of Sudbury.

Exposed timbers, partly jettied upper storey, and a three-storey stair-tower.

OLD RECTORY, ¾ m. S. Timber-framed, of C16–C17 origins, partly faced in brick. Additions by *John Whiting*, 1841.

ROGERS FARM, ¾ m. E. Timber-framed and plastered house of c. 1600, jettied on the S front. Inside, excellent wall paintings dated 1623: scenes from the Life of Samson and Martyrdom of St Stephen.

NORTON

ST ANDREW. Chancel of c. 1300 – see e.g. the lancet window above the priest's doorway. The E window however looks transitional between Dec and Perp. The N aisle (see the doorway) must have been built in the early C14, and the tower at least begun. Money was left for its completion in 1442, and for the bells in 1447. Of that time or later most of the windows. The S aisle has at its base some flushwork chequerboard patterning. S porch with flushwork decoration and a niche above the entrance. The arcade of three bays has concave-sided octagonal piers, each side provided with a shallow blank ogee-arched head (cf. Walsham-le-Willows). Double-hollow-chamfered arches. Roofs renewed in 1897. – FONT. Perp, octagonal, and richly carved. The stem is square and has panels and four figures carrying shields, one of them a Wild Man. On the bowl the four Emblems of the Evangelists, and in addition a double eagle, a unicorn, a pelican and a griffin. Supporting the bowl the usual angels with outstretched wings, but here alternating with winged hearts. – STALLS. Three sections are preserved. They have exceptionally good MISERICORDS, including the Martyrdom of St Edmund, the Crucifixion of St Andrew, a pelican, a woman carding wool, a monk writing, a lion devouring a Wild Man, and on the arms various figures including a boy being beaten on the buttocks. – BENCHES. In the aisles, with poppyheads and animals on the arms. In the nave, good, plain, early C20, perhaps by *William Weir* as part of his restoration of 1913–14. – CHEST. A very early oak dug-out chest. A date of 1199 has been claimed, linked to a papal order for chests to be placed in churches. Money slot in the convex lid. – STAINED GLASS. In the chancel on the S side, whole figures in the tracery, including a censing angel, originally in the E window, now upside down. – MONUMENT. Daniel Bales †1625. Standing monument with ogee-headed canopy and obelisks. Within the canopy remains of painted decoration including a skeleton with scythe and hourglass. Painted inscription no longer legible. Placed at the W end, because it was used for the distribution of bread under the terms of Bales's bequest. – Headstone, W of the tower, 1707. With cartouche, winged cherub's head, and skulls.

BAPTIST CHURCH, Woolpit Road. 1843. Red brick. Three-bay front with two tiers of sash windows and round-arched doorway.
OLD RECTORY, N of the church. The back parts timber-framed, probably C16. The front, towards the church, of white brick, early C19. Seven bays and two storeys with hipped roof and three dormers with triangular pediments. Rev. John Ashburne conducted the first known private madhouse here, until he was murdered by one of his patients (his own brother-in-law) in 1661.
MANOR FARM, Norton Little Green, 1 m. E. The front range is mid-C16, with jettied front and exposed timbers on the first floor, sandwiched between big crowstepped gables of diapered red brick. External chimneys, each with two octagonal shafts, also stepped. This range was built as the cross-wing of an open hall, of which little now remains. In the angle between the front range and the old hall, an early C17 chamber block. The ground floor originally an open loggia, and on the upper floor an oriel window running continuously round two sides. To the E of the house a red brick BARN, mid- to late C16, now converted to housing. – HIGH HALL, 500 yds E of Manor Farm, c. 1600, is a lobby-entrance house with exposed timbers. Two storeys and attics. Thatched roof.
CRAWLEY HALL FARM, 1 m. SSE. To the r. a mid-C16 timber-framed house of one storey and attics. To its l. a two-storey in-line parlour block, jettied to the front. Then a gabled parlour cross-wing of the early C17. Against the end wall of this a large red brick chimneystack with three tall octagonal shafts.

LITTLE HAUGH HALL
¾ m. NW

The house was built by Borowdale Mileson, who purchased the property in 1641; in 1674 it was taxed on sixteen hearths. His grandson sold it to Thomas Macro Jun., the Bury St Edmunds apothecary or grocer who lived at Cupola House (*see* p. 154), for the use of his son *Rev. Dr Cox Macro* (1683–1767), student of medicine at Cambridge and Leiden, D.D. of Cambridge, chaplain to George II, and a distinguished antiquary and virtuoso. *Peter Tillemans*, who was a family friend and died at Little Haugh Hall in 1734,[*] painted a picture of the house (now in Norwich Castle Museum)[†] soon after he and Cox Macro first met in 1715, which shows that it then had a third storey, dormers in the roof, and an off-centre cupola. But that same year, 1715, Macro had already begun altering the house, work which continued for at least thirty years. He seems to have been his own architect, but knew *Sir James Burrough* and received advice from him on

---
[*] He was buried at Stowlangtoft.
[†] Also two paintings by *Francis Hayman* commissioned by Macro, probably overdoors.

plasterwork in 1745. Payments are recorded as being made to *George Bottomley* of Bury, stonemason; *William Hasty*, for roughcasting, and *Newton* for painting the front of the house, indicating that it was Macro who at least began the process of transforming the exterior, although additions were made in the C19. *Thomas Ross* (later of Bath) worked as Tillemans's assistant, painting overmantels and doors, and may also have been responsible for woodcarving, although *Davis* is also recorded as carver. Further remodelling in the 1830s for Peter Huddleston.

The exterior is very reticent, not to say deceptive. Long stuccoed and painted entrance (E) side with a two-pillar two-column porch, probably of the 1830s, spanning three bays. To the l. of this three bays, to the r. two bays, then a later section that has a pronounced little bow, and then, set back, a lower, white brick service range. Short S side of white brick, its windows higher and taller than those on the E, and part of Huddleston's remodelling. On the W side the main part is of red brick and it is clear that we are looking at the core of Mileson's house. Just to the l. of the centre, inserted by Macro, a doorway with Gibbs surround and a fine Venetian window above it. Two windows to the l., three to the r.

It is only inside that the house reveals its true character, with the finest interiors of their date in the county. Behind the Venetian window is a splendid staircase. Three slender balusters to each tread, decorated at the foot. Carved tread-ends, richly carved underside of the upper flight. Equally rich the plaster on the underside of the top landing, and the doorcases. On the top landing, that is in a place not usually seen by visitors, the greatest splendour. Between the doorways a pedimented façade with Corinthian pilasters framing a niche; superbly carved, loosely bunched garlands. In the niche stood a bust of Tillemans which *Rysbrack* had modelled in 1727 but which was not installed until after Tillemans' death (now in the Yale Center for British Art). The ceiling over the stairs coved and with an oval dome. Paintings by *Francis Hayman*, 1743–5. In the dome Apollo and the Muses crowning Archimedes. In the frieze medallions of Galileo, Sir Isaac Newton and the mathematician Nicholas Saunderson, surrounded by putti and the instruments or tokens of the sciences, architecture, sculpture, writing, mechanics (the lever principle), etc. Next to the staircase on the ground floor the dining room, and in this room and the room above it decoration of equally high quality. The dining room has a magnificent plasterwork ceiling, and an ornate, delicately carved pine fire surround and overmantel, perhaps by *Ross*. The fireplace in the room above, whose walls were intended to take tapestries, is almost as fine. In the entrance hall, overdoors by *Tillemans*.

Macro was equally active in improving the surroundings of the Hall, but little evidence of this remains. Tillemans' painting shows a timber-framed house very close to the S side of the Hall, which Macro presumably removed. Farm buildings to the NE, including a tall rectangular dovecote, have been rebuilt. E of the house is the Black Bourn, widened into a serpentine lake, and crossed by a two-arched BRIDGE of C16–C17 red brick. SW of the house a MOUND, probably C18 and probably once carrying a summerhouse or gazebo.

NOWTON

ST PETER. Neo-Norman N aisle of 1842–3 by *Salvin*.* The window in the E wall is a copy of one in the original N wall. The N doorway is genuinely Norman, with one order of shafts and crockety capitals, as is the simpler S doorway. Salvin also renewed the nave S windows. Chancel of c. 1300, restored 1876, when the S vestry was added. Three-light intersected E window, a circle in the top field. Inside, two big niches l. and r. Dec W tower, with battlements and pinnacles of 1749. – FONT. Of c. 1876. An updated version of the old font, now in the grounds of Nowton Court (*see* below). – SCREEN. The N side, with broad one-light divisions, is medieval. – MISERICORDS. In chancel, a set of six by *Henry Wormald*, 1876, carved with the arms of earlier rectors. – STAINED GLASS. A remarkable assemblage of C16–C17 glass, 'collected from the monasteries at Brussels' by Col. Robert Rushbrooke of Rushbrooke Hall (*see* Rushbrooke) between 1801 and 1804. He sold it to Orbell Ray Oakes, for whom it was inserted c. 1816–19 by a Norwich glazier, presumed to be *S. C. Yarington*. Forty-nine roundels in the E window, thirty-five in other windows; mostly Netherlandish, one Swiss or German dated 1643. In addition early C19 figures of knights from brasses illustrated by J. S. Cotman, 1819, and Oakes' arms. The bottom panel of the E window contains glass from Dagnams, Essex (dem.; *see Buildings of England: London 5: East*, pp. 164–5), added in 1970. – MONUMENTS. Many to members of the Oakes family, the best to Elizabeth †1811, wife of Orbell Ray Oakes. By *John Bacon Jun.* Praying woman by a sarcophagus set at an angle. – The rest very ordinary, by *Theakston* and others.

NOWTON HALL, W of the church. Timber-framed and plastered house. Main range jettied. Cross-wing at W end. On the main range a chimneystack with four shafts dated 1595. Internal painted decorations of c. 1610, including imitation linenfold panelling (*ex situ*), and imitation oak panelling and cloth hangings in hall chamber.

ALMSHOUSES, ¼ m. WNW. 1877 by *H. F. Bacon*. A terrace of four. Two storeys. Tudor-Gothic. Red brick with stone dressings. In the centre of the row a little lean-to porch with a seat between two of the doors; stone inscription panel with arms

---

*Pevsner found it 'painful'.

etc. by *T. Earp*. Bacon may also have designed the former SCHOOL, 1879, ¼ m. NE of the church.

OVERWAY HOUSE, 700 yds NNE. Built as the rectory by *Frank Whitmore*, 1888–9. Red brick. Large and not especially attractive.

NOWTON COURT, ¾ m. N. Orbell Ray Oakes was given a piece of land here by his father, James Oakes, the Bury banker, in 1801, and between then and his death in 1837 gradually expanded his property and created a series of gardens and pleasure grounds. The house itself, then called Nowton Cottage, was particularly picturesque, a *cottage orné* on a large scale. His son H. J. Oakes engaged *G. R. French* to rebuild the house, renamed Nowton Court, 1837–9; it was further enlarged by *H. F. Bacon*, 1880–2, for J. H. P. Oakes. The result is rather restless, long and low, in a sort of Tudor style. Red brick with stone dressings. Tall ornate chimneys of white brick. On the entrance front a little polygonal porch joined to the entrance by a short passage. To the r. of that what looks like a chimneybreast but with a door in it and above that a bell-turret. On the corner a single polygonal turret. Inside, some fine panelling and a fireplace surround dated 1607. Is it Flemish? Now part of a retirement village, with various additions broadly in keeping. – STABLES by *Bacon*, dated 1879. With bell-turret and tall weathervane. – Most of the grounds are preserved as a COUNTRY PARK, with much of the C19 planting. Large

Nowton Cottage.
Engraving, 1835

WALLED GARDEN NE of the house by *Bacon*, 1877–8, including GARDENER'S HOUSE. Red brick with tile-hanging on the upper storey. Jettied porch supported on heavy rustic posts. Also by Bacon the LODGE in similar style. – In a corner of the park s of the house a stone ARCHWAY, remains of the s porch of St Mary, Bury St Edmunds, of which O. R. Oakes was churchwarden; removed in 1831 for road widening. Beside it the old FONT from St Peter, Nowton. Square bowl, Norman-looking, but with little scrolls at the corners carved with roses.

At LOW GREEN, ½ m. NE of the church, a picturesque group including two thatched *cottages ornés*, one of *c.* 1840 and another late C17 but dressed up at about the same date.

OFFTON

ST MARY. Simple Norman s doorway. Unbuttressed Dec w tower. Flushwork arcading on the battlements. Nave and chancel with Dec and Perp windows. In one Perp s window the soffit is nicely panelled inside. The s porch is of timber; Dec. The tracery of the side openings differs between E and W (cf. Somersham). Nave N extension by *D. Whymark*, 2002. Nice little oriel under the projecting gable. Chancel restored by *F. Barnes*, 1861, including rebuilt E wall; further restoration by *R. M. Phipson*, 1869 and 1887. Tie-beam roof with crown-posts and four-way struts. Spandrels carved with foliage and faces. – FONT. Octagonal, Perp. With four lions against the stem and four angels and four flowers against the bowl. – PULPIT. Jacobean. – SCREEN. Only the dado, made into benches (chancel and W end). Money was left for painting the rood beam in 1515. – STAINED GLASS. Three chancel windows, and tower window, by *Lavers, Barraud & Westlake*, 1869. – E window by *Hardman*, 1870. – MONUMENT. In churchyard, on s side, John and Sarah Wyard †1867 and †1848. Chest tomb with, on top, a horse and a weeping woman leaning over a figure lying on the ground under a blanket. Based on J. G. Lough's sculpture The Mourners (1844).

Former SCHOOL, 100 yds W. By *Phipson*, 1871. Tudor. Red brick with diapering and stone dressings.

OFFTON PLACE. ¾ m. SE. Georgian. Red brick. Two storeys. Three bays, the windows with segmental heads. Mansard roof, the lower section of which curves slightly, with the gables following the curve. Little finials at the corners.

CASTLE, ¼ m. S, on high ground. All that remains is a square moat.

TOLLEMACHE HALL, 1 m. WNW. Timber-framed and plastered house of *c.* 1550, with jettied front. Formerly the manor house of Little Bricett, reduced in size in the C19; the parish church stood nearby.

OLD NEWTON
Old Newton with Dagworth

ST MARY. The remaining medieval work is entirely Dec, with good tall two-light windows. The W tower has Y-tracery in the bell-openings and flushwork arcading on the battlements. To the l. and r. of the E window inside two ogee niches. PISCINA and SEDILIA also with ogee heads. E window and chancel S windows replaced in the early C19, the latter in cast iron. WEST GALLERY on cast-iron pillars probably of the same date. General restoration by *E. F. Bisshopp*, 1892–9. – FONT. Octagonal. Against the stem four lions and four Wild Men. Against the bowl four lions and four angels. – BENCHES. At the back and on the gallery. Plain, C17, with poppyheads. Otherwise of 1898–9. – ROYAL ARMS. Of George II, dated 1751. On panels. – STAINED GLASS. Some in the heads of the nave N windows.

OLD NEWTON HALL, ½ m. SE. Late C16 timber-framed front range, encased in early C19 white brick. Prominent semicircular porch. The back of the house plastered, with two projecting wings, one nearly twice the width of the other, both with jettied gables supported on brackets with drop finials. Early C17. There was formerly a third wing, making a symmetrical façade, with the narrower wing in the centre. This has an oriel window below the jetty. The room with the oriel is fully panelled and has an overmantel with clusters of three colonnettes. Although the panelling is contemporary with the C17 additions, it does not look to be *in situ*; the suggestion that it came from Gipping Hall is plausible. The little Gothick SUMMERHOUSE next to the house seems to have been built at the same time as the refronting.

ROOKYARD FARM, ⅔ m. NW. L-plan timber-framed and plastered house. The N–S range an early C15 hall house, downgraded to a backhouse when the E–W range was built *c.* 1570. The two ranges were not actually joined, it seems, until *c.* 1630. Remains of painted decoration of the latter date in the parlour and chamber of the C16 range.

WARD FARM, 1 m. NNW, developed in a similar way to Rookyard Farm: early C15, with a range added at right angles in the early C17. Plank-and-muntin cross-passage screen in the later range.

DAGWORTH HALL, 1¼ m. WSW. C15 with C16 parlour crosswing at the W end. W front jettied. Red brick crowstepped S gable. Farm buildings NE of the house include an OAST HOUSE, dated 1846, of clay lump, and a HORSE ENGINE HOUSE, of similar date, of flint with white-brick dressings, both rare survivals.

ONEHOUSE

ST JOHN THE BAPTIST. Round tower, probably later than Norman. A disastrous attempt at restoration in the 1980s resulted in the upper two-thirds being demolished, and rebuilt without the top third. Nave and chancel; C16 s porch of pale red brick. *H. J. Green* worked on the church, 1887–93, restoring the interior and rebuilding the chancel with a rather odd transomed E window. – FONT. Norman, of cauldron shape, with sharp angles and some ornament. – STAINED GLASS. Chancel N and S windows apparently by *Lucy Marriott*, whose husband was curate in the 1840s (cf. Woolpit).

Former SCHOOL (now community centre), 1899, and HOUSE, 1900. Built by R. J. Pettiward of Great Finborough in the same style as a number of buildings in that village: red brick with white-brick decoration, and on the school friezes of moulded bricks.

ONEHOUSE LODGE, 500 yds ENE. Early C18, of five bays and two storeys, plastered. Doorway with segmental pediment on pilasters. The shape of the cross-windows and doorhead is unusual: segmental, but with little shoulders.

STOW LODGE, 1 m. ESE, on the edge of Stowmarket. Built as the Stow Hundred House of Industry or workhouse by *Thomas Fulcher*, 1779–81. It was described in 1816 as having 'rather the appearance of a gentleman's seat than of a receptacle for paupers' (Abraham Rees, *The Cyclopaedia*). Red brick, the façade seventeen bays wide with projecting three-bay centre and two-bay ends. Arched windows to the ground floor, set in arched recesses, and also on the outer bays of the first floor of the three-bay centre. Three-bay pediment with sundial and motto 'Orimur Morimur' (we have risen and we set). Latterly a hospital; closed 1991, now flats.

OUSDEN

ST PETER. Norman nave and central tower. The latter is unusually complete, including bell-openings with engaged angle shafts. S doorway partly blocked to form window. Without shafts. The lintel chip-carved with saltires. In the tympanum *opus reticulatum* of large square blocks unevenly set. One S window next to it. The N doorway is curious. The l. shaft with a Norman capital, the r. shaft with a moulded C13 capital. Pointed arch with a recurrent ornament in the roll moulding which is like a collar of turned wood. Mid-C18 red brick chancel and N chapel, Gothicized in the restoration of 1861–2 by *J. F. Clark* (*Clark & Holland*). At the same time the nave was extended some 19 ft (5.8 metres) to the W. Further restoration by *Crickmay & Son*, 1909, including the rather good N porch. Inside, the two Norman tower arches have on their w faces simple shafts with carved capitals and roll mouldings. To the r. of the E arch of the nave a C13 niche. Neo-Norman arch to N chapel. – FONT. Octagonal, Perp. Unusual stem of eight engaged shafts that radiate outwards to support the bowl. – COMMUNION RAIL. Late C17; with turned balusters. – ROYAL ARMS. Large, on board. Of 1714–1801, but painted over an earlier set. – PAINTING. Crucifixion by *Redvers Taylor*, early 1960s. – MONUMENTS. Laeticia Moseley †1619. Corinthian columns supporting a broken segmental pediment with obelisks and reclining female figures. In the tympanum an hourglass. At the foot, a gruesome three-quarter skeleton in a shroud. Attributed to *William Wright* (GF; cf. Hengrave). – T. J. Ireland of Ousden Hall †1863 (N chapel). Large, Gothic, with crockets and finials and three cusped 'lights'. By *J. E. Thomas*.

OUSDEN HALL, demolished in 1955, was a Late Tudor or Early Jacobean house, rebuilt and enlarged in stages in the mid C18 and early C19, and further enlarged in 1835–6 by *Thomas Rickman* for T. J. Ireland and by *Sir Arthur Blomfield & Sons* in 1914. It stood to the w of the church, and the sunken garden just beyond the churchyard wall is the remains of the E arm of the moat. N of the church a mid-C19 CLOCK TOWER that stood at the E end of the house. Red brick, with square bell-turret. Beyond it OUSDEN HOUSE, converted from the stable block. Also red brick. Two storeys. Seven-bay w front with three-bay centre breaking forward slightly and now with pediment. Lower wings to the rear. To the E a square DOVECOTE of flint with red brick dressings. Probably mid-C19. In the village, EAST LODGE, about ½ m. ESE, is presumably associated with Ousden Hall. Mid-C19, Y-plan, thatched, of flint with red brick dressings (cf. Mouse House, Lidgate).

CEMETERY, Front Street. Opened 1912. With small red brick chapel. Timber LYCHGATE by *Sir Reginald Blomfield*, 1922 (war memorial).

Former PRIMITIVE METHODIST MEMORIAL CHAPEL, nearly 1 m. ESE. 1872. A jolly sight. Red brick with decorative white-brick dressings, including quoins, eaves, and along the gable-ends (like bargeboards). Round-headed windows with panes of brightly coloured glass. On the E wall, as well as the main window, blind panels filled with knapped flint. Porch with shaped gable.

PAKENHAM

ST MARY. A church with long transepts and crossing tower, something decidedly rare in Suffolk. But the transepts date only from 1847–50, part of the restoration by *S. S. Teulon*. The Norman church was of the type with nave, central space and chancel. The survivals of this church are the w and s doorways

Pakenham, St Mary, before restoration.
Print by W. Hagreen of drawing by S. S. Teulon, 1850

(one order of shafts, scalloped capitals, heavy roll moulding) and the chancel arch (nook-shafts, saltire crosses in the abacus, moulded arch with one hollow and one half-roll). There was another such arch at the E end of the nave which was replaced by Teulon. The E.E. arch on the s side of the central space led into a chapel rather than a transept, which was later demolished. The chancel in its present form is of the same date, late C13 (see the window shapes), as are two nave windows with plate tracery. E window of 1887, a copy (by *Hanchet*) of the old one. The upper part of the tower is C14 and turns octagonal, a design used by Teulon when he came to build St Margaret, Hopton-on-Sea (E). White-brick top of *c.* 1805. Panelled and painted ceiling over crossing by *Walter Hagreen*, 1880. Transepts reordered by the *Whitworth Co-Partnership*, 2002–3, including inserted floor in s transept. – FONT. Exceptionally good Perp piece. Four seated figures against the stem (somewhat re-cut *c.* 1850?), against the bowl the Emblems of the four Evangelists, a lion with a cross-shaft, a lamb, a unicorn and a pelican. – FONT COVER. By *Geoffrey Webb*, 1932, in the Suffolk tradition. – REREDOS. By *Teulon*, 1868, executed by *Thomas Earp*. Cusped arches and quatrefoils, filled with gold mosaic by *Salviati & Co.* – COMMUNION RAIL. With twisted balusters, late C17. STALLS. Simple, with poppyheads. – SCREEN. Simple, and not all original. – STAINED GLASS. E window by *G. M. McDowell*, 1887, executed by *Heaton, Butler & Bayne*. Chancel N and S: one-light windows by McDowell, 1907, three-light windows by *T. F. Curtis, Ward & Hughes*, 1913. – MONUMENTS. In churchyard, two very large vaults of the Matthew family, *c.* 1806 and 1852. Slate, with low sides. – Sarah Spicer †1999. Ball on column, the lower part octagonal, echoing the church tower. By *Jamie Sargeant*.

On the N side of the churchyard, MULBERRY HOUSE (former vicarage), mid-C16, altered and enlarged *c.* 1816. Painted on the glass of a first-floor window the figure of an C18 parson; by *Rex Whistler*, one of his last works before he was killed in 1944. Lower down Church Hill, on the W side, the former SCHOOL, 1842, enlarged 1872. Knapped flint with red brick dressings. Front with three small gables. At the bottom on the E side, LINDEN HOUSE. Early C19 white brick. Greek Doric porch on the S side, but the house looks W, along the village street. Three bays and two storeys. A few nice houses along THE STREET, including on the S side PIP'S COTTAGE, a hall house of the 1480s with some C17 painted decoration inside, and on the N side No. 8, a timber-framed house with brick front in Flemish bond, the stretchers red and headers white.

NEWE HOUSE, NE of the church. Built by Sir Robert Bright of Nether Hall for his second son, Henry. It is described as new built in 1621 but the date on the porch is 1622. Red brick. Completely symmetrical, with three large shaped gables. Windows mullioned-and-transomed of three and four lights, with cemented surrounds. In the middle a canted two-storey porch. Round-arched and thinly pedimented doorway, pedimented windows above, and crowned with little lunettes – a rather earlier motif. Square, diagonally placed chimneys. Although the façade is impressive, the house was not particularly large – only one room deep – but in its layout it was up-to-date, with the hall in the middle entered almost centrally without a screens passage. Kitchen to one side, parlour to the other. On the first floor two chambers and, over the hall, a dining chamber opening into the bay, although the original layout has not survived. Smaller rooms on the floor above and garrets above that. Extensions to the rear sympathetically rebuilt by *David Carnwath*, 2006–7.

NETHER HALL, 400 yds SW. The manor was acquired by Robert Bright (*see* above) in 1601; the house had been built in the previous century. It is timber-framed, and it was very probably Bright who encased it in red brick. The entrance was on the S side, with a row of four gables; the middle two have been replaced with a pitched roof, probably in the C18, leaving a centre with cross-wings. In 1874 the estate was purchased by Edward Greene, M.P. and brewer, who engaged *Philip Webb* to carry out alterations and additions, 1874–5 (cf. Manor Farm, Thurston). Further alterations were made by his son, E.W. (later Sir Walter) Greene, who succeeded in 1891, was also M.P. (for Bury St Edmunds) and died in 1920. Webb moved the entrance to the N side, where three of the original gables can still be seen, filled with black weatherboarding. In the middle he added a single-storey brick porch, with a round-arched entrance and little weatherboarded gable. There were few if any windows on this side of the house and Webb tucked one under one side of the porch, with a larger one beside it. On the E side of the new entrance court he added a two-storey, six-bay service range. On the E side of this range, three three-storey gabled projections, like narrow cross-wings, the middle one heightened *c.* 1891–2 as a water tower, with castellated top; there was a fourth, making a symmetrical façade, but this was subsumed in later additions. Also on the E side a kitchen court, much altered, and a single-storey addition (after 1920) described as a ballroom. The S front has a five-bay centre and two two-bay cross-wings. The brickwork of the gabled fronts of the cross-wings is clearly later than the brickwork that first encased the timber-framed house. The windows were replaced in stone, *c.* 1891–2, with canted bays added to the cross-wings and an addition made to the SE corner. This has a shallow pedimented bay on the S front and a canted bay and garden entrance on the E. On the W front, towards the S end, what appears to be an original projection, although the diagonal buttresses rising to pinnacles, and gable with chimney where one might expect a finial, could be Webb's work. Canted bay added *c.* 1891–2, and the whole thing duplicated at the N end of the W front, with a single-storey link between them. Chimneys of various dates, but all with corbelled tops, perhaps added by Webb. Good C19 and early C20 interiors, especially the dining room, which seems to be largely of 1874–5. It has a 'breakfast recess' on one side and, across the end wall, a large built-in sideboard with coved canopy. Ancillary buildings probably all for E. W. Greene, including the STABLES at the N end of the service range (flint with red brick dressings, upper storey with brick-nogging, and clock turret over the entrance); FARMHOUSE, NE, C17 timber-framed and plastered on its S side but remodelled with false half-timbering on the W; and LODGE COTTAGE, at the main entrance from the village (picturesque false half-timbering, on a plinth of knapped flint with red brick dressings).

REDCASTLE FARM, 2 m. NW. L-plan timber-framed and plastered farmhouse, with moat on three sides. The front part late C16, the rear wing C15 and C17. Behind the house a DOVECOTE, also timber-framed and plastered. Hipped roof with gablets. Probably early C17, perhaps soon after 1619 when the law was changed to allow freeholders to build dovecotes.

BARTON MERE HOUSE. *See* Great Barton.

MILLS. Pakenham is unique in Suffolk in having both a working windmill and a working watermill. The former, a TOWER MILL, stands 1½ m. N of the church. Built 1830, of tarred white brick. Five floors, with four patent sails and fantail. Dome-shaped cap with an attractive finial, and two pairs of stones (originally three) on the second floor. The gallery was added as part of the first major restoration in 1950. The WATERMILL, 700 yds to its E, is mentioned in Domesday Book. Foundations of a Tudor building have been found but the mill was rebuilt in the late C18 and again, according to a datestone, in 1814. Ground floor of tarred brick, and two weatherboarded upper storeys with loft and weatherboarded lucam. Three pairs of millstones driven by a cast-iron breastshot wheel (by *Walter Peck* of Bury St Edmunds, 1902), as well as a Blackstone oil engine of 1904. It was the last watermill in Suffolk to cease commercial production, in 1974; acquired by the Suffolk Buildings Preservation Trust in 1978, and repaired for them by *Michael & Sheila Gooch*. Attached two-storey HOUSE at the N end. Early C17, timber-framed and plastered.

PALGRAVE

ST PETER. Dec W tower, unbuttressed. Chancel arch of *c.* 1300, well detailed. The rest of the chancel mentioned by Tom Martin (*see* below) as new in 1729, but restored in 1851. N aisle 1861 by *Henry Angold* of Diss, its arcade based on the chancel arch. The rest Perp. Ornate S porch. Two-storeyed. Flush-panelled front; flushwork battlements. Entrance with crowns, fleurons, etc., in the arch. Spandrels with St Michael and the Dragon. Niches l. and r. Nave roof* with hammerbeams carrying arched braces that meet at the ridge. The rafters prettily painted with tracery patterns. The roof has no hammerposts so that the arched braces rest directly on the hammerbeams. Money was left for painting the roof in 1471, for painting the canopy in 1518, and for leading the church in 1518–35. – FONT. Late Norman, square, with four big heads at the corners and four crosses in the four fields. Five supports, four with scalloped capitals. Considered by Pevsner a South-Western rather than East Anglian type (e.g. Bodmin), but comparable also to the NW Norfolk group (Sculthorpe, Shernborne, South Wootton, Toftrees). – ARMOUR. Some parish armour above the S doorway. – STAINED GLASS. Three chancel windows of 1851, assigned by Birkin Haward to *Ward & Nixon*. Also two nave windows †1849 and 1850. Nave S by *Rowland & Surinder Warboys*, 1995. – MONUMENTS. In porch, 'that able and indefatigable antiquary' Thomas Martin †1771. With urn and arms. Erected by Sir John Fenn of East Dereham. – In the churchyard, headstone to John Catchpole, waggoner, †1787. It shows his six-horse team pulling a wagon, with verse:

> My horses have done Running.
> My Waggon is decay'd.
> And now in the Dust my Body is lay'd
> My whip is worn out & my work It is done
> And now I'm brought here to my last home.

– Chest tomb of Joseph Farrow †1838. With Tudor arches in the panels and little Gothic buttresses with pinnacles.

The church is in the middle of the village, at the bottom of a green that runs N from the main road. In the NW corner of the

---

*Measured and drawn by Raphael and J. Arthur Brandon for their *Open Timber Roofs of the Middle Ages* (1849).

green THE PADDOCKS. It has a red brick shaped gable dated 1720 added to a C17 timber-framed house. Late C19 extension to the l. with another shaped gable. Opposite the church, on the s side of the road, BRACKENDALE, originally the guildhall. Early C16. Five bays with jettied front and exposed timbers on the upper storey. To its W ORME HOUSE, *c.* 1835. Two storeys, three bays, with hipped slate roof. Clay lump and brick, rendered and painted. Pronounced quoins and door and window surrounds. Then WEAVER'S MARK, mid-C16, timber-framed and plastered, with single cross-wing. C19 porch and bargeboards. Pargetted panels of fleur-de-lys, lion and unicorn.

THE PRIORY, 200 yds SW. Partly C16 and C17, but mainly of 1836, when it was remodelled and enlarged for three Harrison sisters. Tudor-Gothic, with hoodmoulds and bargeboarded gables. Main range with two-storey canted bay at the s end and two-storey gabled porch in the middle of the E front. Oriel over the entrance.

ST JOHN'S HOUSE, 1¼ m. SW. Rebuilt in the early C19, probably by Charles Harrison †1820. White brick. Five bays with a semicircular porch on Doric columns. Tripartite window above it, with a segmental arch. Behind this front range, remains of the earlier house, part timber-framed, dating back to the C17. Early C19 STABLE BLOCK and GROOM'S HOUSE to E. Red brick with white-brick fronts. GARDEN to NW with red brick walls, crinkle-crankle on three sides. Now a private hospital, with numerous additional buildings.

(STACKYARD HOUSE, 400 yds NW. By *Mole Architects*, 2010–12. Two-storey 'low-energy' house, clad in western red cedar.)

POLSTEAD

ST MARY. Blocked Norman windows in the chancel N and s walls give a clue to the age of the church, and the bricks that form their arches hint of the church's principal point of interest. This becomes fully apparent within. Arcades of three bays with a further W bay separated from the others by a short section of wall. The three-bay arcades have square Norman piers of limestone with nook-shafts at the angles. These have small capitals. The arches are rough, single-stepped, and constructed partly of tufa but mainly of brick. The bricks are most intriguing. They measure 10 to 11 in. by 5 to 7 in. by 1¾ in. (25.4 to 28 cm. by 12.7 to 17.8 cm. by 4.4 cm.), so they cannot be reused Roman bricks: the Roman size is 18 in. by 12 in. (45.7 cm. by 30.5 cm.). They are very close in size to the 'great bricks' made by the monks at Coggeshall Abbey, Essex, which are 12 by 6 by 1¾ in. (30.5 by 15.2 by 4.4 cm.). These are not thought to have been made before about 1160, and Polstead is thought to have been built at just this time by

Henry of Essex, before he fell from grace in 1163. It seems futile to attempt to determine whether Polstead bricks are older than Coggeshall bricks, and bricks at Bradwell, also in Essex, may be yet older.* A more interesting question is, what led the builders here to make and use brick? Above the arcade are the blocked windows of the original clerestory, also of brick. Brick and Norman also the plain chancel arch and its imposts, and the W doorway and window above it. The W door now leads into the tower, but was originally external. The doorway has to the W two orders of shafts and divers chevrons in the arches. Of the western bays of the arcade, only the arch on the N side is Norman. That on the S is pointed and probably of the same date as the tower, i.e. *c.* 1300. The tower has lancets and Y-tracery. The spire is later. Of the Dec style the S doorway, the S aisle E window with reticulated tracery, and also the N aisle E window with a depressed arch. Most of the rest is Perp. The development of the building is uncertain. The separate bays at the W end suggest an extension to the original church, with the aisles being added at the same time. But the blocked windows in the chancel show that the arcades are contemporary with the chancel, suggesting that the church was built with aisles from the start, *c.* 1160, but that the aisles were rebuilt higher in the C14, at which point the clerestory became blocked. The slight separation of the W end may possibly be connected with a tower that was proposed but never built in the C12. Dormers on the S side belong to repairs of 1983–8. – FONT. Octagonal, on five supports. C13 in origin but completely reconstructed in 1961 with a brick bowl. Fibreglass COVER made by a member of the Community of St Clare. – WALL PAINTING. Fragment of a Bishop (N aisle). – COMMUNION RAIL. Three-sided, C18. – STAINED GLASS. Many fragments, C15 and later, in a chancel window. – MONUMENTS. Brass to a Priest, *c.* 1430. 19-in. (48-cm.) figure. – Brasses to a Civilian and Wife, *c.* 1490, and five sons, the main figures 21 in. (54 cm.). – Jacob Brand †1630, with son Benjamin. Kneeling figures. – War memorial (in churchyard). By *Hunt & Coates*, 1920. Clipsham stone. Similar to Lutyens' Cenotaph, but smaller and less subtle.

POLSTEAD HALL stands close to the church to the W. The two-storey main front can be clearly seen from the churchyard. It is rendered, with a one-storey porch *in antis* and two two-storey canted bay windows, and attics behind a parapet that is partly balustraded. The appearance is due to *William Pilkington*, who made alterations and additions for T.W. Cooke, 1816–19.[†] The return fronts are long and monotonous, but were longer until large parts of the back were demolished in the 1950s – on the N side seven bays, originally eleven. But behind Pilkington's front, apart from the r.-hand bay, the structure of the original early C17 house remains, probably

---

* See *Buildings of England: Essex*, p. 163.
[†] Although 188 balusters and 52 half-balusters were ordered from *Coade* in 1814.

built by John Brand, who purchased the estate from the Waldegraves in 1598. Behind the front rooms are mid-C17 additions and the original stair-turret. On the first floor an outstanding scheme of painted decoration of the early C17. Grisaille, with antiquework decoration, fighting figures and grotesque creatures. Entrance hall by Pilkington with Ionic columns and an elegantly curved geometrical staircase in one of the mid-C17 additions.

Below the church and hall, to the NE, the ponds or pools which give the village its name. PONDS FARM has a red brick front of 1760, seven bays wide. The back timber-framed and earlier. Close by a square DOVECOTE, also red brick, with pyramidal roof and louvre. Most of the village lies on the slope above the ponds, the best house CORDERS with exposed timbers and gabled cross-wings. At the top of the village the former BOARD SCHOOL and house by *Robert Hawkins*, 1876, of red brick with stone and black-brick dressings, and off ROCKALLS ROAD housing for Cosford Rural District Council by *Raymond Erith*, 1949–50 (cf. Cockfield, Hitcham).

Former PRIMITIVE METHODIST CHAPEL, Polstead Heath, 1¼ m. NNE. 1880 by *W. Baalham*. Red brick, with bands of white brick outlining and linking the round-arched doorway and windows. Gabled front with scalloped bargeboard.

OLD RECTORY, ½ m. S. Timber-framed, of the C16 or C17, with gabled cross-wings. Clad in mathematical tiles by *Kingsbury* of Boxford, *c.* 1832–4. Large single-storey entrance hall between the cross-wings.

ROCKALLS HALL, ¾ m. NE. A good-quality compact Neo-Georgian house of 1905. Red brick with stone dressings. Two storeys and attics. Asymmetrical five-bay entrance front, with a further two bays set slightly back. Stone frontispiece with pediment and porch with segmental hood and coupled Corinthian columns, and stone corner pilasters. Square bays on the garden front.

WATERMILL, 700 yds S. C18. Timber-framed, clad in red brick, with weatherboarded gables. Both it and the house with high mansard roofs.

POSLINGFORD

ST MARY. Much restored, in 1853 and then in 1882 by *A. A. G. Colpoys*. Norman nave with one N window, a fragment of the N doorway, and a good S doorway with one order of shafts with finely decorated capitals and some geometrical decoration on the abaci. Tympanum with stars, rosettes and interlace, similar to the motifs on the font at Preston St Mary (q.v.). W tower of the late C13 with triple-chamfered arch towards the nave. Chancel with late C13 windows; E wall rebuilt 1882. In the nave one Dec window with reticulated tracery and a Perp

Poslingford, St Mary, E end of nave.
Based on drawing by A. A. G. Colpoys, 1881

window with niche inside. Nice Perp S porch of red brick with three niches above the entrance (two with pairs of cusped arches), crowstepped gable, and brick windows. – FONT. Norman, completely plain. Restored 1882, when it was made square, having been cut down to octagonal at some time. – SCREEN. Tall, with two-light division, segmental arches, and tracery over. – CHEST. Oak, with the remains of good-quality ironwork. Dated by dendrochronology to the last quarter of the C13, thus the oldest known in Suffolk (but cf. Norton). – WALL PAINTING. C13 scrolls in a chancel window and a nave window. More paintings have been recorded, including a Doom on the tympanum of the chancel arch, which collapsed

during the 1882 restoration, and figures on the chancel s wall.
– ROYAL ARMS. Stuart, probably James I. Painted on board.
– STAINED GLASS. Chancel s by *Ward & Hughes*, 1883; probably also the nave N †1865. – MONUMENT. Frances Golding †1641 and husband Thomas †1652. Tablet in decorated surround with cherubs reclining on the sides of the broken pediment, all quite crudely done.

Former SCHOOL and teacher's house, opposite. 1877 by *Colpoys*. Red brick with white-brick dressings. The classroom window echoes the E window of the church, i.e. three lancets within an arch.

POSLINGFORD HALL, s of the church. Timber-framed and plastered L-plan house of the C17, with C18 sash windows.

OLD VICARAGE, 300 yds E. By *William Dudley* of Bury, 1838, for Rev. W. L. Suttaby. Brick and flint, mostly rendered. Two storeys. Three-bay front with gabled centre and single-storey canted bay to the l. Hoodmoulds to some windows. Half-hipped roof.

POSLINGFORD HOUSE, 1¼ m. NNE. Large stuccoed house of *c.* 1820, rebuilt for Col. Thomas Weston. Two storeys. Main range of five bays with Greek Doric portico on the E front and single-storey bow on the w. Nine-bay N wing.

CHIPLEY ABBEY, 1 m. NNW. Farmhouse on the site of Chipley Priory, an Augustinian house founded before 1235. It incorporates a small part of the w range of the claustral buildings, but is entirely C19 in appearance. Modest farm buildings dated 1880. Remains of the church survived until 1818.

PRESTON ST MARY

9050

ST MARY. The C14 W tower was struck by lightning in 1758 but did not finally collapse until 1863, when it did much damage to the nave. The tower was rebuilt and the nave restored (including new roof and seating) by *A. W. Blomfield*, 1867–8. He also practically rebuilt the chancel, which is otherwise Dec bec one old s window and the PISCINA in the E jamb of the SE window. Perp aisles and tracery, although some of the windows were renewed in 1846 – they are, unusually, dated The arcade piers have four filleted shafts and squares in the diagonals. Low tomb recess in the N aisle. N porch with rich flushwork panelling. Three-light windows with tracery. Three niches above the entrance. – FONT. Norman, square, with rosettes, stars, intersected arches, a tree of life and interlace (cf. Poslingford, s doorway). – REREDOS. By *Powell & Sons*, 1883. Alabaster, mosaic, etc., with Emblems of the Evangelists. Also by Powell the large mosaic panels either side of the E window, 1890–1. – SCREEN. Base only of former chancel screen, now in tower arch. Restored 1907; *Rev. E. Geldart*'s proposal for restoring the upper parts was not executed, but the design hangs nearby. – ROYAL ARMS and COMMANDMENTS. Elizabethan. Spectacular pieces, and exceptionally early as these things go. They were commissioned by the antiquary *Robert Ryece* (1555–1638), the church's patron, and painted either by him or by *William Milles* of Lavenham. Painted triptychs; there was formerly a third, with an inscription celebrating the defeat of Armada in 1588. Elizabeth's arms are fancifully elaborated to suggest her descent from, among others, Brutus. – STAINED GLASS. Fifty-two heraldic pieces in various windows, installed by Ryece, probably painted by *Milles*. There were originally 160, depicting the arms of Suffolk and other local families. – By *Ward & Hughes* the E window, tower window, and angels in tracery of other windows, 1868; also the terrible S aisle Nativity, 1884. – MONUMENT. J. E. Wright †1908. Alabaster, mosaic and *opus sectile* panel by *Powell & Sons*. With two kneeling angels.

PRESTON HALL, SE of the church. Good late C16 house with most timbers exposed. Projecting cross-wings at each end of the front. They are hipped rather than gabled, presumably a later modification. Fine chimneystacks, of six and four octagonal shafts with star tops.

Former SCHOOL, 500 yds NW. 1843, enlarged 1883. White brick, with straight gables and hoodmoulds. Next to it OLD SCHOOL HOUSE by *G. B. Williams*, 1855–6. Painted brick with quoins and deep eaves on brackets.

SHELFORD HOUSE (former rectory), 700 yds NW. 1834–6 by *John Penrice* of Colchester. White brick with slate roof and deep eaves. Main front with full-height canted bays either side of recessed entrance.

DOWN HALL, nearly 1 m. N. Raised-aisle hall house of c. 1400. Plastered, with jettied and gabled cross-wing. Crown-post roofs.

RATTLESDEN

ST NICHOLAS. Quite big, with a Dec W tower with clasping buttresses terminating in gables. Shingled splay-foot spire behind the parapet. Finely detailed S doorway of c. 1300 with a circular window over. In the window a cusped quatrefoil. The S porch has a fine stone-faced front with a tall entrance. It has been attributed by John Harvey to *John Wastell*, and money was left for the 'south entrance' in 1472. The front is panelled and has one niche over the entrance. The sides are roughly chequered flint and stone. The battlemented parapet, characteristic of Wastell, is decorated with cusped lozenges and shields in cusped panels. This is continued along the S aisle. The clerestory (which has single, not double windows per bay) also has battlements, decorated on the S side only with flushwork tracery and saints' emblems. The clerestory on the N side was rebuilt in 1883, part of the restoration by *A. W. Blomfield*, who had repaired the chancel in 1879. He added the pretty spirelets on the corners of the aisles, and the battlemented parapet on the N aisle; stonework by *Lot Jackaman*. C15 N vestry, originally two-storeyed. Wide interior, C14 arcades of five bays with octagonal piers, decorated with blank cusped arches at the top, and arches with two hollow chamfers. Good C14 AUMBRY in the chancel N wall. Arched top, crocketed gable, and pinnacles. The tower arch is triple-chamfered. The arch dies into the imposts. Nave roof with false double hammerbeams, renewed in 1883, when the carved figures (ninety in all) were added; by *Henry Plummer* of Rattlesden, who did all the woodwork for Blomfield's restoration. The arch-braced, lean-to aisle roofs, also reconstructed in 1883, also have angels: one original, in the NE corner of the S aisle, the rest 1894–6. Large window above the chancel arch. The chancel roof is single hammerbeam, boarded over. – FONT. C14, octagonal. Panels with thickly decorated ogee arches resting on heads (cf. Brettenham, Walsham-le-Willows). Castellated top. – SCREENS. Six panels of the dado of an original screen are preserved at the W end, and there are painted panels, almost unrecognizable, in the back wall of the C19 sedilia. The present screen is a masterly piece by *G. H. Fellowes Prynne*, the rood screen of 1909 followed by the Lady Chapel parclose screen of 1916. Wide single-light divisions with delicate tracery. Coved lofts to both screens, neatly connected by Prynne to the original stair in the S aisle wall. – PULPIT. Jacobean. Cut down in 1883. – REREDOS. 1895. Caen stone, with the Last Supper. – BENCHES. Some with poppyheads. Also CHOIR STALLS, restored 1893 as part of a reordering of the chancel by *W. Bassett-Smith*. Original fronts with traceried panels. – COMMUNION RAIL. Later C17, originally three-sided, altered in 1893. At the W end of the nave, C17 communion rails from Kettlebaston, acquired in 1903. – ORGAN CASE. By *Jack Penton*, 1963. Plain wood, simply treated, contemporary in style. – STAINED GLASS. Original bits in the W window (rearranged by *Heaton, Butler & Bayne*, 1897) and the second N window from the E. E window 1895 by *Clayton & Bell*. Chancel S 1928, S aisle E 1936, S aisle war memorial window 1920 and 'children's window' 1921, by *W. Aikman*. Another S aisle window †1913 by *J. Hardman*. – BRASS. Rev. John Barney †1893. Mural, with decorated cross. By *Hart, Son, Peard & Co*.

The church lies in the middle of the village, looking down over it from a slight eminence. On the N side of the churchyard, the former RECTORY (now Glebelands House) by *M. M. Smith*, 1892–3. Red brick. Three shaped gables with semicircular tops and ball finials. Outside the SW corner, HALL COTTAGE and CARTREF, C16 timber-framed and plastered with longwall jetty and large red brick chimney. Then THE OLD WORKHOUSE, also C16. Three-bay hall, floored in the C17, with crown-post roof. At the SE entrance to the churchyard

The Old Moot House, C15 with exposed close studding. Hall house with cross-wing at the S end jettied on three sides. Hall with smoke-blackened timbers and cross-quadrate crown-post, floored in the late C16 or early C17. A little to the S, at Birds Green, an attractive assortment of thatched cottages.

Primary School. By *F. Barnes*, 1872–3, with additions by *J. S. Corder*, 1897. Red brick with bands of black. Gabled porch with Gothic doorway and windows.

Clopton Hall, ⅔ m. NE. Half-H-plan house, the late C17 remodelling of a late C16 timber-framed hall house with cross-wings at each end. In the process of the remodelling the gables of the cross-wings became hipped roofs, and the corners were given quoins. New entrance in the middle of the three-bay centre, with giant pilasters and segmental pediment. Paired sashes with mullions. Early C17 red brick chimneys (one has a date that appears to be 1631) with moulded terracotta friezes against the return walls. S front remodelled in the late 1970s, in the manner of the entrance front, following the removal of large additions of *c.* 1834. The interior considerably altered at the same time and since, including the introduction of panelling, fireplaces etc. Partial moat.

Hollybush Farm, 1½ m. SW. Picturesque C17 timber-framed and plastered house. Hall range, cross-wing with jettied gable to l., and l. of that a lower, C18 service range.

At Hightown Green, 1¾ m. SSW, a group of interesting timber-framed houses, including Friar's Hall, Pantiles and St Margaret's Priory, all dating back to the C15.

Windmill, ¾ m. SW (Hitchcock's Mill). Tower mill by *John Whitmore, c.* 1840. Small white-brick four-storey tower, tarred, its top removed. Shallow-pitched aluminium roof added 2002. Three-bay, two-storey white-brick house to the N, and then extensive former steam mill buildings, up to three storeys, now converted to housing.

RAYDON

St Mary. Mostly late C13 to early C14 – see the chancel windows, the nave windows, the N and S doorways and the priest's doorway (thin shafts and big moulded capitals). The chancel N windows have normal late C13 tracery with quatrefoiled circles. The piscina inside has the same design – unusual and handsome. In the tracery on the S side the quatrefoils are stretched to make crosses. Other differences are the chancel buttresses, square on the S side with cusped gables, V-shaped on the N (cf. Thorpe Morieux). Between the latter, a shallow protuberance to take a low tomb recess; this and hoodmoulds of the chancel windows inside confirm the early C14 date. At the E end are diagonal buttresses with traceried and crocketed finials. Below the NE pinnacle a carving of a dragon. Low timber-framed belfry at w end; the tower fell *c.* 1750. Restoration by *Robert Hawkins* under the direction of the rector, *Rev. J. W. Tomkin*, 1883. E window renewed, N vestry added, and nave re-seated. – MONUMENTS. Brass of Elizabeth Reydon †1479. Figure originally 8 in. (20 cm.); top half lost. – Rev. John Mayer †1664. Black marble tablet detailing his career and many publications. Alabaster surround with broken segmental pediment and flaming urn. Attributed to *Jasper Latham* (GF). – Mary Hopes †1870. Gothic. By *Watts* of Colchester. – Eliza Agnes Coyle †1907. By *G. Spurr*, Pontefract. Honed and polished granite, looking very far from home.

Former SCHOOL (now village hall) and teacher's house, NE of the church. By *F. Barnes*, 1878. Red brick. Pointed windows with white-brick voussoirs. Open timber porch, and timber bellcote perched on a gable.

Former RAILWAY STATION, 1¼ m. NNE. 1847 by *Barnes*. Red brick with white-brick dressings. Two storeys. Prominent chimneystack with an arch between the two stacks. Line closed 1994.

LAYHAM HALL, 1 m. NNW. Timber-framed house, formerly Mason's Bridge Farm, and much altered *c.* 1930. Exposed timbers on the ground floor. Gabled cross-wings, partly jettied. Central range partly rebuilt, it seems, and enlarged, yet surviving painted decoration inside of the 1630s, including imitation panelling with strapwork panels, and imitation textile in the hall chamber. C20 gabled porch and, on the rear elevation, additional gables between the cross-wings.

SPIDER HALL, ½ m. WSW. L-plan timber-framed and plastered house of the C16, refurbished in the C17. Two-storey main range with extended cross-wing at N end. The ground-floor room at the s end of the main range was painted in the first half of the C17 with imitation panelling, now visible on only one wall. s of the house a six-bay BARN, now converted to a house, and to the W an early C19 circular LODGE. Timber-framed and plastered, with conical slate roof and central chimney of moulded white brick. Round-arched windows with Y-tracery.

SULLEYS MANOR, ⅔ m. SW. 1704. Seven-bay front of red brick with timber cross-windows. Large additions to the rear by *James Blackie* (*Tricker Blackie Associates*), *c.* 2004. Two large BARNS to s of house, both early C17; one aisled, of six bays, now a house, the other, of five, now a care home.

REDE

ALL SAINTS. The nave walls are probably Norman – see one window in the NW corner. W tower of *c.* 1300 (see the bell-openings). s porch C15, heavily restored in 1877, with pinnacles and a niche crowned by a nodding arch. Restored by *Thomas Farrow*, 1855. Chancel rebuilt by *J. D. Wyatt*, 1873–4. – PULPIT. C17, with scrolls for the book-rest. – BENCHES. Some with poppyheads. – STAINED GLASS. E window †1872. The first recorded work of *W. F. Dixon*, a pupil of Clayton & Bell, and very much in their style. It commemorates a son of the rector, depicted as the centurion Cornelius (Acts 10).

THE GREEN, 300 yds S, is worth a stroll: GREEN FARMOUSE on the E side, late C18 or early C19 white brick; THE PLOUGH on the S, mid-C16 timber-framed and plastered with thatched roof; and the former SCHOOL on the N, 1843, flint with red brick dressings.

PYKARDS HALL, ½ m. S. Mid-C15 timber-framed and plastered hall house with smoke-blackened crown-post roof. Floored in the C16 and extended to the l., with cross-wing, in the late C17. The service end, to the r., was rebuilt and extended in the late C17 or early C18.

REDGRAVE

The manor of Redgrave was owned by the abbots of Bury and, following the Dissolution, bought from the Crown in 1542 by Sir Nicholas Bacon, later Lord Keeper of the Great Seal and father of Sir Francis. It remained in the family until 1702, when it was bought by Sir John Holt, Lord Chief Justice, whose great-nephew Rowland Holt made great changes to the house and park. The house has been demolished, but both families left a considerable mark on the church.

ST MARY THE VIRGIN (Churches Conservation Trust). Mostly Dec. The chancel has N and S windows with elongated reticulated tracery, and a glorious seven-light E window, treated very elaborately and not at all harmoniously. Chancel buttresses with niches and pitched roofs. Very fine S aisle doorway with two orders of delicate shafts with naturalistic leaf capitals. One arch moulding with fleurons etc. Hoodmould on heads. Perp S aisle windows and the fine clerestory of double windows with panel tracery. The arcade piers quatrefoil with, in the diagonals, slender shafts with fillets. Arches with wavy mouldings. The chancel arch is of the same design. Perp SEDILIA of beautifully inventive design. Each seat has a canted canopy with a small lierne vault inside. The canopies are decorated with charming three-light windows. Straight top to the whole sedilia. Perp also the nave roof, with alternating hammerbeams carrying arched braces to the cambered collars and tie-beams carrying queenposts with arched struts. NE vestry of red brick, built *c.* 1626 as an aisle or chapel over the Bacon family vault (*see* below). Its roof has timber ribs and pendant. Rowland

Holt rebuilt the W tower in the same Woolpit brick as his house; inscribed at the top '[*Richard*] *Todd* built me in 1784'. S porch rebuilt 1819. Repairs and re-seating by *Thomas Farrow*, 1849–50, the BENCHES with low doors.

FURNISHINGS. FONT. Octagonal, Dec. At the bottom of the bowl eight heads. The panels have gables with many small quatrefoils. – Top of the former REREDOS. Early C18, with Commandments and PAINTINGS of Moses and Aaron and crazily huge (eight-turn) volutes l. and r. – PULPIT. 1874–5 by *J. P. Seddon*. Stone, octagonal, with richly carved panels. – WALL PAINTINGS. On N wall, early C15. Probably a fragment of the Three Living and the Three Dead. Another fragment, unidentified, by the S door. – ROYAL ARMS. Stuart. Carved wood, in oval frame. Identical to Wortham's, but here painted. – CHESTS. Oak, with iron bands; early C15. Another, C16 with linenfold panels, from Badley. – CURIOSA. Desk from the grammar school at Botesdale (q.v.). – Carved wood Holt arms from Redgrave Hall; early C18. – STAINED GLASS. E window by *N. J. Cottingham*, 1853, installed by *Farrow*. – In S aisle, E window by *Powell & Sons*, 1913, and another signed 'Taylor late O'Connor', i.e. *W. G. Taylor*, c. 1872. – N aisle E †1915 by *A. L. Moore & Son*.

MONUMENTS. An important series, headed by the outstandingly noble monument to Sir Nicholas Bacon 1st Bt †1624 and his wife Anne †1616 at the E end of the N aisle. This is by *Nicholas Stone*, and one of his best works. It was commissioned by Sir Nicholas, son of the Lord Keeper and premier baronet of England, in 1616. In 1620/1 Sir Nicholas's son Edmund entered into a separate contract with Stone and *James White* for the effigies, for which they were to be paid £200. A further bill was issued in 1627. The architectural parts are by *Bernard Janssen*, no doubt to Stone's design. White and black marble. Restrainedly but tellingly carved effigies. Against the tall tomb-chest inscriptions in cartouches no longer with any memories of strapwork, but in rounded doughy forms characteristic of the mid-C17 future. – Anne Butts (Sir Nicholas's mother-in-law) †1609. Brass on the chancel floor, but originally on a tomb-chest. Still in the medieval tradition, with 38-in. (96-cm.) figure. At her feet the following inscription:

> The weaker sexes strongest precedent
> Lyes here belowe; seaven fayer yeares she spent
> In wedlock sage; and since that merry age
> Sixty one yeares she lived a widdowe sage.
> Humble as great, as full of grace as elde,
> A second Anna had she but beheld
> Christ in his flesh whom now she glorious sees
> Belowe that first in time not in degrees.

– By *Nicholas Stone* also the simple tablet to Dorothy, Lady Gawdy †1621, daughter of Sir Nicholas (chancel S). Oval tablet with thick garlands, segmental pediment at the top, cherub's head at the foot. – Philippa, Lady Bacon, †1626. Wife of Sir Edmund 2nd Bt, who commissioned a monument from *Stone* and built the N chapel over a vault to contain it. This monument was mostly destroyed *c.* 1710 but the paving and raised cross at the W end of the N aisle were probably part of it.* Other Bacon monuments were moved at the same time, including Sir Edmund 4th Bt †1685 and his wife Elizabeth †1690. – In the chancel, a monument to their children, buried 'on this side of that tombe for Mrs Anne Butts', erected 1660. – Robert Bacon †1652. Attributed to *John Stone* (AW). Tablet with arms and a little drapery. – Sir John Holt †1710. Prominently placed on the N side of the sanctuary, in front of what may have been an opening from the N chapel, and accompanied by the removal of the Bacon monuments to the N aisle. By *Thomas Green* of Camberwell, his most impressive work, and boldly signed. Large tripartite composition. He is seated in the centre between coupled Corinthian columns. To either side stand Justice (with scales and sword) and Prudence (with serpent). On the cornice putti, standing alone (one holding his helm, the other his crest) and seated in pairs. The centre is raised and contains a coat of arms under a segmental top.

REDGRAVE HALL stood about ¾ m. SSW of the church. Sir Nicholas Bacon rebuilt the house in 1545–54. It remained largely unchanged until the ownership of Rowland Holt, who inherited in 1739 and died in 1786. Between 1763 and 1773 he employed *Capability Brown*, who remodelled the house by encasing it in white Woolpit brick (work subcontracted to *Henry Holland* and *John Hobcroft*, who received £9,440 of the £10,000 that was paid to Brown). *Basil Oliver* produced a scheme for updating the house in 1937, but most of it was demolished in 1947, leaving only the Tudor core; this in turn was demolished in 1968–70. Brown's work also included red brick STABLES E of the Hall, of which an L-plan corner survives (converted to a house after 1971); and detached conservatory (dem.) N of the Hall. His principal legacy is the fine PARK, including a large serpentine LAKE to the S of the house. At the SE end a BOATHOUSE, altered and enlarged in the C19 and now ruinous. On the hill above it, standing in front of trees and still an excellent eyecatcher, an octagonal domed PAVILION used as a cottage. White brick. Pedimented Tuscan doorcase. ICE HOUSE 600 yds N of the site of the Hall. Single-storey white-brick LODGE to W by *Beadel, Son & Chancellor*, 1859.

The VILLAGE is ¾ m. W of the church. In the middle a small green with, on the W side, TUDOR LIMES, a five-bay house of the late C17 with wooden cross-windows and pedimented doorcase. Along the street to the NW the former BARN of IVYHOUSE FARM with a shaped red brick gable. Opposite, STREET FARM, C17, with three tall straight gables, and THE

---

*I am grateful to Adam White and the late Norman Scarfe for elucidating this.

PINK HOUSE, late C15, thatched, with jettied end facing the road.

RED LODGE

Ribbon development along the Norwich road began in 1926, on land that had previously consisted mostly of rabbit warrens. A grant of free warren was made to the Bishop of Rochester in 1249, and the RED LODGE INN, mainly Tudor brick, incorporates a stone structure that may have been the warrener's lodge. Outline planning permission was given in 2003 for 1,250 homes on land E of Warren Road, and development began there in 2007, led by *Crest Nicholson*. A new village centre is planned.

PRIMARY SCHOOL, Bellflower Crescent. 2011–12 by *Suffolk County Council* (lead designer *Charles Coulson*). Two storeys, with the classrooms in a S-facing line. Mainly timber construction, fabricated off site. Vertical and horizontal larch cladding, as well as large areas of brightly coloured render. Natural ventilation with prominent 'chimneys'.

MILLENNIUM CENTRE (community centre), Lavender Close. By *Wilkinson Pratt Partnership*, 1997–9. Blockwork and large expanses of slate roof. Five interlocking sections, diminishing in height from the middle and slightly angled to make a crescent.

RICKINGHALL INFERIOR

Inferior and Superior refer to the relative elevation of the two Rickinghall churches, which are ⅓ m. apart: one is about 45 ft (14 metres) higher above sea level than the other. The boundary between the parishes runs erratically along the main street, and for the sake of simplicity the village houses of Rickinghall Superior are described here with their Inferior neighbours.

ST MARY. Norman round tower with arch on plain imposts to the nave. The octagonal top is early C14, with elaborate flushwork battlements with quatrefoils, shields etc., to which bequests of 1455 and 1463 probably relate. Early C14 also the chancel and chancel arch (one leaf capital) and the S aisle and S porch. The porch has an upper storey, added in the C15. The sides have two small windows with Y-tracery, and between them, a little higher up, a quatrefoil window. On the upper floor below the window flushwork emblems, very worn. Inside, heavy two-bay arcading with a semi-octagonal middle shaft. The S aisle is curious. The four-bay arcade with its piers of quatrefoiled section, the lobes with fillets, and spurs in the diagonals, and with its arches of one chamfer and one sunk quadrant moulding, looks early C14. But the s windows are of a type more late C13 than early C14. Two cusped lights and in the head three circles with quatrefoils (cf. Thelnetham). The SE window has in addition pointed trefoils at the top of the cusped lights, and dainty foliage in the various spandrels that is of the knobbly kind of after 1300. The S aisle E window is Perp and also has a little foliage in its spandrels. The W window is of a rather muddled early C14 design, still without any ogees. Inside the E window the shafting of its Dec predecessor and a charming leaf frieze below the sill. Angle PISCINA with crocketed gables. The aisle has diagonal buttresses with crocketed gables and spirelets. General restoration by *J. D. Wyatt*, 1858–9. – FONT. Octagonal, early C14, with fine tracery patterns of the various types found in windows. One of them is remarkably similar to the S aisle W window. – REREDOS. Of c. 1870. With tracery from the rood screen and C19 painted figures. – STAINED GLASS. Medieval fragments in chancel SE window. Chancel SW †1888 by *Lavers, Barraud & Westlake*; no doubt also the E window †1870. – S aisle E (central light) by *Eric Eckersley*, 2000. – MONUMENTS. The archaeologist Basil Brown †1977. Plaque by *Gilbert Burroughes*, 2009–12, with portrait. Made in Roman Samian-type pottery. – Lt R. C. F. Maul †1874. Churchyard cross on steps.

Former NATIONAL SCHOOL, N of the church. By *F. Barnes*, 1853, including two-storey teacher's house. Enlarged 1873. Knapped flint with red brick dressings. Lancet windows, in groups of two or three. Fish-scale tiles and delicate ridge tiles. Lots of gables and a little timber flèche.

The VILLAGE lies along the main road, with the more interesting houses towards the Botesdale end. On the SE side, about 700 yds NE of the church, THE GABLES and GABLE END, C16 timber-framed and plastered with three bargeboarded gables facing the street. At one end an early C18 shaped gable of red brick with burnt headers. A little further on, on the other side, JESSAMINE LODGE, early C18. Timber-framed with a broad front of blue-brick header bond with red brick dressings (cf. Broomhills, below), the ends breaking slightly forward. Windows with unorthodox Gothic heads. Doorway with segmental pediment. On the NE side again, after about 200 yds, RIDGE HOUSE, c. 1840, timber-framed and plastered. Two storeys, five bays, with a reused late C18 Doric porch. Finally on the NW side HAMBLYN HOUSE. Mid-C17, timber-framed and plastered. Doorway with big hood on scrolled brackets. Early C18 cross-wing to l. with red brick front and shaped gable; exposed timbers in the return wall. For buildings NE of here *see* Botesdale.

SNAPE HILL HOUSE, 650 yds NW of the church. Large whitebrick house, mostly of c. 1820. Five-bay E front with Tuscan porch. Two storeys, a third added later in the C19. Full-height canted bay on S front. Red brick crinkle-crankle garden wall.

OLD RECTORY, ½ m. NNW. Rebuilt by *Daniel Penning* of Eye, 1850. White brick. Two storeys. Four-bay E front with central and corner pilasters strips. Canted bay to l.

BROOMHILLS, ¾ m. N. Formerly the dower house of Redgrave Hall (*see* Redgrave), perhaps built by Sir John Holt after he purchased the estate in 1702. Dark brick in header bond with red brick dressings. Seven bays, two storeys, with pedimented doorway and pitched roof. Lower rear ranges. Garden with crinkle-crankle wall.

RICKINGHALL SUPERIOR

ST MARY (Churches Conservation Trust). W tower Dec, with battlements panelled in flushwork and small quatrefoil windows to the middle chamber. Chancel Dec with a delightful E window. Intersected tracery finely filled in with smaller patterns. Ogee-headed priest's doorway. Perp PISCINA with crenellated top. Nave with rough stone and flint chequer patterns. Very large Perp three-light windows with small and busy tracery under four-centred arches. At the base flushwork frieze with shields. A will of 1445 left 40s. for the dedication and sanctification of the church, which may refer to this rebuilding. Two-storey S porch with flushwork decoration. Crowned 'IHC' and 'MR' above the entrance. Tierceron vault inside. At its SW corner a fragment of wall and moulded stone jamb that appear to relate to a substantial vanished structure and must be connected with the blocked arch in the nave S wall W of the porch. A chantry or Lady Chapel has been suggested, but it would be a strange position for such a thing. The nave is wide. All along the N and S walls run stone seats. On these stand shafts which carry arches embracing the windows. Restoration by *W. M. Fawcett*, 1868, including new nave roof, PULPIT and BENCHES. The chancel was said then to have been restored 'a few years ago'. – FONT. Octagonal, Dec, with elaborately cusped blank tracery patterns. – BIER. Oak, dated 1763. – BELLS. Of the six, three were cast by *John Goldsmith* of Redgrave, 1712. – STAINED GLASS C15 fragments in a nave N window, re-set as part of general reglazing by *Herbert Orsbourne*, 1868. E window †1868 by *O'Connor*. Chancel S probably by *Heaton, Butler & Bayne*. It commemorates Samuel Speare †1873 aged twenty, having already spent five years as a missionary in Zanzibar. He is portrayed as the biblical Samuel; in the tracery four black angel heads. – MONUMENTS. In churchyard, N of the church, nine headstones to members of the Mills family †1782–1858. Each carved with the same scene of a weeping cherub, one hand resting on a skull, with a pyramid in the background.

For the VILLAGE, *see* Rickinghall Inferior.

RINGSHALL

A scattered village, a large part of which is occupied by Wattisham Airfield, opened on the eve of the Second World War and still operational.

ST CATHERINE. Unbuttressed Norman W tower with two set-offs in its upper stages. An original S window on the ground floor, and an altered N window. Norman windows in the nave, two on the N side (visible only inside), one altered on the S. The tower was completed and remodelled *c.* 1300 – see the arch towards the nave with triple chamfering dying into the imposts. Of the same time the simple S doorway and the chancel S doorway. Dec E window, its restoration discussed by the rector, C. F. Parker, in a letter to *The Ecclesiologist*, 1842; further work in 1853, but the main restoration came in 1878–9, by *R. M. Phipson*, including a new S porch in convincing Dec style.* The restoration also revealed the PISCINA, unusually positioned in the E wall. Very rough nave roof with anchor-beams inserted in the C15 to hold the side walls together. They are placed uncommonly low and go right through the walls. On them crown-posts with two-way struts. That further support was needed in the C18 is shown by the broad brick buttress against the N wall. In the chancel, a hammerbeam roof with arched braces to collar-beams. Arched braces also connecting the wall-posts from W to E. These braces are carved. The moulded wall-plate is continued across the E wall, interrupted by the E window. – FONT. C13; Purbeck marble, octagonal. With the usual two shallow blank pointed arches on each side. – WALL PAINTING. Fragments of the Seven Works of Mercy (nave S wall). – STAINED GLASS. Chancel S, and no doubt also the E window, by *Clayton & Bell*, 1879.

RINGSHALL HALL, S of the church. Mid-C16 timber-framed and plastered house, perhaps dating from the acquisition of the manor by Sir Richard Gresham, father of Sir Thomas, between 1524 and 1548. SW of the house, parallel to the approach, a BARN (now converted) dating to the second half of the C16. Its original purpose is not clear, but it may have been a manorial court hall. It was partly storeyed, and built to a higher specification than one would expect of an agricultural building.

RINGSHALL GRANGE (former rectory), 650 yds S. Low, timber-framed and plastered range of the mid C17. Red brick front range, of five bays and two storeys, added in the early C19, with a further modest addition of 1879 by *Phipson*. Moated. The grounds were laid out in the C18, perhaps by Rev. William Peppen, rector 1707–44, with linear ponds and a long raised terrace walk with a belvedere mound at one end.

---

* Pevsner thought it original.

RINGSHALL HOUSE, 1⅓ m. SSE. C19 white brick front, including two-storey porch with ball finials. But on the return walls are carved tie-beams with a frieze of fishes, the gables plastered above the beams, betraying the house's C17 origins. Lobby-entrance plan. Inside, plaster ceilings of *c.* 1620 and a good dog-leg stair with pierced splat balusters.

RISBY

ST GILES. Norman round tower. Two tiers of arched openings at the top. Rude arch with one order of shafts into the nave. Also Norman the top of one former window visible inside on the nave N wall. Other windows mostly *c.* 1300; also of that date the doorway. The nave originally reached just E of the N lancet, with the chancel within the present nave, before being extended: the present Dec chancel arch reused stones from the old one, with Norman imposts and abaci and a whole order of late Norman arch decoration on the E face. To the l. and r. of the wide pointed arch, richly Dec niches, two l. and two r., with crocketed ogee gables, vaulting inside, and backgrounds of diaperwork. The chancel is clearly Dec. The tracery is of the reticulated kind. To the l. and r. of the E window niches with ogee arches. Also ogee-arched PISCINA. Contemporary a small and pretty N doorway with hoodmould on headstops. Restored by *William Dudley* of Bury St Edmunds, 1840–2; N vestry (site of former chapel) 1843. – FONT. Octagonal, Perp, with the Emblems of the Evangelists, the Annunciation and a pelican. – ALTAR and REREDOS. Made by members of the family of the rector, Rev. S. H. Alderson, 1860–2; miscellaneous carving elsewhere by the same hands. – PULPIT. Jacobean. – NAVE ALTAR of the same date. – SCREEN. Narrow but uncommonly fine. One three-light division either side of the entrance (three-light divisions are unusual in Suffolk). Crocketed ogee lights with a trellis of cusped tracery over. Money was left for the new rood loft in 1436. – BENCHES. With poppyheads and decorated seat backs. – WALL PAINTINGS. A memorable series, though only dimly recognizable. On the N wall, near the W end, a large figure of an ecclesiastic, perhaps Thomas Becket, *c.* 1200 or a little later. Of the same time scenes in arcades a little further E: the Nativity story above (e.g. Massacre of the Innocents, Flight into Egypt), very faded scenes from the Miracles of the Virgin below. Much scrollwork of the C13. Noli me tangere, W of the W window, late C14; also a late C15 St Christopher. – STAINED GLASS. In the E and chancel S windows, many fragments of C14 and C15 glass, arranged in the 1840s and restored in 1928 by *Townshend & Howson*. Chancel N, 1887, and nave S, 1892, by *Kempe*.

Opposite the church, CHURCH HOUSE, C17 timber-framed and plastered with C18 additions including a two-storey bay to the street, and a row of C18 thatched, brick and flint cottages. To the w the former SCHOOL of 1865 by *Lot Jackaman*. Flint, with stone dressings. NW, the OLD RECTORY by *William Dudley*, 1839–40, for Rev. S. H. Alderson. Red brick. ⅓ m. further w THE GREEN, in fact two triangular greens shaped like an hourglass, with a few good houses scattered around them.

PRIMARY SCHOOL, Aylmer Close. By *West Suffolk County Architect's Dept* (job architect *Brian Grayling*), 1967–8, based on a design by *David & Mary Medd*, and using the timber-framed Derwent system. Stained horizontal weatherboard cladding. Three classrooms with sliding partitions grouped round a central hall with clerestory.

WEST SUFFOLK CREMATORIUM, 1 m. ESE. 1987–9 by *Hugh Thomas Architects*. Chapel, cloistered wreath court and free-standing chapel of remembrance. Cream-coloured blockwork and red pantiles.

BARROWS. At Barrow Bottom, 1¾ m. w, a round barrow was partly cut through by roadworks in 1771 and several inhumation burials, an urned cremation and two iron spears, probably Anglo-Saxon, were found. The remainder was excavated in 1975 before its removal to widen the A14. A central Bronze Age primary grave contained the crouched inhumation of a female (aged 40–45; radiocarbon date 1900–1740 B.C.) with 151 jet beads, a bronze awl, a collared urn and flint tools; an extended male (aged 20–35) secondary inhumation in the barrow ditch had an axe or sword cut on the skull and is probably Anglo-Saxon. In a nearby streambed some twenty-five Late Upper Palaeolithic long blades were found in 1975. There were another two barrows at the w end of Risby Poor's Heath, towards the s end of the Black Ditches. Both were excavated in 1869 and again in 1959, and are now virtually flat. One produced both Bronze Age and Anglo-Saxon cremation urns, the other a probably primary crouched inhumation and a cremation in a Bronze Age collared urn, as well as an empty Iron Age pot. *See also* Flempton.

ROUGHAM

ST MARY. S aisle and the very special s porch, chancel, and N aisle all Dec; tower and much remodelling Perp. The s porch has three-light side openings not with mullions but with strong shafts. Ogee arches and straight top. Finely moulded entrance arch. In the aisle wall to its E two low blocked arches, former burial recesses. The s and N aisles both have simple Dec E windows. W lancet in the s aisle. The other s aisle windows Late Perp without tracery. Aisles and clerestory embattled with enriched lozenges as decoration. Perp N aisle windows. Inscriptions on the N aisle buttresses include a date, 1514, and the name of John Smith, 'curator' of the church. The chancel is not embattled. It has a large five-light window with reticulated tracery. The W tower has below the top a lively frieze of tracery motifs and a parapet with flushwork decoration. This, together with the evidence of wills, documents its construction. The mason William Leyr (Layer) of Bury left 20 marks (£13 6s. 8d.) for the tower in the will he made in 1444, although the bequest was not payable until 1460; his apprentice *John Forster* may have been responsible for the early stages, and *Layer* himself may have designed it. Further bequests were made in 1458–88; inscriptions and devices on the parapet acknowledge those of Roger Tillot (1458) and John Nunne Sen. (1459) or Jun. (1472), as well as the Drury family, and there is also the *Aldryche* device. Dec arcades with piers of four strong shafts and in the diagonals four thin ones without capitals. Double-chamfered arches. The chancel arch is of the same design. Nave roof with hammerbeams with arch braces joining moulded principals and cambered collars. Headless angels against them. Wall-plate decorated with quatrefoil friezes. Restorations by *John Johnson* of Bury, 1856, and *J. D. Wyatt*, c. 1873, the latter including new N vestry. Monstrous S vestry and organ chamber of 1900, with reused windows. – FONT. C14. Octagonal, with simple arches of different forms. – BENCHES. A whole set, mostly C16. Ends with tracery patterns of great variety. Poppyheads. The figures on the arms of the older benches have been cut off. The first three rows C19, and also the benches in the aisles, which have low doors. – PANELLING. At E end of N aisle. Jacobean, perhaps from a former pulpit. – TOWER SCREEN. By *Potter & Hare*, 1958, the glazed upper part by *Whitworth, Hall & Thomas*, 1986. – STAINED GLASS. C15 bits in the N aisle E window. Chancel E of 1884 probably by *Hardman*. N aisle N by *Burlison & Grylls*, 1904. – MONUMENT. Fine large brass of Sir Roger Drury †1420 (although the date is left blank) and his wife Margery †1405. The figures 49 in. (124 cm.) long. – Sir Robert Drury †1625 and wife Elizabeth †1621. Marble, with arms in cartouche. Below the inscription a separate plate with incised depiction of a corpse in a woollen shroud.

BRADFIELD AND ROUGHAM BAPTIST CHURCH, Kingshall Green. 1979–80 by *Vivian Thrower*. Dark red brick and prominent pitched roof. – STAINED GLASS. Two windows by *Pippa Blackall*.

RECTORY, E of St Mary's. 1934 by *Cautley & Barefoot*. Modest and conservative. Rendered walls, a delicate shade of pink, with red brick plinth and chimneys and tiled roof.

ROUGHAM HALL. The original hall stood about 700 yds N of St Mary's, and an avenue of limes still leads to the site. It had probably been built in the late C17, and was demolished in the 1850s. A new hall was built a further ½ m. N by *Thomas Hopper* for Philip Bennet, who inherited the estate in 1818. Work was under way in 1821 and largely complete in 1826; in 1827 the house was described as being 'in a forward state, and presents an elegant and singular diversity of Gothic architecture' (*Concise Description of Bury St Edmund's, and its Environs*). Additions for E. J. Johnstone, who bought the estate in 1893 (including electricity generating house and numerous estate cottages), and in 1904–5 for (Sir) George Agnew by *J. Macvicar Anderson*. The house was severely damaged by a German bomb in 1940 and remains a picturesque shell. Local red brick, with stone and cement dressings, in a Tudor-Gothic style. Large polygonal towers, of which one still stands at the E end of the S front. At the W end a block with polygonal buttresses and pinnacles. It has a square two-storey bay on the S front, decorated with shields, and an oriel on the W front, both of stone. The bomb damage revealed much use of cast iron in the original construction, including I-beams and tie-rods. Intact STABLE BLOCK to the N, also red brick (brick with carved date 1824). Gateway with four-centred arch. Loopholes with hoodmoulds, and machicolations. Polygonal tower at one corner with a later stone clock turret. On the N side of the park ROUND HOUSE, a circular C19 cottage. Flint rubble, with white-brick dressings, and conical slate roof. BATTLIES LODGE, on the W side, is Y-plan, red brick, its doorway with four-centred arch and hoodmould. Within the arch a stone arch on clustered columns, perhaps reused. Steep-pitched gable with decorative bargeboards.

RAVENWOOD HALL (hotel), ¾ m. NW. Early to mid-C16 timber-framed house, incorporating a single-cell house of perhaps the C15 at the S end. Five-bay front, jettied, with carved bressumer and a few other exposed timbers. Jettied gables l. and r. The upper part tile-hung, probably in the early C20, with a large central dormer. At the rear a late C17 service wing and C19 extension. In a ground-floor room remains of a scheme of painted decoration, and elsewhere Jacobean panelling.

LAYERS BRECK, ¾ m. WNW. Late C15 Wealden house, of which the parlour (S) end has been rebuilt. The N end retains its original appearance, with exposed timbers and jetty, as does half the recessed hall. Crown-post roof. Contemporary kitchen wing to the rear. The name derives from William Layer (*see* above) who owned property in Rougham.

JAMES STIFF COTTAGES, 700 yds SW. By *John Taylor* of London, dated 1876. Terrace of six single-storey almshouses. Mainly red brick, but with terracotta decoration from *James Stiff & Sons*' Lambeth pottery. Stiff was a native of Rougham; the foundation stone was laid on the fiftieth anniversary of his leaving the village. Additions at both ends.

ROUGHAM AIRFIELD, 1½ m. NW. Opened 1942. The principal survival is the CONTROL TOWER, converted to a house after 1948 but restored as a museum, 1993–2003. Two storeys, of rendered brick. Replacement 'glasshouse' on flat roof. Former RADAR BUILDING to the S.

ROMAN BARROW, known as EASTLOW HILL, 1 m. SW, at the junction of the Rougham Green road with the old Roman route now taken by the road from Little Whelnetham; the only survivor of a group of four, originally forming a line NE–SW, and excavated in 1843–6. The three now destroyed were c. 50 ft (15.25 metres) in diameter, the southernmost being intersected by the modern road. Two of them contained cist burials, glassware and early C2 A.D. *terra sigillata*. The Eastlow Hill barrow, which is larger, covered a brick-gabled burial chamber on a mortared footing. In it was an unaccompanied extended male skeleton contained in a lead coffin which probably had a wooden inner casing. The absence of finds may point to a Christian burial. About 300 yds SE, remains of a Roman building with white stucco flooring were also found in the 1840s, the site re-defined by field survey in 1975–82 with finds dating from the C1 to the late C4.

RUSHBROOKE

A small estate village, but hardly a typical one. Rushbrooke Hall, a C16 U-plan house comparable to Melford and Kentwell, was demolished in 1961 – a tragedy. It had been built by the Jermyn family, passed through the female line to the Davers of Rougham, and after a couple of years in the hands of the 5th Earl of Bristol was acquired by the Rushbrookes in 1808, in exchange for their estate at Little Saxham. They sold Rushbrooke in 1919, and in 1938 it was bought by Lord Rothschild, who made considerable improvements to the house and other estate buildings before the Second World War, but after it did not live in the house and in 1961 decided on demolition. By then he had already taken the remarkable step of rebuilding the village.

ST NICHOLAS. A small church, with a Dec W tower (but a bequest of 1407 'for making the tower'), otherwise Perp and much of it, under the render, of red brick (see the N windows). There is a S but no N aisle. Sir Thomas Jermyn left £66 3s. 4d. in 1497 to have the aisle extended so that he could be buried on the S side of the chancel. Crowstepped gables to nave, chancel and S porch. The interior is very strange, largely the result of reordering by *Col. Robert Rushbrooke* in the 1820s. The S aisle proper is of two bays, followed by one which was the family pew and is now a vestry, followed by yet one more which is the funeral chapel. A tunnel-like passage at the W end gives access to the tower and organ loft. The nave is treated in its furnishings as a chancel, or as a college chapel, i.e. with STALLS facing each other instead of pews. They curve round at the W end, with elaborate canopied backs, and against the W wall is a set of false organ pipes, brightly painted. It is all Rushbrooke's handiwork, carved and assembled himself (not always very expertly), much of it reusing old materials, including some BENCH ENDS with poppyheads, bits of a Commandment board cut up for battening, and a good deal of Tudor panelling from Rushbrooke Hall. He also made the timber PULPIT and FONT; the latter has been abandoned in favour of a reclaimed stone one, but Rushbrooke's COVER remains. The excellent roofs appear to be original: arch-braced in the nave, and with cambered tie-beams in the chancel. Also original is the ROOD BEAM, a rare survival, carved and supported by arched braces, standing on small figures which themselves stand on bases beneath which is the top of a further canopy. Above the rood beam is a TYMPANUM, again a rarity, and displayed on it the carved and painted ROYAL ARMS of Henry VIII, with dragon and greyhound supporters, portcullis and Tudor rose. These were almost certainly introduced by Rushbrooke, although they may be partly or wholly genuine. – CHEST. North Italian, made of cypress wood; probably late C17. Decorated in low relief with panels of figures, on the front and on the underside of the lid. – STAINED GLASS. Fragments in the S and N windows, and especially the E window, where there are two complete figures (cf. Nowton). Some or all of the glass is thought to have come from Little Saxham Hall. – MONUMENTS. Against the chancel N wall, fronts of two tomb-chests, of Sir Thomas Jermyn †1645 (with Ionic pilasters) and Thomas Jermyn †1659 (with fluted pilasters). – Henry Jermyn, Earl of St Albans, †1683/4. Standing monument of white marble, the upper part with swan-neck pediment and arms. Against the sides scrolls, and the heads of cherubs or plump angels, enclosed by their wings. It is a crude copy of the tablet that records the rebuilding of the church at Euston (q.v.) in 1676. – Thomas Jermyn †1692 aged 15, 'a Hopefull Youth' (S chapel). White and black standing monument. Reclining figure, diminutive but completely adult in dress, one hand resting on a skull. Background with open and broken pediment on Composite columns. – Thomas Lord Jermyn †1703. With broken pediment, otherwise surprisingly plain. – Sir Robert Davers †1722 and sons †1723 and 1743. No effigy. Grey sarcophagus below open pediment with festoon. It is a second-rate copy of the monument in Westminster Abbey to the Marchioness of Annandale by *James Gibbs*, 1723 (GF). – Robert Rushbrooke †1829 and his son Col. Robert †1845 (S aisle). Identical grey marble monuments with scrolly tops, the later one signed by *James Emerson* of Bury.

Lord Rothschild's new VILLAGE was commissioned in 1950 and designed by *Llewelyn-Davies & Weeks* (job architect *John Weeks*, executive architect *Michael Huckstepp*). It consists of THE HAMLET, a street NW of the church, and a smaller group (POPLAR MEADOW) to its S. The latter was built first: a linked pair, 1952–5, and a further cottage of 1955–6. The Hamlet followed in two phases, 1956–9 and 1960–3, with five houses and a clubhouse on the S side and six houses on the N. Single-storey, but with a storeroom or playroom in the roof. White-painted brick with monopitch slate roofs and windows of (originally) black-painted timber. The layout is asymmetrical and staggered, the houses of varying size and

Rushbrooke Hall.
Engraving

plan, with the middle ones along each side set back. They are connected by high walls so as to emphasize the privacy of the individual houses from inside, and the unity of the whole village from outside. The paintwork no longer sparkles as it does in early photographs, and Norman Scarfe thought the development 'more Cumbernauld than East Anglian', but the houses create a real sense of place. Focus is provided by a C16 red brick, octagonal WELL-HOUSE, with conical roof and a superfluity of buttresses, in the middle of the street, and at the far end three pairs of traditional cottages of painted brick with thatched roofs by *W. H. Mitchell*, 1939. N of the street HOME FARM, with a model thatched dairy farmstead of *c.* 1938–9 designed and constructed by *George W. King Ltd*, Hitchin. Courtyard of white-painted brick with thatched roofs; even the gatepiers are thatched.

RUSHBROOKE HALL stood ¼ m. SW of the church. It was fully moated, and the moat remains. Two doorcases and a marble chimneypiece were reused at St Edmund (R.C.), Bury St Edmunds (see p. 141). More might have been saved if fire had not broken out during the demolition; as noted above, some Tudor panelling had already found its way into the church.

RUSHFORD HALL

2¼ m. NE of Euston*

Early C18 seven-bay house, extended by five bays in matching style in the early C20. Rendered brick and black pantile roof.

*For Rushford village, *see Buildings of England: Norfolk 2: North-West and South*, pp. 622–3.

Two storeys and attics, with parapet and dormers. Flat-roofed porch added to the older part, 1983.

SANTON DOWNHAM

'Santon Downham' means Downham near Santon, which is just over the Little Ouse in Norfolk. Santon refers simply to sand, and Santon Downham was the unfortunate victim of a 'sand flood' in 1668 which all but buried the village. The dominant position once occupied by Downham Hall has been assumed by the Forestry Commission, which bought the estate in 1924.

ST MARY. Small, Norman, with an unbuttressed Perp W tower. At the foot of the tower, symbols in stone-carved panels and the names of those who gave money for its erection between 1473 and 1503: John Watts, John Reve, Sir John Downham, Margaret Reve, Jafrey Skitte and William Toller. A similar inscription can be seen nearby at West Tofts, Norfolk. Some flushwork panelling too. Norman S doorway with spiral-fluted shafts and roll-moulded arch; the N doorway the same but with altered arch. Above the S doorway an interesting carved panel, variously interpreted, but most likely a lion in profile, its tail ending in a kind of fleur-de-lys. Norman window splay on the N side converted into a lancet. Priest's doorway into the chancel Norman, but with some dogtooth in the arch. Not *in situ*. Similar dogtooth on a section of re-set string course in the chancel N wall. Chancel with C13 N windows and low tomb recess. One Dec S window. The church had a N chapel, the archway to it blocked with C19 work, its PISCINA remaining outside. The moulding of the arch looks *c.* 1300. On the nave S wall, high up, part of a pointed arch has been uncovered, its origins unexplained. On its soffit C13 WALL PAINTING of thin scrolls. Restored 1893, including new roofs. – PULPIT. Jacobean. – SCREEN. Very early C14. Shafts, not mullions. Wide ogee-arched entrance with tracery over. – STAINED GLASS. Tower window, 1880, and three N windows (Faith, Hope and Charity), 1895, by *Kempe*. E window by *Clayton & Bell*, 1897. Nave S †1893 by *Heaton, Butler & Bayne*. Chancel S by *Harcourt M. Doyle*, 1952. – MONUMENTS. Two coped coffin-lids set in chancel floor. C14. – Lt-Col. the Hon. Henry Cadogan †1813 at the Battle of Vittoria. With profile head in relief and trophies.

DOWNHAM HALL was demolished in 1925. It had been rebuilt in the C18, with alterations and additions by *L. Vulliamy*, 1836. It stood at the N end of Hall Drive, and some fragments remain, including the billiard room, coach house and tack room (now private houses), and ice house. Mile-long avenues of lime trees run SW and SE towards Brandon and Thetford, with flint and white-brick lodges where they meet the main road.

HOUSING, W of the church. By *Hughes & Bicknell*, 1948–9, for the Forestry Commission: detached houses for foresters, semi-detached for forest workers. White brick, well laid out round a former paddock to the hall, but bland. Of more interest is a group of four semi-detached prefabricated Swedish timber bungalows erected as part of the same scheme. N of the church, on the site of the Home Farm, Forestry Commission OFFICES and stores by *Kenneth Wood*, 1967. Mainly single-storey, with monopitch and butterfly roofs, divided horizontally: black stained unwrought timber above rough, over-burnt stock bricks.

BARROW. 1⅓ m. ESE, a round barrow about 5 ft 2½ in. (1.59 metres) high and 88 ft 6 in. (27 metres) in diameter on the edge of a Forestry Commission plantation, just S of the Little Ouse River. Nearby, and in the plantations around the High Lodge Forest Centre, are long rabbit warren banks of sand, probably constructed in the C18.

SAPISTON

ST ANDREW (Churches Conservation Trust). Nave, chancel and W tower; S porch. All *c.* 1300 and a little later. The only older element is the S doorway: Norman, with two orders of shafts, single-scalloped capitals, and an arch with an unusual ornamental motif like tongues or leaves. Restored 1847, which is probably when the thatched roof was replaced with tiles. – FONT. Octagonal, plain, with octagonal stem and four circular shafts. Pretty C17 COVER. – WALL PAINTING. Faint traces, on N wall, above an arched recess. The subject is possibly the Martyrdom of St Edmund. – MONUMENT. John Bull †1643. Of the usual type, with pilasters and obelisks.

The setting of the church is delightful, outside the village in meadows with just a few buildings around but not too close to it. Prominent among these THE GRANGE, C17 timber-framed and plastered with C19 bargeboards and other detailing. To its W MILL HOUSE, also C17, encased in red brick in the late C19, and former WATERMILL, C18, red brick and render. At a discreet distance, towards the village, the former VICARAGE. 1866. Red brick with many little bays and gables. Black and red arches over the windows filled with red brick laid herringbone-wise. Recessed porch with Gothic archway.

In the village, NEW COTTAGES, Coney Weston Road. A terrace of seven estate cottages, dated 1867. Red brick with white-brick dressings and roof of black glazed pantiles. Decorative cast-iron casements. Gabled centre, projecting slightly. Triangular windows in this and the end gables.

SEMER

ALL SAINTS. In a meadow by the River Brett amid old trees. C14, with W tower, much renewed. Chancel rebuilt 1872–3 by *George Hewitt* of Ipswich, with a small porch against the priest's door. S porch and internal alterations (including SCREEN) by *J. S. Corder*, 1899. – FONT. Square, plain, C14. With Jacobean COVER. – PAINTINGS. Moses and Aaron, C18. – MONUMENTS. Rev. John Bruning †1663. Tablet in alabaster surround with broken pediment and achievement, cherubs' heads and scrolls. – Rev. Charles Cooke †1838. Tudor-Gothic. By *Benjamin Backhouse*.

Former SCHOOL, W of the church. 1871, with alterations by *Corder*, 1898. Red brick, rather plain.

SEMER MANOR, NW of the church. Timber-framed and plastered. Four-bay front with Georgian doorcase and sashes, some with sidelights. Hipped roof with dormers.

BRIDGE FARM, Ash Street. ¾ m. ESE. Attractive timber-framed farmhouse of the C16 with a two-storey gabled and jettied porch and a jetty to the road. The timbers are exposed, but colourwashed.

COSFORD UNION WORKHOUSE, 1 m. SE, opened in 1781 and closed in 1923, when most of it was demolished. The NE corner survives as part of a house, as does the HOSPITAL of 1869–70. Red brick with white-brick dressings. Single-storey. Nine bays wide with two large and three small gables.

SHELLAND

KING CHARLES THE MARTYR. The unusual dedication is due to Thomas Cropley †1659, whose ledger stone records (in Latin) his devotion to the cause of the Martyr King. The main changes to the medieval fabric were made in 1767, the date over the E window: see for example the plastered bell-turret with ogee cap, supported by little scrolls, and the S vestry window. The windows must have been altered after 1767. The chancel inside, on the other hand, retains a pretty Gothick cornice. The strong colour scheme apparently dates from the end of the C19, as does perhaps the strange patterned moquette covering the lower part of the chancel walls. – FONT. Octagonal, with big, coarse leaf panels and three shields; C14. – BOX PEWS and TRIPLE-DECKER PULPIT. Presumably of 1767. – RAILS. With turned balusters. At the entrance to the chancel, as well as across the sanctuary. – HOUSEL BENCHES, i.e. for the use of communicants. Two, in the chancel. – BARREL ORGAN. By *H. Bryceson*, 1810. Still in regular use. Three original barrels; a fourth by *John Budgen*, 2006.

SHELLEY*

ALL SAINTS. An irregular group. Nave and chancel plastered; tower flint and stone with brick battlements, and brick N chapel. The chancel is E.E. – see the S lancet. The nave projects beyond the N tower. The latter is early C14, and has, unusually, a N doorway. Top probably rebuilt with the 40s. bequeathed by Thomas Tylney in 1557. S aisle also C14 (see one window with intersected tracery). Low arcade with octagonal piers and double-chamfered arches. N chapel (now vestry) added by Sir Philip Tylney and described as new in his will of 1532. Red brick, with brick windows, originally plastered to imitate stone. Small polygonal buttresses at the corners with little stone heads at the top of them. The windows have hoodmoulds with stone headstops. Small stone panel with the Tylney arms. Another stone panel, finely carved with the Tylney arms, on the N wall inside. On the W wall inside, a projecting pole probably used to display a heraldic tabard. Rectangular opening from the chancel into the chapel (partly blocked in the C18) lined with various ornamental panels, including the Tylney arms. General restoration 1882–3, including removal of W gallery and re-seating. – CHANCEL STALLS with poppy-heads and the Tylney arms; probably made for the N chapel. – PULPIT. With linenfold panels. More linenfold panels used in BENCH FRONTS. – STAINED GLASS. Nave S by *William Warrington*. It commemorates Henry Partridge †1864, whose family lived at Shelley Hall, and who was apprenticed to Warrington. – MONUMENTS. Sir Philip Tylney †1533 (chancel N wall). Front of tomb-chest. Three arched panels containing shields of arms for Tylney and his wife Jane Teye. The coloured shields above it belong to the tomb-chest of Dame Margrett Tylney †1597 (beneath nave N window). Recumbent effigy. Stumps of flanking columns for the missing canopy on which the shields once stood. – Hannah Norman and others †1866. By *Watts* of Colchester. Gothic, richly decorated.

SHELLEY HALL. Important fragment of the mansion built by Sir Philip Tylney between 1517 and 1533. Red brick with blue diapering. It seems to have been a courtyard house, with the hall on the E side and a gatehouse in the middle of the W side. It is this gatehouse, or rather the gateways and the S side of the gatehouse, that is the most recognizable part of Tylney's house. The gateways (blocked on the W side) have panelled polygonal buttresses with three tiers of niches. Terracotta plaques in the spandrels with the Tylney griffin. Stone plaque with the Tylney arms on the N wall (not *in situ*) similar to the one in the N chapel of All Saints. S range joined at the SE corner of the gatehouse, with stair-turret in the outer angle

---

*This account of the church and hall owes much to the researches of Edward and Joanna Martin.

between the two ranges, around which a larger stair-turret was built in the early C17. This contains a newel stair with original dog-gate at the bottom. The room (now dining room) at what was the N end of the original S range, until another room was added to the N end in 1813, has a large fireplace with original chimneystack, and may have been the kitchen. More polygonal buttresses on both sides of the S range, and some brick windows. Other additions at the S end. From the middle of the E side of the S range a wall running E with a polygonal buttress, probably the remains of the outer S wall of the courtyard. E of this a moated enclosure, described as a garden in 1533 and thought to have been built as such rather than being the site of an earlier house. It is reached by a brick bridge that is aligned with the gatehouse. Outbuildings SW of the house including a large contemporary brick BARN.

CHAPEL HOUSE, NE of the church. C15, with exposed timber and long-wall jettied front with moulded bressumer.

SHELLEY HOUSE, 400 yds N. C16, with a tall, three-storey range on the l. and two-storey range on the r. The taller range has exposed timbers and brick-nogging on the upper floors. The lower range is plastered and has an C18 pedimented doorcase.

SHIMPLING

ST GEORGE. Reached along an avenue of lime trees and a bridge over Chad Brook. Mostly Dec – see the E window with a usual pattern of flowing tracery, the segment-headed S aisle windows, the N windows, and the arcade inside of low octagonal piers and arches with one chamfer and one hollow chamfer. The chancel S doorway has a frieze of dogtooth inside, reused from an earlier chancel; fragments also in the jambs of the E window. Restoration by *James Fowler* of Louth, 1867–8, including new nave and aisle roofs, new S porch and re-seating. The E side of the tower was also rebuilt. – FONT. Odd, octagonal, probably C14. Stem with eight attached shafts. Bowl shallow, with quatrefoils and tracery. – PULPIT. 1868, with carving by *Emma Tyrwhitt-Drake*. – SCREENS at E end of the S aisle. 1868, forming a private pew (with its own chimney) for Ellen Hallifax, who largely paid for the restoration. – STAINED GLASS. E window by *Warrington*, 1842, including the arms of Thomas Hallifax. S aisle E by *Powell & Sons*. Three main lights originally of 1864 by *Henry Holiday*, replaced *c.* 1890 by Powells; Holiday's tracery remains, and two lights (only) of his window were moved to a S window. – S aisle W by *Heaton, Butler & Bayne*, 1869, designed by *Richard Almack* of Long Melford. – Tower window of 1868 by *Baillie & Mayer*, who also re-set the C14 glass in the tracery of the chancel N and S windows. – MONUMENTS. Elizabeth Plampin †1771. By *R. Westmacott Sen.*

Woman standing by an urn on a sarcophagus. – Ellen Susanna Caldecott †1828. By *Garland & Fieldwick*. Heavy tablet of grey and white marble. – Thomas Hallifax †1850. Arched recess in wall of s aisle, with two angels in profile kneeling against an altar with a cross over it. Unsigned, but an almost exact copy of a monument by *R. Westmacott Jun.* at Marham, Norfolk, *c.* 1847. – In churchyard, SE of the chancel, the Hallifax family MAUSOLEUM, 1842. Stone, with arched panels and buttresses, and a rather utilitarian pitched roof. On the southern boundary, a small white-brick building of 1842. Tudor-Gothic, with a bay window in the E wall. It may have been a schoolroom, but is also said to have been built as a room for the Misses Hallifax to rest in after the walk from Chadacre House (*see* below).

SHIMPLING HALL, W of the church. Timber-framed and plastered, dating from *c.* 1475. Gabled and jettied cross-wings. Doric portico, but the entrance still in its original position.

VILLAGE. Mainly at Shimpling Street, 1¼ m. NE. Former SCHOOL, originally of 1841 (erected by Thomas Hallifax Jun.), doubled in 1871 (by Ellen Hallifax). Tudor-Gothic, of white brick, with non-Tudor-Gothic clock turret and weathervane. SCHOOL HOUSE opposite. To the W, set back, former ALMSHOUSES, dated 1777. Timber-framed and plastered. Then a modest red brick structure of social rather than architectural interest: the parish COAL HOUSE, 1861, erected by Maria and Ellen Hallifax (cf. Haughley). Finally SHIMPLING PLACE, an C18 timber-framed and plastered farmhouse with mansard roof.

CHADACRE HOUSE, 1 m. NNW. Attractively set in the valley of Chad Brook. Seat of the Plampin family, bought by Thomas Hallifax (cf. Cavendish) following the death of Rev. John Plampin in 1823. Hallifax engaged *Philip Hardwick* to rebuild the house, work that was in progress in 1834. In 1919 the estate was bought by Lord Iveagh (cf. Elveden) and established as an agricultural institute; alterations and additions by *Cyril E. Power*, *c.* 1920–2.* The institute closed in 1990 and the house returned to private use. It is stuccoed, and a bit dull. Two and a half storeys, with five windows on the entrance front (W) and six on the E. Large square porch with pilasters. Shaped brackets supporting the eaves. Lower ranges to the N, including C20 additions. (Entrance hall with arcaded screen. Cantilevered staircase, its cast-iron balustrade of the same pattern as at Hardwick's City of London Club of 1833–4.) S of the main house, the DOWER HOUSE has round-arched windows with Gothick tracery, repeated in the dormers. HOME FARM, about ½ m. S, is of flint with red brick dressings, including a house and model farm buildings. TOWER LODGE, ½ m. W, 1849, of the same materials, has a 40-ft (12.2-metre) red brick tower. Of numerous estate cottages, the most picturesque is

---

*Power's linocut, 'The Carcase', *c.* 1929, shows his new library under construction.

KEEPERS HOUSE, ½ m. SE of the church. White brick, dated 1846 with Thomas Hallifax's initials. Windows with decorative cast-iron glazing bars.

SOMERSHAM

ST MARY. Unbuttressed W tower of c. 1300–40. Nave and chancel, with rendered walls, of the same time. S porch of timber, perhaps not later; the timbers of the arched entrance may even be earlier. The simple tracery in the side windows, of which little remains, differs between W and E (cf. Offton). Tie-beam in the chancel with sanctus bell bracket still attached. Restoration by *E. F. Bisshopp*, 1882, including re-seating and removal of W gallery; carving by *John Groom & Son*. – REREDOS. Made of panelling, dated 1601.– COMMUNION RAIL. Mid-C17. – WALL PAINTING. Unidentified fragment on nave S wall. – PAINTINGS. Moses and Aaron, still in their original positions, l. and r. of the reredos. The painting is surprisingly good, done with considerable brio. One suspects a painter who knew London, and Sebastiano Ricci in particular. They were given to the church in 1750. COMMANDMENT BOARDS of similar date. – ROYAL ARMS. Two sets. One of Charles II, in a frame with fretwork border on the sides. The other Hanoverian (1714–1801), cut to the outline of the design. – CURIOSUM. A First World War bomb. – STAINED GLASS. In upper part of N doorway, by *Rowland & Surinder Warboys*, 1997.

PRIMARY SCHOOL, SW of the church. By *B. Binyon*, 1876–7; alterations and additions by *H. J. Wright*, 1898. Red brick.

TUDOR GRANGE. *See* Nettlestead.

SOMERTON

ALL SAINTS. Norman nave. Small N doorway (blocked) with one order of shafts carrying scalloped capitals and an undecorated arch. Early C14 chancel and S chapel, surprisingly spacious. Cusped lancet in S wall of chapel; that in the chancel, W of the chapel, belongs to the restoration by *James Fowler* of Louth, 1882–3, but may be an accurate replacement. The arcade pier has big filleted shafts and spurs in the diagonals. Segment-headed S window. The E window is a Perp insertion, but has the early C14 shafting preserved inside. A curious device is the shafted squint which leads into the chancel PISCINA. The chapel may once have extended further W: its W wall is later, and there is evidence of a third archway in the nave S wall. W tower also C14. Battlements with flushwork quatrefoils and chequerboarding. C16 S porch, largely of brick. N vestry of 1882–3; Fowler also rebuilt the nave S wall and re-seated the nave. – FONT. Perp, octagonal, simple. – PULPIT. Jacobean. – COMMUNION RAIL, now in the place of the rood screen. Jacobean or early Stuart. With turned balusters. – MONUMENT. War memorial by *Powell & Sons*, 1921. Oval alabaster tablet in painted wooden wreath.

OLD RECTORY, opposite. 1857–8 for Rev. James Ford. Red brick with very strong diapering, almost like a trellis. Gothic detailing, including windows with applied cusped tracery.

SOMERTON HALL, ¾ m. SSE. Two-storey timber-framed house, given an excessively grand white-brick, two-and-a-half-storey front and sides in the early C19. Five-bay front, the central bay breaking forward slightly. Doorway with unfluted Greek Doric columns *in antis*. No windows in the side walls. The back of the house still simply plastered, with the deep tiled roof curving out at the edges to meet the high side walls. Stables to the r. of the front, of white brick (with a row of blind arches) towards the road, and red brick towards the yard. Lower timber-framed wing to the rear, extended in red brick in the early C19.

ALMSHOUSES, N of Somerton Hall. 1912. Two semi-detached pairs. Red brick with stone dressings. Single-storey. Windows in straight gables rising through the eaves, and porches.

SPROUGHTON

Separated from Ipswich by the A14, which has also taken the traffic that used to go through Sproughton towards Stowmarket and Bury. Between the old main road (High Street) and the River Gipping runs Lower Street, still quite villagey with the church towards the bottom beside the river.

ALL SAINTS. Essentially of one build, around the turn of the C14. Unbuttressed W tower. Excellent three-bay arcades. The piers deeply moulded with four filleted shafts and four keeled shafts in the diagonals. The hollows between are continuous. Deeply moulded capitals and arches. S doorway with two orders of filleted shafts. Chancel arch of two broad continuous chamfers. Chancel N doorway more nicely designed, with two pretty headstops. The DOUBLE PISCINA opposite has bar tracery and a gable. E window Perp. A bequest of 1389, for making the N aisle like the S, may refer to new windows. Restoration by *F. Barnes*, 1863 (internal) and 1868–9, including rebuilt S porch and tower battlements; heads restored to the angels on the nave's hammerbeam roof. Aisles extended E in 1870, for chapel on S side (existing windows reused) and organ chamber on N; also N vestry. – BENCHES. With poppyheads. In chancel, by *H. Ringham*, 1844, incorporating and copying C15 originals. In nave, 1863, copying Ringham's.

– STAINED GLASS. An unusually rich collection of C19 glass. By *Alexander Gibbs* the E window (1864), two in the S aisle (†1864 and 1869) and the S aisle W window (*c.* 1866); probably also the S chapel E window (†1866) and a N aisle N window (Christ and St John the Baptist, *c.* 1866), and perhaps the N aisle W (†1859). – By *M. & A. O'Connor* the chancel S (1850). By *Ward & Hughes* the S chapel S window (1881). – By *W. G. Taylor* a N aisle window (1885). – N aisle (St Christopher etc.) by *Christopher Whall*, 1924, the year of his death; sidelights by *Veronica Whall* and *Edward Woore*. – MONUMENTS. Elizabeth Bull †1634. Kneeling figure. Two standing angels pull away a curtain. Attributed to *Maximilian Colt* (GF; cf. Lambe monument, East Bergholt (E)). – Rev. Joseph Waite †1670. Beautifully simple punning inscription incised on black stone; probably composed by Waite himself. At the top, Chi-Rho in a circle of cloud. Below that 'Behold I come' (Revelation 16:15). Then a winged hourglass on a skull. At the bottom 'I Waite' and a reference to Job 14:14, which should be followed. – Rev. Edmund Beeston †1713. 'A Man of primitive Integrity'. Also 'his good & Virtuous Wife' Mary †1724 and their son Rev. Edmund †1735, 'a steady Friend Sound Divine and good Christian'. Nice lettering. – Metcalfe Russell of The Chantry, Ipswich,* †1785. Good. No effigies. Urn against a black relief obelisk. Excessively elongated poplar trees l. and r. of the inscription.

Former SCHOOL, S of the church. 1851. Gothic. Knapped flint with red brick dressings.

CHURCH CLOSE, W. Former rectory. Late C15 timber-framed and plastered house with jettied gable towards the road and a gabled and jettied cross-wing. Brick porch with reused carved spandrels. Then a C17 extension. Altered and further enlarged by *John Whiting*, 1836. Subdivided 1961. Its replacement, 750 yds SSE, by *A. B. Whittingham*, now the OLD RECTORY.

TITHE BARN, NW. Late C16 or early C17. Weatherboarded. Eight bays. Converted to community use by the *Whitworth Co-Partnership*, 2005–10. Behind it SPROUGHTON HALL, also *c.* 1600. Timber-framed and plastered with large external brick chimneystacks.

MILL, N. Late Georgian red brick watermill. Five bays and four storeys. Hipped roof with glazed black pantiles. Set across the mill stream. Converted to residential use; no remaining machinery. MILL HOUSE of *c.* 1600, timber-framed and plastered, the front altered and partly encased in brick.

ABBEY OAKS, 850 yds WSW. Large Edwardian house by *J. S. Corder* for A. C. Churchman (later Lord Woodbridge). Many gables and much half-timbering. GATEHOUSE on the main road by *H. R. Hooper*, 1928. Also half-timbered, with a jettied gable over the brick archway.

SPROUGHTON COURT, 450 yds SW. Four blocks of flats and maisonettes by *Basil & David Hatcher*, 1966. End walls and

---

* See *Suffolk: East*, p. 377.

intermediate pillars of white brick, with curtain walling largely hung with green tiles. Pleasantly laid out in a New Town sort of way, but unexpected on the edge of a village, albeit one that in 1966 was still on a busy main road.

SPROUGHTON HOUSE, 750 yds SSW. Early C19 white-brick range facing the Gipping valley. Three broad bays, separated by pilasters, although the centre bay has two windows on the first floor; deep eaves carried up into a pediment. Two-storey canted bay to the r., single-storey square bay to the l. and another on the l. return. Greek Doric porch. Later C19 and early C20 red brick addition to the rear.

SPROUGHTON MANOR, 700 yds NE. By *W. E. Nesfield*, 1863, for Col. Henry Phillipps. White brick. Decoration is provided by herringbone and chequered brickwork in tympana over the windows, and moulded brick panels on the main chimneystack; also by stone panels carved with Phillipps's arms and his and his wife's initials, which look old-fashioned by contrast with the otherwise stripped character of the house. Entrance front with two gables, one half-hipped, the other set back with a large window lighting the staircase hall. In front of the latter a single-storey bow and then a projecting wing, both additions of *c.* 1900. Single-storey service range and then stable yard to the r. Symmetrical garden front overlooking the Gipping valley. Three storeys. Two full-height bays with half-hipped gables and some tile-hanging. The gardens are said to have been laid out by *W. A. Nesfield*, the architect's father.

RED HOUSE, ¾ m. SSE, and now separated from the village by the A14. Georgian red brick front of six bays with pedimented doorway. Two storeys, parapet, pitched roof with little dormers. The core is C16; painted grotesque work decoration from the house now in Christchurch Mansion, Ipswich. Lower, later range to the r. and parallel C19 range at the back. C17 BARN SE of the house. Red brick with some burnt headers. Tumbled gables with little semicircular pediments. Ventilation slits.

STANNINGFIELD

ST NICOLAS. Norman nave. Preserved one N and one S window and the N doorway. Shafts with decayed capitals, arch with slightly decorated chevron. Uncommonly interesting chancel of *c.* 1300. The designer certainly liked personal tracery – see the E window with cusped intersections broken by a quatre-foiled circle at the top, the N windows with double-cusped quatrefoils in circles, and particularly the S windows with four pointed trefoils radially in a circle. Squint in the form of a quatrefoil diagonally from the chancel to the outside, that is really a lowside window. Nice, modest contemporary S doorway into the nave, with two orders of closely set fleurons in jambs and arches and a hoodmould with ballflower. John Rokewood left 20 marks (£13 6s. 8d.) for the new tower and bells in 1415; its top stage was taken down in the late C19. Nave and porch restored 1880–1. – FONT. Octagonal, C14. Panelled stem. Bowl with traceried panels and shields with arms of Rokewood and the three crowns of East Anglia. – SCREEN. Simple, with one-light divisions. – WALL PAINTING. Big C15 Doom over the chancel arch. Conserved by *Donald Smith*, 1994–5. – STAINED GLASS. E window by *Pippa Blackall*, 2003. – MONUMENT. Thomas Rokewood †1521 (chancel N wall). Tomb-chest with shields in quatrefoils. The canopy, with segmental arch and cresting, seems to be later, perhaps C18; the little angels by *Rattee & Kett*, 1895.

OLD RECTORY, opposite. By *Ewan Christian*, 1872. Red brick. Recessed porch with arched entrance. Gables like open pediments. Nice stables with half-hipped roof and weather vane.

COLDHAM HALL. See p. 199.

STANSFIELD

ALL SAINTS. On high ground at the edge of the village. Nave of *c*. 1300, W tower (with three niches round the W window) Dec. Chancel Dec. The side windows with tracery including the motif of the four-petalled flower. E end with two niches outside to l. and r. of the window and PISCINA with ogee arch squeezed into the corner of the SE window. Polygonal battlemented stair-turret on N side leading to rood loft and roof. Early C16 S porch, its roof with moulded beams and brattishing. Nave roof with carved spandrels, e.g. of a maiden in a castle threatened by a dragon. Nave and chancel restored by *J. P. St Aubyn*, 1886; tower restored 1896. – PULPIT. Jacobean. – SCREEN. The base only, much restored. – STAINED GLASS. Fragments in the chancel. – MONUMENTS. Frances Kedington †1715. Nicely lettered, with arms, like a ledger stone. – Rev. Beriah Brook †1809. By *Steggles & Sons*.

Former CONGREGATIONAL CHAPEL, Upper Street. Rebuilt 1859. Red brick with white-brick dressings and front. Tall and austere. Gabled front, with projecting gabled two-storey porches to l. and r. Lancet windows with iron glazing bars. The builder, if not the architect, was *John Sudbury* of Halstead, Essex.

ELM HALL, ½ m. SSE. Much-restored timber-framed house of the C15–C16 with brick-nogging. Jettied cross-wing at one end.*

PURTON GREEN, ½ m. N. Late C13 timber-framed aisled hall house. Thatched, with exposed timbers, jettied at both ends. The hall was of two full bays, of which one and a half survive,

---

*C16 wall paintings on the upper floor are said to survive, but have been covered over.

with a third two-storey bay at the N end that was rebuilt in the C15. Both aisles of the hall remain, but were reduced in width later in the medieval period, probably to allow the walls to be heightened and more windows inserted. The aisle originally continued round the N end of the building. Both the open truss of the hall and closed truss at its N (low) end have passing braces. The closed truss has an arcade of six pointed arches (cf. The Hall, Great Bricett): three blind and three open, giving access to two ground-floor service rooms and to a staircase. The high end of the hall was rebuilt and extended in the C16. Also in the C16 a floor was inserted in the hall, but this was removed as part of restoration by the Landmark Trust, who acquired the house in 1969.

CORDELL HALL, NNE of Purton Green. C17 timber-framed and plastered house. Front with three gables of equal size, two on projecting cross-wings. The wings have two-storey canted bays running up to the bressumers of the gables. Central hall and cross-passage. Above the house, a chain of six PONDS.

WINDMILL, 300 yds NE of the church. Tower mill, built for William Everard, 1840. Red brick, some render remaining. Cap and sails removed; shallow-pitched aluminium roof added 2006.

STANSTEAD

ST JAMES. Early C14 W tower with small lancets, also the chancel doorway and blocked N doorway. The remainder mostly Perp, including battlemented S porch with pinnacles, angle buttresses and outer stoup in arched niche. Chancel restored 1865, the remainder in 1877 by *James Fowler*, who re-seated the nave and opened up the tower arch. – ROYAL ARMS. Of Queen Anne, nicely painted. – BELL. By *Stephen Tonni* of Bury St Edmunds, 1544. On floor of tower. – STAINED GLASS. Chancel S window by *Heaton, Butler & Bayne*, 1907. The E window and two nave windows of *c.* 1856 look like early work of *Heaton & Butler*. – MONUMENT. Rev. Samuel Sheen †1867. Crocketed stone tabernacle enlivened with coloured marbles and mosaic, good of its kind.

STANSTEAD HALL, S of the church. A convincingly Neo-Jacobean house of the 1830s, built next to the site of an earlier hall. Red brick, with shaped gables, and a two-storey gabled porch. Lower wing extending towards the church. At the end of this wing, equally convincing additions by the *Morton Partnership*, 2008–10, with more shaped gables.

Former SCHOOL, N of the church. By *James Fowler*, 1871. Well-detailed red brick. Window in arched recess with herringbone infill, and chimneystacks with tumbling-in.

BRETTESTON HALL, ¼ m. N. Early C17 timber-framed house cased in C18 red brick. Seven-bay front, with segmental heads to the windows. C20 single-storey bays on entrance and S fronts, and various additions to N and E. Heavily beamed and panelled interiors, with carved date 1617.

THE OAKLANDS, Lower Street, ½ m. S. C15 timber-framed and plastered house, in two phases. Hall range with wall-plate projecting as in Wealden houses. Gabled and jettied parlour cross-wing added to one end. The gable itself is jettied, with carved bressumer. Adjacent weatherboarded BARN with crown-post roof, built as a house (possibly guildhall) in the first half of the C16. Original doorway and diamond-mullioned windows.

STANTON

Stanton has two parish churches: All Saints, and St John, 600 yds NW and now outside the bypass. Both are recorded in Domesday. They shared the same parson from 1554 but were not officially consolidated until 1756. St John's declined in the C19 but was not finally abandoned until 1962, when the roof was removed.

ALL SAINTS. The nave is Dec – see the N windows. Fine spacious Dec chancel (spoilt by the organ) with reticulated E window (renewed 1875–6), ogee-headed PISCINA, and SEDILIA, three seats in the window opening plainly separated by stone arms. Ornate Dec S aisle with segment-headed three-light E window, also with reticulated tracery; S windows straight-headed. Ballflower frieze all along the outside. Four-bay arcade, not high, with octagonal piers and double-chamfered arches. Low clerestory with quatrefoil windows. In the aisle a tall damaged tomb recess, cusped and subcusped and crowned by a big crocketed ogee gable. It may have been intended for the putative builder of the aisle, Hervey de Stanton †1327, founder of Michaelhouse (now Trinity College), Cambridge. Pretty PISCINA in the window corner, in the same style. At the W end the buttresses of the S porch tower, suggesting that it pre-dates the aisle and was originally free-standing. Double-chamfered entrance with continuous moulding. Inside originally two-bay blank arcading. The top two-thirds of the tower fell in 1906. Timber-framed belfry by *Marshall Sisson*, 1956. General restoration of 1875–6 by *S. S. Markham*, including new roofs to nave and chancel and the usual furnishings. – STAINED GLASS. Fragments in S aisle E window, including C15 figures of St Margaret and St Elizabeth. – Chancel E by *Luxford Studios*, 1955 (Light of the World). – MONUMENTS. Elizabeth Bidwell †1791. White sarcophagus on black ground by *E. Gaffin*. Copied for her husband Rev. G. Bidwell †1865 by *William Sharp* of Thetford.

ST JOHN (Churches Conservation Trust). W tower with a passage through from S to N, to allow for processions (cf. Combs). The mouldings look *c.* 1300 or a little later. Nave of about the same time. Tall two-light windows. C15 S porch with flushwork base. Chancel E wall rebuilt 1616 with crowstepped gable; it carries also the date of another restoration, 1858.

VILLAGE. All Saints stands at the crossroads in the centre. 150 yds W the OLD RECTORY by *Thomas Jeckyll*, 1864–5. Red brick with a band of white, and stone keystones. Two storeys. The main part of five bays with off-centre porch. Windows with depressed arched heads. E of All Saints, on the corner of Duke Street, WILLOW HOUSE, C16 with a C17 stair-wing added to the front, and further along Old Bury Road FOUNDRY HOUSE, with jettied front, dated 1576. To the S, in Bury Lane, the PRIMARY SCHOOL of 1877. Gothic, with polychromatic brickwork. Extensions by the *County Architect's Dept*, 1980.

GRUNDLE HALL, 400 yds SSE of All Saints. Timber-framed and plastered hall house with two jettied cross-wings, built between *c.* 1480 and 1520. Crown-post roof with smoke-blackened timbers. Trusses painted with cresting, more like church than domestic work. Oliver Rackham's analysis of the timbers (1972) concluded that some 330 trees were needed to provide the house's 730 components.

ROSE AND CROWN, Bury Road, ½ m. WSW of All Saints. Early C19. Painted brick front and thatched roof. Shallow two-storey canted bays. The eaves overhang at the front in a curve, supported on slender posts, and attached to the eaves is a large wrought-iron frame that carries the inn sign over the forecourt.

UPPER CHURCH HOUSE, N of St John's. Former rectory. Timber-framed and plastered. Early C17. Two storeys and attics with two gabled dormers the full height of the roof.

WINDMILL, Upthorpe Road, 700 yds ESE of All Saints. Post mill. Originally 1751, moved to its present site *c.* 1818, the brick roundhouse added later in the C19. Restored to full working order in stages from 1986. White weatherboarded buck, four patent sails and fantail. In Barningham Road, ¼ m. N of St John's, the two-storey brick roundhouse of another post mill.

WYKEN HALL, 1¼ m. S of All Saints. Timber-framed and plastered house, the oldest parts of *c.* 1540, restored and extended by *J. S. Corder*, 1920.* Basically Z-plan, with the centre running W–E. Across the NW corner of this range (which once extended further W) an entrance porch added by Corder, leading into a late C17 section that may originally have been a Great Hall with chamber above. Off this to the S, replacing a late C18 service range, Corder's principal addition, for drawing room and smoking room, with red brick ground floor. At the E end of the centre, an early C17 room, probably a kitchen, converted by Corder into the dining room. Against its S wall a massive brick chimney. Running N of this a range containing the oldest

---

*This account is based principally on a survey of the house by Philip Aitkens.

parts of the house, extended by Corder at the N end, as well as an early C17 gabled cross-wing to the E duplicated on its N side by Corder. Tall red brick chimneys, both C17 and 1920. The overall effect is very attractive, complemented by the surrounding gardens laid out by *Kenneth* and *Carla Carlisle* from 1979, with formal herb and knot gardens by *Arabella Lennox-Boyd*, 1983.

STOKE-BY-CLARE

ST JOHN THE BAPTIST. Big Perp church with N and S aisles and clerestory, N and S chancel chapels, and two-storey N vestry. The tower is Dec. It belonged to an earlier church that was rebuilt in the C15 and placed somewhat further N, so that the former nave S wall became the S wall of the aisle, and the W respond of the S arcade stood against the middle of the blocked former tower arch. The arch can still be seen inside the tower. The transeptal S chapel is probably also part of the old church, which may indeed have been cruciform. The Perp windows are nearly all of the same design, with straight-sided arches to the individual lights. The arcade piers quatrefoil with keeled foils; castellated capitals of the same design as at Clare. Also as at Clare, the piers may be reused, but the old church seems not to have had aisles, so it is unclear where they would have been reused from. Double-hollow-chamfered arches. Chancel arch of the same design. Bequests of 1475–80 for the rood loft, paving etc., suggest that the rebuilding was nearing completion at that time, but there was a bequest of *c.* 1501 for the 'new aisle', and Matthew Parker, Dean of Stoke College 1535–48 (*see* below), is said to have restored the nave. Interior restored and re-seated 1871. – FONT. Perp, octagonal. On the bowl quatrefoils with shields etc. Much restored. – PULPIT. Richest Perp, the richest in the county, and very small, only about 20 in. (50 cm.) across. Two tiers of tracery panels. Money was left towards its making in 1498. – BENCHES. With traceried fronts and poppyheads. There was a bequest for 'new stools' in 1477. – CHEST. Oak, with excellent iron scrollwork. The ironwork is late C13 or early C14, but the chest itself has been altered, perhaps in the C16. – WALL PAINTING. Doom, at the E end of the N chapel. It seems to belong to the Counter-Reformation during the reign of Queen Mary I (1553–8), quite a rare thing. On the nave W wall, remains of a large painted text of *c.* 1700. – STAINED GLASS. Fragments of the C15 in the S transept, including a windmill. – S chancel chapel S †1942 by *Thomas Derrick*. Derrick was principally an illustrator, which is especially apparent in the cartoon-like face of St George. Inscription below by *Peter Watts*, 1948, his first work as a professional carver. – BRASSES. Unknown Lady, *c.* 1530. 18-in. (46-cm.) figure. – Alice Talkarne †1605. 20½-in.

(56-cm.) figure. – Edward Talkarne †1597. 22½-in. (57-cm.) figure.
N of the churchyard a small GREEN and the entrance to Stoke College (*see* below). Along the E side a row of timber-framed houses, mistaken for the Cellarer's Hall of the College but probably built as a hostelry or inn in the late C15 or early C16. Pleasant, wide village street leading to a second, larger green; it is hard to believe that the railway used to cross it, but the STATION is still there (opened 1865, closed 1967). At the S end on the W side GREEN FARM. Early C18, red brick, two storeys, five bays. Roof hipped to the N only; lower timber-framed and plastered S range. On the E side, set back, the OLD VICARAGE of 1843. Painted brick. Two storeys. Three-bay front divided by pilasters. Greek Doric portico.
On the corner of Ashen Lane and Church Park, E of the church, three traditional houses by *Stephen Mattick*, 1988–90. Two with pargetting, one weatherboarded.
BAYTHORNE GROVE, 1 m. W. Unusual and pretty early C19 house of three wide bays. It is of knapped flint with white-brick trim in vertical as well as horizontal divisions. Wide porch with Doric columns. White brick parapet. Curved screen walls to either side. On the l. return wall a shallow two-storey canted bay with canopy over the ground-floor window.

STOKE COLLEGE

The College of St John the Baptist was founded in 1415 and governed by statutes of 1423. It occupied the buildings of a Benedictine priory that had been founded in Clare but moved to Stoke in 1124. The priory was naturalized in 1395, and there is record of a serious fire at about that time, but it is not known how much damage was done, nor is it known whether the priory church was demolished then or later. What does seem clear is that Matthew Parker, the last Dean of the college (and future Archbishop of Canterbury), remodelled part of the buildings as his lodgings during his time in office, 1535–48. After its suppression the college was granted to Sir John Cheke and Walter Mildmay. In about 1660 it was acquired by Sir Gervase Elwes; by 1674 it had again been remodelled, and tax was paid on eighteen hearths. The house remained in the Elwes family until 1897, when it was purchased by Lord Loch, who employed his wife's niece's husband, *Edwin Lutyens*, to make alterations and additions, 1897–9. Further alterations were made in 1922–3 by *H. S. Goodhart-Rendel* for Lord Loch's daughter-in-law. In 1954 it became a private school.

At first sight there is no evidence of the medieval structure, so effectively was it masked from the C16 onwards, mostly in red brick. Careful investigation* has established, however, that the core of the building is the Dean's Lodging occupied by Parker

---
*By Leigh Alston, 2007.

and, most probably, created by him out of the existing buildings. The age of those buildings is less easy to establish but is probably early C15. The core is built mainly of flint and runs N–S through the middle of the present house. There is little doubt that it was the Cellarer's Hall, and that this lay (like the comparable building at Clare Priory) on the W side of the cloister. Of the other monastic buildings not a trace remains, but building work in the 1920s revealed what were probably the foundations of the priory church to the N of the present house, exactly where one would expect it to be. The hall was open to the roof but floored in the early C16, with a series of chambers being created on the first floor. At the same time a two-storey gallery, probably timber-framed, was built against the W wall, allowing separate access to each of the chambers and also to rooms in a new wing that extended W from the N end of the range. This wing probably contained Parker's private apartment on the first floor. Original stone windows, walling and a stone doorway are exposed on the S side, partly now internal. Remarkably similar alterations were made to the prior's lodging at Castle Acre Priory, Norfolk, whose overall layout is similar to the presumed layout of Stoke College.

The next major changes were made c. 1670, when the red brick S wing was added and other parts were faced in the same brick. S wing two storeys and attics, originally of seven bays, extended by one bay to the W in the late C18. Its rounded end, and that on the end of the N wing, were added c. 1800, probably by John Timms Elwes, who inherited in 1796. Some flint walling has been found within the S wing and it may incorporate a medieval structure. The stair-tower in the angle between the N wing and the main range was probably added in the C19, superseding the smaller tower in the corner against the S wing. Also of c. 1670 is the block at the N end of the main range, including a chamber N of the entrance and the entrance itself, although the latter was remodelled and extended by *Lutyens*. By him the outer doorway with Ionic pilasters and open pediment projecting on carved brackets, convincingly 'Early Georgian'; inner stone doorway with Ionic columns and semicircular fanlight of c. 1780, brought from Dublin c. 1919. On the E side of the house Lutyens added a single-storey billiard room at the end of the S wing, and a two-storey bachelor's wing round a small internal courtyard to its N. The latter has characteristic sweeping tiled roofs and tile-hanging. The former was top-lit by an extraordinary skylight, like a giant glazed dormer, that was taken down as part of *Goodhart-Rendel*'s alterations of 1922–3.

Inside, most of the structure of the medieval building is concealed, although some of the moulded beams of the C16 alterations are exposed. A number of rooms have good panelling of c. 1720. The ground-floor room in the N wing has a fine late C18 marble chimneypiece, purchased by Lady Loch in Dublin and installed in 1919, replacing one by *Lutyens*. She also, in

1920, replaced the staircase with one purchased from a London dealer and said then to have come from Pallant House, Chichester, West Sussex. Early C17. Twisted balusters, two to each tread, with carved tread-ends.

E of the house, red brick STABLES (now classrooms, etc.) of *c.* 1670. Two storeys, with wings projecting towards the house. Parallel range added on the E side in the early C19, its windows and doors with Gothick pointed tops. S of the house, a small WALLED GARDEN by *Lutyens* with the Chinese motif of a circular landscape window in the S wall. The original planting by *Gertrude Jekyll* has not survived. N of the house, at the entrance from the village, a highly unusual late C15 DOVECOTE. Red brick, rectangular, with hipped roof and gablets. The lower storey has wide four-centred arches on the two sides open towards the park, and was presumably intended as a sort of pavilion. On the two sides towards the village the brickwork has emblems in dark brick: a portcullis (first adopted as a badge by Henry VII in 1485), an initial I for John the Baptist, and an E (made to look like a mitre on its side) for Richard Edenham, Bishop of Bangor, Dean of the college 1470–93, indicating a date of construction between 1485 and 1493. A similar dovecote, but with a gatehouse on the ground floor, is recorded as having stood on the other side of the entrance, the site of the present C19 flint and white-brick LODGE with arched windows and rustic veranda. The red brick WALL along the N side of the park is documented as having been built by William Welflet, Dean 1461–9, a remarkably early date for such a structure, albeit one that has been partly rebuilt.

STOKE-BY-NAYLAND

9030

A large parish, including separate settlements at Withermarsh Green and Thorington Street; until 1868 it also included Leavenheath (q.v.). The village sits on the ridge between the Stour and Box rivers, with the church at its highest point.

ST MARY. Large Perp church, whose rebuilding probably began in 1421 when Sir John Howard and his wife Alice Tendring succeeded to the lordship of the manor. Their impaled arms appear over the W door, in the S porch and on the font steps. The church is 168 ft (51.2 metres) long, the substantial W tower 120 ft (36.6 metres) high. The tower, which is remarkably ornate, is in its upper parts mostly of brick. Money was left for its building by local merchants between 1439 and 1476. Stone frieze with shields at the base. Up the jambs and arch of the W doorway oblong panels with lions' heads and foliage. Ogee gable, buttresses on corbels l. and r. carrying supporters. Big four-light W window. Three two-light windows, and above these three-light bell-openings. The tower has four stages in all. Very big polygonal buttresses with diagonal buttress attachments, the latter decorated with niches with nodding ogee canopies. Decorated battlements and pinnacles. Chancel with transomed five-light (E) and three-light windows. Nave with clerestory and aisles; three-light aisle windows, clerestory windows renewed 1865. The chancel also has clerestory windows. Of the early C14, left from the previous church, are the N chapel, N of the N aisle, mentioned in the will of its founder, Sir John de Peyton, in 1317, and the two-storey S porch, restored 1879. Rib-vaulted with carved bosses. On the N side a simpler porch of brick, early C16. Six-bay arcades inside with thin piers with eight thin attached shafts, the four main ones carrying fillets. Eight individual capitals, many-moulded arches. String course at the sill level of the clerestory with angel figures and fleurons (renewed 1865). Very tall tower arch. Chancel chapels of two bays with simpler piers: four attached shafts and four thin filleted shafts without capitals in the diagonals.

FURNISHINGS. FONT. Perp, octagonal. It stands on a curious arrangement of three steps, the lower two octagonal, the uppermost in the form of a cross with shields on the risers. Stem with eight niches with nodding ogee arches. Bowl with the Emblems of the Evangelists and four other figures. Whom do they represent? – REREDOS. 1865. – SCREENS. To the N and S chapels; simple, Perp. Money was left for painting the rood loft in 1476. – STALLS. A variety, in various parts of the church, some with little figures against the ends of the arms, some with poppyheads, some with MISERICORDS, and some with reused painted and gilded panels from the rood screen. – DOORS. W door with tracery, S door with tracery and small figures of saints in canopied niches and a larger Virgin Mary at the top. – STAINED GLASS. W window †1865 by *M. & A. O'Connor*, E window †1876 by *O'Connor & Taylor*. E windows of N and S chapels by *J. B. Capronnier* of Brussels, 1868 and 1869. – MONUMENTS. S chapel: brasses to a Lady in mantle, possibly Katherine, widow of Sir Thomas Clopton and wife of Sir William Tendring, †1402, 47-in. (120-cm.) figure; Sir William Tendring †1408, 71-in. (180-cm.) figure, in armour, bare-headed with beard; double canopy, possibly for Sir John Howard †1426 and wife Alice; Lady Catherine Moleyns, wife of John Howard, Duke of Norfolk, †1452, made *c.* 1535, 38-in. (97-cm.) figure in heraldic mantle. – John, son of Lord Windsor, †1588. Incised slab, with figure in chrisom robe. – Lady Waldegrave †1600. Pilasters and two kneeling figures. – Her daughter Ann, Lady Windsor, †1615. Standing wall monument with recumbent alabaster effigy, children kneeling at her head and feet. Background architecture of no special interest. Attributed to *William Wright* (GF). – Many monuments to the Rowley family, including Admiral Sir William †1768 and Vice-Admiral Sir Joshua †1790, erected 1813, by *John Bacon Jun.*; and to the six children of Sir Charles Rowley

Stoke-by-Nayland, St Mary, brass to Sir William Tendring †1408.
Rubbing by M. Stuchfield, 2014

†1833–57 by *Austin & Seeley*. – N chapel: brasses to Francis Mannock of Giffords Hall †1590 (two groups of children only); and Dorothy Sanders, wife of Sir Francis Mannock, †1632, 28-in. (71-cm.) figure set in a black marble slab with incised architectural surround, attributed to *Edward Marshall*. – Sir Francis Mannock †1634. Recumbent alabaster effigy. Columns of touch l. and r. carrying a coffered vault and two small, well-carved figures. On the base thick garlands, a sign of the coming of the new, classical Inigo Jones style. Attributed to *Edward Marshall* (GF). – N aisle: Louise Matilda Forbes †1856. Small but elaborately Gothic. By *Watts* of Colchester. – In churchyard, war memorial by *W. D. Caröe*, 1921. Stone crucifix on stepped base.

ST EDMUND (R.C.), Withermarsh Green. 1825–7. The builder was *Robert Kingsbury* of Boxford. White brick. Simple E.E. with castellated W porch. W gallery on cast-iron columns. The C17 timber-framed house, adjoining to the N, was refaced in white mathematical tiles, presumably at the same time, for use as the presbytery.

CHAPEL OF ST NICHOLAS. *See* Giffords Hall, p. 247.

PERAMBULATION. The most spectacular houses at Stoke-by-Nayland stand W of the church in SCHOOL STREET, both with exposed timbers. Facing the W end is the former GUILDHALL (Guildhall Cottages), C16, close-studded and jettied along the whole front, the ground floor with moulded shafts with capitals at intervals and a massive corner-post at the N end. Chimneystack with six moulded shafts, dated 1619. NW of the church MALTINGS COTTAGES comprises a hall house of *c.* 1480 with gabled and jettied cross-wings, extended to the N in the C16. Further N, the red brick PRIMARY SCHOOL, 1848.

In the NE corner of the churchyard, red brick ROWLEY ALMSHOUSES, rebuilt 1875, while from the SE corner runs CHURCH STREET. On the S side the OLD VICARAGE, timber-framed and plastered, dating back to the mid C16 but adorned in the C19 with ornamental bargeboards. On the N side a later vicarage, built in 1782 for the curate. Red brick, five bays and two storeys. On the SE side of the triangular green, THE COTTAGE is timber-framed and plastered and of uniform C18 appearance, but the N end was originally gabled and jettied, *c.* 1370. Further S, on The Downs, a low terrace of four ALMSHOUSES, founded 1603, with exposed studding and tall chimneys. Across the road DOWNS HOUSE, C16, timber-framed and plastered. Good carved and moulded ceiling to the hall. To their N HILL HOUSE, with rainwater head dated 1803. White brick, with two gables to the road, and three-bay, two-storey S front. Unfortunate late C20 additions.

Back up the hill, Church Street continues NE; on the S side the VILLAGE HALL, 1911, and on the N side STREET HOUSE, timber-framed and plastered with two gables on the front and a gabled cross-wing behind. Partly jettied, with moulded wall-plate and castellated doorhead. Mainly mid-C16, but with a late C14 two-bay hall with evidence of a smoke louvre. At the crossroads, POLSTEAD STREET runs N, PARK STREET S; no individual houses of great importance, but pleasantly varied and unspoilt, mainly C17 and C18 timber-framed and plastered.

SCOTLAND PLACE, ½ m. NE. C15 timber-framed and plastered hall house, with jettied dairy range added to the service cross-wing *c.* 1600. Inside, a wooden overmantel dated 1566 with the arms of the Merchant Adventurers and Sir Thomas Rivett, salvaged from Tendring Hall (*see* below). NE of the house a late C18 red brick DOVECOTE or pigeon tower, only the upper of its two storeys being for birds. Square, with pyramidal roof, dormer and later louvre. It has moulded eaves of imported pine, a rare survival on such a building and indicating its high status.

TENDRING HALL. The house, which was demolished in 1954, stood about ½ m. SE of the church. It came to the Howards with Alice Tendring's marriage to Sir John (*see* above), and building work by John Howard, Duke of Norfolk, in 1482 may have been for the timber-framed house recorded in 1783. This had at one corner a red brick TOWER, the base of which survives. D-plan, with Tudor-style door and windows. In 1784–8 a new house was built for Admiral Sir Joshua Rowley about 250 yds NW; by *John Soane*, his largest commission up to then.

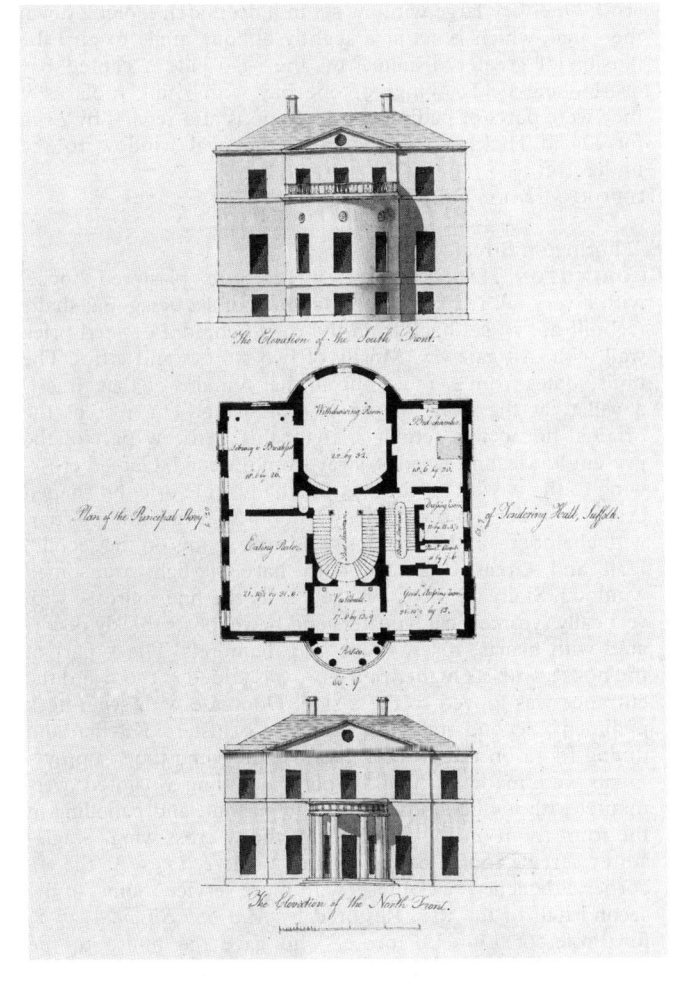

Stoke-by-Nayland, Tendring Hall.
Design by J. Soane, 1784

Humphry Repton prepared a Red Book for the landscaping in 1790–1. The house was enlarged in 1809–11, and in 1950 *Raymond Erith* prepared a scheme for reducing it to a manageable size, but nothing came of this. All that remains is the brick and stone PORTICO with paired Ionic columns, not part of Soane's design. The most important survival, however, is THE TEMPLE or fishing lodge, a small extravaganza by the main road to Nayland SW of the house, attributed to *Sir Robert Taylor*. It stands at the head of a canal. Mid-C18, perhaps following the acquisition of the estate by the Rowley family in 1764; the canal is shown on an estate map of 1723. Symmetrical and pretty with a very deep-eaved roof. It consists of one principal room with good Rococo plasterwork over an undercroft. One very large window set in a deep arch looking down the canal, which is set at a slightly oblique angle to give the illusion of greater distance; on the road side a canted bay overlooking fields. Wings of one bay with rising roofs as if they were parts of pediments. Alterations and repairs by *Erith* for David Hicks, 1956, including the oval window to the undercroft.

GIFFORDS HALL. *See* p. 245.

At Thorington Street, 1½ m. ESE:
THORINGTON HALL. A large, picturesque, plastered house, with a very tall red brick chimneystack of six octagonal shafts (rebuilt 2007), set back from the road behind a C17 red brick wall with C18 gateway. Mostly of two storeys and attics. The house dates from *c.* 1500, but all that remains of that time is a cellar, at the front of the W cross-wing. The rest of the original house was rebuilt *c.* 1630; this is the W part of the present house, and faced N, away from the road. Gabled cross-wing to the W with, at the N end, a handsome oriel on shaped brackets under the bressumer. Ground-floor hall and parlour, with chambers on the first floor and attic rooms on the second. Hall and Great Chamber both have six-light transomed windows. Staircase tower on the S side, the fine staircase with vertically symmetrical balusters and newel posts thickly decorated with hearts, roses, tulips and diamonds. The E part of the house, with its higher roof-line, was added *c.* 1700, and the entrance was moved to the S side. Doorcase with swan-neck pediment. Second staircase, with vase balusters. Kitchen and dining room on the ground floor. At the same time improvements were made to the older part, including a painted overmantel with idyllic landscape in the parlour, and panelling in the front room on the first floor of the W cross-wing. Single-storey service rooms added on the E side *c.* 1730. At the NE corner a detached backhouse, with more service rooms, of the second half of the C16. Restored by *Marshall Sisson*, 1937–8, for Professor Lionel Penrose, who gave the house to the National Trust in 1940.*

---

*Not regularly open.

THORINGTON HOUSE, to its W. White brick. Two storeys. Front range, 1815, of three bays by three, with pilaster strips on the entrance front. Behind this a lower three-bay range, an earlier house to which the front range was added. Then a one-bay range, 1998–2000, of the same height as the front.

WATERMILL, N of Thorington Hall. Weatherboarded. Three storeys, with lucam over the road. Dated inside 1760. Machinery intact. Red brick house of *c.* 1850.

STOWLANGTOFT

9060

ST GEORGE. A fine Perp building, tall and aisleless, and vigorous in the simplicity of its decorative enrichments. The church was under construction in 1387 and is said to have been built by Robert de Ashfield, who was buried in the chancel in 1401. Flushwork chequerboarding on buttresses and parapets, on the base of the walls and on the front of the S porch. The porch has in addition flushwork panelling. Its entrance is still entirely C14 in its responds and arch. Single niche above the entrance. E window of five lights with much panel tracery; nave and chancel with very tall two-light windows, also with panel tracery. Cambered roof with tie-beams in the church. Ceilure above the rood screen; money was left for its painting (which survives) in 1520. General restoration by *William White*, 1855–6. – FONT. Octagonal, early C14. Bowl with eight defaced figures under crocketed gables. – REREDOS. Alabaster and marble, with a deep relief carving of the Last Supper. Perhaps of 1855. To l. and r., panelling with eight carved oak PANELS with scenes of the Passion, Crucifixion, Resurrection and Ascension, and a separate panel of the Harrowing of Hell. Flemish, 1500 or a little earlier; given in 1887. – PULPIT. By *White*, 1856. Stone, with figures of the Evangelists. – SCREEN. Only the dado. Tall and traceried. The panels painted red and green. – STALLS. With close tracery on the ends and instead of poppyheads small standing figures: a preacher in the pulpit, a deacon, a man holding a candlestick, men holding shields, etc. Traceried fronts, and small seats with quatrefoil openings that served as resonating chambers. Also some misericords (a dragon, Emblems of the Evangelists, etc.). Probably not made for the church, and installed after the Reformation; Ixworth Priory has been suggested as their possible origin. – BENCHES. Fine set with traceried ends, poppyheads, and animals on the arms, also seated and kneeling figures. In chancel, a long bench with C17 carving. – ORGAN. Chancel organ by *Gray & Davison*, supplied in 1869. High Victorian Gothic, the oak case inlaid with texts and decoration, and brilliantly decorated pipes. It is almost identical to the organs designed for the firm by *J. P. Seddon* and shown at the International Exhibition, 1862. – DOOR. To the tower stair.

Completely iron-clad, in a wickerwork pattern; *c.* 1400. – WALL PAINTING. Huge St Christopher on the N wall. Almost completely faded, but a heron, lobster and fishing hermit have been noted. – STAINED GLASS. E window by *M. & A. O'Connor*, 1853–4. Chancel N and S by *A. L. Moore*, 1913 and †1906. Nave S †1934 by *Hugh Easton*. – Remaining nave windows by *Lucy Rickards*, daughter of Rev. Samuel Rickards, rector 1832–64. Mainly decorated quarries, with panels copied from illuminated works in the British Museum. She is said to have made and fixed the glass as well as designing it. – MONUMENTS. Paul D'Ewes by *Jan Janssen*, the contract of 1624 preserved (for £16 10s.). Stone, painted. Two kneeling wives facing each other beneath an arch. Between them, kneeling frontally, the husband within a smaller arch. Children in the 'predella'. Flat architecture ending in a flat broken segmental pediment. – Sir Willoughby D'Ewes †1685. Handsome, with twisted Composite columns and broken segmental pediment. Attributed to *Thomas Cartwright I* (GF). Relegated to the base of the tower. – War memorial. By *F. E. Howard*, 1920. Painted and gilded rood group, set in the blocked N doorway. Made by *A. R. Mowbray & Co.*, the figures carved by *Alec Miller*. – In churchyard, E of the chancel, chest tomb of the Cocksedge family, erected 1740. Bulbous, fluted corner pilasters and cherubs' heads. – In SE corner, Peter Fuller and stillborn son †1990 by *Glynn Williams*. Portland stone sculpture of an opening chestnut bud.

OLD RECTORY, W of the church. Under construction in 1832, for Rev. Samuel Rickards. White brick with cast-iron lintels. Two storeys. Five-bay S front, three-bay returns, with Doric portico on the W and two single-storey bays on the E. Single-storey LODGE.

ALMSHOUSES, opposite the church. Early C17. Red brick, single-storey with attics. Four doors and four three-light windows, all with cemented pediments. Pitched roof with three dormers.

READING ROOM COTTAGE, 250 yds E. Tudor-Gothic. Knapped flint with white brick dressings. Two storeys, with single-storey battlemented polygonal bays to l. and r. Gable with elaborate bargeboards and, at the apex, a book carved with the date, 1830.

STOWLANGTOFT HALL. By *J. H. Hakewill*, 1859, for Henry Wilson, and built by *Cubitt & Co.*; now a nursing home. White Woolpit brick with stone dressings. Symmetrical main block of seven bays with projecting wings to entrance and garden. Two storeys, with flat roof behind balustrade. Segment-headed windows, Ionic porch. Big asymmetrically placed Italianate tower between house and offices. Domed conservatory facing the offices towards the garden. Fine C18 fireplace in the entrance hall, presumably from the old house. STABLE YARD to the NE. On the E side of the yard a timber clock tower and below it a recessed balcony with open pediment and dovecote. About 350 yds S a large WALLED GARDEN near the site of the old hall. Partly dated 1829, partly 1862, but also including fragments of various dates, presumably from the old house.

STOWMARKET

A small market town midway on the road between Ipswich and Bury, alongside the River Gipping. The river was the key to Stowmarket's prosperity in the C19, for it was made navigable as far as the town in 1793. A large number of maltings sprang up as a result, as well as other industry. The arrival of the railway in 1846 provided another boost. Although most of the old maltings have been demolished and those remaining have been converted, the large CEDARS MALTINGS still operates on the SE edge of the town (Needham Road), in buildings designed by *Feilden & Mawson*, 1977. The plan of the town was very simple, with the main through road running SE–NW and lesser roads crossing it in the middle. Most of the through traffic was removed in 1975 when the A14 bypass opened, but an inner relief road was still thought necessary and opened in 1992 (Gipping Way). This benefited the centre but had a devastating effect on the E side of the town, cutting through it and destroying the old relationship between the town and the river.

The market place lies just to the S of the central crossroads, and the parish church, whose spire is visible from all parts of the town, just to the E of the market in a little close.

CHURCHES

ST PETER AND ST MARY. The unusual dedication commemorates a separate church, St Mary, that stood SE of St Peter and was demolished *c.* 1546. Dec W tower with flushwork arcading on the battlements. The timbers at the top of the tower and the base of the spire have been tree-ring-dated 1362–3. The extremely slender recessed spire was rebuilt in 1674 (with gallery part-way up), blew down in 1703, was replaced in 1712, taken down in 1975, and rebuilt (by *Andrew Anderson*) in 1994. Dec also the embattled N aisle and the chancel windows; the E window is shafted inside. Below the W window of the N aisle, three odd seven-foiled windows in a row. S aisle later than the N, and narrower, but reusing Dec windows from the old S wall. These have reticulated tracery with flowing motifs in the reticulation units, and flowing tracery. Of the same time the N and S porches, the former described as newly built in 1443, and the two-storey N vestry, originally a chapel on the ground floor. The front of the S porch decorated with flushwork arcading below, with flushwork diapering above. The N porch is similar, but less elaborate. Arcades of seven bays, Dec on the N, with quatrefoil piers with spurs in the diagonals and arches with wave mouldings. Hoodmoulds on leaf crockets. Perp S arcade, as the different details of the piers show. Restoration by *R. M. Phipson*, 1864–5, including partial re-roofing, re-seating and renewal of a number of the windows. New organ chamber and choir vestry by *H. J. Green*, 1884–5, extending the N aisle by a bay and joining up with the existing vestry. – PULPIT. Part of the C18 three-decker, dismantled in 1864–5, and incorporating bits from the rood screen. – REREDOS, ALTAR and COMMUNION RAILS. By *H. M. Cautley*, 1952, executed by *Ernest Barnes*. – S chapel REREDOS 1921 (war memorial). Panels with painted figures on gilded gesso backgrounds by *Eleanor Gribble*, with gilded gesso work. – DOOR to the vestry. C15, with carved leaf border. – BENCHES. Four traceried ends, with poppyheads, reused in 1864–5. – WIG STAND. Of iron, 1675. – STAINED GLASS. E window by *Camm Bros*, Birmingham, 1875. Chancel S by *Clayton & Bell*, 1878, and *A. L. Moore*, 1909. Four S aisle windows by *Helen Whittaker*, 2005–6, with *Keith Barley* (*Barley Studio*) and *Charles Smith* (lettering). – MONUMENTS. Many to the Tyrell family; there was no consecrated churchyard at Gipping, where they had their seat. In the E bay of the N aisle a low tomb-chest with indent of the brass of a female figure, probably Margaret Tyrell †1449. Big ogee arch, panelled inside. A variety of tracery in the spandrels. – Margaret English (*née* Tyrell), her brother and sister-in-law Thomas and Mary Tyrell and their ten children. Erected 1604. Kneeling figures, Margaret facing the rest of them across a prayer-desk. – Ann Tyrell †1638, aged eight. Brass. In her little shroud, crowned. The inscription runs:

> Deare Virgine Child Farewell Thy Mothers teares
> Cannot advance thy Memory, wch beares
> A Crowne above the Starres: yet I mvst Movrne,
> And shew the World my Offrings at thine Vrne.
> And, yet, nor meerly, as a Mother, make
> This sad Oblation for a Childs deare sake:
> For (Readers) know, shee was more, then a Child,
> In Infant-Age shee was as grave as Mild,
> All, that, in Children, Dvty call'd Might be,
> In her, was Frendship and trwe Pietie.
> By Reason and Religion Shee at Seaven,
> Prepar'd her selfe & Fovnd her way to Heaven.
> High Heaven thov hast her & didst take her hence
> The Perfect Patterne of Obedience,
> At those Few yeares, as onely lent to show,
> What Dvty yovng ones to their Parents owe,
> And (by her early Gravity, Appearing
> Fvll ripe for God, by serving & by Fearing)
> To teach the Old, to Fixe on Him their Trvst,
> Before their Bodies shall retvrne to Dvst.

– Dorothy, Lady Forth, †1641. Demi-figures of Dorothy and her third husband, William Tyrell (who erected the monument), turning to each other. Open books and a skull on the parapet between them. Their three children, already deceased, below them: one girl kneeling, two infants reclining. Attributed to *Edward Marshall* (AW). – Edmund Tyrell †1799. White marble tablet with urn and drapery, on black pyramid. By *John de Carle* (cf. Wollaston monument, Great Finborough).

OUR LADY (R.C.), Stricklands Road. By *A. E. Purdie*, 1883–4. Dec. Red brick with stone dressings. Small octagonal campanile at one corner. Only part of a very ambitious scheme, to include what would have been the largest R.C. church in Suffolk; the present church, two storeys, was planned as the school. Reordered by *Eric Sandon*, 1968–70, with single-storey extension along one side, creating a new worship area on the ground floor with first-floor hall.

BAPTIST CHURCH, Bury Street. 1813. Red brick. Two bays by three, extended to the rear 1836, under hipped roof of black pantiles. Gallery on three sides. New entrance and hall 1966.

METHODIST CHURCH, Regent Street. 1836. White brick. Gabled front with three round-arched windows, side with two tall arched windows. Extension to front 1965.

UNITED REFORMED CHURCH, Ipswich Street. 1953–5 by *A. D. Cooke*, replacing the Congregational chapel of 1861 by *F. Barnes* (destroyed 1941). Red brick, with a bold square tower asymmetrically decorated at the top. Brick front to the r. of this with three canted balconies above the three entrances and a further extension to the r. In the interior, oak in its natural colour dominates. The church has a recessed chancel with oak slatting up its back wall and along its ceiling. Pulpit and reading desk at the l. and r. angles of the chancel.

CEMETERY, Violet Hill Road. 1855. Two similar chapels by *E. G. Pennington* not, as is usually the case, placed symmetrically. E.E. Knapped flint with red and white-brick dressings and large timber porches.

PUBLIC BUILDINGS

MILTON HOUSE (Town Council offices), Milton Road South. The vicarage until the 1860s and council offices since 1974. Timber-framed, possibly C14 in its oldest parts but predominantly C17, enlarged to picturesque effect in the mid C19 and less picturesquely in the 1990s. The C19 alterations were due to Rev. A. G. H. Hollingsworth, vicar 1837–59 and author of a history of Stowmarket (1844): first in 1837 by *Ephraim Rednall* with *Daniel Revett*, then in 1850 by *Francis Betts*, the latter including a single-storey extension with an ornamental square bay at the s end. Rev. Thomas Young, vicar 1628–55, was tutor to John Milton, and the large mulberry tree in the garden is said to have been planted by the poet.

MUSEUM OF EAST ANGLIAN LIFE. See p. 510.

HIGH SCHOOL, Onehouse Road. 1955–6 by *East Suffolk County Architect's Dept.* Three storeys. Red brick. Curtain-walled front with continuous glazing.

Former HOSPITAL, originally workhouse. *See* Onehouse.

Stowmarket, Milton House.
Etching by W. Hagreen after F. Russel, 1844

RAILWAY STATION. An elaborate piece of Jacobean architecture by *F. Barnes*, 1846–9. Red brick with yellow dressings. Symmetrical, with two-storey houses at either end of the broad frontage, and in the middle a lower entrance block. Shaped gables to all parts, and polygonal towers at the outer ends.

PERAMBULATION

The layout of Stowmarket means that there is little alternative but to make a series of forays from the centre. From the s door of the church there is an enticing view along Buttermarket to the Market Place, but it would be as well to walk first round the CHURCHYARD, a pleasant backwater. In the SW corner the former CORN EXCHANGE (now John Peel Centre for Creative Arts), rebuilt by *F. Barnes* in 1872. White brick with red brick decoration and rows of narrow round-arched windows. Lofty interior with decorative cast-iron roof trusses. Along the s side ST PETER'S HALL, first built as a school in 1835 with various alterations and additions. Red brick with hoodmoulded windows. Nice pedimented doorway (late C19?) with pilasters and architrave of tiles on edge. Terrace of early C19 white-brick houses along the E side.

STATION ROAD runs along the N side of the churchyard. No. 3, on the bend opposite the NW corner of the church, is late C14, timber-framed and plastered, with gabled range to the l. over carriage entrance added in the early C15. Nos. 7–9

STOWMARKET: PERAMBULATION

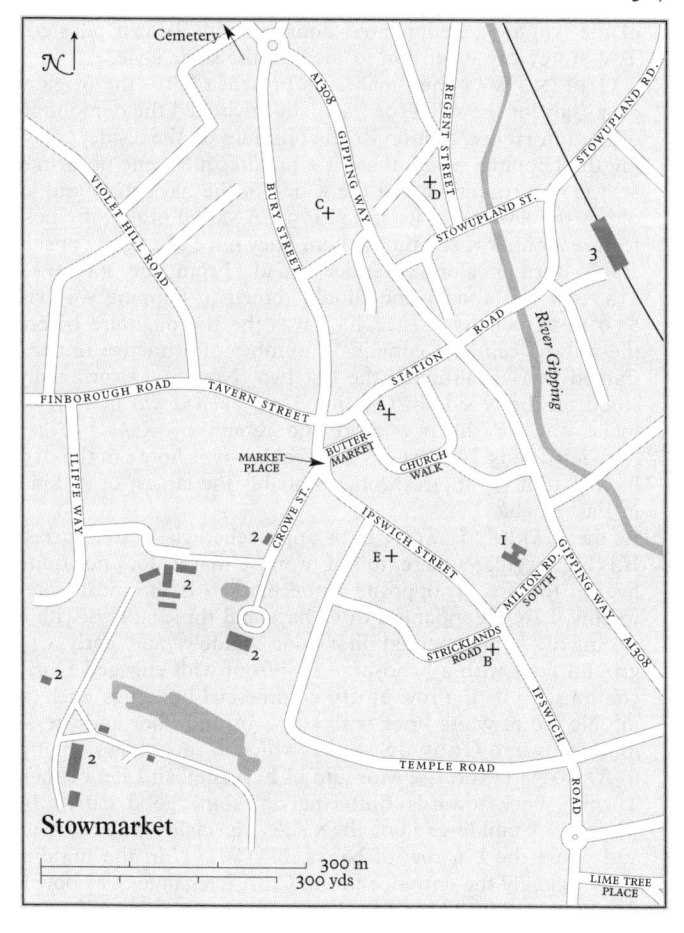

A St Peter & St Mary
B Our Lady (R.C.)
C Baptist Church
D Methodist Church
E United Reformed Church

1 Milton House
2 Museum of East Anglian Life
3 Railway Station

is a timber-framed C16 house with two cross-wings, Nos. 11–13 also C15 or C16 but entirely hidden behind red brick and tile-hanging of 1903. Further E, just where the road starts to slope down towards the Gipping, No. 17, built as Stevens' Brewery. Mid-C19. Two storeys. White-brick front with pilasters and sunk panels where there are not windows. Down the hill, on the s side, LYNTON HOUSE, the Stowmarket house of the Tyrell family of Gipping. Early Georgian, of five bays and two and a half storeys, the half storey being above the cornice. White brick, with red brick dressings and red vertical lacing of the windows. Pedimented doorway with Tuscan pilasters. Two-storey C19 extension to the l. in the same style.

GIPPING WAY then makes its presence felt – the original proposals for the relief road actually envisaged the demolition of Lynton House. Station Road continues on the E side, crossing the Gipping, where there is a picturesque scene of former MALTINGS running along the E side of the navigation and as old as the navigation itself, i.e. 1793. A varied group, the best feature a rather rustic timber kiln. They once extended considerably further along Prentice Road. From the RAILWAY STATION (*see* above) one should return to Gipping Way via STOWUPLAND STREET, which was the thoroughfare before the railway came. It contains a number of attractive timber-framed houses, although the last two (Nos. 11–13) originally stood on the w side of Gipping Way; taken down in 1991 to make way for the new road and rebuilt by *Ronald Geary Associates*, 1995. Nos. 22–26 is a Wealden-type house of the C15, its hall 56 ft (17 metres) long, probably the largest of its kind in East Anglia.

Now the MARKET PLACE can be approached via Buttermarket. It is an irregular square, full of promise that it does not quite live up to. No. 14, opposite Buttermarket, is the most noteworthy, Late Georgian, of three bays and three storeys with a pediment, a pedimented first-floor window, and early C19 ground floor with a handsome shopfront with engaged Doric columns. To its l. a row of C19 commercial buildings, including No. 20 of white brick with stone ground floor and dressings, leads into CROWE STREET, which in turn draws one up to ABBOT'S HALL (*see* Museum of East Anglian Life, below). Turning back towards Buttermarket, some good early C19 white-brick buildings along the N side, especially on the corner, and along the E a row of banks. NATWEST, in the middle, was originally the entrance to the Corn Exchange (*see* above), first built *c.* 1835. Three bays. Upper storey with Ionic pilasters. Ground floor remodelled in ashlar by *J. A. Sherman*, 1927. But opposite here, along the sw side, the picture is very different, with mediocre shops of the mid 1960s, an impression sustained along IPSWICH STREET to the SE, even though there are some older buildings along its NE side, e.g. the seven-bay front of the former Fox Hotel (OLD FOX YARD). The United Reformed church (*see* p. 505), although good in itself, does not look right in the narrow street of a market town, any more than the rather plain REGAL THEATRE (originally cinema) of 1935 with its boxy red brick front, 250 yds SE. Rather better, between the church and the theatre, is the POST OFFICE of 1937: the usual *Office of Works* Neo-Georgian, of red brick with stone dressings and urns on the corners of the parapet, and no doubt by *D. N. Dyke*. MILTON ROAD SOUTH, opposite the Post Office, was originally the drive to the vicarage (*see* above, Milton House).

Just beyond the Regal, at the beginning of IPSWICH ROAD on the NE side, THE LIMES (No. 27), a C16 timber-framed and plastered house with a mid-C18 front. Two storeys and attics. Five bays with Tuscan porch. Single-storey early C19 additions to l. and r., one with an arched doorway, the other with an arched Gothick window. Down a lane to the side former MALTINGS, a late C16 timber-framed barn converted in the late C18. It was originally served by a cut to the Gipping. s of Hollingsworth Road, on the same side, LIME TREE PLACE, described in White's *Directory* of 1874 as 'a handsome modern suburb'. White brick. Large detached houses and more modest terraces. Opposite, a large red brick house in extensive grounds, RED GABLES, originally Woodfield, *c.* 1858–9. Red brick. Two storeys and attics. Front with two tall, narrow straight gables and a lower, gabled, two-storey porch. Another tall gable on the s return and a two-storey canted bay with polygonal roof. Additions on the N side by *Eade & Johns*, 1893.

Back now to the crossroads N of the Market Place. BURY STREET runs N, winding, with nice houses here and there, but nothing special. The most prominent building is No. 12, by *P. J. Turner* for the Co-operative Society, 1902–3. Two plastered gables project over two storeys of red brick. Below the projection three shallow curved oriels. w from the crossroads is TAVERN STREET. On the N side the former COURT HOUSE of 1850–1. Tudor-Gothic, of red brick with white-brick dressings. On the s side THE ROOKERY (No. 15), early C17 but altered in 1770. Five bays, two storeys. Pedimented doorway with Tuscan pilasters. Two-storey bow against the r. gable. Inside, a panelled Adam-style room and handsome staircase with three fluted balusters to each tread. Further out, on the N side, STOW HOUSE, mid-C18, restored 1986. Two storeys and attics. Five-bay front of plastered brick. Doorcase with open pediment. Across Violet Hill Road, at the start of FINBOROUGH ROAD, WELLINGTON HOUSE. Timber-framed, encased in red brick. Five bays and two storeys with early C20 gabled porch. The house is said to have been built in 1660, but some of its timbers seem older, possibly mid-C15, and it contains remains of painted decoration in the form of imitation textile. Early C19 staircase with two turned balusters to each tread.

CEDARS HOTEL, Needham Road, 1 m. SE of the church. Timber-framed and plastered, dating back to the late C15. Early C18 front of three widely spaced bays with a jolly doorway. Fluted Composite pilasters and swan-neck pediment. Early C17 range to the l. of painted brick, and further additions of 1977.

THE STRICKLANDS, Stricklands Road. Once on the s edge of the town. Two parallel blocks, both of three bays and two storeys. On the NE side, C17 timber-framed and plastered with C18 sashes and doorcase, framed by the overhanging eaves and projecting white-brick return walls added in the late C18 or early C19. On the SW side, white brick with pilaster strips. The building in the grounds to the N (KENSINGTON COURT) was built by *Frend & Keogh*, 1887–9, for St Ursula's Convent, which then occupied The Stricklands.

VALLEY FARM, Combs Lane, ⅔ m. SW. Lobby-entrance house of *c.* 1630, with timbers partly exposed, extended by one bay to the r. in the C18. Two storeys and attics. Two-storey porch, originally central, with balustraded sides originally open. Jettied, with carved bressumer. On the rear elevation a three-storey staircase tower, also originally central. The porch and the staircase were probably added some ten or twenty years after the house was built. In the hall chamber, a wall painting of the Sacrifice of Isaac, based on Holbein's *Icones*. – EDGAR'S FARM (*see* below) stood about 300 yds ESE.

MUSEUM OF EAST ANGLIAN LIFE, Iliffe Way. Established in 1962, and occupying nearly 80 acres (33 ha) on what was part of the Abbot's Hall estate. ABBOT'S HALL itself was given to the museum in 2004. It is of the early C18 (detached brick with incised date 1709). Until the Reformation the estate belonged to St Osyth Priory, Essex, and after passing through various hands came in 1681 to Charles Blosse, of a family of Ipswich cloth merchants. It was he who rebuilt the house, which is of brown brick with red brick dressings. Five bays and two storeys, with a hipped roof and five dormers, the dormers with alternating triangular and segmental pediments. Stone doorcase with swan-neck pediment and a festoon between the two ends. Staircase with two twisted balusters to each tread. Additions on the W side of *c.* 1880 and *c.* 1910. Red and white-brick STABLES to the W, also *c.* 1880. W of that the aisled TITHE BARN. C15, but reusing some older timbers. Six bays, formerly longer. C19 weatherboarding. E of Abbot's Hall a WALLED GARDEN, and S a CANAL with a small rectangular island on which stands a square red brick SUMMERHOUSE that is probably contemporary with the Hall. Raised terrace walk round the canal, and a smaller square pond separated from the canal by a causeway. N of the house, by the entrance from the town, CROWE STREET COTTAGES, of about the same date as Abbot's Hall. Timber-framed and plastered, preserved in their state as servants' cottages.

Beyond the gardens of Abbot's Hall is an area containing a number of historic buildings moved from other places in East Anglia. These include:

ALTON WATERMILL. Early C19 timber-framed and weather-boarded mill. Two storeys and attic, with lucam at one end. Cart lodge of the same date. Red brick mill house dating from 1765, with C19 addition. From Stutton (E), moved in 1973 by *John Weller* in advance of the construction of Alton Water.

EASTBRIDGE WINDPUMP. Weatherboarded smock mill. Mid-C19, probably by *Robert Martin* of Beccles. From Leiston (E); rescued following collapse in 1977.

EDGAR'S FARM. Just the windowless hall of a mid-C14 house. Two bays, aisled, open to the crown-post roof. Good moulded capitals to the octagonal arcade posts. There was formerly a

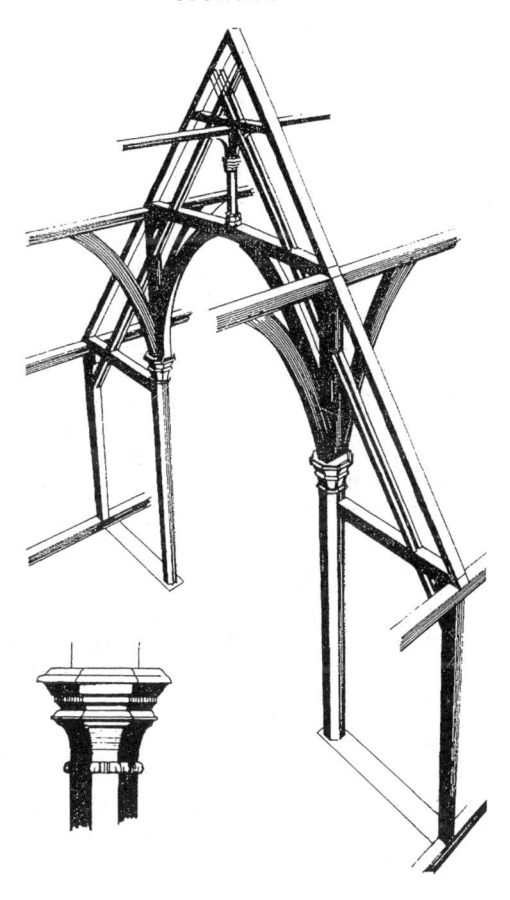

Stowmarket, Edgar's Farm, timber framing, details.
Drawing by C. Hewett

third bay at the lower end. Moved in 1971 from Combs Lane, about 700 yds s of its present location.

GREAT MOULTON CHAPEL. Tin tabernacle of *c.* 1890 by *Boulton & Paul*. From Great Moulton, Norfolk. Reopened 1995.

GRUNDISBURGH SMITHY. Timber-framed and weatherboarded blacksmith's shop of *c.* 1750.

MORTLOCK BUILDING. Timber-framed workshop, clad in corrugated iron, *c.* 1920, built for Frank Mortlock & Sons, engineers, Lavenham. Dismantled 1994, re-erected 2002–5.

ROBERT BOBY BUILDING. Large engineering workshop of *c.* 1877 from Robert Boby's St Andrew's Works, Bury St Edmunds (closed 1972). Two storeys. Weatherboarding, with ground floor of flint with red brick dressings. Rebuilt 1984–5 by *James Blackie*.

SETTLING HOUSE. Octagonal timber pavilion from the cattle market, Bury St Edmunds. 1864, dismantled 2007, rebuilt 2011.

STOWUPLAND

Described by White's *Directory* (1844) as 'a pleasant suburb to Stowmarket'; until the previous year it had not had a church of its own.

HOLY TRINITY. 1842–3 by *T. M. Nelson*. White brick, in the lancet style, with a short chancel and a W tower-cum-porch with splay-foot spire. W gallery on cast-iron columns. – FONT. C14, octagonal. From Creeting All Saints, dem. 1800. – PULPIT. Very ornate, Flemish, early C17, with scenes from the life of Christ and fantastical caryatids. Five sides of an original six. – STALLS and ALTAR RAIL. By *H. M. Cautley*, 1956, made by *Ernest Barnes*. They also did much of the nave seating, 1956–65. – ROYAL ARMS. Of 1816–37. Cast iron, painted, probably by *Coleman & Wallis* of Colchester. – MONUMENT. War memorial by *Miss Rope* (Ellen Mary?) of Blaxhall (E), 1927. Prettily painted board with a semicircular top in which is set a relief panel of two kneeling angels holding a tablet inscribed 'These held not their lives dear'.

OLD VICARAGE, almost opposite. By *R. M. Phipson*, 1873–4. Rather plain red brick.

HIGH SCHOOL. By *Suffolk County Architect's Dept*, 1976–80 (job architects *Derek Coverdale* (in succession to *Jos Dalley*) and *Peter Brooks*). Steel frame construction (SEAC system), and ground floor of blockwork, but otherwise deferring to its semi-rural setting with black weatherboarding on the first floor and steeply pitched pantile roofs.

COLUMBINE HALL, ½ m. NNW. Enchanting moated house, once larger. What remains of the original, dating from *c*. 1390, is an L-plan block in the NW corner of the site, built on the very edge of the moat. The ground-floor is of brick and flint, the jettied upper storey timber-framed and plastered. Near the S end of the W wing a gatehouse passageway, now blocked towards the moat, but formerly leading to a bridge; this was probably originally the main entrance, with a hall range opposite. Flint revetting continues E along the N side, suggesting that the house extended further in this direction; now there is a lower timber-framed structure, once detached, perhaps a kitchen or chapel, added in the early C17. Dog-leg stair with robust balusters of the same date. Mid-C19 E range, red brick with white-brick dressings. Outside the moat, to the S, farm buildings including two early C18 timber-framed and weather-boarded barns; also the C17-style CLOCK TOWER, a conversion by *Melvyn Smith*, 2000, of a plain C20 brick farm office.

STOWUPLAND HALL, ½ m. NE. Early C19 white brick. Two and a half storeys. Three-bay entrance front with Ionic portico.

STRADISHALL

ST MARGARET. Small, but with a clerestory. Norman nave and chancel, the chancel enlarged in the mid C13 and further improved with Dec windows. N aisle (see the E window) and W tower of c. 1300, S aisle mid-C14. S porch of raw timber, C14 but mostly renewed. Main restoration by *Robert Last* of Melton, 1857–8, including re-seating. N aisle restored and re-roofed by *Detmar Blow*, 1914. – FONT. Octagonal, Perp, very closely decorated. – SCREEN. Only the dado remains, and of the l. part only the back. Parts of the tracery framed nearby.* – BENCH ENDS and COMMUNION RAIL. Fragments built into the chancel stalls. Some bench ends also at the W end of the nave. – WALL PAINTING. St Christopher (N wall), fragments of a decorative scheme in the chancel, and a ?C17 text. – ROYAL ARMS. Dated 1788, but originally of James I. – MONUMENTS. Two pairs of tablets by *de Carle* of Bury for the Ranger family, c. 1822–30 and 1835–45, the later pair especially elegant.

Former SCHOOL, 100 yds ENE. 1880–1, by *Lot Jackaman*. Red brick, small. Curious gables, with stepped brickwork like bargeboards.

HIGHPOINT PRISON, 1½ m. WSW. On the site of RAF Stradishall, opened 1938, and adapted for use as a prison in 1973–7. The N part of the site includes three H blocks originally built as RAF officers' accommodation. On the S side of the road, as well as various former RAF buildings, a so-called 'house-block' of 1985 comprising four pairs of short wings with central dining and association areas. Additional blocks by the *Directorate of Works*, 1991–2.

STRATFORD ST MARY

Church and village are now separated by the A12, an unfortunate consequence to set against the benefits of removing the traffic from the doorsteps of both. The church lies immediately along what was the old main road, E of the new one.

ST MARY. Large, Perp, restored 1876–9 by *Henry Woodyer*. W tower, nave with tall clerestory and aisles, chancel and chancel

---

*Some panels formerly incorporated in the windows of the adjacent rectory (now Bridge House), but these appear to be no longer *in situ*.

chapels. Much flushwork, especially on the N side towards the road. The Perp building history is known from bequests and from flushwork inscriptions. Bequests for the S aisle by William Clerk, clothworker, 1458, and John Smyth, 1468, and for the S door by John Leyre of Shotley, 1478. N aisle paid for by the clothier Thomas Mors, who in his will of 1500 asked to be buried in it, which he 'did make of new'. He also left money for making the clerestory. His wife Margery, who died in 1510, left money for building the porch, as did Joan Norcott in 1523 and Margery Marler in 1526; it is dated 1532 and carries the initials of another merchant, John Smyth. The N chapel was given by Thomas Mors' son Edward, who died in 1526. He left money for his father's N aisle to be extended E to match the S chapel. Flushwork on the walls of the N chapel, dated 1530, asks for prayers for Edward and Alys Mors, continued along the N aisle for Thomas and Margaret Mors, dated 1499. In addition Mors' merchant's mark can be seen, and the unusual feature of an almost complete alphabet. Woodyer continued the tradition by dating the W tower, which he largely rebuilt, 1878. NW stair-turret corbelled out and ending in a square turret with its own pinnacles. The stone details of the body of the church also much renewed. Chancel E wall rebuilt, also the S aisle and S chancel aisle with new windows on this side. Nave roof repaired and clerestory renewed, and battlements added to nave and S aisle to match the Perp battlements on the N aisle. The elaborate tracery in the E and W arches of the N porch is also Woodyer's; they were previously open, to allow processions round the church (cf. Aldeburgh (E)).

Interior with four-bay arcade. Thin piers with four thin shafts carrying small capitals. The broad hollows between the shafts are carried into the arches without capitals. The apex of each arch an ogee point. On these rise shafts between each pair of clerestory windows. Shafts also stand on the pier shafts towards the nave, so that all clerestory windows are framed by shafts (cf. Dedham, Essex). Low-pitched roof. Angel figures against the middles of the tie-beams added by *Woodyer*, carved by the clerk of works, *Giles Vinnell*. Chancel arch rebuilt by Woodyer, higher and wider than the old one. The chancel chapels have piers similar to those in the nave, but four-centred instead of two-centred arches.

FURNISHINGS. REREDOS. By *Woodyer*, carved by *Wheeler Bros* of Reading; also SEDILIA, CREDENCE and PULPIT. Stone, the reredos and pulpit with panels of Devonshire marble. – FONT. 1858. Stone and coloured marbles, a showy affair. – SCREENS. By Woodyer; fragments of an original screen displayed in the S chapel (bequest for rood figures, based on those at Dedham, 1500). – WALL PAINTING. By *Alexander Jamieson*, 1904. Oil on canvas, above the chancel N arcade. Three scenes on the theme of the Eucharist. Jamieson may also have been responsible for painted decoration elsewhere in the church, e.g. on the small W gallery, dated 1905. – TILES. In chancel, by *Minton*. – STAINED GLASS. E window by *Powell & Sons*, 1898. Other windows with Powells' patterned glass, that at the W end of the N aisle incorporating C15 fragments. – BRASS. Edward Crane †1558 in civilian dress, and wife Elizabeth. 20 in. (51 cm.) figures.

In UPPER STREET, W of the A12, on the S side of the road, ANCIENT HOUSE and PRIEST'S HOUSE, *c.* 1500, similar but of slightly different heights, one bay wide, with exposed timbers and jettied gables facing the road. Window tracery and W porch not original, probably part of the mid-C20 restoration by *Grace Faithfull Roper*. On the N side, further W, TALLY HO CORNER, a 1930s housing scheme by *Maurice Chesterton*. Painted brick. Two-storey houses and 'semi-bungalows'. After another 275 yds the road turns sharply S. On the corner, the former KINGS ARMS pub, facing S, C16 with a large early C19 canted bay, and facing E, GOOSE ACRE (formerly Corner House), with exposed timbers and two projecting cross-wings, also C16. The road continues S as LOWER STREET; on the r. a large concrete PUMPING STATION, *c.* 1935, in the Modern Movement style of the South Essex Waterworks Co. (cf. Langham, Essex). In front, a cast-iron MILEPOST by *J. Garrett* of Ipswich, 1831. 200 yds S on the E side, VALLEY HOUSE, early C19 white brick. Two storeys and three bays with Doric porch. Hipped slate roof with octagonal glazed lantern. On the same side, 150 yds further S, large former MALTINGS at right angles to the street, red brick with white-brick front. Then BAY HOUSE, early C19 painted brick, with two Doric porches and between them a full-height bow. At the end of the village, back on the W side, WEAVERS HOUSE, a good early C16 house with exposed timbers and jettied front with moulded bressumer. Restored in the 1930s, incorporating windows and other features from elsewhere.

GLEBE HOUSE, ½ m. WNW. Former rectory, dated 1870. Tudor-Gothic. Red brick with stone dressings. Arched windows, paired, with hoodmoulds. Straight gables and tall chimneys. The N range incorporates the remains of the previous rectory by *Thomas Fulcher*, 1783–4. Halfway between it and the church the former BOARD SCHOOL (now offices) by *F. Barnes*, 1877. Red brick. Central feature of a large gable with two pointed windows separated by a buttress. The buttress supports a gabled panel with weathervane.

LOWE HILL HOUSE (formerly Brook Farm), ⅝ m. WNW. L-plan house with exposed timbers. Early C15 four-bay range, to which were added, at its W end and at right angles, a hall and cross-wing, *c.* 1480. The cross-wing was demolished *c.* 1590 and some of its timbers reused to construct a new parlour and solar, jettied to the W, in place of the two western bays of the original range. The ground-floor room of this part contains a surviving section of Tudor wall painting of intricate strapwork. The adjoining room, in the older part of the house, has early C17 panelling painted with imitative marquetry.

STRATFORD HILLS, ½ m. NNW. By *Eric Sandon* (job architect *R. A. Miller*), c. 1960.* Brick, with timber-framed and timber-clad upper storey. This projects, and Sandon saw the house as being in the tradition of medieval timber-framed houses, with a central full-height hall flanked by two-storey wings. The wings are slightly canted to catch the sun.

Two good timber-framed houses SE of the church, on the road to Dedham: RAVENYS, late C15 or early C16, and WHALLEYS, mainly mid-C16. Both plastered. Ravenys has some brick-nogging, and a large bargeboarded gable. Underbuilt jetty. Whalleys is still jettied, with moulded bressumer, and has a gabled cross-wing with two jetties.

STUSTON

ALL SAINTS. Round tower with contemporary Dec octagonal top. Chancel rebuilt 1861–2, including N transept on the foundations of a medieval oratory; probably by *Thomas Jeckyll*, although *E. B. Lamb* had prepared a scheme for rebuilding the whole church. The notable feature of the new work, described by Pevsner as 'truly terrible', is the use internally of red, yellow and black brick for the chancel arch and rere-arches. Thatched roof replaced with slate. Nave windows renewed 1864, N vestry 1865. – PULPIT. By *Rev. J. Barham Johnson*, rector of Welborne (Norfolk), 1862. Octagonal, with traceried panels. – STAINED GLASS. E and tower windows by *Heaton & Butler*, 1862. Two nave windows by *William Wailes*, 1864. Nave S †1888 by *J. & J. King* of Norwich, 1912. – MONUMENT. Sir John Castleton Bt †1705 and wife Bridget †1726; erected 1727. Standing monument. Two busts standing on a ledge and above them, against the pedimented back wall, three oval medallions with the portraits of their children, who predeceased them.

OLD RECTORY, W of the church. C16, refaced and enlarged 1864–5 by *Jeckyll* for Rev. E. H. Paget. Tall thin panels of flint in a framework of red brick, and quirky detailing to the windows and eaves.

SUDBURY

Sudbury sits comfortably in a loop of the River Stour, an elevated spot that was settled by Early Bronze Age farmers c. 2000 B.C. The site was fortified in the Iron Age and again in the C1 A.D.;

---

*Described and illustrated in Sandon's *Suffolk Houses* (1977), where it is dated on different pages 1960 and 1965.

the influence of the banks and ditches on the layout of the town centre is still apparent. By the C8 the town had become an important ecclesiastical centre; Bishop Ælfhun of Dunwich died here *c.* 798, and Æthelred II established a mint which was active from 978 until the C12. From the C14 Sudbury prospered greatly from the wool and cloth trade, thanks to its location on the Stour; and although the wool trade declined in the C17, the town's fortunes revived at the end of the C18 with the arrival of silk weaving, for which Sudbury is still famous. Both wool and silk have left their mark on the town's buildings.

CHURCHES

There are three medieval parish churches: St Gregory, the mother church, by the green at the W end of the town; St Peter, a chapel of ease that grew in importance after the market was moved near it in the C14; and All Saints, built to service a suburb that developed near the Stour.

ST GREGORY. There was a church here in the C10, and very possibly before that, and it was at least partially rebuilt in the C14; but in its present form its history is closely connected with the Thebaud or Theobald family, and in particular Simon (known as Simon Sudbury), consecrated Bishop of London in 1362, and Archbishop of Canterbury from 1375 until 1381, when he was beheaded by the rebels during the Peasants' Revolt. He and his brother John founded a college W of the church (*see* below), which led to the church being remodelled, with the old chancel being rebuilt as a chapel for the college during the mastership of William Wood, 1467–91. Archbishop Sudbury's HEAD is preserved in the vestry.

The church is Perp, built mainly of flint. W tower with diagonal buttresses with five set-offs, and taller SE stair-turret; money for its building was bequeathed in 1384, although it was probably started at least fifty years before that. Much brick among the stone and flint, thought to be Saxon brick reused from the earlier church. At the foot of the tower on the S side a MONUMENT, clearly not *in situ*. Tomb-chest with shields in lozenges and recessed niche above with indents of brasses. Nave and aisles, clerestory not with doubled windows. N aisle rebuilt by Simon Sudbury, the eastern bay (built to house his parents' tomb) completed in 1365. The bosses on the roof are of terracotta, an unusually early and probably isolated use of the material in England. S aisle widened as part of the college rebuilding scheme, after *c.* 1425, which meant rebuilding the S porch with, on its E side, a chapel (cf. St Peter and St Paul, Clare, and St Botolph, Cambridge). There is evidence to suggest that the chapel (St Anne's) already existed as a freestanding building and that the reused windows on the W side of the porch and the E side of the chapel came from it. The later C15 chancel, which is as long as the nave, has tall transomed windows, the lower parts blind to accommodate high stalls and reredos (no longer extant). Brick vestry to the N of the E end, early C16. Inside, C14 arcades of four bays remaining from the earlier church. Polygonal attachments to the piers towards nave and aisle without capitals, semicircular shafts with capitals towards the arch openings. The capitals on the S side simpler and earlier, on the N finer. Nice cambered nave roof, the E bays ceiled. Flat chancel ceiling, panelled with a pattern of squares and elongated hexagons, and elaborately carved cornice, more Renaissance than Gothic in character; painted decoration by *Campbell, Smith & Co.*, 1966, as part of restoration by *Potter & Hare*. Partial restoration by *William Butterfield*, 1860–2, including nave BENCHES* and ALTAR RAIL.

FURNISHINGS. FONT. Perp, octagonal. Bowl shallow with tracery motifs, probably late C14. – FONT COVER. Of *c.* 1450, and one of the finest medieval font covers in the country. Tall, with two tiers of panels with ogee arches and gables, the upper tier placed so that its panels stand above the edges of the panels below. Money was left towards painting and gilding it in 1533. – SCREEN. One surviving panel from the medieval screen, with a painting of Master John Schorne trapping the devil in his boot (bequest for painting rood beam 1457). More panels of the dado (with C19 painted figures) used for the return backs of the cut-down STALLS. These have heads on the arms, MISERICORDS with heads, etc. – PULPIT. By *F. P. Earee*, 1925, made by *Ernest Beckwith*. Octagonal, with Perp tracery. – SOUTH DOOR. With tracery and a trail border. – STATIONS OF THE CROSS. By *Nicholas Mynheer*, 1999, installed 2001. Small stone panels carved in deep relief. – PAINTINGS. Figures of saints by *Aveling Green*, brother of the rector; remains of a more general scheme of decoration, 1885. – LIGHT FITTINGS. Elegant wrought-iron brackets by *J. S. Corder*, 1888. Gas, converted to electricity. – STAINED GLASS. S aisle E window †1880 by *Lavers, Barraud & Westlake*; also no doubt the chancel E window. Two S windows by *Heaton, Butler & Bayne*, 1897 and 1921 (war memorial). – MONUMENTS. Incised slab with Normano-French inscription to Segeyna, wife of Robert de Quintin; early C14 (S aisle). – Thomas Carter †1706 (S chapel). Fine tomb-chest with backplate, the latter with cherubs reclining on a broken scrolly pediment. – John Newman †1814 by *John Bacon Jun.* and Capt. Rodney Sims †1834 by *Charles Harding* of Ballingdon. Both with draped urn.

To the W of the church the GATEWAY to the college founded by Archbishop Sudbury and his brother John Theobald in 1375. Stone arch in brick surround, much restored; the top, with its stone cresting, was rebuilt *c.* 1836. The college was surrendered to the king in 1544 and the surviving buildings were demolished in 1836 for the workhouse (*see* Walnuttree Hospital, p. 522). – WAR MEMORIAL, S of the church, by *Sir Reginald Blomfield*, 1921, executed by *F. J. Lindley*. Stone 'Cross

---

*Now replaced with chairs.

of Sacrifice' with bronze sword. E of the church, overlooking The Croft, STATUE of Bishop Ælfhun (*see* above). Seated stone figure by *Alan Micklethwaite*, 1998.

ST PETER (Churches Conservation Trust). Although large and convincingly expressing the wealth of a prosperous wool-manufacturing town, this church was built as a chapel of ease to St Gregory, originally in the mid C12, but rebuilt as part of Elizabeth de Burgh's expansion of the town and the formation of a new market place after 1322 (*see* Perambulation 1). Work was interrupted by the Black Death and the church was not finished until about 1450, proceeding as usual from E to W. Earlier parts Dec (chancel clerestory, chancel arch), the later parts Perp. A will of 1467 specified that money was to be spent on panelling, paving, a ringing loft and a large bell, indicating that the basic structure was then complete. The W tower, with its angle buttresses and stepped battlements, stands proudly at the top of the market place, embraced by the N and S aisles. A pretty copper spirelet of 1810 was taken down in 1968. Clerestory with no doubling of windows. Two-storey S porch with three niches in the front, the figures added as part of restoration by *C. G. Hare*, 1911. The ground floor was intended to be vaulted. No N porch. Chancel with N and S chapels and vestry below. Tall arcades of five rather narrow bays, the piers with four attached shafts and four small hollows in the diagonals. Nave roof original, ceiled and panelled with fan-shaped coving between the tie-beams. The church was restored by *William Butterfield* in 1854–9, including the removal of C18 furnishings, and the chancel by *Bodley* in 1897–8. Unfortunately most of Bodley's decoration was destroyed in 1964, part of a restoration by *Potter & Hare*.

FURNISHINGS. FONT. Octagonal, Perp. The bowl with cusped pointed quatrefoils. Money was left for the 'new' font in 1456. – REREDOS. By *Bodley*. Tall, gilded and coloured. – CHANCEL SCREEN. Probably by *Thomas Gooch*, i.e. of the last quarter of the C15. Base with panels of saints, heavily restored by *Charles Castell* for *Butterfield*. The cresting of the screen also survives, fixed above the chancel arch. – PARCLOSE SCREENS. Also by *Gooch*. Very rich, though with only one-light divisions. But the arches are broad and there is much cusped tracery. – PULPIT. By *Butterfield*. Oak. – DOORS. S and N doors with tracery. – PAINTINGS. Moses and Aaron by *Robert Cardinall*. From the former reredos of 1715.* – STAINED GLASS. By *Hardman*: E window 1854, W 1860–1, N aisle 1862 and 1880. – MONUMENT. Rev. H. W. Wilkinson †1851. By *Keogh* of Sudbury. Elaborately Gothic (behind organ).

ALL SAINTS, Church Street. At the foot of the town, built to serve the new parish that was created when nearby Ballingdon Bridge was constructed in the mid C12, and rebuilt in the early C14. Perp W tower with big angle buttresses and big SE stair-turret. Nave and aisles with clerestory, the rebuilt N aisle

---

*Other parts of the reredos reused in the rectory, Great Waldingfield (q.v.).

referred to in bequests of 1459 and 1465. Early C14 chancel with family chapels N (Eden family) and s (Felton family). The former was building in 1465, but was remodelled after the Felton chapel was built, *c.* 1480: the eastern portion was adapted as a two-storey vestry, with barred E windows, and the arch into it from the chancel was blocked. Arcades of five bays, the piers of the same design as at St Peter (*see* above), but here in the arch moulding small suspended shields and fleurons. Good cambered roofs in nave and aisles. Chancel roof raised in 1882 during restoration by *W. M. Fawcett* to accommodate the new E window. – FONT. Octagonal, Perp, simple. – PULPIT. A fine Perp piece. Traceried panels. Restored 1848 by *Henry Ringham*, who added the IHS motif and stairs, following a design by *C. F. Sprague*. – READER'S DESKS. With some Perp tracery panels. – SCREENS. To N and s chapels. Large, with one-light divisions and much cusped and crocketed detail. Probably by *Thomas Gooch* (cf. St Peter). – LECTERN. 1921 (war memorial), carved by *H. C. Mauldon*. Oak angel. – DOORS. N and W doors with tracery. – WALL PAINTING. Entertaining but deteriorating family tree of the Eden family in the N chapel; early C17. – STAINED GLASS. E window by *Cox, Sons, Buckley & Co.*, 1882. Tower window by *Kempe & Co.*, 1927. – MONUMENTS. Rev. John Gibbon †1744. Ornately decorated with swags, cherubs' heads, etc. Open pediment. In tower; originally against E wall of s chapel. – Thomas Fenn of Ballingdon †1818. Draped tablet with medallion of the Good Samaritan. By *Bacon & Manning*.

OUR LADY AND ST JOHN (R.C.), The Croft. Brick with stone dressings and banding. E (ritual W) front with a pretty recessed porch turret on the l., carrying a fancy spirelet, very typical of *c.* 1900, but designed in 1893 by that excellent architect *Leonard Stokes*. Plainer sides and blank W (ritual E) wall. Interior of less interest and much altered.

BAPTIST CHURCH, Church Street. By *Eade & Johns*, 1889–90. White brick with stone dressings. Bold E.E. front. Large central gable with rose window above arched loggia. Short flanking towers with pyramidal roofs (and Tudor doorways). Flèche.

FRIENDS' MEETING HOUSE, Friars Street. 1804, enlarged 1818 and (by *F. Barnes*) 1859. Red brick, with half-hipped roof; addition of white brick. Single-storey extension with glazed entrance and canopy by *Tricker Blackie Associates*, 2012–13.

ST JOHN'S METHODIST CHURCH, York Road. 1901–2 by *Gordon & Gunton*. Large Perp W window. Flint, with red brick and Bath stone dressings. Nave, chancel, transept and organ chamber; no tower.

UNITED REFORMED CHURCH (Congregational), School Street. 1839, enlarged and refronted 1891. The earlier part red brick. White-brick front with stone dressings, asymmetric with tall Dec window and gabled tower with octagonal spirelet to one side.

CEMETERY, Newton Road. Opened 1859, with buildings by *J. P. Pritchett Jun.* Flint, with white-brick and stone dressings.

Domestic Gothic lodge and Dec chapels, the usual pair but here joined by an archway supporting a bellcote.

CHAPEL OF ST BARTHOLOMEW, 1 m. NNE of St Gregory. Former chapel of a small cell or grange of Westminster Abbey, established c. 1115. Perp, flint, nave and chancel in one. One doorway and the window surrounds survive, but little tracery. Beside it a C16 timber-framed and plastered FARMHOUSE with two gabled and jettied cross-wings and C19 half-timbered gables on the rear elevation. It seems to incorporate remains of the priory house, mostly demolished in 1779. To the SE stood a C14 thatched and weatherboarded BARN, of six bays, with aisles, burnt down in 2011.

PUBLIC BUILDINGS

TOWN HALL, Market Hill. 1828 by *A. J. Johnston*, a former clerk of works to Thomas Hardwick; previously assumed to have been designed by the builder, *Thomas Ginn*. White Ballingdon brick with stuccoed front. Modest but dignified. Three generously spaced bays, the middle one projecting a little and enriched at first floor level by tall coupled unfluted Ionic columns carrying a pediment. Assembly room on first floor. Formerly a courtroom on the ground floor, with gaol to the rear. The imposing entrance to this survives (in Gaol Lane), now leading to an extension of 1982. Doric portico *in antis*.

PUBLIC LIBRARY, Market Hill. Built as the Corn Exchange by *H. E. Kendall Sen.*, 1841. An essay in Early Victorian security, superiority and prosperity. Four giant Tuscan columns carry projecting parts of the entablature. A scrolly top line with wheat sheaves instead of urns. The group of resting reapers above the façade is by *F. L. Coates* of Lambeth. Inside, a nave-and-aisles plan, with five bays of tall cast-iron columns supporting a clerestory and tall arched windows at each end. Mezzanine floor loosely inserted as part of conversion to library in 1968 by *West Suffolk County Architect's Dept* (job architects *Adrian Palmer* and *Henk Pieksma*).

KINGFISHER LEISURE CENTRE, Station Road. 1987 by *The Charter Partnership* (project architect *Paul Weston*). Swimming pool etc. with large expanse of slate roof relieved, on the N side, by a weatherboarded tower. Low red brick walls broken up by buttress-like projections and semicircular windows.

ORMISTON SUDBURY ACADEMY (former Upper School), Tudor Road. By *West Suffolk County Architect's Dept* (job architects *Hugh Thomas*, *Jos Dalley*, *Dudley Baylis*, *Brian Grayling*, *J. Blackie*), 1969–72. Constructed on the SEAC system, with aggregate-faced concrete slabs and coloured panels. Of one and two storeys on a sloping site. Long block with three internal courts.

ST LEONARD'S HOSPITAL, Newton Road. By *Edward Salter*, 1867–8. Red brick with black-brick decoration. Two-storey, three-bay central block flanked by what were originally single-storey, four-bay wings containing the wards – the first cottage hospital to use this pavilion plan, adopted by Horace Swete as the model in his *Handy Book of Cottage Hospitals* (1870). Band of decorative tiles between the two storeys and distinctive red and black voussoirs to the windows. Upper floors added to the W wing in 1906 (by *Alfred Howard*) and to the E wing 1927–8. Single-storey extensions to rear, including operating theatre, by *Paul Waterhouse*, 1922–3; King George V Memorial Ward by *Cautley & Barefoot*, 1937–8.

WALNUTTREE HOSPITAL, Walnut Tree Lane. Built as the workhouse, 1836–7, by *John Brown* of Norwich. Red brick, gabled in Tudor style. Central boardroom and kitchen block and, N and S of it, two sets of cruciform ranges, one for men, the other for women (cf. Wickham Market (E)). The plan now obscured by additions. Separate hospital block to the NW by *Salter & Firmin*, 1875–6.

PERAMBULATIONS

1. Market Hill and south-west

The church of St Peter is the centrepiece of the expanded town laid out by Elizabeth de Burgh after 1322. This was a masterful piece of town planning. The main open space, present-day Market Hill, was a large piazza with shops down both sides and the church at the E end. On the N side of the church was the poultry and butter market, approached by a new street of shops and houses (now North Street). On the SE side was another market area, once wider, with the butchers' shambles down the centre (now King Street). The creation of two new manors, in addition to a third already existing, defined the site and helped prevent encroachment upon the open spaces. Today most of the interest lies to the SW of St Peter's, so we shall consider this direction first before returning to the remainder. MARKET HILL slopes gently down from the W door of the church. Immediately in front is the bronze STATUE of Thomas Gainsborough, who was born at Sudbury. By *Bertram Mackennal*, 1913. On the NW side the BLACK BOY HOTEL stands out, with its picturesque half-timbered front of 1901 by *J. S. Corder*. This replaced a Georgian refronting of the kind seen elsewhere round the market place (e.g. Nos. 3–4 on the same side, with early C19 plastered front and four roundheaded windows on the first floor); behind the façade is a C15 timber-framed structure. On the SE side, across from the S porch of St Peter's, Nos. 23–24 has a good late C19 shopfront, and above it the front of 1819 added by *Thomas Ginn* to a medieval merchant's house that has moulded beams and carved doorway inside. No. 28 is also medieval and timber-framed but with an attractive Regency façade, especially the wide first-floor window with delicate pointed tracery. Then No. 30 (LLOYDS BANK), a handsome brick house of *c.* 1768. Five bays and three storeys with a broad pedimented Ionic porch at the foot of a canted bay. Two doors down the

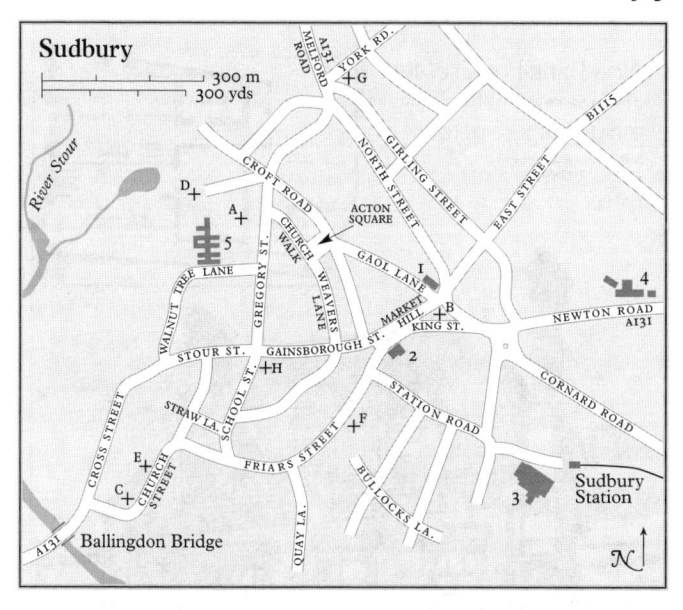

A St Gregory
B St Peter
C All Saints
D Our Lady & St John (R.C.)
E Baptist Church
F Friends' Meeting House
G St John's Methodist Church
H United Reformed Church

1 Town Hall
2 Public Library
3 Leisure Centre
4 St Leonard's Hospital
5 Walnuttree Hospital

NATWEST by *Cheston & Perkin* for the London & County Bank, 1907. Red and blue brick with stone dressings in an imitation Early Georgian style. Next to it the former Corn Exchange, now Public Library (*see* above), then BARCLAYS of 1879 by *Brightwen Binyon*. Red brick, fashionably 'Queen Anne', with a frieze of triglyphs and roundels below modillioned cornice. Adjoining it to the r., and now part of the same premises, a narrow Grecian front with giant columns *in antis*. It began life as a THEATRE, built by *T. Jones* in 1815 and later part of David Fisher's circuit.

At the bottom of Market Hill the road divides, with Friars Street branching off to the l. and Gainsborough Street to the r. We descend by the latter and return by the former. On the corner, HSBC, originally London, City & Midland Bank, by their house architect *T. B. Whinney*, c. 1917–18. Red brick with stone dressings, although the dressings are so elaborate that they predominate. Single-storey, the standard branch design with a domed turret on the corner and entrance with scrolly pediment set in it. The most prominent house in GAINSBOROUGH STREET is No. 46 on the N side, where Gainsborough was born in 1727. Since 1961 it has been a

Sudbury, Market Hill, bank.
Design by B. Binyon, 1879

museum devoted to his work (GAINSBOROUGH'S HOUSE, refurbished by *Alan Cox*, 2005–6), but it is of greater interest architecturally as the home of his father John, a successful cloth dealer and weaver, who bought the house in 1722 and added the present façade. It is of red brick (headers only) with rubbed brick trim. Five bays, two storeys, parapet. Segment-headed windows. Doorway with Doric pilasters and straight entablature. It conceals what were originally two timber-framed houses, joined together *c.* 1520; further alterations were made in the 1790s after the house had passed out of the Gainsborough family's hands. At the back of the house, large windows show that parts of it were used as workshops, and the house was joined to the three-storey block of workshops and warehouse on the corner of Weavers Lane.

WEAVERS LANE is worth a short detour, as it leads to an attractive backwater, ACTON SQUARE, with a mix of modest houses and, on the W side, No. 1 CHURCH WALK, the eccentric offices of the builders Grimwood & Sons, *c.* 1891, presumably designed by *Arthur Grimwood*. Mainly flint rubble, with brick and stone dressings, doorcase with scrolled pediment, two oriels, and half-timbered eaves and gables. On the E side of Acton Square, a former silk factory of *c.* 1870. White brick with red brick dressings. Large segment-headed windows on the ground floor and almost continuous glazing on the first. Manager's house at one end. To its NW, in CROFT ROAD, Nos. 1–4 (GARDENSIDE) by *A. Grimwood*, 1896. Picturesque vernacular style in red brick with tile-hanging, half-timbered gables, etc.

Back in GAINSBOROUGH STREET a few more nice houses, including No. 19 (early C19 white brick, two storeys and five bays with central arched doorway), and also the DRILL HALL by *Arthur Grimwood*, 1881. Red brick with stone dressings and an oriel over the Neo-Tudor entrance. Three gables with a deep coved cornice; the top-floor windows cut through this, but the gutter is allowed to run straight across: is this deliberate whimsy or desperate expediency? Then a crossroads is reached that was the centre of the Saxon town. Little of interest in GREGORY STREET that runs N towards St Gregory's church. Just before the church, inside No. 47 (probably C17) a landscape wall painting with houses and a church. To the S, in SCHOOL STREET, first the United Reformed church (*see* p. 520), then the main building (including headmaster's house) of the former GRAMMAR SCHOOL by *R. P. Pope*, 1857–8, closed 1972 and converted to sheltered housing (WILLIAM WOOD HOUSE). Red brick with bands of black, and stone dressings. Opposite, a good row of early C19 cottages, flint and white brick.

STOUR STREET is the continuation W of Gainsborough Street. It contains the town's finest medieval houses, beginning on the corner of School Street with Nos. 1–2 with gabled and jettied cross-wings, then No. 16 (ST MARY'S) with a large C18 pedimented doorcase. Opposite them HARDWICKE HOUSE, C17 with an elaborate faux-medieval front of 1870. The climax is reached back on the S side with The Chantry and Salter's Hall, originally three houses, all with exposed timbers. First THE CHANTRY, on the corner of Plough Lane, consisting of a hall and two cross-wings, both jettied. C15, with a good corner-post carved with the figure of an angel, and thin buttress-shafts. Then a second house of cross-wing and hall, the latter modified in the C18. Finally SALTER'S HALL, the finest of the lot. Built *c.* 1450, with buttress-shafts, a pretty oriel and windows with delicate tracery. Carved on the soffit of the oriel a group of St James the Less (with his fulling club) between an elephant and a lion. A fourth house was demolished *c.* 1855 and the exposed W façade was then faced in flint with brick dressings probably by *William Butterfield*, then restoring St Peter's, for Rev. John Molyneux, rector of Sudbury, whose house this was. At the same time a courtyard was created with a single-storey building (schoolroom?) on the S side and retaining wall with cast-iron railings by *J. Hawkins* of Ballingdon. The interior also remodelled, with a C16 chimneypiece brought from the Black Boy, Market Hill. CLEVE HALL (formerly Stour Hall), opposite Salter's Hall, is C16 but with many alterations and additions, including a late C18 or early C19 veranda on the W front. The jettied cross-wings had their gables removed in the C18 but retain, beneath their plaster, original timber framing and windows.

At the bottom of the hill WALNUT TREE LANE leads off to the N, the main interest here being the MILL HOTEL, converted in 1971 from a four-storey water and steam mill. The main, weatherboarded part dates back to the late C17, although the mill recorded in Domesday may well have been on this site. It still houses the waterwheel by *Whitmore & Binyon*, 1889, which originally worked four sets of stones. The tall front range was the roller mill, added 1892. Painted brick, divided into bays by pilasters.

Stour Street continues S as CROSS STREET, with a number of weavers' houses on the W side. No. 78, a C15 hall house, was acquired by a saymaker in 1695, refronted with prominent pedimented doorcase, and the adjoining property (now Nos. 75–77) was rebuilt as a warehouse. Beyond them a standard C19 terrace of weavers' houses. Red brick with white-brick dressings, three storeys with large windows on the first floor. On the E side, the OLD MOOT HALL. C15, probably used for civic purposes, although the actual moot hall was in Market Hill. Exposed timbers. Big gabled and jettied cross-wing to the l. with oriel window. Inside, remains of a wall painting with the arms of James I.

CHURCH STREET leads back towards the centre; Cross Street continues to Ballingdon (*see* Perambulation 3). On the corner, the OLDE BULL HOTEL, C16 timber-framed and plastered with jettied front. Rear range (facing Cross Street) with exposed timbers, perhaps a malthouse, and a brick extension of 1869. Between it and the church ALL SAINTS TERRACE, 1889, a white-brick frontage with stone dressings, but along the return facing the church a pair of chequered red brick cottages with Neo-Tudor hoodmoulds converted from outbuildings *c.* 1850. At the same time the VICARAGE, which faces on to the N side of the churchyard, was restored by Rev. Charles Badham. This included adding the two-storey porch to the C17 red brick house. Inside, a good C17 staircase *in situ*, but also panelling from a house that stood on the S side of Cross Street, demolished to make way for All Saints School (now CHURCH HALL) in 1847. The school, opened in 1850, was based on a design by *W. B. Westmacott*, executed by *Stephen Webb* of Ballingdon. Flint with stone dressings. Two large gables with smaller gabled porch between them. Headmaster's house to rear demolished.

Church Street turns sharply N after All Saints. No. 25, on the E side, has a mid-C19 Tudor-Gothic front; No. 7, further up, has a gabled and jettied cross-wing with a date of 1673 on the bressumer. Near the top on the W side, Nos. 51 and 52 are a pair of modest late C14 'renters', small timber-framed hall houses for renting out. One has a later brick front. At this point Friars Street leads off to the E, but a short diversion up Plough Lane, to the N, takes one to IVY LODGE, on the corner of STRAW LANE, apparently a red brick house with deep eaves of *c.* 1830 and owned at that time by *Thomas Ginn*. But the elevation along Plough Lane is jettied, and from the E end the steep gables of a medieval timber-framed house can be seen. At the other end of Straw Lane, on the corner of School Street, CORNER HOUSE by *James Blackie (Tricker Blackie Associates)*, 2000–1, extended by *Stephen Thorpe*, 2007–8. Red brick, making full use of the site, and complementing the simple terrace (Nos. 8–11 Straw Lane) of *c.* 1832–3. Most of the windows face inwards, towards the garden, with only high-level openings to the street.

FRIARS STREET, which largely follows the perimeter of the Norman town, can now be approached by way of School Street, which comes out opposite No. 57 (S side). This was the gatehouse to the Dominican priory, founded in the first half of the C13 and suppressed in 1539. The church was demolished very soon afterwards but the prior's house survived until 1820. The timber frame of the mid-C15 gatehouse is largely complete; the carriage entrance is blocked but the lower, pedestrian entrance still functions. Inside, the porter's room is intact, as well as two rooms on the jettied upper storey. The houses on the N side of the street are of the same date and set back to allow easier access to the gatehouse. The only other remains of the priory are parts of the boundary wall, the most visible being along the W side of the cricket ground; other fragments in private gardens, and incorporated in the front wall of the SHIP AND STAR INN.

The character of Friars Street is pleasantly mixed as it curves back towards the town centre. Opposite the cricket ground (opened 1891, with railings by *Burum & Co.*, Station Road) No. 58, a large C18 red brick house with good pedimented doorcase, then an early C19 white-brick two-storey terrace followed by a three-storey one of ten bays, Nos. 42–50. The latter, whose ground-floor windows and doors are set in arched recesses, was built on the site of an C18 house, part of which survives at the back (e.g. Venetian window), as well as medieval cellars. Further on, No. 22 was built as the manse for the Congregational chapel of 1859 (dem. 1964). White brick, surprisingly large, with pedimented gables. On the SE side, an attractive row of timber-framed houses mainly with C18 plastered and sashed fronts (another good doorcase on No. 31), but also Nos. 35–37 still with jettied upper floors. No. 17 (BUZZARDS HALL), also jettied and with exposed timbers, probably dates back to the C15. Beneath the jetty of the r. part are carved brackets with openwork pendants, part of C17 remodelling. Tripartite first-floor window, of which the outer parts are original and have unusual detailing, with downward-curving mullions. Behind the plain front of Nos. 5–9 is the timber frame of a late C15 or early C16 hall house. In a first-floor room of No. 5 a C17 wall painting, an extensive landscape with meadows and a walled town in the background.

Off Friars Street to the SE, first QUAY LANE, leading to the head of the Stour Navigation, dating from the River Stour Act of 1705. Two WAREHOUSES of 1791 and 1807, of three and two storeys respectively. Red brick with stone dressings. Semicircular windows. The 1791 warehouse, which in addition has oculi on its attic storey, was converted to a theatre in 1979–81 by *James Blackie*, with a weatherboarded extension of 1984.

In BULLOCKS LANE (reached by an alley next to No. 31A Friars Street), RED HOUSE, the stateliest Georgian front in Sudbury: five bays, but a very wide centre with Venetian window (later widened) and pedimented gable. C17 timber-framed core, apparent on the N and E elevations. Converted to a retirement home by *Kenneth Lindy & Partners*, 1947–9, with a Neo-Georgian rear extension; further additions of 1953 and 1979. In the garden a square battlemented GAZEBO with paired lancets, crudely built of flint, waste brick, clinker etc., and along Meadow Lane a fine red brick crinkle-crankle wall. In NONSUCH MEADOW, off Meadow Lane to the S of Bullocks Lane, housing by *Modece Architects*, 1988. White brick. Predominantly S-facing, for passive solar gain.

Meadow Lane runs NE to STATION ROAD. The railway reached Sudbury in 1849, but although the line remains open the station has been demolished. OAK LODGE and BANK BUILDINGS, opposite the end of Meadow Lane, were built by *Thomas Ginn c.* 1835 as the beginnings of a development that was no doubt intended to be more select than the railway soon made it. White brick, still Georgian. Turning l. towards Friars Street, on the S side, Nos. 54–55 was built for the Suffolk and Essex Free Press by *T. F. Ray* of Sudbury, 1867. White brick. Gabled front with ornamental brickwork. Opposite, the former POST OFFICE (now Kingdom Hall) by *Alfred Howard*, 1911–12. White brick with red brick and stone dressings. Neo-Georgian, with prominent pedimented doorway. More late C19 commercial buildings where Station Road meets Friars Road.

2. North and east of Market Hill, including Brundon

Facing the E end of St Peter's is No. 2 KING STREET by *T. Jones*, 1816. White brick with stone bands. Two and a half storeys, with projecting eaves. Five bays wide, the centre slightly recessed with a Greek Doric porch. Further E, at the beginning of NEWTON ROAD, BELLE VUE, a large red brick house of 1871 struggling to be picturesque, with deep eaves on brackets and ornate porch. Beyond it St Leonard's Hospital and the cemetery (*see* p. 521 and 520).

On the N side of St Peter's is the OLD MARKET PLACE with the Town Hall (*see* p. 521). No. 10, on its E side, was built in 1908 for Walker & Co., a chain of grocers, by *F. P. Trepess* of Warwick (now Edinburgh Woollen Mill). The first floor, above the shopfront, is almost entirely glazed, with small-paned iron windows; in the middle an arched panel with clock. Above that a tall straight gable. A short distance along EAST STREET, to the N, the former GAINSBOROUGH CINEMA by *Sidney Naish*, 1912. Now a nightclub. Stuccoed front, but constructed mainly of reinforced concrete. Neoclassical detailing, including florid pilasters, swags and segmental pediment. Restrained interior, with balcony, largely unaltered. Further out, across Girling Way, ELIZABETH COURT (sheltered housing) by *Babergh District Council* (principal architect *C. Chestnutt*), 1978. Pinkish-white brick, with an informal array of pitched and monopitch roofs. Beyond that, also on the SE side, good mid-C19 terraces of weavers' houses. White brick with some red brick dressings, and the characteristic large first-floor windows.

Back now to the Old Market Place and NORTH STREET, which has for the most part retained its scale as an C18 and C19 commercial thoroughfare, starting with the WHITE HORSE on the NE side and next to it the taller, more purely C18 No. 96. Further along, No. 90 has an interesting front with two square oriels and mosaic decoration (including the date, 1876) in the Queen Anne Revival style. Nos. 64–65 form an elegant pair, in white brick. The corner, on the ground floor, is rounded, with a datestone of 1833 neatly incorporated. No. 37, on the SW side, is notable as the former premises of the Sudbury stonemason Edward Keogh, established in 1846; the small red brick office on the street has a stone window with cusped Geometrical tracery. Next to it Nos. 38–41 are C16 or C17, timber-framed and plastered with jettied first floor and some exposed timbers. At the far end, on the corner of Girling Street, the rather forbidding MASONIC HALL of 1886, probably built by *Grimwood & Sons*. It has picturesque elements (tile-hanging, a half-timbered gable) as well as a classical doorcase with terracotta detailing, but still lacks charm.

MELFORD ROAD is the continuation of North Street. It is characterized at first by mid-C19 terraces, e.g. VICTORIA TERRACE (Nos. 17–27), 1858 by *George Grimwood*, and some typical three-storey weavers' houses; and, on the higher ground on the NE side of the road, by larger detached houses built from about 1870. The best of these, about 750 yds from St John's Methodist Church, were built by *Grimwood & Sons*, designed by *A. Grimwood*: No. 104, 1890, white brick with twin projecting gabled bays; No. 110, 1908, barely changed in style;

No. 112, 1911, red brick and roughcast with half-timbered gable; and Nos. 118–120, 1906. The chief interest of the latter semi-detached 'bijoux villas' is their roof garden, complete with greenhouse, advertised as providing 'freedom from motor dust'. More by Grimwood round the corner in PRIORY ROAD: Nos. 5–11, 1908, English Vernacular with tile-hung gables (advertised as 'English homes, old yet new'); Nos. 15–17, 1907, painted brick with flat roof; and No. 19, *c.* 1908, red brick with chalet-style balcony and roof. The flat-roofed houses are most unusual for their date, and Grimwood & Sons were perhaps responsible for other groups dotted about the town, in Queen's Road, Girling Street (dated 1911), and Bellevue Road.

By this stage of Melford Road there are no houses on the SW side, with those on the NE side able to enjoy the view across the meadows to the River Stour. On the river is BRUNDON HALL, a medieval timber-framed house enlarged and cased in red brick *c.* 1730. Three bays with central Venetian window and doorcase with open pediment, the irregular and wide spacing of the windows betraying the house's earlier origins. Nearby a row of modest weatherboarded cottages and the former WATERMILL, of painted brick with mansard roof and weatherboarded lucam, form an attractive group. Nothing remains of Brundon's church, already a ruin in the C18.

Back on Melford Road, N of Brundon Lane, SUDBURY HALL, gutted by fire in 2008. Mid-C19 white brick, of three bays and two storeys, with Ionic portico *in antis*. A little to the N, on the NE side and well back from the road, is HIGHFIELD MILL. Two-storey, three-bay house, and the three-storey octagonal base of a smock mill, converted by *Basil Oliver* with *Lawrence Crampton*, 1928. Both parts white brick, with sash windows set in segmental-arched recesses; the millwright was *William Bear*, working in Ballingdon from 1844 and Sudbury from 1855.

3. Ballingdon

The hamlet of Ballingdon, which was part of the Essex parish of Bulmer until the C19, developed after the construction of the BRIDGE across the Stour in the mid C12. Most recently rebuilt 2002–3 by *Brookes Stacey Randall Architects* with *Ove Arup & Partners*. Pre-cast concrete, with open stainless-steel balustrade protected by aluminium-clad bollards. S of the bridge, BALLINGDON STREET presents an attractive picture, a mix of timber-framed and white-brick houses mostly on a modest scale. No. 7, on the SE side, is larger than most, with two jettied cross-wings and pedimented doorcase. On the other side, set back from the road beside the old railway line, SEWAGE PUMPING STATION by the borough engineer, *T. W. A. Hayward*, 1903. Red brick with white-brick dressings. Segment-headed windows and pedimented gable, well detailed for a building with such a mundane purpose. Just past the railway bridge, on the S side, Nos. 10–13 has a twelve-bay front, of which the centre six are recessed and the centre two have an Ionic portico *in antis*. Early C19, white brick. Nos. 14–15, of similar date, rise to three storeys: a one-bay house attached to one of three bays, all of painted brick. No. 93, opposite, was built in 1720, three bays and two storeys with hipped roof and pedimented doorcase, still timber-framed and plastered. Further along some nice C18 shopfronts, e.g. Nos. 74 and 62 on the N side. No. 62, which has a shallow bowed window and fluted half-columns, is on the site of the NE wing of a large C15 timber-framed house, of which Nos. 60–61 were the original hall (refronted with white brick in the C19), with WEST HOUSE forming the SW cross-wing, refronted in the C18. The NW end of this cross-wing is still in something like its original state, gabled and jettied. Much of the S side is dominated by Nos. 47–48, built *c.* 1900 as offices and pub for Mauldons White Horse Brewery. Red brick with oriels that extend upwards into dormers with fretted bargeboards. Over the crossroads at the far end of Ballingdon Road, at the beginning of MIDDLETON ROAD, a C16 timber-framed hall house with two cross-wings, one with conspicuous exposed timbers. The splendid red brick twisted chimney on the NW return is by *Lawrence Minter* of Bulmer, Essex, *c.* 1965.

BALLINGDON HALL, halfway up Ballingdon Hill, is famous for having been moved there in 1972 from its original position some 200 yds nearer Middleton Road. Its brickwork was dismantled but the timber frame was moved intact. The present house is only the N cross-wing of an H-plan house, built by Sir Thomas Eden *c.* 1593 but mostly demolished after a fire in 1741. The main range was at the E end of the cross-wing, facing towards Middleton. The present main façade was built as a side elevation, so while impressive it has no significant entrance. It has four canted bays on brick plinths, each of two storeys but of varied design; jettied gables above three of the bays. Immediately below the eaves is a strip of high-level windows connecting the bays, blocked in the C18 but exposed after the house was moved; this extravagant display of windows was to light the Long Gallery and Great Chamber of the original house. Short return at the W end of the cross-wing, extended in 1972.

BALLINGDON GROVE, Middleton Road, was an early C17 timber-framed house refronted in red brick (now painted) in the mid C18 and greatly enlarged in white brick for Elliston Allen, 1815, probably by *T. Ginn*. The C17–C18 part of three bays and two storeys with parapet; pedimented doorcase. The C19 extensions are of two and three storeys, with a two-storey canted bay. Service range at the N end, with late C20 weatherboarded upper storey. Now flats. Allen owned the adjacent brickfields, connected by a private cut, still extant, to the Stour Navigation. GROVE HOUSE, SE, was built for the works manager; much enlarged.

BALLINGDON MILL, Bulmer Road. C19 smock mill, of which the red brick two-storey octagonal base and miller's house survive. The walls of the base are, unusually, stepped back rather than tapered.

THELNETHAM

ST NICHOLAS. Charmingly situated in a meadow on the edge of the village. All of *c.* 1300 and a little later. In the W tower Perp W window with a niche above. Above this small circular windows with quatrefoils. In the chancel the E (five-light) window is an unusual, clearly Dec, variation of the theme of intersected tracery. The lights have ogee arches to start with, and there are small motifs interpolated in some of the intersecting fields too. Simple angle PISCINA. The fine S aisle was built in the time of Edmund Gonville, rector 1320–6, founder of Gonville Hall (later Gonville and Caius College), Cambridge. Its E (five-light) and W (three-light) windows are intersected-cusped. The arcade of four bays has octagonal piers and arches of one chamfer and one sunk quadrant, both dying into the piers. Good angle PISCINA with naturalistic foliage, a pointed-trefoiled arch with dogtooth enrichment, and a gable with ballflower. Restored and re-seated by *R. M. Phipson*, 1871–2, including well-carved PULPIT and *Minton* TILES, notably in the sanctuary. New chancel roof by *W. M. Fawcett*, 1895, and further restoration including new nave roof and CHANCEL SCREEN, 1906–8. – SCULPTURE. Good circular relief of the Flight into Egypt. Walnut on mahogany. C18, probably Italian. – PAINTING. C19 copy by *Luigi Pompignoli* of St James the Greater by *Benvenuto Tisi da Garofalo* (1481–1559). Oil on canvas. – STAINED GLASS. Small bits in the S aisle E window and a chancel S window. – MONUMENT. Sir Henry Bokenham †1648 and wife Dorothy †1654. Two demi-figures in an arched niche, with books and a skull. Looped-up curtains l. and r. Above them a broken segmental pediment with achievement of arms. In the 'predella' son and daughter, small, frontal, in oval niches. The quality of the monument is poor.

THE MANOR HOUSE, W of the church. Built as the rectory, 1841. Large, stuccoed, double pile house.

Former SCHOOL (now village hall), 400 yds W. By *Phipson*, 1872. Picturesquely Gothic. Stone rubble and flint with stone dressings. Three-light windows with cusped tops. Small octagonal corner turret with open belfry and conical roof.

EVERGREEN OAK, ½ m. W. Early C16 timber-framed and plastered house. Gabled cross-wing to the l. (service end). Cross-passage with plank-and-muntin screen. In the garden, the base and small part of the shaft of the VILLAGE CROSS, erected in accordance with the will of John Cole, 1527. He left 10s. for it.

WINDMILL, ⅔ m. NW. Tower mill, 1819, and very likely by *George Bloomfield*, millwright and engineer of Thelnetham. Tarred brick. Cast-iron windshaft by *J. Aickman* of King's Lynn, 1832. Fully restored 1979–87.

THORNHAM MAGNA

ST MARY. The W tower appears Dec, although bequests of 1429 and 1440 suggest it was then still under construction. The chancel also originally Dec – see the S doorway and the angle PISCINA. The rest Perp, especially the S porch. Front with flushwork panelling. Entrance with shields in the spandrels and niches l., r. and above. The latter has a little vault. Hammerbeam roof in nave. Restoration, including vestry through old nave N door, by *Daniel Penning* of Eye, 1851. – SCREEN. With single lights and canopy. Made by *Henry Ringham* and designed by *Joseph Clarke* for a church in Surrey; exhibited at the Great Exhibition and purchased by Lord Henniker in 1856. – COMMUNION RAILS, PULPIT, large READING DESK, and BENCHES with poppyheads; of similar date and quality. – STAINED GLASS. A number of windows of *c.* 1851 to the Hennikers. Probably by *William Miller* (cf. the E window at Worlingworth (E), another Henniker church, and similar designs at Thornham Parva). Nave S †1870 by *W. G. Taylor*, 1885. – Nave S †1901 by *Morris & Co*. Three large figures with angels in the tracery. – MONUMENTS. Robert Killigrew †1707 at the Battle of Almanza, Spain. Cartouche with helmet and gauntlets. – John Henniker Major, 2nd Baron Henniker, †1821 and wife Emily †1819. By *J. J. P. Kendrick*, one of his major works. Standing monument. Two large female figures representing Piety and Hope by an urn on a high pedestal. On the urn the profiles of Lord and Lady Henniker, on the pedestal their arms. – Also by *Kendrick* Frances Emilia Henniker †1823. Simple hanging monument. – Hon. Major Henniker †1842. By *W. F. Woodington*. Marble sarcophagus with drapery, helmet and sword. – Maj. Gen. A. H. Henniker †1912. Bronze plaque with portrait medallion. By *Gawthorp & Sons*.

THORNHAM HALL. The E-plan Tudor house was purchased from the Killigrews by John Major, who was created a baronet in 1765 and whose monument is at Worlingworth (F). On his death in 1781 it passed via his daughter Ann to the Hennikers and remains in the family. Alterations and additions were made for the 4th Lord Henniker (†1870) by *Sydney Smirke*, 1837–9, and *c.* 1856–7 *E. B. Lamb* added ranges to the inner sides of the Tudor court, with corner and central towers, in a style part Jacobean and part Loire chateau. The house was greatly reduced for the 6th Lord Henniker in 1937–8 by *G. D. Gordon Hake*, leaving just the E wing, but this was destroyed by fire in 1954. A modest house, L-plan with a two-storey, four-bay front facing S across the park towards the church, was built on the site by *T. A. Bird & R. M. T. Tyler*, 1955–6. To its NW a WATER TOWER, in its present form by *J. K. Colling*, 1872–3, who heightened and clad an existing structure; its top, with pyramidal roof and cupola, is in the same style as the central tower of Lamb's additions. Red brick, the upper stages faced in white brick. To its W an ICE HOUSE. STABLES (now converted to housing) NE of the house by Smirke. Red brick with stone and cement dressings. Archway with pyramidal roof and turret. Shaped gables at each end of the front. WALLED GARDEN to the N, with a range of greenhouses along the N side. To its W a C19 FOLLY, built mainly of stone rubble with reused doorway, restored as a 'hermitage' by *Jack Penton*, 1997–9. Beside it a MONUMENT to the 6th Lord Henniker †1956 by *John A. Green*, 1999. Standing stone with slate panels, including bas-relief heads of dogs. – NORTH LODGE, ½ m. NE. Timber-framed (or apparently so) with brick-nogging. Gables with decorative bargeboards and finials.

THE RED HOUSE, 600 yds W of the church. C17 or C18 red brick with burnt headers, probably older internally. Five bays and two storeys with C20 porch. Three gables to the rear. Behind it extensive ranges of mid-C19 model farm buildings (RED HOUSE YARDS), converted to domestic and commercial use.

VILLAGE. Along THE STREET, running S from the church, a number of nice houses and cottages. On the W side ANSTED, a traditional-looking house of 1983 by *Elaine Denby & Gordon Badnell*. Largely of concrete, rendered and painted 'Suffolk pink', with pantile roof. On the same side but set further back the OLD RECTORY by *Joseph Morris* of Reading, 1873. White brick with some stone dressings. Gothic porch and three-light staircase window. At the S end of The Street, THE FOUR HORSESHOES pub, picturesquely timber-framed and thatched. Two-bay open hall of the second half of the C15, floored in the late C16. Crown-post roof. In a ground-floor room a wall painting of a spread eagle.

THORNHAM PARVA

ST MARY. Nave and chancel and short unbuttressed W tower. All thatched. N and S doorways Norman, that on the N completely plain, that on the S with one order of shafts, scalloped capitals and one roll moulding. One Norman S window, discovered during the restoration of the church in 1883. Good example of Norman walling on the N side, never even repointed. The circular W window high up is attributed by Cautley to the Saxon period, because of its splay. The chancel seems Dec; the nave also has one Dec window. The tower was built *c.* 1485–6 by *Richard Cutting* and *John Tilley*, remembered only because their work was defective; there are records of the action brought against them. – FONT. Octagonal, Dec, with simple tracery patterns. – RETABLE. The Thornham Parva Retable is deservedly famous. It was found in a stable loft at Thornham Hall (*see* Thornham Magna) and given to the church by Lord Henniker in 1927. It had been purchased by his ancestor, Sir John Major, in 1778, and before that was in a house at Stradbroke. For what church or for whom it was originally made is a matter of conjecture, but it has been convincingly argued that it was an altarpiece for the Dominican priory (Blackfriars) at Thetford, Norfolk, founded in 1335. Tree-ring dating of the oak support shows that it was made from timbers felled within a few years of 1322, and stylistically the painting is East Anglian, most likely from Norwich, *c.* 1330–40. A frontal by the same workshop, in the Musée de Cluny in Paris, may well have been a companion piece. The retable consists of a row of cusped arches framing painted and gilded panels, with the Crucifixion in the centre. To either side are four saints, the two outer figures Dominicans: St Dominic himself on the l., St Peter Martyr on the r. Facing them are, respectively, St Catherine of Alexandria and St Margaret of Antioch. Nearer the centre stand St John the Baptist, St Peter and St Paul, and St Edmund. The figures are thin and swaying. The drapery folds have deep troughs across the waist and then fold diagonally. The background is treated in fine patterns cast from tin moulds in paste, alternately chequered and gilded all over. The spandrels have various flowers and leaves in relief, also painted and gilded. Some retouching has occurred over the years, especially to the figure of St Catherine in the C18, and the whole retable was cleaned and conserved by the *Hamilton Kerr Institute* in 1994–2003. – PANELLING below retable. Arched panels of a Jacobean pulpit; from Stradbroke. – SCREEN. With simple one-light divisions. Two cut-off ends of the rood-loft beam remain in the wall. – CHESTS. C14, of imported pine with curved poplar lid. Another, Elizabethan. – WEST GALLERY. Early C19. Bow-fronted. – WALL PAINTINGS. Early C14. On the nave N wall, one of only two complete cycles of the life of St Edmund (the other, mid-C13, is in St Helen, Cliffe, Kent). On the S wall, scenes from the Infancy of Christ. – STAINED GLASS. Nave N †1849 by *William Miller*. The nave s and chancel windows may be his also (cf. Thornham Magna). – ENGRAVED GLASS. Two roundels in a nave S window by *Laurence Whistler*, *c.* 1975. – MONUMENT. Sir Basil Spence †1976 and Joan Spence †1989 (in churchyard, ESE of chancel; cf. Yaxley). Large double slab, designed by their son *John Spence*. Originally carved by *John Skelton*; replica by *Gary Breeze*, 2006. Kilkenny limestone.

CHANDOS FARM, 100 yds NNW. Timber-framed and plastered house, *c.* 1600, altered in the early C18 and again in the mid C19. To the latter belong two canted bays, the porch, and the windows with arched casements and hoodmoulds.

THORPE MORIEUX

ST MARY THE VIRGIN. All C13 to C14. The chancel PISCINA in the angle of the SE window with its angle shaft and stiff-leaf foliage must be C13. The tower looks *c.* 1300, the nave *c.* 1320–30. Chancel windows renewed, presumably in 1870, but representing an original date of *c.* 1300. The nave buttresses are V-shaped (cf. Raydon). Fine C14 timber porch with traceried bargeboards and simply traceried three-plus-three side openings. Its lower walls rebuilt by *J. D. Wyatt* as part of his restoration, 1868–70, which also included new roofs, new N vestry on old foundations, and re-seating. – FONT. Plain, square, C13, on five supports. – PULPIT. By *Wyatt*. Oak, on stone base, with colonnettes of Irish green marble. – DOORS. S and W doors with quatrefoil borders. – SCULPTURE. An elaborately carved bracket with embattled cresting. Late Perp. Presumably an image stool. – STAINED GLASS. E window by *O'Connor*, 1870. Re-set with a good deal of plain glass. – A nave S window †1927 (St George and St Francis) by *A. L. & C. E. Moore*. Another by *Meg Lawrence* (St Peter and St Paul), 2002. – MONUMENTS. Rev. John Fiske †1764. Nice restrained standing wall monument. No figures. The centre is a cartouche with a coat of arms. – His granddaughter S. T. Harrison †1825. By *John Soward*. Large hanging monument with upturned torches.

THORPE HALL. Early C16, mainly timber-framed and plastered. Not big, but with a showy jettied E front facing a lake. Two-storey brick porch with stone windows and steep arched gable.

THRANDESTON

ST MARGARET. The exterior all Perp, although the chancel has good C13 detail in the rere-arches of the windows on N and S. N of the chancel a two-storey vestry. Money was left for repairing the roof in 1475, and for leading the roof of the nave and S aisle in 1491. A bequest of 1452 mentions the tower, but others of 1525–30 probably provide a more accurate date for its construction, confirmed by the arms on the frieze of shields below the W window (Cornwallis and Stamford, Cornwallis and Sulyard, Herbert alias Yaxley and Brome). The tower is of knapped squared flint. Base and buttresses with flushwork decoration. Three-light bell-openings. N and S aisles with arcades of four bays with octagonal piers and double-chamfered arches. An ogee-headed niche in the N wall. Nave roof with tie-beams on arched braces alternating with hammerbeams. Coving boarded and decorated with shields. – FONT. Octagonal, Perp. Four lions against the stem, and the Emblems of the Evangelists and four Tudor roses against the bowl. Restored 1846, according to an inscription on the base;

this seems to refer to a general restoration, not just the font. The COVER may well be original. – REREDOS. 1870. Carved stone surround with Lamb and Pelican; also painted panels with flowers and texts, and glazed tiles on the N and S sanctuary walls. – SCREEN. Dado of a rhythm different from that of the upper one-light divisions, suggesting a made-up piece. Ogee-arched lights. – STALLS. With traceried fronts, but incorporating also some Jacobean panelling and two curiously primitive figures. – BENCHES. With poppyheads, and two with small figures (St Peter and St Paul) facing the gangway. – STAINED GLASS. Canopies in a N aisle window. Chancel windows of about the same date as the reredos, and attributed by Birkin Haward to *Wailes*. – MONUMENTS. Elisabeth Cornewaleys (Cornwallis) †1537. Brass; inscription only. Now mural, in stone frame of 1847. – Rev. Nathanael D'Eye †1844. By *R. Ruffels*. With arms. – In churchyard, on N side of chancel, three chest tombs of the Blakely family of Goswold Hall; *c.* 1776–1817.

OLD RECTORY, W of the church. Large, elegant addition of 1844 by *George Brooks* of Eye, to a timber-framed house of *c.* 1700. Rendered brick. Two storeys. E front of four bays with two-bay pedimented centre. Tuscan pilasters. Two-bay return to S with pedimented gable. Windows with round-arched lights and floating cornices to the ground floor. In the older W range a reused C15 stone doorway. Pointed arch under square head and hoodmould.

Opposite the Old Rectory CHURCH FARM HOUSE, early C17, timber-framed and plastered. Set back behind a red brick wall. Gatepiers with pyramidal caps. To the W LITTLE GREEN, with a few nice houses scattered round it; on the N side AMPNERS, C16 or C17 with C19 Gothick windows and hoodmoulds, and STYLES PIECE, early C16. Thatched. Hall range jettied with brick-nogging, cross-wing plastered. At the SW corner THE MANOR HOUSE, late C16. Four bays, jettied. The quality of the internal woodwork indicates that this is only a fragment of something much larger and grander.

GOSWOLD HALL, ⅔ m. SE. Reached by a brick bridge across the moat. Late C16 cross-wing to r. Main range rebuilt in the C17. Timber-framed, but the exposed timbers and brick-nogging are not genuine. To the r. of the entrance a two-storey bow of *c.* 1820 projects beyond the cross-wing. In the field in front of the house a red brick DOVECOTE with shaped gables. Late C17. Restored *c.* 2004–5, with louvre and pipe (to deter sparrowhawks) on ridge.

THURSTON

ST PETER. Flint rubble walls with dressings of Barnack and Ancaster stone. W tower, nave and aisles rebuilt by *J. H.*

Thurston, St Peter, collapsed tower.
Drawing by Rev. R. S. Fox, 1860

Hakewill, 1860–1, following the collapse of the tower for which Hakewill had already advised urgent restoration. The new building kept to the footprint of the old, except that the tower was made 2 ft (0.6 metres) wider on each side and the ridge of the roof was raised to its original C14 height. Wall arcading in the aisles, echoing the arches of the arcades, an original feature kept by Hakewill. Perp chancel, restored by *Rev. E. Geldart*, 1892–3, including fine roof with angels. Nice SEDILIA and DOUBLE PISCINA reaching evenly to the sill frieze below the windows, original but restored. The piscina has two arches and a shelf across. – FONT. Octagonal, probably C14. Fluted octagonal stem. Big leaf panels of different species, with two Green Men (cf. Tostock). – REREDOS. By *Geldart*. Carved, with the Annunciation and angels bearing Emblems of the Passion. – ROOD SCREEN. 1897, by *Ward & Hughes*. Tall, single-light divisions with elaborate tracery, cresting and cross. The richly carved PULPIT, with figures of saints in nodding ogee canopies, of about the same date. – STALLS. By *Geldart*, but including some original C15 stalls. These have traceried fronts, the ends with simple poppyheads. – STAINED GLASS. Fragments in aisle and chancel windows. – E window †1891 perhaps by *Ward & Hughes*, who sign the other chancel windows. S and N at the E end 1912 and 1922 (*T. F. Curtis*). The western window on the S side, 1895, is based on Axel Ender's altarpiece in Molde Cathedral, Norway ('He is not here but is risen'). – S aisle E by *Powell & Sons* (*E. L. Armitage*), 1950. – MONUMENT. Sir William Gage †1864. By *T. Gaffin*.

Two standard-looking tablets to accommodate the very long inscription.

Two contrasting SCHOOLS by *West Suffolk County Architect's Dept*: PRIMARY SCHOOL of 1965–6, built on the timber-framed Derwent system, with dark-stained hardwood boarding and white-painted metal-framed windows; and THURSTON COMMUNITY COLLEGE (former Upper School), Norton Road (main job architect *Bob Edwards*), 1969–73 and 1979, built on the SEAC system, with brick cladding, weather-boarded fascia and continuous clerestory.

RAILWAY STATION. 1846–7 by *F. Barnes*. Built against a 20-ft (6.1-metre) embankment, so that what appears from the platform to be a single-storey building turns out to be of three. Red brick with white-brick dressings. Two gabled towers project forward from the centre, linked by a single-storey porch of two small arches and one larger arch. Two-storey wings to either side. The lower floors no longer in railway use. A corresponding but simpler building on the opposite platform was demolished in the 1970s. The neighbouring bridge, and others in the vicinity, are equally well detailed. The FOX & HOUNDS across the road must have been built at about the same time. White brick, with somewhat erratic red brick dressings. Tudor-style, with hoodmoulds, a corbel table below the eaves, and decorative chimneys.

THURSTON HOUSE, ½ m. SW. Early Georgian. Of seven bays, red brick. Large, fully glazed semicircular porch covering the three centre bays. Dormer windows with alternating triangular and segmental pediments. Late C19 three-bay extension to the r.

THURSTON GRANGE, 1¼ m. NW. 1895. Ground floor red brick with stone dressings. Upper floor half-timbered. On the garden front two projecting gabled 'cross-wings' and a central gabled dormer. Now a hotel.

MANOR FARM, ¼ m. N. By *Philip Webb*, 1875–6. The client was Edward Greene of Nether Hall, Pakenham (q.v.), where Webb was then working, and the house was for Greene's estate manager. Red brick. Two bays and attics, with pronounced string course. Three bays square. Hipped roof with central lead flat; late C20 balustrade. Dormers and four tall chimneys. Entrance front with recessed porch behind a broad round arch. Relieving arches over ground-floor windows with herringbone brickwork in the tympana. The canted bay on the E front may not be original. Single-storey service range to N and then a group of weatherboarded farm buildings, also by Webb.

THWAITE

ST GEORGE (redundant 2007; in community use). Nave and chancel. The W tower fell about 1800. 'Much improved and beautified' c. 1846, according to White's *Directory*, including rebuilding of the W wall with bellcote; restored and re-seated 1870. In the chancel one slit lancet, i.e. of c. 1200. Early C16 brick S porch, its roof on big wooden head corbels. The nave roof is called by Cautley a hammerbeam roof, but it is more likely that it has tie-beams that were cut off at a later date. The remaining tie-beam (serving as chancel arch), the apparent hammers and the collar-beams are embattled. – FONT. Octagonal. With various cusped tracery patterns. Late C14. – PULPIT. An excellent Perp piece, each side with two ogee-arched panels and quatrefoils below. – READER'S DESK. Made up of Early Renaissance pieces, perhaps domestic. – STAINED GLASS. Some C14 bits in several windows. W window †1846 typical of its date, and attributed by Haward to *Clutterbuck*. – MONUMENT. In churchyard, E of the chancel, Orlando Whistlecraft †1893, 'weather prophet & poet'. Cast-iron cross.

Former NATIONAL SCHOOL, on NE side of churchyard. 1853. Very small. Knapped flint with stone dressings. Straight gables and arched doorway. Of the same year a pair of COTTAGES NW of the church. Pebble and flint with white brick dressings. Said to have been built with materials from the collapsed tower.

WILLOW HALL, ¼ m. NE, by the Norwich Road. Timber-framed, with some exposed timbers, especially on the jettied front along the road. Long cross-wing on the N side, of which the W part is the original C15 open hall. C17 additions, including the rest of the cross-wing and parlour block to the S.

TIMWORTH

ST ANDREW. In the middle of fields, and no village to speak of. Restored in 1868 by Rev. E. R. Benyon, on whose estate it lay (*see* Culford). The architect is not recorded, but the tracery of the W window, as inventive as it is unarchaeological, and the curious lobed archway of the priest's door, are sufficiently roguish to evoke *Teulon* (cf. Wordwell). Much is clearly of the old building, especially the S porch tower and the early C14 doorway. Flushwork arcading at the base of the tower. Dec nave, E.E. chancel. – PULPIT. C18, said to be from St James, Bury St Edmunds, and if so removed as part of *Scott*'s reordering. Some Gothic tracery seems to have been added along the way. – COMMUNION RAILS. With twisted balusters.

TOSTOCK

ST ANDREW. Chancel of the late C13, restored by *J. D. Sedding* in 1889. The E window has three lights and quatrefoiled circles.

The chancel arch is well detailed. Dec w tower with buttresses decorated with flushwork panelling. Wide Perp nave, with dressed stone in the flint giving a rough chequer effect. In the E wall, outside, where the nave spreads either side of the chancel, a recess, of stone on the s side and brick on the N. S porch with very strange side windows, now largely blocked. They are oblong, and have one reticulation motif in the middle, with four mouchettes, two above, two below. The nave roof alternates between arch-braced principals and false double hammerbeams. The latter have pendant hammerposts below, and arched braces springing from the upper hammerbeams. Figures on the pendants. Tracery in the spandrels. Nave restored in 1848–51 (by *T. Farrow*) and 1872–3. N vestry 1989 by *John Pamment*, who also designed and built the w ringing gallery, 1999. – FONT. Octagonal, early C14. Fluted stem, leaf or flower panels on the bowl, some with Green Men (cf. Thurston). The carving crude, but the leaves intended to be true to nature. – BENCHES. Sixteen original C15, with poppyheads and beasts and birds on the arms and carved backs. Restored in 1848–9, when the front four rows were made to match. – COMMUNION RAIL. Of *c.* 1660. With turned balusters. – STAINED GLASS. Bits of original glass in the E window. – MONUMENTS. G. J. E. Brown †1857. White marble oblong with a raised cross, with the inscription on a wavy ribbon around it. By *T. Gaffin*, copied for W. T. Brown †1905. – War memorial. By *Hon. Marion Saumarez*, 1924. Painting, 'The Altar of Sacrifice', in niche by chancel arch.

TOSTOCK OLD HALL, 600 yds NE. Mainly C16, with jettied front. Remodelled in the mid C19, with gabled porch and dormers (two large, three small), all with finials. Windows with small panes, diamond-wise round the edges. Good late C16 six-bay barn, weatherboarded, to N.

The village centre lies 600 yds W of the church, round a GREEN. On the way the OLD SCHOOL of 1874, a lively bit of Domestic Gothic, mainly of red brick but with white and black brick and stone. On the N side of the green CHAPEL HOUSE, a Wesleyan chapel of 1856 converted by *Doug Patterson*, 1982–5, for his own occupation. It connects to an adjoining cottage and incorporates fragments from other buildings. Beyond the W end of the green THE OLD RECTORY, built by Rev. James Oakes, appointed rector in 1796. His father, the Bury banker James Oakes, helped both with acquiring the living and building the house, which was ready in 1798. The road was also diverted away from it that year. White brick. Two storeys. Five-bay with three-bay pedimented centre. Giant Ionic pilasters. Enlarged in 1812.

TOSTOCK PLACE, 300 yds SSW. Rebuilt for George Brown of Bury, 1811–12. White brick. Two storeys. Full-height three-bay bow in the middle of the garden front, with two further bays l. and r. Enlarged 1904, with wings to N and S, but the S wing has been demolished, leaving a single-storey colonnade. N of the house a KITCHEN GARDEN with red brick crinkle-crankle wall on all four sides. Brown, like Oakes, diverted the road, in 1814; hence 'New Road', dead straight, W of the house.

TOSTOCK HOUSE, ½ m. WSW. C16 timber-framed core, encased in flint and white brick in the early C19. Doorway with segmental pediment. Extensive early C19 barns to N, also of flint with white-brick dressings, mostly now converted.

TICEHURST, ½ m. SW. Lobby-entrance house. To the l. of the main range, which was refronted in brick in the C19, a short cross-wing, gabled and jettied with two carved bressumers (including the date, 1599) and carved bargeboards.

TROSTON

ST MARY. E.E. chancel with N and S lancets (broad rere-arches inside) and E window with three stepped lancets. C14 nave and W tower. Fine, steep tower arch. Dec tracery in the nave; the two-light windows have in the tracery head the favourite figure of the four-petalled flower. The nave roof has scissor-bracing above as well as below the collar-beams. Perp S porch with flushwork panelling, very similar to the porch at neighbouring Honington (q.v.). Entrance with fleurons etc. Three niches above it, the pedestal in the central niche supported by an angel. Battlements with initials. General restoration supervised by the patron, *Robert Emlyn Lofft*, 1869, including new nave roof on top of the medieval one. – FONT. Norman. Originally round, later made octagonal. – PULPIT. Two-decker, made up of various parts, probably in 1869. The pulpit itself Jacobean, the reader's desk with parts in similar style, probably domestic. – SCREEN. Of one-light divisions, with ogee arches and tracery over. Money was left in 1459 for the making of the rood beam. Partially restored *c*. 1886–91 and painted brown, the base repainted 1930. The E front of the ROOD LOFT reused as panelling behind the altar, a rare survival. – COMMUNION RAIL. Jacobean. – BENCHES. At the W end, with poppyheads and animals on the arms. The remainder of 1869, carved by *Lofft*, who also made the wainscoting. – WALL PAINTINGS. A very fine group, mostly on the nave N wall. The earliest component, *c*. 1350–70, is a small and rather crude St George, very soon covered over. Next to it a large St Christopher, to the E the Martyrdom of St Edmund, and to the W an exceptionally good St George and the Dragon, all of *c*. 1370–90. Above the arch, remains of a late medieval Doom. Uncovered and partly overpainted in 1869; conserved by *Andrea Kirkham*, 2009. – ROYAL ARMS. Of James I, on board, with George I's initials added. – STAINED GLASS. Canopies etc. in the nave N windows, contemporary with the larger wall paintings. E window by *Harry Stammers*, 1964. A bold piece, excellent of its date. – MONUMENTS. Anne Lofft †1801, daughter of Henry Emlyn of Windsor, architect. Lengthy inscription. – Henry Capel Lofft

†1811. 'Fell in a most gallant charge on the French line in the great battle of Albuhera near Badajoz in Spain.'

TROSTON HALL, 600 yds s. Late C16 timber-framed house with jettied and gabled cross-wings. Late C17 staircase wing. In the early C19 it belonged to the radical writer Capel Lofft (1751–1824), who, according to White, 'greatly improved' the house and grounds, but his grandson *Robert Emlyn Lofft*, who inherited in 1866, had other ideas. He covered the front and s side with small ornamental red tiles laid diamond-wise, and added strips of boarding carved with a similar pattern as well as a porch. The effect is pretty, if incongruous. (Inside, three excellent plaster ceilings, one in the middle room above the hall, and two in the wings, one above and one below. In the middle room patterns of curved ribs and a frieze with unicorns, goats, and a man trying to club a lion. In the other upper room the walls have pretty Chippendale panelling. Fine dog-leg staircase of *c.* 1680 with twisted balusters. Good Elizabethan fireplaces.)

R. E. Lofft's penchant for unusual wall surfaces is apparent elsewhere. The former SCHOOL (now house and village hall; 300 yds w of the church), which he built in 1873, has walls of moulded red bricks with intermittent courses of black bricks, also moulded but of a different pattern. Roofs tiled to similar effect, with a subtle sweep to them, and fancy chimneys. Estate cottages at TROSTON HEATH, ¾ m. NNW, have walls of red moulded bricks, and round-arched doors and windows. Lofft was very likely the architect as well as the client. TROSTON COTTAGE, immediately E of the church, also betrays a certain eccentricity, but is entirely of white brick.

TUDDENHAM

7070

ST MARY. Mostly Dec. The w tower has a pretty front with two niches flanking a circular window with a quatrefoil. Dec nave N and (less good) s aisle windows. Interesting E window with reticulation, in which, however, the top reticulation motif is wilfully replaced by a circle enclosing three cusped spherical triangles. Inside, the window is flanked by niches. Tall gabled s porch of the same date (side windows with Y-tracery). The s arcade has the typical C14 octagonal piers and double-chamfered arches. Tomb recess in the N wall. Perp clerestory and hammerbeam roof, the latter replaced in 1876 as part of restoration by *Charles Kirk*.

Facing the triangular GREEN, 225 yds NW of the church, the former SCHOOL by *L. N. Cottingham*, 1846. Tudor-Gothic. Black flint with stone dressings and red brick quoins and red pantiles. Straight gables with finials. On the N side of the green NETHER HALL, a C16 timber-framed house altered in the C17. Cross-wing at the w end with exposed timbers. In a first-floor room of the cross-wing a painted overmantel with strapwork cartouches.

WATERMILL, 700 yds NW. Part white brick, part weatherboarding. Late C18 and C19. Tall chimney for the steam engine installed by 1844. Now a restaurant; the cast-iron breast-shot wheel is preserved. On the N side of the mill pond OLD MILL FARMHOUSE. White brick, early C19, with a semicircular porch on fluted columns.

WALSHAM-LE-WILLOWS

A pretty village, enhanced by landowners John Martineau in the C19 and Sir Nicholas (later Lord) Cayzer in the C20. Most of the buildings, including many medieval timber-framed houses, are along the main street, with the church at the W end on the S side.

ST MARY THE VIRGIN. Perp throughout. W tower with flushwork panelling on the battlements and at the corners the armorial beasts of Henry IV (lions, bull and griffin), probably added by his brother-in-law John de la Pole c. 1475. N porch with a flushwork lozenge pattern all over. The N aisle has a base of the same flushwork lozenge pattern. The clerestory has doubled windows and flushwork emblems between them, including the device of *Thomas Aldryche*. Money was left in 1473 for glazing a clerestory window. The S aisle is more modest and has no porch. Seven-bay arcades. Concave-sided octagonal piers, double-hollow-chamfered arches. The piers, which are of clunch, have on each side at the top a small cusped blank ogee arch (cf. Norton). The bases are reused from an earlier church: see the NE pier, with a piece of C11 or C12 carving. Beautiful roof of low pitch with alternating tie-beams and short hammerbeams, both very delicately ornamented; c. 1400. Remains of original colouring, mostly red and green. The shafts for the hammerbeams and braces go down between the windows. On the spandrels sunbursts, presumably also added by John de la Pole. General restoration by *E. H. Martineau*, 1877–8. – FONT. C14, octagonal. Crocketed ogee gables in the panels (cf. Brettenham, Rattlesden). Defaced heads below the bowl. Panelled stem. – SCREEN. Tall one-light divisions with ogee arches. Original coving and cresting. The dado is red and dark green with flowers on; the N side was redone in 1842. Money was left for the new rood beam in 1441 and 1448. – BENCH ENDS. A few, incorporated in the re-seating of 1878. New 'stools' are mentioned in wills of 1498 and 1504. – REREDOS. Last Supper, by *George Tinworth*, in terracotta. Dated 1883, and additionally signed *H. Doulton*, Lambeth. An exceptionally lively piece. The standing figure on the r., watching the events, seems to be a self-portrait of Tinworth. – DOOR. The inner door to the vestry is leather-covered. – PANELLING. At E end of N aisle, dated 1620. Probably from the churchwardens' pew. In porch, with Roman lettering and the date 1541; not *in situ*. – ALTAR. By *Rev. John Rutherford* (vicar 1970–86), 1978. – PAINTING. 'Christ walking on the water / Not of Gennesareth, but Thames'. By *Rosemary Rutherford*, 1943. – TILES. C13, some with crude faces. At E end of S aisle, placed there in 1878. – STAINED GLASS. In the E window, C15 fragments rearranged by *Hardman & Co.* Chancel S by *Lavers, Barraud & Westlake*, 1878; no doubt also the tower window, which records the restoration. – S aisle E and S by *W. G. Taylor*, 1884 and 1885. – Chancel N by *Rosemary Rutherford* (†1972), erected as her memorial. – MONUMENTS. Coffin-lid with floriated cross and double-omega ornament on stepped base. C13? – Mary Boyce †1685. A small disc, of elm, with a little heart on top. Hanging in the nave. – John Hunt †1726. By *Thomas Singleton* of Bury. Erected by Hunt's daughter Elizabeth †1758; nearer to 1758 than 1726. – Harriet Golding †1877. Stone slab with inset metal plaque and bold raised lettering. By *William Garrad*, Birmingham (churchyard, S side).

SE of the church THE PRIORY, early to mid-C16 with large additions of 1904 at the E end. S of the church, on The Causeway, THE PRIORY ROOM, 1901–2, built as a Sunday School by John Martineau, and designed by his cousin *E. H. Martineau*. With timber framing, brick-nogging and much decorative detail, including improving texts carved into the timbers. In the same style, for John and presumably also by E. H. Martineau, and built by *Harry Nunn* of Walsham, two groups of cottages further S along The Causeway, 1879 and 1900, and 450 yds N in Summer Road, 1890 and 1896; also the lychgate to the CEMETERY, 100 yds NW, 1890. Opposite the W side of the churchyard, CHURCH VIEW, semi-detached red brick cottages initiated by John's father, Richard Martineau, and completed in 1866.

NW of the church, on the corner of The Street and Summer Road, WILLOW HOUSE, and N along Summer Road WILLOW COURT (formerly Lawrence House), both by *Raymond Erith* for Sir Nicholas Cayzer, 1967–8, on the site of Walsham Hall. Neo-Georgian. Roughcast. Willow House of four bays with the front door squeezed into the middle. Willow Court is grander. Seven bays with a little three-bay pediment set against the tall hipped roof. Arched alcove over the front door. Quoins. N of Willow Court and a foil to it is HALL FARM HOUSE, restored by Erith at the same time. Early C18 with roughcast panels. Five bays. Pedimented doorcase. End walls of chequered brick.

On the N side of THE STREET, E of Summer Road, the SIX BELLS, 'newly built' in 1523, and then the former GUILDHALL of *c.* 1500, now three cottages. Timber-framed and weatherboarded. Roof hipped at the W end, with gablet. Opposite, the BLUE BOAR, red brick and C19 on the outside, on the inside a Wealden house of *c.* 1420. Smoke-blackened roof timbers, including crown-post with fluted octagonal shaft. Further E, on the same side, the former READING ROOM & PUBLIC HALL of 1858. Red brick with ornate white-brick dressings and moulded white-brick chimneys. Back on the N side, the former INFANT SCHOOL, 1871, and CONGREGATIONAL CHAPEL, 1844. Pedimented gabled front of red brick with pilasters and the outline of the pediment in white brick. Doric porch. Finally, on the corner of Wattisfield Road, MALTINGS HOUSE, early C19 white brick with pilasters and Tuscan porch. It goes with the former MALTINGS, round the corner, built between 1817 and 1844 and sensitively converted to housing by *Charles Morris*, 1979–80.

THE GROVE, 375 yds SE. Early C19 white-brick house. Three bays with Doric tetrastyle portico. Semicircular domed bay on the S front. Alterations and additions by *Erith* for Sir Nicholas Cayzer, 1967–8, including clock tower on STABLE BLOCK to N and elliptical domed SUMMERHOUSE. In 1973–4 *Erith & Terry* restored BROOK HOUSE, on the N side of Grove Road.

THE LAWN, ½ m. W. Timber-framed and plastered, of the first half of the C17. Bought by Richard Martineau in 1853, the front remodelled later in the C19 by *E. H. Martineau*.

THE ROOKERY, 750 yds NE. Timber-framed and plastered house of *c.* 1530, enlarged in the C17. Tall red brick chimneys with frieze of diaper-patterned tiles at the base. Part of the S front faced in white brick in the C19, with a gable and crenellated wings.

POUND for stray animals, 950 yds ESE. 1819. Red brick.

At CRANMER GREEN, 1¼ m. E, THE GREEN FARMHOUSE, mid-C16. It has a chimneystack of octagonal shafts with a frieze identical to that on The Rookery. CRANMER LODGE, E, is mostly C16 but retains parts of its original late C14 frame.

WANGFORD

ST DENIS. 'Thoroughly restored' in 1875 (Kelly's), perhaps amounting to rebuilding; very likely by *R. M. Phipson*, who had just built a new church at nearby Whittington, Norfolk, for the same donor, Mrs Norman. Dec W tower. Norman N and S doorways with one order of shafts with scalloped capitals and altered arches. Handsome E window of *c.* 1300, renewed. Three lights, a big circle and in it a finely cusped pointed trefoil and three little circles. In the N wall a pretty niche with a nodding ogee arch in the canopy. Declared redundant 1990.*

The church lies in heathland on the N side of Lakenheath Airfield, with what is left of the village: a few C19 cottages and WANGFORD HALL, late C16 timber-framed and plastered with two gabled cross-wings. Mid-C19 windows, porch and bargeboards.

---

*No access possible in 2013.

WASHBROOK

ST MARY (Churches Conservation Trust). In a sheltered position in a valley, away from all traffic. Norman nave with two windows preserved. Surprisingly ornate Dec chancel. On the S as well as the N six seats in niches with crocketed ogee gables. Also in the jambs of the windows blank ogee arches. A bigger such arch for the Easter sepulchre on the N side, and opposite PISCINA and SEDILIA. The date is probably *c.* 1340–50. The E window was originally larger (see the external outline), the present one 1828. Upper part of E wall rebuilt by *Henry Freeland*, 1993–4. Perp W tower, its base with flushwork decoration. Some large chunks of septaria, and a glacial stone at the base. Early C19 red brick battlements. C19 S porch. Restoration by *E. B. Lamb*, 1865–6, including addition of N baptistery and vestry, and re-seating. – FONT. Octagonal, Perp. On the bowl four panels with demi-figures of angels and four with flowers. Restored and re-cut 1866, when the lions against the stem were replaced. – Fine iron HOURGLASS STAND. – ROYAL ARMS. Of Queen Victoria. Painted plaster. – STAINED GLASS. E window and others of 1866, attributed by Birkin Haward to *Ward & Hughes*. It replaced armorial glass of 1828, which was re-set in the W window.

WATTISFIELD

ST MARGARET. Unbuttressed W tower, the tower arch of *c.* 1300 or earlier. Base outside with flushwork panelling. The bell-openings are Perp, of two lights with tracery. Nave and chancel Perp with two- and three-light windows. The S porch (now vestry) must once have been quite an ambitious piece with flushwork decoration, but it fell on evil days and was extensively repaired in brick. Above the door a terracotta shield with the arms of de la Pole. Good C14 timber N porch. Restoration by *Satchell & Edwards*, 1872–9, including new chancel roof and re-seating. – FONT. Octagonal, Perp, with panelled stem and shields on the bowl. – FONT COVER. C17 Pyramidal, with scrolly ribs and finial. – SCREEN. Parts in the prayer-desk and lectern; also a portion of tracery, with remains of colour, in S porch. Money was left for the rood beam and loft between 1522 and 1533. – STAINED GLASS. E and two chancel windows of 1864–5, typical of their date, and probably by *Ward & Hughes*. – MONUMENTS. Elizabeth Moody †1746 and her sister Anne Thompson †1747. Similar adjacent monuments, of grey and white marble, the later one a little more elaborate with winged cherub's head, consoles, etc.

The church is nicely sited halfway up the gently sloping curving village street. Immediately to its E ORCHARD HOUSE, built as the rectory by *Ephraim Rednall*, 1855–6. Red brick with black headers, both diapered and chequered. Tudor-style chimneys. Plenty of good timber-framed cottages along THE STREET, as well as the former SCHOOL, S of the church, by *John Johnson* of Bury, 1861–2. Red brick with white-brick dressings, claiming to be in the style of the early C14. Also two larger houses: THE OLD MANSE, 100 yds N of the church, late C16 with gabled cross-wings. Mid-C18 alterations, including doorcase with Gibbs surround and, perhaps, the whole of the r. cross-wing. THE CROFT, near the top of the hill to the S, is C17, with exposed timbers.

WATTISFIELD HALL, 500 yds SSW. Probably built by John Osborne, who bought the manor in 1592 and died in 1619. Long early C17 range, timber-framed and plastered, with a two-storey porch in the centre. Four fine chimneystacks, one with five chimneys, one with three, and two with two each. Twenty-one hearths were recorded in 1674. The chimneys are polygonal and have star tops. The porch, which is jettied on three sides, has pretty balustrading in the side walls. Three short gabled wings at the back. In the centre wing a six-light oriel window with original mullions and transom. At the S end a later C17 extension, also gabled to the rear. At the SE corner a single-storey red brick outhouse of the C18. C17 walled front garden. Gateway with rusticated piers opposite the porch.

Former CONGREGATIONAL CHURCH, S of the Hall. By *Alfred Conder*, 1876–7, including school. Red brick with white-brick dressings. Two tiers of paired windows between pilasters. Now flats; school extended and converted for worship by the United Reformed church.

HENRY WATSON'S POTTERIES, Pottery Hill, ½ m. NE of St Margaret. The land on which the pottery was built was purchased by Thomas Watson in 1800, but was already in active use for pottery manufacture. Most of the C19 factory burnt down in 1963 but a simple red brick industrial building of 1889 survives, as well as a brick down-draught kiln and chimney of 1940–1. Also associated with the works is a house (FIELDINGS) built by *James Cornish* for the pottery owners, 1976. Two storeys, flat roof. Frame of Douglas fir with infill panels of glass and red brick. The main rooms are on the upper storey, with the main entrance at this level because the house is built against a bank.

The surrounding land has produced a great many archaeological finds, many of them associated with earlier potteries. Between 1935 and 1962 eighteen Roman kilns were excavated around Pottery Hill; the clay for them was probably extracted from Calke Wood. Six more kilns have been excavated in the vicinity, as well as five medieval kilns at Grundle Farm, about ½ m. S of the village, and a C16–C17 kiln was recorded in Honeypot Lane, near an Iron Age site where hearths and hut sites were excavated in 1948.

WATTISHAM

ST NICHOLAS. Redundant 1977; now in community use.* Nave and chancel. Unbuttressed W tower with battlements. They are panelled in flushwork. Money was left for the tower in 1416. The rest early C14 or Dec, except for the two unexpectedly domestic chancel dormers with their bargeboarded gables. These belong to the restoration of 1847–8, as do presumably the S porch and N vestry. The restoration included re-roofing, and benches by *H. Ringham*. – STAINED GLASS. Seven windows, mostly patterned, by *John King* of Ipswich, 1847–8.

The church stands on one side of a green, with weatherboarded barns on the other side (some converted) and at the top WATTISHAM HALL. C16–C17, timber-framed and plastered. In two attic rooms, interesting remains of C17 painted decoration, one scheme red, the other yellow. Complete moat with series of outer drainage ditches.

STRICT BAPTIST CHAPEL, 650 yds N. The rebuilding, 1825, of a meeting house of 1763. Red brick with hipped roof. Two tiers of sash windows. Later porch to front. Galleried interior. A complete group, with later C19 attached MANSE on the E side, with white brick front; separate SCHOOLROOM, 1868; burial ground; and former STABLE opposite.

THE CASTLE, opposite the chapel. A large Gothick farmhouse of *c.* 1770, much altered. Stuccoed walls with crenellated parapet. Mostly two storeys. On the W front two round towers, one at the SW corner, the other of three storeys with octagonal roof. To the N another tower containing the entrance to a barn, now converted, that formed the N side of the yard.

WESTHORPE

ST MARGARET. A fragment of Norman stonework set in the jamb of the S doorway. Otherwise basically C14, but Elizabeth Elmham left money in 1419 for completing the aisles and tower. Thus, Dec W tower with Perp W window. Dec N aisle with Perp N windows. Dec chancel with renewed E window and ogee-arched PISCINA and SEDILIA. The arches to the latter have been cut away in front of the window (cf. Cotton). Dec W window in the S aisle, but Perp S windows and S porch. Perp clerestory. Attached to the N side the Barrow Chapel, of red brick but (like most of the N side of the church) rendered. Polygonal clasping buttresses suggest C16 origins, but inside it has a Jacobean ceiling with pendants and C18 window surrounds. Dec arcades of four bays with octagonal piers and

---

*Various fittings removed to Bildeston and Little Finborough.

double-chamfered arches. Remains of original colouring. Dec tomb recess in the S aisle. Perp roof of simple hammerbeams alternating with tie-beams on big arched braces. Chancel restored 1896, nave and aisles (by *William Weir*) in 1912. – PARCLOSE SCREEN. Dec, and quite an important piece because so much of its original colour is preserved. With shafts instead of mullions and three circles with two mouchettes each as tracery. – PULPIT. With Perp traceried panels and C17 additions. – BENCHES. A couple of ends with poppyheads; the rest mainly C17. – Also an isolated C17 BOX PEW. – DOORS. S door with tracery. – Door to tower stair covered with iron straps (cf. Cotton). – TILES. At E end of S aisle, a number of C14 encaustic tiles. – WALL PAINTING. Traces on the N aisle N wall. – ROYAL ARMS. Of George II, 1751, but closer examination reveals earlier dates, for Charles II and Anne, overpainted. Also detached boards of another Stuart set. – MONUMENTS. William Barrow †1613. Kneeling figure of Barrow, in armour, with his son, facing his two wives and a daughter across a prayer-desk. – Maurice Barrow †1666. Large standing monument against the E wall of his chapel. Reclining white marble figure, hand on heart. Two flying cherubs hold curtains back from a circular inscription plate. Top entablature with segmentally raised centre on which stand two more cherubs supporting his achievement of arms. Attributed to *Edward Pearce* (GF). A monument was initially commissioned from *Diacinto Cawcy* (cf. Hawstead, Mildenhall), whose work was started but not finished; the paving slabs in the chapel, decorated with vases of flowers in scagliola and originally intended to be upright rather than laid on the floor, seem to have been part of this aborted scheme. – Nathaniell Fox †1679. Black marble inscription plate against a pier of the N arcade. Below it another to his sister Mary †1676 with incised cherub's head. Below that a skull and crossbones.

WESTHORPE HALL was the residence of Mary Tudor (1496–1533), daughter of Henry VII, widow of Louis XII of France and third wife of Charles Brandon, Duke of Suffolk. She had been married to Louis XII at the age of seventeen, and he died after two years. Her love had belonged to Charles Brandon, to whom, when widowed, she was secretly married in France. They had to pay Henry VIII £2,000 a year for twelve years to reconcile him. She died at Westhorpe and is buried in St Mary, Bury St Edmunds. The house that Brandon built, between *c.* 1526 and Mary's death, was a red brick courtyard house, claimed by Brandon to have cost £12,000, i.e. more than three times the cost of Hengrave Hall (q.v.). It is notable for its use of terracotta, both for hoodmoulds and for other architectural features, and for decorative panels; fragments have been recovered from the moat. The house also had an internal corridor round the courtyard, similar to that at Hengrave. Westhorpe reverted to the Crown in 1535 and was demolished in the C18, probably in phases (Thomas Martin of Palgrave left a good description of the destruction he witnessed): final(?) demolition is recorded *c.* 1765, but the present modest red brick house is earlier C18. Over the doorway a reused stone pediment and terracotta panels with the arms of Brandon and his fourth wife, Katherine Willoughby. At right angles, originally detached, an earlier (late C16 to early C17) timber-framed and plastered range along the E arm of the moat, E of the site of the Great Hall. Across the centre of the W arm of the moat a C16 red brick BRIDGE of three arches.

WESTLEY

ST MARY. 1835–6 by *William Ranger*. In the lancet style. Nave and shallow chancel, with a similar narrowing at the W end. NE vestry and SW tower; the latter's spire* crumbled in 1959 and was replaced by the present top section, with pyramidal roof, by *Cecil B. Smith*. The church and churchyard walls are built of concrete, a material with which Ranger made various experiments ('Ranger's patent stone'), and faced in stucco with masonry lines. Most of the concrete is poured, but some (e.g. on the belfry) is blockwork. Cast-iron hammerbeam roof. – SCULPTURE. Carved wooden grotesque, C15. – ROYAL ARMS of Hanover. Cast in plaster. – MONUMENTS. A few by *de Carle*, †1822–42.

Of the medieval church of ST THOMAS À BECKET there remains in a field, 400 yds W of the new church, the E wall with the void of the E window.

WESTLEY HALL, 200 yds N. Gault brick. Early C19 two-storey entrance front, three bays wide and one bay deep with pedimented recessed porch. Behind this an early C16 timber-framed house, enlarged and remodelled in the C18 and given a hipped roof.

WEST STOW

ST MARY. Norman N doorway, inside the vestry of 1903. With primitive volute capitals and a roll moulding. One N lancet, but the nave and chancel mainly Dec, as is visible in the fine four-light reticulated E window, and PISCINA in the angle of the SE window which is elaborately crocketed and finialled. Perp nave N windows; also the battlemented W tower, with chequered flushwork on the buttresses and base. Restoration by *William Butterfield*, 1849–50, including new roofs and woodwork

---

*Described by Pevsner as 'very crude and ignorant': cf. Ranger's St John, Bury St Edmunds.

throughout. – STAINED GLASS. E window by *Ward & Nixon*, 1850, and perhaps also the nave S windows. Other chancel windows by *Hardman*, commemorating Rev. E. R. Benyon †1883 and his wife Jane †1876.

West Stow was part of the Culford estate (q.v.) from 1795 to 1935. There are a number of estate cottages etc., including a pair of flint and white-brick LODGES to Culford Hall, and the red brick READING ROOM (now West Stow and Wordwell Club), 1894, designed by *George Johnson*, clerk of works on the Culford estate, and built by estate staff. White-brick OLD RECTORY, W of the church, by *James Ilsley*, estate carpenter, 1833.

WEST STOW HALL. The precise date is not known, nor is it certain whether this was the principal manor of West Stow, but the indications are that the house was built *c.* 1530 by the last abbot of Bury, John Reeve (1513–39), probably as a hunting lodge. It was bought in 1540 by John Crofts, later owner of Little Saxham Hall, knighted in 1553. The house is dominated by the splendid three-storey red brick GATEHOUSE. The E front has battlemented polygonal turrets with two stages of blank panels with double trefoil tops. Between them, a four-centred arch with quatrefoils in the spandrels. Above it a panel of quatrefoils forming a lattice, originally painted with flowers. Above this a window once larger than the present one, then a recessed terracotta panel with the arms of Mary Tudor †1533 (*see* Westhorpe Hall, p. 550). It is clumsily framed by moulded bricks, suggesting a later insertion. Trefoiled panels to either side. Two-light attic window above that and then a stepped gable with a finial on which sits a dog or ape holding a shield. The turrets have domed caps ending in brick finials on which sit further terracotta figures: a man playing a pipe and a squatting animal with a human face. The W wall of the gatehouse has a similar arrangement of turrets and finials. In the room above the gateway is an interesting and very naïve WALL PAINTING of *c.* 1575: a hunting scene, and the Four Ages of Man represented by a young man out hunting (inscription: 'Thus do I all the day'), a man embracing a woman ('Thus do I while I may'), a middle-aged man looking on ('Thus did I when I myght'), and a bent old man leaning on his stick ('Good Lord, will this worlde last ever').

The gatehouse originally crossed the moat, on two arches. Its timber-framed upper storey is jettied, with brick-nogging. It stood detached from the house, but was connected to it, probably in the early C17, by a two-storey passageway whose ground floor is a brick arcade, plastered and provided with Tuscan demi-columns. The same motif was extended to the inside of the gatehouse itself. Gatehouse and passageway repaired for Lady Cadogan by *William Weir*, 1906.

After all this grand display, the house itself is surprisingly modest. Parts were lost in a fire in the C19 and major alterations were carried out in 1839 by *James Ilsley* for Rev. E. R.

Benyon. The moat was filled in and the S range was encased in white brick (with blind windows of knapped flint on the end walls). Reception rooms were formed out of what was originally the kitchen and, in the SE corner, what seems to have been a viewing room, with raised floor and high-level windows, perhaps associated with hunting. The hall lay to the N of this, but its S end was cut off in 1839 to form an entrance hall. The remainder of the hall has moulded beams and, in the NW corner, a wide Tudor-arched opening that probably led to a staircase. Behind the hall is a fragment of the parlour, with a fine carved beam and stone chimneypiece. Chimneystack with trefoiled brick decoration.

WEST STOW COUNTRY PARK, about 1½ m. WNW of the church. Opened in 1979 following the excavation of an entire Anglo-Saxon village between 1965 and 1972. It stood on a small hill on the N bank of the Lark and was occupied between *c.* A.D. 420 and 650. It was known from earlier excavations that the site had been used since at least the Mesolithic period (*c.* 8000 B.C.), and a Neolithic round barrow (*c.* 2000 B.C.) has been identified. Farmers were present during the Iron Age (*c.* 200 B.C.) and during the Roman period pottery was made here. A group of nine kilns has been excavated, which produced imitation *terra sigillata* of the early C2 A.D. date, a sherd of which was found during the 1953 excavations of the Roman road by Baylham Mill (*see* Coddenham (E)) with a fibula of A.D. 100–20.

The village consisted of three or four groups of houses with a hall at the centre of each group. Since 1974, a number of buildings have been reconstructed, each using different construction methods, in order to determine how the original buildings might have looked. The halls were rectangular, about 30–35 ft (10 metres) long, with wall-posts sunk into the ground and a central hearth. The houses were smaller, with internal posts, of the type usually referred to as 'Grubenhäuser', i.e. 'sunken huts'. Whereas it was previously thought that the occupants used the dug-out base of the house as the floor, with the eaves of the roof coming down to the ground like a tent, excavation and experimental rebuilding have demonstrated that the houses had suspended plank floors above a hollow storage or air space, with vertical plank walls and thatched roofs. Some were provided with internal hearths with a thick clay base to protect the floor. These houses were clearly used for a number of purposes: as weaving sheds, for storage, and for sleeping quarters. Apart from the early boundary ditches on the N side of the settlement there are no ditches or apparent boundaries between the properties within the village. VISITOR CENTRE by *N. Badcock* of *St Edmundsbury Borough Council*, 1988. Timber, in the form of a hall with aisles on all four sides. ANGLO-SAXON CENTRE, 1999, and COLLECTIONS STUDY BUILDING, 2008, also by the council. Timber, with pyramidal roofs. In the SE corner of the park a former PUMPHOUSE, built *c.* 1886 for Bury

St Edmunds sewage works. Red brick with white-brick dressings.

CHIMNEY MILL, ½ m. S of the church. Large, white-brick mill house, mainly early C19 but of earlier origins, and surprisingly elegant for its purpose: one wing has a curved wall and large sash windows. The name pre-dates the tall, white-brick octagonal chimney of *c.* 1840, part of a watermill demolished in 1932.

WETHERDEN

ST MARY. Dec W tower and Dec chancel with an E window which has reticulated tracery and a niche over. Inside it has niches l. and r. The PISCINA is contemporary too. The rest is Perp, i.e. the other windows of the chancel, the sacristy N of the chancel with a curious heavy half-tunnel vault with closely set single-chamfered ribs, the tower doorway and the window above it, and the spectacular S aisle and S porch. The S aisle was begun by Sir John Sulyard, justice of the King's Bench, in the 1480s, but was unfinished at his death in 1488; the western bay, and the porch which is attached to the W end of the aisle and forms part of it, were added by his widow, Dame Anne Bourchier, some thirty years later. This can be deduced from their wills, made in 1487 and 1519 respectively, and from the heraldry that adorns both the exterior and interior. On the porch a base with a frieze of shields and flushwork panelling. Also a frieze of shields above the entrance. On the buttress between the porch and the aisle a lily in a vase, emblem of the Virgin Mary. The S arcade inside is Perp too, with capitals only to the shafts towards the arch openings. False double hammerbeam roof, the lower hammerbeams tenoned into the hammerposts, arch braces springing from the upper hammerbeams. Three-tier decorated wall-plate. Figures (not original) on the pendants. True single hammerbeam roof in the chancel. The aisle roof has cambered tie-beams and figures at the springing of the arched braces. The outer rafters continue to the nave wall; the inner rafters are really a ceiling. – PULPIT. Perp panels are reused. – SCREEN. Part of the tracery (between chancel and S aisle). – BENCHES. Some on the N side with carved backs, poppyheads and, on the arms, beasts and birds. Restored and multiplied in the C19. – BOX PEWS. In the S aisle, early C19. Lined with straw-work. – STAINED GLASS. E window and chancel S by *H. Hughes*. The E window, dated 1863, reuses in its tracery interesting C14–C15 glass including several figures. In a nave N window, tracery remaining from a window of 1861 by *Willement*, the rest blown out during the Second World War. – MONUMENTS. Sir John Sulyard †1488. Tomb-chest with three lozenges with shields. Very damaged. – Sir John Sulyard †1575. Tall tomb-chest with fluted pilasters and shields. On it a stone panel with a framed shield with foliage flanked by two columns. Below the panel four small kneeling figures, Sir John and his family. Not a convincing composition. As a rule such monuments as this have no figures at all. – Edward Sulyard of Haughley Park †1799. Very elegant, with urn and garlands. – Elizabeth Crawford †1828 and Rev. William Henry Crawford †1868. Identical to their monuments at Haughley (q.v.).

SCHOOL MEADOW and WHITES MEADOW, W of the church, is a housing scheme promoted by the Suffolk Building Preservation Trust, 1978–9. By *David Luckhurst* of *Feilden & Mawson*. Ten houses, mostly detached, of pale brick with steep-pitched roofs of dark pantiles.

OLD RECTORY. ¼ m. NE. 1816 by *Robert Heffer* of Ixworth. Two storeys. Three-bay entrance front with projecting centre and semicircular portico.

ROOKYARD FARM, ½ m. NE. Timber-framed and plastered hall house of *c.* 1500 with gabled and jettied cross-wings.

BRICKWALL FARM, ½ m. SE. Three-bay, two-storey house of *c.* 1530–50; cross-wing to r. added *c.* 1600. Both parts jettied with exposed timbers. Carved bressumer and tie-beam on the cross-wing.

WHATFIELD

ST MARGARET. In the middle of the village, but set back from the street and approached by a little lane between thatched cottages. Entirely stuccoed. Low broad W tower of the C13, with later pyramid roof. Nave of *c.* 1300, window with Y- and intersected tracery, one with pretty little quatrefoils in two of the intersections. The stoup inside belongs to the same date. Dec chancel with reticulated windows, although the three-light E window is early C20. Simple C16 brick S porch. Tie-beam roof with crown-posts in the nave, wagon roof in the chancel. Restored 1869, including re-seating of chancel and part of the nave. Nave N vestry 1955. – PULPIT. Jacobean. Plain panelled pulpit; backboard and tester carved in the style of the day but quite coarsely. – Plain BENCHES, the date 1589 on one of them, of a pattern different from the others. – COMMUNION RAIL and WEST GALLERY, probably *c.* 1700, with turned balusters, in effect similar to twisting. – MONUMENT. William Vesey †1699. Handsome black and white marble tablet with Ionic columns and achievement at the top. Attributed to *William Stanton* (GF).

OLD RECTORY, ½ m. SW. Timber-framed and plastered house, moated. Rebuilt in whole or part in 1657, and remodelled by Rev. John Clubbe, rector 1735–73. The main part of the front symmetrical. Straight gables l. and r. with ground-floor bays, a tripartite window above them, and Diocletian windows in the gables. Clubbe tunnelled through the chimney of the lobby-entrance house to lead through to a new staircase at the back. In one room a compartmented ceiling with C17 plasterwork. Clubbe, who was painted by Gainsborough, wrote a spoof *History and Antiquities of the ancient Villa of Wheatfield*, and had the frontispiece of another satirical work drawn by Hogarth, also laid out the grounds, including canals; two very fine cedars remain. Rev. John Plampin, rector 1794–1823, erected a rustic flint SUMMERHOUSE to his memory in 1797.

BARRARD'S HALL, ½ m. SSW. Two-storey, three-bay chequered brick front of 1704. Pedimented doorcase. Timber-framed, with a Jacobean plaster ceiling in one room.

WHEPSTEAD

ST PETRONILLA. A unique dedication, although it dates only from *c.* 1883. Before the Reformation the church was dedicated to St Thomas. Fragmentary W tower with three niches round the W window. Its spire is traditionally said to have blown down in 1658, on the night of Oliver Cromwell's death. Nave and chancel *c.* 1300 (intersected and Y-tracery). But inside, the imposts of the chancel arch with nook-shafts are Norman. The arch itself collapsed during *H. M. Cautley*'s restoration of the church in 1925–8, and was rebuilt; some original stones reused for the door to the ringers' gallery. At the same time the rood stair was discovered, climbing up in the window recess as at Barningham, the S porch restored, N vestry added and ringers' gallery erected. – PULPIT. By *George Mingay*, 1925. Made up of Elizabethan panels from Plumpton House, including some marquetry work. – STAINED GLASS. Fragments in a chancel S window. – E window by *Powell & Sons*, 1908. Lower panels (designed by *J. Hogan*) added 1925–6. Also by Powells the nave S armorial window, 1927–8, and tower window, 1931–2, the latter predominantly blue and inspired by Chartres. – Chancel N (St Peter and St Petronilla) by *F. C. Eden*, 1926. – MONUMENTS. John Ryley †1673. With broken pediment and shield of arms. – Gen. Sir Francis Hammond †1850. By *M. W. Johnson* and, unusually for this date, C17 in style, of black and white marble with Corinthian columns and achievement in a segmental pediment. – In churchyard, chest tomb of Jane Brown †1818. On the chest a stone casket with tapered sides, on feet.

BAPTIST CHURCH, ⅓ m. SE. 1844, and very charming in its rustic-Gothick way. Flint and septaria rubble with white-brick dressings. Lancet windows with hoodmoulds. Gabled front with brick pinnacles. The centre projects slightly, with its own smaller pinnacles, and has a large quatrefoil window. Below this a porch, also with pinnacles.

Former BOARD SCHOOL, E of St Petronilla. By *Frank Whitmore*, 1874. Red brick with white-brick and stone dressings. Adjoining arched entrances to schoolroom and teacher's house, separated by an attached shaft; above the schoolroom entrance a short tower with pyramidal roof. Triple-arched window to schoolroom set in arched recess with circular plaque in tympanum.

DOVEDEN HALL, ¾ m. NW. Facing the road, a mid-C19 painted brick front of four bays and two storeys, added to the S crosswing of a C15 hall house. Behind this front, all is evidently timber-framed and plastered. The cross-wing was rebuilt and extended E in the late C16, when the hall was floored and the tall chimneys erected. In the E extension a ground-floor panelled room with arcading over the fireplace. The inserted hall floor was mostly removed in the C20, leaving only a gallery. Complete moat.

MANSTON HALL, I m. S. Main range mid-C16 with jettied front and chimneystack of four octagonal shafts. Exposed timbers on front and back. In the parlour and chamber at the N end black-letter inscriptions over fireplaces. Cross-wing to the S added early in the C17. Timbers exposed on the front only. At the NE of the main range a short C18 wing, timber-framed and plastered, and running N from this an extension by *Basil Oliver*, 1938, who also restored the older parts. All thatched. Incomplete moat.

PLUMPTON HOUSE, I m. W. Odd-looking. John Gage observed that as a result of alterations and additions by Maj.-Gen. (Sir) Francis Thomas Hammond, who acquired the property in 1800, the place had the character of a French chateau, with its

Whepstead, Plumpton House.
Engraving by G. Hollis, 1838

steeply pitched roofs and flanking pavilions with hipped roofs. The age of the original structure is uncertain, early C18 or older. H-plan. Red brick, mostly now rendered. A number of cross-windows, but on the main garden front (SE) arched French windows on the ground floor and shutters; also a canted bay on the end of the S cross-wing, the window above it with segmental head cutting into the eaves, both early C20 alterations. The N cross-wing carries a slender bell-turret with spirelet. To the N one of the pavilions, extended in the early C20, connected to the main house by a single-storey range. The S pavilion was replaced by large red brick additions of *c.* 1911–15, with a very rich panelled interior. Now subdivided. Gatehouse 700 yds N (NORTH LODGE), *c.* 1911. Rendered and with false half-timbering, the entry spanned by a hammerbeam roof, and cottages on either side. Well-house to the E. Of about the same date SOUTH EAST LODGE and SOUTH WEST LODGE (semi-detached), 600 yds SE, timber-framed and thatched, very picturesque, apparently a C16 house restored and enlarged.

WICKHAMBROOK

ALL SAINTS. Mostly Dec, and with a fine chancel. In the E window large circle with figure of six-petalled flower; in the side windows figures of four-petalled flowers. Finely moulded chancel arch. N aisle N windows with cusped and uncusped intersected tracery. Earlier N doorway with two orders of shafts and dogtooth decoration in the hoodmould. PISCINA at E end of N aisle also with dogtooth. Somewhat later E window with reticulation. S doorway with two quadrant mouldings, though the windows here are Perp. Tall two-light reticulated window in the W tower belongs to the restoration of 1862–3 by *Clark & Holland*, but may be correct. Chequerboard flushwork on the panelling. Arcades with octagonal piers but semicircular responds. Double-chamfered arches. On the N side hoodmould with defaced figures. In the N aisle an arch was planned or built to the N. There seems to be no reason for it. The nave roof is of the hammerbeam type, but Jacobean. – BENCHES. Of an unusual shape; C16 or C17. – SCULPTURE. Outside in the N wall, a stone panel with the crude figure of a man with a shield. C11 or C12. – HELM. Above the Higham monument (replica). – MONUMENTS. Brass to Thomas Burrough †1597, two wives, and children. Behind a wooden grating. – Sir Thomas Higham †1630. By *Nicholas Stone*. Good alabaster monument. He is lying on his side, his hand on his sword. Broad beard. Plain back wall. The inscription is worth reading. Original railings. – Mirable Cradock †1631. Slate tablet with round-arched top within a steep open pediment. Composite capitals. Attributed to *William Wright* (AW). – Ruth Partridge †1693. Good headstone, re-set in the N porch.

In the NW corner of the churchyard, former SCHOOLROOM of 1835. Flint with red brick dressings. Next to it a row of former ALMSHOUSES built by Anthony Sparrow, Bishop of Norwich †1685, baptized at Wickhambrook in 1612. Timber-framed and plastered with thatched roof. On the E side of the churchyard THE OLD VICARAGE, timber-framed and plastered, dating back to the C15. C16 gabled and jettied cross-wing at the E end with C19 bargeboards.

COMMERCE HOUSE, 600 yds NW. Probably c. 1740–50. Timber-framed and plastered with thatched roof. Two storeys and attics. Three-bay W front with Gibbs door surround. Four-bay front with early C19 shop window.

In the main part of the village, about 1 m. NW of the church, the PRIMARY SCHOOL by *Clark & Holland*, 1877–8. Red brick with white-brick dressings. Separate teacher's house. A little further on the PRIMITIVE METHODIST CHAPEL of 1850. Red brick. Tall gabled front of three bays separated by pilasters. NE along Cemetery Road the CEMETERY of 1891 with war memorial by *W.C. Waymouth*, 1924. Portland stone cross on stepped base. At the top of Cemetery Road the UNITED REFORMED CHURCH of 1733–5 (originally Presbyterian, then Congregational). Red brick. Three-bay front, spoilt by the addition of a porch in 1989. Hipped roof, rebuilt in 1889. In the back wall two tall round-arched windows. Original W gallery, with side galleries added 1814. Schoolroom of that date on N side. To its W, in NUNNERY GREEN, HOUSING for Clare Rural District Council by *A. E. Richardson* (*Richardson & Houfe*), 1950. Six semi-detached pairs, of the same type as at Barnardiston and Hundon (qq.v.).

WAKELINS, Genesis Green, 2 m. N. A relatively modest C16 timber-framed house, restored and extended by *James Gorst Architects*, 2002–3. The new wing, an in-line extension of the old house, is uncompromising, with flat roof and large windows, but clad in vertical oak boarding. At the far end a formal pond with Carrara marble sculpture (Bird) by *Jessica Walters*.

There are four good houses round Wickhambrook, the best known being GIFFORDS HALL, 1 m. ESE of the church. The manor is recorded in 1272 and was acquired by Thomas Higham in the mid C15; the house was probably built c. 1485 by his son Clement, who died in 1521. Significant alterations and additions were made in the C16. It was sold by Higham's descendants in 1698 and declined until, according to Basil Oliver, it was saved from demolition by John Seymour Lucas R.A., c. 1903 (cf. The Priory, Blythburgh (E)). It was then rented by painters John and Mary Young Hunter, and appears in a number of their works. In about 1908 the house was acquired by A. H. Fass, who had a South African fortune, a degree in history, and a taste for the antique. He restored the old part of the house and extended it to the N; he may have acted as his own architect.

The house is exceptionally picturesque, even by the high standard of moated Suffolk houses, with exposed timbers.

The moat is on three sides, its S arm crossed by a red brick bridge of three arches. Across the bridge is the oldest part of the house, facing W, of two storeys and attics with crown-post roof. It must once have been larger – there are no original services – and may have extended further W; Edward Martin suggests a hall range opposite the bridge, with services W of that. As it is, the core part of the house consists of a hall (single-storey from the start, and perhaps originally a grand parlour to the lost hall) with parlour at the N end. The hall has a five-light W and seven-light S window, although the latter is not original but part of Fass's restoration. At the S end of the W front is a two-storey gabled porch, added in the C16, and at the N end a later C16 stair-tower, also gabled. On the E side of the hall and parlour are gabled extensions, added at different times in the C16. Beyond the NE corner is a block of 1909, jettied to the E, which convincingly imitates the older work and may indeed have reused old materials: there was a detached building on the site. This was soon (c. 1912–13) followed by the N range, of painted brick, with a polygonal stair-tower on the N front; this seems to have been a more or less self-contained wing for Fass's private occupation. These C20 additions created a little courtyard open to the W, with a single-storey passage linking the old and new parts.

Inside, the best room is over the hall, which has a splendid cambered ceiling with moulded beams, and a fireplace decorated with fleurons. It is carved with graffiti including the names of Highams and Cloptons. The adjoining smaller room has a similar ceiling, but the corresponding ground-floor room has early C18 panelling.

WICKHAM HOUSE, 500 yds SE of Giffords Hall. Timber-framed and plastered house of c. 1610, updated c. 1630. Gabled cross-wing at one end. Chimneystack with four circular shafts. In the parlour, hall chamber, parlour chamber and circulation areas an important sequence of C17 decorative painting, including an overmantel of imitation panelling in the hall chamber.

CLOPTON HALL, ⅔ m. NNW of Giffords Hall. Mainly mid-C17, but with early C16 elements that seem to be *in situ*, notably carved and moulded beams in the parlour. Timber-framed and plastered. Front with three equal gables and a (modern) one-storeyed gabled central porch. Star-topped chimneys in three symmetrically arranged stacks. Return wing at NW end with two-storey gabled porch.

BADMONDISFIELD HALL, 1½ m. NNW of the church. A moated house of the C16, with a block of c. 1530 to which were added, about fifty years later, a hall and cross-wing. The cross-wings project slightly at the front but are deeper at the back, where the W cross-wing is double pile. The house was remodelled in about the second quarter of the C19, when a third storey was removed and the cross-wings were given hipped roofs instead of gables. Something of the original character was restored in the mid C20, including exposed timbers and some brick-nogging, and a single-storeyed gabled porch.

(Inside, two beautiful doorways remain in the hall, one larger than the other, both with angels in spandrels playing musical instruments. In the r. wing an original fireplace, in the l. wing the kitchen fireplace and oven.). The NW arm of the moat appears to have been straightened in the C18; at its N end a little Georgian SUMMERHOUSE with half-hipped roof and turret.

WICKHAM SKEITH

ST ANDREW. Dec W tower. Diagonal buttresses with chequer flushwork panelling. Perp N porch with tall side windows, a front with arched flushwork panelling, a niche above the entrance, a flushwork frieze of shields in stars below the battlements, and flushwork-panelled buttresses. Less important Perp S porch, for which 6s. 8d. was left in 1459. Two-storeyed. Knapped front with flushwork on the lower storey. Nave windows Perp, with stepped embattled transoms, characteristic of the work of *Hawes* of Occold; copied in the chancel (replacing Dec windows) as part of the restoration by *Daniel Penning* of Eye, 1856–7. Broad chancel arch on head corbels, reinforced with an inner arch on outsize head corbels, probably also in 1856–7. To its N three narrow niches, to its S one broad one. Single hammerbeam roof in the nave. Good bosses including a Green Man. – FONT. Badly preserved. The stem had the Emblems of the Evangelists and four Wild Men. Against the bowl a variety of tracery patterns. – BENCHES. A nice set, of 1856–7, with poppyheads. – WEST GALLERY. 1808. It cost £25. The tracery was added later. – DOORS. S door with linenfold. On the W door, tracery that might once have formed part of the rood screen. – COMMUNION RAIL. With turned balusters, probably mid-C17. – STAINED GLASS. Chancel S by *Rev. Walter Wilson*, 1998. The design is mostly in the leading, with some lettering and etching and a little very pale colouring. – MONUMENTS. Brass of a Lady and her daughters. Fragments, c. 1530, the kneeling lady in widow's dress 13 in. (33 cm.) in length. – Ledger stone of Jane Harvey †1644. Stones for other family members on either side, the three joined together by incised buckles.

WICKHAM HALL, SW of the church. Built in 1846 by Rev. Castell Garrad, patron of the living and between 1844 and 1868 the vicar. The architects may have been *Whiting & Woolnough*, who oversaw the sale and demolition of the old hall. Tudor-Gothic. Red brick, with straight gables, hood-moulds and tall decorative chimneys. THREE WAYS, 350 yds SW, was the vicarage, said by White's *Directory* to have been built in 1570. Alterations by *F. Rednall*, 1868; considerably enlarged by *A. P. McAlister*, 1897.

STREET FARM, ¾ m. NW. Small C15 hall house, extended to the s and w in the C17. The hall, with sooted crown-post roof, retains its screen. The main interest of the house lies in the narrow wing that extends E from the service end. This has a continuous jetty linking the wing and service rooms parallel to the road. On the inside wall at the E end is a painting of *c.* 1500: most of a Christ in Majesty, a whole figure of a pilgrim to the r., and space for another figure to the l. The room may have been an oratory, and the house a pilgrims' hostel on a route from the coast to Bury St Edmunds. An alternative suggestion is that the wing was built for a priest attached to the household.

WILLISHAM

ST MARY. Completely rebuilt by *H. J. Green*, 1877–8. On the site of, and the same size as, its predecessor. Nave, chancel and bellcote. Flint with stone dressings. The style is late E.E. to early Dec. – FONT. The only relic of the medieval church. Four lions against the stem, four angels with shields and four hanging shields against the bowl.

WISSINGTON
Nayland-with-Wissington

Wissington (until the mid C19 generally, and by some still, known as Wiston) was unwillingly joined to Nayland in 1884.

ST MARY. A delightful group, with the church above the farm buildings and next to the hall. Pretty weatherboarded bell-turret with pyramid roof and weathervane carrying the date 1722. Nave, chancel and apse all Norman, although made more Norman in 1853, when the apse was rebuilt on its original foundations and the nave windows were made grander externally than they had been. But their inner splays are all right. It is possible that the Norman church had a tower over the chancel space, such as still survives in many Norman churches (e.g. Ousden). Chancel arch with one order of shafts and chevron in the arch. Sumptuous tall S doorway. One order of shafts with odd spiral fluting on the l., horizontal chevrons on the r. Tympanum on a segmental lintel stone, with chip-carving. Chevron and other decoration in the arch. Simpler N doorway (inside C19 vestry) with chevron decoration in the arch of the tympanum. S porch rebuilt 1861. – FONT. Perp, octagonal, of the usual Suffolk type but unrestored and with remains of colouring. Bowl with castellated rim. Angels with shields and two playing musical instruments, frieze of angels with overlapping wings below. Traceried stem. – Neo-Norman FURNISHINGS introduced by Rev. C. E. Birch as part of his restoration of the church, begun in 1848. Wooden ALTAR RAILS and stone PULPIT and LECTERN of 1853; stone-carving by *Thomas Crisp*. Timber WEST GALLERY by *William Hawkins* of Monks Eleigh, 1862. – DOOR. In S doorway, C19, but with late C12 ironwork. – WALL PAINTINGS. Discovered by Birch, covered over again, and rediscovered in 1932. They are a comprehensive cycle of *c.* 1250–75, of which much survives, even if only fragmentarily. The quality can never have been more than provincial. On the S wall of the nave two tiers, the upper with stories from the childhood of Christ, the lower with stories from the lives of St Margaret and St Nicholas. The scenes of the upper tier are framed by arcading with trefoiled arch-heads and roofs and turrets over; the lower panels are simply rectangular. On the upper tier Annunciation (only part of the angel remains), Nativity, Annunciation to the Shepherds (two scenes), Adoration of the Magi, Dream of the Magi (three men naked in one bed), Flight into Egypt, Massacre of the Innocents (two scenes), then a window, then Presentation in the Temple and Christ among the Doctors. Among the scenes below, St Nicholas with the three boys in the pickling barrels is recognizable, as is the Miracle of the Cup (ship with sail). St Margaret is seen spinning, then part of the body in the scene of the Passion, the Beheading, Burial(?), Ascension to Heaven(?). On the N wall W of the doorway stories of St John the Baptist. The Beheading can be recognized. Other parts covered by a splendid dragon over the doorway, probably C15. In the tympanum of the doorway a devil tempting a gossiping woman, as a warning to janglers. E of the doorway three tiers. In the upper tier St Francis's Sermon to the Birds. The tree on which the birds are perched has a stylized scrolly shape, as if it were done in metalwork. The Passion of Christ is in the middle tier. Entry into Jerusalem, Last Supper (both much defaced), Christ washing the Apostles' feet, Betrayal(?), Christ carrying the Cross, Crucifixion, Pietà, Resurrection. The stories in the bottom tier have almost completely disappeared. On the W wall the Last Judgment in three tiers, very faint. – STAINED GLASS. Three apse windows by *Wilmshurst & Oliphant*, 1853–4. Nave and tower windows by *T. Baillie*, 1869–70. – MONUMENT. Dr Jane Walker, founder of the East Anglian Sanatorium (*see below*), †1938. Bronze with profile relief by *John Mansbridge*. In vestry; originally in sanatorium chapel.

WISTON HALL. Built in 1791 by *Sir John Soane* for Samuel Beachcroft, a director of the Bank of England. Simple two-storey house of three by one bays; red brick. Doorway with Tuscan pilasters and heavy entablature. Windows without any surrounds. Joined on to an existing timber-framed house that was rebuilt in the 1860s.

WISTON MILL, ½ m. E. Timber-framed and weatherboarded watermill. Four storeys and loft. C18–C19, although the mill race has Tudor brickwork. Ground and first floors converted by *A. S. G. Butler*, 1927, connecting with what were three cottages on the W side. This part partly brick, partly timber-framed and plastered. Surviving machinery includes sluice gear by *Alfred Clubb*, millwright, Colchester, 1864.

Former EAST ANGLIAN SANATORIUM, ¾ m. NNW. By *Smith & Brewer*, 1899–1901. Founded by Dr Jane Walker as a TB sanatorium, and designed along the latest lines, i.e. two long blocks facing SE, at an obtuse angle, with patients' rooms at the front on two storeys for maximum exposure to the sun and fresh air. Three-bay centre with cupola and large weathervane. Large windows divided by broad pilasters, deep eaves, and dormers. T-plan block to rear with entrance courtyard on one side and beyond it the CHAPEL, a homely roughcast affair with battered buttresses, low windows under the eaves, and a small timber bellcote. Also a BOILER HOUSE and LAUNDRY with integral water tower and tapered chimney. Part of the sanatorium closed in the 1950s, the remainder in 1991; principal buildings converted to housing by *Lexden Restorations*, 1995–6.

NEW MALTINGS and MALTINGS CHASE, Bures Road, ½ m. NNW. Two houses by *Edward Cullinan* built for the same clients, Rosemary and Gerald Knox, on part of the site of the East Anglian Sanatorium. NEW MALTINGS, 1963–4, is mainly single-storey with the roof-line broken irregularly by sleeping accommodation. Large windows on brick plinth with weather-boarding above. Extended by Cullinan with semi-underground guest rooms. Large additions to the rear, making new entrance and hall, 1990, by *Penoyre & Prasad*, who also remodelled the interior. Pavilion alongside by *Knox Bhavan Architects*, 2002, predominantly timber with curved copper roof. MALTINGS CHASE, to the NE, 1969–71 (with *Julyan Wickham*), remains unaltered. Load-bearing buff brick with exposed timber joists on concrete beams. Single-storey, U-plan, with separate parents' and children's wings with communal linking block. Flat roof with deep overhang. CHASE COTTAGE, S of Maltings Chase, restored by *Jeremy Stacey Architects* for the same clients, 2007–8, with a bold cuboid extension, the walls part timber-clad, part rendered and brightly painted. Sunand Prasad, Simon Knox and Jeremy Stacey have all worked in Cullinan's office.

WITHERSFIELD

ST MARY. Essentially Perp. Chancel rebuilt and S aisle added by *Clark & Holland*, 1867; the aisle replaced a S chapel, of which the Dec E window was reused. W tower with higher SE stair-turret, S doorway with Perp decoration. The N aisle was built with money bequeathed by Robert Wyburgh (see the brass inscription) in 1497. In its roof, carved bosses including the mullet of the de Veres (cf. Lavenham), a Tudor rose and a grotesque face. Arcade of four bays, quatrefoil piers, double-hollow-chamfered arches. This is Perp, and was copied for the s arcade. The former Dec s arcade is perhaps represented by the stoup, which seems to be a reused respond. – FONT. Octagonal, probably late C16. Decoration with shields and pointed quatrefoils. – SCREEN. Good, still with its gates. Two-light divisions with pendants instead of intermediate mullions. Trefoiled ogee arches and tracery above them. Carvings of animals, etc., in the spandrels, especially on the E side. Money was bequeathed in 1468/9 to light the rood. Unusually embellished in the C17 with cherubs' heads and other classical carving. Repainted in 1867. – PULPIT. Jacobean. – BENCHES. Some straight-headed with buttresses, others with figured poppyheads: St Michael weighing a soul, two animals fighting among vines, youth with shield of St George, the Pelican in its piety, collared and chained swan, mermaid, St George and the Dragon. – STATUE. In niche on S porch, St Mary by *Alexander Wenham*, 2007. – RING HANDLE on S door of two salamanders, against a circular pierced backplate. C13. – STAINED GLASS. N aisle E window †1972 by *Philippa Heskett (Pippa Blackall)*. – MONUMENTS. J.W. Mayd †1848. By *Green* of Haverhill. Plain, heavy Gothic. – A. E. Choat †1916. Cast brass. By *S. Rampling*, Cambridge.

JACOB'S MANOR, E of the church. Built as the rectory, 1726, for Rev. Abraham Oakes, paid for by his father-in-law, Sir John Jacob. Red brick, five bays, two storeys. String course and heavy cornice, also brick. Pitched, not hipped, roof behind parapet. The pedimented doorway is Later Georgian. Extension and stables of *c*. 1800.

TURNPIKE HOUSE, 200 yds SE. C15. Jettied front with exposed timber framing. Cross-wing at N end. Altered in the mid C16.

VILLAGE HALL, 300 yds ESE. Former school, 1865 by *Clark & Holland*; enlarged 1908. Red brick, with depressed-pointed windows and castellated porches.

HALL FARM, beyond the village hall. Late Georgian house of five bays and two and a half storeys. Red brick, with stone plinth, string course and cornice on the front only. Hipped roof. Behind it, a large timber-framed BARN, probably C15, partly weatherboarded but with brick-nogging and evidence of window openings in the E side; it seems to have been converted to a house in the C16, reverting to a barn when the present house was built. Inside some arched doorways opening into rooms on the W side, which is aisled. The manor house lay to the SE, a moated site now ploughed out.

WIXOE

ST LEONARD. Nave and chancel with weatherboarded bell-turret. Nave and chancel are Norman, as is seen in the treatment of the flint walling and also the S doorway, with one order of shafts with scalloped capitals and a chevron in the arch, and the plain arch of the blocked N doorway. The chancel, originally apsidal, was rebuilt in the C14. Restoration by *W.M. Fawcett*, 1898–9, including re-seating and new N vestry. – STAINED GLASS. E window by *Cakebread, Robey & Co.*, 1898. – MONUMENTS. The following inscription appears in large and dignified letters on a slab in the chancel floor: 'The Entrance Into the Vault of Henry Berkeley Esq. and Dorothy his Wife Containing Ten Foot Square'. Good hanging monument nearby with arms, flaming lamps, cherubs' heads, winged skull, etc.; she †1735, he †1751. – William Payne †1843. By *C. Harding* of Ballingdon. With draped urn.

Former SCHOOL and detached two-storey house. 1877–8 by *Frank Whitmore*. Red brick with white-brick dressings. Plain.

FLORISTON HALL, ¼ m. NE. Early C19 white-brick house. Two storeys. Four-bay front with one-bay stuccoed addition to the l. Tuscan porch flanked by single-storey bows. LODGE of painted brick with Gothick windows. Polygonal centre with veranda on slender columns.

WATER HALL, ¾ m. NW. C17 timber-framed and plastered house with Georgian front. Behind it an exceptionally large BARN. A timber on the midstrey, elegantly dated 1795, presumably refers to alterations. A contract survives for *John Whyghte* of Sible Hedingham, Essex, to build a stable and shippon at Water Hall in 1473, but unfortunately this cannot refer to any of the present buildings.

WIXOE MILL, ¼ m. SW. C18 timber-framed and weatherboarded watermill. Timber-framed house also C18 but remodelled in the C19 and later. To the W a sweet little Gothick summerhouse of *c.* 1840.

BAYTHORNE GROVE, ½ m. ENE. *See* Stoke-by-Clare, p. 493.

WOOLPIT

Woolpit is perhaps most famous for the bricks it produced: 'a very white and durable kind of brick, equal in beauty to stone ... Many mansions in various parts of the county have been built of it', according to White's *Directory*. Brickmaking in Woolpit is first recorded in the C16, and the BRICKWORKS, which lay ½ m. E of the village on Old Stowmarket Road, operated until the 1950s. The most visible evidence is the large pit, now flooded, as well as a range of early C20 buildings. Another pit, on the N side of the road, provided earth for red bricks. The focus of the village is once more the church and the very pleasant triangular square known as Green Hill – more pleasant now that the A14 no longer passes through it.

ST MARY. The W tower with its conspicuous spire was built by *R. M. Phipson* in 1853–4, the previous one having been struck by lightning. Cobble flint, with Bath stone dressings. With its openwork parapet and the double-curved flying buttresses helping to hold up the spire, it is Nene Valley rather than Suffolk, but makes an attractive feature. The tower has a timber vault of 1854 and a sexfoiled circular window into the nave. The medieval church of Woolpit is Perp, except for the modest Dec s aisle and the Dec chancel. This has a five-light E window with reticulated tracery, niches with ogee heads in the diagonal buttresses l. and r., and a shafted doorway. The s porch can be dated *c.* 1430–55 (money given for it between 1430 and 1452). It is extremely opulent, much taller than the aisle, with a stone-faced front panelled all over, an entrance with a big crocketed ogee gable and five stepped niches above, and the mouldings of the entrance arch beset with the repeated motif of a beast with a big leaf coming out of its mouth. The side windows have crocketed ogee gables too. The w wall is of rubble but the E wall has excellent flint and stone chequerwork. The porch has openwork cresting of quatrefoils and, inside, a lierne vault with many bosses. A will of 1474 left money for five images for the porch – presumably to go in the gable niches.

Many legacies are recorded for rebuilding the rest of the church. They run from 1403 to 1500, and show that throughout that period the N aisle was under contemplation: John Cooke in 1500 left 10 marks (£6 13s. 4d.), on condition that *William Abrey* or *Albry* started work within two years. Perp arcade inside, of five bays, surprisingly quiet (octagonal piers, arches with one hollow chamfer and one wave moulding). Fine Perp clerestory with double windows. The windows are of two lights with panel tracery. The wall has flushwork decoration: panelling, chequerboard pattern, and emblems. When the clerestory was built, the splendid roof was also made, one of the proudest in Suffolk. The roof stands on wall-posts which in their turn rest on angel brackets. Small figures against the wall-posts. The roof has principal rafters, false double hammerbeams throughout with angels against both hammers, and arch-braced collar-beams. The wall-plate is decorated with two tiers of demi-figures of angels. All the spread-out wings make a glorious feathery, spiky pattern. Decorated spandrels and crestings of both hammerbeams and collars. In the aisle roofs also angels on the wall-posts. Large angels in addition against every second pair of principals so that their heads are separated only by big bosses. Against the other pairs wall-posts with demi-figures in niches and angels below them. Of the angels, some are original, but most date from a general restoration of the roofs by *Henry Ringham* in 1843–4, his first major commission.

FURNISHINGS. FONT. By *Comper*, 1904. Octagonal, plain. – SCREEN. Of one-light divisions with ogee arches and some panel tracery above. A will proved in 1469 left 20 marks (£13 6s. 8d.) for the rood beam. Upper part restored and partly repainted 1750. On the dado eight figures, repainted in 1892 by *G.W. Ostrehan*. – High up, below the nave E window, a CANOPY OF HONOUR. Five bays of finely ribbed coving with lierne patterns. It was placed there in the mid C19 and probably came from another church. – PULPIT. 1883, by *G. G. Scott Jun.*, on a slender marble column. Woodwork executed by *James Elwell* of Beverley. – BENCHES. Some medieval, but mainly by *E. F. Bisshopp*, 1878, based on the old ones. They have poppyheads, animals (and a few saints) on the arms, and traceried ends with a variety of patterns. Carved backs as well. – LECTERN. A fine brass eagle on a substantial base and shaft. It may date from *c*. 1525. It belongs to a group with Cavendish (q.v.), Upwell (Norfolk), Croft (Lincs.), Chipping Camden (Glos.) and Corpus Christi College, Oxford. – STAINED GLASS. Various medieval fragments, especially in the E window. – W window by *Lucy Marriott*, 1849. It survived the fall of the tower. – *Willement* supplied glass in 1843. This may be the nave E window (over chancel arch), or may form part of the chancel E window, rearranged 1962. – MONUMENTS. Rev. J. S. Cobbold †1837. Gothic, with ogee arch and pinnacles, but restrained. By *William Milligan*. – Rev. H. S. Marriott †1875 and wife Lucy †1899. Painting of an angel, 1901, by their daughter *Lucy Marriott*, who seems to have inherited some of her mother's talent. – NE of the chancel, a gravestone protected by a heavy iron cage; probably mid-C19 (cf. Elmswell).

PRIMARY SCHOOL, Heath Road. 1892–5 by *Frank Whitmore*. Red brick with white-brick dressings. With tall windows rising into gables through the eaves, and a spiky bell-turret at one end.

GREEN HILL breaks prettily into the SW corner of the churchyard in the form of the gable-end of TUDOR ROSE COTTAGE. This is of red brick, jettied, with tile-hanging in the gable and a plaster panel decorated with flowers between brick-nogging, and above that coving supporting the top part of the gable. More flowers in a blind window. It is very 'Queen Anne' of the 1870s and rather surprising in this situation. The front is more conventional: earlier C19 brick on a C16 timber-framed house. Green Hill is utterly unspoilt. The N and E sides consist almost entirely of timber-framed houses of the C15 and C16, but varied in that some have their original fronts, with or without exposed timbers, and others C18 or C19 brick fronts, painted or not. The SW side is different. At the S end is GREEN HILL HOUSE. C17 with early C19 alterations. Two storeys, four bays, with a Doric porch. Next to it the early C19 white-brick front of HILL HOUSE conceals the remains of a Wealden-type house, including a crown-post roof with smoke-blackened timbers. It may be as early as the third quarter of the C14, that is to say, exceptionally early for a Wealden house. Then, as a reminder that Woolpit used to be on the main Ipswich–Bury road, the SWAN INN, with a lower part dated 1759 and a higher dated 1826. Both are of red brick. The lower is of two storeys with quoins and a niche not quite in the centre – the irregularity is due to this being the refronting of a C16 timber-framed building. The higher part is of two and a half storeys and six bays, and has at one end a tall archway leading through to the coach yard. At the back the walls are of white brick, and on them is painted RING FOR OSTLER. In the middle of Green Hill a VILLAGE PUMP, 1897. Circular wooden shelter with conical roof supported on four posts that carry small figures of Boudica, Queen Elizabeth I, Queen Anne and Queen Victoria.

THE STREET leads out of the NW corner of Green Hill and contains more good timber-framed houses, some – notably the row on the SW side after Rags Lane – fronted in brick, others – notably WEAVER HOUSE on the NE side and GRANMOR opposite – with exposed timbers. Weaver House is jettied along the front and side. Inside are two mid-C16 black-letter inscriptions over fireplaces. TIMBERS, further out on the SW side, is jettied to the front, and contains a ceiling with apotropaic candle-smoke marks. At the SE end of Green Hill, on the corner of Mill Lane, TYRELLS, with jettied upper storey and exposed timbers, is the gabled cross-wing of a C15 hall house, the hall part now a separate house and faced in painted brick.

OUR LADY'S WELL, 300 yds NE. Moat, roughly oval and up to about 215 ft (66 metres) wide, fed by a spring. It was reputed to be the site of a chapel of Our Lady, a popular place of pilgrimage before the Reformation, but this is now thought to have been on the N side of the parish church and taken down in 1551.

WORDWELL

ALL SAINTS. Nave and chancel, restored by Rev. E. R. Benyon (cf. Culford). The W bellcote is dated 1866, but this feature was not part of S. S. Teulon's design of 1857 and it is not certain how much of the restoration is by him. To it belong the W wall, more heavily buttressed than would seem necessary, S porch, canopied priest's door, over-sized PULPIT and arched REREDOS. The pulpit and reredos are Neo-Norman, but the rest is the real thing, and quite out of the ordinary. The two Norman doorways both have one order of shafts, primitive volute capitals, and carved tympana. That on the S side represents the Tree of Life with two affronted hounds l. and r. The branches and leaves spread and intertwine. On the eastern capital is carved the small figure of a man, perhaps a priest. The N tympanum is a puzzle. It has been reversed, so faces inwards, and has carving apparently by the same hand that did the figure in the S doorway. It shows two standing figures, one with arms raised, the other holding up a ring in one hand. Between them an obscure object, perhaps a bush. Many theories have been advanced as to what is represented, but the figure with raised arms is standing in the classic pose of the orant, and the ring may be the consecrated wafer being

Wordwell, All Saints, before restoration.
Engraving after J. G. Lenny, 1824

elevated by a priest. The date is probably late C11, the S tympanum about fifty years later. Norman also the chancel arch, again with volute capitals. The arch has one big roll moulding and no other mouldings. Imposts with chip-carved lozenges continuing as a frieze. Two large Dec niches l. and r., no doubt for side altars. – BENCHES. A fine set. The ends have tracery, and poppyheads with seated animals. The seat backs are carved (not in openwork) with tracery, foliage and figures (grotesques, a jester, etc.).

WORDWELL HALL, NNW of the church. C16 timber-framed and plastered, altered in 1841 by Benyon (bay window, hoodmoulds).

TRAVELLER'S HILL, 1¾ m. NE. Bronze Age round barrow, 120 ft (36.6 metres) in diameter and 4 ft 6 in. (1.4 metres) high, in Forestry Commission woodland.

WORLINGTON

ALL SAINTS. E.E. chancel, with one N lancet and an E window with three cusped lancet lights under one arch. Dec W tower with a pretty W window with flowing tracery. Niches l. and r. of it. Finely moulded W doorway. Dec arcade of five bays with concave-sided octagonal piers and double-chamfered arches. The sides of the piers have pointed trefoils applied to the tops (cf. Lakenheath). Perp S aisle and clerestory, with vestry (originally two-storey) at the W end of the aisle. Simple nave roof, although with hammerbeams alternating with tie-beams supporting vertical struts. C18 white-brick S porch. Chancel restored 1879; general restoration by *W.M. Fawcett*, 1900–11. – FONT. Probably Norman, remodelled with attached columns at the corners. It appears to be standing on the original S wall (cf. Great Ashfield). – FONT COVER by *Jack Penton*, 1966. – ROOD BEAM. The original cambered beam is preserved. 20s. was bequeathed in 1475 for painting the rood loft. – BENCH ENDS. Square-headed, with three little stepped cusped lancets or big flowers. – WALL PAINTINGS. Fragments only, but indicative of an extensive and colourful display, that included a St Christopher on the N wall. C14. – ROYAL ARMS. Of George III, ordered in 1762. – STAINED GLASS. Some C15 pieces in the chancel side windows. E window †1909 by *J. Dudley Forsyth*. – MONUMENTS. Rice James †1822. Obelisk with a mourning female, kneeling over an urn. Unsigned, but good of its kind. – Rev. Sir William Henry Cooper Bt †1835. By *H. Hopper*. With open book, cross and a palm frond.

OLD RECTORY, 250 yds SE. By *George Maliphant*, 1819–20, for Rev. James Gibson. White brick. Two storeys. Three bays with corner pilaster strips and slightly projecting centre. Further enlivened by a stuccoed surround to the entrance, and external shutters.

WORLINGTON HALL (hotel), 650 yds E. Late C16, timber-framed, with some exposed timbers at the rear. The front was clad in red brick *c.* 1900. Pilasters, and terracotta pediments to the windows. Other alterations and additions of various dates. The OLD HALL, opposite, is early C16 with an early C18 plastered front and a broad semicircular Doric porch.

KING'S STAUNCH (flash lock). *See* Mildenhall, p. 412.

WORTHAM

ST MARY THE VIRGIN. The broadest Norman round tower in England, 29 ft (9 metres) in diameter. About 62 ft (19 metres) high and now open to the sky. The top collapsed in 1789. Peeping out from behind the awe-inspiring rotundity of the tower is an engaging little weatherboarded bell-turret with an ogee top. The tower is contemporary with the W wall, i.e. C12, but the church itself is mainly Perp (although the chancel S doorway, as is so often the case, is Dec). The E window is of five lights. NE vestry, originally of two storeys with a chapel on the ground floor. The clerestory has double windows, and between them emblems in flushwork (including the *Aldryche* device) with much use of brick. C14 arcades of three bays. Octagonal piers, double-chamfered arches. Nave and aisles repaired 1891–3 by *E. F. Bisshopp*, who also re-roofed the chancel, 1903. s porch rebuilt 1907–8 by *Albert Bartrum*, builder and churchwarden, based on a report by *Arthur J. Lacey* of Norwich. – FONT. Dec, octagonal. With gables and much decoration with small quatrefoils. Heads at the lower corners of the bowl, battlements at the top. – ALTAR SURROUND. Stone. With verses from the Gospels in broad frames with thick vine leaves and grapes. Below, a frieze of gables copied from the font. Ten Commandments l. and r. of the E window. Variously dated 1856 and 1867, so perhaps not all of a piece.* – SCREEN. Fragments of tracery reused in the front of the altar. – PULPIT. By *Bartrum*, 1909. – BENCHES. 1892. By *Bartrum*, with poppyheads by *John Groom* and figures and animals by *Arthur C. James*, brother of the rector. – ROYAL ARMS. Stuart. Carved wood, in oval frame (cf. Redgrave). – STAINED GLASS. C15 fragments in the E window. Also ornamental quarries of *c.* 1830, attributed by Birkin Haward to *Robert Allen* of Lowestoft. N aisle N by *G. King & Son*, 1986 (Four Seasons), and *Deborah Lowe*, 2012. – MONUMENTS. Two stone coffin-lids with floriated crosses by the font; a third built into the base of the tower. – Rev. Richard Cobbold †1877, author of the novel *The History of Margaret Catchpole* and rector for fifty-two years. Brass lozenge with decorated border. By *Barkentin & Krall*. – LYCHGATE. By *Bartrum*, 1911. Hipped roof with gablets.

TITHE MONUMENT, 600 yds W. Concrete monolith with inscription recording 134 pigs and fifteen cattle seized for tithe in 1934 (cf. Elmsett).

Former RECTORY, ¼ m. E. White-brick range of 1827–8, added by Rev. Richard Cobbold. Two tall storeys. Five bays, the centre slightly projecting, and corner pilaster strips. But the entrances are inconspicuously placed round the sides. At the back, at right angles, a modest, timber-framed C16 range, and between the two a C17 extension. In the latter a small dog-leg staircase of *c.* 1700–10 behind a typical arch.

RASH'S CRESCENT, ½ m. NE. A curved terrace of ten houses for Suffolk Rural Housing Association, 1992, by *Mid Suffolk District Council* (group architect *Jonathan Wainwright*; project architect *Colin Hart*). Further interest is provided by a mix of materials and roof heights.

MANOR HOUSE, ¾ m. NW. Timber-framed and red brick. C17 with an C18 front with two steep straight gables and a regular two-and-a-half-storey centre. In the middle a blank-arched niche or former window. Under the gables canted bays. To the l. round the corner a C17 shaped gable. Square chimneys with arched panels. W of the house a large thatched BARN. Mid-C16. Converted to a house by *Simon Conder Associates*, *c.* 1987–9.

LING FARM, E of the Manor House. Early C17, timber-framed, with an early C19 white-brick front. Also early C19 the red brick

---

*In 1868, according to White's *Directory*, the church was 'somewhat improved, and quaintly ornamented'.

WALL enclosing the garden in front of the house. Central entrance with sturdy brick piers and stone ball finials.

PRIMARY SCHOOL, Long Green, 1 m. s. 1870, later enlarged and partly rebuilt. From the original building the classical façade of three pedimented bays with three arched entrances, *à la* Arch of Constantine. Above them the inscriptions Faith, Charity, Hope. Red brick with stone dressings. Hall immediately behind this of 2001, with prominent hipped slate roof.

THE ROOKERY, 1¼ m. SE. C17 timber-framed farmhouse, enlarged and fronted in white brick for C. Harrison of Palgrave, 1815. Front range of two storeys and three bays with Doric porch.

WYVERSTONE

ST GEORGE. Dec W tower with a tier of small quatrefoil windows. At the belfry stage to the S and W openings of two lights with square heads, to the N and E cusped vesicas. S porch of timber with carved bargeboards and a crown-post roof, restored as the First World War memorial. Perp nave and chancel, clerestory, though no aisles. Good roof with alternating single hammerbeams and arched braces joining at the high collar-beams. General restoration by *E. F. Bisshopp*, 1900. – FONT. Octagonal, Perp, simple. Panelled stem; bowl with shields in quatrefoils etc. – C17 FONT COVER with curved braces radiating from a central baluster. – SCREEN. Dado with remains of carved, not simply painted, scenes: Annunciation, Nativity, Magi, Mass of St Gregory, Visitation. Money was left for the rood beam in 1491. At the S end, two C17 panels, perhaps part of a reading desk. – PULPIT. Early C16, with linenfold panelling. – COMMUNION RAIL. Jacobean. – BENCHES. Some ends with medieval poppyheads, some strengthened with C17 carved posts; also one dated 1616. – ROYAL ARMS. A fine set, for William and Mary, carved in wood. – Another dated 1812, painted on boards. STAINED GLASS. A little in the NW and more in the NE window of the nave. E window by *William Glasby*, 1926.

THE MANOR, 350 yds W. Built as the rectory, 1830. White brick. Two storeys and three bays with Doric porch.

LODGE FARM, 1,000 yds W. Mid-C16, timber-framed and plastered. Hall with moulded ceiling and cross-passage screen. SE of the house extensive farm buildings, converted in 2009–10 by the *Whitworth Co-Partnership* from designs by *Keith Day Architects*. They included a weatherboarded barn contemporary with the house and, at right angles to it, a small plastered building of the early C16 moved to its present site in the mid C19. It seems to have been a public building (such as a guildhall or market house), albeit unusually small, rather than an agricultural one.

YEW TREE COTTAGE, 900 yds sw. *Cottage orné*, dated 1831, with the initials of W. C. Steggall. Roughly rendered. Thatched two-storey centre in the shape of an elongated octagon. Lower wings to l. and r.

YAXLEY

ST MARY. Early C14 W tower with an ogee niche in the W side. Tower arch to the nave with two continuous chamfers. Extremely ornate N porch, one of the most swagger in Suffolk. In 1459 John Herberd *alias* Yaxley asked to be buried in it, and for the rest to be paved at his expense. Two-storeyed front with flushwork panelling and symbols for Mary and Jesus. Entrance with spandrels showing a man, a monster, a Wild Man and a lion. Niches l. and r. A frieze of shields l. and r. below them. Two upper two-light windows with three niches. Parapet with shields. Pinnacles. Tierceron-vaulted interior with carved bosses, including what was probably an Annunciation scene. Perp nave with large windows to the N, to the S an aisle and a clerestory with doubled windows. There is also an E window at clerestory level. The S arcade has octagonal piers and double-chamfered arches. Nave roof with long arched braces up to the castellated collar-beams. Traces of colouring on the easternmost bay. S porch (now vestry) by *John Johnson* of Bury, 1854. General restoration by *E. L. Blackburne*, 1867–8, including almost complete rebuilding (and heightening) of the chancel. The notion of a flying buttress running up in front of the priest's door was borrowed from neighbouring Eye (E). – PULPIT. Dated 1635, with the churchwardens' initials. With canted back panel and tester, very richly carved. – SCREEN. The dado painted badly with saints. But there is attractive gilding of the ornamental parts. Of the upper part of the screen all the finery has gone except for the extremely rich carved entrance arch, with cusping and subcusping (cf. Eye, almost certainly made by the same workshop). Original also the cresting. The gates, and tympanum above the beam, were removed in 1868. The position of the rood beam is indicated by its ends remaining in the walls. – WALL PAINTING. Doom above the chancel arch, discovered in 1868; no longer recognizable. – CURIOSUM. Over the S door a SEXTON'S WHEEL, dating from not long before the Reformation. One of only two surviving; the other is at Long Stratton, Norfolk. In fact a pair of iron wheels, used to choose the Lady Day for starting a fast that lasted for a year, one day a week. – HATCHMENT. Rev. Seymour Leeke of Yaxley Hall †1786. Painted by *William Johnson*. – STAINED GLASS. E window made up with fragments of medieval glass (of 1199–1549, if the inscription is to be believed) in 1886. It was done by *Horace Burrows* of Eye at the behest of Rev. W. H. Sewell, vicar 1861–96, a profile portrait of whom is concealed in the inscription. Other fragments incorporated in the tower screen. – Nave N by *Jones & Willis* (Light of the World), 1900, as a memorial to Sewell. Cf. the porch W window by *Powell & Sons*, 1898. – MONUMENTS. In the chancel, C14 effigy of an Ecclesiastic. – William Yaxley †1588. Another sad loss from 1868. It was a painted wooden monument, with inscription, shields of arms and columns. Parts survive, displayed in the S aisle, and built into cupboards in the vestry. – Brass of Andrew Felgate †1598. 19-in. (48-cm.) figure in civilian dress. Figure of wife missing.

N of the church, on the corner of Church Lane, SEWELL HOUSE (originally Rose Cottage) by *W.A. Tagg-Arundell* (*Arundell & Tarte*), 1882–3, for W. H. Sewell, who as a bachelor preferred not to live in the large vicarage (now Yaxley House) S of the church. Red brick, single-storey with attics. L-plan with canted corner; against the splay a pretty porch with decorated bargeboards and pointed doorway. Tudor-style chimneys of moulded brick. To its N WELL COTTAGE, with pyramidal roof, also red brick, and timber WELL HEAD dated 1875.

GUILDHALL COTTAGE, 250 yds N. Early C16 guildhall, later almshouses, now a single dwelling. Timber-framed and plastered. Two storeys from the start, the upper floor originally an open hall with smoke-hood at the S end. Parlour with large brick chimney added to the S end in the late C16.

YAXLEY MANOR, ¾ m. WNW. Timber-framed, with exposed timbers on the upper floor. Main range *c.* 1520, with jettied front. Service wing at E end added *c.* 1600. Good internal features including moulded beams, original doorways, crown-post roof and C17 panelling.

BULL'S HALL, ¾ m. SSW. Timber-framed and plastered farmhouse, built *c.* 1580 on an older site. Facing SW, with the parlour wall at the SE end jettied. At the NW end a detached mid-C17 building, perhaps a kitchen, joined to the main house in the C20. Original windows with diamond mullions. Service stairs with solid treads. Remains of a scheme of grey painted decoration in the C17 part. 'True and perfect' inventories of the house survive from 1661 and 1686.

YAXLEY HALL, 600 yds SE, now separated from the village by the bypass. The unusual appearance of the house – more like a terrace of three separate ones – is partly explained by a fire in 1922, which destroyed two further ranges at the NW end; until then it was symmetrical. *R. C. Wrinch* rebuilt the end wall, 1923, with a new front door and staircase. What is now the l.-hand portion of the house was the centre, and is a Gothick refronting of 1772. Red brick. Three bays. Conventional sashes and pedimented doorway on the ground floor. Above them two small windows and one large Gothick window. The latter has an ogee top and is an accurate replacement by *Nicholas Jacob*, 2006, of the original that was taken out in 1905. The top lights are blind, as the upper part of the wall is a deep parapet, with battlements, concealing the steep-pitched roof. Open timber cupola on ridge. To the r. of this the plastered gable-end of a C16 extension to a timber-framed cross-wing of the original U- or E-plan house. Then a second cross-wing, later C16, of red brick, the gable-end rendered in imitation of stone. On the ground floor a four-light window with transom, repeated on the first floor but larger. In the gable a blind three-light window with transom, and over it a pediment with three square pinnacles. The sides of the gable are concave and then convex, with moulded kneelers carrying pinnacles. Owned by *Sir Basil Spence*, 1975–6, who reinstated the first-floor room of the outer r. wing, with C16-style plasterwork on the barrel-vaulted ceiling. Also by Spence an octagonal timber GAZEBO with open fretwork sides ('The Teahouse of the August Moon'), 1976, that must be one his last works.* 300 yds S of the house, a mid-C19 FOLLY in the form of a church tower, now very dilapidated. Flint and red brick with stone dressings, and a reused C15 arch. It formed part of a Romantic 'Nun's Walk' from the Hall.

---

*He and his wife are buried at Thornham Parva (q.v.).

GLOSSARY

Numbers and letters refer to the illustrations (by John Sambrook) on pp. 586–593.

ABACUS: flat slab forming the top of a capital (3a).

ACANTHUS: classical formalized leaf ornament (4b).

ACCUMULATOR TOWER: see Hydraulic power.

ACHIEVEMENT: a complete display of armorial bearings.

ACROTERION: plinth for a statue or ornament on the apex or ends of a pediment; more usually, both the plinth and what stands on it (4a).

AEDICULE (*lit.* little building): architectural surround, consisting usually of two columns or pilasters supporting a pediment.

AGGREGATE: *see* Concrete.

AISLE: subsidiary space alongside the body of a building, separated from it by columns, piers, or posts.

ALMONRY: a building from which alms are dispensed to the poor.

AMBULATORY (*lit.* walkway): aisle around the sanctuary (q.v.).

ANGLE ROLL: roll moulding in the angle between two planes (1a).

ANSE DE PANIER: *see* Arch.

ANTAE: simplified pilasters (4a), usually applied to the ends of the enclosing walls of a portico *in antis* (q.v.).

ANTEFIXAE: ornaments projecting at regular intervals above a Greek cornice, originally to conceal the ends of roof tiles (4a).

ANTHEMION: classical ornament like a honeysuckle flower (4b).

APRON: raised panel below a window or wall monument or tablet.

APSE: semicircular or polygonal end of an apartment, especially of a chancel or chapel. In classical architecture sometimes called an *exedra*.

ARABESQUE: non-figurative surface decoration consisting of flowing lines, foliage scrolls etc., based on geometrical patterns. Cf. Grotesque.

ARCADE: series of arches supported by piers or columns. *Blind arcade* or *arcading*: the same applied to the wall surface. *Wall arcade*: in medieval churches, a blind arcade forming a dado below windows. Also a covered shopping street.

ARCH: Shapes *see* 5c. *Basket arch* or *anse de panier* (basket handle): three-centred and depressed, or with a flat centre. *Nodding*: ogee arch curving forward from the wall face. *Parabolic*: shaped like a chain suspended from two level points, but inverted. Special purposes. *Chancel*: dividing chancel from nave or crossing. *Crossing*: spanning piers at a crossing (q.v.). *Relieving or discharging*: incorporated in a wall to relieve superimposed weight (5c). *Skew*: spanning responds not diametrically opposed. *Strainer*: inserted in an opening to resist inward pressure. *Transverse*: spanning a main axis (e.g. of a vaulted space). *See also* Jack arch, Triumphal arch.

ARCHITRAVE: formalized lintel, the lowest member of the classical entablature (3a). Also the moulded frame of a door or window (often borrowing the profile of a classical architrave). For *lugged* and *shouldered* architraves *see* 4b.

ARCUATED: dependent structurally on the arch principle. Cf. Trabeated.

ARK: chest or cupboard housing the

tables of Jewish law in a synagogue.

ARRIS: sharp edge where two surfaces meet at an angle (3a).

ASHLAR: masonry of large blocks wrought to even faces and square edges (6d).

ASTRAGAL: classical moulding of semicircular section (3f).

ASTYLAR: with no columns or similar vertical features.

ATLANTES: *see* Caryatids.

ATRIUM (plural: atria): inner court of a Roman or C20 house; in a multi-storey building, a toplit covered court rising through all storeys. Also an open court in front of a church.

ATTACHED COLUMN: *see* Engaged column.

ATTIC: small top storey within a roof. Also the storey above the main entablature of a classical façade.

AUMBRY: recess or cupboard to hold sacred vessels for the Mass.

BAILEY: *see* Motte-and-bailey.
BALANCE BEAM: *see* Canals.
BALDACCHINO: free-standing canopy, originally fabric, over an altar. Cf. Ciborium.

BALLFLOWER: globular flower of three petals enclosing a ball (1a). Typical of the Decorated style.

BALUSTER: pillar or pedestal of bellied form. *Balusters*: vertical supports of this or any other form, for a handrail or coping, the whole being called a *balustrade* (6c). *Blind balustrade*: the same applied to the wall surface.

BARBICAN: outwork defending the entrance to a castle.

BARGEBOARDS (corruption of 'vergeboards'): boards, often carved or fretted, fixed beneath the eaves of a gable to cover and protect the rafters.

BAROQUE: style originating in Rome c.1600 and current in England c.1680–1720, characterized by dramatic massing and silhouette and the use of the giant order.

BARROW: burial mound.

BARTIZAN: corbelled turret, square or round, frequently at an angle.

BASCULE: hinged part of a lifting (or bascule) bridge.

BASE: moulded foot of a column or pilaster. For *Attic* base *see* 3b.

BASEMENT: lowest, subordinate storey; hence the lowest part of a classical elevation, below the *piano nobile* (q.v.).

BASILICA: a Roman public hall; hence an aisled building with a clerestory.

BASTION: one of a series of defensive semicircular or polygonal projections from the main wall of a fortress or city.

BATTER: intentional inward inclination of a wall face.

BATTLEMENT: defensive parapet, composed of *merlons* (solid) and *crenels* (embrasures) through which archers could shoot; sometimes called *crenellation*. Also used decoratively.

BAY: division of an elevation or interior space as defined by regular vertical features such as arches, columns, windows etc.

BAY LEAF: classical ornament of overlapping bay leaves (3f).

BAY WINDOW: window of one or more storeys projecting from the face of a building. *Canted*: with a straight front and angled sides. *Bow window*: curved. *Oriel*: rests on corbels or brackets and starts above ground level; also the bay window at the dais end of a medieval great hall.

BEAD-AND-REEL: *see* Enrichments.

BEAKHEAD: Norman ornament with a row of beaked bird or beast heads usually biting into a roll moulding (1a).

BELFRY: chamber or stage in a tower where bells are hung.

BELL CAPITAL: *see* 1b.

BELLCOTE: small gabled or roofed housing for the bell(s).

BERM: level area separating a ditch from a bank on a hill-fort or barrow.

BILLET: Norman ornament of small half-cylindrical or rectangular blocks (1a).

BLIND: *see* Arcade, Baluster, Portico.

BLOCK CAPITAL: *see* 1a.

BLOCKED: columns, etc. interrupted by regular projecting

blocks (*blocking*), as on a Gibbs surround (4b).

BLOCKING COURSE: course of stones, or equivalent, on top of a cornice and crowning the wall.

BOLECTION MOULDING: covering the joint between two different planes (6b).

BOND: the pattern of long sides (*stretchers*) and short ends (*headers*) produced on the face of a wall by laying bricks in a particular way (6e).

BOSS: knob or projection, e.g. at the intersection of ribs in a vault (2c).

BOWTELL: a term in use by the C15 for a form of roll moulding, usually three-quarters of a circle in section (also called *edge roll*).

BOW WINDOW: *see* Bay window.

BOX FRAME: timber-framed construction in which vertical and horizontal wall members support the roof (7). Also concrete construction where the loads are taken on cross walls; also called *cross-wall construction*.

BRACE: subsidiary member of a structural frame, curved or straight. *Bracing* is often arranged decoratively e.g. quatrefoil, herringbone (7). *See also* Roofs.

BRATTISHING: ornamental crest, usually formed of leaves, Tudor flowers or miniature battlements.

BRESSUMER (*lit.* breast-beam): big horizontal beam supporting the wall above, especially in a jettied building (7).

BRICK: *see* Bond, Cogging, Engineering, Gauged, Tumbling.

BRIDGE: *Bowstring*: with arches rising above the roadway which is suspended from them. *Clapper*: one long stone forms the roadway. *Roving*: *see* Canal. *Suspension*: roadway suspended from cables or chains slung between towers or pylons. *Stay-suspension* or *stay-cantilever*: supported by diagonal stays from towers or pylons. *See also* Bascule.

BRISES-SOLEIL: projecting fins or canopies which deflect direct sunlight from windows.

BROACH: *see* Spire and 1c.

BUCRANIUM: ox skull used decoratively in classical friezes.

BULL-NOSED SILL: sill displaying a pronounced convex upper moulding.

BULLSEYE WINDOW: small oval window, set horizontally (cf. Oculus). Also called *œil de bœuf*.

BUTTRESS: vertical member projecting from a wall to stabilize it or to resist the lateral thrust of an arch, roof, or vault (1c, 2c). A *flying buttress* transmits the thrust to a heavy abutment by means of an arch or half-arch (1c).

CABLE OR ROPE MOULDING: originally Norman, like twisted strands of a rope.

CAMES: *see* Quarries.

CAMPANILE: free-standing bell-tower.

CANALS: *Flash lock*: removable weir or similar device through which boats pass on a flush of water. Predecessor of the *pound lock*: chamber with gates at each end allowing boats to float from one level to another. *Tidal gates*: single pair of lock gates allowing vessels to pass when the tide makes a level. *Balance beam*: beam projecting horizontally for opening and closing lock gates. *Roving bridge*: carrying a towing path from one bank to the other.

CANTILEVER: horizontal projection (e.g. step, canopy) supported by a downward force behind the fulcrum.

CAPITAL: head or crowning feature of a column or pilaster; for classical types *see* 3; for medieval types *see* 1b.

CARREL: compartment designed for individual work or study.

CARTOUCHE: classical tablet with ornate frame (4b).

CARYATIDS: female figures supporting an entablature; their male counterparts are *Atlantes* (*lit.* Atlas figures).

CASEMATE: vaulted chamber, with embrasures for defence, within a castle wall or projecting from it.

CASEMENT: side-hinged window.

CASTELLATED: with battlements (q.v.).

CAST IRON: hard and brittle, cast in a mould to the required shape.

Wrought iron is ductile, strong in tension, forged into decorative patterns or forged and rolled into e.g. bars, joists, boiler plates; *mild steel* is its modern equivalent, similar but stronger.

CATSLIDE: *See* 8a.

CAVETTO: concave classical moulding of quarter-round section (3f).

CELURE OR CEILURE: enriched area of roof above rood or altar.

CEMENT: *see* Concrete.

CENOTAPH (*lit.* empty tomb): funerary monument which is not a burying place.

CENTRING: wooden support for the building of an arch or vault, removed after completion.

CHAMFER (*lit.* corner-break): surface formed by cutting off a square edge or corner. For types of chamfers and *chamfer stops see* 6a. *See also* Double chamfer.

CHANCEL: part of the E end of a church set apart for the use of the officiating clergy.

CHANTRY CHAPEL: often attached to or within a church, endowed for the celebration of Masses principally for the soul of the founder.

CHEVET (*lit.* head): French term for chancel with ambulatory and radiating chapels.

CHEVRON: V-shape used in series or double series (later) on a Norman moulding (1a). Also (especially when on a single plane) called *zigzag*.

CHOIR: the part of a cathedral, monastic or collegiate church where services are sung.

CIBORIUM: a fixed canopy over an altar, usually vaulted and supported on four columns; cf. Baldacchino. Also a canopied shrine for the reserved sacrament.

CINQUEFOIL: *see* Foil.

CIST: stone-lined or slab-built grave.

CLADDING: external covering or skin applied to a structure, especially a framed one.

CLERESTORY: uppermost storey of the nave of a church, pierced by windows. Also high-level windows in secular buildings.

CLOSER: a brick cut to complete a bond (6e).

CLUSTER BLOCK: *see* Multi-storey.

COADE STONE: ceramic artificial stone made in Lambeth 1769–c.1840 by Eleanor Coade (†1821) and her associates.

COB: walling material of clay mixed with straw. Also called *pisé*.

COFFERING: arrangement of sunken panels (coffers), square or polygonal, decorating a ceiling, vault, or arch.

COGGING: a decorative course of bricks laid diagonally (6e). Cf. Dentilation.

COLLAR: *see* Roofs and 7.

COLLEGIATE CHURCH: endowed for the support of a college of priests.

COLONNADE: range of columns supporting an entablature. Cf. Arcade.

COLONNETTE: small medieval column or shaft.

COLOSSAL ORDER: *see* Giant order.

COLUMBARIUM: shelved, niched structure to house multiple burials.

COLUMN: a classical, upright structural member of round section with a shaft, a capital, and usually a base (3a, 4a).

COLUMN FIGURE: carved figure attached to a medieval column or shaft, usually flanking a doorway.

COMMUNION TABLE: unconsecrated table used in Protestant churches for the celebration of Holy Communion.

COMPOSITE: *see* Orders.

COMPOUND PIER: grouped shafts (q.v.), or a solid core surrounded by shafts.

CONCRETE: composition of *cement* (calcined lime and clay), *aggregate* (small stones or rock chippings), sand and water. It can be poured into *formwork* or *shuttering* (temporary frame of timber or metal) on site (*in-situ* concrete), or *pre-cast* as components before construction. *Reinforced*: incorporating steel rods to take the tensile force. *Pre-stressed*: with tensioned steel rods. Finishes include the impression of boards left by formwork (*board-marked* or *shuttered*), and texturing with steel brushes (*brushed*) or hammers (*hammer-dressed*). *See also* Shell.

CONSOLE: bracket of curved outline (4b).
COPING: protective course of masonry or brickwork capping a wall (6d).
CORBEL: projecting block supporting something above. *Corbel course*: continuous course of projecting stones or bricks fulfilling the same function. *Corbel table*: series of corbels to carry a parapet or a wall-plate or wall-post (7). *Corbelling*: brick or masonry courses built out beyond one another to support a chimneystack, window, etc.
CORINTHIAN: *see* Orders and 3d.
CORNICE: flat-topped ledge with moulded underside, projecting along the top of a building or feature, especially as the highest member of the classical entablature (3a). Also the decorative moulding in the angle between wall and ceiling.
CORPS-DE-LOGIS: the main building(s) as distinct from the wings or pavilions.
COTTAGE ORNÉ: an artfully rustic small house associated with the Picturesque movement.
COUNTERCHANGING: of joists on a ceiling divided by beams into compartments, when placed in opposite directions in alternate squares.
COUR D'HONNEUR: formal entrance court before a house in the French manner, usually with flanking wings and a screen wall or gates.
COURSE: continuous layer of stones, etc. in a wall (6c).
COVE: a broad concave moulding, e.g. to mask the eaves of a roof. *Coved ceiling*: with a pronounced cove joining the walls to a flat central panel smaller than the whole area of the ceiling.
CRADLE ROOF: *see* Wagon roof.
CREDENCE: a shelf within or beside a piscina (q.v.), or a table for the sacramental elements and vessels.
CRENELLATION: parapet with crenels (*see* Battlement).
CRINKLE-CRANKLE WALL: garden wall undulating in a series of serpentine curves.

CROCKETS: leafy hooks. *Crocketing* decorates the edges of Gothic features, such as pinnacles, canopies, etc. *Crocket capital*: *see* 1b.
CROSSING: central space at the junction of the nave, chancel, and transepts. *Crossing tower*: above a crossing.
CROSS-WINDOW: with one mullion and one transom (qq.v.).
CROWN-POST: *see* Roofs and 7.
CROWSTEPS: squared stones set like steps, e.g. on a gable (8a).
CRUCKS (*lit.* crooked): pairs of inclined timbers (*blades*), usually curved, set at bay-lengths; they support the roof timbers and, in timber buildings, also support the walls (8b). *Base*: blades rise from ground level to a tie- or collar-beam which supports the roof timbers. *Full*: blades rise from ground level to the apex of the roof, serving as the main members of a roof truss. *Jointed*: blades formed from more than one timber; the lower member may act as a wall-post; it is usually elbowed at wall-plate level and jointed just above. *Middle*: blades rise from half-way up the walls to a tie- or collar-beam. *Raised*: blades rise from half-way up the walls to the apex. *Upper*: blades supported on a tie-beam and rising to the apex.
CRYPT: underground or half-underground area, usually below the E end of a church. *Ring crypt*: corridor crypt surrounding the apse of an early medieval church, often associated with chambers for relics. Cf. Undercroft.
CUPOLA (*lit.* dome): especially a small dome on a circular or polygonal base crowning a larger dome, roof, or turret.
CURSUS: a long avenue defined by two parallel earthen banks with ditches outside.
CURTAIN WALL: a connecting wall between the towers of a castle. Also a non-load-bearing external wall applied to a C20 framed structure.
CUSP: *see* Tracery and 2b.
CYCLOPEAN MASONRY: large irregular polygonal stones, smooth and finely jointed.

CYMA RECTA and CYMA REVERSA: classical mouldings with double curves (3f). Cf. Ogee.

DADO: the finishing (often with panelling) of the lower part of a wall in a classical interior; in origin a formalized continuous pedestal. *Dado rail*: the moulding along the top of the dado.
DAGGER: *see* Tracery and 2b.
DALLE-DE-VERRE (*lit.* glass-slab): a late C20 stained-glass technique, setting large, thick pieces of cast glass into a frame of reinforced concrete or epoxy resin.
DEC (DECORATED): English Gothic architecture c. 1290 to c. 1350. The name is derived from the type of window tracery (q.v.) used during the period.
DEMI- or HALF-COLUMNS: engaged columns (q.v.) half of whose circumference projects from the wall.
DENTIL: small square block used in series in classical cornices (3c). *Dentilation* is produced by the projection of alternating headers along cornices or stringcourses.
DIAPER: repetitive surface decoration of lozenges or squares flat or in relief. Achieved in brickwork with bricks of two colours.
DIOCLETIAN OR THERMAL WINDOW: semicircular with two mullions, as used in the Baths of Diocletian, Rome (4b).
DISTYLE: having two columns (4a).
DOGTOOTH: E.E. ornament, consisting of a series of small pyramids formed by four stylized canine teeth meeting at a point (1a).
DORIC: *see* Orders and 3a, 3b.
DORMER: window projecting from the slope of a roof (8a).
DOUBLE CHAMFER: a chamfer applied to each of two recessed arches (1a).
DOUBLE PILE: *see* Pile.
DRAGON BEAM: *see* Jetty.
DRESSINGS: the stone or brickwork worked to a finished face about an angle, opening, or other feature.
DRIPSTONE: moulded stone projecting from a wall to protect the lower parts from water. Cf. Hoodmould, Weathering.
DRUM: circular or polygonal stage supporting a dome or cupola. Also one of the stones forming the shaft of a column (3a).
DUTCH or FLEMISH GABLE: *see* 8a.

EASTER SEPULCHRE: tomb-chest used for Easter ceremonial, within or against the N wall of a chancel.
EAVES: overhanging edge of a roof; hence *eaves cornice* in this position.
ECHINUS: ovolo moulding (q.v.) below the abacus of a Greek Doric capital (3a).
EDGE RAIL: *see* Railways.
E.E. (EARLY ENGLISH): English Gothic architecture c. 1190–1250.
EGG-AND-DART: *see* Enrichments and 3f.
ELEVATION: any face of a building or side of a room. In a drawing, the same or any part of it, represented in two dimensions.
EMBATTLED: with battlements.
EMBRASURE: small splayed opening in a wall or battlement (q.v.).
ENCAUSTIC TILES: earthenware tiles fired with a pattern and glaze.
EN DELIT: stone cut against the bed.
ENFILADE: reception rooms in a formal series, usually with all doorways on axis.
ENGAGED or ATTACHED COLUMN: one that partly merges into a wall or pier.
ENGINEERING BRICKS: dense bricks, originally used mostly for railway viaducts etc.
ENRICHMENTS: the carved decoration of certain classical mouldings, e.g. the ovolo (qq.v.) with *egg-and-dart*, the cyma reversa with *waterleaf*, the astragal with *bead-and-reel* (3f).
ENTABLATURE: in classical architecture, collective name for the three horizontal members (architrave, frieze, and cornice) carried by a wall or a column (3a).
ENTASIS: very slight convex deviation from a straight line, used to prevent an optical illusion of concavity.
EPITAPH: inscription on a tomb.
EXEDRA: *see* Apse.

EXTRADOS: outer curved face of an arch or vault.
EYECATCHER: decorative building terminating a vista.

FASCIA: plain horizontal band, e.g. in an architrave (3c, 3d) or on a shopfront.
FENESTRATION: the arrangement of windows in a façade.
FERETORY: site of the chief shrine of a church, behind the high altar.
FESTOON: ornamental garland, suspended from both ends. Cf. Swag.
FIBREGLASS, or glass-reinforced polyester (GRP): synthetic resin reinforced with glass fibre. GRC: glass-reinforced concrete.
FIELD: *see* Panelling and 6b.
FILLET: a narrow flat band running down a medieval shaft or along a roll moulding (1a). It separates larger curved mouldings in classical cornices, fluting or bases (3c).
FLAMBOYANT: the latest phase of French Gothic architecture, with flowing tracery.
FLASH LOCK: *see* Canals.
FLÈCHE or SPIRELET (*lit.* arrow): slender spire on the centre of a roof.
FLEURON: medieval carved flower or leaf, often rectilinear (1a).
FLUSHWORK: knapped flint used with dressed stone to form patterns.
FLUTING: series of concave grooves (flutes), their common edges sharp (arris) or blunt (fillet) (3).
FOIL (*lit.* leaf): lobe formed by the cusping of a circular or other shape in tracery (2b). *Trefoil* (three), *quatrefoil* (four), *cinquefoil* (five), and *multifoil* express the number of lobes in a shape.
FOLIATE: decorated with leaves.
FORMWORK: *see* Concrete.
FRAMED BUILDING: where the structure is carried by a framework – e.g. of steel, reinforced concrete, timber – instead of by load-bearing walls.
FREESTONE: stone that is cut, or can be cut, in all directions.
FRESCO: *al fresco*: painting on wet plaster. *Fresco secco*: painting on dry plaster.
FRIEZE: the middle member of the classical entablature, sometimes ornamented (3a). *Pulvinated frieze* (*lit.* cushioned): of bold convex profile (3c). Also a horizontal band of ornament.
FRONTISPIECE: in C16 and C17 buildings the central feature of doorway and windows above linked in one composition.

GABLE: For types *see* 8a. *Gablet*: small gable. *Pedimental gable*: treated like a pediment.
GADROONING: classical ribbed ornament like inverted fluting that flows into a lobed edge.
GALILEE: chapel or vestibule usually at the W end of a church enclosing the main portal(s).
GALLERY: a long room or passage; an upper storey above the aisle of a church, looking through arches to the nave; a balcony or mezzanine overlooking the main interior space of a building; or an external walkway.
GALLETING: small stones set in a mortar course.
GAMBREL ROOF: *see* 8a.
GARDEROBE: medieval privy.
GARGOYLE: projecting water spout often carved into human or animal shape.
GAUGED or RUBBED BRICKWORK: soft brick sawn roughly, then rubbed to a precise (gauged) surface. Mostly used for door or window openings (5c).
GAZEBO (jocular Latin, 'I shall gaze'): ornamental lookout tower or raised summer house.
GEOMETRIC: English Gothic architecture *c.* 1250–1310. *See also* Tracery. For another meaning, *see* Stairs.
GIANT or COLOSSAL ORDER: classical order (q.v.) whose height is that of two or more storeys of the building to which it is applied.
GIBBS SURROUND: C18 treatment of an opening (4b), seen particularly in the work of James Gibbs (1682–1754).
GIRDER: a large beam. *Box*: of hollow-box section. *Bowed*: with its top rising in a curve. *Plate*: of I-section, made from iron or steel

plates. *Lattice*: with braced framework.
GLAZING BARS: wooden or sometimes metal bars separating and supporting window panes.
GRAFFITI: *see* Sgraffito.
GRANGE: farm owned and run by a religious order.
GRC: *see* Fibreglass.
GRISAILLE: monochrome painting on walls or glass.
GROIN: sharp edge at the meeting of two cells of a cross-vault; *see* Vault and 2c.
GROTESQUE (*lit.* grotto-esque): wall decoration adopted from Roman examples in the Renaissance. Its foliage scrolls incorporate figurative elements. Cf. Arabesque.
GROTTO: artificial cavern.
GRP: *see* Fibreglass.
GUILLOCHE: classical ornament of interlaced bands (4b).
GUNLOOP: opening for a firearm.
GUTTAE: stylized drops (3b).

HALF-TIMBERING: archaic term for timber-framing (q.v.). Sometimes used for non-structural decorative timberwork.
HALL CHURCH: medieval church with nave and aisles of approximately equal height.
HAMMERBEAM: *see* Roofs and 7.
HAMPER: in C20 architecture, a visually distinct topmost storey or storeys.
HEADER: *see* Bond and 6e.
HEADSTOP: stop (q.v.) carved with a head (5b).
HELM ROOF: *see* IC.
HENGE: ritual earthwork.
HERM (*lit.* the god Hermes): male head or bust on a pedestal.
HERRINGBONE WORK: *see* 7ii. Cf. Pitched masonry.
HEXASTYLE: *see* Portico.
HILL-FORT: Iron Age earthwork enclosed by a ditch and bank system.
HIPPED ROOF: *see* 8a.
HOODMOULD: projecting moulding above an arch or lintel to throw off water (2b, 5b). When horizontal often called a *label*. For label stop *see* Stop.
HUSK GARLAND: festoon of stylized nutshells (4b).

HYDRAULIC POWER: use of water under high pressure to work machinery. *Accumulator tower*: houses a hydraulic accumulator which accommodates fluctuations in the flow through hydraulic mains.
HYPOCAUST (*lit.* underburning): Roman underfloor heating system.

IMPOST: horizontal moulding at the springing of an arch (5c).
IMPOST BLOCK: block between abacus and capital (1b).
IN ANTIS: *see* Antae, Portico and 4a.
INDENT: shape chiselled out of a stone to receive a brass.
INDUSTRIALIZED or SYSTEM BUILDING: system of manufactured units assembled on site.
INGLENOOK (*lit.* fire-corner): recess for a hearth with provision for seating.
INTERCOLUMNATION: interval between columns.
INTERLACE: decoration in relief simulating woven or entwined stems or bands.
INTRADOS: *see* Soffit.
IONIC: *see* Orders and 3c.

JACK ARCH: shallow segmental vault springing from beams, used for fireproof floors, bridge decks, etc.
JAMB (*lit.* leg): one of the vertical sides of an opening.
JETTY: in a timber-framed building, the projection of an upper storey beyond the storey below, made by the beams and joists of the lower storey oversailing the wall; on their outer ends is placed the sill of the walling for the storey above (7). Buildings can be jettied on several sides, in which case a *dragon beam* is set diagonally at the corner to carry the joists to either side.
JOGGLE: the joining of two stones to prevent them slipping by a notch in one and a projection in the other.

KEEL MOULDING: moulding used from the late C12, in section like the keel of a ship (1a).
KEEP: principal tower of a castle.
KENTISH CUSP: *see* Tracery and 2b.

KEY PATTERN: *see* 4b.
KEYSTONE: central stone in an arch or vault (4b, 5c).
KINGPOST: *see* Roofs and 7.
KNEELER: horizontal projecting stone at the base of each side of a gable to support the inclined coping stones (8a).

LABEL: *see* Hoodmould and 5b.
LABEL STOP: *see* Stop and 5b.
LACED BRICKWORK: vertical strips of brickwork, often in a contrasting colour, linking openings on different floors.
LACING COURSE: horizontal reinforcement in timber or brick to walls of flint, cobble, etc.
LADY CHAPEL: dedicated to the Virgin Mary (Our Lady).
LANCET: slender single-light, pointed-arched window (2a).
LANTERN: circular or polygonal windowed turret crowning a roof or a dome. Also the windowed stage of a crossing tower lighting the church interior.
LANTERN CROSS: churchyard cross with lantern-shaped top.
LAVATORIUM: in a religious house, a washing place adjacent to the refectory.
LEAN-TO: *see* Roofs.
LESENE (*lit.* a mean thing): pilaster without base or capital. Also called *pilaster strip*.
LIERNE: *see* Vault and 2c.
LIGHT: compartment of a window defined by the mullions.
LINENFOLD: Tudor panelling carved with simulations of folded linen. *See also* Parchemin.
LINTEL: horizontal beam or stone bridging an opening.
LOGGIA: gallery, usually arcaded or colonnaded; sometimes freestanding.
LONG-AND-SHORT WORK: quoins consisting of stones placed with the long side alternately upright and horizontal, especially in Saxon building.
LONGHOUSE: house and byre in the same range with internal access between them.
LOUVRE: roof opening, often protected by a raised timber structure, to allow the smoke from a central hearth to escape.
LOWSIDE WINDOW: set lower than the others in a chancel side wall, usually towards its W end.
LUCAM: projecting housing for hoist pulley on upper storey of warehouses, mills, etc., for raising goods to loading doors.
LUCARNE (*lit.* dormer): small gabled opening in a roof or spire.
LUGGED ARCHITRAVE: *see* 4b.
LUNETTE: semicircular window or blind panel.
LYCHGATE (*lit.* corpse-gate): roofed gateway entrance to a churchyard for the reception of a coffin.
LYNCHET: long terraced strip of soil on the downward side of prehistoric and medieval fields, accumulated because of continual ploughing along the contours.

MACHICOLATIONS (*lit.* mashing devices): series of openings between the corbels that support a projecting parapet through which missiles can be dropped. Used decoratively in post-medieval buildings.
MANOMETER or STANDPIPE TOWER: containing a column of water to regulate pressure in water mains.
MANSARD: *see* 8a.
MATHEMATICAL TILES: facing tiles with the appearance of brick, most often applied to timber-framed walls.
MAUSOLEUM: monumental building or chamber usually intended for the burial of members of one family.
MEGALITHIC TOMB: massive stone-built Neolithic burial chamber covered by an earth or stone mound.
MERLON: *see* Battlement.
METOPES: spaces between the triglyphs in a Doric frieze (3b).
MEZZANINE: low storey between two higher ones.
MILD STEEL: *see* Cast iron.
MISERICORD (*lit.* mercy): shelf on a carved bracket placed on the underside of a hinged choir stall seat to support an occupant when standing.

586

GLOSSARY

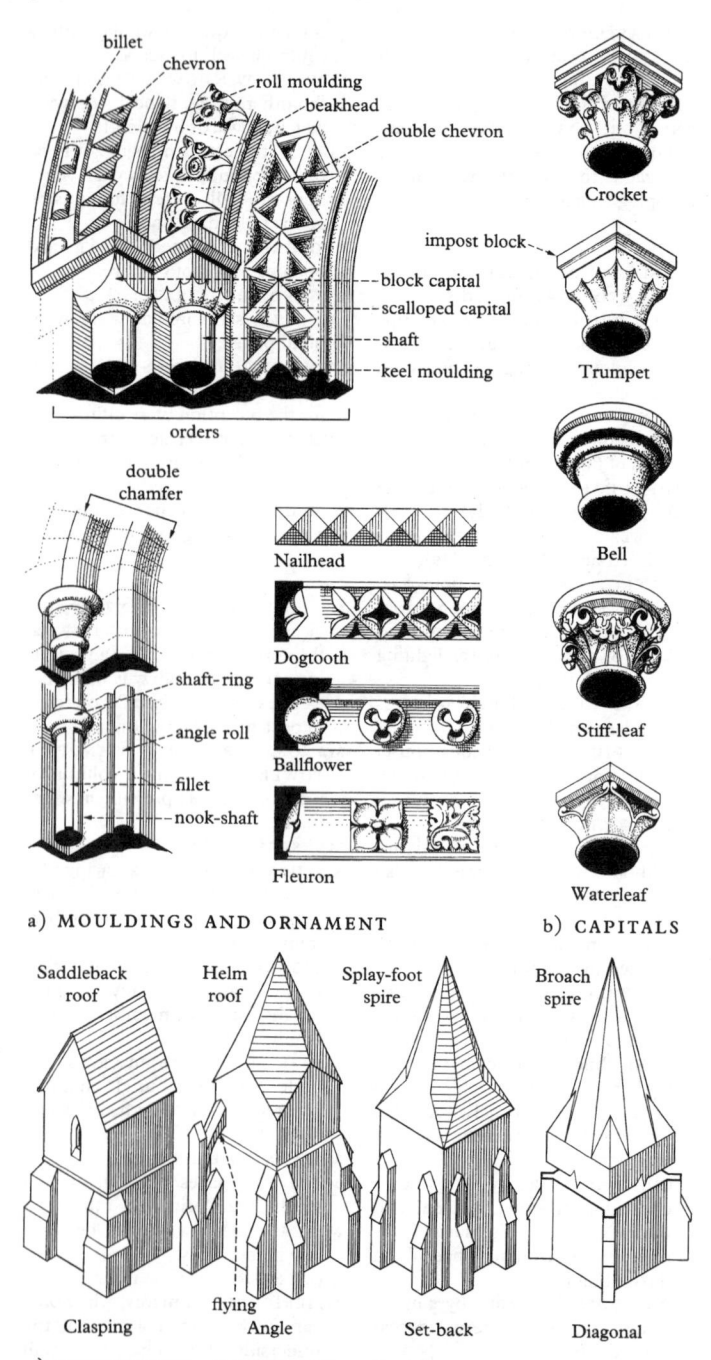

a) MOULDINGS AND ORNAMENT

b) CAPITALS

c) BUTTRESSES, ROOFS AND SPIRES

FIGURE 1: MEDIEVAL

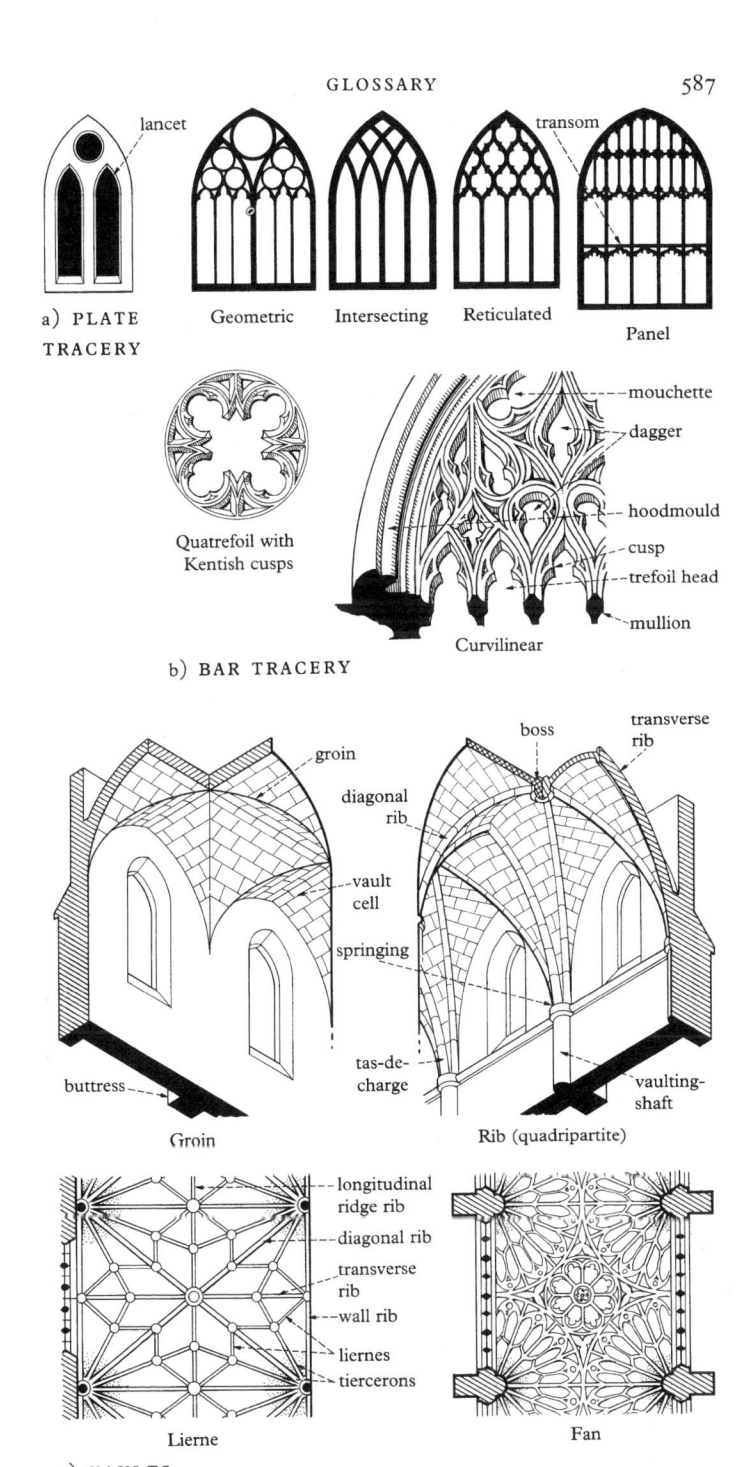

GLOSSARY

a) PLATE TRACERY — lancet; Geometric; Intersecting; Reticulated; Panel (transom)

b) BAR TRACERY — Quatrefoil with Kentish cusps; Curvilinear (mouchette, dagger, hoodmould, cusp, trefoil head, mullion)

c) VAULTS — Groin (groin, vault cell, buttress); Rib (quadripartite) (boss, transverse rib, diagonal rib, springing, tas-de-charge, vaulting-shaft); Lierne (longitudinal ridge rib, diagonal rib, transverse rib, wall rib, liernes, tiercerons); Fan

FIGURE 2: MEDIEVAL

GLOSSARY

ORDERS

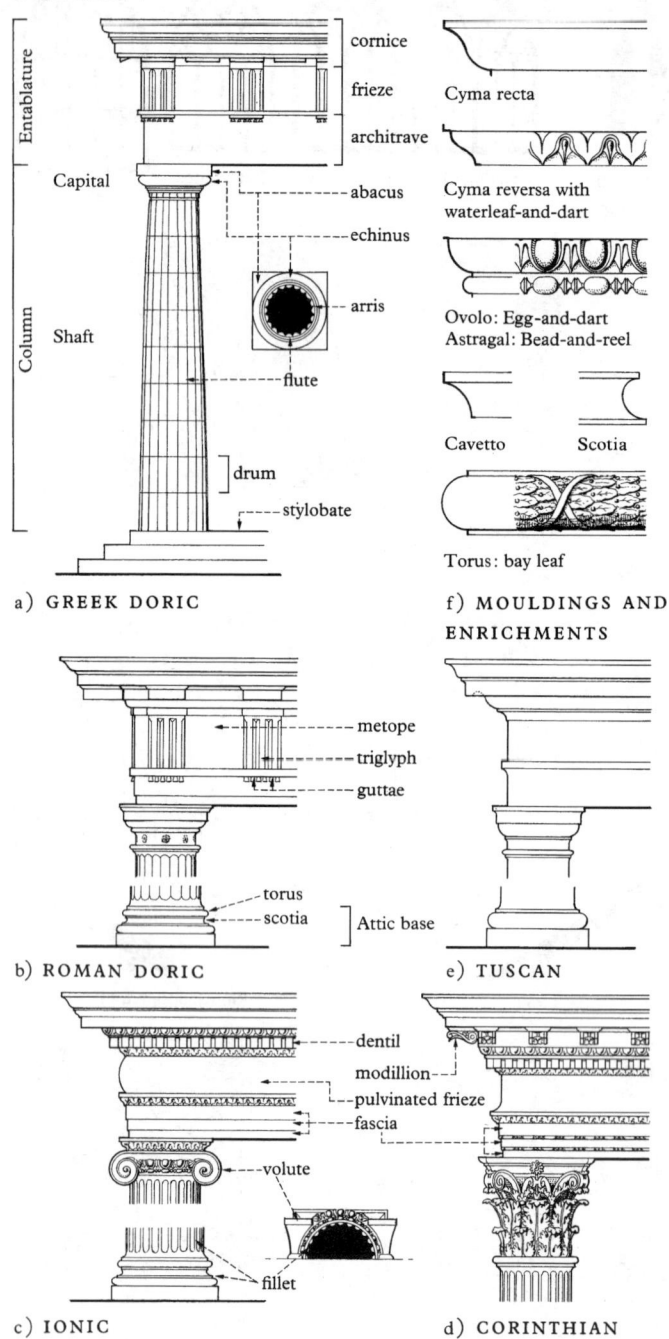

a) GREEK DORIC

- Entablature: cornice, frieze, architrave
- Capital: abacus, echinus
- Column / Shaft: arris, flute, drum
- stylobate

b) ROMAN DORIC

- metope
- triglyph
- guttae
- torus
- scotia } Attic base

c) IONIC

- dentil
- modillion
- pulvinated frieze
- fascia
- volute
- fillet

d) CORINTHIAN

e) TUSCAN

f) MOULDINGS AND ENRICHMENTS

- Cyma recta
- Cyma reversa with waterleaf-and-dart
- Ovolo: Egg-and-dart
- Astragal: Bead-and-reel
- Cavetto
- Scotia
- Torus: bay leaf

FIGURE 3: CLASSICAL

GLOSSARY

a) PORTICO

- acroterion
- tympanum
- antefixa
- column
- anta
- naos
- pronaos
- Distyle in antis
- Prostyle

b) ORNAMENTS AND FEATURES

- Anthemion & Palmette
- Guilloche
- Key pattern
- Rinceau
- Husk garland
- Vitruvian scroll
- Console
- Diocletian window
- Acanthus
- Broken pediment
- Lugged architrave
- Segmental pediment
- Shouldered architrave
- Venetian window
- console
- cartouche
- keystone
- blocking
- Open pediment
- Swan-neck pediment
- Gibbs surround

FIGURE 4: CLASSICAL

GLOSSARY

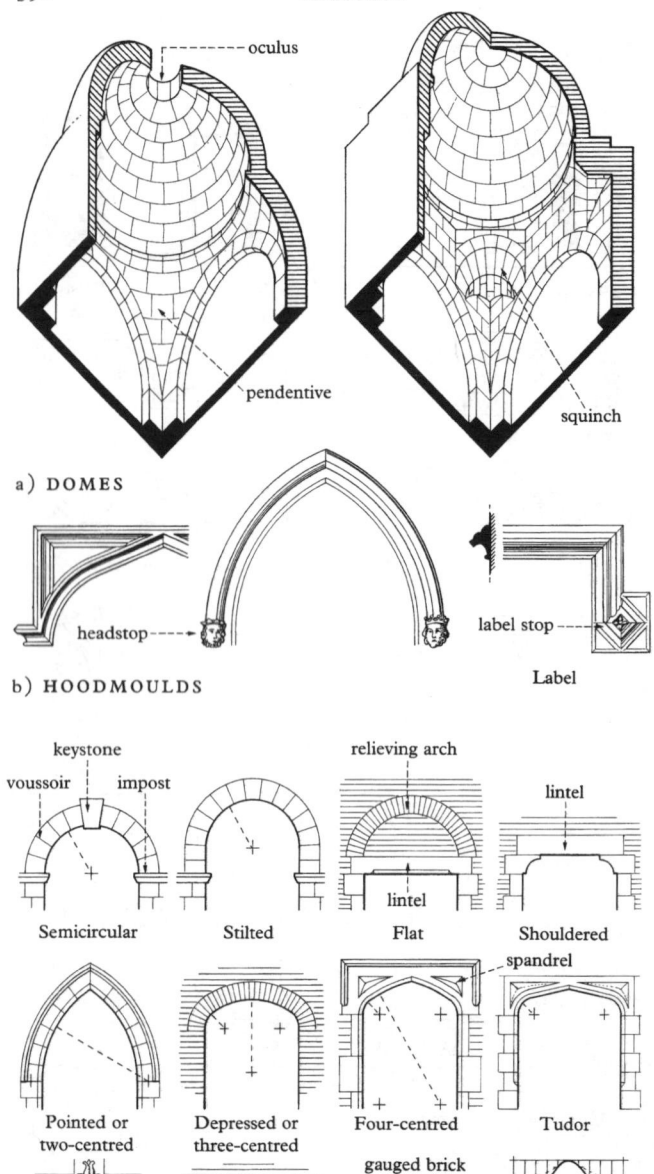

a) DOMES

- oculus
- pendentive
- squinch

b) HOODMOULDS

- headstop
- label stop
- Label

c) ARCHES

- Semicircular (keystone, voussoir, impost)
- Stilted
- Flat (relieving arch, lintel)
- Shouldered (lintel)
- Pointed or two-centred
- Depressed or three-centred
- Four-centred (spandrel)
- Tudor
- Ogee
- Segmental
- Basket (gauged brick voussoirs)
- Parabolic

FIGURE 5: CONSTRUCTION

GLOSSARY 591

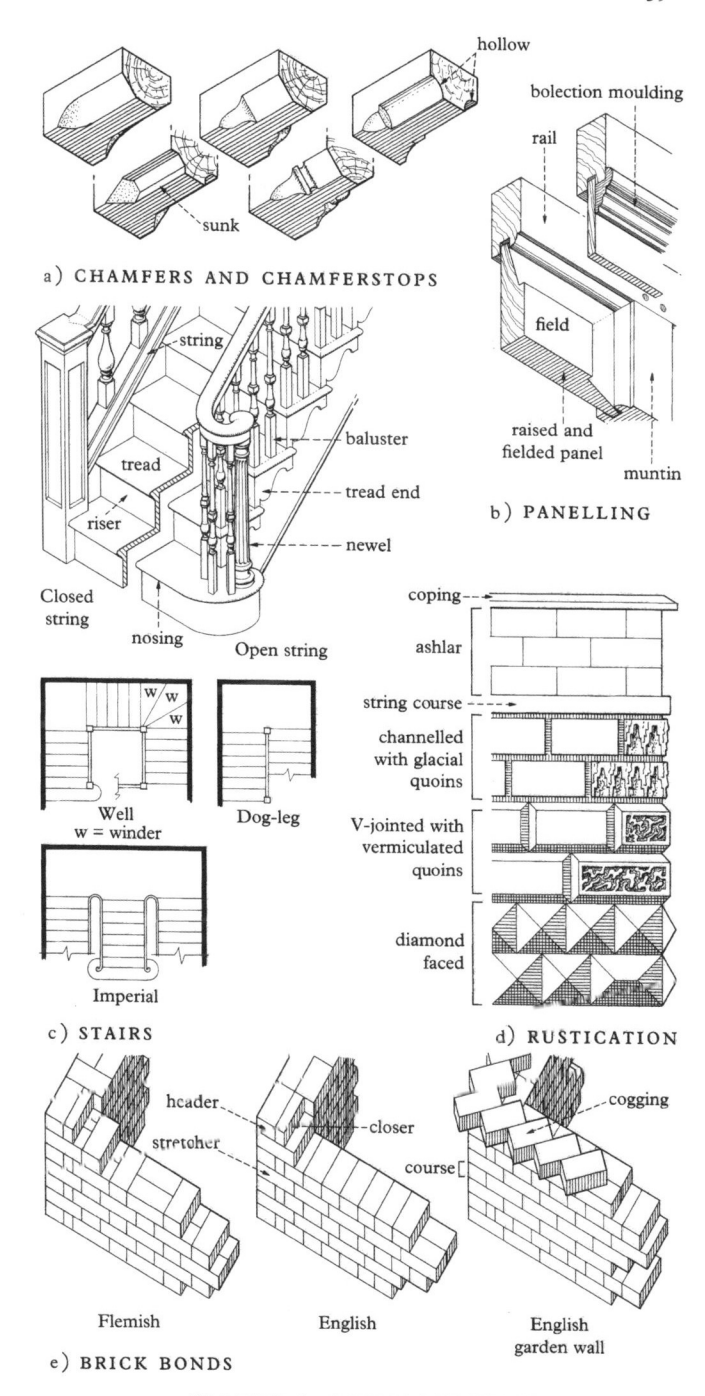

a) CHAMFERS AND CHAMFERSTOPS

(labels: hollow, sunk)

b) PANELLING

(labels: bolection moulding, rail, field, raised and fielded panel, muntin)

c) STAIRS

(labels: string, baluster, tread, tread end, riser, newel, Closed string, nosing, Open string, Well w = winder, Dog-leg, Imperial)

d) RUSTICATION

(labels: coping, ashlar, string course, channelled with glacial quoins, V-jointed with vermiculated quoins, diamond faced)

e) BRICK BONDS

(labels: header, stretcher, closer, course, cogging, Flemish, English, English garden wall)

FIGURE 6: CONSTRUCTION

GLOSSARY

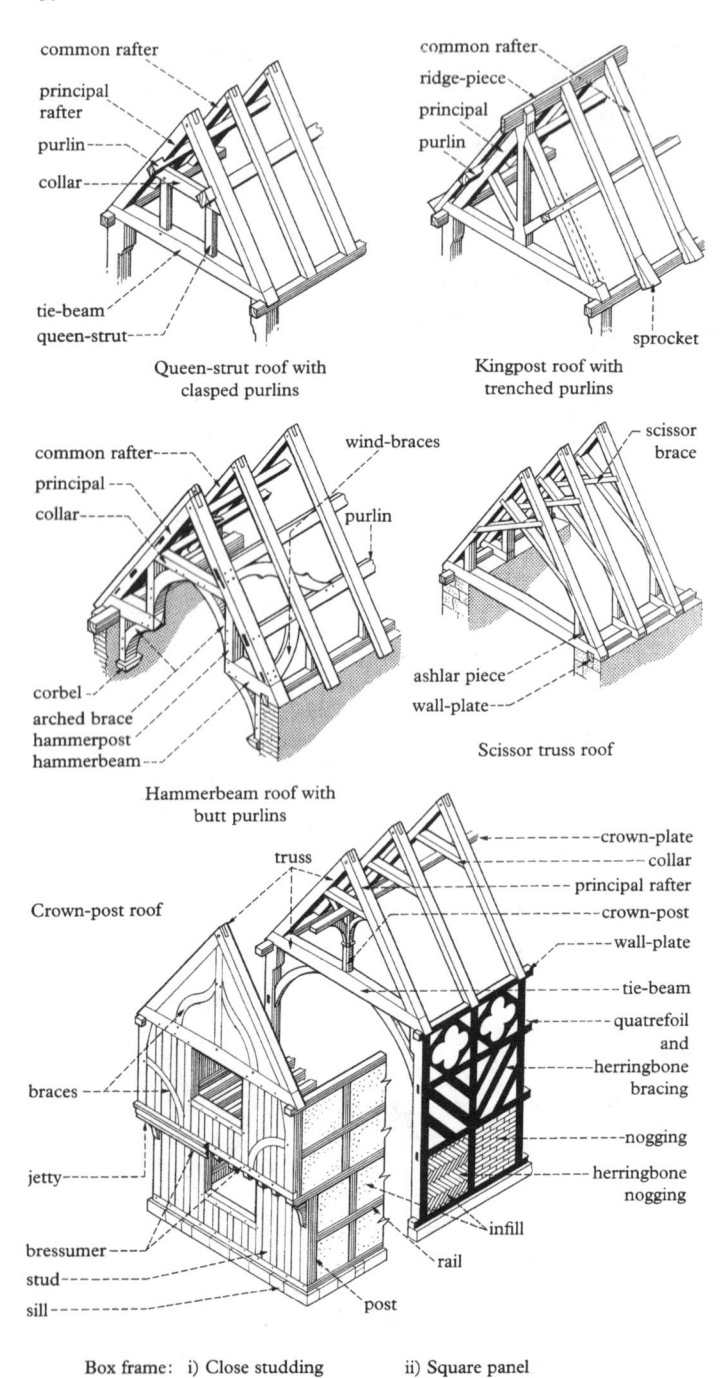

Queen-strut roof with clasped purlins

Kingpost roof with trenched purlins

Hammerbeam roof with butt purlins

Scissor truss roof

Crown-post roof

Box frame: i) Close studding ii) Square panel

FIGURE 7: ROOFS AND TIMBER-FRAMING

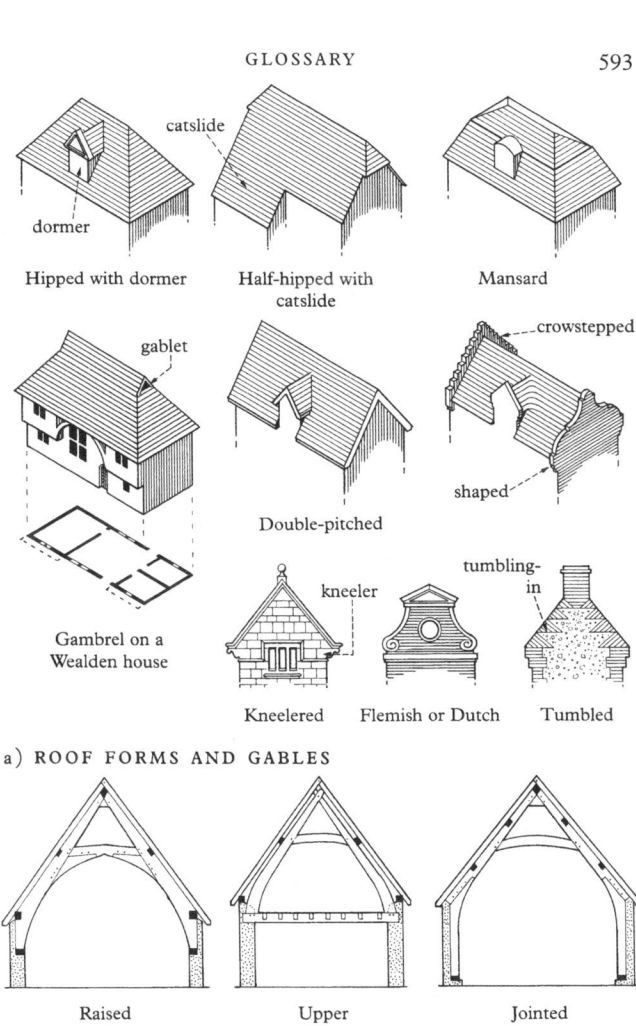

GLOSSARY

Hipped with dormer — catslide, dormer
Half-hipped with catslide
Mansard

gablet
Double-pitched
crowstepped, shaped

Gambrel on a Wealden house
Kneelered — kneeler
Flemish or Dutch
Tumbled — tumbling-in

a) ROOF FORMS AND GABLES

Raised
Upper
Jointed

Full — blade
Base

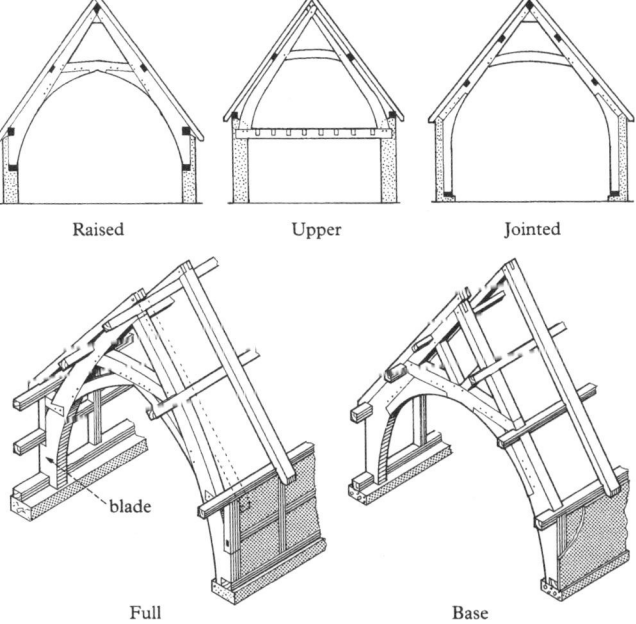

b) CRUCK FRAMES

FIGURE 8: ROOFS AND TIMBER-FRAMING

MIXER-COURTS: forecourts to groups of houses shared by vehicles and pedestrians.

MODILLIONS: small consoles (q.v.) along the underside of a Corinthian or Composite cornice (3d). Often used along an eaves cornice.

MODULE: a predetermined standard size for co-ordinating the dimensions of components of a building.

MOTTE-AND-BAILEY: post-Roman and Norman defence consisting of an earthen mound (motte) topped by a wooden tower within a bailey, an enclosure defended by a ditch and palisade, and also, sometimes, by an internal bank.

MOUCHETTE: see Tracery and 2b.

MOULDING: shaped ornamental strip of continuous section; see e.g. Cavetto, Cyma, Ovolo, Roll.

MULLION: vertical member between window lights (2b).

MULTI-STOREY: five or more storeys. Multi-storey flats may form a *cluster block*, with individual blocks of flats grouped round a service core; a *point block*, with flats fanning out from a service core; or a *slab block*, with flats approached by corridors or galleries from service cores at intervals or towers at the ends (plan also used for offices, hotels etc.). *Tower block* is a generic term for any very high multi-storey building.

MUNTIN: see Panelling and 6b.

NAILHEAD: E.E. ornament consisting of small pyramids regularly repeated (1a).

NARTHEX: enclosed vestibule or covered porch at the main entrance to a church.

NAVE: the body of a church W of the crossing or chancel often flanked by aisles (q.v.).

NEWEL: central or corner post of a staircase (6c). Newel stair: see Stairs.

NIGHT STAIR: stair by which religious entered the transept of their church from their dormitory to celebrate night services.

NOGGING: see Timber-framing (7).

NOOK-SHAFT: shaft set in the angle of a wall or opening (1a).

NORMAN: see Romanesque.

NOSING: projection of the tread of a step (6c).

NUTMEG: medieval ornament with a chain of tiny triangles placed obliquely.

OCULUS: circular opening.

ŒIL DE BŒUF: see Bullseye window.

OGEE: double curve, bending first one way and then the other, as in an *ogee* or *ogival arch* (5c). Cf. Cyma recta and Cyma reversa.

OPUS SECTILE: decorative mosaic-like facing.

OPUS SIGNINUM: composition flooring of Roman origin.

ORATORY: a private chapel in a church or a house. Also a church of the Oratorian Order.

ORDER: one of a series of recessed arches and jambs forming a splayed medieval opening, e.g. a doorway or arcade arch (1a).

ORDERS: the formalized versions of the post-and-lintel system in classical architecture. The main orders are *Doric, Ionic*, and *Corinthian*. They are Greek in origin but occur in Roman versions. Tuscan is a simple version of Roman Doric. Though each order has its own conventions (3), there are many minor variations. The *Composite* capital combines Ionic volutes with Corinthian foliage. *Superimposed orders*: orders on successive levels, usually in the upward sequence of Tuscan, Doric, Ionic, Corinthian, Composite.

ORIEL: see Bay window.

OVERDOOR: painting or relief above an internal door. Also called a *sopraporta*.

OVERTHROW: decorative fixed arch between two gatepiers or above a wrought-iron gate.

OVOLO: wide convex moulding (3f).

PALIMPSEST: of a brass: where a metal plate has been reused by turning over the engraving on the back; of a wall painting: where one overlaps and partly obscures an earlier one.

PALLADIAN: following the examples and principles of Andrea Palladio (1508–80).

PALMETTE: classical ornament like a palm shoot (4b).

PANELLING: wooden lining to interior walls, made up of vertical members (*muntins*) and horizontals (*rails*) framing panels: also called *wainscot*. *Raised and fielded*: with the central area of the panel (*field*) raised up (6b).

PANTILE: roof tile of S section.

PARAPET: wall for protection at any sudden drop, e.g. at the wall-head of a castle where it protects the *parapet walk* or wall-walk. Also used to conceal a roof.

PARCLOSE: *see* Screen.

PARGETTING (*lit.* plastering): exterior plaster decoration, either in relief or incised.

PARLOUR: in a religious house, a room where the religious could talk to visitors; in a medieval house, the semi-private living room below the solar (q.v.).

PARTERRE: level space in a garden laid out with low, formal beds.

PATERA (*lit.* plate): round or oval ornament in shallow relief.

PAVILION: ornamental building for occasional use; or projecting subdivision of a larger building, often at an angle or terminating a wing.

PEBBLEDASHING: *see* Rendering.

PEDESTAL: a tall block carrying a classical order, statue, vase, etc.

PEDIMENT: a formalized gable derived from that of a classical temple; also used over doors, windows, etc. For variations *see* 4b.

PENDENTIVE: spandrel between adjacent arches, supporting a drum, dome or vault and consequently formed as part of a hemisphere (5a).

PENTHOUSE: subsidiary structure with a lean-to roof. Also a separately roofed structure on top of a C20 multi-storey block.

PERIPTERAL: *see* Peristyle.

PERISTYLE: a colonnade all round the exterior of a classical building, as in a temple which is then said to be *peripteral*.

PERP (PERPENDICULAR): English Gothic architecture *c.* 1335–50 to *c.* 1530. The name is derived from the upright tracery panels then used (*see* Tracery and 2a).

PERRON: external stair to a doorway, usually of double-curved plan.

PEW: loosely, seating for the laity outside the chancel; strictly, an enclosed seat. *Box pew*: with equal high sides and a door.

PIANO NOBILE: principal floor of a classical building above a ground floor or basement and with a lesser storey overhead.

PIAZZA: formal urban open space surrounded by buildings.

PIER: large masonry or brick support, often for an arch. *See also* Compound pier.

PILASTER: flat representation of a classical column in shallow relief. *Pilaster strip*: *see* Lesene.

PILE: row of rooms. *Double pile*: two rows thick.

PILLAR: free-standing upright member of any section, not conforming to one of the orders (q.v.).

PILLAR PISCINA: *see* Piscina.

PILOTIS: C20 French term for pillars or stilts that support a building above an open ground floor.

PISCINA: basin for washing Mass vessels, provided with a drain; set in or against the wall to the S of an altar or free-standing (*pillar piscina*).

PISÉ: *see* Cob.

PITCHED MASONRY: laid on the diagonal, often alternately with opposing courses (*pitched and counterpitched* or *herringbone*).

PLATBAND: flat horizontal moulding between storeys. Cf. stringcourse.

PLATE RAIL: *see* Railways.

PLATEWAY: *see* Railways.

PLINTH: projecting courses at the

foot of a wall or column, generally chamfered or moulded at the top.

PODIUM: a continuous raised platform supporting a building; or a large block of two or three storeys beneath a multi-storey block of smaller area.

POINT BLOCK: *see* Multi-storey.

POINTING: exposed mortar jointing of masonry or brickwork. Types include *flush*, *recessed* and *tuck* (with a narrow channel filled with finer, whiter mortar).

POPPYHEAD: carved ornament of leaves and flowers as a finial for a bench end or stall.

PORTAL FRAME: C20 frame comprising two uprights rigidly connected to a beam or pair of rafters.

PORTCULLIS: gate constructed to rise and fall in vertical grooves at the entry to a castle.

PORTICO: a porch with the roof and frequently a pediment supported by a row of columns (4a). A portico *in antis* has columns on the same plane as the front of the building. A *prostyle* porch has columns standing free. Porticoes are described by the number of front columns, e.g. tetrastyle (four), hexastyle (six). The space within the temple is the *naos*, that within the portico the *pronaos*. *Blind portico*: the front features of a portico applied to a wall.

PORTICUS (plural: porticūs): subsidiary cell opening from the main body of a pre-Conquest church.

POST: upright support in a structure (7).

POSTERN: small gateway at the back of a building or to the side of a larger entrance door or gate.

POUND LOCK: *see* Canals.

PRESBYTERY: the part of a church lying E of the choir where the main altar is placed; or a priest's residence.

PRINCIPAL: *see* Roofs and 7.

PRONAOS: *see* Portico and 4a.

PROSTYLE: *see* Portico and 4a.

PULPIT: raised and enclosed platform for the preaching of sermons. *Three-decker*: with reading desk below and clerk's desk below that. *Two-decker*: as above, minus the clerk's desk.

PULPITUM: stone screen in a major church dividing choir from nave.

PULVINATED: *see* Frieze and 3c.

PURLIN: *see* Roofs and 7.

PUTHOLES or PUTLOG HOLES: in the wall to receive putlogs, the horizontal timbers which support scaffolding boards; sometimes not filled after construction is complete.

PUTTO (plural: putti): small naked boy.

QUARRIES: square (or diamond) panes of glass supported by lead strips (*cames*); square floor slabs or tiles.

QUATREFOIL: *see* Foil and 2b.

QUEEN-STRUT: *see* Roofs and 7.

QUIRK: sharp groove to one side of a convex medieval moulding.

QUOINS: dressed stones at the angles of a building (6d).

RADBURN SYSTEM: vehicle and pedestrian segregation in residential developments, based on that used at Radburn, New Jersey, USA, by Wright and Stein, 1928–30.

RADIATING CHAPELS: projecting radially from an ambulatory or an apse (*see* Chevet).

RAFTER: *see* Roofs and 7.

RAGGLE: groove cut in masonry, especially to receive the edge of a roof-covering.

RAGULY: ragged (in heraldry). Also applied to funerary sculpture, e.g. *cross raguly*: with a notched outline.

RAIL: *see* Panelling and 6b; also 7.

RAILWAYS: *Edge rail*: on which flanged wheels can run. *Plate rail*: L-section rail for plain unflanged wheels. *Plateway*: early railway using plate rails.

RAISED AND FIELDED: *see* Panelling and 6b.

RAKE: slope or pitch.

RAMPART: defensive outer wall of stone or earth. *Rampart walk*: path along the inner face.

REBATE: rectangular section cut out of a masonry edge to receive a shutter, door, window, etc.

REBUS: a heraldic pun, e.g. a fiery cock for Cockburn.

REEDING: series of convex mouldings, the reverse of fluting (q.v.). Cf. Gadrooning.

RENDERING: the covering of outside walls with a uniform surface or skin for protection from the weather. *Limewashing*: thin layer of lime plaster. *Pebbledashing*: where aggregate is thrown at the wet plastered wall for a textured effect. *Roughcast*: plaster mixed with a coarse aggregate such as gravel. *Stucco*: fine lime plaster worked to a smooth surface. *Cement rendering*: a cheaper substitute for stucco, usually with a grainy texture.

REPOUSSÉ: relief designs in metalwork, formed by beating it from the back.

REREDORTER (*lit.* behind the dormitory): latrines in a medieval religious house.

REREDOS: painted and/or sculptured screen behind and above an altar. Cf. Retable.

RESPOND: half-pier or half-column bonded into a wall and carrying one end of an arch. It usually terminates an arcade.

RETABLE: painted or carved panel standing on or at the back of an altar, usually attached to it.

RETROCHOIR: in a major church, the area between the high altar and E chapel.

REVEAL: the plane of a jamb, between the wall and the frame of a door or window.

RIB VAULT: *see* Vault and 2c.

RINCEAU: classical ornament of leafy scrolls (4b).

RISER: vertical face of a step (6c).

ROACH: a rough-textured form of Portland stone, with small cavities and fossil shells.

ROCK-FACED: masonry cleft to produce a rugged appearance.

ROCOCO: style current *c.* 1720 and *c.* 1760, characterized by a serpentine line and playful, scrolled decoration.

ROLL MOULDING: medieval moulding of part-circular section (1a).

ROMANESQUE: style current in the CII and CI2. In England often called Norman. *See also* Saxo-Norman.

ROOD: crucifix flanked by the Virgin and St John, usually over the entry into the chancel, on a beam (*rood beam*) or painted on the wall. The *rood screen* below often had a walkway (*rood loft*) along the top, reached by a *rood stair* in the side wall.

ROOFS: Shape. For the main external shapes (hipped, mansard, etc.) *see* 8a. *Helm* and *Saddleback*: *see* 1c. *Lean-to*: single sloping roof built against a vertical wall; lean-to is also applied to the part of the building beneath.

Construction. *See* 7.

Single-framed roof: with no main trusses. The rafters may be fixed to the wall-plate or ridge, or longitudinal timber may be absent altogether.

Double-framed roof: with longitudinal members, such as purlins, and usually divided into bays by principals and principal rafters.

Other types are named after their main structural components, e.g. *hammerbeam*, *crown-post* (*see* Elements below and 7).

Elements. *See* 7.

Ashlar piece: a short vertical timber connecting inner wall-plate or timber pad to a rafter.

Braces: subsidiary timbers set diagonally to strengthen the frame. *Arched braces*: curved pair forming an arch, connecting wall or post below with tie- or collar-beam above. *Passing braces*: long straight braces passing across other members of the truss. *Scissor braces*: pair crossing diagonally between pairs of rafters or principals. *Wind-braces*: short, usually curved braces connecting side purlins with principals; sometimes decorated with cusping.

Collar or *collar-beam*: horizontal transverse timber connecting a pair of rafter or cruck blades (q.v.), set between apex and the wall-plate.

Crown-post: a vertical timber set centrally on a tie-beam and supporting a collar purlin braced to it longitudinally. In an open truss lateral braces may rise to the collar-beam; in a closed truss they may descend to the tie-beam.

Hammerbeams: horizontal brackets projecting at wall-plate level like an interrupted tie-beam; the inner ends carry *hammerposts*, vertical timbers which support a purlin and are braced to a collar-beam above.

Kingpost: vertical timber set centrally on a tie- or collar-beam, rising to the apex of the roof to support a ridge-piece (cf. Strut).

Plate: longitudinal timber set square to the ground. *Wall-plate*: plate along the top of a wall which receives the ends of the rafters; cf. Purlin.

Principals: pair of inclined lateral timbers of a truss. Usually they support side purlins and mark the main bay divisions.

Purlin: horizontal longitudinal timber. *Collar purlin* or *crown plate*: central timber which carries collar-beams and is supported by crown-posts. *Side purlins*: pairs of timbers placed some way up the slope of the roof, which carry common rafters. *Butt* or *tenoned purlins* are tenoned into either side of the principals. *Through purlins* pass through or past the principal; they include *clasped purlins*, which rest on queenposts or are carried in the angle between principals and collar, and *trenched purlins* trenched into the backs of principals.

Queen-strut: paired vertical, or near-vertical, timbers placed symmetrically on a tie-beam to support side purlins.

Rafters: inclined lateral timbers supporting the roof covering. *Common rafters*: regularly spaced uniform rafters placed along the length of a roof or between principals. *Principal rafters*: rafters which also act as principals.

Ridge, ridge-piece: horizontal longitudinal timber at the apex supporting the ends of the rafters.

Sprocket: short timber placed on the back and at the foot of a rafter to form projecting eaves.

Strut: vertical or oblique timber between two members of a truss, not directly supporting longitudinal timbers.

Tie-beam: main horizontal transverse timber which carries the feet of the principals at wall level.

Truss: rigid framework of timbers at bay intervals, carrying the longitudinal roof timbers which support the common rafters. *Closed truss*: with the spaces between the timbers filled, to form an internal partition.

See also Cruck, Wagon roof.

ROPE MOULDING: *see* Cable moulding.

ROSE WINDOW: circular window with tracery radiating from the centre. Cf. Wheel window.

ROTUNDA: building or room circular in plan.

ROUGHCAST: *see* Rendering.

ROVING BRIDGE: *see* Canals.

RUBBED BRICKWORK: *see* Gauged brickwork.

RUBBLE: masonry whose stones are wholly or partly in a rough state. *Coursed*: coursed stones with rough faces. *Random*: uncoursed stones in a random pattern. *Snecked*: with courses broken by smaller stones (snecks).

RUSTICATION: *see* 6d. Exaggerated treatment of masonry to give an effect of strength. The joints are usually recessed by V-section chamfering or square-section channelling (*channelled rustication*). Banded rustication has only the horizontal joints emphasized. The faces may be flat, but can be *diamond-faced*, like shallow pyramids, *vermiculated*, with a stylized texture like worm-casts, and *glacial* (frost-work), like icicles or stalactites.

SACRISTY: room in a church for sacred vessels and vestments.

SADDLEBACK ROOF: *see* 1c.

SALTIRE CROSS: with diagonal limbs.

SANCTUARY: area around the main altar of a church. Cf. Presbytery.

SANGHA: residence of Buddhist monks or nuns.

SARCOPHAGUS: coffin of stone or other durable material.

SAXO-NORMAN: transitional Romanesque style combining Anglo-Saxon and Norman features, current c. 1060–1100.

SCAGLIOLA: composition imitating marble.

SCALLOPED CAPITAL: see 1a.

SCOTIA: a hollow classical moulding, especially between tori (q.v.) on a column base (3b, 3f).

SCREEN: in a medieval church, usually at the entry to the chancel; see Rood (screen) and Pulpitum. A *parclose screen* separates a chapel from the rest of the church.

SCREENS or SCREENS PASSAGE: screened-off entrance passage between great hall and service rooms.

SECTION: two-dimensional representation of a building, moulding, etc., revealed by cutting across it.

SEDILIA (singular: sedile): seats for the priests (usually three) on the S side of the chancel.

SET-OFF: see Weathering.

SETTS: squared stones, usually of granite, used for paving or flooring.

SGRAFFITO: decoration scratched, often in plaster, to reveal a pattern in another colour beneath. *Graffiti*: scratched drawing or writing.

SHAFT: vertical member of round or polygonal section (1a, 3a). *Shaft-ring*: at the junction of shafts set *en delit* (q.v.) or attached to a pier or wall (1a).

SHEILA-NA-GIG: female fertility figure, usually with legs apart.

SHELL: thin, self-supporting roofing membrane of timber or concrete.

SHOULDERED ARCHITRAVE: see 4b.

SHUTTERING: see Concrete.

SILL: horizontal member at the bottom of a window or door frame; or at the base of a timber-framed wall into which posts and studs are tenoned (7).

SLAB BLOCK: see Multi-storey.

SLATE-HANGING: covering of overlapping slates on a wall. *Tile-hanging* is similar.

SLYPE: covered way or passage leading E from the cloisters between transept and chapter house.

SNECKED: see Rubble.

SOFFIT (*lit*. ceiling): underside of an arch (also called *intrados*), lintel, etc. *Soffit roll*: medieval roll moulding on a soffit.

SOLAR: private upper chamber in a medieval house, accessible from the high end of the great hall.

SOPRAPORTA: see Overdoor.

SOUNDING-BOARD: see Tester.

SPANDRELS: roughly triangular spaces between an arch and its containing rectangle, or between adjacent arches (5c). Also non-structural panels under the windows in a curtain-walled building.

SPERE: a fixed structure screening the lower end of the great hall from the screens passage. *Spere-truss*: roof truss incorporated in the spere.

SPIRE: tall pyramidal or conical feature crowning a tower or turret. *Broach*: starting from a square base, then carried into an octagonal section by means of triangular faces; and *splayed-foot*: variation of the broach form, found principally in the south-east, in which the four cardinal faces are splayed out near their base, to cover the corners, while oblique (or intermediate) faces taper away to a point (1c). *Needle spire*: thin spire rising from the centre of a tower roof, well inside the parapet: when of timber and lead often called a *spike*.

SPIRELET: see Flèche.

SPLAY: of an opening when it is wider on one face of a wall than the other.

SPRING or SPRINGING: level at which an arch or vault rises from its supports. *Springers*: the first stones of an arch or vaulting rib above the spring (2c).

SQUINCH: arch or series of arches thrown across an interior angle of a square or rectangular structure to support a circular or polygonal superstructure, especially a dome or spire (5a).

SQUINT: an aperture in a wall or through a pier usually to allow a view of an altar.

STAIRS: see 6c. *Dog-leg stair*: parallel flights rising alternately in opposite directions, without an open well. *Flying stair*: cantilevered from the walls of a stairwell, without newels; sometimes called a *Geometric* stair when the inner edge describes a curve. *Newel stair*: ascending round a central supporting newel (q.v.); called a *spiral stair* or *vice* when in a circular shaft, a *winder* when in a rectangular compartment. (Winder also applies to the steps on the turn.) *Well stair*: with flights round a square open well framed by newel posts. *See also* Perron.

STALL: fixed seat in the choir or chancel for the clergy or choir (cf. Pew). Usually with arm rests, and often framed together.

STANCHION: upright structural member, of iron, steel or reinforced concrete.

STANDPIPE TOWER: *see* Manometer.

STEAM ENGINES: *Atmospheric*: worked by the vacuum created when low-pressure steam is condensed in the cylinder, as developed by Thomas Newcomen. *Beam engine*: with a large pivoted beam moved in an oscillating fashion by the piston. It may drive a flywheel or be *non-rotative*. *Watt* and *Cornish*: single-cylinder; *compound*: two cylinders; *triple expansion*: three cylinders.

STEEPLE: tower together with a spire, lantern, or belfry.

STIFF-LEAF: type of E.E. foliage decoration. *Stiff-leaf capital see* 1b.

STOP: plain or decorated terminal to mouldings or chamfers, or at the end of hoodmoulds and labels (*label stop*), or stringcourses (5b, 6a); *see also* Headstop.

STOUP: vessel for holy water, usually near a door.

STRAINER: *see* Arch.

STRAPWORK: late C16 and C17 decoration, like interlaced leather straps.

STRETCHER: *see* Bond and 6e.

STRING: *see* 6c. Sloping member holding the ends of the treads and risers of a staircase. *Closed string*: a broad string covering the ends of the treads and risers. *Open string*: cut into the shape of the treads and risers.

STRINGCOURSE: horizontal course or moulding projecting from the surface of a wall (6d).

STUCCO: *see* Rendering.

STUDS: subsidiary vertical timbers of a timber-framed wall or partition (7).

STUPA: Buddhist shrine, circular in plan.

STYLOBATE: top of the solid platform on which a colonnade stands (3a).

SUSPENSION BRIDGE: *see* Bridge.

SWAG: like a festoon (q.v.), but representing cloth.

SYSTEM BUILDING: *see* Industrialized building.

TABERNACLE: canopied structure to contain the reserved sacrament or a relic; or architectural frame for an image or statue.

TABLE TOMB: memorial slab raised on free-standing legs.

TAS-DE-CHARGE: the lower courses of a vault or arch which are laid horizontally (2c).

TERM: pedestal or pilaster tapering downward, usually with the upper part of a human figure growing out of it.

TERRACOTTA: moulded and fired clay ornament or cladding.

TESSELLATED PAVEMENT: mosaic flooring, particularly Roman, made of *tesserae*, i.e. cubes of glass, stone, or brick.

TESTER: flat canopy over a tomb or pulpit, where it is also called a *sounding-board*.

TESTER TOMB: tomb-chest with effigies beneath a tester, either free-standing (tester with four or more columns), or attached to a wall (*half-tester*) with columns on one side only.

TETRASTYLE: *see* Portico.

THERMAL WINDOW: *see* Diocletian window.

THREE-DECKER PULPIT: *see* Pulpit.

TIDAL GATES: *see* Canals.

TIE-BEAM: *see* Roofs and 7.

TIERCERON: *see* Vault and 2c.

TILE-HANGING: *see* Slate-hanging.

TIMBER-FRAMING: *see* 7. Method of construction where the structural frame is built of interlocking timbers. The spaces are filled with non-structural material, e.g. *infill* of wattle and daub, lath and plaster, brickwork (known as *nogging*), etc. and may be covered by plaster, weatherboarding (q.v.), or tiles.

TOMB-CHEST: chest-shaped tomb, usually of stone. Cf. Table tomb, Tester tomb.

TORUS (plural: tori): large convex moulding usually used on a column base (3b, 3f).

TOUCH: soft black marble quarried near Tournai.

TOURELLE: turret corbelled out from the wall.

TOWER BLOCK: *see* Multi-storey.

TRABEATED: depends structurally on the use of the post and lintel. Cf. Arcuated.

TRACERY: openwork pattern of masonry or timber in the upper part of an opening. *Blind tracery* is tracery applied to a solid wall.
Plate tracery, introduced *c.* 1200, is the earliest form, in which shapes are cut through solid masonry (2a).
Bar tracery was introduced into England *c.* 1250. The pattern is formed by intersecting moulded ribwork continued from the mullions. It was especially elaborate during the Decorated period (q.v.). Tracery shapes can include circles, *daggers* (elongated ogee-ended lozenges), *mouchettes* (like daggers but with curved sides) and upright rectangular *panels*. They often have *cusps*, projecting points defining lobes or *foils* (q.v.) within the main shape: *Kentish* or *split-cusps* are forked (2b).
Types of bar tracery (*see* 2b) include *geometric(al)*: *c.* 1250–1310, chiefly circles, often foiled; *Y-tracery*: *c.* 1300, with mullions branching into a Y-shape; *intersecting*: *c.* 1300, formed by interlocking mullions; *reticulated*: early C14, net-like pattern of ogee-ended lozenges; *curvilinear*: C14, with uninterrupted flowing curves; *panel*: Perp, with straight-sided panels, often cusped at the top and bottom.

TRANSEPT: transverse portion of a church.

TRANSITIONAL: generally used for the phase between Romanesque and Early English (*c.* 1175–*c.* 1200).

TRANSOM: horizontal member separating window lights (2b).

TREAD: horizontal part of a step. The *tread end* may be carved on a staircase (6c).

TREFOIL: *see* Foil.

TRIFORIUM: middle storey of a church treated as an arcaded wall passage or blind arcade, its height corresponding to that of the aisle roof.

TRIGLYPHS (*lit.* three-grooved tablets): stylized beam-ends in the Doric frieze, with metopes between (3b).

TRIUMPHAL ARCH: influential type of Imperial Roman monument.

TROPHY: sculptured or painted group of arms or armour.

TRUMEAU: central stone mullion supporting the tympanum of a wide doorway. *Trumeau figure*: carved figure attached to it (cf. Column figure).

TRUMPET CAPITAL: *see* 1b.

TRUSS: braced framework, spanning between supports. *See also* Roofs and 7.

TUMBLING or TUMBLING-IN: courses of brickwork laid at right-angles to a slope, e.g. of a gable, forming triangles by tapering into horizontal courses (8a).

TUSCAN: *see* Orders and 3e.

TWO-DECKER PULPIT: *see* Pulpit.

TYMPANUM: the surface between a lintel and the arch above it or within a pediment (4a).

UNDERCROFT: usually describes the vaulted room(s), beneath the main room(s) of a medieval house. Cf. Crypt.

VAULT: arched stone roof (sometimes imitated in timber or plaster). For types see 2c.
Tunnel or *barrel vault*: continuous semicircular or pointed arch, often of rubble masonry.

Groin-vault: tunnel vaults intersecting at right angles. *Groins* are the curved lines of the intersections.

Rib-vault: masonry framework of intersecting arches (ribs) supporting *vault cells*, used in Gothic architecture. *Wall rib* or *wall arch*: between wall and vault cell. *Transverse rib*: spans between two walls to divide a vault into bays. *Quadripartite* rib-vault: each bay has two pairs of diagonal ribs dividing the vault into four triangular cells. *Sexpartite* rib-vault: most often used over paired bays, has an extra pair of ribs springing from between the bays. More elaborate vaults may include *ridge ribs* along the crown of a vault or bisecting the bays; *tiercerons*: extra decorative ribs springing from the corners of a bay; and *liernes*: short decorative ribs in the crown of a vault, not linked to any springing point. A *stellar* or *star* vault has liernes in star formation.

Fan-vault: form of barrel vault used in the Perp period, made up of halved concave masonry cones decorated with blind tracery.

VAULTING SHAFT: shaft leading up to the spring or springing (q.v.) of a vault (2c).

VENETIAN or SERLIAN WINDOW: derived from Serlio (4b). The motif is used for other openings.

VERMICULATION: *see* Rustication and 6d.

VESICA: oval with pointed ends.

VICE: *see* Stair.

VILLA: originally a Roman country house or farm. The term was revived in England in the C18 under the influence of Palladio and used especially for smaller, compact country houses. In the later C19 it was debased to describe any suburban house.

VITRIFIED: bricks or tiles fired to a darkened glassy surface.

VITRUVIAN SCROLL: classical running ornament of curly waves (4b).

VOLUTES: spiral scrolls. They occur on Ionic capitals (3c). *Angle volute*: pair of volutes, turned outwards to meet at the corner of a capital.

VOUSSOIRS: wedge-shaped stones forming an arch (5c).

WAGON ROOF: with the appearance of the inside of a wagon tilt; often ceiled. Also called *cradle roof*.

WAINSCOT: *see* Panelling.

WALL MONUMENT: attached to the wall and often standing on the floor. *Wall tablets* are smaller with the inscription as the major element.

WALL-PLATE: *see* Roofs and 7.

WALL-WALK: *see* Parapet.

WARMING ROOM: room in a religious house where a fire burned for comfort.

WATERHOLDING BASE: early Gothic base with upper and lower mouldings separated by a deep hollow.

WATERLEAF: *see* Enrichments and 3f.

WATERLEAF CAPITAL: Late Romanesque and Transitional type of capital (1b).

WATER WHEELS: described by the way water is fed on to the wheel. *Breastshot*: mid-height, falling and passing beneath. *Overshot*: over the top. *Pitchback*: on the top but falling backwards. *Undershot*: turned by the momentum of the water passing beneath. In a *water turbine*, water is fed under pressure through a vaned wheel within a casing.

WEALDEN HOUSE: type of medieval timber-framed house with a central open hall flanked by bays of two storeys, roofed in line; the end bays are jettied to the front, but the eaves are continuous (8a).

WEATHERBOARDING: wall cladding of overlapping horizontal boards.

WEATHERING or SET-OFF: inclined, projecting surface to keep water away from the wall below.

WEEPERS: figures in niches along the sides of some medieval tombs. Also called mourners.

WHEEL WINDOW: circular, with radiating shafts like spokes. Cf. Rose window.

WROUGHT IRON: *see* Cast iron.

INDEX OF ARCHITECTS, ARTISTS, PATRONS AND RESIDENTS

Names of architects and artists working in the area covered by this volume are given in *italic*. Entries for partnerships and group practices are listed after entries for a single name.

Also indexed here are names/titles of families and individuals (not of bodies or commercial firms) recorded in this volume as having commissioned architectural work or owned, lived in, or visited properties in the area. The index includes monuments to members of such families and other individuals where they are of particular interest.

Abbott & Co. 241
Abraham, Robert 48, 241, 242
Abrey (Albry), William 567
Acton family 94
Acton, John 110
Acton, Nathaniel Lee 263
Adam, James 144
Adam, Robert 46–7, 49, 126, 144, 174, 264
Adye, Thomas 349
Ælfhun, Bishop 517, 519
Æthelred II 517
Affleck family 212
Affleck, Sir Richard 213
Agnew, Sir George 474
Aickman, J. 51, 533
Aikman, W. 104, 350, 461
Albry see Abrey
Alderson, Rev. S. H. 471, 472
Aldington & Craig 61, 312, Pl. 113
Aldryche, Thomas 29–30, 81, 83, 98, 220, 223, 334, 402, 473, 544, 571
Alexander, Rev. Maurice 202
Allen, Ellioton 331
Allen, James Milner 354
Allen, Robert 572
Almack, Richard 386, 387, 482
Amicia, Dame 338
Anderson, Andrew 64, 95, 285, 503
Anderson, J. Macvicar 474
Anderson, Rev. Thomas 237
Andrews, Frederick 287
Andrews, O. 201
Andrews & Son 201
Anglia Housing Ltd 294, Pl. 111
Angold, Henry 400, 454
Anna, King 22

Anne, Queen 432
Anning Bell, Robert see Bell, Robert Anning
Anselm, Abbot 127, 128
Appleton, John 267
Appleyard, Rev. Benjamin 64, 122
Arber, Richard 433
Archer, Fred 440
Archer, J. W. 349
Arlington, Henry Bennet, 1st Earl of 229–31, 232, 233
Armitage, E. L. 538
Armitage, Joseph 80
Armstrong, Tim 367
Arundell & Tarte 575
Arup Associates 63, 275
Arup (Ove) & Partners 530
Ashburne, Rev. John 443
Ashfield, Robert de 501
Ashley, Henry (knapper) 5, 324
Ashley, Henry 412
Ashmead, R. F. 241
Ashton, Robert 268
Asprucci, Mario 47, 327, Pl. 86
Aston, Marcia 441
Atkins, John 159
Atkinson, T. D. 262
Atkinson & Browne 290
Auchincloss, Janey 219
Audley family 255
Austin & Seely 497

Baalham, W. 457
Babergh District Council 358, 529
Backhouse, Benjamin 53, 144, 164, 480
Bacon family 209, 309, 310, 464–6

INDEX OF ARCHITECTS, ETC.

Bacon, Sir Edmund, 2nd Bt 465, 466
Bacon, Sir Edmund, 4th Bt and wife Elizabeth 466
Bacon, Sir Francis (son of Sir Nicholas) 464
Bacon, H. F. 47, 54, 85, 142, 153, 445, 446–7
Bacon, Jane, Lady 209
Bacon, John (d. 1513) 107, 309
Bacon, John Jun. 43, 80, 222, 299, 400, 409, 445–6, 496, 518
Bacon, John Sen. 43, 79, 237, 299
Bacon, Sir Nathaniel 209
Bacon, Sir Nicholas (d. 1579) 98, 335, 464, 465, 466
Bacon, Sir Nicholas, 1st Bt and wife Anne 42, 209, 465, Pl. 67
Bacon, Percy 290
Bacon, Philippa, Lady 42, 466
Bacon & Bell 142, 169, 324
Bacon (Percy) & Bros 139
Bacon & Manning 233, 520
Badcock, Baynes 120
Badcock, Isabel Baynes 119
Badcock, N. 553
Badham, Rev. Charles 526
Baillie, T. 563
Baillie & Mayer 417, 482
Baily, E. H. 209, 299
Baily, Emily and Louisa 267
Bain, Rev. W. R. 238
Baker, J. W. & F. W. 358
Baker, Thomas 358
Baldwin, Abbot 36, 127, 149
Bales, Daniel 442
Balfour & Turner 78, 79
Ballance, A. W. 308
Banham, Walter de 127
Banting, France & Co. 329
Bardwell, Thomas 82
Barefoot, Peter 291
Barefoot & Gilles 111
Baret, John 27, 139–40, 156
Baret, William 156
Barkentin & Krall 572
Barker family 190
Barley, Keith 504
Barley Studio 504
Barnardiston family 113–14, 190, 338–9
Barnardiston, Lady Elisabeth 338
Barnardiston, Mary 114
Barnardiston, Sir Nathaniel and wife Jane 42, 339
Barnardiston, Sir Samuel 338, 339
Barnardiston, Sir Thomas and Lady Elizabeth 35, 338–9
Barnes, Ernest 64, 240, 371, 408, 504, 512
Barnes, Frederick 52, 53, 54, 93–4, 108, 109, 124, 149, 176, 225, 273, 280, 281, 282, 314, 420, 423, 425, 447, 462, 463, 468, 485, 505, 506, 515, 520, 539, Pl. 93
Barnes & Bisshopp 203
Barrow, Maurice 42, 550
Bartolozzi, Francesco 203
Barton, Sir Henry 408
Barton & Co. 259, 527
Bartrum, Albert 572
Bassett-Smith, W. 461
Bath, Margaret, Countess of 141, 304–5
Bath, John Bourchier, Earl of 304
Baylis, Dudley 286, 521
Beachcroft, Samuel 563
Beadel, Son & Chancellor 466
Beale, Miss H. L. 115
Bear, William 530
Beaumont, P. M. 180, 194
Beckwith, Ernest 518
Bedingfield family 228, 249
Behnes, William 233
Bell, Charles 55, 290, Pl. 102
Bell, Daniel 271, 363
Bell, Henry 232
Bell, M. C. Farrar 309
Bell, Robert Anning 417
Bennet, Philip 473
Bennett, Sir Hubert 62, 259, 293, 411
Bennett, Richard 179
Bennetts 179
Bentham, P. G. 435
Benyon, Rev. Edward Richard and Jane 57, 209, 211, 333–4, 540, 552, 569, 570
Benyon de Beauvoir, Richard 209
Berdewell, Sir William 84–5, Pl. 35
Berry, W. H. Atkin 58, 311, 312–13
Betts, Francis 365, 405, 505
Bicknell, Julian 415
Biddell, William and Mary Anne 361
Binns (George) & Associates 409
Binyon, Brightwen 54, 59, 126, 167, 484, 523
Birch, Rev. C. E. 563
Bird (T. A.) & R. M. T. Tyler 534
Birde, David 100–1
Bisbie, Revd Nathaniel 382, 388
Bisshopp, E. F. 53, 54, 87, 95, 126, 153, 185, 244, 307, 311, 370, 448, 484, 568, 572, 573
Bisshopp & Cautley 87
Black, Rodney 62, 223, 249, 288, 374
Blackall, Pippa (Philippa Heskett) 78, 96, 137, 318, 473, 488, 565
Blackburne, E. L. 574
Blacker, Philip 440
Blackie, James 63, 97, 162, 268, 319, 463, 511, 521, 527, 528, Pl. 94
Blake, Patrick 350
Blakely family 537

INDEX OF ARCHITECTS, ETC.

Blakeman, C. 107
Blanchard, M. H. 161
Bliss, Edward 112
Blomfield, A. C. 47, 328–31, Pl. 87
Blomfield, A. W. 54, 56, 94, 114, 137–8, 168, 211, 240, 241, 307, 416, 459, 461
Blomfield, C. J. 418
Blomfield, Sir Reginald 53, 100, 103, 168, 286, 450, 518
Blomfield (Sir Arthur) & Sons 212, 450
Bloomfield, George 51, 89, 306, 400, 532
Blosse, Charles 510
Blow, Detmar 189–90, 191, 205, 295, 338, 513
Blow (Detmar) & Billerey 322
Blunden, Edmund 391
Boardman (E.) & Son 112
Boby, Robert 511
Bodley, G. F. 56, 91, 135, 139, 221–2, 385, 519
Boehm, Sir Edgar 55, 430
Bonaparte, Joseph 115, 116
Bond, Laurence H. 265, 372
Booth, Benjamin B. 288
Borough Architects' Dept 164
Botetourt family 257
Bottomley, Charles 115
Bottomley, George 444
Boudica 14
Boughton, Henry 369
Boulton & Paul 511
Bourchier family 304
  see also Bath, Earl and Countess of
Bourchier, Dame Anne 554
Bourne, C. J. 257
Bower, S. E. Dykes see Dykes Bower, S. E.
Boyton, Ed. 238
Branch family 27, 351–2
Branch, Simon and Elizabeth 351, 352
Brand family 222
Brand, John 457
Brandon, Charles see Suffolk, Duke of
Brangwyn, Sir Frank 226
Brassey, Thomas 52
Breeze, Gary 535
Brett, Jasper 56, 308
Brettingham, Matthew 46, 230, 233
Brewins, Leslie 298
Brewse family 377–9
Brewse, Sir John 377, 379
Brewse, Thomas and wife Jane 378–9
Bridgeman, Orlando 200–1
Bridgeman, Robert 221
Brierley, Walter H. 440

Bright, Henry 452
Bright, Sir Robert 452
Brightman, Hilary 81
Briscoe, Rodney 181
Bristol, Elizabeth Hervey, Countess of (wife of 1st Earl) 49, 126, 160
Bristol, Earls and Marquesses of 47, 321, 326–8
Bristol, 1st Earl of 185, 186, 325, 331, 332
Bristol, 2nd Earl of 145, 325
Bristol, 4th Earl of (Earl-Bishop) 47, 48, 261, 325, 327, 329, 330, 333
Bristol, 5th Earl of see Bristol, 1st Marquess of
Bristol, Marchioness of (wife of 1st Marquess) 331
Bristol, Marchioness of (wife of 4th Marquess) 121
Bristol, 1st Marquess of (former 5th Earl) 185, 327, 329, 330, 331, 333, 475
Bristol, 3rd Marquess of 329
Bristol, 4th Marquess of 328
Bristol, 7th Marquess of 328
Broad, Gordon L. 345
Brocklebank, C. G. 245
Brooke, A. J. 321
Brooke, W. J. 307
Brookes, W. McIntosh 53, 143
Brookes Stacey Randall Architects 530
Brooks, George 537
Brooks, Peter 512
Brown, Capability 48, 206, 231, 241, 325, 327, 332, 466
Brown, George 541–2
Brown, H. 64, 408
Brown, J. W. 423
Brown, John 54, 522
Brown, R. 85, 141
Brown, William 49, 87, 221, 223
Brown & Burgess 202
Browne, Arthur 49, 307
Browne, Robert 79n.
Bruff, Peter 52, 149
Bryans, H. W. 212
Bryceson, H. 480
Buck, William 162
Buckingham, Duke of 302
Buckler, J. C. 349
Buckler, J. C. & G. 238
Bucknall, John 136
Budgen, John 480
Building Design Partnership 64, 172
Bullen, C. H. 269
Bunbury family 254, 255, 409
Bunbury, Sir H. 409
Bures family 75, 118
Bures, Sir Robert de 35, 75–6
Burgate family 122–3
Burgate, Sir William de and wife Eleanor 35, 122–3

INDEX OF ARCHITECTS, ETC.

Burgh (de) family 195
Burgh, Elizabeth de *see* Ulster, Countess of
Burgkmair, Hans (school of) 136
Burlington, Lord 231
Burlison & Grylls 56, 78, 138, 222, 244, 269, 285, 298, 340, 473
Burne-Jones, Sir Edward 81, 254, 429n.
Burrell, Benjamin 212, 213
Burrell, C. 231
Burrough, Sir James 49, 160, 443
Burroughes, Gilbert 468
Burrows, Horace 574
Bury, S. J. 175
Butler, A. S. G. 564
Butler, Rev. Harold 343–4
Butterfield, William 54, 81, 267, 362, 518, 519, 526, 551
Buxbaum, Tim 411
Byfield, George 14, 49

Cadge, T. 78
Cadge, Thomas 182
Cadogan, Beatrix Jane Craven, Countess 56, 209, 552
Cadogan, 5th Earl 57, 209–11, 334
Cakebread, Robey & Co. 566
Calthorpe family 79, 297
Calthorpe, Dorothy (d. 1693) 79
Calthorpe, Sir Henry and wife Dorothy (mon. 1638) 42, 79
Calthorpe, James (d. 1702) 79
Calthorpe, James (d. 1784) 48, 79, 263
Cambridge Stained Glass 308
Cameron, J. 266, 271
Camm Bros 504
Campbell, Smith & Co. 136, 517
Canham, John 406
Canham, Mary 406
Canute, King 130
Capon, George 342
Capronnier, J. B. 56, 496
Carabelli, Casimiro 328
Carabelli, Donato 328
Caracciolo, Giovanni Battista 429
Carausius 16
Cardinall, Robert 519
Cardozo-Kindersley Workshop 238
Carle (de) family 132, 409
Carle, de 104, 107, 198, 209, 215, 217, 222, 264, 287, 337, 345, 513, 551
Carle, Benjamin de 327
Carle, John de 44, 156, 160, 260, 327, 333, 505
Carle, Robert de 44, 140, 160
Carle, Robert de IV 212, 299
Carlisle, Carla 492
Carlisle, Kenneth 492
Carnac, Lt-Col. John 115

Carnwath, David 452
Caröe, W. D. 55, 109, 136, 225, 346, 351, 353, 497, Pl. 108
Caröe & Passmore 271
Carpenter, R. C. 367, 368
Carpenter, R. H. 55, 429, Pl. 104
Carter & Co. (Poole Pottery) 163
Carter, George 312
Cartwright, Thomas I 502
Carwardine family 120
Carwardine-Probert, Col. W. G. *see* Probert, W. G.
Castell, Charles 519
Catalano 161
Catchpole, Edmund 54, 238
Cathedral Studio, The 387
Cattee, Peter 234
Cattermole & Eade 109, 205
Cautley, H. M. 32, 64, 77, 122, 138, 163, 195, 203, 226, 240, 253, 273, 346, 371, 386, 408, 426, 427–8, 504, 512, 556
Cautley, Mabel S. 64, 408
Cautley & Barefoot 473, 522
Cavendish, Sir John 177
Cawcy, Diacinto 43, 298, 408, 550, Pl. 72
Cayzer, Lord (former Sir Nicholas Cayzer) 544, 545, 546
Cazalet, Mark 346
Chadwick, Enid 343
Chamberlain, Ralph 283
Chamberlain, Sir Robert 245
Chamberlain, Rev. Samuel 283
Chambers, W. O. 429
Chambers, Sir William 255
Chance Bros 96, 109
Chantrey, Francis 137
Chapel Studio 139, 273
Chaplin, Alice 308
Chapman, Robert and Rose 249
Charles II, King 46, 229, 428, 431, 433
Charter Partnership, The 521
Cheere, Sir Henry 76, 137, Pl. 74
Cheke, Sir John 493
Chesterton, Maurice 515
Chestnutt, Christopher 392, 529
Cheston & Perkin 59, 108, 523
Chiffney, Samuel Jun. 438
Childs & Sulzmann 328, 330
Christian, Ewan 77, 108, 114, 117, 267, 374, 402–3, 488
Christiani & Nielsen 231
Christmas, Gerard 42, 187, 298
Christmas, John & Matthias 41, 42, 79, 80, 214
Churchman, A. C. *see* Woodbridge, Lord
Clare, Gilbert de 188, 192
Clare, Richard de (Richard fitz Gilbert, d. 1090) 36, 188

Clare, Richard de (d. 1262) *see* Gloucester, 6th Earl of
Clark, J. F. 53, 340, 414, 428, 430, 431, 449
Clark, J. M. 240
Clark, James 56, 257, 259, 308, 403
Clark & Holland 53, 88, 193, 428, 429, 431, 440, 449, 558, 559, 564, 565
Clarke, Sir Caspar Purdon 57, 227
Clarke, Geoffrey 147, 286
Clarke, I. A. 205
Clarke, Isaac 314
Clarke, Jonathan 137
Clarke, Joseph 55, 533
Clayton & Bell 56, 80, 91, 94, 137, 139, 141, 226, 232, 238, 260, 310, 311, 320, 365, 374, 387, 430, 461, 464, 470, 478, 504
Cleere, William 267
Clerk, Simon 29, 215, 308, 351, 382
Clerk, William 514
Cleveland, Barbara Villiers, Duchess of 229
Cleverly, C. F. M. 297
Cleverly, Peter 92, 200, 237
Clopton family 27, 28, 132, 215, 382–4, 385, 387, 393, 396, 496, 560
Clopton, Francis 396
Clopton, John (d. 1497) 35, 382, 383, 384, 386, 387
Clopton, Dr Poley 132
Clopton, Sir William (d. 1446) 35, 384, 387
Clopton, William (fl. c. 1500) 383
Clopton, William (fl. 1579) 396
Clubb, Alfred 564
Clubbe, Rev. John 49, 555–6
Clutterbuck, C. E. (stained glass) 139, 244, 367, 540
Coade (stone) 144, 174, 216, 221, 264–5, 328, 329, 456n.
Coade & Sealy 48, 176, 265
Coates, F. L. 521
Coates, Richard 50
Cobbett, William 125
Cobbold, Felix 283
Cobbold, Rev. Richard 572
Cockedge family 502
Codington family 335
Codington, Richard 41, 334, 335
Coket family 78
Coket, John 78
Cole, John 532
Coleman, Benjamin 278
Coleman & Wallis 416, 512
Collier, R. W. 110
Colling, J. K. 534
Colman family 113
Colman, Edward 43, 113, 114
Colman, Samuel 113

Colpoys, A. A. G. 457, 459
Colt, Maximilian 486
Comper, J. B. S. 64, 430
Comper, Sir Ninian 56, 138, 139, 178, 344, 567
Concordia, Mother, OSB 191
Conder, Alfred 548
Conder (Simon) Associates 572
Connolly, Simon 410
Constable (stained glass) 198
Constable, John 41, 359, 416
Constable, W. H. 139, 198, 270, 429
Conway, Jennifer 109
Cooke family 263
Cooke, A. D. 64, 505
Cooke, John 567
Cooke, T. W. 456
Cooke, Rev. William 244, 310
Cooper, C. H. 369
Cooper, C. J. Harold 440
Cooper, Sir Daniel 57, 436
Cooper, Francis 91
Cooper & Peck 142
Copinger family 175, 354
Copinger, William 175
Coppyng, Ricardus 116
Cordell, Robert 393
Cordell, Sir William 41, 45, 387–8, 392–3, Pl. 61
Corder, John Shewell 59, 126, 153, 175, 236, 291, 296, 306, 308, 355, 357, 361, 377–9, 421, 462, 480, 486, 491–2, 518, 522
Cordova, Denise de 144
Cornerthe (de) family 118
Cornerthe, Sir Richard de 118
Cornewalys *see* Cornwallis
Cornish, James 548
Cornish, Richard 313
Cornwallis/Cornewaleys family 209, 536, 537
Cornwallis, 1st Marquess 209
Cory & Ferguson 220, 256
Cottingham, L. N. 51, 54, 59, 90, 126, 128, 137–9, 156, 400, 543
Cottingham, N. J. 56, 90, 465
Cottingham (L. N.) & Son 51, 320, 400
Cotton family 348–9
Cotton, Sir John 41, 348–9
Cotton, Walter 348
Coulson, Charles 467
Couper, Thomas *see* Cowper, Thomas
Coverdale, Derek 512
Cowper, William 107
Cowper/Couper, Thomas 382
Cox, Alan 524
Cox & Sons 178, 271
Cox, Sons, Buckley & Co. 520
Crace, J. D. 329–30
Crampton, Lawrence 530

Crane family 42, 187, 515
Crane, Robert (d. 1500) 186–7
Crane, Robert IV (d. 1591) 187
Crane, Sir Robert (d. 1643) 42, 187
Crawford family 287
Crawford, Elizabeth 287, 555
Crawford, Rev. William Henry 287, 288–9, 555
Crawford, William 287, 288
Creed, Rev. H. K. 182
Crest Nicholson 467
Crickmay & Son 449
Crisp, F. A. 377
Crisp, G. E. 377
Crisp, Thomas 563
Crofts family 337, 369–70
Crofts, William, Baron 42–3, 369
Crofts, Cecilia and Elizabeth 85
Crofts, Sir Charles 85, 337
Crofts, Sir John 552
Cromwell, Oliver 228, 556
Cropley, Thomas 480
Croughton, Michael 223
Crowe, J. 287
Crowe, Richard 224
Crowe, Thomas 225
Crowfoot, Leonard 178, 259, 354
Crowley, Abraham 83
Cselko, Tibor 143
Cubitt, William 51, 114, 145, 196
Cubitt & Co. 502
Cullinan, Edward 61, 564, Pl. 112
Cullum family 173, 298–9
Cullum, Dean 308
Cullum, Sir Dudley 43, 173, 299
Cullum, Sir Thomas (d. 1664) 43, 298, 300, Pl. 72
Cullum, Rev. Sir Thomas Gery (d. 1855) 47, 171, 173, 174, 299, 321, 412
Cunobelinus 14, 15
Cure, Cornelius 388
Currie (sculptor) 237
Curtis, T. F. 273, 304, 538
Curtis (T. F.), Ward & Hughes 238, 403, 451
Cushing, Joshua 85
Cutting, Richard 534

Dalley, Jos 512, 521
Darby, John and Mary 249, 250
Darcy family 302, 304
Darkin, John 85, 310, 407
Darlington, Lord 438
Darmanin (J.) & Sons 387
Davenport, J. L. 302
Davers family 475
Davers, Sir Robert and sons 43, 476
Davies, H. E. M. 180, 307–8
Davis (carver) 444
Davy (carver) 302
Davy, Rev. Charles 87

Dawber, E. Guy 347
Dawe, William 421
Dawson family 222
Dawson, Charles 222
Day, Charles 40, 141
Day, Richard 256
Day (Keith) Architects 573
Daye, John 367
Daymond (John) & Son 109
Deanes, W. S. 118
Dearle, J. H. 81
Debenham, Gilbert de 379
de Carle see Carle, de
Defoe, Daniel 124, 125
Delafosse, Charles 141
de la Pole *see* Pole
Denby (Elaine) & Gordon Badnell 534
Denman (sculptor) 388
Denman, T. 206
Denston, John 215
Densy, William 334
Dent, Giles 382, 383
Derby, Earl of 439
Derrick, Thomas 492
de St Philibert *see* St Philibert, Sir John de
Desmond, Earl of 229
Despenser family 90
Devey, George 432–3
D'Ewes family 354, 502
D'Ewes, Paul 41–2, 502
D'Ewes, Sir Simonds 397
Dickins, Ambrose 206
Dickins, Francis 43, 205, 206, Pl. 78
Digby, Jack 62–3, 146, 147, 255, 286
Dinkel, E. M. 144
Directorate of Works 513
Dister family 354, 383
Dix, A. J. 259, 298, 308
Dixon, Frampton & Hean 214
Dixon, W. F. 464
Donne, John 298
Doulton, H. 544
Doulton & Co. 61, 163
Downes family 259
Downham, Sir John 478
Dowson, Philip 61, 399, 413
Doyle, Harcourt M. 478
Drew, W. J. 343
Drury family 173, 215, 297, 298, 300, 473
Drury, Edward Dru 206
Drury, Elizabeth 41, 298
Drury, Henry 362
Drury, Sir Robert 42, 173, 298, 300
Drury, Roger 300
Drury, Sir William (d. 1558) 362
Drury, Sir William (d. 1589/90) 298
Dudley, William 49, 95, 182, 269, 459, 471–2
Dufficey, Paul 398

INDEX OF ARCHITECTS, ETC. 609

Duleep Singh *see* Singh, Maharajah Duleep
Dunford, J.W. 141
Dunn, John 115
Dunn, Thomas 43, 113
Dürer, Albrecht 386
Durham, Earl of 59, 234
Dyke, D. N. 508
Dykes Bower, S. E. 65, 134, 135–7, Pl. 115
Dyriche, Thomas 302

Eade, William 171, 176, 336
Eade & Johns 55, 171, 190, 225, 274, 276, 359, 509, 520
Earee, F. P. 518
Earee, Paul 420
Earee & Haslewood 259, 368
Earp, Thomas 111, 446, 451
East Suffolk County Architect's Dept 505
Eastawe, John 302
Eastland, James 150
Easton, Hugh 141, 226, 502
Eckersley, Eric 468
Eden family 520
Eden, F. C. 176, 182, 190, 238, 305, 386, 387, 556
Eden, Sir Thomas 531
Edenham, Richard, Bishop of Bangor 495
Edge (stained glass) 254
Edge, Rev. William 415, 421
Edis, R.W. 58, 435, 436, 438
Edmund, St 117, 125, 127, 130, 132
Edmund, King 125, 127
Edward II, King 127, 132
Edward VI, King 134
Edward VII, King 58, 436
Edward, Thomas 240
Edward, William 240
Edwards, Bob 539
Edwards, Eliza 89, 202
Eldred, John 42, 264
Eliot, Rev. William 207
Elizabeth I, Queen 121, 300, 362, 393, 460
Elliott, C. 408
Elliott, Patrick 192
Ellis & Woodward 53, 144–5
Elliston, Thomas 80
Elmes, J. H. 97
Elmham, Elizabeth 549
Elmslie & Franey 290, 291
Elwell, James 568
Elwes family 493
Elwes, Sir Gervase 493
Elwes, John Timms 494
Ely, Reginald 29, 177, 384
Elys, John 383
Emerson, James 476

Erith, Raymond 62, 199, 269, 317, 328, 329, 405, 457, 500, 545, 546
Erith & Terry 546
Erskine, Ralph 62, 440
Erswell, Charles 373
Evans, Samuel 109
Evans & Son 163
Evelyn, John 229, 231, 433
Everard, Henry 215, 216
Everard, Richard and Dorothy 104, 295
Everard, William 489
Everett, Rosemary 198

Faber, Oscar 126
Fairweather, Robert 175
Faith Craft 338
Farmer, William 273, 310
Farmer & Brindley 136, 222, 227, 273, 297, 386
Farrar Bell, M. C. *see* Bell, M. C. Farrar
Farrow, Mrs Elizabeth 198, 224
Farrow, Thomas 54, 59, 85, 126, 156, 186, 226, 320, 407, 464, 465, 541
Fass, A. H. 559–60
Fawcett, W.M. 53, 54, 75, 77, 95, 106, 107, 178, 197–8, 234, 254, 265, 267, 313, 314, 324, 363, 367, 469, 520, 532, 566, 571
Fawcett & Atkinson 185, 318, 423
Feilden & Mawson 503, 555
Fellows, John 319
Felton family 520
Fenn, Sir John 454
Fenton, J. 423
Fenwick family 312n.
Field, John 327, 329–30, Pl. 87
Field, William 310
Fiennes, Celia 154
Fincham, John and Margaret 83
Firebrace, Sir Cordell 393, 396
Firmin, W. R. 53
Fisher, Alfred 273
Fisher, David 434, 523
Fisk, Henry 336
Fison, Joseph 110
Fitzbrian, Ralph and Emma 257
FitzRoy family 233
 see also Grafton, Dukes of
Fitzroy Robinson & Partners 235
Flatman, John 53, 236, 238, 269, 428, 432, 433, 435, 436, 437, 439, 440
Flatman, Nat 428, 437
Flaxman, John 328, 329, Pl. 87
Foggo, Peter 61, 399
Foote, Geoffrey 384
Ford, Rev. James 485
Fordham, William 388, 392
Forrest & Bromley 140
Forster, John 28, 473

Forsyth, J. Dudley 209, 408, 409, 571
Forsyth, W. A. 87, 364
Fortescue-Brickdale, Eleanor 269
Forth, Dorothy, Lady, and William Tyrell 42, 504–5
Fowler, James 238, 482, 484, 489
Fradan, Cyril 403
Francis, Rev. W. F. 224, 228
Fraser, J. O. 201
Freeland, Henry 136, 547
Freeland Rees Roberts Architects 136, 331, 432–3
Freeman, Charles 437
French, G. R. 47, 173, 364, 446
Frend & Keogh 510
Frende, Richard 190
Frere family 237–8
Frere, Augustus 287
Frere, E. C. 58, 238
Frere, John 8–9, 237
Frere, Rev. L. H. 238
Frere, Rev. Temple 238
Frink, Elisabeth 65, 132, 136, 265, 372
Frink, Brig. H. A. C. 372
Frost, Harvey G. 121, 174
Fulcher, Thomas 50, 449, 515
Furneaux, Norman 136
Fyrmage, Nicholaus 253
Fyrmage, William 252

Gaffin, E. 97, 490
Gaffin, T. 222, 538, 541
Gaffin & Co. 233, 368
Gage family 302, 305, 538
Gage, Sir Edward Rokewode 302, 362
Gage, John (historian) 65, 557
Gage, Peter 182
Gage, Sir Thomas 302, 306
Gage, Sir Thomas Rokewood 306
Gainsborough family 523–5
Gainsborough, Jack 419
Gainsborough, John 524
Gainsborough, Thomas 49, 57, 259, 276, 318, 419, 522, 523–4, 556
Gardener, Sir Robert 41, 224
Garland & Fieldwick 483
Garofalo, Benvenuto Tisi da 532
Garrad, Rev. Castell 561
Garrad, William 545
Garrard, David 295
Garrard, Frederick 429
Garrett, J. 515
Garrett, J. S. 178, 179
Garrett (R.) & Son 266
Gawthorp (sculptor) 89, 400
Gawthorp & Sons 533
Gayer-Anderson, R. G. (John) 354, 357
Gayer-Anderson, Col. T. G. 357
Geary, Ronald 216

Geary (Ronald) Associates 508
Gedge, Rev. Joseph 98
Geldart, Rev. Ernest 78, 343, 349, 459, 538
Gérente, Alfred 56, 139
Gibberd, Sir Frederick 290, 293–4
Gibbons, James 220, 256
Gibbons (G. B.) & Co. 225
Gibbs, Alexander 224, 267, 486
Gibbs, C. A. 429
Gibbs, James 76, 476
Gibbs & Howard 290
Gibson, Rev. James 571
Gibson, John 59, 154
Gifford family 245
Gilbert family 261
Gilbert, Sir John 261
Gill, Eric 58, 90, 238n., 274, 355
Gillick, Ernest G. 57, 164, 254
Gillows (furnishers) 394
Gilstrap, William 242
Ginn, Thomas 521, 522, 527, 528, 531
Glasby, William 573
GLC see Greater London Council
Gleichen, Countess Feodora 56, 209
Gloucester, Earls of 188, 190
Gloucester, Richard de Clare, 6th Earl of (and 5th Earl of Hertford) 190
Goate, Edward 114
Goater, Jenny 81
Goche, Thomas see Gooch, Thomas
Goche, Robert and Agnes 81
Godbold, Robert 220, 256
Goddard, F. H. 85, 403
Goddard & Gibbs 95, 137
Goddard Wybor Practice, The 64, 440, Pl. 114
Godfrey, Henry 207, 208
Godfrey, Neil 354
Goff, Leonard 136
Golden, John 43, 237
Goldie & Child 96
Golding family 27, 251, 459
Golding, John and Joan 250–1
Goldschmidt, A. B. H. 180
Goldsmith, John 469
Goldsmith, N. C. 62, 171
Gonville, Edmund 532
Gooch, Michael & Sheila 454
Gooch, Thomas 27, 33, 189, 341, 441n., 519, 520
Gooden, R. Y. 416
Goodey & Cressall 291
Goodhart-Rendel, H. S. 213, 493–4
Goodman, Howard 63, 148
Gordon, Bronwen 307
Gordon & Gunton 430, 520
Gorst (James) Architects 62, 559, Pl. 116
Gothic Design Practice 65, 134–5, Pl. 115

INDEX OF ARCHITECTS, ETC. 611

Grafton, Henry FitzRoy, 1st Duke of 229
Grafton, Charles FitzRoy, 2nd Duke of 230, 231
Grafton, Augustus FitzRoy, 3rd Duke of 133, 231
Grafton, Charles Alfred Euston FitzRoy, 10th Duke of 230
Graham & Joslin 363
Gray, George Kruger 61, 163, 251
Gray, John 223
Gray, Robert 415
Gray & Davison (organ builders) 56, 501
Grayling, Brian 339, 472, 521
Greater London Council (GLC) 62, 259, 293, 294, 411
Green (sculptor, Haverhill, C19) 565
Green, Aveling 518
Green, Benjamin 162
Green, E. M. 290
Green, H. J. 200, 214, 236, 304, 426, 449, 504, 562
Green, John A. 207, 534
Green, Percy 359
Green, Samuel 416
Green, Thomas 43, 466, Pl. 73
Greene, Edward, M.P. 162–3, 452, 539
Greene, Sir (Edward) Walter, M.P. 163, 452, 453
Gresham, Sir Richard 93, 470
Gresham, Sir Thomas 93, 470
Grey (de) family 203
Grey, Hon. and Rev. Frederick de 203
Grey, Rev. Thomas 179
Grey, Bishop William 422
Gribble, Eleanor 504
Grigby, Joshua 218
Grimshaw 256
Grimwood, Arthur 259, 525
Grimwood, George 187, 529–30
Grimwood & Sons 529
Groom, John 572
Groom (John) & Son 95, 370, 484
Gurdon family 42, 57, 80
Gurdon, Brampton 42, 80
Gurdon, Rev. Philip 80
Gurteen, Daniel 289, 290, 291, 292
GWP Architecture 433

Habershon, W. G. 209, 210, 310, 333
Habershon, W. G. & E. 210, 333
Haggar, D. & E. 109
Hagreen, Walter 451
Hake, G. D. Gordon 533
Hakewill, E. C. 217–18
Hakewill, H. 234
Hakewill, J. H. 57, 88, 141, 224, 267, 334, 349, 422, 429, 502, 537–8, Pl. 36

Hall, Rev. W. B. 370
Hall, William 327
Hallifax family 483
Hallifax, Ellen 482, 483
Hallifax, Maria 483
Hallifax, Thomas 56, 179, 482, 483–4
Hallifax, Thomas Jun. 483
Hambling, Maggi 273
Hamilton Kerr Institute 535
Hammond, Gen. Sir Francis Thomas 556, 557
Hamvyll, Thomas 367
Hanchet, A. H. 132, 142, 165, 180, 451
Hanmer, Sir Thomas 410
Hardgrave, C. 95
Harding, Charles 187, 518, 566
Harding, J. L. 276
Harding & Horsman 294
Hardman, John 137, 183, 209, 240, 242, 295, 447, 461, 473, 519, 552
Hardman & Co. 545
Hardwick, Philip 483
Hardy, James 80, 379
Hardy, Richard 440
Hardy, Cochrane & Partners 292
Hare, Cecil G. 56, 92, 221, 251, 519
Hare & Pert 428
Harper (colourist, London) 221
Harrison sisters 455
Harrison, Charles 455, 573
Harrison, Henry 278
Hart, Colin 572
Hart, Son, Peard & Co. 388, 415, 421, 461
Harvey, F. 425
Harvey, Harry 266
Harvey, James 198
Hasty, William 444
Hatcher, Basil 97
Hatcher, Basil & David 223, 292, 486
Havard, Birkin 63
Hawes (of Occold, master mason) 28, 95, 304, 311, 561
Hawkins, E. R. 173
Hawkins, J. 526
Hawkins, Robert 221, 374, 457, 463
Hawkins, William 363
Hawkins Brown 161
Hawks (William) & Sons 51, 210
Hayman, Francis 443n., 444
Hayward, H. W. 422
Hayward, T. W. A. 530
Heathcote (sculptor, London) 200
Heaton Abbott Swales 158
Heaton & Butler 139, 298, 489, 516
Heaton, Butler & Bayne 75, 84, 89, 91, 111, 124, 139, 140, 183, 215, 217, 234, 254, 266, 318, 323, 324, 331, 347, 367, 369, 429, 451, 461, 469, 478, 482, 489, 518

Heaton & Gibb 59, 234, 439, 440, Pl. 105
Hedge, John 224
Hedgeland, George 56, 273
Heffer, Robert 49, 263, 555
Heigham family 90, 244, 323
Hemgrave, Sir Thomas de 304
Hems, Harry 291, 353
Hemsworth, Rev. A. B. 82
Henniker family 533–4, 535
Henniker, John Henniker Major, 2nd Baron, and wife Emily 55, 533, Pl. 95
Henry VII, King 495
Henry of Essex 456
Herberd (*alias* Yaxley), John 574
Hersent, John 198
Hert, William 223
Hertford, Earls of 188, 190
Hervey family 160–1, 325, 331
Hervey, John (d. 1751) see Bristol, 1st Earl of
Heseltine, Richard 80
Heskett, Philippa see Blackall, Pippa
Hewitt, George 480
Hicks, David 500
Hicks & Charlewood 139
Higham family 559–60
Higham, Clement 559
Higham, Thomas 559
Hill family 175
Hill, Agnes Emily 175
Hill, Rev. Copinger 8, 175, 176
Hill, Rev. Henry 175
Hill, John 158
Hill, Oliver 92
Hill, Rev. Dr Thomas 175
Hills, Daniel 385
Hindson, Denis 339
Hitch, Nathaniel 56, 226
Hobart, Sir James 81
Hobcroft, John 466
Hogan, J. 311, 556
Holden, Rev. J. R. 345
Holebrok, Master Roger de 375
Holiday, Henry 298, 311, 345, 482
Holland, Henry 466
Holland, J. W. 257, 432
Holland (Percy) & Son 206, 429, 430
Hollingsworth, Rev. A. G. H. 505
Hollins, R. S. 116
Holt family 464–5
Holt, Sir John 43, 464, 466, 469, Pl. 73
Holt, Rowland 48, 464–5, 466
Holt-Lomax, Richard 199
Holzer (carver, Titisee) 273
Holzmann (colourist and gilder) 226
Hoo, John 308
Hoo, Robert and Agnes 309
Hooper, H. R. 171, 486

Hopkins, Michael 64, 164
Hopkins, Michael & Patty 61, 163
Hopkins Architects 64, 165, 328, 330, Pl. 117
Hopkins (Michael) Architects 164
Hopper, H. 571
Hopper, Thomas 47, 49, 392, 393–6, 397–8, 473
Hopwood, James 355
Hore, John 85
Hornblower, G. 206
Horrex, William 346
Horsfall, Alan 62, 320
Horwood Bros 362
Hospital Design Partnership 148
Houghton, John Sanderson 61, 126
Houk, Necolai 34, 220
Howard family 499
  see also Norfolk, Dukes of
Howard, Alfred 522, 528
Howard, F. E. 65, 136, 351, 388, 502
Howard, John 145
Howard, Sir John and Lady (Alice Tendring) 495, 496, 499
Howe, James 305
Howe, William 54, 101
Howson, Joan 200, 266
Hubert, Alfred 205
Huckstepp, Michael 476
Hucton, John 295
Huddleston, Peter 444
Hudson Architects 216
Huggins & Bromage 116
Hughes, H. 91, 139, 203, 221, 387, 408, 554
Hughes, H. C. 244
Hughes & Bicknell 479
Hull, Charlie 234
Humphry, A. G. 207
Hunt, Archie Ainsworth 53, 54, 139, 143, 159, 167, 170, 400, 430
Hunt, Derek 290
Hunt, Elizabeth 545
Hunt & Coates 75, 78, 254, 456
Hurwood, George 280
Hyde Parker see Parker/Hyde Parker family

Ilsley, James 211, 552
Image, Selwyn 440
Ingleton, Thomas 158
Inkpen Downie 64, 192
Ireland, T. J. 450
Iveagh, Countess 226
Iveagh, Edward Cecil Guinness, 1st Earl of (d. 1927) 57, 225, 228, 229, 483

Jack, George 338
Jackaman, Lot 59, 126, 145, 162, 164, 180, 224, 252–3, 372, 461, 472, 513

INDEX OF ARCHITECTS, ETC. 613

Jackson, J. Brian 62, 146, 147
Jackson, Stephen 426
Jacob, Sir John 565
Jacob, Nicholas 575
Jacob (Nicholas) Architects 130
Jacob, William 357
James I, King 46, 431, 435
James, Arthur C. 572
James, Paul 148
Jamieson, Alexander 514
Janssen, Bernard 465, Pl. 67
Janssen, Jan 42, 372, 502
Jarman, Derek 182, 273
Jeckyll, Thomas 229, 401n., 491, 516
Jekyll, Gertrude 495
Jelfe, Andrews 234
Jennens, Ann 75–6
Jennens, Robert 75–6, Pl. 74
Jennings, Frank 60
Jennings, John 107
Jennings, Mark 163
Jermyn family 475, 476
Jermyn, Sir Robert 113
Jermyn, Sir Thomas (fl. 1497) 475
Jermyn, Thomas (d. 1692) 43, 476
Jessop, William 50
Joan of Acre 191
Johns, E. T. 423
Johns Practice 411
Johns & Slater 171
Johns, Slater & Haward 63, 147, 148, 276, 289, 430
Johnson, George 552
Johnson, Rev. J. Barham 516
Johnson, John (1732–1814) 350, 435, 436
Johnson, John (1811–91) 52, 53, 94, 98, 126, 144, 178, 250, 254, 401, 473, 548, 574
Johnson, M. W. 84, 238, 339, 556
Johnson, William 574
Johnston, A. J. 50, 521
Johnstone, E. J. 474
Johnstone, W. M. 440
Jones, Catrin 291
Jones, Inigo 46, 431, 497
Jones, T. 523, 528
Jones, William 416
Jones & Willis 85, 180, 259, 573
Josselyn, John 174
Judde, Andrew 93

Kaines, Nigel 166
Kedington, Rev. Robert 267
Kemp & How 60, 357
Kempe 96, 109, 135, 137, 140, 198, 207, 212, 226, 319, 471, 478
Kempe & Co. 417, 429, 520
Kempe (C. E.) & Co. 207
Kendall, H. E. Jun. 54, 147, 159, 172
Kendall, H. E. Sen. 53, 217, 521
Kendrick, J. J. P. 43, 533, Pl. 95

Kendrick, Joseph 218
Kennedy, Lewis 263
Kent, Charles 241
Kent, R. 54, 339
Kent, William 46, 51, 230–2, Pl. 82
Kenyon, Capt. J. P. M. and Mrs 112
Keogh, Edward (sculptor, Sudbury) 190, 519, 529
Keogh & Son 187
Keppel, Admiral Augustus Keppel, 1st Viscount 226
Kersey, Gale & Spooner 173
Killigrew family 533
Kilpatrick, Elsa 298
King, Dennis 295
King, Frederick 162
King, H. A. 171
King, J. & J. 287, 516
King, John 56, 208, 549
King, Laurence 338
King, R. B. 183
King, Rob 276
King, Robert 258
King (George W.) Ltd 477
King (G.) & Son 387, 572
Kingsbury, Robert 312, 457, 498
Kingston, Duke of 435
Kirk, Charles 543
Kirk & Parry 133
Kirkham, Andrea 542
Kitchener, Herbert Kitchener, 1st Earl 347
KLH Architects 62, 219
Knight (stained glass) 254
Knight, W. Frank 266
Knox, Rosemary and Gerald 61, 564
Knox, Simon 61, 564
Knox Bhavan Architects 61, 564
Knyvet, John 35, 403–4
Kohler, C. J. 207
Krimpen, Jan van 362
Kyrbe, Richard 302
Kytson family 304
Kytson, Sir Thomas (d. 1540) 301–2, 304, 335
Kytson, Sir Thomas II (d. 1603) 41, 302–3, 304, 306

Lacey, Arthur J. 572
Ladds, S. I. 310
Lake, John 327
Lamb, E. B. 48, 57, 203, 401n., 516, 533–4, 547
Lambert, William 49, 236
Lambton, Hon. George 439
Lane, Danny 289
Lang (sculptor) 176
Langley, Batty 265
Langley, John 296
Langton, Stephen, Archbishop of Canterbury 119

Larnach, James 414
La Rochefoucauld, François de 174
Last, Robert 513
Last, W. N. 199
Latham, Jasper 232, 258, 463
Lavers & Barraud 56, 183, 211, 218, 224, 244, 334, 354
Lavers, Barraud & Westlake 106, 122, 267, 268, 354, 447, 468, 518, 545
Lavers, Westlake & Co. 429
Lawrence, Meg 536
Layer (Leyr), William 28, 137, 473, 474
LCC see London County Council
Leach (F. R.) & Sons 56, 221–2
Lee, Baptist 48, 263
Lee, J. T. 112
Lee, Lawrence 226
Lee, Thomas 263
Leeks, John & Henry 78
Leeper, Leonard 260
Legget, John 249
Lennard, P. D. 413
Lennox-Boyd, Arabella 492
Lenny, Isaac 50
Leonard, A. W. 409
Leonardo da Vinci 89
Levitt Bernstein Associates 146, Pl. 91
Lewis, Thomas 268
Lewkenor, Sir Edward and wife Susan 41, 214
Lexden Restorations 564
Leyr, William see Layer, William
Leyre, John 514
Limbrick Architecture & Design 440
Lindley, F. J. 194, 222, 388, 518
Lindy (Kenneth) & Partners 528
Little, Owen C. 439
Llewelyn-Davies & Weeks 62, 476, Pl. 110
Lloyd family 315
Lloyd, Richard 315
Lloyd-Anstruther family 315
Lobb Partnership 440
Loch, Lady 493, 494–5
Loch, Lord 58, 493
Lockwood, William 8
Lofft family 542–3
Lofft, Capel 543
Lofft, Robert Emlyn 542, 543
Logan, Robert Hart 397
London County Council (LCC) 62, 259, 293, 294, Pl. 111
Lonsdale, H. W. 242
Loomes, Nick 148, 270
Louder, Alexander 142
Lough, J. G. 137, 447
Louise, Princess 60, 360
Lovegrove, Henry 54, 201, 347, 410
Lowe, Deborah 572
Lowe, John 337
Lowndes & Drury 95, 100, 198

Lucas, John Seymour, R.A. 559
Lucas, Sir Thomas 369, 370
Luckhurst, David 555
Ludlam, Rev. William 197
Lutyens, Sir Edwin 58, 114, 213, 312, 439, 456, 493–5
Luxford Studios 308, 490
Lydgate, John 365, 387
Lyon, Samuel 158
Lyster, Grillet & Harding 64, 164

McAlister, A. P. 561
McCalmont, Harry 438
McCulloch, John 222, 297
McDowell, G. M. 451
MacGregor, J. E. M. 179
Mackennal, Bertram 57, 522
McKillop, Iain 140
Mackintosh, A. 138
McMorran, Donald 143
McMorran & Whitby 63, 143
Macro, Rev. Dr Cox (d. 1767) 154, 443–4
Macro, Thomas Jun. and Susan 154, 443
Macro, Thomas Sen. 154
Magnus (sculptor, London) 254
Maile, G. 226, 258
Maile (G.) & Son 176
Major, Sir John, Bt 533, 535
Major, John Henniker see Henniker, 2nd Baron
Major, William Dench 269
Malcher, Thomas 267
Maliphant, George 571
Mallows, C. E. 58, 213
Mallows & Grocock 213
Mann (stained glass) 298
Manning, A. S. 430
Manning, S. Jun. 299, 403
Manning, S. Sen. 43, 233, 299
Manning, W. C. 53, 59, 428, 438
Manning, W. C. & A. S. 429
Mannock family 245–7, 312, 497
Mannock, George 245
Mannock, John 247
Mannock, Philip 245
Mansbridge, John 563
Markham, S. S. 490
Marks, H. Stacy 244
Marler, Margery 514
Marriott, Lucy (daughter) 56, 568
Marriott, Lucy (mother) 56, 449, 568
Marsh, John 430
Marshall, Edward 42, 264, 314, 497, 505
Marshall, Joshua 209, 408
Marshall (T. J.) & Co. 429
Martin see also Martyn
Martin, Robert (carpenter) 189
Martin, Robert (millwright) 510
Martin, Roger (c16) 386

INDEX OF ARCHITECTS, ETC. 615

Martin, Thomas (d. 1771) 454, 550
Martineau, E. H. 544, 545, 546
Martineau, John 544, 545
Martineau, Richard 545, 546
Martyn/Martin family 382, 383, 384, 387, 388–9
Martyn, Richard 382, 383
Martyn, Roger (d. 1542) 383, 389
Martyn (H. H.) & Co. 429
Mary Tudor, Princess 139, 140, 550, 552
Mason, Alfred R. 299
Mathew, Hugh 65, 134, 136, Pl. 115
Mathews, Rev. J.W. 317
Mattick, Stephen 196, 493
Maufe, Edward 156
Mauldon, H. C. 520
Maw & Co. (ceramics) 93–4, 226
Mawson, T. H. 213
Maxwell-Gumbleton, Rt Rev. M. H. 316
Mayer & Co. 232, 325, 403
MEB Partnership 430
Medd, David & Mary 472
Melford, John 29, 100, 177–8, 384
Mesdag, J. B. van 362
Metcalfe family 298, 299, 300
Metcalfe, Philip 299
Micklethwaite, Alan 519
Mid Suffolk District Council 572
Middleton, G. A. T. 78
Mikhail (David) Architects 321
Milburn Leverington Thurlow (MLT Architects) 143, 144, 167, 171
Mildmay, Walter 493
Mileham, C. H. M. 422
Mileson family 443
Mileson, Borowdale 443, 444
Miller, Alec 502
Miller, H. A. 122
Miller, R. A. 516
Miller, William 271, 365, 533, 535
Milles, William 460
Milligan, J. 342
Milligan, William 568
Mills family 263, 269
Mills, Anne 265
Mills, Thomas 263, 264
Mills, William (architect) 198
Mills, William (Great Saxham Hall) 264
Milner, Victor 304
Milner-Gibson-Cullum, Gery 298
Milnes, Thomas 254
Milton, John 505
Mingay, George 556
Minter, Lawrence 531
Minton (tiles) 362, 515, 532
Mitchell, William Henry 61, 62, 64, 126, 143, 147, 163, 165, 477
Mitchell & Houghton 61, 62, 126, 163, 164, 171

Mitchell & Weston 61, 230
MLT Architects see Milburn Leverington Thurlow
Modece Architects 62, 141, 175, 286, 294, 362, 528
Mody, Richard and Leticia 441
Mole Architects 455
Molyneux, Rev. John 526
Montfort, Hugh de 36, 287
Montrose, Caroline Agnes, Duchess of 429, 438
Moore, A. L. 502, 504
Moore, Leslie T. 429
Moore, Richard 397
Moore, Temple 233, 353
Moore, Thomas (C17) 285
Moore, Thomas (C18, clockmaker) 246, 387
Moore, A. L. & C. E. 536
Moore (A. L.) & Son 465
Morant & Co. 394
Morgan & Phipson 110, 165
Morland, Sir Samuel 231
Morley, Martin 314
Morley, Matthew 409
Morris, Sir Cedric 283
Morris, Charles 159, 265, 336, 546
Morris, Joseph 534
Morris & Co. 81, 254, 533
Mors family 27, 514
Mors, Edward (d. 1526) 514
Mors, Edward and Alys (fl. 1530) 514
Mors, Margery 514
Mors, Thomas and Margaret 514
Mortimer family 118, 195
Mortlock, John 292
Mortlock, Thomas and Anne 292
Morton Partnership 489
Moryell/Moriell, Roger 382, 383
Moseley, Rev. Richard 218
Moser & Co. 396
Moss, Aaron 358
Moundevyle, Sir William 223
Mowbray (A. R.) & Co. 502
Moÿe, J. S. 97, 101
Munday (George) & Sons 424
Mundys family 27, 251
Mundys, John and family 251
Munnings, Robert and Elizabeth 413
Mure, Hutchison 264
Murillo, Bartolomé Esteban 89
Murray, Keith 64, 185
Murray Ward & Partners 292
Muthesius, Hermann 57, 180
Mynheer, Nicholas 518

Naish, Sidney 53, 61, 126, 152, 164, 168, 170, 211, 529
Naish & Mitchell 61, 126, 143, 164
Nash, S. A. 139

INDEX OF ARCHITECTS, ETC.

Needham, Joseph 5, 324
Neker, Thomas 302
Nelson, T. M. 512
Nesfield, W. A. 487
Nesfield, W. E. 57, 106, 487
Nevill, Isobel 409
Newton (painter) 444
Nicholls, Maryanne 427
Nicholson, A. K. 88, 253, 298, 331
Nicholson, Sir Charles 320
Nicholson & Corlette 320
Norcott, Joan 514
Norfolk, Dukes of 315
Norfolk, John Howard, 1st Duke of 499
Norfolk, Bernard Edward Howard, 12th Duke of 241, 242
Norman, Mrs 546
North family 408–9
Northwold, John, Abbot 132
Norton, John 57, 225, 226
Notyngham, John 138
NPS Group 290
Nunn, Harry 545
Nunne, John Sen. and Jun. 473
Nuttgens, J. E. 320, 338

Oakes family 445, 446
Oakes, Rev. Abraham 565
Oakes, H. J. 296, 446
Oakes, J. H. P. 446
Oakes, Rev. James (fl. 1796) 541–2
Oakes, James (banker, Bury St Edmunds) 140, 150, 158, 446, 541
Oakes, Orbell Ray 445, 446, 447
O'Brien, Emmanuel 166
O'Connor, Michael (stained glass) 81, 85, 113, 271, 310, 465, 469, 536
O'Connor, John 273
O'Connor, M. & A. 334, 486, 496, 502
O'Connor & Taylor 496
Odeham, Margaret 125
Office of Works 430, 508
Oliver family 60
Oliver, Basil 60–1, 64, 80, 95, 126, 137, 143, 150, 165, 168, 183, 270, 272, 296, 466, 530, 557
Orchard, Philip 198
Orr, A. A. 298
Orridge, John 145
Orsbourn, Herbert 81, 469
Osborne, James 440
Osborne, John 548
Osborne, Patrick 343
Ostrehan, G. W. 568
Otley, Michael 160
Ouida (Marie Louise de la Ramée) 57, 164
Overbeck 56, 273
Oxford, Earls of 120, 352
Oxford, Robert de Vere, 5th Earl of 35, 120
Oxford, John de Vere, 13th Earl of 351

Packard family 109–11
Packard, E. Sylvia 65, 109
Packard, Sir Edward 109, 110
Paget, Rev. E. H. 516
Palmer, Adrian 358, 359, 521
Palmer, Benjamin 305
Palmer, W. 370
Pamment, John 541
Park, Robert 141
Parker/Hyde Parker family 387, 388, 393, 394
Parker, A. H. 391
Parker, Rev. C. F. 470
Parker, Sir Harry 393
Parker, Sir Hyde 393, 396
Parker, Matthew, Archbishop of Canterbury (formerly Dean of Stoke College) 492, 493–4
Parker, Sir William 393
Parker, Sir William Hyde 393
Partridge family 481
Partridge, Henry 481
Paske, Edward 208
Patience, Joseph 47, 264
Patrick, Bishop of Ely 212
Patterson, Doug 541
Paty, Thomas 140
Pawling, Mark A. 144
Pearce, Edward 550
Pearce, J. B. 153
Pearson, F. L. 107
Peck, Walter 453
Pellegrini, G. A. 210
Pemberton, Rev. William 122
Penning, Daniel 401, 469, 533, 561
Pennington, E. G. 368, 505
Penoyre & Prasad 61, 564
Penrice, John 460
Penrose, F. C. 105, 327, 329, 351–4
Penrose, Professor Lionel 500
Penton, Jack 242, 251, 353, 461, 534, 571
Penwarden (stained glass) 84, 298, 307
Peppen, Rev. William 470
Pepper, Messrs 236
Perry, William 372
Perry Lithgow Partnership 345
Pert, K. G. 428
Pertwee, Charles 259
Pethers, Warwick 65, 134, 135, Pl. 115
Pettiward family 260–1
Pettiward, Jane 260, 285
Pettiward, R. J. 260, 449
Pettiward, Roger (d. 1833) 260–1, 285
Petto, Edmund 249

INDEX OF ARCHITECTS, ETC. 617

Peyton, Sir John de 496
Philibert *see* St Philibert, Sir John de
Philipps, Sir Laurence 212
Philipson, John 285
Phillipps, Col. Henry 487
Phillips, Patrick 397, 399
Phipson, R. M. 53, 54, 55, 121, 260, 426, 447, 470, 504, 512, 532, 546, 566, Pl. 101
Physick, E. G. 113
Physick, E. J. 363
Pick Everard 144, 147
Pie, John 383
Pieksma, Henk 146, 521
Pierse, Samuel 394, 396
Pietzsch, Siegfried 346
Pilkington, Hugh 399
Pilkington, William 456–7
Pite (William A.), Son & Fairweather 65, 140
Plampin family 482–3
Plampin, Rev. John 483, 556
Pleasant, Henry 217
Plesance, Thomas 90
Plume, Edward 104
Plummer, Henry 461
Pole (de la) family 401, 547
Pole, John de la (*c.* 1475) 544
Poley family 35, 82, 103–4
Poley, Dame Abigail 43, 104, Pl. 71
Poley, Alice 426
Poley, Edmund 83
Poley, Sir John 43, 104, Pl. 71
Pompignoli, Luigi 532
Ponyard, William 302–3, 304
Poole, Henry 57, 353, 436
Pope, R. P. 54, 525
Porter, Roy 166
Potter, Robert 138
Potter, T. W. 439
Potter, Thomas 400
Potter & Hare 473, 517, 519
Potter & Son 122
Powell family 298
Powell, Charles 304
Powell, Hugh B. 334
Powell, James 298
Powell, John 298
Powell, W. O. 297, 298
Powell, William 56, 221
Powell & Sons 79, 80, 84, 91, 95, 106, 115, 183, 190, 207, 226, 232, 233, 257, 270, 271, 298, 307, 311, 331, 345, 347, 423, 429, 459, 460, 465, 482, 485, 515, 538, 556, 575
Power, Cyril E. 483
Powys family 315
Powys, A. R. 357
Powys, Richard, M.P. 315
Prasad, Sunand 61, 564
Prasutagus 15

Pratt (T.) & Sons 409
Preedy, Frederick 82, 263–4, 372
Prentice, A. N. 57–8, 180, 181, 347–8, 436–7
Pretyman, George 82
Price, William the Younger 266
Pritchett, G. E. 273, 316, 341, 363
Pritchett, J. P. Jun. 520
Probert family 118, 119, 120
Probert, W. G. (later *Carwardine-Probert*) 60, 119, 120
Project Orange 163, 358
Prycke, John 90
Prynce, John 396
Prynne, E. A. Fellowes 107
Prynne, G. H. Fellowes 56, 461
Pulham, John 8
Purcell 154n.
Purcell & Johnson 330
Purdie, A. E. 55, 505
Pykenham, Archdeacon William 39, 274, 276, 281

Quail, Paul 183, 305
Queensberry, 4th Duke of (former Earl of March) 436
Quilter, Sir Cuthbert 357
Quilter, Cuthbert (Jun.) 357

Rampling, Clark 49, 112
Rampling, S. 565
Randall, Charles 215
Ranger, William 8, 55, 140–1, 327, 551
Ransome & Son 50–1, 114, 196
Ransomes 278
Ransomes & Sims 145, 413
Rattee & Kett 136, 198, 221, 224, 297, 310, 488
Rawlins, Rev. Charles 56, 208
Ray, T. F. 268, 528
Read family 409
Read (designer) 79
Rebecca, Biagio 210
Redgrave, John 49, 152, 160
Rednall, Ephraim 201, 505, 548
Rednall, F. 561
Rednall, John Y. 218
Rednall, Richard 249
Rednall, William 130, 156
Reeve, J. A. 237
Reeve, John, Abbot 392, 552
Reeve, William 93
Reeves, Denzil J. 388
Regnart, Charles 274, 311, 403
Rennie, John 50
Repton, Humphry 48, 210, 262n., 263, 363, 500
Reve, John 478
Reve, Margaret 478
Revett, Daniel 505
Reynolds, James 43, 137

Reynolds, John 236–7
Reynolds, W. Bainbridge 222
RH Partnership Architects 328
Rhodes family 212
Rhodes, Cecil 58, 212, 213
Rhodes, Col. E. F. 213
Ribbans, W. P. 53, 275
Richardson, Sir Albert Edward 62, 64, 88, 322, 393, 396, 435, 437, 559, Pl. 109
Richardson & Gill 64, 110, 435, Pl. 109
Richardson & Houfe 62, 88, 322, 437, 559
Riches Hawley Mikhail Architects 62, 225
Rickards, E. A. 57, 436
Rickards, Lucy 56, 400, 502
Rickards, Rev. Samuel 56, 502
Rickman, Thomas 450
Rickman & Hutchinson 386
Ridley, J. C. 171
Riley, Athelstan 56, 178
Ringham, Henry 55, 57, 354, 380, 426, 485, 520, 533, 549, 567, Pl. 52
Rivers, Countess 393
Rivett, Sir Thomas 498
Robert, Abbot of Bury (Robert Scot alias Ixworth) 224, 334
Roberts & Way 436
Robinson family 215
Robinson, Sir John 216
Robinson, Sir Thomas 397, 398
Rogers, John 29, 351
Rogers, William 77, 244
Rokewode Gage family 199
Rokewode family see Rokewood (or Rokewood) family
Rokewood, John 487
Rolfe, Samuel 242
Romaine-Walker & Jenkins 439
Rome, Alan 136
Rome, Richard 320
Rookwood (or Rokewood) family 199, 229, 233, 488
Rookwood, Ambrose 199
Rookwood (or Rokewood), Robert 199
Roote, William P. 54, 431
Rope, Miss 65, 512
Rope, Ellen Mary 512
Roper, F. W. 54, 437
Roper, Grace Faithfull 515
Roper, William W. 350, 356, 360
Rose, Joseph 210
Ross (carver) 444
Ross, Thomas 444
Rossellino, Antonio 212
Rothschild, 3rd Baron 62, 475, 476
Rothschild, Leopold de 433
Rothschild, Baron Mayer de 432

Rous family 309
Rouw, H. 183
Row, C. J. N. 389
Rowley family 496–7, 500
Rowley, Admiral Sir Joshua 363, 496, 499
Rowley, Sir William 363, 496
Rownson, Drew & Co. 119
Royce, N. 43, 198
Ruddock, Edward 319
Ruddock, T. 319
Ruffels, R. 537
Rusel, John 249
Rush, Roger 358
Rushbrooke family 475
Rushbrooke, Col. Robert 41, 396, 445, 475, Pl. 96
Russel, F. B. 57, 426
Russell, Charles 149
Russell, Giles 93
Russell, Hugh 366
Russell, Metcalfe 486
Rust & Co. 91
Rutherford, Rev. John 313, 545
Rutherford, Neil 355
Rutherford, Rosemary 65, 100, 313, 545
Ryece, Robert 460
Rysbrack, J. M. 43, 444
Rysby, John 351

St Albans, Earls of 476
St Aubyn, J. P. 189, 488
St Aubyn & Wadling 341
St Clare (or Cleers) family 106
St Davids, Lord 349
St Edmundsbury Borough Council 553
St Philibert, Sir John de 183, Pl. 15
Salter, Edward 53, 54, 119, 178, 179, 259, 521
Salter & Firmin 53, 54, 251, 271, 522, Pl. 100
Salviati & Co. 56, 430, 451
Salvin, Anthony 54, 445
Samson, Abbot 127, 170, 392
Samwell, William 46, 229, 431–3
Sanders, J. J. 299
Sandon, Eric 61, 239, 274, 281, 289, 306, 505, 516, Pl. 66
Sandon & Harding 61, 413
Sandys, Francis 47, 49, 150–2, 161, 261, 327, Pl. 86
Sandys, Rev. Joseph 47, 327, Pl. 86
Sarel, Walter 349
Sargeant, Jamie 451
Sarin, Sophie 398
Satchell & Edwards 89, 202, 319, 364, 547
Saumarez, Hon. Marion 65, 541
Saunders (Ipswich) 343
Saunders, Bryan 343

INDEX OF ARCHITECTS, ETC.

Saunders, E. E. 97
Saunders (Frank) & Partners 222
Savage, Sir Thomas Savage, Viscount 386, 393
Sayers, Samuel and Thomasine 42, 426
Sayet, Salamon 243
Scarfe, Norman 126–7
Scheemakers, Henry 76, Pl. 74
Scheemakers, Peter 43, 206, Pl. 78
Scheuermann see Sherman, J. A.
Schmidt, Bernard (Father Smith) 222, 273
Schofield, Muriel 60, 280, 371
Schofield, Sydney 60, 280, 371
Scholz, Henry 330
Schorne, Master John 518
Schultz, R. W. 283–4
Scoles, Rev. I. C. 141
Scot, Robert see Robert, Abbot of Bury
Scott, George Gilbert 54–5, 134, 136, 146, 243, 258, 267, 310, 540, Pl. 97
Scott, G. G. Jun. 135, 568
Scott, Giles Gilbert 91
Scott, T. J. 287
Scrope family 416
SEArch Architects 101
Searle & Son 291
Sears, J. E. 141
Sedding, E. H. 258
Sedding, J. D. 540
Seddon, Major H. C., R. E. 167
Seddon, J. P. 56, 465, 501
Self, Matthew 295
Seliger, Léonie 387
Sewell, Rev. W. H. 574–5
Sewell, W. A. E. & Rosemary W. 116
Sharman, Edward 53, 291
Sharp, William 490
Shearman, E. C. 112, 430
Sheldon, Percy J. 400
Sheppard, Jeremy 159
Sheriff, John see Shrive, John and Juliana
Sherman, J. A. (formerly Scheuermann) 60, 508
Shoolbred (James) & Co. 354
Shrigley & Hunt 290
Shrive (or Sheriff), John and Juliana 98
Sidney, Rev. Edwin 367, 368
Simmons, Edgar 436
Simpson (sculptor) 287
Simpson, Edward 218
Simpson (W. B.) & Sons 350
Singh, Maharajah Duleep 57, 225, 226–7, 228
Singleton, Robert 43, 161, 299
Singleton, Thomas 43–4, 132, 144, 160, 320, 545

Sisson, Marshall 115, 279, 282, 318, 490, 500
Skeaping, John 435, 440
Skelton, John 535
Skitte, Jafrey 478
Sly, Allan 441
Smirke, Sydney 48, 533–4
Smith, Father see Schmidt, Bernard
Smith, C. R. 190, 417
Smith, Cecil B. 113, 140, 551
Smith, Charles 504
Smith, Donald 488
Smith, F. J. 257
Smith, G. E. R. 238
Smith, J. Campbell 146
Smith, James 50
Smith, John (Rougham 'curator') 473
Smith, M. M. 461
Smith, Melvyn 512
Smith, Robert 89
Smith, T. H. 438
Smith, W. H. 270
Smith (Andrew) Associates 99
Smith & Brewer 564
Smyth family 27, 178, 382
Smyth, Jankyn see Smyth, John (Jankyn)
Smyth, John (C15, Long Melford) 382
Smyth, John (C15, Stratford St Mary) 514
Smyth, John (C16) 514
Smyth, John (Jankyn) 125, 137, 140, 142–3
Smyth, Robert 384
Smyth, Roger 382, 384
Soame family 371–2
Soame, Sir Stephen 371, 372, 373
Soane, Sir John 47, 158, 499, 563
Soward, John 178, 536
Spark, John 302, 303
Sparrow, Anthony, Bishop of Norwich 559
Spear, Francis 348
Spence, Sir Basil and Lady (Joan) 535, 576
Spence, John 535
Spiller, James 317
Spooner, Charles 55, 65, 273, 274, 281
Spooner, Minnie Dibdin 55, 65, 274
Spourne, Thomas 353
Sprague, C. F. 520
Sprigge, Rev. J. D. 117
Spring family 27, 351
Spring, Sir Francis 353
Spring, Thomas II (d. 1486) and Margaret 351, 352, 354
Spring, Thomas III (d. 1523) and Alice 351, 352, 353
Spurgeon, John 273

Spurr, G. 463
Stacey, Jeremy 61, 564
Stacey (Jeremy) Architects 564
Stammers, Harry 542
Standley, George S. 144
Stannard, Joseph 355
Stansfield, J. J. 280
Stanton, Hervey de 490
Stanton, Thomas 42, 209, 349
Stanton, William (photographer) 153
Stanton, William (sculptor) 79, 104, 555, Pl. 71
Stayner, Thomas 339
Steane, Shipman & Cantacuzino 61, 413
Steele, Thomas 49, 132
Steggall, W. C. 574
Steggles family 132
Steggles, William Jun. (1777–1859) 53, 196, 252, 266
Steggles, William Sen. (1752–1834) 49, 53, 126, 140, 141, 152, 156, 158, 159, 167, 171, 172, 218
Steggles (W.) & Sons(s) 159, 168, 488
Stepien & Winiarski 63, 147
Stiff, James 474
Stiff (James) & Sons 474
Stirgess, Lionel 181
Stirling-Crawfurd, William Stuart 429
Stokes (stained glass) 254
Stokes, Isaac Newton Phelps 60
Stokes, Leonard 55, 520, Pl. 103
Stone, John 42, 90, 310, 466
Stone, Nicholas 42, 79, 209, 298, 465–6, 558, Pl. 67
Stopher, Thomas 124
Storey, Abraham 42–3, 369
Stow, E. M. 254
Streater, Robert 267
Street, G. E. 242
Studio MGM 62, 165
Sturgeon, George 297
Stuteville family 212
Stuteville, Sir Martin 42, 212
Stuteville, Thomas 212
Sudbury, John 488
Sudbury, Simon, Archbishop of Canterbury 35, 517, 518
Suffling, E. R. 369
Suffolk County Architect's Dept 62, 145, 146, 147, 259, 293, 294, 410, 423, 491, 512
Suffolk County Council 145, 295, 467
Suffolk, Charles Brandon, Duke of 140, 550–1
Sulyard family 288, 536, 554–5
Sulyard, Sir John (d. 1488) 288, 554
Sulyard, Sir John (d. 1575) 288, 554–5
Sulyard, Sir John (fl. 1620) 288
Surrey, Meg & Kit 146

Suttaby, Rev. W. L. 459
Swale, John 409
Swete, Horace 54
Sword, Robert 314
Syer, Rev. Barrington 374
Syer, Maria E. 338
Syer, W. H. 224, 228
Symonds, John 174

Tagg-Arundell, W. A. 401, 575
Talman, William 46, 325, 330, 331, Pl. 84
Tanner, H. 154
Tanner, John 392
Tanner, Matthew 249
Tany, Sir Gilbert de 119
Tapper, Walter 302–4, 408
Tapster, T. 398
Tatham, C. H. 327n.
Tattersall, George 59, 439
Tattersall, Richard 436
Taylor, Alfred 349
Taylor, John 54, 474
Taylor, Redvers 450
Taylor, Sir Robert 48, 500, Pl. 83
Taylor, Rev. Rowland 283
Taylor, W. G. 78, 190, 465, 486, 533, 545
Taylor & Clifton 78, 343
Tendring family 495, 496–7
Tendring, Alice *see* Howard, Sir John and Lady (Alice Tendring)
Tendring, Sir William 35, 496–7
Terry, Quinlan 311–12
Teulon, S. S. 54, 78, 79, 450–1, 540, 569
Thake, H. B. 290
Theakston, J. 233, 445
Thebaud (or Theobald) family 517
Theobald, Sir Francis 425
Theobald, John 517, 518
Thomas, Brian 207
Thomas, Hugh 521
Thomas, J. E. 450
Thomas (Hugh) Architects 472
Thompson, Francis 348
Thompson, Frederick 354
Thompson, M. G. 49, 102–3, 118–19, 285
Thorpe, John 393–4
Thorpe, Stephen 527
Thrower, Vivian 473
Thurlow, Edward Thurlow, 1st Baron 253
Thurlow, Rev. Thomas 102
Thurston, John 377
Thurston, William 377
Tillemans, Peter 43, 443–4
Tilley, John 534
Tillot, Roger 473
Timperley/Tymperley/Tympley family 314, 315

INDEX OF ARCHITECTS, ETC.

Timperley, Henry 315
Timperley, Capt. John 42, 314
Tinworth, George 544
Titchmarsh & Goodwin 282
Titcomb (stained glass) 254
Todd, Richard 465
Toller, William 478
Tomkin, Rev. J.W. 463
Tomson (sculptor) 237
Tomson, T. 372
Tonge, G.A. 206
Tonni, Stephen 489
Tovell (sculptor, Ipswich) 175
Tovell, George 323
Townshend & Howson 248, 471
Travers, Martin 215
Treleaven, M.V. 59, 154
Trepess, F.P. 529
Trevethan, John 327, 330
Tricker Blackie Associates 463, 520, 527
Tristram, Professor E.W. 338
Troup, F.W. 283
Turner, E.W. 158
Turner, John 40, 403, Pl. 70
Turner, Laurence 143, 304
Turner, P.J. 236, 509
Turner, Thomas 356
Tylney family 481
Tylney, Sir Philip 481
Tylney, Thomas 481
Tymperley family *see* Timperley family
Tympley family *see* Timperley family
Tympley, Thomas 315
Tyrell family 247–9, 504–5, 507
Tyrell, Lady (Anne Arundel) 248
Tyrell, Charles 285
Tyrell, Dorothy *see* Forth, Dorothy, Lady
Tyrell, Sir James 247–8
Tyrell, William 504–5
Tyrwhitt, Thomas 415
Tyrwhitt-Drake, Emma 482

Ulster, Elizabeth de Burgh, Countess of 188, 191, 192, 519, 522
Uvedale, Robert 87
Uvius, Abbot 132

Valognes (de) family 236
Valognes, Peter de 236
Vanbrugh, Sir John 325, 330
Vaughan & Co. 362
Vaux (de) family 376
Vaux, Sir John de 375, 376
Vere (de) family 35, 118, 120, 351–3, 361, 564
Vere, Aubrey de 35, 120
Vere, Robert de *see* Oxford, 5th Earl of

Vernon, James 266
Verrio, Antonio 229
Vestey family 265–6
Victoria, Queen 139, 225
Vinnell, Giles 514
Vortigern 22
Vulliamy, L. 478
Vyal, Thomas 334

Waddington, H.S. 180
Wadling, H.J. 341
Wailes 137, 537
Wailes, William 180, 241, 516
Wailes & Strang 96, 241
Wainwright, Jonathan 572
Wakerley, Arthur 245
Waldegrave family 118, 121, 217, 245, 317, 457, 496
Waldegrave, Sir Richard 118
Waldegrave, Sir William (d. 1527/8) 117, 118
Waldegrave, Sir William (d. 1613) 121
Wales, Prince of *see* Edward VII, King
Walker, A.G. 57, 154
Walker, Dr Jane 563, 564
Walker, Leonard 56, 111
Wallace, Caroline 415
Walsh, J. 372
Walsham, Sir Alexander de 117
Walter, Edmund 223
Walter, Margery 223, 224
Walters, Jessica 559
Walters, Sir Roger 62, 293, 411
Warboys, Rowland & Surinder 253, 313, 401, 454, 484
Ward, D. 388
Ward, John (C16–C17) 290
Ward, John (C20) 148
Ward(e), Richard 396
Ward & Hughes 91, 111, 115, 117, 118, 139, 190, 212, 221, 304, 319, 387, 412, 459, 460, 486, 538, 547
Ward & Nixon 454, 552
Ward & Silver 196, 339, 381, 388, 390
Warham Guild 190
Warner family 115
Warner, Sir Courtenay 115
Warner, Sir Henry 411
Warner, Dr Thomas 212
Warren family 265
Warren, E.P. 297–8
Warrington, William 137, 310, 481, 482
Wastell, John 29, 134, 135, 142, 254, 351, 416, 460
Waterhouse, Paul 522
Watling, H.S. 157, 171
Watling, Hamlet 220
Watson (stained glass) 254

INDEX OF ARCHITECTS, ETC.

Watson, John 155
Watson, Robert 302
Watson, Thomas 548
Watts, James 213
Watts, John 478
Watts, L. J. (sculptor) 463, 481, 497
Watts, Peter 274, 492
Watts & Co. 222
Waymouth, W. C. 559
Wearing & Hastings 171
Weaver, Robin 358
Webb, Christopher 205, 429
Webb, Geoffrey 372, 451
Webb, Lankester 201
Webb, Philip 58, 234, 452-3, 539
Webb, Stephen 527
Wedgwood 210
Weeks, John 476
Weir, William 60, 219, 338, 360, 442, 550, 552
Welflet, William 495
Weller, George (later Weller Poley; C18) 104-5
Weller, John 97, 510
Weller Poley family *see* Poley family
Weller Poley, Mrs 105
Weller Poley, George (C19) 104, 105
Wenham, Alexander 565
Wentworth family 426
Wenyeve family 115
Wenyeve, Sir George 115
Wesley, John 236
West Suffolk County Architect's Dept 63, 97, 147, 162, 254, 268, 286, 294, 319, 339, 472, 521, 539
Westlake, Nathaniel 183, 334, 354
Westmacott, Henry 285
Westmacott, Sir Richard 43, 260, 349, 482
Westmacott, R. Jun. 57, 483
Westmacott, W. B. 527
Weston, Norman 61
Weston, Paul 521
Weston, Col. Thomas 459
Westwater, Norman 358
Whall, Christopher 56, 307-8, 486
Whall, Veronica 486
Whalley, Rev. Daniel 268
Whalley (Maurice) & Partners 142
Wharncliffe, Caroline, Lady 328
Wheeler Bros 514
Whettell, William 42, 79
Whewell, Rev. William 278
Whiffen, C. 65, 140
Whinney, T. B. 153, 523
Whistler, Laurence 535
Whistler, Rex 452
Whitby, George 143
White, James 42, 264, 465, Pl. 67
White, Rev. Stephen 318
White, William 178, 501
Whitefriars 139

Whitelaw, William 388
Whiting, John 49, 208, 442, 486
Whiting & Woolnough 561
Whitmore, Frank 53, 54, 58, 172, 293, 336, 410n., 430, 446, 557, 566, 568
Whitmore, John 53, 462
Whitmore & Binyon 343, 526
Whittaker, Helen 504
Whittingham, A. B. 486
Whittle, George 390
Whitworth Co-Partnership 81, 95, 135, 139, 140, 141, 176, 178, 192, 198, 217, 218, 224, 240, 270, 290, 334, 338, 362, 380, 426, 451, 486, 573
Whitworth, Hall & Thomas 64, 94, 117, 185, 429, 473
Whyghte, John 566
Whymark, D. 287, 447
Wickham, Geoffrey 439-40
Wickham, Julyan 61, 564, Pl. 112
Wiles, John 97
Wiley, Michael 320
Wilkins, Henry 143
Wilkins, William 49, 144, 146, 162, Pl. 91
Wilkins, William Sen. 146
Wilkinson, Horace 77, 118, 119
Wilkinson & Parsons 279
Wilkinson Pratt Partnership 467
Willement 212, 304, 554, 568
Willement, Thomas 139
Williams, Alfred 289
Williams, G. B. 460
Williams, Glynn 502
Williams, John 139
Williams, M. Meredith 95
Williams, Neil 293
Williams, Ray 103
Willmington, H. 343-4
Willoughby, Katherine 551
Willson, D. W. 80
Willson, T. J. 115
Wilmshurst & Oliphant 563
Wilson, Harry 154
Wilson, Henry 502
Wilson, Rev. Walter 561
Wincer Kievenaar 97, 115, 116, 278, 315-16, 355, 358
Wingfield, Thomas 426
Winters, Eric 352, 358
Winthrop family 271
Winthrop, John 271
Winthrop, Robert C. 271
Wirth, Abraham 298
Withers, R. J. 224
Wollaston family 260-1
Wollaston, William (fl. 1656) 261
Wollaston, Col. William, M.P. (fl. 1794) 261
Wolverton, Lord 436

INDEX OF ARCHITECTS, ETC.

Wood, Sir John, 1st Baronet 302, 304
Wood, John (painter) 429
Wood, Kenneth 479
Wood, Sancton 52, 148
Wood, William 517
Woodbridge, A. C. Churchman, Lord 486
Woodington, W. F. 533
Woodroffe, Paul 56, 308
Woods, Richard 306
Woods & Co. 50
Woodyer, Henry 207, 386, 513–14
Woodzell, H. 440
Wooldridge, H. E. 232
Woolner, Thomas 317
Woore, Edward 486
Worlledge, John 186
Wormald, Henry 445
Wormald, James 218
Wren, Sir Christopher 40, 46, 232
Wright, G. F. 297
Wright, George E. 122
Wright, H. J. 54, 281, 343, 484
Wright, Robert 304
Wright, Thomas 48, 210
Wright, William 224, 305, 450, 496, 558
Wrinch, R. C. 575
Wuffingas 22

Wyatt, George 210n.
Wyatt, J. D. 53, 54, 55, 111, 140, 224, 228, 242, 243, 273, 285, 310, 320, 362, 380, 407–8, 409, 464, 468, 473, 536, Pl. 97
Wyatt, James 47, 152, 210n., 241
Wyatt, Samuel 47, 51, 209–10, 263, Pl. 90
Wyatt, T. H. 321
Wyburgh, Robert 564
Wykes, Margaret 98
Wythes, George 121

Yarington, S. C. 217, 445
Yaxley family 401, 575
  see also Herberd
Young family 106
Young, Arthur (agriculturalist) 106, 263, 359
Young, Arthur John 106
Young, Clyde 65, 209, 227
Young, Rev. Thomas 505
Young, William 57, 210, 227, 229, 438, Pl. 106
Young, Witherden 82
Young (J.) & Son 410
Young Hunter, John and Mary 559

Zeller, Dom Hubert van 274

INDEX OF PLACES

Principal references are in **bold** type; demolished buildings are shown in *italic*.

Abbas Hall *see* Great Cornard
Acton **75–7**
  All Saints 35, **75–6**, Pl. 74
Aldham **77**
  Aldham Mill *see* Hadleigh
  St Mary 23, **77**
Alpheton **77–8**, 399
  Old Hall Farm 39, **78**
Ampton **78–9**
  Ampton Hall 48, 78, **79**
  St Peter 42, 54, **78–9**
Assington **79–81**
  Assington Hall xvi, 80
  St Edmund 42, 43, 57, **79–80**

Babergh Hall *see* Great Waldingfield
Babwell *see* Bury St Edmunds
Bacton **81–2**
  St Mary 30, 31, 54, **81–2**
Badley **82–3**
  Badley Hall **83**, 201
  St Mary 33, **82**, 465, Pl. 27
Badwell Ash **83–4**
  St Mary 26, 30, 31, **83–4**, 334
Ballingdon *see* Sudbury
Bardwell **84–6**
  guildhall (former) 39, **86**
  St Peter and St Paul 31, 34, **84–5**, Pl. 35
Barking 36, **86–7**, 425
  Barking Hall 17, **87**
  Creeting Lock 50, **87**
  Old Rectory 49, **87**
  St Mary 30, 33, 44, **86–7**, 425, Pl. 48
Barnardiston **88**
  council housing 62, **88**, 559
Barnham 9, 12, 13, **88–9**
  atomic bomb store (former) 21, **88–9**
Barningham 8, **89–90**
  St Andrew 29, 32, 51, **89**, 556
Barrow **90–1**
  All Saints 42, 56, **90–1**

Barton Mills **91–2**
  Bronze Age barrow, Chalk Hill **92**
  St Mary 26, 32, **91–2**, 324
  Street Farm 38, **92**
Battisford **92–3**
  St John's Manor House 24, **93**
Baylham **93–4**
  Baylham Hall 45, **94**
  lock 50, **94**
  National School (former) 54, **94**
  watermill 51, **94**
Beyton **94–5**
  Beyton House 61, **95**
  Old Rectory 49, **95**
Bildeston **95–8**
  Bildeston Hall 38, **98**
  Chapel Street houses 38, **98**
  Market Place 36, **97**, 98
  primary school 63, **97**
  St Mary Magdalene 28, 64, **95–7**, 311, 549n.
Bosmere Mill and Lock *see* Needham Market
Botesdale 36, **98–9**, 465, 468
  Chapel of St Botolph **98–9**, 421
  Tollgate House 50, **99**
Boxford 13, 21, **99–103**
  Boxford House (former rectory) 49, **102–3**
  primary school 54, **101**
  St Mary 26, 27, 29, 40, 65, **100–1**, 366, Pl. 17
Boxted **103–5**
  Boxted Hall 48, 103, **104–5**
  Holy Trinity 35, 40, 41, 43, **103–4**, Pl. 71
Boynton Hall *see* Capel St Mary
Bradfield Combust **105–6**
  Bradfield Hall 57, **106**
Bradfield St Clare **106–7**
  St Clare Hall 37, **107**
Bradfield St George 59, **107–8**
  St George **107**, 309

INDEX OF PLACES

Bramford 5, **108–11**
  Bramford House 48, **110**
  St Mary 33, 65, **108–9**
Brandon 1, 4, 5, 12, 35, 52, **111–12**
  Brandon Park 57, **112**
  flint industry 5, 50, 111
  Foord House (former rectory) 49, **112**
  Middle Saxon settlement site 22–3
  North Court Lodge 57, **112**
  overspill housing 21, 62, 111
  rabbit industry 3, 50
  Roman remains 15, 18–19
  St Peter 56, **111**
Brent Eleigh **112–14**
  bridge 50–1, **114**
  Colman Cottages 50, **114**
  St Mary 33, 41, 43, **112–13**
Brettenham **114–16**
  Brettenham Park (now Old Buckenham Hall School) 45, **115–16**
  St Mary the Virgin 34, **114–15**, 461, 544
Brockley **116–17**
  St Andrew 38, **116–17**
Brundon *see* Sudbury
Bures (Bures St Mary) 10, **117–21**
  Dunstead House 60, **120**
  Great Bevills 60, **120**
  mill 51, **119**
  St Mary 29, 35, 41, **117–18**
  St Stephen's Chapel 35, **119–20**
  Smallbridge Hall 45, **121**
  vicarage (former) 49, **118–19**
Burgate **121–3**
  St Mary of Pity 35, 64, **121–3**
Burstall **122–4**
  St Mary 26, 31, 33, **122–4**
Bury St Edmunds 1, 2, 4, 20, 22, 50, 51, 53, 59, **124–75**, 511
  churches, monastic buildings etc. **137–42**, **161**, **169**, **172**, **175**
    Abbey 2, 5, 23, 24, 125, **127–34**, 149; St Edmund statue (Frink) 65, **132**, 372; Great Gate 26, 127, 128, **133**, 150, Pl. 7; Norman Tower 24, **128**, 129, 149–50, Pl. 6
    All Saints **140**
    Babwell Priory (Franciscan house) 24, 170–1
    Cathedral Church of St James (St Edmundsbury Cathedral) 2, 5, 24, 27, 29, 43, 54, 65, 126, 127, 128, 131, **134–7**, 146, Pl. 115
    Christ Church **175**
    Franciscan house see Babwell Priory above
    Friends' Meeting House 40, **141**
    Hospital of St Nicholas 169
    Hospital of St Petronilla 169
    St Edmund (R.C.) 40, **141**, 477
    St George **171**
    St James *see* Cathedral *above*
    St John the Evangelist 55, **140–1**, 172, 55in.
    St Mary 5, 26–7, 28, 31, 48, 54, 56, 65, 128, **137–40**, 447, Pl. 28
    St Peter **141**
    St Saviour's Hospital **170**
    Unitarian Meeting House 40, **142**, Pl. 75
    United Reformed church, Whiting Street 40, **142**
  public buildings 49, 53, 63, 125–7, **142–9**, 512
    assembly room *see* Athenaeum *below*
    Athenaeum (former assembly room) 49, 126, **150–2**
    Blomfield House Health Centre 63–4, **148**
    Boer War Memorial 57, **154**
    Borough Offices (former) 61, 63, **143–4**
    Clopton Asylum (now Deanery) 49, **132**
    College Square almshouses 54, **159**
    corn exchanges (former) 53, 126, **144–5**, 164
    county offices *see* Old Shire Hall *and* Shire Hall *below*
    Fennell Memorial Homes 54, 126, **167–8**
    gaol (former) 49, 126, **145**
    Great Market 125, 150
    Guildhall 29, 125, **142–3**
    Guildhall Feoffment School 54, **147**, 159
    hospital (1826) 54, 126, 164
    Howard Primary School 63, **147**
    King Edward VI (Grammar) School: former premises 54, **168**, **170**; Grove Road 63, **147**
    Market Cross 49, 53, 126, **144**, 146
    Maynewater House 63, **162**
    medieval hospitals see churches *above*
    Moyse's Hall (Museum) 36, 125, 143, **145–6**, 172
    Old Shire Hall **143**
    Ouida monument 57, **164**
    Pillar of Salt (road sign) 61, **150**

INDEX OF PLACES

Bury St Edmunds, public buildings *cont.*
    Poor Girls' School (former) 172
    railway station 52, 126, **148–9**
    Shire Hall 53, 63, **143**
    Theatre Royal 49, 144, **146**, 162, Pl. 91
    town gates 150
    Westley Middle School 63, **147**
    West Suffolk College **147**, 167
    West Suffolk County Club (former) 126, **153**
    West Suffolk Hospital (current) 63, **148**
    West Suffolk Hospital (former) 61, 63, **164**
    West Suffolk House 143, **144**
    William Barnaby Almshouses 49, **159**
    workhouses 53, 126, **159**, 164
  streets, commercial buildings and houses 35, 36, 45, 49, 63–4, 125–7, **149–72**
    Abbeygate Street 150, 151, **152–3**
    Alliance Assurance Co. 59, 126, **153**
    Angel Hill 61, **150–2**, 169, Pl. 2
    Angel Hotel 49, **152**, 160
    Angel Lane 149–50, **152**
    ARC shopping centre 64, 127, **165**, Pl. 117
    Baret House, Chequer Square 45, **156**
    Boots store (former), Cornhill 59, **154**
    Chequer Square 45, 49, **156**
    Churchgate Street 125, 149–50, **157**
    Clarice House (former Horringer Court) **173**
    College Street 125, **157**, 159
    Cornhill 145, **154**, 165
    Cornhill Walk shopping centre 64, **172**
    Crown Street 49, **160**, 163
    Crystal Palace 61, **163**
    Cupola House 46, *154–5*, 443
    Farrow's premises *see* Tower Cottage *below*
    Fox Inn 61, **168**
    Guildhall Street 149–50, **158**
    Hardwick House 47–8, **173–4**, *199, 299, 300, 321*, Pl. 98
    Hatter Street 150, **157**
    Honey Hill 45, 49, 126, 132, **160–1**
    Jackaman's premises 59, **164**
    King's Road 62, **165**
    maltings 126, **171**
    Manor House, Honey Hill 49, 126, 132, **160–1**
    Maynewater Lane 63, **162**
    Mildenhall Estate 62, 126, **171**
    Moreton Hall (preparatory school) 46, **174–5**
    Moreton Hall development 126, **175**
    Moyse's Hall *see* public buildings *above*
    National Provincial Bank (former) 59, **154**
    Norman House 36, 125, **158**
    Norman Tower House *see* Savings Bank *below*
    Northgate Street 49, 149, **169–70**
    Parkway 62, **165**
    Priors Estate 126, **165**
    Prior's Inn 64, **165**
    St Andrew's Street 149, **167–8**
    St Margaret's House **132**, 143
    St Mary's Square 47, 149, **161–2**, 163
    Savings Bank (now Norman Tower House) 59, 126, **156**
    Sparhawk Street 45, 149, 160, **161**
    sugar beet factory 126, 127
    Tower Cottage (Farrow's premises) 59, **156**
    Westgate Brewery 64, 126, 146, 160, 161, **162–3**
    Westgate Street 149, **162–4**
    Whiting Street 45, 149–50, 153, **158–9**
Buxhall 8, **175–6**

Camboricum 16
Capel St Mary 19, **176–7**
  Boynton Hall 37, **177**
  Lattinford Bridge roadside settlement 19
  Old Hadleigh 60, **177**
Cavendish **177–80**, Pl. 3
  primary school 52–3, **178–9**
  St Mary 26, 29, 31, 35, 56, **177–8**, 384, 568
Cavenham 12, **180–1**
  Black Ditches 22, **181**
  Cavenham Hall 57, *180–1*
Chattisham **181–2**
Chedburgh **182**
Chelsworth **182–5**
  All Saints **182–3**, Pl. 15
  Grange, The 61, **183–4**
Chevington **185–6**
  All Saints 34, 35, 64, **185–6**, Pl. 20
  palace of the abbots of Bury 36, *186*

INDEX OF PLACES

Chilton **186–8**
  Chilton Brickworks 53
  St Mary 42, **186–7**
Chilton Street *see* Clare
Clare 22, 52, **188–97**
  castle 36, 188, **192**, 194, **195**, 287
  Chilton Street **197**
  churches etc. **189–92**
    Benedictine house 24
    Clare Priory (Austin Friars) 24, 188, **190–2**, 494
    Our Lady of Good Counsel (R.C.) 64, **192**
    St Peter and St Paul 27, 33, 34, 35, 40, 44, **189–90**, 492, 517, Pl. 19
  Clare Camp 188, **197**
  public buildings 188, **192–6**
    bridge 50–1, 114, **196**
    police station (former) 53, **196**
    railway station (former) 192, **194–5**
    school (now community centre) 53, **193–4**
  streets and houses 35, 38, **192–7**
    Ancient House 6, **192**
    Cliftons 7, **196**, Pl. 63
    Cock Inn 38, **194**
Clopton Hall *see* Rattlesden
Cockfield **197–9**
  Church Cottage (former church house) 39, **198**
  council housing 62, **198–9**, 317, 457
  St Peter 43, **197–8**
Coldham Hall 45, 173n., **199–200**
Columbine Hall *see* Stowupland
Combs **200–1**
  Board School (former) 54, **201**
  Combs Hall 83, **200–1**
  St Mary **200**, 490
  tannery (former) 50, **201**
Coney Weston 25, 32, **201–2**
Copdock **202–4**
  Felcourt (former rectory) 57, **203**
  St Peter 27, **202–3**
Cosford Union workhouse see Semer
Cotton **204–5**
  St Andrew 25, 26, 31, **204–5**, 549, 550
Cowlinge **205–6**
  Branches Park 47, 48, **206**
  St Margaret 26, 40, 43, **205–6**, Pl. 78
Creeting Lock *see* Barking
Creeting St Mary **207–8**
  All Saints 207, **512**
  St Mary 56, **207**, 208
Creeting St Peter 207, **208**
  Old Rectory 49, **208**

St Peter 56, **208**
Culford **208–11**
  Culford Hall 7, 21, 44, 47, 48, 51, 57, **208–11**, 333, 552, Pls. 90, 106
  St Mary 42, 43, 56, **209**, 333
  St Peter, Culford Heath 56, **211**

Dagworth *see* Old Newton
Dalham **211–14**
  Dalham Hall 58, **211–13**
  St Mary 42, **212**, 340
Darmsden **214**
Denham **214**
  Denham Castle *see* Gazeley
  St Mary 41, **214**
Denston **214–16**
  St Nicholas 29, 32, **214–15**
Depden 3, **216–17**
Devil's Dyke 22, **441**
Down Hall *see* Preston St Mary
Drinkstone **217–19**
  All Saints 34, **217–18**
  Drinkstone Park 218
  Holm House 62, **219**
  Old Rectory 49, **218**
  windmills 51, **219**

Earl Stonham **219–21**
  Earl Stonham House (former rectory) 49, **221**
  St Mary the Virgin 25, 27, 30, 31, 34, **219–21**, 256, 421
Eastern Union Railway 401
Edwardstone **221–2**
  Benedictine house 23
  St Mary the Virgin 43, 56, **221–2**
Elmsett **222–3**
  Old Rectory 49, **223**
  St Peter 41, **222–3**
  tithe monument **223**, 572
Elmswell **223–5**
  Clay Field 62, **225**
  St John the Divine 30, 41, **223–4**, 568
Elveden 1, 21, **225–7**
  Elveden Hall 57, 225, **226–7**
  estate village **227**, Pl. 107
  St Andrew and St Patrick 55, 56, **225–6**, Pl. 108
  war memorial 65, **227**
Eriswell 22, **227–9**
  St Laurence 25, 33, **228**
  St Peter 227, **228**, 346
Euston **229–33**, 236
  Euston Hall 46, 48, **229–32**, 233, 335n.
    King Charles's Gate 46, **231**
    Temple, The 46, **231–2**, Pl. 82
    watermill 51, **231**
  St Genevieve 40, 41, 46, **232–3**

Exning xvii 4, 21, 36, 51, 53, **233–5**
    Exning Cemetery *see* Newmarket
    Exning House 58, **234–5**
    Harraton Court 59, **234**, Pl. 105
    Landwade Villa site 18
    stables 59, **234–5**

Fakenham Magna **235–6**
    St Peter 23, **235**
Felsham **236–7**
    Old Rectory 49, **236**
Finborough Hall *see* Great Finborough
Finningham **237–8**
    National School (former) 54, **238**
    Old Rectory 58, **238**
    St Bartholomew 32, 33, 34, 43, **237–8**
    Yew Tree House and Amberley 46, **238**
Flempton **238–9**
Flowton **239–40**
    St Mary 26, **239–40**
Fornham All Saints 50, **240**
    causewayed enclosures and cursus 10, **240**
Fornham Hall see Fornham St Genevieve
Fornham St Genevieve **241**
    Fornham Hall 47, 48, **241**
    Park Farm 48, **241**, 242
Fornham St Martin 125, **241–2**
    Hall Farm 48, **242**
    St Martin 34, **241**, Pl. 49
Freckenham **242–3**
    Beacon Mound (castle) 36, **243**

Gazeley **243–4**
    All Saints 32, 54, **243–4**
    Denham Castle (Castle Holes) 36, **244**
    Desning Hall barn 39, **244**
Gedding **244–5**
    Gedding Hall 39, **245**
    St Mary 23, **244**
Giffords Hall, Stoke-by-Nayland 31, 37, 39, **245–7**, 312, 497, Pl. 55
Giffords Hall, Wickhambrook 37, **559–60**
Gipping **247–9**
    Chapel of St Nicholas 30, 41, **247–8**, Pls. 39, 77
    Gipping Hall 247, 448
    Wood Farm 62, **249**
Gipping Navigation *see* Ipswich & Stowmarket Navigation
Gislingham **249–50**
    St Mary 28, 41, **249–50**
    Templars' preceptory 24
Glemsford 20, 21, 195, **250–2**
    Board School (former) 54, **251**, Pl. 100
    St Mary the Virgin 27, 52, **250–1**, 382
Great Ashfield **252–3**
    All Saints 23, 40, **252–3**, 571, Pl. 69
    Ashfield Lodge (former) and Ashfield House **253**
    Castle Hill motte 36, **253**
Great Barton **253–5**
    Holy Innocents 29, 52, **253–4**
    Manor Farm 39, **255**
Great Blakenham **255–6**
    Benedictine house 24
Great Bradley **256–7**
    St Mary 30, **256–7**, Pl. 50
Great Bricett **257–8**
    Hall, The **258**, 489
    Old Vicarage 55, **258**
    St Mary and St Lawrence and *priory remains* 24, 25, 32, **257–8**
    prior's house 36–7, **258**
Great Cornard 11, **259–60**
    Abbas Hall 5–6, 36–7, **259–60**, 418
    mill buildings 51, **259**
    overspill housing 21, 62, **259**
Great Finborough **260–2**
    Finborough Hall 47, **261**
    St Andrew 43, 55, **260–1**, 505, Pl. 101
Great Livermere **262–3**
    Livermere Hall (former rectory) 49, **263**
    Livermere Hall (original) 7, 47, 48, 79, 262, **263**, 368
    St Peter 33, 40–1, **262–3**, 368n.
Great Saxham **263–5**
    Great Saxham Hall 46–7, 48, 263, **264–5**, 370
    St Andrew 42, **263–4**
Great Thurlow **265–6**
    All Saints 25, 65, **265–6**
Great Waldingfield **266–7**
    Babergh Hall 267, **268**
    Old Rectory **267–8**, 519n.
    primary school 63, **268**, 320
    St Lawrence 40, 54, **266–7**
Great Wenham **268–9**
Great Whelnetham **269–70**
    Old Rectory 61, **270**
    Rushbrooke Arms 61, **270**
    St Thomas à Becket 34, **269–70**
    Sicklesmere **270**
    toll house (former) 50, **270**
Great Wratting **270**
Groton **271–2**
    Castling's Hall 61, **272**
    Pitches Mount castle mound 36, **271–2**

Hadleigh 1, 20, 51, **272–84**
    Aldham Mill Hill ring ditches 12

churches **272-4**
  Row Chapel 55, **274**
  St Mary 26, 55, 56, 65, **272-4**, 276
public buildings **274-6**
  Babergh District Council Offices 63, **275-6**, 280
  Deanery Tower 39, **276-8**, Pl. 42
  Guildhall (and Market Hall) 36, 39, **274-5**, 276
  National School (former) 54, **280**
  primary schools 63, **276**
  Pykenham Almshouses 54, **281**
  railway station (former) 52, 272, **282**
  town hall 53, **275**
  war memorial 65, **281**
streets and houses 272, **276-84**
  George Street 60, **177**, 280
  High Street 275, **279**, 281
  Peyton Hall 37, **283**
  Sun Courts 60, **279-80**
Hardwick House *see* Bury St Edmunds
Hargrave **283**
Harleston **285**
  St Augustine 33, **285**
Hartest **285-7**
  Hartest and Boxford Club (village hall) 53, **286**
  primary school 63, **286**
  rectory (former) 49, **285**
Haughley **287-9**
  castle 36, **287-8**
  Haughley Park *xvi*, 45, **288-9**, Pl. 66
  St Mary 27, 44, **287**, 555
Haverhill 20, 22, 52, **289-95**
  Old Independent Church 55, **290-1**, Pl. 102
  public buildings **291**
    Board School (former) 54, **293**
    corn exchanges (former) 53, **291**, 293
    town hall (former) 53, **291**
  streets and houses 21, 35, **291-5**
    overspill estates 21, 62, 290, **293-5**
    prefabricated 'Anglia' houses 259, **294**, Pl. 111
    Teasel Close 62, **294**
Hawkedon **295-7**
  Langley's Newhouse 61, **296**
  St Mary 32, 104, **295**, 372
Hawstead 60, **297-301**
  All Saints 31, 41, 42, 43, **297-9**, 409, Pl. 72
  Guildhall (former) 39, **299**

Hawstead Place 173-4, **300**, Pl. 76
Metcalfe Almshouses 50, **299-300**
school (former) and estate cottages 47, **299**, 321, Pl. 99
Hengrave 238, **301-6**
  bus shelter 239, **306**
  Hengrave Hall 7, 44, 109, **301-6**, 307, 550, Pls. 59, 60
    St John Lateran 28, 41, **304-5**
Hepworth **306-7**
  Old Rectory 49, **307**
  St Peter 31, 51, **306-7**, Pl. 23
Herringswell **307-8**
  St Ethelbert 56, **307-8**
Hessett **308-10**
  St Ethelbert 28, 29, 32-3, 35, 42, 107, **308-10**
Higham (near Gazeley) **310-11**
  Old Parsonage House 55, **310**
  St Stephen 54-5, **310**, Pl. 97
Higham (near Stratford St Mary) **311-13**
  Chauffeurs Cottage 58, **312-13**
  Higham Place (formerly Barhams Manor) **312**
  Ketelfield 61, **312**, Pl. 113
  St Mary 28, **311**
Hinderclay **312-14**
  St Mary 25, 44, 65, 190, **312-13**
Hintlesham **314-16**
  Hintlesham Hall 45, 46, **315-16**, Pl. 80
  St Nicholas 25, 42, **314**
Hitcham **316-17**
  All Saints 31, 64, **316-17**
  council housing 62, 199, **317**, 457
  Wetherden Hall 270, 288, 289, **317**
Holton St Mary **318**
Honington 22, **318-19**
  All Saints 25, **318-19**, 542
Hopton 2, **319-20**
  All Saints 35, **319**
  Cottage Hall 62, **320**
  National School (former) 54, **320**
  primary school 63, **319-20**
Horringer **320-2**, 332, 333
  Clarice House (former Horringer Court) *see* Bury St Edmunds
  estate buildings 47, 299, **321**
  St Leonard 43, 54, **320**
Hundon **322**
  council housing 62, 88, **322**, 559
  Highpoint Prison *see* Stradishall
Hunston **322-3**
  St Michael 23, 25, 34, **322-3**

Icklingham 19, 227, **323–5**
  All Saints 32, 34, 91, **324**
  How Hill earthworks 11, **325**
  Roman settlement and Christian cemetery 16, 19–20, 22
  St James 5, 34, **324–5**
Icknield Way 21, 22, 428
Ickworth **325–33**
  Dower House (Ickworth Lodge) 325, **331–2**
  Ickworth House 44, 47, 48, 185, 261, 321, **325–31**
    gardens 44, 46, 48, **330–1**
  Ickworth Park **332–3**
  St Mary 25, **331**
Ingham 211n., **333–4**
  estate buildings 57, 209, **333–4**
Ipswich & Stowmarket (or Gipping) Navigation 50, **87**, **94**, 421, **425**, 503, **508**, Pl. 88
Ixworth 15, 35, **334–7**
  council houses 58, **336**
  Ixworth Abbey 24, 302, **334–6**, 501
  Roman 18, 334
  St Mary 30, 41, **334**
Ixworth Thorpe, All Saints 30, 34, 41, 85, **337**

Jacob's Manor *see* Withersfield

Kedington 10, **337–40**
  Kedington Hall 114, 338
  Ketton House 49, **340**
  National School (former) 54, **339**
  St Peter and St Paul 23, 31, 35, 41, 42, **337–9**, Pl. 68
  watermill 51, **339**
  workhouse 53, 340
Kentford **340**
Kentwell Hall *see* Long Melford
Kersey 3, 60, **340–3**, Pl. 1
  Kersey Mill 51, **343**
  priory 24, **342**
  St Mary 27, 31, 33, **340–2**, 366, Pls. 30, 31
Kettlebaston **343–4**
  St Mary 32, **343–4**, 461
Ketton House *see* Kedington
Knettishall 334, **344**

Lackford 19, 22, 181, **344–5**
Lakenheath 4, 14, 22, 229, **345–8**, 546
  airfield 21, 345
  Lakenheath Hall (formerly The Retreat) 57, **347–8**
  railway station 52, **348**
  St Mary 24, 26, 31, 32, 33–4, 35, 41, 180, 228, **345–7**, 571, Pl. 12
  school (former) 54, **347**
  Undley bracteate 22
Landwade xvii 21, **347–9**
  Roman site *see* Exning
  St Nicholas 41, **348–9**
Langham **349–50**
  St Mary 26, 33, **349–50**
Lanwades Park *see* Moulton
Lark Navigation 50, **171**, **411–12**
Lavenham 20, 21, 51, 52, 60, **350–61**, 511
  public buildings **354–9**
    Guildhall 39, 60, 61, **357–8**, Pl. 46
    Wool Hall 60, 350, **360–1**, Pl. 45
  St Peter and St Paul 5, 21, 27, 28, 29, 31, 33, 34, 189, 350, **351–4**, 564, Pls. 51, 54
  streets and houses 5, 21, 38, 60, 350–1, **355–61**
    De Vere House 60, **360**
    High Street 37, **355–6**
    Lady Street 38, 60, **360**, Pl. 45
    Little Hall 6, **357**
Lawshall **361–2**
  All Saints 199, **361–2**
  Foundry, The 62, **362**
Layham **362–4**
  Layham Hall *see* Raydon
  St Andrew 32, **362–3**
Leavenheath **364**, 495
Lidgate 18, **364–5**
  castle 36, 365
  Mouse House **365**, 450
Lindsey **365–6**
  castle 36, 366
  St Peter 41, **365–6**
Little Blakenham **366**
  St Mary 25, **366**
Little Bradley **367**
  All Saints 23, **367**
Little Bricett *see* Offton
Little Cornard **367–8**
Little Finborough **368**
  St Mary **368**, 549n.
Little Haugh Hall *see* Norton
Little Livermere **368**
  St Peter and St Paul 23, 263, **368**, 369
  Seven Hills barrows 11, **368**
Little Saxham **369–70**, 475
  Little Saxham Hall 370, 476, 552
  St Nicholas 25, 43, 310, 368n., **369–70**, Pl. 8
Little Stonham **370–1**
  Clock House 45, 60, 280, **371**
  St Mary 31, **370–1**
Little Thurlow **371–3**
  St Peter 32, 41, 65, 295, **371–2**
  schoolhouse (former) 45, **373**, Pl. 64

INDEX OF PLACES

Little Waldingfield **373–5**
Little Wenham **375–9**
   All Saints 25, 33, **377–9**, Pl. 13
   Little Wenham Hall (Wenham Castle) 7, 36, **375–7**, Pls. 10, 11
Little Whelnetham **379–80**
   Crutched Friars 24, **380**
   Sicklesmere *see* Great Whelnetham
Little Wratting **380–1**
   Holy Trinity 23, **380–1**
Livermere Hall *see* Great Livermere
Long Melford 21, 52, **381–400**
   churches **381–8**
      Holy Trinity 5, 27, 28, 29, 31, 34, 35, 41, 135, 187, 188, 351, **381–8**, Pls. 18, 37, 38, 61
      United Reformed church 40, **390**
   public buildings **388–92**
      railway station (former) 52, 381, **400**
      Trinity Hospital 54, **388**
   Roman settlement 15, 18, 19, 334, **400**
   streets and houses 381, **388–99**
      Kentwell Hall 44–5, 47, 325, 385, 392, **396–9**, Pl. 56
      Little St Mary's (street) **389**, 400
      Long Wall 61, **399**
      Lutons 396–7
      maltings (former) 52, 381, **399–400**
      Melford Hall 44–5, 47, 391, **392–6**, Pl. 58
      Old Rectory 49, **392**

Market Weston **400**
   St Mary 43, 51, 56, **400**
Melford Hall *see* Long Melford
Mellis **401–2**
   St Mary the Virgin 35, 41, 52, **401**
Mendlesham 36, **402–5**
   St Mary 25, 28, 30, 35, 40, 44, **402–4**, Pl. 70
Milden **405–6**
   castle 36, 406
   St Peter 41, 43, **405–6**
Mildenhall 3, 4, 9, 12, 22, **406–12**
   churches **406–9**
      St John the Evangelist, Beck Row 53, **409**
      St Mary 25, 27, 28, 31, 43, 64, 346, **406–9**, 421, Pl. 14
   Hurst Fen Neolithic settlement 10
   Mildenhall Treasure 20
   public buildings **409–11**
   airbase 21, 406
      Beck Row Primary School 54, **410**
      locks 50, **411–12**
      Mildenhall College Academy (former Upper School) 63, **410**
      workhouses (former) 53–4, **410**
   rabbit warrens 3, 50, 406, **411**, Pl. 4
   streets and houses 35–6, **410–12**
      overspill housing 21, 62, 406, **411**
      Wamil Hall 4, **411**
   West Row Fen Bronze Age site 12
Monks Eleigh **412–13**
   Second Pits 61, **413**
   Tye House 61, **413**
Moreton Hall *see* Bury St Edmunds
Moulton 21, **414–15**
   Lanwades Park 58, **414–15**
   packhorse bridge **414**, Pl. 25
   St Peter 25, 53, **414**

Naughton **415**
Nayland 1, 21, 36, **416–20**
   Alston Court 38, **417–18**, 419, Pl. 44
   Court Street 38, **418–19**
   Old Guildhall 39, **419**
   St James 29, 31, 34, 41, **416–17**
Nedging **421**
Needham Market 36, 86, **421–5**
   Bosmere Mill and Lock 50, 51, **425**
   Friends meeting house (former) 40, **424**
   railway station 52, **423**
   St John the Baptist 31–2, **421–3**, Pl. 36
Nettlestead **425–8**
   Nettlestead Chace **426–7**
   St Mary 42, 57, 366, **425–6**
Newmarket 1, 4, 20, 21, 46, 50, 51, 52, 53, 58, **428–41**
   churches **428–30**
      Exning Cemetery **430**
      Our Lady Immaculate and St Etheldreda (R.C.) 64, **430**
      St Agnes 55, 56, **429–30**, Pl. 104
   Devil's Dyke 22, **441**
   public buildings 46, 58, 428, **430–3**
      Cooper Memorial Fountain 57, **436**
      covered ride, Exeter House Stables 59, **439**
      Jockey Club Rooms 58, 64, **435–6**, Pl. 109

INDEX OF PLACES

Newmarket, public buildings *cont.*
    Machell Place Stables 59, **438**
    National Horseracing Museum 433, **435**
    racecourses 21, 64, 428, **440–1**; Rowley Mile Course (with Millennium Grandstand etc.) 64, **440**, Pl. 114
    Rous Memorial Court 54, **437–8**
    Tattersalls 64, **436–7**
    workhouse (former) 54, **431**
  streets and houses 36, 46, 49, 58, **433–40**
    Cheveley Park lodges 58, **438**
    High Street 49, **433–6**
    James I's lodgings 46, *431*, 435
    Murray Lodge 58, **436–7**
    Palace House 46, 49, **431–3**; Kings Yard Stables **433**
    Prince's Lodging 46, *431*
    'Queen Anne' houses 58, **436**
    Rutland Arms Hotel 49, 433, **434**
    Stanley House and stables 59, **439**
    Studlands Park 62, **440**
Newton **441–2**
  All Saints 33, 34, 35, **441**
Norton **442–5**
  Little Haugh Hall 43, 46, **443–5**, Pl. 81
  St Andrew 26, 34, **442**, 458, 544
Nowton **445–7**
  almshouses 54, **445**
  Nowton Court (former Nowton Cottage) 47, 48, 138, 445, **446–7**
  St Peter 41, 43, 54, **445**, 447, 476

Offton **447–8**
  Tollemache Hall, Little Bricett 258, **447–8**
Old Buckenham Hall School *see* Brettenham
Old Newton **448**
Onehouse **449**
  St John the Baptist 56, **449**
  Stow Lodge (former Stow Hundred House of Industry) 50, **449**
Ousden **449–50**
  East Lodge 365, **450**
  Primitive Methodist chapel (former) 55, **450**
  St Peter 24, 53, **449–50**, 562

Pakenham 15, **450–4**
  mills 51, **453–4**, Pls. 89, 92
  Roman fort and villa 15, 16, 18
  St Mary 24, 25, 32, 54, **450–1**, Pl. 33
  settlement (C5) 22
  streets and houses **451–4**
    Nether Hall **452**, 539
    Newe House 45, **452**, Pl. 65
    Redcastle Farm 18, **453**
Palgrave 8, **454–5**
  St Peter 31, **454**
Peddars Way 381
Peyton Hall *see* Hadleigh
Polstead 13, **455–7**
  council housing 62, 199, 317, **457**
  St Mary 7, 24, 25, 26, 41, **455–6**, Pl. 9
Poslingford **457–9**
  Chipley Priory 24, *459*
  Old Vicarage 49, **459**
  St Mary 25, 34, **457–9**
Preston St Mary **459–60**
  Down Hall 37, **460**
  St Mary 25, 32, 40, 457, **459–60**, Pl. 62
Purton Green *see* Stansfield

Rattlesden **460–2**
  Clopton Hall 46, **462**
  St Nicholas 29, 31, 56, 115, **460–1**, 544
Raydon **462–3**
  Layham Hall **463**
  railway station (former) 52, **463**
  St Mary **462–3**, 536
Rede **463–4**
Redgrave 36, **464–7**
  Redgrave Hall 45, 48, *464*, 465, **466**, 469
  St Mary the Virgin 30, 31, 40, 42, 56, 82n., 421, **464–6**, 572, Pls. 67, 73
Red Lodge xvii 63, **467**
Rickinghall Inferior **467–9**
  St Mary 25, 26, 32, 33, **467–8**, Pl. 21
Rickinghall Superior 467, **468–9**
Ringshall **470–1**
Risby **471–2**
  barrows 239, **472**
  Old Rectory 49, **472**
  primary school 63, **472**
  St Giles 33, 310, **471**
Rougham 28, **472–5**
  James Stiff Cottages (almshouses) 54, **474**
  Roman barrow 19, **474–5**
  Rougham Hall 47, *473*
  St Mary 27, 28, 30, 31, 52, **472–3**
Rushbrooke **475–7**
  estate village 62, 475, **476–7**, Pl. 110

INDEX OF PLACES

Rushbrooke Hall xvi, 44–5, *141*, 475, 476, 477
  St Nicholas 31, 34, 40, 41, 43, **475–6**, Pl. 96
Rushford Hall **477–8**

St Clare Hall *see* Bradfield St Clare
Santon Downham **478–9**
  St Mary 33, **478**
Sapiston **479**
  New Cottages 319, **479**
Semer **480**
  Cosford Union workhouse 50, 460
Seven Hills *see* Ingham; Little Livermere
Shelland **480**
  King Charles the Martyr 40, 41, **480**, Pl. 79
Shelley **481–2**
  Shelley Hall 38, 39, **481–2**
Shimpling **482–4**
  coal house 288, **483**
  St George 43, 56–7, **482–3**
Sicklesmere *see* Great Whelnetham
Smallbridge Hall *see* Bures
Somersham **484**
  St Mary 26, 100, 447, **484**
Somerton **484–5**
Sproughton 9, **485–7**
  All Saints 26, **485–6**
  mill 51, **486**
  Sproughton Manor 57, **487**
Stanningfield 199, **487–8**
  St Nicholas 33, **487–8**
Stansfield **488–9**
  All Saints 26, **488**
  Purton Green 5, 36–7, 258, **488–9**, Pl. 24
Stanstead 19, **489–90**
Stanton 18, **490–2**
  St John 27, **490–1**
  windmill 51, **491**
Stoke-by-Clare **492–3**
  St John the Baptist 34, **492–3**, Pl. 47
  Stoke College (Benedictine priory) 24, 58, **493–5**
  dovecote 39, **495**, Pl. 43
Stoke-by-Nayland **495–501**
  St Edmund (R.C.) 40, **498**
  St Mary 27, 34, 35, 41, 43, 56, **495–7**
  Tendring Hall 47, 48, 306, 498, **499–500**, Pl. 83
  see also Giffords Hall
Stour Navigation 50, **528**, 531
Stowlangtoft **501–3**
  St George 27, 33, 34, 35, 42, 56, 443n., **501–2**
  Stowlangtoft Hall 57, **502–3**
Stowmarket 1, 14, 20, 50, **503–12**
  churches **503–5**

  Our Lady (R.C.) 55, **505**
  St Peter and St Mary 42, 64, 247n., 260, **503–5**
  United Reformed church 64, **505**, 508
  maltings 50, **503**, **508**, **509**, Pl. 88
  public buildings **505–8**
    corn exchange (now John Peel Centre for Creative Arts) 53, **506**
    Ipswich & Stowmarket Navigation 50, 503, **508**, Pl. 88
    Milton House (Town Council offices) **505**
    Museum of East Anglian Life **510–11**; Robert Boby Building **511**, Pl. 94
    railway station 52, 423, 503, **506**
  streets and houses 35, 50, 503, **506–12**
    Edgar's Farm 37, **510–11**
    Stowupland Street 38, **508**
Stowupland **512–13**
  Columbine Hall 47, **512**, Pl. 26
  high school 63, **512**
  Holy Trinity 65, 207n., **512**
Stradishall **513**
  Highpoint Prison **513**
  St Margaret 33, **513**
Stratford St Mary xvii 10, **513–16**
  Board School (former) 54, **515**
  St Mary 27, **513–15**, Pl. 53
  Stratford Hills 61, **516**
Stuston 401n., **516**
Sudbury 2, 20, 22, 50, 52, 53, **516–32**
  churches etc. **517–21**
    All Saints 33, 259, 517, **519–20**
    Baptist church 55, **520**
    Chapel of St Bartholomew 23, **521**; *barn* 39, 521
    Dominican priory 24, 527
    Friends Meeting House 40, **520**
    Our Lady and St John (R.C.) 55, **520**, Pl. 103
    St Gregory 6–7, 33, 35, 43, 189, 259, **517–19**
    St Peter 33, 54, 267, 517, **519**, 520
  public buildings **521–30**
    corn exchange (now public library) 53, 63, **521**
    Gainsborough statue 57, **522**
    grammar school (former) 54, **525**
    Ormiston Sudbury Academy (former Upper School) 63, **521**

INDEX OF PLACES

Sudbury, public buildings *cont.*
  St Leonard's Hospital 54, **521–2**
  Town Hall 50, **521**
  workhouse (now Walnuttree Hospital) 54, 518, **522**
  streets, commercial buildings and houses 21, 35, 516–17, 519, **522–32**
    Ballingdon 50, **530–1**
    Barclays Bank 59, **523–4**
    Brundon 51, **530**; mill 51, **530**
    Church Street 38, **526–7**
    Gainsborough's House 48–9, **523–5**
    Natwest (former London & County Bank) 59, **523**
    Salter's Hall 38, **525–6**, Pl. 40
    silk mills 21, 517, 525

Tendring Hall *see* Stoke-by-Nayland
Thelnetham **532–3**
  St Nicholas 25, 468, **532**
  windmill 51, **532–3**
Thorington *see* Stoke-by-Nayland
Thornham Hall *see* Thornham Magna
Thornham Magna **533–4**
  St Mary 25, 43, 55, **533**, 535, Pl. 95
  Thornham Hall 47–8, **533–4**, 535
Thornham Parva **534–5**
  St Mary 23, 34, 533, **534–5**, 576n., Pl. 16
Thorpe Morieux **536**
  St Mary the Virgin 34, 462, **536**
Thrandeston **536–7**
Thurston **537–9**
  Manor Farm 452, **539**
  railway station 52, **539**, Pl. 93
  St Peter 250, **537–9**, 541
  schools 63, **539**
Thwaite 60, **539–40**
Timworth 57, 209, **540**
Tollemache Hall *see* Offton
Tostock **540–2**
  Old Rectory 49, **541**
  St Andrew 31, 65, 538, **540–1**
Troston **542–3**
  St Mary 26, 34, 318, **542–3**, Pl. 22
  Troston Hall 45, **543**
Tuddenham **543–4**
  school (former) 54, **543**

Walsham-le-Willows **544–6**
  Blue Boar 38, **545**
  Guildhall (former) 39, **545**
  St Mary the Virgin 26, 30, 31, 33, 43, 65, 115, 442, 461, **544–5**

Wangford 12, **546**
  Benedictine priory 24
Washbrook **547**
  St Mary 5, **547**
Washmere Green **361**
Wattisfield **547–8**
  Roman kiln sites 19, **548**
  school (former) 53, **548**
Wattisham **549**
  St Nicholas 55, 96, **549**
  Wattisham Airfield *see* Ringshall
Wenham Castle *see* Little Wenham
Westhorpe **549–51**
  St Margaret 33, 42, 43, 205, **549–50**
  Westhorpe Hall 44, **550–1**
Westley **551**
  St Mary 8, 51, 55, **551**
  St Thomas à Becket 551
West Row Fen *see* Mildenhall
West Stow 57, 209, **551–4**
  Anglo-Saxon village (West Stow Country Park) 22, **553–4**, Pl. 5
  West Stow Hall 39, 45, 210, 245–6, **552–3**, Pl. 57
Wetherden **554–5**
  Old Rectory 49, **555**
  St Mary 31, 287, 288, **554–5**
  Wetherden Hall *see* Hitcham
Whatfield **555–6**
  Old Rectory 49, **555–6**
  St Margaret **555**
Whepstead **556–8**
  Baptist church 55, **556**
  Board School (former) 54, **557**
  Manston Hall 61, **557**
  St Petronilla 29, **556**
Wickhambrook **558–61**
  All Saints 23, 26, 40, 53, **558**
  council housing 62, 88, **559**
  Giffords Hall 37, **559–60**
  primary school 53, **559**
  United Reformed church 40, **559**
  Wakelins 62, **559**, Pl. 116
Wickham Skeith **561–2**
  Benedictine house 23
Willisham **562**
Wissington **562–4**
  Chase Cottage 61, **564**
  mill 51, **563–4**
  New Maltings and Maltings Chase 61, **564**, Pl. 112
  St Mary 24, 25, 33, **562–3**
  Wiston Hall 47, **563**
Wiston Hall *see* Wissington
Withermarsh Green *see* Stoke-by-Nayland
Withersfield **564–5**
  Jacob's Manor 49, **565**
  St Mary 34, 53, **564–5**, Pl. 34
  school (former) 53, **565**

Wixoe **565–6**
  mill 51, **566**
Woolpit 7, **566–9**
  Hill House 38, **568**
  St Mary 27, 28, 31, 32, 35, 56, 178, **566–8**, Pls. 29, 52
Wordwell 57, 209, **569–70**
  All Saints 25, 54, 209, 540, **569–70**
Worlington **570–1**
  All Saints 26, 252, 346, **570–1**

Wortham **571–3**
  St Mary the Virgin 25, 30, **571–2**
  tithe monument 223, **572**
Wyverstone **573–4**
  St George 27, 31, 33, **573**

Yaxley **574–6**
  guildhall (former) 39, **575**
  St Mary 27, 31, 35, 40, 52, 574–5, Pl. 32
  Yaxley Hall 48, **575–6**